ACTIVE CHEMISTRY

Project-Based Inquiry Approach

SECOND EDITION

TEACHER'S EDITION

VOLUME 2

Chapter 5 Ideal Toy
Chapter 6 Cool Chemistry Show
Chapter 7 Cookin' Chem
Chapter 8 CSI Chemistry

IT's ABOUT TIME®

HERFF JONES EDUCATION DIVISION

Developed in association with

AIChE®

American Institute of
Chemical Engineers

IT's ABOUT TIME ®

HERFF JONES EDUCATION DIVISION

84 Business Park Drive, Armonk, NY 10504
Phone (914) 273-2233   Fax (914) 206-6444
www.its-about-time.com

Print Components

Student Edition

Teacher's Edition – Two-Volume Set

Periodic Table of the Elements

Technology Components

Student Edition Online

Teacher's Edition Online

Durable Kits

Consumable Kits

Chemical Kits

Teacher Resources CD – Blackline Masters and Color Overheads

Teacher Resources Online – Blackline Masters and Color Overheads

Multimedia DVD – Content Videos and Spreadsheets

EXAMVIEW® Test Generator

LESSONVIEW® Planner

Professional Development Videos

Printed and bound in the United States of America.

ISBN 978-1-60720-401-5
Two-Volume Set ISBN 978-1-60720-402-2

1 2 3 4 5 6   15 14 13 12 11

This project was supported, in part, by the
National Science Foundation under Grant No. 0352516.
Opinions expressed are those of the authors and not necessarily
those of the National Science Foundation.

Contents

Acknowledgements vii

Welcome to *Active Chemistry*: Your Guide to Success xii

Features of *Active Chemistry* xvii

Overview of Meeting the Needs of All Students: Differentiated Instruction xxii

Students' Prior Conceptions: Overview and 7E Tools xxiv

Pacing Guides for Teachers xxv

Active Chemistry and the National Science Education Standards xxvi

Active Chemistry Curriculum Strengths xxx

Active Chemistry—A Research-Based Curriculum xxxii

Expanding the 5E Model xxxvii

Artist as Chemist Article xxlii

Safety Contract: Safety in the Chemistry Classroom xlvii

Chapter 5 Ideal Toy 1

Chapter Overview 2

Key Science Concepts and Skills 3

Chapter Concept Map 4

Understanding by Design 5

Pacing Guide 6

Materials, Equipment, and Chemicals 8

Teacher Resources 12

Chapter Challenge 14

Sample Criteria for Excellence 17

    Section 1: Electrochemistry and Batteries 18

    Section 2: Intermolecular Forces in Solids, Liquids, and Gases 34

    Section 3: Boyle's Law and the Cartesian Diver 52

    Section 4: Charles's Law and Hot-Air Balloons 74

    Chapter Mini-Challenge 94

    Section 5: Types of Reactions and Gas Production 96

    Section 6: Ideal Gas Law for the Ideal Toy 118

Section 7: Kinetic Molecular Theory and Graham's Law 132

Section 8: Properties of Polymers and Plastics 150

Chem You Learned 170

Chem Chapter Challenge 171

Sample Assessment Rubric 173

Chem Connections to Other Sciences 176

Chem at Work 177

Chem Practice Test 178

Chapter 6 Cool Chemistry Show **181**

Chapter Overview 182

Key Science Concepts and Skills 183

Chapter Concept Map 184

Understanding by Design 185

Pacing Guide 186

Materials, Equipment, and Chemicals 188

Teacher Resources 194

Chapter Challenge 196

Sample Criteria for Excellence 199

Section 1: Solutions: Chemical or Physical Change? 200

Section 2: Characteristics of Chemical Change 222

Section 3: Chemical Names and Formulas 240

Section 4: Reaction Types and Chemical Equations 260

Chapter Mini-Challenge 284

Section 5: Reaction Diagrams and Conservation of Energy 286

Section 6: Factors in Reaction Rates 306

Section 7: Acids, Bases, and Indicators – Colorful Chemistry 324

Section 8: Oxidation and Reduction of Metals 352

Chem You Learned 366

Chem Chapter Challenge 367

Sample Assessment Rubric..369

Chem Connections to Other Sciences...372

Chem at Work 373

Chem Practice Test 374

Chapter 7 Cookin' Chem...**377**

Chapter Overview...378

Key Science Concepts and Skills..379

Chapter Concept Map...380

Understanding by Design 381

Pacing Guide...382

Materials, Equipment, and Chemicals..384

Teacher Resources..388

Chapter Challenge 390

Sample Criteria for Excellence 393

Section 1: Heat Transfer: What Is Heat? 394

Section 2: Combustion Reactions and Hydrocarbons 418

Section 3: Thermochemistry and Cooking Fuels 440

Chapter Mini-Challenge 458

Section 4: Phase Changes and the Heating Curve of Water 460

Section 5: Phase Changes and the Cooling Curve of Water 476

Section 6: Calorimetry and Specific Heat Capacity 494

Section 7: Denaturation: How Do Proteins in Foods Change? 510

Section 8: Modeling Organic Molecules: Soap...526

Chem You Learned 550

Chem Chapter Challenge 551

Sample Assessment Rubric...553

Chem Connections to Other Sciences...556

Chem at Work 557

Chem Practice Test 558

Active Chemistry

Chapter 8 CSI Chemistry..**561**

Chapter Overview 562

Key Science Concepts and Skills 563

Chapter Concept Map..564

Understanding by Design 565

Pacing Guide...566

Materials, Equipment, and Chemicals..568

Teacher Resources 572

Chapter Challenge 574

Sample Criteria for Excellence 577

    Section 1: Groups, Periods, and the Properties of Elements: Clue Me In 578

    Section 2: Physical Properties: Density of Glass 594

    Section 3: Atomic Structure and Chemiluminescence: The Luminol Reaction 616

    Section 4: Solubility and Qualitative Analysis: White Powders 638

    Chapter Mini-Challenge 660

    Section 5: Double-Replacement Reactions and Fingerprints.........................662

    Section 6: Reactions with Transition Metals: Metal Activity Series 686

    Section 7: Using the Metal Activity Series to Etch a Serial Number...........................712

    Section 8: Paper Chromatography: Separating Molecules 730

    Chem You Learned 750

    Chem Chapter Challenge 751

    Sample Assessment Rubric 753

    Chem Connections to Other Sciences...756

    Chem at Work 757

    Chem Practice Test 758

Acknowledgements

Development Partner

The American Institute of Chemical Engineers (AIChE) is the world's leading organization for chemical engineers. AIChE played a pivotal role in the development of *Active Chemistry*. AIChE's involvement has helped to ensure the accuracy of the program's chemistry content as well as its engineering design principles.

Project Director

Dr. Arthur Eisenkraft has taught high school physics for over 30 years and is currently the Distinguished Professor of Science Education and a Senior Research Fellow at the University of Massachusetts, Boston.

Dr. Eisenkraft has been recognized with numerous awards, including: Presidential Award for Excellence in Science Teaching, 1986, from President Ronald Reagan; the American Association of Physics Teachers (AAPT) Distinguished Service Citation for "excellent contributions to the teaching of physics," 1989, the Excellence in Pre-College Teaching Award, 1999, and the Robert A. Millikan Medal for "notable and creative contributions in physics education," 2009; Disney American Teacher Award for Science Teacher of the Year, 1991; Honorary Doctorate of Science, Rensselaer Polytechnic Institute, 1993; National Science Teachers Association (NSTA) Distinguished Service Award to Science Education, 2005, and the NSTA's most prestigious award, the Robert H. Carleton Award for "notable and creative contributions in physics education" in 2010.

In 1999, Dr. Eisenkraft was elected to a three-year cycle as the President-Elect, President and Retiring President of the National Science Teachers Association (NSTA), the largest science teacher organization in the world. He also served on the content committee and helped to write the National Science Education Standards for the National Research Council. In 2003, he was elected a fellow of the American Association for the Advancement of Science (AAAS). Dr. Eisenkraft has been involved with a number of projects and chaired many competition programs, including: the Toshiba/NSTA ExploraVisions Awards (1991 to the present); the Toyota TAPESTRY Grants (1990 to 2005); the Duracell/NSTA Scholarship Competitions (1984 to 2000). In 1993, he served as Executive Director for the XXIV International Physics Olympiad after being Academic Director for the United States Team for six years.

Dr. Eisenkraft is a frequent presenter and keynote speaker at National Conventions. He has published over 100 articles and presented over 200 papers and workshops. He has been featured in articles in *The New York Times, Education Week, Physics Today, Scientific American, The American Journal of Physics* and *The Physics Teacher* and has appeared on *The Today Show*, ESPN's *Sports Figures,* and NPR and many other radio and television broadcasts.

Content Specialists

Gary Freebury has been teaching chemistry for more than 35 years. He has been the Safety Advisor for Montana Schools, director of the Chemistry Olympiad, chairman of the Montana Section of the American Chemical Society (ACS), member of the Executive Committee of the Montana Section of the ACS, and a member of the Montana Science Advisory Council. Mr. Freebury has been the regional director and author of *Scope, Sequence and Coordination (SS&C) – Integrated Science Curriculum* and co-director of the NSF-supported Chemistry Concepts four-year program. He earned a B.S. degree at Eastern Montana College in mathematics and physical science, and an M.S. degree in chemistry at the University of Northern Iowa.

Dr. Gary Hickernell earned a B.S. degree in chemistry at Allegheny College and his Ph.D. in organic chemistry at the University of Washington in Seattle. He spent 19 years as a research scientist, studying the chemistry of food flavors at General Foods Technical Center in Tarrytown, NY. During this period, he was awarded two patents, a U.S. patent for "Novel Sweetener Effects," and a Canadian patent for the "Resin Decaffeination of Coffee." His second career began at Vassar College in Poughkeepsie, where he taught general and organic chemistry as an associate professor. During this period, he co-authored chapters in the NSF-funded series of engineering and environmental books, *Accident and Emergency Management: Problems and Solutions* and *Pollution Prevention: Problems and Solutions*. After two years at Vassar, Dr. Hickernell joined the science faculty at Keuka College, where he participated in the MADCAP project to bring project-based chemistry to college freshmen. Dr. Hickernell joined the staff at It's About Time in 2002 as the Project Coordinator for NSF-funded projects.

NSF Program Officer

Gerhard Salinger
Instructional Materials
Development (IMD)

Principal Investigators

Arthur Eisenkraft
University of Massachusetts,
Boston, MA

Gary Freebury
Kalispell High School
Kalispell, MT

Darlene Schuster
American Institute of
Chemical Engineers
Washington, D.C.

Barbara Zahm,
It's About Time
Armonk, NY

Project Coordinators

Gary Hickernell
Project Coordinator
It's About Time,
Armonk, NY

Jean Pennycook
Field Test Coordinator
Fresno Unified School District,
Fresno, CA

Writers

David Barry,
Chelsea High School
Chelsea, MA

Kristen Cacciatore
Dedham High School
Dedham, MA

James Clements
Atlantic High School
Port Orange, FL

Paul D. Dunbar
University of Kentucky
Paducah, KY

L.S. Fan*
Ohio State University
Columbus, OH

Mary Gromko
Colorado Springs
School District II
Colorado Springs, CO

Himanshu Gupta
Ohio State University
Columbus, OH

Robert Hartshorn*
University of Tennessee
Martin, TN

Carl Heltzel*
Transylvania University
Lexington, KY

Lydia Islan
Dartmouth College
Hanover, NH

Diane Johnson
Lewis Co. High School
Vanceburg, KY

Maggie Matthews
Shorewood High School
Shoreline, WA

Sean Muller
Merrimack High School
Merrimack, NH

John Parson
Ohio State University
Columbus, OH

Stanford N. Peppenhorst
Germantown H.S.
Germantown, TN

Josh Pretzer
Culver Academy
Culver, IN

Brian Radcliffe
Bryan Station High School,
Lexington, KY

John Roeder
The Calhoun School
New York, NY

Hannah Sevian*
University of Massachusetts,
Boston, MA

Peggy Sheets
Upper Arlington H.S.
Arlington, OH (Retired)

Sandra Smith
Colorado Springs, CO

Michael Tinnesand
American Chemical Society,
Washington, D.C.

Alissa Watson
Bardstown High School
Bardstown, KY

Melissa Wickenkamp
San Rafael H.S.,
San Rafael, CA

Doug Yenney
Dayton High School
Dayton, WA

Board of Advisors

Jerry Bell
Senior Scientist International
Activities Division of ACS
(American Chemical Society)

Rodger Bybee
Executive Director of BSCS
(Biological Sciences
Curriculum Study)

James Davis
Chemistry Professor Emeritus
Harvard University

Marilyn Decker
Senior Program Director
of Science for Boston
Public Schools

Dianne Dorland
Former President, AIChE
and Dean of Engineering
Rowan University

Maria Alicia Lopez Freeman
Executive Director
of CSP (California
Science Project)

Mary Gromko
Science Supervisor K-12
for the Colorado Springs
School District 11

David Lavallee
Provost Vice President of
Academic Affairs
SUNY, New Paltz

Carlo Parravano
Executive Director
Merck Institute for Science
Education and AAAS Fellow

Harold Pratt,
NSTA President
and BSCS Advisory
Board member

Bryan Roberts,
NSF Site Visitor,
University of Pennsylvania, PA

Ethel Schultz,
Science Education
Consultant CESAME,
trustee of the Noyce
Foundation

Consultants

William Berlinghoff
Colby College, ME

Audrey Champagne
SUNY Albany, NY

Michael Hacker
Loudonville, NY

Martin Hughto
Ridgefield H.S.
Ridgefield, CT

Inna Krasminskaya
Pace University, NY

Ronald Klemp
Secondary Literacy Coodinator
Los Angeles USD
Los Angeles, CA

Steve Long
Rogers High School, AR

George Miller
University of California
at Irvine, Irvine, CA

Sr. Mary Virginia Orna
College of
New Rochelle, NY

James Pellegrino
U. Illinois Chicago, IL

Maren Reeder
Merck Institute for
Science Education
Rahway, NJ

Vladimir Shafirovich
New York University, NY

Ellen Weiser
Pace University, NY

Evaluation Team

Rachelle Haroldson
University of
Minnesota, MN

Frances Lawrenz
University of
Minnesota, MN

Nate Wood,
University of
Minnesota, MN

Field Test Teachers

Dawn Arnett
Titusville H.S., FL

Rachel Badnowski
Southfield H.S., MI

Team Leaders

Patricia Barker
Hollywood H.S., CA

Nora Ann Bennett
Mt. Tabor H.S., NC

Kristen Cacciatore
Dedham H.S., MA

Isabel Camille
Coral Gables H.S., FL

Connie Celestine
Crossland H.S., MD

Ann Chatfield
Dalton H.S., GA

Jody Christophe
Lincoln H.S., PA

Grant Clark
Newton N. H.S., MA

James Clements
Atlantic H.S., FL

Linda Craig
Butler H.S., PA

Jeanene Crenshaw
Jeff. Davis H.S., AL

Carol Durso
Haverford H.S., PA

Frances Dziuma
St. Barnabas H.S., NY

Valerie Felger
DATA, TX

Brian Gagne
Newton N. H.S., MA

Marci Harvey
W. Forsythe H.S., NC

Gail Hermann
Quincy H.S., IL

Oscar Hernandez
Robert E.Lee H.S., TX

Angela Holcomb
Mt. Tabor H.S., NC

Solona Hollis
Miller Grove H.S., GA

Ray Hulse
Haverford H.S., PA

John Paul Jones
Crestview H.S., FL

James Kopchains
Flushing H.S., NY

Stephanie Levens
N. Broward Prep., FL

Arthur Logan
Clio Area H.S., MI

Charlotte Lum
Summit Prep. H.S., CA

Dan Mader
Kaukauna H.S., WI

Maggie Matthews
Shorewood H.S.,WA

Catherine McCluskey
E. Wake H.S., NC

Mitzi Moore
International School, TX

Sharona Moss
Selma High School, AL

Amy Murphy
Spain Park H.S., AL

Gerard Pepe
North Babylon H.S., NY

Alicia Peterson
Haverford H.S., PA

Vince Santo Pietro
Shorecrest H.S., WA

Richard Pimentel
Coachella Valley
H.S., CA

Joshua Pretzer
Culver Academies, IN

Candace Purdom
Washington County H.S., KY

Richard Redman
Franklin H.S., CA

Veronica Riffle
Lake Ridge Acad., OH

Rosemary Riggs
Roosevelt H.S., TX

Brenda Rinehart
Thompson H.S., AL

Jocelyn Roger
Squalicum H.S., WA

Carol Smith
Van Alstyne H.S., TX

David Smith
Battle Creek H.S., MI

Karen Tokos
Newton N. H.S., MA

Jane Wallace
Dalton H.S., GA

Alissa Watson
Bardstown H.S., KY

Janice Weaver
Culver Academies, IN

Shanan Wheeler
Churchill H.S., MI

Rodney White
Shorecrest H.S., WA

Melissa Wickenkamp
San Rafael H.S., CA

James Wicks, Sr.
Garfield H.S., CA

Sarah Wilson
Caldwell H.S., ID

Doug Yenney
Dayton H.S., WA

Pilot Testers

Rob Adams
Wyoming, DE

Ina Ahern,
Plymouth Regional H.S.
Plymouth, NH

Yolanda Anderson
Wingfield H.S., MS

Susan Auld
Squalicum H.S., WA

Linda Barry
Skyview H.S., WA

Arthur Beauchamp
Will C. Wood H.S., CA

John Bibb
Georgetown, DE

Amy Biddle
Pinkerton Academy, Derry, NH

Heidy Boyd
Grand Island H.S., NE

Fran Burkett
Forest Hill H.S., MS

Kristin Cacciatore
Dedham H.S., MA

Christine Carlson
Randolph H.S., NJ

Kelly Chaney
Cabot High School, AZ

Chris Clermont
Largo High School, MD

Sue Coluccio
Seattle Preparatory
High School, WA

Melissa Conrad
Hartford Academy of
Math & Science, CT

Marsha Crawford
Perry H.S., MI

Mary Cummane
Perspectives Charter School, IL

Robert Dayton
Rush-Henrietta H.S.
Henrietta, NY

Deb Ditkowsky
Carl Schurz H.S., IL

Barbara Duch
Education Resource Ctr.
Newark, DE

Robert Dutch
South Shore Vocational
Tech, MA

Gabriel Duque
North Miami Sr. H.S.
Miami, FL

Kathleen Dwyer
Maplewood Richmond
Heights H.S., MO

Debra Edelman
Pueblo East H.S., CO

Julia Eichman
McDonald County
High School, MO

Louis Fraga
Hopedale H.S., MA

David Frantz
Bayshore H.S., FL

Shauna Friend
Webb City H.S., MO

Suzanne Fudold
Bowie High School, MD

Liz Garcia
Carson High School, CA

Bill Green
E.O. Smith H.S., CT

Jennifer Grivens
Eaton Rapids H.S., MI

Laura Hajdukiewicz
The Bromfield School
Harvard, MA

Jonathon Haraty
SAGE School
Springfield, MA

Curt Hart
Corbin High School, KY

Rachel Hechtman
Lyman Hall H.S., CT

Bill Heeren
D.C. Everest H.S., WI

Carl Heltzel
Transylvania University
Lexington, KY

Bernie Hermanson
Harlan Community
High School, IA

Alison Hess
Northwestern H.S., MD

Natalie Hiller
Philadelphia Public Schools, PA

Nick Hoffman
Wallace Senior H.S., ID

Bronwyn Hogan
Meadowcreek H.S., GA

Penny Hood
Stanwood H.S., WA

Peg Huben
Somerville H.S., MA

Ray Hulse
Haverford H.S., PA

Tamilyn Ingram
Menifee County H.S.
Frenchburg, KY

John Jacoby
Upper Scioto Valley, OH

Amy James
Public Academy for the
Performing Arts, NM

Barbara Jeffries
Casey Co. High School
Liberty, KY

Diane Johnson
Lewis County High School
Vanceburg, KY

Lorraine Kelly
Hull High School, MA

Mary Kennedy
Texas Military Inst., TX

Elizabeth Kirkham
Chemawa Indian
School, OR

Steve Knight
Winthrop H.S., ME

Gerry LaFontaine
Toll Gate High School
Warwick, RI

Jo Larmore
Laurel, DE

Maria Lee-Alverez
Western Hills Design
Technology, OH

Jeffery Little
Pikeville H.S., KY

Kathy Lucas
Casey Co. High School
Liberty, KY

Neva Lyon
Jefferson H.S., OR

Barbara Malkas
Taconic H.S., MA

JoAnn Manor
Orchard View H.S., MI

Barbara Martin
Reading H.S., MA

Earl Martin
Garfield Sr. H.S., CA

Maggie Matthews
Shorewood H.S.,WA

Robert Mayton
Allen Central High School
Eastern, KY

Peggy McCoy
Alternative #1, CO

Jill McNew
Street School, OK

Vicki Mockbee
Caesar Rodney H.S.
Camden, DE

Dr. Judy Moody
Starkville H.S., MS

Guillermo Muhlman
PVPA High School, MA

Brenda Mullins
Knott Co. Central H.S.
Hindman, KY

Amy Murphy
Spain Park H.S., AL

Barbara Murphy
Benjamin School, FL

Barry North
Rivendell Interstate Regional
High School Orford, NH

Mary Ollie
Caldwell H.S., ID

Angela Pence
Wolfe County H.S.
Campton, KY

Roy Penix
Prestonburg H.S., KY

Gerard Pepe
North Babylon H.S., NY

Alicia Peterson
Haverford H.S., PA

Frank Petkunas
Bradley-Bourbonnais
Community H.S., IL

Lou Pompilli
Abington Senior H.S., PA

Marcia Powell
Central City School District, IA

Cindy Powell-Burgess
Affton H.S., MO

Genevieve Prendergast
Benedictine Academy, NJ

Hilary Reilly
Capitol Region Career
& Technical School, NY

Robin Ringland
Stanwood H.S., WA

George Robertson
Stanwood H.S., WA

Jocelyn Roger
Squalicum H.S., WA

Dena Rosenberger
El Capitan H.S., CA

Lance Rudiger
Potsdam H.S., NY

John Scali
Newark, DE

Noreen Scarpitto
Reading H.S., MA

Sarah Schenk
East Syracuse-Minoa
High School, NY

Fred Schiess
Stanwood H.S., WA

James Senicola
Baldwin Senior H.S., NY

Hannah Sevian
Chelsea H.S., MA

Margaret Showalter
El Dorado H.S., NM

Angela Skaggs
Magoffin County H.S.
Salyersville, KY

Karin Skipper
Mid-Carolina H.S., SC

Mark Smith
Arcola High School, IL

Valerie Stone
Whitnall H.S., WI

Mary Stoukides
Toll Gate High School
Warwick, RI

Jim Swanson
Saugus H.S., MA

Kathy Swingle
Rehoboth, DE

Mary Thomaskutty
Owensboro H.S., KY

Karen Tokos
Newton North H.S., MA

Jeffert Scott Townsend
Powell Co. High School
Stanton, KY

Betsy Uhing
Grand Island Sr.
H.S., NE

Josh Underwood
Deming High School
Mount Olivet, KY

Andrew Uy
Venice H.S., CA

Amy Voss
Grand Island Sr.
H.S., NE

Elaine Weil
Berlin, MD

Jen Wilson
Wilmington, DE

Sarah Wilson
Caldwell H.S., ID

Carrie Woolfolk
Louisa Country H.S., VA

Doug Yenney
Dayton H.S., WA

Corey Zirker
Wahluke H.S., WA

Bruce ZuWalick
Lymann Hall H.S., CT

Special Features

Chem at Work
Todd Fishlin
Mount Kisco, NY

Chem Poetry
Mala Radhakrishnan
MIT, Cambridge, MA

Welcome to Active Chemistry: Your Guide to Success

A Five-Minute Introduction

Active Chemistry is different from a traditional chemistry program. It contains all the chemistry content you need to teach, but it is presented in an excitingly innovative and meaningful way. It has qualitative analysis, quantitative analysis, electrochemistry, thermodynamics, and kinetics, as you would expect—but not where you would expect to find them. In a traditional course, you might teach atomic structure in the fall, chemical reactions in the winter, and polar molecules in the spring. In *Active Chemistry*, students are introduced to chemistry concepts on a need-to-know basis and they begin by exploring *Movie Special Effects*, *Fun with the Periodic Table*, and *Artist as Chemist*.

In this eight-chapter textbook, you will find all the chemistry you need to teach in a school year. You will also find that the important concepts that your students need are covered in several chapters in a spiraling process that allows students to see the concepts in a variety of contexts and at a variety of depths.

It is recommended that you start the year with the first chapter, *Movie Special Effects*. Your students will be introduced to many of the basic chemistry concepts that they will need to understand in the following chapters. When you start a chapter, for example, *Chapter 2, Fun with the Periodic Table*, your students learn about the **Chapter Challenge**, which will be the focus of their work. At the outset of *Fun with the Periodic Table*, students are challenged to develop a game based on the periodic table. This game will be a learning tool for the students as they develop the game and also a tool for review as they play the game.

To meet their challenge, students must:

- Devise a game that uses facts about the elements found in the periodic table.

- Decide what kind of a game they will model their game after—a card game, a computer game, a board game—there are no limitations.

- Decide on the rules of the game so that advancement toward a goal is achievable.

Determine how to structure the game, so that it is a useful learning tool, and fun to play within a reasonable time frame

How can the students get started? How can they complete such a challenge without the necessary chemistry knowledge? That's what makes *Active Chemistry* unique. Students are introduced to the chemistry they can use to complete the challenge on a need-to-know basis.

Before the chapter activities begin, a classroom discussion takes place to determine the **Criteria for Success**. The class decides what is expected in an excellent game and how those components should be graded. For instance, they may decide that the rubric for grading should rate the following qualities:

- How well the game shows an understanding of the periodic table.

- How well the game enables players to learn about the periodic table.

- How interesting the game is to play.

They will also need to decide whether each factor carries equal weight, or if some have a greater value. In this way, students will be aware of what is required for an excellent presentation before they begin and have a sense of ownership. They will revisit the criteria for readjustments before work on the challenge is finalized.

The second day begins with the first of nine sections. As one section is completed, the next one starts. *Active Chemistry* is an investigation-based curriculum.

For example, look at *Chapter 2, Section 1: Periodicity and Trends: Organizing a Store*. Each section begins with an illustration that you can use to introduce some of the aspects of the coming section. More importantly, the illustration is used to engage the interests of the students with a simple *What Do You See?* question. Students' answers to this question need not be correct, but it is important that they provide some response to the question.

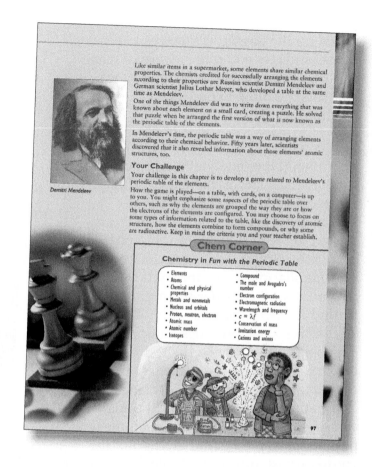

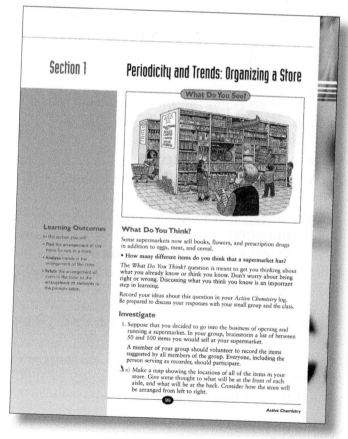

Active Chemistry

Based on the cognitive sciences, the question alerts you to be aware of what students think. You can then enhance students' learning experience based on that knowledge.

This is followed by the *What Do You Think?* question: "How many different items do you think that a supermarket has?" This question is directly related to the activity of supermarket organization and indirectly related to the periodic table. The point of this activity is to have students think about how a very familiar place (a supermarket) is organized and consider the organization behind the periodic table. The *What Do You Think?* response provides an opportunity for a writing assignment in the *Active Chemistry* log or a brief classroom discussion. For you, the teacher, this section is an opportunity to find out what students know. Formally, you can say that these questions elicit the students' prior understanding and are part of the constructivist approach. Typically, students write a response for one minute, followed by two minutes of discussion. You should not try to reach closure here. The question opens the conversation.

Students then begin the *Investigate*. In *Section 2: Elements and Their Properties* in *Chapter 2*, they are involved in a number of investigations that teach them about physical and chemical properties of some elements. From the results of these experiments, the students begin to see the differences between metals and nonmetals and how they would apply this knowledge to the organization of a periodic table. At the same time, they learn laboratory skills and safety procedures.

Chem Talk summarizes the chemistry principles and provides some historical background to enhance the experience, presenting students with text, illustrations, and photographs that provide greater insight into the chemistry concepts.

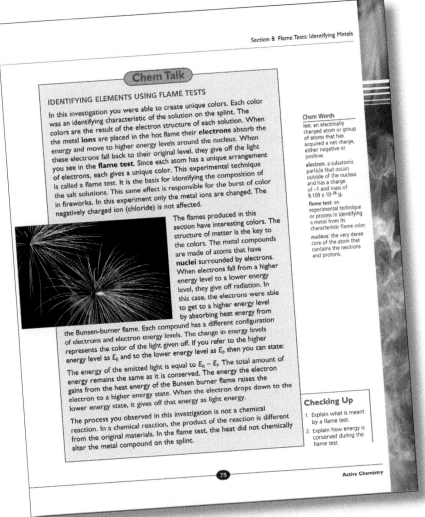

Words that may be unfamiliar to the student are highlighted. To provide reading support, the words are also defined in *Chem Words. Checking Up* questions are designed to guide student reading toward the highlights of the text.

What Do You Think Now? revisits the original *What Do You Think?* question and provides an opportunity for the student to reflect on any changes in understanding. You can use this exercise in a similar manner with a written response in the *Active Chemistry* log, followed by a short classroom discussion.

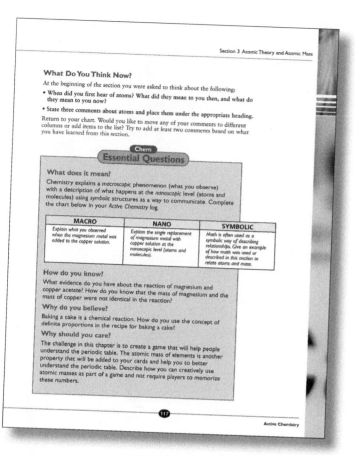

This is also an appropriate time to return to the **What Do You See?** illustration, so the students can reinterpret it in light of their investigations.

One of the inherent difficulties in learning chemistry is the perceived disconnect between observations in the lab, relating the observations to what is happening at the atomic level, and how this is communicated in equations and formulas.

Active Chemistry bridges these issues and makes them relevant with **Chem Essential Questions.** First, **What does it mean?** leads the students to make connections through questions about what is observed at the **MACRO** level, what is happening at the **NANO** level, and how this is shown in **SYMBOLIC** terms. A **How do you know?** question asks the students to describe observations from their investigations that led to this new knowledge. **Why do you believe?** asks the students to use the new knowledge in everyday applications. Finally, **Why should you care?** makes this new knowledge immediately relevant by asking the student to place it in the context of the **Chapter Challenge.**

Reflecting on the Section and the Challenge provides a brief summary of the section and again relates the section to the larger challenge of developing a game based on the periodic table.

Students are asked about the specifics of the section and required to apply their knowledge of physical and chemical properties of elements in the **Chem to Go** homework assignment. Often, the homework will include an additional investigation, **Preparing for the Chapter Challenge**, which enables students to do some background work toward their final challenge.

Following the **Chem to Go** homework, many sections have **Inquiring Further** exercises. These exercises often require the student to design and carry out an experiment. Typically, the **Inquiring Further** option will be more challenging and can be used for extra credit or as extensions for highly motivated students.

In the middle of each chapter you will find a *Chapter Mini-Challenge*. This provides the students an opportunity to try out one or two ideas that they are considering using for their challenge. Having this chance to see what works and what doesn't work makes the final challenge much more successful. Such feedback is important for the *Engineering Design Cycle* process.

The *Chem You Learned* lists key concepts from the chapter in the meaningful context of a sentence. The *Chem Chapter Challenge* section begins with a review of the sections and the key concepts. Before the students present their periodic table game, the *Criteria for Success* should be reviewed by the class and finalized. *Preparing for the Chapter Challenge* outlines the steps that the students may follow in completing the challenge.

The chapter concludes as the students share their periodic table games and spend time playing the games developed by other groups. The creation of the game requires the students to transfer knowledge from their weeks of investigation into a new context. This facilitates learning and each team's creativity makes each project unique.

Chem Connections to Other Sciences helps students appreciate that the fundamental science principles they are learning are used across the breadth of scientific inquiry. Modern scientific research depends on interaction between disciplines, and this feature allows students to gain insight into that interaction. *Extending the Connection* offers a more comprehensive look at the issues of our times and some of the major scientific breakthroughs that have altered the direction of history.

In addition to the *Chapter Challenge,* there are traditional assessment questions provided in the *Chem Practice Test*. These are in addition to the hundreds of questions asked throughout each chapter.

Chem at Work introduces the students to people who use the chemistry in the chapter as part of their careers. Reading about their lives and jobs starts students thinking about their own future careers.

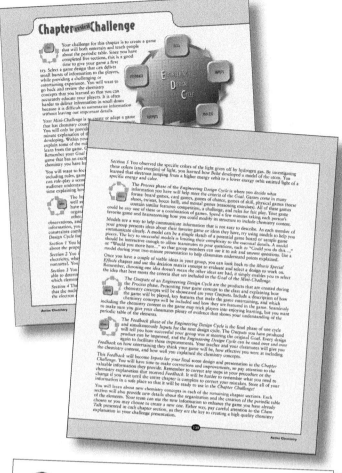

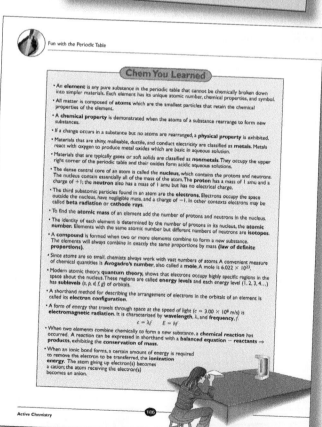

Features of Active Chemistry

1. Scenario

Each *Active Chemistry* chapter opens with an engaging *Scenario*. Students from diverse backgrounds and localities have been interviewed in order to find situations which are not only realistic but meaningful to the high school population. The *Scenario* sets the stage for the *Chapter Challenge* that immediately follows. Many teachers choose to read the *Scenario* aloud to the class as a way of introducing the new chapter.

2. Chapter Challenge

The heart and soul of *Active Chemistry* are the *Chapter Challenges*. They provide the students a purpose for all of the work and provide the rationale for learning. One of the most common complaints that teachers hear from students is, "Why am I learning this?" In *Active Chemistry*, students do not raise this question. Similarly, teachers do not have to answer, "Because someday it will be useful to you." The complaint is avoided because on day one of the chapter students are presented with a challenge that, in essence, becomes their job for the next few weeks.

The beauty of the challenges lies in the variety of tasks, which allows students of different interests and skills to excel. Students who express themselves artistically will have an opportunity to shine in a chapter such as *Artist as Chemist*. Students who enjoy games may find *Fun with the Periodic Table* a favorite. Other students who enjoy being "on-stage" may find their niche with *Cool Chemistry Show* and *Cookin' Chem*.

The challenges are not contrived situations. For example, the basis of many extravagant special effects in movies are the chemical principles in *Movie Special Effects*. The actual techniques of crime investigations are used in *CSI Chemistry*. The students will see that they are doing real projects and learning the chemistry to understand their work.

3. Chem Corner

The chemistry content in each chapter is summarized in a preview illustration. The illustration shows the students focused on the activities and the challenge, while the teacher sees the chemistry that the students will learn.

4. Criteria for Success

In creating *Active Chemistry*, the original thought was that the generation of the challenge was enough and that all else would fall in place. Upon reflection, we soon realized that the criteria for success must also be delineated. When students agree to the rubric by which their work will be measured, research has shown that the students perform better and achieve more. It makes sense. In the simplest situation of cleaning a lab room, the teacher may simply state, "Please clean up the lab." The results are often a minimal cleanup. If the teacher begins by asking, "What does a clean lab room look like?" and students and teacher jointly list the attributes of a clean lab room (no paper on the floor, all beakers put away, all materials placed on the back of the lab tables, all power supplies unplugged and all water wiped up) the students respond differently and the cleanup is better.

Thus, the discussion of grading criteria and the creation of a grading rubric is a crucial ingredient for student success. After the introduction of the challenge, *Active Chemistry* requires a class discussion about the grading criteria. How much is required? What does an "A" challenge product look like? Should creativity be weighed more than delivery? When students are asked to include chemical principles in their explanations, is the expectation for three chemical principles or five? The criteria will be visited again at the end of the chapter, but at this point it establishes an expectation level that the students have set for themselves.

5. What Do You See?

An illustration introduces each section and asks the question *"What Do You See?"* The students are given a humorous preview of some of the concepts and tasks in that section. You can use this to engage the students' attention and interest. From the discussion, you can also observe what the students already know about the topics. It is not important at this point that students responses are correct or completely relevant.

6. Chem Poetry

Chem Poetry is yet another opportunity to present the chemistry content to students with different learning styles in a way that is meaningful and engaging. Through the use of language, rhyme and metaphor, the poems bring to life the chemistry concepts in a way that is playful, alive, and imaginative. The students will find the poems even more meaningful if they return to them at the *What Do You Think Now?* stage of the section.

7. What Do You Think?

During the past few years much has been written about a constructivist approach to learning. Videos of Harvard graduates, in caps and gowns, show that many are not able to explain correctly why it is colder in the winter than it is in the summer. These students have no doubt previously answered these questions correctly in fourth grade, in middle school, and then again in high school. How else would they have been accepted to Harvard? We believe that they never internalized the logic and understanding of the seasons. One reason for this problem is that they were never confronted by their misconceptions, and were never adequately shown why they should give up that belief system. Certainly, it is worth writing down a "textbook answer" on a test to secure a good grade, but to actually believe that answer requires a more thorough examination of competing explanations.

The best way to ascertain a student's prior understanding is through extensive interviewing. Much of the research in this area includes the results of such interviews. In a classroom, however, this one-on-one dialogue is rarely possible. The *What Do You Think?* question introduces each section in a way that elicits prior understandings. It gives students an opportunity to verbalize what they think about elements, atoms, or reactions before they embark on an investigation. The brief discussion of the range of answers brings the students closer to that part of his/her brain that understands elements, atoms, or reactions. The *What Do You Think?* question is not intended to produce a correct answer or a discussion of the features of each question. It is not intended that you bring the discussion to closure. The investigation that follows will provide that closure as experimental results are analyzed. The *What Do You Think?* question should take no more than a few minutes of class time. It is a critical lead into the chemistry investigation.

Students should be strongly encouraged to write their responses to the questions in their logs to ensure that they have, in fact, addressed their prior conceptions. After students have discussed their responses in their small groups, activate a class discussion. Ask students to comment on other students' answers which they found interesting. This may encourage students to exchange ideas without the fear of personally giving a "wrong" answer.

8. Investigate

Active Chemistry is a hands-on, minds-on curriculum. Students do chemistry; they do not read about doing chemistry. Each *Investigate* has instructions for each part of the investigation. Students are reminded that data, hypotheses, and conclusions should be recorded in their logs or laboratory manuals.

Investigations are the opportunity for students to garner the knowledge that they will need to complete the *Chapter Challenge*. Students will understand the chemical principle involved because they have investigated it. In *Active Chemistry*, if a student is asked, "How do you know?" the response is, "Because I did an experiment!"

Recognizing that many students know how to read, but do not like reading, *Background Information* often is provided within the context of the section. Students have demonstrated that they will read when the information is required for them to continue with their investigation.

Occasionally, the investigation will require the entire class to participate in a large, group activity. On other occasions, you may decide that a specific investigation is best done as a demonstration. This would be appropriate if there is limited equipment for that one investigation, or the facilities are not available for every student to do the activity. Viewing demonstrations on an ongoing basis, however, is not what *Active Chemistry* is about.

Icons throughout the investigations alert students to safety issues that should be given full attention. Students are reminded of all safety rules throughout the program. An overview of safety rules for the chemistry classroom, as well as a safety contract, is available at the end of this *Teacher's Edition* Introduction and on the *Teacher Resources CD*.

Most of the *Investigates* and on your Teacher Resources CD require between one and two 45-minute class periods. Considering current trends in class scheduling, there are so many time structures that it is difficult to predict how *Active Chemistry* will best fit your schedule. Another effect on pacing is the achievement and preparation level of your students. For example, in a given investigation students may be required to complete a graph of their data. If the students have never been exposed to graphing, this could require a two-period lesson to teach the basics of graphing.

Active Chemistry is accessible to all students. You are in the best position to make accommodations that reflect the needs of your students.

9. Chem Talk

Sometimes it is difficult for students to make the conceptual leap from doing an investigation to connecting the ideas to a chemical principle. Indeed, if you consider the theory of multiple intelligences, some students grasp concepts more easily by reading. *Chem Talk* summarizes the chemistry principles and includes chemical formulas and equations when appropriate. It presents students with text, illustrations, photographs, and a historical perspective that provide greater insight. If sample problems or important laws are integral to the lesson, they will be thoroughly explained in *Chem Talk*.

10. Chem Words

Science has a language of its own, and some concepts are more efficiently communicated when vocabulary is introduced. Certainly, in order to fully participate in science, students need to have an understanding of this language. As a part of *Chem Talk*, *Chem Words* highlights the important terms. These words are pulled outside the text area and redefined. Such support helps students understand the process of learning as they note important ideas within the text. *Chem Words* will also be found in the *Glossary*.

As in the world of science, the introduction of vocabulary follows the understanding of the concept. ABC (Activity Before Concept) and CBV (Concept Before Vocabulary) model the science and the sequence of learning practiced in *Active Chemistry*.

11. Checking Up

Another important part of the *Chem Talk* is the *Checking Up*. Each section has several of these questions about the section in the margins.

The student can use these for self-examination. In addition, you can assign these as homework or as Chem Log entries for the students to answer as the *Chem Talk* section is read.

12. What Do You Think Now?

This section offers the student (and you) the opportunity to return to the *What Do You Think?* questions to informally assess changes in knowledge and understanding. This reflection is beneficial to both the students and to you. If you see widespread lapses in understanding, you may spend some time helping the students or you might wait for the opportunity to use the spiraling design of the curriculum to foster greater understanding. This is also an appropriate time to return to the *What Do You See?* illustration as an opportunity for students to reinterpret the illustration in the light of their investigations.

13. Chem Essential Questions

Chemistry can be a difficult subject for many students. One of the reasons for this is the lack of organizing principles as it is traditionally taught. For many students, chemistry is a vast collection of unrelated facts that one needs to memorize for the test. *Active Chemistry* has developed four questions that capture the organizing principles of chemistry and make understanding more holistic and accessible.

- What does it mean?
- How do you know?
- Why do you believe?
- Why should you care?

If the students can answer these four questions (and they can), they will likely keep their newly learned principles and concepts forever.

The first essential question, *What does it mean?* requires the students to describe the content

of the section and frame it at three levels of understanding. At the MACRO level, the students will be able to describe what they observed during the investigation. At the NANO level, the students will be able to describe what is happening at the atomic level that causes the macroscopic observations. The NANO level then is translated into the shorthand of chemistry, the SYMBOLIC level. This is the level of formulas, graphs, models, diagrams, and the letters representing the elements.

The second essential question, *How do you know?* is answered by a description of the experiment that they performed during the *Investigate*.

The third essential question, *Why do you believe?* requires the students to link the investigation and its results to an everyday phenomenon or event in the world outside the chemistry lab.

Finally, the last question, *Why should you care?* requires the students to make a direct link from the section to the *Chapter Challenge*. This serves two purposes: students have an immediate need to know this information and can begin planning a response to the *Chapter Challenge*.

14. Reflecting on the Section and the Challenge

At the close of each section, the students are often so involved with the completion of the single experiment that the larger context of the investigation is lost. *Reflecting on the Section and the Challenge* is the opportunity for students to place their new insights into the context of the chapter and the *Chapter Challenge*. If the *Chapter Challenge* is considered a completed puzzle, each section is a jigsaw piece.

When students complete half of the *Investigates*, they will be able to fit jigsaw pieces together and complete the *Mini-Challenge*. This section ensures that the students do not forget about the larger context and continue their personal momentum toward completion of the challenge.

15. Chem to Go

This section provides additional questions and problems that can be completed outside of class as homework. Some of the problems are applications of the principles involved in the preceding section. Others are replications of the work in the *Investigate*. Still others provide an opportunity to transfer the results of the investigation to the context of the *Chapter Challenge*. Often, the homework will include an additional question, *Preparing for the Chapter Challenge*, which provides students with the chance to do some background work toward their final challenge. You may wish to assign these questions to the entire class or to those students who would benefit most from the extra work.

16. Inquiring Further

Following the *Chem to Go* sections, many sections have *Inquiring Further* exercises. These exercises often require the student to design and carry out an experiment. Students can put into practice the technique, approaches, and knowledge they have acquired in the section and expand upon it to gain new information. The *Inquiring Further* exercises can be assigned as independent study or as a class extension to the investigation.

17. Chapter Mini-Challenge

In *Active Chemistry*, the challenges require students to use an *Engineering Design Cycle*. The *Mini-Challenge* helps students familiarize themselves with design principles. It allows students to set some preliminary goals for their challenge. Using the input from the first four sections, students can integrate the input and goals to design a product for testing. The *Mini-Challenge* presentation serves as the output for their plan. Students will receive feedback from the experience (from the other students and from you), and use this feedback later when they refine the design of their product, the *Chapter Challenge*.

18. Chem You Learned

This section provides a list of chemistry concepts that were studied in the context of the *Investigate* and the *Chem Talk*. It provides students with a sense of accomplishment and serves as a quick review of all that was learned. Students also can use this list to select those chemical principles that are appropriate for their *Chapter Challenge* project.

19. Chem Chapter Challenge

The *Chapter Assessment* is the return to the *Chapter Challenge* and *Criteria*. The students are ready to complete the challenge. They are able to view the challenge with a clarity that has emerged from the completion of the *Investigate* activities and the feedback from the *Mini-Challenge*. Students are able to review the chapter as they discuss the synthesis of the information into the required context of the challenge. They should have some class time to work together to complete the challenge and to present their project.

In many chemistry courses, all students are expected to converge on the same solution. In *Active Chemistry*, each group is expected to have a unique solution. All solutions must have correct chemistry, but there is ample room for creativity on the students' part. This is one of the features that captures the imagination of students who often have previously chosen not to enroll in chemistry classes. In addition, business leaders want to hire people who know how to work effectively in groups and how to complete projects. This is exactly what is required in each *Chapter Challenge*.

20. Chem Connections to Other Sciences

The *Chem Connections to Other Sciences* highlights how the fundamental ideas students learn in each chapter relate to many of the other sciences students will study. By appreciating the connections among various science disciplines, scientists develop a more in-depth understanding of nature.

21. Extending the Connection

The *Chem Connections to Other Sciences* shows students that the chemistry concepts they studied in each chapter are also basic to many other sciences. The chemistry they are learning is fundamental in the understanding of the concepts that they will study in all the other sciences. *Extending the Connection* delves deeper into one or two of these connections. It gives students an opportunity to examine a particular relationship to another science in greater depth.

22. Chem at Work

This section highlights three individuals whose work or hobby is illustrative of the chemistry in the *Chapter Challenge*. *Chem at Work* speaks to the authenticity of the challenge. The profiles show how important chemistry can be in a variety of careers requiring varying educational backgrounds.

23. Chem Practice Test

The *Chem Practice Test* provides additional assessment opportunities in the format of the traditional state assessments. Students can use the *Chem Practice Test* as a gauge to find out how well they learned the chemistry contained in each chapter. Before beginning the test, students should be reminded to go back to their *Active Chemistry* logs and homework to review the hundreds of traditional questions and problems they have answered throughout the chapter in the form of the *Chem to Go*, *Checking Up*, *What Do You Think Now?* and *Chem Essential Questions*.

Overview of Meeting the Needs of All Students: Differentiated Instruction

Augmentation and Accommodations

This section is designed to help you to help struggling students. Every section has its own table with specific information that identifies learning issues you may encounter. The table also gives the location of the issue within each section and recommends instructional and management strategies for helping students compensate for their difficulties. The teaching of necessary skills has been labeled *Augmentation*. Compensation techniques have been labeled *Accommodations*.

LEARNING ISSUE	REFERENCE	AUGMENTATION AND ACCOMMODATIONS

To understand how augmentation and accommodation can be used as tools by teachers to help struggling students access each section, take an example from **Section 1** in the chapter *Cookin' Chem*. Assume some students in the class cannot follow complex multi-step directions. What will these students learn about conduction, convection and radiation, if they cannot read the text or follow the specific directions embedded in it? Their confusion quickly results in the cessation of their learning and probably the distraction of other students. To prevent this, you can either provide the students with directions they can understand (accommodation) or you can teach them direction-following skills (augmentation). Whether you augment students' skills or find ways to accommodate their weaknesses depends upon your goal in the each lesson.

Augmentation of prerequisite skills involves the direct teaching of the skill. In this example, the you might take the group and show them where the directions are written for **Part A: Transferring Heat Energy** and help the students read them one at a time, completing each task as they go. The advantages of augmentation are that the students begin to develop the skills they need to learn independently. The disadvantage is that other students who are allowed to move through **Part A** independently will finish sooner, possibly losing interest or motivation, as they wait for the other group. The best plan is to differentiate the investigation at that point, providing the independent students a related **extension** or **anchor activity** while the other students learn to read the directions. Extensions have been provided in the lesson under the heading *"Inquiring Further."* Anchor activities are those tasks that can be done independently by everyone. For example, taking notes on the *Chem Talk* or creating flash cards from the new vocabulary could serve as anchor activities for this lesson.

Accommodation of students has the advantage of allowing the student to move along with the group using a teacher-provided scaffold that helps the student compensate for the difficulty in direction reading. In this case, the accommodation might be to place the student with poor reading skills with other students who are better in that area. You could provide a different set of directions in which the language is simpler, each step is labeled, and space is provided for the tasks required. The disadvantage of doing this is that the student will likely need this accommodation for every set of directions until the skill is learned.

Strategies for Students with Limited English Language Proficiency

The *Strategies for Students with Limited English Language Proficiency* allow you to adjust your teaching to differentiate for English-language learners. The augmentations (broken down to the section level) offer suggestions and also indicate potential interference points which could disrupt the students' engagement in the activities. By focusing on words and their derivations, which may not be in the student's receptive or expressive vocabulary, teachers can help students meet the linguistic challenges of the particular subject. Also, the use of discussion as a means of bridging the oral language development to the content development can add to a richer experience for the students and facilitate the teacher's instruction. As teachers plan their instruction, they can consult the augmentations to determine at which points to best incorporate these considerations.

NOTES _____

_____

_____

Students' Prior Conceptions: Overview and 7E Tools

Research in cognitive learning and how students establish foundations for understanding science have identified various categories of student conceptions that are alternative frameworks for understanding science. Definitions for these categories are cited below:

Preconceived notions—Popular conceptions rooted in everyday experiences.

Example: Many people believe that water flowing underground must flow in streams because the water they see at Earth's surface flows in streams.

Nonscientific beliefs—Include views learned by students from sources other than scientific education, such as religious or mythical teachings.

Example: Some students have learned through religious instruction about an abbreviated history of Earth and its life forms. The disparity between this widely held belief and the scientific evidence for evolution, dating back to pre-historical times, has led to considerable controversy in the teaching of science.

Conceptual misunderstandings—Arise when students are taught scientific information in a way that does not motivate them to confront paradoxes and conflicts resulting from their own preconceived notions and nonscientific beliefs.

Example: To deal with their confusion, students construct faulty models that usually are so weak that the students themselves are insecure about the concepts.

Vernacular misconceptions—Arise from the use of words that mean one thing in everyday life and another in a scientific context (e.g., "work").

Example: A geology professor noted that students have difficulty with the idea that glaciers retreat, because they picture the glacier stopping, turning around, and moving in the opposite direction. Substitution of the word "melt" for "retreat" helps reinforce the correct interpretation that the front end of the glacier simply melts faster than the ice advances.

Factual misconceptions—False conceptions often learned at an early age and retained unchallenged into adulthood.

Example: The idea that "lightning never strikes twice in the same place" is clearly nonsense, but that notion may be buried somewhere in a student's belief system.

In order for teachers to break down student prior conceptions and align their knowledge to current theory they must:

- Identify students' prior knowledge.
- Provide a forum for students to confront their misconceptions.
- Help students reconstruct and internalize their knowledge, based on scientific models.

The *What Do You Think?* and *Investigates* and sections presented in *Active Chemistry* are designed so that teachers are informed about basic student prior knowledge and have the tools with which to break down alternative ideas that may be strongly held by students.

Each chapter of *Active Chemistry* identifies lists of commonly held student preconceptions and offers opportunities for students to test their conceptual ideas. Students continually are asked to explain their reasoning, which enables you to work with students to root out prior conceptions.

Active Chemistry uses a 7E learning-cycle model. The steps (phases) of the 7E learning cycle are Elicit, Engage, Explore, Explain, Elaborate, Extend, and Evaluate.

The Elicit, Explain, Elaborate, and Extend phases of this learning cycle offer valuable tools for you to interview students to ascertain if prior belief systems leading to misconceptions continue to exist. You have the opportunity to encourage students to compare their preconceptions with their data analysis of the Explore stage of the learning cycle. The critical question, *"Why do you believe?"* and the Evaluate phase enable students to root out personally held misconceptions and to align new conceptual knowledge with current scientific thinking. Constant and open classroom discussions are powerful tools when wielded wisely through the listening and evaluative ear of a classroom educator. The more you understand about how students learn, the more effective you become at crafting classroom interactions to deliver the most effective learning.

Pacing Guides for Teachers

A chart showing the approximate number of weeks and days required to cover each *Active Chemistry* chapter is provided below. Your pace may be slower or faster depending on a number of variables, including the grade level of your students and your experience in using the *Active Chemistry* curriculum. The chart is based on an academic year of 36 weeks (180 days).

The eight chapters are listed in order across the first row, beginning with *Movie Special Effects*. The second row indicates the approximate number of weeks to complete each chapter in a typical classroom setting. Weeks are translated into days in the third row. In general, the average time for each chapter is about 22 days, though *Chapter 1* and *Chapter 2* likely will take longer than others. As you can see, this chart accounts for only 176 days, which allows time for school events, review and testing periods, and other interruptions to the schedule.

This chart is only intended to provide an overview of the time required for the entire year. For a more detailed description of what is suggested for each chapter, see the *Pacing Guide* that accompanies each chapter.

PACING GUIDE OVERVIEW

Chapter	1 Movie Special Effects	2 Fun with the Periodic Table	3 Artist as Chemist	4 Chemical Dominoes	5 Ideal Toy	6 Cool Chemistry Show	7 Cookin' Chem	8 CSI Chemistry	Total Weeks/Days
Weeks	4.8	4.8	4.0	4.8	4.2	4.0	4.4	4.2	35.2
Days	24	24	20	24	21	20	22	21	176

Active Chemistry and the National Science Education Standards

Active Chemistry was designed and developed to provide teachers with instructional strategies that model the philosophy from the National Science Education Standards:

Guide and facilitate learning

- Focus and support inquiries while interacting with students.

- Orchestrate discourse among students about scientific ideas.

- Challenge students to accept and share responsibility for their own learning.

- Recognize and respond to student diversity; encourage all to participate fully in science learning.

- Encourage and model the skills of scientific inquiry as well as the curiosity and openness to new ideas and data and skepticism that characterize science.

Engage in ongoing assessment of their teaching and student learning

- Use multiple methods and systematically gather data about student understanding and ability.

- Analyze assessment data to guide teaching.

- Guide students in self-assessment.

Design and manage learning environments that provide students with time, space and resources needed for learning science

- Structure the time available so students are able to engage in extended investigations.

- Create a setting for student work that is flexible and supportive of science inquiry.

- Make available tools, materials, media, and technological resources accessible to students.

- Identify and use resources outside of school.

Develop communities of science learners that reflect the intellectual rigor of scientific attitudes and social values conducive to science learning

- Display and demand respect for diverse ideas, skills, and experiences of students.

- Enable students to have significant voice in decisions about content and context of work and require students to take responsibility for the learning of all members of the community.

- Nurture collaboration among students.

- Structure and facilitate ongoing formal and informal discussion based on shared understanding of rules.

- Model and emphasize the skills, attitudes and values of scientific inquiry.

Use Authentic Assessment Standards

- Features claimed to be measured are actually measured.

- Students have adequate opportunity to demonstrate their achievement and understanding.

- Assessment tasks are authentic and developmentally appropriate, set in familiar context, and engaging to students with different interests and experiences.

- Assesses student understanding as well as knowledge.

- Improve classroom practice and plan curricula.

- Develop self-directed learners.

ACTIVE CHEMISTRY AND THE NATIONAL SCIENCE EDUCATION STANDARDS

Active Chemistry Chapter	Chapter 1 Movie Special Effects	Chapter 1 Fun with the Periodic Table	Chapter 3 Artist as Chemist
Physical Science			
Structure of atoms	•	•	
Structure and properties of matter	•	•	•
Chemical reactions	•	•	•
Conservation of energy			
Increase in disorder			
Interactions of energy and matter		•	
Unifying Concepts and Processes			
Systems, order and organization	•	•	•
Evidence, models and explanations	•	•	
Constancy, change and measurement	•	•	
Science as Inquiry			
Identify questions and concepts that guide scientific investigations	•	•	•
Design and conduct scientific investigations	•	•	•
Use technology and mathematics to improve investigations	•	•	•
Formulate and revise scientific explanations and models using logic and evidence	•	•	
Communicate and defend a scientific argument	•	•	•
Understand scientific inquiry	•	•	•
Science and Technology			
Identify a problem or design an opportunity	•	•	•
Propose designs and choose between alternate solutions	•	•	•
Implement a proposed solution	•	•	•
Evaluate the solutions and their consequences	•		•
Communicate the problem, process, and solution	•	•	•
Understand science and technology	•	•	•
Science in Personal and Social Perspectives	•	•	•
History and Nature of Science			
Science as a human endeavor	•	•	•
Nature of scientific knowledge	•	•	•
Historical perspectives	•	•	•

ACTIVE CHEMISTRY AND THE NATIONAL SCIENCE EDUCATION STANDARDS

Chapter 4 Chemical Dominoes	Chapter 5 Ideal Toy	Chapter 6 Cool Chemistry Show	Chapter 7 Cookin' Chem	Chapter 8 CSI Chemistry
	•	•		•
		•		•
•	•	•	•	•
•		•		
•				
•		•	•	•
•	•			•
•	•	•	•	•
•	•	•	•	
•	•	•	•	•
•	•	•	•	•
•	•	•	•	•
•	•			•
•	•	•	•	•
•	•	•	•	•
•	•	•	•	•
•	•	•	•	•
•	•	•		•
•	•		•	•
•	•	•	•	•
•	•	•	•	•
•	•	•	•	•
•	•	•	•	•
•	•	•	•	•
•	•		•	•

Active Chemistry Curriculum Strengths

Problem-Based Learning Model

Each chapter begins with an engaging scenario that challenges the students and sets the stage for the learning activities and assessments to follow. Chapter content and *Investigates* are selectively aimed at providing students with the knowledge and skills needed to respond effectively to the challenge. This scenario-challenge framework provides the students with a new focus and topic in successive chapters and covers a wide variety of student interests.

Multiple Exposure Curriculum

The thematic nature of the course requires students to continually revisit fundamental chemistry principles throughout the semester, extending and deepening their understanding of these principles as they apply them in new contexts. This repeated exposure fosters the retention of content and process as well as the transfer of learning. The development of critical-thinking skills also is promoted by multiple exposure and application.

Inquiry-Based Learning

All of the 7–9 sections per chapter routinely involve inquiry at some level. In some sections, students are required to design an experiment to explore a concept. At other times, they collect data and interpret that data to formulate a new concept. Students regularly are asked to answer questions about what they think and what they do, as well as to support their statements with concrete data. "Activity Before Concept" (ABC) is at the heart of inquiry-based learning. The students always have a common lab experience on which to base their understanding of the concept. For the same reason, it is important to demonstrate a concept before exposing students to the vocabulary associated with the concept, as in "Concept Before Vocabulary" (CBV).

Constructivist Approach

Students continually are asked to explore how they think about certain situations. As they investigate each new situation, they are challenged to either explain observed phenomena using an existing paradigm, or to develop a more consistent one. This approach can be used to help students recognize previous notions and to abandon these in favor of more powerful ideas offered by scientists.

Authentic Assessment

As the culmination of each chapter, students are required to demonstrate their ability to use their newly acquired knowledge by adequately meeting the challenge posed in the chapter introduction. Students are then evaluated on the degree to which they accomplish this performance task using a rubric based on their own input. The curriculum also includes other methods and instruments for authentic assessments, as well as nontraditional procedures for evaluating and rewarding desirable achievements.

Cooperative Grouping Assignments

Use of cooperative groups is integral to the curriculum as students work together in small groups to acquire the knowledge needed to address the series of challenges presented through the chapter scenarios. Today's business model requires employees to work cooperatively in small groups to accomplish business goals. Students learn to value the abilities and contributions of others while maintaining a focus on the group goal of providing a meaningful response to the *Chapter Challenge*.

Problem Solving

For the curriculum to be both meaningful and relevant to students, problem solving related to technological applications is an essential component. Problem solving ranges from simple numerical calculations in which a single result is expected, to more involved decision-making situations where multiple alternatives must be compared. In some sections, students are asked to compare class data and determine which data is useful and valid and to suggest reasons for other data falling short of this goal. Seen in its entirety, each chapter is a large problem to be solved with multiple correct solutions and opportunities for design change before completion.

Challenging Learning Extensions

Throughout the text, a variety of *Inquiring Further* and *Preparing for the Chapter Challenge* exercises are provided for more motivated students. These extensions range from more challenging design tasks, to enrichment readings, to intriguing and unusual problems. Many of the extensions provide additional opportunities for the oral and written expression of students' ideas.

Research-Based Model

Active Chemistry relies upon the proven NSF developmental process as well as the most up-to-date research in pedagogy and learning theory. The research-based NSF process, with its strict criteria and standards, usually takes three to four years to complete. The curriculum is written and tested in the classroom in the pilot test. Following data collection and evaluation, the curriculum is rewritten and retested in the field test classrooms. Following a second evaluation by a nationally recognized independent evaluation team, the curriculum is rewritten again. Expert review panels guide the process at each stage.

Response to Equity Concerns

A diverse classroom is a wonderful place for exposure to the various cultures and experiences of other students. However, in most cases, it is unrealistic to expect a teacher to become "expert" in every culture represented and to be able to integrate these cultural perspective and expression into a comprehensive teaching program. *Active Chemistry* honors the diversity of students by allowing them creatively to bring their individual cultures and backgrounds into the classroom in the format of the *Chapter Challenge* — for example, through games, art, and cooking.

Active Chemistry—A Research-Based Curriculum

Active Chemistry has been funded by the National Science Foundation (NSF) and exemplifies the NSF's goals and objectives to improve science, mathematics, and technology education for all students. It is aligned with the National Science Education Standards (NSES) and follows the guidelines of the NSES to improve science content knowledge, thinking skills, and problem-solving abilities for all students, regardless of background or ability. The National Science Education Standards are guided by certain principles:

- Science is for all students.
- Learning science is an active process.
- School science reflects the intellectual and cultural traditions that characterize the practice of contemporary science.
- Improving science education is part of systemic education reform.

Adhering to these principles, *Active Chemistry* relies on the rigorous research of the NSF research on pedagogy and learning theory. The *Active Chemistry* curriculum consequently promotes positive student attitudes toward science and positive perceptions of the student as learner. It engages students through its use of real-world contexts and provides a deeper understanding of the role of science and technology in the workplace.

The NSF Research-Based Curriculum Development Process

The NSF Instructional Materials Development Program ensures that each of the curriculum development programs it has funded follows strict *research-based* criteria throughout the development process. The projects are extremely competitive and only awarded to development teams who have established themselves to be distinguished leaders in science education. The embedded *research-based* development process, with the strict criteria and standards for all NSF-funded programs, usually takes at least three to four years to complete.

A crucial component to all NSF development projects is the ongoing research and evaluation of the development process and materials by a nationally recognized independent evaluation team. The research and evaluation of the *Active Chemistry* project was comprehensive and provided both formative and summative information to the development team as well as to the NSF for review. The formative feedback and information is used to optimize the curricular revision process, and the summative evaluation examines the effectiveness of the curricular materials on teachers and students throughout the three-year process.

First Year of the Curriculum Development Process

Under the direction of a distinguished, active, and dynamic Advisory Board, the *Active Chemistry* Principal Investigators selected and then oversaw teams of writers chosen from top university science education departments, content-based science departments, specially selected high school teachers, and industry scientists to collaborate on the development of the first drafts of the curriculum materials. These lead authors, each a distinguished content specialist and/or educator from a leading university, also served as part of the Review Committee for *Active Chemistry* to assess each other's works for pedagogical strategies and content accuracy. The curriculum was then reviewed and evaluated by other leading educational specialists for pedagogy, content, safety, equity, readability, cognitive effectiveness, and efficacy. Based on those results, the curriculum was revised again. All new materials proceeded through the following system for development and revision:

- Approval by Content Review Committee, comprised of leading content experts
- Approval by the following consultants: science educators, master teachers, and cognitive scientists
- Microtesting by the development group. (A microtest is a series of tests of a few students with careful observation and follow-up interviews by the developers.)

Second Year of the Curriculum Development Process

The curriculum was then ready to be pilot-tested by a select group of high school teachers from across the country. After an extensive summer training course, these teachers spent the next year piloting the *Active Chemistry* program in their classrooms.

- The curriculum was pilot-tested by master teachers in their classrooms.
- Pilot materials, classes, teachers, and students were studied and evaluated based on an established evaluation and research design model.
- Materials were also reviewed by leading content experts and science educators to evaluate if the materials appropriately prepare students for later study in these subjects.
- Materials were then revised based on the pilot feedback, experts' reviews and evaluation and research reports.

Third Year of the Curriculum Development Process

The *Active Chemistry* curriculum was now ready to be field-tested by a broad range of high school teachers from across the country. After an extensive summer training course, these teachers spent the next year field-testing the materials in their classrooms. Like the pilot test, the research/evaluation component of the revision process is designed to inform the next iteration and revision of the materials.

- Field-testing of the materials was conducted in a wide range of classrooms by teachers with a wide range of experience and expertise.
- Field-test materials, classes, teachers, and students were studied and evaluated based on the evaluation and research-design model.
- Materials were then revised again based on the field-test feedback, experts' reviews and evaluation and research reports.

Fourth Year of the Curriculum Development Process

Additional consultant-specialists in cognitive psychology, assessment, technology, science education and equity continued to be brought into the *Active Chemistry* project to review the materials and secure its pedagogical approach and content basis. Finally, the product was turned over to the commercial publisher to mold into a commercial product.

The Active Learning Research-Based Instructional Model

The *Active Learning Instructional Model* has evolved out of this rigorous research-based development process. Much of the success of the *Active Learning Model* is attributed to the adherence to research on how people learn, what motivates students intellectually, and the National Science Education Standards. The *Active Learning Model* resonates strongly with some of the key findings in the cognitive psychology research (Bransford, J.D., M.S. Donovan, Pellegrino, 1999 and Bransford, J.D., A.L. Brown, and R.R. Cocking, 2000) as well as in the motivational processes in learning literature (Marzano, R., D. Pickering, G. Blackburn, D. Arrendondo, 1997, H. Dembo, R.Rueda, 1995). Many of the key authors, advisors, and consultants who worked on this curricula also have served as members on the committees that developed the National Science Education Standards (the Standards). Consequently, these curricula programs match the intent of the Standards in content, pedagogy, and assessment and are not retrofitted to meet the Standards. Two of the central components to the *Active Learning Instructional Model* are the *project-based learning model* (Delisle, R., 1997) and a directed inquiry approach (National Research Council, 2000). Each chapter centers around the need for the students to accomplish an authentic performance-task project that deals with real life situations. The students then do the directed inquiry-based activities within the chapter in order to learn the science necessary to complete their summative project. Although the cornerstone of the program is this authentic performance project, the **Chapter Challenge**, more traditional assessment tools, such as quizzes, tests and prompts, journal writing and lab books, are also provided and encouraged.

The *Active Learning Instructional Model* also has built into its curriculum design a number of additional features that point to greater learning and deeper understanding, such as:

• An approach to the curriculum design that assures student engagement in inquiry and promotes discovery in order to make understanding of the big ideas more likely

• Eliciting prior understandings from the students

• A continuum of methods for appropriately assessing the degree of student understanding

• Consideration of the role of predictable student misconceptions that need to be incorporated into the design of curriculum and its assessment tools.

Elaborating on the well-known 5E learning cycle instructional model (Bybee, 1997), with its discrete elements of: *engage, explore, explain, elaborate*, and *evaluate*, Dr. Arthur Eisenkraft, the Project Director of *Active Chemistry*, has proposed the *7 E model* that expands the *engage* element into two components—*elicit and engage*. Similarly, he expands the *elaborate* and *evaluate* element into three components—to include *extend*, the transfer of knowledge from one domain to another (Eisenkraft, 2003). As stated by Dr. Eisenkraft, "Eliciting prior understandings is determining what students know prior to a lesson and is imperative. Recognizing that students construct knowledge from existing knowledge, teachers need to find out what existing knowledge their students possess. Failure to do so may result in students developing concepts very different from the ones the teacher intends." In the *Active Learning model*, teachers elicit prior understandings from their students by the **What Do You Think?** question that initiates each section. This direct and simple task asks students to jot down some of their thoughts and ideas about the content area they are about to investigate. Comparing their prior ideas about the subject with the ideas learned during the investigation creates the environment for deeper and more meaningful learning.

The *7E learning cycle* asks students to apply their knowledge in a new context, a new domain (transfer of learning). This is a central component to *Active Chemistry*. Each chapter begins with a **Chapter Scenario** and **Challenge**. For example, in the chapter called *Fun with the Periodic Table*, the students are asked to design a game based on Mendeleev's Periodic Table of the Elements. They then work with their classmates and teacher to create a rubric for assessing each other's games. Nine sections (guided-inquiry, hands-on labs) then follow, with each investigation taking a day or two to complete, which helps the students learn the chemistry necessary to complete their challenge. The students then transfer the content knowledge learned in their lab experiences to a new domain, the **Chapter Challenge**, in this case a game based on the periodic table. The public display of these games by each group of students, as well as playing each other's games, engages the students creatively and intellectually. It also serves as a format for multiple exposure and review of the content.

"What an AWESOME week! We 'kinda' finished *Section 8* in *Fun with the Periodic Table*. The reason I say 'kinda' is because I could hardly contain my kids' enthusiasm! It was as if they all had a breakthrough in understanding all the concepts covered up to this point. Suddenly, electron configuration was a concept they understood and the kids that didn't understand it were overwhelmed by peer teachers eager to share their newfound understanding. Not only do they understand e-configuration, but NOW the arrangement of the periodic table makes sense to them. They also started (on their own) to predict how different elements would react with other elements to form compounds. It was incredible!" *(Rosemary Riggs, Roosevelt H.S., San Antonio, Texas)*

A 1997 study (*Dimensions of Learning*) conducted extensive examination on what constitutes students' positive responses toward certain characteristics of instruction and curriculum. This study revealed a listing of attributes titled: "What Engages Students Intellectually." Key attributes from this study include:

• Students helping define content and task

• Students having time to wonder—to find a particular direction that interested them

• Teachers permitting—even encouraging—different forms of expression and respect for student views.

• Students creating original and public products

• Students sensing that the results of their work were not predetermined or fully predictable.

Although students in the *Active Learning Model* do not define the science or content they will be asked to learn, they will be encouraged to use the science, transferring the knowledge learned, in creative and unpredictable ways.

"As a veteran chemistry teacher of 22 years, and after having tried numerous programs, I feel that I have the experience to identify quality programs. *Active Chemistry* is a quality program for several reasons. It's engaging, it develops higher order thinking skills, and it is applicable to students' lives. I am excited about this new and different approach. But more importantly, my students are excited! And that is really a testimony when you consider the population that I teach. (My students come from a very rural, poverty-stricken area where education is not valued.) I wholeheartedly endorse the program." *(Diane Johnson, Lewis County High School, Kentucky Department Head, KSTA President)*

The *Active Learning Model* also follows the theoretical approach that advocates a *Backward Design Process*, (G. Wiggins and J. McTighe, 2001). In this approach, the developer first identifies the desired learning results, then determines what would be considered acceptable evidence toward demonstrating those results, and then designs the curriculum to orchestrate learning experiences that will best lead toward those desired learning outcomes.

"My student teacher and I have found the **Reflecting on the Section and the Challenge** of each section to be an enormously helpful wrap-up and review of each section. One of my students put it into his own words as "What did we do?" "What did we see?" "What does it mean?" I feel like we are building meaningful relationships between the investigations, students' observations and interpretations." (*Karen Tokos, Newton North High School, Newtonville, Massachusetts*)

Thus, the *Active Chemistry* curriculum is accessible and engaging to all students, including students who are historically low-achieving and those who have previously shown little interest in science. It is a blueprint for learning that takes a content subject and shapes it into a format for effective teaching and learning for students of a diverse range of abilities.

Indicators of Success

Studies on student performance are important indicators of success. In the Cincinnati Public Schools, for example, where *Active Physics*, *Active Chemistry* and *EarthComm* make up the 9th grade science course, Dr. Robert Endorf from the Physics Department of the University of Cincinnati has conducted a study of effectiveness on students in the course. His data is preliminary, but the initial results show significant promise. This study included the administering of the FCI (Force Concept Inventory) exam to these 9th-grade students, on a pre-and-post basis, as well as to the entering first-year college engineering students, and the study shows the *Active Learning Instructional Model* to be remarkably effective.

Newton's Third Law

Question of FCI

	Pre-Test – 9th grade	Post-Test – 9th grade	1st year college
	Active Physics students	Active Physics students	engineering students pre-test
Item # 4	13%	67%	27%
Item # 15	25%	48%	20%
Item # 16	13%	70%	64%
Item # 29	13%	26%	32%

Cincinnati Public Schools (FCI Study)
Robert Endorf, Ph.D., University of
Cincinnati, Professor of Physics
Robert.endorf@UC.edu

Another noteworthy indicator of success consists of teacher responses. In Seattle, for example, on a survey administered to teachers who have completed a year of their Integrated Program (*Active Physics*, *Active Chemistry* and *EarthComm*), 70% responded that these programs had "supported and/or facilitated their teaching."

In Florida, a teacher captured her enthusiasm.

"This year at my school, the Dean of Faculty is using me as one the models for our Faculty Recognition Program since I'm using innovative, research-based models in my classroom. (Yes, my administrators are up to date on the research!) I can also report that I am LOVING *Active Chemistry* and I have never enjoyed teaching more in my life! I can't remember a school year that I worked this hard but was THIS happy!" (*Stephanie Levens, North Broward Preparatory School, Florida*)

References:

American Association for the Advancement of Science, 1993, *Science for All Americans*, Washington D.C.

Bransford, J.D., A.L. Brown, and R.R. Cocking, 2000, *How People Learn: Brain, Mind, Experience, and School*, Washington, D.C.: National Academy Press

Bransford, J.D., M.S. Donovan, Pellegrino, 1999, *How People Learn: Bridging Research and Practice*, Washington, D.C.: National Academy Press

Brooks, J.G., Brooks, M.G., Brooks, M., 2000, *In Search of Understanding: The Case for Constructionist Classrooms*, New York: Prentice Hall

Bybee, R. W. 1997, *Achieving Scientific Literacy*, Portsmouth, N.H.: Heinemann

Chudowsky, N., R. Glaser, J. Pellegrino, 2001, *Knowing what Students Know: The Science and Design of Educational Assessment*, Washington D.C.: National Academy Press

Colburn, A., and M.P. Clough. 1997, *Implementing the Learning Cycle. The Science Teacher* 64(5): 30-33

Delisle, R., 1997, *How to Use Problem-Based Learning in the Classroom*, Alexandria, VA: Association for Supervision and Curriculum Development

H. Dembo, R.Rueda, 1995, *Motivational Processes in Learning: A Comparative Analysis of Cognitive and Sociocultural Frameworks, Advances in Motivation and Achievement*, Vol. 9, 255-289

Eisenkraft, A., 2003, *Expanding the 5E Model, The Science Teacher* 70(6): 56-59

Hilgard E.R., and G.H. Bower. 1975, *Theories of Learning*, Englewood Cliffs, N.J.: Prentice Hall

Lawson, A.E., 1995, *Science Teaching and the Development of Thinking*, Belmont, Calif.: Wadsworth.

Marzano, R., D. Pickering, G. Blackburn, D. Arrendondo, 1997, *Dimensions of Learning*, Alexandria, VA: Association for Supervision and Curriculum Development

National Research Council, 1999, *Designing Mathematics or Science Curriculum Programs: A Guide for Using Math and Science Education Standards*, Washington, D.C.: National Academy Press

National Research Council, 2000, *Inquiry and the National Science Education Standards: A Guide for Teaching and Learning*, Washington, D.C.: National Academy Press

National Research Council, 1996, *National Science Education Standards*, Washington, D.C.: National Academy Press

Wiggins, G., J. McTighe, 2001, *Understanding by Design*, Prentice Hall

Expanding the 5E Model

the

A proposed 7E model emphasizes "transfer of learning" and the importance of eliciting prior understanding

Arthur Eisenkraft

Sometimes a current model must be amended to maintain its value after new information, insights, and knowledge have been gathered. Such is now the case with the highly successful 5E learning cycle and instructional model (Bybee 1997). Research on how people learn and the incorporation of that research into lesson plans and curriculum development demands that the 5E model be expanded to a 7E model.

MIKE OLLIVER

The 5E learning cycle model requires instruction to include the following discrete elements: *engage, explore, explain, elaborate,* and *evaluate.* The proposed 7E model expands the *engage* element into two components—*elicit* and *engage.* Similarly, the 7E model expands the two stages of *elaborate* and *evaluate* into three components—*elaborate, evaluate,* and *extend.* The transition from the 5E model to the 7E model is illustrated in Figure 1.

These changes are not suggested to add complexity, but rather to ensure instructors do not omit crucial elements for learning from their lessons while under the incorrect assumption they are meeting the requirements of the learning cycle.

Eliciting prior understandings

Current research in cognitive science has shown that eliciting prior understandings is a necessary component of the learning process. Research also has shown that expert learners are much more adept at the transfer of learning than novices and that practice in the transfer of learning is required in good instruction (Bransford, Brown, and Cocking 2000).

The *engage* component in the 5E model is intended to capture students' attention, get students thinking about the subject matter, raise questions in students' minds, stimulate thinking, and access prior knowledge. For example, teachers may engage students by creating surprise or doubt through a demonstration that shows a piece of steel sinking and a steel toy boat floating. Similarly, a teacher may place an ice cube into a glass of water and have the class observe it float while the same ice cube placed in a second glass of liquid sinks. The corresponding conversation with the students may access their prior learning. The students should have the opportunity to ask and attempt to answer, "Why is it that the toy boat does not sink?"

The engage component includes both accessing prior knowledge and generating enthusiasm for the subject matter. Teachers may excite students, get them interested and ready to learn, and believe they are fulfilling the engage phase of the learning cycle, while ignoring the need to find out what prior knowledge students bring to the topic. The importance of *eliciting* prior understandings in ascertaining what students know prior to a lesson is imperative. Recognizing that students construct knowledge from existing knowledge, teachers need to find out what existing knowledge their students possess. Failure to do so may result in students developing concepts very different from the ones the teacher intends (Bransford, Brown, and Cocking 2000).

A straightforward means by which teachers may elicit prior understandings is by framing a "what do you think" question at the outset of the lesson as is done consistently in some current curricula. For example, a common physics lesson on seat belts might begin with a question about designing seat belts for a racecar traveling at a high rate of speed (Figure 2, p. 58). "How would they be different from ones available on passenger cars?" Students responding to this question communicate what they know about seat belts and inform themselves, their classmates, and the teacher about their prior conceptions and understandings. There is no need to arrive at consensus or closure at this point. Students do not assume the teacher will tell them the "right" answer. The "what do you think" question is intended to begin the conversation.

The proposed expansion of the 5E model does not exchange the *engage* component for the *elicit* component; the engage component is still a necessary element in good instruction. The goal is to continue to excite and interest students in whatever ways possible and to identify prior conceptions. Therefore the elicit component should stand alone as a reminder of its importance in learning and constructing meaning.

Explore and explain

The *explore* phase of the learning cycle provides an opportunity for students to observe, record data, isolate variables, design and plan experiments, create graphs, interpret results, develop hypotheses, and organize their findings. Teachers may frame questions, suggest approaches, provide feedback, and assess understandings. An excellent example of teaching a lesson on the metabolic rate of water fleas (Lawson 2001) illustrates the

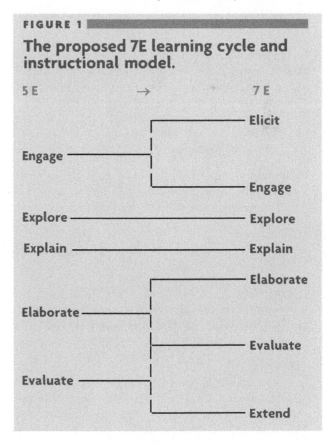

FIGURE 1

The proposed 7E learning cycle and instructional model.

5E	→	7E
		Elicit
Engage		Engage
Explore		Explore
Explain		Explain
		Elaborate
Elaborate		Evaluate
Evaluate		Extend

FIGURE 2

Seatbelt lesson using the 7E model.

Elicit prior understandings

◆ Students are asked, "Suppose you had to design seat belts for a racecar traveling at high speeds. How would they be different from ones available on passenger cars?" The students are required to write a brief response to this "What do you think?" question in their logs and then share with the person sitting next to them. The class then listens to some of the responses. This requires a few minutes of class time.

Engage

◆ Students relate car accidents they have witnessed in movies or in real life.

Explore

◆ The first part of the exploration requires students to construct a clay figure they can sit on a cart. The cart is then crashed into a wall. The clay figure hits the wall.

Explain

◆ Students are given a name for their observations. Newton's first law states, "Objects at rest stay at rest; objects in motion stay in motion unless acted upon by a force."

Engage

◆ Students view videos of crash test dummies during automobile crashes.

Explore

◆ Students are asked how they could save the clay figure from injury during the crash into the wall. The suggestion that the clay figure will require a seat belt leads to another experiment. A thin wire is used as a seat belt. The students construct a seat belt from the wire and ram the cart and figure into the wall again. The wire seat belt keeps the clay figure from hitting the wall, but the wire slices halfway through the midsection.

Explain

◆ Students recognize that a wider seatbelt is needed. The relationship of pressure, force, and area is introduced.

Elaborate

◆ Students then construct better seat belts and explain their value in terms of Newton's first law and forces.

Evaluate

◆ Students are asked to design a seat belt for a racing car that travels at 250 km/h. They compare their designs with actual safety belts used by NASCAR.

Extend

◆ Students are challenged to explore how airbags work and to compare and contrast airbags with seat belts. One of the questions explored is, "How does the airbag get triggered? Why does the airbag not inflate during a small fender-bender but does inflate when the car hits a tree?"

effectiveness of the learning cycle with varying amounts of teacher and learner ownership and control (Gil 2002).

Students are introduced to models, laws, and theories during the *explain* phase of the learning cycle. Students summarize results in terms of these new theories and models. The teacher guides students toward coherent and consistent generalizations, helps students with distinct scientific vocabulary, and provides questions that help students use this vocabulary to explain the results of their explorations. The distinction between the explore and explain components ensures that concepts precede terminology.

Applying knowledge

The *elaborate* phase of the learning cycle provides an opportunity for students to apply their knowledge to new domains, which may include raising new questions and hypotheses to explore. This phase may also include related numerical problems for students to solve. When students explore the heating curve of water and the related heats of fusion and vaporization, they can then perform a similar experiment with another liquid or, using data from a reference table, compare and contrast materials with respect to freezing and boiling points. A further elaboration may ask students to consider the specific heats of metals in comparison to water and to explain why pizza from the oven remains hot but aluminum foil beneath the pizza cools so rapidly.

The elaboration phase ties directly to the psychological construct called "transfer of learning" (Thorndike 1923). Schools are created and supported with the expectation that more general uses of knowledge will be found outside of school and beyond the school years (Hilgard and Bower 1975). Transfer of learning can range from transfer of one concept to another (e.g., Newton's law of gravitation and Coulomb's law of electrostatics); one school subject to another (e.g., math skills applied in scientific investigations); one year to another (e.g., significant figures, graphing, chemistry concepts in physics); and school to nonschool activities (e.g., using a graph to calculate whether it is cost effective to join a video club or pay a higher rate on rentals) (Bransford, Brown, and Cocking 2000).

Too often, the elaboration phase has come to mean an elaboration of the specific concepts. Teachers may provide the specific heat of a second substance and have students perform identical calculations. This practice in transfer of learning seems limited to near transfer as opposed to far or distant transfer (Mayer 1979). Even though teachers expect wonderful results when they limit themselves to near transfer with large similarities between the original task and the transfer task, they know students often find elaborations difficult. And as difficult as near transfer is for students, the distant transfer is usually a much harder road to traverse. Students who are quite able to discuss phase changes of substances and their related freezing points, melting points, and heats of fusion and vaporization may find it exceedingly difficult to transfer the concept of phase change as a means of explaining traffic congestion.

Practicing the transfer of learning

The addition of the *extend* phase to the *elaborate* phase is intended to explicitly remind teachers of the importance for students to practice the transfer of learning. Teachers need to make sure that knowledge is applied in a new context and is not limited to simple elaboration. For instance, in another common activity students may be required to invent a sport that can be played on the moon. An activity on friction informs students that friction increases with weight. Because objects weigh less on the moon, frictional forces are expected to be less on the moon. That elaboration is useful. Students must go one step further and extend this friction concept to the unique sports and corresponding play they are developing for the moon environment.

The *evaluate* phase of the learning cycle continues to include both formative and summative evaluations of student learning. If teachers truly value the learning cycle and experiments that students conduct in the classroom, then teachers should be sure to include aspects of these investigations on tests. Tests should include questions from the lab and should ask students questions about the laboratory activities. Students should be asked to interpret data from a lab similar to the one they completed. Students should also be asked to design experiments as part of their assessment (Colburn and Clough 1997).

Formative evaluation should not be limited to a particular phase of the cycle. The cycle should not be linear. Formative evaluation must take place during all interactions with students. The *elicit* phase is a formative evaluation. The *explore* phase and *explain* phase must always be accompanied by techniques whereby the teacher checks for student understanding.

Replacing *elaborate* and *evaluate* with *elaborate, extend,* and *evaluate* as shown in Figure 1, p. 57, is a way to emphasize that the transfer of learning, as required in the extend phase, may also be used as part of the evaluation phase in the learning cycle.

Enhancing the instructional model

Adopting a 7E model ensures that eliciting prior understandings and opportunities for transfer of learning are not omitted. With a 7E model, teachers will *engage* and *elicit* and students will *elaborate* and *extend*. This is not the first enhancement of instructional models, nor will it be the last. Readers should not reject the enhancement because they are used to the traditional 5E model, or worse yet, because they hold the 5E model sacred. The 5E model is itself an enhancement of the three-phrase learning cycle that included exploration, invention, and discovery (Karplus and Thier 1967.) In the 5E model, these phases were initially referred to as explore, explain, and expand. In another learning cycle, they are referred to as exploration, term introduction, and concept application (Lawson 1995).

The 5E learning cycle has been shown to be an extremely effective approach to learning (Lawson 1995; Guzzetti et al. 1993). The goal of the 7E learning model is to emphasize the increasing importance of eliciting prior understandings and the extending, or transfer, of concepts. With this new model, teachers should no longer overlook these essential requirements for student learning. ■

Arthur Eisenkraft is a project director of Active Physics and a past president of NSTA, 60 Stormytown Road, Ossining, NY 10562; e-mail: eisenkraft@att.net.

References

Bransford, J.D., A.L. Brown, and R.R. Cocking, eds. 2000. *How People Learn.* Washington, D.C.: National Academy Press.

Bybee, R.W. 1997. *Achieving Scientific Literacy.* Portsmouth, N.H.: Heinemann.

Colburn, A., and M.P. Clough. 1997. Implementing the learning cycle. *The Science Teacher* 64(5): 30–33.

Gil, O. 2002. Implications of inquiry curriculum for teaching. Paper presented at National Science Teachers Association Convention, 5–7 December, in Alburquerque, N.M.

Guzzetti B., T.E. Taylor, G.V. Glass, and W.S. Gammas. 1993. Promoting conceptual change in science: A comparative meta-analysis of instructional interventions from reading education and science education. *Reading Research Quarterly* 28:117–159.

Hilgard, E.R., and G.H. Bower. 1975. *Theories of Learning.* Englewood Cliffs, N.J.: Prentice Hall.

Karplus, R., and H.D. Thier. 1967. *A New Look at Elementary School Science.* Chicago: Rand McNally.

Lawson, A.E. 1995. *Science Teaching and the Development of Thinking.* Belmont, Calif.: Wadsworth.

Lawson, A.E. 2001. Using the learning cycle to teach biology concepts and reasoning patterns. *Journal of Biological Education* 35(4): 165–169.

Mayer, R.E. 1979. Can advance organizers influence meaningful learning? *Review of Educational Research* 49(2): 371–383.

Thorndike, E.L. 1923. *Educational Psychology, Vol. II: The Psychology of Learning.* New York: Teachers College, Columbia University.

Artist as Chemist

Students link art and chemistry through problem-based learning activities

Arthur Eisenkraft, Carl Heltzel, Diane Johnson, and Brian Radcliffe

*a*ll artists are chemists. Artists understand and study the properties of specific materials and find ways to explore these properties to express views of themselves and the world around them. In this curriculum unit, chemistry students create an original artwork and describe the chemistry principles involved in their work. Before beginning the challenge, students learn the chemistry concepts and related art techniques through a series of eight activities.

The five-week chemistry unit centers on the Artist as Chemist and uses a problem-based learning model. We have found that students in class and teachers in professional development workshops become equally engaged in this chemistry unit. As part of an NSF-supported curriculum project (Eisenkraft 2006), the project leans on the National Science Education Standards (NRC 1996), the research findings of cognitive science (Bransford 2000) and assessment (Pellegrino 2001), and is cohesively structured using novel curriculum design strategies (Wiggins and McTighe 1998).

The curriculum

On day one of the class, students are exposed to the unit challenge: "Art is the result of the human need to express ourselves. It tells stories of societies, eras, and individuals. Your challenge is to create a work of art that represents you and/or your times using appropriate artistic techniques. You will also need to create a museum display that includes: a demonstration of the techniques involved; your original artwork; and a museum placard that explains the chemistry involved."

After hearing the challenge, students discuss the criteria of an excellent unit challenge. Facilitated by their teacher, students discuss the qualities that must be present in the work of art as well as the number of chemical principles that will be required for the museum placard. This discussion leads to the development of a scoring rubric that will be used to evaluate the projects at the close of the unit. The rubric delineates the expectations for each level of success. Examples of "exemplary" criteria are shown in Figure 1.

As our introduction to the high school chemistry course, students will have to learn some chemistry over the next month in order to succeed. In the problem-based learning model, students learn the chemistry because they are confronted with a challenge that requires knowledge of chemistry to complete (Delisle 1997). Students learn chemistry on a need-to-know basis. Students never ask, "Why are we learning this?" because the premise of the challenge and their engagement in the challenge presupposes the response. Students are learning chemistry because they want to create an original piece of artwork for a museum display.

Students learn chemistry through a series of eight activities. The philosophy of Artist as Chemist demands that all activities follow a structure to strengthen inquiry (NRC 2000). The 7E instructional model (an enhancement of the 5E model) (Eisenkraft 2003) includes eliciting prior understandings, engaging the students, exploration of the concepts through an activity, elaboration of the content, extending the concept (transfer of knowledge to the unit) with evaluation throughout all aspects of the lesson.

Throughout the unit, the overarching theme is that chemistry is about change. Threaded through each activity are discussions of these changes at the macro and nano level. Students are encouraged to view all chemical interactions from the observable properties of the material substances before and after the reaction (macro) and the atomic level explanation of what is occurring (nano). Students are also introduced explicitly to the symbolic structures that are used throughout chemistry including formulas and equations, math, molecular models, dot diagrams, graphs, and computer images.

FIGURE 1

Rubric: Exemplary criteria.

	Excellent
Demonstration of techniques	• Display contains a thorough and accurate description of the artistic techniques used, which includes the chemistry involved. • Display contains accurate and key information concerning how techniques were applied to your work.
Original work	• Original work employs techniques described accurately and with craftsmanship. • Original work is creative. • Original work is an excellent representation of yourself or your times.
Placard	• All information on the placard is accurate. • All information on the placard is clearly written and easy to understand. • Seven or more chemical principles are addressed. • Placard is neat and correct. • All sources of information are correctly documented. • Placard is very creative.
Effectiveness of display	• The layout of the display has visual appeal. • The layout is engaging and interesting to a wide range of audiences. It is very creative. • Display is realistic; it could appear in a museum. • Display shows insight and understanding of art and chemistry.

The content

One of the early activities in The Artist as Chemist challenge focuses on the choice of artistic media for durability. Students are shown images of statues that have suffered the effects of acid rain ("engage" in the 7E model). The *What Do You Think* question ("elicit" in the 7E model) asks students what is in the air that can cause this damage.

In the *Investigate* section ("explore" in the 7E model), students generate sulfur dioxide and determine the effects of both sulfur dioxide and carbon dioxide on the pH of water; this is related to the effects of weathering on outdoor artworks. Students are also are asked to design a procedure to determine which media will best hold up under acidic conditions.

The *Chem Talk* section ("explain" in the 7E model) then leads students through a discussion of Arrhenius acids, their dissociation, and the chemical equations representing the reactions that they carried out. The *What Do You Think Now* question ("explain" in the 7E model) asks them to revisit their original response to the statue deterioration question and how their understanding has changed.

In the *Reflecting on the Activity and the Challenge* ("elaborate" in the 7E model) section, students review what they have experienced in light of the Unit Challenge. Students are prompted to develop an understanding of the chemistry concepts learned in terms of the macroscopic observations, nano level explanations, and symbolic structures used. At the macroscopic level students saw gases form, visible color changes of water as pH changed, and the effects of acids on marble, limestone, and other materials. On the nanoscopic level students learned about the formation of hydrogen ions and chemical reactions between acids and various materials. Symbolically, students used chemical equations to represent these changes.

The *Chemistry to Go* ("elaborate" in the 7E model) section provides students with homework problems that focus on the topics learned. A final section, titled *Preparing for the Unit Challenge* ("extend" in the 7E model), asks students to sketch a sculpture that would be placed outdoors. Students need to describe the material they would use and explain how it would resist

Throughout the unit, the overarching theme is that chemistry is about change. Threaded through each activity are discussions of these changes at the macro and nano level.

deterioration caused by exposure to the elements. Once again, students are reminded that they are learning chemistry concepts because they will be required to create an original piece of art.

This approach and 7E instructional model is then used in subsequent activities to illustrate the connections between chemistry and art. Two activities, centered on the use of metals for artwork and tools, help develop the concepts of the metal activity series and valence electrons. Students practice electroplating and form alloys as well as annealed, tempered, and hardened steel.

Artists use a variety of materials and chemicals and there is a kinesthetic activity to allow students to understand bonding and how compounds are named. A further activity covers ceramics in terms of anhydrates and hydrates where mass percent and the mole concept are examined. Paints are investigated by carrying out precipitation reactions in an activity that incorporates the solubility rules. Intermolecular forces and polarity are investigated in an activity on typical solvents that artists encounter. In another activity students extract dyes from natural sources and gauge the effect of pH on colorfastness. The final activity is on the use of metals for coloring glass.

Figure 2 (p. 36) includes details of each of the activities and their related chemistry principles. Some of the labs are those traditionally done in chemistry classes. In this unit, these labs are not an end in themselves but rather necessary content to complete the unit challenge—creating a work of art that represents you and your times using appropriate artistic techniques.

The unit's impact

A successful problem-based learning unit should be able to challenge all who attempt it. Teachers experienced the Artist as Chemist unit during workshops and the unit was then field tested with students in their classes. Both groups experienced similar positive reactions to the unit.

The field test of the Artist as Chemist unit began with teacher professional development at Ohio State University during July 2004. Twenty-four high school teachers from across the United States participated in the training. Working in teams, all of the teachers proceeded through each of the eight activities to get a

FIGURE 2

Summary of activities.

[**Editor's Note:** These procedures are not intended to be full descriptions; be sure to follow normal safety guidelines. For two complete activities for the Artist as Chemist chapter of *Active Chemistry*, visit the online version of this article at *www.nsta.org/highschool#journal*.]

Title and summary of activity	Chemistry principles
What is Art? Present images of art—important and questionable work. Broad term discussion of the chemistry behind art.	• create a definition of art • materials that are used in art • How is chemistry related to art?
Choice of media for durability. Generation of sulfur dioxide in plastic bag, examining the effect of this gas and CO_2 (from breath) on the pH of water. Students design experiment to test how acids react with various metals, carbonates, silicates and sulfates (environmental impact on sculpture).	• acid/base chemistry • pH scale • chemical reactions • single displacement reactions • synthesis reactions
Chemical behavior of metals. Students determine relative activity of various metals (testing combination of metals in a solution with voltmeter to see which way current flows). Discussion of properties of metals based on electron arrangement. Electroplating; copper coating a nickel.	• chemical reactivity of metals • atomic structure–valence electrons
Physical behavior of metals. Make brass from a post-1982 penny.	• physical properties of metals • metallic bonding • alloys
Clay. (a) make observations of changes in crystalline structure, color (b) determine molar ratio of water in an unknown hydrate (c) conservation of mass–mass before and after dehydration. Why is clay "fired"? What happens when clay is fired?	• chemical reactions • hydrated and anhydrous compounds • mole concept • molar mass • percent by mass
Paints. Production of pigments from double displacement reactions. Testing of precipitates (and other compounds provided, i.e., metal oxides) in water, guar gum and oil to determine usefulness as pigments for paints. Produce a painting.	• chemical reactions • double displacement reactions • solubility
Dyes extracting and testing (effect of pH) natural dyes from plant sources on various fabrics (with and without a mordant).	• solubility • organic molecules • chromophore • auxochrome • mordants • dyes
Glazes and glass. Students make borax beads and show how the beads take up metal compounds and become colored. Discussion of glazes.	• naming compounds

feel for what their students would be doing in the fall.

Each group then produced an original work of art and a presentation explaining the various chemical concepts that were involved in the production of the artwork. The artwork included wire sculptures, multimedia mobiles, clay sculptures decorated with homemade paints, colored borax beads and heat-treated bobby pins, dyed yarn and painted paper sculptures, and jewelry made from copper-plated nickels and brass pennies. All teachers were excited about the works of art, the process of discovery and inquiry in the activities, and the prospect of getting their students involved in chemistry though art.

One group of teachers presented a sculpture using one piece of clay molded into three female figures. The teachers explained that the physical features and uniqueness of each of them was represented in the art with the common base denoting that they are all strong and independent. Another group of teachers created a wire mobile with ceramics. The meaning of the art was described as the need that people have to be kept in balance and the changes that occur during life.

Student projects during the year were just as creative. One student group created a bracelet and described it in this way, "The bracelets represents us in a material form. The strings represent us and the beads represent important moments of our lives. These events range from deaths in our family to moving to a new town. The color of the beads also symbolically represent that no matter how bad an experience may seem, there is always a good lesson to be learned from it."

What is outstanding about the displays of artwork, but not surprising from a problem based learning model, is that the chemistry concepts are correctly explained while the artistic aspects are original and creative. As the student teams display their work, the pride comes not in their correct explanations of dehydration or suspensions but in the novel ways in which they applied the chemistry to express themselves. The creativity of the teams emerges in ways that we usually don't see in a science class. We find out more about each other as individuals while we continue to learn the science content.

The nature of the challenge also provides an opportunity to respect and celebrate the different cultures in our classroom. In schools throughout the country, a wide diversity of students work side by side, often ignorant of their neighbors' ethnic backgrounds and cultures. The art project encourages students to create a meaningful art project that may indeed reflect their backgrounds. Research on equity issues recommends that we bring the cultural backgrounds of our students into the lessons. Here is an approach that fosters such inclusion in our chemistry classes.

Artwork created for the unit challenge by the teachers and students was creative and much broader than the writers of the unit had originally envisioned while working. For example, the writing team had anticipated that the bobby pins would be used for a metal sculpture but never imagined that pieces could be used for hair as part of a pottery figurative sculpture. The glass beads, originally intended for ceramics, became jewelry. Student engagement increases when the results of student work are not predetermined or fully predictable (Perrone 1994.) During the presentation of the artwork, teachers realize that they did not anticipate their students' level of creativity and this adds to student pride and satisfaction.

Artist as Chemist rewards both knowledge of chemistry and student creativity. It fosters collaborations among students and provides an opportunity for all students to succeed. Through their creation of an original artwork and the accompanying museum placard, students communicate their knowledge of chemistry. They become artists because of their chemistry knowledge in much the same way that they realize that all artists have become chemists as a necessary component of their need to understand materials and their interactions. ∎

Arthur Eisenkraft is distinguished professor of science education at the University of Massachusetts Boston and is a past-president of NSTA; Carl Heltzel is the editor of ChemMatters Magazine of the American Chemical Society; Diane Johnson is instructional supervisor for Lewis County Schools in Vanceburg, KY; and Brian Radcliffe is an educational consultant for the Tracy Farmer Center for the Environment at the University of Kentucky in Lexington, KY.

References

Bransford, J.D., A.L. Brown, and R.R. Cocking, eds. 2000. *How people learn.* Washington, DC: National Academy Press.

Delisle, R. 1997. *How to use problem-based learning in the classroom.* Alexandria, VA: Association for Supervision and Curriculum Development.

Eisenkraft, A. 2003. Enhancing the 5E model. *The Science Teacher* 70(6): 56–59.

Eisenkraft, A. 2006. *Active chemistry.* Armonk, NY: It's About Time, Herff Jones Education Division.

National Research Council (NRC). 1996. *National science education standards.* Washington, DC: National Academy Press.

Olson, S., and S. Loucks-Horsley, eds. 2000. *Inquiry and the national science education standards.* Washington, DC: National Academy Press.

Pellegrino J.W., N. Chudowsky, and R. Glaser, eds. 2001 *Knowing what students know.* Washington, DC: National Academy Press.

Perrone, V. 1994. How to engage students in learning. *Educational Leadership* 51(5): 11–13.

Wiggins, G., and J. McTighe. 1998. *Understanding by design.* Alexandria, VA: Association for Supervision and Curriculum Development.

Safety Contract: Safety in the Chemistry Classroom

Chemistry is a laboratory science. During this course you will be doing many investigations in which safety is a factor. To ensure the safety of all students, the following safety rules will be followed. You will be responsible for abiding by these rules at all times. After reading the rules, you and a parent or guardian must sign a safety contract acknowledging that you have read and understood the rules and will follow them at all times. The safety contract is provided as a Blackline Master in the *Teacher Resources* CD.

General Rules

1. Never work in the lab unless your teacher or an approved substitute is present.

2. You must follow all directions carefully and use only materials and equipment provided by your teacher. Only activities approved by your teacher may be carried out in the chemistry laboratory.

3. Identify and know the location of a fire extinguisher, fire blanket, emergency shower, eyewash, gas and water shut-offs, and telephone.

4. All spills and accidents must be reported to your teacher immediately.

5. No loose clothing is allowed in the laboratory; long sleeves must be rolled up; bulky jackets, as well as jewelry, must be removed.

6. Eating, drinking, chewing gum, or applying cosmetics is strictly prohibited.

7. There will be no running, jumping, pushing, or other behavior considered inappropriate in the science laboratory. You must behave in an orderly and responsible way at all times.

Equipment Rules

1. All equipment must be checked out and returned properly.

2. Do not touch any equipment until you are instructed to do so.

3. Do not use glassware that is broken or cracked. Alert your teacher to any glassware that is broken or cracked.

Working with Chemicals

1. Safety goggles and lab aprons must be worn at all times.

2. Contact lenses can absorb certain chemicals. Advise your teacher if you wear contact lenses.

3. Keep your hands away from your face and thoroughly wash with soap and water before exiting the classroom.

4. Never touch or smell chemicals unless specifically instructed to do so by your teacher. Never taste chemicals.

5. Carefully read all labels to make sure you are using the correct chemicals and use only the amount of chemicals instructed by your teacher.

6. Follow your teachers' instructions for the correct disposal of chemicals. Do not dispose of any chemical waste, including paper towels used for chemical spills, in the trash basket or down a sink drain unless specifically to do so.

Flame Safety

1. Use extreme caution when using any type of flame. Keep your hands, hair, and clothing away from flames. Long hair must be tied back at all times.

2. Keep all flammable materials away from open flames. Some winter jackets are extremely flammable and should be removed before entering the laboratory.

3. Extinguish any flame as soon as you are finished using it.

4. When heating a substance over a flame, always point the mouth of a test tube away from yourself or any other person.

5. Always use heat-resistant gloves or tongs when working with an open flame.

Work Area

1. When working in the laboratory all materials should be removed from the workstation except for instructions, chem notebooks and data tables. Materials should not be placed on the floor because this is a hazard for someone walking with glassware or chemicals.

2. The work area should be kept clean at all times. After completing an investigation, wipe down the area.

3. Notify your teacher of any spills immediately so they can be properly taken care of.

Safety Contract

The following contract may be reproduced and must be signed by each student and a parent or guardian before participating in laboratory activities.

I have read **Safety in the Chemistry Classroom** and understand the requirements fully. I recognize that there are risks associated with any chemistry activity and acknowledge my responsibility in minimizing these risks by abiding by the safety rules at all times.

Please list any known medical conditions or allergies:

_____

_____

_____

I do / do not wear contact lenses. (Circle one)

Emergency phone contact _____

Student signature _____ **Date** _____

Parent or guardian _____ **Date** _____

Teacher _____ **Date** _____

Chapter 5

CHAPTER 5
IDEAL TOY
Chapter Overview

Chapter Challenge

This chapter challenges students to create a toy that operates on chemical and/or gas principles. It may be powered by a chemical reaction or even a phase change. The challenge is flexible in that the toy may be a mock prototype or simply a series of design sketches. You may want your students to be involved in the decision process of what is acceptable for the final product. The challenge also requires students to provide a plan for the manufacturing of the toy with a rudimentary cost analysis and waste-removal program. Students should be encouraged to consider "green" chemistry concepts in their plan.

In order to complete the challenge, students will need to draw from the gas laws and chemical principles they will learn through the sections and apply them to their toy. The chapter begins with an investigation exploring something they have often used in toys – batteries. The students will then be guided through a series of sections involving phase changes, gas laws, and the kinetic molecular theory. The final section is focused on polymers to give the students an opportunity to incorporate the housing or shell of their toy into their toy design plan.

Chapter Summary

- Learn how chemical concepts can be incorporated into everyday objects; in this case a toy.

- Learn how to use scientific inquiry and how to develop conclusions from the data and evidence collected.

- Learn how to use instruments and make precise measurements.

- Understand how to carry out mathematical calculations.

- Gain awareness that chemistry is all around us and that an understanding of chemical principles can enrich our lives.

KEY SCIENCE CONCEPTS	
SECTION SUMMARIES	**CHEMISTRY PRINCIPLES**
Section 1: Electrochemistry and Batteries In this three-part investigation, prior information about batteries is explored and several types of batteries are examined. Starting on a macroscopic level, observations about commercial batteries are made. The Metal Activity Series is used to guide the construction of electrochemical cells. The nanoscopic concepts of redox reactions and electrochemical cell chemistry are explored. Then, the discussion returns to the macroscopic level in order to power a toy with the electrochemical cells that were previously built.	Metal activity series Electrochemistry, Half-reactions Redox reactions Matter–energy interactions Spectator ions, Cathode Anode, Voltage, Current
Section 2: Intermolecular Forces in Solids, Liquids, and Gases In this two-part investigation, the free *ChemSketch* and *3-D viewer* programs from the ACD Labs are used to create representations of different molecules. The focus is on the fact that the size and shape of a molecule have an important effect on the properties of the molecule. Properties that are examined are boiling points and melting points of organic compounds.	Molecular motion Particle nature of matter Molecular size and shape Polar, Nonpolar, Electronegativity Intermolecular forces London dispersion forces
Section 3: Boyle's Law and the Cartesian Diver This investigation involves two parts. In Part A, the effect of pressure on gas volume is examined by measuring volume changes with pressure changes using a syringe. In Part B, the change in buoyancy is observed with pressure changes in a Cartesian diver.	Natural laws Units of pressure Boyle's law mm Hg, Atmospheres Kinetic theory of matter
Section 4: Charles's Law and Hot-Air Balloons An indirect measure of gas volumes at decreasing temperatures is used to determine the relationship between gas volume and temperature. From this data, absolute zero is graphically determined as well as an understanding of the Kelvin scale versus the Celsius scale. Then, the understanding of temperature and gas volumes is applied by constructing and testing hot-air balloons.	Kelvin scale Charles's law Kinetic theory of matter Absolute zero
Section 5: Types of Reactions and Gas Production In this two-part investigation, hydrogen, oxygen, and carbon dioxide are generated and tested. Then, an effective ratio of hydrogen/oxygen gases to use in the propulsion of a small rocket is determined.	Molar relationships, Moles Reaction types, Catalysts Decomposition reactions Single-replacement reaction Double-replacement reaction Balanced equations Precipitation reactions Acid–base reactions, Redox reactions Law of conservation of mass
Section 6: Ideal Gas Law for the Ideal Toy This investigation uses the knowledge gained from the preceding investigations in order to determine the volume of one mole of oxygen gas. With this information, the gas law constant "*R*" is calculated	Standard temperature and pressure (STP) Combined gas law, Ideal gas law Avogadro's gas law Universal gas constant Intermolecular forces
Section 7: Kinetic Molecular Theory and Graham's Law First, the rate of diffusion of a gas is experienced based on how fast a perfume odor travels across a room. Stoichiometric calculations are performed to determine the amount of reagents needed to fill one plastic bag with hydrogen and another with carbon dioxide. After filling and sealing the two bags, the size of each bag is measured over several days to determine which gas effuses out of its bag faster.	Kinetic molecular theory Graham's law of effusion Limiting reagents Balanced equations Diffusion, Effusion, Stoichiometry Dalton's law of partial pressures
Section 8: Properties of Polymers and Plastics This investigation has three parts. In Parts A and B, a thermoplastic and a thermoset polymer are made. The differences between the two types of plastics are noted and an item, which could be part of the prototype, from each type is constructed. In Part C, the different types of plastics are tested to determine the better choice for its function. Two important criteria of the plastic needed for the toy are identified and tests are designed to determine which plastic best fits the criteria.	Types of polymers Thermoset, Thermoplastic Organic compounds, Polymers, Monomers, HDPE, LDPE, Polyethylene, Chain branching Proteins, DNA, Nucleotides Amino acids, Molecular clock Recyclable plastics

Chapter Concept Map

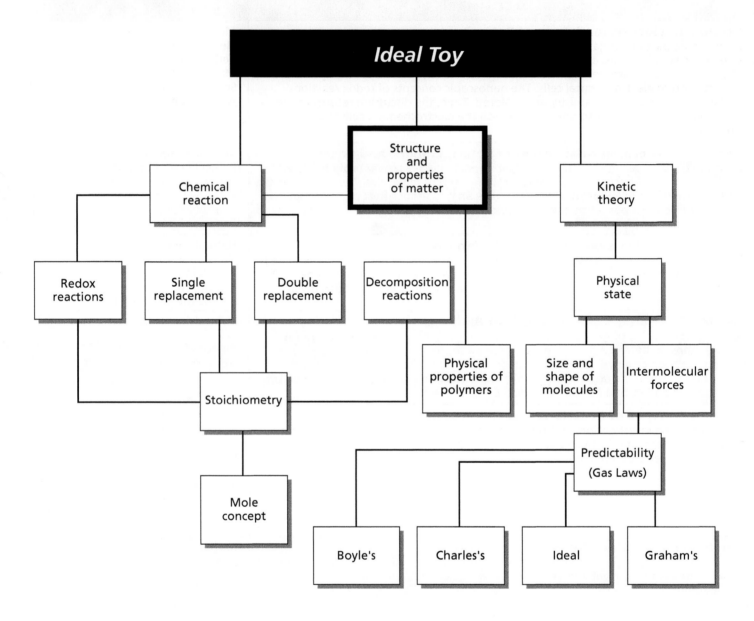

UNDERSTANDING BY DESIGN*

The *Understanding by Design* template focuses on the three stages of backward design:
- **Identify desired results**
- **Determine acceptable evidence**
- **Plan learning experiences**

What overarching understandings are desired?

- Chemical principles are involved in many toys.
- The nature of matter determines its use.
- The behavior of gases is predictable.
- Energy can be transferred in many ways; energy is transformed in chemical reactions.

What are the overarching "essential" questions?

- How are chemical principles used by the toy industry?
- How do physical and chemical properties of matter relate to its use?
- How do gases behave?
- How is energy released from matter?
- How can energy be harnessed to do useful work?

What will students understand as a result of this chapter?

- Chemistry is involved in everyday life.
- Toys involve numerous chemical principles.
- Energy conversions in chemical reactions.
- Various types of chemical reactions and their products.
- Oxidation-reduction reactions.
- Laws have been determined that allow us to predict the behavior of gases.
- The properties of matter influence its use.
- Kinetic theory and the particulate nature of matter.
- Matter is conserved in chemical reactions.

What "essential" questions will focus this chapter?

- How is chemical energy converted to other forms?
- How can we use metals to produce electricity?
- How are materials chosen in product design?
- How does the size and shape of molecules affect their physical phase?
- Can we use kinetic theory and knowledge of the particulate nature of matter to predict the behavior of gases?
- What types of chemical reactions produce gases?
- How do changes in pressure, temperature, volume, and concentration affect the behavior of gases?
- How can these gases be used in product design?
- What happens to matter during a chemical reaction?
- Can we predict the quantities of products produced from chemical reactions?
- What are polymers?

* Grant Wiggins and Jay McTighe, *Understanding by Design* (Merrill/Prentice Hall, 1998), 181.

Pacing Guide

This chapter will take about 4 weeks to complete, assuming a full 5-day school week. Keep in mind that a *Pacing Guide* is merely a suggestion and that you should adjust your pace to your students' needs and the school schedule.

A sample outline is shown below. It assumes that you will assign homework every day and that class time will be used to discuss homework and special topics. *Inquiring Further* activities, if assigned, will allow students to do research or investigations outside regular class time.

Note: Each "Day" assumes a 45-minute class period, or one-half of a 90-minute block.

DAY	SECTION	HOMEWORK
1	Discuss *Scenario, Your Challenge,* and *Criteria for Success.* Develop a scoring rubric. **Section 1** Discuss *What Do You See?* and *What Do You Think?*	Read *Investigate* and write a summary. At home, answer *Investigate* Part A, Step 1a.
2	Students complete *Investigate* Parts A and B. Review results of investigation.	Read *Chem Talk* and answer *Checking Up.* Answer *What Do You Think Now?* Battery-operated toy for *Investigate* Part C.
3	Complete *Investigate* Part C. Discuss *Chem Talk* and *Checking Up* answers. Discuss *What Do You Think Now?* and *Chem Essential Questions.* Answer *Chem to Go* problems 1 and 2.	Read *Reflecting on the Section and the Challenge.* Answer *Chem to Go* problems 3-9.
4	Review *Chem to Go* answers. **Section 2** Discuss *What Do You See?* and *What Do You Think?* Students complete *Investigate* Parts A and B. Review results of investigations.	Read *Chem Talk* and answer *Checking Up* questions. Answer *What Do You Think Now?* questions.
5	Discuss *Chem Talk* and review *Checking Up* answers. Discuss *What Do You Think Now?* and *Chem Essential Questions.* Answer *Chem to Go* problems 1 and 2.	Answer *Chem to Go* problems 3-7. Read *Reflecting on the Section and the Challenge.*
6	Review *Chem to Go* answers. **Section 3** Discuss *What Do You See?* and *What Do You Think?* Students complete *Investigate* Parts A and B. Review results of investigations.	Read *Chem Talk* and answer *Checking Up* questions. Answer *What Do You Think Now?* questions.
7	Discuss *Chem Talk* and the *Checking Up* answers. Discuss *What Do You Think Now?* and the *Chem Essential Questions.* Answer *Chem to Go* problems 1 and 2 in class.	Answer *Chem to Go* problems 3-8. Read *Reflecting on the Section and the Challenge.*
8	Review the *Chem to Go* answers. **Section 4** Discuss *What Do You See?* and *What Do You Think?* Students complete the *Investigate* Part A Steps 1 and 2. Discuss the results of the *Investigate.*	Read *Investigate* Parts B and C and summarize in an outline.
9	Students complete *Investigate* Part B. Review results of the investigation. Discuss *Investigate* Part C.	Read *Chem Talk* and answer *Checking Up.* Answer *What Do You Think Now?* Read *Reflecting on the Section and the Challenge.*

DAY	SECTION	HOMEWORK
10	Discuss the *Chem Talk* and the *Checking Up* answers. Discuss the *What Do You Think Now?* and the *Chem Essential Questions*. Students complete *Investigate* Part C. Discuss results of the investigation.	Answer *Chem to Go* questions. Read the *Chapter mini-Challenge*. Work with group on the *Chapter Mini-Challenge*.
11	Review *Chem to Go* answers. Students present *Chapter Mini-Challenges* and receive feedback on *Chapter Mini-Challenges*.	Read and summarize the *Investigate* for *Section 5*.
12	**Section 5** Discuss *What Do You See?* and *What Do You Think?* Review measurements and discuss precision and accuracy. Students complete *Investigate* Part A. Review results of the investigation.	Read *Investigate* Part B and summarize in an outline. Read *Chem Talk* and answer *Checking Up* questions.
13	Discuss *Chem Talk* and review *Checking Up* answers. Students complete *Investigate* Part B. Review results of the investigation. Discuss *Chem Essential Questions*.	Answer *What Do You Think Now?* and *Chem to Go* problems. Read *Reflecting on the Section and the Challenge*.
14	Review *What Do You Think Now?* and *Chem to Go* answers. **Section 6** Discuss *What Do You See?* and *What Do You Think?* Students complete *Investigate* Steps 1-7. Review results of investigation.	Read *Chem Talk* and answer *Checking Up* questions. Complete *Investigate* Steps 8-10.
15	Discuss *Chem Talk* and review *Checking Up* answers. Review results from *Investigate* Steps 8-10. Discuss *Chem Essential Questions* and *What Do You Think Now?*	Answer *Chem to Go* problems. Read *Reflecting on the Section and the Challenge*.
16	Review *Chem to Go* answers. **Section 7** Discuss *What Do You See?* and *What Do You Think?* Students complete *Investigate*. Review investigations.	Read *Chem Talk* and answer *Checking Up* questions. Answer the *What Do You Think Now?* question.
17	Discuss *Chem Talk* and review *Checking Up* answers. Review the *What Do You Think Now?* responses. Discuss the *Chem Essential Questions*.	Answer *Chem to Go* problems. Read *Reflecting on the Section and the Challenge*.
18	Review the *Chem to Go* answers. **Section 6** Discuss *What Do You See?* and *What Do You Think?* Students complete *Investigate* Parts A and B. Review investigation. Answer *Chem to Go* problems 1-3.	Complete *Investigate* Part C. Read *Chem Talk* and answer *Checking Up*. Answer *What Do You Think Now?* questions.
19	Discuss *Investigate* Part C and carry out approved procedure. Discuss *Chem Talk* and review *Checking Up* answers. Discuss *What Do You Think Now?* and *Chem Essential Questions*.	Answer *Chem to Go* problems 4-6. Read *Reflecting on the Section and the Challenge*. Read *Preparing for the Chapter Challenge*.
20	Review *Chem to Go* answers. Discuss *Preparing for the Chapter Challenge*. Work on the *Chapter Challenge*.	Work on the *Chapter Challenge* in groups.
21	*Chapter Challenge* presentations by students.	

CHAPTER 3

Chapter 5
Materials, Equipment, and Chemicals

The following tables contain lists of materials, equipment, and chemicals needed to do all of the investigations. The tables are organized as follows:

- **Table 1:** Durables per group (4 Students)
- **Table 2:** Durables per class
- **Table 3:** Consumables per group (4 Students)
- **Table 4:** Consumables per class
- **Table 5:** Chemicals

Durables are items which are not consumed during the investigation and which can be used for several classes over several years. **Consumables** are items that are used up during each class and must be re-supplied for future classes. Both the durables and consumables are broken down by group and by class. A **group** consists of four students. While the groups size will be determined by the teacher based upon logistics and availability of equipment, the information in **Table 1** and **Table 3** is based upon the recommended group size of four students.

Materials and Equipment

The first table contains the **durable** items needed per group. The right column, **Quantity**, contains the number of items needed per group. The left column, **Section**, gives the section number(s) in which each item will be used. The item quantities given are considered to be a minimum but, in some cases, if more are available, that would be ideal.

The second table contains the information on **Durables** needed per class. In some cases, these will be items that are shared by the class. In other cases, the item will be used for a demonstration.

The third and fourth tables contain the items which are **consumable**. The third table contains **consumables per group** (recommended group size is four students) and the fourth table contains **consumables per class**.

TABLE 1: DURABLES PER GROUP (4 STUDENTS)		
Section	Materials and Equipment (Durables)	Quantity
All	Lab aprons	4
All	Safety goggles	4
1	Porous cup	1
1	Wire leads with alligator clips	2
1	Voltage sensor	1
1	Toy (battery-operated to run with electrochemical	1
1	Battery holder, D-cell	2
1, 5	Beaker, 250 mL	1
3	Syringe, 50-60 mL, graduated	1
3, 4, 6	Ringstand	1
3	Bottle, 2 liter, plastic	1
3, 4, 6	Burette clamp	1
3	Eye dropper	1
4, 8	Beakers, 600 mL	2
4, 8	Wire gauze squares for hot plate	2
4, 8	Crucible tongs	1
4	Thermometer (or temperature probe)	1
4, 5, 6	Scissors	1
4, 8	Hot plate	1
5	Scoopula	1
5	Watch glass (250-mL beaker cover)	1
5	Launch pad (board with nail)	1
5	Test tubes, large	2
5	Test tube rack	1
5	Rubber stoppers, solid (to fit large test tubes)	2
5	Rubber stoppers, one hole (to fit large test tubes)	2
6	Wire, #22, bare copper, 1 foot	1
6	Gas collection tube, graduated, 50 mL	1
6	Rubber stopper, one hole (for gas tube)	1
6	Graduated cylinder, 10 mL	1
6	Beaker, 1 L	1
6, 7	Ruler or tape measure	1
7	Graduated cylinder, 100 mL	1

CHAPTER 3

TABLE 2: DURABLES PER CLASS		
Section	**Materials and Equipment (Durables)**	**Quantity**
2	Computer with *ChemSketch*™ and *3D Viewer* (available from acdlabs.com)	1 (optional)
5	Tesla coil, hand-held	1
6, 7	Balances, 0.01 g	2
7	Bottle of perfume (or other strong scent)	1

TABLE 3: CONSUMABLES PER GROUP (4 STUDENTS)		
Section	**Materials and Equipment (Consumables)**	**Quantity**
1	Set of assorted batteries (AA, AAA, 2D, 9-V)	1
4	Sheet of white paper	1
4	Dry-cleaner bags	2
4, 5	Beral pipettes, 3 mL	10
7	Resealable plastic bags, quart-size	2
7	Marking pen, indelible	1
7	Weighing boats	5
8	Rubber gloves (pairs)	4
8	Stick of epoxy putty	1

TABLE 4: CONSUMABLES PER CLASS		
Section	**Materials and Equipment (Consumables)**	**Quantity**
1	Distilled water	5 gal
1	Battery, 6-volt	1
3	Graph paper, pad of 50 sheets	1
4	Roll of clear, wide postal tape	1
4	Boxes of paper clips	2
5	Box of wooden splints	1
5	Box of matches	1
7	Paper, 8.5" x 11" white (for sketches)	50
8	Roll of paper towels	1
8	Thermoplastic strips'	1 lb
8	Various items to mold with, such as plastic toys, kitchen utensils, etc., and each group should have two or more	15 assorted

Chemicals

In this fifth table, the **Chemicals** required for each section are listed. By their nature, most chemicals are consumable, of course. The amounts given in the right-hand column under **Quantity** are calculated for 5 classes of 24 students, or 120 students. Most teachers will find that these amounts (when divided by 5 to give the amount

needed for one class) will still provide ample excess for repeat experiments or student error. It should be noted that the metal strips in *Section 1* are meant to be used in other sections and in other chapters. After use as electrodes or testing with hydrochloric acid, they can be recovered, rinsed and used again.

Section	Chemicals	Quantity
	TABLE 5: CHEMICALS FOR FIVE CLASSES (24 students)	
1	Strips of iron	7
1	Strips of magnesium	7
1	Strips of copper	7
1	Strips of zinc	7
1	1.0 M iron (III) nitrate solution	3 L
1	1.0 M magnesium nitrate solution	3 L
1	1.0 M copper (II) nitrate solution	3 L
1	1.0 M zinc nitrate solution	3 L
5	Manganese dioxide, MnO_2	25 g
5	Mossy zinc, approx.105 pieces	25 g
5	3% Hydrogen peroxide, H_2O_2	1 L
5, 7	1.0 M Hydrochloric acid, HCl	4 L
5, 7	Baking soda, sodium bicarbonate, $NaHCO_3$	625 g
6	3.0 M Hydrochloric acid, HCl	500 mL
6	Magnesium ribbon	5 m
7	Zinc, granular	100 g
7	Vinegar, 5-6% acetic acid, CH_3COOH	1.75 L
8	Isopropyl (rubbing) alcohol	500 mL

Teacher Resources

Blackline Masters

- Blackline Masters

Available on the *Teacher Resources CD*.

- Color Overheads

Available on *Teacher Resources CD*.

Blackline Masters

Chapter Supports

	POINT OF USE	BLACKLINE MASTER LABEL
Sample Criteria for Excellence	*Chapter Challenge* Introduction	5a
Chem at Work: Profile 1	Chem at Work	5b
Chem at Work: Profile 2	Chem at Work	5c
Chem at Work: Profile 3	Chem at Work	5d
Sample Assessment Rubric	*Chapter Challenge* Conclusion	5e

Section Quizzes

Section 1 Quiz	Section 1	5-1a
Section 2 Quiz	Section 2	5-2a
Section 3 Quiz	Section 3	5-3d
Section 4 Quiz	Section 4	5-4b
Section 5 Quiz	Section 5	5-5a
Section 6 Quiz	Section 6	5-6a
Section 7 Quiz	Section 7	5-7a
Section 8 Quiz	Section 8	5-8a

Section Supports

	POINT OF USE	BLACKLINE MASTER LABEL
Volume/Pressure Data Table	Section 3 – *Investigate*	5-3a
Pressure vs. Volume Graph	Section 3 – *Investigate*	5-3b
Pressure vs. 1/Volume Graph	Section 3 – *Investigate*	5-3c
Volume/Temp. Blank Data Table	Section 4 – *Investigate*	5-4a

Chapter Assessment

Chem Practice Test	Chapter Conclusion	5f

Color Overheads

	POINT OF USE
What Do You See?	Section 1
Variety of batteries diagram	Section 1 – *Investigate*
What Do You See?	Section 2
Page 1-halogen molecules	Section 2 – *Investigate*
Page 2-CX_4 molecules	Section 2 – *Investigate*
Page 3-hydrocarbons	Section 2 – *Investigate*
Page 4-alcohols	Section 2 – *Investigate*
Melting and Boiling Points of Halogens	Section 2 – *Investigate*
Melting and Boiling Points of CX_4	Section 2 – *Investigate*
Graph of Boiling Points	Section 2 – *Investigate*
What Do You See?	Section 3
What Do You See?	Section 4
What Do You See?	Section 5
What Do You See?	Section 6
What Do You See?	Section 7
What Do You See?	Section 8

CHAPTER 5

Chapter Challenge

Scenario

Read, or have a student read aloud, the *Scenario*. Ask them about their favorite toys and if any of those toys operated on chemical principles. You might also ask if any students ever tried to invent a toy. The subject of toys can easily get students eager to talk. It is your responsibility as the teacher to engage them but not to devote too much time to this discussion. You may want to expand on the *Scenario* by using videos, or by inviting people from the industry to give presentations.

Your Challenge

You may wish to lead a class discussion about the challenge and the expectations. Review the titles of the sections in the Table of Contents at the front of the *Student Edition*. Point out that the content of the sections aligns with the content expected for the *Chapter Challenge* and ask students for ideas as to how this content might relate to the challenge at hand. The students should be aware that there are three main parts to the challenge. These can be written on the board:

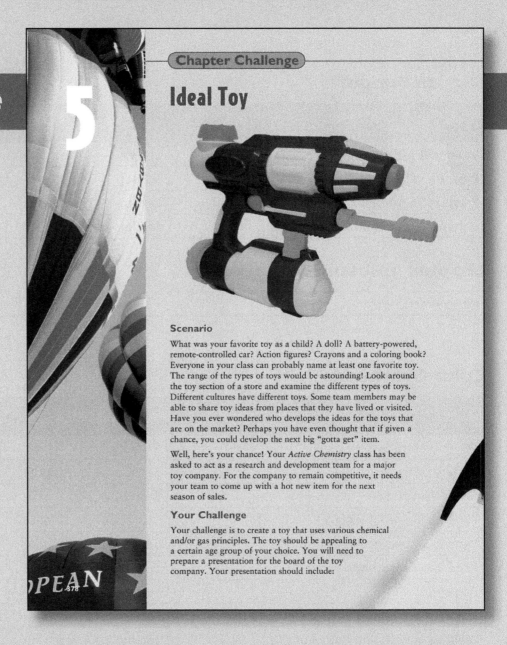

Chapter Challenge

Ideal Toy

Scenario

What was your favorite toy as a child? A doll? A battery-powered, remote-controlled car? Action figures? Crayons and a coloring book? Everyone in your class can probably name at least one favorite toy. The range of the types of toys would be astounding! Look around the toy section of a store and examine the different types of toys. Different cultures have different toys. Some team members may be able to share toy ideas from places that they have lived or visited. Have you ever wondered who develops the ideas for the toys that are on the market? Perhaps you have even thought that if given a chance, you could develop the next big "gotta get" item.

Well, here's your chance! Your *Active Chemistry* class has been asked to act as a research and development team for a major toy company. For the company to remain competitive, it needs your team to come up with a hot new item for the next season of sales.

Your Challenge

Your challenge is to create a toy that uses various chemical and/or gas principles. The toy should be appealing to a certain age group of your choice. You will need to prepare a presentation for the board of the toy company. Your presentation should include:

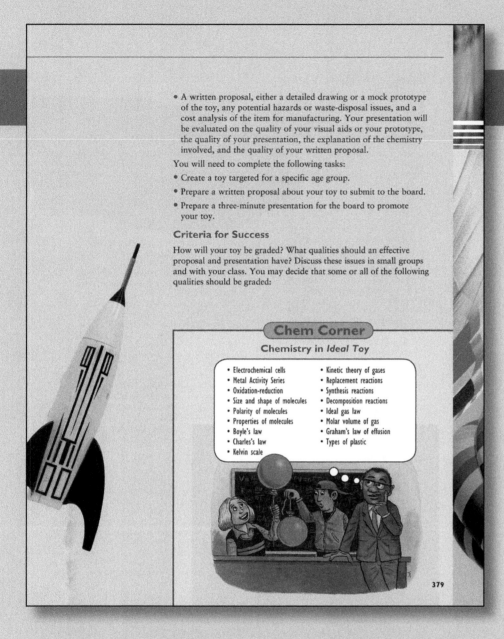

• A written proposal, either a detailed drawing or a mock prototype of the toy, any potential hazards or waste-disposal issues, and a cost analysis of the item for manufacturing. Your presentation will be evaluated on the quality of your visual aids or your prototype, the quality of your presentation, the explanation of the chemistry involved, and the quality of your written proposal.

You will need to complete the following tasks:

• Create a toy targeted for a specific age group.

• Prepare a written proposal about your toy to submit to the board.

• Prepare a three-minute presentation for the board to promote your toy.

Criteria for Success

How will your toy be graded? What qualities should an effective proposal and presentation have? Discuss these issues in small groups and with your class. You may decide that some or all of the following qualities should be graded:

Chem Corner

Chemistry in *Ideal Toy*

- Electrochemical cells
- Metal Activity Series
- Oxidation-reduction
- Size and shape of molecules
- Polarity of molecules
- Properties of molecules
- Boyle's law
- Charles's law
- Kelvin scale
- Kinetic theory of gases
- Replacement reactions
- Synthesis reactions
- Decomposition reactions
- Ideal gas law
- Molar volume of gas
- Graham's law of effusion
- Types of plastic

379

Chem Corner

This section is a preview of the basic science principles and skills that will be presented in the various sections in this chapter. It may be useful to find out how many of these terms are familiar to your students by asking for a show of hands to indicate whether they know the meaning, are unsure, or are unfamiliar with the word. Encourage them to offer ideas as to how these principles and skills might relate to the design and operation of a toy. Remember to help students keep track of the concepts and skills they are learning as they will need to apply them once they begin work on the *Chapter Challenge*.

CHAPTER 3

• Create or design a toy that uses various chemical and/or gas principles and is targeted for a specific age group. It can be produced either as a detailed drawing or as a mock prototype.

• Prepare a written proposal about the toy to submit to the board of a toy company. This proposal should include any potential hazards or waste-disposal issues and a cost analysis of the item for manufacturing.

• Prepare a three-minute presentation to promote your design and submit the written proposal to the board.

As you discuss the challenge, reassure students that while they might not feel able to complete the assignment now, by the end of the chapter they will have the necessary skills and experience to respond adequately.

Chapter Challenge

Criteria for Success

After the class has read the *Scenario* and the *Chapter Challenge*, you can take a few moments as a class to develop the assessment. Students should be asked, "What should the toy design, the proposal and the presentation have to be like to earn an A?" Remind them that the toy must help people understand certain chemical principles. One way to get started is to make a list of the important criteria that must be included in the *Chapter Challenge*. List some suggestions they might consider, including the number and variety of chemical principles incorporated in the toy's operation, the accuracy and clarity of the explanation, the quality of the prototype or schematic of the toy, etc. (As they volunteer ideas, it is important that all suggestions be recognized, so consider this a brainstorming session.)

Then ask the class what an "ideal" toy would look like and how it might operate. Ask what a proposal worthy of an A grade would have to include. By soliciting the students' opinions, the class will create an assessment tool that is written in language the students can understand. When you have a thorough description of each part of the *Chapter Challenge*, you can have the class vote on how much each part is worth.

A sample rubric for assessing the *Chapter Challenge* is provided at the end of this chapter. You can copy and distribute the rubric as is, or use it as a baseline for developing scoring guidelines and expectations that suit your needs. For example, you might wish to ensure that core concepts and abilities derived from your local or state science frameworks also appear on the rubric. You might also wish to modify the format of the rubric to make it more consistent with your evaluation system. However you decide to evaluate the *Chapter Challenge*, keep in mind that all expectations should be

---

Chapter Challenge

Presentation
- Visual aid
- Schematic or prototype of toy
- Explanation of how the toy works
- Hazard and waste-disposal issues
- Cost analysis

Quality of Presentation
- Organization
- Audience appeal
- Eye contact
- Time limit
- Clarity of explanation

Chemical Principles
- Variety used

- Explanation of chemistry involved
- Accuracy of explanation

Written Proposal
- Rationale
- Visuals
- Explanation
- Cost analysis

Once you have determined the list of qualities for evaluating the toy, presentation, and proposal, you and your class should also decide how many points should be given for each criterion. How many points should be awarded for the presentation and how many for the proposal? Should more points be awarded if more chemistry is involved? How many different chemical principles should be incorporated into your toy? Determining the grading criteria in advance will help you focus your time and effort on the most important aspects of your work.

Since you will be working with other students in small groups, you will need to determine grading criteria that reward each individual in the group for his or her contribution and also reward the group for the final presentation. What is a fair contribution of each person? How can the group be judged fairly for their toy, presentation, and proposal? Your teacher may provide you with a sample rubric to help you get started.

Set your imagination free, this *Chapter Challenge* requires you to design the toy of your dreams! In addition to your new chemistry knowledge, you will use a simplified *Engineering Design Cycle* to help your group complete this design challenge. Understanding the *Goal* is the first step in any *Engineering Design Cycle*. Creating your new toy design is the *Goal* for this challenge, so you have already completed the first step. Each chapter section you complete will provide you with potential technologies to include in your design.

As you experience each one of the chapter sections you will be gaining *Inputs* to use in the *Engineering Design Cycle*. These *Inputs* will include new chemistry concepts, vocabulary, and techniques that might be incorporated into the toy that your group envisions. Each section of this chapter will provide you with a different potential technology to include in your toy design. When your group prepares the *Mini-Challenge* presentation and the *Chapter Challenge*, you will be completing the *Process* step of the *Engineering Design Cycle*. During the *Process* step you will establish and consider criteria for your toy design, compare and contrast potential solutions, and most importantly make decisions about the types of chemistry that your group you will use to design their *Ideal Toy*.

The *Outputs* of your *Engineering Design Cycle* will be the presentation of your *Ideal Toy* design. You will need to include your written proposal, diagrams or models, and a cost analysis as part of your presentation. Finally, you will receive *Feedback* from your classmates and your instructor about what parts of your toy are good and which parts need to be refined. You will repeat the *Engineering Design Cycle* two times during the course of the chapter. The first will be when you complete the *Mini-Challenge* halfway through the chapter. The second is when you complete the second half of the chapter, gain more *Inputs*, finalize your design, and complete your written proposal.

380

---

communicated to students at the start of their work. Be sure that the students actively participate in deciding the criteria for evaluation. *The Sample Criteria for Excellence* is also provided as a Blackline Master on the *Teacher Resources CD*.

5a | **Blackline Master**

SAMPLE CRITERIA FOR EXCELLENCE

It is important for students to decide on the criteria for grading the *Chapter Challenge* themselves. This provides them with the opportunity to take part in determining how their projects will be judged. You can help them arrive at a list of criteria by outlining those aspects of the project that could be rated. Some aspects to be considered are the actual toy design (prototype or detailed drawing), the variety of chemical principles employed and their explanation, the quality and thoroughness of the written proposal, and the quality and peripherals of the presentation. You may want to help them by sharing some of the sample criteria that are listed below. Bear in mind that at this point, students are only establishing the criteria needed to earn a top grade in order to motivate them to succeed.

As the *Chapter Challenge* approaches, you will need to develop a more comprehensive assessment rubric for evaluating the projects. For an example, you can refer to the *Sample Assessment Rubric* at the end of the chapter in this *Teacher's Edition.*

MEETS THE STANDARD OF EXCELLENCE FOR CHAPTER CHALLENGE

Aspect	Criteria of Excellence
Chemistry concepts	• at least three chemical and/or gas principles are applied in the design and operation of the toy
Quality of prototype	• prototype or schematic is well-designed and well-crafted • an effective and entertaining demonstration of the chemical and/or gas concepts as applied to the toy
Scientific explanations	• clear explanations for each chemical concept are provided
Written proposal	• presentation is professional, well-rehearsed and contains sufficient visuals • provides all the information needed for the board to make a decision

SECTION 1
Electrochemistry and Batteries

Section Overview

In this three-part section, students first review and explore what they already know about batteries, then examine several types of them. Starting at the macro level, they make observations about commercial batteries. They use the Metal Activity Series as a guide as they build their own electrochemical cells. Students will learn the microscopic concepts of redox reactions and electrochemical cell chemistry. They then return to the macroscopic level as they attempt to power a toy with the cells they have created.

Background Information

A battery is one or more electrochemical cells that may be interconnected as one unit. Each cell has two electrodes (cathode and anode) and contains electrolytes. Redox reactions (oxidation-reduction) occur in the cells and this converts chemical energy into electrical energy.

The electrolyte is used to transfer ions between the electrodes in the body of the battery. When the battery is attached to a load (something to be powered), electrons flow from the anode to the cathode outside of the electrolyte solution. The cathode goes through reduction and the anode goes through oxidation, the pair making a redox reaction.

One type of common cell introduced in the 1860s is the Leclanché cell, named after its inventor, French electrical engineer Georges Leclanché. The Leclanché cell is also known as a zinc-carbon cell and has a zinc anode and a manganese dioxide cathode, though graphite is often added to the cathode to improve conductivity. The electrolyte is ammonium chloride or zinc chloride. The zinc chloride version has been used more in recent times, because it performs better when needed for heavy use.

Another commonly used cell introduced a century later, in the 1960s, is the alkaline cell, which is now more popular than the Leclanché cell. Its anode is zinc and the cathode is manganese dioxide, both in powder form. No added graphite (carbon) is needed for the cathode, because this MnO_2 is synthetic, which makes it more conductive than naturally occurring MnO_2 that is used in the Leclanché. The electrolyte is potassium hydroxide (KOH), which allows for higher conductivity than ammonium chloride. Additives like zinc oxide (added to the anode) and cellulose (a gelling agent) make alkaline cells more expensive than Leclanché cells, but they do perform much better. Most of the batteries found in stores today are alkaline cells.

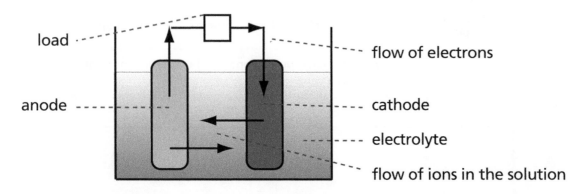

load ---- flow of electrons

anode ---- cathode

---- electrolyte

---- flow of ions in the solution

LEARNING OUTCOMES

LEARNING OUTCOMES	LOCATION IN SECTION	EVIDENCE OF UNDERSTANDING
Make observations about commercial batteries.	*Investigate* Part A	Observations recorded in students' *Active Chemistry* logs are similar to what is listed in this *Teacher's Edition*.
Make an electrochemical cell.	*Investigate* Part B *Chem Talk*	Students use the activity series to build an electrochemical cell with the greatest voltage.
Understand the chemistry of an electrochemical cell.	*Investigate* Parts B-C *Chem Talk, Chem to Go* Questions 1-7 *Preparing for the Chapter Challenge, Inquiring Further*	Students are able to carry out the investigation and draw conclusions about voltage from their data. Answers match those listed in this *Teacher's Edition*. Summary is similar to the one in this *Teacher's Edition*.
Use an electrochemical cell to power a toy.	*Investigate* Part C	Answers to questions are similar to those listed in this *Teacher's Edition*.

NOTES

_____

_____

_____

_____

_____

_____

_____

_____

_____

_____

_____

_____

_____

_____

_____

_____

_____

_____

CHAPTER 3

Section 1
Materials, Chemicals, Preparation, and Safety

("per Group" quantity is based on group size of 4 students)

Materials and Equipment

Materials (and Equipment)	Quantity per Group (4 students)
Beaker, 250 mL	1
Porous cup (or salt bridge)	1
Wire leads with alligator clips	2
Voltage sensor	1
Toy (battery-operated to run with electrochemical cell)	1
Set of assorted batteries (AA, AAA, 2D, 9-V)	1
Battery holder, D-cell	2
Materials (and Equipment)	Quantity per Class
Battery, 6-volt	1
Distilled water	5 gal

Chemicals

Chemicals	Quantity per Class (24 students)
1.0 M iron (III) nitrate solution	750 mL
1.0 M magnesium nitrate solution	750 mL
1.0 M copper (II) nitrate solution	750 mL
1.0 M zinc nitrate solution	750 mL
Strips of iron	7
Strips of magnesium	7
Strips of copper	7
Strips of zinc	7

Teacher Preparation

1.0 M Iron (III) nitrate, $Fe(NO_3)_3$:
Dissolve 303.0 g of $Fe(NO_3)_3 \cdot 9H_2O$ in 650 mL of distilled water and dilute to 750 mL.

1.0 M Magnesium nitrate, $Mg(NO_3)_2$:
Dissolve 192.3 g of $Mg(NO_3)_2 \cdot 6H_2O$ in 650 mL of distilled water and dilute to 750 mL.

1.0 M Copper (II) nitrate, $Cu(NO_3)_2$:
Dissolve 181.2 g of $Cu(NO_3)_2 \cdot 3H_2O$ in 650 mL of distilled water and dilute to 750 mL.

1.0 M Zinc nitrate, $Zn(NO_3)_2$:
Dissolve 192.3 g of $Zn(NO_3)_2 \cdot 6H_2O$ in 650 mL of distilled water and dilute to 750 mL.

Safety Requirements

- Goggles and aprons are required in the laboratory area.

- Solutions can be saved for another class or washed down the sink, except for copper (II) nitrate. This should be evaporated back to the hydrated salt and reused or saved for waste disposal.

- The porous cups can be cleaned by soaking them overnight in 6 M HNO_3. Then rinse them with water. Dilute the used nitric acid and flush down the drain with copious amounts of water.

- At the completion of the laboratory work the students should wash arms and hands with soap and water before they leave the lab area.

NOTES

Meeting the Needs of All Students
Differentiated Instruction
Augmentation and Accommodations

LEARNING ISSUE	REFERENCE	AUGMENTATION AND ACCOMMODATIONS
Selecting and organizing data in a table	*Investigate* Part A, 2.	**Augmentation** • Teach students to read carefully and think about what criteria they need to record in their tables. **Accommodations** • Provide students who have difficulty selecting criteria for observation with a list of categories they should include in their charts, including battery name, size, shape, voltage, and other markings. • Provide students with a blank, formatted table. • Provide a formatted table with category titles inserted.
Mastering vocabulary	*Investigate, Chem Talk*	**Augmentation** • Students must interact at least six times with an unfamiliar term before it becomes part of their working vocabularies. Each interaction gives them another representation or context through which to understand the term. Understanding comes in stages as the term becomes more familiar. Not until the final stage is it likely that they will be able to use it in new contexts independently. Until then they need scaffolds and direct instruction to enhance their understanding. This instruction is best embedded in the meaningful context of their work. Therefore, mastering the 20 or so vocabulary terms in this section should begin during the investigation where words like volt, voltmeter, battery, electrochemical cell, ion, porous cup, electrode and others are first used. • Have students set aside a place in their *Active Chemistry* logs for these words, even those they have seen in other chapters, so they can reference them as they read. This will mean that the class will have to stop at certain points during the investigation so that students can focus on vocabulary as they learn content. If not done strategically, stopping can sometimes disrupt the flow and momentum of a session. • Strategies students should be taught as they read and investigate include skipping the unfamiliar word, finding its meaning using the context or a definition in the text, asking a group member for its meaning, taking time to write its meaning verbatim or an example of its use in their *Active Chemistry* logs, and looking in the *Chem Talk* section under *Chem Words* to locate a concise definition even before they have read that section. Stop the investigation at convenient points to have students focus on learning vocabulary. • Another strategy for making meaningful representations of the terms in this section is to have students label them in a diagram. Consider using some form of the diagram of the energy cell in the *Chem Talk* section, which students can label with terms they learned. This will allow them to meaningfully organize the terms that belong together. They should label the positive and negative charges, the anode, cathode, oxidation half-reaction, reduction half-reaction, and direction of electron flow.

LEARNING ISSUE	REFERENCE	AUGMENTATION AND ACCOMMODATIONS
Accessing previous learning	*Chem Talk*	**Augmentation** • Students need to review electron-releasing tendencies of various elements in order to understand why certain combinations of metals create more voltage than others. That involves helping them recall the significance of the number of electrons in an outer shell of an element and the relative ease with which it releases electrons. This could be done by helping students access information from previous chapters in their *Active Chemistry* logs or by leading a class review. The first method fosters independence. This could be differentiated by placing competent students together. Those groups could move to the *Inquiring Further* section while instruction is given to others. **Accommodations** • Place students in mixed groups so students who have mastered electron-releasing tendencies can help those in their group who have not.

Strategies for Students with Limited English Language Proficiency

LEARNING ISSUE	REFERENCE	AUGMENTATIONS
Background knowledge Vocabulary Project work	*Chapter Challenge, Scenario, Your Challenge*	Consider inviting students to bring in a toy from their own childhood or from a younger sibling. A variety of toys from different cultures will increase interest and serve as a springboard for an open discussion. Students should develop oral language skills as they describe their toys and how they are used. Set up the arrangements for students to work in carefully coordinated teams to develop their *Chapter Challenge* projects. Ensure that the word "targeted" is understood in this context. Students will need a model of what a proposal looks like and how it is structured. Check for understanding of the listed criteria for the presentation and proposal.
Background knowledge	*What Do You Think?*	Check to make sure that students know the term "*come to life*," and give examples of things that are "animated."
Vocabulary	*Investigate* Part A, 1. Part B, 3.,6.	Students may not be aware of the use of the term "*commercially*" as a word associated with "*commerce*." Check for understanding of the term "*porous*" as well as the word "*determine*" used in Step 6. Derivations such as "*determination*" might be helpful. Students might benefit from having a partner or team member paraphrase the directions as they intensify in complexity.
Background knowledge Vocabulary Comprehending text	*Chem Talk*	Have students put new words in their personal dictionaries or *Active Chemistry* logs. Check for understanding of the word "*current*" and share other meanings and derivations. Check for recognition and understanding of periodic table abbreviations such as "Zn" and "Cu." Reference to "*LEO the lion*" may not be clear for some students.
Background knowledge	*What Do You Think Now?*	Point out to students that this is a two-part question requiring two answers.
Background knowledge Vocabulary Comprehending text	*Chem Essential Questions*	Check for understanding of "*phenomenon*" in the context of what is observed. Have students work with partners to write their explanations, possibly having one student dictate to the other.
Comprehension Vocabulary	*Chem to Go*	Make sure students understand questions that are stacked, where there is more than one response (2,4,5). Make sure students understand when a question is a multiple-choice response (7,8,9).
Application Comprehension	*Inquiring Further*	Help students with the concept of "*design.*"

Section 1
Teaching Suggestions and Sample Answers

What Do You See?

This section serves as a strategy to engage students via the illustration, which is based on the upcoming section. The question *What Do You See?* can be answered on several levels. One student may report literally what she sees, e.g., "There are nuts and bolts coming out of the back of the car!" Another may try to interpret the intent of the artist, e.g., "It looks like a remote-controlled electric car." Both responses are valid and should be acknowledged as such. Later, you may wish to return to the illustration so that the students will have a better understanding of the significance to the investigation and recognize that they have progressed in content understanding and knowledge.

Students will certainly mention the vehicle, the screws and nuts falling out the back and other details. You may encourage them to notice that it is a battery-operated car and that there is battery "information" on the board in the background. You can ask them if anything on this board is familiar to them.

What Do You Think?

Students will most likely say that batteries are a source of electricity. They may know that they are based on chemical reactions inside the battery. Value all of their comments and encourage them to share among the groups their ideas of how batteries operate. You should not expect correct answers at this point. The purpose here is to gauge the level of understanding and background knowledge that you will be building upon. You will be returning to this question after the section for a more comprehensive discussion.

STUDENTS' PRIOR CONCEPTIONS

Electrochemistry is regarded as one of the most difficult topics for teachers to teach and for students to learn. This may be due in part to the fact that two challenging concepts – redox reactions and electricity – are simultaneously presented.

Students may have the idea that a battery is a can of electrons that are released on demand.

From this overall misconception, the following statements, taken from a review of chemistry misconceptions[1], are derived:

The current flows because there is a difference in charge at the anode and cathode.

This statement confuses "charge" with "voltage" or "potential difference." There is a difference in potential between the anode and cathode which is the driving force for the flow of current.

The anode is positively charged because it loses electrons; the cathode is negatively charged because it gains electrons.

In fact, the anode gives up electrons because it is more easily oxidized than the cathode. This is relative and the anode can become the cathode by changing the cathode to a more active metal.

Electrons move through the electrolyte to complete the circuit.

This is more an oversimplification than a misconception. The electrons do move through the electrolyte, not as naked electrons, but by "piggybacking" on an anion.

[1]. Garnett, Pamela J. & Hackling, M.W. "Students' Alternative Conceptions in Chemistry: A Review of Research and Implications for Teaching and Learning." *Studies in Science Education, v.25* (1995): 69-95

Section 1

Electrochemistry and Batteries

What Do You See?

Learning Outcomes

In this section you will

• Make observations about commercial batteries.

• Make an electrochemical cell.

• Understand the chemistry of an electrochemical cell.

• Use an electrochemical cell to power a toy.

What Do You Think?

Many toys use batteries. You pop these small metal containers into a toy and it "comes to life."

• What is a battery and how does it work?

The *What Do You Think?* question is provided to get you engaged in the section. It is meant to grab your attention. It is also used to find out what you already know or think you know. Don't worry about being right or wrong. Discussing what you think you know is an important step in learning.

Record your ideas about this question in your *Active Chemistry* log. Be prepared to discuss your responses with your small group and the class.

Investigate

Part A: Commercial Batteries

1. There are many different *batteries* available commercially. Your teacher will provide you with some examples.

 a) List all the types of batteries that you can think of (AA, C, D, and so on). Record your observations of the physical properties of the batteries, such as size, shape, markings, and so on.

381

Active Chemistry

What Do You Think?
A CHEMIST'S RESPONSE

A battery is one or more electrochemical cells that may be interconnected as one unit. Each cell has two electrodes (cathode and anode) and contains electrolytes. The electrodes are connected in series so that the voltage of the entire battery is boosted. For instance, six 1.5 volt cells connected in series will provide 9 volts. The voltage difference between the electrodes is caused by a difference in electrical potential. Redox reactions (oxidation-reduction) occur in the cells and this converts chemical energy into electrical energy.

Investigate

Part A: Commercial Batteries

1.a)

Students should list the types of batteries they are familiar with and make observations about some commercial batteries. Have them look at a number of different sizes of batteries from AAA to D (all have about 1.5 volts) and a 9-V as well.

CHAPTER 5

2.

Have students determine the voltage of three different batteries using a simple voltmeter. Encourage them to make their predictions about what is inside a 9-V battery after they see that the other batteries are 1.5-V each. They may be surprised to realize that there are 6 small batteries inside the 9-V, each producing 1.5 volts in a serial arrangement.

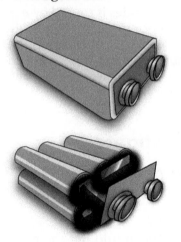

Inside a standard 9-volt battery

3.a)

Voltage: The measurement of electrical potential between two metals, representing the "push" that drives electrons through the wire connecting the two metals.

3.b)

Two 1.5-V batteries connected in series would have 3.0 volts.

3.c)

The voltage should be about 3-V, depending on the batteries. Partially depleted batteries may be slightly less.

Part B: Electrochemical Cells

1.

If a porous cup is not available, a salt bridge (U-tube) will work very well also. Two beakers will be required in this case.

2.-3.

The Zn/Cu combination is suggested. Other possible anode/cathode combinations are: Mg/Cu, Mg/Fe, Zn/Fe, etc.

Note: Metals higher in the activity series should be used as anodes and metals lower in series should be used for cathodes.

4.

Be sure that students get a positive reading on their voltmeter.

5.

To save time and chemicals, you might wish to consider having each group of students set up only one of the metal electrode pairs. After each group measures the voltage at their station, they can rotate through the class to measure the voltage at stations set up by the other groups.

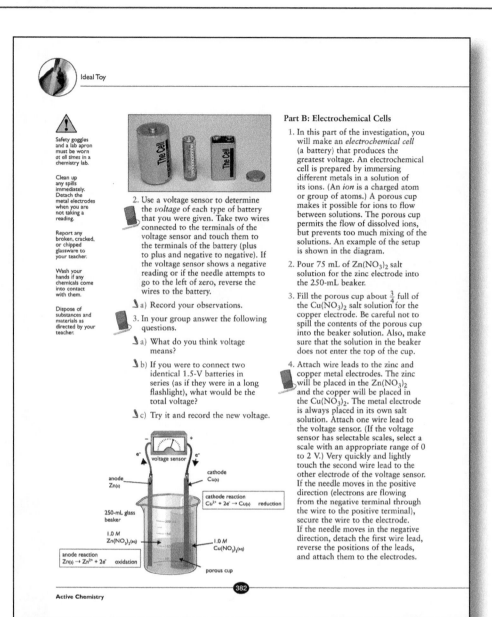

Ideal Toy

Safety goggles and a lab apron must be worn *at all times* in a chemistry lab.

Clean up any spills immediately. Detach the metal electrodes when you are not taking a reading.

Report any broken, cracked, or chipped glassware to your teacher.

Wash your hands if any chemicals come into contact with them.

Dispose of substances and materials as directed by your teacher.

2. Use a voltage sensor to determine the *voltage* of each type of battery that you were given. Take two wires connected to the terminals of the voltage sensor and touch them to the terminals of the battery (plus to plus and negative to negative). If the voltage sensor shows a negative reading or if the needle attempts to go to the left of zero, reverse the wires to the battery.

   a) Record your observations.

3. In your group answer the following questions.

   a) What do you think voltage means?

   b) If you were to connect two identical 1.5-V batteries in series (as if they were in a long flashlight), what would be the total voltage?

   c) Try it and record the new voltage.

Part B: Electrochemical Cells

1. In this part of the investigation, you will make an *electrochemical cell* (a battery) that produces the greatest voltage. An electrochemical cell is prepared by immersing different metals in a solution of its ions. (An *ion* is a charged atom or group of atoms.) A porous cup makes it possible for ions to flow between solutions. The porous cup permits the flow of dissolved ions, but prevents too much mixing of the solutions. An example of the setup is shown in the diagram.

2. Pour 75 mL of $Zn(NO_3)_2$ salt solution for the zinc electrode into the 250-mL beaker.

3. Fill the porous cup about $\frac{3}{4}$ full of the $Cu(NO_3)_2$ salt solution for the copper electrode. Be careful not to spill the contents of the porous cup into the beaker solution. Also, make sure that the solution in the beaker does not enter the top of the cup.

4. Attach wire leads to the zinc and copper metal electrodes. The zinc will be placed in the $Zn(NO_3)_2$ and the copper will be placed in the $Cu(NO_3)_2$. The metal electrode is always placed in its own salt solution. Attach one wire lead to the voltage sensor. (If the voltage sensor has selectable scales, select a scale with an appropriate range of 0 to 2 V.) Very quickly and lightly touch the second wire lead to the other electrode of the voltage sensor. If the needle moves in the positive direction (electrons are flowing from the negative terminal through the wire to the positive terminal), secure the wire to the electrode. If the needle moves in the negative direction, detach the first wire lead, reverse the positions of the leads, and attach them to the electrodes.

anode
Zn(s)

voltage sensor

cathode
Cu(s)

cathode reaction
$Cu^{2+} + 2e^- \rightarrow Cu(s)$ reduction

250-mL glass beaker

1.0 M
$Zn(NO_3)_2(aq)$

1.0 M
$Cu(NO_3)_2(aq)$

anode reaction
$Zn(s) \rightarrow Zn^{2+} + 2e^-$ oxidation

porous cup

382

Active Chemistry

5. You will now vary the metal strips (electrodes) in your cell to find the combination that produces the greatest voltage. Every time a new metal is used as an electrode, the salt solution must also be changed.

Electrode choices	Salt solutions (1 M)
Mg	Mg(NO$_3$)$_2$
Zn	Zn(NO$_3$)$_2$
Fe	Fe(NO$_3$)$_3$
Cu	Cu(NO$_3$)$_2$

To achieve any voltage, one metal must release electrons and the other metal must capture electrons. The metals you will use in this investigation are listed in a specific order (Mg, Zn, Fe, Cu). Magnesium has the greatest tendency to release electrons, while copper has the least tendency to release electrons. This information may guide you in your selection of metals for your battery.

Remember, in this part of the investigation you are to create the electrochemical cell with the greatest voltage (electrical potential difference). You will only be permitted to test three electrode combinations, so choose wisely!

6. Determine what information you will need.

🔌 a) Construct an appropriate data table in your *Active Chemistry* log.

7. Test your three electrode pairs, making sure to rinse the beaker and the porous cup thoroughly between each test. Check with your teacher about the proper disposal of the liquids.

8. Answer the following questions in your log.

🔌 a) Which electrode pair produced the greatest voltage?

🔌 b) Share your data with the other groups.

🔌 c) Explain the observed order in terms of the activity series of metals (the tendency of metals to release electrons).

🔌 d) Describe any modifications to the setup that you used that might affect the voltage.

Part C: Powering a Toy

1. Bring a battery-powered toy from home. Your teacher may supply you with some examples. Examine the toy that you have chosen.

🔌 a) What voltage does it require to power it? Record this in your *Active Chemistry* log.

2. Determine how many of the electrochemical cells that you tested in *Part B* will be needed in a series to power your toy. The total voltage of batteries in series is equal to the sum of the voltages of each battery. In order to connect batteries in a series, you must connect a wire between the negative terminal of the first battery and the positive terminal of the second battery and then the negative terminal of the second battery to the positive terminal of the third battery, and so on. Then you will have a lead coming off of the positive terminal of the first battery and a negative lead coming off of your last battery.

A series battery setup is shown in the diagram on the next page.

383

Active Chemistry

8.a)

Answers will vary according to the metals and solutions each group tests. The results should mirror the activity series of metals.

8.b)

This provides an opportunity for discussion of experimental error.

8.c)

The results from the class should duplicate the information in the Metal Activity Series. Any large discrepancies should be reviewed and discussed.

8.d)

Answers will vary.

Part C:
Powering a Toy

1.

If bringing in toys is not possible, you may wish to check with your physics department to get a simple motor or fan to complete this section. If you are the supplier, local garage sales can provide an inexpensive supply of toys that run on batteries.

Have students look at the battery compartment of the toy or device to see how the wires are connected.

1.a)

Most simple toys will run on some multiple of 1.5 volts.

2.

Hopefully, the toy will run on 1.5 or 3.0 volts. An extended series of cells is discouraged for a variety of reasons.

This will avoid a lot of cross-contamination of the solutions and you will be able to save the solutions for other purposes or for future classes.

6.

Students may create a data table similar to the one below.

Electrode Choices	Salt solutions (1 *M*)	Voltage

7.

Rinsing in deionized water is very important. Most results which deviate from the expected values are due to contaminated solutions. Various responses are acceptable.

3.

If necessary, students can put each group's cell in series to generate greater voltage.

4.a)

The students should recognize that the voltages are cumulative when connected in series.

4.b)

Answers will vary. It is likely that the students will notice a decline in activity over the class period.

Chem Talk

This section explains the basic operation of an electrochemical cell and then places that information into the context of the Metal Activity Series. Oxidation and reduction are reviewed with several examples given. Spectator ions are defined as are variations in electrochemical cells (wet cell and dry cell batteries).

Ideal Toy

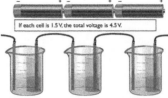

If each cell is 1.5 V, the total voltage is 4.5 V.

⚠️ Wash your hands and arms thoroughly after the investigation.

Save solutions and rinse metal strips for future use.

3. Use alligator clips to hook the electrode from one electrochemical cell to the different metal electrode of the next electrochemical cell. Continue in this fashion until you have enough voltage to power your toy. You will have to share your cell with other teams to get enough voltage to run some toys.

4. Compare your setup to the battery arrangement in the toy.

📝 a) How many electrochemical cells were required?

📝 b) How long do you think it will take for your battery to die?

Chem Words

electrochemical cell: a cell or a battery that uses chemical reactions to generate electricity.

voltage: a measure of the difference in electrochemical potential between two electrodes.

volts: the electrical potential of an electrochemical cell. They represent the "push" that drives electrons through the wire connecting the two metals.

current: the amount of electric charge flowing past a specified circuit point per unit time. The unit used is the ampere (A) = 1C/s.

battery: a system that directly converts chemical energy to electrical energy.

Chem Talk

OXIDATION-REDUCTION REACTIONS AND ELECTROCHEMICAL CELLS

Electrochemical Cell

An **electrochemical cell** is a cell or a battery that uses chemical reactions to generate electricity. When two metals of differing electron-releasing tendencies are connected, an electrical potential is created between the two metals. The electrical potential (**voltage**) is measured in **volts** (V) and represents the energy that drives electrons through the wire connecting the two metals. A 9-V battery has a larger electrical potential than a 1.5-V battery. **Current** describes the amount of flow of electric charge. Larger batteries can generate larger currents than smaller batteries.

Some metals tend to lose electrons (become oxidized) more readily than other metals. Examine the metal activity series shown on the next page. A metal that is higher in the activity series will "give up," or release, electrons more readily than one that is lower. You can make use of these differing tendencies to convert chemical energy to electrical energy. As you may have found in the investigation, metals that are furthest apart in the activity series will produce the largest voltages.

Metal Activity Series

A **battery** is a system that directly converts chemical energy to electrical energy. The Consumer Electronics Association claims that

384

Active Chemistry

*decreasing tendency
to release electrons*

| Li |
| K |
| Ba |
| Ca |
| Na |
| Mg |
| Al |
| Mn |
| Zn |
| Cr |
| Fe |
| Cd |
| Co |
| Ni |
| Sn |
| Pb |
| Cu |
| Ag |
| Hg |
| Au |

there are over 4.9 billion dollars worth of batteries sold in the United States in one year. The typical batteries used in toys are more correctly called electrochemical cells.

If you examine any commercial battery you will see two terminals. One terminal is marked ($+$), or positive, while the other is marked ($-$), or negative. These are typically located at the ends of the battery.

Electrons (which are negative) flow from the negative terminal of the battery. If connected to the positive terminal, the electrons will flow toward the positive. Wires and a **load** provide the path for the electrons. The load may be a motor or a light or something else that runs on electricity (the flow of electrons).

Before considering how your chemical batteries worked, look at a simpler system.

Consider the following reactions:

$$Zn_{(s)} \rightarrow Zn^{2+}_{(aq)} + 2e^-$$

In certain situations, neutral zinc (Zn) loses two electrons. When that happens, a Zn **ion** and two free electrons are formed. Since the zinc has lost two electrons, the charge on the Zn ion is $+2$.

$$Cu^{2+}_{(aq)} + 2e^- \rightarrow Cu_{(s)}$$

In certain situations, a copper (Cu^{2+}) ion tends to gain two electrons. When that happens, a neutral copper atom is formed. The Cu ion had a charge of $+2$ so it needed two electrons to become electrically neutral.

When the neutral zinc and the copper ion interact, as shown by these reactions, the neutral zinc supplies electrons to the copper ion. This flow of electrons is produced by the potential difference (voltage) and the result is a battery.

The zinc reaction of *losing* electrons is called **oxidation**. The copper reaction of *gaining* electrons is **reduction**. Each of the two reactions are called **half-reactions**.

$$Zn_{(s)} \rightarrow Zn^{2+}_{(aq)} + 2e^-$$
(loss of electrons = oxidation, occurs at the anode)

$$Cu^{2+}_{(aq)} + 2e^- \rightarrow Cu_{(s)}$$
(gain of electrons = reduction, occurs at the cathode)

A mnemonic device to remind you of these two processes is:

LEO the lion says **GER**
Lose **E**lectrons **O**xidation   **G**ain **E**lectrons **R**eduction

Chem Words

load: a motor, light bulb, or other device that runs on electricity (the flow of electric charge).

ion: an atom or molecule that has acquired a charge by either gaining or losing electron(s).

oxidation: the process of a substance losing one or more electrons.

reduction: the process of a substance gaining one or more electrons.

half-reactions: two separated parts of a redox reaction. One part is the oxidation reaction and the other part is the reduction reaction.

oxidation-reduction (redox) reaction: a chemical reaction in which the valence electrons of one substance are transferred to the valence shell of the second substance.

oxidized: the acquiring of a positive charge on an atom or molecule by losing electron(s).

reduced: the acquiring of a negative charge on an atom or molecule by gaining electron(s).

spectator ions: ions that are present in solution but do not chemically react in the overall reaction.

dry cell: an electrochemical cell in which the electrolyte is a paste instead of a solution.

385

Active Chemistry

CHAPTER 5

Checking Up

1.

Ca will lose electrons more readily than Mg.

2.

Ca and Cu will produce the greater voltage since they are further apart on the activity series scale.

3.

Volts are used to measure electrical potential.

4.

Spectator ions get their name because they do not participate in the reaction but merely serve to balance the electrical charge of the solution. NO_3^- serves this purpose in an electrochemical cell.

5.

Reduction is the gain of electrons by an atom or a group of atoms. Oxidation is the loss of electrons by an atom or a group of atoms.

6.

OIL RIG: "Oxidation Is Loss" (of electrons); "Reduction Is Gain" (of electrons).

7.

A dry cell operates on the same principles as a wet cell, but the solutions are replaced by a paste. This makes the cell more manageable and smaller.

What Do You Think Now?

Have students revisit the *What Do You Think?* question at the beginning of this section and see how their experience with

Ideal Toy

Checking Up

1. Which metal will lose electrons more easily, Ca or Mg?
2. Which combination of metals will produce the greater voltage, Ca and Al or Ca and Cu?
3. What units are used to measure electrical potential?
4. Why is the NO_3^- ion in an electrochemical cell called a spectator ion?
5. Define reduction and oxidation.
6. Another memory "trick" for remembering oxidation and reduction is "OIL RIG." What do the letters in this device stand for?
7. What is the difference between a dry cell and the one you built in this investigation?

The pair of reactions occurring at the same time is called an **oxidation-reduction** (often called **redox**) reaction.

$$Zn_{(s)} + Cu^{2+}_{(aq)} \rightarrow Zn^{2+}_{(aq)} + Cu_{(s)}$$

One of the characteristic properties of metals is that they tend to lose or "give up" electrons more easily compared to nonmetal atoms. When an atom has lost electrons, it has been **oxidized**. No atom or particle can be oxidized unless some other particle is simultaneously reduced. An atom is **reduced** when it gains electrons.

In the investigation, the Zn metal and the Cu^{2+} ions were kept separated by using a porous barrier. This separation forces the electrons to flow through the wire and the load from the anode (Zn) to reach the cathode (Cu). In this way electricity is produced that can do useful work. The Zn anode is bathed in a solution of $Zn(NO_3)_2$ while the Cu cathode sits in a solution of $Cu(NO_3)_2$ in the porous cup. Because the nitrate ions (NO_3^-) do not participate in the reaction, they are referred to as **spectator ions**. Typically, they are not written into the equation.

When the wire is connected, the zinc metal is oxidized to Zn^{2+} ions, which dissolve into the solution. The Cu^{2+} ions are converted to neutral copper atoms that come out of the solution as copper metal.

As the reaction takes place, the zinc half-cell becomes positive and the copper half-cell becomes negative. This would slow and eventually stop the reaction unless the two sides can become electrically neutral. The porous cup allows for the negative NO_3^- ions to move from the copper half-cell to the zinc half-cell. This keeps both sides neutral and the reaction continues.

Your car battery is a wet cell battery that functions similarly to the electrochemical cells that you created. However, most toy batteries are **dry cell** batteries. They operate on exactly the same principles as your electrochemical cells, but the electrolytic substances are in a paste form.

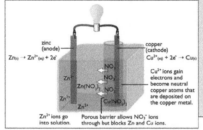

zinc (anode)
$Zn_{(s)} \rightarrow Zn^{2+}_{(aq)} + 2e^-$
copper (cathode)
$Cu^{2+}_{(aq)} + 2e^- \rightarrow Cu_{(s)}$
Cu^{2+} ions gain electrons and become neutral copper atoms that are deposited on the copper metal.
Zn^{2+} ions go into solution.
Porous barrier allows NO_3^- ions through but blocks Zn and Cu ions.

What Do You Think Now?

At the beginning of this section you were asked the following:

• **What is a battery and how does it work?**

Take a look at your original thoughts on the nature of batteries. How have they changed? How would you answer the question now?

386

Active Chemistry

batteries has changed their answers. You may want to provide them with the answer contained in *A Chemist's Response* and open a discussion of their reactions and opinions.

This is also an opportunity for students to reflect on the *macro/nano/symbolic* theme. On the macro scale, they examined and made observations about batteries. On the microscopic level, they examined the chemistry involved, and used the *macro/nano/symbolic* theme to describe different systems. They returned to the macro scale when they powered a toy using the electrochemical cells they created.

You may also want to return to the *What Do You See?* illustration and have students identify features that have more significance now that they have completed the section. You can ask them if the writing on the board in the illustration makes any more sense to them now.

Reflecting on the Section and the Challenge

Many students may choose to use batteries to power their *Chapter Challenge* projects. Encourage them to incorporate their new understanding of how batteries operate into the design of their toys.

Chem Essential Questions

What does it mean?

Chemistry explains a *macroscopic* phenomenon (what you observe) with a description of what happens at the *nanoscopic* level (atoms and molecules) using *symbolic* structures as a way to communicate. Complete the chart below in your *Active Chemistry* log.

MACRO	NANO	SYMBOLIC
How do you know that a battery is working?	*Describe what is occurring at the nanoscopic level when a cell is producing electrical energy.*	*Make a sketch of a cell. Be sure to label all of the important parts.*

How do you know?

What evidence do you have to support the idea that your battery actually produced electrical energy?

Why do you believe?

Batteries are such an important part of your life. The electronics that are part of the items you use every day are, for the most part, limited only by the batteries that power them. Propose future breakthroughs that could take place as technology continues to improve batteries, making them more powerful, longer lasting, and smaller/lighter.

Why should you care?

Many toys are powered by batteries. Write an explanation of how the battery works as part of your toy explanation. Include a labeled diagram.

Reflecting on the Section and the Challenge

In this section, you explored how batteries work. You know that metals tend to give up electrons. If an electrical charge difference can be created between the electrodes (terminals), then a current can be generated and chemical energy is converted to electrical energy! You were able to witness this using the voltage sensor. By connecting batteries in a series more energy is available, thus increasing the electrical potential. You may decide that the new toy product that you propose will require batteries. Your new knowledge of batteries should assist you in the design of your toy.

CHAPTER 3

Chem Essential Questions

What does it mean?

A battery converts chemical energy to electrical energy.

MACRO—The successful operation or functioning of a toy or device is an indication that a battery is working; voltage readings also supply evidence.

NANO — Electrochemical reactions are occurring at the nanoscopic level. Oxidation-reduction reactions generate the voltage needed.

SYMBOLIC —
Electrochemical cell

Voltmeter
Zinc Anode
Copper Cathode
−
+
Cu²⁺
Zn²⁺
Glass beaker
Porous cup

At the anode: $Zn \rightarrow Zn^{2+} + 2e^-$
At the cathode: $Cu^{2+} + 2e^- \rightarrow Cu$

How do you know?

The electrochemical cells generated voltage which could be measured and also operated a toy or device.

Why do you believe?

Answers will vary. Some of the students' projections about future breakthroughs in battery design could be ahead of the current technology.

Why should you care?

Being able to explain and diagram how a battery works will be of significant value in the written proposal and the presentation for the *Chapter Challenge*.

Chem to Go

1.

For the highest electrochemical potential, the two metals should be far apart on the activity series.

The voltage obtained from an electrochemical cell is dependent upon the oxidation potentials of the cathode and anode. The greater the difference between the two electrodes, the greater the voltage that will be obtained. For example, if both the anode and the electrode were the same metal, then the voltage obtained would be zero.

2.

Answers will depend on which metal pairings the students selected.

3.

Silver (Ag), platinum (Pt), and gold (Au) have good reduction potential but they are prohibitively expensive.

4.

Direction of electron flow:

a) Mg to Cu

b) Zn to Cu

c) Mg to Ag

5.a)

a) Mg = anode, Cu = cathode

b) Zn = anode, Cu = cathode

c) Mg = anode, Ag = cathode

5.b)

a) $Mg \rightarrow Mg^{2+} + 2e^-$
$Cu^{2+} + 2e^- \rightarrow Cu$

b) $Zn \rightarrow Zn^{2+} + 2e^-$
$Cu^{2+} + 2e^- \rightarrow Cu$

c) $Mg \rightarrow Mg^{2+} + 2e^-$
$2Ag^+ + 2e^- \rightarrow 2Ag$

6.

Pros: portable, convenient

Cons: disposal issues, cost, limited life span, technology hindered by space required for battery, etc.

7.

b) $Au^{3+} + 3e^- \rightarrow Au$

8.

b) $Cu + 2AgNO_3 \rightarrow Cu(NO_3)_2 + 2Ag$

9.

c) at the anode

 Ideal Toy

Chem to Go

1. For the highest electrical potential, should an electrochemical cell's two metals be close together or far apart on the activity series? Explain.

2. Predict whether the electrical potential of cells composed of these metal pairings will be higher or lower than that of the pairs you tested:
   a) Zn and Cr   b) Zn and Ag   c) Sn and Cu

3. Notice that silver, platinum, and gold have good reduction potential. Why are these elements not generally found in batteries?

4. Predict the direction of electron flow in an electrochemical cell made from each pair of metals in solutions of their ions.
   a) Mg and Cu   b) Zn and Cu   c) Ag and Mg

5. a) Identify the anode and the cathode for the metal pairs in *Question 4*.
   b) Write the half-reactions for each metal pair in *Question 4*.

6. List some of the pros and cons of batteries. Consider cost, size, and disposal issues, among others.

7. Which half-reaction correctly represents reduction?
   a) $Ag \rightarrow Ag^+ + e^-$ b) $Au^{3+} + 3e^- \rightarrow Au$
   c) $F_2 \rightarrow 2F^- + 2e^-$ d) $Fe^{2+} \rightarrow Fe^{3+} + e^-$

8. Which reaction is an example of an oxidation-reduction reaction?
   a) $AgNO_3 + KI \rightarrow AgI + KNO_3$
   b) $Cu + 2AgNO_3 \rightarrow Cu(NO_3)_2 + 2Ag$
   c) $2KOH + H_2SO_4 \rightarrow K_2SO_4 + 2H_2O$
   d) $Ba(OH)_2 + 2HCl \rightarrow BaCl_2 + 2H_2O$

9. Where does oxidation occur in an electrochemical cell?
   a) at the cathode
   b) at the cathode and the anode in the electrolytic cell
   c) at the anode
   d) neither the cathode nor the anode

Inquiring Further

1. Storing batteries
Design and conduct a test for determining the best way to store batteries in order to extend their life.

2. Best battery competition
Find advertising materials for two different brands of Type AA batteries (or any comparable types, AAA, C, D, 9-volt) that provide data for comparison of value. Determine which battery is the better value based on cost and on longevity. If possible, estimate disposal costs if the batteries use different materials in their manufacture.

 388

Active Chemistry

Inquiring Further

1. Storing batteries

The students will come up with their own thoughts and plans for this. You should review their design and procedures for safety and potential for success. Their research design should contain a control and at least one variable. Some options for a control could be a disconnected battery, a battery left in a circuit with the switch on, or a battery left in a circuit with the switch off.

The most useful control would probably be the last option.

For variables, the students might choose to turn the switch off and leave it at room temperature. This would test whether being in the circuit, even with the switch off, would still permit some current to be drawn. Another variable could be temperature. The battery could be stored in a refrigerator to extend its life. A problem will be how to determine whether the life of a battery has been extended.

For this to be measured in a relatively short period of time, they would need to test each battery in a circuit that draws a lot of current.

2. Best battery competition.

The greatest challenge for students in this study will be to determine comparable costs. Batteries are often "on sale" but students should attempt to compare batteries that are at normal retail prices.

SECTION 1 – QUIZ

5-1a	Blackline Master

1. Which half-reaction correctly represents oxidation?

   a) $Sn^{2+} + 2e^- \rightarrow Sn^{4+}$ b) $Cu^{2+} + 2e^- \rightarrow Cu$

   c) $Cl_2 \rightarrow 2Cl^- + 2e^-$ d) $Zn \rightarrow Zn^{2+} + 2e^-$

2. What are the correct half-reactions for an electrochemical cell made from Zn and Ag?

   a) $Ag^+ + e^- \rightarrow Ag$ and $Zn \rightarrow Zn^{2+} + 2e^-$

   b) $2Ag \rightarrow 2Ag^+ + 2e^-$ and $Zn^{2+} + 2e^- \rightarrow Zn$

   c) $Ag^+ + e^- \rightarrow Ag$ and $Zn^{2+} + 2e^- \rightarrow Zn$

   d) $Ag \rightarrow Ag^+ + e^-$ and $Zn \rightarrow Zn^{2+} + 2e^-$

3. In an electrochemical cell, _____ occurs at the anode and _____ occurs at the cathode.

   a) oxidation, reduction

   b) reduction, oxidation

   c) oxidation, oxidation

   d) reduction, reduction

4. Why are two different metals needed to produce a potential difference in an electrochemical cell?

5. Reduction is the opposite of oxidation. Why do oxidation-reduction reactions always occur together?

SECTION 1 – QUIZ ANSWERS

❶ d) $Zn \rightarrow Zn^{2+} + 2e^-$

❷ a) $2Ag^+ + 2e^- \rightarrow 2Ag$ and $Zn \rightarrow Zn^{2+} + 2e^-$

❸ a) oxidation, reduction

❹ Two different metals are used because one of the metals has to give up electrons (be oxidized) more easily than the second metal. The second metal accepts the electrons and is reduced. The difference in metals produces the potential difference of the battery terminals.

❺ Oxidation-reduction reactions always occur in pairs because if electrons are lost by one substance, they have to go somewhere (Law of Conservation of Matter); the electrons have to be picked up by some other substance.

SECTION 2
Intermolecular Forces in Solids, Liquids, or Gases

Section Overview

In Part A of this section, students look at representations of four different sets of molecules. They compare shapes and sizes of molecules and learn to identify similarities and differences. In Part B, students look at tables of data for melting points and boiling points of these molecules. From this, they deduce molecular reasons for the physical state of one molecule when compared to another. Polarity is explored on a very basic level.

Background Information

Intermolecular forces are the forces of attraction that exist between molecules of a substance. These forces cause the substance to exist in a particular state of matter: solid, liquid, or gas; they affect the melting and boiling points of compounds, as well as the solubilities of one substance in another.

The stronger the attractions between particles (molecules or ions), the more difficult it is to separate the particles. When substances melt into a liquid phase, the particles are still close to one another but the forces of attraction that held the particles rigidly together in the solid state have been sufficiently overcome to allow the particles to move. When substances boil, the particles become separated from one another and the attractions between molecules are completely overcome by their kinetic energy.

Intermolecular attractions are based on molecular polarity, shape, and size.

Polarization of bonds and molecules depends on differences in the relative electronegativity of the atoms involved. Electronegativity is the intrinsic property of an atom describing its affinity for electrons. The greater the electronegativity of an element, the greater its affinity for electrons. The general trend regarding the electronegativity of elements is that it increases in the directions of left to right → and bottom to top ↑ of the periodic table. A table of electronegativity values for the elements was developed by Linus Pauling and can be found in most textbooks or online. When a covalent bond involves two atoms of different electronegativities, a polar covalent bond is the result.

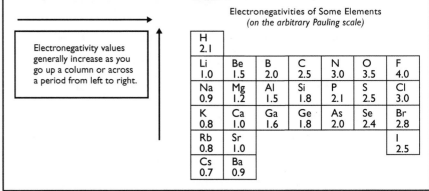

Electronegativity values generally increase as you go up a column or across a period from left to right.

Electronegativities of Some Elements
(on the arbitrary Pauling scale)

H 2.1						
Li 1.0	Be 1.5	B 2.0	C 2.5	N 3.0	O 3.5	F 4.0
Na 0.9	Mg 1.2	Al 1.5	Si 1.8	P 2.1	S 2.5	Cl 3.0
K 0.8	Ca 1.0	Ga 1.6	Ge 1.8	As 2.0	Se 2.4	Br 2.8
Rb 0.8	Sr 1.0					I 2.5
Cs 0.7	Ba 0.9					

A water molecule is polar because its O-H bonds are significantly polar, and its bent geometry makes the distribution of those polar bonds asymmetrical. The side of the water molecule containing the more electronegative oxygen atom is partially negative (δ^-), and the side of the molecule containing the less electronegative hydrogen atoms is partially positive (δ^+).

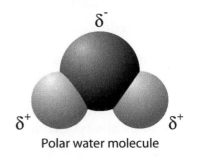

Polar water molecule

Polar molecules, with their different regions of partial positive and negative charges, have attractions for one another that are described as dipole-dipole interactions.

When there are no polar bonds in a molecule, there is no permanent charge difference between one part of the molecule and another, and the molecule is nonpolar. For example, the H_2 molecule does not have a polar bond because the electron charge is identical on both atoms. It is therefore a non-polar molecule. None of the bonds in hydrocarbon molecules, like pentane, C_5H_{12}, are significantly polar, so hydrocarbons are non-polar molecular substances.

Molecular polarity is dependent on bond polarity *and* molecular geometry. For small molecules, if all the regions surrounding an atom are similar in electronegativity, the molecule is non-polar. If the regions are different, then the molecule will be polar.

For large molecules, there may be both polar and non-polar regions in the molecule.

The size of a molecule also plays a role in intermolecular attractions. In general, the larger the molecule, the more surface area it has, and the greater attraction between molecules, even if they are non-polar. The weak intermolecular attractions in non-polar molecules are referred to as dispersion forces.

LEARNING OUTCOMES

LEARNING OUTCOMES	LOCATION IN SECTION	EVIDENCE OF UNDERSTANDING
Describe how the size and shape of molecules affect their physical state.	*Investigate* Part A *Investigate, Chem Talk, Chem to Go* Question 1	Four pages of molecular representations are similar to those shown in this *Teacher's Edition*. Students make informed guesses as to which molecules are solids, liquids, or gases. Answers match those found in this *Teacher's Edition*.
Classify molecules as polar or non-polar.	*Investigate* Part B *Investigate, Chem Talk, Chem to Go* Questions 2-4	Conclusions match those found in this *Teacher's Edition*. Answers in students' *Active Chemistry* logs match those found in this *Teacher's Edition*.

NOTES

_____

_____

_____

_____

_____

_____

_____

Section 2
Materials, Chemicals, Preparation, and Safety

("per Group" quantity is based on group size of 2 students)

Materials and Equipment

Materials (and Equipment)	Quantity per Group or per Class
Computer with *ChemSketch*™ and *3D Viewer* (available from acdlabs.com)	1 (optional)
Materials (and Equipment)	**Quantity per Class**
None	None

Chemicals

Chemicals	Quantity per Class (24 students)
None	None

Teacher Preparation

You can download the free software from the Internet at *www.acdlabs.com/download* or at any other Web site that offers it. After you become familiar with it, you can share it with your class in either of two ways. The more time-efficient way is to project it from your computer onto a screen for students to observe. If, however, you would like to have students extend their own skills with the programs, you can load the software onto computers in your school's computer lab, thereby allowing students to draw their own molecules. It is best to have no more than two students per computer. Finally, if Internet access or computer resources are not available, copies of the four pages of molecules are provided as overheads on the *Teacher Resources CD*.

This software has features called *ChemSketch* and *3D Viewer* that allow the user to create a variety of molecules and view them in different forms and at various angles. Open the *3D Viewer* program, go to *ChemSketch* at the bottom left corner, and you will be able to draw the molecules needed for this investigation. If you are going to project the images onto a screen for the entire class, it is advisable to draw the molecules in advance and save them in a file.

In the *ChemSketch* program, a menu appears on the left side. This menu has default elements. As an example, the following steps can be followed to "create" the ethane (CH_3CH_3) molecule:

- Place cursor on 'carbon' and click in the sketchpad area to produce a molecule of CH_4.

- Repeat to create another identical molecule.

- Click and drag to connect the two. A bond will form between the two. To correspond to the proper bonding, two of the hydrogen atoms will disappear. You now have CH_3CH_3.

- Toward the upper right corner is an icon similar to the ball-and-stick model of methane. Click on this icon to optimize the structure's properties. The molecule can then be viewed by clicking on the **Copy to 3D** icon at the bottom left, bringing up the *3D Viewer* screen. You should now see several icons displaying various viewing configurations and options. The most instructional view for this investigation may be the space-filling models.

NOTES

Meeting the Needs of All Students
Differentiated Instruction
Augmentation and Accommodations

LEARNING ISSUE	REFERENCE	AUGMENTATION AND ACCOMMODATIONS
Understanding diagrams of molecules	*Investigate* Part A	**Augmentation** • Be sure students understand that they are looking at four different examples of halogen molecules. Define halogen. • Give students a pattern for making good observations by modeling observations of the shape and size of a molecule not included in the text samples. **Accommodations** • Provide students with more specific criteria for making observations: size, number of atoms, shape, and symmetry. Be sure students understand the meaning of *symmetry*.
Understanding the relationship between temperature and state from reading and numerical data	*Investigate* Part B	**Augmentation** • Have students draw a simple number line to record different temperatures of water. The only numbers they need to label are the melting point, boiling point and room temperature. Have them label the areas on the number line where water is a solid, a liquid and a gas. Ask them to check their diagrams to be sure that water is liquid at room temperature. Then have students repeat this procedure for each of the molecules listed to determine its state at room temperature. Doing so will provide visual reinforcement of the concept originally taught linguistically and numerically.
Reading a graph	*Investigate* Part B, 3.	**Augmentation** • Check to be sure that every student understands how to correctly pull the numerical data from the graph to determine its state at room temperature. Help those who have difficulty or ask other members of each group to assist.
Organizing information provided in text	*Chem Talk, Chem Essential Questions, What does it mean? Nano*	**Augmentation** • Divide the characteristics of solids, liquids, and gases into sections of a visual organizer to make it more meaningful and easier to remember. Have students read the first section of *Chem Talk* and create a visual organizer which clearly shows the differences between solids, liquids, and gases. The visual organizer could be a three-column chart, a table coordinating characteristics with the three states across the top, or a cluster diagram. **Accommodations** • Give students the areas of comparison such as structure, motion, attraction space between molecules, and examples.
Organizing information provided in text	*Chem Talk*	**Augmentation** • Break down and organize the information in a similar fashion, but this time categorize by the effects of size and symmetry on boiling point, attraction and charge. Include examples of each substance and information that distinguishes polar from non-polar molecules. **Note:** Since the value of making a visual organizer comes from students being required to organize the information, avoid giving them a prepared table to simply record their data.
Applying sources of information to solve problems	*Chem Essential Questions, What does it mean? Symbolic, Chem to Go* 1., 2.	**Augmentation** • Suggest that students refer to the visual organizer they made comparing the three states and the water molecule diagram in *Chem Talk* to create their symbolic drawing of water. • Refer students to the Non-polar Molecules section of *Chem Talk* to answer Question 1. • Refer students to their table comparing non-polar and polar molecules to answer Question 2.

Strategies for Students with Limited English Language Proficiency

LEARNING ISSUE	REFERENCE	AUGMENTATIONS
Background knowledge	*What Do You Think?*	The term "substances gases" might sound confusing as there are two plurals. Have students answer questions in small groups.
Vocabulary	*Investigate*	Make sure students know what to do when asked to "notice," as in Part A. Acquaint students with the "If…then…" structure as used in Part B. Familiarize students with the signal words "since" and "simply." Make sure students are familiar with the word "thus" as a transition word. Check for understanding of the word "based" as a synonym for "in conclusion."
Background knowledge Vocabulary Comprehending text	*Chem Talk*	Have students put new words in their personal dictionaries or *Active Chemistry* logs. Review the use of the prefix *"non-"* as in "non-polar." Check for understanding of prefix, *"di-"* as in "dipole." Assist students with pronunciation of technical terms.
Background knowledge Vocabulary Comprehending text	*Chem Essential Questions*	Check for understanding of the phrase, "draw a conclusion," and the word "regarding."
Comprehension Vocabulary	*Chem to Go*	Make sure students understand questions that are stacked, where there is more than one response. Have students work with a partner or in small groups to discuss answers prior to writing them down.

CHAPTER 3

NOTES

_____

_____

_____

_____

_____

_____

_____

_____

_____

_____

_____

Section 2
Teaching Suggestions and Sample Answers

What Do You See?

The *What Do You See?* serves to engage students' interest with an illustration based on the coming section. The question, *What Do You See?* can be answered at more than one level. One student may report literally what she sees, e.g., "I saw *Fatal Attraction!*" Another may try to interpret the intent of the artist, e.g., "This must have something to do with attraction between atoms." Both responses are valid and should be acknowledged as such. Later, you may wish to return to the illustration so that the students will have both a better understanding of the artist's intent and recognize how they have progressed in content understanding and knowledge.

The students will recognize the parallel between the molecules on the screen and the romantic dog and cat on the floor. Since the title of the section is Solid, Liquid, or Gas? you can ask the students how they think that the "fatal attraction" of molecules is related to solids, liquids and gases.

What Do You Think?

There are many misconceptions related to gases. Some people think that gases have no mass. You will want to listen to students' responses to these *What Do You Think?* questions and not try to correct or reach closure. The section will help the students with their understanding. If all the discussion has to do with macroscopic properties, you might want to ask them about gases, liquids, and solids from the nanoscopic (molecular) level to ascertain what they know.

What Do You Think?
A CHEMIST'S RESPONSE

Gases differ from liquids and solids in that they have no definite volume or shape. Those properties are defined by the container which holds the gas. At the NANO level, gas particles move much more freely and randomly than liquids and solids. Whether a substance is a gas at room temperature is determined by the forces of attraction between the particles (atoms or molecules) of the gas. Helium atoms, for example, have very little attraction for each other and will remain a gas even at very low temperatures. The water molecule, on the other hand, is a very small molecule with much stronger forces of attraction between molecules. Thus, it is a liquid at room temperature.

STUDENTS' PRIOR CONCEPTIONS

Students have a difficult time visualizing the three-dimensional shapes of molecules. Relating molecular shape to physical properties is also very likely a foreign concept to them. This section is designed to provide the visuals to begin the process of understanding the relationships between chemical formulas and the actual shapes of the compounds and molecules that the formulas represent. It is also designed to help the students understand the concept of polarity and how the shape of molecules affects the physical properties of the substance.

Section 2

Intermolecular Forces in Solids, Liquids, and Gases

What Do You See?

Learning Outcomes

In this section you will

• Describe how the size and shape of molecules affect their physical state.

• Classify molecules as polar or nonpolar.

What Do You Think?

A number of toys use gases.

• What makes a gas different from a liquid or a solid?

• Why are some substances gases at room temperature, while others are not?

Record your ideas about these questions in your *Active Chemistry* log. Be prepared to discuss your responses with your small group and the class.

Investigate

Part A: Size and Shape of Molecules

1. Look at the following computer-drawn diagrams of molecules.

Shape and relative size of diatomic halogen molecules

| fluorine | chlorine | bromine | iodine |
| F_2 | Cl_2 | Br_2 | I_2 |

389

Active Chemistry

Investigate

Part A:
Size and Shape of Molecules

1.-2.

At the beginning of the section, students are asked to look at some computer-drawn molecules. There are four pages of computer-rendered molecules provided as overheads on the *Teacher Resource CD*. The molecules are shown on separate pages for comparison purposes. It will avoid confusion to show them Page 1 first – fluorine, chlorine, bromine and iodine – followed by the questions in Step 2.a).

If using the *ChemSketch*™ software, do the molecules in the order listed or instruct students to do so. Clicking on fluorine and then in the sketch area will bring up HF (hydrogen fluoride). Clicking again and connecting the two makes F_2 (fluorine). Optimizing the fluorine creates the correct bond length, F-F. The same should be done to generate the chlorine molecule. This time, however, it is necessary to use the "lasso" icon in the upper left to capture just the chlorine (Cl_2), before optimizing. This should always be done when multiple molecules are on the same sketch area. Follow the same procedure with bromine and iodine and then **Copy to 3D**. On the *3D Viewer* page, the space-filling icon should be used. Find the color option under the options button at the top of the page. You can set the background color to white (for printing) and the colors of the halogens can also be selected. If spacing is a problem, corrections can be made by going back to *ChemSketch* and fixing them,

or just starting a new page. When completed, you should have molecules similar to those shown here.

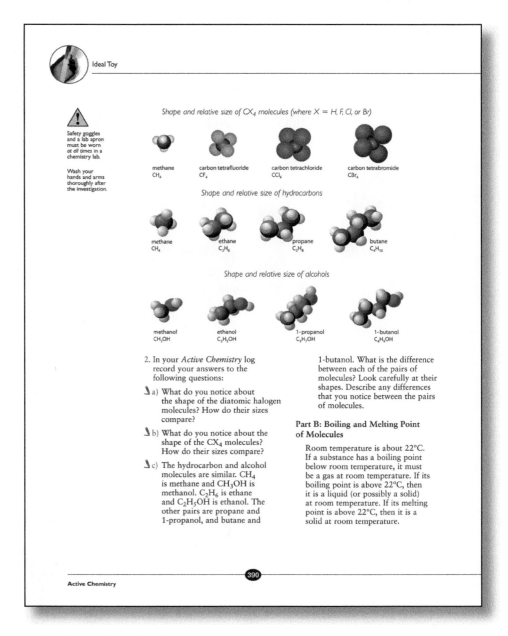

Shape and relative size of CX₄ molecules (where X = H, F, Cl, or Br)

methane CH_4 carbon tetrafluoride CF_4 carbon tetrachloride CCl_4 carbon tetrabromide CBr_4

Shape and relative size of hydrocarbons

methane CH_4 ethane C_2H_6 propane C_3H_8 butane C_4H_{10}

Shape and relative size of alcohols

methanol CH_3OH ethanol C_2H_5OH 1-propanol C_3H_7OH 1-butanol C_4H_9OH

Safety goggles and a lab apron must be worn *at all times* in a chemistry lab.

Wash your hands and arms thoroughly after the investigation.

2. In your *Active Chemistry* log record your answers to the following questions:

a) What do you notice about the shape of the diatomic halogen molecules? How do their sizes compare?

b) What do you notice about the shape of the CX₄ molecules? How do their sizes compare?

c) The hydrocarbon and alcohol molecules are similar. CH₄ is methane and CH₃OH is methanol. C₂H₆ is ethane and C₂H₅OH is ethanol. The other pairs are propane and 1-propanol, and butane and

1-butanol. What is the difference between each of the pairs of molecules? Look carefully at their shapes. Describe any differences that you notice between the pairs of molecules.

Part B: Boiling and Melting Point of Molecules

Room temperature is about 22°C. If a substance has a boiling point below room temperature, it must be a gas at room temperature. If its boiling point is above 22°C, then it is a liquid (or possibly a solid) at room temperature. If its melting point is above 22°C, then it is a solid at room temperature.

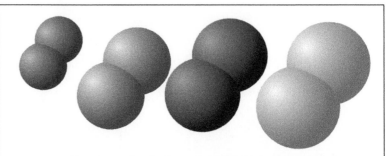

Page 1 – Shape and relative size of halogen molecules: fluorine F_2, chlorine Cl_2, bromine Br_2, iodine I_2 (also provided as an overhead transparency)

The second page of the overheads compares the shape and sizes of CH_4, CF_4, CCl_4, and CBr_4 molecules and should be referred to for the questions in 2.b). These molecules start with CH_4 with the halogens added and optimized before moving on to the next molecule. The results should look similar to those below.

Page 2 – Shape and relative size of CX_4 molecules: methane CH_4, carbon tetrafluoride CF_4, carbon tetrachloride CCl_4, carbon tetrabromide CBr_4 (also provided as an overhead transparency)

Page 3 compares the shape and sizes of CH_4, C_2H_6, C_3H_8, and C_4H_{10} molecules with Page 4 of the corresponding alcohols. It may work best to provide both handouts with images of all eight molecules for comparison purposes.

The related questions are found in Step 2.c).

Start by creating CH_4, then add additional carbons and optimize before moving on to the next molecule. The results should look similar to the ones below.

Page 3 – Shape and relative size of hydrocarbons: methane CH_4, ethane C_2H_6, propane C_3H_8, butane C_4H_{10} (also provided as an overhead transparency)

Page 4 compares the shape and sizes of CH_3OH, C_2H_5OH, C_3H_7OH, and C_4H_9OH molecules. All of these start with CH_3 with the additional carbons added. An OH is added by clicking on the oxygen and connecting it to a carbon. Each molecule is optimized before moving on to the next molecule. The results should look similar to the ones below.

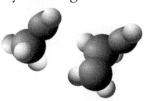  

Page 4 – Shape and relative size of alcohols: methanol CH_3OH, ethanol C_2H_5OH, 1-propanol C_3H_7OH, 1-butanol C_4H_9OH (also provided as an overhead transparency)

CHAPTER 3

2.a)

Overhead Page 1: Students should notice that the shape of all of the halogens is the same, only the size differs. The diatomic molecules get larger from fluorine to iodine. Emphasize that the colors are not the color of the atoms, although iodine is a purplish solid, bromine is a reddish-brown liquid, and chlorine is a greenish-yellow gas.

2.b)

Overhead Page 2: Again, the students should notice that all of the CX_4 compounds have the same shape (tetrahedral) but the molecules increase in size through CBr_4 due to the increasing size of the halogens.

2.c)

Overhead Pages 3 and 4: The pairs of molecules having the same number of carbon atoms are similar in shape. The difference is due to an oxygen molecule on one end of the alcohols on page 4. This changes the shape of the molecules. On page 3 the molecules are symmetrical; both ends are the same. On page 4, one end of each molecule is different from the other end.

Part B:
Boiling and Melting Point of Molecules

For your convenience, the tables of melting and boiling points are also provided as overheads on the *Teacher Resources CD*.

After reading the data in the labels and a discussion, students should be able to respond with the following answers:

1.a)

Fluorine and chlorine are gases at room temperature (22°C). Bromine is a liquid and iodine is a solid at this temperature.

1.b)

Size is the only difference between the molecules. The gas molecules are smaller than either the liquid or solid ones. The solid substance is also the largest molecule.

2.a)

CH_4 and CF_4 are gases at room temperature, while CCl_4 is a liquid, and CBr_4 is a solid.

2.b)

The gas molecules are smaller than either the liquid or solid ones. The solid one is the largest molecule.

NOTES _____

_____

_____

_____

_____

_____

_____

Section 2 Intermolecular Forces in Solids, Liquids, and Gases

1. Look at the table showing the melting and boiling points of halogens.

Melting and Boiling Points of Halogens (Group 7A)		
Substance	Melting point (°C)	Boiling point (°C)
F_2 (fluorine)	−220	−188
Cl_2 (chlorine)	−101	−34
Br_2 (bromine)	−7	59
I_2 (iodine)	114	185

Answer the following in your *Active Chemistry* log:

 a) Fluorine will be a solid at any temperature less than its melting point of −220°C. At −220°C, fluorine melts and becomes a liquid. The liquid then heats up until it reaches the boiling point of −188°C. At that temperature the fluorine becomes a gas and remains a gas for all higher temperatures. Which of the halogens are gases at room temperature of 22°C? Which are liquids? Which are solids?

b) Since all of the halogens have the same shape, what is the difference between those that are gases and the ones that are liquids or solids at room temperature?

2. Look at the table showing the melting and boiling points of CX_4 compounds.

Melting and Boiling Points of CX_4 Compounds		
Substance	Melting point (°C)	Boiling point (°C)
CH_4 (methane)	−183	−161
CF_4 (carbon tetrafluoride)	−184	−128
CCl_4 (carbon tetrachloride)	−23	77
CBr_4 (carbon tetrabromide)	90	190

Answer the following in your *Active Chemistry* log:

a) Of the CX_4 compounds, which are gases, liquids, and solids at room temperature?

b) Since all of the CX_4 compounds have the same shape, what is the difference between those that are gases at room temperature and the ones that are liquids or solids?

3. Hydrocarbons are simply molecules made up of carbon and hydrogen. Alcohols are molecules containing an –OH group. Note the difference between methanol (CH_3OH) and sodium hydroxide (NaOH). Both have an OH in the formula, but the alcohol is a covalently bonded molecule and NaOH is an ionic compound, not a molecule.

391

CHAPTER 5

3.a)

All of the hydrocarbons are gases at room temperature (hydrocarbons of less than 5 carbons are gases at room temperature). The four alcohols are all liquids at room temperature.

3.b)

As the number of carbon atoms and the size of the molecules increases, so does the boiling point.

3.c)

Except for the presence of the oxygen atom, the alcohols are identical to the hydrocarbons in structure. The presence of the highly electronegative oxygen atom changes the shape of the molecule slightly, but makes a huge difference in polarity.

4.

The size, shape, and polarity of molecules can be used to determine if a substance is a solid, liquid or a gas. Smaller, non-polar molecules have lower boiling points and tend to be gases at room temperature. Larger molecules tend to be liquids or solids. Polar molecules containing electronegative atoms tend not to be gases at room temperature.

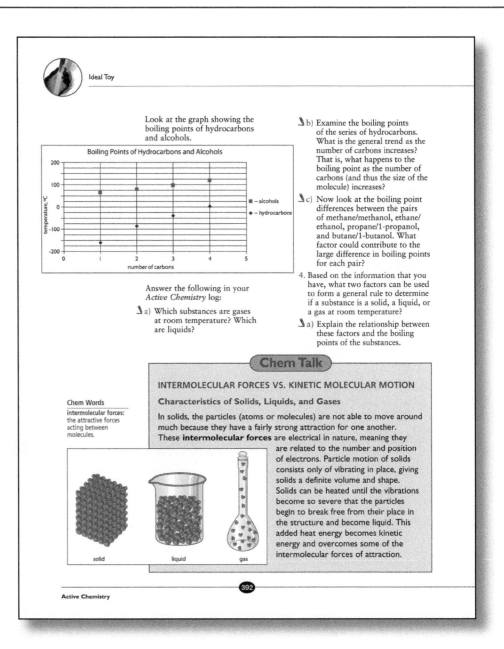

Ideal Toy

Look at the graph showing the boiling points of hydrocarbons and alcohols.

Boiling Points of Hydrocarbons and Alcohols

Answer the following in your *Active Chemistry* log:

a) Which substances are gases at room temperature? Which are liquids?

b) Examine the boiling points of the series of hydrocarbons. What is the general trend as the number of carbons increases? That is, what happens to the boiling point as the number of carbons (and thus the size of the molecule) increases?

c) Now look at the boiling point differences between the pairs of methane/methanol, ethane/ethanol, propane/1-propanol, and butane/1-butanol. What factor could contribute to the large difference in boiling points for each pair?

4. Based on the information that you have, what two factors can be used to form a general rule to determine if a substance is a solid, a liquid, or a gas at room temperature?

a) Explain the relationship between these factors and the boiling points of the substances.

Chem Talk

Chem Words

intermolecular forces: the attractive forces acting between molecules.

INTERMOLECULAR FORCES VS. KINETIC MOLECULAR MOTION

Characteristics of Solids, Liquids, and Gases

In solids, the particles (atoms or molecules) are not able to move around much because they have a fairly strong attraction for one another. These **intermolecular forces** are electrical in nature, meaning they are related to the number and position of electrons. Particle motion of solids consists only of vibrating in place, giving solids a definite volume and shape. Solids can be heated until the vibrations become so severe that the particles begin to break free from their place in the structure and become liquid. This added heat energy becomes kinetic energy and overcomes some of the intermolecular forces of attraction.

solid   liquid   gas

392

Active Chemistry

Chem Talk

The physical state of a substance is discussed in terms of intermolecular forces and molecular size. Small, non-polar molecules tend to be gases and liquids. Larger, polar molecules tend to be liquids and solids. Completely non-polar molecules have only weak London dispersion forces between molecules. Polar molecules will have one or more atoms with high electronegativity and, in some cases, hydrogen bonds. The result is that the intermolecular forces are stronger and boiling points are higher.

In the liquid phase, the particles are still attracted to each other and are still in contact with each other. However, they are not locked into a fixed place by the attractive forces. The liquid particles are free to move past each other, as well as vibrate. Liquids have a definite volume but not a definite shape. A liquid can be heated until the kinetic energy of its particles overcomes remaining forces of attraction and the substance becomes a gas.

Gases are different from liquids and solids because there are relatively large distances between the particles (atoms or molecules). This makes gases compressible, whereas the compressibility of liquids and solids is negligible. A gas is characterized as being composed of fast-moving particles in constant, random motion. Gases have neither definite shape nor definite volume.

The intermolecular forces of attraction have not been changed by these phase changes. The process of going from solid to liquid to gas by adding heat energy can be reversed by cooling. By removing heat energy, a gas will become a liquid, and a liquid will become a solid. This happens because the particles are slowed enough that the still-present intermolecular forces of attraction exert their effect.

Intermolecular Forces of Attraction and Non-polar Molecules

Nonpolar molecules, such as the halogens, oxygen, nitrogen, carbon dioxide, and the CX_4 molecules have shapes and bonds that are symmetrical. The electrons of these molecules are distributed evenly in such a way that there are no permanent electrical charges anywhere on the molecules and the intermolecular forces are small. The symmetrical shapes of nonpolar molecules cause them to have very little attraction to each other. Small, nonpolar molecules tend to be gases or liquids with low boiling points. For these same reasons, the noble gases have very small forces between atoms of these elements.

As the size of nonpolar molecules increases, the attractive forces between molecules also begin to increase. You saw this for the series of hydrocarbon molecules. Larger molecules have more electrons. When there are more electrons they may, at one instant, be distributed unevenly. One part of the molecule briefly may have an increased number of electrons. This distortion of electrons gives rise to a temporary partial negative charge (represented by the Greek letter delta, δ^-). Since one part of the molecule has an overabundance of electrons another part of the molecule must have a deficiency of electrons, creating a partial positive charge (δ^+). The molecule becomes a temporary dipole (meaning two poles or two charges). This in turn triggers (induces) a similar dipole in neighboring molecules and this process spreads from molecule to

Chem Words

nonpolar molecule: a molecule that has small intermolecular forces due to symmetry of charge distribution.

distortion of electrons on a molecule

$\delta^+ \qquad \delta^-$

Active Chemistry

CHAPTER 5

Checking Up

1.

Polarity is the unequal distribution of charge throughout a molecule. This can be due to the molecule's shape, to the electronegativity of some of its atoms, or both.

2.

London dispersion forces are temporary dipoles that form due to a transient unequal distribution of electrons on the surface of an atom or molecule.

3.

Heptane, C_7H_{16}, would have the higher boiling point due to its greater size and surface area, and therefore, greater intermolecular forces of attraction.

 Ideal Toy

Chem Words

London dispersion forces: weak intermolecular forces that cause the electrons of an atom or a molecule to shift slightly to form a temporary dipole moment. These forces are also called London forces.

electronegativity: the ability of an atom of an element to attract electrons in a chemical bond.

polar bond: the difference in the electronegativity of neighboring atoms causes the electrons to be attracted more to one of the atoms of the bond, making one atom slightly negative and the other slightly positive.

hydrogen bond: the intermolecular attraction of a polarized hydrogen atom to a nearby highly electronegative atom, such as oxygen, nitrogen, or fluorine.

van der Waals forces: weak intermolecular attraction forces between molecules.

molecule. These attractive forces, called **London dispersion forces,** are much weaker than ionic or covalent bonds which hold atoms together. The polarity causes a greater attraction between molecules. The molecules are difficult to separate, which is what takes place when a substance boils. The larger molecules tend to have higher boiling points and can be liquids or solids at room temperature.

Intermolecular Forces of Attraction and Polar Molecules

Other molecules have permanent, separated charges as a result of their shape and the types of atoms in the molecule. Some atoms, particularly oxygen, nitrogen, and fluorine, have a greater tendency to pull the electrons of a covalent bond toward themselves. This property is called **electronegativity**. For example, oxygen is more electronegative than hydrogen so the electrons in the O–H bond are pulled closer to the oxygen atom. This makes a **polar bond** with a partial negative charge on oxygen and a partial positive charge on the hydrogen atoms. These partial charges are permanent, not fleeting, like the London dispersion forces.

Water molecules have two hydrogen atoms attached to a central oxygen atom at an angle of about 108°. The polar bonds and its shape cause water to be a

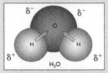

polar molecule. The positive hydrogen atoms are attracted to the negative oxygen atoms of nearby water molecules and form **hydrogen bonds**. While hydrogen bonds are not real bonds, they are important intermolecular forces. In strength, they stand intermediate between real covalent bonds and the weak London dispersion forces. On a scale of 0 to 100, the relative strengths of these attractive forces are 1:5:100, with 100 representing a covalent bond. The term, **van der Waals forces**, is sometimes used to cover the attractive interactions of both hydrogen bonding and dispersion forces.

The red dashed lines represent hydrogen bonds.

Three-Dimensional Orientation of Water Molecules

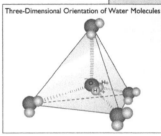

Many of the unique properties of water are a result of hydrogen bonding. A water molecule has only three atoms with a low total mass of 18 amu. Even so, it has a relatively high freezing point of 0°C and a high boiling point of 100°C. A nonpolar molecule of comparable size, such as methane, CH_4, has a boiling point of –161°C. Even ammonia, NH_3, which also has hydrogen bonding between molecules, boils at –33°C. Water also is unique for its high heat capacity and its ability to dissolve a variety of organic and inorganic compounds. All of these properties make life possible on Earth.

 394

Active Chemistry

Chem Essential Questions

What does it mean?

MACRO — A solid will have a specific volume and shape; a liquid will flow, having specific volume but not shape; a gas will have neither specific volume nor shape.

NANO — At the NANO level, a solid will have a defined position for each atom or molecule.

Vibration is allowed but no real linear movements. A liquid is capable of some relatively slow linear motion and has an undefined structure. A gas has extensive linear motion and no defined structure.

SYMBOLIC — Students' sketches should be similar to the drawings featured at the beginning of *Chem Talk*. The water molecules will have a regular pattern and will be very close to one

another in the solid state. In the liquid state, the molecules will be randomly organized, but still close together. In the gas phase, the molecules will show no organization and will be far apart.

How do you know?

The shape of a molecule can have some effect on the physical state. For example, butane, a non-polar molecule, has a molecular weight of 58 and a boiling point of about 0°C. It is a gas at room

When there is a strong attraction between molecules, the substances are probably liquids or solids at room temperature. The alcohols discussed in this investigation have one –OH group that makes these molecules somewhat polar in nature. Just like water, this polarity increases the amount of heat energy needed to separate the molecules, as seen in the higher boiling points of alcohols compared to the hydrocarbons.

Checking Up

1. What is meant by a molecule's polarity?
2. What are London dispersion forces?
3. Which would have a greater boiling point: C_5H_{12} or C_7H_{16}?

What Do You Think Now?

At the beginning of this section you were asked the following:

• What makes a gas different from a liquid or a solid?
• Why are some substances gases at room temperature, while others are not?

Revisit your initial responses to these questions. Now add to or modify your thoughts in light of what you learned in this section.

Chem Essential Questions

What does it mean?
Chemistry explains a *macroscopic* phenomenon (what you observe) with a description of what happens at the *nanoscopic* level (atoms and molecules) using *symbolic* structures as a way to communicate. Complete the chart below in your *Active Chemistry* log.

MACRO	NANO	SYMBOLIC
Explain the visible macroscopic features of a solid, a liquid, and a gas.	*Compare and contrast the nanoscopic nature of a solid, a liquid, and a gas.*	*Make sketches of water molecules in the solid state (ice), the liquid state, and the gas state.*

How do you know?
What conclusions can you draw regarding the shape of a molecule and its physical state? Use data from this section to support your ideas.

Why do you believe?
It is important to have an understanding about the nature of matter in its different states. In this section there was a discussion of how cooling a gas could cause it to liquefy by slowing the molecules enough to allow them to attract each other. In boiling, the increase in energy allows the molecules to move apart despite their intermolecular attractive forces. Provide a similar discussion of what happens at the molecular level when a chocolate bar melts or how ice forms on a windshield overnight even though it didn't rain. Be sure to include intermolecular forces in your discussion.

Why should you care?
Your toy design may include the use of a gas, such as you find in toy rockets, or some high-tech water guns. Explain the nature of gas particles as you would in your toy project, if a gas were involved in your toy.

395

What Do You Think Now?

Have students reconsider the *What Do You Think?* questions and reflect on their original responses. This is an opportunity to discover if their understanding at the molecular level has been altered in a positive way. You may point out that what goes on at the molecular level determines what can be "seen" at the macro level. Have their ideas of the molecular behavior of gases changed? You can share the answer found in *A Chemist's Response* and elicit their opinions and reactions. This is an introduction to Kinetic Molecular Theory, which will be revisited in *Sections 3, 4,* and *7* of this chapter.

Now is also a good time to return to the *What Do You See?* illustration and have students identify features that have more significance now. You can ask them what the attraction of molecules has to do with solids, liquids, and gases.

CHAPTER 3

---

temperature. Even though it has a higher molecular weight (71 amu), chlorine is a gas at 0°C and doesn't liquefy until the temperature drops to –34°C. The shape of the molecule is the major difference between the two molecules.

Why do you believe?

Water molecules are present in air in the form of a gas – water vapor. During a cold night when the temperature drops below 0°C, the kinetic energy of the molecules is decreased and the molecules slow down enough until their intermolecular forces of attraction predominate. When this happens, they "stick" together. When enough water molecules stick together on a cold surface, such as a windshield, frost is formed.

Why should you care?

Some toys function on the principles of a compressed gas, such as air. Gases are compressible because they have a great deal of space between the molecules. When confined in a space containing a piston, the air particles (largely O_2 and N_2) can be squeezed together, increasing the potential energy of the system. When the volume confining the gas (air) is released quickly, the potential energy can be transferred to a rocket or the water of a water gun.

Reflecting on the Section and the Challenge

Students should now understand that the size and shapes of molecules affect their physical state. The concept of Kinetic Molecular Theory has been introduced and will be further developed in the following sections. This is an excellent opportunity for students to assess their new level of understanding and spend some time thinking about how to incorporate what they have learned into some aspect of their *Chapter Challenge*.

Chem to Go

1.

Most gases are made up of small, non-polar atoms and molecules. As such, the intermolecular attractive forces are quite weak and not strong enough to overcome the translational kinetic energy of the gas particles. Weak London dispersion forces are the major source of intermolecular attraction and these forces only operate at close distances and with increasing surface area. Due to their small size, gas molecules have relatively little surface area.

2.

a) non-polar, b) polar,
c) non-polar

3.a)

c), a), b)

3.b)

b) is a liquid at room
   temperature

Ideal Toy

Reflecting on the Section and the Challenge

You now understand that the size and shape of molecules determine whether or not the substance is a gas at room temperature. The molecules of most gases at room temperature show very little attraction for one another, and there is a lot of space between the molecules. Because of this, gases are easily compressed, which is something that is not easily done with most liquids and solids. Your toy may take advantage of the compressibility of gases.

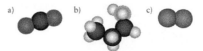

1. Explain why most gases have very little attraction between their molecules.

2. Ignoring the electronegativity values of the atoms, label each molecule as polar or nonpolar based on shape alone.

   a)   b)   c)

3. a) Rank the molecules listed in *Question 2* from lowest to highest boiling points.

   b) Only one is a liquid at room temperature. Which one is it?

4. Water is a liquid at room temperature while methane is a gas. Which of the following statements correctly describes the intermolecular forces between these molecules?

   a) Water and methane basically have no intermolecular forces.

   b) The intermolecular forces in water are stronger than those of methane.

   c) The intermolecular forces in methane are stronger than those of water.

   d) More information is needed in order to compare the intermolecular forces.

5. Under which conditions do you think you could dissolve the most gas in a liquid: (Hint: Think of a carbonated soda—carbon dioxide dissolved in water.)

   a) low pressure and high temperature   c) high pressure and low temperature

   b) low pressure and low temperature   d) high pressure and high temperature

6. Draw sketches and compare:

   a) methane and methanol

   b) methane and carbon tetrachloride

   c) fluorine and carbon tetrachloride

7. *Preparing for the Chapter Challenge*

   Prepare a list of all of the toys you know that use a gas in some manner. List the gases used and the purpose of each gas.

Active Chemistry

4.

b) The intermolecular forces in water are stronger than those of methane.

5.

c) high pressure and low temperature

6.a)

Sketches should resemble those in the text. Methane is symmetrical with little bond polarity and is non-polar.

Methanol has an electronegative oxygen atom, is unsymmetrical and is therefore polar.

6.b)

Sketches should resemble those in the text. Methane is symmetrical with little bond polarity and is non-polar. Carbon tetrachloride is symmetrical with some bond polarity due to the presence of chlorine atoms. However, because it is symmetrical, the molecule is non-polar.

6.c)

Sketches should resemble those in the text. Fluorine is very electronegative but symmetrical and non-polar. Carbon tetrachloride is symmetrical with some bond polarity due to the presence of chlorine atoms. However, because it is symmetrical, the molecule is also non-polar.

7.

Preparing for the Chapter Challenge

Answers will vary. This may work better as a group activity or a discussion. You might want to first establish a definition of a "toy," since students may suggest an air rifle or a bicycle as items that use gas.

SECTION 2 – QUIZ

5-2a   **Blackline Master**

1. Do hydrocarbons or their alcohols have higher boiling points? How could you explain this?

2. What are London dispersion forces and how do they affect molecules of different sizes?

3. A molecule is more likely to be polar if

    a) its shape is not symmetrical.

    b) its shape is symmetrical.

    c) its size is not small.

    d) its size is small.

4. Of the following molecules, which would you predict to be non-polar?

    a) CH_3Cl b) CH_3CH_3

    c) HCl d) H_2O

5. Liquids may be turned into gases (vaporized) by adding heat energy. Why is it necessary to add the energy?

    a) to change the molecules into different molecules.

    b) to break the forces of the crystalline structure.

    c) to break the attractive forces between the molecules.

    d) to break the bonds between atoms in the molecules.

SECTION 2 – QUIZ ANSWERS

❶ The alcohols have higher boiling points than the corresponding hydrocarbons. The alcohols have an oxygen atom in their structure which makes them more polar. The greater polarity increases the intermolecular attraction forces between molecules and increases the boiling point considerably.

❷ London dispersion forces are weak intermolecular forces that cause the surface electrons of an atom or molecule to shift slightly to form a temporary dipole. This transient distribution of uneven charges creates forces of attraction between molecules. As a surface phenomenon, larger molecules with their larger surface area have stronger London dispersion forces and higher boiling points.

❸ a) its shape is not symmetrical.

❹ b) CH_3CH_3

❺ c) to break the attractive forces between the molecules.

SECTION 3
Boyle's Law and the Cartesian Diver

Section Overview

This section involves two parts. In Part A, students simply explore pressure changes on volume using a syringe. Then, students explore pressure changes on buoyancy of a Cartesian diver. In Part B, students can use a pressure sensor probe and their graphing calculators, if available, to derive Boyle's law ($P_1V_1 = P_2V_2$). Alternative procedures are provided if you do not have pressure sensors and graphing calculators.

Background Information

Boyle's law states that under conditions of constant temperature and quantity, there is an inverse relationship between the volume and pressure for an ideal gas.

Robert Boyle is responsible for specifically investigating the relationship between volume and pressure of a gas while fixing all other variables. He found that increasing volume caused pressure to decrease, leading to the mathematical formula $PV = k$, where P is pressure, V is volume and k is constant. If one is given the pressure and volume of a gas, and then one of those conditions is changed, one can use Boyle's Law to calculate the change in the other variable:

$$P_1V_1 = P_2V_2$$

A simple example is squishing an inflated balloon. If you apply pressure to the balloon, it decreases in volume. In addition, the air particles inside of the balloon are exerting more pressure on the walls of the balloon. The functioning of the lungs is also a good example of Boyle's law. Air moves, or is pushed, from high-to-low-pressure environments. When the body desires to inhale air, the diaphragm flattens, which increases the volume of the lungs. This causes the pressure in the lungs to be lower than the pressure of air outside of the body, which causes air to be pushed into the lungs. Thus, high volume results in low pressure. When the body desires to exhale, the diaphragm becomes curved again, which lowers the volume of the lungs. This causes higher pressure inside the lungs than outside of the body. The air is thus pushed out of the lungs. Lowered volume results in higher pressure.

LEARNING OUTCOMES		
LEARNING OUTCOMES	**LOCATION IN SECTION**	**EVIDENCE OF UNDERSTANDING**
Investigate the relationship between the volume and pressure of gases at constant temperature.	*Investigate* Parts A-B *Chem to Go* Questions 1-4 *Chem Talk, Inquiring Further* 1-2	Explanation of observations and answers to questions in *Active Chemistry* logs match those listed in this *Teacher's Edition*. Answers to questions match those listed in this *Teacher's Edition*.
Quantify changes in volume or pressure with changes in the other.	*Investigate* Part B	Explanation of observations and answers to questions in *Active Chemistry* logs match those listed in this *Teacher's Edition*.
Interpret data concerning gas, volume, and pressure.	*Investigate* Parts A-B *Chem to Go* Question 4 *Section Quiz*	Explanation of observations and answers to questions in *Active Chemistry* logs match those listed in this *Teacher's Edition*. Answers match those presented in this *Teacher's Edition*.

NOTES

CHAPTER 5

Section 3
Materials, Chemicals, Preparation, and Safety

("per Group" quantity is based on group size of 4 students)

Materials and Equipment

Materials (and Equipment)	Quantity per Group (4 students)
Syringe, 50-60 mL, graduated	1
Ringstand	1
Burette clamp	1
Bottle, 2 liter, plastic	1
Eye dropper	1
Books for pressure	4
Pressure sensor, probeware (optional)	1
Materials (and Equipment)	**Quantity per Class**
Graph paper, pad of 50	1

Chemicals

Chemicals	Quantity per Class (24 students)
None	None

Teacher Preparation

Nearly 2 L of tap water will be required for each group.

Balancing books on the syringe plunger can be tricky. You might wish to have a piece of paneling glued to the syringe plunger to save time.

Safety Requirements

- Goggles and aprons are required in the laboratory area.

- Wash arms and hands before leaving the laboratory area.

NOTES

_____

_____

_____

_____

_____

_____

_____

_____

_____

Meeting the Needs of All Students
Differentiated Instruction

Augmentation and Accommodations

LEARNING ISSUE	REFERENCE	AUGMENTATION AND ACCOMMODATIONS
Generating applications of a principle	*Investigate* Part A, 1.d)	**Accommodations** • Some students may have difficulty thinking of toys that use this principle. Give them a list of toys which includes some that use this principle and some that don't. Have them select appropriate examples from your list. • Use guiding questions to elicit examples from the students who have difficulty generating their own lists. For example, you could ask "What toys do you have to fill with air?"
Writing precise and accurate responses to questions	*Investigate* Part A, 3. *Investigate* Part B, 4.b-c) *Chem Words, Boyle's law, Chem Essential Questions, What does it mean?, Macro*	**Augmentation** • Throughout this section, students are asked to express relationships and effects of volume and pressure on gases. They must also learn Boyle's law. These questions provide the perfect opportunity to teach them to write with precision and accuracy by using the scientific vocabulary and appropriate formats for their written answers. • In Part A, Step 3., ask students to identify scientific words that would make their answers more precise. They should use the words they identify in their answers. These might include: pressure, volume, increase, and decrease. This is also an opportunity to reinforce writing "if, then" statements that identify the effects of pressure on volume. • In Part B, Step 4.b-c), students should use the same techniques to write the verbal statements in b), and the generalization required in c). The words used might include: pressure, increase, volume, decrease, constant and inverse. • In the *Chem Words* section, students are given Boyle's law. Later they are asked to apply it, give examples, etc. The law is interpreted in the *Chem Talk* in the sentence immediately after it is defined. Before students read the *Chem Talk*, ask them to preview the *Chem Words*. Ask them to rewrite Boyle's law in their own words. One way to do this is to teach them to underline key words and phrases in the original statement, write substitute words/phrases above those they underlined, and then rewrite the statement maintaining the structure of the statement but substituting their words and phrases for the ones in the original. Then they should read the *Chem Talk* section and compare the interpretation given in the text with the ones they wrote. • In the *Macro* section of the *Chem Essential Questions*, students are asked to express the effect of pressure changes in the syringe on the volume of gas in the syringe. They should generate their own list of key words and phrases and use those words they generate and a cause/effect sentence structure in their answers. **Accommodations** • Give students a list of words to use in the answers to the questions and a sentence frame that they fill in.
Following directions	*Investigate,* Part B, 1.	**Augmentation** • Students must use a syringe, books, a pressure sensor, and/or probeware to take good measurements. Since the equipment varies, the directions in the text are not detailed. This complex procedure will require you to generate specific, clear sequential directions that students can carry out one at a time. • Check to see that each group has followed the directions correctly.

CHAPTER 3

LEARNING ISSUE	REFERENCE	AUGMENTATION AND ACCOMMODATIONS
Drawing a graph	*Investigate* Part B, 1.b) *Chem to Go,* 1.	**Augmentation** • Model the steps to set up axes, range and domain for graphs. Then, have students practice with some guidance from you. **Accommodations** • Give them a simple picture model with the x and y axes labeled. • Give them the values they should graph in the range and domain. • Give students a pre-made graph and ask them to plot the line.
Calculating inverse proportions	*Investigate* Part B, 3.	**Augmentation** • Students may need help with the math involved. Some might need a formula in which to plug in values in order to answer the questions in this part, but the investigation is asking them to calculate the relationship first, before they are given the equation which expresses that relationship. Some students will intuit answers immediately. Others may not understand how to interpret the questions. Take students having difficulty through 1.a), carefully illustrating and verbalizing each mental step. Then have them try. This instruction should only include the students who are having difficulty. Let others move on independently or work on a related activity while you work with the small group who needs help.
Interpreting numerical and mathematical labels	*Chem Talk*	**Augmentation** • Be sure to explain to students that the subscripts which follow V and P are used to differentiate two different volumes and two different pressures. Students may see those subscripts as indicating the number of volumes as subscripts are used in chemical formulas. Assuming students will know this can be confusing and embarrassing.
Finding information in a text	*Checking Up*	**Augmentation** • Ask students what strategies they will use to find the answers in the text. One of them will suggest that they look in order. Ask all students to try that strategy when looking for the information. After they have finished, ask them if the answers were in order. In this instance, the answers to Questions 1-6 follow the same order in the text as they do in the questions.

NOTES

_____

_____

_____

_____

_____

_____

_____

_____

_____

Strategies for Students with Limited English Language Proficiency

LEARNING ISSUE	REFERENCE	AUGMENTATIONS
Background knowledge	*What Do You Think?*	Students might benefit from a demonstration of a water pump-action squirt gun.
Vocabulary	*Investigate*	For words such as "*observe*," and "*explore*," and "*examine*," ask students to do certain things. Check for understanding of these terms. Make sure students understand the use of the word "*based*" (Part B, Step 2.). Check for understanding of use of term, "*halved*" (Part B, Step 3.b)
Background knowledge Vocabulary Comprehending text	*Chem Talk*	Have students put new words in their personal dictionaries or *Active Chemistry* logs. Review the use of prefix, "*non*" as in "*non-polar*." Point out use of the word "*simply*" as a signal word of an alternative explanation.
Comprehension	*What Do You Think Now?*	Explain that a "*why*" question can have more than one answer.
Background knowledge Vocabulary Comprehending text	*Chem Essential Questions*	Check for understanding of phrase "*representation of a relationship*" in the *Symbolic* section.
Comprehension Vocabulary	*Chem to Go*	Check for understanding of use of "*sketch*" as a verb. At the end of some of the questions is the one word direction "*explain*." Make sure that students know what to do at that point. Allow students to work in small groups to discuss questions and answers. Check for understanding of the terms "*specs*" and the related term "*specifications*."
Application Comprehension Research skills	*Inquiring Further*	Students may need help in accessing research on SCUBA diving, etc. When students are asked to "*research*," they may need some assistance in how to access information. Also, the phrase "*taken into account*" may not be familiar.

CHAPTER 3

NOTES

_____

_____

_____

_____

_____

_____

_____

_____

_____

Section 3
Teaching Suggestions and Sample Answers

What Do You See?

The question *What Do You See?* can be answered at more than one level. One student may report literally what she sees, e.g., "The cat is bored." Another may try to interpret the intent of the artist, e.g., "The kids are pushing so hard that they're sweating." Both responses are valid and should be acknowledged as such. Later, you may wish to return to the illustration so that the students will both have a better understanding of the artist's intent and observe that they have progressed in content understanding and knowledge.

As the students describe the students in the illustration pushing on the plunger, you may wish to ask them why they think the students have to exert so much effort. You can also ask them what they think the girl on the right is recording from the gauge. Finally, it appears that the cat is able to read without any distraction. Does the compression of the air cause any noise?

What Do You Think?

You might assume that everybody has seen an air-powered water gun but it's probably an incorrect assumption. If you are able to bring one in to show the students, they will enjoy it and provide better answers to the *What Do You Think?* question. This question is a good formative assessment opportunity. Student responses will help you gauge if they have an intuitive feel for pressure-volume relationships. This intuitive feel will be especially important as students derive the relationship and use it to make predictions.

What Do You Think?
A CHEMIST'S RESPONSE

By pumping the water gun, air is being compressed. The more pumps, the more compressions and the higher pressure the gas exerts. When this potential energy is released to the water, it makes a stream of water travel out of the gun. The greater the pressure when released, the farther the water stream will travel. Water itself is essentially noncompressible. Temperature may play a small factor in that the compression of air tends to heat it up and this, too, would increase the pressure.

STUDENTS' PRIOR CONCEPTIONS

Students tend to intuitively know that increasing the pressure at a constant temperature will decrease the volume of a gas. Because this is an inverse relationship, they may have trouble interpreting their data. Have students visualize or act out what is happening to pressure and volume at each data point. Discuss the advantages of graphing pressure versus the inverse of the volume, as this step will confuse students.

The kinetic theory of matter was introduced in *Section 2*. Reinforce the premises of this theory by helping the students apply them to the observations they are making in this section. This is a good opportunity to reinforce the particulate nature of matter and the implications of this nature, especially as it relates to compressibility of gases. Discuss the applications of this property of gases in the context of student's everyday life. Examples could be spray cans, atmospheric pressure, internal combustion engines, altitude sickness, and inhaling and exhaling.

Section 3

Boyle's Law and the Cartesian Diver

What Do You See?

Learning Outcomes

In this section you will

• Investigate the relationship between the volume and pressure of gases at constant temperature.

• Quantify changes in volume or pressure with changes in the other.

• Interpret data concerning gas, volume, and pressure.

What Do You Think?

Have you ever had a chance to play with the ever-popular air-powered water gun? The more you pump the water gun, the more water comes out, and the further it goes! Squirting someone on a hot day sounds like a lot of fun.

• Why do you think pumping the water gun makes the water that comes out of the gun travel further?

Record your ideas about this question in your *Active Chemistry* log. Be prepared to discuss your responses with your small group and the class.

Investigate

In this investigation, you will observe the effect of *pressure* on the volume of a *gas*. Then, you will explore this effect further by using a gas-pressure probe to better quantify your observations. As you examine this relationship, consider all the application possibilities for toys.

397

Active Chemistry

Investigate

Part A: Boyle's Toys

Have students explore what happens to the volume of air in the syringe as they apply pressure on the plunger.

1.a)

Students should note that the volume of air decreases as the plunger is depressed.

1.b)

Students should note that the plunger is harder to depress when they hold their finger over the hole in the end. Thus, it is harder to effect a change on the volume.

1.c)

Students should note the plunger returns to its original position when they stop depressing the plunger.

1.d)

Answers will vary.

2.a)

Students should note that the dropper sinks when they squeeze the bottle.

2.b)

Students should note that the dropper rises when they release pressure on the bottle.

2.c)

Students should note that the volume of water in the dropper increases as they squeeze and decreases when they release the pressure on the bottle. The volume of air in the dropper decreases as they squeeze and increases when they release the bottle.

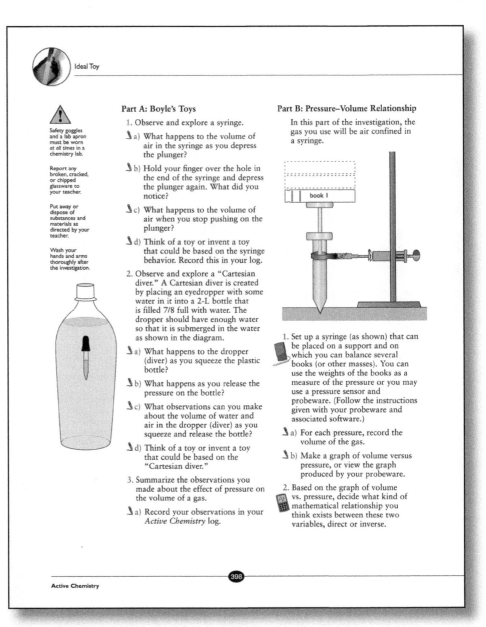

2.d)

Answers will vary.

3.

Answers should be a summary of students' observations from Step 2.

Part B: Pressure–Volume Relationship

The student instructions in the textbook use a large calibrated gas syringe upon which books are stacked to provide the needed variations in pressure. Alternatively, commercial data collection labware can be used, if available. The sample data that follows on the next page was obtained using commercial data collection labware and a pressure probe. However, data from a simple setup as shown in the student text will provide usable, but less precise numbers.

1.

It will make the experiment a bit easier if the series of books used to depress the syringe plunger are of the same mass.

1.a)

Have the students prepare a data table in advance. The mass of the books can be converted to atm (14.7 psi). You will need to calculate (or estimate) the surface area of the internal plunger of the syringe.

For your convenience, the following table, without the numeric values, is provided as a Blackline Master in the *Teacher Resources CD*.

5-3a	Blackline Master

Sample Volume-Pressure Data

Volume (mL)	Pressure (atm)	Constant, *k* (*P•V*)
5.0	2.02	10.1
7.5	1.35	10.1
10.0	1.02	10.2
12.5	0.81	10.1
15.0	0.69	10.4
17.5	0.58	10.2
20.0	0.50	10.0

1.b)

A sample graph is shown below.

The graph is also provided as a Blackline Master in the *Teacher Resources CD*.

5-3b	Blackline Master

2.

Pressure and volume have an inverse relationship.

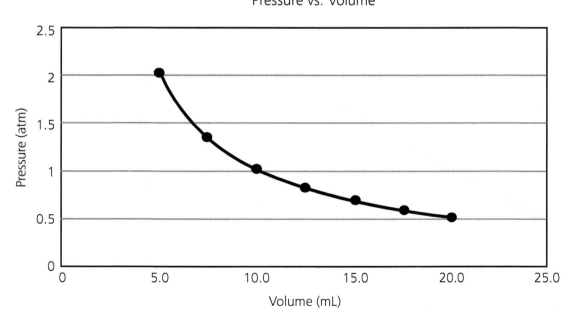

Pressure vs. Volume

3.a)

When the volume was doubled, the pressure was halved (pressure went from 2.02 atm to 1.02 atm).

3.b)

When the volume was halved, the pressure doubled (pressure went from 0.50 atm to 1.02 atm).

3.c)

The pressure is reduced by a factor of $\frac{1}{3}$ (pressure went from 2.02 to 0.69 atm).

3.d)

If the volume is increased to 40.0 mL, one would expect the pressure to be half of what it was at 20.0 mL. This would be a pressure of approximately 0.25 atm.

3.e)

If the volume were reduced to 2.5 mL, one would expect the pressure to be double what it was at 5.0 mL. This would be a pressure of approximately 4.00 atm.

3.f)

The temperature (K) and the number of molecules (moles) in the gas sample are assumed to be constant.

4.

The students should find an inverse relationship, as P increases, V decreases. When P is plotted vs. $\frac{1}{V}$, a straight line is obtained. The slope of this line is the constant, k.

The following graph of pressure vs. inverse volume is also provided as a Blackline Master on the *Teacher Resources CD*.

5-3c | **Blackline Master**

4.a)

Values for k should be quite constant with very little deviation.

4.b)

The equation represents Boyle's law, k $P \cdot V$. At constant temperature, the pressure of a confined gas varies inversely with the volume of the gas.

4.c)

The equation should support the summary statement from *Part A*. A student statement might read as follows:

At constant temperature and moles of any gas, there is an inverse relationship between the volume of that gas and its volume, $PV = k$.

Pressure vs. 1/Volume

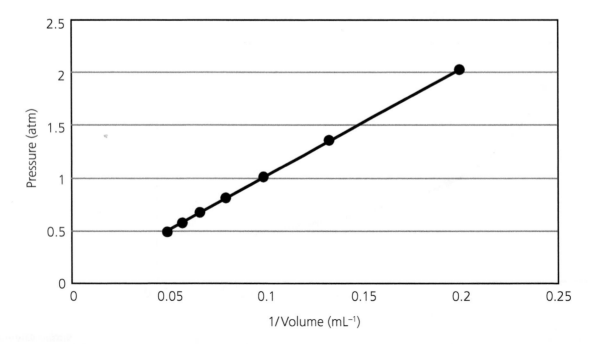

(Reminder: In a direct relationship, as the pressure increases, the volume increases. In an inverse relationship as the pressure increases, the volume decreases.)

3. In the experiment, you varied the pressure and recorded volume. You could have changed the volume and measured the pressure required to maintain that volume. This would be equal to the pressure of the gas.

Record your answers to the following in your *Active Chemistry* log:

a) If the volume doubled from 5.0 mL to 10.0 mL, what does your data show happens to the pressure?

b) If the volume is halved from 20.0 mL to 10.0 mL, what does your data show happens to the pressure?

c) If the volume is tripled from 5.0 mL to 15.0 mL, what does your data show happened to the pressure?

d) Based on your data, what would you expect the pressure to be if the volume of the syringe was increased to 40.0 mL? Explain or show your work to support your answer.

e) Based on your data, what would you expect the pressure to be if the volume of the syringe was decreased to 2.5 mL? Explain or show your work to support your answer.

f) What experimental factors are assumed to be constant in this experiment?

4. One way to determine if a relationship is inverse or direct is to find a proportionality constant, k, from the data. If this relationship is direct, $P = kV$. If it is inverse, $P = k/V$. Based on your data, choose one of these formulas and calculate k for each ordered pair in your data table (divide or multiply the P and V values). Record your answers in your log.

a) How *constant* were the values for k you obtained? Good data may show some minor variation, but the values for k should be relatively constant.

b) Using P, V, and k, write an equation representing their relationship. Write a verbal statement that correctly expresses this relationship.

c) Does this equation support your summary statement from your *Part A* observations? Write a generalization about the effect of the pressure on the volume of a gas at a constant temperature.

399

Chem Talk

Robert Boyle's contribution to the gas laws is discussed and the physics of gas pressure being a function of force and area is highlighted as $P = F/A$. The conversion of pressure units between atmospheres (atm), mm Hg, and Pascals (1 atm = 101.325 kPa) is covered. Several examples of everyday examples of Boyle's law are presented.

Ideal Toy

BOYLE'S LAW

Pressure

As you saw in this investigation, **gas** is easily compressed. It will fill any container, and mixes completely with other gases.

The observation and study of gases have led to various natural laws. A natural **law** is a summary of observed and measurable behavior. An Irish chemist, Robert Boyle (1627–1691), was one of the scientists whose work played a valuable part in the development of the natural laws of gases. Robert Boyle was the fourteenth child of the first Earl of Cork, Ireland. He wrote *The Sceptical Chymist* in 1661, saying that supposed elements must be tested to see if they were indeed simple. If a substance could be broken down into simpler substances, it was not an element. Boyle is also credited with carrying out the first quantitative experiments on gases. He presented to the scientific community a law that relates the pressure and the volume of gases.

One familiar property of gases is that they exert **pressure** on their container. When you blow up a balloon, the air molecules inside the balloon collide with the sides of the balloon, exerting pressure to keep it inflated.

Pressure is defined as the force exerted per unit of surface area:

$$\text{Pressure } (P) = \frac{\text{force } (F)}{\text{area } (A)}$$

As you pushed on the syringe to compress the gas, you could feel the pressure of the gas on your finger.

Chem Words

gas: a state of matter in which the molecules are free to move without fewer restrictive forces. A gas has neither definite shape nor definite volume.

law: a concise verbal or mathematical statement of a relation that is always the same under the same conditions.

pressure: force applied over a surface area. $P = F/A$.

Enough air for many minutes of breathing can be compressed into a tank.

Pressure can be measured by using devices like a barometer, as shown in the diagram.

A glass tube is filled with mercury and inverted into a pool of mercury that is open to the air. The mercury in the tube falls, but only a short distance. The air is exerting pressure on the pool of mercury and keeps the mercury in the tube. Under normal conditions, the pressure of the air pushes the mercury to a height of 760 mm. The units of measurement for pressure are **atmospheres** (atm) or **mm Hg** (millimeters of mercury). The relationship between the two is:

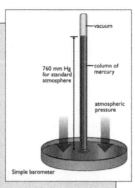

vacuum

column of mercury

760 mm Hg for standard atmosphere

atmospheric pressure

Simple barometer

$$1 \text{ atm} = 760 \text{ mm Hg}$$

In SI, which stands for *Système International d'Unités*, a modern, international version of the metric system, the unit used for pressure is kilopascals (kPa).

$$1 \text{ atm} = 101.325 \text{ kPa}$$

Relationship between the Pressure and the Volume of a Gas

Boyle studied the relationship between the gas pressure and the volume of a gas trapped in a tube. He described what is now called **Boyle's law.** *For a given amount of a gas at a constant temperature, the volume of the gas varies inversely with its pressure.* That simply means that when the pressure increases, the volume decreases; when the volume increases, the pressure decreases.

Imagine a group of 15 students. They are all running in straight lines in the classroom at top speed, hitting and bouncing off the walls. The additional pressure on one classroom wall will be determined by the speeds of the students and how often the students hit that wall. If the same 15 students now moved to the gymnasium and ran in straight lines at top speed, the number hitting one wall in a given time would be less than in the classroom. This is because the walls are larger and also because it takes a longer time for the students to get from one wall to the opposite wall.

The **kinetic theory of matter** provides a way to understand what is happening to gases at the nano or molecular level. The particles of

Chem Words

atmosphere: a measurement of the pressure being exerted on a surface. One atmosphere will support a column of mercury 760 mm high.

mm Hg: a unit commonly used in barometers to measure the height of a mercury column that the atmospheric pressure will support.

Boyle's law: a gas law that states that for a given amount of a gas at a constant temperature, the volume of the gas varies inversely with its pressure. $P \times V = k$, where k is a constant.

kinetic theory of matter: states that the particles that make up matter (atoms and molecules) are always in constant motion.

401

CHAPTER 3

Ideal Toy

a gas are moving about with a range of speeds and corresponding kinetic energy. These particles can collide with the walls of the container. These collisions create the pressure, or force per area, on the walls of the container. When you increase the volume (the size of the container), the number of gas particles hitting any section of the wall in a given time decreases and the pressure then decreases. It's similar to the students going from the classroom (small volume) to the gym (large volume). When you decrease the volume (make the container smaller), the gas particles have less distance to go before they hit the walls and so the particles will strike the container walls more often and create a greater pressure.

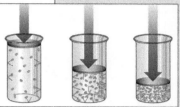

This behavior can be represented mathematically as:

$$\text{pressure} \times \text{volume} = \text{a constant}$$
$$\text{or}$$
$$PV = k$$

Chem Words

constant:
a mathematical value that does not change under controlled conditions.

where k is a **constant** for a given sample of air at a constant temperature. It can also be represented graphically as shown. The pressure $\times$ volume of each point on the graph is identical.

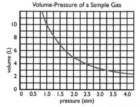

Volume-Pressure of a Sample Gas

In this investigation you started with a fixed amount of air in a syringe. When you pushed the plunger in, you squeezed the air into a smaller volume. The molecules of air inside the syringe were then colliding with the sides of the syringe more often and the pressure increased. You felt that pressure on your finger. You measured the additional pressure with the number of books that could be supported by the gas.

You can use the following equation to calculate the new volume of a gas when the pressure has been changed, or the new pressure of a gas when the volume has undergone a change. The equation compares the initial and final pressures and volumes.

$$P_1V_1 = P_2V_2$$

P_1 and V_1 are the initial pressure and volume, and P_2 and V_2 are the final pressure and volume at constant temperature.

Example:

Suppose you have a 1.0 L sample of oxygen gas at a pressure of 1.0 atm. If the pressure were increased to 2.0 atm, what would be the resulting volume?

$$P_1 = 1.0 \text{ atm} \qquad P_2 = 2.0 \text{ atm}$$
$$V_1 = 1.0 \text{ L} \qquad V_2 = ?$$

Rearrange Boyle's law equation to solve for V_2.

$$V_2 = \frac{P_1 V_1}{P_2}$$

$$V_2 = \frac{(1.0 \text{ atm})(1.0 \text{ L})}{(2.0 \text{ atm})}$$

$$V_2 = 0.50 \text{ L}$$

The final volume would be 0.50 L. This is the volume you would predict. The pressure was doubled, so the volume was decreased by one half.

The Cartesian diver toy can also be explained using Boyle's law. When you squeeze the container, the volume of the air decreases, causing an increase in the pressure of the air. This increased pressure drives the diver down into the water. If the diver is an eyedropper, you can see how the extra pressure on the water drives more water into the eyedropper. This increases the density of the eyedropper and it sinks.

Pressurized airplane cabins, tennis balls, and scuba diving are some of the applications of this pressure-volume law.

Checking Up

1. Define pressure.
2. What units are used to measure pressure?
3. What units are usually used to measure the volume of a gas?
4. State Boyle's law.
5. Determine the change in pressure if 1.0 L of gas at 1.0 atm was reduced to 0.25 L.
6. Give two practical applications of Boyle's law.

What Do You Think Now?

At the beginning of this section you were asked the following:

• Why do you think pumping the water gun makes the water that comes out of the gun travel further?

Diagram and explain the pressure-volume changes in a water gun. How does the change in pressure affect the volume of the gas and how the toy operates? Compare this response to your ideas at the beginning of the section.

CHAPTER 3

What Do You Think Now?

Have the students revisit the *What Do You Think?* section of their *Active Chemistry* logs. After a more thorough examination of the relationship between pressure and volume for gases, their explanation of the air-powered water gun should now be more sophisticated and detailed. They may include the effect of pressure changes on gas volumes in their explanations of how this toy works. Be sure to insist that the students use the words "pressure" and "volume" with care and precision. Having them provide the equation will show them how much they have learned from this section.

As you return to the *What Do You See?* illustration, you can ask your students why the students in the illustration are pushing so hard on the piston. You can also ask which direction the pressure gauge will go as the gas is compressed.

Checking Up

1.

Pressure is the force exerted per unit area of surface, $P = F/A$.

2.

Pressure can be expressed as atmospheres, mm Hg, psi, and kPa. 1 atm = 760 mm Hg = 101.325 kPa = 14.7 psi.

3.

Liters, L.

4.

"For a given amount of gas at constant temperature and quantity, the volume of the gas varies inversely with its pressure."

5.

The pressure would be 4.0 atm.

6.

Car tires, pressurized airplane cabins, tennis balls, basketballs, and SCUBA diving tanks are a few examples.

Chem Essential Questions

What does it mean?

MACRO — The pressure change in the syringe showed an inverse relationship to the volume in the syringe, $PV = k$. As pressure increased, volume decreased.

NANO — The drawings should reflect an understanding of kinetic theory and the particulate nature of matter. The gas particles should be closer together at Point B than at Point A.

SYMBOLIC — $PV = k$

This tells us that as the pressure increases, the volume will decrease in a proportional manner. Temperature and moles of gas must remain constant.

How do you know?

Using the syringe or the pressure probe, variations in volume were observed and recorded as the pressure on the system changed. An inverse relationship between P and V was observed. Temperature and moles of gas were the constants, $PV = k$.

Why do you believe?

Answers will vary. Most students will relate this question to a balloon, one of the most common experiences for everyone. Be alert and receptive for novel student experiences to show other students a new aspect of this phenomenon.

Why should you care?

Using a gas under pressure is a likely choice for a toy design. One choice might be the propulsion of a rocket under gas pressure. Another might be the use of gas pressure to move players about a board in a simulation of hockey or (American) football.

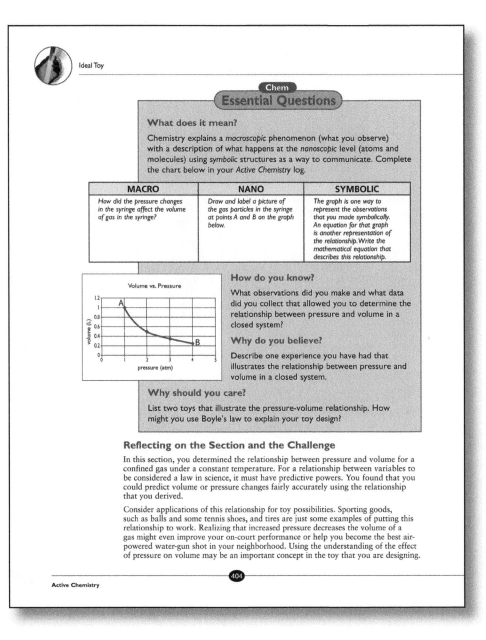

Reflecting on the Section and the Challenge

Although there are no questions in this section for students to answer or to use for discussion, this is an important opportunity to consider the section with respect to the *Chapter Challenge*. Students now know Boyle's law and the relationship between pressure and volume. This can be used in the design and the explanation of their toy.

NOTES

CHAPTER 5

Chem to Go

1.a)

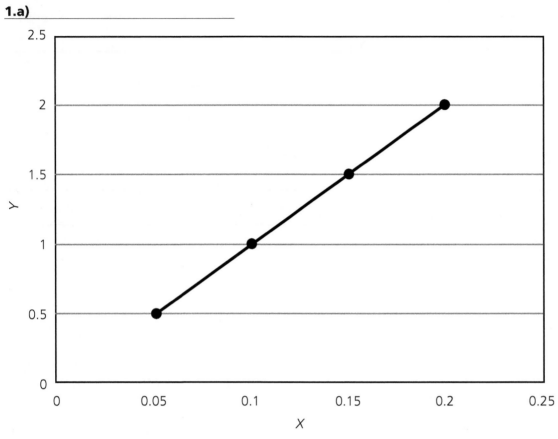

1.b)

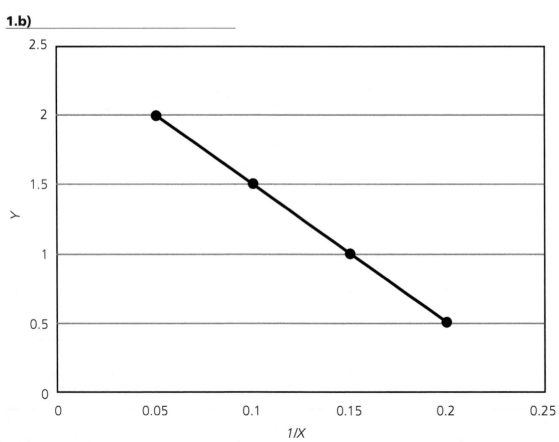

Section 3 Boyle's Law and the Cartesian Diver

Chem to Go

1. a) Sketch a graph that shows a direct relationship between two variables.

   b) Sketch a graph that shows an inverse relationship between two variables.

   c) Which of your graphs best depicts the relationship between pressure and volume? Explain.

2. What is the mathematical relationship for pressure and volume of a confined gas at constant temperature?

3. What pressure would be required to decrease the volume of a balloon from 1200 cm³ to 750 cm³ if the original pressure was 1 atm?

4. A tire gauge actually expresses the difference in pressure between air inside the tire and the atmospheric pressure. Therefore, if a tire gauge reads 30 lb/in.² on a day when the atmospheric pressure is 14 lb/in.², the total tire pressure is 44 lb/in.². Determine the volume of atmospheric air (at 14 lb/in.²) needed to fill your bike tires (assuming it holds 500 mL of air) to the pressure recommended by the manufacturer (70 lb/in.²).

5. If the pressure of a gas in a 1-liter system was increased fourfold (4 times), the volume of the gas would:

   a) increase 4 times   b) increase 2 times   c) decrease by $\frac{1}{4}$ d) decrease by $\frac{1}{2}$

6. Describe how a tennis ball bounces by commenting on the pressure and volume changes during the bounce.

7. Which pressure change would cause the volume of a sample of gas to double when the temperature stays the same?

   a) from 1 atm to 2 atm   b) from 2 atm to 1 atm

   c) from 4 atm to 1 atm   d) from 1 atm to 4 atm

8. Describe the motion of molecules of a gas in terms of kinetic molecular theory.

9. At constant temperature, a bicycle tire pump contains 525 mL of air at 995 kPa pressure. The plunger of the pump is pushed down until the volume is 95.0 mL. What is the new pressure of the air inside the pump?

10. A balloon containing 1.00 L of nitrogen gas is stretched and expanded until it has a volume of 22.4 L with no change in temperature. If its new pressure is 1.10 atm, what was its original pressure?

11. **Preparing for the Chapter Challenge**

    Select a toy that applies Boyle's law. Draw the specifications for the toy and include any changes in volume that might result due to pressure changes.

405

Active Chemistry

---

decreasing. This increases the pressure exerted by the gas on the interior surface of the tennis ball, pushing it away from the ground. The pressure returns to its original value until the next bounce.

7.

b) from 2 atm to 1 atm

8.

The molecules of all gases behave the same at normal temperatures and pressures. They move independently of each other in a constant and random fashion, colliding with each other and with the walls of the container. These collisions are elastic, that is, no energy is lost. Distance between molecules is very large, relative to the diameter of the molecules.

9.

$P_1V_1 = P_2V_2$ at constant temperature.

995 kPa × 525 mL = P_2 × 95.0 mL

P_2 = (995 kPa × 525 mL)/95.0 mL = 5.50×10^3 kPa

10.

$P_1V_1 = P_2V_2$ at constant temperature.

P_1 × 1.00 L = 1.10 atm × 22.4 L

P_1 = (1.10 atm × 22.4 L)/1.00 L = 24.6 atm

11.

Preparing for the Chapter Challenge

Answers will vary depending upon the students' choices of toys. Examine their specs for proper pressure-volume relationships.

1.c)

Graph b) describes the relationship between pressure and volume. This shows an inverse relationship where one variable increases while the other decreases linearly.

2.

$k = PV$

3.

$P_1V_1 = P_2V_2$

(1 atm) (1.2 L) = (X atm) (0.75 L)

$P_2 = 1.6$ atm

4.

$P_1V_1 = P_2V_2$

(84 lb/in²) (500 mL) = (14 lb/in²) (X mL)

V_2 = 3000 mL or 3.0 L

5.

c) decrease by $\frac{1}{4}$

6.

Initially, the pressure and volume of the gas inside a tennis ball are constant. Upon initially hitting the ground, the sphere is distorted with the volume of the gas inside of the ball

CHAPTER 3

Inquiring Further

1. SCUBA diving and the bends

Both Boyle's law and Henry's law are applicable here. Boyle's law describes how these gas volumes respond to changes in pressure. Henry's law describes the relationship between gas pressure and gas solubility in a liquid.

2. Mars rover

Students' answers will vary. The rover landed on air bags that inflated at the last minute and then had to deflate quickly. The NASA engineers would need to know how much gas to store in order to inflate the bags to the proper pressure. Specific information on the landing gear of the rover and general information about the mission, pictures, and links to other useful information can be found on the Internet using the search words "Mars rover."

3. Crushing a soda can

The student explanation should include the following:

- Boiling the water inside the can caused the formation of water vapor which displaced the air and filled the can.

- Inverting the can into cold water caused the water vapor to condense and the pressure inside the can was no longer 1 atm but much below 1 atm.

- The atmospheric pressure on the outside walls of the can crushed the can because the opposing pressure inside the can was much less than the outside pressure.

 Ideal Toy

Inquiring Further

1. Scuba diving and the bends

Research scuba diving and a condition known as the bends. Explain how pressure changes while descending and then ascending in the ocean affect your lungs.

2. Mars rover

Research the Mars rover. It deployed a unique landing tactic. What did NASA engineers have to take into account in order for this landing to succeed?

3. Crushing a soda can

Follow these steps to crush a soda can without exerting any physical force on your part!

Step 1: Place about 10 mL of water in an empty soda can.

Step 2: Heat the can on a hot plate until water is steaming out of the can.

Step 3: When steam is seen coming out of the can, use beaker tongs to quickly invert the can into a tub of cold water.

Use Boyle's law to explain what happens.

Do this experiment only with adult supervision. Never use a hot plate without adult supervision.

SECTION 3 – QUIZ

5-3d	Blackline Master

1. For a gas at constant temperature and number of particles, describe the relationship between volume and pressure.

2. If the pressure of a gas is tripled, what will be the effect of the volume of the gas (assuming no change in temperature)?

    a) increase by a factor of 3

    b) decrease by a factor of 3

    c) increase by a factor of 9

    d) decrease by a factor of 9

3. If 1.5 L of a gas in a balloon at 750 mm Hg is allowed to expand at constant temperature to 2.5 L, what will the resulting pressure be?

    a) 300 mm Hg   b) 450 mm Hg

    c) 1250 mm Hg   d) 1875 mm Hg

4. If 5.00 L of a gas at 1.20 atm has a change in pressure to 3.00 atm, what will the resulting volume be (assuming constant temperature)?

    a) 2.00 L   b) 4.17 L

    c) 12.5 L   d) 18.0 L

5. Use Boyle's law to explain how a simple toy cork gun works (this is basically a tube with a piston and handle at one end and a cork at the other).

SECTION 3 – QUIZ ANSWERS

1 As the volume decreases, the pressure of a gas increases and vice versa. There is an inverse relationship between the volume and pressure of a gas (at constant temperature and number of particles). $PV = k$

2 b) decrease by a factor of 3

3 b) 450 mm Hg

$$P_2 = \frac{P_1 V_1}{V_2} = \frac{(750 \text{ mm Hg}) (1.5 \text{ L})}{(2.5 \text{ L})}$$

$$P_2 = 450 \text{ mm Hg}$$

4 a) 2.00 L

$$V_2 = \frac{P_1 V_1}{P_2} = \frac{(1.20 \text{ atm})(5.00 \text{ L})}{(3.00 \text{ atm})}$$

$$V_2 = 2.00 \text{ L}$$

5 When the piston is pushed in, the volume of air in it suddenly decreases. As the volume decreases, the pressure increases. Once the pressure is greater than the force holding the cork in, the cork will pop out.

CHAPTER 3

SECTION 4
Charles's Law and Hot-Air Balloons

Section Overview

In Part A of this section, students will derive Charles's law and absolute zero. Indirect measure is used to collect data on gas volumes at several temperatures. This data is recorded on a graph set up so that the x-axis extends from –350°C to 150°C. Students will draw a line of best fit through their data points intersecting both the y and x-axis. The interception on the x-axis should be close to –273°C (absolute zero). The equation of the line shows the mathematical relationship between volume and the temperature of a gas (Charles's law). From this exercise, students graphically determine absolute zero and gain an understanding of the Kelvin scale versus the Celsius scale.

In Part B, students will apply the relationship they just derived to the construction and testing of hot-air balloons made from plastic dry-cleaning bags or thin garbage bags. This provides an opportunity to further develop their understanding of the kinetic molecular theory.

Background Information

Charles's law (named for Jacques Charles) states that the temperature and volume of a gas are directly proportional. Under constant pressure and moles of gas, as temperature increases, so does the volume. Likewise, as the temperature decreases, the volume decreases. This relationship is represented by the formula for an ideal gas: $\frac{V}{T} = k$, where k is constant, V is volume in liters, and T is temperature in Kelvin. When volume and temperature of a gas are plotted on a line graph, a straight line is formed.

A working example of Charles's law is a hot-air balloon. When the air in the balloon is heated, the gas particles start to move more rapidly. As they do, they exert more pressure on the walls of the balloon, which causes it to inflate, thereby increasing the volume of air in the balloon. Cold air surrounding the balloon is displaced as the balloon expands, filling with hot air. This causes a buoyant force which makes the balloon rise.

LEARNING OUTCOMES		
LEARNING OUTCOMES	**LOCATION IN SECTION**	**EVIDENCE OF UNDERSTANDING**
Investigate the relationship between temperature and volume of a gas.	*Investigate* Part A *Chem Talk, Chem to Go* Questions 2,4-6 *Inquiring Further, Preparing for the Chapter Challenge*	Answers to questions in Part A are similar to those presented in this *Teacher's Edition*. Answers match those shown in this *Teacher's Edition*. Proposed ideas and solutions correctly apply the principle of Charles's law. Proposed ideas are reasonable.
Understand why the Kelvin scale is used for temperature relationships.	*Investigate* Part A *Chem Talk, Chem to Go* Question 3	Answers to questions in Part A are similar to those presented in this *Teacher's Edition*. Answers match those shown in this *Teacher's Edition*.
Apply Charles's law to launch a hot-air balloon.	*Investigate* Part B, Step 3	Explanation includes correct application of Charles's law.

Section 4
Materials, Chemicals, Preparation, and Safety

("per Group" quantity is based on group size of 4 students)

Materials and Equipment

Materials (and Equipment)	Quantity per Group (4 students)
Beakers, 600 mL	2
Beral pipettes, 3 mL	4
Wire gauze squares for hot plate	2
Crucible tongs	1
Hot plate	1
Ringstand	1
Beaker clamp	1
Burette clamp for thermometer	1
Thermometer (or temperature probe)	1
Scissors	1
Dry-cleaner bags	2
Materials (and Equipment)	Quantity per Class
Roll of clear, wide postal tape	1
Boxes of large paper clips	2

Chemicals

Chemicals	Quantity per Class (24 students)
None	None

Teacher Preparation

None

Safety Requirements

- Goggles and aprons are required in the laboratory area.

- Wash arms and hands before leaving the laboratory area.

Meeting the Needs of All Students
Differentiated Instruction

Augmentation and Accommodations

LEARNING ISSUE	REFERENCE	AUGMENTATION AND ACCOMMODATIONS
Interpreting directions	*Investigate* Part A, 6.-8.	**Accommodations** • Give students an additional drawing of the pipette in the room-temperature bath. • Differentiate the process by suggesting that each group select someone who understands the directions to perform the procedure outlined in Steps 6-8. Other group members should follow along in the directions as they observe, but require that three others repeat the process as required in the text, so that more students get practice in following lab procedures.
Finding the average Constructing a data table	*Investigate* Part A, 9.	**Augmentation** • Check to see that students know how to find the average from the four measurements by writing them in the class chart. If necessary, teach students to find the average using a different example and redo their calculation. **Accommodations** • The above exercise and the data table of the class volumes and temperatures will serve as a model of the data students must transfer to their *Active Chemistry* logs in 9.a).
Designing a graph	*Investigate* Part A, 10.,11.	**Augmentation** • By this chapter, you may know which students will have difficulty determining the scale and labeling each axis. Circulate in class during this step to help those students. Teach them a procedure they can use next time. For example, they might determine a relationship between the change in temperature if they plot the number of lines on the *x*-axis. **Accommodations** • You may determine that being able to set up a graph independently is not currently a realistic goal for a particular student. In such a case, provide a labeled graph and ask the student to plot the points.
Writing with accuracy and precision	*Investigate* Part A, 10.a)	**Accommodations** • The goal of the investigation is for students to understand the relationship between temperature and volume of a gas. Expressing this relationship clearly reflects clear thinking. Give students words such as temperature, volume, and increase to include in their answers. • Suggest that students use an "if… then" sentence structure.
Converting Celsius to Kelvin	*Investigate* Part A, 11.	**Augmentation** • Draw a number line on the board that clearly designates –273°C to 100°C above hash marks on the line. Have students copy it and label the absolute zero location. Then show them the Kelvin equivalents. Once they see that –273°C is equivalent to 0 K, give them another temperature in Celsius and ask them to determine the Kelvin equivalent. Most will intuit that they must simply add 273 to the Celsius measurement.
Determining the slope of a line Solving equations	*Investigate* Part A, 11.b)-c)	**Augmentation** • Keep in mind that the purpose of having students determine slope using this equation is to see how Charles's law was derived. Some students may not have the prerequisite skills needed to apply this equation. Teaching them to find slope using the rise over run method allows them to find the slope, but it may not help them understand Charles's law or the reason the Kelvin scale must be used. There are two alternatives: Teach students the skills they need to do the math, or explain that Kelvin must be used because using Celsius would yield impossible volumes.

LEARNING ISSUE	REFERENCE	AUGMENTATION AND ACCOMMODATIONS
Writing with precision and accuracy Explaining how the balloon worked	*Investigate* Part B, 3.	**Accommodations** • Refer students to the description of Charles's experiment in the beginning of *Chem Talk* or to the section titled Applying Charles's law in *Chem Talk*. • Write your own answer. Then remove some words and phrases. Use them to create a word bank. Have students reconstruct your answer.

Solving problems using Charles's law	*Chem Talk, Chem to Go* 4.-6.	**Augmentation**
		• Some students understand real numbers more readily than they understand manipulation of variables in an equation. Those students might solve problems more easily without manipulating the unknowns in the equation. They may benefit from a set sequence of steps that they can use in all cases. Teach them this series of steps:
		    • Convert all temperatures from Celsius to Kelvin.
		    • Copy the formula.
		    • Express the values given in the problem, $V_1 = 2.8$ L, etc.
		    • Substitute the givens in the formula.
		    • Cross multiply.
		    • Solve the equation algebraically.
		Have students record these steps on an index card, called a procedure card they use when solving these types of problems.

Strategies for Students with Limited English Language Proficiency

LEARNING ISSUE	REFERENCE	AUGMENTATIONS
Background knowledge	*What Do You Think?*	Help students define the word "*affect.*"
Vocabulary	*Investigate*	Build background knowledge on the idea of "*inventing*" something; provide derivations of the word and explore other uses. Check for understanding of the phrase, "based on this relationship." Check for understanding of the term "*half-fill.*"
Background knowledge Vocabulary Comprehending text	*Chem Talk*	Have students put new vocabulary words into their personal dictionaries or *Active Chemistry* logs. Check for understanding of multiple uses of the word "*contract(s).*" Refer students to sidebars on the pages as points for discussion (*Chem Words, Checking Up*). Have students work together as you direct them to read portions of the text and then take turns paraphrasing what is being stated as well as what is being asked in the form of questions.
Comprehension	*What Do You Think Now?*	Point out that there is more than one question here.
Background knowledge Vocabulary Comprehending text	*Chem Essential Questions*	Check for understanding of the words "*predictable*" and "*prediction.*"
Comprehension Vocabulary	*Chem to Go*	Check for understanding of the word "*install.*" Make sure students also understand the one-word direction, "Explain," which appears at the end of some of the questions. In *Question 6.*, the phrase, "To what temperature..." might be a structure with which they are not familiar. Allow students to work in small groups to discuss questions and answers.
Application Comprehension Research skills	*Inquiring Further*	Students may not understand the term "*guide*" as a piece of writing and might need examples. Derivations of this word will help build background knowledge as well. Also, the criteria for writing a guide should to be shared. Check for understanding of use of the word "*tips*" in this context.

CHAPTER 5

Section 4
Teaching Suggestions and Sample Answers

What Do You See?

Allow students a few minutes to contemplate the illustration. The purpose here is to engage their interest; you should not expect correct answers at this time. One student may point out irrelevant features, e.g., "The bird caught a fish." Another may try to interpret the intent of the artist, e.g., "If the kid lets go, the balloon will go up in the air." Both responses are valid and should be acknowledged as such. Later, you may wish to return to the illustration to give students another chance to assess the artist's intent and observe how they have progressed in content understanding and knowledge.

The illustration may lead to the question of whether anyone in the class has ever been in or seen a hot-air balloon. After students finish sharing their observations, you can ask if they have ideas about the purpose of the flame beneath the balloon.

What Do You Think?

Before eliciting students' responses to the *What Do You Think?* question, ask if any of them ever had an experience with a helium-filled balloon appearing to deflate when taken outside on a cold day (as mentioned in the text). If not, you may want to describe it to them, or better yet—have a helium-filled balloon ready in a freezer. You can then remove the balloon and let the students see it expand. This demonstration should encourage them to share their understandings of the relation between temperature and the balloon (and the gases in the balloon).

Temperature and pressure effects on volume are rather intuitive. Students' thinking here will provide some insight into their preconceptions about volume and temperature relationships.

What Do You Think?
A CHEMIST'S RESPONSE

A decrease in temperature will decrease the volume of a balloon. This will be a linear relationship using the absolute temperature scale. Temperature is a measure of the average kinetic energy of all of the gas particles. As the temperature falls, the average kinetic energy falls and the gas particles do not move as fast. As a result, their collisions with the inside surface of the balloon are less forceful and the exterior pressure of the atmosphere pushes the walls of the balloon in.

STUDENTS' PRIOR CONCEPTIONS

Although this section will derive Charles's law and determine absolute zero, students will need to discuss the meaning of the data they are collecting. Because the volume of the gas must be determined by indirect measure, many students will make the measurements and follow the directions without understanding why they are collecting that data. Take time to discuss the meaning of the data and why they are measuring gas volumes indirectly.

There will be numerous errors in this procedure unless you caution the groups about the need for carefully counting the drops. This lab will be a good opportunity to discuss data techniques, multiple trials, etc. If the class does not end up with –273°C as absolute zero, you will need to discuss possible sources of error in this rather crude technique. Help students to verbalize what the relationship means when it is directly proportional. For example, ask students what would happen to the volume of the gas if the temperature were doubled (the volume would double). Then ask what would happen to the volume if the temperature were halved (the volume would be halved).

Determination of absolute zero is an appropriate time to talk about limits. Their graph suggests that there

Section 4 — Charles's Law and Hot-Air Balloons

What Do You See?

Learning Outcomes

In this section you will

• Investigate the relationship between temperature and volume of a gas.

• Understand why the Kelvin scale is used for temperature relationships.

• Apply Charles's law to launch a hot-air balloon.

Safety goggles and a lab apron must be worn at all times in a chemistry lab.

Report any broken, cracked, or chipped glassware to your teacher.

What Do You Think?

A young child takes a helium-filled balloon outside the store on a cold, wintry day and the balloon seems to deflate.

• How might a decrease in temperature affect an inflated balloon?

Record your ideas about this question in your *Active Chemistry* log. Be prepared to discuss your responses with your small group and the class.

Investigate

In this investigation, you will explore the effects of temperature on a gas's volume under constant pressure. You will then invent a toy that can be based on this relationship.

Part A: Volume and Temperature of a Gas

1. Completely fill an empty pipette with water.

2. Count and record the number of drops it takes to empty the pipette.

    a) This number represents the volume of the pipette. It also represents the volume of gas at room temperature in the empty pipette in this investigation. Record this as the volume of the empty pipette.

3. Half fill a 600 mL-beaker with H_2O (approximately 20°C).

407

Active Chemistry

Investigate

Part A: Volume and Temperature of a Gas

TEACHING TIP

Metal washers or nuts can be used to keep the pipette submerged. Slip the washer or the nut onto the "barrel" of the pipette. This way, students will only have to keep the tip closed until the pipette is submerged.

1.

Explain to students that because it is difficult to get a Beral pipette completely full, they will be using an average number of drops for each test.

2.

This number will vary widely. Students should use the class average in their calculations to help reduce error.

2.a)

Compile each group's number of drops on the board or overhead. Remember to calculate the average number of drops. For the sample data to be used in this *Teacher's Edition*, the pipette holds 64 drops at 20°C.

is an absolute coldest temperature. However, because air molecules (or any other gas or mixture of gases) have mass, they cannot be reduced to zero volume, even though this is shown on their graph.

Buoyancy is a factor to consider with the hot-air balloons, and students often find this concept confusing. Explain Charles's law in terms of the kinetic theory of gases. When air in the balloon is heated, molecules of nitrogen, oxygen, and other atmospheric gases move more rapidly. These molecules collide with each other and the walls of the balloon, resulting in an increase in local pressure. Since the balloon is open at the base, pressure inside the balloon equilibrates with that outside, as warmer, higher-pressure air flows out into the cooler lower-pressure air surrounding it. As air exits the balloon, the composite density of the balloon drops below that of the surrounding air, and the balloon rises. You may wish to explain hot-air balloons in terms of Archimedes's Principle, which states that a force equal to the weight of the fluid it displaces buoys up any object completely or partially submerged in air, water or other fluid. The hot-air balloon rises because the composite weight of the balloon (plus the air it contains) is less than the weight of the outside air it displaces.

3.

Measurement of the water is not necessary. It should be deep enough to completely submerge the Beral pipette.

4.

Have students use caution when using thermometers, hot plates and hot water. Assign each group of students a different temperature for their beaker of hot water. For example, if you have six groups of students, assign water temperatures of 90°C, 80°C, 70°C, 60°C, 50°C and 40°C. Using their thermometer, they should try to keep the temperature close to the assigned value. The groups with lower temperatures will be able to begin collecting data sooner and should have less trouble maintaining the temperature.

5.

Steel washers will help keep the pipette bulbs underwater as they are heated.

6.

Plastic dish tubs work well for the room temperature water bath. Large beakers (600-1000 mL) can also be used. The main point is to have the entire pipette submerged.

7.

Students should see water being drawn into the stem of the pipette as the temperature drops.

8.

Upon cooling, greater amounts of water will be drawn into the pipettes that were immersed in water of higher temperatures. Have the students monitor their hot-water temperatures carefully so that the data is as good as possible.

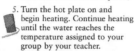

Safety goggles and a lab apron must be worn at *all times* in the chemistry lab.

Wear protective gloves when handling heated objects. Hot plates may remain hot for some time after they are turned off.

Wipe up any spills immediately.

4. Half fill a second 600 mL-beaker with water and place it on a hot plate. Place a temperature sensor in the beaker. Do not allow the temperature sensor to rest on the bottom of the beaker. Do not turn the hot plate on until the entire setup is ready to go. (Your teacher may supply you with pre-heated water instead of the hot plate.)

5. Turn the hot plate on and begin heating. Continue heating until the water reaches the temperature assigned to your group by your teacher.

6. Use tongs to hold the bulb of the pipette under water in the beaker being heated. The stem of the pipette should be above the water level. Keep the pipette immersed for 2 minutes. After 2 minutes, squeeze and seal the tip of the pipette with tweezers. Then lift the pipette out of the water.

This traps the hot air in the pipette. Quickly transfer the pipette to your room-temperature water bath and, removing the tweezers, completely submerge the pipette bulb and stem. Hold it in place with your tongs.

7. Notice that water is entering the pipette. Keep the pipette submerged until no further changes are noted (about 1 minute).

8. Remove the pipette from the water and dry the outside. Count the number of drops of water that were drawn into the pipette. This number allows you to calculate the volume of the air in the pipette when the pipette is at room temperature (20°C). Subtracting the number of drops of water from the total volume of the pipette (found in *Step 2*) gives you the volume of the air at 20°C.

a) Complete this calculation and record the volume of the 20°C air in the pipette in your log.

b) When the hot air in the pipette cooled in the room temperature (20°C) water, it took up less space and water got sucked into the pipette. Write a statement summarizing this observation using the terms temperature and volume.

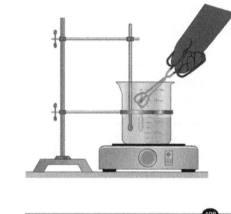

9. Repeat these measurements three times.

a) Calculate and record the average.

b) Your class will now share the data and complete the first three columns of the following data chart:

Active Chemistry

8.b)

The student statement may be similar to this: When the heated pipette full of air was placed under water and cooled, water was drawn into the pipette. This happened because as the air cooled, the pressure in the pipette became less and less. Atmospheric pressure on the water forced water into the pipette until the pressure inside the pipette matched the pressure outside the pipette.

9.a)

Sample Data and Answers to Data Analysis

Temperature (°C)	Volume of air (drops of water)
90	80
75	75
60	71
45	69
30	65
20	64

9.b)

A Blackline Master of the blank chart for student data is available on the *Teacher Resources CD*.

| 5-4a | Blackline Master |

Temperature of hot air (equal to the temperature of the heated water bath)	Volume of hot air (equal to the total volume of the pipette from Step 2.)	Volume of room temperature 20°C air	Ratio of volumes (hot air to room temperature 20°C air)	Volume of hot air corresponding to 100 drops of room temperature 20°C air

NOTES

_____

_____

_____

_____

_____

_____

_____

_____

_____

_____

_____

CHAPTER 5

9.c)

The volume of hot air is larger than the volume of air at 20°C. As the temperature increases, the volume becomes larger.

9.d)

Using sample data from the table on the previous page, the ratio of hot air volume to 20°C air is:

90°C 80/64 = 1.25

75°C 75/64 = 1.18

60°C 71/64 = 1.11

45°C 69/64 = 1.08

30°C 65/64 = 1.02

20°C 64/64 = 1.00

9.e)

If the volume of room temperature 20°C air was 100 drops, the following hot air volumes would apply:

90°C = 125 drops

75°C = 118 drops

60°C = 111 drops

45°C = 108 drops

30°C = 102 drops

20°C = 100 drops

10.

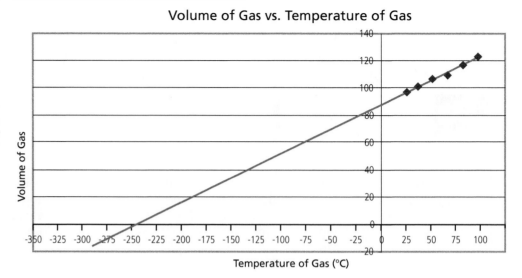

Volume of Gas vs. Temperature of Gas

10.a)

The relationship between the volume and the Celsius temperature is a positive, direct relationship.

10.b)

Based on the graph, the temperature would be about −250°C at zero volume. It's not actually possible to have zero volume and therefore, difficult to imagine what it would look like.

10.c)

Using the data above, the temperature on this new scale would be equal to 250°C.

Section 4 Charles's Law and Hot-Air Balloons

Temperature of hot air (equal to the temperature of the heated water bath)	Volume of hot air (equal to the total volume of the pipette from Step 2)	Volume of room temperature 20°C air	Ratio of volumes (hot air to room temperature 20°C air)	Volume of hot air corresponding to 100 drops of room temperature 20°C air

c) What is the relationship between the volume of hot air and the volume of room temperature 20°C air for different temperatures of hot air?

d) It would be very helpful to compare the volume of hot air if each group had an identical amount of room temperature 20°C air. This is not possible with one size pipette and your procedure. However, a bit of math can help you. You can calculate what the volume of hot air would have been for any volume of room temperature 20°C air. For example, if your volume of hot air was 200 drops and your volume of room temperature 20°C air were 80 drops, you can see that the volume of hot air is 200/80 or 2.5 times larger than the volume of room temperature air.

Calculate the ratio of your hot air to room temperature 20°C air and place this in the class data chart.

e) Use the ratio to calculate what the volume of hot air would be if the volume of room temperature 20°C air was 100 drops. Record this in the class data chart.

10. Prepare a graph of your class data, with temperature (in degrees Celsius) on the horizontal axis (x-axis) and the volume of hot air corresponding to 100 drops of room temperature 20°C air on the vertical axis (y-axis). Although your temperature data goes from 0°C to 100°C, the x-axis should be numbered from –350°C to 150°C for reasons that will be clear soon. Draw the line with the best fit through all the data points. Answer the following questions in your Active Chemistry log:

a) What is the relationship between the volume and the Celsius temperature as shown on your graph?

b) Based on the graph, at what temperature would the volume be zero? What would a zero volume look like?

c) Your temperature estimate was probably close to –273°C. If you created a new temperature scale where the volume becomes zero at a temperature of zero, what would 0°C be on this new scale? This presumes that both temperature scales have the same scale units.

409

Active Chemistry

CHAPTER 3

Ideal Toy

11. You are now going to graph your class data on the Kelvin temperature scale where the lowest possible temperature is 0 K (called absolute zero). To do so, you need to add 273 to your Celsius temperatures.

$$K = {}^{\circ}C + 273$$

a) Set up a graph in your *Active Chemistry* log with volume on the *y*-axis and temperature (in K) on the *x*-axis from 0 to 400 K. Draw the line with the best fit for the class data points.

b) Determine the slope of the line, making sure to include the units on the slope value. The slope intercept equation of a straight line is:

$$y = mx + b,$$
where *b* is the *y*-intercept and *m* is the slope.

You can use this form of the equation to calculate the slope:

$$m = \frac{\Delta y}{\Delta x} = \frac{y - b}{x - 0} = \frac{y - b}{x}$$

c) In your graph, label the *y*-values as volume and the *x*-values as temperature. Using the Kelvin scale, the *y*-intercept or "*b*" in the equation is 0. The equation for your straight line is $V = mT$. This relationship is identical to the one expressed in *Charles's law*.

Part B: Hot-Air Balloon Challenge

In this part of the investigation, you will apply your understanding of the relationship between temperature and volume by constructing a "hot-air balloon," and competing to find the balloon that can lift the most mass.

1. For your first trial with a hot-air balloon, use a plastic dry-cleaning bag or a lightweight trash bag.

Place about 12 regular-sized paper clips, evenly spaced, around the opening of the bag. This added weight will help to maintain stability in the hot-air balloon.

2. As shown in the picture, use at least three people to hold the bag over a hot plate turned to "High." Be careful not to let the bag touch the hot surface of the hot plate.

3. Within a minute or two, you can release the hot-air balloon and it will drift slowly to the ceiling.

a) In your *Active Chemistry* log, use the change in air volume with respect to temperature to explain how your hot-air balloon worked.

4. You can experiment with more weight, taping the holes in the dry cleaning bag, or a variety of other options. Use your imagination!

a) What variables do you think will affect the performance of your hot-air balloon?

5. If your teacher permits a competition in "lifting power" between groups, design a balloon that you think will win. After your teacher's approval, build your hot-air balloon and let the event begin!

Be careful not to let the plastic touch the hot plate.

Wear protective gloves when handling heated objects. Hot plates may remain hot for some time after they are turned off.

Dispose of all materials as directed by your teacher.

410

Active Chemistry

11.a)

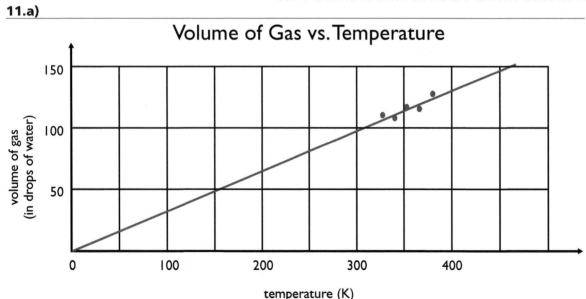

Volume of Gas vs. Temperature

volume of gas (in drops of water)

temperature (K)

The volume of the gas is on the *y*-axis. The temperature of the gas is on the *x*-axis, using an absolute temperature scale.

11. b-c)

Volume of a gas = kT (K) where k is the slope. ($k = 0.33$).

Note that depending on range of accuracy, data may vary from what is shown. The investigation provides a good visual for the relationship between the temperature and volume of gases (the amount of water drawn into the pipette represents the volume).

Part B:
Hot-Air Balloon Challenge

1.

Any light-weight plastic bag will work. Popular choices are dry-cleaning bags or transparent trash bags. The balloon will rise even if there are a few small holes in the bag. The number of paper clips is variable but 10-12 seems to work well. They must be evenly spaced or the balloon will tip over on liftoff.

2.

If the hot plate is pre-heated, the procedure heating of the air in the bag often takes less than a minute. It is important to use three students so that the bag does not touch the hot surface of the hot plate. If it touches the hot plate, the plastic will melt. Two students should hold the open end of the bag around the hot plate and against the table. The third student support the top of the bag until it is inflated with hot air.

3.

The student holding the top can let go first. The other two students will release when they are certain the balloon will rise.

3.a)

Heating the air causes the molecules to move faster and apply more pressure to the walls of the bag, thus inflating it. At the same time, the volume of the air increases causing further inflation and also a loss of air through the open end. This loss of air causes the internal density of the air to be less than the external density of air in the room. The difference in density causes the balloon to rise.

4.

If using dry-cleaning bags, there will be holes in the top. Although the bag will rise when heated, it may be more effective if students tape over the holes. This has the disadvantages of making the balloon heavier, and also, top-heavy. Greater weight can be added with more paper clips or other objects. Students may propose using a collar on the bottom to limit the size of the opening. If so, the collar should be larger than the hot plate surface so that it does not touch it.

4.a)

As factors affecting their hot-air balloon, students may suggest the size of the bag, the mass of the bag, the use of tape to close holes, a collar, the temperature of the hot plate, the length of time the air is heated, and many others. One that they may not consider is the temperature (and density) of the air in the classroom or the atmospheric pressure of the day.

5.

Closely monitor student ideas for safety. If the gymnasium is available, you might want to do the competition there, as there will be more room. For even more excitement, you might allow the students to do their competition while other classes watch in the gymnasium.

CHAPTER 3

NOTES

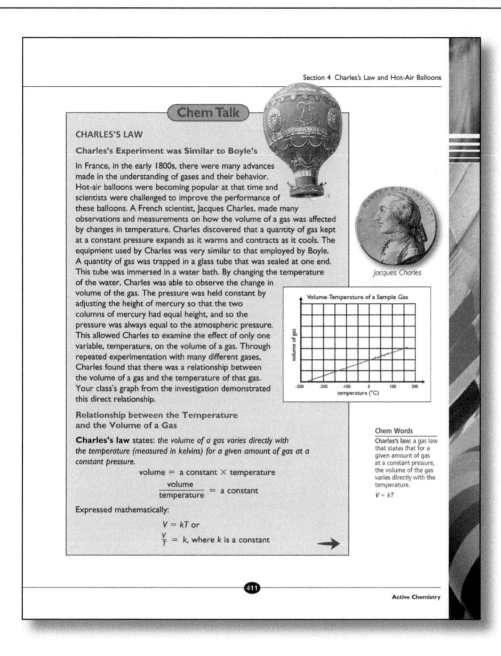

Chem Talk

CHARLES'S LAW

Charles's Experiment was Similar to Boyle's

In France, in the early 1800s, there were many advances made in the understanding of gases and their behavior. Hot-air balloons were becoming popular at that time and scientists were challenged to improve the performance of these balloons. A French scientist, Jacques Charles, made many observations and measurements on how the volume of a gas was affected by changes in temperature. Charles discovered that a quantity of gas kept at a constant pressure expands as it warms and contracts as it cools. The equipment used by Charles was very similar to that employed by Boyle. A quantity of gas was trapped in a glass tube that was sealed at one end. This tube was immersed in a water bath. By changing the temperature of the water, Charles was able to observe the change in volume of the gas. The pressure was held constant by adjusting the height of mercury so that the two columns of mercury had equal height, and so the pressure was always equal to the atmospheric pressure. This allowed Charles to examine the effect of only one variable, temperature, on the volume of a gas. Through repeated experimentation with many different gases, Charles found that there was a relationship between the volume of a gas and the temperature of that gas. Your class's graph from the investigation demonstrated this direct relationship.

Jacques Charles

Volume-Temperature of a Sample Gas

Relationship between the Temperature and the Volume of a Gas

Charles's law states: *the volume of a gas varies directly with the temperature (measured in kelvins) for a given amount of gas at a constant pressure.*

$$\text{volume} = \text{a constant} \times \text{temperature}$$

$$\frac{\text{volume}}{\text{temperature}} = \text{a constant}$$

Expressed mathematically:

$$V = kT \text{ or}$$

$$\frac{V}{T} = k, \text{ where } k \text{ is a constant}$$

Chem Words

Charles's law: a gas law that states that for a given amount of gas at a constant pressure, the volume of the gas varies directly with the temperature.

$V = kT$

Chem Talk

Charles's law $(V = kT)$ is examined from several different perspectives. From a historical perspective, Charles's work is compared with Boyle's findings on the same subject. Next, the mathematical equations are revisited and explained. The kinetic theory of matter is described as a way to understand the relationship between the temperature and volume of a gas and the relationship to Charles's law is shown. Finally, the concept of zero volume (which is impossible) and zero temperature (also impossible) are related, followed by an application of Charles's law in everyday life – balloons.

CHAPTER 5

Ideal Toy

You can compare the volumes of the same gas at two different temperatures:

$$\frac{V_1}{T_1} = \frac{V_2}{T_2}$$

Kinetic Theory of Matter and Charles's Law

A mass weighing 10 N (newtons), approximately 2 lb, is supported by a column of air in a piston. The air must be supplying a force of 10 N to keep the mass from falling down. When the air is heated to a higher temperature, the mass rises due to the increase in volume of the air. The piston stops moving when once again, the air is supplying a force of 10 N to keep the mass from falling.

The kinetic theory of matter provides a way to understand this relationship between the temperature and the volume of a gas at the nanoscopic or molecular level. The particles of a gas are moving about with a range of speeds and corresponding kinetic energy. These particles can collide with the walls and the moveable piston. These collisions create the pressure, or force per area, on the piston. The particles hit the piston so that the average force on the piston is 10 N. When you increase the temperature of the air, you are increasing the speed and kinetic energy of the air molecules. These molecules hit the piston more often and with a greater force. If the average increased force is 12 N, then the mass will move up. When the piston moves up, it increases the volume. As the volume increases, these energetic air particles don't hit the piston as often because of the extra distance they must travel. The average force of the energetic particles once again becomes 10 N and the piston remains in its elevated position. When the air cools, the particles have a decrease in their kinetic energies. They hit the piston less often and the average force is now less than 10 N and the mass descends again.

Absolute Zero and the Kelvin Temperature Scale

If a decrease in temperature results in a decrease in volume, what happens if the temperature is lowered to a point where the volume drops to zero? A negative volume is impossible, so the temperature at which the volume drops to zero must be the lowest temperature that can be achieved. This temperature is called absolute zero. **Absolute zero** is the lowest possible temperature. It is 0 K, or –273°C. Whenever determining the effect of a temperature change on the volume of a gas, you must first convert from the

Chem Words

absolute zero: a theoretical temperature at which molecular motion is minimal. 0 K, or –273°C

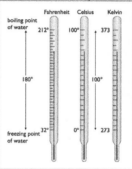

	Fahrenheit	Celsius	Kelvin
boiling point of water	212°	100°	373
	180°	100°	100°
freezing point of water	32°	0°	273

Celsius temperature to the Kelvin temperature. You do this by adding 273 to the Celsius temperature.

$$K = °C + 273$$

Applying Charles's Law

The mass of your plastic hot-air balloon is the mass of the plastic plus the mass of the air. To get the balloon to fly, you have to decrease the mass of the air in the balloon. In the hot-air balloon investigation that you conducted, you found that the hot air takes up more volume than the cool air. Filling your plastic balloon required less hot air than cool air. With less air in the balloon, the balloon had a smaller total mass and it could fly.

Example:

A balloon is in a room at 25°C. The volume of the balloon is 2.0 L. Suppose that the balloon is taken outside at a temperature of –5°C. What will be the new volume of the balloon?

Charles's law lets you predict what the volume of the balloon will be.

$$\frac{V_1}{T_1} = \frac{V_2}{T_2}$$

$V_1 = 2.0 \text{ L}$ $V_2 = ?$

$T_1 = 25°C \text{ (298 K)}$ $T_2 = -5°C \text{ (268 K)}$

Notice that temperature in kelvin must be used to solve problems with Charles's law.

Rearrange Charles's law equation to solve for V_2.

$$V_2 = \frac{V_1 T_2}{T_1}$$

$$= \frac{2.0 \text{ L (268 K)}}{298 \text{ K}}$$

$$= 1.8 \text{ L}$$

Checking Up

1. What is the relationship between the temperature and the volume of a gas?
2. What is absolute zero on the Kelvin and Celsius temperature scales?
3. What problems would you encounter in your calculations if you did not convert the Celsius temperature to the Kelvin scale?
4. How might the temperature in the gym affect the volume of a basketball and thus its bounce?
5. Determine the effect on the volume of a basketball if the initial volume is 6.4 L at 20°C and the ball is taken outside to a temperature of 27°C.

What Do You Think Now?

At the beginning of this section you were asked the following:

• **How might a decrease in temperature affect an inflated balloon?**

Now that you have investigated Charles's law, how would you answer this question? How would an increase in temperature affect the balloon?

 413

Checking Up

1.

The relationship between the temperature and volume of a gas is a direct relationship as an increase in temperature results in an increase in volume, $V = kT$, when pressure and moles are constant. In a system where either the volume or the temperature is changed, the final conditions can be calculated using $\frac{V_1}{T_1} = \frac{V_2}{T_2}$ as long as the pressure and moles of gas remain constant.

2.

Absolute zero on the Kelvin scale is 0; absolute zero on the Celsius scale is –273°C.

3.

The calculations using $\frac{V_1}{T_1} = \frac{V_2}{T_2}$ would not work using the Celsius scale. Celsius temperatures of 0°C or below (–values) would lead to impossible numbers as final results.

4.

In a cold gym, a basketball would have a smaller volume (lower gas pressure) and less bounce than in a warm or hot gym.

5.

$$\frac{V_1}{T_1} = \frac{V_2}{T_2} \qquad \frac{6.4 \text{ L}}{293} = \frac{V_2}{300}$$

$V_2 = 6.6$ L, an increase of 0.2 L. And a lot more bounce!

What Do You Think Now?

Have students revisit the *What Do You Think?* question at the beginning of the section and ask how they might revise their initial responses. You may want to share the answer found in *A Chemist's Response* and allow them to discuss their opinions and reactions. Also have them consider the effect temperature changes would have on a balloon, as suggested in this section.

This is an opportune time to return to the *What Do You See?* illustration as well. Ask students to comment about the function of the fire beneath the balloon, and how it relates to the chemistry just learned.

CHAPTER 3

Reflecting on the Section and the Challenge

Although there are no questions in this section for students to answer or to use for discussion, this is an important opportunity for students to consider the section with respect to the *Chapter Challenge*. Students should now be familiar with Charles's law and the relationship between temperature and volume. This principle can be critical in the design and explanation of their toy.

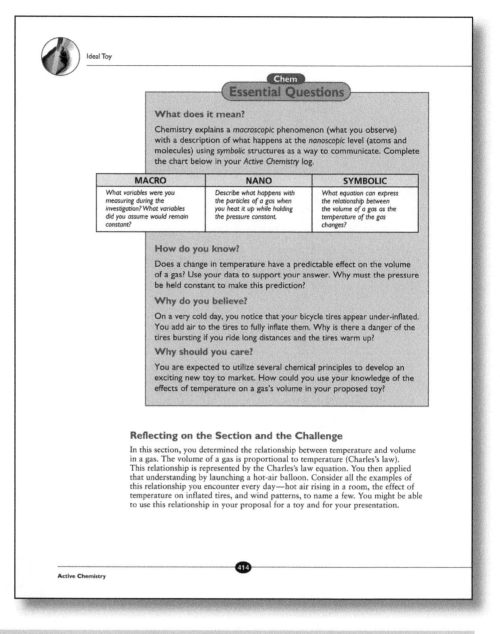

Ideal Toy

Chem Essential Questions

What does it mean?

Chemistry explains a *macroscopic* phenomenon (what you observe) with a description of what happens at the *nanoscopic* level (atoms and molecules) using *symbolic* structures as a way to communicate. Complete the chart below in your *Active Chemistry* log.

MACRO	NANO	SYMBOLIC
What variables were you measuring during the investigation? What variables did you assume would remain constant?	Describe what happens with the particles of a gas when you heat it up while holding the pressure constant.	What equation can express the relationship between the volume of a gas as the temperature of the gas changes?

How do you know?

Does a change in temperature have a predictable effect on the volume of a gas? Use your data to support your answer. Why must the pressure be held constant to make this prediction?

Why do you believe?

On a very cold day, you notice that your bicycle tires appear under-inflated. You add air to the tires to fully inflate them. Why is there a danger of the tires bursting if you ride long distances and the tires warm up?

Why should you care?

You are expected to utilize several chemical principles to develop an exciting new toy to market. How could you use your knowledge of the effects of temperature on a gas's volume in your proposed toy?

Reflecting on the Section and the Challenge

In this section, you determined the relationship between temperature and volume in a gas. The volume of a gas is proportional to temperature (Charles's law). This relationship is represented by the Charles's law equation. You then applied that understanding by launching a hot-air balloon. Consider all the examples of this relationship you encounter every day—hot air rising in a room, the effect of temperature on inflated tires, and wind patterns, to name a few. You might be able to use this relationship in your proposal for a toy and for your presentation.

414

Active Chemistry

Chem Essential Questions
What does it mean?

MACRO—Volume and temperature were measured. It was assumed that pressure and the number of gas molecules remained constant.

NANO — At constant pressure, the gas particles travel faster as they are heated up. This increases the volume of the gas and whatever container the gas is in must expand.

SYMBOLIC — Charles's law is $V = kT$, or for calculation of changing variables,
$$\frac{V_1}{T_1} = \frac{V_2}{T_2}$$

How do you know?

Yes, a change in temperature has a predictable effect on the volume of a gas. $\frac{V_1}{T_1} = \frac{V_2}{T_2}$. This relationship was determined in this experiment.

Why do you believe?

It is fairly intuitive that gases expand upon heating, which is why tires fully inflated on a cold day might be at risk once heated. While they may not actually explode (tire manufacturers take temperature changes into account), there is a chance that they might burst their seal, allowing air to be released and resulting in flat tires.

Why should you care?

Students' answers will vary but should relate to the use of Charles's law and involve volume and temperature. They may think of some way to heat a gas under controlled conditions (constant pressure) to inflate an expandable object.

Chem to Go

1. If you could install only one thermostat in a two-story toy factory, should it be placed on the first or second floor? Explain.

2. Predict the effect of hot temperatures on car tires. Will they appear fuller or flatter? Predict the effect of cold temperatures on car tires. How will their appearance change? Explain your answer.

3. Why must the temperature measurements used in Charles's law be in kelvin? Show an example that supports your reasoning.

4. Using Charles's law, what would the volume of a gas be if 2.8 L at 25°C were heated to 75°C?

5. If 5.5 L of a gas at 78°C were cooled to 25°C, what would the resulting volume be?

6. To what temperature would you need to heat 750 mL of a gas at 25°C in order to increase its volume to 2500 mL?

7. In a hot-air balloon, the balloonist may have to light the propane torch for a few minutes. Using Charles's law, explain why he might need to do this.

8. As the temperature of a given sample of gas decreases at constant pressure, the volume of the gas:

   a) decreases   b) increases   c) remains the same

9. *Preparing for the Chapter Challenge*

   Think of a toy or a sporting goods product that uses or is affected by the relationship between volume and temperature. Explain how Charles's law is applied and how temperature changes in the environment could affect the product. Brainstorm ways the designer could minimize the effect of temperature on this product.

Inquiring Further

1. The motorists' guide to temperature and volume

Write a short, practical guide for motorists explaining changes in their automobile tire volume during different seasons. Provide them with tips on how to prolong the life of their tires by keeping them properly inflated. Explain to them why these changes in volume occur. Your article could be publishable as "consumer help" for your local paper.

2. Balloon storage

The prom committee has decided to use lots of balloons in this year's décor. Write a memo to the committee suggesting how the inflated balloons should be stored in order to minimize deflation prior to the prom. They're a hard committee to convince, so back up your suggestions with calculations.

CHAPTER 5

Chem to Go

1.

You would want to install the thermostat on the second floor. Since hot air rises, you would want the higher level to determine when the thermostat should turn on the air conditioning or the heat.

2.

The higher the temperature, the fuller the tires will appear. The colder the temperature, the less inflated the tires will appear. You can usually see the difference. Tires often appear flatter in the winter. According to Charles's law, the same amount (moles) of air will have greater volume when heated and less volume when cold. However, it is important to follow the manufacturer's directions regarding tire inflation and temperature. You would not want to over-inflate in cold weather or under-inflate in hot weather.

3.

There are two reasons for using the Kelvin (absolute temperature) scale. First, the volume has a linear relationship with the Kelvin scale and using it gives the correct answer. For example, in *Question 5* of *Checking Up*, the correct volume is 6.6 L using Kelvin. But according to the Celsius scale,

$$\frac{V_1}{T_1} = \frac{V_2}{T_2} \qquad \frac{6.4 \text{ L}}{23} = \frac{V_2}{27}$$

$V_2 = 7.5$ L, an increase of 20% for a 4-degree change in temperature, which is clearly incorrect.

Also, when the temperature is at 0°C then you would have an undefined value since you cannot divide by zero.

4.

$$\frac{V_1}{T_1} = \frac{V_2}{T_2}$$

$25°C + 273 = 298$ K
$75°C + 273 = 348$ K

$$\frac{2.8 \text{ L}}{298 \text{ K}} = \frac{V_2}{348 \text{ K}} \qquad V_2 = 3.3 \text{ L}$$

5.

$$\frac{V_1}{T_1} = \frac{V_2}{T_2}$$

$78°C + 273 = 351$ K
$25°C + 273 = 298$ K

$$\frac{5.5 \text{ L}}{351 \text{ K}} = \frac{V}{298 \text{ K}} \qquad V = 4.7 \text{ L}$$

6.

$$\frac{V_1}{T_1} = \frac{V_2}{T_2}$$

$25°C + 273 = 298$ K

$$\frac{0.75 \text{ L}}{298 \text{ K}} = \frac{2.5 \text{ L}}{T_2}$$

$T_2 = 993$ K $= 720°C$

7.

The balloonist would need to light the propane torch periodically to keep the temperature of the gas (air) in the balloon higher, and thereby less dense, than the atmosphere. If he does not do this, the air in the balloon will cool, eventually reaching the same temperature as that of the atmosphere, and the balloon will descend. This is based on Charles's law which dictates that heating a gas makes it expand. This expansion makes it less dense, which means that the denser atmospheric air can support it.

8.

a) decreases

9.

Preparing for the Chapter Challenge

Students' answers will vary depending upon the toy, temperature conditions, and how temperatures are to be regulated. If a decrease in volume is not desirable for their toy, students might need to address storage or insulation measures. They may suggest temperature ranges to maintain optimal volume, or provide for increasing or decreasing the volume as needed by use of valves, pumps, etc.

Inquiring Further

1. The motorists' guide to temperature and volume

The guide should contain references to basic temperature-volume relationships. It should suggest that tires might seem over-inflated during warmer months or after long driving periods and under-inflated during cooler months. Students should include researched information concerning recommended pressure readings correlating to tire volume. Such recommendations will be different for different-sized tires and cars; that information should be included in the guide.

2. Balloon storage

This can be a tricky question depending upon what gas is used to inflate the balloons. Since gases of lower molecular weight will diffuse out of the balloon more quickly than gases of higher molecular weight, the molecular weight is key information.

Temperature can be used as a variable in the diffusion of a gas through a membrane. Balloons stored in a cooler room will "re-inflate" when brought out to the warmer environment.

NOTES

SECTION 4 – QUIZ

5-4b	Blackline Master

1. Describe the relationship between volume and temperature for a gas at constant pressure and number of particles.

2. For a gas at constant pressure, if the absolute temperature is increased by a factor of 3, what happens to the volume?

    a) increase by a factor of 3

    b) decrease by a factor of 3

    c) increase by a factor of 9

    d) decrease by a factor of 9

3. Convert 25°C to Kelvin.

    a) −273 K

    b) −248 K

    c) 298 K

    d) 323 K

4. If 1.5 L of a gas with an initial temperature of 35°C is heated to 55°C, what will the resulting volume be (assuming no change in pressure)?

    a) 0.95 L

    b) 1.4 L

    c) 1.6 L

    d) 2.4 L

5. You go outside in January to play basketball and the temperature is 30°F. The last time you played basketball was in August when the temperature was 92°F. Assuming you have not done anything to the ball since summer, what will happen when you first try to dribble it? Explain.

SECTION 4 – QUIZ ANSWERS

1 As the temperature of a gas increases, so will its volume and vice versa. There is a direct relationship between the volume and temperature of a gas at constant pressure and number of particles.

    4. $\dfrac{V}{T} = k$

2 a) increase by a factor of 3

3 c) 298 K

4 c) 1.6 L

$$\frac{V_1 T_2}{T_1} = \frac{(1.5\ \text{L})(328\ \text{K})}{308\ \text{K}} = 1.6\ \text{L}$$

5 The basketball will not dribble well. It will be "flat" because the pressure of the air inside the ball has decreased. It will not bounce well at the lower pressure.

Chapter Mini-Challenge

This marks the midpoint of *Chapter 5*. The students have been introduced to new chemistry concepts in the first four sections and now is a good time for them to review these principles and consider how they can be applied to their *Chapter Challenge* projects. The *Mini-Challenge* provides an opportunity for students to implement and test some of these ideas. Any problems or obstacles that they encounter with this smaller project will better prepare them for the bigger challenge ahead.

The *Mini-Challenge* will give you an opportunity to coach students in the design of their toys and help them focus on developing procedures that adequately represent the chemistry concepts they have learned. Remind them that safety is a critical component of both the design and operation of their toy. This is also a great time for you to address misconceptions that will arise as students compose their written presentations and attempt to explain the chemical processes related to their toys. Remind students to refer to their list of criteria for grading the *Chapter Challenges* when they design their *Ideal Toy*.

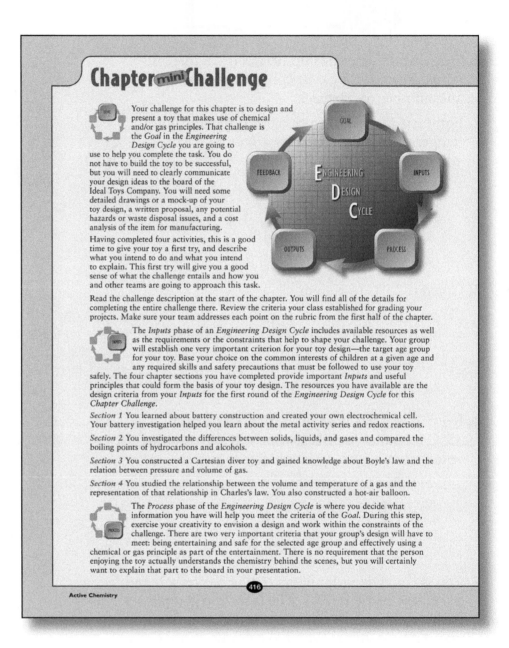

Chapter mini Challenge

Your challenge for this chapter is to design and present a toy that makes use of chemical and/or gas principles. That challenge is the *Goal* in the *Engineering Design Cycle* you are going to use to help you complete the task. You do not have to build the toy to be successful, but you will need to clearly communicate your design ideas to the board of the Ideal Toys Company. You will need some detailed drawings or a mock-up of your toy design, a written proposal, any potential hazards or waste disposal issues, and a cost analysis of the item for manufacturing.

Having completed four activities, this is a good time to give your toy a first try, and describe what you intend to do and what you intend to explain. This first try will give you a good sense of what the challenge entails and how you and other teams are going to approach this task.

Read the challenge description at the start of the chapter. You will find all of the details for completing the entire challenge there. Review the criteria your class established for grading your projects. Make sure your team addresses each point on the rubric from the first half of the chapter.

The *Inputs* phase of an *Engineering Design Cycle* includes available resources as well as the requirements or the constraints that help to shape your challenge. Your group will establish one very important criterion for your toy design—the target age group for your toy. Base your choice on the common interests of children at a given age and any required skills and safety precautions that must be followed to use your toy safely. The four chapter sections you have completed provide important *Inputs* and useful principles that could form the basis of your toy design. The resources you have available are the design criteria from your *Inputs* for the first round of the *Engineering Design Cycle* for this *Chapter Challenge*.

Section 1 You learned about battery construction and created your own electrochemical cell. Your battery investigation helped you learn about the metal activity series and redox reactions.

Section 2 You investigated the differences between solids, liquids, and gases and compared the boiling points of hydrocarbons and alcohols.

Section 3 You constructed a Cartesian diver toy and gained knowledge about Boyle's law and the relation between pressure and volume of gas.

Section 4 You studied the relationship between the volume and temperature of a gas and the representation of that relationship in Charles's law. You also constructed a hot-air balloon.

The *Process* phase of the *Engineering Design Cycle* is where you decide what information you have will help you meet the criteria of the *Goal*. During this step, exercise your creativity to envision a design and work within the constraints of the challenge. There are two very important criteria that your group's design will have to meet: being entertaining and safe for the selected age group and effectively using a chemical or gas principle as part of the entertainment. There is no requirement that the person enjoying the toy actually understands the chemistry behind the scenes, but you will certainly want to explain that part to the board in your presentation.

416

Active Chemistry

The *Mini-Challenge* should take about one class period to prepare and another for all teams to share their presentations. Each team should receive written feedback from the class after the *Mini-Challenge* presentation is made. You may choose to have each student write at least two positive comments and one suggestion for improvement for each presentation.

Begin your search for the *Ideal Toy* by considering how you might use each of the chapter section technologies—chemical cells, phase changes of materials, fluid densities, and heating air—to create an entertaining toy. Your group could brainstorm, considering the chemistry principle from each chapter section individually, or have each person create a toy idea to go with each principle and then present ideas to each other. Focusing on the recent information will help your group reach a usable design idea in the short amount of time you have available.

Next, try to combine ideas from different sections. Maybe you can use a liquid that becomes a gas by adding heat and then continues to be heated within your toy? Perhaps the heat source can come from a chemical cell that is part of the toy? Compare and contrast different ideas until you have one or more ideas that sound interesting. Now try to determine the appropriate age group for your toy design. Remember, your toy does not have to entertain a teenager to meet the criteria of the challenge.

Finally, consider what skills and safety precautions are required to operate your toy. Are they appropriate for the age group you think will find your toy entertaining? Do you need to make changes to your toy design to make it more entertaining? Do you need to make it easier or safer to operate? Engineers face these types of compromises every time they design something. Some dangers are not even obvious until an object is built and tested. Models and prototypes are an inexpensive way to find unintended design flaws before too much money is spent on building an inadequately designed product.

The *Outputs* of an *Engineering Design Cycle* are the products that are created during the *Process* step of the cycle. Your product will be a comprehensive presentation of your toy design to the board of directors from the Ideal Toys Company. You will need to present your ideas in the form of sketches or models and clear explanations describing the chemistry involved in the function of your design. The presentation of your ideas is part of the product you are creating, so you should set aside some time to practice presenting and coordinating who will present which information. Everyone should be involved in the *Process* so that everyone will be satisfied with your resulting grade. Working in a group is often harder than working alone, but with an effective team you can accomplish much more than any person can alone.

The *Feedback* phase of the *Engineering Design Cycle* is the final phase of one cycle and simultaneously the *Inputs* for the next design cycle. The information you get about the *Outputs* will tell you how successful your group was at meeting the original *Goal*. Your instructor and your classmates will give you *Feedback* on your *Ideal Toy* design, how well you described the chemistry that it employs, the safety considerations, and disposal issues. This *Feedback* will become one of the *Inputs* you will use in the final *Chapter Challenge* presentation. You will have enough time to make corrections and improvements before the *Chapter Challenge*, so pay attention to the valuable information they provide. Remember to make any necessary changes in the chemistry explanation that received *Feedback*. Also note any ideas you may have gotten by viewing other presentations. It will be harder to remember what you need to change if you wait until the entire chapter is complete to go back and correct your mistakes. When you are finished revising, store all of your information in a safe place so that it will be ready to use in the *Chapter Challenge*!

You will learn about new chemistry concepts in each of the remaining chapter sections. Each section will introduce new chemistry principles you can use to design your *Ideal Toy*. Your team can use the new information to enhance the toy design you have already chosen or you may choose to create a new one. Either way, pay careful attention to the *Chem Talk* presented in each chapter section, as they are the key to creating a high-quality chemistry explanation in your challenge presentation.

417

Active Chemistry

Engineering Design Cycle

Remind students that this is a first try and that they should use the feedback to improve upon their projects for the *Chapter Challenge*. The feedback is essential in providing guidance to students in areas they need to focus on to make their final chapter projects more effective. After all the presentations are completed, review the *Engineering Design Cycle* to help students see other ways to put their chemistry knowledge into use.

At the end of the chapter as the *Chapter Challenge* approaches, have students reflect on their successes and disappointments from the *Mini-Challenge*. The experience and information will be vital for making the necessary modifications to their design cycle in order to have success with the *Chapter Challenge*.

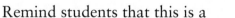

SECTION 5
Types of Reactions and Gas Production

Section Overview

In this section, students will generate and test for hydrogen, oxygen, and carbon dioxide gases. They will then determine the most effective ratio of hydrogen:oxygen to use in the propulsion of a small rocket.

Background Information

Common Types of Chemical Reactions

Being able to identify a particular type of reaction is often useful in writing chemical equations. Most chemical reactions can be placed into one or more of the following five categories.

1. Combustion reactions. Organic hydrocarbons can burn in the presence of oxygen to produce CO_2 and water. The burning of methane (CH_4), the chief component of natural gas, is an example of a combustion reaction:

$$CH_{4(g)} + 2O_{2(g)} \rightarrow CO_{2(g)} + 2H_2O_{(l)}$$

2. Synthesis reactions. Also called *combination reactions*, these reactions occur when one element or compound combines with another element or compound to produce a new compound. This process can be generally represented as:

$$A + B \rightarrow AB$$

When H_2 gas reacts with O_2, water is synthesized:

$$2H_{2(g)} + O_{2(g)} \rightarrow 2H_2O_{(l)}$$

Hydrogen can also react with ethylene (C_2H_4), using a palladium catalyst, to produce ethane (C_2H_6):

3. Decomposition reactions. When a compound has broken down into two or more simpler materials, a decomposition reaction has occurred. The general equation for this type of reaction is:

$$AB \rightarrow A + B$$

An example of a decomposition reaction is the decomposition of dinitrogen pentoxide:

$$2N_2O_{5(g)} \rightarrow 4NO_{2(g)} + O_{2(g)}$$

4. Single-replacement reactions. When a metal will react with an acid and produce hydrogen gas we can say that one element replaced another element from a compound. This phenomenon is commonly called a single-replacement reaction, but is also an oxidation-reduction reaction.

$$Zn_{(s)} + 2HCl_{(aq)} \rightarrow ZnCl_{2(aq)} + H_{2(g)}$$

Other reactions that are also classified as single-replacement reactions are those where we place a metal strip in a metallic ionic solution and, again, have an oxidation-reduction type reaction. An example of this type of reaction is when zinc metal is placed in a solution of copper (II) sulfate. The copper is reduced to the metal and plates out on the zinc strip. The equation for this reaction is:

$$Zn_{(s)} + CuSO_{4(aq)} \rightarrow Cu_{(s)} + ZnSO_{4(aq)}$$

The *total ionic equation:*

$$Zn_{(s)} + Cu^{2+}_{(aq)} + SO_4^{2-}_{(aq)} \rightarrow$$
$$Cu_{(s)} + Zn^{2+}_{(aq)} + SO_4^{2-}_{(aq)}$$

We can see that the sulfate ion does not have a role in the reaction, so if we remove the sulfate ion (called a *spectator ion*) we will then have the *net ionic equation:*

$$Zn_{(s)} + Cu^{2+}_{(aq)} \rightarrow Cu_{(s)} + Zn^{2+}_{(aq)}$$

Single-replacement reactions are used to identify which elements will be displaced from their compounds by other metals. This order of reactivity is often called the *activity series of metals*.

5. Double-replacement reactions (also called metathesis). These reactions usually involve ionic solutions. In the reaction, cations are thought of as exchanging anion partners. A reaction will take place if we see a solid dissolve, a precipitate form, or a gas being evolved. If we were to mix sodium sulfate solution with barium nitrate solution, the formation of a white precipitate is observed, barium sulfate. The equation for this reaction is:

$$Na_2SO_{4(aq)} + Ba(NO_3)_{2(aq)} \longrightarrow$$
$$BaSO_{4(s)} + 2NaNO_{3(aq)}$$

The total ionic equation:

$$2Na^+_{(aq)} + SO_4^{2-}_{(aq)} + Ba^{2+}_{(aq)} + 2NO_3^-_{(aq)} \longrightarrow$$
$$BaSO_{4(s)} + 2Na^+_{(aq)} + 2NO_3^-_{(aq)}$$

Note that the equation is balanced with a net charge of 0 on both sides. We should also note that the sodium and nitrate ions are spectators in this reaction and thus the net ionic equation is:

$$Ba^{2+}_{(aq)} + SO_4^{2-}_{(aq)} \longrightarrow BaSO_{4(s)}$$

CHAPTER 3

LEARNING OUTCOMES		
LEARNING OUTCOMES	**LOCATION IN SECTION**	**EVIDENCE OF UNDERSTANDING**
To produce and test for three different gases.	*Investigate* Part A *Chem Talk, Preparing for the Chapter Challenge*	Answers to questions in Part A are similar to those presented in this *Teacher's Edition*. Ideas proposed are reasonable.
Use chemical reactions to make gases to use as a rocket fuel.	*Investigate* Part B *Chem Talk, Checking Up*	Answers to questions are similar to those presented in this *Teacher's Edition*.
To investigate four types of chemical reactions.	*Investigate* Parts A-B *Chem to Go* Questions 1-3	Answers match those shown in this *Teacher's Edition*.

NOTES

_____

_____

_____

_____

_____

_____

_____

_____

_____

Section 5
Materials, Chemicals, Preparation, and Safety

("per Group" quantity is based on group size of 4 students)

Materials and Equipment

Materials (and Equipment)	Quantity per Group (4 students)
Beaker, 250 mL	1
Scissors	1
Scoopula	1
Test tubes, large	2
Test tube rack	1
Rubber stoppers, solid (to fit large test tubes)	2
Rubber stoppers, one-hole (to fit large test tubes)	2
Watch glass (250-mL beaker cover)	1
Beral pipettes, 3 mL	6
Launch pad (board with nail)	1
Materials (and Equipment)	**Quantity per Class**
Box of wooden splints	1
Tesla coil, hand-held	1
Box of matches	1

Chemicals

Chemicals	Quantity per Class (24 students)
Baking soda, sodium bicarbonate, $NaHCO_3$	100 g
Mossy zinc, 25 pieces	5 g
3% Hydrogen peroxide, H_2O_2	200 mL
Manganese dioxide, MnO_2	5 g
1.0 M Hydrochloric acid, HCl	200 mL

Teacher Preparation

1.0 M Hydrochloric acid, HCl: Slowly and carefully, in a fume hood, with stirring, add 16.6 mL of concentrated (12 M) hydrochloric acid to 100 mL of distilled water. Dilute to 200 mL.

Safety Requirements

- Goggles and aprons are required in the laboratory area.

- The hydrochloric acid, sodium bicarbonate solution, and hydrogen peroxide can be rinsed down the sink. Any zinc remaining can be filtered, dried and reused. If not reused, then it and the manganese dioxide can be safely disposed of in the trash.

- Wash arms and hands before leaving the laboratory area.

NOTES

Meeting the Needs of All Students
Differentiated Instruction

Augmentation and Accommodations

LEARNING ISSUE	REFERENCE	AUGMENTATION AND ACCOMMODATIONS
Recording observations and writing summaries accurately and precisely	*Investigate* Part A, 4.	**Augmentation** Memory and understanding are tied to details that differentiate events. In this investigation three gases were produced that reacted differently to a hot splint. While it is true that all three splints were hot, describing them in that way is not accurate enough. Two splints were lit; one was glowing. That was important in observing the reactions. Point out that example in the directions and require students to consider the following when writing precise answers: • Ask students what they did with the splints. They may say they put them in the test tubes. Point out that they inserted two splints in the tubes to test for oxygen and carbon dioxide, but they brought the mouth of the test tube to the match when testing for hydrogen. To write with precision and accuracy, they must closely analyze the text and use specific words/phrases from the text. • Help students develop a list of words/phrases they should use in their descriptions by examining the text for them. Such a list might include lit splint, glowing splint, carbon dioxide, oxygen, hydrogen, extinguished the flame, ignited the flame, and ignited the gas. • Another way to encourage precise writing is by using a specific sentence structure that reflects the idea that under certain conditions, a specific result occurred. Ask students to structure their sentences so that they begin with the word "when" followed by the conditions which is followed with a description of the results. A student might write, "When a lit splint was placed into the mouth of the test tube containing sodium hydrogen carbonate and hydrochloric acid, the flame was extinguished." Note that this response incorporates specific vocabulary and phrases from the text.
Interpreting directions from a text and diagram	*Investigate* Part B	**Augmentation** • This is another task that requires specific analysis of the text. The diagram provides supplementary visual information that helps students interpret the directions. Consider the following issues that may require your clarification: • Only the stem of the Beral pipette is shown in the diagram. Students may take the diagram literally and not see the match between the Beral pipette they are given and the pictured piece. • The diagram corresponds only to making hydrogen. Some students may need clarification about making the oxygen. • Students may not understand how to get an equal amount of both gases into the Beral pipette. **Accommodations** • Create heterogeneous groups such that students with difficulty interpreting directions are with others who can. • Create homogeneous groups and work with the group of students who have difficulty with interpreting directions.

LEARNING ISSUE	REFERENCE	AUGMENTATION AND ACCOMMODATIONS
Mastering scientific vocabulary	*Chem Talk*	**Augmentation** • The *Chem Talk* uses several specific words not included in the *Chem Words* section, such as numerical coefficients, subscripts, molecules and ionic compounds. Review strategies with the class for dealing with unfamiliar words in a text. Strategies include skipping the unfamiliar word, finding its meaning using the context or a definition in the text, asking a group member for its meaning, and looking in the *Chem Talk* section under *Chem Words*. Ask students to read the two paragraphs at the top of the second page in the *Chem Talk* section which include those words. Check for understanding. Can they balance an equation? Can they explain the difference between an ionic compound and a molecule? What strategies did they use when they came to those terms? Were their strategies successful? What should they do next?

Organizing and summarizing learning	*Chem Essential Questions*	**Augmentation**
		• Structure an section around the *Macro, Nano, Symbolic* charts that will help students organize the information about the four types of reactions they studied, differentiate among them and remember them for future use. For each type of reaction have students:
		  • Name the type of reaction (single replacement, decomposition, double replacement, and synthesis).
		  • Define the reaction according to the text.
		  • Answer the *Macro* question.
		  • Explain what was happening on the *Nano* level.
		  • Answer the *Symbolic* questions.
		  • Write the general equation for each type of reaction.
		  • Give an example of the equation for each type of reaction.

Strategies for Students with Limited English Language Proficiency

LEARNING ISSUE	REFERENCE	AUGMENTATIONS
Background knowledge	*What Do You Think?*	Make sure students understand the phrase "*frontier of space,*" as well as the word "*propel*" and provide derivatives for background knowledge such as "*propulsion,*" and "*propellant.*"
Vocabulary Following directions	*Investigate*	Check for understanding of the meaning of "*producing.*" Have students work with partners to allow for following of directions. Point out the sections where directions change to questions.
Background knowledge Vocabulary Comprehending text	*Chem Talk*	Have students put new words in their personal dictionaries or *Active Chemistry* logs. Review meaning of "*moles.*" Refer to *Checking Up* questions to check for understanding and comprehension.
Comprehension	*What Do You Think Now?*	Question that begins with "How are..." might be vague, and might need to be paraphrased for some students.
Background knowledge Vocabulary Comprehending text	*Chem Essential Questions*	Students will need to look back to a previous section of the text in order to answer the questions. Use some small group discussion to make sure everyone has the same understanding. Oral language development will help students with comprehension and confidence in their own answers.
Comprehension Vocabulary	*Chem to Go*	Check for understanding of the term "*balance*" in reference to equations and the pronunciation of "*coefficients.*"
Application Comprehension Research skills	*Inquiring Further*	Have students discuss ways to find out about *propellants*. Students may need to see models of articles to understand the structure and create an idea of what to include. Partner work might help in the production of the article.

CHAPTER 5

Section 5
Teaching Suggestions and Sample Answers

What Do You See?

The *What Do You See?* section is designed to engage students through the illustration which brings to life the chemistry concepts they will learn in the upcoming section. The question, *What Do You See?* can be answered based on various degrees of understanding. One student may report literally what she sees, e.g., "Wouldn't the explosion hurt the boys' hands?" Another may try to interpret the intent of the artist, e.g., "The bottles on the floor must contain gases." Both responses are valid and students should be encouraged to think and respond imaginatively. Later, you may wish to return to the illustration so that the students will both have a better understanding of the artist's intent and observe that they have learned the chemistry knowledge and skills to understand what is being illustrated from a chemistry perspective.

The students should be able to tell the story from the illustration of the three students using the gases shown in the tank to propel a rocket. The passenger heading to the moon is a mouse. As the teacher and one of the students wave good-bye, another student is noting the time of flight.

Ideal Toy

Section 5   Types of Reactions and Gas Production

What Do You See?

Learning Outcomes

In this section you will

- Produce and test for three different gases.
- Use chemical reactions to make gases to use as a rocket fuel.
- Investigate four types of chemical reactions.

Safety goggles and a lab apron must be worn at all times in a chemistry lab.

Hydrochloric acid is caustic.

Wash your hands immediately if any chemical makes contact with them and notify your teacher.

Tie back hair and loose clothing. Do not reach across an open flame.

What Do You Think?

A rocket is a vehicle that gets its propulsion from the discharge of a fast-moving gas from an engine. Rockets have helped to open the frontier of space to humankind.

- How are the gases that can propel a rocket generated?

Record your ideas about this question in your *Active Chemistry* log. Be prepared to discuss your responses with your small group and the class.

Investigate

Part A: Producing Gases

A toy that is powered by a gas certainly could be entertaining. Let's take a look at how various gases can be produced.

1. *Producing and testing hydrogen gas*
   Obtain two test tubes. Fill one test tube about a third of the way with hydrochloric acid (1 *M* HCl). Add a piece of zinc and invert the second test tube over the first one.

   After a few minutes, use rubber stoppers to cap the test tubes. Have your lab partner light a match. With the test tube still inverted, carefully bring the mouth of the test tube to the match. Remove the stopper and see what happens.

418

STUDENTS' PRIOR CONCEPTIONS

Some students may have a good background in rocket propulsion from having worked with model rockets and from watching NASA launches. Others, however, may not know many of the fundamentals of rockets, fuels, and oxidizers. The latter group may not know that rockets carry their own oxidizer and can function outside the Earth's atmosphere. Others may believe that rockets can only function in space. The small rocket that they use in this section is propelled by an uncontrolled small explosion and it is important that the students do not pick up the notion that all rockets are propelled in this fashion.

What Do You Think?

Students might list hydrogen gas produced by the reaction of acid with metals and carbon dioxide generated from baking soda and vinegar. They may list other gases as well. Listen carefully to determine if the students are aware that the gases in storage tanks are highly compressed.

What Do You Think?
A CHEMIST'S RESPONSE

The simplest answer to the question is that chemical rockets generate their propulsion gases by the combustion of a fuel. Both jet planes and rockets are propelled by the discharge of fast-moving gases. However, a rocket carries its own oxidizing agent, often liquid oxygen, while a jet plane is dependent upon using the air in the atmosphere. Some common fuels for rockets include liquid hydrogen, hydrazine, and kerosene.

Investigate

Part A:
Producing Gases

1.

Students will be producing and testing hydrogen gas from zinc and hydrochloric acid. The concentration of hydrochloric acid should be about 1 M. The reaction is exothermic and the test tube will get a little warm. If acid comes into contact with their skin, rinse with plenty of water. The test for hydrogen should produce a loud pop as the hydrogen reacts with oxygen to produce water. Best results are obtained if the test tube is kept inverted.

CHAPTER 3

NOTES

_____

_____

_____

_____

_____

_____

_____

_____

_____

_____

_____

_____

_____

_____

2.

Students will be producing and testing oxygen gas from the decomposition of hydrogen peroxide, which is catalyzed by MnO_2. The key to testing for oxygen is to quickly insert a glowing splint into the mouth of the test tube. The splint should relight and burn brightly.

3.

Students will be producing and testing carbon dioxide gas by the reaction of an acid with baking soda (sodium hydrogen carbonate, $NaHCO_3$). The gas production will be vigorous and may spill over the beaker. Provide paper towels to contain spills. The watch glass on top of the beaker is to contain the carbon dioxide. The lit splint will go out as it is pushed into the carbon dioxide in the beaker. Students can test more than once if they quickly replace the watch glass.

4.a)

In the presence of a lit match, hydrogen gas gave a "pop" sound.

In the presence of a glowing splint, oxygen caused it to burst into flame.

In the presence of a burning splint, carbon dioxide extinguished the flame.

4.b)

Test the unknown gas with a burning splint. If it makes a sudden "pop" sound, the gas is most likely to be hydrogen. If the splint is extinguished, the gas is most likely carbon dioxide. If the gas is oxygen, it will probably briefly flare up. Test another

sample of the gas with a glowing splint. If the splint bursts into flame, the gas is probably oxygen.

Part B:
Gas-Powered Rockets

Hydrogen and oxygen are used as the fuel for the rocket because they explode when mixed and ignited.

$$2H_{2(g)} + O_{2(g)} \rightarrow 2H_2O_{(l)}$$

The rocket is the bulb end of a Beral pipette (not the thin stem type). Cut as many as needed and save the stems for the nozzles in the gas-generating tubes. Carefully push the stem through a one-hole stopper that fits the test tube. Two test tubes are needed for each group of students.

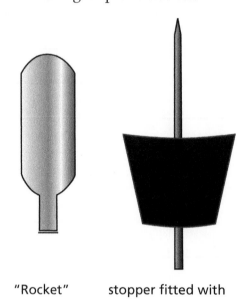

"Rocket"   stopper fitted with
              pipette stem

1.

The rocket should be filled with water to start by submerging the bulb, stem up, in a beaker of water. Squeeze several times to fill.

2.

The students should begin generating hydrogen gas with 1 *M* HCl and two small pieces of zinc in a test tube. They should let it generate gas for a few minutes before collecting any hydrogen in order to sweep out as much air as possible from the test tube. The rocket should be filled halfway with hydrogen gas as shown in the text and then removed from the hydrogen generator. The rocket is best handled with the open end down and pinched off.

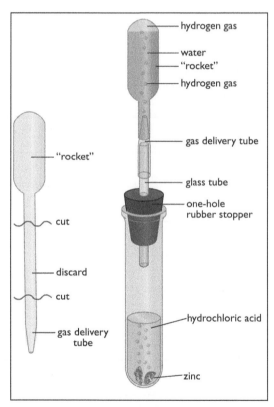

Paper towels should be placed under the test-tube rack to absorb excess water as the gases are collected. If generation of hydrogen gas is too slow, you will need to adjust the concentration of hydrochloric acid.

a) Record what happened in your *Active Chemistry* log.

2. **Producing and testing oxygen gas**

Oxygen gas can be obtained by decomposing hydrogen peroxide. Fill a test tube about one third full with 3% aqueous hydrogen peroxide. Add a small scoop of manganese (IV) dioxide (MnO_2) to the test tube. When a gas is being produced, light a wooden splint and blow out the flame. Quickly insert the glowing splint into the test tube.

a) Record what happens in your *Active Chemistry* log.

3. **Producing and testing carbon dioxide gas**

Carbon dioxide gas can be produced by the reaction of an acid with baking soda (sodium hydrogen carbonate). Put two scoops of sodium hydrogen carbonate in a 250-mL beaker. Add 10 mL of hydrochloric acid (1*M* HCl) and cover the beaker with a watch glass. Test the gas by lighting a splint and then quickly inserting it into the mouth of the beaker (after removing the watch glass).

a) Record what happens in your *Active Chemistry* log.

4. Answer the following in your *Active Chemistry* log.

a) Describe how each gas behaved in the presence of a lit or glowing splint.

b) Summarize the positive test for determining if an unknown gas is H_2, O_2, or CO_2.

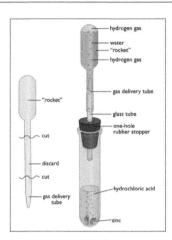
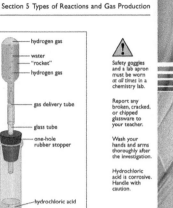

Labels: hydrogen gas; water; "rocket"; hydrogen gas; gas delivery tube; glass tube; one-hole rubber stopper; hydrochloric acid; zinc; "rocket"; cut; discard; cut; gas delivery tube

Safety goggles and a lab apron must be worn *at all times* in a chemistry lab.

Report any broken, cracked, or chipped glassware to your teacher.

Wash your hands and arms thoroughly after the investigation.

Hydrochloric acid is corrosive. Handle with caution.

Part B: Gas-Powered Rockets

In this part of the investigation, you will use two of the gases that you produced to provide the propellant for a small rocket. You will use hydrogen and oxygen gases as the fuel for your rocket.

1. For your rocket, you will use the bulb end of a Beral pipette. Fill the pipette (rocket) completely with water by immersing it in a beaker of water.

2. To make hydrogen gas, fill one test tube one-third full with 3*M* HCl. Build the gas collection system shown in the diagram above. Add two pieces of zinc and place the stopper in the test tube. Fill a half of the rocket with hydrogen.

3. To make oxygen gas, fill the other test tube one-third full with 3% aqueous hydrogen peroxide. Add a small scoop of MnO_2 and cover the tube with a stopper and nozzle. Fill a half of the rocket with oxygen gas.

Active Chemistry

3.

The rocket should then be moved to the oxygen generating tube which also has been operating for a few minutes. The students should fill the other half of the rocket by displacing the remaining water. However, they must leave a drop of water in the narrow neck of the pipette to provide a plug to prevent the escape of gases and to provide some friction for propelling the rocket.

Ideal Toy

4. Place the rocket on a nail. The rocket should contain equal amounts of the two gases. Leave a water plug in the neck of the rocket and bring it to the launch pad, open end down.

5. Place the Beral pipette on a nail and use the Tesla coil (a device that produces an electrical spark) to jump a spark through the plastic to the tip of the nail.

a) Record the results in your *Active Chemistry* log.

Wash your hands and arms thoroughly after the investigation.

a) Collect the two gases in the rocket, noting the relative amounts of each gas in your *Active Chemistry* log. Leave a water plug in the neck of the rocket and bring it to the launch pad, open end down.

b) Launch your rocket and compare this launch to the first trial.

Repeat the procedure as often as time allows.

7. Answer the following in your *Active Chemistry* log:

a) Were both gases necessary in order for the rocket to launch? Explain your answer.

b) Was there a combination of gases that worked best? What was the ratio?

c) The reaction in the rocket was a synthesis reaction. In a synthesis reaction, one product is made from two simpler reactants. In this case, the reactants were hydrogen and oxygen. What was the product? Write a word equation and a balanced chemical equation for the reaction in the rocket.

8. Clean up your workstation as directed by your teacher. Rinse and save copper wire for future use.

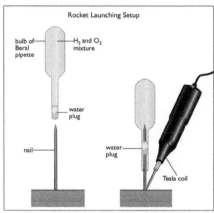

Rocket Launching Setup

bulb of Beral pipette

H_2 and O_2 mixture

water plug

nail

water plug

Tesla coil

6. Now that you know the proper procedure, you can perform an inquiry investigation to determine the optimum hydrogen-to-oxygen gas ratio for a successful rocket. Should there be one part hydrogen to one part oxygen as you first tried? Should there be more hydrogen or more oxygen?

4.

Direct students to carry the rocket stem end down, preferably sealed with a fingertip when they are moving to the launch pad. The launch pad consists of nails driven through wood. See diagram.

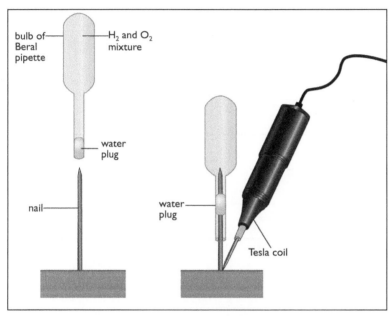

Tesla coil – jump a spark through the plastic to the nail tip

5.

The students should place the rocket on the "launch pad" as shown in the sketch in their text. Make sure everyone is wearing safety goggles and ignite the rocket with a Tesla coil as shown in the sketch.

6.a-b)

The first launch serves as a "run-through" of the procedure. The students can now begin experimentation with various ratios of the two gases. If the board is tilted slightly in one direction, it may be possible to judge which ratio of gases is best by measuring the distance traveled. Students should record relative amounts of each gas

collected (half and half, one-third hydrogen, two-thirds oxygen etc.) in their *Active Chemistry* logs.

7.a)

Yes, both gases are necessary. In order to answer this question based upon data, the students will have to fire the rocket twice, once with only hydrogen and once with only oxygen.

7.b)

Results will vary. Theoretically, the best ratio will be 2:1 hydrogen to oxygen, but it will be difficult to measure this ratio exactly.

7.c)

The product of the synthesis reaction is water.

Two moles of hydrogen gas reacts with one mole of oxygen gas to form 2 moles of water which, at room temperature, is a liquid.

$$2H_{2(g)} + O_{2(g)} \rightarrow 2H_2O_{(l)}$$

You can make the launching a contest by providing a prize to the first one to get the rocket in a target. A plastic sink insert works well as the target. The distance should be about 15–20 feet from the launch pad.

NOTES

Chem Talk

The different types of chemical reactions – single and double replacement, decomposition, and synthesis – are discussed in this *Chem Talk*. In addition, examples of each, with balanced equations, are shown.

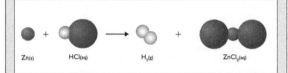

KINDS OF CHEMICAL REACTIONS

Single-Replacement Reactions

The reaction in this investigation that produces hydrogen gas was a **single-replacement reaction**. In this type of reaction, substances are rearranged and one element takes the place of another in a compound. The result is two new products. The general equation for this type of reaction can be written as follows:

$$\underset{reactants}{A + BC} \rightarrow \underset{products}{B + AC}$$

The reaction you carried out to produce hydrogen gas was:

zinc + hydrochloric acid → hydrogen + zinc chloride

You can see how it fits the pattern in the general equation. The zinc replaced the hydrogen. It can be written as a formula equation as follows:

$$Zn_{(s)} + HCl_{(aq)} \rightarrow H_{2(g)} + ZnCl_{2(aq)}$$

Using models, the equation would look like this:

Zn(s)   HCl(aq)   H₂(g)   ZnCl₂(aq)

You probably noticed that there is something wrong with the equation and drawing. When writing chemical equations representing reactions, it is important that the numbers of atoms on both sides of the equation are equal because mass cannot be created or destroyed in a chemical reaction. In the above reaction as written, you see that there are two atoms of hydrogen on the right side of the equation, while there is only one on the left. You must adjust the proportions of the reactants and products to satisfy the **law of conservation of mass**. Remember, in a chemical reaction, atoms are rearranged to form different compounds when bonds are broken and new bonds are formed. The atoms are not changed or destroyed. They are simply rearranged. Therefore, you must balance the equation.

Chem Words

single-replacement reaction: a reaction in which an element displaces or replaces another element in a compound.

law of conservation of mass: the law that states that the total mass of the products of a chemical reaction is the same as the total mass of the reactants entering into the reaction.

421

Active Chemistry

Ideal Toy

You can do this by placing numeral coefficients in front of the different reactants and products. In this reaction, you could place a 2 in front of the HCl. That would give two hydrogen atoms on each side of the equation. There are also equal numbers of atoms of zinc and chlorine on both sides of the equation. The balanced equation is represented as:

$$Zn_{(s)} + 2HCl_{(aq)} \rightarrow H_{2(g)} + ZnCl_{2(aq)}$$

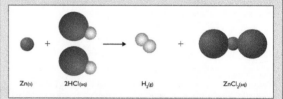

$Zn_{(s)}$ $2HCl_{(aq)}$ $H_{2(g)}$ $ZnCl_{2(aq)}$

This tells you that one atom of zinc reacts with two molecules of hydrochloric acid to yield one molecule of hydrogen gas and one unit of zinc chloride (zinc chloride is an ionic compound so it cannot be called a molecule). It should be noted that you balance equations *only* by placing coefficients in front of the reactants and products. You cannot change the subscripts in the molecular formulas. The subscripts cannot change, because then you would change the compound you were representing. If there is only one chemical unit in the balanced equation, then you do not write the numeral 1 as a coefficient. The coefficient is understood.

Since single molecules are so small, chemists use a larger quantity when referring to chemical reactions. Chemists use **moles** to represent large quantities of small particles. A mole of molecules (or anything, for that matter), is equal to 6.022×10^{23} of those molecules. Since the number of particles in a mole is constant, the ratio in the balanced equation does not change. The equation can now be read as:

One mole of zinc reacts with two moles of hydrochloric acid to produce one mole of hydrogen gas and one mole of zinc chloride.

This is a much larger quantity than individual molecules and is one that can be easily measured in the laboratory. You will find out more about this in the next section.

Redox Reactions

All single-replacement reactions are also called redox reactions because they involve both reduction and oxidation. Reaction of a metal with an

Chem Words

mole: the number equal to the number of carbon atoms in exactly 12 g of pure ^{12}C. It is represented by Avogadro's number, 6.022×10^{23}.

acid is an example of one atom being oxidized (losing electrons) and an ion being reduced (gaining electrons) to become an atom.

Decomposition Reactions

The reaction in this investigation that produced oxygen gas was a **decomposition reaction**. In a decomposition reaction, a more complex compound breaks down into simpler substances. The general equation for a decomposition reaction is:

$$AB \rightarrow A + B$$

reactants   products

The products of decomposition reactions may be two elements, an element and a compound, or two compounds. In any case, they will be simpler than the reactant.

The reaction you used to produce oxygen gas was the decomposition of hydrogen peroxide. It was catalyzed (sped up) by adding manganese dioxide. Since the manganese dioxide is a catalyst and not a reactant, it is shown above the arrow in the equation.

The word equation is:

hydrogen peroxide $\longrightarrow$ oxygen + water

and the chemical equation is:

$$H_2O_{2(aq)} \xrightarrow{MnO_2} O_{2(g)} + H_2O_{(l)}$$

This equation is not balanced. Placing a 2 in front of H_2O changes the odd number of oxygen atoms to an even number. This now gives a total of four oxygen atoms in the products. If a 2 is placed in front of the H_2O_2 on the reactant side, it too will now have four oxygen atoms. Checking the number of hydrogen atoms indicates that there are four on each side. The equation is now balanced and shows the correct coefficients for the reactants and the products.

Chem Words

decomposition reaction:
a chemical reaction
in which a single
compound breaks
down into two or
more simpler substances.

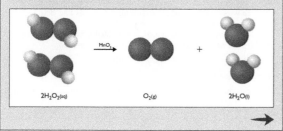

$2H_2O_{2(aq)}$ $O_{2(g)}$ $2H_2O_{(l)}$

Ideal Toy

It can now be read as "Two moles of hydrogen peroxide decompose to produce one mole of oxygen and two moles of water."

Double-Replacement Reactions

Carbon dioxide gas was produced by a **double-replacement reaction**. In a double-replacement reaction, parts of two compounds in solution switch places with each other. The general equation for a double-replacement reaction is:

$$AB + CD \rightarrow AD + CB$$
reactants   products

The word equation for the reaction that you did is:

hydrochloric acid + sodium hydrogen carbonate →
sodium chloride + carbonic acid

The carbonic acid decomposed into water and carbon dioxide, so the entire equation would be:

hydrochloric acid + sodium hydrogen carbonate →
sodium chloride + water + carbon dioxide

Note: If you are talking about the gas then HCl is called hydrogen chloride, but if the gas is dissolved in water then HCl is called hydrochloric acid ($HCl_{(aq)}$).

The chemical equation would be:

$$HCl_{(aq)} + NaHCO_{3(aq)} \rightarrow NaCl_{(aq)} + H_2O_{(l)} + CO_{2(g)}$$

By counting the number of H, Cl, Na, C, and O atoms of the reactants and products, you can see that the equation is balanced.

Acid–Base Reactions

When double-replacement reactions involving an acid and a base produce water and a salt, they can also be classified as acid–base reactions. For example, the simple reaction between hydrochloric acid, HCl, and sodium hydroxide, NaOH, is a double-replacement reaction. At the same time, it is an example of an acid–base reaction:

$$HCl + NaOH \rightarrow NaCl + H_2O$$

Precipitation Reactions

Reactions that produce a precipitate, a solid that comes out of solution, are also double-replacement reactions. For example, the reaction when

Section 5 Types of Reactions and Gas Production

Chem Words

synthesis reaction: a chemical reaction in which two or more substances combine to form a single product.

two solutions of salts are mixed—silver nitrate ($AgNO_3$) and sodium chloride ($NaCl$)—yields a solid precipitate, $AgCl$. The other ions in the solution, sodium and nitrate, remain as a salt solution.

Synthesis Reactions

In the rocket, a mixture of hydrogen and oxygen was made to react. The reaction was a **synthesis reaction** in which two simple substances combine to form a more complex substance. The general equation for a synthesis reaction is:

$$A + B \rightarrow AB$$
reactants   product

The word equation for the reaction in the rocket is:

hydrogen + oxygen → water

The balanced chemical equation is:

$$2H_{2(g)} + O_{2(g)} \rightarrow 2H_2O_{(l)}$$

The ratio of hydrogen to oxygen is 2 mol to 1 mol in the balanced equation. You might have noticed as you were testing your rockets that more hydrogen than oxygen was needed for the rocket to work well. The balanced equation gives you a clue as to why.

Analysis of Reaction Types

Reactions can be categorized as follows:

• Single-replacement reactions—usually redox reactions in which one substance is oxidized and another substance is reduced. Metal–acid reactions are a common example of this.

• Decomposition reactions—there are only a few examples of these, but they are characterized by a more complex compound breaking down to simpler compounds.

• Double-replacement reactions—this type of reaction is recognizable by two reactants going to two products. The reason they go to products is the formation of water (acid–base), a gas (often CO_2), or a precipitate. Acid–base reactions are common examples.

• Synthesis reactions—reactions where two elements react to form a new, single compound. Combustion reactions are common examples. Often, these also can be redox reactions.

Checking Up

1. Why do chemists use moles to describe quantities involved in chemical reactions?

2. Distinguish between a single- and a double-replacement reaction.

3. Give an example of a decomposition reaction.

4. The reaction in the rocket was a synthesis reaction. In a synthesis reaction, one product is made from two simpler reactants. In this case, the reactants were hydrogen and oxygen. What was the product? Write a word equation for the reaction in the rocket.

5. Identify each reaction as a synthesis, decomposition, single-replacement, or double-replacement reaction. What information from the reaction did you use to help you categorize them?
a) $NaOH_{(aq)} + AgNO_{3(aq)} \rightarrow AgOH_{(s)} + NaNO_{3(aq)}$
b) $Mg_{(s)} + CuBr_{2(aq)} \rightarrow Cu_{(s)} + MgBr_{2(aq)}$
c) $NH_4OH_{(aq)} + HBr_{(aq)} \rightarrow H_2O_{(l)} + NH_4Br_{(aq)}$
d) $Pb_{(s)} + O_{2(g)} \rightarrow PbO_{2(s)}$
e) $Na_2CO_{3(s)} \rightarrow Na_2O_{(s)} + CO_{2(g)}$

425

Active Chemistry

3.

An example of a decomposition reaction is the reaction of hydrogen peroxide in the presence of the catalyst, manganese dioxide, MnO_2:

$$2H_2O_{2(l)} \rightarrow 2H_2O_{(l)} + O_{2(g)}$$

4.

The product was water. The word equation is "Hydrogen and oxygen react to yield water."

5.

a) double replacement – a precipitate, AgOH was formed

b) single replacement – magnesium was oxidized and copper was reduced

c) double replacement – water was formed, irreversibly

d) synthesis – one product was formed from two reactants

e) decomposition – two products were formed from one reactant

CHAPTER 5

Checking Up

1.

Chemicals react in molar ratios and it is convenient to use moles when comparing chemicals in a reaction equation. Since atoms and molecules are so small, it is useful to use the mole to represent a large number of particles (Avogadro's number).

2.

In a single-replacement reaction, one element takes the place of another in a chemical compound. The first element is oxidized while the second is reduced. A double-replacement reaction occurs between two ionic compounds, usually in solution. Typically, a precipitate or gas is formed.

What Do You Think Now?

Have students revisit their original *What Do You Think?* ideas. You can lead a discussion of the microscopic view of the formation of gases and the macroscopic use of them in rocket launching. You may also want to ask them if they know anything about the technology of mixing gases or releasing gases during an actual launch.

In referring back to the *What Do You See?* illustration, you can ask students how much gas each of the canisters may hold.

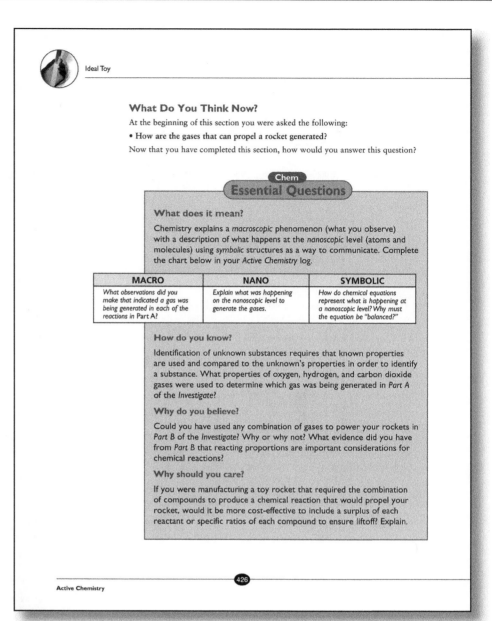

Ideal Toy

What Do You Think Now?

At the beginning of this section you were asked the following:

• How are the gases that can propel a rocket generated?

Now that you have completed this section, how would you answer this question?

Chem
Essential Questions

What does it mean?

Chemistry explains a *macroscopic* phenomenon (what you observe) with a description of what happens at the *nanoscopic* level (atoms and molecules) using *symbolic* structures as a way to communicate. Complete the chart below in your *Active Chemistry* log.

MACRO	NANO	SYMBOLIC
What observations did you make that indicated a gas was being generated in each of the reactions in Part A?	Explain what was happening on the nanoscopic level to generate the gases.	How do chemical equations represent what is happening at a nanoscopic level? Why must the equation be "balanced?"

How do you know?

Identification of unknown substances requires that known properties are used and compared to the unknown's properties in order to identify a substance. What properties of oxygen, hydrogen, and carbon dioxide gases were used to determine which gas was being generated in *Part A* of the *Investigate?*

Why do you believe?

Could you have used any combination of gases to power your rockets in *Part B* of the *Investigate?* Why or why not? What evidence did you have from *Part B* that reacting proportions are important considerations for chemical reactions?

Why should you care?

If you were manufacturing a toy rocket that required the combination of compounds to produce a chemical reaction that would propel your rocket, would it be more cost-effective to include a surplus of each reactant or specific ratios of each compound to ensure liftoff? Explain.

426

Active Chemistry

Chem Essential Questions

What does it mean?

MACRO — Bubbles of gas going through a solution showed that a gas was generated.

NANO — Hydrogen was formed as it was reduced by zinc in a single-replacement reaction. Oxygen was formed in a decomposition reaction from the reactant, H_2O_2.

SYMBOLIC — A chemical equation shows the substances which react and the products of the reaction. The equation must be balanced to show that matter is neither created nor destroyed and to be able to predict how much of each reactant is needed.

How do you know?

Hydrogen gave a small explosion with air, oxygen was able to relight a glowing splint, and carbon dioxide extinguished a burning splint. All of these are unique properties of the three gases.

Why do you believe?

No, 100% of either gas would not power the "rocket." The rocket traveled the greatest distance with 2:1 hydrogen:oxygen mixture. Other proportions gave shorter distances traveled.

Why should you care?

It would be more cost-effective to include only the minimum amounts of each reactant to assure a successful rocket flight. Excess reagent is wasted.

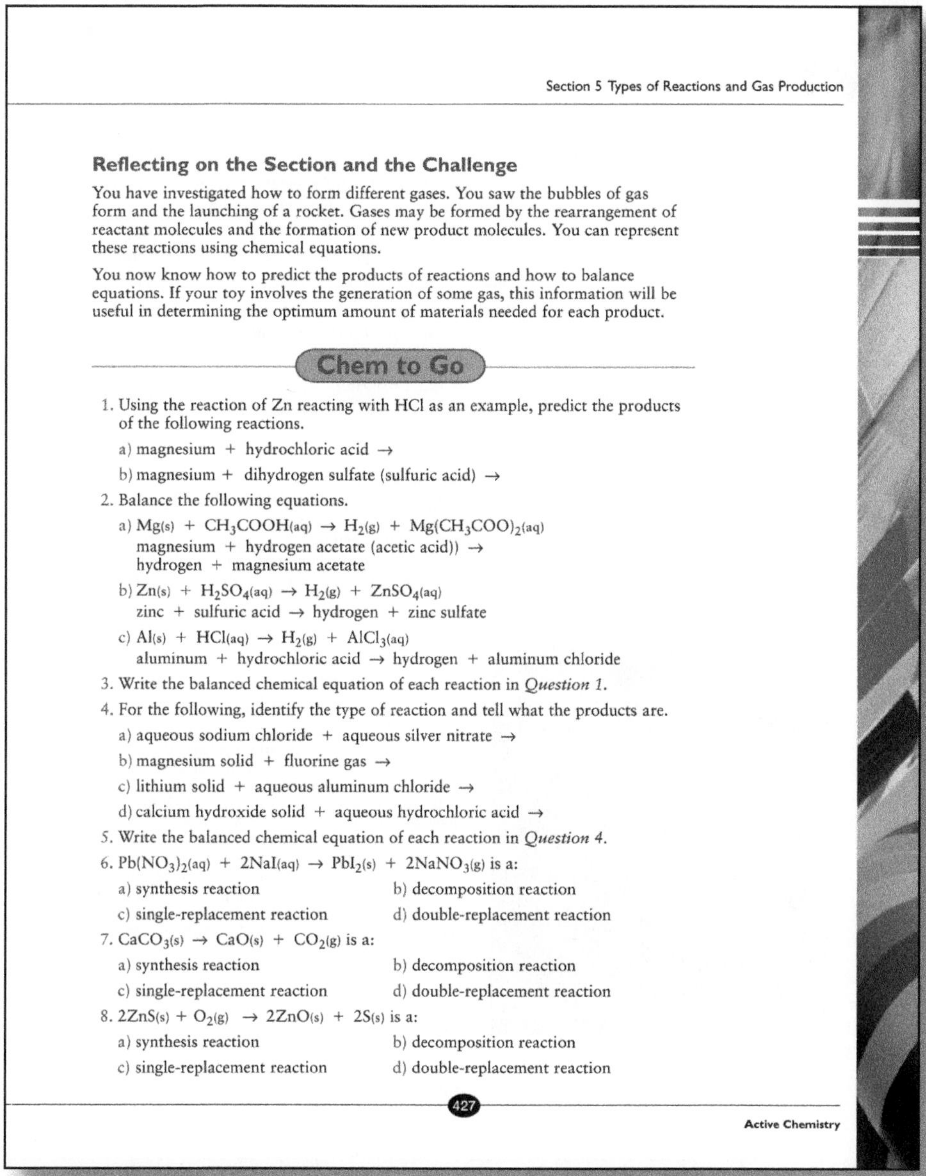

Reflecting on the Section and the Challenge

You have investigated how to form different gases. You saw the bubbles of gas form and the launching of a rocket. Gases may be formed by the rearrangement of reactant molecules and the formation of new product molecules. You can represent these reactions using chemical equations.

You now know how to predict the products of reactions and how to balance equations. If your toy involves the generation of some gas, this information will be useful in determining the optimum amount of materials needed for each product.

Chem to Go

1. Using the reaction of Zn reacting with HCl as an example, predict the products of the following reactions.
   a) magnesium + hydrochloric acid →
   b) magnesium + dihydrogen sulfate (sulfuric acid) →
2. Balance the following equations.
   a) $Mg(s) + CH_3COOH(aq) \rightarrow H_2(g) + Mg(CH_3COO)_2(aq)$
   magnesium + hydrogen acetate (acetic acid)) → hydrogen + magnesium acetate
   b) $Zn(s) + H_2SO_4(aq) \rightarrow H_2(g) + ZnSO_4(aq)$
   zinc + sulfuric acid → hydrogen + zinc sulfate
   c) $Al(s) + HCl(aq) \rightarrow H_2(g) + AlCl_3(aq)$
   aluminum + hydrochloric acid → hydrogen + aluminum chloride
3. Write the balanced chemical equation of each reaction in *Question 1*.
4. For the following, identify the type of reaction and tell what the products are.
   a) aqueous sodium chloride + aqueous silver nitrate →
   b) magnesium solid + fluorine gas →
   c) lithium solid + aqueous aluminum chloride →
   d) calcium hydroxide solid + aqueous hydrochloric acid →
5. Write the balanced chemical equation of each reaction in *Question 4*.
6. $Pb(NO_3)_2(aq) + 2NaI(aq) \rightarrow PbI_2(s) + 2NaNO_3(g)$ is a:
   a) synthesis reaction b) decomposition reaction
   c) single-replacement reaction d) double-replacement reaction
7. $CaCO_3(s) \rightarrow CaO(s) + CO_2(g)$ is a:
   a) synthesis reaction b) decomposition reaction
   c) single-replacement reaction d) double-replacement reaction
8. $2ZnS(s) + O_2(g) \rightarrow 2ZnO(s) + 2S(s)$ is a:
   a) synthesis reaction b) decomposition reaction
   c) single-replacement reaction d) double-replacement reaction

Reflecting on the Section and the Challenge

Although there are no questions in this section for students to answer or to use for discussion, this is an important opportunity to consider the section with respect to the *Chapter Challenge*. Students now know three ways to generate a gas and how to use two of the gases in a toy. This knowledge can be used in the design and the explanation of their toy.

Chem to Go

1.

a) magnesium + hydrochloric acid → **hydrogen + magnesium chloride**

b) magnesium + dihydrogen sulfate → **hydrogen + magnesium sulfate**

2.

a) $Mg(s) + 2CH_3COOH(aq) \rightarrow H_2(g) + Mg(CH_3COO)_2(aq)$

magnesium + hydrogen acetate →hydrogen + magnesium acetate

b) $Zn(s) + H_2SO_4(aq) \rightarrow H_2(g) + ZnSO_4(aq)$

zinc + sulfuric acid → hydrogen + zinc sulfate

c) $2Al(s) + 6HCl(aq) \rightarrow 3H_2(g) + 2AlCl_3(aq)$

aluminum + hydrochloric acid → hydrogen + aluminum chloride

3.

a) $Mg(s) + 2HCl(aq) \rightarrow H_2(g) + MgCl_2(aq)$

b) $Mg(s) + H_2SO_4(aq) \rightarrow H_2(g) + MgSO_4(aq)$

4.

a) sodium chloride + silver nitrate → **sodium nitrate(aq) + silver chloride(s)**

double replacement

b) magnesium + fluorine → **magnesium fluoride(s)**

synthesis

c) lithium + aluminum chloride → **aluminum(s) + lithium chloride(aq)**

single replacement

d) calcium hydroxide + hydrochloric acid → **calcium chloride(aq) + water**

double replacement

CHAPTER 5

5.

a) $NaCl_{(aq)} + AgNO_{3(aq)} \rightarrow$
$NaNO_{3(aq)} + AgCl_{(s)}$

b) $Mg_{(s)} + F_{2(g)} \rightarrow MgF_{2(s)}$

c) $3Li_{(s)} + AlCl_{3(aq)} \rightarrow$
$Al_{(s)} + 3LiCl_{(aq)}$

d) $Ca(OH)_{2(s)} + 2HCl_{(aq)} \rightarrow$
$CaCl_{2(aq)} + 2H_2O_{(l)}$

6.

d) double-replacement reaction

7.

b) decomposition reaction

8.

c) single-replacement reaction

9.

a) synthesis reaction

10.

c) the subscripts represent the proportions of the reactants and the products.

11.

c) 3

12.

Preparing for the Chapter Challenge

Acetic acid (vinegar) would be a natural choice for this household acid.

Ideal Toy

9. $SO_{3(g)} + H_2O_{(l)} \rightarrow H_2SO_{4(l)}$ is a:
   a) synthesis reaction
   b) decomposition reaction
   c) single-replacement reaction
   d) double-replacement reaction

10. In a correctly written chemical equation, all of the following are true **except**:
    a) the number of atoms of the reactants equals the number of atoms of the product.
    b) the coefficients indicate the proportions of the reactants and the products.
    c) the subscripts represent the proportions of the reactants and the products.
    d) the mass of the reactants is equal to the mass of the products.

11. Given the unbalanced equation:
    _____ $Al_{(s)}$ + _____$O_{2(g)} \rightarrow$ _____$Al_2O_{3(s)}$
    When this equation is correctly balanced using *smallest* whole numbers, what is the coefficient of $O_{2(g)}$?
    a) 6   b) 2   c) 3   d) 4

12. *Preparing for the Chapter Challenge*
    Your toy design may require the production of a gas from a chemical reaction. The reaction you carried out in this investigation had you use $HCl_{(aq)}$ (hydrochloric acid) for the production of hydrogen gas. Propose a reaction that generates carbon dioxide gas using a common household acid, one that would be less dangerous than hydrochloric acid for storage in a toy. Make a sketch of a toy that might use this chemical reaction.

Inquiring Further

History of rockets

Explore the different types of propellants that have been used throughout history. (The Chinese are credited with creating the first rockets hundreds of years ago for fireworks and as weapons.) What are some commonalities of these propellants? What are some differences? What are some of the newest propellants being tested currently? Select two or three different types of commercial toy-rocket propellants. Design a test to determine which propellant is the best. Write up a short article detailing your findings that might be of interest to local rocket clubs and other rocket enthusiasts.

Inquiring Further

History of rockets

The crucial part of this assignment is the design of a test to determine which of three commercial rocket propellants is the "best." Some of the criteria that students might consider are expense, safety, convenience, size (mass) of payload, and distance traveled per gram of fuel.

SECTION 5 – QUIZ

5-5a | **Blackline Master**

1. What is the general equation for a decomposition reaction?

    a) $A + B \rightarrow AB$ b) $AB \rightarrow A + B$

    c) $A + BC \rightarrow B + AC$ d) $AB + CD \rightarrow AD + CB$

2. What is the general equation for a double-replacement reaction?

    a) $A + B \rightarrow AB$ b) $AB \rightarrow A + B$

    c) $A + BC \rightarrow B + AC$ d) $AB + CD \rightarrow AD + CB$

3. Complete the following word equations by identifying the type of reaction and then predicting the products (the reactions are done at room temperature).

    a) copper (II) chloride + silver nitrate $\rightarrow$

    b) hydrogen peroxide $\rightarrow$

    c) aluminum + oxygen $\rightarrow$

4. Explain why chemical equations must be balanced and balance the following equation.

$$Al_{(s)} + H_2SO_{4(aq)} \rightarrow H_{2(g)} + Al_2(SO_4)_{3(aq)}$$

aluminum + dihydrogen sulfate $\rightarrow$ hydrogen + aluminum sulfate
                (sulfuric acid)

5. Avogadro's number of particles (6.022×10^{23}) is equal to what quantity in chemistry?

SECTION 5 – QUIZ ANSWERS

❶   b) $AB \rightarrow A + B$

❷   d) $AB + CD \rightarrow AD + CB$

❸   a) double replacement:

    copper (II) chloride + silver nitrate $\rightarrow$ silver chloride + copper (II) nitrate

    b) decomposition: hydrogen peroxide $\rightarrow$ water + oxygen

    c) synthesis: aluminum + oxygen $\rightarrow$ aluminum oxide

❹   Chemical equations must be balanced because matter cannot be created or destroyed in ordinary chemical reactions. The amount you start with is what you will end up with, just arranged differently.

    $2Al_{(s)} + 3H_2SO_{4(aq)} \rightarrow 3H_{2(g)} + Al_2(SO_4)_{3(aq)}$

❺   A mole

CHAPTER 5

SECTION 6
Ideal Gas Law for the Ideal Toy

Section Overview

This section gives students an opportunity to use knowledge gained from the preceding sections combined with new knowledge in order to determine the volume of one mole of hydrogen gas. Using a gas-collecting tube, students will collect the hydrogen formed from the reaction of magnesium with hydrochloric acid. The magnesium will be the limiting reagent.

With this new information they will be able to calculate the gas law constant R.

Background Information

While there is no "ideal gas" in actuality, the inert gases do approach that concept in many cases. Over a range of temperatures, most gases, such as O_2 and N_2, can be considered to be ideal for the purposes of doing calculations. However, at very low temperatures and very high pressures, none of the gases have the properties of an ideal gas.

The first condition for an ideal gas is that there be no intermolecular forces of attraction. This relates to the second condition, which specifies that all collisions of an ideal gas be perfectly elastic. Since all gases can be liquefied with high pressure and low temperature, this is where they fail as ideal gases. In order to become a liquid, there has to be some small, finite amount of attraction between the atoms and molecules. A third condition for an ideal gas is that it must have no volume. Clearly, that is impossible for any matter in our world.

There is a mathematical equation that combines the three variables—pressure, temperature, and volume—into one expression. This is called the Ideal Gas Law and, as mentioned above, can be used for calculations involving most gases at reasonable temperatures and pressures.

$$\text{Ideal Gas Law: } PV = nRT$$

Where
n = number of moles and
R = universal gas constant = $\dfrac{0.08206 \text{ L·atm}}{\text{mol·K}}$.

For energy calculations such as the Arhenius equation, use $R = \dfrac{8.3145 \text{ J}}{\text{mol·K}}$.

Temperature must be expressed in kelvins.
One mole of an ideal gas is 22.4 liters at STP.

LEARNING OUTCOMES		
LEARNING OUTCOMES	**LOCATION IN SECTION**	**EVIDENCE OF UNDERSTANDING**
Determine the volume of one mole of a gas.	*Investigate,* *Chem Talk,* *Chem to Go* Questions 1-3 *Checking Up,* *Preparing for the Chapter Challenge,* *Section Quiz*	Answers to questions in the *Investigate* section are similar to the answers in this *Teacher's Edition*. Answers match those found in this *Teacher's Edition*. Ask students the type of gas they intend to generate and to show calculations for the reaction. Answers match those found in this *Teacher's Edition*.
Calculate the gas law constant *R*.	*Investigate,* *Chem Talk*	Answers to questions in *Investigate* are similar to those presented in this *Teacher's Edition*.
Derive the Ideal Gas Law equation.	*Investigate*	Answers match those found in this *Teacher's Edition*.

Section 6
Materials, Chemicals, Preparation, and Safety

("per Group" quantity is based on group size of 4 students)

Materials and Equipment

Materials (and Equipment)	Quantity per Group (4 students)
Gas collection tube, graduated, 50 mL	1
Rubber stopper, one-hole (for large tubes)	1
Graduated cylinder, 10 mL	1
Ringstand	1
Burette clamp	1
Wire, #22, bare copper, 1ft	30 cm
Scissors	1
Ruler or tape measure	1
Beaker, 1 L	1
Materials (and Equipment)	Quantity per Group
Balances, 0.01 g	2

Chemicals

Chemicals	Quantity per Class (24 students)
Magnesium ribbon	1 m
3 M Hydrochloric acid, HCl	100 mL

Teacher Preparation

Obtain the mass of 1.00 m of magnesium ribbon and then cut into approximately 2.50 cm pieces.

Cut copper wire into 15 cm pieces and thread through one-hole stoppers.

3 M Hydrochloric acid, HCl: Slowly, carefully, with stirring, in a fume hood, add 25.0 mL of concentrated (12 M) HCl to 50 mL of distilled water. Dilute to 100.0 mL.

Safety Requirements

- Goggles and aprons are required in the laboratory area.

- Do not place unreacted magnesium in the trash or sink. The hydrochloric acid solution can be rinsed down the sink. The copper wire can be rinsed and saved for future use. Be careful that no magnesium remains unreacted and is disposed of in the trash. Any magnesium fragments should be treated with additional hydrochloric acid.

- Wash arms and hands before leaving the laboratory area.

Meeting the Needs of All Students
Differentiated Instruction

Augmentation and Accommodations

LEARNING ISSUE	REFERENCE	AUGMENTATION AND ACCOMMODATIONS
Determining values needed for the investigation	*Investigate*	**Augmentation** • Give specific directions for converting mass in grams to moles. The text stipulates that one mole of any element is equal to its gram atomic weight, but some students will not make this inference. • Explain the purpose and values in the equation given in Step 3.b). • Remind students how to convert Celsius to Kelvin in Step 9.b). • Clarify how to derive the values in the table students must make in Step 9.

Distinguishing between values and unit for each variable	*Investigate*	**Augmentation**
		• This investigation is somewhat complex due to the number of variables and associated units and values used to derive and apply the Ideal Gas Law. Students will need help to organize their thinking. Take time to help students clarify and organize these variables and associated units and their derivations.
		• Set up a table showing the following information assembled by the class in small groups or as a class:
		    • Symbol of the variable
		    • Name of the variable
		    • Unit used to measure variable
		    • Examples that show students how to derive desired units from other units

Using an equation to find values of an unknown	*Investigate* 9.	**Augmentation** • Model for the class the steps involved in converting the first equation (with the left side containing the first pressure, volume and temperature) to the second equation shown under 9.b) which contains only the second volume on the left side. Do not assume all students understand that they are equivalent. **Accommodation** • Have students who are more adept at working with real numbers solve the problem using the first version of the equation (instead of manipulating the variables to isolate the volume on one side of the equation).
Using an equation to find values of an unknown Distinguishing among different forms of the Ideal Gas Law equation	*Chem Talk, Checking Up* 3. *Chem to Go*	**Augmentation** • Teach students to begin with the standard form of the Ideal Gas Law and manipulate the variables according to the questions asked. Some students may benefit from learning the algebraic steps to move a variable from one side to the other. • Have students use the standard form of the equation, substitute known values and then solve for the unknown. • Give students a chance to choose the method that works for them. Provide guided practice using one of these methods after having exposed them to each.

LEARNING ISSUE	REFERENCE	AUGMENTATION AND ACCOMMODATIONS
Determining how a toy company knows how many times a CO_2 cartridge can be used Applying a scientific law to a real-life problem Habits of mind: Accessing prior knowledge, taking risks, and persistence	*What Do You Think Now?*	**Augmentation** Successful students exhibit certain habits of mind to determine an answer to a problem when they do not see the solution at the outset. Their approach includes use of past knowledge, taking risks like guessing, and persisting even when the solution is not apparent. Students who have struggled need to be taught these habits. Determining how a toy company knows how many times a CO_2 cartridge can be used is likely to be a problem that requires these qualities of students. • Ask students what they do when confronted with a problem whose solution is not apparent. Reinforce responses that exemplify the three habits above. • Explain to other students how to incorporate these habits in solving the problem at hand. • Think about what they learned in the investigation. How could the Ideal Gas Law be used to answer the question? • Even if they do not see how it could be used, ask them to consider taking a risk and trying to use it by substituting known values for the variables in the equation. • Persistence will lead students to discoveries that will eventually lead to an answer.

Strategies for Students with Limited English Language Proficiency

LEARNING ISSUE	REFERENCE	AUGMENTATIONS
Background knowledge	*What Do You Think?*	Give students examples to illustrate the word "*ideal*" found in the title. Students may not have background experience with darts or with a CO_2 cartridge and may need an example or explanation.
Vocabulary Following directions	*Investigate*	Make sure students are able to paraphrase the directions in the first paragraph as a means of understanding what they are going to do in the investigation.
Background knowledge Vocabulary Comprehending text	*Chem Talk*	Check for understanding of the prefix "*inter*" as in *intermolecular forces*. Give students time to discuss the table in this section.
Comprehension	*What Do You Think Now?*	There are a series of questions following the initial *What Do You Think?* question. It may be helpful to isolate each one and have the students discuss possible answers.
Background knowledge Vocabulary Comprehending text	*Chem Essential Questions*	In the *How do you know?* section, the phrase "What does your experimental data suggest?" may need some explanation in terms of the use of the word "*suggest*."
Comprehension Vocabulary	*Chem to Go*	Check for understanding of the term "*occupy*" in Question 1. In *Preparing for the Chapter Challenge*, help students set up a discussion protocol and clarify the use of the word "*generate*."

CHAPTER 5

Section 6
Teaching Suggestions and Sample Answers

What Do You See?

The illustration featured here is based on the upcoming section and is designed to engage students' interest. The question should prompt a range of responses ranging from "one picture is winter and one is summer" to "the balloon inflates better when it is warm outside." Both responses are valid and should be acknowledged as such. Later, you may wish to return to the illustration so that students have a chance to reassess the artist's intent and to recognize how they have progressed in content understanding and knowledge.

As the students try to make sense of the two pictures, you can ask them to compare and contrast them. Based on the knowledge they gained from the last section, you can expect to hear comments on how the temperature affects the volume of the enclosed hydrogen gas.

What Do You Think?

This question is designed to focus interest on the section topic and to gauge students' prior conceptions. It is not important that they arrive at a correct answer although their responses should be plausible.

An obvious response to the question might be that the company would conduct tests on a large number of cartridges and calculate an average as to how many darts each cartridge could support.

What Do You Think?
A CHEMIST'S RESPONSE

Toy companies conduct hundreds if not thousands of studies and tests on their products before releasing them to the market. Their data would include mathematical calculations based on the Ideal Gas Law to determine the amount of CO_2 needed for each discharge. This data, combined with specifications as to how much compressed gas can be contained in a cartridge, would give a predictable number of shots for each CO_2 cartridge.

STUDENTS' PRIOR CONCEPTIONS

Students' conceptions about gases have been mentioned in the preceding sections. Some of the most common ideas they might have include:

- Molecules of gases are somehow smaller and softer than those of solids.

- Vapor molecules have less mass than solid molecules, even to the point that gaseous molecules have no mass.

- Molecules expand when heated.

NOTES

_____

_____

_____

_____

_____

_____

_____

Section 6   Ideal Gas Law for the Ideal Toy

What Do You See?

Learning Outcomes

In this section you will

• Determine the volume of one mole of a gas.

• Calculate the gas-law constant "R."

• Derive the ideal gas law equation.

What Do You Think?

A toy dart gun uses a CO_2 cartridge to shoot darts.

• How does a toy company know how many times a CO_2 cartridge can be used to shoot the darts in a dart gun before it runs out?

Record your ideas about this question in your *Active Chemistry* log. Be prepared to discuss your responses with your group and the class.

Investigate

From previous sections, you know that pressure and temperature affect gas volumes. In this investigation you will explore another variable that influences the behavior of gases—the number of particles. Then you will combine the relationships from all of these variables in order to derive an equation that allows you to more accurately predict changes in a gaseous system.

1. Measure the mass of 100 cm of polished magnesium ribbon. Your teacher may provide you with this mass.

 a) Record this mass in your *Active Chemistry* log.

2. Obtain a small piece of polished magnesium ribbon (approximately 2.5 cm) and carefully measure its length to the nearest 0.05 cm.

 a) Record the length of your piece of magnesium.

3. Set up a ratio to determine the mass of your small piece of

429

Active Chemistry

Investigate

The lab will go more quickly if you cut the magnesium pieces ahead of time. See *Teacher Preparation*.

1.

The mass of 100 cm of polished magnesium ribbon could measure anywhere from 1.95-2.2 g, depending on the thickness.

2.

If you have accurate balances available, students can skip the length measurement and just calculate the mass of magnesium. A measure of 2.5 cm of magnesium should produce between 35 and 45 mL of hydrogen gas. If the magnesium ribbon is thick, adjustments will need to be made.

CHAPTER 5

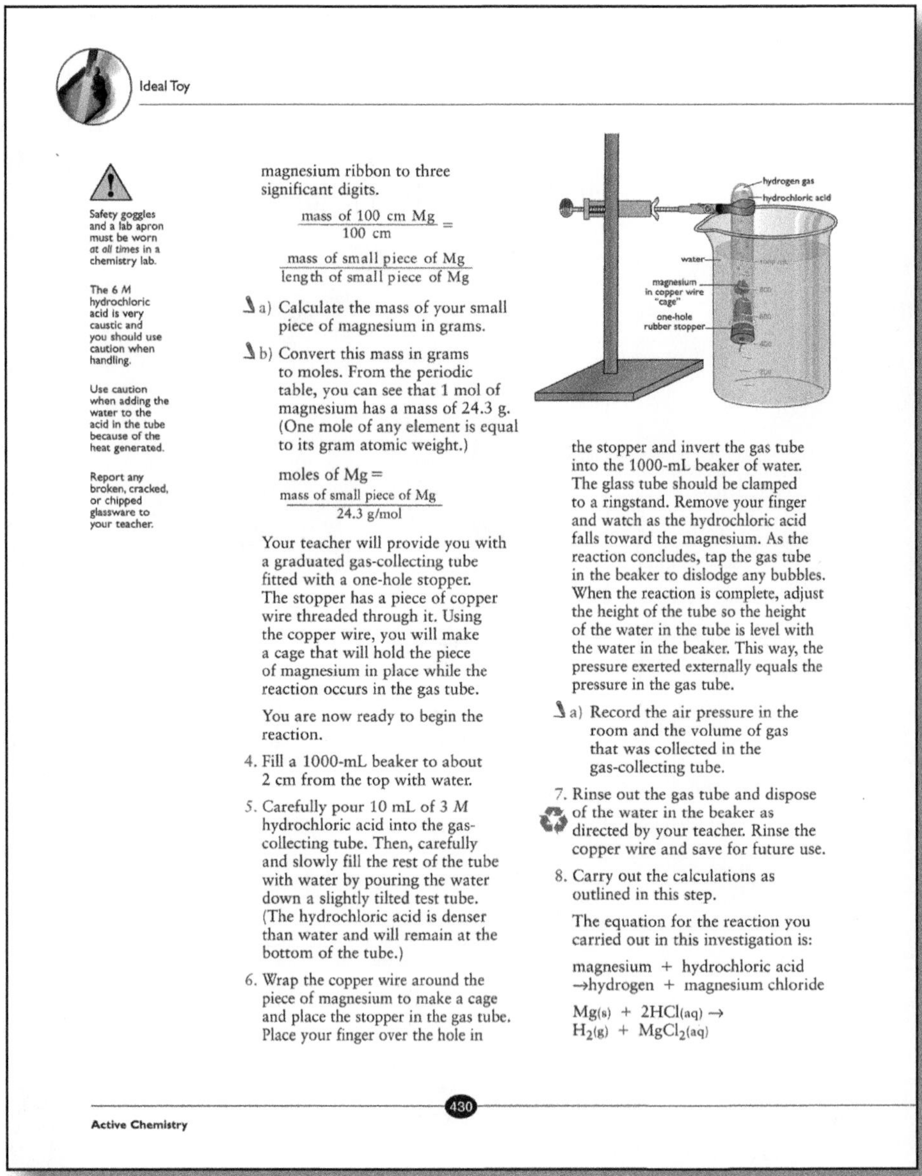

Ideal Toy

Safety goggles and a lab apron must be worn *at all times* in a chemistry lab.

The 6 *M* hydrochloric acid is very caustic and you should use caution when handling.

Use caution when adding the water to the acid in the tube because of the heat generated.

Report any broken, cracked, or chipped glassware to your teacher.

magnesium ribbon to three significant digits.

$$\frac{\text{mass of 100 cm Mg}}{\text{100 cm}} = \frac{\text{mass of small piece of Mg}}{\text{length of small piece of Mg}}$$

a) Calculate the mass of your small piece of magnesium in grams.

b) Convert this mass in grams to moles. From the periodic table, you can see that 1 mol of magnesium has a mass of 24.3 g. (One mole of any element is equal to its gram atomic weight.)

$$\text{moles of Mg} = \frac{\text{mass of small piece of Mg}}{\text{24.3 g/mol}}$$

Your teacher will provide you with a graduated gas-collecting tube fitted with a one-hole stopper. The stopper has a piece of copper wire threaded through it. Using the copper wire, you will make a cage that will hold the piece of magnesium in place while the reaction occurs in the gas tube.

You are now ready to begin the reaction.

4. Fill a 1000-mL beaker to about 2 cm from the top with water.
5. Carefully pour 10 mL of 3 *M* hydrochloric acid into the gas-collecting tube. Then, carefully and slowly fill the rest of the tube with water by pouring the water down a slightly tilted test tube. (The hydrochloric acid is denser than water and will remain at the bottom of the tube.)
6. Wrap the copper wire around the piece of magnesium to make a cage and place the stopper in the gas tube. Place your finger over the hole in the stopper and invert the gas tube into the 1000-mL beaker of water. The glass tube should be clamped to a ringstand. Remove your finger and watch as the hydrochloric acid falls toward the magnesium. As the reaction concludes, tap the gas tube in the beaker to dislodge any bubbles. When the reaction is complete, adjust the height of the tube so the height of the water in the tube is level with the water in the beaker. This way, the pressure exerted externally equals the pressure in the gas tube.

a) Record the air pressure in the room and the volume of gas that was collected in the gas-collecting tube.

7. Rinse out the gas tube and dispose of the water in the beaker as directed by your teacher. Rinse the copper wire and save for future use.
8. Carry out the calculations as outlined in this step.

The equation for the reaction you carried out in this investigation is:

magnesium + hydrochloric acid →hydrogen + magnesium chloride

$Mg_{(s)} + 2HCl_{(aq)} \rightarrow H_{2(g)} + MgCl_{2(aq)}$

430

Active Chemistry

3.a)

A typical conversion of centimeters of magnesium to grams of magnesium:

$$2.26\text{ cm}\left(\frac{1.98\text{ g}}{100\text{ cm}}\right) = 0.0447\text{ g}$$

3.b)

A measure of 2.26 cm of magnesium, calculated at 0.0447 g, would be 0.0018 mol of magnesium.

$$0.0447\text{ g}\left(\frac{1\text{ mole}}{24.3\text{ g}}\right) = 0.0018\text{ mol}$$

If you do not have calibrated gas-collection tubes, you can have the students do a crude calibration using water, a 10-mL graduated cylinder, and a wax pencil. Alternatively, a 100-mL graduated cylinder can be used. The gas-collection tube should hold 45-50 mL.

4.

The 1000-mL beaker is used to place the gas-collection tube in.

5.

Be sure to supervise the pouring of the 3 *M* hydrochloric acid into the gas-collection tubes. Eight to 10 mL should be more than sufficient. As noted in the *Student Edition*, the hydrochloric acid is denser than water and will remain at the bottom of the tube as the rest of the tube is filled with water.

6.

Wrapping the copper wire around the magnesium will keep the magnesium in place while the reaction occurs. If the magnesium works loose, it will continue to react as it floats in the hydrochloric acid. There is a possibility that it will stick to the sides of the tube. If it does, simply tilting the tube should cause the reaction to continue. Be sure that there are no air bubbles in the tube before it is inverted into the beaker of water.

6.a)

Students may be able to equalize the pressure before recording the volume by moving the gas-collection tube up or down until the liquid level inside is equal to the level of water in the beaker. You might want them to bring the tube to a larger container of water (a 1000-mL graduated cylinder provides plenty of depth) to equalize the pressure. There will be a slight error introduction if this is not done, but it is not great enough to affect the conclusions.

Some hypothetical calculations that students might make are shown in the data table on the opposite page.

The balanced equation shows that one mole of magnesium reacts with two moles of hydrochloric acid to produce one mole of hydrogen gas and one mole of magnesium chloride.

a) Record the balanced equation. Notice that one mole of magnesium will produce one mole of hydrogen gas. The number of moles of magnesium you used is therefore equal to the number of moles of hydrogen gas that forms.

$$\_\text{ mol Mg} \frac{1 \text{ mol } H_2}{1 \text{ mol Mg}} = \_\text{ mol } H_2$$

b) From the volume of gas collected and the number of moles of hydrogen gas, calculate the volume of one mole of hydrogen gas.

$$\frac{\_ \text{ L of } H_2}{\_ \text{ mol of } H_2} = \_\frac{\text{L}}{\text{mol}}$$

This is the number of liters in a mole of hydrogen gas at the present conditions of room temperature and pressure.

9. You can use a combination of Boyle's and Charles's laws to determine the volume at any given temperature and pressure.

You learned in earlier sections that the pressure and volume of gases are inversely related and the volume and temperature are directly related (as long as the number of particles remains constant).

By combining the two equations you get:

$$\frac{\text{(pressure) (volume)}}{\text{(temperature)}} = \text{constant}$$

For the same gas, if temperature and pressure conditions are changed, you can calculate the expected change in volume using this combined gas law.

$$\frac{P_1 V_1}{T_1} = \frac{P_2 V_2}{T_2}$$

This states that the pressure × volume/temperature of a gas at any one time is equal to the pressure × volume/temperature of that gas under any other conditions.

Using this equation, you can calculate the molar volume of hydrogen under the conditions of standard temperature (0°C or 273 K) and standard pressure (1 atm or 760 mm Hg), also called STP conditions.

a) Record the room temperature and pressure as provided by your teacher.

b) Convert the temperature to kelvins by adding 273 to the Celsius degrees.

	In your lab	At STP
P		760 mm Hg
V		
T		273 K

Using the above equation, you know the pressure, volume, and temperature for the hydrogen gas you collected. You also know the temperature and pressure at STP.

Using this information, calculate the molar volume of hydrogen at STP.

$$V_2 = \frac{P_1 V_1 T_2}{P_2 T_1}$$

Where P_1 is room pressure, T_1 is room temperature, V_1 is your calculated volume of hydrogen, P_2 is standard pressure (1.0 atm) and T_2 is standard temperature (0°C). Remember to change Celsius degrees to kelvins.

Wash your hands and arms thoroughly after the investigation.

431

Active Chemistry

As noted in the *Student Edition*, the balanced equation shows that one mole of magnesium reacts with two moles of hydrochloric acid to produce one mole of hydrogen gas and one mole of magnesium chloride.

8.a)

Converting the mass of a piece of magnesium to moles:

$$0.0447 \text{ g} \left(\frac{1 \text{ mole}}{24.3 \text{ g}} \right) =$$

0.00184 mole Mg

Converting the mole of magnesium to moles of hydrogen:

$$0.00184 \text{ mole Mg} \left(\frac{1 \text{ mole } H_2}{1 \text{ mol Mg}} \right) =$$

00.00184 mole H_2

8.b)

Calculating the volume of one mole of hydrogen gas:

$$\frac{(0.0465 \text{ liter of } H_2)}{(0.00184 \text{ mole } H_2)} =$$

25.3 Liters/mole

9.

Using the Combined Gas Law to find the volume at STP conditions:

$$\frac{P_1 \times V_1}{T_1} = \frac{P_2 \times V_2}{T_2}$$

$$V_2 = \frac{P_1 V_1 T_2}{P_2 T_1}$$

9.a)

Room temperature should be in degrees Celsius.

Pressure can be in atm, mm Hg, or psi, as long as the same units are used for P_1 and P_2.

Mass of 100 cm Mg ribbon	Length of Mg ribbon, cm	Mass of Mg ribbon, g	Moles of Mg ribbon	Room pressure, mm Hg	Room temperature, °C and K	Volume of hydrogen produced, mL and L
1.98 g	2.26 cm	0.0447 g	0.00184 mol	755 mm Hg	23.0°C 296 K	46.5 mL 0.0465 L

7.

When the lab is finished, the beaker will contain a diluted solution of hydrochloric acid. Dispose of this in the sink with plenty of water.

8.

Work with the students through the calculations. Sample data can be inserted as students do their own data.

$$Mg_{(s)} + 2HCl_{(aq)} \rightarrow$$

$$H_{2(g)} + MgCl_{2(aq)}$$

CHAPTER 5

9.b)

$$V_2 = \frac{(755 \text{ mm Hg})(25.3 \text{ L})(273 \text{ K})}{(760 \text{ mm Hg})(296 \text{ K})}$$

9.c)

$$V_2 = 23.2 \text{ L}$$

9.d)

It should be close, within 2-3 liters of the accepted value.

9.e)

Finding the percent error:

$$\left(\frac{22.4 - 23.2}{22.4}\right)(100) = -3.57\%$$

Students should get results with less than a 10 – 15% error.

9.f)

Students may feel that any error is the result of faulty work. This may sometimes be the case, but it is important for them to realize that any work with measurements in it will have a "percent error," regardless of how meticulous the researcher may be. Some common sources of error are:

- Measuring the temperature
- Measuring the volume
- Measuring the atmospheric pressure
- Weighing the magnesium
- Solubility of hydrogen gas in water

10.

You may need to work with the students through this section.

Pressure is proportional to $\frac{1}{V}$ (at constant temperature and number of particles). It is an inverse relationship.

$$PV = k$$

Volume is proportional to the absolute temperature (at constant pressure and number of particles). It is a direct relationship. You might mention to the students that "k" stands for a constant ("konstant" in German).

$$\frac{V}{T} = k$$

It may be confusing to students that the first k does not equal the second k. They stand for an undefined constant at this point.

Before inserting the number of particles into the equation, ask students what increasing the number of particles would do to the pressure of a gas (it increases it – they are directly related). Then ask what increasing the number of particles would do to the volume of a gas (it increases

---

Ideal Toy

c) Record the molar volume at STP in your *Active Chemistry* log.

d) The accepted value for the molar volume of *any* gas at STP is 22.4 L/mol. How close was your value?

e) Find your percent error by finding the difference between your value and 22.4 and then dividing by 22.4. Multiply by 100 to get a percent. Record this information in your *Active Chemistry* log.

f) What are some factors that may account for your percent error?

10. You now have all the information you need to compare changes in pressure, temperature, and volume for gases. The Combined Gas Law allows you to look at changes in these three variables that affect gases. The fourth variable is the number of particles—the number of moles of gas involved. How does it fit into the equation?

You know the combined gas law:

$$\frac{(\text{pressure})\,(\text{volume})}{(\text{temperature})} = \text{constant}$$

or more simply: $\frac{PV}{T} = k$

Using the conditions of STP, you can add the number of particles to the equation. The unit for molar volume is liters per mole, so the number of moles will go into the denominator in the equation. Using n for the number of moles you get:

$$\frac{PV}{Tn} = k$$

Substituting the conditions for STP into the equation you get:

$$\frac{(1 \text{ atm})\,(22.4 \text{ L})}{(273 \text{ K})\,(1 \text{ mole})} = R$$

By convention, "R" is called the *ideal gas law constant*.

a) What is the value and unit of "R"? Record this in your *Active Chemistry* log.

b) What would be the value and unit for "R" if the pressure were measured in 760 mm Hg? Calculate and record this in your *Active Chemistry* log.

Chem Talk

Chem Words

ideal gas: a gas in which all collisions between atoms or molecules are perfectly elastic and in which there are no intermolecular attractive forces.

intermolecular forces: the attractive forces acting between molecules.

IDEAL GAS LAW

Temperature, pressure, and the number of particles must be considered when talking about a gas. An **ideal gas** is defined as one in which all collisions between atoms or molecules are perfectly elastic and in which there are no **intermolecular forces**. The molecules/atoms of an ideal gas have no volume. You can picture the ideal gas as a number of perfectly hard spheres that collide but that otherwise do not interact with each other. Many common gases exhibit behavior very close to that of an ideal gas at high temperature and low pressure.

In spite of their different masses, all ideal gases have similar characteristics, as shown in the table.

432

Active Chemistry

Section 6 Ideal Gas Law for the Ideal Toy

Gas	Number of moles	Volume (L)	Number of particles	Mass (g)
hydrogen (H_2)	1	22.4	6.02×10^{23}	2
oxygen (O_2)	1	22.4	6.02×10^{23}	32
krypton (Kr)	1	22.4	6.02×10^{23}	84

Note: Molar volumes of real gases vary a little, but they are close to the molar volume shown in the table. As examples, a mole of chlorine gas (22.1 L) and carbon dioxide gas (22.3 L) are a little less than the volume of an ideal gas (22.4 L). You can think of a real gas as being close to an ideal gas under standard conditions. This is due to attractive forces.

The **ideal gas law** relates the pressure, temperature, volume, and number of moles of an ideal gas. The ideal gas law was originally derived from the experimentally measured Charles's law, Boyle's law, and **Avogadro's gas law**.

The ideal gas law states:

$$PV = nRT$$

where P = pressure in atmospheres
        n = the number of moles of gas
        R = the **universal gas constant**
        (62.4 L · mm Hg/mol · K, or 0.0821 L · atm/mol · K)
        T = temperature in kelvins

(Notice that the R values differ depending upon the units of pressure, volume, temperature, and mass of the gas. However, the preferred and most convenient units are liter, atmosphere, moles, and kelvins, in which R has the value of 0.0821 L · atm/mol · K.)

Example:

The ideal gas law can be used to make predictions about the pressure, temperature, volume, and number of particles of a gas. For example, you might want to find the pressure of 2.5 mol of hydrogen gas at 25.0°C if its volume is 8.55 L.

Using $PV = nRT$, rearrange the equation to solve for pressure:

$$P = \frac{nRT}{V}$$

Substituting values into the equation:

$$P = \frac{(2.5 \text{ mol})(0.0821 \text{ L} \cdot \text{atm/mol} \cdot \text{K})(298 \text{ K})}{8.55 \text{ L}}$$

$$P = 7.2 \text{ atm}$$

By using the ideal gas law, you are able to make predictions about the behavior of a gas based upon the data you have measured.

Chem Words

ideal gas law: a law relating the pressure, temperature, and volume of an ideal gas. $PV = nRT$.

Avogadro's gas law: states that equal particles (molecules or atoms) of gases at equal temperatures have equal volumes.

universal gas constant: a constant factor in the ideal gas equation. $R = 0.0821$ L·atm/mol·K.

Checking Up

1. Explain how pressure, temperature, and the number of particles affect the behavior of a gas.

2. What are the differences between an ideal gas and most common gases under normal room conditions? Why do we distinguish between ideal and non-ideal gases?

3. What is the volume of 6.5 moles of oxygen gas if the temperature is 40.0°C and the pressure is 6.2 atm?

Active Chemistry

Chem Talk

This section discusses the significance of the Ideal Gas Law along with an explanation of the equation. A hypothetical example is provided to demonstrate the calculations involved.

Checking Up

1.

At constant temperature and moles, the pressure of a gas is inversely proportional to the volume. As pressure increases, the volume decreases.

At constant pressure and moles, the volume of a gas is directly proportional to the absolute temperature. As temperature increases, the volume increases.

At constant temperature and pressure (STP), the volume of a gas is directly proportional to the number of particles (moles).

2.

An ideal gas is assumed to have no volume; it is also assumed that there are no forces of attraction between the particles of the gas. This is accurate for the majority of gases at most temperatures and pressures. However, at low temperatures and/or high pressures, these assumptions become invalid since forces of attraction and volume cause deviation from the Ideal Gas Law.

3.

$PV = nRT$, or,

on rearranging, $V = \dfrac{nRT}{P} =$

$$\frac{(6.5 \text{ mol})(0.0821 \text{ L} \bullet \text{atm})(313 \text{ K})}{(\text{mol} \bullet \text{K})(6.2 \text{ atm})}$$

$V = 27$ L

it – they are also directly related). These two are intuitive, and you can show that since they are both direct relationships, the number of moles (n) would go in the denominator of the combined gas law equation.

$$\frac{PV}{Tn} = k$$

Substituting the conditions of standard temperature and pressure into the equation, you can calculate the value of the Ideal Gas Law constant.

$$\frac{(1 \text{ atm})(22.4 \text{ L})}{(273 \text{ K})(1 \text{ mole})} = R,$$

R being the accepted symbol for the Ideal Gas Law.

10.a)

$$R = \frac{0.082 \text{ atm} \bullet \text{L}}{\text{K} \bullet \text{mol}}$$

10.b)

$$R = 62.4 \quad \frac{\text{mm Hg} \bullet \text{L}}{\text{K} \bullet \text{mol}}$$

It may be advisable to work through these problems with the class.

What Do You Think Now?

Have students revisit the *What Do You Think?* question and, if possible, recall their original answers. Do they have a more concrete understanding now of how the volume of a gas might be measured? You may want to share the answer provided in *A Chemist's Response* and have students discuss their opinions.

Now is also a good time to revisit the *What Do You See?* illustration. Ask if students can explain the significance of the cold vs. warm weather settings depicted by the artist. Now that they are familiar with the Ideal Gas Law, they may appreciate the double entendre in the chapter title.

Chem Essential Questions
What does it mean?

MACRO — The mass of the magnesium determined the amount of hydrogen gas generated.

NANO — According to the balanced equation, one atom of magnesium will generate one molecule of hydrogen gas.

SYMBOLIC —

$Mg_{(s)} + 2HCl_{(aq)} \longrightarrow MgCl_{2(aq)} + H_{2(g)}$

Yes, one would expect to get the same value for R for another gas. All gases occupy the same volume at the same conditions of temperature and pressure.

How do you know?

The experimental data suggests that the behavior of gases can be predicted from measurements of pressure, volume, and temperature. Calculations based upon the collection of hydrogen gas under controlled conditions gave answers that corroborated accepted values for the volume of a mole of gas and for the value of the Ideal Gas constant, R.

Why do you believe?

The Ideal Gas Law states that there is a very predictable relationship between P, V, and T and that this relationship is valid for most gases at reasonable pressures and temperatures.

Why should you care?

If a gas is used in the toy project, information gained from this section will be of great help in the chemistry explanation. If the propellant for the toy is being generated in the toy, then it is important to know the amounts of reactants to bring together to produce the desired effect. A balanced equation will guide the calculations in determining the number of moles needed to generate a given number of moles of gas. If, on the other hand, the propellant is a stored gas, then a knowledge of the Ideal Gas Law will be useful in determining the conditions of storage.

 Ideal Toy

What Do You Think Now?

At the beginning of this section you were asked the following:

- How does a toy company know how many times a CO_2 cartridge can be used to shoot the darts in a dart gun before it runs out?

Do toy companies just guess as to how many times a cartridge can be used to shoot darts before it runs out? Do they just test several cartridges and use an average to manufacture the rest of their cartridges? Or is there a better, more predictable method to determine how much CO_2 to put in their cartridges? Explain.

Chem
Essential Questions

What does it mean?

Chemistry explains a *macroscopic* phenomenon (what you observe) with a description of what happens at the *nanoscopic* level (atoms and molecules) using *symbolic* structures as a way to communicate. Complete the chart below in your *Active Chemistry* log.

MACRO	NANO	SYMBOLIC
What determined the volume of hydrogen gas collected in the investigation?	How did the number of magnesium atoms impact the number of molecules of hydrogen produced?	Write the formula equation for the reaction between Mg and HCl. Would you expect to get the same value for R under the same room conditions for another gas, for example, O_2 from the decomposition of H_2O_2? Explain.

How do you know?

What does your experimental data suggest about the behavior of gases?

Why do you believe?

What does the ideal gas law suggest about the predictability of gas behavior?

Why should you care?

You will be creating a toy for your challenge in this unit. You have seen that many toys are designed to use gases in some way. It could be as simple as inflating the tires to something more complicated, like generating a propellant. Write a short explanation for how determining the amounts of materials to include as a gas propellant can be determined.

 434

Active Chemistry

> ### Section 6 Ideal Gas Law for the Ideal Toy
>
> #### Reflecting on the Section and the Challenge
>
> You have now discovered a way to relate the pressure, volume, amount, and temperature of a gas. You saw the formation of hydrogen gas in this investigation. You know that when the magnesium reacted with the acid, H_2 gas formed. You are able to symbolically represent the reaction with a balanced chemical equation.
>
> If your toy was designed to employ a CO_2 gas cartridge to inflate a balloon, propel a car, or blast a rocket, you should include information telling the consumer how many times the toy can be used with one CO_2 cylinder.
>
> ##### Chem to Go
>
> 1. A sample of dry gas weighing 1.05 g is found to occupy 1.43 L at 23.5°C and 0.951 atm. How many moles of the gas are present?
>
> 2. What is the mass of one mole of the gas in *Question 1*?
>
> 3. Let's say that you are designing a toy that requires the generation of 1.0 L of oxygen gas to operate it. What reagents would you use, and how many moles would be required if the gas was being produced at 1.0 atm and 20°C? (See *Section 5* for help.)
>
> 4. Many gases are stored in their compressed form (under pressure). Calculate the mass of N_2 that could be stored at 22°C and 125 atm in a cylinder with a volume of 45.0 liters. The molecular mass of N_2 is 28.0 g/mole.
>
> 5. Calculate the mass in grams of the air in a hot-air balloon that has a volume of 4.0×10^5 L when the temperature of the gas is 90.0°C and the pressure is 750 mm Hg. Assume that the average molecular mass of air is 30.0 g/mole.
>
> 6. A 2.0 L soda bottle is used as a water rocket. If 0.30 L of water is in the bottle and it is pumped with air to a pressure of 3.8 atm at a temperature of 25°C, how many moles of air are in the rocket?
>
> 7. Explain how you could determine the identity of an unknown gas by using the ideal gas law.
>
> 8. A balloon is to be filled with 30.0 kg of helium gas. What volume can be filled to a pressure of 1.15 atm if the temperature is 20.0°C?
>
> 9. You want to send chlorine gas, Cl_2, safely across your state. Chlorine gas is very poisonous and corrosive. You have a 5000-L truck cylinder that will withstand a pressure of 100 atm. The cylinder will be kept at 2°C throughout the trip. How many moles of chlorine gas can you safely ship?
>
> 10. *Preparing for the Chapter Challenge*
>
>   Discuss with your group how you might use a gas in your toy. Try to decide how much gas will need to be generated, how you will generate this gas, and the quantity of reactants that will be required to produce the desired amount of gas. Keep in mind that you will probably be forming the gas under normal atmospheric conditions and room temperatures.
>
> 435
>
> *Active Chemistry*

Reflecting on the Section and the Challenge

Although there are no questions in this section for students to answer or to use for discussion, this is an important opportunity to consider the section with respect to the *Chapter Challenge*. Students now know the Ideal Gas Law and how to use it to determine any of the four variables –pressure, volume, temperature, and number of moles. This knowledge can be used in the design and the explanation of their toy.

Chem to Go

1.

$$n = \frac{PV}{RT}$$

$$n =$$

$$\frac{(0.951 \text{ atm})(1.43 \text{ L})}{(0.0821 \text{ atm} \cdot \text{L/mol} \cdot \text{K})(296.5 \text{ K})}$$

$$n = 0.0559 \text{ mol}$$

2.

$$1.05 \text{ g}/0.0559 \text{ mol} = 18.8 \text{ g/mol}$$

3.

The reagents to use would be hydrogen peroxide and manganese dioxide.

The equation is

$$2H_2O_{2(aq)} \longrightarrow O_{2(g)} + 2H_2O_{(l)}$$

To find the moles of oxygen needed:

$$n = \frac{PV}{RT}$$

$$n =$$

$$\frac{(1.0 \text{ atm})(1.0 \text{ L})}{(0.0821 \text{ atm} \cdot \text{L/mol} \cdot \text{K})(293 \text{ K})}$$

$$n = 0.042 \text{ mol oxygen needed}$$

To find the mol of hydrogen peroxide needed:

0.042 mol oxygen

$$\left| \frac{2 \text{ moles } H_2O_2}{1 \text{ mole } O_2} \right| =$$

0.084 mol of hydrogen peroxide

Note: The quantity of manganese dioxide is not important because it is the catalyst.

4.

$$n = \frac{PV}{RT}$$

$$n =$$

$$\frac{(125 \text{ atm})(45.0 \text{ L})}{(0.0821 \text{ atm} \cdot \text{L/mol} \cdot \text{K})(295 \text{ K})}$$

$$n = 232 \text{ moles } N_2$$

232 moles N_2 (28.0 g/mole) = 6500 g of N_2 or 6.50×10^3 g or 6.50 kg

5.

$$n = \frac{PV}{RT}$$

$$n =$$

$$\frac{(750 \text{ mm Hg})(4.0 \times 10^5 \text{ L})}{(62.4 \text{ mm Hg} \cdot \text{L/mol} \cdot \text{K})(363 \text{ K})}$$

$n = 13{,}244$ moles air
(1.3×10^4 to two significant figures)

$$1.3 \times 10^4 \text{ mol air} \times \frac{30 \text{ g air}}{\text{mol air}} =$$

$397{,}200$ g of air =
4.0×10^5 g of air

6.

$2.0 \text{ L} - 0.30 \text{ L} = 1.7 \text{ L}$

$$n = \frac{PV}{RT} =$$

$$\frac{(3.8 \text{ atm})(1.7 \text{ L})}{(0.0821 \text{ atm} \cdot \text{L/mol} \cdot \text{K})(298 \text{ K})} =$$

0.26 mol

7.

You will need to know the pressure, mass, volume, and temperature of the unknown gas. Then use $n = \frac{PV}{RT} =$ to find number of moles. Divide mass by the number of moles and look at the periodic table to find the element whose molar mass matches your answer. Remember that many gases are diatomic (O_2, N_2, F_2, Cl_2) and will have twice the mass of the element.

8.

$$\text{mol He}: 30.0 \text{ kg} \times \frac{1000 \text{ g}}{\text{kg}} \times \frac{1 \text{ mol}}{4.0 \text{ g}} =$$

7.50×10^3 mol

$$V = \frac{nRT}{P} =$$

$$\frac{(7.50 \cdot 10^3 \text{ mol})(0.0821 \text{ atm} \cdot \text{L})(293 \text{K})}{(\text{mol} \cdot \text{K})(1.15 \text{ atm})} =$$

$= 1.57 \times 10^5$ L

9.

$$n = \frac{PV}{RT} =$$

$$\frac{(100 \text{ atm})(5000 \text{ L})}{(0.0821 \text{ atm} \cdot \text{L/mol} \cdot \text{K})(275 \text{ K})}$$

2.2×10^4 mol of Cl_2 gas.

10.

Preparing for the Chapter Challenge

Answers will vary depending on the choices each group makes. There are three possible gases that they might generate—oxygen, carbon dioxide, and hydrogen. Check to make certain that they are aware of the safety issues with each gas.

NOTES

SECTION 6 – QUIZ

5-6b   **Blackline Master**

1. What is the volume of one mole of any gas at standard temperature and pressure?

   a) 0.0821 L

   b) 1 L

   c) 22.4 L

   d) $6.02 \cdot 10^{23}$

2. If you are pumping air into a rigid container (in which the volume can't change), the pressure will _____.

   a) rise

   b) fall

   c) stay the same

   d) fluctuate, but return to the initial pressure

3. What is the pressure of 6.55 moles of carbon dioxide gas in a 12.50 L fire extinguisher at 20.0 °C?

4. What volume would the same 6.55 moles of carbon dioxide occupy at STP?

5. Many gases are stored in their compressed form (under pressure). Calculate the mass of O_2 that could be stored at 25.0°C and 135 atm in a cylinder with a volume of 45.0 liters. The molecular mass of O_2 is 32.0 g/mole.

SECTION 6 – QUIZ ANSWERS

❶ c) 22.4 L

❷ a) rise

❸ $P = \dfrac{nRT}{V} =$

$$\frac{(6.55 \text{ mol})(0.0821 \text{ atm} \bullet \text{L/mol} \bullet \text{K})(293 \text{ K})}{(12.5 \text{ L})}$$

$P = 12.6$ atm

❹ $V = \dfrac{nRT}{P} =$

$$\frac{(6.55 \text{ mol})(0.0821 \text{ atm} \bullet \text{L/mol} \bullet \text{K})(273 \text{ K})}{(1 \text{ atm})}$$

$V = 147$ L

Or $V = (22.4 \text{ L/mol})(6.55 \text{ mol}) = 147$ L

❺ $n = \dfrac{PV}{RT} =$

$$\frac{(135 \text{ atm})(45.0 \text{ L})}{(0.0821 \text{ atm} \bullet \text{L/mol} \bullet \text{K})(298 \text{ K})}$$

$n = 248$ mol

mass = 248 mol (32.0 g/mol) = 7945 g
(7.95×10^3 to two significant figures.)

CHAPTER 5

Kinetic Molecular Theory and Graham's Law

Section Overview

Students will use pictorial and physical models to determine the effect of mass on gas effusion rates. Then they will apply stoichiometric relationships to determine the amount of $NaHCO_3$ and Zn needed to completely inflate two plastic bags with carbon dioxide and hydrogen gas. Finally, students will explain the observations made using the balloon/bag model and the molecular weights of the gases generated.

Background Information

Interested in the diffusion of atoms and molecules, Thomas Graham (1805-1869) studied gases and liquids in his native Scotland. His work was rewarded with the Keith Medal from the Royal Society of Edinburgh in 1833. Later, he was awarded the prestigious Royal Medal of the Royal Society in 1838. The methods he developed for the study of diffusion are still used today in the purification of the blood of kidney patients by dialysis.

The two phenomena to be investigated in this section are often confused because they have similar names and describe similar processes.

Diffusion – The process by which two gases (or liquids, solids) mix and which is caused by a concentration gradient.

Effusion – The process by which a contained gas escapes through a pinhole into a vacuum. The pinhole must be smaller than the mean free path of the gas particles.

Graham's Law of Diffusion

The equation that follows describes the relationship of the rate at which a gas diffuses and the density of the gas. An example of this would be the rate at which the molecules of a perfume scent travel across a room. This rate is proportional to the inverse square root of the gas's density.

$$\text{Diffusion Rate} \; \alpha \; 1/(\text{density})^{1/2}$$

The calculations are made simpler by the fact that all gases occupy the same volume (22.4 L/mol) under equal conditions of temperature and pressure. Therefore, the density is proportional to the atomic mass (for the noble gases) or the molecular mass of the gas. It follows that the density of a gas is directly proportional to its molar mass.

$$\text{Diffusion Rate} \; \alpha \; 1/(\text{molar mass})^{1/2}$$

Graham's Law of Effusion

In a like manner, the rate of the effusion of a gas is inversely proportional to the square root of either the density or the molar mass of the gas.

$$\text{Effusion Rate} \; \alpha \; 1/(\text{molar mass})^{1/2}$$

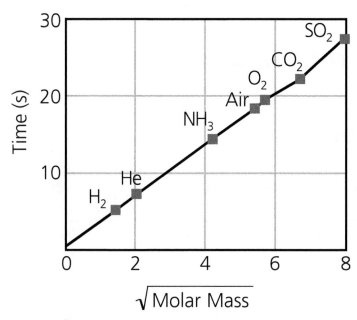

The time required for 25-mL samples of different gases to diffuse through a pinhole into a vacuum.

LEARNING OUTCOMES		
LEARNING OUTCOMES	**LOCATION IN SECTION**	**EVIDENCE OF UNDERSTANDING**
To determine the effect of molecular size on molecular motion.	*Investigate* Steps 1-3, 7-10 **Chem Talk, Checking Up** Questions 1-4 **Chem to Go** Questions 1-5	Answers from students are similar to those in this *Teacher's Edition*.
To predict the quantities of gas produced in chemical reactions.	*Investigate* Steps 4–6 **Inquiring Further**	Answers from students are similar, if not identical, to those in this *Teacher's Edition*.

NOTES

_____

_____

_____

_____

_____

_____

_____

CHAPTER 5

Section 7
Materials, Chemicals, Preparation, and Safety

("per Group" quantity is based on group size of 4 students)

Materials and Equipment

Materials (and Equipment)	Quantity per Group (4 students)
Marking pen, indelible	1
Ruler or tape measure	1
Graduated cylinder, 100 mL	1
Resealable plastic bags, quart-size	2
Weighing boats	2
Materials (and Equipment)	**Quantity per Class**
Bottle of perfume (or other strong scent)	1
Paper, 8.5 x 11, white (for sketches)	50
Balances, 0.01 g	2

Chemicals

Chemicals	Quantity per Class (24 students)
1.0 M Hydrochloric acid, HCl	600 mL
Zinc, granular	25 g
Vinegar, 5-6% acetic acid, CH_3COOH	350 mL
Baking soda, $NaHCO_3$, sodium bicarbonate	25 g

Teacher Preparation

1.0 M Hydrochloric acid, HCl: Slowly, carefully, with stirring, in a fume hood, add 83.3 mL of concentrated (12 M) HCl to 800 mL of water. Dilute to 1.0 L.

Safety Requirements

- Goggles and aprons are required in the laboratory area.

- The hydrochloric acid, sodium bicarbonate, and vinegar can be rinsed down the sink. Any zinc remaining can be recovered, rinsed, and reused.

- Wash arms and hands before leaving the laboratory area.

NOTES

CHAPTER 5

Meeting the Needs of All Students
Differentiated Instruction

Augmentation and Accommodations

LEARNING ISSUE	REFERENCE	AUGMENTATION AND ACCOMMODATIONS		
Showing an equation is balanced	*Investigate* 5.b) and 6.b)	**Accommodations** • Ask students to place their observations of the three substances in a table. Students may first look to see if the equation is balanced. They will count the number of atoms of each element on each side and realize it is balanced, but they may not understand how they should show it is balanced. The question for you is: Are students' difficulties related to their misunderstanding of the concept of balancing or of not knowing how they are expected to show the equation is balanced? • To find out, ask students how they know when an equation is balanced. If they cannot answer appropriately, re-teach the concept. If their answer includes the idea of the law of conservation of mass, then proceed to one of the other accommodations below which addresses expressing their answers. • Ask students to give you an example of a balanced element from this equation. If they can give an example, tell them to write down what they told you and do the same for each element in the equation. • Suggest they make a T-chart similar to the one below or provide a student with one.		
		Element	$Zn + 2HCl$	$ZnCl_2 + H_2$
		Zn		
		H		
		Cl		
Determining the mass of zinc needed to make a mole of H_2 Solving problems using proportions	*Investigate* 5.d)-e)	**Augmentation** • Students may need to be reminded how to set up proportions. Use a familiar example from their everyday lives or an earlier problem to re-teach the concept of proportions. It is important that students learn the skill in a familiar context first. Students who already know how to do this should be given an alternative investigation they can do independently. It is important not to "waste" their time by asking them to sit through instruction they have already mastered. After everyone understands proportions, return to the problem at hand. Model setting up a proportion to solve Step 5.d). Then, ask the students to read Step 5.e) and create their own proportions they can use to determine the mass of zinc needed to make a mole of H_2. • Meet with students having difficulty with these steps. Read Step 5.d) together. Help them transfer the information from the narrative form to a proportion. Guide them as they do Step 5.e). **Accommodation** • Have students work in heterogeneous groups to provide help for students who need it.		

LEARNING ISSUE	REFERENCE	AUGMENTATION AND ACCOMMODATIONS
Determining the amount of baking soda that will be necessary to fill a bag with CO_2 Solving complex problems using a procedure card strategy Reading comprehension	*Investigate* 6.c)	**Augmentation** • In Step 5 of the *Investigate* section, students followed a complex set of steps in the text to determine the amount of zinc necessary for their reaction. In Step 6.c) they are asked to repeat this procedure to determine the amount of baking soda they will need. Ask groups of students to go back through Step 5 and the solutions they wrote, making a set of directions to follow. It is important to name this investigation and tell students why they are doing it. Call it "The Procedure Card Strategy" and explain that writing down the steps helps them know exactly what to do, develop analytical reading skills they need to solve complex problems independently, and will help them solve the next problem in this investigation. Circulate among the groups to oversee the work. When students have completed their cards, choose students with good models to share them with the class. Then ask the groups to use the cards to solve Step 6.c). **Accommodation** • Give students a procedure card you have made and ask them to use it to solve Step 6.c).

Strategies for Students with Limited English Language Proficiency

LEARNING ISSUE	REFERENCE	AUGMENTATIONS
Background knowledge	*What Do You Think?*	Make sure students understand what to do when they "*predict*" that something will occur.
Vocabulary Following directions	*Investigate*	Students may not be familiar with the term "*tally*" and may need a synonym. Check for understanding of "*circumference*." Give explicit instructions as to how students are to "*describe*" differences.
Background knowledge Vocabulary Comprehending text	*Chem Talk, Checking Up*	Have students put new words in their personal dictionaries or *Active Chemistry* logs. Review meaning of "*velocity*" and provide derivations. Refer to *Checking Up* questions to check for understanding.
Comprehension	*What Do You Think Now?*	Check to see if students understand why the hyphenated interjection is in the bold sentence.
Background knowledge Vocabulary Comprehending text	*Chem Essential Questions*	Students will need to look back to a previous section of the text in order to answer the questions. In the *Symbolic* section there is specific reference to Graham's law of effusion that may require some location skill. Use some small group discussion to make sure everyone has the same basic understanding and comprehension of the chemistry concepts.
Comprehension Vocabulary	*Chem to Go*	Have students work together as they "*rank*" the information. Explain the use of the word "*rank*," and provide different examples of how things are "*ranked*."
Application Comprehension Research skills	*Inquiring Further*	Check students' understanding of the word "*assume*."

CHAPTER 5

Section 7
Teaching Suggestions and Sample Answers

What Do You See?

This illustration is an artistic representation of the section the students are about to investigate, and its purpose is to spark students' imagination and interest. The illustration can be interpreted on various levels. One student may attempt a literal interpretation of what she sees, while another student may try to interpret the intent of the artist, or the chemical principle that's being illustrated, e.g., "It looks like one balloon is heavy and one is light." There is no correct response, and at this time students should be encouraged to participate and think freely. Later, you may wish to return to the illustration so that students are able to fully understand the artist's intent as well as measure how much they have progressed, based on the chemistry content and knowledge they've gained after completing the section.

Ideal Toy

| Section 7 | Kinetic Molecular Theory and Graham's Law |

What Do You See?

Learning Outcomes

In this section you will:

• **Determine** the effect of molecular size on molecular motion.

• **Predict** quantities of gas produced in chemical reactions.

What Do You Think?

Party balloons are often filled with air or helium.

• Predict which balloons — ones filled with air or ones filled with helium — will stay inflated longer. Explain why you predicted this.

Record your ideas about this question in your *Active Chemistry* log. Be prepared to discuss your responses with your small group and the class.

Investigate

1. If your teacher were to open a bottle containing a substance with a strong perfume odor at the front of the class, estimate how much time it would take before you could smell it. Have your teacher tally the estimates at the board.

 a) Explain why you think the time for someone in the front of the class would or would not be different from someone in the back of the class.

2. Your teacher will now open the bottle. Raise your hand when you smell the odor so that the entire class can observe how the odor is traveling.

a) Measure and record the time that elapses before you can smell the odor.

436

STUDENTS' PRIOR CONCEPTIONS

Although students will intuitively predict that higher molecular weight gases travel slower than lower molecular weight gases, they will have a difficult time understanding that the mass differences are significant at all. A common misconception among all ages is that "air" does not have mass. Because the substance is not visible under normal conditions, then that substance must not have mass, is a commonly held misconception. Have students discuss how they know that gases are being generated in the baggies and that those gases have mass. Have the students brainstorm ways in which the mass of the gas could affect its behavior. Discuss the equation for determining kinetic energy and help students to understand that it applies to all size particles. Reinforce the postulates of the kinetic theory. Help students understand the implications of different masses by allowing them to construct or draw scale models of the different gases being tested and explain why they have different masses. Because this is such an abstract idea, any methods that you can use to make it more concrete will be helpful. Students often have difficulty understanding relationships expressed as a ratio. Help students to verbalize what the ratio means once it is calculated.

Students may note that somehow Gas A has a different result than Gas B. Students can try to explain what the differences may be. You can also ask the students if they think that there is any significance to the label of Gas A being red and its balloon being red.

What Do You Think?

If available, two latex balloons inflated with air and with helium would serve well as a visual cue for discussion. Note if students consider molecule size (mass) in their predictions. This is an opportunity to check the class for prior conceptions. Ask the students to explain their answers, but do not be judgmental. There is no need to come to closure at this point. You might generate a class list of factors that might affect the time the balloon will stay inflated. You will want to return to this list later to assist students' thinking concerning their baggie models.

What Do You Think?

A CHEMIST'S RESPONSE

According to Graham's law of effusion, a balloon filled with helium would be predicted to deflate more quickly than an identical balloon filled with air. Basically, this law reduces to a comparison of the square root of the ratio of the molar mass of each gas. In this case, taking the molar mass of air to be about 29 g/mol and that of helium to be 4 g/mol, the ratio is 29/4 or 7.25. The square root of 7.25 is 2.7. Helium has an effusion rate which is 2.7 times as great as air and so the air-filled balloon, although less buoyant, will stay inflated longer. Keep in mind that this value, 2.7, is not exact because Graham's law relates to the effusion of a gas through a hole into a vacuum. In this specific case of two balloons, the effusion is into one atmosphere of air and certainly not into a vacuum. But, this does not affect the fact that helium effuses faster than air and that the helium-filled balloon will deflate more quickly.

Investigate

1.

Obtain a sampling of student opinions about how fast an odor will travel across the room and tabulate these for later reference.

1.a)

Explanations will vary but most students will understand that some time must lapse between the actual opening of the bottle and any student smelling the odor. Most will also understand that students at the rear of the room will smell the odor later than students at the front of the room.

2.

The class should observe a wave-like raising of hands from front to back. If there are strong air currents from heating, cooling, or open windows, the pattern may be interrupted or completely disrupted.

2.a)

Use this moment to ask the students how they visualize the molecules of the perfume moving across the room. They should remember the kinetic molecular theory of how gases move – fast-moving particles with many, many collisions before traversing the room.

CHAPTER 5

NOTES

_____

_____

_____

_____

_____

Compare the student guesses with the actual time elapsed and discuss any anomalies, such as a student in back smelling the perfume before a student in front.

3.a)

Ask the students to use only one gas to represent air, for example, nitrogen molecules. The nitrogen molecules should be drawn larger than the helium atoms. Since nitrogen moves more slowly at a given temperature, the arrows representing its direction and speed should be shorter. The directional arrows for both gases should be randomly distributed in all directions.

4.

One type of sandwich bag will hold about 0.85 L of gas. You should measure the volume of your sandwich bags in advance and insert that value into their calculations. It is important that the bag not burst its seal so the students should only use the calculated amounts of reagents, not more.

5.a-b)

Students should be quite adept at writing an equation and making certain that it is balanced.

5.c)

At STP, it will take $\frac{0.85 \text{ L}}{22.4 \text{ L/mol}} = 0.038$ mol H_2 gas.

5.d)

Since 1 mole of zinc will generate 1 mole of H_2 gas, the moles of zinc required is

0.038 mol $H_2 \times \frac{1 \text{ mol zinc}}{1 \text{ mol } H_2} = 0.038$ mol of zinc

5.e)

0.038 mol zinc $\times 65.4$ g/mol = 2.5 g of zinc will be needed.

CHEM TIP

If desired, here is the correction for temperature, assuming the classroom is at 22°C:

At 1 atm and 295 K, 1 mol of gas has a volume of $\frac{V_1}{T_1} = \frac{V_2}{T_2}$ and solving for V_2,

$$V_2 = \frac{V_1 T_2}{T_1}$$

$V_2 = 22.4$ L $\times$ 298 K/273 K = 24.2 L

Under conditions of 1 atm and 295 K, it will take 0.85 L/24.2 L/mol = 0.035 mol H_2 gas.

Since 1 mole of zinc produces 1 mole of H_2, then 0.035 mol zinc will produce 0.035 mol H_2.

0.035 mol Zn $\times$ 65.4 g/mol = 2.30 g Zn are required to inflate a 0.85 L bag at 295 K.

Under these conditions, 0.85 L of H_2 can be generated from 2.30 g of zinc and 70 mL of 1 M HCl. Have the students use 100 mL of HCl to drive the reaction to completion and to make zinc the limiting reagent.

6.a-b)

Students should be quite adept at writing an equation and making certain that it is balanced.

$NaHCO_3 + HC_2H_3O_2 \longrightarrow$
$NaC_2H_3O_2 + H_2O + CO_2$

6.c)

At STP, it will take
0.85 L/22.4 L/mol = 0.038 mol CO_2 gas.

Since 1 mole $NaHCO_3$ generates 1 mole of CO_2 gas, 0.038 mole $NaHCO_3$ are needed.

0.038 mol $NaHCO_3 \times$ 84.0 g/mol = 3.2 g $NaHCO_3$ will be needed.

CHEM TIP

If desired, here is the correction for temperature, assuming the classroom is at 22°C:

At 1 atm and 295 K, 1 mol of gas has a volume of $\frac{V_1}{T_1} = \frac{V_2}{T_2}$ and solving for V_2,

$$V_2 = \frac{V_1 T_2}{T_1}$$

$V_2 = 22.4$ L $\times$ 298 K/273 K = 24.2 L

Under conditions of 1 atm and 295 K, it will take 0.85 L/24.2 L/mol = 0.035 mol CO_2 gas.

Since 1 mole of $NaHCO_3$ produces 1 mole of CO_2, then 0.035 mol $NaHCO_3$ will produce 0.035 mol CO_2.

0.035 mol $NaHCO_3 \times$ 84.0 g/mol = 2.94 g $NaHCO_3$ are required to inflate a 0.85 L bag at 295 K.

Under these conditions, 0.85 L of CO_2 can be generated from 2.9 g of $NaHCO_3$ and 35 mL of 1 M $HC_2H_3O_2$ (acetic acid, vinegar). Have the students use 50 mL of 1 M $HC_2H_3O_2$ to drive the reaction to completion and to make $NaHCO_3$ the limiting reagent.

You will need to help students think through what they are being asked to calculate. Help them recall that in the previous section they found that 1 mole of any gas occupies 22.4 L at STP. Since room conditions are not STP, they will need to determine the volume of 1 mole under room conditions.

For the most part, students can assume that room conditions would be 1 atm of pressure and about 22°C. So, they will need to use the volume – temperature relationship (Charles's law) they learned in *Section 4* to determine the volume of 1 mole of a gas under room conditions.

3. Dry air is composed of 79% nitrogen, 20% oxygen, 1% argon, 0.3% carbon dioxide, and trace amounts of other elements.

a) Draw pictures of the internal views of two latex balloons. One balloon is filled with pure helium (He) and one is filled with air from your breath. Your pictures should show the size of the molecules as well as arrows depicting the speed and direction of the particles. The greater speeds will be represented by the longer arrows.

4. You are going to examine two gases under identical conditions to help you understand what might be happening in the balloons. You will use sandwich-sized plastic bags to represent the balloons. Before beginning, you must determine the amounts of chemicals required to fill the plastic bags with gas.

5. In one plastic bag, you will generate H_2 by reacting Zn with HCl (hydrochloric acid).

a) In your *Active Chemistry* log, write down the balanced equation for reacting Zn and HCl.

$Zn_{(s)} + 2HCl_{(aq)} \rightarrow ZnCl_{2(aq)} + H_{2(g)}$

b) Show that this equation is balanced.

c) If you wish to fill the plastic bag with 0.85 L of H_2 gas, you will need to calculate the amount of zinc that will be necessary to do this. (Too much gas could burst the bag.) Since 1 mol of H_2 fills a volume of 22.4 L, calculate how many moles of H_2 will be required to fill a volume of 0.85 L.

d) Since the mole ratio in the reaction shows that 1 mol of Zn produces 1 mol of H_2, write

down the number of moles of Zn that will be required to create the number of moles of H_2 that will fill the volume of 0.85 L.

e) Since 1 mol of zinc is 65.4 g (see the atomic mass on the periodic table), determine the mass of zinc to add to the HCl to produce the volume of 0.85 L of gas. You can also determine the required mass of HCl, but that is not necessary. If you have extra HCl, then the reaction will be limited by the amount of zinc. Zinc is called the limiting reactant. Record the amount of zinc needed to add to the HCl to produce the volume of 0.85 L of gas.

6. In the other plastic bag, you will generate CO_2 by reacting $NaHCO_3$ (baking soda) with CH_3COOH (vinegar).

a) In your *Active Chemistry* log, write down the balanced equation for reacting $NaHCO_3$ and vinegar (CH_3COOH).

$NaHCO_{3(s)} + CH_3COOH_{(aq)} \rightarrow CO_{2(g)} + H_2O_{(l)} + NaC_2H_3O_{2(aq)}$

b) Show that the equation is balanced.

c) Since you wish to fill the plastic bag with 0.85 L of CO_2 gas, calculate the amount of baking soda that will be necessary to do this.

7. Have your teacher approve your calculations. Set up your labeled plastic bags, and generate the different gases in each. Then measure the circumference of each bag.

a) Record the circumference in your *Active Chemistry* log.

8. Dispose of the materials as directed by your teacher. Clean up your workstation. Rinse and save zinc for future use.

Safety goggles and a lab apron must be worn *at all times* in a chemistry lab.

Hydrogen gas is very flammable. Keep the bag away from sparks or a flame.

Hydrochloric acid is corrosive. Handle with caution.

Wash your hands and arms thoroughly after the investigation.

7.a)

Using a flexible tape measure will allow greater ease in measuring the circumference of the baggie in cm. (An alternative would be to use string and wrap it around the baggie, then measure it on a ruler or meter stick.)

8.

Make sure to let students know of any particular disposal needs that may be specific to your lab.

$$\frac{V_1}{T_1} = \frac{V_2}{T_2}$$

$$\frac{V_2}{298 \text{ K}}$$

22.4 L/273 K =

$V_2 = 24.5$ L

Students can now use the molar relationship from the balanced equation to determine how much $NaHCO_3$ and Zn they will need to use to fill their baggie.

Instruct students to use 50 mL of vinegar, which will be in excess. An excess of HCl is about 75 mL. Liquids should

be placed in the baggies first, followed by the solids at which time the bag should be sealed immediately.

You might provide an incentive for working through these calculations by offering a "prize" to the group who can get their baggie inflated the most without bursting. However, bursting bags may be messy and will certainly slow the class down.

9.a)

Have the students make observations and take measurements daily.

10.a)

Refer to the pre-lab discussion, where the class generated a list of ideas that might affect how long a balloon (and in this case a baggie) will stay inflated and which gas would deflate the quickest.

10.b)

Help students use a process of elimination to determine that the only thing different in the baggie is the size of the molecules.

Chem Talk

The kinetic molecular theory of gases is reviewed in depth and then the topic of diffusion is introduced. Diffusion rates are shown to be related to the kinetic energy of the gas particles and then to molar mass. Finally, Graham's law of effusion is discussed in the context of two balloons inflated with two different gases. It is shown mathematically that the relative rates of effusion out of the balloon is related to the square root of the ratio of the molar masses of the two gases.

 Ideal Toy

9. Allow the bags to sit for several days.

a) Record your observations and new circumference measurements in your *Active Chemistry* log each day.

10. Your teacher may have generated the gases in the balloons a few days earlier so that you can compare the volume of the balloons after several days. A pair of balloons is shown in the diagram, so that you can complete this investigation rather than halt everything for the days it may take for your balloons to change.

a) Describe the differences between the gases you generated that might account for the differences you observe in the two models.

b) How could these differences explain your observations?

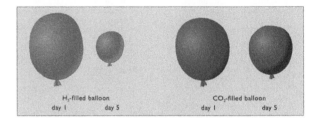

H_2-filled balloon
day 1   day 5

CO_2-filled balloon
day 1   day 5

Chem Talk

MOLECULAR SIZE AND MOLECULAR MOTION OF GASES

Kinetic Molecular Model of Gases

Scientists have adopted the following model for gases:

- Gases consist of tiny particles (atoms or molecules) that are separated by relatively large distances. For water, the particles are about 1000 times further apart in the gas phase than in the liquid phase.

- Gas molecules are in constant, random motion and travel in a straight line between collisions. They do collide frequently with other gas molecules and with the walls of their container. Gas pressure is related to the sum of all of these collisions with the walls during a given time.

- At any given temperature (Kelvin scale), the average kinetic energy of all the molecules of gas is directly proportional to that temperature. However, some of the molecules will be moving faster than the average, some slower.

• At the same temperature, all gases have the same average kinetic energy in their molecules. As the temperature increases, so do the average velocities and kinetic energies of the molecules.

Dalton's Law of Partial Pressures

Because gas molecules are so far apart, all gases behave the same way at ordinary temperatures. This is stated by the kinetic molecular model of gases, in which the properties of gases are discussed and, regardless of the gas in question, the properties are the same.

John Dalton recognized this behavior and, in 1801, proposed that in a mixture of gases, such as air, the total pressure exerted by the gas mixture can be found by adding the pressures exerted by each of the gases in the mixture. Mathematically, this is expressed as:

$$P_{total} = P_1 + P_2 + P_3 + \ldots\ldots$$

Example: For air, $P_{total} = P_{nitrogen} + P_{oxygen} + P_{argon} + \ldots = 760$ mm Hg at standard conditions.

Diffusion

When the perfume or other odors left the bottle and traveled about the room, you observed that the students closest to the teacher smelled the perfume first. **Diffusion** is the spontaneous mixing of one gas (or liquid) with another that occurs because of the random movement of the molecules. This occurs with perfumes because the fragrant gaseous molecules move freely through the widely spaced air molecules to reach your nose. (In typical classrooms, with radiators, air conditioners, open windows, students moving around, etc., convection currents are much more important in distributing gases than diffusion.) The process of diffusion is complete when the molecules of the gases are evenly spread within the room. Diffusion is purely a physical phenomenon. The rate of diffusion has to do with the speed of the gas molecules. All gases at the same temperature have the same average kinetic energy. However, gases with a large molar mass have slow speeds while gases with small molar mass have fast speeds. The velocity (v) of a gas molecule is related to its kinetic energy (KE):

$$KE = \frac{1}{2}mv^2$$

where m is the mass of the molecule.

Since two gases have the same kinetic energy, you can derive the relationship from the above equation. Assume that you have a

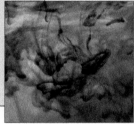

Chem Words

diffusion: the spontaneous mixing of one gas (or liquid) with another that occurs because of the random movement of the molecules.

439

CHAPTER 5

Ideal Toy

gas with a large mass, m_L and one with a small mass, m_S. Since their kinetic energies are equal:

$$\tfrac{1}{2}m_L v^2_L = \tfrac{1}{2}m_S v^2_S$$

$$\frac{v_L}{v_S} = \sqrt{\frac{m_S}{m_L}}$$

The velocity of large-mass gases is smaller than the velocity of small-mass gases and its diffusion is also slower. For example, if the ratio of the masses of the gases is 1:9, then the ratio of speeds will be 1:3. If you make the mass of the particles nine times larger, the speed decreases by a factor of 3.

Effusion

When the balloon deflated over time, it was because the interior gas was leaking through tiny openings in the balloon latex. These holes in the material are molecular in size, and much, much smaller than a pin puncture would be. The **effusion** of a gas is its movement through tiny holes from a region of higher pressure (inside the balloon) to a region of lower pressure (outside the balloon). Even though the hole in the latex that they escape from is microscopic, it is still much larger than either of the gas molecules. A smaller molecule, such as H_2, effuses faster than a larger molecule, such as CO_2. In addition, even though the two kinds of gas molecules have the same kinetic energy at the same temperatures, the hydrogen has less mass, which gives it greater speed. The major reason that hydrogen effuses faster than carbon dioxide is that it strikes the inner surface of the balloon more frequently, giving it a better chance of hitting one of those tiny holes.

A Scottish scientist, Thomas Graham (1805–1869), studied the rates at which various gases effused through a tiny hole. He found that the higher the density of a gas (greater mass), the more slowly it effuses through a hole. He was able to develop a mathematical expression for the effusion of gases now called **Graham's law of effusion**. It is very similar to the expression for diffusion and is usually used to compare two different gases.

Graham's law states that the rate of effusion of a gas is inversely proportional to the square root of the density of the gas. Since equal volumes of gas at the same temperature and pressure contain equal numbers of gas molecules, the rate of effusion is also inversely proportional to the square root of the molar mass of the gas. The gas with the lowest molar mass effuses the fastest.

Chem Words

effusion: the movement of a gas through an extremely tiny opening into a region of lower pressure.

Graham's law of effusion: a law that states that the rate of escape of a gas from a container through a pinhole (effusion) is inversely proportional to the square root of the molar mass of the gas.

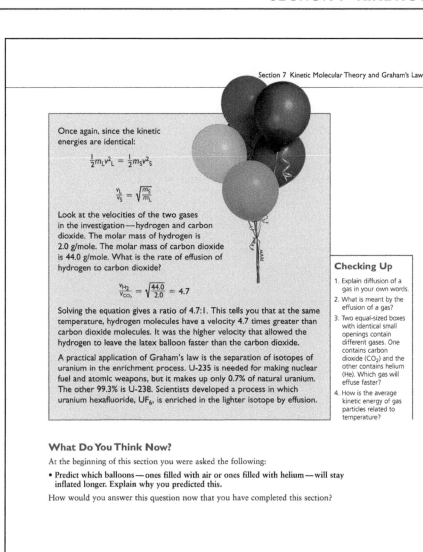

Once again, since the kinetic energies are identical:

$$\frac{1}{2}m_L v^2_L = \frac{1}{2}m_S v^2_S$$

$$\frac{v_L}{v_S} = \sqrt{\frac{m_S}{m_L}}$$

Look at the velocities of the two gases in the investigation—hydrogen and carbon dioxide. The molar mass of hydrogen is 2.0 g/mole. The molar mass of carbon dioxide is 44.0 g/mole. What is the rate of effusion of hydrogen to carbon dioxide?

$$\frac{v_{H_2}}{v_{CO_2}} = \sqrt{\frac{44.0}{2.0}} = 4.7$$

Solving the equation gives a ratio of 4.7:1. This tells you that at the same temperature, hydrogen molecules have a velocity 4.7 times greater than carbon dioxide molecules. It was the higher velocity that allowed the hydrogen to leave the latex balloon faster than the carbon dioxide.

A practical application of Graham's law is the separation of isotopes of uranium in the enrichment process. U-235 is needed for making nuclear fuel and atomic weapons, but it makes up only 0.7% of natural uranium. The other 99.3% is U-238. Scientists developed a process in which uranium hexafluoride, UF_6, is enriched in the lighter isotope by effusion.

Checking Up

1. Explain diffusion of a gas in your own words.
2. What is meant by the effusion of a gas?
3. Two equal-sized boxes with identical small openings contain different gases. One contains carbon dioxide (CO_2) and the other contains helium (He). Which gas will effuse faster?
4. How is the average kinetic energy of gas particles related to temperature?

What Do You Think Now?

At the beginning of this section you were asked the following:

• Predict which balloons—ones filled with air or ones filled with helium—will stay inflated longer. Explain why you predicted this.

How would you answer this question now that you have completed this section?

4.

Temperature is a direct measurement of the average kinetic energy of gas particles. At a given temperature, all gases have the same kinetic energy. Particles with larger molar mass will have correspondingly lower velocities according to the equation, $KE = \frac{1}{2}mv$.

What Do You Think Now?

Have students calculate effusion ratio for He and N_2 (since air is mostly N_2) and discuss the significance of the ratio. Discuss their predictions with what the calculations show and explain any discrepancies.

In returning to the *What Do You See?* illustration, ask the students to predict which gas may be Gas A, and which gas may be Gas B.

Checking Up

1.

Student answers to a request that they express their understanding of diffusion will vary. Answers should include a mention of how gases move (kinetic molecular theory) and how the rate of diffusion (velocity) is related to the molar mass of the gas at a given temperature.

2.

Effusion of a gas is how a gas leaves a closed container through a hole into a vacuum. In real terms, it is the loss of gas particles through small holes in a membrane, such as a balloon.

3.

According to Graham's law of effusion, helium will effuse faster than carbon dioxide because it has a smaller molar mass.

Reflecting on the Section and the Challenge

Although there are no questions in this section for students to answer or to use for discussion, this is an important opportunity to consider the section with respect to the *Chapter Challenge*. Students now know both Graham's law of diffusion and law of effusion. This knowledge can be used in the design and the explanation of their toy.

Ideal Toy

Chem Essential Questions

What does it mean?

Chemistry explains a *macroscopic* phenomenon (what you observe) with a description of what happens at the *nanoscopic* level (atoms and molecules) using *symbolic* structures as a way to communicate. Complete the chart below in your *Active Chemistry* log.

MACRO	NANO	SYMBOLIC
What visual evidence do you have that supports Graham's Law of Effusion?	Describe what is happening at the nanoscopic level when two gases of different masses are escaping from tiny holes in their containers.	Use an equation to represent Graham's law of effusion.

How do you know?

Using the molar mass of H_2 of 2.0 g and an approximation of the molar mass of air to be 28.6 g, what is the rate of effusion of H_2 to air? From this information, what would you predict for the "leak rate" of air-filled and hydrogen-filled balloons?

Why do you believe?

A tennis ball contains a mixture of gases. Why does a tennis ball lose its bounce over time?

Why should you care?

If your toy uses a gas to propel or otherwise support the way it is used, what considerations will you need to keep in mind as you design it? If the toy must contain a constant amount of some gas, will choosing the heaviest gas available always be the best decision? Explain your answer using examples to support your thoughts.

Reflecting on the Section and the Challenge

In this section you explored the effect of gas size on effusion rates. You found that the more massive the gas, the slower its rate of effusion. For example, H_2 has a molar mass of 2; He has a molar mass of 4; and N_2 has a molar mass of 28. Using Graham's law, you would predict that H_2 would effuse at a faster rate than helium or nitrogen.

You have probably seen the effect of mass on effusion with party balloons lots of times, but had never really tested what might be occurring. You might apply your new knowledge of what is occurring to the toy model your team is proposing. Your proposal will have to explain the advantages and disadvantages of using one particular gas over another. The use of different gases might impact the behavior of your toy. Consider how you could make that knowledge work to your advantage in the toy design.

Active Chemistry

442

Chem Essential Questions

What does it mean?

MACRO — The bag filled with hydrogen gas deflated more quickly than the bag filled with carbon dioxide gas.

NANO — In each bag, the gas molecules randomly hit the walls and keep the bag inflated. However, the smaller molecule, H_2, is moving faster and hits the walls and the holes more often.

SYMBOLIC — Rate of Effusion α $1/(\text{molar mass})^{1/2}$

How do you know?

The relative rate of effusion of hydrogen to air is 3.8 times as fast. The hydrogen balloon will deflate almost four times as fast as the air-filled balloon.

Why do you believe?

The interior gases in a tennis ball effuse out over time and leave it in a less inflated state with less "bounce."

Why should you care?

Some of the considerations that the students should keep in mind are the volumes and pressures involved, as well as the temperature if there are large changes involved. Safety, of course, is always at the top of the list. If the gas is stored in a container before release, its rate of effusions and thus its molecular mass, must be considered.

If the amount of gas must be constant, as in a balloon, a heavy gas will effuse more slowly and might be considered. However, if buoyancy is a consideration, a heavy gas will not work well.

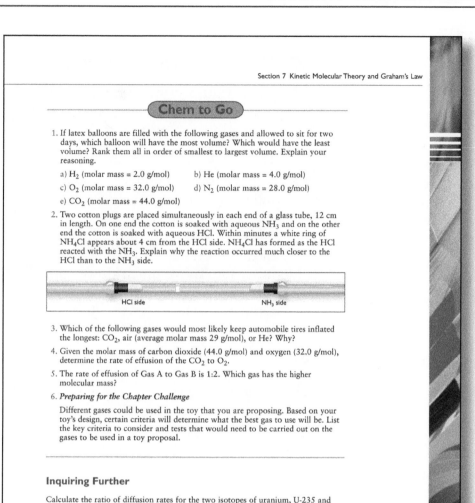

Chem to Go

1. If latex balloons are filled with the following gases and allowed to sit for two days, which balloon will have the most volume? Which would have the least volume? Rank them all in order of smallest to largest volume. Explain your reasoning.

   a) H_2 (molar mass = 2.0 g/mol)   b) He (molar mass = 4.0 g/mol)

   c) O_2 (molar mass = 32.0 g/mol)   d) N_2 (molar mass = 28.0 g/mol)

   e) CO_2 (molar mass = 44.0 g/mol)

2. Two cotton plugs are placed simultaneously in each end of a glass tube, 12 cm in length. On one end the cotton is soaked with aqueous NH_3 and on the other end the cotton is soaked with aqueous HCl. Within minutes a white ring of NH_4Cl appears about 4 cm from the HCl side. NH_4Cl has formed as the HCl reacted with the NH_3. Explain why the reaction occurred much closer to the HCl than to the NH_3 side.

   HCl side NH_3 side

3. Which of the following gases would most likely keep automobile tires inflated the longest: CO_2, air (average molar mass 29 g/mol), or He? Why?

4. Given the molar mass of carbon dioxide (44.0 g/mol) and oxygen (32.0 g/mol), determine the rate of effusion of the CO_2 to O_2.

5. The rate of effusion of Gas A to Gas B is 1:2. Which gas has the higher molecular mass?

6. *Preparing for the Chapter Challenge*

   Different gases could be used in the toy that you are proposing. Based on your toy's design, certain criteria will determine what the best gas to use will be. List the key criteria to consider and tests that would need to be carried out on the gases to be used in a toy proposal.

Inquiring Further

Calculate the ratio of diffusion rates for the two isotopes of uranium, U-235 and U-238. At slightly elevated temperatures (greater than 57°C and 1 atm), uranium hexafluoride is a gas.

443

Chem to Go

1.

Least volume – a) hydrogen, next b) helium, next d) nitrogen, then c) oxygen, and finally e) carbon dioxide – most volume.

Since carbon dioxide is the most massive of these gases, it would effuse the slowest. Since hydrogen is the least massive, it would effuse the quickest. The other gases would be somewhere in between, depending on their molar mass.

2.

Students should predict that the ammonia molecule is less massive than hydrogen chloride; therefore it diffused more quickly across the tube before it met the HCl molecules and reacted. If students are familiar with calculating molar mass, then they should be able to explain using differences in molar mass. (HCl is 36.5 g/mol and NH_3 is 17 g/mol.)

3.

Theoretically, it would be carbon dioxide because it has more massive molecules. It would effuse out of the tire at a slower rate.

4.

$$\frac{v_{CO_2}}{v_{O_2}} = \sqrt{\frac{32.0 \text{ g/mol}}{44.0 \text{ g/mol}}} = 0.85$$

Carbon dioxide would effuse about 0.85 times slower than oxygen.

5.

Gas A has the higher molecular weight, because it effuses $\frac{1}{2}$ as quickly as Gas B.

6.

Preparing for the Chapter Challenge

Students' answers will vary but should include considerations of molecular weight and effusion rates. Safety is also an important consideration.

Inquiring Further

Using the equation for the diffusion ratio of two gases, the problem sets up as:

$$\frac{v_{235}}{v_{238}} = (m_{238}/m_{235})^{1/2}$$

The mass of UF_6 for the U-235 isotope is 349.0 g/mol and the mass of UF_6 for the U-238 isotope is 352.0 g/mol.

$$\frac{v_{235}}{v_{238}} = (352/349)^{1/2} = 1.004,$$

or the U-235 hexafluoride will diffuse 1.004 times as fast as the U-238 hexafluoride.

CHAPTER 5

SECTION 7 – QUIZ

5-7a	Blackline Master

1. In the front of a room where the air is completely still, you open two bottles of different gases. One has a very pleasant odor, the other stinks. People in the back of the room smell the pleasant odor first, but the stinky gas takes much longer. What conclusion can you draw about the two gases?

2. A balloon filled with which of the following gases would stay inflated the longest? Explain. He (molar mass = 4.0 g/mol); CO_2 (molar mass = 44.0 g/mol); N_2 (molar mass = 28.0 g/mol)

3. Determine the rate of effusion of helium to carbon dioxide. He (molar mass = 4.0 g/mol); CO_2 (molar mass = 44.0 g/mol)

    a) 120   b) 3.3

    c) 0.30   d) 0.0082

4. The rate of effusion of Gas A to Gas B is 2:1. Which gas has the higher molecular mass?

    a) Gas A

    b) Gas B

    c) neither, they are the same

5. If the molecular mass of Gas A is 36.0 g/mol, determine the molecular mass of Gas B (given that the rate of effusion of Gas A to Gas B is 2:1).

    a) 9.00 g/mol   b) 25.5 g/mol

    c) 50.9 g/mol   d) 144 g/mol

SECTION 7 – QUIZ ANSWERS

❶ Since it diffuses more rapidly, the gas that has the pleasant odor must have a lower molar mass than the one that stinks.

❷ The one filled with CO_2 would stay inflated the longest because it is the heaviest molecule. The rate of effusion is dependent on the mass of the molecules. More massive molecules move much slower than less massive ones (at the same temperature).

❸ b) 3.3

❹ b) Gas B

❺ d) 144 g/mol

NOTES

SECTION 8
Properties of Polymers and Plastics

Section Overview

This section has three parts. In Part A, students explore the properties of a thermoplastic polymer by making a small object and allowing it to harden by cooling. In Part B, students learn to make a thermosetting polymer by mixing the ingredients. They create another object and examine the differences between that and the object made from the thermoplastic polymer. Finally, in Part C, students identify two important criteria for the plastic needed for their toy, and then design tests to determine which plastic best fits those criteria.

Background Information

Plastics are polymers. A polymer is a chain of monomers. Monomers are molecules composed of carbon, hydrogen and oxygen, and can have other elements attached, such as silicon. Each "mer" is "polymerized," or bonded together with other "mers," to form the polymer. This is called polymerization and is much like linking paper clips together into one long chain.

The polymers that exist in nature have been used by humans in many ways. Many of them can be modified to create useful products. Celluloid and vulcanized rubber are examples of modified natural polymers, and amber, which is hardened tree sap, is often used to make jewelry.

Synthetic polymers such as rayon that imitate the construction of natural polymers are commonly manufactured. The need for synthetic polymers began during World War II, when natural resources were scarce. Nylon, acrylics and polyethylene were invented to replace latex, wool and silk. Since that time, the manufacture of synthetic polymers has evolved into one of the fastest-growing industries in the world.

The Structure of Polymers

Hydrocarbons are the principal backbone of almost all polymers. They are simply chains of carbons with hydrogen atoms branching off of them. They can be arranged in a variety of ways and have other atoms added on in various places to make an incredibly large assortment of polymers. One of the simplest polymers is polyethylene, $(C_2H_4)_n$, the monomer of which is two carbons double-bonded with two hydrogens bonded to each carbon:

Many polymers only contain carbon and hydrogen, such as polystyrene and polypropylene, but others can contain other elements. An example is polyvinyl chloride, PVC, which contains carbon, hydrogen and chlorine. Other nonmetals and metalloids (forming inorganic polymers) can also be added to hydrocarbons to make a variety of polymers.

Characteristics of Polymers

Polymers can be structured in many ways, which give them distinct physical properties. Polymer chains can be arranged in a variety of ways if the polymerization process is controlled and manipulated. Amorphous polymers can result, which appear transparent, or crystalline arrangements can result, which would show up as various degrees of opaqueness. Other characteristics can be created with engineering. Fillers, reinforcements and other additives can make polymers useful for a variety of purposes.

There are two main types of polymers: thermoplastics and thermosets. Thermoplastic polymers have a structure that allows for melting and reshaping, and are ideal for recycling. Their unlinked structure allows for this:

Thermoset polymers cannot be melted and reshaped due to their linked structure:

Some other characteristics of polymers include resistance to chemicals. This makes them useful as containers for household and industrial chemicals. They are also useful as insulators of heat and electricity. Plastics are often found around wires, covering handles of pots and pans, in microwave cookware and as fibers in winter coats. Polymers are also strong, lightweight, and can be used as additives to make other materials more versatile.

The characteristics of thermoplastic polymers also make them highly recyclable. There are many ways in which they can be recycled. Not only can they be melted and reused for similar purposes, but they can be melded with new plastics, used for outdoor items that would normally be constructed of wood, and some can even be burned for heat energy. The recycling of plastics is environmentally sound and cost-effective.

CHAPTER 5

LEARNING OUTCOMES

LEARNING OUTCOMES	LOCATION IN SECTION	EVIDENCE OF UNDERSTANDING
Distinguish between thermoset and thermoplastic polymers.	*Investigate* Parts A-B *Chem Talk,* *Checking Up* Question 2 *Chem to Go* Questions 1– 2	Answers to questions in the *Investigate* section are similar to those listed in this *Teacher's Edition*. Answers match those listed in this *Teacher's Edition*.
Test materials for product design.	*Investigate* Part C	Students' designs for testing plastics are reasonable. Answers are similar to those in this *Teacher's Edition*.

NOTES

_____

_____

_____

_____

_____

_____

_____

_____

Section 8
Materials, Chemicals, Preparation, and Safety

("per Group" quantity is based on group size of 4 students)

Materials and Equipment

Materials (and Equipment)	Quantity per Group (4 students)
Beakers, 600 mL	1
Hot plate	1
Wire gauze squares for hot plate	2
Rubber gloves (pair)	4
Thermoplastic strips	1 lb
Crucible tongs	1
Materials (and Equipment)	**Quantity per Class**
Roll of paper towels	1
Various items to mold with, such as plastic toys, kitchen utensils, etc. (enough for each group to have a few if needed)	
Stick of epoxy putty	1

Chemicals

Chemicals	Quantity per Class (24 students)
Isopropyl (rubbing) alcohol	100 mL

Teacher Preparation

Cut each epoxy putty stick into approximately 2 cm strips.

Safety Requirements

- Goggles and aprons are required in the laboratory area.

- Remind students that the putties will harden on skin or counters, so they should use the gloves and paper towels provided.

- Isopropyl alcohol is flammable. Do not use near flames or place paper soaked in it into the trash. Allow the alcohol to evaporate in a fume hood. Plastic and epoxy putty can be put into the trash.

- Wash arms and hands before leaving the laboratory area.

NOTES

Meeting the Needs of All Students
Differentiated Instruction
Augmentation and Accommodations

LEARNING ISSUE	REFERENCE	AUGMENTATION AND ACCOMMODATIONS
Describing observations Writing comparisons	*Investigate* Parts A-B	**Augmentation** • In Part A, use the think-pair-share procedure to elicit from students a list of words that would appropriately describe their observations. Remind the class that precise scientific writing includes specific terms. • Help students structure their comparisons in Part B. Find out beforehand if there is a structure for writing comparisons taught in their English or Social Studies classes that can be applied here. If not, teach students to refer to the paragraph they wrote describing their observations in Part A as a structure for their comparisons in Part B. For each observation about thermoplastic polymers in Part A, they should write a sentence or two which compares that characteristic with the thermoset polymers in Part B. Remind students to clearly refer to the terms "thermoset" and "thermoplastic" as they use them in Part B. Have students make a T-chart which includes their word lists. • Encourage students to see that Parts A and B are like the first two paragraphs of a comparison essay in which they describe one situation, compare it to another, and finally, analyze and apply their observations. Part C is the analysis. Explain that analysis includes their opinions based on observable facts.
Identifying and evaluating desirable criteria of a plastic toy Organizing data	*Investigate* Part C	**Augmentation** • Ask students to identify each possible characteristic in the reading and set up a table their group can use to determine which characteristics are important and how they could test for them. The following table is an example: <table><tr><td>Characteristic</td><td>Possible importance in a toy</td><td>Ways to test for this characteristic</td></tr><tr><td>Strength</td><td></td><td></td></tr><tr><td>Impact</td><td></td><td></td></tr><tr><td>Bendable</td><td></td><td></td></tr><tr><td>Durability</td><td></td><td></td></tr><tr><td>Other?</td><td></td><td></td></tr></table> **Accommodations** • Give students this table to use.

NOTES

_____

_____

_____

_____

_____

LEARNING ISSUE	REFERENCE	AUGMENTATION AND ACCOMMODATIONS
Distinguishing characteristics of plastics and polymers Taking good notes from a reading Building vocabulary	*Chem Talk*	**Augmentation** • The *Chem Talk* section explains the relationships among plastics, polymers and types of polymers. Unless the information is processed further, students may read it without clearly understanding. Ask them to organize notes on this passage using one of the differentiated methods listed below. Students will need models of each type. Create three models using types of fruit instead of polymers to teach students about the structures. Elicit comments about the advantages and disadvantages of each. Point out that different information-processing structures appeal to different types of learners: • Students could make a standard outline where the topics and indentations show the relationships among the terms. • Students could make a circle diagram showing the relationships. This type of graphic organizer may be unfamiliar to students, but may effectively show the relationships in this particular reading. It would begin with a big circle labeled "plastics." Within the boundaries of the original circle would be three non-overlapping circles labeled "plastic," "cellulose" and "starches." This illustrates the concept in the second paragraph of *Chem Talk* that all plastics are polymers, but not all polymers are plastics. At the next level, inside the polymer circle would be circles labeled "thermoset" and "thermoplastic." Inside the thermoplastic circle would be high and low density polyethylene. • Students could also make a graphic organizer. An example appears below: 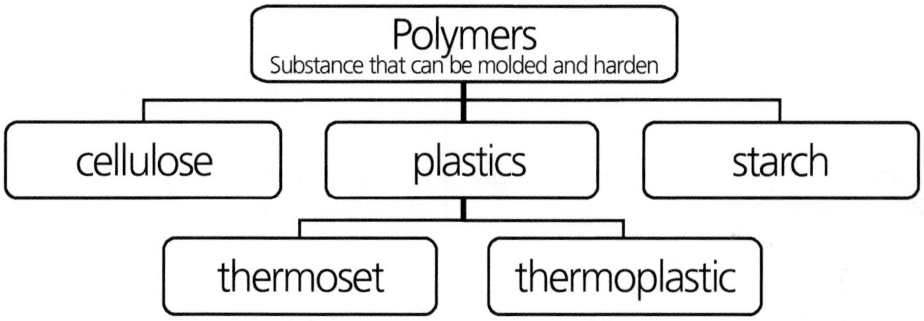

NOTES

_____

_____

_____

_____

_____

_____

_____

_____

Strategies for Students with Limited English Language Proficiency

LEARNING ISSUE	REFERENCE	AUGMENTATIONS
Background knowledge	*What Do You Think?*	Make sure students have background knowledge of all of the objects listed in the first part of this section. Pictures or examples will help build background knowledge. Check for understanding of the use of the word "*properties*."
Vocabulary Following directions	*Investigate*	Pair students with partners as a support for following directions. Point out where questions are in the steps of the *Investigate*. Make sure students understand the use of "*shape*" and "*mold*" as verbs. Check for understanding of the word "*component*" in Step 3 of Part A. In Step 5.b) of Part B, be specific on how they are to "*describe*." When students are asked to "*identify*" in Step 2 of Part C, they may need specific directions.
Background knowledge Vocabulary Comprehending text	*Chem Talk*	Review meaning of the word "*synthetic*" and give examples. Explain the term "*patent*."
Comprehension	*What Do You Think Now?*	Describe for students how to approach this task when there are several questions asked at once. Explain the use of the word "*properties*" in this context.
Background knowledge Vocabulary Comprehending text	*Chem Essential Questions*	The word "*derived*" may not be in students' expressive vocabulary and may deserve some attention. Examples of derivations of words from this text might build background knowledge and language development.
Comprehension Vocabulary	*Chem to Go*	Check for understanding of those questions that begin with the word "*was.*"
Application Comprehension Research skills	*Inquiring Further*	Ensure that students are familiar with the word "*slime.*" Help with pronunciation of the word "*gluep.*" Explain what it means to "*determine*" something.
Comprehension Application	*Chem You Learned*	Have students work in small groups to discuss aspects of these items to check for oral language and comprehension.

NOTES

_____

_____

_____

_____

_____

_____

_____

NOTES

CHAPTER 5

Section 8
Teaching Suggestions and Sample Answers

What Do You See?

The illustration featured on the opening page is designed to capture students' attention and focus their interest on the upcoming section. There could be any number of responses to the question, *What Do You See?*. Whereas some students may only address what is evident on a surface level, others may try to interpret the intent of the artist. All responses are valid and should be acknowledged as such. After the section is completed, you may wish to return to the illustration so students have a chance to reassess the significance of the illustration and recognize how they have progressed in content understanding and knowledge.

You can ask students if they can think of a "story" that connects the two illustrations.

Ideal Toy

Section 8   Properties of Polymers and Plastics

What Do You See?

Learning Outcomes

In this section you will

* Distinguish between thermoset and thermoplastic plastics.
* Test materials for product design.

What Do You Think?

In 1909, Leo Baekeland developed the polymer, Bakelite. The polymer industry hasn't stopped growing since! The term "plastics" was introduced in the 1920s to describe these new materials that were being introduced. Here is a *partial* list of common items that contain polymers.

* 2-L soda bottles
* balloons
* carpet
* caulk
* cellophane tape
* coffee stirrers
* combs
* computers
* contact lenses
* credit cards
* disposable razors
* epoxy glue
* erasers
* foam cups

* foam rubber
* food wrap
* football helmet
* garbage bags
* guitar strings
* hairspray
* hockey puck
* insulation
* margarine tubs
* milk jugs
* non-stick coating
* paint
* pantyhose
* playground balls

* raincoat
* rubber bands
* sandwich bags
* shampoo bottles
* shoe laces
* slime
* snorkle and swim fins
* sunglasses
* tennis ball
* thread
* tires
* toothbrush
* umbrella
* vinyl car top

* What properties of plastics have made their use so widespread?

 a) Record your ideas about this question in your *Active Chemistry* log. Be prepared to discuss your responses with your small group and the class.

444

STUDENTS' PRIOR CONCEPTIONS

Many students will be unaware of the two categories of plastics and will be under the impression that all plastics are re-moldable and recyclable. This section provides an opportunity to discuss the differences between the two types and how molecular structure impacts the function of plastics. You might want to use paper clips in a demonstration of the different types of linkages between polymer chains.

It is likely that students will also be unaware of the array of natural polymers that exist. You may want to discuss proteins, starches, DNA, RNA,

cotton, flax, hemp fibers, silk, spider webs, etc. Discuss the definition of polymer and how these natural molecules fit the definition. This section also provides an opportunity to discuss petroleum distillates as sources of the raw materials for the production of many plastics. The increase in the amount of plastics in our trash and the waste-disposal issues it engenders is another area that might be discussed. If you are involved in a career component, you may want students to know that over half of the nation's chemists and chemical engineers work in polymer-related industries.

What Do You Think?

Guide students to consider the properties of plastics that make them so versatile. Compile a class list of these. Get them to speculate about the nature of the structure of plastics that results in such a range of diverse properties. Offer incentives for students to explore the costs of producing plastics vs. other types of materials (e.g., metals, composites, wood, etc.). This information will be beneficial as they begin to develop a cost analysis for their *Chapter Challenge* toy projects.

What Do You Think?
A CHEMIST'S RESPONSE

In a word, it is "versatility" that makes polymer use so widespread. Once a need is created and a purpose is defined, a new polymer can usually be designed to meet that purpose. Some of the variables that chemists have to work with in polymer engineering are: chain length, degree of cross-linking, monomers, mixture of monomers, composite materials, color and shape.

NOTES

_____

_____

_____

_____

_____

_____

_____

_____

_____

_____

_____

_____

_____

CHAPTER 5

Investigate

You may want to conduct the following demonstration before beginning this investigation in order to expand upon the class list of properties of plastics:

Boil 400 mL of water in a 600-mL beaker. Place a clear plastic cup (that is not made of styrene foam or recycle code No. 6 plastic) and the handle end of a kitchen tool (such as a spatula) into the boiling water and keep the water boiling for 2-3 minutes. Remove the cup with tongs and show that it can be molded into a new shape. Then remove the kitchen tool and demonstrate that the handle does not soften or bend. These are examples of the two types of polymers.

Part A: Thermoplastic Activity

Before beginning this part of the investigation, remind students that they should not make bracelets, rings or anything touch the skin from these polymers, since the plastic will harden and become very difficult to remove. Students must also be warned against putting any of the polymer material in their mouths, because it will stick to any metal (such as orthodontic braces). Provide rubbing alcohol (isopropyl alcohol) for cleaning hands after using the epoxy putty. Caution students that rubbing alcohol is flammable and *not* drinkable.

1.

You can save time by preheating the water. Provide beaker tongs or gloves for the students to protect their hands. The water does not necessarily have to be boiling as the polymer softens at 65-70°C.

2.

Alternatively, the entire piece can be submerged and removed with tongs.

3.

A variety of shapes and forms can be made using common kitchen equipment, such as a garlic press, strainer, cups, cookie cutters, etc.

4.

Cooling time will vary with the mass of the polymer. It can be softened again by heating in hot water.

5.

The polymer can be discarded in the trash.

Part B: Thermoset Activity

1.

There are many types of epoxy putty for various purposes. You may want to share this information with students in case any are interested in researching a specific type of polymer for their project.

2.

All epoxy putties are composed of two parts which must be mixed immediately before use.

3.

Caution the students not to make an object such as a ring or bracelet. Once the putty hardens, it may not come off easily.

4.

Most epoxy putties are made to stick to the surface of whatever they are applied to.

5.a)

The temperature increases as the putty hardens.

5.b)

Thermoplastics can be remolded by reheating while thermosetting polymers cannot.

5.c)

Thermoset polymers would be more desirable where strength and heat resistance are important. Thermoplastic would be more desirable where flexibility is an important consideration.

6.

The polymer can be discarded in the trash.

Section 8 Properties of Polymers and Plastics

Investigate

Part A: Thermoplastic Activity

1. Pour about 300 mL tap water into a 400 mL-beaker. Place the beaker on a hot plate. Turn on the hot plate and bring the water to a boil. Then turn off the hot plate.

2. Wearing gloves, hold one end of a strip of thermoplastic modeling material, and dip the other end into the hot water until it softens. Keep it away from the sides of the beaker. Remove it from the water. With wet gloved fingers, grasp the softened end. Dip the other end in the water until it is also softened.

3. Remove the strip from the water bath, and quickly mold the thermoplastic modeling material into a design of your own choosing. *Do not mold it on yourself as a bracelet or a ring as the final product could be difficult to remove!* You might mold it into

some component of the toy model your group is going to propose. If the polymer becomes too hard, dip it in hot water to soften it.

4. Let the material cool on the countertop.

5. Clean up your workstation and return all equipment as directed.

Part B: Thermoset Activity

1. Get a 2 cm piece of epoxy putty. Note that it is composed of two colored components.

2. Knead the putty until the two components are thoroughly mixed.

3. Quickly shape the putty into a design of your choosing. Again, you might want to shape it into something that you could use in your toy model.

4. Let the putty harden on a paper towel or piece of plastic bag. Do **not** let the putty harden on the countertop; it may be difficult to remove.

5. As the putty is hardening, test its temperature with your fingertips.

   a) Does the sample change temperature? Describe what you observe.

   b) Describe the difference between the thermoplastic and thermoset polymers.

   c) In what applications would a thermoset polymer be most desirable? Thermoplastic? Explain your reasoning.

6. Clean up your workstation.

Safety goggles and a lab apron must be worn *at all times* in a chemistry lab.

Report any broken, cracked, or chipped glassware to your teacher.

Hot plates may remain hot for some time after they are turned off.

Wash your hands and arms thoroughly after the investigation.

445

CHAPTER 5

Part C:
Testing Plastics to Determine Product Use

Because students may be using hammers, pendulums, or blunt-end darts, they should wear goggles at all times while conducting tests on plastics.

1.

Sources of plastics could include plastic bags of various types, old toys, old kitchen utensils, old radio or electronic casings, etc. Each group should consider what properties of plastic they need for their toy when determining what type of plastics to bring in for testing.

2.

Each group should identify two criteria to test – tensile strength, impact resistance, flexibility, heat resistance, etc.

3.

It is important for students to put together a workable procedure for their tests and to locate the necessary testing items – clamps, spring scales, hammers, etc.

4.

Check students' equipment and procedural plans before they begin testing.

4.a)

Students should justify their choice of plastic for their toy on the basis of their test results. Cost considerations should also be included in their justification.

5.

Set aside a specific amount of time for groups to share their findings. You might have each group report briefly on what they tested and what they found, so that all groups have access to the information gathered by the whole class.

Ideal Toy

Part C: Testing Plastics to Determine Product Use

1. Think carefully about the plastics that may be a part of your toy model. How will it be used, and what type of wear and tear could be expected on each part? How strong will the parts need to be? What type of impact might the parts be subjected to? How bendable will the parts need to be? What other conditions will be important in considering the durability and the quality of your toy? Brainstorm these questions with members of your group.

   a) Record your thoughts in your *Active Chemistry* log.

2. Identify two important criteria that will need to be considered for your toy model. Now, determine a way to test the types of plastic that you are considering, so that you can justify that choice on more than availability and costs. For example:

   • If strength of the plastic is important, then you will need to design a method to determine the strength of the material by measuring how large a constant force the plastic can withstand without breaking.

   • If resistance to impact is important, then you will need to design a method to determine the amount of impact force the plastic you will be using can take.

   • Perhaps your plastic will need to withstand lots of flexing, bending, stretching, compressing, and twisting. Design a valid method to determine the fatigue resistance of your plastic.

3. Design the procedure of the tests you will conduct. Use good experimental design. Collect both quantitative and qualitative data.

   a) Record your procedure in your *Active Chemistry* log.

4. When your teacher has approved your procedure, carry out the tests.

   a) Based on your results, justify the best plastic(s) to use in your toy model. (Use your data.)

5. Share your results with other groups. What else did you learn about some of the materials you were considering using?

446

Active Chemistry

Chem Talk

POLYMERS

Polymers Are Long Chains of Monomers

Often referred to as macromolecules, **polymers** are enormously long molecules made up of many repeating smaller molecules. The smaller molecules that make up a polymer are called **monomers** (from the Greek *mono*, meaning one). Polymers may be made of tens of thousands of repeating monomer units with molecular weights reaching to millions of daltons (one dalton is equal to one atomic mass unit). Monomers are the building blocks of polymers; the links that make up the polymer chains. These molecular chains may be branched or unbranched, interconnected at various points, or interconnected at a great many points so that they form rigid solids. At the molecular level, they may be long chains, or sheets, or even a complicated three-dimensional lattice.

Natural Polymers

Long before there were any synthetic polymers, natural polymers existed in starch, cellulose, **proteins**, and **DNA** (deoxyribonucleic acid). Starch is made by plants as a food source, and the **repeating unit** is the glucose molecule, which is a sugar. Cellulose is a plant polymer that also is based on the **glucose** molecule, but is arranged in a different configuration. Proteins are another class of organic compounds that contain nitrogen and in which the repeating units are **amino acids**. Meats, beans, and eggs are familiar foods that are mostly made of proteins.

DNA is a category of organic compounds that are found in cells. DNA contains the genetic instructions used in the development and functioning of all living things. DNA is a polymer made up of repeating units called **nucleotides**. While each nucleotide may have a molecular mass of about 200 amu, each DNA molecule may contain millions of nucleotides. For example, the largest human chromosome is chromosome 1, and it contains 220 million nucleotides.

Every trait that is characteristic of a type of plant or animal is determined by its DNA pattern. The basis of heredity and the transmission of traits from one generation to the next are based on DNA replication during cell division. However, sometimes an "error" is made in the coding of DNA. That these occasional mistakes are passed on from one generation to the next provides evidence for the theory of evolution. Because these genetic errors seem to occur on a regular statistical basis, the historical point at which species with common ancestors separated can be

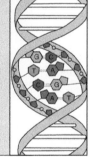

Chem Words

polymers: very large molecules made up of smaller repeating units (called monomers).

monomers: the smallest repeating unit of a polymer.

protein: an organic substance made of long chains of amino acids.

DNA: deoxyribonucleic acid; a polymer made up of repeating units called nucleotides that contains the genetic instructions used in the development and functioning of all living things.

repeating unit: one or more monomers chemically linked end-to-end to form immense molecules called polymers.

glucose: a soluble crystalline sugar, $C_6H_{12}O_6$, digestible by animals.

amino acid: an organic molecule that has both a carboxyl acid and amine functional group.

nucleotide: repeating units of molecules that, when linked together, form the basic structure of DNA.

447

Chem Talk

This section discusses polymers at the molecular level, explains how plastics are related to polymers and briefly reviews the different properties of thermoset and thermoplastic polymers. The two principal types of polyethylene, high-density (HDPE) and low-density (LDPE) are introduced, with a brief description of the various uses for each.

CHAPTER 5

TEACHING TIP

Although there are numerous plastics that could be produced in a high school lab using simple materials and chemical reactions, these procedures have students take a more practical approach to exploring plastics. Within the constraints of a lab setting, it is more important for students to consider which plastic is best to use in their toy, than it is to try to "create" different plastics. However, if there is time, you may consider having students explore latex, nylon, or any of the commercial polymer modeling compounds popularized by toy companies to better understand the polymerization process.

Checking Up

1.

The term "macromolecule" usually refers to a polymer containing thousands of monomer units and is very large with molecular weights going into the millions. Proteins and starch are natural macromolecules.

2.

Thermoplastic polymers can be remolded by reheating while thermosetting polymers cannot be remolded.

3.

A linear-chain molecule has no branching and the monomer units extend in only one direction. A branched-chain molecule has the same linear features but also has short lengths of the molecule attached to the linear "trunk."

 Ideal Toy

Chem Words

molecular clock: the historical point at which species with common ancestors separated can be calculated on a regular statistical basis.

phenol: a toxic, white, crystalline derivative of benzene having the hydroxyl functional group; carbolic acid.

formaldehyde: the common name for methanal, the smallest organic compound having the aldehyde functional group.

thermoset polymer: a polymer that is a hard, non-conducting material that cannot be melted and remolded.

thermoplastic polymer: a polymer that can be softened by heat and then remolded.

polyethylene: a thermoplastic polymer of the monomer ethene (ethylene).

plastic: any of various organic compounds produced by polymerization, capable of being molded into objects.

calculated. This technique is called the **molecular clock**. For example, the DNA of humans and chimpanzees differs by approximately 1 percent, which means the two species are very similar. For comparison, the range of human DNA variation is twenty times less than this. Evolutionary scientists estimate that humans and chimpanzees had a common ancestor 4 to 7 million years ago. Other examples show that dogs and gray wolves parted ways, genetically, about 1 million years ago. Asian and African elephants separated about 7.6 million years ago. Although such estimates are approximate and may contain significant error, the information generally is consistent with some geologic or prehistoric data.

Synthetic Polymers

The first synthetic polymer was developed in response to a call for a synthetic substitute for ivory. In 1909, Leo Baekeland received a patent for the first fully synthetic polymer, which he named Bakelite. Bakelite is a three-dimensional resin network made from the polymerization of **phenol** and **formaldehyde**, two organic chemicals. This polymer is a hard, non-conducting material that cannot be melted and remolded. Such a polymer is called a **thermoset polymer**—one that is soft enough to be molded when first prepared, but once it hardens, it remains hard. Other thermoset polymers include rubber tires, urea-formaldehyde foam (used in insulation and in plywood), and melamine for countertops. When heated, these types of polymers will decompose before melting and generally are not recyclable.

Thermoplastic polymers, on the other hand, are recyclable because they can be softened by heat and remolded to make new objects. **Polyethylene**, a polymer of ethylene, is the simplest and cheapest thermoplastic polymer. Over 20 million tons of polyethylene is produced in the United States each year. There are two principal types of polyethylene—low-density polyethylene (LDPE) and high-density polyethylene (HDPE). LDPE has many side chains branching off from the main polymer chain. This structure makes it lighter (low density) and more flexible. The sturdier HDPE has fewer side chains, which allows the chains to pack together more tightly, giving it rigidity and a higher melting point.

HDPE   LDPE (branching)

There are many other types of synthetic polymers in use today and the list continues to grow. A list of recyclable **plastics** with their corresponding codes is shown in the table on the following page.

Checking Up

1. What is meant by the term "macromolecule"?

2. How does a thermoset polymer differ from a thermoplastic polymer?

3. Explain the difference between a branched-chain and a linear-chain molecule.

448

Recyclable Plastics			
Code	Abbreviation	Name	Uses
01 PET	PET (or PETE)	polyethylene terephthalate	polyester fibers, thermoformed sheet, strapping, soft drink bottles
02 PE-HD	HDPE	high-density polyethylene	bottles, grocery bags, recycling bins, playground equipment, plastic lumber
03 PVC	PCV (or V)	polyvinyl chloride	pipe, fencing, non-food bottles, auto seat covers
04 PE-LD	LDPE	low-density polyethylene	plastic bags, 6-pack rings, containers, tubing
05 PP	PP	polypropylene	auto parts, industrial fibers, food containers, dishware
06 PS	PS	polystyrene	desk accessories, cafeteria trays, plastic utensils, toys, insulation (as a hardened foam)
07 O	Other (or O)	other plastics, including acrylic (PMMA), polyacrylonitrile (PAN), polybutadiene (PBD), nylon, polycarbonate (PC), polylactic acid (PLA)	PMMA-reading glasses; PAN-clothing, tents, sails; PBD-tires, hoses, gaskets; Nylon-fabrics, carpets, rope; PC-windows, headlights, safety glasses; PLA-sutures, stents, compost bags

What Do You Think Now?

At the beginning of this section you were asked the following:

- What properties of plastics have made their use so widespread?

How have your ideas about the properties of polymers changed after having completed this section? List three important properties of polymers that you did not have in your original list.

Chem
Essential Questions

What does it mean?

Chemistry explains a *macroscopic* phenomenon (what you observe) with a description of what happens at the *nanoscopic* level (atoms and molecules) using *symbolic* structures as a way to communicate. Complete the chart below in your *Active Chemistry* log.

MACRO	NANO	SYMBOLIC
What important properties of polymers did you observe in this section?	Take two of the properties from the macro box and describe how the structure of the polymers gives rise to these properties.	Show symbolically how LDPE and HDPE differ. Then draw two polymer chains with cross-linkers that reduce the mobility of a polymer.

→

449

What Do You Think Now?

Have students revisit the *What Do You Think?* question as well as the *What Do You See?* section of their notebooks. Ask them to review their lists of properties of plastics. Now that they have completed the section, they should be able to add some properties that they tested for. You can provide them with the answer found in *A Chemist's Response* and ask them to share their opinions. You may also invite discussion on the pros and cons of the widespread use of plastics and have them debate the issues.

CHAPTER 5

Chem Essential Questions

What does it mean?

MACRO — Answers will vary. Example: Strength and flexibility are the important properties that were observed.

NANO — Answers will vary. Example: Strength is due to a high degree of cross-linking of the polymer chains. Flexibility is due to the low degree of cross-linking in the polymer chain.

SYMBOLIC — Answers should resemble the drawings featured in the *Chem Talk* section.

How do you know?

Answers will vary. Example: According to the tests, brittleness increases as the degree of cross-linking in the polymer increases; flexibility is related to a high degree of branching in the polymer chain.

Why do you believe?

Answers will vary. Example: Trees could provide an alternative source of carbon for future polymers.

Why should you care?

Answers will vary. If plastic is to be used, the type of plastic chosen is critical for the toy design and students should be prepared to provide an explanation for their choice.

Reflecting on the Section and the Challenge

Although there are no questions in this section for students to answer or to discuss, this is an important opportunity to consider the section with respect to the *Chapter Challenge*. Students now know how to use two types of polymers and how the properties are related to molecular structure. This knowledge should be very useful in designing and making their toy.

Chem to Go

1.

Thermoplastics

a) Heating provides the energy needed to weaken the intermolecular forces, which allows the chains to slip and slide over one another.

b) An endothermic change.

c) A physical change.

d) Thermoplastics are ideal for industrial molds and for sculpting material.

Thermosets

e) To prevent premature reaction.

f) The putty felt hot.

g) An exothermic reaction.

h) A chemical change.

i) No, a thermoset polymer cannot be remolded once it has "set."

j) A thermosetting plastic can be used for forming the body of an object with a permanent shape, of which there is an endless variety. It is also ideal for making objects that need to withstand high temperatures (e.g., kitchen equipment, etc.).

2.

Students' drawings should show that they understand that thermoplastics are exhibiting physical change and that the thermosets are undergoing a chemical change. Their drawings should illustrate the cross-linking differences between the two types.

 Ideal Toy

How do you know?
Explain how your tests for two properties of a polymer related to the structure of the polymer.

Why do you believe?
Plastics are a large part of everyday life; Americans use an astounding amount of polymers each year. Most of these materials are derived from petroleum, a limited natural resource. The polymers are made mostly of carbon as well as other elements. Propose an alternative source of carbon for the creation of future polymers.

Why should you care?
It seems reasonable to assume that your toy design may include the use of some plastic. Understanding the nature of, and being able to clearly explain, your choice of polymer will improve your toy design.

Reflecting on the Section and the Challenge

In this section, you compared two types of plastics, thermoplastic and thermoset. You found that they had very different properties, which would help determine which type of plastic to use for different design purposes. Thermoplastics can be recycled as long as the polymer chain remains intact. On the other hand, thermoset plastics cannot be recycled. After examining these two types of plastics, you conducted some material tests, much like those that would be done in an industrial setting, to help you determine which plastic would be best for your toy model. Now, you can use your plastic test results to help you complete your toy model and determine a cost analysis for your product.

 Chem to Go

1. Let's consider the first part of this section where you compared two types of plastics.

   Thermoplastics

   a) Why was it necessary to heat the thermoplastic modeling material in order to shape it?

   b) Was this an exothermic or endothermic change?

   c) Was this a chemical or physical change, or both?

   d) How could thermoplastics be used?

   Thermosets

   e) Why are the two epoxy putty components separated?

   f) As the epoxy putty sets, did it feel hot or cold?

   g) Was this an exothermic or endothermic reaction?

   h) Was this a chemical or physical change, or both?

   i) Could you remold the material if you did not like the first thing you made? Explain.

   j) How could thermoset plastics be used?

450

Active Chemistry

2. Draw pictures of what was occurring at the molecular level as you worked with the thermoplastic modeling material and the epoxy putty.

3. Are all polymers products of chemical industries? Explain.

4. What are the advantages and disadvantages of using plastic rather than other materials in your toy model?

5. Speculate as to why so many products today are made of polymers.

6. *Preparing for the Chapter Challenge*

Consider how you might use plastics in your toy model. Draw a scale model of your toy and label the components and the materials that it is made of. Determine how much of each material will be required to manufacture one of your toys, and develop a cost analysis sheet for your toy that could be included in your final presentation.

Inquiring Further

1. The cost of toys

Investigate toys at a local store. Determine the percentages that are made mostly of plastics. Compile a list of the other materials in the toys. Estimate the cost of manufacturing each item based on the materials and compare that to the retail cost. Discuss the markup that toy products have and what other costs are involved in their manufacturing.

2. Exploring other plastics

Make Slime

Mix 20 mL of a 4% polyvinyl alcohol (PVA) solution with 5 mL of 4% borax solution in a small disposable cup. Stir with a wooden stirring stick. Test its properties (for example, density, viscosity, malleability, resistance to pressure). Determine how this might be used in a toy product.

Make "Gluep"

Mix 15 mL each of white glue and water in a small disposable cup. Add food coloring if desired. Add 10 mL of 4% borax solution and stir vigorously with a wooden stirring stick. Knead the gluep and observe its properties and compare them to the properties of slime. Determine how gluep might be used in a toy product.

⚠️ Do not inhale or ingest borax!

451

Active Chemistry

be an important investigation to prepare students to successfully complete the project. You may need to advise students regarding the design and execution of a scale drawing. Provide a sample sheet for doing a cost analysis and resources or websites for finding information about pricing for raw materials.

Students might contact chemical plants and their materials suppliers to get an estimate on the cost of raw materials for developing a cost-analysis sheet. They might consult science supply catalogs to get price information for the materials needed. Another source of information might be to contact chemical engineers or chemical engineering societies for assistance with cost analysis.

Inquiring Further

1. The cost of toys

Students' answers will vary.

2. Exploring other plastics— Slime and Gluep

Student answers will vary depending upon the tests that they conduct. Slime and Gluep are both thermoplastics.

3.

No, many polymers are biomolecules, such as proteins and starch – long chains of repeating units that can have varying degrees of cross-linking as well.

4.

Students' answers will vary, but advantages should reference cost, versatility, light weight, accessibility, etc.

5.

Students' answers will vary, but should include low cost, versatility, durability, and non-conductivity.

6.

Preparing for the Chapter Challenge

Students' answers will vary depending upon their toy. Drafting a scale model and identifying the components and the materials it is made of will

SECTION 8 – QUIZ

5-8a	Blackline Master

1. Why are polymers considered to be macromolecules? What are monomers?

2. What is **not** a characteristic of a thermoset polymer?

  a) cannot be softened and remolded

  b) conducts electricity

  c) soft enough to be molded when first prepared

  d) made up of many linked molecules

3. What is **not** a characteristic of a thermoplastic polymer?

  a) cannot be softened and remolded

  b) does not conduct electricity

  c) soft enough to be molded when first prepared

  d) made up of many linked molecules

4. Polyethylene comes in two forms – high density (HDPE) and low density (LDPE). Describe the differences in their properties and the differences at the molecular level.

SECTION 8 – QUIZ ANSWERS

❶ Polymers are extremely long chains of smaller sub-units strung together. They are very large molecules or macromolecules. Monomers are the individual sub-units that make up a polymer.

❷ b) conducts electricity

❸ a) cannot be softened and remolded

❹ High-density polyethylene (HDPE) is harder and less pliable. It is made of long, linear chains of polyethylene packed tightly together. Low-density polyethylene (LDPE) is flexible and pliable. It has more side chains branching off the polymer chains that prevent the molecules from packing.

NOTES

Chapter Assessment

Chem You Learned

For your convenience, all of the chemistry content that was covered in this chapter is listed in the *Student Edition* at the end of the chapter. This may be a good time to evaluate your students' comprehension of the material. You may then want to suggest that they help each other in reviewing those concepts that may need reinforcement.

You may also want to point out to students that they can use the *Chem You Learned* section as a handy checklist of the chemistry concepts they might want to incorporate into their *Chapter Challenge*.

Ideal Toy

Chem You Learned

- **Electrochemical cells** (batteries) produce **voltage** based on the relative **metal activities** of the **electrodes**.
- The **half-reactions** that are taking place at the **anode** and **cathode** can be explained in terms of **oxidation** and **reduction**.
- **Oxidation** is the loss of electrons in a reaction; **reduction** is the gain of electrons. **LEO** the lion says **GER**rrrr is a helpful mnemonic device.
- The size and shape of a molecule depends on what atoms are contained in the molecule.
- **London dispersion forces** are the weak **intermolecular forces** in **nonpolar** molecules, such as the **hydrocarbons**.
- In **polar covalent** molecules the strength of the intermolecular forces depend on the **electronegativity** of the atoms and their intramolecular orientation.
- Some **physical properties**, like **melting point** and **boiling point**, increase regularly as the molecular size of a family of compounds becomes larger.
- **Boyle's law** states that the product of the pressure and volume of a sample of gas will equal a constant when the temperature is constant. $P_1V_1 = P_2V_2$
- **Charles's law** states that the volume of a sample of gas is directly related to the temperature (**kelvins**) when the pressure is constant. $\frac{V_1}{T_1} = \frac{V_2}{T_2}$
- Producing rocket fuels requires an understanding of the following type of reactions: **synthesis**, **single-** and **double-replacement**, and **decomposition**.
- Using Avogadro's gas law with Charles's and Boyle's laws allows for the development of the **combined gas law:** $\frac{P_1V_1}{T_1} = \frac{P_2V_2}{T_2}$
- From the **combined gas law** the **ideal gas equation** can be developed: $PV = nRT$. This equation allows the determination of any one of the variables (P, V, T, n) when the other three are known.
- At the same temperature, all gases have the same **kinetic energy**. $KE = \frac{1}{2}mv^2$. It follows that a heavier gas moves more slowly than a lighter gas.
- **Graham's law of effusion** states that the rate of **effusion** is inversely proportional to the square root of the density of the gas. In comparing the effusion rate of two gases, $\frac{v_1}{v_2} = \sqrt{\frac{m_2}{m_1}}$, note that since the volume is constant, then molecular mass values can be used instead of density.
- **Thermoset** plastics are rigid and cannot be remolded after they set.
- **Thermoplastics** differ from the thermoset plastics since they can be reheated and reformed to different shapes.
- Plastics are **polymers** and built from **monomers**. An example is **polyethylene**, which contains ethylene monomers.

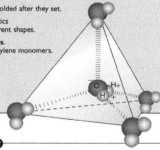

452

Active Chemistry

Chem Chapter Challenge

As you assemble ideas and information for your *Chapter Challenge* you will be completing a second round of the *Engineering Design Cycle*. The *Goal* and criteria remain unchanged; however, your list of *Inputs* has grown. You now have much more chemistry information and new concepts that may help you envision a new toy idea. You also have the *Feedback* your group received during the *Mini-Challenge* to help guide your efforts. You may have had new ideas while you watched other presentations that could make use of the new techniques you have learned!

Goal

Your *Chapter Challenge* is to make a toy that uses various chemical and/or gas principles. You have already created one *Ideal Toy* design. As you complete the *Chapter Challenge* you will use the *Engineering Design Cycle* to improve that toy or create a brand new one. The *Goal*, remember, is the objective you are trying to reach or the problem you need to solve in the *Engineering Design Cycle*. Go back and quickly read the challenge description at the start of the chapter. In there you will find all of the details for completing the entire challenge. You should also review the rubric your class generated to determine the way your toy design presentation

and proposal will be graded. You should make sure you address each aspect of the rubric completely so that your team can earn the highest possible grade.

Your group will need to include all four major components to completely satisfy the requirements of this challenge. In your presentation to the Ideal Toys Company board of directors you will need to:

- Describe your design using clear drawings or a model.
- Describe the chemistry and/or gas principles used by your design, including any potential hazards or waste disposal issues.
- Provide a cost analysis for manufacturing your toy.
- Provide a written proposal clearly organizing all of the information in your presentation.

A successful presentation will draw on the combined strength of your team members and address each one of these components completely.

Inputs

The *Inputs* for the *Engineering Design Cycle* include all of the resources you have to help you complete the *Chapter Challenge*. Each section of the chapter has provided you with chemical principles that you can use to design your *Ideal Toy*. You can also use some of the techniques presented in the section activities to improve your toy model and clarify your ideas for the board. Your team will also provide a critical design constraint by identifying the target age group for your toy. You will want to make sure your toy is both entertaining and safe for the age group you specify.

All of the *Inputs* for this challenge will shape the ultimate product you develop. As your group reviews the chemistry you have learned, be sure to pay special attention to the *Reflecting on the Section and the Challenge*, *Chem Essential Questions*, and *Preparing for the Chapter Challenge* portions of the text. You should also

---

Chem Chapter Challenge

A brief review of the *Chapter Challenge* reminds students that the toy they will be creating must operate on chemical and/or gas principles and target a specific age group. The prototype or detailed drawing of the toy should be presented with a written proposal that addresses manufacturing costs and environmental issues. The evaluation of the projects will be based on the explanation of the chemistry involved as well as the quality of the proposal, presentation and prototype.

Chemistry Content

A list reviewing the various sections contained in this chapter provides a convenient summary of the chemical concepts that were covered by these investigations. This list can be useful in generating ideas for the *Ideal Toy* and for locating material related to specific concepts.

Criteria for Success

Students should be preparing to start their *Chapter Challenge* projects now that they have completed all the sections and the *Mini-Challenge*. They will need to develop a comprehensive assessment rubric to determine how their projects will be graded. It is critical that they be responsible for deciding the criteria and scoring system so they know exactly what is expected and how their projects will be judged.

On the facing page is a sample assessment rubric for the *Chapter Challenge*. You can copy and distribute the rubric as is, or use it as a foundation for developing scoring guidelines and expectations that suit your own particular needs. For example, you might wish to ensure that core concepts and abilities derived from your local or state science frameworks also appear on the rubric.

Students may decide to vary the point value of the different criteria categories. In the example, Content value is potentially worth 60 points, Presentation value is worth 30 points and Group interaction is worth 10 points. Students may decide to change the balance and put a higher value on Group interaction.

However you decide to evaluate the *Chapter Challenge*, it is essential that all expectations be communicated to students before they begin work on the *Chapter Challenge*.

Be sure that the students actively participate in deciding the criteria for evaluation and the guidelines for scoring.

The *Sample Assessment Rubric* is also provided as a Blackline Master on the *Teacher Resources CD*.

5c **Blackline Master**

 Ideal Toy

review your *Active Chemistry* log for notes that you recorded during each section. The brief section summaries listed here will give you an overview of the information you have learned to help get you started.

Section 1 You learned about battery construction and created your own electrochemical cell. Your battery investigation helped you learn about the metal activity series and redox reactions.

Section 2 You investigated the differences between solids, liquids, and gases and compared the boiling points of hydrocarbons and alcohols.

Section 3 You constructed a Cartesian diver toy and gained knowledge about Boyle's law and the relation between pressure and volume of a gas.

Section 4 You studied the relationship between the volume and temperature of a gas and the representation of that relationship in Charles's law. You also constructed a hot-air balloon.

Section 5 You produced and tested three different gases. You then used two of these gases to power a toy rocket.

Section 6 You determined the volume of one mole of gas. You then developed the ideal gas law relating the pressure, temperature, and volume of gas.

Section 7 You predicted the quantities of gas produced in a chemical reaction.

Section 8 You investigated the differences between thermoset and thermoplastic plastics.

 Process

The *Process* step of the *Engineering Design Cycle* is where you turn your ideas into products. During this step you will compare and contrast design solutions, choose hypothetical materials for manufacturing the toy, and document all of your work in a clearly written design proposal. Fortunately, you have your experience with the *Mini-Challenge* to build on. You can repeat each one of the steps you followed to complete your original toy design, incorporating the chemistry principles from the second half of the chapter. You definitely want to consider new toy designs and compare them to the design you previously created. You may find that your original design

cannot incorporate any of the new chemical principles from the second half of the chapter, and continuing with that toy would not allow you to demonstrate your understanding of any of that new material. Repeating your analysis will ensure that you select the best design your group can provide.

Your challenge requirements include presenting information about any potential hazards associated with using your product, any waste disposal issues, and creating a manufacturing cost estimate. When engineers design a new product they have to consider the entire "life cycle" of the product. This means they think about the raw materials that are extracted from the earth to create the product, the energy that goes into manufacturing the product, how the product will travel from the factory to the consumer (including stops along the way), how long the product will be used (its useful life), and what happens to the product when it is no longer useful to the consumer. How long will your toy last? Can it be recycled? Will your product end up in landfill? Can it be made with recyclable materials?

While your chemistry explorations have not directly addressed these topics, chemistry principles are used to manufacture materials, to provide fuel for shipping, to create materials for packaging, to recycle materials, and even to decompose landfill materials. You should rely on information you learned directly through the chapter sections to address your challenge requirements. When you create your cost analysis, you may want to consider your product's life cycle and present some ideas about how you would try to incorporate concerns for the environmental effect of your toy and issues related to recycling. It will not be possible to put dollar figures on your ideas, but the chemistry principles you are learning are the science behind how these questions can be answered.

454

Active Chemistry

SAMPLE ASSESSMENT RUBRIC FOR CHAPTER 5

CHAPTER 5

CONTENT CRITERIA

	MEETS THE STANDARD OF EXCELLENCE	APPROACHES THE STANDARD OF EXCELLENCE	MEETS AN ACCEPTABLE STANDARD	BELOW ACCEPTABLE STANDARD
Chemistry Concepts	At least three chemistry concepts are effectively applied in the design and operation of the toy **30**	At least two chemistry concepts are applied in the design and operation **20-29**	At least one chemistry concept is effectively applied **10-19**	The chemistry is not effectively incorporated in the toy design and operation **0-9**
Scientific Explanations	Clear explanations for each chemical concept are provided **15**	Explanations of the chemical concepts are provided, but they lack somewhat in clarity **10-14**	Explanations of chemical concepts are incomplete or unclear **5-9**	Explanations are inaccurate or are not provided **0-4**
Quality of Prototype or Drawing	Prototype or schematic of toy is well-designed, well-crafted and an effective demonstration of the chemical concepts **15**	Prototype or schematic is theoretically sound but construction is somewhat lacking or some chemical concepts are not well incorporated **10-14**	Prototype or schematic needs more work for concepts to be effectively incorporated **5-9**	Prototype or schematic lacks rationale, is poorly crafted and does not adequately demonstrate chemical concepts **0-4**

PRESENTATION CRITERIA

Presentation	Presentation is professional and well-rehearsed with entertaining visuals, and covers all the relevant material needed for the board to make a decision **15**	Presentation is coherent, but not well-polished and lacks some components **10-14**	Presentation is somewhat disorganized, misses vital points that should be included **5-9**	Presentation is very disorganized and incomplete **0-4**
Written Proposal	Proposal is clear, complete, organized, and well-written **15**	Proposal is clear but does not adequately address all issues or lacks organization and style **10-14**	Proposal is not well organized, has some errors and lacks some important components **5-9**	Proposal is disorganized, incomplete and poorly written **0-4**

GROUP INTERACTION

Teamwork Skills	All group members work effectively in a joint cooperative effort, each member contributing equally **10**	All group members showed effort to work constructively, but lacked cooperative coordination **6-9**	Some group members more engaged than others; lack of team effort and coordination **3-5**	There is little indication of any team effort or coordination **0-2**

Preparing for the Chapter Challenge

The *Chapter Challenge* is the opportunity for students to review all the material in the chapter and find a creative way of interpreting that content. The *Preparing for the Chapter Challenge* sections in the textbook guides the students toward a successful project. The pages in the front matter of this *Teacher's Edition* provide the instructional rationale for this problem-based learning model.

In this challenge, remind students that the "ideal" toy is one that not only functions properly and appeals to the target age group, it should also demonstrate the students' understanding of the chapter content. It should be possible to include several of the concepts learned in this chapter into the design and/or operation of the toy. Also remind them that since the project is essentially a proposal for a toy design, it is very important that their presentation include data pertaining to the manufacturing (cost analysis), safety, and waste-disposal issues for their product.

Before students begin their projects, you should review some of the discussion you had at the start of the chapter and make sure the rubric and standards for excellence are still endorsed by the class.

Have the student teams review the *Manage Your Time* section at the end of the chapter. Make certain that they have a realistic plan for accomplishing all the tasks in the time allocated and that it includes full participation by the entire group.

NOTES
_____

_____

_____

_____

_____

_____

_____

_____

_____

_____

_____

_____

Each *Chapter Challenge* toy design is allotted a three-minute presentation which is evaluated on the quality of the toy design, the quality of the visual aids, the explanation of the chemistry, the written proposal, and the presentation itself.

It is highly unlikely that students will be successful in their first attempts to design a toy that works successfully each time. They will have to improvise, troubleshoot, and sometimes, go back to the drawing board and make modifications. For example, they may find that their toy does not operate reliably each time. They will need to isolate the problem, make adjustments and retest to ensure that their modifications were effective.

Emphasize teamwork and encourage students to organize their efforts to overcome obstacles or difficulties. By now they should be able to make intelligent predictions and approach modifications with a deeper understanding of why results will change when conditions are altered by reviewing the *Engineering Design Cycle*.

Engineering Design Cycle

Have students reflect on the successes and disappointments from the *Engineering Design Cycle* they applied to the *Mini-Challenge*. Students should use the feedback they received to make improvements and adjustments to their ideal toy design.

The *Chapter Challenge* asks students to design a toy for a toy company that utilizes some of the chemistry and/or gas principles covered in this chapter. The toy design is to be rendered as a mock prototype or a detailed drawing along with a written proposal that contains data regarding the potential hazards, waste-disposal issues, and a cost analysis for manufacturing.

Inset page (455)

Outputs

The products that you deliver during an *Engineering Design Cycle* are the *Outputs*. The *Output* for this challenge is your design presentation to the Ideal Toys Company board of directors. Your presentation will need to address four distinct components to be successful:

• Describe your design using clear drawings or a model.

• Describe the chemistry and/or gas principles used by your design, including any potential hazards or waste disposal issues.

• Provide a cost analysis for manufacturing your toy.

• Provide a written proposal clearly organizing all of the information in your presentation.

Your group should make sure that you have included each component listed in the class rubric for your presentation. The rubric will clearly describe the products you must deliver to earn the points associated with that component. To get all of these tasks done in the time you have available you will need to divide the tasks among your group members. Make sure each person is comfortable with their task and understands how they will be contributing to the success of the group. In addition, set deadlines for each product so that you will have time to review everybody's work as a group and make any necessary corrections prior to your final presentation. Planning a project well does not ensure success, but poor planning almost always leads to a disappointing product. Make sure you plan for success!

Feedback

Your classmates will give you *Feedback* on your *Ideal Toy* design based on the criteria of the chapter challenge. This *Feedback* will likely become part of your grade, indicating how successful your group was at meeting the *Chapter Challenge*, but could also be useful for additional design iterations. Don't forget, you will be viewing other design solutions for the same challenge. The different group presentations may represent *Feedback* in the form of presenting alternatives you may have included in your toy design. The variety of design solutions should reflect the fact that there are endless ways to satisfy the challenge criteria.

Active Chemistry

Chem Connections to Other Sciences

Students gain understanding of the interdisciplinary aspects of chemistry when they are actively engaged in thinking about the connections between the sciences. This section provides a glimpse of the interconnections between the content in this chapter and other scientific disciplines. Brief sketches relate students' study of chemistry concepts to biology, physics, and Earth science.

Encourage students to draw analogies with science connections they are familiar with while discussing the science connections. The chemistry concepts discussed in this chapter hold true in every branch of science, and can provide scientists in other fields with new insights. Emphasize the growing interdisciplinary approach to science and the need for scientists who have a broader view of science. Discuss how scientists try to understand phenomena by studying a problem from different points of view. Encourage the appreciation for chemistry in relation to the broader framework of science by describing the increase in demand for scientists with interdisciplinary backgrounds (for example, geochemistry, biochemistry, and chemical physics).

Consider developing an interdisciplinary lesson plan that investigates how key chemistry concepts are applied in different sciences. Groups would select a topic and determine how it relates to biology, physics, and Earth science based on their reading of *Chem Connections to Other Sciences*, and how it relates to the key chemistry concepts. A set of questions can be constructed for students to focus on, allowing them to build a constructive inquiry. A group member could write down the highlights of their discussion. Once students have recorded the focal points of their group discussions, bring together the whole class and have a volunteer from each group share the major points of their discussion of science connections.

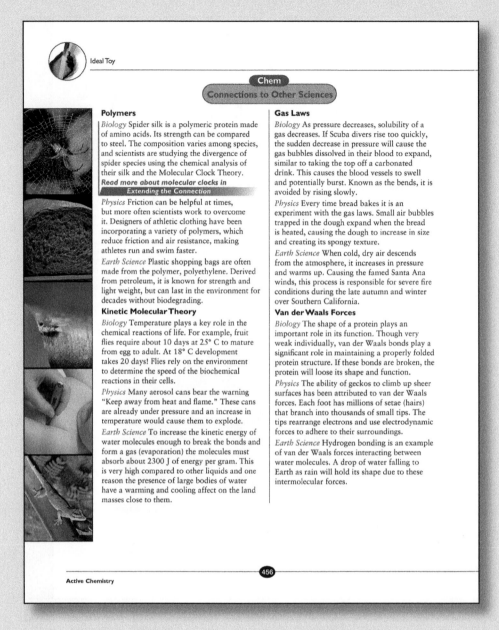

Ideal Toy

Chem Connections to Other Sciences

Polymers

Biology Spider silk is a polymeric protein made of amino acids. Its strength can be compared to steel. The composition varies among species, and scientists are studying the divergence of spider species using the chemical analysis of their silk and the Molecular Clock Theory.
Read more about molecular clocks in Extending the Connection

Physics Friction can be helpful at times, but more often scientists work to overcome it. Designers of athletic clothing have been incorporating a variety of polymers, which reduce friction and air resistance, making athletes run and swim faster.

Earth Science Plastic shopping bags are often made from the polymer, polyethylene. Derived from petroleum, it is known for strength and light weight, but can last in the environment for decades without biodegrading.

Kinetic Molecular Theory

Biology Temperature plays a key role in the chemical reactions of life. For example, fruit flies require about 10 days at 25° C to mature from egg to adult. At 18° C development takes 20 days! Flies rely on the environment to determine the speed of the biochemical reactions in their cells.

Physics Many aerosol cans bear the warning "Keep away from heat and flame." These cans are already under pressure and an increase in temperature would cause them to explode.

Earth Science To increase the kinetic energy of water molecules enough to break the bonds and form a gas (evaporation) the molecules must absorb about 2300 J of energy per gram. This is very high compared to other liquids and one reason the presence of large bodies of water have a warming and cooling affect on the land masses close to them.

Gas Laws

Biology As pressure decreases, solubility of a gas decreases. If Scuba divers rise too quickly, the sudden decrease in pressure will cause the gas bubbles dissolved in their blood to expand, similar to taking the top off a carbonated drink. This causes the blood vessels to swell and potentially burst. Known as the bends, it is avoided by rising slowly.

Physics Every time bread bakes it is an experiment with the gas laws. Small air bubbles trapped in the dough expand when the bread is heated, causing the dough to increase in size and creating its spongy texture.

Earth Science When cold, dry air descends from the atmosphere, it increases in pressure and warms up. Causing the famed Santa Ana winds, this process is responsible for severe fire conditions during the late autumn and winter over Southern California.

Van der Waals Forces

Biology The shape of a protein plays an important role in its function. Though very weak individually, van der Waals bonds play a significant role in maintaining a properly folded protein structure. If these bonds are broken, the protein will loose its shape and function.

Physics The ability of geckos to climb up sheer surfaces has been attributed to van der Waals forces. Each foot has millions of setae (hairs) that branch into thousands of small tips. The tips rearrange electrons and use electrodynamic forces to adhere to their surroundings.

Earth Science Hydrogen bonding is an example of van der Waals forces interacting between water molecules. A drop of water falling to Earth as rain will hold its shape due to these intermolecular forces.

456

Active Chemistry

Extending the Connection

MOLECULAR CLOCKS

DNA and Evolution

Polymers are the foundation of all life forms. Deoxyribonucleic acid, or DNA, is a polymer with unequalled importance. Heredity is a function of living organisms, and DNA is the molecule that controls it. DNA is composed of billions of smaller building blocks called nucleotides. There are only four nucleotides that are used to build DNA in all living organisms: cytosine (C), guanine (G), adenine (A) and thymine (T). The structure of a DNA molecule consists of two separate chains of nucleotides, each held together by a series of strong covalent bonds. These two chains are then bound to each other by hydrogen bonds. A always forms a hydrogen bond with T, and C always bonds with G, to ensure the pairings mentioned above. In a strand of DNA that looks like this: AATCGCCCCGTA, its complimentary strand will look like this: TTAGCGGGGCAT. The last part of this complicated polymer structure involves the DNA strands coiling into a structure called a double helix.

DNA is passed down from parent to offspring during reproduction. The number and order of nucleotides within a DNA molecule is extremely important because it codes for, another group of vital polymers called proteins, which distinguish one species from another. In essence, the major role of DNA is to provide the instructions that "tell" cells how to make proteins. These proteins account for all variations within a species, such as whether one human has blonde or brown hair, or how fish can extract oxygen from water but birds cannot. As DNA is passed down from generation to generation, sometimes there is an error (mutation) in the code. These errors can be 1) fatal, the organism does not survive, 2) beneficial, the organism has a new trait that makes it easier to survive, or 3) neutral, neither favors nor disfavors the survival of the organism. This process is how new species evolve. The rate of mutations (changes in the sequence of the code) has been estimated for many species and is used as a "molecular clock" to estimate the time when organisms diverged from each other.

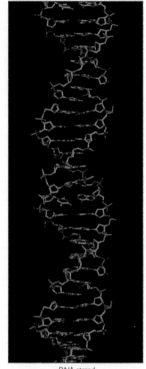

DNA strand

Extending the Connection

The *Chem Connections to Other Sciences* show students that the chemistry concepts they studied in each chapter are also basic to many other sciences. The chemistry they are learning is fundamental in the understanding of the concepts that they will study in all the other sciences. *Extending the Connection* delves deeper into one or two of these connections. It gives students an opportunity to examine a particular relationship to another science in greater depth.

Ideal Toy

DNA Sequencing

The combination of proteins distinguishes one species from another, and DNA codes for these proteins. Scientists have recently been working to identify the geologic timescale of species divergence based on differences in DNA sequences. Before DNA sequencing became available, scientists relied on the fossil record. Scientists looked at morphology (the shared physical characteristics) to classify fossils as different species and would reconstruct the timescale of when species broke off from a common ancestor producing the evolutionary tree seen in textbooks today. Within the last forty years, scientists have begun to use sophisticated techniques to compare the DNA sequences of different organisms, a process known as DNA taxonomy or the molecular clock theory. This process has redesigned the current "evolutionary tree" based on morphology alone. Scientists are hoping that the addition of DNA techniques to the complicated process of biological classification will add concrete molecular evidence to what some argue has been a partial guessing game to this point.

The molecular clock theory states that there is a direct relationship between the genetic differences between two species that indicates the geologic date the two species diverged. If this is true, then the amount of similarity (or difference) between two gene sequences would be proportional to the time the two species shared a common ancestor. The more closely related species are the more similar their DNA strands. For instance, many animals have hemoglobin in their blood. There is a part of the DNA strand that codes for this protein. That code, made up of repeating units of ATCG is more similar between a gorilla and a human than a horse and a human, because the gorilla and human are more closely related. It is estimated that a common ancestor for horses and humans was about 100 million years ago (mya) and humans and gorillas about 11 mya. The more mammals diverged from each other in their evolutionary paths, the more the DNA code for their hemoglobin changed. Added to the fossil record, it helps establish evolutionary time scales of speciation and fills in the blanks where the fossil record failed.

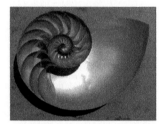

Using the knowledge of exactly how often a change in DNA occurs, scientists can analyze a piece of DNA from two different species and pinpoint roughly when they diverged. Reliance on DNA as a molecular clock requires the assumption that it keeps relatively precise evolutionary time. While this technique has gained popularity over the past 40 years as a means of estimating evolutionary timescales, scientists must still use caution as the rates of molecular evolution can vary significantly among different species. Nevertheless, the molecular clock is an extremely valuable tool that, if perfected, may help answer the complicated question: "Where do we all come from?"

Chem at Work

Susan Stamats
Hot-Air Balloon Pilot, Cedar Rapids, IA

When Susan Stamats saw her first hot-air balloon, she was captivated. The vision of the beautiful, multi-colored ball floating overhead filled her with excitement and she knew instantly that hot-air balloons would become part of her life.

She got a job with a balloon crew and learned about the mechanics of ballooning. Without even realizing it, she was learning a lot of science! Eventually, she worked her way up to becoming pilot of a hot-air balloon.

Over the past two decades, Susan has flown over 1,600 hours. "It's magical," she says. "Every time you fly is different—the conditions always change... It's great for me... I get bored easily!"

Now, Susan is an instructor, teaching other balloon pilots. Pilots have to learn to use complicated equipment, including altimeters, variometers, and thermisters, (heat sensors.) The sensors measure the temperature at the top of the envelope, which is what the balloon is called. Heat is a key factor in balloon piloting because it is what causes the balloon to rise. Heat also controls the altitude.

There are many principles of chemistry that apply to the flight of a hot-air balloon. The fuel is combusting propane and the envelope is made out of nylon (a polymer) with a polymer heat-seal on the inside. Although she hasn't taken chemistry since she was in high school, Susan is very aware of the important part it plays in every flight she takes.

Susan enjoys participating in balloon races and competitions all over the world. So far, she and her balloon have soared high above Mexico, France, Zimbabwe and South Africa.

Kay Gonzales
Owner, Costume and Magic Store, Orlando FL

Kay Gonzales owns a Florida store where you can buy magic tricks. Many of these tricks are just simple chemistry experiments. "Flash paper," for example, is made by altering the hydroxyl groups in papers' natural cellulose to act as an oxidizing agent. Like magic, the paper burns up completely in seconds.

Ron Bonnstetter
Video Game Developer, Lincoln, NE

Teacher and scientist, Ron Bonnstetter worked with students to develop a video game called *Nano*. This game features a laser-toting microscopic robot who patrols the inside of the human respiratory system. It incorporates the fun of blasting "bad guys" with the chemistry and biology used in fighting cancer.

457

Active Chemistry

Chem at Work

The *Chem at Work* section provides students with examples of how chemistry is applied by working people in the real world. These profiles might help students realize that the very challenges they are attempting to master for their *Chapter Challenge* projects are likely to be routine procedures for people who work in professions such as those featured here. As a matter of fact, most of the chemical procedures that students have performed in the previous sections are employed every day by average people such as those featured here.

Students should also note from these profiles that chemistry relates to a wide range of professions practiced by an equally broad range of people. Scientists and science teachers are not the only ones who practice chemistry. Nor are there any geographic, ethnic, gender, or educational specifications for people who apply chemistry in their professions. As the *Chem at Work* profiles show, people from all backgrounds use chemistry for a wide range of purposes as part of their jobs.

The *Chem at Work* profiles demonstrate that many common occupations that don't seem to be chemistry related actually are. For example, one wouldn't generally associate chemistry with a hot-air balloon pilot or a video game developer, but obviously, there are connections. You may want to open a discussion on various connections that chemistry might have to some occupations that students are interested in.

For your convenience, all three full-length *Chem at Work* profiles are provided as Blackline Masters on the *Teacher Resources CD*.

5b	Blackline Master
5c	Blackline Master
5d	Blackline Master

Chem Practice Test

The *Chem Practice Test* is provided as a Blackline Master on the *Teacher Resources CD*.

5f	Blackline Master

1. b

2. b

3. d

4. b

5. d

6. c

7. c

8. b

9. c

10. d

11. c

Ideal Toy

Chem
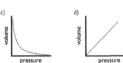
Practice Test

Content Review

On a separate sheet of paper answer the following.

1. Zinc has two valence electrons. Which equation shows the oxidation of an atom of zinc?

   a) $Zn + 2e^- \rightarrow Zn^{2+}$
   b) $Zn \rightarrow Zn^{2+} + 2e^-$
   c) $Zn^{2+} \rightarrow Zn + 2e^-$
   d) $Zn^{2+} + 2e^- \rightarrow Zn$

2. Which of the following would you expect to have the highest boiling point?

   a) H_2
   b) CH_3OH
   c) CH_4
   d) O_2

3. Polar molecules

   a) have little attraction for each other.
   b) are all solids.
   c) are symmetrical.
   d) are asymmetrical.

4. A substance with strong intermolecular forces

   a) is most likely a gas at room temperature.
   b) is most likely a liquid or solid at room temperature.
   c) is also a very large molecule.
   d) is not possible to predict the phase at room temperature.

5. Which graph below best shows the change in volume of 1 mole of chlorine as pressure increases and temperature remains constant?

   a)

   volume / pressure

   b)

   volume / pressure

   c)

   volume / pressure

   d)

   volume / pressure

Use the table below to answer *Question* 6:

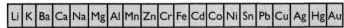

| Li | K | Ba | Ca | Na | Mg | Al | Mn | Zn | Cr | Fe | Cd | Co | Ni | Sn | Pb | Cu | Ag | Hg | Au |

decreasing tendency to release electrons $\longrightarrow$

6. Which pair of metals will produce the greater electrical potential in an electrochemical cell?

   a) K and Ba
   b) Ca and Mg
   c) Cr and Ag
   d) Mg and Fe

458

Active Chemistry

7. A 1 L container of gas (at constant temperature and number of particles) is at 1 atm of pressure. If the volume were to suddenly increase from 1 L to 5 L, what would the new pressure be?

a) 5 atm

b) 1 atm

c) $\frac{1}{5}$ atm

d) impossible to predict

8. As the temperature of a gas decreases and the pressure and quantity of gas remain constant, the volume of the gas will

a) increase.

b) decrease.

c) remain the same.

d) not be predictable.

9. What is the Kelvin equivalent of 35°C?

a) 35 K   b) 238 K

c) 308 K   d) –308 K

10. Which of the following shows the general equation for a single-replacement reaction?

a) A + B → AB

b) AB → A + B

c) AB + CD → AD + CB

d) A + BC → B + AC

11. Which of the following shows the general equation for a double-replacement reaction?

a) A + B → AB

b) AB → A + B

c) AB + CD → AD + CB

d) A + BC → B + AC

12. When iron is dropped in a beaker of hydrochloric acid (aqueous hydrogen chloride), bubbles are produced. What is in the bubbles?

HCl
bubbles
iron nails

a) hydrogen gas

b) chlorine gas

c) both hydrogen and chlorine gas

d) oxygen gas

13. Which of the following equations is correctly balanced?

a) $2Al + 3H_2SO_4 \rightarrow 3H_2 + Al_2(SO_4)_3$

b) $ZnCl_2 + AgNO_3 \rightarrow Zn(NO_3)_2 + AgCl$

c) $2Fe + Ca(NO_3)_2 \rightarrow 2Ca + Fe(NO_3)_2$

d) $Al + S \rightarrow Al_2S_3$

14. The volume of one mole of any gas at standard temperature and pressure conditions is how many liters?

a) 24.2   b) 22.4

c) 62.4   d) 0.082

15. Which of the following statements is **not** true?

a) The pressure of a gas is directly related to the number of particles (constant V, T).

b) The temperature of a gas is inversely related to the number of particles (constant P, V).

c) The volume of a gas is directly related to the number of particles (constant P, T).

d) The volume of a gas is dependent on the temperature (constant n, P).

Active Chemistry

12. a

13. a

14. b

15. b

16. a

17. c

18. b

19. b

20. b

CHAPTER 5

Critical Thinking

21.a)

Zn is oxidized.

22.b)

Copper will come out of the solution.

22.c)

The sulfate ion is the spectator ion. It doesn't do anything in the reaction.

22.a)

$V_2 = P_1V_1/P_2 =$
$2.0 \text{ atm} \times 5.5 \text{ L}/4.5 \text{ atm} = 2.4 \text{ L}$

22.b)

$V_2 = P_1V_1/P_2 =$
$4.5 \text{ atm} \times 5.5 \text{ L}/6.5 \text{ atm} = 3.8 \text{ L}$

22.c)

$V_2 = P_1V_1/P_2 =$
$6.5 \text{ atm} \times 5.5 \text{ L}/1 \text{ atm} = 36 \text{ L}$

22.d)

Volume increases by a factor of 2, $V_2 = 11 \text{ L}$.

23.a)

$V_2 = V_1T_2/T_1 =$
$(2.85 \text{ L} \times 363 \text{ K})/293 \text{ K} = 3.53 \text{ L}$

23.b)

$V_2 = V_1T_2/T_1 =$
$(2.85 \text{ L} \times 383 \text{ K})/293 \text{ K} = 3.73 \text{ L}$

23.c)

$V_2 = V_1T_2/T_1 =$
$(2.85 \text{ L} \times 283 \text{ K})/293 \text{ K} = 2.75 \text{ L}$

Ideal Toy

Practice Test (continued)

16. The rate of effusion of Gas A to Gas B is 1:4. Which of the following is true?

   a) The molecular mass of Gas A is greater than the molecular mass of Gas B.

   b) The molecular mass of Gas A is less than the molecular mass of Gas B.

   c) Gas A will effuse more quickly than Gas B.

   d) Gas B will effuse more slowly than Gas A.

17. Gas A has a mass four times greater than that of Gas B. Which of the following would you expect to happen?

   a) Gas A will effuse 2 times faster than Gas B.

   b) Gas A will effuse 4 times faster than Gas B.

   c) Gas B will effuse 2 times faster than Gas A.

   d) Gas B will effuse 4 times faster than Gas A.

18. Long, linear polymer chains packed tightly together describes the structure of

   a) low-density polyethylene (LDPE).

   b) high-density polyethylene (HDPE).

   c) thermoset plastic.

   d) thermoplastic plastic.

19. A polymer that can be softened by heat and remolded is a

   a) thermoset polymer.

   b) thermoplastic polymer.

   c) starch.

   d) protein.

20. A polymer that is made from a hard, non-conducting material and cannot be melted or remolded is known as

   a) a thermoplastic polymer.

   b) a thermoset polymer.

   c) ethylene.

   d) cellulose.

Critical Thinking

On a separate sheet of paper answer the following.

21. In an electrochemical cell with copper and zinc electrodes, the two solutions are zinc sulfate and copper (II) sulfate.

   a) Which metal will be oxidized?

   b) Which metal will come out of the solution?

   c) Identify the spectator ion and tell what it does.

22. At constant temperature and number of particles, the volume of a gas is 5.5 L. What is the new volume of the gas if

   a) the pressure is changed from 2.0 atm to 4.5 atm?

   b) the pressure is changed from 4.5 atm to 6.5 atm?

   c) the pressure is changed from 6.5 atm to 1.0 atm?

   d) the pressure is decreased by one-half?

23. A gas is in a cylinder with a movable piston. The original volume is 2.85 L at 20.0°C. If pressure is constant as the piston moves what will the new volume be when

   a) the cylinder is heated to 90.0°C?

   b) the cylinder is heated to 110°C?

   c) the cylinder is cooled to 10°C?

24. In a cork gun, the cylinder has a volume of 135 mL. How many moles of air does it contain at 20.0°C and 1.00 atm of pressure?

25. Calculate the relative rate of effusion between nitrogen gas (28.0 g/mol) and argon gas (40.0 g/mol).

24.

$$n = \frac{PV}{RT} =$$
$$\frac{1 \text{ atm} \times 0.135 \text{ L}}{0.0821 \text{ L} \cdot \text{atm}/(\text{mol} \times \text{K}) \cdot 293 \text{ K}} =$$
$$5.61 \times 10^{-3} \text{ mole}$$

25.

$$v_{\text{nitrogen}}/v_{\text{argon}} = \sqrt{40/28} = 1.2 \, ;$$
N_2 effuses 1.2 times faster.

Chapter 6

000 mL
± 5%

900

700

600

CHAPTER 6
COOL CHEMISTRY SHOW
Chapter Overview

Chapter Challenge

How often have you heard the statement that you learn more in the first year of teaching chemistry than you did in all of the years that you studied chemistry? This chapter takes this thought and has your students learn chemistry concepts and then do a demonstration (a *Cool Chemistry Show*) at the local elementary school for the fourth and fifth-grade students. They will enjoy working with the younger students and will find that they will gain poise and, hopefully, an appreciation for all the work that their teachers must do in order to be successful teachers. Who knows! Your students may find that they love to teach!

Students should draw on the chemistry they learned through the sections and investigations to help them complete the challenge. The chapter starts with a review of physical and chemical properties. As the students continue working through the sections, they learn more about chemical changes and factors that influence the chemical reaction. At the same time they start naming compounds and balancing chemical equations. A strong understanding of how ionic and covalent compounds differ is also stressed. At the midpoint of the chapter, following *Section 4*, students will get the opportunity to give their *Cool Chemistry Show* a first try. Encourage students to use the feedback they will receive on their trial demonstration from their classmates to improve on their show for the *Chapter Challenge*. In the final sections they study the energy of the reaction, factors that affect the rate of reactions, and how acids and bases react with each other. The final section leads them through an understanding of how redox reactions take place which leads to a review of metal activities.

Chapter Summary

- Learn to differentiate between chemical and physical changes.

- Balance chemical equations and name chemical formulas and compounds by using written equations.

- Predict the charges of ions of some elements and the formulas of ionic compounds.

- Determine whether energy changes are endothermic or exothermic from a particular point of reference.

- Discover conditions that make a reaction proceed faster or slower, and understand why this happens at the molecular level.

- Identify characteristic properties of acids and bases and learn to tell the difference between acids and bases.

- Determine what materials can react with metals, causing the metal to corrode or rust.

KEY SCIENCE CONCEPTS

SECTION SUMMARIES	CHEMISTRY PRINCIPLES
Section 1: Solutions: Chemical or Physical Change? The conditions that are necessary in order to determine whether a process is a physical or chemical change is discussed. First, a series of simple tests on fifteen different materials is performed. Then, the data are organized to determine which tests indicate a physical change and which tests indicate a chemical change.	Chemical change, Physical change Chemical reaction, Chemical tests Reactant, Product Solution, Solvent, Solute Molarity, Concentration Saturated solution, Unsaturated Precipitate, Polymer, Dilution Moles per liter
Section 2: Characteristics of Chemical Change Students learn what characteristics are used to identify a chemical reaction taking place, how indicators are used to identify acids and bases, and tests used to identify gases.	Chemical tests Acid-Base indicators Precipitates Carbon dioxide test
Section 3: Chemical Names and Formulas The section shows how to use the symbols from the periodic table and how to write the correct formulas for a compound. In addition to writing formulas, the section also explains how to name compounds.	Chemical symbols, Chemical names Chemical formulas Compounds, Molecules Anions, Cations, Polyatomic ions Covalent bonds, Ions Oxidation number Electrolyte, Non-electrolyte
Section 4: Reaction Types and Chemical Equations The writing of chemical changes by using word equations and chemical equations is practiced. In addition, single-replacement reactions and double-replacement reactions are examined.	Chemical equations Balancing equations Single replacement Double replacement Synthesis, Salts Decomposition Metal activity series Solubility rules
Section 5: Reaction Diagrams and Conservation of Energy The section shows how to use chemical thermodynamics to generate products from either endothermic or exothermic reactions.	Heat energy, Kinetic energy Endothermic reaction Exothermic reaction, Potential energy Gravitational energy, Activation energy Law of Conservation of Energy Heat vs. temperature
Section 6: Factors in Reaction Rates The factors tat can alter the rate of a chemical reaction are explained. These factors include temperature, concentration, and the nature of the reactants.	Reaction rates Concentration Kinetic energy Collision theory Catalysts, Surface area
Section 7: Acids, Bases, and Indicators—Colorful Chemistry The special properties of acids and bases are explored. These properties include how these compounds feel and how they taste (however, remember that chemicals are not to be tasted in the laboratory). The section also shows how they can be tested for, using indicators.	Acids, bases, pH scale Indicators, Buffers, Endpoint Titration, pOH, Neutralization Hydronium ion, Kw, Arrhenius Brønsted and Lowry, Lewis acids Strong acids and bases Weak acids and bases Equilibrium
Section 8: Oxidation and Reduction of Metals The activity of metals is investigated. Oxidation and reduction and how they might be controlled to benefit people are discussed.	Redox reactions, Corrosion Ions, Spectator Ions Polyatomic ions Single replacement Galvanization Metal plating, Rust

CHAPTER 6

Chapter Concept Map

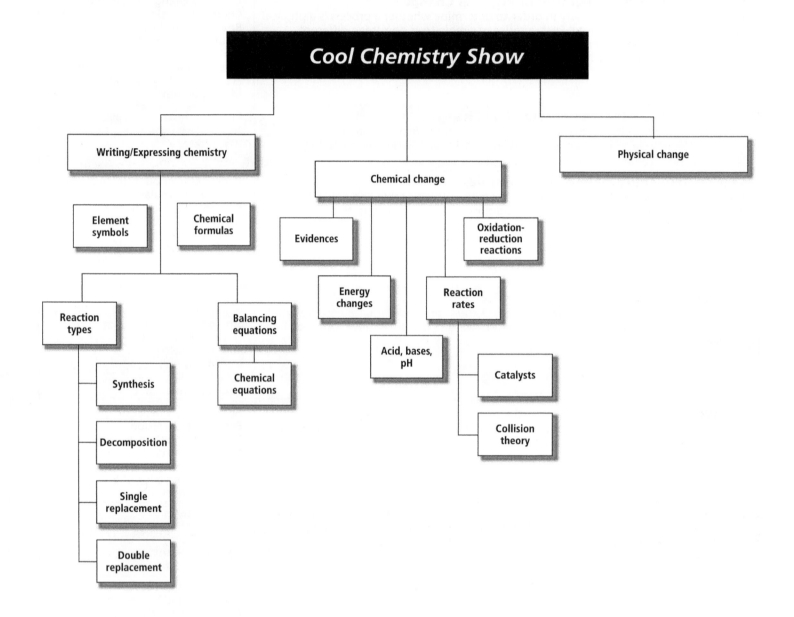

UNDERSTANDING BY DESIGN*

The *Understanding by Design* template focuses on the three stages of backward design:
- **Identify desired results**
- **Determine acceptable evidence**
- **Plan learning experiences**

What overarching understandings are desired?

- There are two basic types of changes that matter can undergo: chemical and physical.
- When chemical change occurs, new substances are produced.
- Pure substances are assigned chemical names with specific chemical formulas.
- Chemical change can be represented using word equations and chemical equations.
- Heat energy is either absorbed or released during chemical change.
- The rate of chemical reactions can vary.
- Aqueous solutions can be classified as acids or bases.
- Chemical change occurs when atoms or molecules collide with each other.
- During chemical change, electrons are transferred from one substance to another.

What are the overarching "essential" questions?

- How can changes in matter be demonstrated in an exciting way?
- How does matter change?
- How can chemical change be expressed in writing?
- How can chemical change be classified?
- Why does chemical change occur?

What will students understand as a result of this chapter?

- Give examples of chemical and physical changes.
- Cite evidences that a chemical change has occurred.
- Write symbols and formulas for elements and compounds.
- Write chemical equations for chemical reactions.
- Classify chemical reactions as synthesis, decomposition, single displacement or double displacement.
- Determine whether a chemical reaction is endothermic or exothermic.
- List some ways that the rate of chemical change can be increased.
- Classify solutions as either acids or bases.
- Explain how electrons are transferred during chemical change.

What "essential" questions will focus this chapter?

- How does matter undergo change?
- How do chemists express substances and how substances undergo change?
- What happens to the energy of substances during chemical change?
- How long does it take for chemical change?
- Can we influence the rate of chemical change?
- What are some common substances that are acids and bases?
- What is meant by the pH of a substance?
- What happens to electrons during chemical change?

* Grant Wiggins and Jay McTighe, *Understanding by Design* (Merrill/Prentice Hall, 1998), 181.

CHAPTER 6

Pacing Guide

This chapter will take about 4 weeks to complete, assuming a full 5-day school week. Keep in mind that a *Pacing Guide* is merely a suggestion and that you should adjust your pace to your students' needs and the school schedule.

A sample outline is shown below. It assumes that you will assign homework every day and that class time will be used to discuss homework and special topics. *Inquiring Further* activities, if assigned, will allow students to do research or investigations outside regular class time.

Note: Each "Day" assumes a 45-minute class period, or one-half of a 90-minute block.

DAY	SECTION	HOMEWORK
1	Discuss *Scenario, Your Challenge,* and *Criteria for Success.* Develop a scoring rubric. **Section 1** Discuss *What Do You See?* and *What Do You Think?* Students complete *Investigate* Steps 1-4. Review results of investigations. Perform teacher demo with sodium acetate, Step 5. Students complete *Investigate* Step 6. Review results of demonstration and investigation.	Read *Chem Talk* and answer *Checking Up* questions. Answer *What Do You Think Now?* questions.
2	Discuss *Chem Talk* and review *Checking Up* answers. Discuss *What Do You Think Now?* responses and *Chem Essential Questions.* Answer *Chem to Go* problems 1 and 2.	Answer *Chem to Go* problems 3-7. Read *Reflecting on the Section and the Challenge.*
3	Review *Chem to Go* answers. **Section 2** Discuss *What Do You See?* and *What Do You Think?* Students complete *Investigate.* Review results of investigations.	Read *Chem Talk* and answer *Checking Up* questions. Answer *What Do You Think Now?* questions.
4	Discuss Chem *Talk* and review *Checking Up* answers. Discuss *What Do You Think Now?* responses. Discuss *Chem Essential Questions.* Answer *Chem to Go* problem 1.	Answer *Chem to Go* problems 2-4. Read *Reflecting on the Section and the Challenge.*
5	Review *Chem to Go* answers. **Section 3** Discuss *What Do You See?* and *What Do You Think?* Students complete *Investigate.* Review results of investigations.	Read *Chem Talk* and answer *Checking Up* questions. Answer *What Do You Think Now?* questions.
6	Discuss *Chem Talk* and review *Checking Up* answers. Discuss *What Do You Think Now?* and *Chem Essential Questions.* Answer *Chem to Go* problems 1.a), 2.a), and 4 in class.	Answer *Chem to Go* problems 1.b-d), 2.b-d), 3, 5-9. Read *Reflecting on the Section and the Challenge.*
7	Review *Chem to Go* answers. **Section 4** *What Do You See?* and *What Do You Think?* Students complete the *Investigate.* Review results of the investigation.	Read *Chem Talk* and answer *Checking Up* questions. Answer *What Do You Think Now?* questions.
8	Discuss *Chem Talk* and review *Checking Up* answers. Discuss *What Do You Think Now?* and *Chem Essential Questions.* Answer *Chem to Go* problem 1.	Answer the *Chem to Go* problems 2-4. Read *Reflecting on the Section and the Challenge* and the *Chapter Mini-Challenge.* Work with group on the *Chapter Mini-Challenge.*

DAY	SECTION	HOMEWORK
9	Review the *Chem to Go* answers. Discuss the *Chapter Mini-Challenge*. Students present their *Chapter Mini-Challenge* and receive feedback.	Read and summarize the *Investigate* for *Section 5*.
10	**Section 5** Discuss *What Do You See?* and *What Do You Think?* Students complete *Investigate*. Review results of investigation.	Read *Chem Talk* and answer *Checking Up* questions. Answer *What Do You Think Now?* questions.
11	Discuss *Chem Talk* and review *Checking Up* answers. Discuss *Chem Essential Questions*. Answer *Chem to Go* problems 1.a-c) and 2 in class.	Answer *Chem to Go* problems 1.d-f), 3-8. Read *Reflecting on the Section and the Challenge*.
12	Review *Chem to Go* answers. **Section 6** Discuss *What Do You See?* and *What Do You Think?* Students complete *Investigate* Step 1. Perform teacher demo in Step 10 as students record data. Review results of investigations.	Read *Investigate* Steps 2-9. Outline your ideas for Steps 2, 5 and 8.a).
13	Students complete *Investigate* Steps 2-9. Discuss the results of the investigations.	Read *Chem Talk* and answer *Checking Up* questions. Answer *What Do You Think Now?* questions.
14	Discuss *Chem Talk* and review *Checking Up* answers. Discuss *What Do You Think Now?* and *Chem Essential Questions*. Answer *Chem to Go* problems 1 and 2	Answer *Chem to Go* problems 3-8. Read *Reflecting on the Section and the Challenge*.
15	Review *Chem to Go* answers. **Section 7** Discuss *What Do You See?* and *What Do You Think?* Students complete *Investigate*. Discuss results of the investigations.	Read *Chem Talk* and answer *Checking Up* questions. Answer *What Do You Think Now?* questions.
16	Discuss *Chem Talk* and review *Checking Up* answers. Discuss *What Do You Think Now?* and *Chem Essential Questions*. Answer *Chem to Go* problems 1, 2.a), and 3.a).	Answer *Chem to Go* problems 2.b), 3.b), 4-10. Read *Reflecting on the Section and the Challenge*.
17	Review *Chem to Go* answers and discuss *Reflecting on the Section and the Challenge*. **Section 8** Discuss *What Do You See?* and *What Do You Think?* Students complete the *Investigate*. Review the results of the investigation.	Read *Chem Talk* and answer *Checking Up* questions. Answer *What Do You Think Now?* questions.
18	Discuss *Chem Talk* and review the *Checking Up* answers. Discuss *What Do You Think Now?* and *Chem Essential Questions*. Answer *Chem to Go* problems 1 and 3.	Answer *Chem to Go* problems 2, 4-8. Read *Reflecting on the Section and the Challenge*. Read *Preparing for the Chapter Challenge*.
19	Review *Chem to Go* answers. Discuss *Preparing for the Chapter Challenge*. Work on the *Chapter Challenge*.	Work on the *Chapter Challenge* as a group.
20	*Chapter Challenge* presentations by students.	

CHAPTER 6

Chapter 6
Materials, Equipment, and Chemicals

The following tables contain lists of materials, equipment, and chemicals needed to do all of the sections. The tables are organized as follows:

- **Table 1:** Durables per group (4 Students)
- **Table 2:** Durables per class
- **Table 3:** Consumables per group (4 Students)
- **Table 4:** Consumables per class
- **Table 5:** Chemicals

Durables are items which are not consumed during the section and which can be used for several classes over several years. **Consumables** are items that are used up during each class and must be re-supplied for future classes. Both the durables and consumables are broken down by group and by class. A **group** consists of four students. While the groups size will be determined by the teacher based upon logistics and availability of equipment, the information in **Table 1** and **Table 3** is based upon the recommended group size of four students.

Materials and Equipment

The first table contains the **durable** items needed per group. The right column, **Quantity**, contains the number of items needed per group. The left column, **Section**, gives the section number(s) in which each item will be used. The item quantities given are considered to be a minimum but, in some cases, if more are available, that would be ideal.

The second table contains the information on **Durables** needed per class. In some cases, these will be items that are shared by the class. In other cases, the item will be used for a demonstration.

The third and fourth tables contain the items which are **consumable**. The third table contains **consumables per group** (recommended group size is four students) and the fourth table contains **consumables per class**.

TABLE 1: DURABLES PER GROUP (4 STUDENTS)		
Section	**Materials and Equipment (Durables)**	**Quantity**
All	Lab aprons	4
All	Safety goggles	4
1	Beaker, 1 L	1
1	Crucible tongs	1
1	Pencil	1
1	Pencil sharpener	1
1, 5	Graduated cylinder, 100 mL	1
1, 6	Beakers, 250 mL	4
1, 3, 6	Hot plate	1
1, 3, 6	Wire gauze for hot plate	2
2, 5, 6	Graduated cylinder, 50 mL	1
2, 3, 5, 8	Scoopula	1
2, 4, 6, 7	Large microwell plates, 24 well	2
2, 3, 5, 6, 8	Test tubes, large	9
2, 3, 5, 6, 8	Test-tube rack	1
3	Graduated cylinder, 10 mL	1
3, 6	Mortar and pestle	1
6	Glass stirring rod	1
6	Stopwatch	1
7	Beakers, 100 mL	3
7	Artist brush	1
8	Scissors	1
8	# 2 Rubber stopper with no hole	1

CHAPTER 6

TABLE 2: DURABLES PER CLASS

Section	Materials and Equipment (Durables)	Quantity
1, 5	Erlenmeyer flask, 250 mL**	1
1, 5	# 8 Rubber stopper with no hole**	1
3, 6	Beakers, 600 mL**	10
3, 5	Balances, 0.01 g	2
4	Beakers, 100 mL**	3
4, 5	Graduated cylinder, 50 mL**	1
5	Board, 1" × 6" × 8"**	1
6	Graduated cylinder, 100 mL**	3

TABLE 3: CONSUMABLES PER GROUP (4 STUDENTS)

Section	Materials and Equipment (Consumables)	Quantity
1	Disposable diaper	1
1	Glass jar with screw-top lid, 32 oz	1
1	Birthday candle	1
1, 4, 7	Beral pipettes	20
1, 6, 7, 8	Steel wool pad, fine mesh	1
2, 5	Resealable plastic bags, quart-size	3
3, 5	Weighing boats	5
3, 6	Antacid tablets, effervescent	7
5	Disposable rubber gloves, pairs	4
6	Tea bags	2
7	Vial of blue litmus paper	1
7	Vial of red litmus paper	1
8	Pie plates, aluminum	6

**teacher demonstration

TABLE 4: CONSUMABLES PER CLASS		
Section	**Materials and Equipment (Consumables)**	**Quantity**
1	Marble chips or limestone, lb.	1
1	Box of table salt, NaCl	1
1, 6	Spray can of starch	1
1, 2, 3	Boxes of baking soda	2
1, 3	Box of wood splints	1
1, 3	Box of matches	1
1, 3, 7	Bottles of household ammonia, pint	2
1, 3, 6, 7	Bottles of vinegar, pint	2
1, 6	Bucket of ice	1
1, 7	Bottle of lemon juice, pint	1
1, 7	Milk, pint	2
2	Straws, box	1
3	Baking powder, box	1
6	Bottle of hydrogen peroxide, H_2O_2, 3%, pint	1
7	Bottle of mineral water (or soda), 12 oz	1
7	Bottle of dishwashing fluid	1
7	Bottle of milk of magnesia, pint	1
7	Bottle of apple juice, pint	1
7	Window cleaner with ammonia	1
7	Distilled water, gal	1

CHAPTER 6

Chemicals

In this fifth table, the **Chemicals** required for each section are listed. By their nature, most chemicals are consumable, of course. The amounts given in the right-hand column under **Quantity** are calculated for 5 classes of 24 students, or 120 students. Most teachers will find that these amounts (when divided by 5 to give the amount needed for one class) will still provide ample excess for repeat experiments or student error. It should be noted that the metal strips in this list are meant to be used in other sections and in other chapters. After use as electrodes or testing with hydrochloric acid, they can be recovered, rinsed and used again.

TABLE 5: CHEMICALS FOR FIVE CLASSES (of 24 students each)		
Section	**Chemicals**	**Quantity**
1	Lugol's reagent	100 mL
1	Sodium silicate, 37.5% aqueous ("water glass")**	750 mL
1	Cobalt chloride, $(CoCl_2)$**	7.5 g
1	Copper (II) chloride, $(CuCl_2)$**	7.5 g
1	Nickel chloride, $(NiCl_2)$**	7.5 g
1	Iron (III) chloride, $(FeCl_3)$**	7.5 g
1	Manganese chloride, $(MnCl_2)$**	7.5 g
1	Sodium hydrogen sulfate, $(NaHSO_4)$, 0.1 M	200 mL
1	Sodium acetate, $(CH_3CO_2Na \cdot 3H_2O)$**	500 g
1, 2, 4	Sodium hydroxide, $(NaOH)$, 0.1 M	1600 mL
1, 2, 4	Copper (II) sulfate, $(CuSO_4)$, 0.1 M	1800 mL
1, 2, 6, 7	Hydrochloric acid, (HCl), 0.1 M	1700 mL
1, 4, 7	Phenolphthalein solution, 1%	200 mL
1	Zinc pieces	75 g
2	Phenol red indicator	100 mL
2	Iron (III) nitrate, $[Fe(NO_3)_3]$, 0.1 M	250 mL
2	Barium nitrate solution, $[Ba(NO_3)_2]$, 0.1 M	250 mL
2	Sodium bicarbonate, $(NaHCO_3)$ 0.1 M	250 mL
2, 4	Potassium iodide solution, (KI), 0.1 M	750 mL
2, 4	Silver nitrate solution, $(AgNO_3)$, 0.1 M	750 mL
2	Calcium chloride, $(CaCl_2)$	250 g

**teacher demonstration

TABLE 5: CHEMICALS FOR FIVE CLASSES (of 24 students each)

2, 7	Saturated solution of calcium hydroxide, [Ca(OH)$_2$]	5 L
4	Ammonia hydroxide, (NH$_3$), 2.0 M**	700 mL
4	Potassium carbonate, (K$_2$CO$_3$), 0.1 M	600 mL
4	Iron (III) chloride, (FeCl$_3$), 0.1 M	600 mL
4	Magnesium sulfate solution, (MgSO$_4$), 0.1 M	600 mL
4	Magnesium sulfate solution, (MgSO$_4$), 1.0 M**	100 mL
4, 8	Copper (II) sulfate, (CuSO$_4$), 1.0 M	700 mL
5	Ammonium nitrate, (NH$_4$NO$_3$)	350 g
5	Ammonium thiocyanate, (CH$_3$N$_2$SH)	100 g
5	Barium hydroxide, [Ba(OH)$_2$]	200 g
5	Sodium hydroxide pellets, (NaOH)	50 g
5	Sodium carbonate, (NaCO$_3$)	750 g
6, 7	Magnesium ribbon	3 m
6	Manganese dioxide, (MnO$_2$)	50 g
6	Potassium iodate, (KIO$_3$) 0.1 M	5 L
6	Sodium hydrogen sulfite, (NaHSO$_3$), 0.25 M	600 mL
6, 7	Zinc pieces	50 g
7	Magnesium hydroxide [Mg(OH)$_2$], 1.0 M	175 mL
7	Sulfuric acid solution, (H$_2$SO$_4$), 1.0 M	175 mL
7	Potassium hydroxide, (KOH), 1.0 M	175 mL
7	Sodium hydroxide, (NaOH), 1.0 M	175 mL
7	Universal indicator solution	100 mL
7	Bromothymol blue indicator solution	100 mL
7	0.3% methyl red indicator solution	100 mL
8	Zinc granules	60 g
8	Copper strips	7
8	Zinc strips	7
8	Copper (II) nitrate, [Cu(NO$_3$)$_2$], 1.0 M	500 mL
8	Aluminum nitrate, [Al(NO$_3$)$_3$], 1.0 M	500 mL

**teacher demonstration

CHAPTER 6

Teacher Resources

Blackline Masters

- Blackline Masters
Available on the *Teacher Resources CD*.

- Color Overheads
Available on the *Teacher Resources CD*.

Blackline Masters

Chapter Supports

	POINT OF USE	BLACKLINE MASTER LABEL
Sample Criteria for Excellence	*Chapter Challenge* Introduction	6a
Sample Assessment Rubric	*Chapter Challenge* Conclusion	6b
Chem at Work: Profile 1	Chem at Work	6c
Chem at Work: Profile 2	Chem at Work	6d
Chem at Work: Profile 3	Chem at Work	6e

Section Quizzes

Section1 Quiz	Section 1	6-1b
Section 2 Quiz	Section 2	6-2b
Section 3 Quiz	Section 3	6-3c
Section 4 Quiz	Section 4	6-4c
Section 5 Quiz	Section 5	6-5c
Section 6 Quiz	Section 6	6-6a
Section 7 Quiz	Section 7	6-7d
Section 8 Quiz	Section 8	6-8a

Section Supports

	POINT OF USE	BLACKLINE MASTER LABEL
Chemical vs. Physical Changes Table	Section 1 – *Investigate*	6-1a
Chemical Reactions Blank Data Table I	Section 2 – *Investigate*	6-2a
Common Polyatomic Ions Table	Section 3 – *Investigate*	6-3a
Chemical Reactions Blank Data Table II	Section 3 – *Investigate*	6-3b
Chemical Reactions Blank Data Table III	Section 4 – *Investigate*	6-4a
Bond Energies Table	Section 5 – *Chem Talk*	6-5a
Solution Reactions Data Table	Section 7 – *Investigate*	6-7a
Sample Data Table-pH of Household Substances	Section 7 – *Investigate*	6-7b
Titration Graph	Section 7 – *Chem Talk*	6-7c

Chapter Assessment

Chem Practice Test	*Chapter Conclusion*	6f

Color Overheads

	POINT OF USE
What Do You See?	Section 1
What Do You See?	Section 2
What Do You See?	Section 3
What Do You See?	Section 4
What Do You See?	Section 5
What Do You See?	Section 6
pH scale	Section 7 – *Chem Talk*
What Do You See?	Section 8

CHAPTER 6

Chapter Challenge

Scenario

Read, or have a student read aloud, the *Scenario*. You may wish to expand on the *Scenario* by using videos, or by inviting persons from the field to present the *Scenario*.

Your Challenge

You may wish to lead a class discussion about the challenge and the expectations. Review the titles of the sections in the *Table of Contents*. To remind students that that the content of the sections corresponds to the content expected for the *Chapter Challenge*, ask them to explain how the title of each section relates to the expectations. Familiarize the students with the structure of each section. When you come to the *Reflecting on the Section and the Challenge*, point out that each section contributes to the challenge in some way. As you discuss the challenge, reassure students that while the challenge may seem overwhelming now, by the end of the chapter they will have the necessary skills and vocabulary to respond adequately.

Chapter Challenge

6 Cool Chemistry Show

Scenario

The fourth- and fifth-grade students at a local elementary school have been studying chemistry in their classes. Because of the students' overwhelming interest, their teachers have asked your class to present a chemistry science show to their students. The elementary teachers have requested that the show be both interesting and informative. For the chemistry science show, the fourth-grade teachers are asking your class to include demonstrations and explanations about chemical and physical properties. The fifth-grade teacher wants the students to learn more about acids and bases, and about chemical reactions that involve color changes.

Your Challenge

You and your classmates are being challenged to present an entertaining and informative chemistry science show to fourth- and fifth-grade students.

- The content of the show should meet the needs and interest of your audience. Keep in mind that you will need to tailor your shows to address the specific needs of both the fourth- and fifth-grade teachers' requests. Your class may choose to add other presentations to enhance the show.

- All presentations must include a demonstration and an audience-appropriate explanation of the chemistry concepts involved.

- You must provide the teachers with a written summary including directions for your chemistry show with explanations of the chemistry. Although you are giving a presentation to elementary students, your understanding of your chosen demonstrations should be appropriate for high-school students.

- As always, safety is a top priority. You and your classmates will wear safety gear, including safety goggles, appropriate to the presentation being conducted. Presentations including flammable or explosive reactions are not appropriate for the elementary audience and may not be included in the show.

The class as a whole is responsible for putting on this *Cool Chemistry Show*. You will need to coordinate your selection of presentations to provide a show that addresses a variety of chemistry concepts in an entertaining and informative manner.

462

Criteria for Success

How will your involvement in the *Cool Chemistry Show* be graded? What qualities should a good presentation have? Discuss these issues in small groups and with your class. You may decide that some or all of the following qualities of your presentation should be graded:

- Knowledge of chemistry content beyond what is presented
- accuracy
- meets teacher needs (fourth or fifth grade)
- number of concepts addressed

Demonstration
- carefully planned
- safety
- explanation (age-appropriate)
- adherence to assigned time limits
- showmanship

- creativity
- clarity
- organization
- appeal
- written summary
- directions for experiment
- explanation of chemistry
- appropriateness for an elementary school teacher with limited chemistry background
- statements concerning safety needs

Chem Corner

Chemistry in *Cool Chemistry Show*

- Physical properties
- Chemical properties
- Concentrations of solutions
- Chemical tests
- Chemical names
- Chemical formulas
- Valence electrons
- Ionic compounds
- Polyatomic ions
- Covalent and ionic bonds

- Chemical equations
- Single-replacement reactions
- Double-replacement reactions
- Exothermic and endothermic reactions
- Chemical kinetics
- Acids, bases, indicators
- Acid/base definitions
- Acid–base reactions
- Oxidation-reduction reactions

463

Chem Corner

This is a list of the basic science concepts and skills that will be covered in the various sections in this chapter. It may be useful to elicit definitions of the terms from the class. Canvas your students to see how many of the terms are familiar to them before the chapter begins and which ones they will have to learn about. Encourage them to offer ideas as to how these principles and skills might be incorporated in a chemistry show.

CHAPTER 6

Chapter Challenge

Criteria for Success

Before the students read this section, you can ask them what they think their *Chapter Challenge* chemistry show should be like to earn a top grade. You can take a few moments as a class to decide on the criteria for judging their projects. It is important for students to actively participate in this exercise to instill a sense of ownership and to motivate them to succeed.

List some suggestions on the board of criteria they might consider, such as number of concepts addressed, accuracy, creativity, etc. The students should be able to come up with others. It may be helpful to organize the criteria into categories, such as content, demonstration, presentation, teamwork, etc. You can use a voting system to narrow down and finalize the list.

After having this 10 minute discussion with the students, you can read aloud the *Criteria for Success* section. It should help reinforce the discussion and may also add some interesting points that did not emerge earlier.

Students should now try to develop a rough rubric for grading the *Chapter Challenge*. This can be as simple as ascribing points to each of their criteria.

Chapter Challenge

Once your class has determined the list of criteria for judging the presentations, you should also decide how many points should be given for each criterion. Determining grading criteria in advance will help you focus your time and effort on the various aspects of the presentation. How many points should be assigned to the content and how many should be assigned to the actual presentation? Will each high school student be involved in only one presentation, or more? For each criterion, you should decide on how excellence is defined and how it compares to a satisfactory effort.

Because you will be working with other students in small groups, you will need to determine grading criteria that reward each individual in the group for his or her contribution and also reward the group for the final presentation. You should discuss different strategies and choose the one that is best suited to your situation. Your teacher may provide you with a sample rubric to help you get started.

This challenge is going to feel a lot like ordering one pizza to satisfy five different people. Creating one coordinated *Cool Chemistry Show* will require a lot of cooperation and compromise. The simplified *Engineering Design Cycle* you have been using for each *Chapter Challenge* will help your class complete this design challenge. Understanding the *Goal* is the first step in any *Engineering Design Cycle*. You know that compiling a *Cool Chemistry Show* for fourth- and fifth-graders is your challenge, so you are already on the path to success. Each chapter section you complete will provide you with potential additional ideas that can become part of your show.

As you experience each one of the chapter sections you will be gaining *Inputs* to use in the *Engineering Design Cycle*. These *Inputs* will include new chemistry concepts, new chemical reactions, and even techniques that might be incorporated in your class show. Each section of this chapter will help you learn important information you can use to teach the younger students about chemical reactions. When your class prepares the *Mini-Challenge* presentation and the *Chapter Challenge,* you will be completing the *Process* step of the *Engineering Design Cycle*. During the *Process* step you will consider different potential reactions, compare and contrast potential ideas, and, most importantly, make decisions about the types of chemistry demonstrations your class will perform as part of your show.

The *Output* of your *Engineering Design Cycle* will be the performances of your show and the chemistry explanations that go along with it. Remember, you will provide explanations targeted at fourth- and fifth-grade students as well as written explanations that demonstrate your thorough understanding of the chemistry. Finally, you will receive *Feedback* from your audience and your instructor about what parts of show are good and which parts need to be refined. You will repeat the *Engineering Design Cycle* two times during the course of the chapter. The first will be as you complete the *Mini-Challenge* halfway through the chapter. The second is after you complete the second half of the chapter and gain more *Inputs*, finalize your show, and complete your written explanations.

464

For example, the content could be worth 30 points, the explanation worth 20, the presentation worth 30, and the teamwork effort worth another 20 points. A sample assessment rubric for assessing the *Chapter Challenge* is provided at the end of this chapter. This can be shared with the students as a guide for their own creation, or used as a standard to compare theirs with. Be sure to encourage active participation; the more input the students have in the criteria and the rubric, the more commitment they are likely to have for the work and the expectations.

At the end of the chapter, you can copy and distribute the rubric as it is designed, or use it as a baseline for developing scoring guidelines and expectations that suit your needs. For example, you might wish to ensure that core concepts and abilities derived from your local or state science frameworks also appear on the rubric. You might also wish to modify the format of the rubric to make it more consistent with your evaluation system. However you decide to evaluate the *Chapter Challenge*, keep in mind that all expectations should be communicated to the students at the start of their work.

The Sample Criteria for Excellence is also provided as a Blackline Master in your *Teacher Resources CD*.

| 6a | **Blackline Master** |

SAMPLE CRITERIA FOR EXCELLENCE

It is important for students to determine the criteria for grading the *Chapter Challenge* themselves so they know what to expect and what to strive for. You can help them compile a list of criteria by outlining those aspects of the project that you consider important and by ascribing a value to each. Some aspects that might be considered are accuracy and knowledge of the chemistry content that is displayed in the show, whether it meets your specific needs, and making sure the proper safety measures are practiced at all times. You may want to share some of the sample criteria below to help

students make their own list they feel meets the standard of excellence for this particular *Chapter Challenge*. Remember, at this time students are simply establishing the criteria to be considered for earning an A in order to motivate them to succeed.

As the *Chapter Challenge* approaches, you will need to develop a more comprehensive assessment rubric for evaluating the projects according to your own grading system. For an example, you can find a complete *Sample Assessment Rubric for Chapter 6* at the end of the chapter in this *Teacher's Edition*.

MEETS THE STANDARD OF EXCELLENCE FOR CHAPTER CHALLENGE

Aspect	Criteria of Excellence
Chemistry concepts	• at least six chemistry concepts are accurately incorporated into the show • procedures for the chemistry show are safe, accurate, and effectively demonstrate the chemical principles
Quality of science show	• chemistry show demonstration is creative, well-crafted, rehearsed, and has high entertainment value • is appropriate for the grade level it is targeting
Scientific explanations	• appropriate and correct science vocabulary is used for the grade level that is being targeted • clear explanations detailing how each chemical procedure works are provided
Written summary	• a thorough and well-written summary of all procedures and related chemical principles is provided for the teacher

CHAPTER 6

SECTION 1
Solutions: Chemical or Physical Change?

Section Overview

At the beginning of the section, 15 very brief and simple procedures are carried out, after which the students determine whether the observed results are due to physical or chemical changes. Students will make predictions about the absorptive power of a disposable diaper, and them observe. After you conduct a teacher demonstration of the precipitation of sodium acetate from a supersaturated solution, students will mix a "water-glass" solution and observe the effects of ion movement. This solution should be monitored and observed over a period of several days.

Background Information

The properties of matter can be grouped into two categories: physical and chemical. Color, density, freezing point, melting point, boiling point, hardness, and odor are all examples of a substance's physical properties. In all cases, these properties can be observed without changing the identity and composition of the material. Chemical properties show how each substance can react to produce a different substance or substances. Flammability or the decomposition of a substance are examples of chemical properties because new substances are formed. The new substances will have new physical and chemical properties.

Some properties of matter are independent of the amount of matter. We call these properties intensive properties. Among these properties are temperature, density, melting point, and boiling point. Whether you have one gram or a thousand grams, the intensive properties of a substance are the same. Sometimes these properties are listed on the periodic table, and can be used to help identify an element or material. More often the student will have to consult tables of data to find this information. The extensive properties of a material, like mass and volume, will always depend on the amount of material present.

Physical changes can alter a material's physical appearance but will not change its composition. If ice is melted into water, the physical state changes from a solid to a liquid, but the chemical composition of the water does not change. It is still H_2O. The same is true when liquid water evaporates into the gas phase. The gaseous H_2O still has the same composition as the liquid water.

When a substance undergoes a chemical reaction (or we could say a chemical change), it loses its original characteristics and becomes a new substance. An example is water, a liquid at room temperature, when it decomposes into hydrogen gas and oxygen gas. Another example is zinc metal reacting with hydrochloric acid to produce hydrogen gas and zinc chloride. The chemical and physical properties of the products, hydrogen gas and zinc chloride, are far different than the reactants, zinc metal and hydrochloric acid.

Solutions

Many of the chemicals in our bodies are dissolved in water – that is, they occur in aqueous solution. Solutions are typically described in terms of *solute* and *solvent*. The solvent is the component of a solution that is present in the greatest amount. Solutes are substances dissolved in a solution, and the components are present in smaller amounts than the solvent. The solubility of a solute is the amount of solute that will dissolve in a given amount of solvent at a given temperature. This is often described in terms of grams of solute per

100 g of solvent. Since solubility is temperature-dependent, the temperature must be specified with any solubility data. When a solution contains the maximum amount of solute for the conditions, the solution is said to be *saturated* with regard to the solute at that temperature. If it contains more solute than would be expected, then the solution is *supersaturated*. This is an unstable condition that is likely to change spontaneously to a stable condition by solute being released from solution. This is true of solutes that are solid, liquid, or gas.

Quantifying concentrations (the ratio of amount of solute to solvent) of solutions is used to define a solution. Molarity is the most common chemical term for concentration and is defined as the number of moles of solute per liter of solution.

For example, the most concentrated solution of sulfuric acid (H_2SO_4), a strong acid that you can obtain commercially, is about 18 molar. For each liter of solution, there are 18 moles (1764 grams) of sulfuric acid present.

Another way to express concentration is percent, or parts per hundred. This is probably the most familiar concentration term in non-scientific situations. Common vinegar solutions are about 5-6% acetic acid in water, which indicates that the solution contains about 5-6 g of acetic acid for every 100 g of vinegar solution. Changing these numbers to molarity, 60 g of acetic acid in 1000 mL (1 L) of solution would be about a 1 molar solution. Conveniently, in this example, the molar mass of acetic acid is 60 g/mol.

LEARNING OUTCOMES		
LEARNING OUTCOMES	**LOCATION IN SECTION**	**EVIDENCE OF UNDERSTANDING**
Learn to differentiate between chemical and physical changes.	*Investigate* Step 1	Students' observations are similar to those given in this *Teacher's Edition*.
Make observations and cite evidence to identify changes as chemical or physical.	*Investigate* Steps 2-3 *Chem to Go* Questions 1-4	Students are able to organize evidence for the types of changes and identify the types of changes observed. Students' conclusions match those outlined in this *Teacher's Edition*.
Give examples of chemical and physical changes you encounter in everyday life.	*Investigate* Step 1	Students can provide appropriate examples that correlate with the investigation.
Explore the new properties exhibited when new materials are made from combinations of two or more original materials as a result of a chemical change.	*Investigate* Steps 4-6	Students can focus on the difference between the starting materials and the ending materials to identify the type of change occurring.
Design an experiment to test properties of different combinations of materials.	*Chem to Go* Question 5 *Inquiring Further*	Students can describe how to differentiate two solutions that appear similar. Students are able to design and carry out an experiment to determine the effects of different factors on solubility.

CHAPTER 6

NOTES

_____

_____

_____

_____

_____

Section 1
Materials, Chemicals, Preparation, and Safety

("per Group" quantity is based on group size of 4 students)

Materials and Equipment

Materials (and Equipment)	Quantity per Group (4 students)
Beaker, 1 L	1
Tongs	1
Pencil	1
Pencil sharpener	1
Graduated cylinder, 100 mL	1
Beaker, 250 mL	1
Hot plate	1
Wire gauze for hot plate	1
Birthday candle	1
Marble chip or limestone	1
Disposable diaper, polyacrylate	1
Glass jar with screw-top lid, 32 oz	1
Steel wool, pad, fine	1

Materials (and Equipment)	Quantity per Class
Baking soda, $NaHCO_3$, sodium bicarbonate, box	1
Wooden splints, box	1
Starch, spray can	1
Ammonia, household, NH_3(aq), pint	1
Bucket of ice	1
Table salt, NaCl	50 g
Lemon juice, pint	1
Milk, pint	1
Vinegar, pint	1
Beral pipettes	100
250-mL Erlenmeyer flask w/ rubber stopper*	1
Box of matches	1

Chemicals

Chemicals	Quantity per Class (24 students)
Sodium acetate, $NaC_2H_3O_2$*	100 g
Lugol's solution	20 mL
Zinc, Zn, small pieces	15 g
Sodium silicate, 37.5% aqueous*	150 mL
Cobalt chloride*	1.5 g
Copper (II) chloride*	1.5 g
Nickel chloride*	1.5 g
Iron (III) chloride*	1.5 g
Manganese chloride*	1.5 g
Sodium hydrogen sulfate, 0.1 M	40 mL
Sodium hydroxide, 0.1 M, NaOH**	120 mL
Copper (II) sulfate, 0.1 M, $CuSO_4$**	120 mL
Hydrochloric acid, 0.1 M, HCl**	120 mL
1% Phenolphthalein solution, PHTH**	20 mL

*Materials, equipment, or chemicals for teacher demonstration only
**These solutions should be stored in dropper bottles. Many are used in later experiments.

Teacher Preparation

Sodium silicate, 37.5%: This is best purchased as a solution which is then diluted for use. In this section, each 100 mL will be diluted with 400 mL of distilled water.

Lugol's solution for the starch test: For 120 mL of solution, dissolve 2.4 g of KI in 100 mL of distilled water. Add 1.2 g of elemental iodine, I_2. Stir and dilute to 120 mL. Store in brown bottles. To make 1.0 liter, dissolve 20 g of KI in 200 mL of distilled water. Add 10 g of iodine and stir to dissolve. Dilute to 1.0 L and store in 6 brown dropper bottles.

Sodium hydroxide, 0.1 *M*: With care and stirring, add 0.48 g of NaOH to 100 mL of distilled water. When dissolved, dilute to 120 mL. Store in 6 dropping bottles. To make 1 liter, dissolve 4.0 g of NaOH in 1000 mL (1 L) of distilled water.

Copper sulfate, 0.1 *M*: Dissolve 30.0 g of $CuSO_4 \bullet 5H_2O$ in 100 mL of distilled water. When dissolved, dilute to 120 mL. Store in 6 dropping bottles. To make 1.0 liter, dissolve 300 g and dissolve in about 700 mL of distilled water. Dilute to 1.0 L.

Hydrochloric acid, 0.1 *M*: Slowly and carefully, with stirring and in a fume hood, add 8.3 mL of concentrated HCl (12 *M*) to 800 mL of distilled water. Dilute to 1.0 L. Store in 6 dropping bottles

Phenolphthalein, 1% in alcohol: Dissolve 1.2 g of phenolphthalein in 50 mL of 95% ethanol, then dilute to 120 mL with additional ethanol. Store in 6 dropping bottles.

Sodium acetate solution, supersaturated: Place 100 g of $NaC_2H_3O_2 \bullet 3H_2O$ in a 250 mL Erlenmeyer flask. Add 10 mL of distilled water and heat, with stirring, until all the solid has gone into solution. Cover and allow to cool slowly to room temperature without any disturbances. Save one crystal of the sodium acetate to perform the demonstration.

Starch solution, 1%: With stirring, spray a can of commercial spray starch into 100 mL of distilled water for about 1 minute. This will make approximately a 1% solution.

Safety Requirements

- Goggles and aprons are required in the laboratory area.

- Solutions can be disposed of down the drain.

- Solids can be placed in the trash.

- Save the supersaturated sodium acetate solution.

- Save the sodium silicate solution with the metal ions.

- Wash hands and arms before leaving the laboratory area.

NOTES

_____

_____

_____

_____

_____

_____

CHAPTER 6

Meeting the Needs of All Students
Differentiated Instruction

Augmentation and Accommodations

LEARNING ISSUE	REFERENCE	AUGMENTATION AND ACCOMMODATIONS
Organizing skills	*Scenario, Your Challenge, Chem Corner, and Criteria*	**Accommodation** • Some students may be overwhelmed by the amount and different types of information they must think about in planning the *Chapter Challenge*. Provide a task that helps organize the ideas presented. After students have read *Your Challenge*, ask them to list all characteristics in the reading having to do with chemistry content. They should then make separate lists for criteria related to project format and a third list of rules they must follow. The project format list will give students a separate, concrete description of what their final project includes. They will see that the *Chem Corner* list on the next page fits nicely with their content-related list, and the criteria they are asked to consider for evaluation of their projects is probably a separate list.

Class participation	*What Do You Think?*	**Accommodations**
		• Differentiating the *What Do You Think?* discussion will increase the engagement of students and the willingness of reluctant learners to share their prior understandings with the class.
		Ten ways to engage and elicit:
		  o Begin by asking the most reluctant participant to break one match and light the other.
		  o Ask other students who don't often share, questions that require them to report simple observations.
		  o Offering an opinion may be a greater academic risk for some. Save those questions for students ready to take such risks.
		  o Encourage everyone by accepting every answer, since being right or wrong is part of learning at this step of the lesson.
		  o Acknowledge students taking greater risks than they usually take.
		  o Create an environment safe for participation by making sure everyone knows he/she will not be humiliated when participating in class.
		  o Call on students. Depending on students to raise hands usually leads to class discussions dominated by your most verbal learners.
		  o Have students record their ideas and share them with the person next to them. Strategic seating assignments will allow less verbal students to gain confidence by sharing their answers in small groups.
		  o Pair less capable students with more capable students and ask the less capable student to report what he and his partner shared. Doing so allows him to share his answer or his partner's depending on his confidence level.
		  o When students are thinking or in a paired discussion, alert a student that when the class discussion reconvenes, you will call on him/her. That gives him longer wait time and a chance to prepare.

Differentiating instruction to match readiness and interests	*Investigate* 1.	**Accommodations** • There are many changes students could observe in the procedures in addition to the ones listed. Using stations instead of doing demonstrations for the class as a whole allows you to differentiate for students ready for more difficult challenges or who will engage more in a subject of interest. • Look at the list of procedures and changes to be observed. Find a variety that are easy and include both chemical and physical changes. Consider assigning your weakest students to observe those along with some of interest to them. • Have your weakest students begin at the easiest stations. • Create some additional procedures with changes that might be tougher to identify. Mix some of those in with the standard procedures you assign your most capable students. • Find out the interests of your least motivated learners and set up procedures related to their interests. The procedures could involve cars, music or cosmetics.

LEARNING ISSUE	REFERENCE	AUGMENTATION AND ACCOMMODATIONS
Organizing observations Classifying changes	*Investigate* 2.a)	**Augmentation** • Teach students to form their charts based on careful reading and highlighting of the paragraph to determine chart headings. **Accommodations** • Have students read the instructions and set up their table before they observe the changes in the first procedure. • Have students add two columns to their table so they can record whether the change is physical or chemical and the rationale for their choice in Step 3.a. • Give students a table they can use to record their observations.
Design an investigation	*Investigate* 4.b)	**Accommodation** • Give students a rubric or an outline that includes information they can reformat into their own investigation.
Distinguishing characteristics of physical and chemical changes Taking good notes from a reading Developing vocabulary	*Chem Talk*	**Augmentation** • The *Chem Talk* explains the differences between chemical and physical changes. Ask students to organize notes on this reading using one of the differentiated methods that follow. Students will need models of each type. Create four models using types of fruit to teach students about the structures. Elicit comments about the advantages and disadvantages of each. Point out that different models will appeal to different types of learners. • Students could make a standard outline where the topics and indentations show the relationships among the terms. • Students could make a circle diagram showing the relationships. This type of graphic organizer may be unfamiliar to students, but one that can clearly show the relationships in this particular reading. It would begin with a big circle labeled Changes. Within the boundaries of the original circle would be two overlapping circles labeled Physical and Chemical. Inside the Chemical and Physical circles would be Definition, Characteristics and Examples. • Some students may prefer to make flash cards with the vocabulary term on the front and a definition and example on the back. But add an important requirement that students include a final step in which they organize all the cards on a table in a way that shows the relationships among them. • Students could also make a graphic organizer like the partial one below:

CHAPTER 6

Strategies for Students with Limited English Language Proficiency

LEARNING ISSUE	REFERENCE	AUGMENTATIONS
Background knowledge	*Chapter Challenge*	Students will benefit from a discussion about the term, *"audience appropriate"* as they begin to plan their presentations. When students are writing summaries for their presentations they would benefit from having a model from which to craft their own. If students have no prior experience with rubrics, there is potential for students to learn the process through creating a rubric.
Background knowledge	*What Do You Think?*	Students might benefit from a discussion of the various uses of the word *"matter."*
Vocabulary	*Investigate*	Check for understanding of the word *"substances."* Students might benefit from working in teams or with partners to carry out each of the steps. Some background knowledge of the word *"precipitates"* might help with understanding. Help with pronunciation of some of the chemical names and labels. Check for use of *"disposable."*
Background knowledge Vocabulary Comprehending text	*Chem Talk*	Check for understanding of bold-type words. Multiple uses are helpful to apply understanding, such as the explanation of the uses of *"concentration."* Refer students to sidebar material for further explanations of the isolated words.
Background knowledge	*What Do You Think Now?*	There are many questions stacked in this section. Help students isolate the various questions prior to answering. Also, explain what it means to *"support"* an answer.
Background knowledge Vocabulary Comprehending text	*Chem Essential Questions*	Have students work with partners to write their explanations, possibly having one student dictate to another. Help students compare the differences between physical and chemical changes, and suggest a format since they will have an audience.
Comprehension Vocabulary	*Chem to Go*	Make sure students understand questions that are stacked, where there is more than one response. Make sure students understand when a question is a multiple-choice response.
Application Comprehension	*Inquiring Further*	Make sure that students are clear on the concept of *"solubility."* Explain how the results are either independent or dependent and ensure that those words are understood.

NOTES

_____

_____

_____

_____

_____

_____

_____

_____

NOTES

Section 1
Teaching Suggestions and Sample Answers

What Do You See?

In this illustration, several students are shown mixing solutions as part of a chemistry show. Ask your students to analyze what the artist was attempting to reveal in the depiction. You may want to make this part of a regular routine to be kept in their *Active Chemistry* logs. Depending on your students' abilities, this illustration will invoke a wide range of responses from a simple, "The kids are putting on a show," to "Doing chemistry is scary, like Halloween." Use the responses you get from the *What Do You See?* illustration and the *What Do You Think?* questions as means to elicit prior knowledge and engage your students in this section. Keep in mind that there are no wrong answers and that the goal is student response and engagement.

What Do You Think?

This section and the *What Do You See?* section preceding it provide students with an opportunity to demonstrate prior learning of the subject matter. Good instruction elicits prior understanding and allows students to practice the transfer of what they already know to the concepts to be learned during the section. Engaging students in topics associated with the section that they already know something about generates enthusiasm in the learner and gives you a chance to evaluate their prior conceptions. You must be careful not to be judgmental and to accept all responses. It is important, however, that students provide specific reasons for their choice between chemical and physical change in the *What Do You Think?* questions.

What Do You Think?
A CHEMIST'S RESPONSE

Chemical changes occur when substances are converted into new substances. The ignition of the match causes a chemical change. It irreversibly changes the form and properties of the match because new substances are produced. Water (H_2O), carbon dioxide (CO_2), and carbon have been produced from the wooden match, which is mostly cellulose, and oxygen (O_2). Breaking a match is a physical change because it only makes the pieces smaller. The properties are unchanged because the substances remain the same.

STUDENTS' PRIOR CONCEPTIONS

Students tend to focus on the tangible, visual features accompanying chemical changes. Molecular changes are usually not visible, and are therefore abstract chemical concepts. Students often believe that the particles possess the same properties associated with the macroscopic matter. (For example, they might believe gold atoms are shiny and hard, that water molecules are tiny droplets of water.)

Students often do not understand that new substances can form by recombining the atoms in the former substances. They tend to see chemical change as resulting from a separate change in the original substance, and believe that properties exhibited after a chemical change result from a material gaining or losing matter. For example, many students will believe that the mass of rust from a completely rusted iron nail will be less than that of the original nail.

Section 1 | Solutions: Chemical or Physical Change?

What Do You See?

What Do You Think?

Chemistry is the study of matter and how matter changes. Changes in matter are described as physical changes and chemical changes. Consider two wooden matches. One is broken in half and the other is lit on fire by striking it along the side of the matchbox. In both of these instances matter has changed.

• **Which match has undergone a chemical change? Which has undergone a physical change? Give specific reasons to support your answer. How did you make your decision?**

The *What Do You Think?* questions are meant to get you thinking about what you already know or think you know. Don't worry about being right or wrong. Discussing what you think you know is an important step in learning.

Record your ideas about these questions in your *Active Chemistry* log. Be prepared to discuss your responses with your group and the class.

Investigate

1. Here are 15 opportunities for you to observe changes in matter. Your teacher may choose to do some or all of these as a demonstration or set up stations for you to visit. Notice that the directions call for small amounts of substances.

Learning Outcomes

In this section you will

• Learn to differentiate between chemical and physical changes.

• Make observations and cite evidence to identify changes as chemical or physical.

• Give examples of chemical and physical changes you encounter in everyday life.

• Explore the new properties exhibited when new materials are made from combinations of two or more original materials as a result of a chemical change.

• Design an experiment to test properties of different combinations of materials.

465

Active Chemistry

The following are common misconceptions regarding physical changes:

• As a material goes from solid to liquid to gas, the molecules change in size.

• Expansion is due to the expansion of particles rather than the spacing of the particles.

• Covalent bonds are broken in the process of melting and boiling.

• When a material dissolves in solution, that material changes from a solid to a liquid.

• The bubbles in boiling water are composed of air. Changes in the solid/liquid/gas phase of a substance involve chemical change.

Many students do not make a distinction between a solution and a pure liquid. Having them evaporate a pure liquid and then a liquid solution will be instructive because they will be able to see the residue left behind from the solution. Most students will be unaware that solutions are not limited to liquids, but can also be gaseous or solids.

CHAPTER 6

Investigate

1.

You may choose to do all or to select the most instructive procedures for the students to do. The first five procedures on the list work well as demonstrations and can be followed by questions. Most students will know what will happen in each case, but the question and answer period will enable them to see the pattern and to apply it to the last 10 procedures. Also, conducting the first five as demonstrations will save class time.

2.

Even as a demonstration, the students should record their observations in their *Active Chemistry* logs.

2.a)

The table on the next page can serve as a model. It is provided for you as a Blackline Master on the *Teacher Resources CD*.

6-1a	Blackline Master

 Cool Chemistry Show

Safety goggles and a lab apron must be worn *at all times* in a chemistry lab.

Report any broken, cracked, or chipped glassware to your teacher.

Hot plates may remain hot for some time after they are turned off.

Hydrochloric acid is corrosive. Handle with caution.

Copper sulfate contains a heavy metal. Dispose of it as directed by your teacher.

Before you begin the *Investigate*, make a data table to organize your observations. You will want to record what was done and detailed observations for changes that take place.

a) Heat an ice cube in a beaker until it melts. Continue heating the ice cube after it melts.

b) Boil a small amount of water.

c) Melt a small amount of candle wax. Allow the wax to cool.

d) Break a wooden splint into several pieces.

e) Hold a wooden splint in a flame.

f) Add a few drops of lemon juice to a small amount of milk.

g) Add a few drops of vinegar to a small amount of baking soda ($NaHCO_3$).

h) Add a small amount of table salt to water. Stir. Consider what would happen if you allowed the water to evaporate from this mixture.

i) Add several drops of iodine solution to a small amount of starch.

j) Add a small piece of polished zinc to a small amount of hydrochloric acid (0.1 *M* HCl).

k) Add a drop of phenolphthalein indicator *solution* to a solution of sodium hydroxide (0.1 *M* NaOH).

l) Add two drops of sodium carbonate (0.1 M Na_2CO_3) to two drops of sodium hydrogen sulfate (0.1 *M* $NaHSO_4$).

m) Add a few drops of household ammonia to a small amount of a copper (II) sulfate (0.1 *M* $CuSO_4$) solution.

n) Add a few drops of vinegar to a small piece of chalk or marble chips.

o) Sharpen a pencil and collect the shavings.

Save the zinc and dispose of the materials as directed by your teacher. Clean your workstation.

2. Look at your observation notes in your data table.

a) Prepare and complete a chart table that organizes your observations into separate columns. Create a separate column for each type of observation made, such as color changes observed, the formation of *precipitates* (sometimes visible as a cloudy solution), gas formation (fizz), and any other changes. Use one column to note where no visible change occurred.

3. A *physical change* involves changes in the appearance of the material, but does not involve creation of new substances. A *chemical change* involves the formation of new substances. Chemical reactions are characterized by a number of changes, including color changes and the formation of precipitates or gases.

a) Which of the interactions you observed were chemical changes? Write the words "chemical change" next to each of these interactions. Explain your answer.

b) Which of the interactions you observed were physical changes? Write the words "physical change" next to each of these interactions. Explain your answer.

c) When you placed the wooden splint into a flame, what other evidence (besides the color change) indicated that a chemical change took place?

A discussion of results may include the following observations:

a) *Heating an ice cube:* This is a physical process since the solid water changes to the liquid state.

b) *Boiling water:* This change of liquid water into gaseous water is a physical process. Make certain students understand that "steam" refers to water in the gas state. Gaseous water is invisible; what most people call steam is small water droplets suspended in air. A good example is boiling water in a whistling teapot. The invisible steam comes out through the opening and then condenses farther out in the cooler air.

c) *Melting a candle:* The wax still has the same properties even though it has gone through physical changes from solid to liquid and back to solid.

d) *Breaking a wood splint:* Breaking the splint does not change its chemical properties, so it is a physical change.

e) *Burning the splint:* Combustion of the wood splint changes its original properties and forms new substances— in this case, carbon dioxide, soot, and water. This is a chemical change.

f) *Adding lemon juice to milk:* The acidic lemon juice lowers

Section	Color changes	Formation of precipitates	Is gas produced?	Other changes	No visible change	Type of change
a) Heat an ice cube				Ice melts		Physical
b) Boil water			Yes	Liquid amount decreases		Physical
c) Melt candle wax				Wax melts, then hardens		Physical
d) Break wood splint				Smaller pieces		Physical
e) Burn wood splint	Wood turns black		Possibly (in smoke)	Heat		Chemical
f) Add lemon juice to milk		White precipitate of proteins				Chemical
g) Add vinegar to baking soda			Yes	Baking soda "dissolves"		Chemical
h) Add salt to water, stir				Salt dissolves		Physical
i) Add Lugol's solution to starch	Starch turns dark purple					Chemical
j) Add zinc to HCl			Yes	Zinc "dissolves"		Chemical
k) Add phenolphthalein to NaOH	Solution turns pink/red					Chemical
l) Add sodium carbonate to sodium hydrogen sulfate			Yes			Chemical
m) Add ammonia to copper sulfate	Solution turns dark blue	Yes				Chemical
n) Add vinegar to marble chips			Yes	marble chips "dissolves"		Chemical
o) Sharpen a pencil; collect shavings				Pencil gets smaller as shavings collect		Physical

the pH of the milk. This causes the precipitation of proteins, a chemical change.

g) *Adding vinegar to baking soda:* The acetic acid in vinegar reacts with the sodium hydrogen carbonate to produce carbon dioxide, water and sodium acetate. This is a chemical change.

h) *Adding salt to water:* The salt dissolves in the water and makes a conductive solution

containing sodium and chloride ions. You can recover the salt by evaporating the water. Dissolving is a physical change.

i) *Adding Lugol's to starch:* The polymer of glucose has two forms: cellulose or starch. The iodine test identifies the starch form. This chemical process will also be used later for the clock reaction.

j) *Adding zinc to hydrochloric acid:* The hydrochloric acid oxidizes the zinc to form hydrogen gas and zinc chloride. This change is chemical.

k) *Adding PHTH solution to sodium hydroxide:* Phenolphthalein is a very weak acid. The sodium hydroxide neutralizes this acid to form the anion that changes the solution to a pink or red color. This is a chemical change.

CHAPTER 6

Active Chemistry 211

l) *Adding sodium carbonate to sodium hydrogen sulfate:* Sodium carbonate is a base and sodium hydrogen sulfate is an acid. The two react to form carbon dioxide gas and sodium sulfate. This is a chemical reaction.

m) *Adding ammonia to copper sulfate:* When copper sulfate is dissolved in water, the copper ions it forms are hydrated, which produces the blue color. If ammonia is added, it displaces the water molecules and forms an even deeper blue $[Cu(NH_3)_4]^{2+}$ complex. This is probably a chemical change.

n) *Adding vinegar to marble chips:* Vinegar contains an acid, acetic acid. Marble chips (or calcium carbonate) are a base. They react to form carbon dioxide gas and calcium acetate. This is a chemical reaction.

o) *Sharpening a pencil:* This changes the physical shape of the pencil, producing shavings. The chemical properties of the pencil and the shavings remain the same, so this is a physical change.

CHEM TIP

If you use a microscale setup, a piece of white paper placed under a clear plastic well plate can make it easier to observe the changes. As an alternative to well plates, you could perform each step on a sheet of plastic, such as a blank overhead transparency. Alternatively, if you use small test tubes to observe changes, there is a better opportunity to detect heating and cooling changes.

3.a)

Chemical changes: e, f, g, i, j, k, l, m, n. See preceding table and notes.

3.b)

Physical changes: a, b, c, d, h, o. See preceding table and notes.

3.c)

Smoke was released, the wood glowed, and then crumbled into black soot.

NOTES

_____

_____

_____

_____

_____

_____

_____

_____

_____

d) Imagine a situation in which two colorless solutions are mixed together. There is no color change, no precipitate is formed, and no gas is released. However, heat is released as the solutions are mixed. Even though dissolving is a physical process, it very often results in a change in temperature, which can be either positive or negative, depending on the solute and solvent. Is this an example of a chemical or physical change? Explain your choice.

4. Each group will be given some of the material used in disposable diapers. Place the material in a beaker.

a) Predict how much liquid the diaper material will be able to hold. Record your prediction in your log.

b) Design an investigation to measure the amount of liquid that the diaper material can absorb. Record your procedure in your log.

c) With the approval of your teacher, carry out your investigation. Record your results.

d) Explain how your prediction compared with your observations.

e) The diapers contain a material called sodium polyacrylate. When it absorbs water, is this a physical or chemical change? Explain your answer.

5. Your teacher will show you a solution of sodium acetate in a 250-mL flask. Observe the solution carefully.

a) Record your observations in your *Active Chemistry* log.

   Your teacher will then add one crystal of sodium acetate to the flask.

b) What happens? Record your observations in your log.

c) Was this a chemical or physical change?

6. In a large disposable glass jar, mix 150 mL of sodium silicate (sometimes called liquid-glass solution) and 400 mL of water. Carefully drop solid-colored crystal compounds of cobalt, copper, nickel, iron, and/or manganese in different locations inside the jar.

a) Is there evidence of a change immediately? In several minutes? In several hours? In several days? In your *Active Chemistry* log, describe the results.

b) Is the phenomenon you see the result of a physical or a chemical change? Explain your answer.

Wash your hands and arms thoroughly after the investigation.

467

Active Chemistry

4.a)

Students' predictions will vary widely.

4.b)

They will judge the amount of absorption based on the visible size of the diaper. This may vary from 50 mL to 1 L. The amount of diaper material will determine the amount of water that it will absorb.

4.d)

There will probably be a marked discrepancy between students' predictions and reality, and they will likely be surprised that diapers can absorb so much water. Generally, 1 g of sodium polyacrylate can absorb 800 mL of distilled water, and a somewhat lesser amount of tap water.

4.e)

This is a physical change. This material has found commercial applications for diapers. Plant nurseries also encase roots and seeds with saturated sodium polyacrylate as a means of providing water to the roots.

CHEM TIP

Sodium polyacrylate is a chemical compound called a polymer. It is made up of many (poly) repeating units of a smaller group of elements (the monomer called acrylate). The monomer unit is $-CH_2-CH(CO_2Na)-$). A single gram of sodium polyacrylate will absorb 800 mL of distilled water, but only about 300 mL of tap water.

3.d)

This question should elicit some discussion. Heat is released if you add acid to water. This is a heat of hydration reaction and is usually classified as a physical change. However, adding sodium hydroxide solution to hydrochloric acid solution also releases heat, and this is a chemical reaction. Allow students to express their thoughts on this question. Their background at this time is weak and they will find it difficult to arrive at an acceptable answer that covers all situations. Another example of a physical reaction that releases heat is when you dissolve sodium hydroxide pellets in water. You can evaporate the water and recover the sodium hydroxide. You can also dissolve barium nitrate in water and the temperature of the solution will drop. Caution students to avoid the conclusion that all processes that release or absorb heat are chemical reactions.

CHAPTER 6

5.a)

This is a clear solution. To supersaturate the solution, dissolve 100 g of sodium acetate trihydrate ($NaC_2H_3O_2 \bullet 3H_2O$) in about 60 mL of boiling water. Allow to cool slowly without agitation. Although the solution cools to room temperature, an excess of sodium acetate will remain dissolved in the water. You can then carefully add a crystal of sodium acetate to the solution and it will immediately cause the excess sodium acetate to crystallize. This is an exothermic process.

5.b)

When the crystal of sodium acetate is added to the supersaturated solution of sodium acetate, it will cause solid sodium acetate to form and fill the flask.

5.c)

A physical change has occurred. If the water is evaporated, the sodium acetate can be recovered without change.

6.a)

Yes, there is immediate change that continues for hours. When the solids sink to the bottom, they start to develop stringy substances that grow upwards.

CHEM TIP

It is advisable to purchase prepared sodium silicate solution because it is difficult to make. The commercial product is usually 40% sodium silicate that you can dilute to about a 10% solution.

6.b)

The metal cations combine with the silicate ion and the process is a chemical reaction. However, there is no way for the students to know this in advance.

Almost any soluble transition-metal salt that is placed in a silicate solution will develop columns of colored crystals starting at the bottom and extending upward. The reason is that as the salts dissolve, they release positively charged metallic ions. These ions combine with the negatively charged silicate polyatomic ions to form a partially insoluble silicate membrane (or gel-like structure) around the precipitating metal ion. The pressure on the sides causes this membrane to rise upward. The structural precipitates that form are quite complex. If you were to use an iron salt, you would form a mixture of iron silicates and iron hydroxides. This mixture forms the gel-like structure.

NOTES

NOTES

Chem Talk

The differences between physical and chemical changes are examined, followed by a review of saturated and supersaturated solutions. The subject of polymers is briefly revisited in reference to the sodium polyacrylate material used in the section.

 Cool Chemistry Show

Chem Talk

CHANGES IN MATTER

Physical and Chemical Changes

In this investigation, you observed a number of situations that involved changes in matter, both physical and chemical. A **physical change** involves changes in the appearance of the material but does not involve creation of new materials. A change of a solid to a liquid is a physical change. When the candle wax melted it may have appeared different, but it was still wax. After it solidified, it had a similar appearance to the initial product. When the ice cube melted it may have appeared different, but it was still water. Dissolving is also a physical change. When you added the salt to the water, the salt crystals seemed to disappear as they dissolved in the water. However, they had only

spread out into a solution. A **solution** is a **homogeneous** mixture of at least two different materials. The materials forming a solution are called the **solute** and **solvent**. The material usually present in the largest amount is called the solvent. When the solvent (water) evaporated away, the solute (salt crystals) remained the same as it was originally.

A **chemical change** involves the formation of new materials. The new materials are called **products** and the starting materials are called **reactants**. The process that brings about a chemical change is called a **chemical reaction**. Chemical reactions are characterized by a number

of changes, including color changes, the formation of a **precipitate** or gas, and in many cases a release of heat or light. Chemical changes are usually not easy to reverse. When you burned the wooden splint you could not put the charcoal and gases back together to form the original splint as you could when you simply broke the splint into pieces.

Chem Words

physical change: a change that involves changes in the state or form of a substance but does not cause any change in chemical composition.

solution: a homogeneous mixture consisting of two or more substances and at least one solute.

homogeneous: a word used to describe a substance which appears to contain only one type of matter.

solute: the substance that interacts with a solvent to form a solution.

solvent: a substance present in a larger amount that interacts with the solute to make a solution.

chemical change: a change that converts the chemical composition of a substance into different substance(s) with different chemical composition.

product: a substance formed by a chemical reaction.

reactant: a starting substance in a chemical reaction.

chemical reaction: a process in which new substance(s) are formed from starting substance(s).

precipitate: an insoluble solid formed in a liquid solution as a result of a chemical reaction.

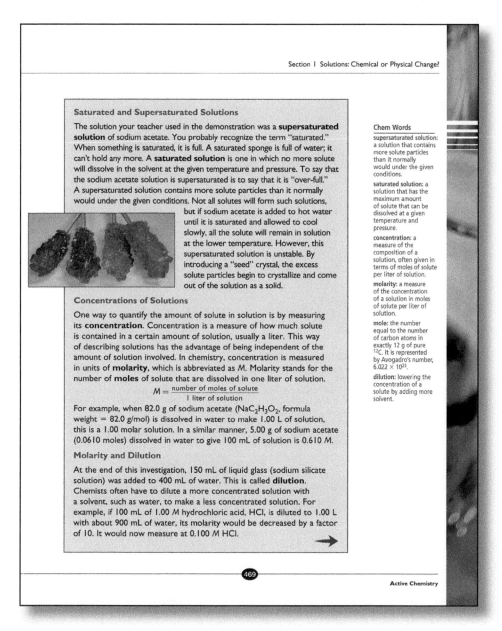

Saturated and Supersaturated Solutions

The solution your teacher used in the demonstration was a **supersaturated solution** of sodium acetate. You probably recognize the term "saturated." When something is saturated, it is full. A saturated sponge is full of water; it can't hold any more. A **saturated solution** is one in which no more solute will dissolve in the solvent at the given temperature and pressure. To say that the sodium acetate solution is supersaturated is to say that it is "over-full." A supersaturated solution contains more solute particles than it normally would under the given conditions. Not all solutes will form such solutions, but if sodium acetate is added to hot water until it is saturated and allowed to cool slowly, all the solute will remain in solution at the lower temperature. However, this supersaturated solution is unstable. By introducing a "seed" crystal, the excess solute particles begin to crystallize and come out of the solution as a solid.

Concentrations of Solutions

One way to quantify the amount of solute in solution is by measuring its **concentration**. Concentration is a measure of how much solute is contained in a certain amount of solution, usually a liter. This way of describing solutions has the advantage of being independent of the amount of solution involved. In chemistry, concentration is measured in units of **molarity**, which is abbreviated as M. Molarity stands for the number of **moles** of solute that are dissolved in one liter of solution.

$$M = \frac{\text{number of moles of solute}}{1 \text{ liter of solution}}$$

For example, when 82.0 g of sodium acetate ($NaC_2H_3O_2$, formula weight = 82.0 g/mol) is dissolved in water to make 1.00 L of solution, this is a 1.00 molar solution. In a similar manner, 5.00 g of sodium acetate (0.0610 moles) dissolved in water to give 100 mL of solution is 0.610 M.

Molarity and Dilution

At the end of this investigation, 150 mL of liquid glass (sodium silicate solution) was added to 400 mL of water. This is called **dilution**. Chemists often have to dilute a more concentrated solution with a solvent, such as water, to make a less concentrated solution. For example, if 100 mL of 1.00 M hydrochloric acid, HCl, is diluted to 1.00 L with about 900 mL of water, its molarity would be decreased by a factor of 10. It would now measure at 0.100 M HCl.

→

Chem Words

supersaturated solution: a solution that contains more solute particles than it normally would under the given conditions.

saturated solution: a solution that has the maximum amount of solute that can be dissolved at a given temperature and pressure.

concentration: a measure of the composition of a solution, often given in terms of moles of solute per liter of solution.

molarity: a measure of the concentration of a solution in moles of solute per liter of solution.

mole: the number equal to the number of carbon atoms in exactly 12 g of pure ^{12}C. It is represented by Avogadro's number, 6.022×10^{23}.

dilution: lowering the concentration of a solute by adding more solvent.

469

Active Chemistry

Checking Up

1.

In a physical change, the substance may change from one state to another, or from highly organized to less organized, but it remains the same substance chemically. Dissolving a salt in water will change its appearance but the salt can be recovered by evaporating the water. The scrambling of an egg is another form of physical change although it is impossible to "unscramble" it.

2.

If a material is dissolved in water, the water acts as the solvent and the material is the solute. The dissolved material plus the water is a solution. It is customary to consider the material present in the greatest amount as the solvent.

3.

A chemical change is a process in which one material chemically reacts with another to form new materials, or a single substance decomposes into new materials. The new materials have different chemical properties from the original material. One example is the decomposition of potassium chlorate, which yields potassium chloride and oxygen. Another example is the addition of a barium nitrate solution to a solution of sodium sulfate, which yields a barium sulfate precipitate and a solution of sodium nitrate.

4.

Some clues to a chemical reaction are the formation of precipitate, the release of gas, and color changes. The exchange of heat can accompany either a chemical change or, as with salt dissolving in water, a physical change.

5.

The amount of solute that is dissolved in a solvent can be expressed as grams per 100 milliliters, percent of solution, or as moles of solute per liter of solution.

6.

At a given temperature and pressure, a solvent can dissolve only a certain amount of solute. Elevating the solvent temperature will allow a greater amount of solute to dissolve. If it is then cooled and no solute precipitates from the solution, the solution is called supersaturated. If a solution contains exactly the full amount that it can dissolve under given conditions, the solution is saturated.

CHAPTER 6

What Do You Think Now?

This section allows students to assess, explain and elaborate on their learning from the section. Students are asked to summarize what happened during the lab section by connecting what they already knew with the new concepts and vocabulary introduced in this section. See how students' initial responses to the *What Do You Think?* questions compare with those they have now. You may want to present students with the answers found in *A Chemist's Response* and invite them to share their opinions.

Now is also a good time to revisit the *What Do You See?* illustration and determine how the artist's depiction relates to their own lab experience. Students' ability to recognize significant features they missed before should provide them with a sense of accomplishment for what they have learned in the section.

Both the lighting of a match and the frying of an egg signify chemical changes. Ask students to explain why.

Cool Chemistry Show

Chem Words

polymer: a substance that is a macromolecule consisting of many similar smaller repeating units (monomers) covalently bonded together in long chains.

Checking Up

1. What is a physical change? Provide two examples.
2. Explain the meaning of a solution, a solute, and a solvent.
3. What is a chemical change? Provide two examples.
4. What "clues" can you look for to determine if a chemical change has occurred?
5. How do you describe the concentration of a solution?
6. Explain the difference between a saturated and a supersaturated solution.

There is a simple relationship between molarity and volume, which is used to calculate dilutions.

$$M_1V_1 = M_2V_2$$

M_1 and V_1 are the initial molarity and volume of Solution 1, the more concentrated solution. M_2 and V_2 represent the final molarity and volume of Solution 2, the less concentrated solution. The dilution of 1.00 M HCl above can be stated as "What volume of 1.00 M HCl is needed to make 1.00 L of 0.100 M HCl?" Using the equation,

$$1.00\ M \times V_1 = 0.100\ M \times 1.00\,L$$

Solving for V_1, $V_1 = 0.100$ L or 100 mL.

Polymers

The chemical material that you were working with when you investigated the absorbency of the diaper was sodium polyacrylate. It is a chemical compound called a **polymer**. It is made up of many (poly) repeating units of a smaller group of elements (the monomer called acrylate). This particular polymer has a unique property. It will absorb more than 800 times its own mass in distilled water. The fascinating ability of this polymer (sodium polyacrylate) to absorb large amounts of water has led to its use in a number of commercial endeavors.

What Do You Think Now?

At the beginning of this section you were asked to consider a match broken in half and one lit on fire.

• Which match has undergone a chemical change? Which has undergone a physical change? Give specific reasons to support your answer. How did you make your decision?

Did you have difficulty at the beginning of this section in telling the difference between physical and chemical changes?

A match is lit. Is this an example of a chemical or physical change? An egg is fried. Is this an example of a chemical or physical change?

Chem Essential Questions

What does it mean?
Chemistry explains a *macroscopic* phenomenon (what you observe) with a description of what happens at the *nanoscopic* level (atoms and molecules) using *symbolic* structures as a way to communicate. Complete the following chart in your *Active Chemistry* log.

470

Chem Essential Questions
What does it mean?

MACRO — When a physical change occurs, the substance may change in appearance while retaining the same chemical composition.

NANO — During a chemical change, a substance changes at the atomic level; combining with other substances or otherwise changing in atomic composition to form new substances.

SYMBOLIC —
$H_2O(l) \rightarrow H_2O(g)$
This is a physical change.

$2H_2O(l) \rightarrow 2H_2(g) + O_2(g)$
This is a chemical change.

How do you know?

Answers will vary but students should be able to pick "best examples" and defend their choices. For example, good examples from this section of physical change are melting or boiling water, breaking a wood splint, and adding salt to water. Examples of chemical change are the reactions involving baking soda and vinegar, burning the wood splint, and the reaction between zinc and hydrochloric acid.

Why do you believe?

When we use water in our daily lives, we sometimes change it physically, in the freezer or in a tea kettle, but not chemically. Boiling, freezing, and

MACRO	NANO	SYMBOLIC
What does it mean when substances undergo physical change?	What happens at the atomic level during a chemical change?	Determine which equation is representing a chemical change and which is representing a physical change $H_2O_{(l)} \rightarrow H_2O_{(g)}$ $2H_2O_{(l)} \rightarrow 2H_{2(g)} + O_{2(g)}$

How do you know?
Refer to the data collected in this investigation and pick a "best example" for a physical change and a "best example" for a chemical change.

Why do you believe?
Water is a substance that you use in many different ways. When you use water in your daily life, are you changing it chemically? Explain.

Why should you care?
Giving a demonstration of chemistry in your *Cool Chemistry Show* will probably include both physical and chemical changes. How will you explain the difference between a physical change and a chemical change to your audience?

Reflecting on the Section and the Challenge

In this section, you investigated the two types of changes in matter. A physical change is a change in the appearance of the material without creating a new substance. The result is the creation of a solution or homogenous mixture. You also learned that solutions are commonly described in terms of concentration, which is the ratio of the quantity of solute to the quantity of solution expressed in molarity (*M*). The difference between a saturated and supersaturated solution is discussed. A chemical change, on the other hand, does involve the creation of new products from reactants. Chemical reactions are characterized by a color change or the formation of a precipitate or gas. You further investigated a type of physical reaction by testing the absorbency of a diaper made of sodium polyacrylate, a type of polymer. You can now use this knowledge of chemical and physical changes to amaze the fourth- and fifth-grade students.

Chem to Go

1. Which of the following are chemical changes and why?
   a) Toast turns black after being in the toaster too long.
   b) Water condenses on the outside of a glass of iced tea.
   c) Green leaves turn orange, yellow, and red in the fall.
   d) Green bananas become yellow.
   e) Milk becomes sour if left at room temperature.
   f) Butter melts on a hot summer day.

471

Active Chemistry

using water in mixtures are examples of physical changes of water. There are some chemical changes involving water that take place during metabolic processes.

Why should you care?

Answers will vary but students will be including physical and chemical changes in their chemistry show demonstration. It is important to be able to describe changes in matter in terms that a younger audience can understand.

Reflecting on the Section and the Challenge

In this phase of the section, students are asked to extend their learning by transferring their new knowledge to a new situation. For example, students should be able to describe which color-changing procedures from this section, such as the addition of sodium hydroxide to phenolphthalein, would be best to show a group of fifth-grade students.

Chem to Go

1.

a) *Chemical change –* New materials such as carbon are produced.

b) *Physical change –* Water retains the same properties, and has only changed in state.

c) *Chemical change –* The changing colors in the leaves are due to new materials being formed.

d) *Chemical change –* The ripening of fruit, such as bananas, is due to new materials being formed.

e) *Chemical change –* Microbes metabolize the milk and produce lactic acid as a byproduct, thus causing the milk to "sour."

f) *Physical change –* In the evening, when the butter cools, it will return to its solid form.

2.

Answers will vary. Allow students to discuss their responses.

Chemical changes: Enzymes within their digestive systems change the food they eat into new materials; stomach acids also break down food into new materials; cooking food brings about chemical change.

Physical changes: Food is physically changed when it is cut with a knife or chewed; melting ice cubes are also undergoing physical change.

3.

Making a cake: Have the students select a specific cake recipe. They can identify which

CHAPTER 6

steps represent physical and chemical changes.

Driving a car: Students begin by describing how a car is started and explain the various changes involved as the car starts, is put into gear, and begins moving.

4.

The first and third sentences, referring to the melting point and density of aluminum, exemplify are physical properties. The second and last sentences, relating to reactions with hydrochloric acid and oxygen, are chemical properties.

5.

You could attempt to dissolve a small amount of sugar in the liquid. If it dissolves, the solution is not saturated. To determine if the liquid is "just water," test the density of the liquid. Another method might be to take a small sample, evaporate the water and see if a residue of sugar remains. For safety reasons, tasting samples in the laboratory is never an option.

6.

9.0 g of NaCl is $(9.0 \text{ g})/(58.4 \text{ g/mol}) = 0.15$ mol of Na Cl

$M = \text{mol/L} = 0.15 \text{ mol}/1.00 \text{ L} = 0.15 \, M$

7.

$V_1 = M_2 V_2 / M_1$

$V_1 = (0.15 \, M \times 0.150 \text{ L})/(0.50 \, M)$

$V_1 = 0.045 \text{ L or } 45 \text{ mL}$

8.

The decomposition equation represents the electrolysis of water (a chemical process).

Chemical bonds are broken and formed. The products, hydrogen and oxygen, have far different physical and chemical properties than water.

9.

Preparing for the Chapter Challenge

Students' answers will vary. They might think of reactions that emit gas, such as when vinegar reacts with baking soda. A "cooler" idea would be the sublimation of dry ice.

 Cool Chemistry Show

2. Think back to a recent lunch or dinner. Describe two physical and two chemical changes that were involved in preparing and consuming the meal and explain why you think each was a physical or chemical change.

3. Write a paragraph describing the process of making a cake or driving a car. Indicate the physical changes and chemical changes taking place within each process.

4. The following information is obtained for the element aluminum. Identify which are physical and which are chemical properties.

Aluminum is a shiny silver metal and melts at 660°C. When a strip of aluminum is placed in hydrochloric acid, hydrogen gas is released. The density of aluminum is 2.70 g/cm³. When polished aluminum is exposed to oxygen over a period of time it forms aluminum oxide (Al_2O_3) on the surface of the metal.

5. How would you determine whether a clear liquid in a beaker is saturated sugar water or just water? Remember, you do not taste samples in the laboratory.

6. The concentration of salt in human blood is about 9.0 g per liter. How many moles of sodium chloride, NaCl, are in 9.0 g? If this mass were dissolved in water to make 1.00 L of stock solution, what would the molarity be?

7. A scientist has 1.00 L of a sodium chloride solution that is 0.50 *M*. What volume of this solution does she need to make 150 mL of a salt solution that has the same molarity as blood?

8. The decomposition of water is shown in the following equation:
$$2H_2O_{(l)} + \text{energy} \rightarrow 2H_{2(g)} + O_{2(g)}$$
What type of process is this, physical or chemical? Explain.

9. *Preparing for the Chapter Challenge*

Describe how you would demonstrate the difference between a physical and a chemical change in a "cool" way.

Inquiring Further

Factors affecting solubility and the rate of dissolving

Understanding the factors that affect how quickly a solute dissolves in a solvent is important in many practical applications in manufacturing. Design an investigation to determine the factors that affect solubility. Consider the following:

- nature of the solute and solvent
- temperature
- agitation (stirring or shaking)
- surface area (for example, try using a sugar cube, granulated sugar, and icing sugar)
- pressure of gases.

Remember that your investigation must be controlled if your results are to be reliable. What will be your independent (manipulated) variables and what will be your dependent (responding) variables?

CHEM TIP

Younger students might enjoy the following demonstration with sodium polyacrylate:

1. Prepare three styrene foam cups in advance by marking them A, B, and C. Put 1 g of sodium polyacrylate into cup B.

2. Set the "empty" cups on a table and turn them so that only you see the letters. Pour 10 mL of water into cup A as students watch. Explaining that "the hand is faster than the eye," shuffle the cups

around and ask them which one contains the water.

3. Pour the water into cup C and repeat the process. Again, they should easily identify the correct cup. Now pour the water into cup B. The sodium polyacrylate will absorb it (which students will not know).

4. Repeat the shuffling and ask which one contains the water. They will be surprised when you tip it upside down. Let them then lead you in a discussion about what happened.

Inquiring Further

Factors affecting solubility and the rate of dissolving

• **nature of solute and solvent**
The general rule is that like materials will dissolve each other. Ionic compounds will dissolve in water. Gasoline or hydrocarbons are insoluble in water.

• **temperature**
Increasing temperature should cause a greater amount of solute to dissolve in the solvent.

• **agitation (stirring or shaking)**
The more the agitation, the more the solute contacts the solvent and the faster the rate of dissolving.

• **surface area**
The greater the surface area of the solute, the greater the contact of individual particles with the solvent and the faster the dissolving will occur.

• **pressure of gases**
If you increase the pressure on a gas over a liquid by decreasing the volume of the container, the gas molecules will be more concentrated and have greater odds of colliding with the surface of the solvent and then dissolving.

The amount of solvent should remain constant. In some cases, the amount of solute should remain constant. Collect data at room temperature and room pressure. Then vary the factors above to see the effect of each.

SECTION 1 – QUIZ

| 6-1b | Blackline Master |

1. Which of the following does NOT indicate that a chemical change has occurred?
   a) formation of a precipitate   b) formation of a gas
   c) melting of a solid   d) color change

2. The materials forming a solution are called _____.
   a) the solute and the solvent   b) reactants and products
   c) molarities   d) solvents

3. Which of the following situations represents a chemical change?
   a) A blue solution is mixed with a yellow solution and a green solution results.
   b) A blue solution is mixed with a yellow solution and a brown solid is formed.
   c) Ice is placed in a beaker and heated until it melts.
   d) A strip of magnesium ribbon is broken into many small pieces.

4. When two different substances are mixed, does a chemical reaction always take place? Explain.

5. What is a chemical test? Give an example.

SECTION 1 – QUIZ ANSWERS

❶ c) melting of a solid.

❷ a) the solute and the solvent.

❸ b) A blue solution is mixed with a yellow solution and a brown solid is formed.

❹ No, mixing two substances will not usually cause a chemical reaction. For example, the mixing of oxygen and nitrogen gas does not cause a reaction. There are thousands of examples.

❺ A chemical test is a type of diagnostic test that is dependent upon the chemical properties of a substance. The glowing splint test is a test for oxygen gas, a burning splint test can be used for both hydrogen and carbon dioxide, and acid-base indicators are used to test the pH of a solution. All of these are types of chemical tests.

CHAPTER 6

SECTION 2
Characteristics of Chemical Change

Section Overview

In this section, students learn what conditions are necessary for classification as a chemical reaction. They will be provided with a selection of chemical solutions which they will be mixing in pairs. Some of these combinations will result in chemical reactions; others will not. Students will gain an understanding of how to determine when a chemical reaction has taken place.

Background Information

When you have a chemical reaction, you have a chemical change. Recall that a chemical change is the process that changes materials into new materials.

Chemical reactions that occur in solutions usually involve ions. For example, if you combine silver nitrate and hydrochloric acid you get a precipitate of silver chloride:

$HCl_{(aq)} + AgNO_{3(aq)} \rightarrow$

$HNO_{3(aq)} + AgCl(s)$

But if you combine sodium hydrogen carbonate with hydrochloric acid, you get carbon dioxide gas:

$HCl_{(aq)} + NaHCO_{3(aq)} \rightarrow$

$H_2CO_{3(aq)} + NaCl_{(aq)}$

$H_2CO_{3(aq)} \rightarrow H_2O_{(l)} + CO_{2(g)}$

Generally, solutions of carbonates, bicarbonates, sulfides, sulfites and hydrogen sulfites will yield gas when you mix them with strong acids like hydrochloric acid.

You can predict which solutions will form precipitates if you consult a solubility product table. However, it is simpler to gain familiarity with the general solubility rules for aqueous solutions:

1. All nitrates and acetates are soluble.

2. All common compounds of alkali metals and ammonium ions are soluble.

3. All chlorides, bromides, and iodide salts are soluble with the exception of those combined with silver, lead or mercurous (Hg_2^{2+}) cations.

4. All sulfates are soluble except those of lead, Mercury (I), barium, strontium, and calcium (note that calcium sulfate is slightly soluble).

5. The normal carbonates, phosphates, and sulfides are insoluble with the exception of the alkali metals and ammonium ions (Rule 2).

6. All hydroxides and all metal oxides are insoluble with the exception of the alkali metals, ammonium, calcium, barium, and strontium ions.

	LEARNING OUTCOMES	
LEARNING OUTCOMES	**LOCATION IN SECTION**	**EVIDENCE OF UNDERSTANDING**
Observe several typical examples of evidence that a chemical change is occurring.	*Investigate* Steps 1-2	Students' observations match those given in this *Teacher's Edition.*
Make generalizations about the combinations of materials that result in the same evidence.	*Investigate* Steps 4-5 *Chem to Go* Questions 1-3	Students' observations and answers to questions are similar to those given in this *Teacher's Edition.*
Make generalizations about materials that tend to react with everything and materials that tend not to react with anything.	*Investigate* Step 3	Students' answers match those given in this *Teacher's Edition.*
Practice careful laboratory techniques, such as avoiding contamination of reactants, to ensure that results observed are repeatable and unambiguous.	*Investigate* Step 2	Students are able to follow laboratory procedure.

NOTES

_____

_____

_____

_____

_____

_____

_____

_____

_____

_____

_____

_____

CHAPTER 6

Section 2
Materials, Chemicals, Preparation, and Safety

("per Group" quantity is based on group size of 4 students)

Materials and Equipment

Materials (and Equipment)	Quantity per Group (4 students)
Graduated cylinder, 50 mL	1
Large microwell plates, 24 well**	2
Plastic bag, resealable, quart-size	1
Scoopula	1
Test tube, large	1
Test-tube rack	1

Materials (and Equipment)	Quantity per Class
Box of baking soda, $NaHCO_3$, sodium bicarbonate	1
Straws, box	1

Chemicals

Chemicals	Quantity per Class (24 students)
Sodium hydroxide, NaOH 0.1 M*	100 mL
Copper (II) sulfate, $CuSO_4$ 0.1 M*	100 mL
Hydrochloric acid, HCl 0.1 M*	100 mL
Phenol red indicator*	20 mL
Iron (III) nitrate, $Fe(NO_3)_3$ 0.1 M*	50 mL
Barium nitrate, $Ba(NO_3)_2$ 0.1 M*	50 mL
Sodium bicarbonate, $NaHCO_3$ 0.1 M*	50 mL
Potassium iodide solution, KI 0.1 M*	50 mL
Silver nitrate solution, $AgNO_3$ 0.1 M*	50 mL
Calcium chloride, $CaCl_2$	250 g
Saturated solution of calcium hydroxide (limewater)	500 mL

**As an alternative, 28 small test tubes can be used to test the solutions. This has the advantage of allowing the students to feel any exothermic or endothermic reactions directly.

*These solutions should be stored in dropper bottles; many are used in later experiments.

NOTES _____

_____

_____

_____

_____

_____

_____

Teacher Preparation

*Sodium hydroxide, 0.1 M: With care and stirring, add 0.48 g of NaOH to 100 mL of distilled water. When dissolved, dilute to 120 mL. To make 1 liter, dissolve 4.0 g of NaOH in 900 mL of distilled water. Dilute to 1.0 L.

*Copper sulfate, 0.1 M: Dissolve 30.0 g of $CuSO_4 \bullet 5H_2O$ in 100 mL of distilled water. When dissolved, dilute to 120 mL. To make 1.0 liter, dissolve 300 g and dissolve in about 700 mL of distilled water. Dilute to 1.0 L.

*Hydrochloric acid, 0.1 M: Slowly and carefully, with stirring and in a fume hood, add 8.3 mL of concentrated HCl (12 M) to 800 mL of distilled water. Dilute to 1.0 L.

*Phenol red, 0.02% in alcohol: Dissolve 0.1 g of phenol red in 400 mL of 95% ethanol and then dilute to 500 mL with additional 95% ethanol.

*Iron (III) nitrate, 0.1 M: Dissolve 4.8 g of $Fe(NO_3)_3 \bullet 9H_2O$ in 80 mL of distilled water. Dilute to 120 mL. To make 1.0 liter, dissolve 40.4 g in 500 mL of distilled water and then dilute to 1.0 L.

*Barium nitrate, 0.1 M: Dissolve 3.1 g of $Ba(NO_3)_2$ in 80 mL of distilled water. Dilute to 120 mL. To make 1.0 liter, dissolve 26.1 g in 500 mL of distilled water and then dilute to 1.0 L.

*Sodium hydrogen carbonate, 0.1 M: Dissolve 1.0 g of $NaHCO_3$ in 80 mL of distilled water. Dilute to 120 mL. To make 1 liter, dissolve 8.4 g in 500 mL of distilled water and then dilute to 1.0 L

*Potassium iodide, 0.1 M: Dissolve 2.0 g of KI in 80 mL of distilled water. Dilute to 120 mL. To make 1 liter, dissolve 16.6 g in 500 mL of distilled water and then dilute to 1.0 L.

*Silver nitrate, 0.1 M: Dissolve 2.0 g of $AgNO_3$ in 80 mL of distilled water. Dilute to 120 mL. To make 1 liter, dissolve 17.0 g in 500 mL of distilled water and then dilute to 1.0 L. Store in brown bottles.

Calcium hydroxide, saturated (limewater): Add 1.0 g of $Ca(OH)_2$ to 500 mL of distilled water. Stir for 1 hour and then filter.

Safety Requirements

- Goggles and aprons are required in the laboratory area.

- All solutions can be washed down the sink.

- All students should wear gloves when handling chemicals. Caution students that silver nitrate will stain skin and clothing.

- Caution them on the use of the soda straw. Students must not inhale, should only blow into the limewater.

- Wash hands and arms before leaving the laboratory area.

*These solutions should be stored in dropper bottles; many are used in later experiments.

NOTES

_____

_____

_____

_____

_____

Meeting the Needs of All Students
Differentiated Instruction

Augmentation and Accommodations

LEARNING ISSUE	REFERENCE	AUGMENTATION AND ACCOMMODATIONS
Copying a chart to scale	*Investigate* 1.a)	**Accommodations** • Students with fine motor or visual-spatial disabilities may not be able to copy and scale a chart of this complexity. For some students, copying a visual design is a difficult task. Provide those students with a chart with boxes large enough for them to fill in legibly.
Observing chemical changes Reading for detail	*Investigate* 2.	**Augmentation** • Have students read the second paragraph of Step 2 very carefully. In it, they will find the changes they should observe. Ask students to work with their group to identify a list of changes they should look for before they begin mixing pairs of solutions. **Accommodations** • Give students these observations to watch in the form of a checklist.

Developing vocabulary	*Checking Up* 1., 5., 6.	**Augmentation**
		• Each of these questions essentially requires students to define a *Chem Word* used in the *Chem Talk*. Give students a mnemonic device for organizing information about vocabulary they define which includes a Definition, Rewrite of the definition, Importance and Example or DRIE.
		  o Definition: Teach students to find the words that provide the definition in the passage. In this text, two of the words are defined in the *Chem Words* sidebars, but "precipitate" is not. Using "chemical test" as an example will help students learn to avoid simply finding the highlighted term in the text and copying the sentence in which it appears. The definition of "chemical test" is not given in the sentence where the words are bolded, but in the sentence after. Encourage students to read the entire paragraph to determine the definition and capture its nuances. They can compare the definition in the passage with the formal definition in the sidebar. Students will have to draw an inference from their observations to define "precipitate." Ask students to find another source for the formal definition they can use, such as the glossary or a dictionary. It is important that terms be defined verbatim in student notes.
		  o Rewrite: It is also important that students write their own definitions of terms. Doing so gives them a chance to process what they have copied. This promotes deeper understanding. If students have difficulty, have them copy the formal definition of the term, underline the key words and phrases in the definition, and write their own substitute words and phrases above those they have underlined. Then they should rewrite the definition with their own words but retain the sentence structure of the original definition.

LEARNING ISSUE	REFERENCE	AUGMENTATION AND ACCOMMODATIONS
Identifying evidence of chemical changes Making inferences from more than one example	*Chem Essential Questions*	**Augmentation** • Some students will automatically make inferences from the investigation and reading they have completed. Making inferences does not come naturally to other students who need help identifying the facts on which to base their thinking. They may also need the process broken into smaller steps to make it easier to follow. • Explain that inferences require students to think of answers that are not given directly in the text. Surprisingly, this may not occur to students, who will assume they must keep looking for the answer in the text until they find it or give up. • For the *Macro* and the *How do you know?* questions, refer students to *Investigate* Step 2 where the evidence of chemical changes is detailed. Tell them to base their thinking on this passage. Students may also have the list of those changes in their notes from the augmentation described above. • For the Macro and the *How do you know?* questions, use scaffolding questions to break the process into simpler steps. Ask a student to pick one chemical change he remembers well. Ask him to name the change. He will probably name evidence in his answer. Identify the evidence he named. Ask him to use that pattern of recalling a chemical change, identifying what changed, and labeling the change as evidence. • In the *Nano* section, struggling students should base their thinking on *Investigate*, Step 4.d). • In the *Nano* section, additional questions that would provide scaffolding to students are, "Where did the steam come from when you boiled water?" and "How does that compare to where the gas came from when you mixed calcium chloride and sodium hydrogen carbonate?" Another question could be, "Did the water change state or was a new substance created?"

Strategies for Students with Limited English Language Proficiency

LEARNING ISSUE	REFERENCE	AUGMENTATIONS
Background knowledge	*What Do You Think?*	Check for understanding of the word "*involve*" in this context. Also, check for understanding of the directions, "*explain*" and "*describe*."
Vocabulary	*Investigate*	Check for understanding of the phrase "*organized manner*." Students might benefit from working in teams or with partners to carry out each of the steps. Some background knowledge of the word "*precipitates*" might help with understanding of that concept. Help with pronunciation of some of the chemical names and labels. For Step 3, students would benefit from a discussion, as many of the questions are stacked with multiple questions. Specify how they are to answer the questions and demonstrate the use of the chart. Check for recognition of the word, "*reactants*."
Background knowledge Vocabulary Comprehending text	*Chem Talk*	Check for understanding of bold type words. Explain the term "*indicators*" in this context. Refer students to sidebar material for further explanations of the isolated words.
Background knowledge	*What Do You Think Now?*	Help students understand what is meant by "*evidence*."
Background knowledge Vocabulary Comprehending text	*Chem Essential Questions*	In the *Why do you believe?*, students may benefit from hearing examples from other class members to help realize the multitude of examples in everyday experiences.
Comprehension Vocabulary	*Chem to Go*	Make sure students understand the phrase "*pretty cool*" as an idiom and not as a description of temperature.

CHAPTER 6

Section 2
Teaching Suggestions and Sample Answers

What Do You See?

To begin the section, ask students to study the illustration at the beginning of the section. You might ask a question such as, "Why is the fish jumping from the tank?" or "What is the meaning of $CuSO_4$?" Another strategy would be to ask how they think the fish tank might look if the artist followed the sequence with a third frame. By listening to your students' responses, you may be able to assess their prior understanding about the concepts as well as any misconceptions they might have about solutions. Be careful not to judge their responses because the main goal now is to engage the students and to encourage participation.

What Do You Think?

This section and the preceding *What Do You See?* section provide you with the opportunity to *elicit* prior knowledge and *engage* the learner, and provide students with the opportunity to *demonstrate* prior learning and to practice the transfer of what they already know to the concepts to be learned during the section.

Ask students to consider the two processes described and discuss the questions. You are not looking for correct answers at this point; the discussion should allow you to evaluate students' prior conceptions of the topics found in the section. Have students record their ideas in their *Active Chemistry* logs.

What Do You Think?
A CHEMIST'S RESPONSE

Both processes involve chemistry. Students may predict that only the second set of directions b) will result in a chemical change. Their prediction may be based on the use of the formulas for sodium carbonate (0.1 M Na_2CO_3) and sodium hydrogen sulfate (0.1 M $NaHSO_4$) since they represent the language of chemistry. However, the first set of instructions a), describing a recipe, will also result in chemical reactions. The key to the first process (the recipe) is the oven and heat. Up to that point, the procedures in the recipe represented mostly physical changes. The second process b) will produce a reaction that generates bubbles of CO_2 (carbon dioxide) immediately.

One similarity is that both a) and b) include specific directions to follow. One difference is that the first set of directions does not provide chemical formulas while the second set of directions is very specific about the chemicals.

STUDENTS' PRIOR CONCEPTIONS

When students explain chemical changes, they often do not understand the differences between parts and wholes. They may not realize, for example, that compounds made of combined elements have different properties than the individual elements. In other words, students think that "wholes are like their parts." The example of a recipe (parts) becoming a cake (whole) is an excellent strategy to help students understand how the "whole" is nothing like the "parts."

Another common misconception is that when there is a change in color, it must be the result of chemical change. Often, simple physical mixing of substances produces a color change, such as when blue and yellow mix to form green.

In addition, students might think that the way a substance is represented somehow determines whether it will change chemically. Many students will believe that the process of adding sodium carbonate to sodium hydrogen sulfate sounds "scientific" and thus must produce a chemical reaction. In this particular case, it does. But if either salt were changed to sodium chloride, there would be no reaction, although the procedural description would still have a scientific connotation.

Section 2

Characteristics of Chemical Change

What Do You See?

What Do You Think?

Read the following sets of instructions for two different processes:

a) Mix 1 cup flour, 1/3 cup sugar, and 1 teaspoon of baking powder with a cup of milk and 1 well-beaten egg. Pour the mixture into a baking pan and place in an oven for 30 minutes.

b) Add two drops of sodium carbonate (0.1 M Na_2CO_3) to two drops of sodium hydrogen sulfate (0.1 M $NaHSO_4$).

• Which of the instructions above involve chemistry? Explain your answer.

• Describe one similarity and one difference in the above instructions.

Record your ideas about these questions in your *Active Chemistry* log. Be prepared to discuss your responses with your group and the class.

Investigate

1. The following eight solid materials have been dissolved in distilled water to make solutions. You will combine the solutions (one to one) with each other in an organized manner in order to observe their interactions.

• barium nitrate ($Ba(NO_3)_2$)

473

Active Chemistry

Investigate

1.

Have students make a chart similar to the one in their text or use a blank version of the chart on the next page, which is provided as a Blackline Master in your *Teacher Resources CD*.

1.a)

The cells blocked out with "X" represent unnecessary combinations of the same solutions. It would be a waste of time and materials to mix identical solutions. The notation "N Rx" can be used to indicate that no apparent reaction takes place. All solutions are 0.1 *M* in concentration.

6-2a | **Blackline Master**

CHEM TIP

These solutions must be handled with extreme care. Silver nitrate can easily stain skin and clothing. All students must wear gloves when handling chemicals. Solutions for removing silver nitrate stains are available online or from chemical supply facilities.

2.a)

Students should record observations in their *Active Chemistry* logs as they work. Most observations will refer to precipitate (color), presence of gas bubbles, color changes, and "N Rx" for no reaction.

Cool Chemistry Show

Silver nitrate will stain skin and clothing. Handle with care.

Wash your hands and arms thoroughly after the investigation.

- sodium hydroxide (NaOH)
- sodium hydrogen carbonate (NaHCO₃)
- copper (II) sulfate (CuSO₄)
- potassium iodide (KI)
- silver nitrate (AgNO₃)
- iron (III) nitrate (Fe(NO₃)₃)
- hydrochloric acid (HCl(aq))

a) Begin by making a chart to record your data. Your chart will require an entire page of your notebook. Allow plenty of room to record your observations. A sample chart has been provided. You will have to replace the numbers with the names of the other chemicals. Notice that some of the blocks in this chart are marked with an X, indicating there is no need to mix those particular chemicals. Why do you suppose those particular blocks have an X?

2. Now it is time to mix the solutions.

Begin with barium nitrate. Add three drops of the barium nitrate solution to each of seven wells of a well plate. Add three drops of sodium hydroxide solution to the first well. After mixing the two solutions, make notes on your chart of any changes you observe. Do not overlook any color changes,

the formation of a precipitate (sometimes observed as a cloudy solution), the formation of a gas (fizzing or bubbles), or a change in temperature. Using another dropper, continue by adding three drops of the sodium hydrogen carbonate to the second well. It is important that you do not allow the tip of the dropper of one solution to come in contact with another solution. Your attention to this detail will prevent contamination of the solutions. Continue by adding copper (II) sulfate to the third well, and so on.

a) After mixing the pairs of solutions, make note on your chart of any changes you observe.

You have now completed the first row of your chart. Next, you should begin the second row. Continue by putting three drops of sodium hydroxide into each of the other seven wells and adding the other solutions.

You may have noticed that adding barium nitrate to the sodium hydroxide (in the second row of the chart) produced the same result as adding sodium hydroxide to the barium nitrate (in the first row of the chart).

	Ba(NO₃)₂	NaOH	NaHCO₃	4	5	6	7	8
Ba(NO₃)₂	x							
NaOH		x						
NaHCO₃			x					
4				x				
5					x			
6						x		
7							x	
8								x

474

Active Chemistry

	Barium nitrate	Sodium hydroxide	Sodium hydrogen carbonate	Copper (II) sulfate	Potassium iodide	Silver nitrate	Iron (III) nitrate	HCl
Barium nitrate	XX	Cloudy ppt	Cloudy ppt	Blue/White ppt	NRx	NRx	NRx	NRx
Sodium hydroxide		XX	NRx	Blue ppt	NRx	Brown ppt	Brown ppt	Slight heat
Sodium hydrogen carbonate			XX	Lt. blue ppt	NRx	Yellow ppt	NRx	Gas
Copper (II) sulfate				XX	Brown ppt	Light ppt	Green Soln	NRx
Potassium iodide					XX	Yellow ppt	NRx	NRx
Silver nitrate						XX	NRx	White ppt
Iron (III) nitrate							XX	Light yellow
HCl								XX

NOTES

_____

_____

_____

_____

_____

_____

_____

_____

_____

_____

_____

_____

_____

_____

_____

_____

_____

CHAPTER 6

3.a)

The following combinations produced no reactions:

Barium nitrate/potassium iodide

Barium nitrate/silver nitrate

Barium nitrate/iron (III) nitrate

Barium nitrate/hydrochloric acid

Sodium hydroxide/ sodium hydrogen carbonate (a reaction occurs but it can't be seen)

Sodium hydroxide/ potassium iodide

Sodium hydrogen carbonate/ potassium iodide;

Sodium hydrogen carbonate/ iron (III) nitrate;

Copper sulfate/ hydrochloric acid;

Potassium iodide/ iron (III) nitrate;

Potassium iodide/ hydrochloric acid;

Silver nitrate/iron (III) nitrate

3.b)

Gas is formed in the combination of sodium hydrogen carbonate and hydrochloric acid. Carbon dioxide gas is formed.

Overall reaction:

$$NaHCO_{3(aq)} + HCl_{(aq)} \rightarrow$$
$$NaCl_{(aq)} + H_2CO_{3(aq)}$$

$$H_2CO_{3(aq)} \rightarrow$$
$$CO_{2(g)} + H_2O_{(l)}$$

3.c)

The following combinations form color changes:

Blue: Copper (II) sulfate combined with barium nitrate, sodium hydroxide or sodium hydrogen carbonate.

Brown: Sodium hydroxide combined with silver nitrate or iron nitrate, copper (II) sulfate with potassium iodide.

Yellow: Silver nitrate combined with sodium hydrogen carbonate or with potassium iodide, iron (III) nitrate combined with hydrochloric acid.

Green: Copper (II) sulfate with iron (III) nitrate.

White: silver nitrate combined with hydrochloric acid.

3.d)

The following reactants form precipitates quickly:

Barium nitrate/ sodium hydrogen carbonate

Barium nitrate/copper (II) sulfate

Sodium hydroxide/copper sulfate

Sodium hydroxide/silver nitrate

Sodium hydroxide/ iron (III) nitrate

Sodium hydrogen carbonate/ copper (II) sulfate

Sodium hydrogen carbonate/ silver nitrate

Potassium iodide/silver nitrate

Copper sulfate/potassium iodide

Silver nitrate/hydrochloric acid

The following precipitates form slowly:

Barium nitrate/ sodium hydroxide

Copper sulfate/silver nitrate

3.e)

Yellow precipitate:

potassium iodide/silver nitrate

Brown precipitate:

Sodium hydroxide/silver nitrate;

sodium hydroxide/iron nitrate

White precipitate:

Silver nitrate/hydrochloric acid;

barium nitrate/ sodium hydroxide;

copper sulfate/ silver nitrate

Blue precipitate:

Barium nitrate/copper sulfate;

sodium hydroxide/ copper sulfate;

sodium hydrogen carbonate/ copper sulfate

3.f)

The sodium hydroxide/ hydrochloric acid combination released heat, which can be sensed if using test tubes for collecting the combinations.

3.g)

Evidence of a chemical change could include:

formation of a precipitate

release of heat

formation of a gas

change of color

4.a)

When mixed together, the powders cause no apparent reaction.

4.b)

When the phenol red solution was added, the color changes from red to a yellow color.

4.c)

Yes, a chemical reaction took place in the plastic bag. In addition to the color change, the contents become very warm and carbon dioxide gas is produced.

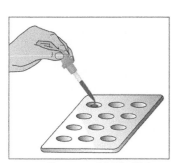

If you can explain why this is so, you can shorten the time needed for your investigation by not repeating other mixtures. After completing your *entire* chart in this fashion and mixing all possible one-to-one combinations of solutions, clean up your workstation. Your teacher will provide disposal information.

3. Use your chart to answer the following questions:

a) Which combination of reactants seems to produce no reaction when mixed together?

b) Which combination of reactants forms a gas? Can you guess which gas is formed? Try to deduce this from the reactants' names and chemical formulas.

c) Which combination of reactants produces a color change when mixed together?

d) Which combination of reactants forms precipitates quickly? Slowly?

e) Which combination of reactants forms a yellow precipitate? A muddy brown precipitate? A white precipitate? A blue precipitate?

f) Which combination of reactants produces heat? How could you tell?

g) What evidence indicates that a chemical change is occurring?

4. Place the following chemicals in a quart-size resealable plastic bag with a zipper seal:

One teaspoon (scoop) of calcium chloride ($CaCl_2$)

One teaspoon (scoop) of baking soda ($NaHCO_3$)

Seal the bag and mix the powders.

a) Record your observations in your *Active Chemistry* log. Did a chemical reaction occur? Pour 10 mL of phenol red indicator solution into the bag and seal quickly. Make sure the solids come in contact with the indicator solution.

b) Observe the reaction and, in your *Active Chemistry* log, describe what you see.

c) Did a chemical reaction occur in the plastic bag? If so, identify all of the evidence of the chemical change.

d) For this particular reaction, calcium chloride and sodium hydrogen carbonate combined to produce an aqueous solution of sodium chloride and calcium carbonate in addition to the carbon dioxide, water, and heat. The balanced equation is
$$CaCl_{2(aq)} + 2NaHCO_{3(aq)} \rightarrow 2NaCl_{(aq)} + CaCO_{3(s)} + H_2O_{(l)} + CO_{2(g)}$$

What do you think are the names of the reactants? What do you think are the names of the products?

Barium nitrate contains a heavy metal. Dispose of it as directed by your teacher.

475

4.d)

$$CaCl_{2(aq)} + 2NaHCO_{3(aq)} \rightarrow$$
$$2NaCl_{(aq)} + CaCO_{3(s)} +$$
$$CO_{2(g)} + H_2O_{(l)}$$

Reactants	Products
Calcium chloride	Sodium chloride
Sodium hydrogen carbonate	Calcium carbonate Carbon dioxide Water

5.a)

Yes, a chemical reaction occurred as shown by the formation of a precipitate. The carbon dioxide from a student's breath caused the solution to become cloudy due to production of insoluble calcium carbonate. Carbon dioxide combines with water to produce carbonic acid, which then reacts with the basic solution to form calcium carbonate and water:

$$CO_{2(g)} + H_2O_{(l)} \rightleftarrows H_2CO_{3(aq)}$$

$$H_2CO_{3(aq)} + Ca(OH)_{2(aq)} \rightleftarrows$$

$$CaCO_{3(s)} + 2\ H_2O_{(l)}$$

Chem Talk

Chemical tests for gases, as implemented in this section, are reviewed. Testing for the presence of acids and bases is generally conducted with substances that change color when they react with an acid or a base. These substances are called acid-base indicators.

Cool Chemistry Show

Report any broken, cracked, or chipped glassware to your teacher.

Wash your hands and arms thoroughly after the investigation.

5. Your teacher will provide you with a small amount (~25 mL) of limewater, a solution of calcium hydroxide $(Ca(OH)_2)$, in a test tube. One end of a straw should be submerged in the solution.

Gently blow through the straw into the solution for a minute or so. *Caution! Blow gently, and be careful to only blow out through the straw.* Avoid ingesting any of the solution. You are actually bubbling some carbon dioxide through the solution.

a) Did a chemical reaction occur? What is the evidence?

6. Clean up your workstation and dispose of the chemicals as directed by your teacher.

Chem Words

chemical test: a procedure or chemical reaction used to identify a substance.

Chem Talk

TESTS FOR CHEMICALS

Chemical Tests for Gases

In this investigation, you focused on chemical reactions, those processes that result in the formation of new products. You also tested for the presence of some of the new materials. You used **chemical tests** to identify the unknown substances. A chemical test is a form of a diagnostic test. To test for the presence of oxygen, you introduce a glowing splint into a test tube with a small amount of gas. If the splint bursts into a flame, you then know that the gas is oxygen. When you introduce a burning splint into a test tube and hear a loud pop, you assume the gas present to be hydrogen. In this investigation you tested for the presence of carbon dioxide. Since carbon dioxide does not burn or support burning, by using a glowing or burning splint, you could not tell if a gas was carbon dioxide. (If the splint is extinguished you can say that the gas is neither oxygen nor hydrogen and therefore could be carbon dioxide.)

The test for carbon dioxide uses limewater, a clear, colorless solution of calcium hydroxide in water. When you blew bubbles into the test tube you were actually blowing some carbon dioxide from your lungs into the limewater. The carbon dioxide reacted with the calcium hydroxide forming a precipitate. The precipitate caused the limewater to turn cloudy in appearance.

CO_2 + limewater

limewater

Indicators for Acids and Bases

When acids and bases are involved in a chemical reaction the appearance of the products is often very similar to the appearance of the reactants. (You will learn more about acids and bases in a later section.) Therefore, indicators are used to determine the presence of an acid or base. Substances that change color when they react with an acid or a base are called **acid-base indicators**. In this investigation you used phenol red, an acid-base indicator that turns yellow in the presence of an acid. Chemists use a great variety of acid-base indicators. You may also have used litmus in previous science classes. It is a very common indicator used in school laboratories.

Chem Words

acid-base indicator: a substance that changes color when exposed to either an acid or a base.

Checking Up

1. What is a chemical test?
2. Describe how you can use a burning or glowing splint to test for hydrogen or oxygen.
3. Why is a glowing splint extinguished with carbon dioxide?
4. What test is used to identify the presence of carbon dioxide?
5. What is a precipitate?
6. What are acid-base indicators and how are they useful?

What Do You Think Now?

At the beginning of this section you were given two procedures and asked which ones involve a chemical reaction and/or chemistry.

Look back at your answers and compare them to what you think now. Are chemical changes usually carried out in a laboratory? What is the most common evidence that a chemical change is taking place?

477

Checking Up

1.

A chemical test is a diagnostic test based on a chemical reaction which is specific to a compound or a class of compounds. Chemical tests can be used to identify a substance or to eliminate a substance from consideration.

2.

Oxygen supports combustion. If you place a glowing splint in a tube that contains oxygen, it will burst into flame. If you are testing for hydrogen gas and you bring a burning splint to the mouth of the test tube, it should produce a loud "pop."

3.

Carbon dioxide does not support combustion and is not explosive, so the glowing (or burning) splint test would produce negative results. In fact, a burning splint would be extinguished, which would be a positive indicator for the presence of carbon dioxide.

4.

The presence of carbon dioxide is generally detected by bubbling a given gas through limewater, which is a calcium hydroxide solution.

5.

A precipitate is the solid that forms in solution when two soluble chemicals react.

6.

Acid-base indicators are substances that change color when they react with an acid or a base. They are particularly useful in determining the pH of a solution.

What Do You Think Now?

This is a good time to go back to the opening illustration *What Do You See?* and the *What Do You Think?* questions. The students will benefit from this review and realize how their understanding has changed. They should be able to give the correct response to the first question and know that both recipes will result in chemical changes. Coming up with one similarity and one difference in the two sets of instructions should also be easier now. You may want to provide them with the answer found in *A Chemist's Response* and ask them to share their opinions in a discussion.

CHAPTER 6

Reflecting on the Section and the Challenge

Students should spend some time here to develop a specific, direct connection between the section and the *Chapter Challenge*. You might wish to have the students work in their groups briefly in order to complete this task. Feedback to the entire class might be useful for those groups having difficulty in developing a connection.

 Cool Chemistry Show

Chem Essential Questions

What does it mean?

Chemistry explains a *macroscopic* phenomenon (what you observe) with a description of what happens at the *nanoscopic* level (atoms and molecules) using *symbolic* structures as a way to communicate. Complete the chart below in your *Active Chemistry* log.

MACRO	NANO	SYMBOLIC
What evidence do you see that reactants have undergone a chemical change? What happens to substances as they undergo chemical change?	One evidence of chemical change is the production of a gas. Where did the gas come from in the reaction of calcium chloride and sodium hydrogen carbonate? How is the formation of this gas different from the boiling of water to make vapor? How is a gas different from a liquid at the atomic level?	In the following chemical equation, indicate the symbolic representation for carbon dioxide gas being produced. $NaHCO_{3(aq)} + HCl_{(aq)} \rightarrow$ $NaCl_{(aq)} + H_2CO_{3(aq)} \rightarrow$ $NaCl_{(aq)} + CO_{2(g)} + H_2O_{(l)}$

How do you know?

Refer to your *Active Chemistry* log and develop a list of the evidence revealed in this section that indicates that a chemical reaction has taken place.

Why do you believe?

Give an example of a chemical reaction you have personally witnessed recently. It can involve cooking food. List the evidences of a chemical reaction for your example.

Why should you care?

Chemical changes are often exciting! Your *Cool Chemistry Show* will probably involve some kind of chemical reaction. How can you make your chemistry show more interesting by utilizing the evidences of chemical change?

Reflecting on the Section and the Challenge

Recall that the fourth-grade teacher has specifically requested that your chemistry show addresses chemical and physical properties. You are right on track for the fourth graders. The fifth-grade teacher wants the students to learn more about chemical reactions that involve color changes. You have seen a few of those, too. If you had to conduct the show based on your experiences so far, which investigation would you use? What additional information would you need to be able to explain the chemistry to fourth- and fifth-grade students?

Active Chemistry

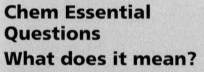

Chem Essential Questions
What does it mean?

MACRO — When it appears that new substances are produced, it is often assumed that a chemical reaction has occurred. The formation of a gas or a precipitate, the generation of heat, or a change of color are clues that this has happened.

NANO — The carbonate anion changed chemically to carbon dioxide, a gas. In the boiling of water, the liquid water is changed to gaseous water but this is not a chemical change. At the atomic level, a gas is different from a liquid because its particles are not confined to a given volume.

SYMBOLIC — $CO_{2(g)}$ represents carbon dioxide gas. Since this symbol appears on the right side of the equation, this gas is a product.

How do you know?

Evidence of a chemical reaction includes the production of new substances (precipitates, gases, change of color) and a change in energy.

Why do you believe?

Students' answers will vary with their selection of an example. When an egg is fried, the chemical structure of the egg is changed and the egg white changes from a clear liquid to an opaque, white solid. The egg yolk undergoes similar changes, becoming a solid.

Why should you care?

Students' answers will vary. By emphasizing the evidences of chemical reactions, the chemistry show will be more interesting and of greater educational value for the audience. For example, instead of mixing small amounts of aqueous solutions, the solutions can be diluted into larger, clear containers so the audience can more easily see the products of the reaction.

Chem to Go

1. In both *Section 1* and *Section 2*, you gathered evidence for chemical changes. However, this evidence does not always indicate a chemical change. For instance, a change in color can be evidence of a chemical change. However, when you add water to a powdered drink mix, the color often changes, but a chemical change has not taken place.

   In each of the following situations indicate whether the evidence suggests a chemical change or not. Include the evidence that you used to make your decision

   a) An acid is dissolved in water and heat is released.

   b) A burning match produces light.

   c) A "seed" crystal is placed in a supersaturated solution and the extra solute particles "join" the crystal and come out of the solution.

   d) The glowing filament of a light bulb produces light.

   e) A small piece of metal is placed into an acid and hydrogen is released.

   f) Solutions of sodium hydroxide and copper (II) sulfate are mixed and a blue precipitate appears.

2. Anhydrous copper (II) sulfate ($CuSO_4$) is a white solid. When it is dissolved in water, the solution becomes blue. Is this a chemical change? Give an explanation to defend your answer.

3. If a glass of carbonated soda drink is allowed to sit out for a period of time, you will find that the drink seems to be flat. Discuss this observation in terms of whether this is a physical or chemical change.

4. *Preparing for the Chapter Challenge*

   Select one of the reactions you observed in this investigation that you thought was pretty cool. Describe how you might incorporate it into a possible event in the *Cool Chemistry Show* you are designing. Would it meet the needs of the fourth-grade teacher, the fifth-grade teacher, or both? What additional information would you need to be able to explain the chemistry to the audience?

479

Active Chemistry

Chem to Go

1.a)

The release of heat when an acid is dissolved in water is an example of a physical process. When substances are dissolved in water they often release, or in some cases, absorb heat.

1.b)

A burning match is a chemical reaction. Heat is released and light is produced. The final products are different materials than what the reactants were.

1.c)

Seeding a supersaturated solution is a physical process as is the evaporation of a saturated solution. Heat may be produced or absorbed. The salt can be recovered unchanged if the water is evaporated from the solution.

1.d)

The glowing filament in a light bulb is a physical process because it is the same substance before, during, and after electricity passes through it. Eventually it will break due to "metal fatigue."

1.e)

A metal such as zinc will react with hydrochloric acid and hydrogen gas will be released. This is an example of a chemical reaction—specifically, a single-replacement reaction.

1.f)

The formation of a precipitate indicates that a chemical reaction has taken place. The reaction equation is:

$$2NaOH_{(aq)} + CuSO_{4(aq)} \rightarrow$$
$$Na_2SO_{4(aq)} + Cu(OH)_{2(s)}$$

2.

This is not a chemical change because if the water is evaporated, the white crystalline solid, $CuSO_4$, will be recovered. The solution turns blue because when anhydrous copper sulfate is dissolved in water, the Cu^{2+} ion will associate strongly with the water molecules, which gives a blue color to the solution.

3.

Although the carbon dioxide was introduced into the soda drink with pressure, it is not a chemical reaction. (A small amount of the carbon dioxide does react with water, but very little.) When the carbonated solution is allowed to stand at room temperature over a period of time, the carbon dioxide will "escape" and the soda will taste flat. While a gas is "generated," we classify this as a physical process overall.

4.

Preparing for the Chapter Challenge

Answers will vary. Have the students discuss these questions in their groups and report back to the class, if time permits.

CHAPTER 6

SECTION 2 – QUIZ

6-2b	Blackline Master

1. Which of the following is NOT a physical process?

   a) sharpening a pencil   b) melting ice

   c) an explosion of dynamite   d) popping a balloon with a needle

2. Which of the following is evidence of a chemical reaction?

   a) formation of a gas   b) disappearance of a liquid

   c) formation of smaller pieces   d) formation of crystals from a supersaturated solution

3. Which of the following is a test for carbon dioxide?

   a) a burning splint causing a "pop"   b) a glowing splint bursting into flame

   c) forming a white precipitate with limewater   d) global cooling

4. Insert the last product of the reaction of calcium chloride with sodium hydrogen carbonate and balance the equation.

   $CaCl_{2(aq)} + NaHCO_{3(aq)} \rightarrow NaCl_{(aq)} + CaCO_{3(s)} + H_2O_{(l)} + ?$

5. What are acid-base indicators and why are they useful?

SECTION 2 – QUIZ ANSWERS

❶ c) an explosion of dynamite

❷ a) formation of a gas

❸ c) forming a white precipitate with limewater

❹ b) $CaCl_{2(aq)} + 2NaHCO_{3(aq)} \rightarrow 2NaCl_{(aq)} + CaCO_{3(s)} + H_2O_{(l)} + CO_{2(g)}$

❺ Indicators are useful to determine pH. An acid-base indicator is a substance that changes color in the presence of an acid or a base.

NOTES

SECTION 3
Chemical Names and Formulas

Section Overview

In this section, students return to the periodic table to better understand the language of chemistry. They will learn the names of different ions, how these ions combine in order to form ionic compounds as well as how to write the correct formula for compounds and how to name ionic compounds. Toward the end, they will conduct some simple tests with baking soda, baking powder, and antacid tablets to determine if chemical changes occur every time reactants are mixed.

Background Information

Each element of the periodic table each has a different atomic number. The atomic number not only tells us how many protons an element contains, but also the number of electrons in the neutral atom. All isotopes of a given element have the same number of protons. Chlorine-35 and chlorine-37 are examples of isotopes. They both contain 17 protons and 17 electrons, but they differ in the number of neutrons. The symbols for these two isotopes are $^{35}_{17}Cl$ and $^{37}_{17}Cl$.

Ionic compounds

There are two main types of compounds – ionic and covalent. Ionic compounds result when electrons transfer from one element to another. This electron transfer creates ions (an atom or group of atoms that carries an electrical charge). Ionic compounds are held together by electrostatic forces which are the forces of attraction between positively and negatively charged particles. Electrostatic forces are relatively strong and as a result, ionic compounds have high melting points. Sodium chloride (NaCl) and sodium hydroxide (NaOH) are examples of ionic compounds.

Elements from group IA of the periodic table are metals that form positively charged ions (cations) with a charge of +1. Elemental metals from group IIA form ions with a charge of +2. These ions form as a result of the metals giving up one and two electrons, respectively. On the right side of the periodic table in Group VIIA are the halogens (F, Cl, Br, I), which tend to accept an electron to form negatively charged ions (anions) with a –1 charge. Sodium, a highly poisonous metal, gives up an electron to chlorine, a highly poisonous gas, which accepts the electron to form ordinary table salt. The sodium becomes a cation, the chlorine becomes an anion, and the two ions are held together as an ionic compound. The chemical and physical properties are dramatically changed.

When NaCl is placed in a container of water, the compound separates, or dissociates, into Na^+ and Cl^- ions. Ionic compounds are electrolytes – they dissociate in solution, enabling the solution to conduct electricity.

Simple ionic compounds are named by first listing the positive ion (as the name of the element; Na^+ is called sodium) followed by the anion (by taking the root of the element name and adding -ide; Cl^- is called chloride). Subscripts are used to denote multiple ions in the formula. For example, magnesium chloride requires two chlorine ions and is $MgCl_2$.

Sometimes ions are composed of more than one element and are called polyatomic ions. The elements are covalently bonded together and when a polyatomic ion is placed in an aqueous solution, the polyatomic ion stays together as a unit. For example, if you dissolve KNO_3 (potassium nitrate) in water, the compound dissociates into K^+ and NO_3^- ions.

The following table of common polyatomic ions is also provided as a Blackline Master for use with *Investigate* Step 4.

Ion	Name	Examples	
$C_2H_3O_2^-$	acetate	$NaC_2H_3O_2$	Sodium acetate
NH_4^+	ammonium	NH_4Cl	Ammonium chloride
CO_3^{2-}	carbonate	Li_2CO_3	Lithium carbonate
HCO_3^-	hydrogen carbonate	$NaHCO_3$	Sodium hydrogen carbonate (sodium bicarbonate)
CN^-	cyanide	KCN	Potassium cyanide
OH^-	hydroxide	$Ca(OH)_2$	Calcium hydroxide
NO_2^-	nitrite	$NaNO_2$	Sodium nitrite
NO_3^-	nitrate	$Fe(NO_3)_2$	Iron (II) nitrate
PO_4^{3-}	phosphate	$Ba_3(PO_4)_2$	Barium phosphate
SO_3^{2-}	sulfite	$BeSO_3$	Beryllium sulfite
SO_4^{2-}	sulfate	K_2SO_4	Potassium sulfate

If a metal can form cations with different charges, a Roman numeral in parentheses (I, II, III) follows the name of the metal to specify the positive charge intended. Traditionally, the different charges are indicated by adding the endings -ous and –ic but this practice is slowly being discontinued. The lower of the two possible charges on the ion is indicated using the -ous ending, and the higher charge is specified using the -ic ending.

Monoatomic ions with two possible charges

Ion	Name	Historic, or common name
Fe^{2+}	iron (II)	Ferrous ion
Fe^{3+}	iron (III)	Ferric ion
Cu^{1+}	copper (I)	Cuprous ion
Cu^{2+}	copper (II)	Cupric ion
Co^{2+}	cobalt (II)	Cobaltous ion
Co^{3+}	cobalt (III)	Cobaltic ion
Cr^{2+}	chromium (II)	Chromous ion
Cr^{3+}	chromium (III)	Chromic ion

Covalent compounds

Covalent compounds occur when elements are joined by shared electrons. Water and carbon dioxide are examples of covalent compounds. Simple binary covalent compounds (composed of only two elements) form between two nonmetals. The less electronegative element appears first in the formula. These elements would be farther to the left in the periodic table, and/or closer to the bottom within any group. Examples: SO_2, CCl_4, OF_2. Hydrogen is written as the second element in the compounds it forms with elements in Groups IA to VA (LiH, CH_4, NH_3), and first in the compounds with the Groups VIA and VIIA elements (H_2S, HF).

Covalent compounds are named as follows: The first element in the formula is named first, using the full element name. The second element is named as if it were an anion. Prefixes (mono-, di-, tri-, tetra-, etc.) are used to denote the numbers of each element present. We do not use the prefix mono- for naming the first element.

Simple binary covalent compounds

CO	Carbon monoxide	SF_6	Sulfur hexafluoride
CO_2	Carbon dioxide	SO_3	Sulfur trioxide
CCl_4	Carbon tetrachloride	AsI_3	Arsenic triiodide
N_2O_4	Dinitrogen tetroxide*	SeO_2	Selenium dioxide

Covalent compounds do not dissociate in solution. They may dissolve, of course, but the molecular unit remains intact. Therefore, solutions containing covalent compounds are unable to conduct electricity and are called non-electrolytes.

*It is common practice to drop the last letter of a prefix that ends in 'a' or 'o' before anions that begin with a vowel.

CHAPTER 6

LEARNING OUTCOMES		
LEARNING OUTCOMES	**LOCATION IN SECTION**	**EVIDENCE OF UNDERSTANDING**
Predict the charges of ions of some elements.	*Investigate* Steps 1-2, 5 *Chem to Go* Questions 4-5	Students' answers match those given in this *Teacher's Edition*.
Determine the formulas of ionic compounds.	*Investigate* Steps 3-4 *Chem to Go* Questions 2-3, 6-8	Students' answers match those given in this *Teacher's Edition*.
Write the conventional names of ionic compounds.	*Chem to Go* Question 1	Students' answers match those given in this *Teacher's Edition*.
Make observations to determine whether there is evidence that chemical changes occur when combining two ionic compounds.	*Investigate* Steps 6-10	Students' observations and conclusions match those given in this *Teacher's Edition*.

NOTES

_____

_____

_____

_____

_____

_____

_____

_____

_____

_____

_____

_____

_____

Section 3
Materials, Chemicals, Preparation, and Safety

("per Group" quantity is based on group size of 4 students)

Materials and Equipment

Materials (and Equipment)	Quantity per Group (4 students)
Graduated cylinder, 10 mL	1
Test tubes, large	9
Test-tube rack	1
Box of matches	1
Antacid tablets, effervescent	3
Mortar and pestle	1
Scoopula	1
Weighing boats	3

Materials (and Equipment)	Quantity per Class
Baking soda, $NaHCO_3$, sodium bicarbonate	1 box
Baking powder	1 box
Wood splints	1 box
Ammonia, household, NH_3	1 pint
Vinegar, 5% acetic acid	1 pint
Beaker, 600 mL*	1
Hot plate*	1
Wire gauze for hot plate	2
Balances, 0.01 g	2

*Materials or equipment for teacher demonstration only

Chemicals

Chemicals	Quantity per Class (24 students)
None	None

Teacher Preparation

To save time and equipment, the effervescent antacid tablets could be ground up with mortar and pestle in advance.

Safety Requirements

- Goggles and aprons are required in the laboratory area.
- All solutions can be disposed of in the sink.
- Wash hands and arms before leaving the laboratory area.

CHAPTER 6

Meeting the Needs of All Students
Differentiated Instruction

Augmentation and Accommodations

LEARNING ISSUE	REFERENCE	AUGMENTATION AND ACCOMMODATIONS
Identifying atomic numbers from a visual organizer (the periodic table)	*Investigate* 1.	**Augmentation** • Be sure all students have their periodic tables out for this investigation. After students finish reading the first paragraph of *Investigate*, ask them to write the atomic number for Ca. Check answers. Refer students who are unsure of the number to the legend in the periodic table.

Understanding positively and negatively charged ions	*Investigate* 2.	**Augmentation**
		• Some students become confused by positive and negative numbers and the language connected with them. Visual anchors help them keep this information correctly organized.
		  o Use a diagram to illustrate an atom with an equal number of protons and electrons. Symbolize each proton with a plus sign and each surrounding electron with a negative sign. Then show the same atom diagram with one electron missing. Ask students to count the number of plus signs and negative signs. This will help them understand why removing a negatively charged electron creates an ion with a positive charge of one.
		  o Repeat this procedure using an atom which gains an electron.
		  o Summarize by helping students use the proper nomenclature to explain what they learned.
		  o To differentiate while you help those who are learning this concept, ask students who understand the charges of ions, to name the charges of ions in a list of compounds you assign.

Finding information in a graphic organizer Reading the periodic table	*Investigate* 2.a, 3.	**Augmentation** • Despite their previous experiences, students may not be familiar with their periodic tables. Show students where to find the group labels. Explain the oxidation numbers of atoms and show students where that information is in the table. Ask students to explain how the oxidation numbers, the charges and the group an element is in on the periodic table are related. • Some students have difficulty remembering rules and labels, but base their understanding on reasons *why* something works. Show these students a model of atoms with levels of electrons in the outer shells and explain why they tend to lose or gain a specific number of electrons.
Understanding a graphic organizer (the periodic table)	*Chem Talk*	**Augmentation** • Be sure to use the periodic table to illustrate the information in this paragraph. Point out the positive ions on the left and the negative ions on the right. Remind students that the elements that form ionic bonds are color coded; blue elements are metals and yellow elements are nonmetals. Names read from left to right. The positive ion is named first, followed by the negative ion from the right side. Provide extra practice.

Comparing ionic compounds with molecular compounds	*Chem Talk*	**Augmentation**
		• Ask students to set up a T-chart comparing ionic compounds with molecular compounds.
		Accommodation
		• Give students the following comparisons to include:
		  o Effect on electrons (gained, lost or shared)
		  o Name of the bond (covalent or ionic)
		  o Names of components (anions, cations, molecules)
		  o Types of elements involved (metals or nonmetals)
		  o Type of charge (real or imagined)
		  o Electrical conductivity

LEARNING ISSUE	REFERENCE	AUGMENTATION AND ACCOMMODATIONS
Understanding subscripts	*Investigate,* 3. *Chem Essential Questions*	**Augmentation** • In the explanation of how three iodine atoms combine with one aluminum atom in the *Investigate* section, subscripts are explained but not named. Some students may remember the term from previous chapters or be able to determine the meaning from context when answering the *Symbolic* question, but others need that connection made explicitly by naming it when they first encounter it.

Strategies for Students with Limited English Language Proficiency

LEARNING ISSUE	REFERENCE	AUGMENTATIONS
Background knowledge	*What Do You Think?*	Students might benefit from listing or brainstorming all of the symbols they see in everyday life such as stop signs, flashing lights, directional signals or signs, etc.
Vocabulary	*Investigate*	Check to see that students pronounce the letters correctly for the symbols of the various chemical formulas, as they may be used in reference. Check for understanding of the word "*apparatus*."
Background knowledge Vocabulary Comprehending text	*Chem Talk*	Check for understanding of bold-type words. Multiple uses are helpful to apply understanding, such as the explanation of the uses of "*property*." Refer students to sidebar material for further explanations of the isolated words.
Background knowledge	*What Do You Think Now?*	Ensure that students understand what is meant by "*represented*." Questions are reflective and might merit some discussion.
Background knowledge Vocabulary Comprehending text	*Chem Essential Questions*	Have students work with partners to write their explanations, possibly having one student dictate to another. Students might not be familiar with the term "*dazzle*."
Comprehension Vocabulary	*Chem to Go*	Students may not be familiar with the use of the parentheses and may need further explanation.

NOTES

_____

_____

_____

_____

_____

_____

_____

_____

CHAPTER 6

Section 3
Teaching Suggestions and Sample Answers

What Do You See?

To engage students' interest, ask them to take a look at the illustration at the beginning of the section and share their reactions. You can do this as part of a class discussion or by having students respond directly in their *Active Chemistry* logs. You might prompt with a question such as, "How would it be possible to create a multi-colored image simply by spraying with one bottle?"

Keep in mind that you are not looking for correct answers at this point; all answers are helpful. By listening to students' responses you may be able to assess their prior understanding about the section as well as any misconceptions they might have about the related chemistry.

 Cool Chemistry Show

Section 3   Chemical Names and Formulas

What Do You See?

Learning Outcomes

In this section you will:

- Predict the charges of ions of some elements.
- Determine the formulas of ionic compounds.
- Write the conventional names of ionic compounds.
- Make observations to determine whether there is evidence that chemical changes occur when combining two ionic compounds.

What Do You Think?

Your ability to understand chemistry is determined by how well you can understand and write the language of chemistry. Just as there are only 26 letters in the English alphabet and thousands of words, there are only 92 elements found in nature and hundreds of thousands of materials. These elements and their symbols make up the language of chemistry. To make it easier to communicate, the elements are assigned symbols and the symbols are organized into the periodic table of elements.

- How is water represented in the language of chemistry?
- How are symbols useful when communicating?

Record your ideas about these questions in your *Active Chemistry* log. Be prepared to discuss your responses with your small group and the class.

Investigate

1. The periodic table lists the elements in order of their atomic number. The atomic number is the number of protons (positively charged particles) in the nucleus of one atom of that element. For a neutral atom, the number of protons also equals the number of electrons (negatively charged particles).

20   1.0
2
Ca
40.078
[Ar]4s²
Calcium

480

STUDENTS' PRIOR CONCEPTIONS

Many students will not understand formulas–how to decode a formula, and especially what subscripts indicate. Students often want to insert a coefficient into the formula to balance the equation, without understanding how the chemical change occurs, or what the formula represents.

It is helpful to have students build simple compounds using a model kit or even using gumdrops and toothpicks. They can then rearrange the "atoms" for a chemical change by literally breaking and reforming bonds, and represent this change in writing and finally, in symbolic form.

Sometimes it is effective to use personification as a device in explaining ion formation. For example, you might say, "The alkali metals 'love to' give up one electron each (to achieve noble gas electron configurations)." It is important to emphasize that all alkali metals require energy to be ionized.

Many consumer products list sodium or potassium as ingredients. What the product actually contains are the ions, Na^+ and K^+, and not the elements. Students are often unaware that elements and ions of the same elements have very different properties. For example, while sodium and potassium ions are necessary for life, the elemental substances are highly toxic.

Section 3 Chemical Names and Formulas

Electrons are found outside the nucleus. A helium atom, with an atomic number of 2, has 2 protons in its nucleus and 2 electrons surrounding the nucleus.

For each of the following elements, write the symbol for the element and indicate the number of protons and electrons an atom of that element would have. (Refer to the periodic table.)

- a) copper
- b) sulfur
- c) zinc
- d) gold
- e) oxygen
- f) carbon
- g) silver
- h) chlorine
- i) nitrogen
- j) hydrogen
- k) magnesium
- l) iodine
- m) iron
- n) calcium
- o) aluminum
- p) sodium
- q) potassium
- r) lead

2. Elements can combine to form *compounds*. A compound results when two or more different elements bond. Some compounds are comprised of positive and negative *ions* that are bound by their mutual attraction. An ion is an atom that has lost or gained electrons, and therefore is charged because its protons and electrons no longer balance and cancel each other. For example, when a chlorine atom gains 1 electron, it becomes a chloride ion with a charge of –1 (remember electrons have negative charge). When a sodium atom loses 1 electron, it becomes a sodium ion with a charge of +1 (because now there is one more proton than the number of electrons). The resulting compound is sodium chloride (NaCl), which you know as table salt and it is an *ionic compound*.

a) The chemical formula for the compound of potassium and bromine is KBr. Look at where potassium is located on the periodic table (Group 1) and also where bromine is located (Group 17). Each of these has an ionic charge of 1. Potassium is +1, and bromine is –1.

List four other compounds that are created from elements in Group 1 combining with elements in Group 17.

b) Magnesium forms an ion with a charge of +2 and oxygen forms an oxide ion with a –2 charge. The chemical formula for magnesium oxide is MgO.

List four other compounds that are created from elements in Group 2 combining with elements in Group 16.

3. The charges for the positive ions in a compound must equal the charges of the negative ions in that compound. If the values of the charge on a positive ion and a negative ion are the same, the formula of the resulting compound is simply the chemical symbols of each element (NaCl, MgO). If the values of the charge on a positive ion and a negative ion are not the same, subscripts can be used to balance them. For example, aluminum loses 3 electrons to become an ion with a charge of +3. An iodine atom gains only 1 electron to form an ion with a charge of –1. It takes 3 iodine atoms to accept the 3 electrons given up by aluminum. This is reflected in the formula AlI_3. (Note where the 3 is placed for the 3 iodine atoms.) Another example is $CaCl_2$, where 2 chloride ions (each gaining 1 electron) and 1 calcium ion (having lost 2 electrons) combine.

481

Active Chemistry

What Do You Think?
A CHEMIST'S RESPONSE

Water is represented as H_2O in the language of chemistry. Similarly, table salt is NaCl, and carbon dioxide is CO_2. Symbols are helpful in communication as symbols can often give more information than words can, or can shorten the amount of space used in written communication.

Investigate

1.

a) copper	Cu	(29)
b) sulfur	S	(16)
c) zinc	Zn	(30)
d) gold	Au	(79)
e) oxygen	O	(8)
f) carbon	C	(6)
g) silver	Ag	(47)
h) chlorine	Cl	(17)
i) nitrogen	N	(7)
j) hydrogen	H	(1)
k) magnesium	Mg	(12)
l) iodine	I	(53)
m) iron	Fe	(26)
n) calcium	Ca	(20)
o) aluminum	Al	(13)
p) sodium	Na	(11)
q) potassium	K	(19)
r) lead	Pb	(82)

2.a)

KBr. Students should realize that potassium belongs to the same family as sodium, lithium, and cesium. Bromine belongs to the same family as chlorine, iodine, and fluorine. Other compounds that can form from column 1 and column 17 have the formulas: LiF, LiCl, LiBr, LiI,

What Do You Think?

This section and the *What Do You See?* section are key points for students to demonstrate prior learning and to become engaged. Good instruction elicits prior understanding and gives students a chance to practice the transfer of what they already know to the concepts to be learned during the section. Engaging students in topics they already know about and which are

associated with the section both generates enthusiasm in the learner and gives the teacher a chance to evaluate students' prior conceptions.

At least some of the students will know that water is represented as H_2O, that table salt is NaCl, and carbon dioxide is CO_2. It might be useful to have a periodic table displayed to provide a hint to the answers to the two questions.

NaF, NaBr, NaI, KF, KCl, KI, CsF, CsCl, CsBr, and CsI. Due to their limited understanding of the periodic table, students may require help.

2.b)

MgO. The alkaline earth metals can lose two electrons and will then have an ionic charge of 2+ and the group 16 (or VIA) family can gain two electrons and have an ionic charge of 2–. Examples of these ion combinations are: BeO, BeS, BeSe, BeTe, MgS, MgSe, MgTe, CaO, CaS, CaSe, CaTe, SrO, SrS, SrSe, SrTe, BaO, BaS, BaSe, and BaTe. Make certain that students understand that the net charge on the ionic compound must be zero.

3.a)

CaO. Calcium is in the same family as magnesium (alkaline earth metals). The name is calcium oxide.

3.b)

AlF_3. Aluminum has a 3+ charge and fluorine is a halogen with a 1– charge. The name is aluminum fluoride.

3.c)

B_2O_3. Boron is in the same family as aluminum and should then have a 3+ charge and the oxygen has a 2– charge. Then $2(3+) +3(2-) = 0$. This point is actually debatable, because boron, carbon and silicon really do not form ions. However, the formation of boron compounds seems to indicate that it occurs in a 3+ state similar to that of aluminum. Some call the oxidation state of boron a fictitious "oxidation state" so that it won't contradict

---

Cool Chemistry Show

Write the chemical formula and name for the compound formed when the following pairs of elements are combined:

a) calcium and oxygen

b) aluminum and fluorine

c) boron and oxygen

d) strontium and nitrogen

e) barium and selenium

4. Some compounds, like baking soda and sodium hydrogen carbonate ($NaHCO_3$), incorporate *polyatomic ions*. Polyatomic ions are made up of several elements joined together. In the case of baking soda, the sodium (Na^+) ion has a charge of +1 and the hydrogen carbonate ion (the polyatomic ion HCO_3^-) has a charge of −1. (Note: hydrogen carbonate is also called bicarbonate.)

Write the chemical formula for each compound below.

a) potassium nitrate (nitrate: NO_3^2)

b) barium sulfate (sulfate: SO_4^{2-})

c) potassium sulfate

d) sodium acetate (acetate: $C_2H_3O_2^-$)

Write the name for each compound below.

e) $(NH_4)_2SO_4$ (ammonium: NH_4^1)

f) $Al_2(CO_3)_3$

g) $LiHCO_3$

5. You have learned about ionic compounds that are made from positive and negative ions. In another class of compounds, called molecules, the atoms are bound by electrons being mutually attracted to the protons in adjacent atoms.

These bonds are called *covalent bonds*, because atoms are sharing electrons. It is often useful to imagine, however, that the atoms inside of molecules are charged. These "imagined charges" are called *oxidation numbers*.

a) The formula for carbon dioxide is CO_2. If you pretend this is an ionic compound, what is the charge (oxidation number) of carbon?

b) Carbon monoxide is CO. What is the oxidation number of carbon now?

c) Explain how you arrived at your answers.

6. Let's find out if chemical changes occur every time reactants are mixed. Read the directions for this step so you can prepare a data table to record and describe all that you observe.

Put equal amounts of baking soda, crushed effervescent antacid tablet, and baking powder into three separate test tubes respectively. Be sure to label the test tubes!

Add equal amounts of water to each.

a) Record your observations. (Note: You should now know the chemical formula for baking soda is $NaHCO_3$.)

b) Light a wooden splint and blow it out to create a glowing splint. Place the glowing splint into the top of each test tube. Make note of what happens. A glowing splint bursts into flames in the presence of oxygen. A glowing splint is extinguished in the presence of carbon dioxide. Which gases were most likely given off for each reaction?

Safety goggles and a lab apron must be worn *at all times* in a chemistry lab.

Hold the splint with tongs or wear a heatproof glove. Be sure the mouth of the test tube is pointed away from everyone.

Report any broken, cracked, or chipped glassware to your teacher.

Tie back hair and loose clothing. Do not reach across an open flame.

482

Active Chemistry

---

the general nonmetal tendency to gain electrons (while metals lose electrons). The name is boron oxide.

3.d)

Sr_3N_2. Strontium is an alkaline earth metal which can take on a charge of 2+ and nitrogen is a non metal has a charge of 3–. Students may struggle here, due to their inexperience with nitrogen. The name is strontium nitride.

3.e)

BaSe. Barium is an alkaline earth metal and selenium, in the same family as oxygen and sulfur, can take on a 2– charge. The name is barium selenide.

4.

Take time to explain nomenclature and how to name compounds and acids before students start this section. A table of common polyatomic ions, provided as a Blackline Master in your

Teacher Resources CD, will be useful to students for writing the correct formulas and names.

6-3a Blackline Master

4.a)

KNO_3 (Notice that the anion name ends with the name of the ion that was assigned.)

4.b)

$BaSO_4$

4.c)

K_2SO_4

4.d)

$NaCH_3COO$ or $NaC_2H_3O_2$. (The first formula gives more information about the structure of sodium acetate. However, the second form is also perfectly acceptable.)

4.e)

Ammonium sulfate

4.f)

Aluminum carbonate

4.g)

Lithium hydrogen carbonate

5.a)

Carbon would have the oxidation number of 4+ since each oxygen atom has an oxidation number of 2–. Carbon does have 4 valence electrons and shares these 4 electrons with the two oxygen atoms.

5.b)

The carbon in carbon monoxide now has the oxidation number of 2+ and only one oxygen is needed to balance it. This compound is interesting in that it does not satisfy the octet rule. Because of this, carbon monoxide is unstable and will often combine with a metal atom in order to gain stability.

5.c)

The most common method for assigning valences is to assume that oxygen is always 2–. This is generally a reliable assumption since it is almost always true. Students' answers may vary.

6.

A blank table for the following exercise is provided as a Blackline Master in your Teacher Resources CD.

6-3b Blackline Master

6.a)

The first column of the table below indicates the expected results when reactants are mixed with water. Baking soda is only sodium hydrogen carbonate, $NaHCO_3$, and does not contain an acid to react and form carbon dioxide as the other two mixtures do. Baking powder is a mixture of monocalcium phosphate, $Ca(H_2PO_4)_2$, and sodium hydrogen carbonate, and corn starch to prevent caking (non-reactive). The monocalcium phosphate is an acid. The effervescent tablet contains aspirin, citric acid (the necessary acid) and sodium hydrogen carbonate.

6.b)

The 'X' in the first column indicates that the splint is extinguished when exposed to the effervescent tablet solution. This suggests that the gas being tested for is probably carbon dioxide.

CHAPTER 6

	Water	Heated	Vinegar	Ammonia
a. Baking soda	No bubbles	More bubbles	Intense bubbling, X	No bubbles
b. Baking powder	Slow bubbling	Intense bubbling, X	Intense bubbling, X	No bubbles
c. Effervescent antacid tablet	Fast reaction, almost foaming over, X	Fast bubbling, X	Intense bubbling, X	No bubbles

Key: X = Extinguished glowing splint

7.

You only need to use the three test tubes from one group of students for this demonstration. Alternatively, you could have each group test their own test tubes in a beaker of hot water.

Heating the solution with baking powder will produce the most dramatic change as it bubbles furiously. This is the basis for using it as an alternative to baking with yeast; it provides the carbon dioxide for light, fluffy biscuits.

There should be little change in the other two test tubes.

8.

• **vinegar:** Since this reagent provides the needed acid to all of the powders, all tests should result in vigorous bubbling and extinguish the glowing splint.

• **ammonia:** Ammonia is a base and neutralizes the acid in the baking powder and in the effervescent tablet. Therefore, no bubbling or carbon dioxide is produced.

CHEM TIP

Students might ask why the effervescent tablets give off carbon dioxide when placed in water. The answer is that water dissolves the citric acid and the sodium hydrogen carbonate contained in the tablets. The acid-base reaction that occurs releases carbon dioxide. When shown the label from the effervescent tablet packaging, they should note that citric acid is listed as an ingredient.

Ask students which treatment most effectively released the gas from baking soda. (The answer is vinegar, which contains acetic acid.)

The reactions are:

a) Baking soda with water and ammonia – no reaction.
  With vinegar:

$CH_3COOH_{(aq)} + NaHCO_{3(aq)} \rightarrow$
$NaC_2H_3O_{2(aq)} + H_2O_{(l)} + CO_{2(g)}$

b) Baking powder with water and heat:

$Ca(H_2PO_4)_{2(aq)} + 2NaHCO_{3(aq)} \rightarrow$
$CaHPO_{4(aq)} + Na_2HPO_{4(aq)} +$
$2H_2O_{(l)} + 2CO_{2(g)}$

c) Effervescent antacid tablet with water:

$H_3C_6H_5O_{7(aq)} + 3NaHCO_{3(aq)} \rightarrow$
$Na_3C_6H_5O_{7(aq)} +$
$3H_2O_{(l)} + 3CO_{2(g)}$

9.a)

The students will test their unknown powder using the same procedure as with the known powders. Since the results from vinegar and ammonia do not provide enough information to distinguish one powder from another, they do not need to do these reagents.

Testing with water: If there are no bubbles, then it is probably baking soda.

If bubbling is slow, then it is probably baking powder.

If bubbling with water causes rapid bubbling, almost foaming, then it is a groundup effervescent tablet.

Applying heat: If no bubbles form, baking soda is confirmed.

If furious bubbling occurs, baking powder is confirmed.

NOTES

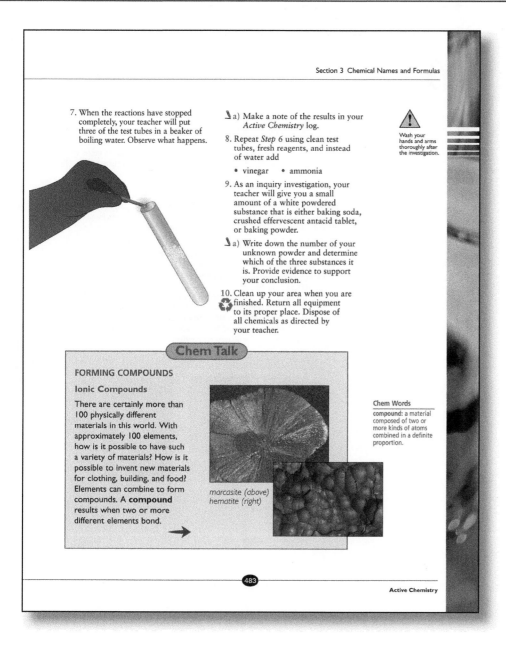

7. When the reactions have stopped completely, your teacher will put three of the test tubes in a beaker of boiling water. Observe what happens.

⟋ a) Make a note of the results in your *Active Chemistry* log.

8. Repeat *Step 6* using clean test tubes, fresh reagents, and instead of water add

   • vinegar   • ammonia

9. As an inquiry investigation, your teacher will give you a small amount of a white powdered substance that is either baking soda, crushed effervescent antacid tablet, or baking powder.

⟋ a) Write down the number of your unknown powder and determine which of the three substances it is. Provide evidence to support your conclusion.

10. Clean up your area when you are finished. Return all equipment to its proper place. Dispose of all chemicals as directed by your teacher.

Wash your hands and arms thoroughly after the investigation.

Chem Talk

FORMING COMPOUNDS

Ionic Compounds

There are certainly more than 100 physically different materials in this world. With approximately 100 elements, how is it possible to have such a variety of materials? How is it possible to invent new materials for clothing, building, and food? Elements can combine to form compounds. A **compound** results when two or more different elements bond. →

marcasite (above) hematite (right)

Chem Words

compound: a material composed of two or more kinds of atoms combined in a definite proportion.

483

Active Chemistry

CHAPTER 6

Chem Talk

The section on Ionic Compounds explores the definitions of ions, compounds, ionic compounds, anions, cations, and polyatomic ions. This is followed by as a brief explanation of molecular compounds, covalent bonds and oxidation numbers.

Cool Chemistry Show

ion: an atom or molecule that has acquired a charge by either gaining or losing electrons.

cation: a positively charged atom or molecule.

anion: a negatively charged atom or molecule.

ionic compound: a compound that contains cations and anions that are held together by electrostatic forces. Example: Sodium chloride is an ionic compound.

Some compounds are made of positive **ions** and negative ions that are bound together by the electrostatic attraction of opposite charges. An ion is an atom that has lost electrons and become positive, or an atom that has gained electrons to become negative. This is in accordance with the octet rule. For example, when a potassium atom loses its one valence electron, it takes on a charge of $+1$ and becomes a **cation**, or potassium ion K^+. A cation is any positively charged ion. Both the potassium atom and the potassium ion contain 19 protons in the nucleus. However, the potassium ion contains only 18 electrons in its orbitals—one less than the potassium ion. This is the reason for its positive charge.

Where does this electron go? It must be accounted for. Typically, a nonmetal such as iodine will take up this electron to become an **anion**. An anion is any negatively charged ion. Iodine takes on the electron to fill its outer valence shell and becomes the iodide ion. Iodine and iodide both have 53 protons in their nucleus, but iodide has one more electron in its orbitals than iodine. The 54 electrons give iodide a net charge of -1. The resulting **ionic compound** is potassium iodide (KI). Small amounts of potassium iodide are added to most common table salt to provide iodine as a dietary supplement. Common table salt, or sodium chloride (NaCl), is another example of an ionic compound.

Elemental sodium is a metal and elemental chlorine is a gas, but the compound sodium chloride is common table salt.

Naming Ionic Compounds

If you refer to the periodic table, you will notice that elements that form cations are metals on the left side. Most elements that form negative ions are non-metals, and are found on the right side of the periodic table. Metals combine with nonmetals to form ionic compounds. To name binary ionic compounds, the positive ion of the metal comes first and its name is unchanged. The negative ion is named second and its name is changed to end in *ide*. In the example given, potassium and iodine will react to form potassium iodide. When ionic compounds are dissolved in water, you find that the ions conduct electricity through the solution. The term **electrolyte** is used for a substance that conducts electricity when dissolved in water.

Polyatomic Ions

In this section, you also investigated some compounds formed with **polyatomic ions**. Polyatomic ions are made of two or more atoms that are covalently bonded together as one particle with a charge. In covalent bonds, the electron transfer is incomplete and the atoms share the valence electrons. For example, some antacids contain magnesium hydroxide ($Mg(OH)_2$). Being in Group 2A, magnesium takes on a charge of $+2$ when it loses its valence electrons. The hydroxide ion, OH^-, is an example of a polyatomic ion. It has a net charge of -1, so it takes two hydroxide ions to make the compound neutral.

Hydroxide is a common anion in all ionic bases. The following table lists some polyatomic ions, their formulas, and their charges. It is important to realize that when a compound containing a polyatomic ion dissolves in water, the atoms of the polyatomic ion remain bonded together, and the charge does not change.

→

Chem Words

electrolyte: a substance that forms ions in water and conducts electricity.

polyatomic ion: an ion that consists of two or more atoms that are covalently bonded.

485

CHAPTER 6

Cool Chemistry Show

Chem Words

molecular compound: two or more atoms bonded together by sharing electrons (covalent bond).

covalent bond: a bond formed when two atoms combine by sharing their paired electrons with each other.

non-electrolyte: a solute that does not form ions in solution and cannot conduct an electric current.

oxidation number: a number assigned to an element in a compound designating the number of electrons the element has lost, gained, or shared in forming that compound.

Polyatomic Ions		
nitrate	NO_3^-	negative one, −1
sulfate	SO_4^{2-}	negative two, −2
hydroxide	OH^-	negative one, −1
carbonate	CO_3^{2-}	negative two, −2
hydrogen carbonate	HCO_3^-	negative one, −1
acetate	$C_2H_3O_2^-$	negative one, −1
ammonium	NH_4^+	positive one, +1

Naming Acids and Bases

Many acids and bases contain a polyatomic portion that, when dissolved in water, retains its identity. However, each acid forms hydrogen ions (hydronium ions) and each base forms hydroxide ions. The naming of most bases follows the same rules as for the naming of ionic compounds: metal, then hydroxide. For example, calcium hydroxide is $Ca(OH)_2$. Acids are a bit more difficult because each has its own name. The following table lists the common acids, their formulas, and their strengths (degree of dissociation).

Table of Common Acids		
nitric acid	HNO_3	strong acid
sulfuric acid	H_2SO_4	strong acid
hydrochloric acid	HCl	strong acid
acetic acid	$HC_2H_3O_2$	weak acid
ammonium chloride	NH_4Cl	weak acid
carbonic acid	H_2CO_3	weak acid

To write the formula of most acids, the acidic "H" is written first because it will become the cation in water. After the H, the anion is written.

Checking Up

1.

There are myriads of combinations of those 100 elements The ionic compounds can form numerous binary compounds, complex compounds, and compounds that have numerous atoms in different arrangements. Covalent compounds also constitute a wide assortment of combinations. Due to the capacity of carbon to form long chains, there are millions of organic compounds.

2.

If an atom gains or loses electrons, it will assume a negative or positive charge. This new substance is called an ion. Notice that only electrons are transferred and no changes occur in the nucleus of the atom. The same number of protons and neutrons remain in the nucleus.

3.

Ionic compounds form due to differences in the electronegativity between two atoms and electrons are transferred to the more

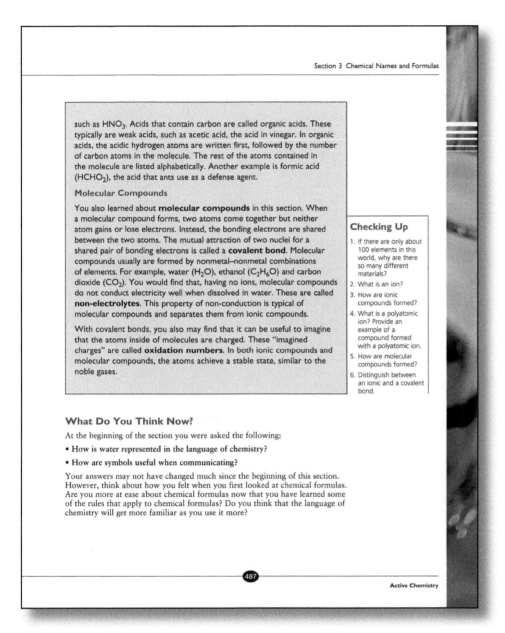

such as HNO_3. Acids that contain carbon are called organic acids. These typically are weak acids, such as acetic acid, the acid in vinegar. In organic acids, the acidic hydrogen atoms are written first, followed by the number of carbon atoms in the molecule. The rest of the atoms contained in the molecule are listed alphabetically. Another example is formic acid ($HCHO_2$), the acid that ants use as a defense agent.

Molecular Compounds

You also learned about **molecular compounds** in this section. When a molecular compound forms, two atoms come together but neither atom gains or lose electrons. Instead, the bonding electrons are shared between the two atoms. The mutual attraction of two nuclei for a shared pair of bonding electrons is called a **covalent bond**. Molecular compounds usually are formed by nonmetal–nonmetal combinations of elements. For example, water (H_2O), ethanol (C_2H_6O) and carbon dioxide (CO_2). You would find that, having no ions, molecular compounds do not conduct electricity well when dissolved in water. These are called **non-electrolytes**. This property of non-conduction is typical of molecular compounds and separates them from ionic compounds.

With covalent bonds, you also may find that it can be useful to imagine that the atoms inside of molecules are charged. These "imagined charges" are called **oxidation numbers**. In both ionic compounds and molecular compounds, the atoms achieve a stable state, similar to the noble gases.

Checking Up

1. if there are only about 100 elements in this world, why are there so many different materials?

2. What is an ion?

3. How are ionic compounds formed?

4. What is a polyatomic ion? Provide an example of a compound formed with a polyatomic ion.

5. How are molecular compounds formed?

6. Distinguish between an ionic and a covalent bond.

What Do You Think Now?

At the beginning of the section you were asked the following:

• How is water represented in the language of chemistry?

• How are symbols useful when communicating?

Your answers may not have changed much since the beginning of this section. However, think about how you felt when you first looked at chemical formulas. Are you more at ease about chemical formulas now that you have learned some of the rules that apply to chemical formulas? Do you think that the language of chemistry will get more familiar as you use it more?

487

Active Chemistry

electronegative atom. The ionic compound is held together by the electrostatic attraction between the positive and negative ions. The charge on the positive ion must balance with the charge on the negative ion. If the positive ion (cation) has a charge of 2+ and the negative ion (anion) has a charge of 1−, then you need two anions to balance the 2+ charge of the cation.

4.

A polyatomic ion is a combination of covalently bonded atoms with a net ionic charge. For example, the carbonate anion has a 2− charge and it is the combination of one carbon and three oxygen atoms (CO_3^{2-}). An example of a compound with a polyatomic ion is potassium carbonate (K_2CO_3).

5.

Molecular compounds are formed when two atoms share electrons to fill their octet.

Neither atom in the bond can totally pull an electron from the other atom as occurs with ionic bonds. Carbon dioxide is a good example of a molecular compound. The carbon and oxygens bond by sharing electron pairs. Since most atoms bond to have eight electrons in the outer shell (with the exception of hydrogen and helium), CO_2 is formed by two oxygen atoms each sharing a pair of electrons with a carbon atom. The carbon atom, in turn, shares a pair of electrons with each oxygen atom.

6.

Ionic bonds are formed by the complete transfer of electrons between two atoms. Covalent bonds form when electrons are shared between atoms.

What Do You Think Now?

Students should be able to easily answer the two questions from the *What Do You Think?* section. This is a good time to return to that section and to review the answers they gave earlier; this review will give students confidence in their growth and ability to use formulas correctly. You may want to provide the answers given in *A Chemist's Response* and allow students to share their opinions.

Now is also a good time to return to the *What Do You See?* section and ask students if they can now explain the significance of the ammonia as depicted in the illustration.

CHAPTER 6

Reflecting on the Section and the Challenge

Students should read this section for a direct connotation between the section and the *Chapter Challenge*. While students do not answer any questions in this section, it will give them a chance to think about how to use the information in this section in composing the explanations for their chemistry shows. You might want to have a short discussion.

 Cool Chemistry Show

Chem Essential Questions

What does it mean?

Chemistry explains a *macroscopic* phenomenon (what you observe) with a description of what happens at the *nanoscopic* level (atoms and molecules) using *symbolic* structures as a way to communicate. Complete the chart below in your *Active Chemistry* log.

MACRO	NANO	SYMBOLIC
How is learning chemistry similar to learning a new language? Describe a chemical reaction that you observed in this investigation.	How do the particles called atoms differ from the particles called ions? How do atoms differ from molecules?	You will see subscripts used frequently in the symbolic representation of substances (as in H_2O). What do these subscripts indicate about a compound?

How do you know?

What experimental evidence from *Step 6* in this *Investigate* can you give that baking powder contains carbon and oxygen?

Why do you believe?

Most people can tell you what H_2O is, but they may not know that water is made from two atoms of hydrogen and one atom of oxygen. List two substances for which you know either the chemical formula or at least what elements they contain.

Why should you care?

As you further develop your knowledge of chemistry, you'll gain more confidence in being able to speak and write the language of chemistry. In your *Cool Chemistry Show*, you'll want to dazzle people with your ability to communicate what you are demonstrating. What would happen if you included too much of the language of chemistry in your demonstration?

Reflecting on the Section and the Challenge

In this section you have learned how to write the formulas for many compounds and how to name some compounds. You also have investigated both ionic and molecular compounds. As you prepare your presentation for your *Cool Chemistry Show*, you will want to include your knowledge of formulas, the names of compounds, and the different kinds of compounds. Remember that you will be providing the teacher with an explanation of why you included certain demonstrations, and you will also want to include explanations that are grade appropriate. Think about how much information you will need to provide for each demonstration.

 488

Chem Essential Questions
What does it mean?

MACRO — Like any language, chemistry uses a system of symbols to convey meaning. In this case, the symbols and numbers represent the various properties and behaviors of the elements. In order to create accurate records and to communicate chemistry findings effectively, it is important to understand the meaning of the symbols, just as in any language. A chemical reaction observed in this section was the decomposition of the effervescent antacid tablet. When treated with water, it produced bubbles (carbon dioxide gas), indicating a chemical reaction.

NANO — Atoms have no net electric charge because they have equal number of protons (+) and electrons (–). Ions have unequal numbers of protons and electrons and will have a positive (more protons) or negative (more electrons) charge. The term "molecule" refers to the smallest unit of a covalent compound. Molecules are composed of atoms.

SYMBOLIC —

The subscripts in a chemical formula indicate the number of atoms or ions that precede the subscript. For example, in H_2O, there are two hydrogen atoms. These subscripts cannot be changed without changing the compound.

How do you know?

The gas generated from the reaction of baking soda with an acid put out the glowing splint used in this section and therefore is probably carbon dioxide. Carbon dioxide is composed of carbon and oxygen.

Section 3 Chemical Names and Formulas

Chem to Go

1. Write the chemical formula and name for the compound formed when the following pairs of elements are combined:
   a) sodium and bromine   b) potassium and sulfur
   c) magnesium and chlorine   d) cesium and iodine

2. Write the chemical formula for each of the following:
   a) nitric acid (hydrogen nitrate)   b) ammonium hydroxide
   c) calcium carbonate   d) acetic acid (hydrogen acetate)

3. a) Write the chemical formula for copper (II) sulfate. The (II) indicates that this copper ion has a +2 charge.
   b) Oxygen ions usually have −2 charge. How would formulas for iron (II) oxide differ from iron (III) oxide?

4. You may have noticed that all the elements in the first column of the periodic table, the alkali metals, have a +1 charge when they combine with negative ions. Another group of positive ions are the alkaline earth metals located in the second column of the periodic table. What charge is typical for ions of the alkaline earth metals?

5. The formula for sodium phosphate is Na_3PO_4. What is the charge on the polyatomic phosphate ion? What information did you use to arrive at your answer?

6. When you write the formula for sodium hydroxide, you do not have to put parentheses around the hydroxide polyatomic ion. However, when writing the formula for aluminum hydroxide, you must put parentheses around the hydroxide polyatomic ion.
   a) Write each formula.
   b) Explain why the parentheses are necessary for aluminum hydroxide.

7. a) If the chemical formula for iron (III) chloride is $FeCl_3$, what is the chemical formula for iron (III) nitrate?
   b) If the chemical formula for lead (II) oxide is PbO, what is the chemical formula for lead (II) sulfate?
   c) If the chemical formula for silver chloride is AgCl, what is the chemical formula for silver nitrate?

8. In *Section 2*, you tested various compounds for chemical changes. (Barium nitrate, sodium hydroxide, sodium hydrogen carbonate, copper (II) sulfate, potassium iodide, silver nitrate, iron (III) nitrate, and hydrochloric acid.) Write the chemical formulas for each of the reactants.

9. *Preparing for the Chapter Challenge*
   Review any chemical reactions you will be including in your *Cool Chemistry Show*. Write the formulas of any compounds that you plan to use.

489

Active Chemistry

Why do you believe?

Answers will vary. Students can locate compounds in the section to use as examples. Carbon dioxide and sodium chloride will be popular choices.

Why should you care?

Students' answers will vary but should include the understanding that too much chemistry language will cause the audience to lose interest. A "cool" chemistry show should focus more on the effects, and less on the language.

Chem to Go

1.

a) NaBr, sodium bromide

b) K_2S, potassium sulfide

c) $MgCl_2$, magnesium chloride

d) CsI, cesium iodide

2.

a) HNO_3, which is usually called nitric acid.

b) NH_4OH; no parentheses are required since the two ionic groups combine in a 1:1 ratio.

c) $CaCO_3$

d) CH_3COOH or $HC_2H_3O_2$, usually called acetic acid (acetic acid is found in vinegar solution).

3.

a) $CuSO_4$

b) Iron (II) oxide is FeO and iron (III) oxide is Fe_2O_3. Iron (II) oxide was formerly called ferrous oxide and iron (III) oxide was called ferric oxide.

4.

The alkaline earth metals have the ionic charge of 2+. They will lose two electrons in order to achieve a noble gas configuration.

5.

Since we know that the charge on sodium is 1+ and it took three sodium atoms to combine with the phosphate anion, then the charge on the phosphate anion must be 3−.

CHAPTER 6

6.

a) Sodium hydroxide is NaOH and aluminum hydroxide is $Al(OH)_3$.

b) Aluminum has a 3+ charge and the hydroxide ion has a 1– charge, so 3 hydroxide ions are needed to balance the aluminum ion. It would be incorrect to put the subscript 3 after the hydrogen atom of hydroxide without parentheses since that would indicate 3 hydrogen atoms but only 1 oxygen atom.

7.

a) If iron chloride is $FeCl_3$ then the iron must have a 3+ charge. The nitrate anion has a charge of 1–, which is the same as a chloride anion. Therefore, the correct formula for iron (III) nitrate is $Fe(NO_3)_3$.

b) If the formula for lead oxide is PbO, then the lead must have a 2+ charge. Since the sulfate anion has a charge of 2–, then the correct formula for lead (II) sulfate is $PbSO_4$.

c) If the formula for silver chloride is AgCl, then the silver must have a charge of 1+. Since the nitrate anion has a charge of 1–, then the correct formula for silver nitrate is $AgNO_3$.

8.

Barium nitrate: $Ba(NO_3)_2$

Sodium hydroxide: NaOH

Sodium hydrogen carbonate or sodium bicarbonate: $NaHCO_3$

Copper (II) sulfate: $CuSO_4$

Potassium iodide: KI

Silver nitrate: $AgNO_3$

Iron (III) nitrate: $Fe(NO_3)_3$

Hydrochloric acid: HCl (Note that hydrogen chloride dissolved in water is called hydrochloric acid.)

9.

Preparing for the Chapter Challenge

Students' answers will vary. Check to make certain that they show their understanding of formulas and reactions through their work.

NOTES

_____

_____

_____

_____

_____

_____

_____

_____

_____

_____

SECTION 3 – QUIZ

6-3c | **Blackline Master**

1. Using the periodic table, fill in the following table:

Name	Formula	Cation	Anion
Sodium fluoride			
	$MgBr_2$		
		Li^+	O^{2-}
	K_2S		
Calcium hydroxide			OH^-
Strontium carbonate	$SrCO_3$		
		Fe^{3+}	CO_3^{2-}
Cesium sulfate			SO_4^{2-}
Ammonium carbonate		NH_4^+	

2. Which of the following statements regarding polyatomic ions is false?

   a) They are made up of several elements joined together.

   b) They can have either a positive or negative charge.

   c) They can combine with other polyatomic ions.

   d) They can only make covalent bonds with metals and nonmetals.

3. Which of the following statements regarding compounds is false?

   a) They can be made up of several elements joined together.

   b) There are approximately 100 known compounds.

   c) They can have either covalent or ionic bonds.

   d) They can react with other compounds.

SECTION 3 – QUIZ ANSWERS

❶

Name	Formula	Cation	Anion
Sodium fluoride	NaF	Na^+	F^-
Magnesium bromide	$MgBr_2$	Mg^{2+}	Br^-
Lithium oxide	Li_2O	Li^+	O^{2-}
Potassium sulfide	K_2S	K^+	S^{2-}
Calcium hydroxide	$Ca(OH)_2$	Ca^{2+}	OH^-
Strontium carbonate	$SrCO_3$	Sr^{2+}	CO_3^{2-}
Iron (III) carbonate	$Fe_2(CO_3)_3$	Fe^{3+}	CO_3^{2-}
Cesium sulfate	Cs_2SO_4	Cs^+	SO_4^{2-}
Ammonium carbonate	$(NH_4)_2CO_3$	NH_4^+	CO_3^{2-}

❷ d) is false. They can only make ionic compounds with metals and nonmetals.

❸ b) is false. There are approximately 100 known compounds. There are millions of compounds. This answer would be better for 100 known elements.

CHAPTER 6

SECTION 4
Reaction Types and Chemical Equations

Section Overview

Students perform single-replacement and double-replacement chemical reactions in this section. They also practice balancing equations and learn the rules for predicting whether a precipitate will form.

Background Information

A chemical equation is a shorthand description of a chemical reaction that uses symbols and formulas to represent the elements and compounds that are involved. Chemical equations provide a wealth of information about reactions. The numbers of atoms of each element before and after the reaction must be equal in a balanced chemical equation. The stoichiometric coefficients in front of formulas in chemical equations are manipulated to balance the equations. These coefficients represent the molar ratios of reactants and products.

Chemical reactions occur in several different forms. Knowing the type of reaction is useful when you write a chemical equation. Most chemical reactions can be placed into one or more of the following four categories:

1. **Synthesis reactions:** Also called combination reactions, these reactions occur when one element or compound combines with another element or compound to produce new compounds. This process can be generally represented as:

$$A + B \longrightarrow AB$$

For example, when H_2 gas reacts with O_2 gas, water is synthesized:

$$2H_{2(g)} + O_{2(g)} \longrightarrow 2H_2O_{(g)}$$

Hydrogen can also react with ethylene (C_2H_4), in the presence of platinum (or palladium) catalyst, to produce ethane (C_2H_6):

Combustion reactions are another example of synthesis reactions. Organic hydrocarbons can burn in the presence of oxygen to produce CO_2 and water. The burning of methane (CH_4), the chief component of natural gas, is an example of a combustion reaction:

$$CH_{4(g)} + 2O_{2(g)} \longrightarrow CO_{2(g)} + 2H_2O_{(g)}$$

In ordinary terms, combustion reactions are not thought of as "synthesis" reactions since the products are not wanted. It is the heat that these reactions provide that make them useful.

2. **Decomposition reactions:** When a compound is broken down into two or more simpler materials, a decomposition reaction has occurred. The general equation for this type of reaction is:

$$AB \longrightarrow A + B$$

An example of a decomposition reaction is the electrolysis of water:

$$2H_2O_{(l)} \longrightarrow 2H_{2(g)} + O_{2(g)}$$

This reaction requires the input of a great deal of energy, as do most decomposition reactions.

3. **Single-replacement reactions:** When a metal reacts with an acid to produce hydrogen gas, the elemental metal displaces the hydrogen from what

is basically an ionic compound. This phenomenon is commonly called a single-replacement reaction and generates hydrogen gas, H_2.

$$Zn_{(s)} + 2HCl_{(aq)} \rightarrow ZnCl_{2(aq)} + H_{2(g)}$$

This can also be classified as an oxidation-reduction reaction.

Another example is when zinc metal is placed in a solution of copper (II) sulfate. Note that the copper is reduced and plates out on the zinc strip. The general equation for this reaction is:

$$Zn_{(s)} + CuSO_{4(aq)} \rightarrow Cu_{(s)} + ZnSO_{4(aq)}$$

The total ionic equation:

$$Zn_{(s)} + Cu^{2+}_{(aq)} + SO_4^{2-}_{(aq)} \rightarrow$$
$$Cu_{(s)} + Zn^{2+}_{(aq)} + SO_4^{2-}_{(aq)}$$

The sulfate ion plays no role in the reaction (called a "spectator ion") and so, it can be removed from the equation to write the net ionic equation:

$$Zn_{(s)} + Cu^{2+}_{(aq)} \rightarrow Cu_{(s)} + Zn^{2+}_{(aq)}$$

Single-replacement reactions are used to identify which elements will be replaced from its compounds by other metals. This order of reactivity is often called the Activity Series of Metals (also called the Metal Activity Series).

4. Double-replacement reactions (also called metathesis): These reactions usually involve ionic solutions. The cations exchange their anion partners in the reaction. A reaction has occurred if you see a solid dissolve, a precipitate form, or a gas evolve. If you mix a sodium sulfate solution with a barium nitrate solution, a white precipitate of barium sulfate will form. The general equation for this reaction is:

$$Na_2SO_{4(aq)} + Ba(NO_3)_{2(aq)} \rightarrow$$
$$BaSO_{4(s)} + 2NaNO_{3(aq)}$$

The total ionic equation:

$$2Na^+_{(aq)} + SO_4^{2-}_{(aq)} + Ba^{2+}_{(aq)} + 2NO_3^-_{(aq)} \rightarrow$$
$$BaSO_{4(s)} + 2Na^+_{(aq)} + 2NO_3^-_{(aq)}$$

Note that the equation is balanced with a net charge of zero on both sides. Note also that the sodium and nitrate ions are spectators in this reaction and thus the net ionic equation is:

$$Ba^{2+}_{(aq)} + SO_4^{2-}_{(aq)} \rightarrow BaSO_{4(s)}$$

If magnesium hydroxide and hydrochloric acid are mixed together, the solid magnesium hydroxide dissolves in the acid solution and produces water and magnesium chloride. Another example, as seen before, is the addition of an acid to sodium hydrogen carbonate. This produces carbon dioxide gas, water, and a soluble salt.

Knowing the solubility charts comes in handy for predicting the identity of precipitates formed when two ionic solutions are mixed. Double-replacement reactions are used to separate ions, for qualitative analysis, and in some cases, for neutralizing acid spills.

CHAPTER 6

LEARNING OUTCOMES		
LEARNING OUTCOMES	**LOCATION IN SECTION**	**EVIDENCE OF UNDERSTANDING**
Represent chemical changes using word equations and chemical equations.	*Investigate* Steps 5-7, 11	Students' answers match those found in this *Teacher's Edition*.
Distinguish between different classes of chemical reactions.	*Investigate* Steps 3-4, 6-7	Students can generalize forms of reactions to match those found in this *Teacher's Edition*.
Predict the possible products of single-replacement and double-replacement reactions.	*Investigate* Step 11 *Chem to Go* Questions 1, 4	Students' answers match those found in this *Teacher's Edition*. Reactions written by students correspond to their observations in experiment.
Determine whether a reaction has occurred based on the evidence observed.	*Investigate* Steps 1-2, 7-11 *Chem to Go* Questions 2-3, 5	Observations closely match those given in this *Teacher's Edition*. Students' answers match those found in this *Teacher's Edition*.
Use the Law of Conservation of Matter to balance chemical reactions.	*Investigate* Steps 4, 6-7, 11 *Chem to Go* Question 4	Reactions are correctly balanced.

NOTES

_____

_____

_____

_____

_____

_____

_____

_____

_____

_____

_____

_____

_____

NOTES

Section 4
Materials, Chemicals, Preparation, and Safety

("per Group" quantity is based on group size of 4 students)

Materials and Equipment

Materials (and Equipment)	Quantity per Group (4 students)
Large microwell plates, 24 well*	2
Beral pipettes	8

Materials (and Equipment)	Quantity per Class
Beakers, 100 mL (Teacher demo)	3
Brown dropping bottles	1
Graduated cylinder, 50 mL (Teacher demo)	1
Clear dropping bottles	10

*As an alternative, small test tubes (16) could be used. If so, a test-tube rack will also be needed for each group.

Chemicals

Chemicals	Quantity per Class (24 students)
Ammonia hydroxide, NH_3, 2.0 M	135 mL (Teacher demo)
Copper sulfate solution, $CuSO_4$, 1.0 M	15 drops (Teacher demo)
Magnesium sulfate solution, $MgSO_4$, 1.0 M	15 drops (Teacher demo)
Phenolphthalein, PHTH, 1% alcoholic solution	20 drops (Teacher demo)
Sodium hydroxide, NaOH, 0.1 M**	100 mL
Copper (II) sulfate, $CuSO_4$, 0.1 M**	100 mL
Potassium iodide solution, KI, 0.1 M**	100 mL
Silver nitrate, $AgNO_3$ solution, 0.1 M**	100 mL
Potassium carbonate, K_2CO_3, 0.1 M**	100 mL
Iron (III) chloride, $FeCl_3$, 0.1 M* **	100 mL
Magnesium sulfate, $MgSO_4$, 0.1 M**	100 mL

**These solutions are placed in small dropper bottles for student use.

Note: Some of these solutions have been prepared for previous sections and may still be available.

NOTES

Teacher Preparation

Ammonia, 2.0 M: In a fume hood, add 27.2 mL of concentrated NH_3 (14.8 M) to 150 mL of distilled water. Dilute to 200 mL.

Copper sulfate, 1.0 M: Dissolve 2.50 g of $CuSO_4 \cdot 5H_2O$ in 6.0 mL of distilled water. When dissolved, dilute to 10.0 mL. Store in a dropper bottle for the teacher demo.

Magnesium sulfate, 1.0 M: Dissolve 2.46 g of $MgSO_4 \cdot 7H_2O$ in 6.0 mL of distilled water. When dissolved, dilute to 10.0 mL. Store in a dropper bottle for the teacher demo.

Phenolphthalein, 1% in alcohol: Dissolve 1.0 g of phenolphthalein in 50 mL of 95% ethanol, then dilute to 100 mL with additional ethanol. Store in dropping bottles for teacher demo and future student use.

Sodium hydroxide, 0.1 M: Dissolve 0.40 g of NaOH in 70 mL of distilled water. When dissolved, dilute to 100 mL. Store in dropping bottles for student use.

Copper sulfate, 0.1 M: Dissolve 2.50 g of $CuSO_4 \cdot 5H_2O$ in 70 mL of distilled water. When dissolved, dilute to 100 mL. Store in dropping bottles for student use.

Potassium iodide, 0.1 M: Dissolve 1.66 g of KI in 70 mL of distilled water. Dilute to 100 mL when dissolved. Store in dropping bottles for student use.

Silver nitrate, 0.1 M: Dissolve 1.70 g of $AgNO_3$ in 70 mL of distilled water. Dilute to 100 mL when dissolved. Store in brown dropping bottles for student use.

Potassium carbonate, 0.1 M: Dissolve 1.38 g of K_2CO_3 in 70 mL of distilled water. When dissolved, dilute to 100 mL. Store in dropping bottles for student use.

Iron (III) chloride, 0.1 M: Dissolve 2.70 g of $FeCl_3 \cdot 6H_2O$ in 70 mL of distilled water. When dissolved, dilute to 100 mL. Store in dropping bottles for student use.

Magnesium sulfate, 0.1 M: Dissolve 2.46 g of $MgSO_4 \cdot 7H_2O$ in 70 mL of distilled water. When dissolved, dilute to 100 mL. Store in dropping bottles for student use.

Safety Requirements

- Aprons and goggles are required in the laboratory area.

- All solution can be disposed of down the drain.

- Minimal solids that remain can be placed in the garbage.

- Caution in preparing ammonia solution as this is an irritant to the respiratory tract.

- Wash arms and hands before leaving the laboratory area.

NOTES

CHAPTER 6

Meeting the Needs of All Students
Differentiated Instruction

Augmentation and Accommodations

LEARNING ISSUE	REFERENCE	AUGMENTATION AND ACCOMMODATIONS
Identification of terms and corresponding symbols	*Investigate* 4.	**Augmentation** • Students need to name, recognize and apply subscripts and coefficients to complete this investigation. Coefficients are clearly defined in the text. The text explains what a subscript tells you, but does not explicitly say which symbol or number is the subscript in $Mg + O_2 \longrightarrow MgO$. Give students a definition similar to the one for coefficients, such as: "The number after and slightly below a chemical element or formula, called a subscript, communicates the number of atoms in the element or compound it follows."
Defining a term in a student's own words	*Investigate* 4.g)	**Accommodations** • Ask students to do this as a "think, pair, share" exercise. • Provide a scaffold for students with inadequate definitions by showing them how to create a general rule from the parenthetical example in the text which precedes the directive to write a definition.

Balancing equations
 	
Working through a complex mathematical procedure systematically
 	
Persistence
	Investigate 4.-7., 11.	**Augmentation**
		• The chart in Step 7 will provide a good scaffold to help students balance equations. Help struggling students with the following steps:
		    o Copy the equation.
		    o Create a table like the one in the text.
		    o List each atom on the left (reactant) side of the equation.
		    o Write the number of atoms of each element before the reaction.
		    o Check the product side. Record the number of each element there.
		    o Add coefficients to balance each element.
		    o Recheck other elements for balance when you have added coefficients.
		    o Persist until all elements are in balance.
		Accommodations
		• Have students create their own procedure cards they can use when balancing equations.
		• Provide extra practice balancing equations requiring more than one step.

Applying order of operations to solve problems involving parentheses	*Investigate* 11.	**Augmentation** • Check to see that every student understands the implications of parentheses followed by a subscript such as those found in $Fe(OH)_3$ and $Fe(NO_3)_3$. Clearly distinguish between those and the meaning of subscripts without parentheses like K_2SO_4. Explain that students must multiply subscripts to determine the number of atoms indicated in formulas like $Fe(NO_3)_3$.

Explaining the reactions students explored
 	
Differentiating among chemical reactions
	Chem Talk	**Augmentation**
		• Ask each group to invent a graphic organizer that represents what they learned about the four types of chemical reactions. Suggest that groups consider using a chart or a cluster diagram as a substitute for the answers to the first three questions in the *Checking Up* section.
		Accommodation
		• Provide students with the types of information they should include:
		    o Name of the reaction
		    o Definition in words
		    o Symbolic form of the reaction
		    o Examples of this type of reaction in both words and chemical symbols.

LEARNING ISSUE	REFERENCE	AUGMENTATION AND ACCOMMODATIONS
Storing information for future use Making decisions about one's own learning needs	*Chem Talk*	**Accommodations** • One or two students may remember the solubility rules and the activity series. Others will remember the principles and where to find the information in the text. Discuss your expectations of them for retaining this information. Given those expectations, encourage students to develop a method for retaining the information. Methods could include memorization, but are more likely to include adding a reference to it in their *Active Chemistry* logs. Notes are like the memory storage of an external drive of a computer. If students think of notes and references that way, it may motivate them to keep good notes.

Strategies for Students with Limited English Language Proficiency

LEARNING ISSUE	REFERENCE	AUGMENTATIONS
Background knowledge	*What Do You Think?*	Students might not understand the phrase, "*in a compact way.*" Specify how they are to "*record*" their ideas.
Vocabulary	*Investigate*	Check for understanding of the idiom, "*cool.*" Students might benefit from working in teams or with partners to carry out each of the steps. Help students with their understanding of "*decomposition*" and "*synthesis*" as these words may not be in their expressive vocabulary. In Step 4.h) there is a reference to the how the chemical equation "*communicate*(s)" the reaction. Students may not understand the word in this context. Check for pronunciation of the word "*aqueous.*"
Background knowledge Vocabulary Comprehending text	*Chem Talk*	Check for understanding of bold-type words. Refer students to sidebar explanations for further assistance.
Background knowledge	*What Do You Think Now?*	The bold-faced question might be confusing. The term "*situation*" might need explanation, as might the terms "*compressed*" and *abbreviated*" in this context.
Background knowledge Vocabulary Comprehending text	*Chem Essential Questions*	Check for understanding of words "*represent,*" and "*simplifies,*" in the *Why should you care?* section.
Comprehension Vocabulary	*Chem to Go*	Give students directions on how they are to "*explain*" their answer.

CHAPTER 6

Section 4
Teaching Suggestions and Sample Answers

What Do You See?

To begin, elicit a response from your students about the illustration introducing the section. You can do this as part of a class discussion or by having students respond directly in their *Active Chemistry* log. You might provide a prompt such as, "What is the theme of this chemistry show and how does it relate to what the figures are doing?" You can also ask if there are other possibilities for themes they could use for their own shows. Remember that student engagement and participation is the primary goal at this point; there are no wrong answers.

Cool Chemistry Show

Section 4   Reaction Types and Chemical Equations

What Do You See?

Learning Outcomes

In this section you will

- **Represent** chemical changes using word equations and chemical equations.

- **Distinguish** between different classes of chemical reactions.

- **Predict** the possible products of single-replacement and double-replacement reactions.

- **Determine** whether a reaction has occurred based on evidence observed.

- **Use** the law of conservation of matter to balance chemical reactions.

What Do You Think?

When people communicate with each other, they often like to do so in a compact way. Below are a few examples. Can you interpret these?

From the Internet: CUl8r   Wat RU ^ 2?   TMI   LOL

License plates: 14U2C   10SNE1   EDUC8R

- **What are some situations (other than the examples given) when language is compressed or abbreviated?**

Record your ideas about this question in your *Active Chemistry* log. Be prepared to discuss your responses with your small group and the class.

Investigate

1. Watch closely as your teacher shows you some cool chemistry.

    a) Record your observations in your *Active Chemistry* log.

2. Here's how the cool chemistry was done. Into each of three beakers that appeared empty, your teacher added about 45 mL of 2.0 *M* ammonium hydroxide solution.

   Before beginning the demonstration, your teacher had also added the following to each beaker:

   Beaker One—20 drops of the indicator phenolphthalein solution;

490

STUDENTS' PRIOR CONCEPTIONS

It is common for students to "give up" when confronted too early with the language of chemistry – formulas and equations. When this occurs, the battle to change the direction of learning is made far more difficult. A seven-step program outlined below can help to alleviate students' concerns.

1. Have students learn the symbols for each element.

2. Given the requirements of the rules for filling orbitals, help them understand the filling of the orbitals and atomic numbers and atomic masses.

3. Clarify the relationship between valence electrons and each element's position on the periodic table.

4. Using the octet rule (aside from hydrogen and helium), help students develop an understanding of how compounds (ionic and covalent) form.

5. Introduce and solidify the concept of formulas.

6. Introduce equations as processes which occur under certain conditions.

7. Explain that to conserve matter, equations must be balanced.

What Do You Think?

Students' responses to this question and the *What Do You See?* above will be strong indicators of what they have already learned about the topic of this section as well as any misconceptions they might have about the related chemistry. It is important not to judge their answers; you want to encourage them to share their opinions, no matter what they are. Engaging students in topics that they already know something about and that are associated with the section generates enthusiasm in the learner and gives you a chance to evaluate prior conceptions for the topics found in the section.

What Do You Think?
A CHEMIST'S RESPONSE

The connection here is between what students know (such as shortened text messages) to what they don't know (chemical symbols, formulas, and equations). The first Internet message, *"CUl8r"* translates to *"See You Later,"* and is a common text message many students use. The second message, *"What are you up to?,"* can be derived with just a little thought. TMI stands for "too much information; LOL stands for "laugh out loud"; 14U2C stands for "one for you to see"; and EDUC8R stands for "educator."
In addition to those listed, there are many examples of abbreviated or compressed language forms. Some possible answers may be text messaging, maps, computer languages, and professional titles and degrees (Ph.D., Dr., etc.).

NOTES

_____

_____

_____

_____

_____

_____

_____

_____

_____

_____

_____

CHAPTER 6

Investigate

1.-2.

Since the ammonium hydroxide is basic, it will have the following effects:

- Beaker One (phenolphthalein solution) – will turn red

- Beaker Two (magnesium sulfate solution) – the magnesium ions will react with the hydroxide ions to produce a white precipitate

- Beaker Three (copper sulfate solution) – the copper ions will react with the ammonium ions to produce a blue copper ammonia complex

The reactions are:

PHTH (clear solutions) + base (OH$^-$) $\rightarrow$ pink/red solution

$Mg^{2+}_{(aq)} + 2OH^-_{(aq)} \rightarrow Mg(OH)_{2(s)}$
a white precipitate

$Cu^{2+}_{(aq)} + 4NH_{3(aq)} \rightarrow Cu(NH_3)_4^{2+}_{(aq)}$
blue to deeper blue

NOTES

___

CHEM TIP

In this red, white, and blue demonstration, the copper ions combine with the ammonia to form copper ammonia complex $[Cu(NH_3)_4]^{2+}_{(aq)}$ as a blue solution. The magnesium hydroxide forms a white precipitate. If silver nitrate is substituted for the magnesium sulfate, silver hydroxide is produced. This is initially a white precipitate, but will turn brownish-black. Also, remember that silver nitrate is not only expensive, it is also sensitive to light and must be stored in a dark bottle. You could substitute barium nitrate and have it react with sodium sulfate solution to obtain a similar white precipitate. If you feel that the white precipitate produced in the reaction between ammonium hydroxide and magnesium sulfate is too weak, you can increase the concentration of the ammonium hydroxide. This should give you a whiter precipitate.

2.a)

Yes, it appeared that a chemical reaction occurred in each of the beakers. The evidence would be:

Beaker One: a color change

Beaker Two: a precipitate formed

Beaker Three: a color change. Whether this is indeed a chemical change might be debated, as the starting materials can be recovered without any chemical changes or reagents.

3.a)

The term "synthesis" means that new compounds have been formed through chemical reaction. Usually, two substances become one new substance. However, in many instances, two compounds can react to form two new substances. An example is combining hydrogen gas with oxygen gas to produce water:

$$2H_2 + O_2 \rightarrow 2H_2O$$

The term "decomposition" refers to a chemical reaction when one more complex substance breaks down into two simpler substances. This usually requires the input of energy, often in the form of heat energy. An example of decomposition is:

$$2KClO_3 + heat \rightarrow 2KCl + 3O_{2(g)}$$

Beaker Two—15 drops of 1 M magnesium sulfate solution;

Beaker Three—15 drops of 1 M copper (II) sulfate solution.

a) Did a chemical reaction take place in each beaker? What evidence do you have to justify your answer?

3. A chemical reaction occurs when substances change to form new substances. There are many chemical reactions that can occur. You have already observed some of them. One way chemists group reactions is into the following four categories.

- *synthesis reactions*;
- *decomposition reactions*;
- *single-replacement reactions*;
- *double-replacement reactions*.

a) What do the words synthesis and decomposition mean?

4. In a synthesis reaction, two or more chemicals combine to form a compound.

$$A + B \rightarrow AB$$

Here is an example of a synthesis reaction. When magnesium and oxygen react, a white solid, magnesium oxide, is formed.

This can be written as a word equation

Magnesium (solid) and oxygen (gas) produce magnesium oxide (solid).

This can also be written using a chemical equation

$$Mg + O_2 \rightarrow MgO$$

(The subscript tells you the number of atoms in one molecule. Oxygen is diatomic. It exists as a molecule made up of two atoms.)

a) What do you think are the advantages of writing a reaction using chemical symbols?

Any equation in chemistry must follow scientific laws or principles. The number of atoms of each element must be equal before and after the reaction.

b) In the equation to the left, how many atoms of oxygen are in the reactants (before the reaction)?

c) How many oxygen atoms are in the product (after the reaction)?

d) What is the problem with the equation?

Write a two in front of the MgO.

$$Mg + O_2 \rightarrow 2MgO$$

(The number in front of a chemical formula, called a coefficient, communicates the number of molecules or formula units that are involved in the reaction. In this equation there are two molecules of magnesium oxide represented. That is, there is a total of two magnesium atoms and two oxygen atoms.)

e) How many magnesium atoms are now represented in the product?

f) How many reactant atoms of magnesium are shown?

g) What is the problem with the equation?

Write a two in front of the Mg.

$$2Mg + O_2 \rightarrow 2MgO$$

h) The chemical equation above is now balanced. (The number of magnesium and oxygen atoms in the product is equal to the number in the reactant.) In your own words, explain the meaning of a balanced equation. How does the chemical equation communicate what happened in the reaction, and how does it follow the law of conservation of matter?

491

Active Chemistry

4.f)

There is only 1 atom of magnesium on the reactant side.

4.g)

It is unbalanced. Inserting a "2" in front of the magnesium on the reactant side will resolve the problem and the equation will be balanced.

4.h)

Students' answers will vary but all should contain the information that:

- A chemical equation tells how much (moles) of each compound reacts to form how much (moles) product.

- The balanced equation is useful for doing stoichiometric calculations of reactants and products because the atoms are conserved from the reactant side to the product side.

4.a)

Using chemical symbols is a shortcut method. This reveals what materials are reacting and also the ratio in which they combine. It also shows us the number of atoms that are conserved from the reactant side to the product side.

4.b)

There are 2 atoms of oxygen on the reactant side.

4.c)

There is 1 atom of oxygen on the product side.

4.d)

The equation is unbalanced. A "2" is needed in front of the magnesium oxide to balance the number of oxygen atoms needed on the product side.

4.e)

There are 2 atoms of magnesium on the product side.

CHAPTER 6

5.a)

Solid carbon combines with oxygen gas to produce carbon dioxide gas.

$$C_{(s)} + O_{2(g)} \rightarrow CO_{2(g)}$$

5.b)

Hydrogen gas combines with oxygen gas to produce liquid water.

$$2H_{2(g)} + O_{2(g)} \rightarrow 2H_2O_{(l)}$$

5.c)

Solid iron reacts slowly with oxygen gas to produce iron (III) oxide solid.

$$4Fe_{(s)} + 3O_{2(g)} \rightarrow 2Fe_2O_{3(s)}$$

5.d)

Solid sodium metal reacts with chlorine gas to produce solid sodium chloride (table salt).

$$2Na_{(s)} + Cl_{2(g)} \rightarrow 2NaCl_{(s)}$$

6.a)

Yes, the equation is balanced. The atoms are conserved on both sides of the equation. A student checks for being balanced by counting the atoms of each substance on each side of the equation and making certain that they are equal.

6.b)

Sodium chloride (solid) and energy produce sodium (metal) and chlorine (gas).

$$2NaCl_{(s)} + energy \rightarrow$$
$$2Na_{(s)} + Cl_{2(g)}$$

6.c)

Potassium iodide (solid) and energy produce potassium metal (solid) and iodine (solid).

$$2KI_{(s)} + energy \rightarrow$$
$$2K_{(s)} + I_{2(s)}$$

6.d)

Magnesium bromide (solid) and energy produce magnesium (solid) and bromine (liquid).

$$MgBr_{2(s)} + energy \rightarrow$$
$$Mg_{(s)} + Br_{2(l)}$$

Cool Chemistry Show

When writing a chemical equation the states of the reactants and products are also given. The following symbols are used:

- (s) for solid
- (l) for liquid
- (g) for gas
- (aq) for aqueous, meaning in a water solution.

The complete balanced chemical equation for the reaction of magnesium and oxygen is

$$2Mg_{(s)} + O_{2(g)} \rightarrow 2MgO_{(s)}$$

5. Write a word equation and a balanced chemical equation for each of the following synthesis reactions. Note that there are eight elements that are diatomic, which means that they exist as a molecule comprised of two atoms. They are hydrogen (H_2), nitrogen (N_2), oxygen (O_2), fluorine (F_2), chlorine (Cl_2), bromine (Br_2), iodine (I_2), and astatine (At_2). If you need to include any of these elements in an uncombined state in a chemical equation, don't forget the 2 as a subscript.

a) Solid carbon (C) burns in air (oxygen gas) to form carbon dioxide gas (CO_2).

b) Hydrogen gas reacts with oxygen gas to form liquid water (H_2O).

c) A piece of solid iron (Fe) over time will react with oxygen to form iron (III) oxide (Fe_2O_3).

d) A piece of solid sodium (Na) is dropped into a container of chlorine gas to produce solid sodium chloride (NaCl).

6. Water can be separated into its elements with an input of energy. The equation for this reaction is

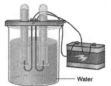

Decomposition of water into $H_{2(g)}$ and $O_{2(g)}$ by electrolysis

Water (liquid) and energy produces hydrogen (gas) and oxygen (gas).

$$2H_2O_{(l)} + energy \rightarrow 2H_{2(g)} + O_{2(g)}$$

a) Is the equation properly balanced? How did you check?

When a substance breaks down into its component parts, the process is called a *decomposition reaction*.

$$AB \rightarrow A + B$$

Write word and balanced chemical equations for the following decomposition reactions:

(Remember that some elements are diatomic—H_2, N_2, and so on.)

b) sodium chloride solid ($NaCl_{(s)}$)

c) potassium iodide solid ($KI_{(s)}$)

d) magnesium bromide solid ($MgBr_{2(s)}$)

7. The reactions mentioned above involve elements combining to form compounds or compounds breaking up to form elements.

There are other reactions that involve elements reacting with compounds to form products. Such was the case when solid zinc was dropped into hydrochloric acid in *Section 1*, forming hydrogen gas and aqueous zinc chloride solution.

The equation for this reaction is:

Zinc (solid) and hydrochloric acid (aqueous) produces hydrogen (gas) and zinc chloride (solution).

$Zn_{(s)} + 2HCl_{(aq)} \rightarrow H_{2(g)} + ZnCl_{2(aq)}$

a) Check to ensure that the chemical equation is properly balanced by completing the table in your log.

The reaction with zinc and hydrochloric acid is called a *single-replacement* reaction because zinc replaces the hydrogen in the acid.

$A + BC \rightarrow B + AC$

Write word and chemical equations for the following:

b) A piece of iron (Fe) metal is added to an aqueous solution of copper (II) sulfate ($CuSO_4$) and produces iron (II) sulfate ($FeSO_4$) and copper metal.

c) Solid lead (Pb) metal is added to an aqueous solution of silver nitrate ($AgNO_3$) and produces lead (II) nitrate ($Pb(NO_3)_2$) and silver metal.

d) Aluminum foil (Al) is placed in a beaker of aqueous copper (II) hydroxide ($Cu(OH)_2$) and produces aluminum hydroxide ($Al(OH)_3$) and copper metal. Balance each of the equations, if you have not done so.

	Number of Atoms		
	Before	After	Balanced
Zn	1	1	yes
H	2		
Cl			

You can use a chart similar to the one above, as you did before.

8. Another type of reaction is a *double-replacement* reaction.

$AB + CD \rightarrow CB + AD$

You may have already done double-replacement reactions in a previous chapter. You will soon try some more with your group. Use the chart below to guide your work. The compounds are in water solution.

a) Record your observations of the reactants before you mix them. For example, record your observations of potassium carbonate and silver nitrate before you mix them.

b) Create a chart in your log to record your observations after you mix the reactants. You may wish to use a chart similar to the one shown below.

Safety goggles and a lab apron must be worn at all times in a chemistry lab.

	Silver nitrate (AgNO₃)	Copper (II) sulfate (CuSO₄)	Magnesium sulfate (MgSO₄)	Sodium hydroxide (NaOH)
potassium carbonate (K₂CO₃)	1.	2.	3.	4.
sodium hydroxide (NaOH)	5.	6.	7.	8.
potassium iodide (KI)	9.	10.	11.	12.
iron (III) chloride (FeCl₃)	13.	14.	15.	16.

493

Active Chemistry

7.c)

Lead (solid) reacts with silver nitrate (aqueous) to produce lead nitrate (aqueous) and silver (solid).

$Pb_{(s)} + 2AgNO_{3(aq)} \rightarrow$
$Pb(NO_3)_{2(aq)} + 2Ag_{(s)}$

7.d)

Aluminum (metal) reacts with copper (II) hydroxide (aqueous) to produce copper (solid) and aluminum hydroxide (aqueous).

$2Al_{(s)} + 3Cu(OH)_{2(aq)} \rightarrow$
$2Al(OH)_{3(aq)} + 3Cu_{(s)}$

8.a)

Observations: The copper sulfate solution is blue and the iron (III) chloride solution is yellow. All other solutions are colorless.

8.b)

A blank data table is provided as a Blackline Master in your *Teacher Resources CD*.

6-4a **Blackline Master**

7.a)

	Reactant	Product	Balanced?
Zn	1	1	Yes
H	2	2	Yes
Cl	2	2	Yes

7.b)

Iron (solid) is added to copper (II) sulfate (aqueous) and reacts to form iron (II) sulfate (aqueous) and copper metal (solid).

$Fe_{(s)} + CuSO_{4(aq)} \rightarrow$
$FeSO_{4(aq)} + Cu_{(s)}$

	Silver nitrate (AgNO₃)	Copper (II) sulfate (CuSO₄)	Magnesium sulfate (MgSO₄)	Sodium hydroxide (NaOH)
Potassium carbonate (K₂CO₃)	1.	2.	3.	4.
Sodium hydroxide (NaOH)	5.	6.	7.	8.
Potassium iodide (KI)	9.	10.	11.	12.
Iron (III) chloride (FeCl₃)	13.	14.	15.	16.

Key: Ppt (precipitate) NRx (no reaction)

Cool Chemistry Show

Safety goggles and a lab apron must be worn *at all times* in a chemistry lab.

Silver nitrate will stain skin and clothing. Handle with care.

The iron, silver, and copper solutions contain heavy metals. Dispose of them as directed by your teacher.

Wash hands and arms thoroughly after the investigation.

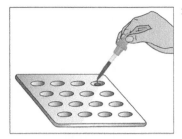

9. Mix three drops of one solution (for example, potassium carbonate) with three drops of another solution (for example, silver nitrate), as indicated by the first box on the chart. You can mix these solutions in a well of a well-plate or on a plastic surface. Do not allow the tip of the dropper of one solution to come in contact with another solution. This is important to prevent contamination of solutions.

a) In the chart in your log, record your observations after mixing the reactants. Continue with the other reactants (potassium carbonate with copper (II) sulfate; then potassium carbonate with magnesium sulfate; and so on).

b) Record all your observations in your *Active Chemistry* log.

10. Clean all equipment and the laboratory bench when you are finished. Dispose of all chemicals as directed by your teacher. Wash your hands.

11. Look at the data from the double-replacement reactions that you observed.

a) Do you think a chemical reaction took place in each case? Explain your answer.

b) Are you able to predict or identify any of the products that were formed? If so, which ones?

c) Write word equations and balanced chemical equations for each reaction that you observed.

In all cases, assume only two reactants are used and only two products are formed. Use the following formulas to help you write your equations

copper (II) carbonate ($CuCO_3(s)$)

* copper (II) iodide ($CuI_2(s)$)

iron (III) hydroxide ($Fe(OH)_3(s)$)

silver carbonate ($Ag_2CO_3(s)$)

* silver hydroxide ($AgOH(s)$)

potassium sulfate ($K_2SO_4(aq)$)

silver iodide ($AgI(s)$)

sodium nitrate ($NaNO_3(aq)$)

copper (II) hydroxide ($Cu(OH)_2(s)$)

iron (III) nitrate ($Fe(NO_3)_3(aq)$)

magnesium carbonate ($MgCO_3(s)$)

silver chloride ($AgCl(s)$)

potassium nitrate ($KNO_3(aq)$)

magnesium hydroxide ($Mg(OH)_2(s)$)

sodium chloride ($NaCl(aq)$)

sodium sulfate ($Na_2SO_4(aq)$)

* These are more complex than indicated above.

494

9.a)

	Silver nitrate ($AgNO_3$)	Copper (II) sulfate ($CuSO_4$)	Magnesium sulfate ($MgSO_4$)	Sodium hydroxide ($NaOH$)
Potassium carbonate (K_2CO_3)	1. Ppt	2. Ppt	3. Ppt	4. NRx
Sodium hydroxide ($NaOH$)	5. Ppt	6. Ppt	7. Ppt	8. XXX
Potassium iodide (KI)	9. Ppt	10. Ppt	11. NRx	12. NRx
Iron (III) chloride ($FeCl_3$)	13. Ppt	14. NRx	15. NRx	16. Ppt

Key: Ppt (precipitate) NRx (no reaction)

Before you complete the following steps, have students read through the *Chem Talk* section. Afterwards, they should be able to explain why these solutions did not precipitate.

10.

Direct students to dispose of chemicals properly.

11.a)

The following combinations did not react. This is derived because no change was noted (no precipitate, no evolution of gas, no color change).

Potassium carbonate and sodium hydroxide

Potassium iodide and magnesium sulfate

Potassium iodide and sodium hydroxide

Iron (III) chloride and copper sulfate

Iron (III) chloride and magnesium sulfate

The following combinations did show a precipitate, providing evidence that they reacted.

Potassium carbonate and silver nitrate

Potassium carbonate and copper (II) sulfate

Potassium carbonate and magnesium sulfate

Sodium hydroxide and silver nitrate

Sodium hydroxide and copper (II) sulfate

Sodium hydroxide and magnesium sulfate

Potassium iodide and silver nitrate

Iron (III) chloride and silver nitrate

Sodium hydroxide and iron (III) chloride

11.b)

Student answers will vary. With a solubility chart, they may be able to predict or identify the following precipitated products:

Silver carbonate

Copper (II) carbonate

Magnesium carbonate

Silver hydroxide

Copper (II) hydroxide

Magnesium hydroxide

Silver iodide

Potassium iodide and copper (II) sulfate

Silver chloride from $FeCl_3/AgNO_3$

Iron (III) hydroxide

It is unlikely that the students will predict a precipitate from potassium iodide and copper (II) sulfate. This reaction is more complex and is actually an oxidation-reduction reaction.

11.c)

Correctly written, the equation for the potassium iodide and copper (II) sulfate reaction is:

$$4KI_{(aq)} + 2CuSO_{4(aq)} \rightarrow Cu_2I_{2(s)} + 2K_2SO_{4(aq)} + I_{2(aq)}$$

It should be acceptable, however, for students to represent it as follows:

$$2KI_{(aq)} + CuSO_{4(aq)} \rightarrow K_2SO_{4(aq)} + CuI_{2(s)}$$

Other equations are:

Silver carbonate:
$$K_2CO_{3(aq)} + 2AgNO_{3(aq)} \rightarrow Ag_2CO_{3(s)} + 2KNO_{3(aq)}$$

Copper (II) carbonate:
$$K_2CO_{3(aq)} + CuSO_{4(aq)} \rightarrow CuCO_{3(s)} + K_2SO_{4(aq)}$$

Magnesium carbonate:
$$K_2CO_{3(aq)} + MgSO_{4(aq)} \rightarrow MgCO_{3(s)} + K_2SO_{4(aq)}$$

Silver hydroxide:
$$NaOH_{(aq)} + AgNO_{3(aq)} \rightarrow AgOH_{(s)} + NaNO_{3(aq)}$$

Copper (II) hydroxide:
$$2NaOH_{(aq)} + CuSO_{4(aq)} \rightarrow Cu(OH)_{2(s)} + Na_2SO_{4(aq)}$$

Magnesium hydroxide:
$$2NaOH_{(aq)} + MgSO_{4(aq)} \rightarrow Mg(OH)_{2(s)} + Na_2SO_{4(aq)}$$

Silver iodide:
$$KI_{(aq)} + AgNO_{3(aq)} \rightarrow AgI_{(s)} + KNO_{3(aq)}$$

Silver chloride:
$$FeCl_{3(aq)} + 3AgNO_{3(aq)} \rightarrow 3AgCl_{(s)} + Fe(NO_3)_{3(aq)}$$

Iron (III) hydroxide:
$$FeCl_{3(aq)} + 3NaOH_{(aq)} \rightarrow Fe(OH)_{3(s)} + 3NaCl_{(aq)}$$

CHAPTER 6

NOTES

Chem Talk

Brief summaries of the four common kinds of chemical reactions are provided: synthesis, decomposition, single- and double-replacement reactions. The Activity Series of Metals is reviewed and a table is provided as a reference for determining how metals will react in a metal solution. A list of five solubility rules for salts is presented as a foundation for predicting whether a mixture will produce a precipitate.

Chem Talk

CHEMICAL REACTIONS

Kinds of Chemical Reactions

A chemical reaction takes place when starting materials (reactants) change to new materials (products). Synthesis, decomposition, single-replacement, and double-replacement reactions are some common kinds of chemical reactions.

Synthesis and Decomposition Reactions

Synthesis means "putting together." In a **synthesis reaction** two or more substances (elements or compounds) combine to form one or more compounds. In this investigation you explored the reaction of magnesium in oxygen to form magnesium oxide. The opposite kind of reaction is a **decomposition reaction**. In chemical decomposition a compound is separated into its elements. Electricity can be used to decompose water into hydrogen and oxygen.

Single-replacement Reactions

A **single-replacement reaction** is one in which an element reacts with a compound to produce a new element and an ionic compound. For example, a single-replacement reaction occurs when you put a strip of zinc into hydrochloric acid. Hydrogen gas and aqueous zinc chloride are formed, as you observed in *Section 1*.

Activity Series

A single-replacement reaction occurs when you put a strip of zinc in a copper (II) sulfate solution. The zinc metal exchanges places with the copper cations.

If you put copper metal in a zinc sulfate solution you would find that no reaction would take place, as expected. Zinc atoms exchange places with copper ions, but copper atoms will not exchange places with zinc ions. You have learned something about a property of copper and zinc. Zinc is more reactive than copper. If you were to experiment with different metals and metallic solutions, you should be able to create an activity series of metals. The activity series of metals can be put into a table that you can use to predict if a reaction will take place.

Chem Words

synthesis reaction: a chemical reaction in which two or more substances combine to form a compound.

decomposition reaction: a chemical reaction in which a compound breaks down into two or more simple substances.

single-replacement reaction: a reaction in which an element displaces or replaces an ion of another element in a compound.

495

Active Chemistry

CHAPTER 6

Before using the Activity Series of Metals table, demonstrate how to use the equations. For example, if you place zinc in copper sulfate solution you can use the following equations from the table:

$$Zn \longrightarrow Zn^{2+} + 2e^-$$
(Oxidation reaction)

$$Cu^{2+} + 2e^- \longrightarrow Cu$$
(Reduction reaction)

$$Cu^{2+} + Zn \longrightarrow Cu + Zn^{2+}$$
(Net ionic equation)

Notice that the electrons subtract out and also that the reduction reaction is the opposite of the reaction given in the table. Many authors like to write the table in reduction form instead of oxidation form. Also, make sure that the students understand that the electron transfer must be equal. Reduction-oxidation reactions are called redox reactions since you can't have reduction without oxidation.

Here is another example that shows what happens if you place copper metal in silver nitrate solution:

$$Cu \longrightarrow Cu^{2+} + 2e^-$$
(Oxidation)

$$2[Ag^+ + e^- \longrightarrow Ag] =$$
$$2Ag^+ + 2e^- \longrightarrow 2Ag$$
(Reduction)

$$Cu + 2Ag^+ \longrightarrow Cu^{2+} + 2Ag$$
Redox reaction

Note that it is necessary to multiply the second equation by 2 in order to transfer the necessary 2 electrons from copper to silver. Once students understand the Activity Series of Metals, they will recognize how and why gold jewelry is often made by plating a gold solution onto a metal like copper.

 Cool Chemistry Show

Activity Series of Metals (most active to least active)
lithium (Li → Li⁺ + e⁻)

Activity Series of Metals (most active to least active)
lithium ($Li \rightarrow Li^+ + e^-$)
potassium ($K \rightarrow K^+ + e^-$)
calcium ($Ca \rightarrow Ca^{2+} + 2e^-$)
sodium ($Na \rightarrow Na^+ + 1e^-$)
magnesium ($Mg \rightarrow Mg^{2+} + 2e^-$)
aluminum ($Al \rightarrow Al^{3+} + 3e^-$)
zinc ($Zn \rightarrow Zn^{2+} + 2e^-$)
iron ($Fe \rightarrow Fe^{2+} + 2e^-$)
lead ($Pb \rightarrow Pb^{2+} + 2e^-$)
hydrogen ($H_2(g) \rightarrow 2H^+ + 2e^-$)
copper ($Cu \rightarrow Cu^{2+} + 2e^-$)
mercury ($Hg \rightarrow Hg^{2+} + 2e^-$)
silver ($Ag \rightarrow Ag^+ + e^-$)
gold ($Au \rightarrow Au^{3+} + 3e^-$)

The table looks like the one on this page. The table permits you to determine how a metal will react in a metal solution. A metal that is more active than another will dissolve into the metal solution and plate out the less active metal. Zinc replaced the copper in the copper (II) sulfate solution and the copper plated the zinc. For example, let's say that you place a strip of copper in a silver nitrate solution. According to the table, the copper will dissolve into copper ions (Cu^{2+}) and the silver ions in the silver nitrate solution will plate out on the copper as silver.

In addition to metals, you will notice that hydrogen gas is also listed in the activity series. You read above that metals can replace less active metals in metal salt solutions. Metals that are more active than hydrogen can replace the hydrogen from water to form metal hydroxides. As an example, if you were to react potassium metal with water, you would get hydrogen gas and potassium hydroxide solution. The equation is

$$2K(s) + 2HOH(l) \rightarrow H_2(g) + 2KOH(aq)$$
(Note: Water, H_2O is written as HOH.)

Double-replacement Reactions

Double-replacement reactions are different from single-replacement reactions in that you start with two aqueous phase solutions and when they are mixed they "switch partners."

Chem Words

double-replacement reaction: a chemical reaction in which two ionic compounds "exchange" cations to produce two new compounds.

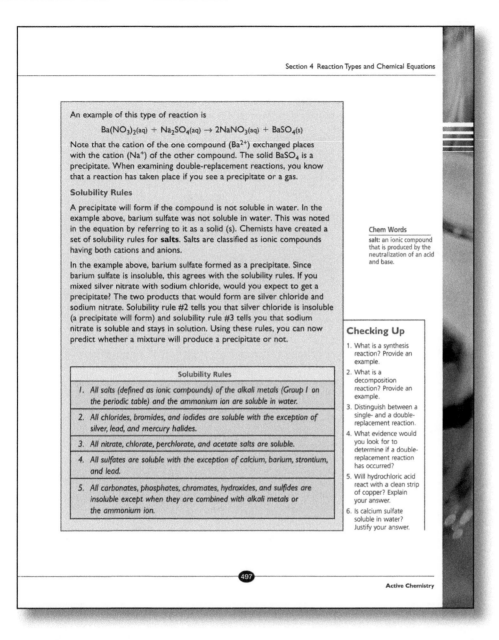

An example of this type of reaction is

$$Ba(NO_3)_2(aq) + Na_2SO_4(aq) \rightarrow 2NaNO_3(aq) + BaSO_4(s)$$

Note that the cation of the one compound (Ba^{2+}) exchanged places with the cation (Na^+) of the other compound. The solid $BaSO_4$ is a precipitate. When examining double-replacement reactions, you know that a reaction has taken place if you see a precipitate or a gas.

Solubility Rules

A precipitate will form if the compound is not soluble in water. In the example above, barium sulfate was not soluble in water. This was noted in the equation by referring to it as a solid (s). Chemists have created a set of solubility rules for **salts**. Salts are classified as ionic compounds having both cations and anions.

In the example above, barium sulfate formed as a precipitate. Since barium sulfate is insoluble, this agrees with the solubility rules. If you mixed silver nitrate with sodium chloride, would you expect to get a precipitate? The two products that would form are silver chloride and sodium nitrate. Solubility rule #2 tells you that silver chloride is insoluble (a precipitate will form) and solubility rule #3 tells you that sodium nitrate is soluble and stays in solution. Using these rules, you can now predict whether a mixture will produce a precipitate or not.

Chem Words

salt: an ionic compound that is produced by the neutralization of an acid and base.

Solubility Rules

I.	All salts (defined as ionic compounds) of the alkali metals (Group I on the periodic table) and the ammonium ion are soluble in water.
2.	All chlorides, bromides, and iodides are soluble with the exception of silver, lead, and mercury halides.
3.	All nitrate, chlorate, perchlorate, and acetate salts are soluble.
4.	All sulfates are soluble with the exception of calcium, barium, strontium, and lead.
5.	All carbonates, phosphates, chromates, hydroxides, and sulfides are insoluble except when they are combined with alkali metals or the ammonium ion.

Checking Up

1. What is a synthesis reaction? Provide an example.
2. What is a decomposition reaction? Provide an example.
3. Distinguish between a single- and a double-replacement reaction.
4. What evidence would you look for to determine if a double-replacement reaction has occurred?
5. Will hydrochloric acid react with a clean strip of copper? Explain your answer.
6. Is calcium sulfate soluble in water? Justify your answer.

497

Active Chemistry

Checking Up

1.

A synthesis reaction makes a new material from other materials.

Example 1: Sodium metal placed in a container of chlorine gas will produce sodium chloride.

$$2Na(s) + Cl_2(g) \rightarrow 2NaCl(s)$$

Example 2: Magnesium burning in the presence of oxygen will produce magnesium oxide.

$$Mg(s) + O_2(g) \rightarrow 2MgO(s)$$

2.

A decomposition reaction breaks a compound into smaller compounds or elements. For example, the electrolysis of molten sodium chloride will produce sodium metal and chlorine gas.

$$2NaCl(l) + energy \rightarrow 2Na(s) + Cl_2(g)$$

3.

A single-replacement reaction is a process in which one material replaces one of the members of a compound. This is usually a redox reaction.

A double-replacement reaction is a process in which the cations of the two binary ionic compounds exchange anions. These reactions are usually driven by the formation of a gas or a precipitate (or water).

4.

Evidence of a double-replacement reaction would be the production of a precipitate, a gas, or water.

5.

Hydrochloric acid and copper metal will not react. The hydrogen proton cannot oxidize copper metal. Hydrogen is above copper in the Metal Activity Series and cannot remove an electron (oxidize) from copper.

6.

Calcium sulfate is insoluble in water according to the solubility rules.

CHAPTER 6

What Do You Think Now?

It is useful for students to return to the original *What Do You See?* illustration and the *What Do You Think?* question to review their original responses. The illustration will be more meaningful to them now as it represents the demonstration that the teacher performed. Also, they will gain confidence in using chemical equations when they realize how far they have come. Refer to the suggestions in *A Chemist's Response* for some examples of answers to the *What Do You Think?* question. Students should now recognize how chemical equations simplify communication by shortening the expression for chemical change.

Cool Chemistry Show

What Do You Think Now?

At the beginning of the section you were asked the following:

• What are some situations (other than the examples given) when language is compressed or abbreviated?

As a student chemist, you know that an obvious answer to this question is chemistry. Do you think the use of chemical equations simplifies the communication of chemical change? Explain. Do you think you understand the basic format for how chemical change is communicated in a compact way?

Chem
Essential Questions

What does it mean?

Chemistry explains a *macroscopic* phenomenon (what you observe) with a description of what happens at the *nanoscopic* level (atoms and molecules) using *symbolic* structures as a way to communicate. Complete the chart below in your *Active Chemistry* log.

MACRO	NANO	SYMBOLIC
If you add silver nitrate solution to sodium chloride solution, what will you observe that convinces you that a chemical reaction has taken place?	Why do chemical equations have to be "balanced"? Explain what occurs on the atomic level when potassium iodide reacts with silver nitrate.	How can you represent the reaction of silver nitrate solution with potassium iodide solution using chemical symbols?

How do you know?

Water can be decomposed to form two products: hydrogen and oxygen. What evidence was given in this section for the chemical composition of water?

Why do you believe?

In mathematics, the = symbol is used to represent "sides" of an equation. In chemistry the symbol → is used in chemical equations. Why do you believe this symbol is better for chemistry than the = symbol?

Why should you care?

Being able to represent chemical changes in a compact way simplifies chemistry. When you perform your chemistry show, how might you use chemical equations to make it easier for your audience to understand the chemical changes that you are demonstrating?

498

Chem Essential Questions
What does it mean?

MACRO — A white precipitate forms when silver nitrate and sodium chloride solutions are mixed. This precipitate is evidence of a chemical reaction.

NANO — A chemical equation must be balanced in order to show that matter is conserved. It is also essential for stoichiometric calculations. On the atomic level, when potassium iodide reacts with silver nitrate, the silver cations are attracted to the iodide anions and form a precipitate. The potassium and nitrate ions stay in solution and are called "spectator ions."

SYMBOLIC —
$Ag^+_{(aq)} + NO_3^-_{(aq)} + K^+_{(aq)} + I^-_{(aq)} \longrightarrow$
$AgI_{(s)} + K^+_{(aq)} + NO_3^-_{(aq)}$

How do you know?

Step 5.b) of *Investigate* defines the reaction of the hydrogen and oxygen gases to form liquid water as a synthesis reaction. Also, Step 6 in *Investigate* outlines the decomposition of water by electrolysis into $H_{2(g)}$ and $O_{2(g)}$.

Why do you believe?

In expressing chemical change, the → symbol represents "yields" or "produces" indicating the end product of the change. These products are new substances and the reactants that combined to form them are gone. Thus, the = symbol would not accurately represent the chemistry that occurred.

Why should you care?

While demonstrating chemical change during the chemistry show, students might find it useful to prepare visual aids, such as posters, describing the reactions taking place. Using chemical equations is a good way to emphasize the symbolic aspect of chemistry for both the presenters and the audience.

Reflecting on the Section and the Challenge

In this section you have learned about a number of different types of reactions: synthesis, decomposition, single-replacement and double-replacement reactions. Knowing these types of reactions can help you predict the products of some chemical reactions. You'll need to decide if you want the audience for the *Cool Chemistry Show* to learn about these reaction types. You also learned how to write balanced equations for some of the reactions you observed. Think about a creative way of showing how you can explain balancing chemical equations to your elementary school audience.

Chem to Go

1. Baking soda ($NaHCO_3$) has been used in several reactions in previous sections. When heat is applied to baking soda, three compounds are produced. Two of the compounds are gases and the other is a solid. If the two gases are water and carbon dioxide, what is the third product? Explain how you arrived at your answer.

2. When solutions of sodium hydroxide and potassium carbonate are mixed together, no apparent reaction takes place. The same is true when you mix sodium hydroxide and potassium iodide together. Explain this observation.

3. If you mix sodium sulfate and barium nitrate solutions together, you get a white precipitate. What is the precipitate that formed? What information did you use to arrive at your answer?

4. Use the solubility rules to explain why these reactions do not form precipitates.

   a) $K_2CO_{3(aq)} + NaOH_{(aq)} \rightarrow$ b) $KI_{(aq)} + MgSO_{4(aq)} \rightarrow$

   c) $KI_{(aq)} + NaOH_{(aq)} \rightarrow$ d) $FeCl_{3(aq)} + CuSO_{4(aq)} \rightarrow$

   e) $FeCl_{3(aq)} + MgSO_{4(aq)} \rightarrow$

Reflecting on the Section and the Challenge

Students should read this section for a specific, direct connection between the section and the *Chapter Challenge*. They do not need to answer any questions, but are encouraged to think about how they might integrate the knowledge they have gained from this section into their *Chapter Challenge* projects. You may want to read this section aloud and spend a few minutes discussing in groups or as a class.

Chem to Go

1.

The third product that is produced when heat is applied to baking soda is sodium carbonate (students might also come up with sodium oxide). Students can explain this as due to conservation of atoms and using the process of balancing the equation in a series of steps:

Step 1:
$NaHCO_{3(s)} + heat \rightarrow$
$CO_{2(g)} + H_2O_{(g)} + ??$

Step 2:
$2NaHCO_{3(s)} + heat \rightarrow$
$CO_{2(g)} + H_2O_{(g)} + ??$
This balances the "H's"

Step 3:
$2NaHCO_{3(s)} + heat \rightarrow$
$CO_{2(g)} + H_2O_{(g)} + Na_2CO_{3(s)}$
            (sodium carbonate)

Alternatively, the students may arrive at:

Step 3: $2NaHCO_{3(s)} + heat \rightarrow$
$2CO_{2(g)} + H_2O_{(g)} + Na_2O_{(s)}$
            (sodium oxide)

2.

According to solubility rules, all compounds of alkali metals are soluble, meaning no reaction will take place when mixed with each other. This includes sodium, potassium, lithium, rubidium and cesium salts.

3.

$Na_2SO_{4(aq)} + Ba(NO_3)_{2(aq)} \rightarrow$
$BaSO_{4(s)} + 2NaNO_{3(aq)}$

Students can cite the solubility rules to explain this reaction. They should recall that all

CHAPTER 6

sodium compounds are soluble, as well as all nitrates. They should also recall that barium sulfate is listed among the insoluble sulfates. This means that barium sulfate must be the identity of the precipitate.

4.

a) $K_2CO_{3(aq)} + 2NaOH_{(aq)} \rightarrow$
$Na_2CO_{3(aq)} + 2KOH_{(aq)}$

All sodium and potassium salts are soluble.

b) $2KI_{(aq)} + MgSO_{4(aq)} \rightarrow$
$MgI_{2(aq)} + K_2SO_{4(aq)}$

All iodides are soluble except AgI, Hg_2I_2, PbI_2. All sulfates are soluble except $BaSO_4$, $PbSO_4$, $SrSO_4$, and $CaSO_4$.

c) $KI_{(aq)} + NaOH_{(aq)} \rightarrow$
$NaI_{(aq)} + KOH_{(aq)}$

All sodium and potassium salts are soluble.

d) $2FeCl_{3(aq)} + 3CuSO_{4(aq)} \rightarrow$
$3CuCl_{2(aq)} + Fe_2(SO_4)_{3(aq)}$

All chlorides are soluble except AgCl, Hg_2Cl_2, $PbCl_2$. All sulfates are soluble except $BaSO_4$, $PbSO_4$, $SrSO_4$, and $CaSO_4$.

e) $2FeCl_{3(aq)} + 3MgSO_{4(aq)} \rightarrow$
$3MgCl_{2(aq)} + Fe_2(SO_4)_{3(aq)}$

All chlorides are soluble except AgCl, Hg_2Cl_2, $PbCl_2$. All sulfates are soluble except $BaSO_4$, $PbSO_4$, $SrSO_4$, and $CaSO_4$.

SECTION 4 – QUIZ

6-4b **Blackline Master**

1. Classify each reaction below as synthesis, decomposition, single replacement, or double replacement:

a) $2K_{(s)} + Fe(SO_{4(aq)} \rightarrow K_2SO_{4(aq)} + Fe_{(s)}$
_____.

b) $CaCO_{3(s)} + energy \rightarrow CaO_{(s)} + CO_{2(s)}$
_____.

c) $P_{4(s)} + 3O_{2(g)} \rightarrow 2P_2O_{3(s)}$
_____.

d) $2AgNO_{3(aq)} + BeCl_{2(aq)} \rightarrow Be(NO_3)_{2(aq)} + 2AgCl$
_____.

2. Complete the reaction:
$Mg + HCl \rightarrow$ _____.

    a) $MgCl_2 + H_2$ b) $Mg + H_2 + Cl_2$

    c) $MgH_2 + Cl_2$ d) $Mg_2H + MgCl_2$

3. Which of the following is soluble?

    a) AgCl   b) MgS

    c) K_2S d) $CaSO_4$

4. $Ca_{(s)} + Au(NO_3)_{3(aq)} \rightarrow Ca(NO_3)_{2(aq)} + Au_{(s)}$

When the equation above is balanced, the correct coefficients are:

    a) 1, 1, 1, 1   b) 1, 2, 1, 2

    c) 3, 1, 3, 1   d) 3, 2, 3, 2

SECTION 4 – QUIZ ANSWERS

❶   a) single replacement
        b) decomposition
        c) synthesis
        d) double replacement

❷   a) $MgCl_2 + H_2$

❸   c) K_2S

❹   d) 3, 2, 3, 2

NOTES

Chapter Mini-Challenge

The students have been busy learning new chemistry principles in the first four sections of this chapter. Although each section reminds the students to consider how the chemistry content might apply to the creation of their *Chapter Challenge*, this is a good opportunity to provide some time for contemplation.

The *Chapter Challenge* promotes learning in that it requires students to transfer their chemistry knowledge to a new domain. The *Mini-Challenge* gives students a chance to review the chemistry they have learned so far as well as to get a sense of what other teams are doing.

This first attempt at the *Chapter Challenge* will help inform students of the challenges involved in putting together a chemistry show that is entertaining, safe, age-appropriate, and uses a number of the chemical concepts in an informative way.

The *Mini-Challenge* should take at most one class period for preparation and one class period for all teams to share the descriptions of their chemistry shows. Some teams may be hesitant to share their ideas at this stage because of their concern for originality and the fear that others might "steal" their ideas. You must address this by explaining how the sharing of ideas could be beneficial. You can

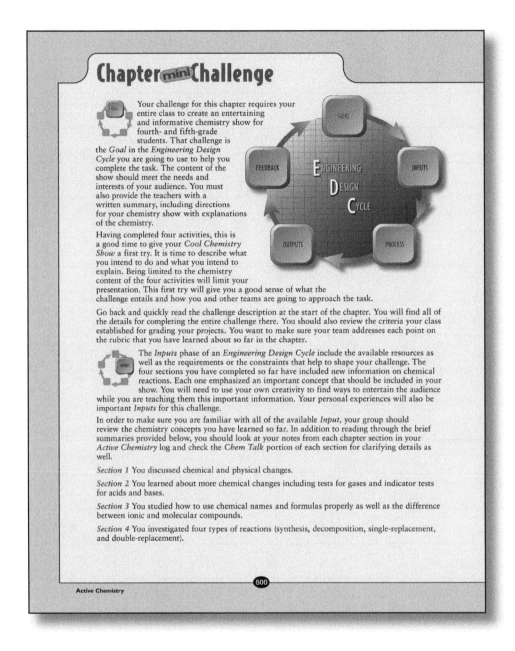

Chapter mini Challenge

Your challenge for this chapter requires your entire class to create an entertaining and informative chemistry show for fourth- and fifth-grade students. That challenge is the *Goal* in the *Engineering Design Cycle* you are going to use to help you complete the task. The content of the show should meet the needs and interests of your audience. You must also provide the teachers with a written summary, including directions for your chemistry show with explanations of the chemistry.

Having completed four activities, this is a good time to give your *Cool Chemistry Show* a first try. It is time to describe what you intend to do and what you intend to explain. Being limited to the chemistry content of the four activities will limit your presentation. This first try will give you a good sense of what the challenge entails and how you and other teams are going to approach the task.

Go back and quickly read the challenge description at the start of the chapter. You will find all of the details for completing the entire challenge there. You should also review the criteria your class established for grading your projects. You want to make sure your team addresses each point on the rubric that you have learned about so far in the chapter.

The *Inputs* phase of an *Engineering Design Cycle* include the available resources as well as the requirements or the constraints that help to shape your challenge. The four sections you have completed so far have included new information on chemical reactions. Each one emphasized an important concept that should be included in your show. You will need to use your own creativity to find ways to entertain the audience while you are teaching them this important information. Your personal experiences will also be important *Inputs* for this challenge.

In order to make sure you are familiar with all of the available *Input*, your group should review the chemistry concepts you have learned so far. In addition to reading through the brief summaries provided below, you should look at your notes from each chapter section in your *Active Chemistry* log and check the *Chem Talk* portion of each section for clarifying details as well.

Section 1 You discussed chemical and physical changes.

Section 2 You learned about more chemical changes including tests for gases and indicator tests for acids and bases.

Section 3 You studied how to use chemical names and formulas properly as well as the difference between ionic and molecular compounds.

Section 4 You investigated four types of reactions (synthesis, decomposition, single-replacement, and double-replacement).

Active Chemistry

500

also assure students that you will be sensitive to cases of outright plagiarism.

Each team should receive written feedback from the class after its *Mini-Challenge* presentation. One effective method is to require each individual to write down two positive comments and one suggestion for improvement.

The *Process* phase of the *Engineering Design Cycle* is where you decide what information you have will help you meet the criteria of the *Goal*. You may have already agreed as a class how you would coordinate each group's contribution to the *Cool Chemistry Show*. If not, that will be an important first step. While everyone has important ideas and experiences to contribute, you simply do not have enough time to have every person involved in every decision for creating the show. Instead, you should focus your efforts on making sure each person contributes fully to their own group's portion of the show.

In the *Process* step of the *Engineering Design Cycle* the design work gets done and the decisions get made. Your group should have a good idea of how your efforts will coordinate with the efforts of other groups. Knowing what will come before and after you will help you structure your part. Will you be continuing a story line in a skit, creating the next color in the rainbow with your chemical reaction, or creating a standalone skit in a variety show? However your part fits, understanding your role is an essential part of coordinating with your class.

The overall format of the show your class agrees on will add constraints to the *Process* step for each group. The more connected each demonstration is to the next, the more constraints each group will have to work within. Engineering design tasks often involve concurrent development of different portions of a design solution. Constant communication is the only way to ensure that each team's product will function well with the products of the other teams. You may need to have a spokesperson—one person who keeps track of what everyone in your group is doing and communicates often with the spokespeople from the other groups. The spokesperson should have other assigned tasks, but also recognize that part of their time is going to be spent communicating with other groups.

The *Outputs* of an *Engineering Design Cycle* are the products that are created during the *Process* step of the cycle. Your product for the *Mini-Challenge* will be an explanation of the demonstration you want to produce for the *Cool Chemistry Show*. You will not have enough time to produce your demonstration, but you will need to describe it and show how you will make it entertaining to the audience. You should also prepare the instructional portion of your demonstration to help you practice explaining chemistry concepts to a younger audience and demonstrate your thorough understanding of the chemistry involved to the fourth- and fifth-grade teachers.

The *Feedback* phase of the *Engineering Design Cycle* is the final phase of one cycle and simultaneously the *Input* for the next design cycle. Your instructor and your classmates will give you *Feedback* on your portion of the show, how well you described the chemistry that it employs, and how well it coordinates with the other groups' work to form a complete show. This *Feedback* will become one *Input* you will use in the final *Chapter Challenge* presentation. You will have enough time to make corrections and improvements before the *Chapter Challenge*, so you will want to pay attention to the valuable information they provide.

Remember to make any necessary changes in the chemistry explanation that received feedback. Also note any ideas you may have gotten by viewing other presentations. Your class may want to revise the way it coordinates the efforts of each group for the *Chapter Challenge* and seeing others may spark your own creative ideas.

You will learn about new chemistry concepts in each of the remaining chapter sections. Each section will teach you new information about acids, bases, or chemical reactions. Pay careful attention to the *Chem Talk* presented in each chapter section, as they are the key to creating a high quality chemistry explanation in your challenge presentation.

501

Active Chemistry

Engineering Design Cycle

The completion of every *Chapter Challenge* utilizes the *Engineering Design Cycle*. The students should use the engineering design in developing this *Mini-Challenge* presentation as well. The design cycle articulated in the *Mini-Challenge* will help students see how these projects are similar to all projects and allows them to see the work from a different angle.

They do not have to have their show ready, but they should have some firm plans for the procedures that they will perform and be able to describe them. They should also be able to explain what chemical principles they are going to emphasize in their chemistry shows. Control the amount of time that each team will have, but encourage classroom participation and feedback on each team's presentation.

CHAPTER 6

SECTION 5
Reaction Diagrams and Conservation of Energy

Section Overview

This section introduces students to thermochemistry. They will learn about endothermic and exothermic reactions and how to make cold and hot packs.

Background Information

Up to this point, the sections in this chapter have covered writing and balancing chemical equations, showing reactants and products in their correct stoichiometric amounts. This section will address the energy changes that accompany chemical reactions. When hydrogen gas reacts with oxygen gas to produce water, energy is released. Where does this energy come from?

Bond Energies

Chemical reactions require breaking the bonds of reactants and forming new bonds in the products. It takes energy to break a bond. On the other hand, energy is released when new bonds form. Energy released during chemical reactions come from the potential energy that was stored in chemical bonds.

For example, when hydrogen gas and oxygen gas combine to produce gaseous water, the standard enthalpy (heat of reaction) is –241.6 kJ/mol.

You can produce this value using the equation:

$2H_{2(g)} + O_{2(g)} \rightarrow 2H_2O_{(g)}$.

The change in heat content of the products and reactants can be expressed in the following equation:

ΔH_f = (Bond energies of reactant bonds broken) – (bond energies of product bonds formed), where

ΔH_f is enthalpy of formation of the product. Then, using values of average bond energies obtained from a table will produce the following results:

Bonds formed = 4(H – O bonds) = 4(463 kJ/mol) = 1852 kJ (Note that this is energy released.)

Bonds broken = 2(H – H bonds) + 1(O = O bond) = 2(436 kJ/mol) + 495 kJ/mol = +1367 kJ (Note that this value is positive.)
Then ΔH_f = 1367 kJ – 1852 kJ = –485 kJ for 2 mol H_2O or –242 kJ/mol.
This value is close to the experimental value (–241.6 kJ/mol). A negative value for ΔH_f indicates an **exothermic reaction** (heat is released). Heat energy is released because the reactants contain less potential energy than the products.

The same approach can determine the heat of reaction for **endothermic reactions**. In an endothermic reaction, the bonds of the reactants are stronger than those of the products. For this type of reaction to begin and continue, more energy must initially be continuously supplied. Endothermic reactions are indicated by positive heat of reaction values.

Representative Bond Energies

Bond	Bond energy (kJ/mol)	Bond	Bond energy (kJ/mol)
H-H	436	C-C	347
C-H	414	C=C	611
N-H	389	C=O	736
O-H	463	O=O	495
Cl-H	431	F-F	159
Br-H	364	Cl-Cl	243
C-N	305	Br-Br	193
C-O	360	I-I	151

Energy Diagrams

Energy diagrams (also called reaction profiles) are a convenient method for describing the energy of a chemical reaction. The y-axis is usually designated as Potential Energy (P.E.) and the x-axis is typically designated as the Reaction Coordinate, or Progress of Reaction. At constant pressure, the potential energy difference between the reactants and products is equal to the **change in enthalpy (ΔH)**, or heat of reaction. The **activation energy (E_a)** is the minimum amount of collision energy required for a reaction to occur. The highest point on the reaction coordinate represents the transitory, unstable arrangement of atoms known as the **transition state**, or activation complex.

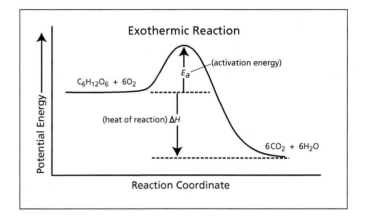

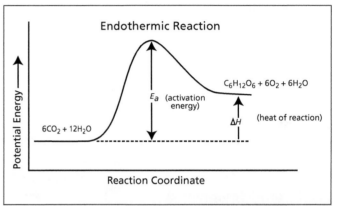

LEARNING OUTCOMES		
LEARNING OUTCOMES	**LOCATION IN SECTION**	**EVIDENCE OF UNDERSTANDING**
Make hot packs and cold packs.	*Investigate* Steps 1-2 *Inquiring Further* Part 1	Students are able to follow careful laboratory procedures safely to make hot and cold packs. Students research commercial uses of hot and cold packs and develop a cold pack from their research.
Observe energy changes when matter changes.	*Investigate* Steps 1-4 *Inquiring Further* Part 2	Students' observations match those given in this *Teacher's Edition*. Students develop investigations to explore colligative properties.
Determine whether energy changes are endothermic or exothermic from a particular point of reference.	*Investigate* Steps 1-4 *Chem to Go* Questions 1-5	Students are able to defend their assignments of endothermic and exothermic changes. Students' answers match those given in this *Teacher's Edition*.

CHAPTER 6

NOTES

_____

_____

_____

_____

_____

Section 5
Materials, Chemicals, Preparation, and Safety

("per Group" quantity is based on group size of 4 students)

Materials and Equipment

Materials (and Equipment)	Quantity per Group (4 students)
Graduated cylinder, 50 mL	1
Test tube, large	1
Test-tube rack	1
Rubber gloves	4 pair
Scoopula	1
Resealable plastic bags, quart size	2
Weighing boats	3

Materials (and Equipment)	Quantity per Class
Balances, 0.01 g	2
Erlenmeyer flask, 250 mL*	1
Rubber stopper, solid, to fit flask*	1
Board, 1" x 6" x 8"*	1
Weighing boats*	2

*Materials, equipment, or chemicals for teacher demonstration only

Chemicals

Chemicals	Quantity per Class (24 students)
Sodium carbonate, Na_2CO_3, anhydrous	150 g
Ammonium nitrate, NH_4NO_3	100 g
Sodium hydroxide pellets , NaOH	10 g
Ammonium thiocyanate, NH_4SCN	16 g*
Barium hydroxide, $Ba(OH)_2$	32 g*

Teacher Preparation

To save time in class, you can have the ammonium thiocyanate and barium hydroxide weighed out in advance.

Safety Requirements

- Goggles and aprons are required in the laboratory area.

- Caution in working with sodium hydroxide pellets. Students should wear rubber gloves to prevent skin burns. Do not allow any spilled pellets to remain unclaimed. Each must be picked up and disposed of in a beaker of water.

- Ammonium nitrate requires security procedures at all times.

- Chemical solutions can be disposed of down the drain.

- Barium salts should be collected for disposal on a periodic basis.

- Wash hands and arms before leaving the laboratory area.

NOTES

CHAPTER 6

Meeting the Needs of All Students
Differentiated Instruction

Augmentation and Accommodations

LEARNING ISSUE	REFERENCE	AUGMENTATION AND ACCOMMODATIONS
Understanding bond breaking and bond formation	*Chem Talk*	**Augmentation** • The concepts of adding energy to a system to break the bonds of the reactants and releasing energy as new bonds are formed is difficult for students to understand. Clarify the process for students using a flow chart that shows energy being added to a system, causing particles to move faster, resulting in collisions that break existing bonds. Label this flow chart Activation Energy. Then create another flow chart labeled Heat of Reaction in which new bonds are formed, causing energy to be released. Combine the two flow charts to explain that reactions contain both processes above. • Explain that when the release of energy in a reaction is greater than the energy needed to activate the reaction (breaks the original bonds of the reactants), the reaction is called exothermic. When more energy is absorbed to break the bonds than is released as new bonds are formed, the reaction is called endothermic. • Then show students diagrams similar to the ones in the text, but not labeled exothermic or endothermic. Reinforce the flow chart and explanation with an analysis of the diagrams of exothermic and endothermic reactions in which students explain the diagram to their groups using the flow chart.
Explaining what is learned Writing summaries of processes	*Checking Up* 1.-3.	**Accommodations** Some students may have difficulties explaining what they have learned: understanding the topic, use of precise language, and structuring their responses. • Help students find the information and think about the topic before they try to write. Refer them to the formal definitions in *Chem Words*, the description in the *Chem Talk* and/or the flow chart from the above section to help them reengage and understand the topic before they try to write an explanation. Use questions to guide their thinking. Most writers do not load their answers in their minds and then write them. They constantly alternate between understanding, determining next steps and referencing sources for more information. This step will occur simultaneously throughout their writing process. • Help students choose precise phrases and terms to use in their answers. The following words and phrases would be appropriate selections: *exothermic, endothermic, reactants, products, less energy, more energy, energy is released,* and *energy is absorbed*. • Give students a sentence format for their answers, such as, "An exothermic/endothermic) reaction is one in which (reactants/products) begin with (less energy/more energy) than the (reactants/products), so that when products are formed, energy is (released/absorbed)." • Be cautious—this type of fill-in can be as confusing to some students as writing their own answers, or students may complete the answer without truly understanding what they have written. As an alternative, ask students to write a draft answer and help them shape it by using the word list above or editing with them for accuracy.

LEARNING ISSUE	REFERENCE	AUGMENTATION AND ACCOMMODATIONS
Organizing the thinking process	*Chem Essential Questions*	**Augmentation** • As a supplemental activity to clarify the processes of exothermic and endothermic reactions, ask groups of students to organize the learning using the *Macro*, *Nano* and *Symbolic* categories for both reactions in a chart like the sample below: • **Exothermic Reactions** **Macro – How do they feel?** hot. **Examples:** hot pack, breathing **Nano – What happens to atoms and molecules?** Heat energy is added, molecules move faster, collisions increase, bonds break, new bonds form, energy is released. **Example:** $C_6H_{12}O_6 + 6O_2 \longrightarrow 6CO_2 + 6H_2O$ + energy **Symbolic –** **Graph of an exothermic reaction:**

Strategies for Students with Limited English Language Proficiency

LEARNING ISSUE	REFERENCE	AUGMENTATION AND ACCOMMODATIONS
Background knowledge	*What Do You Think?*	Students might not have experience with instant ice packs, and may benefit from a demonstration of their use.
Vocabulary	*Investigate*	Check for understanding of the word, "*endothermic*." Use of the prefix, "*endo*" might help build background knowledge as would reference to the root word, "*therm*."
Background knowledge Vocabulary Comprehending text	*Chem Talk*	Check for understanding of bold-type words. Examples of words that use the prefix, "*exo*" may build background knowledge. Refer students to sidebar material for further explanations of the isolated words. Students might need background on the process of photosynthesis.
Background knowledge	*What Do You Think Now?*	Students will benefit from a small group discussion of the questions and answers in this section.
Background knowledge Vocabulary Comprehending text	*Chem Essential Questions*	In the *Why do you believe?* section, students are asked to "*consider*" and may need assistance with this direction.
Comprehension Vocabulary	*Chem to Go*	When students are asked to "*give an explanation*," they may need more explanation of what the term "*give*" means in this context.
Application Comprehension	*Inquiring Further*	Students may need specific directions on how to research cold and hot packs, and may need some examples of what these are. They also may not be aware of what "*anti-freeze*" is. They may require help with the pronunciation and understanding of the term "*colligative*."

CHAPTER 6

Section 5
Teaching Suggestions and Sample Answers

What Do You See?

To begin the section, elicit a response from your students about the illustration at the beginning of the section. You can do this as part of a class discussion or by having students respond directly in their *Active Chemistry* logs. Provide a prompt such as, "Write a paragraph in your log that describes what is taking place in the illustration," or after giving the class some time to look at the illustration, ask the class a question for discussion such as, "The stand in the illustration seems to be selling hot and cold packs – are these real things you can buy?" By listening to your students' responses you may be able to judge both their prior understanding about the chemistry involved in this section as well as any misconceptions they might have. Keep in mind that all responses are acceptable at this point; you are not looking for right answers.

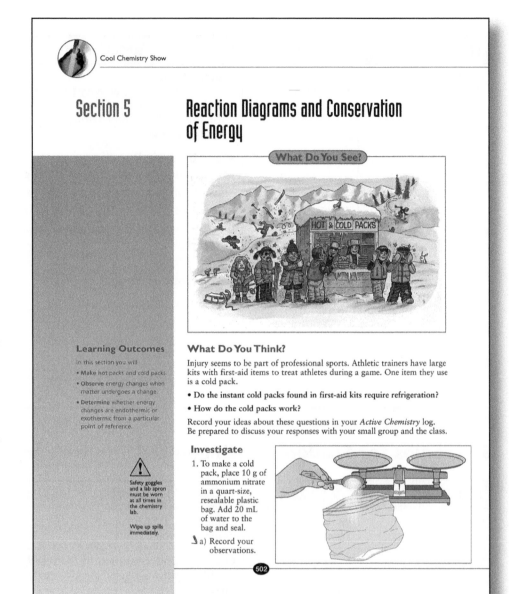

Cool Chemistry Show

Section 5

Reaction Diagrams and Conservation of Energy

What Do You See?

Learning Outcomes

In this section you will

• Make hot packs and cold packs

• Observe energy changes when matter undergoes a change.

• Determine whether energy changes are endothermic or exothermic from a particular point of reference.

⚠️ Safety goggles and a lab apron must be worn at all times in the chemistry lab.

Wipe up spills immediately.

What Do You Think?

Injury seems to be part of professional sports. Athletic trainers have large kits with first-aid items to treat athletes during a game. One item they use is a cold pack.

• Do the instant cold packs found in first-aid kits require refrigeration?

• How do the cold packs work?

Record your ideas about these questions in your *Active Chemistry* log. Be prepared to discuss your responses with your small group and the class.

Investigate

1. To make a cold pack, place 10 g of ammonium nitrate in a quart-size, resealable plastic bag. Add 20 mL of water to the bag and seal.

a) Record your observations.

502

STUDENTS' PRIOR CONCEPTIONS

Although students are generally aware that there are two types of energy, they are not familiar with their numerous forms, such as electrical energy, mechanical energy, light energy, heat energy, nuclear and chemical energy.

It is a common tendency for students to simply misunderstand energy and how it can be transferred. Some students believe that energy is a concrete substance, or that it relates only to living and moving things. Problems with this concept often stem from a poor understanding of atomic structure and the role of electrons in bonding and energy changes. Once again, the issue is one of visualizing and understanding particulate nature.

Many students do not understand that heat has a tendency to move from an area of high heat energy to an area of lower heat energy. They may also believe that "cold" is a form of energy similar to heat. They might derive this thinking from hearing a parent say, "Don't let the cold in."

Additionally, students will often falsely believe that energy is released as bonds break.

What Do You Think?

This section and the *What Do You See?* section in the section serve to elicit prior knowledge and engage the learner. They provide students with an opportunity to demonstrate prior learning and practice the transfer of what they already know to the concepts to be learned during the section. Again, whereas it is important to have the students respond, their actual responses should not be judged but used to assess prior understanding.

What Do You Think?
A CHEMIST'S RESPONSE

As many students will likely know, cold packs do not need to be refrigerated, although some types do require placement in a freezer before use. Athletes and student trainers will know that the "cold" of a cold pack is generated as needed. The principles behind this generation of coldness will not be common knowledge and provide an opportunity for students to learn during this section. Commonly, a salt which dissolves in water endothermically, such as ammonium nitrate, is used in cold packs. Heat is taken from the surroundings to provide the energy to break the ionic bonds, allowing the ions to dissociate into the water.

Investigate

1.a)

Students should detect that the system is absorbing heat. This is an example of a physical change. They should also note that ammonium nitrate is a white solid.

CHEM TIP

You might want to blindfold half of the students on each team. This will emphasize that scientific observations are objective and generally involve four of the five senses (taste is not used in the chemistry laboratory). Most students rely on their sense of sight for their laboratory observations. Visually impaired students will especially appreciate the message here – that scientists also rely heavily on their other senses.

NOTES
_____
_____
_____
_____
_____
_____
_____
_____
_____
_____
_____

CHAPTER 6

1.b)

Since the system is absorbing heat from the environment, the reaction is an endothermic reaction. The overall process is:

$$NH_4NO_{3(s)} + H_2O_{(l)} + energy \rightarrow NH_4^+{}_{(aq)} + NO_3^-{}_{(aq)}$$

CHEM TIP

Ammonium nitrate is a strong oxidizer. In the solid form, it must not be contaminated or heated. At the end of the section, dilute the ammonium nitrate and flush it down the drain. The plastic bag should be rinsed out and placed in the trash.

2.a)

Students should be able to detect that heat is being released by the system. This is an example of a physical change. Be aware that if the anhydrous form of calcium chloride is used, a large amount of heat is generated. In this case, the same results are obtained with a much smaller amount of the salt.

2.b)

The reaction is exothermic. The overall process with sodium carbonate is:

$$Na_2CO_{3(s)} + H_2O_{(l)} \rightarrow 2Na^+{}_{(aq)} + CO_3^{2-}{}_{(aq)}$$

3.a)

You should wear gloves while shaking the flask. The flask will become very cold and freeze to the board. The overall process is:

$$2NH_4SCN_{(s)} + Ba(OH)_2 \bullet 8H_2O_{(s)} \rightarrow Ba(SCN)_{2(aq)} + 2NH_{3(aq)} + 10H_2O_{(l)}$$

The temperature should drop well below 0°C (somewhere between –5°C to –10°C). You can explain to the students that, unlike the cold pack and the cold pack investigations, this represents a chemical change. You can show them the equation for the reaction and they may smell any ammonia that escapes the stoppered bag. Of course, the freezing of the water is a physical process.

3.b)

Students should know that this is an endothermic reaction.

Note: If ammonium thiocyanate is too expensive, ammonium nitrate can be substituted for this reaction. Also note that the barium salts are heavy metals and must be saved for safe disposal by an outside firm.

4.a)

As the sodium hydroxide pellets dissolve, they release heat, indicating an exothermic process. Make sure that students understand how to handle the sodium hydroxide pellets safely. The overall process is:

$$NaOH_{(s)} + H_2O_{(l)} \rightarrow Na^+{}_{(aq)} + OH^-{}_{(aq)} + energy$$

4.b)

The reaction was exothermic.

In an *endothermic chemical reaction*, energy in the form of *heat* is absorbed in the process. In an *exothermic chemical reaction*, energy in the form of heat is given off in the process.

b) Was the cold pack an example of an exothermic or endothermic chemical reaction?

2. Make a hot pack by placing 20 g of sodium carbonate (or calcium chloride) in a quart-size, resealable plastic bag. Add 20 mL of water to the bag and seal.

a) Record your observations.

b) Was the reaction exothermic (heat generating) or endothermic (heat absorbing)?

3. Your teacher will perform the following demonstration.

To a flask containing 16 g of ammonium thiocyanate, 32 g of barium hydroxide is added.

A rubber stopper is placed in the mouth of the flask. The flask is shaken vigorously.

The stoppered flask is placed on a wood board that has been wet down so that there are puddles of water.

a) Record your observations. Cool chemistry!

b) Was the reaction exothermic (heat generating) or endothermic (heat absorbing)?

4. Using a chemical scoop, transfer a few pellets of sodium hydroxide to a test tube half full of water. Carefully feel the side of the test tube.

a) Record your observations.

b) Was the reaction exothermic (heat generating) or endothermic (heat absorbing)?

5. Dispose of materials and solutions as directed by your teacher. Clean up your workstation.

Be careful when working with the sodium hydroxide pellets. Wear rubber gloves and eye protection. If you should accidentally drop a pellet, do not try to pick it up with your bare hands as it may burn them. Use gloved hands to retrieve the pellets.

Wash your hands and arms thoroughly after the investigation.

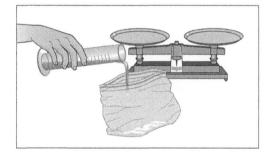

CHAPTER 6

Chem Talk

A thorough discussion of endothermic and exothermic processes is followed by an introduction to energy diagrams. Activation energy is shown to be an important concept for the understanding of a reaction. The importance of the concept of energy conservation in reactions is emphasized. Finally, the difference between heat and temperature is explained.

A table of representative bond energies is provided as a Blackline Master in your *Teacher Resources CD*.

6-5a **Blackline Master**

Cool Chemistry Show

Chem Talk

ENDOTHERMIC AND EXOTHERMIC PROCESSES

Reactions That Absorb and Release Heat Energy

Chem Words

endothermic reaction: a change in which energy in the form of heat is absorbed from the surrounding environment resulting in an increase in the internal energy of the system.

exothermic reaction: a change in which energy in the form of heat is released from a system resulting in a decrease in the internal energy of the system.

kinetic energy: the energy of motion. $KE = \frac{1}{2} mv^2$

activation energy: the minimum energy required for a chemical reaction.

A process is described as **endothermic** when heat energy is absorbed, increasing the internal energy of the system. The cold pack you made with ammonium nitrate is an example of an endothermic process. Another example is the decomposition of potassium chlorate. In this reaction, energy must be added to the system in order to cause the decomposition of the potassium chlorate to form the products of oxygen gas and potassium chloride. If you touch a container that holds a spontaneous endothermic process, it will feel cool to the touch.

An **exothermic** process results when heat energy is released, decreasing the internal energy of the system. If you touch a container that holds an exothermic process, it will feel warm or hot to the touch. The hot pack you made with sodium carbonate is an example of an exothermic process. Another example is the combining of sodium hydroxide solution with hydrochloric acid. This reaction produces sodium chloride and water and releases energy to the environment. The terms endothermic and exothermic can be used when describing both physical and chemical changes.

Importance of Energy

Why is energy so important? In order for a chemical reaction to take place, the particles (reactants) involved in the reaction must interact. Not all collisions result in a chemical reaction. The particles involved must have enough energy to enable them to react with each other. The colliding particles must have enough **kinetic energy** to break the existing bonds in order for new bonds to be formed. (Physics reminder: Kinetic energy is the energy of motion. $KE = \frac{1}{2} mv^2$) The minimum energy required for a chemical reaction is called the **activation energy** for the reaction. Bond breaking is an endothermic process and requires an addition of energy. Bond formation is an exothermic process and is accompanied by a release of energy.

As products form, energy is released as new bonds are created. If this released energy is greater than the energy needed to break the bonds of the reactants (bond-forming > bond-breaking), the reaction is

504

Active Chemistry

---

exothermic, as shown in the graph. The prefix *exo* means "leaving" and *thermo* means heat energy and so, heat energy is leaving. The products have less potential energy than the reactants. For example, the cells

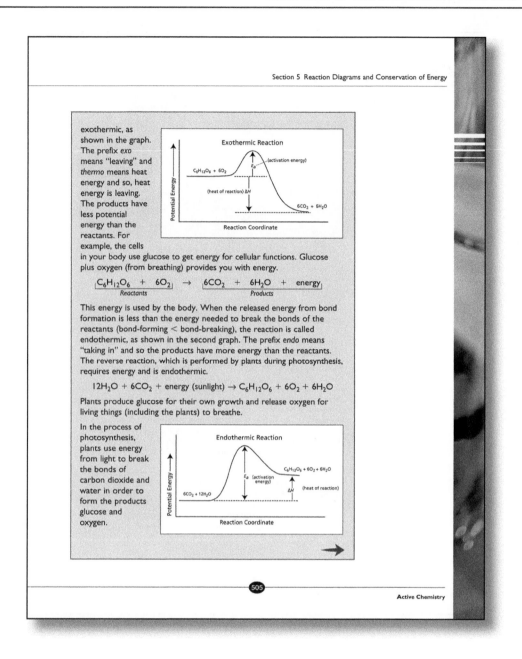

in your body use glucose to get energy for cellular functions. Glucose plus oxygen (from breathing) provides you with energy.

$$\underline{C_6H_{12}O_6 \ + \ 6O_2} \ \rightarrow \ \underline{6CO_2 \ + \ 6H_2O \ + \ energy}$$
$$\text{Reactants} \qquad\qquad \text{Products}$$

This energy is used by the body. When the released energy from bond formation is less than the energy needed to break the bonds of the reactants (bond-forming < bond-breaking), the reaction is called endothermic, as shown in the second graph. The prefix *endo* means "taking in" and so the products have more energy than the reactants. The reverse reaction, which is performed by plants during photosynthesis, requires energy and is endothermic.

$$12H_2O + 6CO_2 + energy \ (sunlight) \rightarrow C_6H_{12}O_6 + 6O_2 + 6H_2O$$

Plants produce glucose for their own growth and release oxygen for living things (including the plants) to breathe.

In the process of photosynthesis, plants use energy from light to break the bonds of carbon dioxide and water in order to form the products glucose and oxygen.

CHAPTER 6

Cool Chemistry Show

Conservation of Energy

Energy transfer is an important feature in all chemical changes. Energy is transferred whether the chemical reaction takes place in the human body, like the metabolism of carbohydrates, or in a car, like the combustion of gasoline. In both of these cases energy is released into the surroundings. The photosynthesis that occurs in living plants and the decomposition of water into hydrogen and oxygen both require energy from the surroundings. Energy is the great organizing principle of all science. The conservation of energy allows you to better understand the world around you.

Energy exists as light energy, heat energy, sound energy, nuclear energy, kinetic energy, and chemical energy, as well as other forms. According to the **law of conservation of energy**, the energy absorbed from the surroundings or released to the surroundings is equal to the change in the energy of the system. The total energy in any isolated (perfectly insulated), closed system remains the same. In the simplest physical systems, it is quite easy to describe the energy changes. When a bowling ball falls, its original **gravitational potential energy** becomes kinetic energy as the ball increases its speed. After the ball hits the ground, this kinetic energy is converted to sound energy (you hear the crash) and heat energy (you can measure a temperature rise of the ball and ground) and the compression and vibration of the ground. Each of these can be measured and it is always found that the total energy before an event is equal to the total energy after the event. When a human being is involved, you notice other energy interactions. A person is able to eat food and digest the food. The energy released from this slow-burn of the food (metabolism) is able to keep the body at about

Chem Words

law of conservation of energy: states that the energy absorbed from the surroundings or released to the soundings is equal to the change in the energy of the system.

gravitational potential energy: is a stored energy determined by an object's position in a gravitational field.

37°C. As all nonliving things in a room cool down to room temperature, humans are able to stay warm in the 22°C room environment. People also use the food energy that they ingest for moving muscles, keeping the heart pumping, and operating all human functions. Living organisms are superb energy conversion systems.

Heat and Temperature

Both **heat** and **temperature** have been mentioned in this section. It is important to note that heat and temperature are not the same, although they are related. Heat is one form of energy. When two materials of different temperatures interact, they exchange heat energy until they arrive at the same temperature. Temperature is a number associated with how hot or cold something is. On a molecular level, temperature is related to the average kinetic energy of the atoms in the material. All particles in a material are in a constant state of motion. The temperature of the material is a measurement of this molecular motion. If the kinetic energy of the particles increases, the temperature increases.

A thermometer is an instrument that measures temperature. Heat is the transfer of energy, which often results in a change in the kinetic energy of particles. That is, it results in a change in the temperature of the system.

Chem Words

heat: a form of energy that results from the motion of atoms and molecules.

temperature: a measure proportional to the average kinetic energy of all the particles of a material.

Checking Up

1. Describe an endothermic reaction.
2. Describe an exothermic reaction.
3. Explain whether each of the following is endothermic or exothermic:
   a) bond breaking
   b) bond forming
4. Distinguish between heat and temperature.

What Do You Think Now?

At the beginning of the section you were asked the following:

• Do the instant cold packs found in first-aid kits require refrigeration?

• How do the cold packs work?

How would you answer these questions now that you have completed this section?

507

Active Chemistry

Checking Up

1.

An endothermic reaction absorbs heat from the surroundings. Dissolving ammonium nitrate in water will cause heat to be absorbed. If you touch the side of the beaker, it will feel cold.

2.

An exothermic reaction releases heat to the surroundings. You will notice heat transferring to your hand if you place it near a burning candle! The burning of a candle is an exothermic reaction.

3.a)

bond breaking – Energy must be absorbed to break a chemical bond. This is an example of an endothermic process.

3.b)

bond forming – When atoms combine they release energy to the surroundings. This is an example of an exothermic process.

4.

Heat is a form of energy. Temperature is the measure of the average kinetic energy of all the particles of the material. So, heat is energy, and temperature is a measure of that energy.

What Do You Think Now?

This is a good time to return to the *What Do You See?* illustration and the *What Do You Think?* questions and review the responses students gave at the outset of the section. They should now understand the principles behind the uses of cold packs to warm cold extremities and hot packs to help heal injuries.

Their answers to the two questions should have more depth now and reflect the concepts learned in the section just completed. You may want to provide the answer given in *A Chemist's Response* and have students discuss their reactions.

CHAPTER 6

Reflecting on the Section and the Challenge

This is a good opportunity for students to think about how they can include one or more elements from this section in their challenge. You might allow them to discuss this in a short group meeting during class time or outside of class. If the time is available, it may be helpful to open up a class discussion and let students share their reflections and ideas on how to utilize the section content for their *Chapter Challenges*.

Cool Chemistry Show

Chem Essential Questions

What does it mean?

Chemistry explains the *macroscopic* phenomenon (what you observe) with an explanation of what happens at the *nanoscopic* level (atoms and molecules) using *symbolic* structures (formulas and measurements) as a way to communicate. Complete the chart below in your *Active Chemistry* log.

MACRO	NANO	SYMBOLIC
What do you observe when heat energy is absorbed during a chemical reaction? What do you observe when heat energy is released during a chemical reaction?	What happens to atoms and molecules as they become heated?	How can you graphically depict an exothermic reaction and the activation energy required for the reaction to take place?

How do you know?

In the investigation, what chemical process did you observe that was an exothermic process? What evidence did you have that the process was exothermic?

Why do you believe?

Consider the chemical reactions that you encounter in daily life. Which are more common, endothermic reactions or exothermic reactions? Hand and feet warmers are used in the winter. Why do you think that hand and feet coolers are not used in the summer?

Why should you care?

Experiences that involve more than one sense (as in sight, sound, etc.) add interest to a presentation. Consider and explain how the concept of chemical energy can safely incorporate the sense of touch in your chemistry show.

Reflecting on the Section and the Challenge

Energy is involved in any process that requires the breaking or making of bonds. The process may be a chemical or physical change. Sometimes energy changes are not noticed or measured, but other times an energy change is significant enough to be detected. In this section you explored both endothermic and exothermic processes. As you select investigations to include in the *Cool Chemistry Show*, you must be aware of any heat energy released or absorbed. The audience may be interested to learn about the energy changes that accompany chemical processes. In addition, your awareness will ensure that the presentations are safe for both the presenters and the audience.

508

Active Chemistry

Chem Essential Questions
What does it mean?

MACRO — When energy is absorbed during an endothermic reaction, the container for the reaction decreases in temperature and feels cold. When energy is released during an exothermic reaction, the container increases in temperature and feels warm.

NANO — As liquid and gaseous substances are heated, their particles move faster and their collisions have more energy. In the case of crystalline solids, the atoms vibrate more vigorously in their fixed positions.

SYMBOLIC —

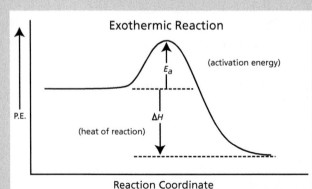

Exothermic Reaction

E_a (activation energy)

P.E.

ΔH (heat of reaction)

Reaction Coordinate

How do you know?

When calcium chloride dissolves in water, the process is exothermic. This was evident because the system increased in temperature.

$$CaCl_{2(s)} + H_2O_{(l)} \longrightarrow$$
$$Ca_2^+{}_{(aq)} + 2Cl^-{}_{(aq)} + energy$$

Why do you believe?

Exothermic reactions are more common in everyday life. This is because it is more likely that exothermic reactions will occur spontaneously, not needing outside energy to keep going.

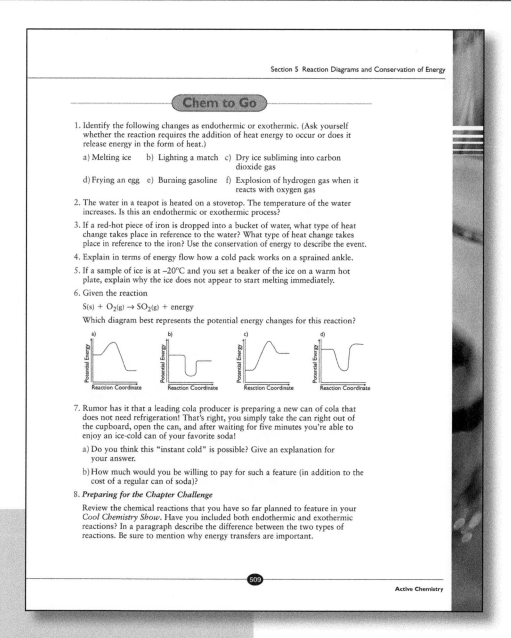

Chem to Go

1. Identify the following changes as endothermic or exothermic. (Ask yourself whether the reaction requires the addition of heat energy to occur or does it release energy in the form of heat.)

   a) Melting ice   b) Lighting a match   c) Dry ice subliming into carbon dioxide gas

   d) Frying an egg   e) Burning gasoline   f) Explosion of hydrogen gas when it reacts with oxygen gas

2. The water in a teapot is heated on a stovetop. The temperature of the water increases. Is this an endothermic or exothermic process?

3. If a red-hot piece of iron is dropped into a bucket of water, what type of heat change takes place in reference to the water? What type of heat change takes place in reference to the iron? Use the conservation of energy to describe the event.

4. Explain in terms of energy flow how a cold pack works on a sprained ankle.

5. If a sample of ice is at –20°C and you set a beaker of the ice on a warm hot plate, explain why the ice does not appear to start melting immediately.

6. Given the reaction

   $S(s) + O_2(g) \rightarrow SO_2(g) + energy$

   Which diagram best represents the potential energy changes for this reaction?

7. Rumor has it that a leading cola producer is preparing a new can of cola that does not need refrigeration! That's right, you simply take the can right out of the cupboard, open the can, and after waiting for five minutes you're able to enjoy an ice-cold can of your favorite soda!

   a) Do you think this "instant cold" is possible? Give an explanation for your answer.

   b) How much would you be willing to pay for such a feature (in addition to the cost of a regular can of soda)?

8. *Preparing for the Chapter Challenge*

   Review the chemical reactions that you have so far planned to feature in your *Cool Chemistry Show*. Have you included both endothermic and exothermic reactions? In a paragraph describe the difference between the two types of reactions. Be sure to mention why energy transfers are important.

509

Active Chemistry

In the winter, the extremities (hands and feet) are the coldest and will need the heat of hand warmers and foot warmers. In the summer, the extremities will be the coolest parts, not the warmest.

Why should you care?

Students might want to include an exothermic or endothermic reaction in their chemistry show. These processes can be done safely in sealed plastic bags. The type of reaction used and the concentration of reactants should be closely monitored.

Chem to Go

1.

a) Endothermic – This physical change is called a change of state.

b) Endothermic – This reaction requires the addition of energy (activation energy) to raise the energy level of the reactants in the match head to the point where reaction begins and can continue without further energy input.

c) Endothermic – Dry ice is unique in that when it absorbs energy it skips the liquid phase and goes directly to the gas phase. This is called sublimation.

d) Endothermic – Energy must be supplied to the egg in order to not only initiate the reactions, but to continue until it is adequately "fried."

e) Exothermic – Energy is released as the hydrocarbons in gasoline react with oxygen to produce carbon dioxide and water.

f) Exothermic – The hydrogen gas combines with the oxygen gas to produce gaseous water and a great deal of energy.

2.

Endothermic – As heat is added to the system, the water's average kinetic energy increases and thus the temperature of the liquid water will increase.

3.

This is an endothermic process with respect to the water as it absorbs heat energy and the temperature rises. With respect to the iron, it is an exothermic process and the temperature of the iron decreases. Energy is conserved as the energy that the iron loses, the water gains.

4.

Since the average kinetic energy of the sprained ankle is greater than the average kinetic energy of the cold pack, energy will flow from the ankle to the cold pack. The cold pack will gain energy and the sprained ankle will lose energy and, hopefully, the swelling will go down.

CHAPTER 6

5.

The ice will not melt until it absorbs enough energy to raise the average kinetic energy to a temperature of 0°C. Then a state change will occur at constant temperature which is a change in potential energy.

6.

Diagram **a**) best represents an exothermic reaction. Diagrams **b**) and **d**) represent negative activation energy terms and have no place in discussions of chemical reactions. The minimum activation energy is zero. Diagram **c**) is endothermic.

7.a)

It is theoretically possible through the application of endothermic chemical or physical changes to produce a self-contained cooling system within a beverage container. Cost and disposal concerns would be factors in the decision about manufacturing such a system.

7.b)

Answers will vary, but students should consider what the relative value would be, in price and in environmental terms, to have self-cooling cans available for their beverages.

8.

Preparing for the Chapter Challenge

Students' answers will vary. Their reviews of the reactions in this section should include both endothermic and exothermic processes with an explanation of the difference between the two, as well as an explanation of the significance of energy transfer from higher energy to lower energy.

Inquiring Further

1. Commercial cold and hot packs

Hot packs are sometimes made with crystals of sodium thiosulfate that are added to a solution, causing it to solidify and release heat. It can be reheated to dissolve the crystals before it is used again as a heat pack. This is an example of a physical change.

Adding barium nitrate or ammonium thiocyanate to water would act as a cold pack. After a certain period, it's necessary to add more crystals to the solution in order

---

 Cool Chemistry Show

Inquiring Further

1. Commercial cold and hot packs

Research several cold and hot packs. What materials are used in the packs, and how is the chemical reaction activated? You should be aware that there are a variety of commercially available hot and cold packs. Some are reusable and some are not. Those that are not reusable typically work by starting chemical reactions. Those that are reusable typically work because of physical changes. Design a process to make a cold pack, using your research. Have your teacher approve your design before you actually try it out.

2. One colligative property of a solvent

A salt solution will depress the freezing point of water. This is commonly known as the colligative property of a solution. When you add anti-freeze (ethylene glycol) to water, you find that the freezing point of the solution is lowered, which prevents the water in the car radiator from freezing at 0°C. It also elevates the boiling point of the solution, which will prevent the water solution from boiling at 100°C. Design an experiment to demonstrate the colligative property of a solvent. With the approval of your teacher, carry out your experiment.

to keep it cold. Proper disposal of these compounds may require storage and the services of a commercial disposal company.

If the entire class performs the inquiry investigation, you may need a large amount of sodium thiosulfate pentahydrate – especially if you choose not to reduce the amount you use. A cup of the compound is approximately 415 g. If sodium thiosulfate is not available, ammonium chloride or barium nitrate could be substituted although barium represents another disposal problem. Solutions of barium compounds should be stored and disposed of periodically through a commercial company.

2. One colligative property of a solvent

To demonstrate a colligative property, students will be using a process of dissolving a salt in water. First, as a control step, determine the freezing point and boiling point of the untreated liquid. (Water is your best choice, and you may choose to skip this step since the data is readily available: freezing point – 0°C; boiling point – 100°C.)

Once the salts are dissolved, the students can determine the freezing and boiling points of the solutions. You will need a cold bath container containing dry ice or salt and ice mixture.

Place a test tube of water in the dry ice (or salt and ice mixture) with a thermometer and record the temperature at which it freezes. Do the same with the saltwater solution. Record the data.

Compare the two solutions at the boiling temperature. The salt solution will boil at a higher temperature than pure water, which boils at 100°C. Record the data.

Making ice cream provides another good example of colligative properties. Ice cream will not freeze in a bath of simple ice water. You must use ice, salt and water to lower the temperature of the cold bath to sub-zero temperatures in order to freeze the ice cream.

NOTE

CHAPTER 6

SECTION 5 – QUIZ

6-5b **Blackline Master**

1. Label the reactants, products, activation energy (E_a), and heat of reaction (ΔH) for the following reaction. Finally, label the reaction as either exothermic or endothermic.

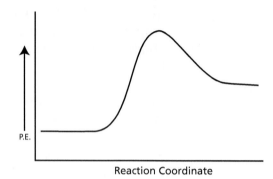

2. Activation energy is _____.

   a) the energy released at bond formation

   b) the net amount of energy gained or lost in a reaction

   c) the minimum energy required for a chemical reaction to begin

   d) another name for temperature

3. Which of the following statements is true? Temperature _____.

   a) is directly related to the kinetic energy of particles

   b) is directly related to the potential energy of particles

   c) increases in the surroundings when the system absorbs energy

   d) can be expressed in moles or percent composition

4. Which situation is endothermic?

   a) a cold pack which has been activated

   b) a hot pack which has been activated

   c) water freezing into ice

   d) explosion of hydrogen gas

SECTION 5 – QUIZ ANSWERS

❶ This represents an endothermic reaction:

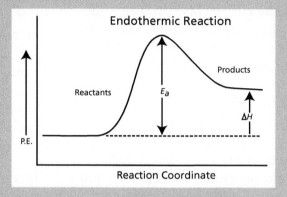

❷ c) the minimum energy required for a chemical reaction to begin

❸ a) is directly related to the kinetic energy of particles

❹ a) a cold pack which has been activated

NOTES

SECTION 6
Factors in Reaction Rates

Section Overview

This section leads students through the various factors that determine the rate of a chemical reaction. They will learn that the speed of a reaction can be altered by changing certain conditions – particle size, temperature, concentration of reactants, and the presence of a catalyst.

Background Information

Thermochemistry is the field of study in chemistry that focuses on the heat of reaction, enthalpy. The term *chemical kinetics* refers to the rates of reaction and the factors that affect different reaction rates.

What circumstances will cause iron to combine with oxygen to produce rust, Fe_2O_3? Five key factors help reactions to proceed:

- temperature of the system

- the ability of the reactants to collide with each other

- the nature of the reactants

- concentrations of the reactants

- the presence of a catalyst.

The key to all successful collisions is for the collision energy to be greater than the activation energy (E_a) of the system. It should seem obvious that as the temperature of the system is increased, the average kinetic energy of the particles will increase. As each particle's average velocity increases, more successful collisions will occur to produce the reaction and the reaction will proceed faster. There are always some particles that lack enough kinetic energy to cause successful collisions and these particles will not react.

In some cases reactants must be oriented in a specific way during collisions for the reaction to occur. Orientation is probably not critical for monoatomic reactants, or if the reactant molecules are small – as when iron reacts with oxygen. On the other hand, consider a double-replacement reaction of the general type:

$$AB + CD \rightarrow AC + BD$$

Different collision orientations may not be equivalent. It is clear that of the three proposed orientations shown below, only case (1) shows the molecules possessing the optimum orientation to form the products AC and BD.

Some possible molecular orientations in a double-replacement reaction:

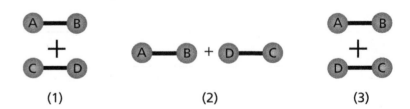

(1)　　　　　　(2)　　　　　　(3)

In the reaction, if iron powder rather than solid iron were used, the reaction would proceed faster. The chances for successful collisions would increase due to the greater surface area of the powder. If you put an iron bar in a fire you get very little change, but if you put iron powder in a flame it reacts with oxygen almost explosively.

You can also increase the chances for successful collisions if you increase the concentration of the reactants. In reactions involving a gas, such as oxygen, by increasing the pressure (concentration),

the number of collisions will increase and thus, the reaction will proceed at a faster rate.

In some cases the activation energy of the system is very large and must be reduced for reactions to occur. This can sometimes be done by using a catalyst. A catalyst can lower the activation energy by changing the path of the reactants, enabling products to form faster. An analogy is to compare the amount of energy it would take to drive your car over a mountainous road versus driving it through a tunnel to get to the other side.

LEARNING OUTCOMES

LEARNING OUTCOMES	LOCATION IN SECTION	EVIDENCE OF UNDERSTANDING
Discover conditions that make a reaction proceed faster or slower.	*Investigate* Steps 1-7 *Chem to Go* Questions 1, 3-5, 7 *Inquiring Further*	Students' observations and explanations for how different factors affect the rate of reaction closely match those outlined in this *Teacher's Edition*. Answers to problems are correct. Students are able to design and carry out an investigation to quantify the relationship between temperature and reaction rate, similar to what is outlined in this *Teacher's Edition*.
Discuss explanations for why this happens at the molecular level.	*Chem Talk, Chem to Go* Questions 2, 6	Students are able to explain the effects of different factors on reaction rates and attribute those effects to molecular phenomena. Students' discussions are similar to those outlined in this *Teacher's Edition*.

NOTES

_____

_____

_____

_____

_____

_____

_____

_____

_____

_____

CHAPTER 6

Section 6
Materials, Chemicals, Preparation, and Safety

("per Group" quantity is based on group size of 4 students)

Materials and Equipment

Materials (and Equipment)	Quantity per Group (4 students)
Graduated cylinder, 50 mL	1
Beakers, 250 mL	2
Hot plate	1
Large microwell plates, 24 well	1
Test-tube rack	1
Glass stirring rod	1
Test tubes, large	3
Stopwatch	1
Mortar and pestle	1
Steel wool, fine	1
Effervescent antacid tablets	4
Tea bags	2

Materials (and Equipment)	Quantity per Class
Bottle of vinegar	1
Bottle of hydrogen peroxide, 3%, H_2O_2	1
Bucket of ice cubes	1
Starch, spray can*	1
Beakers, 600 mL*	10
Graduated cylinders, 100 mL*	3

*Materials, equipment, or chemicals for teacher demonstration only

Chemicals

Chemicals	Quantity per Class (24 students)
Hydrochloric acid, 0.1 M, HCl**	100 mL
Hydrochloric acid, 1.0 M, HCl***	100 mL
Magnesium ribbon	20 cm
Manganese dioxide, MnO_2	10 g
Zinc pieces	50 g
Potassium iodate, 0.1 M, KIO_3*	1 L
Sodium hydrogen sulfite, 0.25 M, $NaHSO_3$*	200 mL

**This solution is placed in a dropper bottle but was prepared in *Section 1* and may be available.
***This solution is placed in a dropper bottle and used again in *Section 7*.

Teacher Preparation

Hydrochloric acid, 0.1 *M*: In a fume hood, with stirring, slowly add 0.83 mL (0.99 g) of concentrated HCl (12.1 *M*) to 80 mL of distilled water. Dilute to 100 mL.

Hydrochloric acid, 1.0 *M*: In a fume hood, with stirring, slowly and carefully add 8.3 mL of concentrated HCl (12.1 *M*) to 80 mL of distilled water. Dilute to 100 mL.

Potassium iodate, 0.1 *M*: Add 21.4 g of KIO_3 to 800 mL of distilled water. Dilute to 1.0 L.

Starch solution: Spray enough starch into 500 mL of very hot (~90°C) distilled water until it becomes cloudy. Alternatively, make a paste of 10 g of starch and distilled water. Pour the paste into 1 L of boiling water and stir until uniform. Cool before using.

Sodium hydrogen sulfite, 0.25 *M*: Dissolve 5.2 g $NaHSO_3$ in 150 mL of distilled water. Dilute to 200 mL.

Safety Requirements

- Goggles and aprons are required in the laboratory area.

- Solutions can be rinsed down the sink.

- MnO_2 can be disposed of in the trash.

- Wash arms and hands before leaving the laboratory area.

NOTES

CHAPTER 6

Meeting the Needs of All Students
Differentiated Instruction

Augmentation and Accommodations

LEARNING ISSUE	REFERENCE	AUGMENTATION AND ACCOMMODATIONS
Designing an experiment Constructing logical sequences of cause and effect relationships	*Investigate* 4., 5.	**Accommodations** • With students, reread the directions carefully. Have students read aloud the sentence which says specifically what their inquiry must prove. Ask them what "reaction" that sentence refers to. Tell them to design their experiments starting with the setup of that reaction. • Refer students to Step 4 for the setup of the reaction of hydrogen peroxide and manganese dioxide. • Once they have set up that part of the experiment, ask them again what they must prove. Follow up by asking how they will determine the manganese dioxide was not used. With this scaffold, they are likely to realize they need to measure the manganese dioxide before and after.
Recording relevant observations	*Investigate* 1.a), 3.a), 4.a), 6.a), 7.a)	**Augmentation** • If students are not recording relevant observations, they probably do not understand what they are testing. Use guiding questions: o What is the title of this section? o What are the tests we are conducting going to determine? o What evidence was there that a reaction took place? o Do the instructions in the text refer to data you must collect?
Explaining the effects of concentration, temperature, use of a catalyst and surface area on reaction rate	*Investigate* 8.	**Accommodations** • Impulsive students may not reflect on the task thoroughly enough to identify the results of the investigation, evaluate the information and make inferences from it. Make this thought process explicit by breaking it into steps that you help students to implement, one at a time. 1. Find the section of the investigation that involved concentration. 2. Compare reaction rates when concentration strength was changed. 3. Form a conclusion about the impact of concentration on reaction rate. 4. Reread Step 8 and evaluate whether their conclusion answers the question. 5. Write the answers.
Reading for information	*Checking Up* 2.	**Augmentation** • The ways which each factor studied increases reaction rate is directly stated in the text. Ask students to think about strategies they use when finding answers to questions in text passages. Encourage them to underline key words or phrases in the question and scan the text for them. Help them realize they must then read and evaluate to determine which part answers the question.
Elaborating on the factors affecting reaction rates by applying them in new domains	*What Do You Think Now?* *Chem Essential Questions*	**Augmentation** • Each of these questions requires students to apply the principles they learned in situations they have not studied. Though they may seem like small steps to experts, students need help to make these cognitive leaps. Give students scaffolding questions to make the distance smaller. o Under what circumstances do nails rust? What are the four factors we studied which affect reaction rate? Which ones affect rusting nails? How are those effects slowed? o Which makes a better fireworks display, fast or slow reaction rates? o Of surface area, temperature, or concentration, which factor do we associate with keeping food in a refrigerator? o How are steel wool and steel ships alike? How are they different? Are there any differences we studied which have to do with concentration, surface area, a catalyst, or temperature? o Does chewing food change the temperature, concentration, surface area or provide a catalyst for digestion?

Strategies for Students with Limited English Language Proficiency

LEARNING ISSUE	REFERENCE	AUGMENTATION AND ACCOMMODATIONS
Background knowledge	*What Do You Think?*	Check again for understanding of the word *"factor"* in the first bullet.
Vocabulary	*Investigate*	Students might not understand what is meant by an *"inquiry activity"* in Step 5. Check for understanding of term *"highlight"* in Step 10.
Background knowledge Vocabulary Comprehending text	*Chem Talk*	Students might benefit from an explanation of the difference between the words *"affect"* and *"effect"* as they are often confused and they do sound similar. Have students survey the text to determine if there are any new words or words with which they are unfamiliar.
Background knowledge	*What Do You Think Now?*	When students are asked to think about their answers, they may be unclear on what they are to actually *"do"* here. Be specific on the directions.
Background knowledge Vocabulary Comprehending text	*Chem Essential Questions*	When students are asked to *"give chemical explanation,"* in the *Why do you believe?* section, they may need more explicit direction.
Comprehension Vocabulary	*Chem to Go*	Help students pronounce the term *"effervescent"* and give a definition, as this may be a new word for some students. Students may not be familiar with the term *"grain elevators"* in Question 6, and may need some background information.
Application Comprehension	*Inquiring Further*	Make sure students are familiar with the term *"quantify"* and provide multiple uses of the term *"quantity"* to build background knowledge. The direction *"explore"* may also need clarification. Ensure that students understand what they are to do based on the directions *"Design"* and *"Conduct."*

NOTES

_____

_____

_____

_____

_____

_____

_____

_____

_____

CHAPTER 6

Section 6
Teaching Suggestions and Sample Answers

What Do You See?

To begin this section, invite discussion about the illustration at the introduction. This is an opportunity to draw the students out and get them interested. You can do this by asking, "Why is the girl on the left cheering?" Take time to listen for prior conceptions and misconceptions.

This is best done as part of a class discussion, but you can also have students respond in their *Active Chemistry* logs. Keep in mind that you are not looking for correct answers, verbal or written. This is a chance to gauge your students' understanding of the concepts that this section will cover.

What Do You Think?

These preliminary questions are designed to elicit prior knowledge, generate enthusiasm among students and give them a chance to transfer what they already know to the concepts to be learned during the section. Their initial answers will serve to demonstrate prior learning; the accuracy of their responses are not of concern at this point.

Students may know one or two of the factors involved in rates of reaction but the most common answer is likely to be the effect of temperature. Raising the temperature will speed up a reaction. Lowering the temperature will slow down a reaction.

What Do You Think?
A CHEMIST'S RESPONSE

Factors that influence the rate of reactions are: particle size of the reactants, concentration of the reactants, temperature, and the presence of a catalyst. A reaction can be speeded up by any of these factors, that is, by the reduction of the particle size of the reactants, an increase in temperature or in the concentration of one or more reactants, or by the introduction of a catalyst. There are known catalysts for only a relatively few reactions, so that option is not generally available. On the reverse side, a reaction could be slowed by increasing the particle size of the reactants, decreasing the concentration of one or more reactants, lowering the temperature, and/or removing any catalyst.

STUDENTS' PRIOR CONCEPTIONS

Students will readily accept that particles must collide in order for a reaction to occur. They probably do not realize, however, that the particles require energy to cause the reaction to occur.

The following are some common misconceptions that students might have:

- Increasing the concentration of any reactant will always increase the reaction rate.
- The rate of the reaction is constant throughout the course of the reaction.

- Adding additional catalyst or substrate will always increase the rate of a reaction.

Students may have a vague conception of catalysts, and when prodded will sometimes propose that catalysts are depleted or altered in the course of a chemical reaction; or that catalysts cause a reaction rather than simply increasing the reaction rate.

If students have previously studied chemical equilibrium, they may incorrectly assume the exponents in the rate law are the coefficients in the balanced equation for the reaction.

Section 6   Factors in Reaction Rates

What Do You See?

What Do You Think?

Have you ever wondered why some chemical reactions, like the burning of a match, take place at a fast rate, while others, like the spoiling of milk, take place slowly? The rate of a chemical reaction is the speed at which the reactants are converted to products.

• What are some factors that influence the rate of a reaction?

• How could you make a reaction take place at a faster rate?

• How could you slow a reaction down?

Record your ideas about these questions in your *Active Chemistry* log. Be prepared to discuss your responses with your group and the class.

Investigate

1. Predict how the concentration (strength) of vinegar will affect how fast it will react with magnesium. One way to study the *rate of a reaction* is to time the reaction with a stopwatch. Try this!

   Place 20 mL of vinegar into a large test tube.

   To a second test tube, add 10 mL of vinegar and 10 mL of water. Mix well using a stirring rod.

   In a third test tube, add 5 mL of vinegar to 15 mL of water. Mix.

511

Active Chemistry

CHAPTER 6

Investigate

1.a)

Students should make a prediction about the rate of reaction before carrying out the experiment.

1.b)

The highest concentration should cause the fastest reaction in all three cases. As the vinegar is diluted, fewer hydrogen ions become available and the oxidation of the magnesium metal decreases. Thus, fewer hydrogen gas bubbles will form. Have them refer to their chart of the Metal Activity Series and see if magnesium is more reactive than the hydrogen. The overall reaction is:

$$Mg_{(s)} + 2HC_2H_3O_{2(aq)} \rightarrow Mg(C_2H_3O_2)_{2(aq)} + H_{2(g)}$$

1.c)

Students should analyze their experimental results and compare them to their initial prediction.

2.

Have students design a microscale experiment duplicating the reaction in Step 1 but using a well plate instead of test tubes. They will need to think about equipment, amount of reactants, and safety procedures.

2.a)

The equipment and reagents may include a well plate, pipettes, a stopwatch, magnesium, acetic acid, and distilled water.

2.b)

Check to make certain the students use a very small piece of magnesium.

Cool Chemistry Show

Prepare three equal-sized pieces of polished magnesium ribbon. Set your stopwatch so that it is ready to start immediately.

Add a piece of polished magnesium ribbon to the first test tube, keeping track of the time the reaction takes.

⚠️

Hydrochloric acid is corrosive. Handle with care. Notify your teacher if any spills occur.

Report any broken, cracked, or chipped glassware to your teacher.

Be sure the mouth of the test tube is pointed away from everyone.

Wash your hands immediately if any chemicals spill on them.

a) Record your observations and the reaction time on a data table. Repeat for the other two test tubes.

b) In this step, you changed the concentration of one of the reactants (the vinegar). The vinegar was less concentrated (more dilute) in each successive test tube. Did this affect the reaction rate? If so, describe the relationship between the concentration of the vinegar and the resulting reaction rate.

c) Compare your experimental results to the prediction you made before conducting the experiment.

2. Using the same reaction above, design a small-scale experiment using a wellplate and smaller amounts of reagents.

a) Record your design. Include the equipment you will need, the amount of reactants, and any safety procedures.

b) With the approval of your teacher, carry out the procedure. Record your data and results.

c) How do the results compare with the reaction in *Step 1*?

3. Place 10 drops of 0.1 *M* HCl (weak concentration) into a small test tube and 10 drops of 1.0 *M* HCl (strong concentration) into a second test tube. Drop a small piece of polished zinc (equal size) into each test tube containing HCl.

a) Record your observations.

b) How do these results compare to your earlier results? Do these results support or refute the relationship you stated in *Step 1.c)*?

4. Hydrogen peroxide (H_2O_2) is sold over the counter in pharmacies to be used as a disinfectant for minor injuries. Because hydrogen peroxide decomposes slowly to form oxygen and water, it is also a source of oxygen gas.

$$2H_2O_{2(aq)} + \text{light energy} \rightarrow O_{2(g)} + 2H_2O_{(l)}$$

Pour a small amount of hydrogen peroxide into each of two test tubes. Add a small amount of manganese dioxide to one of the test tubes.

a) Record your observations.

The manganese dioxide did not actually react with the hydrogen peroxide; it simply acted as a catalyst for the decomposition of the hydrogen peroxide. A *catalyst* is a material that speeds up a reaction without being permanently changed itself. The chemical equation for this reaction is

$$2H_2O_{2(l)} \xrightarrow{MnO_2} O_{2(g)} + 2H_2O_{(l)}$$

5. As an inquiry investigation, design an experiment to prove that the manganese dioxide did not get used up in the reaction. Record your design. Include the equipment you will need, the amount of reagents, and any safety procedures.

512

Active Chemistry

2.c)

Students' answers will vary, depending on their results.

3.

The 1.0 *M* HCl will cause a stronger reaction with the zinc than the 0.1 *M* HCl. Make certain that the zinc pieces are polished. You can substitute magnesium metal if you are having difficulties with the zinc metal.

3.a)

The students should note that zinc is more active than the hydrogen ion.

3.b)

They should report the same type of reaction as with the magnesium metal in acetic acid. The results confirm the earlier observation that increased concentration of acid increases the rate of reaction.

4.a)

The manganese dioxide speeds the dissociation of the hydrogen peroxide into water and oxygen gas. Emphasize that, although a catalyst may interact with the reactants, it can be recovered unchanged at the end of the reaction.

5.

Students should be able to recover the mass of the manganese dioxide. Their experimental technique is key to their success in doing so. Make certain that they let the test tube and its contents cool to room temperature before they filter out the manganese dioxide and determine its mass.

NOTES

_____

_____

_____

_____

_____

_____

_____

_____

_____

_____

_____

_____

_____

_____

_____

_____

_____

_____

CHAPTER 6

5.a-b)

Check students' procedures for safety and effectiveness. Their equipment and chemical list may include a test tube, a balance, a weighing boat, a graduated cylinder, filter paper, funnel, beaker, ringstand, iron ring, a drying oven, hydrogen peroxide, and manganese dioxide.

5.c)

After filtration and drying, they should be able to show that the mass of the manganese dioxide is unchanged. To be absolutely certain that the manganese dioxide is unchanged, they could also retest the dried catalyst with fresh hydrogen peroxide.

5.d)

The catalyst expedites the reaction. In general terms, the catalyst lowers the overall activation energy for the chemical reaction.

6.a)

The hot water beaker shows a tea-color faster than the cold water beaker. This is not really a reaction but an extraction with the tea pigments dissolving more quickly in hot water.

6.b)

The effervescent tablet will react more vigorously in the hot water than in the cold water. As in the extraction of the tea bag, a reactant at a higher temperature has greater average kinetic energy than it has at the lower temperature of ice water.

6.c)

The rate of reaction normally will increase as the temperature increases.

As the kinetic energy of the reactant increases, the motion of the particles and therefore, the number of collisions also increases. Not only do more collisions occur but, due to greater kinetic energy, the violence of the collisions is also increased. These two factors combined increase the number of successful collisions.

7.a)

The powdered tablet reacts faster than the whole tablet. The effect of surface area was the factor being studied.

7.b)

The increased surface area of the powdered tablet helps speed up the rate of reaction. The powdered form allows more particles to collide in the reaction. The greater the number of collisions, the greater the opportunity for a successful reaction to take place.

8.a)

• concentration

Increasing the concentration of one or more of the reactants usually increases the rate of the reaction. Sometimes, however, increasing the concentration of the reactants does not affect the reaction rate because of some other limiting factor.

An example is the burning of steel wool in air. If the amount of steel wool is increased, the reaction rate does not change. However, if you increase the amount of oxygen available, the steel wool will burn faster. This indicates that the concentration of oxygen is a limiting factor in this reaction. In general, however, if you increase the concentration of the reactants, the reaction rate is increased.

• temperature

Increasing the temperature of a reaction usually speeds the rate of reaction.

• catalyst

A catalyst lowers the energy activation path and increases the rate of the reaction. When the reaction is complete, the catalyst can be recovered unchanged.

• surface area

Surface area plays an important role in the reaction rate. A piece of iron put it in a flame will react slowly but powdered iron will react quickly. In general, the smaller the size of the reactant particles, the faster the reaction.

9.

Use normal procedures in disposing the chemicals used in this investigation. The manganese dioxide should be filtered off and disposed of in the trash. All solutions can be rinsed down the sink. Left over magnesium metal should be treated with dilute hydrochloric acid.

- The molecular iodine will then complex with the starch and form a blue solution. The complex probably includes the starch molecule and the I^{3-} ion.

$$Starch + I^{3-}_{(aq)} \rightarrow I^{3-} Starch \ (complex)$$

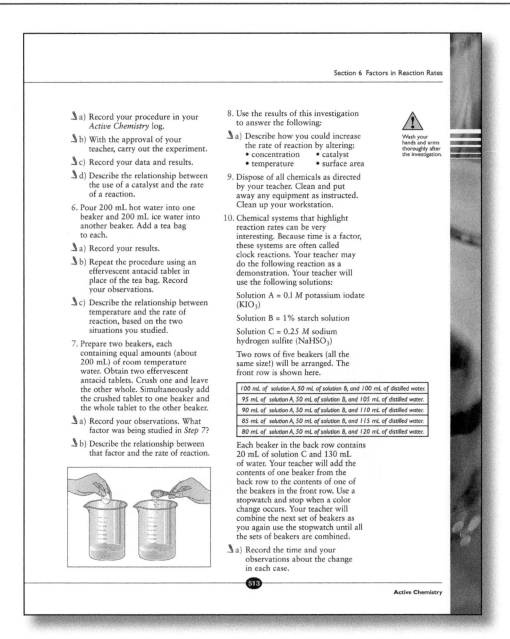

a) Record your procedure in your *Active Chemistry* log.

b) With the approval of your teacher, carry out the experiment.

c) Record your data and results.

d) Describe the relationship between the use of a catalyst and the rate of a reaction.

6. Pour 200 mL hot water into one beaker and 200 mL ice water into another beaker. Add a tea bag to each.

a) Record your results.

b) Repeat the procedure using an effervescent antacid tablet in place of the tea bag. Record your observations.

c) Describe the relationship between temperature and the rate of reaction, based on the two situations you studied.

7. Prepare two beakers, each containing equal amounts (about 200 mL) of room temperature water. Obtain two effervescent antacid tablets. Crush one and leave the other whole. Simultaneously add the crushed tablet to one beaker and the whole tablet to the other beaker.

a) Record your observations. What factor was being studied in *Step 7*?

b) Describe the relationship between that factor and the rate of reaction.

8. Use the results of this investigation to answer the following:

a) Describe how you could increase the rate of reaction by altering:
- concentration
- catalyst
- temperature
- surface area

⚠ *Wash your hands and arms thoroughly after the investigation.*

9. Dispose of all chemicals as directed by your teacher. Clean and put away any equipment as instructed. Clean up your workstation.

10. Chemical systems that highlight reaction rates can be very interesting. Because time is a factor, these systems are often called clock reactions. Your teacher may do the following reaction as a demonstration. Your teacher will use the following solutions:

Solution A = 0.1 *M* potassium iodate (KIO$_3$)

Solution B = 1% starch solution

Solution C = 0.25 *M* sodium hydrogen sulfite (NaHSO$_3$)

Two rows of five beakers (all the same size!) will be arranged. The front row is shown here.

100 mL of solution A, 50 mL of solution B, and 100 mL of distilled water.
95 mL of solution A, 50 mL of solution B, and 105 mL of distilled water.
90 mL of solution A, 50 mL of solution B, and 110 mL of distilled water.
85 mL of solution A, 50 mL of solution B, and 115 mL of distilled water.
80 mL of solution A, 50 mL of solution B, and 120 mL of distilled water.

Each beaker in the back row contains 20 mL of solution C and 130 mL of water. Your teacher will add the contents of one beaker from the back row to the contents of one of the beakers in the front row. Use a stopwatch and stop when a color change occurs. Your teacher will combine the next set of beakers as you again use the stopwatch until all the sets of beakers are combined.

a) Record the time and your observations about the change in each case.

513

10.

The clock reaction is done as a teacher demonstration. Since the reaction rates should be the same if you keep the conditions constant, try using different temperatures for several of the reactions and vary the concentrations in the final two beakers. Keep all temperatures below 50°C to avoid stability problems. Remember to use the first beaker as a control. The reaction mechanism probably has three steps:

- The bisulfite ion and the iodine react to form iodide ion:

$$HSO_3^-_{(aq)} + I_2_{(aq)} + H_2O_{(l)} \rightarrow 2I^-_{(aq)} + SO_4^{2-}_{(aq)} + 3H^+_{(aq)}$$

- When the hydrogen sulfite ions are used up, the iodide ions will react with the iodate ions to produce iodine (I_2):

$$IO_3^-_{(aq)} + 5I^-_{(aq)} + 6H^+_{(aq)} \rightarrow 3I_2_{(aq)} + 3H_2O_{(l)}$$

CHAPTER 6

Chem Talk

This is a detailed discussion of the various factors that affect the rate of a reaction. They include surface area, concentration, temperature, and catalysts.

Cool Chemistry Show

Chem Talk

FACTORS AFFECTING THE RATE OF A REACTION

Chem Words
rate of reaction: the decrease in the concentration of reactants with a corresponding increase in products over time.

surface area: the physical property of a solid which measures its surface in square units. For example, a 1 cm sugar cube has a surface area of 6 cm².

In this investigation you explored several common factors that influence reaction rate. The **rate of reaction** is the decrease in the concentration of reactants over time. This leads to a corresponding increase in products over time. The factors you investigated included surface area, concentration of reactants, temperature, and catalysts. On a molecular level, these factors either increase or decrease the collision frequency of the particles of the materials involved in the reaction or they lower the activation energy of the reaction. In many cases, factors that speed up dissolution in a solution (temperature, particle size, gas pressure, agitation, and the nature of the solute/solvent) also increase the rate of a reaction.

Consider **surface area**. In water, a sugar cube dissolves at a much slower rate than if the same cube is first crushed. The crushed cube has a greater surface area. More parts of the sugar are in contact with the water. In a fireplace, wood chips burn faster than a pile of logs. In your investigation, the crushed effervescent antacid tablet probably reacted faster. In all of these cases, the smaller pieces, with their increased surface area, allow the particles that are reacting to come in contact with each other more often. This increases the collision frequency.

Another factor that influences reaction rate is the *concentration* of the reactants. You investigated increases of concentration with vinegar and with hydrochloric acid. An increase in concentration means an increase in the number of particles in the reaction. This results in an increase in the collision frequency. If a chemist wants to increase the rate of a reaction, an increase in the concentration of one or more of the reactants will do the trick.

Altering collision frequency and efficiency can also be accomplished through *temperature* changes. According to the kinetic theory, particles move faster at higher temperatures and slower at lower temperatures. The faster motion of the particles increases the energy of the particles and increases the probability that particles will collide. In addition, increasing the temperature of the reactants increases the number of

 514

Active Chemistry

Checking Up

1.

The four factors that influence reaction rate are:

- Concentration of the reactants
- Temperature
- Surface area of reactants
- Catalyst

2.

Increasing the concentration increases the number of particles per unit of volume

and therefore increases the chances for more collisions.

Increasing the temperature will increase the average kinetic energy of the reactants and this leads to greater motion and greater probability for more collisions. Because the collisions will have more energy, there will be a higher percentage of successful collisions.

As the size of the reacting particles decreases, the surface area increases. This increases

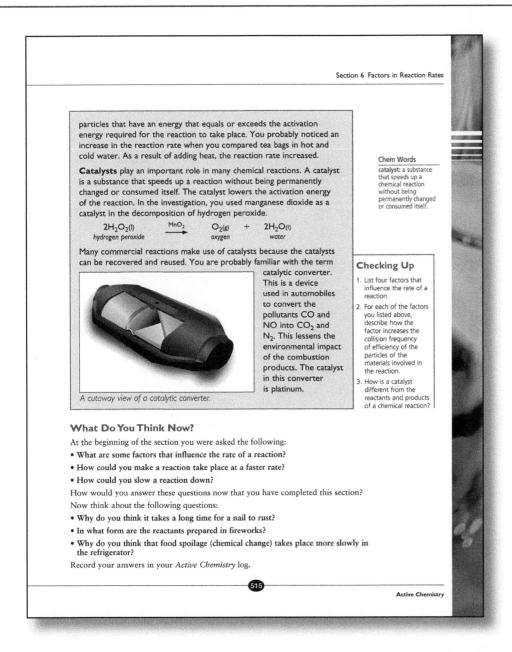

particles that have an energy that equals or exceeds the activation energy required for the reaction to take place. You probably noticed an increase in the reaction rate when you compared tea bags in hot and cold water. As a result of adding heat, the reaction rate increased.

Catalysts play an important role in many chemical reactions. A catalyst is a substance that speeds up a reaction without being permanently changed or consumed itself. The catalyst lowers the activation energy of the reaction. In the investigation, you used manganese dioxide as a catalyst in the decomposition of hydrogen peroxide.

$$2H_2O_{2(l)} \xrightarrow{MnO_2} O_{2(g)} + 2H_2O_{(l)}$$
hydrogen peroxide   oxygen   water

Chem Words

catalyst: a substance that speeds up a chemical reaction without being permanently changed or consumed itself.

Many commercial reactions make use of catalysts because the catalysts can be recovered and reused. You are probably familiar with the term catalytic converter. This is a device used in automobiles to convert the pollutants CO and NO into CO_2 and N_2. This lessens the environmental impact of the combustion products. The catalyst in this converter is platinum.

A cutaway view of a catalytic converter.

Checking Up

1. List four factors that influence the rate of a reaction.

2. For each of the factors you listed above, describe how the factor increases the collision frequency of efficiency of the particles of the materials involved in the reaction.

3. How is a catalyst different from the reactants and products of a chemical reaction?

What Do You Think Now?

At the beginning of the section you were asked the following:

• What are some factors that influence the rate of a reaction?
• How could you make a reaction take place at a faster rate?
• How could you slow a reaction down?

How would you answer these questions now that you have completed this section?

Now think about the following questions:

• Why do you think it takes a long time for a nail to rust?
• In what form are the reactants prepared in fireworks?
• Why do you think that food spoilage (chemical change) takes place more slowly in the refrigerator?

Record your answers in your *Active Chemistry* log.

515

Active Chemistry

---

the number of collisions of the reagents.

A catalyst changes the reaction path by reducing the activation energy. Since less energy is required, the number of particles having this minimum amount of energy will be greater.

3.

A catalyst becomes chemically involved during the reaction, but when the reaction is complete,

the catalyst can be totally recovered unchanged. Products are not there at the beginning and reactants are not present at the end of the reaction.

What Do You Think Now?

This is an opportunity to return to the illustration that began this section and to the *What Do You Think?* questions and review the students' original answers. The illustration should be more

meaningful to students now and they should be able to provide answers that have more depth.

In helping the students to address the three new questions listed here, you can suggest that they try to relate one of the four reaction factors to each situation. You may note that students can provide better answers as a result of this section and you should congratulate them on this progress.

The first question about the rusting of a nail is fairly simple and they may immediately understand that a nail rusts slowly because of the low surface area it provides. The interior of the nail is totally protected from collisions with oxygen.

The second question regarding the form of the reactants in fireworks is more challenging. At first, the only form that students may come up with is simply "solid form." However, since the reaction is very fast, you might prompt them to consider how close the reactants must be to each other. This would lead to the answer, "highly concentrated."

The third question regarding food spoilage is a simple one and relates to temperature. Students should have no problem associating the slowing of food spoilage by the lowering of temperature. The lower temperatures found in the refrigerator decrease the reaction rates found in the biological processes responsible for spoilage.

Reflecting on the Section and the Challenge

The conclusion of a section provides an opportunity for students to take a moment and review the challenge in light of their new knowledge. You might want to have them brainstorm in their group and report back to the class, if time permits.

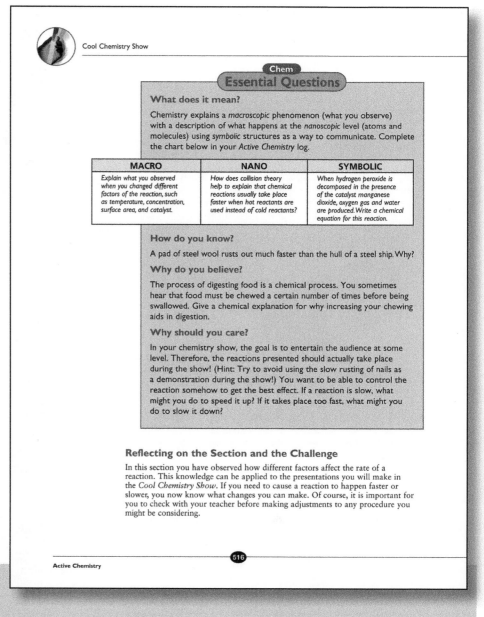

Cool Chemistry Show

Chem Essential Questions

What does it mean?

Chemistry explains a *macroscopic* phenomenon (what you observe) with a description of what happens at the *nanoscopic* level (atoms and molecules) using *symbolic* structures as a way to communicate. Complete the chart below in your *Active Chemistry* log.

MACRO	NANO	SYMBOLIC
Explain what you observed when you changed different factors of the reaction, such as temperature, concentration, surface area, and catalyst.	How does collision theory help to explain that chemical reactions usually take place faster when hot reactants are used instead of cold reactants?	When hydrogen peroxide is decomposed in the presence of the catalyst manganese dioxide, oxygen gas and water are produced. Write a chemical equation for this reaction.

How do you know?

A pad of steel wool rusts out much faster than the hull of a steel ship. Why?

Why do you believe?

The process of digesting food is a chemical process. You sometimes hear that food must be chewed a certain number of times before being swallowed. Give a chemical explanation for why increasing your chewing aids in digestion.

Why should you care?

In your chemistry show, the goal is to entertain the audience at some level. Therefore, the reactions presented should actually take place during the show! (Hint: Try to avoid using the slow rusting of nails as a demonstration during the show!) You want to be able to control the reaction somehow to get the best effect. If a reaction is slow, what might you do to speed it up? If it takes place too fast, what might you do to slow it down?

Reflecting on the Section and the Challenge

In this section you have observed how different factors affect the rate of a reaction. This knowledge can be applied to the presentations you will make in the *Cool Chemistry Show*. If you need to cause a reaction to happen faster or slower, you now know what changes you can make. Of course, it is important for you to check with your teacher before making adjustments to any procedure you might be considering.

516

Active Chemistry

Chem Essential Questions
What does it mean?

MACRO — By changing temperature, concentration, surface area and the addition of a catalyst we changed the rate of reaction; the reactions could be controlled and made to go faster or slower.

NANO — By heating the reactants, the particles begin to move faster and thus have a greater chance for collision and lead to reaction between particles. In addition, the collisions have more energy and are more likely to be successful, leading to product.

SYMBOLIC —

$$2H_2O_{2(l)} \xrightarrow{MnO_2} 2H_2O_{(l)} + O_{2(g)}$$

How do you know?

A pad of steel wool reacts faster than the hull of a steel ship because it has greater surface area per gram of steel.

Why do you believe?

Chewing increases the surface area of food (reactant). Enzymes (also a reactant during digestion) are better able to combine with smaller food particles than with larger bites of food.

Why should you care?

Students should know that the nature of the reactants can be manipulated (warmer, more surface area, greater concentration, addition of a catalyst) to create a faster, and thus more interesting, reaction. The processes can be slowed down by cooling, lowering concentrations, or creating a smaller surface area to make a more easily observed reaction. This knowledge may be useful in planning their challenge and for making their show entertaining.

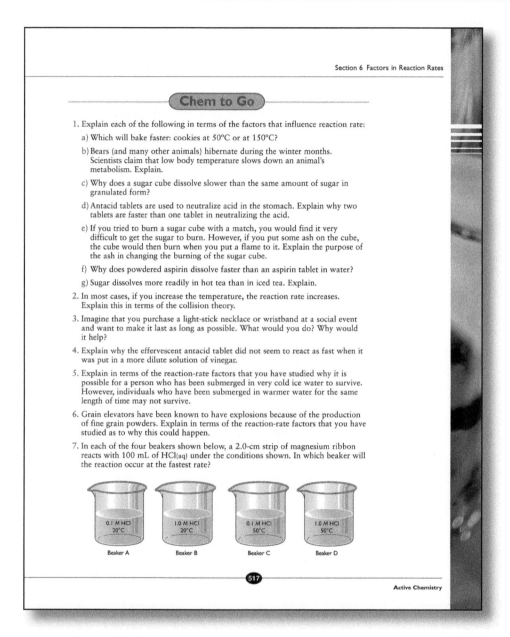

Section 6 Factors in Reaction Rates

Chem to Go

1. Explain each of the following in terms of the factors that influence reaction rate:

   a) Which will bake faster: cookies at 50°C or at 150°C?

   b) Bears (and many other animals) hibernate during the winter months. Scientists claim that low body temperature slows down an animal's metabolism. Explain.

   c) Why does a sugar cube dissolve slower than the same amount of sugar in granulated form?

   d) Antacid tablets are used to neutralize acid in the stomach. Explain why two tablets are faster than one tablet in neutralizing the acid.

   e) If you tried to burn a sugar cube with a match, you would find it very difficult to get the sugar to burn. However, if you put some ash on the cube, the cube would then burn when you put a flame to it. Explain the purpose of the ash in changing the burning of the sugar cube.

   f) Why does powdered aspirin dissolve faster than an aspirin tablet in water?

   g) Sugar dissolves more readily in hot tea than in iced tea. Explain.

2. In most cases, if you increase the temperature, the reaction rate increases. Explain this in terms of the collision theory.

3. Imagine that you purchase a light-stick necklace or wristband at a social event and want to make it last as long as possible. What would you do? Why would it help?

4. Explain why the effervescent antacid tablet did not seem to react as fast when it was put in a more dilute solution of vinegar.

5. Explain in terms of the reaction-rate factors that you have studied why it is possible for a person who has been submerged in very cold ice water to survive. However, individuals who have been submerged in warmer water for the same length of time may not survive.

6. Grain elevators have been known to have explosions because of the production of fine grain powders. Explain in terms of the reaction-rate factors that you have studied as to why this could happen.

7. In each of the four beakers shown below, a 2.0-cm strip of magnesium ribbon reacts with 100 mL of HCl(aq) under the conditions shown. In which beaker will the reaction occur at the fastest rate?

| 0.1 M HCl 20°C | 1.0 M HCl 20°C | 0.1 M HCl 50°C | 1.0 M HCl 50°C |
| Beaker A | Beaker B | Beaker C | Beaker D |

517

Active Chemistry

Chem to Go

1.

a) Cookies will bake faster at 150°C rather than 50°C. The higher temperature makes the reactions go faster by promoting more collisions and more energetic collisions.

b) The lower the temperature of hibernating animals, the slower the biochemical reactions and the less energy required for survival. Of course, in order to support life, there is a minimal temperature required.

c) A sugar cube has less surface area to interact with the water than granular sugar. When the surface area is increased, the rate of the process is increased.

d) Increasing the number of antacid tablets increases the concentration and therefore will increase the probability of successful collisions.

e) The ash acts as a catalyst for the burning of sugar; it lowers the activation energy so that the reaction will take place more easily.

f) Powdered aspirin has more surface area, increasing the chances for collisions and quicker dissolution.

g) An increase in temperature increases the average kinetic energy of the system. Each particle's average velocity increases, leading to more chances for collisions and dissolution.

2.

As you increase the temperature, the average kinetic energy of the system increases, thus increasing the velocity of the particles. The increased velocity leads to more collisions and more energetic collisions. Both factors lead to a faster reaction rate.

3.

The lightstick will glow brighter but not last as long if the temperature is increased. Similarly, if you increase your physical activity, the lightstick will glow brighter, but will last longer if you minimize movement and place some type of material on the backside of the necklace or wristband to deflect body heat. In between uses, you could store it in a refrigerator. These measures work because they effectively reduce the collision rate, thus slowing the reaction of the lightstick.

CHEM TIP

Demonstrate how a lightstick works. Place one lightstick in a beaker of ice water and another in a beaker of boiling or hot water.

CHAPTER 6

4.

As the concentration of the vinegar (acetic acid) decreases, the chances of collisions decrease and the reaction goes slower.

5.

In some cases, a decreased body temperature slows down the biological reaction rates, thus increasing an individual's chance of survival.

6.

The great amount of surface area present on the fine grain increases the chance for successful collisions to occur. More friction increases the possibility of sparks that can lead to a spontaneous combustion reaction.

7.

Beaker D will react the fastest. It has the higher concentration of acid combined with the higher temperature. Both factors will speed up the reaction.

8.

Preparing for the Chapter Challenge

Students' answers will vary. Their answers should include at least one of the four modes of reaction rate control–concentration, surface area, temperature, and catalysis.

Inquiring Further

Quantifying the relationship between temperature and reaction rate

Students can use ice to cool down the room temperature water to at least 10°C or less.

Cool Chemistry Show

8. *Preparing for the Chapter Challenge*

The factors affecting a reaction can be varied to achieve different reaction rates. How could you use this information in developing a presentation for the *Cool Chemistry Show*? Describe one possible scenario.

Inquiring Further

Quantifying the relationship between temperature and reaction rate

You have seen that temperature is a factor that influences the rate of reaction. In general, if the temperature increases, the reaction rate increases. When the temperature decreases, the reaction rate decreases. Can this relationship be quantified? Is there a mathematical relationship between temperature and reaction time? To answer these questions, explore the reaction between magnesium (Mg(s)) and vinegar (CH_3COOH(aq)).

Design and conduct an investigation that will use this reaction to show the relationship between temperature and reaction time in a quantitative way. Have your teacher approve your design before you begin. Remember—the point of the investigation is to see if the relationship between temperature and reaction time is quantifiable. You'll need to monitor both the temperature and the time carefully. Plot your data on a graph to make the relationship explicit. In your notes, include the chemical equation for this reaction.

Active Chemistry

Leave each test tube in the water bath for at least 3 or 4 minutes so that the temperature of the vinegar is the same as the water bath.

Remove the test tube at the desired temperature from the water bath, and add the magnesium ribbon. Record the time it takes for the magnesium to completely react with the vinegar.

Suggest that students use intervals of 10°C in temperature and share their values to develop their graphs.

When students plot the values of the rate of the reaction versus temperature, they will find that they do not produce a linear graph. Show them how to tabulate the rate values into natural logarithm with the reciprocals of the temperatures. Remember that the temperatures must be changed to kelvins before determining the reciprocals. The graph should then be a linear plot.

SECTION 6 – QUIZ

6-6a | **Blackline Master**

1. For each condition, predict whether the chemical reaction will proceed faster or slower as a result. (**F**= Faster, **S**= Slower)

    a) The reactants are made into smaller pieces _____.

    b) The reactants are heated _____.

    c) The reactants are diluted _____.

    d) The reactants are in kept in large pieces _____.

    e) A catalyst is added to the reactants _____.

2. Pick one of the conditions above and explain why it affects the chemical reaction as it does.

3. Look at the diagrams for each beaker on the side. Pick the beaker in which the chemical reaction will proceed faster than the other. Explain your answer.

    reactant A   reactant B

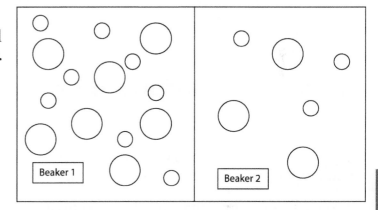

SECTION 6 – QUIZ ANSWERS

❶   a) Faster   b) Faster   c) Slower   d) Slower   e) Faster

❷   a) When reactants are broken into smaller pieces, the surface area increases and more of the reactant is in contact with the other reactant, increasing the collision frequency.

    b) When the temperature is increased, particles have a higher kinetic energy and move faster. This increases the probability that the particles will collide and also increases the number of reactants that have an energy that equals or exceeds the activation energy.

    c) If the reactants are diluted, the concentration goes down, so the collision frequency will decrease.

    d) If the reactants are kept in large pieces, the surface area of the reactant is not as large, and less of it will be in contact with the other reactant, lowering the collision frequency.

    e) A catalyst lowers the activation energy, increasing the number of reactants that have an energy that equals or exceeds the activation energy.

❸   Beaker 1 will most likely react faster due to the increased concentration of the reactants, which provides the possibility for more collisions between reactants.

CHAPTER 6

SECTION 7
Acids, Bases, and Indicators—Colorful Chemistry

Section Overview

This section introduces the students to the properties of acids and bases. A series of tests show how acids and bases react. A series of titrations are used to show how strong and weak acids neutralize strong and weak bases. They will also be able to identify household products that are either an acid or a base solution.

Background Information

You probably use many products around your home – such as vinegar, lemon juice, vitamin C, ammonia, milk of magnesia, and drain cleaner – that are solutions classified as acids or bases.

Taste tests are not recommended for identifying whether a solution is acidic or basic. Acids from lemon juice (citric acid), and ascorbic acid from vitamin C are weak and do no harm, however, practice caution at all times when working with acids and bases. Acids will turn litmus paper red and they have a tart taste. Bases, on the other hand, turn litmus paper blue, they feel slippery or soapy, and they taste bitter.

Acids and Bases Defined

How are acids and bases defined? There are three basic definitions that have been used over the years: (a) Arrhenius, (b) Brønsted-Lowry and (c) Lewis acid-base theory. Historically, when new data is obtained, scientists are forced to develop new definitions to fit the data.

The Arrhenius acid definition calls an acid a substance that releases hydrogen ions (H^+) when dissolved in water. Bases are defined as substances that dissociate to produce hydroxide ions (OH^-) when dissolved in water. Some examples are:

$$HCl_{(g)} \xrightarrow{H_2O} H^+_{(aq)} + Cl^-_{(aq)}$$

$$NaOH_{(s)} \xrightarrow{H_2O} Na^+_{(aq)} + OH^-_{(aq)}$$

Note that the hydrogen chloride releases hydrogen ions in water and the sodium hydroxide releases hydroxide ions in water. This definition only works for certain acids and bases. A broader definition is needed for more complex compounds, or for when the solvent is something other than water.

A Brønsted-Lowry acid is defined as any substance that is a proton (H^+) donor to another substance; and a base is defined as a proton (H^+) acceptor from another substance. For example:

$$CH_3COOH_{(aq)} + H_2O_{(l)} \rightleftharpoons H_3O^+_{(aq)} + CH_3COO^-_{(aq)}$$

$$\text{acid} \qquad + \text{base} \rightleftharpoons \text{conjugate} + \text{conjugate}$$
$$\text{acid} \qquad\qquad \text{base}$$

Acetic acid (CH_3COOH) transfers a hydrogen proton to the water. The water acts as the base and accepts the hydrogen proton from the acetic acid. Also note that the system reaches an equilibrium state. If you read the equation from right to left, then the hydronium ion (H_3O^+) now acts as the acid and will donate its hydrogen proton to the acetate anion that is now acting as the base. The acetic acid and the acetate ion comprise what is called a conjugate pair and the water and hydronium ion make another conjugate pair. Which pair has the strongest acid and base? This question determines which side of the reaction is favored. Remember that the reaction always drives to the weak side. In this example, it will favor the acetic acid side since acetic acid is a weak acid. The reaction equilibrium lies to the left for this reaction.

The Lewis acid-base definition is somewhat different from the others. A Lewis acid is an electron pair acceptor and a Lewis base is an electron pair donor.

When boron trichloride reacts with ammonia, the boron trichloride acts as the acid since it is missing a pair of electrons needed to complete its octet of valence electrons. The ammonia has a pair of nonbonding electrons that allows it to act as the base. In one of the earlier sections, cupric ions were added to ammonia water to produce a bright blue solution of copper ammonium complex $[Cu(NH_3)_4{}^{2+}{}_{(aq)}]$. This was an example of the cupric ion accepting four pairs of electrons from the ammonia molecules and thus acting as a Lewis acid.

Calculations Involving pH

In terms of acid and bases, water is said to be neutral or expressed as $[H^+] = [OH^-]$. The ion product constant of water, K_w, is 1×10^{-14} at 25°C and you can write the expression:

$K_w = [H^+] [OH^-] = 1 \times 10^{-14}$.
Then the $[H^+] = 1 \times 10^{-7}$.

The definition of pH is:

$pH = -\log[H^+]$.

Then if $[H^+] = 1 \times 10^{-7}$,
the $pH = -\log (1 \times 10^{-7}) = 7$.

If you look at the $[OH^-]$, you can say the pOH is also 7 and the $pK_w = 14$. Then you can conclude that the pH + pOH = 14. Therefore, if you know the hydrogen ion concentration of a solution you can easily find the concentration of the hydroxide ions.

Acetic acid is a weak acid and it has an acid dissociation constant (K_a) of 1.8×10^{-5}. The general equation for the dissociation of acetic acid is:

$$CH_3COOH_{(aq)} \rightleftarrows H^+{}_{(aq)} + CH_3COO^-{}_{(aq)}.$$

$[H^+] = [CH_3COO^-]$ since for every H^+ that forms, one CH_3COO^- ion must form.

The equilibrium–constant expression is:

$$K_a = 1.8 \times 10^{-5} = \frac{[H^+][CH_3COO^-]}{[CH_3COOH]}$$

If you had a 1.0 M solution of acetic acid and it was allowed to reach equilibrium, then the hydrogen ion concentration would equal the acetate ion concentration. You could then calculate the pH of the solution by using the above equation. Since acetic acid is weak you can assume that the amount of acid that dissociates into hydrogen and acetate ions must be small and would be insignificant in terms of acid dissociation. Therefore, you can assume that the $[CH_3COOH] \approx 1\ M$. Let X represent the hydrogen and acetate ion concentrations and you can then find the concentration of the hydrogen ion:

$$1.8 \times 10^{-5} = \frac{X \bullet X}{[CH_3COOH]} = \frac{X^2}{1.0}$$
$$1.8 \times 10^{-5} = X^2 \qquad X = 4.2 \times 10^{-3}\ M = [H^+].$$

$pH = -\log[H^+]$ and the pH of the solution is 2.4 and the pOH is 11.6.

Buffers

To keep pH constant you need a buffered solution. Buffered solutions are used for calibrating pH electrodes, biochemistry procedures, and the body chemistries that blood depends on. How do you make a buffered solution? If the ratio of the acid to the anion were 1:1, then the hydrogen ion concentration would equal the acid dissociation constant. For example, if you mix a 1.0 M acetic acid solution with 1.0 M sodium acetate solution then the $[H^+] = K_a = 1.8 \times 10^{-5}$. The pH of this buffered solution will be 4.7. What would happen if you doubled the concentration of the sodium acetate solution?

$$[H^+] = \frac{1.8 \times 10^{-5}\,(1.0)}{2.0} = 0.9 \times 10^{-5},\ pH = 5.05$$

Note that doubling the anion concentration caused very little change to the pH.

Blood has a pH of 7.4 and is buffered. If it were not buffered you could be in big trouble; if the pH dropped down to 6.8 or went above 7.8 you could die. So the next time that you exercise and increase the amount of carbon dioxide (think of CO_2 as an acid anhydride) in your system, be thankful for the buffers in your blood that protect against major pH changes.

CHAPTER 6

LEARNING OUTCOMES

LEARNING OUTCOMES	LOCATION IN SECTION	EVIDENCE OF UNDERSTANDING
Identify common household acids and bases.	*Investigate* Steps 2, 5 *Inquiring Further* Part 3	Students' answers to chemical tests are similar to those listed in this *Teacher's Edition*. Students are able to design and carry out an investigation to explore "pH balancing" in shampoos or deodorants.
Identify characteristic properties of acids and bases and learn to tell the difference between acids and bases.	*Investigate* Steps 1, 3 *Checking Up* Question 1 *Chem to Go* Questions 1-5, 7 *Inquiring Further* Part 2	Students are able to differentiate acids and bases by their reactions with metals and other properties. Students are able to write chemical equations using the Arrhenius definition of acids and bases. Answers are similar to those given in this *Teacher's Edition*. Students research other definitions for acids and bases and relate these to the Arrhenius definition.
See how strong acids and bases behave differently from weak acids and bases.	*Investigate* Steps 4-5	Students test a range of acids and bases and are able to rank them according to their strengths.
Determine the pH of various solutions using indicators.	*Investigate* Steps 2 and 4	Students' observations are similar to those given in this *Teacher's Edition*.
Categorize solutions based on the pH scale.	*Investigate* Steps 4-5 *Chem to Go* Question 6	Students test a range of acids and bases and are able to rank them according to their strengths. Students are able to identify where on the pH scale different solutions should fall.
Use the mathematical definition of pH.	*Chem Talk, Checking Up* Question 6	Students are able to interpret pH readings for different solutions in terms of relative concentrations.

NOTES

NOTES

Section 7
Materials, Chemicals, Preparation, and Safety

("per Group" quantity is based on group size of 4 students)

Materials and Equipment

Materials (and Equipment)	Quantity per Group (4 students)
Large microwell plate, 24 well	1
Beakers, 100 mL	3
Piece of steel wool	1
Bottle of blue litmus paper	1
Bottle of red litmus paper	1

Materials (and Equipment)	Quantity per Class
Bottle of ammonia	1
Bottle of vinegar	1
Bottle of lemon juice	1
Pint of milk	1
Beral pipettes	100
Bottle of mineral water (or soda)	1
Bottle of dishwashing fluid	1
Bottle of milk of magnesia	1
Bottle of apple juice	1
Artist brush	1
Distilled water, 1 gal	1

Chemicals

Chemicals	Quantity per Class (24 students)
Saturated solution of calcium hydroxide**	500 mL
Magnesium ribbon	40 cm
Zinc pieces	50 g
1.0 M Hydrochloric acid solution***	35 mL
1.0 M Sulfuric acid solution*	35 mL
1.0 M Sodium hydroxide solution*	35 mL
1.0 M Potassium hydroxide solution*	35 mL
1.0 M Magnesium hydroxide solution*	35 mL
Universal indicator solution*	20 mL
Bromothymol blue indicator solution*	20 mL
0.3% methyl red indicator solution*	20 mL
Phenolphthalein solution, 1%	20 mL

*These solutions are placed in dropper bottles.
**This solution was prepared in *Section 2*.
***This solution was prepared in *Section 6*.

Teacher Preparation

Collect previously prepared solutions of saturated calcium hydroxide from *Section 2* and 1.0 M hydrochloric acid from *Section 6*.

Safety Requirements

- Goggles and aprons are required in the laboratory area.

- Solutions can be disposed of down the drain.

- Save unused indicator solutions.

- Wash arms and hands before leaving the laboratory area.

NOTES

CHAPTER 6

Meeting the Needs of All Students
Differentiated Instruction

Augmentation and Accommodations

LEARNING ISSUE	REFERENCE	AUGMENTATION AND ACCOMMODATIONS
Eliciting prior understandings	*What Do You Think?*	**Accommodations** It may take more than one or two questions for students to access what they know about acids and bases. Some students who have particular difficulty finding information they have mentally stored, can respond to stimuli that match their learning styles. • Students with relatively strong visual memories may respond best to a visual image of a previous investigation or class experience with acids and bases or pH. Have visual reminders around the classroom that students can use as cues. • Social learners with relative strength in episodic memory may recall information about acids and bases they have stored with an experience they had in a previous class when acids and bases were discussed. Remind them of something funny or dramatic which happened the last time acids and bases were studied in class. • Other students may benefit from a reminder of something they heard or did (auditory or kinesthetic). Give them reminders of the time they said or did something associated with acids and bases. • Ask follow-up questions that lead students to the information you want them to recall.

Creating data tables
 	
Organizing observations
	Investigate 1.a), 2.a), 4.a), 5.	**Augmentation**
		• Teach students the following chart-making strategy:
		  1. Determine what type of information to put in the left-hand column (materials to be tested).
		  2. Determine what type of information goes along the top row of the chart (Observations).
		  3. Determine the number of items of each of the above by a close analysis of the text and brainstorm with their groups.
		  4. Create a table framework.
		  5. Add the labels along the top and left column.
		  6. Collect the data.
		Accommodations
		• Ask students to create a procedure card titled "Creating a Table" that they can keep and use to make tables until they have memorized the process.
		• Allow students with handwriting or visual-spatial difficulties to use a word processor to create their table framework.
		• Provide a blank table as indicated in Step 4.a), with the right number of rows and columns and require students to determine and place the labels.
		• Use the procedure card to create the table required in Step 5.

Determining the limits of indicators Persistence	*Investigate* 4.b)	**Augmentation** • Not immediately recognizing the limitations of using only three indicators, lack of good reading strategies, lack of persistence, low tolerance for frustration and lack of confidence in problem solving will tend to stop students from solving this problem. Tell students to read the paragraph in Step 4.b) carefully and organize the data given. Once they see what the indicators do, they are likely to see the gaps. **Accommodation** • Have those students who still do not see the gaps create a number line for the pH scale from 0-14 and indicate on the number line the ranges where the indicators work.

LEARNING ISSUE	REFERENCE	AUGMENTATION AND ACCOMMODATIONS		
Identifying and drawing comparisons between acids and bases	*Chem Talk, Checking Up* 1. *Chem to Go* 1.	**Augmentation** • Reinforce what students have read comparing acids and bases by organizing the features along familiar lines of study in a T-chart:		

Augmentation (table within cell):

What does it mean?	Acids	Bases
Macro	– Become a distinct color in the presence of indicators – react with metals – taste sour – conduct electricity	– Become a distinct color in the presence of indicators – do not react with metals – taste bitter – feel slippery – conduct electricity
Nano	produce hydrogen ions when dissolved in water	Produce hydrogen peroxide ions when dissolved in water
Symbolic	Produce H^+ or H_3O^+ ions	Produce OH^- ions

Accommodation
• Give students the completed table above and ask them to use it to answer Question 1 in *Chem to Go*.

Strategies for Students with Limited English Language Proficiency

LEARNING ISSUE	REFERENCE	AUGMENTATION AND ACCOMMODATIONS
Background knowledge	*What Do You Think?*	Check again to see that students understand the use of the word *"properties"* in this context.
Vocabulary	*Investigate*	Have students work in partners or in small groups. Suggest that one student dictate the directions while the others read along and then take turns performing the various tasks. Explain the term *"cautious"* in Step 3.a) as this term may not be in the student's expressive vocabulary.
Background knowledge Vocabulary Comprehending text	*Chem Talk*	Some background on the 19th century and Svante Arrhenius may help to build some contextual knowledge and relevance. Have students add the bold face words (*Chem Words*) to their *Active Chemistry* logs or personal dictionaries. Check sidebar text for further elaboration. Check for use of words such as *"express,"* or *"exhibit"* as they may not be in students' expressive vocabulary.
Background knowledge	*What Do You Think Now?*	Students might benefit from a small group discussion of each of the bulleted items.
Background knowledge Vocabulary Comprehending text	*Chem Essential Questions*	In the *How do you know?* section, students are directed to *"make specific references"* and may need some assistance or clarification with this direction.
Comprehension Vocabulary	*Chem to Go*	Students might need to work in small groups to accomplish the answering of the questions prior to writing their own responses.
Application Comprehension	*Inquiring Further*	Help students with the pronunciation of the term *"titration"* and give some background as to its meaning. Students might be able to check their own shampoo for pH as a way of building background. When asked to research specific chemists, they may require some help in how to access that information. Providing background on these scientists may also be helpful.

CHAPTER 6

Section 7
Teaching Suggestions and Sample Answers

What Do You See?

To begin the section, elicit a response from your students about the illustration at the beginning of the section. You can do this as part of a class discussion or by having students respond directly in their *Active Chemistry* logs. Provide a prompt such as "Write a paragraph in your *Active Chemistry* logs that describes what you think is taking place in the illustration." Or, after giving the class some time to look at the illustration, ask the class a question for discussion such as "What kinds of materials are the students in the illustration experimenting with?" By listening to your students' responses you may be able to judge both their prior understanding about the section and also learn some possible misconceptions they have about chemistry.

What Do You Think?

This section and the *What Do You See?* section in the section provide students an opportunity to demonstrate prior learning; to elicit prior knowledge and engage the learner. Good instruction elicits prior understanding and gives students a chance for practicing the transfer of what they already know to the concepts to be learned during the section. Engaging students in topics they already know about and associated with the section generates enthusiasm in the learner and gives you a chance to evaluate students' prior conceptions for the topics found in the section.

> *What Do You Think?*
> ### A CHEMIST'S RESPONSE
>
> Other properties of acids include a sour taste, the ability to change a variety of indicators to a different color, reaction with most metals to form hydrogen gas, and the ability to hydrolyze polysaccharides and proteins.
>
> Other properties of bases include a bitter taste, the ability to change a variety of indicators to a different color, a slippery feel, and the ability to hydrolyze proteins.
>
> You should never taste an acid or a base in the laboratory, nor apply either to your skin. Therefore, taste and feel are not to be considered. The most common ways to distinguish between an acid and a base is with an indicator or a pH probe.

STUDENTS' PRIOR CONCEPTIONS

Many students do not understand that many compounds fall into the three categories of acids, bases, and indicators.

Again, the macro to nanoscale connection is crucial – if a compound has certain macroscopic properties, then what nanoscale properties must be present? What is occurring in a chemical change to cause these color changes? Why do some things cause an indicator to change and others do not? Students may equate these color changes with "magic," and not think about the particulate behavior.

Students will often think that the presence of an -OH group will always indicate a base. Point out that methanol, CH_3OH, and glucose contain -OH groups, yet are not basic. Similarly, students may think that because acids are proton donors, any compound with a proton is an acid. You can tell them that methane, CH_4, has four protons, yet the pK_a of one of these protons is about 50.

It is important to clearly define the term proton as a hydrogen atom without its electron. A proton transfer does not mean that a molecule is losing a proton from its nucleus.

Students will often confuse strength and concentration. Strength relates to the degree of ionization and ion formation in solution. Concentration is the amount of solute per amount of solution. Students might think that a concentrated acid is a pure substance.

Students may be able to give many examples of color changes in cooking or elsewhere in everyday life. Many of these will not have anything to do with acids and bases, but color change is related to the study of acids, bases and indicators. The topic for this section will be using acid/base chemistry to produce interesting color changes. Students will enjoy being able to manipulate the color of indicator solutions by simply changing the solution pH.

Section 7

Acids, Bases, and Indicators—Colorful Chemistry

What Do You See?

Learning Outcomes

In this section you will

• Identify common household acids and bases.

• Identify characteristic properties of acids and bases and learn to tell the difference between acids and bases.

• See how strong acids and bases behave differently from weak acids and bases.

• Determine the pH of various solutions using indicators.

• Categorize solutions based on the pH scale.

• Use the mathematical definition of pH.

Safety goggles and a lab apron must be worn at all times in a chemistry lab.

Hydrochloric acid and sulfuric acid are corrosive. Handle with care. Notify your teacher if any spills occur.

What Do You Think?

If you add red cabbage to boiling water, a special bluish colored solution is made. Vinegar, a common acid, will turn the solution red. Ammonia, a common base, will turn the solution green.

• What are some other properties of acids and bases you know about?

• How can you tell the difference between an acid and a base?

Record your ideas about these questions in your *Active Chemistry* log. Be prepared to discuss your responses with your group and the class.

Investigate

1. Your teacher will provide you with samples of some of the materials listed below. Place a small amount of each solution in a separate well of a well plate. Add a small piece of polished zinc (or magnesium) to each of the solutions.

   • hydrochloric acid ($HCl_{(aq)}$)

   • lemon or orange juice (citric acid)

   • vinegar (acetic acid, $CH_3COOH_{(aq)}$)

   • sulfuric acid ($H_2SO_{4(aq)}$)

519

Active Chemistry

CHAPTER 6

Investigate

1.a)

For your convenience, the data table at the bottom of the page is provided as a Blackline Master in your *Teacher Resources CD*.

6-7a Blackline Master

1.b)

Hydrochloric acid, lemon juice, vinegar, sulfuric acid, carbonated drink, and apple juice. They all contain an acid.

1.c)

Mineral water, milk, dishwashing soap, sodium hydroxide, milk of magnesia, potassium hydroxide, calcium hydroxide and ammonia. They are basic or neutral.

2.a)

Acids turn litmus paper red; react with zinc or magnesium metal and have a tart taste. Bases turn litmus paper blue, do not appear to react with zinc or magnesium metal and they have a somewhat bitter taste.

Cool Chemistry Show

Be careful with the NaOH. Do not get it on your skin!

Do not dispose of magnesium in sink or trash! Dispose of it as directed by your teacher.

- mineral water or carbonated beverage (contains $H_2CO_3(aq)$)
- milk
- dishwashing solution
- sodium hydroxide ($NaOH(aq)$)
- magnesium hydroxide (contains $Mg(OH)_2(aq)$)
- apple juice (malic acid)
- potassium hydroxide ($KOH(aq)$)
- calcium hydroxide ($Ca(OH)_2(aq)$)
- household ammonia ($NH_3(aq)$)

a) Make a data table to record your observations.

b) Which substances reacted with the metal? How could you tell? What do these substances have in common? (Consider the chemical formulas listed for some of the substances.)

c) Which substances did not react with the metal? What do these substances have in common? (Consider the chemical formulas listed for some of the substances.) Wash and save zinc pieces for future use.

2. Place small amounts of each solution you used in *Step 1* in a separate well of a well plate. Test

the solutions with one or more common laboratory indicators. (Your teacher will provide acid-base indicators like blue litmus paper, red litmus paper, phenolphthalein, bromothymol blue, and methyl red.) Indicator papers are activated simply by dipping a small piece of the paper into the solution and noting any color change. If the indicator is a solution, add a drop or two to the substance being tested and note any color change. You will need to use fresh test solutions if you want to test with more than one indicator solution.

a) Make a chart and record your observations.

3. Use your observations as well as previous experiences to answer the following:

a) Make a list of some of the observable properties for *acids* and *bases*. For example:

- How do substances containing acids or bases taste? You should never taste substances in a lab, but you have probably had the opportunity to taste vinegar or lemon juice at home, or you may have accidentally gotten soap in your mouth.

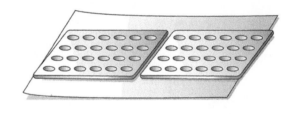

520

Substance	Zn or Mg	Litmus paper	Phenolphthalein
HCl	Bubbles	Red	Clear
Lemon juice	Light bubbles	Red	Clear
Vinegar	Light bubbles	Red	Clear
H_2SO_4	Bubbles	Red	Clear
Mineral water	No Rx	No Rx	Clear
Carbonated drink	Some bubbles	Red	Clear
Milk	No Rx	Slight	Clear
Dishwashing soap	No Rx	Blue	Slight change
NaOH	No Rx	Blue	Red
milk of magnesia	No Rx	Blue	Red
Apple juice	Some bubbles	Red	Clear
KOH	No Rx	Blue	Red
$Ca(OH)_2$	No Rx	Blue	Red
Ammonia	No Rx	Blue	Red

3.a)

Acids and bases will react with skin and eyes. When bases react with the skin it causes the skin to feel slippery.

Discussion: Litmus pH range is 4.7 – 8.3 and phenolphthalein pH range is 8.2 – 10.0. Encourage the students to examine their tests closely.

• How do acids and bases feel?
You must be very cautious
when handling chemicals
both at home and in the lab.
However, you've probably had
the experience of touching
cleaning materials, such as
soaps or floor cleaners. Think
about vinegar or citrus fruits.
How do they feel on a cut on
your skin or a canker sore in
your mouth?

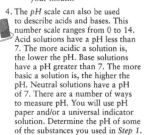

4. The *pH* scale can also be used
to describe acids and bases. This
number scale ranges from 0 to 14.
Acid solutions have a pH less than
7. The more acidic a solution is,
the lower the pH. Base solutions
have a pH greater than 7. The more
basic a solution is, the higher the
pH. Neutral solutions have a pH
of 7. There are a number of ways
to measure pH. You will use pH
paper and/or a universal indicator
solution. Determine the pH of some
of the substances you used in *Step 1*.

a) Make a data table that includes
the name of the substance, the pH
test, and whether the substance
is an acid, a base, or a neutral
substance.

b) You may have used both pH
paper and universal indicator
solution to measure pH. Both
are made from a combination of
indicators to produce a range of
colors throughout the pH scale.

Universal indicator solution
contains four separate indicators,
including the following: Thymol
blue is a chemical that changes
color twice. Between a pH of
1.2 and 2.8, it changes from red
to yellow. Between a pH of 8.0
and 9.6, it changes from yellow
to blue. Methyl red is another

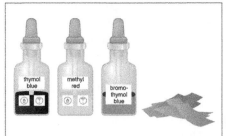

Wash your
hands and arms
thoroughly after
the investigation.

indicator but it changes from red
to yellow in the pH range of 4.8
to 6.0. Bromothymol blue is a
third component which changes
color from yellow to blue in the
pH range 6.0 to 7.6.

How could these three chemicals
be used to create an indicator
scale? What are the limitations of
the pH scale if only these three
chemicals are used?

5. Use the pH paper to test additional
common household substances in
order to determine which are acids
and which are bases. (Hint: Try
carbonated beverages, tea, coffee,
baking powder, mayonnaise, power
drinks, pickle juice, window cleaner,
and stain removers.) Your teacher
may give you some pH paper to
take home with you.

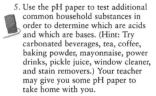

a) Make a list of common acids
and bases found in your school
or home. When possible, include
both the name and formula for
each substance you test.

6. Dispose of all chemicals as directed
by your teacher. Clean and put
away any equipment as instructed.
Clean up your workstation.

521

Active Chemistry

4.

If you choose not to use
universal indicator then it is
suggested that you use pH
hydrion paper to get the pH
range of the different materials
that you choose to test.

4.a)

For your convenience, the
following sample data table is
also provided as a Blackline
Master in your *Teacher
Resources CD*.

| 6-7b | **Blackline Master** |

CHAPTER 6

pH of Household Substances

Substance and pH Range→	Litmus paper (6.5)	pH paper (Full range)	Universal indicator (Full range)	Methyl red (4.2-6.3)	Methyl orange (3.7)	Thymol-phthalein (9.4-10.6)	Thymol blue (1.2-2.8,8.0-9.3)
Cola							
Tea							
Coffee							
Baking powder							
Baking soda							
Mayonnaise							
Pickle juice							

4.b)

To create an indicator scale, the three indicators could be mixed in one solution. This solution would give pH changes at around 2, 5, 8 and 10.

The limitation would be that pH changes between these values would not be measurable. This would be pH values about 3, 4, 6, 7, 9, 11, 12, 13.

5.a)

Household materials will vary but suggest to students that they use hydrion pH paper to do their tests. Do not allow them to take chemicals home. They could make cabbage juice for a universal indicator and that they could take home to test household chemicals.

6.

All chemicals used in this section can be disposed of by normal procedures.

CHEM TIP

If you want the students to use red cabbage as an indicator with the different items tested in Step 1, then the following is a general procedure in making the indicator:

Slice the red cabbage into chunks and place in a blender to chop it into small pieces. Place the chopped cabbage in a large beaker and add an equal amount of water. Place the beaker on a hot plate and bring it to a near boil for 30 minutes. Decant the liquid into a large container or you could pour the mixture through a strainer to remove the solid particles.

The color of the indicator in water is purple, in acids it is red, and in a base it is green. Over the entire pH scale:

pH	Color
1	
2	Red
3	
4	
5	Pink
6	
7	
8	Purple
9	
10	Blue
11	
12	Green
13	
14	Yellow

There are other plants that could also be used as indicators. Blueberries, blackberries, and beets are some examples.

NOTES

CHAPTER 6

7.a)

Make certain that students understand the dangers of using bases. The spray solution of ammonia must be carefully used and students must avoid getting the mist in their eyes.

The disappearing ink part can be done as a demonstration. If the window wash with ammonia is weak, you may have to add 1 or 2 mL of concentrated ammonium hydroxide to the solution. Also, as an alternative use can use a solution of thymolphthalein.

7.b)

The phenolphthalein will be colorless in the "I" beaker when the 50 mL of water is added to it. When the "I" beaker solution is poured into the "A" beaker you should observe no color change. When the contents from beaker "A" are poured into beaker "B" the result will cause the phenolphthalein solution to turn pink or red. In the acid media, phenolphthalein is colorless and when it is in a basic media it will be pink or light red.

Cool Chemistry Show

Caution must be used with these sprays because they can cause eye damage if they get into the eyes.

7. Here are two investigations that display the characteristics of acids and bases in a colorful way. Your teacher may show you these as demonstrations.

- Paint a message on a large sheet of paper or poster board using phenolphthalein indicator solution. (How about painting a message announcing your *Cool Chemistry Show*?) Allow the message to dry completely and hang the paper/poster board where everyone can see it. Use a window glass cleaner that contains ammonia water and when you are ready to reveal the message, lightly spray the design with the basic solution. (The secret message can also be revealed with a dilute ammonia solution. As the ammonia evaporates, the secret message that has been revealed will disappear again.)

- Rinse a small beaker with a strong acid and label it "A." Rinse another small beaker with a strong base and label it "B." Let both beakers air dry. In another beaker (label it "I") add 20 drops of phenolphthalein indicator solution to about 50 mL of distilled water. When you are ready, pour some of the solution from beaker "I" into beaker "A." Then pour the solution from beaker "A" into beaker "B."

a) Record your observations.

b) Account for the observations in each case.

Chem Words

acid: a substance that produces hydrogen ions in water, or is a proton donor.

base: a substance that releases hydroxide ions (OH⁻) in water, or is a proton acceptor.

Chem Talk

ACIDS AND BASES

Arrhenius's Definition of Acids and Bases

Acids and **bases** were first classified according to their characteristic properties. As you've experienced, acids and bases have different, distinct interactions with indicators (substances that change color with changes in the acidic or basic nature of another material). Some acids react with metals, while bases do not. Bases have a characteristic bitter taste and slippery feel, while acids have a characteristic sour taste. In fact, the term acid comes from the Latin word *acidus*, which means sour. Acids and bases are also good conductors of electricity.

In the nineteenth century a chemist named Svante Arrhenius attributed the characteristic properties of acids to their ability to produce hydrogen ions when dissolved in water. If you look at the formulas for many common acids (HCl, H_2CO_3, H_2SO_4), you'll notice that they all have H as a common element. When these

522

Active Chemistry

CHEM TIP

In addition to the Arrhenius acid-base definition, Brønsted and Lowry created a new definition of acids and bases. Their concept was that acid-base reactions dealt with proton-transfer reactions. It also could explain acid-base reactions that did not have water present. Arrhenius's definition was restrictive and required the presence of water. A good example to use is: gaseous hydrogen chloride and gaseous ammonia form ammonium chloride. Place an open bottle of concentrated hydrochloric acid next to an open bottle of concentrated ammonium hydroxide. The cloud produced is ammonium chloride crystals.

Another acid-base theory is the one produced by Lewis. He found that an acid with an empty orbital could accept a pair of electrons to produce a coordinate covalent bond between the two species. The acid species can be ionic or molecular. The base is any ionic or molecular species that can donate a pair of electrons to the forming of a coordinate covalent bond. And neutralization is the formation of the covalent bond between the acid (electron acceptor) and base (electron donor). An example of this type of reaction would be aluminum chloride (acting as the acid) and a chlorine molecule (acting as the base). The aluminum has an empty orbital that can accept a pair of electrons from the chlorine to form a covalent bond.

The general equation is:

$$AlCl_3 + Cl_2(g) \longrightarrow AlCl_4^- + Cl^+$$

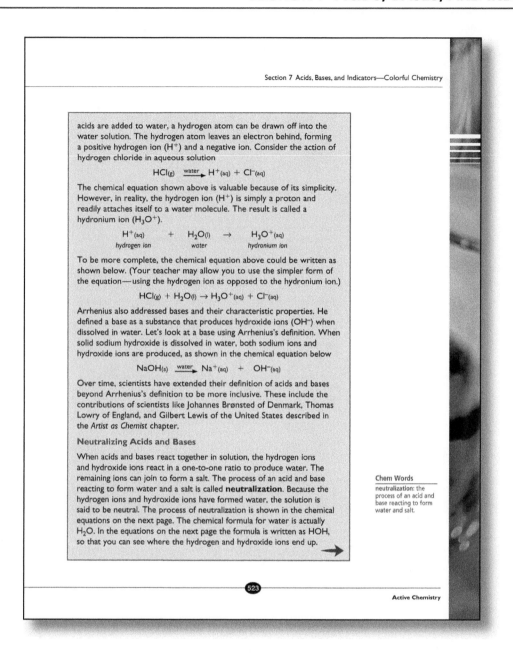

acids are added to water, a hydrogen atom can be drawn off into the water solution. The hydrogen atom leaves an electron behind, forming a positive hydrogen ion (H^+) and a negative ion. Consider the action of hydrogen chloride in aqueous solution

$$HCl_{(g)} \xrightarrow{water} H^+_{(aq)} + Cl^-_{(aq)}$$

The chemical equation shown above is valuable because of its simplicity. However, in reality, the hydrogen ion (H^+) is simply a proton and readily attaches itself to a water molecule. The result is called a hydronium ion (H_3O^+).

$$\underset{\text{hydrogen ion}}{H^+_{(aq)}} + \underset{\text{water}}{H_2O_{(l)}} \rightarrow \underset{\text{hydronium ion}}{H_3O^+_{(aq)}}$$

To be more complete, the chemical equation above could be written as shown below. (Your teacher may allow you to use the simpler form of the equation—using the hydrogen ion as opposed to the hydronium ion.)

$$HCl_{(g)} + H_2O_{(l)} \rightarrow H_3O^+_{(aq)} + Cl^-_{(aq)}$$

Arrhenius also addressed bases and their characteristic properties. He defined a base as a substance that produces hydroxide ions (OH^-) when dissolved in water. Let's look at a base using Arrhenius's definition. When solid sodium hydroxide is dissolved in water, both sodium ions and hydroxide ions are produced, as shown in the chemical equation below

$$NaOH_{(s)} \xrightarrow{water} Na^+_{(aq)} + OH^-_{(aq)}$$

Over time, scientists have extended their definition of acids and bases beyond Arrhenius's definition to be more inclusive. These include the contributions of scientists like Johannes Brønsted of Denmark, Thomas Lowry of England, and Gilbert Lewis of the United States described in the *Artist as Chemist* chapter.

Neutralizing Acids and Bases

When acids and bases react together in solution, the hydrogen ions and hydroxide ions react in a one-to-one ratio to produce water. The remaining ions can join to form a salt. The process of an acid and base reacting to form water and a salt is called **neutralization**. Because the hydrogen ions and hydroxide ions have formed water, the solution is said to be neutral. The process of neutralization is shown in the chemical equations on the next page. The chemical formula for water is actually H_2O. In the equations on the next page the formula is written as HOH, so that you can see where the hydrogen and hydroxide ions end up.

Chem Words

neutralization: the process of an acid and base reacting to form water and salt.

CHAPTER 6

Chem Talk

The Arrhenius definition of acids and bases is thoroughly discussed and the existence of other definitions (Brønsted-Lowry's definition and Lewis's definition) is mentioned. The terms "neutralization" and "titration" are explained in terms of acids and bases.

This is followed by a discussion of buffers and how they work. Finally, the pH scale is shown as it relates to common everyday foods and household items. This is enhanced with a table of various pH indicators and the pH at which they change color.

In your group discussion of the *Chem Talk* section, when referring to titration, you may want to use the Titration Graph is provided as a Blackline Master on the *Teacher Resources CD*.

6-7c | **Blackline Master**

 Cool Chemistry Show

$$H^+_{(aq)} + OH^-_{(aq)} \rightarrow HOH_{(aq)}$$

hydrogen ion   hydroxide ion   water

$$HCl_{(aq)} + NaOH_{(aq)} \rightarrow HOH_{(aq)} + NaCl_{(aq)}$$

acid   base   water   salt

Chem Words

endpoint: the point at which the indicator changes color.

titration: a procedure for determining the concentration of an unknown chemical by having it react with measured amounts of a second chemical of known concentration.

If a suitable indicator is added to the reaction system, it will change colors when neutralization occurs. The point at which the indicator changes color is called the **endpoint**.

Consider the reaction of a strong acid (HCl) and a strong base (NaOH), as shown in the equation above. These substances are described as "strong" because they ionize completely in solution. For every HCl molecule, one hydrogen ion is released. For every NaOH molecule, one hydroxide ion is released. These two ions then combine in a one-to-one ratio to form a neutral water molecule.

Titration

Chemists take advantage of the neutralization process to help determine the concentration of solutions of acids or bases. Suppose you wanted to determine the concentration of an acid solution. You would add measured amounts of a base to the acid until the solution became neutral (pH = 7). The name of this experimental procedure is **titration**. The actual titration technique requires you to know the concentration of the base. It also requires an indicator, such as phenolphthalein, or a pH meter to determine when the solution reaches pH 7. The neutralization point or endpoint of a strong acid titrated with a strong base is at a pH of 7 as shown in graph for hydrochloric acid vs. sodium hydroxide.

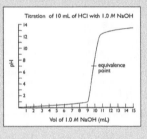

Titration of 10 mL of HCl with 1.0 M NaOH

pH

equivalence point

Vol of 1.0 M NaOH (mL)

Buffers

A **buffer** is a solution that resists changes in pH when a small amount of acid or base is added. Because of this buffering effect, titration of a solution of a weak acid with a strong base is slightly different than the titration of a strong acid. When a weak acid such as acetic acid is titrated with a strong base like NaOH, the endpoint or equivalence point is not pH = 7. Also, the endpoint does not occur as suddenly as with a strong acid. As you neutralize some of the weak acid, some of the acid's conjugate base is formed. In the case of acetic acid, the conjugate base is the acetate ion. The acetate ion is a weak base itself and a buffer solution is created which contains both the weak acid and its conjugate base. The solution now resists a change in pH as more of the strong base is added. The increase in pH is more gradual and the endpoint will be shifted to the basic side. The equivalence point or endpoint of acetic acid titrated with a strong base is 8.72, not 7.00.

$$CH_3COOH \; + \; OH^- \; \leftrightarrows \; CH_3COO^- \; + \; H_2O$$

acetic acid   *base*   *acetic ion*   *water*

This equation shows an **equilibrium,** where acetic acid reacts with the strong base, OH^-, to form an acetate ion (forward reaction with the arrow pointing to the right) and water. It also shows the reverse reaction occurring at the same time (arrow pointing to the left). In the reverse reaction, the acetate ion reacts with water to form acetic acid and a hydroxide ion. In equilibrium, the forward and reverse reactions occur at the same rate.

The titration of a weak base such as ammonia (NH_3) with a strong acid will also show these characteristics. The pH will decrease more slowly and the endpoint will be shifted to a pH less than 7.00.

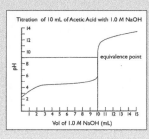

Titration of 10 mL of Acetic Acid with 1.0 M NaOH

Chem Words

buffer: a solution containing a weak acid (or weak base) and the salt of the weak acid (or weak base). A buffer solution will resist large changes in pH when small amounts of acid or base are added to the solution.

equilibrium: a condition that exists when the forward reaction rate equals the reverse reaction rate, such that there appears to be no change in the concentration of products or reactants.

CHAPTER 6

For your convenience, a color diagram of the pH scale is provided as a Color Overhead on the *Teachers Resource CD*.

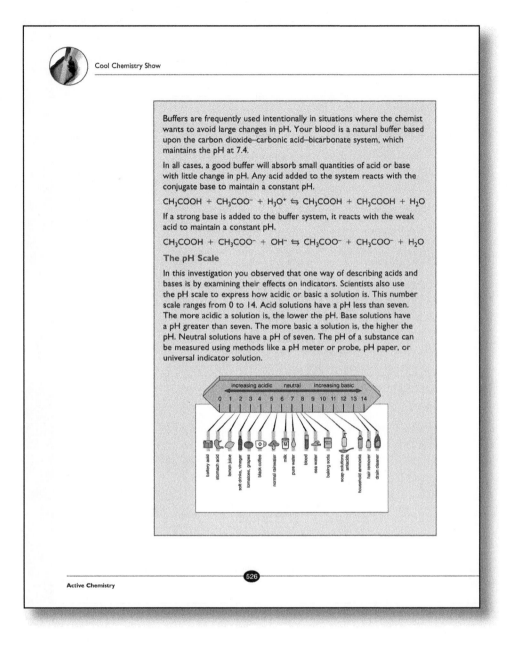

Common Laboratory Acid–Base Indicators		
Indicator	**Color change**	**pH Range**
methyl violet	*yellow to blue*	*0.0 to 1.6*
thymol blue	*red to yellow*	*1.2 to 2.8*
methyl orange	*red to yellow*	*3.2 to 4.4*
bromocresol green	*yellow to blue*	*3.8 to 5.4*
methyl red	*red to yellow*	*4.8 to 6.0*
litmus paper	*red to blue*	*5.5 to 8.0*
bromothymol blue	*yellow to blue*	*6.0 to 7.6*
thymol blue	*yellow to blue*	*8.0 to 9.6*
phenolphthalein	*colorless to pink*	*8.2 to 10.0*
thymolphthalein	*colorless to blue*	*9.4 to 10.6*

Acid and base indicators are compounds that are sensitive to pH. The color of the indicator changes as the pH of the solution changes. Most indicators are weak acids or weak bases that typically exhibit two different colors under varying pH conditions. The table above shows some common laboratory indicators and the colors they display under different pH conditions.

The pH scale ranges from 0 to 14 and is used to express the concentration of the hydrogen (H^+) or hydronium ion (H_3O^+) of a solution at 25°C. Mathematically, it is defined as the negative logarithm of the hydrogen ion concentration in moles per liter (M). The term **pH** stands for **p**ower of **H**ydrogen ion. It can be written as

$$pH = -\log[H^+]$$

where the brackets [ ] stand for "concentration of" (hydrogen ions in solution). Because pH is a logarithmic scale, the concentration of the hydrogen ion $[H^+]$ actually increases or decreases tenfold for each unit on the scale. An acid with a pH of 2 has a $[H^+]$ that is 10 times greater than an acid with a pH of 3 and 100 times the concentration of an acid with pH 4. A base with a pH of 10 has a $[H^+]$ that is 10 times less than a base with a pH of 9.

Chem Words

pH: a measure of the acidity or alkalinity of a solution based on the concentration of hydrogen ions ($pH = -\log[H^+]$).

CHAPTER 6

Checking Up

1.

Chart should show a series of metals that will react with acids. Refer to the Metal Activity Series chart. Students should be able to list the other properties.

Properties of Acids and Bases		
Property	**Acids**	**Bases**
Taste	Sour	Bitter
Feel	Like water	Slippery
pH	Less than a pH of 7	pH greater than 7
Reaction with metals*	Bubbles of hydrogen gas	No reaction**

*All metals higher (more active) than hydrogen on the Metal Activity Series.

**Highly concentrated base (lye, NaOH, KOH) will dissolve aluminum and release a large amount of heat.

2.

Arrhenius's definition of acids was any substance that releases hydrogen ions. Bases release hydroxide ions.

3.

The process is called neutralization. In water, the reaction can be expressed as:
$H^+_{(aq)} + OH^-_{(aq)} \rightarrow H_2O_{(l)}$

4.

The pH at which litmus paper and phenolphthalein change color (the end point) are close enough to the neutral pH of 7. In a titration, one drop of acid or base will shift the pH through this end point when titrating. Example, 10 mL of 0.1 M HCl will be neutralized with 10 mL of 0.1 M NaOH and the next drop will change the indicator of phenolphthalein to the pink side.

5.

pH is defined as the negative log of the hydrogen ion concentration, or pH = $-\log[H^+]$.

6.

If the pH is 3 then the $[H^+] = 10^{-3}$ M and if the pH is 5 then the $[H^+] = 10^{-5}$ M. Or, we can see that the $[H^+]$ of a solution at pH 3 is 100 times more concentrated than at a pH of 5.

7.

$[H^+] = 3 \times 10^{-5} =$
pH of $-\log(3 \times 10^{-5}) = 4.5$

8.

A solution with pH 4.5 has a pOH of $14.0 - 4.5$, or 9.5

Cool Chemistry Show

Checking Up

1. Use a chart to compare the properties of acids and bases. Be sure to include headings like taste, feel, pH, and reaction with metals.
2. What characteristic property did Arrhenius attribute to acids and bases?
3. Describe the process that occurs when an acid reacts with a base.
4. Why are litmus paper and phenolphthalein particularly useful indicators for distinguishing between acids and bases?
5. What does pH stand for?
6. How much more acidic is a solution of pH 3 than one of pH 5?
7. For a solution with a $[H^+]$ of 3×10^{-5}, calculate the pH.
8. What is the pOH of a solution with a $[H^+]$ of 3×10^{-5}?

The pH of Water and Equilibrium

To understand the pH of water, you must remember that water contains very small amounts of H^+ and OH^- according to the reaction: $H_2O_{(l)} \rightleftarrows H^+_{(aq)} + OH^-_{(aq)}$. Pure water has a pH of 7, therefore the concentration of hydrogen ions $[H^+]$, is 1×10^{-7}, calculated from the formula, pH = $-\log[H^+]$. Since the number of H^+ (hydrogen ions) has to be equal to the number of OH^- (hydroxyl ions), $[OH^-]$ is also equal to 1×10^{-7}. Just as the pH can be calculated from the $[H^+]$ in water, the pOH can be calculated from the $[OH^-]$. The values for pH and pOH have an inverse relationship: as one goes up, the other goes down. This means that their product is a constant, which is called K_w. K_w is equal to the product of $[H^+]$ and $[OH^-]$, or 1×10^{-14}.

$$K_w = [H^+][OH^-] \text{ or } (1 \times 10^{-7})(1 \times 10^{-7}) = 1 \times 10^{-14}$$

This will always be true in water. As the $[H^+]$ goes up (solution becomes more acidic) the $[OH^-]$ goes down in proportion (becomes less basic). This makes the calculation of pH and pOH quite simple. Taking the $-\log$ of the equation, $pK_w = pH + pOH = 14$. The sum of the pH and the pOH will always equal 14. For example, if the pH of a solution is 3, the pOH is 11 because $3 + 11 = 14$.

What Do You Think Now?

At the beginning of the section you were asked the following:
- **What are some other properties of acids and bases you know about?**
- **How can you tell the difference between an acid and a base?**

Have your answers changed now that you have completed this section? Think about the following questions:
- Is it accurate to describe a mixture of an acid and a base as in "conflict"?
- What happens when equal amounts of acid are added to equal amounts of a base?
- How would you know how strong an acid is or how strong a base is?

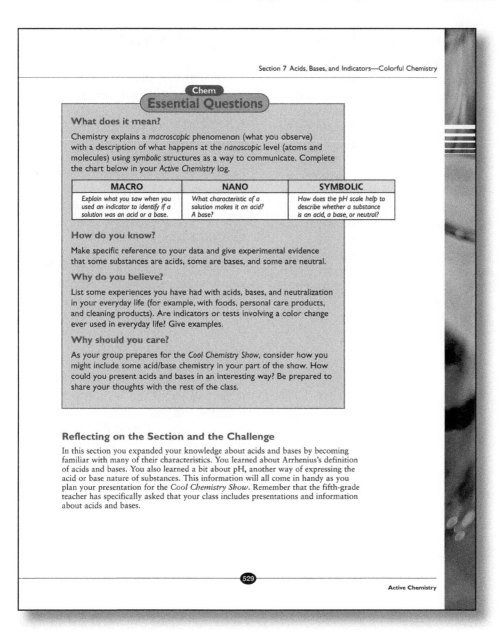

go back and forth between these two bases but will remain with the stronger base, CH_3COO^-, most of the time.

What happens when equal amounts of acid are added to equal amounts of a base?

Assuming the acid and base are of equal strength, then neutralization will occur. For strong acids and strong bases, the reaction would be:

$$H^+(aq) + OH^-(aq) \longrightarrow H_2O(l)$$

How would you know how strong an acid is or how strong a base is?

By determining the pH of the acid or base (test paper, indicator solution, pH meter). You could also determine the strength of an acid or base through titration.

Reflecting on the Section and the Challenge

After each *Investigate* and *Chem Talk* section, it is valuable to stop briefly and have the students place what they have learned in the context of the challenge. This can be done out of class or, if time permits, in class by having the groups meet briefly and summarize their thoughts. If the summary could be done orally in class, then they may receive ideas from others and also help other groups to generate ideas for their own challenge.

What Do You Think Now?

Is it accurate to describe a mixture of an acid and a base as in "conflict"?

While it is not considered "scientific" to attribute human characteristics to inanimate substances, it is sometimes useful, in teaching, to use such a device. An acid and a base could be considered to be competing for the proton of an acid, especially when considering a weak acid or base in aqueous solution. For example, a dilute solution of acetic acid in water is an equilibrium mixture of the following substances:

$$CH_3COOH + H_2O \rightleftarrows$$
$$CH_3COO^- + H_3O^+$$

As shown, the two bases, H_2O and CH_3COO^- are competing for the H^+ and could be considered to be "in conflict." The proton will

CHAPTER 6

Chem Essential Questions

What does it mean?

MACRO — The indicator changed color depending on the acidity or basicity of the solution.

NANO — In the Arrhenius definition for acids and bases, acids have an ability to contribute H^+ ions to aqueous solutions and bases have the ability to contribute OH^- ions to aqueous solutions.

SYMBOLIC — The pH scale provides a quantitative measure for how acidic a substance is.

How do you know?

Acids: hydrochloric acid, lemon juice, vinegar, carbonated beverage. These substances turn litmus red, clear in the presence of phenolphthlalein, yellow in bromothymol blue and red in methyl red. They have measured pH of less than 7. Dishwashing solution, sodium hydroxide, potassium hydroxide, calcium hydroxide, and ammonia turn blue in the presence of litmus, pink in the presence of phenolphthalein, turn blue in the presence of bromothymol blue, and turn yellow in the presence of methyl red. They have a measured pH of greater than 7.

Why do you believe?

Many food items are acidic (citrus fruit, apples, tomatoes, foods containing vinegar.) Many cleaning products are basic (window cleaner, ammonia, soaps, drain cleansers). Personal care products often advertise as "pH balanced." Swimming pools, spas, and aquariums are monitored for pH using indicator solutions and adjusted using a neutralization reaction.

Why should you care?

An entertaining demonstration is how indicators change color as solution pH changes. It's better to have dilute acids and bases in large enough quantities for the audience to see easily. Another interesting way to demonstrate acid/base chemistry is by creating invisible ink which is then dramatically revealed during the show (such as in the illustration for *Section 3*).

NOTES

NOTES

CHAPTER 6

Chem to Go

1.

a) Acid

b) Base

c) Base

d) Acid

e) Base

f) Acid

g) Base

h) Base

2.

a) $H_2SO_{4(aq)} \rightarrow$
$2H^+_{(aq)} + SO_4^{2-}_{(aq)}$
Remember that $H^+_{(aq)}$
means H_3O^+

b) $H_2CO_{3(aq)} \rightleftarrows$
$H^+_{(aq)} + HCO_3^-_{(aq)}$

3.

a) $KOH_{(aq)} \rightarrow K^+_{(aq)} + OH^-_{(aq)}$

b) $Ca(OH)_{2(aq)} \rightarrow$
$Ca^{2+}_{(aq)} + 2OH^-_{(aq)}$

4.

1 M HCl will produce a
$[H^+] = 1\ M$ and 1 M H_2SO_4
will produce a $[H^+] = 2\ M$.
From this we can see that sulfuric
acid will have twice the number
of hydrogen ions as compared
to hydrochloric acid. Therefore,
it will be more acidic and have a
lower pH value.

5.

An indicator is used in a titration
because it will "indicate" the end
point when the amount of base
equals the original amount of
acid in the solution.

6.

The pH would be less than 7.

7.

They should have the properties
of an acid. They may react with
some metals, their pH is less
than 7 and they will change blue
litmus to red.

8.

b) It has a higher concentration
of OH^- than H_3O^+ and causes
litmus paper to turn blue.

Cool Chemistry Show

Chem to Go

1. Identify which of the following characteristics relate to acids and which relate to bases:

   a) taste sour   b) release hydroxide ions (OH^-) when dissolved in water

   c) feel slippery   d) release hydrogen ions (H^+) when dissolved in water

   e) turn pink in the presence of phenolphthalein

   f) react with metals to produce hydrogen gas

   g) taste bitter   h) turn red litmus paper blue

2. Use Arrhenius's definition of an acid to help you write a chemical equation that shows the acidic nature of the following:

   a) sulfuric acid (H_2SO_4)   b) carbonic acid (H_2CO_3)

3. Use Arrhenius's definition of a base to help you write a chemical equation that shows the basic nature of the following:

   a) potassium hydroxide (KOH)   b) calcium hydroxide ($Ca(OH)_2$)

4. If you prepared the same concentration of two strong acids, sulfuric and hydrochloric, why would the pH of the sulfuric acid be lower than the pH of the hydrochloric acid?

5. A chemist will usually add an indicator to a solution before beginning a titration of an acid with a base. Explain the purpose of an indicator in a titration.

6. If you bubbled carbon dioxide through water of pH 7, would the new pH of the solution be greater than or less than 7?

7. Lemon juice, curdled milk, and vinegar all taste sour. What other properties would you expect them to have in common?

8. Which statement correctly describes a solution with a pH of 9?

   a) It has a higher concentration of H_3O^+ than OH^- and causes litmus to turn blue.

   b) It has a higher concentration of OH^- than H_3O^+ and causes litmus to turn blue.

   c) It has a higher concentration of H_3O^+ than OH^- and causes litmus to turn red.

   d) It has a higher concentration of OH^- than H_3O^+ and causes litmus to turn red.

9. Which pH change represents a hundredfold increase in the concentration of H_3O^+?

   a) pH 5 to pH 7   c)   pH 3 to pH 1

   b) pH 13 to pH 14   d)   pH 4 to pH 3

530

Active Chemistry

---

10. *Preparing for the Chapter Challenge*

You have seen a number of interesting color changes using acids, bases, and indicators. Choose one or two different cool investigations to demonstrate in your show. Describe the procedure you will use and explain the chemistry involved. You may also wish to include an interesting scenario to accompany your "presto change-o" demonstrations.

Inquiring Further

1. Titration

Titration is a procedure for determining the concentration of one chemical by having it react with measured amounts of a second chemical. An acid is titrated with a base; a base is titrated with an acid. Research how chemists perform a titration and the importance of indicators. With your teacher's permission, demonstrate titration to your class.

2. The changing definition of an acid and base

The definition of acids and bases has changed through time. You are familiar with the earliest definitions that defined acids and bases in terms of their characteristic properties. The traditional definition has been expanded a number of times to include other substances that behave like acids and bases, but don't fit the traditional definition. Review (from *Artist as Chemist*) and further research the expansion through time of the definition of acids and bases. Identify the scientists involved and the changes that were made. Consider researching chemists such as Johannes Brønsted of Denmark, Thomas Lowry of England, or the American chemist Gilbert Lewis.

3. Is it pH balanced?

You may have heard the term "pH balanced" used to describe a shampoo or a deodorant. What does this term mean? What is the pH of most shampoos? Deodorants? Is it important for a shampoo or deodorant to be "pH balanced"? Conduct some research, both in and out of lab, to get answers to these questions. Describe your research method, explaining how you know the Web sites you chose are reliable. Focus only on shampoos or only on deodorants.

4. Balanced or unbalanced?

Examine the promotional materials for two different brands of "pH balanced" shampoos (or deodorants) to determine what each manufacturer means by using that phrase. Choose the meaning that you feel is most testable, devise a test for "pH balanced," and apply it to each brand. Which truly has the better balance in pH?

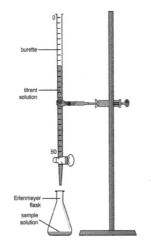

burette

titrant solution

Erlenmeyer flask

sample solution

Inquiring Further

1. Titration

If you decide that you want the students to do titrations, then you will have to take some time to show them how to titrate. The titrations are going to take some patience. They will have difficulty in getting the faint pink color of phenolphthalein without practice. If you have magnetic stirrers available it will help them in getting successful results. Also, if you have CBLs (Calculated-Based Laboratory Systems) available, you can show them how to titrate with them. They must be cautioned as to how to clean the burette. They cannot shake the burettes, as they will snap quite easily.

Strong acid and strong base will have a pH of 7 at the end point. The graph should have a steep slope. The equivalence point is reached when the number of moles of sodium hydroxide equals the number of moles of hydrochloric acid. This is shown on the graph.

CHAPTER 6

9.

c) pH 3 to pH 1

10.

Preparing for the Chapter Challenge

Since this work should be relevant to the challenge, you might want to have the students do this exercise in their group. This will keep them "on the same page" and working together.

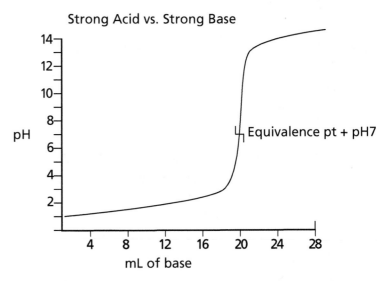

Strong Acid vs. Strong Base

Equivalence pt + pH7

pH

mL of base

Weak acids and bases do not ionize as much as a strong acid or base. Hence, we find that weak acids have a higher pH value than strong acids and weak bases have a smaller pH value than strong bases.

The initial pH of acetic acid is about 2.9, which is higher than the hydrochloric acid that we used in the first part (initial pH of the hydrochloric acid was 1.0).

As the sodium hydroxide is added to the acetic acid we find that it has a gentle slope and at the equivalence point the pH is 8.72, which is greater than the hydrochloric acid titration curve. The reason for this is that you really do not have a neutral solution, but instead the acetate ion is now acting as a base and it is freeing some hydroxide ions and that is the reason why the pH is greater at the equivalence point.

The equivalence point of the acetic acid was higher than the equivalence point of hydrochloric acid. The students should not be able to explain this observation, as they do not understand how the acetate anion is acting as a base. Leave this as an open question and then you may want to explain why the equivalence point's pH shifted to a higher value.

2. The changing definition of an acid and base

See *Chem Tip* after 7.b) in the *Investigate* section of this *Teacher's Edition*.

3. Is it pH balanced?

The normal pH of hair is about 5.5. Shampoos are in the range of 5 to 6. You must pick a shampoo that is compatible to your type of hair. Unfortunately, many do not pay any attention to what they use and they can do damage to their hair. A good example of a poor choice is washing your hair with hand soap, which in most cases is slightly basic. These soaps are not compatible to the human hair. Deodorants are comparable to the pH used in shampoos but they do vary.

4. Balanced or unbalanced?

Students will find a variety of claims by manufacturers of these products. For a more objective viewpoint, they should look for studies done by consumer advocate companies.

It may also be of value to their study to carry out an informal survey of their classmates' experiences with various shampoos.

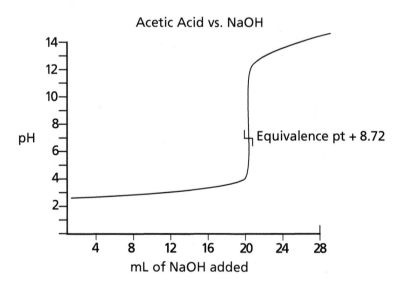

Acetic Acid vs. NaOH

SECTION 7 – QUIZ

6-7d | **Blackline Master**

1. When an acid is dissolved in water, it releases:

   a) H^+ b) OH^- c) HOH   d) M

2. pH is equal to

   a) the concentration of H^+ ions.

   b) the concentration of OH^- ions.

   c) the negative log of the concentration of H^+ ions.

   d) the negative log of the concentration of OH^- ions.

3. List three common acids and three common bases that you could find in your school or home.

4. A titration between strong acids and bases ends at the equivalence point of pH 7. A titration between a weak acid and a strong base will end at an equivalence point that has a pH of greater than 7. Explain why this happens, making sure to use the word "buffer" in your explanation.

SECTION 7 – QUIZ ANSWERS

❶ a) H^+

❷ c) the negative log of the concentration of H^+ ions.

❸ acids: battery acid, citrus fruits, vinegar, soft drinks, tomatoes, black coffee
bases: baking soda, drain cleaner, antacids, ammonia, hair remover

❹ As some of the weak acid is neutralized, some of the acid's conjugate base will be formed. The combination of weak acid and conjugate base creates a buffer solution. If more strong base is added, more conjugate base is formed and the pH changes little. If strong acid is added, the conjugate base reacts with it and again, the pH changes very little. The solution resists a change in pH so the increase in pH is more gradual. The end point will be shifted to the basic side due to the presence of the conjugate base.

CHAPTER 6

SECTION 8
Oxidation and Reduction of Metals

Section Overview

This section investigates oxidation and reduction reactions (redox) using simple Metal Activity Series replacement reactions. The students will also learn how the oxidation of one substance is accompanied by the reduction of another substance. The rusting of iron is an everyday example of a redox reaction.

Background Information

Reactions that involve a transfer of electrons are called oxidation-reduction reactions (often referred to as redox reactions). Combustion reactions, the rusting process, and many reactions that occur in the human body are examples of redox reactions.

Oxidation Numbers

In order to make sense of these reactions, the concept of oxidation numbers must be understood first. An oxidation number is equal to the charge that an atom or ion would have if all of its polar bonds were ionic. This concept is a system of bookkeeping that allows for keeping track of electrons in redox reactions by assigning charges to the various atoms in a compound. In ionic compounds, the charges are obvious because they are already identified. In a covalent compound, imaginary charges are assigned by assuming that the more electronegative atom in the compound keeps both of the bonding electrons. For this electron counting system, ignore the fact that the electrons are shared. In an HCl molecule, for example, "ownership" of the two bonding electrons is assigned to the chlorine atom which is more electronegative than hydrogen. This gives the Cl a total of 8 valence electrons. This total is

one more electron than a neutral Cl atom, so this puts an imaginary charge of 1– on the Cl. In this concept, the H has no electrons, leaving it with an imaginary charge of 1+. For oxidation numbers the ± sign gets placed before the number as opposed to ionic charges where they customarily follow the number indicating the charge. Therefore, the oxidation number of hydrogen in HCl is +1 and the oxidation number of chlorine is –1.

The oxidation number of any atom of an element is zero. For example, the oxidation numbers for oxygen, hydrogen, and bromine in O_2, H_2, and Br_2 are all zero. Similarly, if you have pure carbon in a reaction, its oxidation number is also zero.

Hydrogen has an oxidation number of +1 when bonded to nonmetals and –1 when bonded to metals. Examples are H_2O where it is +1 and LiH where its oxidation number is –1.

Oxygen usually has an oxidation number of –2 except in elemental oxygen as mentioned above. Peroxides (H_2O_2 is hydrogen peroxide) are compounds where the oxidation number of oxygen is –1. Other exceptions occur for oxygen, but these are rare.

The sum of the oxidation numbers of all the atoms in a neutral molecule must be zero, and for a polyatomic ion the sum of the oxidation numbers must equal the charge on the ion. The oxidation number of a monoatomic ion is equal to the charge of the ion.

Some atoms have variable oxidation numbers and the actual oxidation number must be calculated from the other atoms it is bound to. Nitrogen, for example, has the following oxidation numbers:

NH_3 H = +1, N = −3

NO   O = −2, N = +2

NO_2^- O = −2, N = +3

NO_3^- O = −2, N = +5

Examples of Redox Reactions

A highly exothermic process called the thermite reaction is an example of a redox reaction. The chemical equation for this reaction is:

$$2Al_{(s)} + Fe_2O_{3(s)} \rightarrow 2Fe_{(s)} + Al_2O_{3(s)}$$

In this reaction, two aluminum atoms transfer three electrons to each iron atom. The aluminum goes from an oxidation number of zero to +3. Since its oxidation number is increasing, we say it is being oxidized. The oxidation number of the iron atoms goes from +3 to zero, indicating that iron has been reduced.

Remember, a gain of electrons is a reduction (oxidation number decreases), and a loss of electrons is an oxidation. The aluminum causes the iron to be reduced, so Al is the reducing agent. The iron acts as an electron acceptor, allowing the Al to be oxidized, so Fe is the oxidizing agent.

Aluminum displaces iron in a reaction that produces so much heat that the liberated iron is molten. This process is used in the welding of large metal objects, such as the rails of a railroad track.

The thermite reaction involves ionic reactants and products, so it is easy to see the changes in oxidation numbers. It is sometimes difficult to tell whether a covalent material is oxidized or reduced. Let's consider again the combustion of hydrogen gas in the presence of oxygen:

$$2H_{2(g)} + O_{2(g)} \rightarrow 2H_2O_{(l)}$$

This is also a redox reaction where the electron transfer occurs in a different sense from the previous example. Remember that the oxidation number of any material in its elemental form is zero. Therefore, the oxidation number of both reactants is zero. Now let's look at the atoms in the product. Oxygen usually has a −2 oxidation number when combined with other atoms. If this is so (and it is), then each hydrogen atom must have a +1 oxidation number. It can be reasoned that each of the four H atoms involved has given up one electron to the two O atoms to arrive at these oxidation numbers. Knowing the oxidation numbers of all atoms before and after the reaction, you can determine what is being oxidized and what is being reduced. Each hydrogen atom goes from 0 to 1+ so it is being oxidized. The oxygen atoms go from 0 to 2− so they are being reduced.

The following phrase will help you keep oxidation and reduction straight:

OIL RIG. Oxidation Is Loss of electrons, Reduction Is Gain of electrons.

CHAPTER 6

NOTES

_____

_____

_____

_____

_____

_____

LEARNING OUTCOMES		
LEARNING OUTCOMES	**LOCATION IN SECTION**	**EVIDENCE OF UNDERSTANDING**
Cause different metals to rust by oxidation-reduction (redox) reactions.	*Investigate* Steps 1-4	Students' observations match those listed in this *Teacher's Edition*.
Determine what materials can react with metals, causing the metals to corrode.	*Investigate* Steps 1-4	Students' observations match those listed in this *Teacher's Edition*.
Write the word equations and chemical equations for redox reactions.	*Investigate* Steps 1-4 *Chem to Go* Questions 1-5	Students are able to write correct word and chemical equations for the changes they observe. Students' answers to problems match those given in this *Teacher's Edition*.
Identify the materials that react, and the materials that are simply spectators, in a redox reaction.	*Investigate* Steps 1-4	Students are able to write correct net ionic reactions for the changes they observe.
Learn how to impede corrosion.	*Chem to Go* Question 6 *Inquiring Further*	Students are able to formulate a hypothesis about why galvanized nails rust more slowly than regular nails, and then are able to design an investigation to test the hypothesis. Students research the problems with the Statue of Liberty and their resolution.

NOTES

Section 8
Materials, Chemicals, Preparation, and Safety

("per Group" quantity is based on group size of 4 students)

Materials and Equipment

Materials (and Equipment)	Quantity per Group (4 students)
Test tubes, large	4
Test-tube rack	1
Scoopula	1
Scissors	1
#2 Rubber stopper with no hole	1

Materials (and Equipment)	Quantity per Class
Pie plates, aluminum	6
Steel wool pads	6

Chemicals

Chemicals	Quantity per Class (24 students)
Zinc metal, small granules	12 g
Copper strips	7
Zinc strips	7
Copper (II) nitrate, $Cu(NO_3)_2$, 1.0 M*	100 mL
Aluminum nitrate, $Al(NO_3)_3$, 1.0 M*	100 mL
Copper (II) sulfate, $CuSO_4$, 1.0 M*	100 mL

*These solutions are placed in dropper bottles.

Teacher Preparation

Copper (II) nitrate, 1.0 M: Dissolve 24.2 g of $Cu(NO_3)_2 \cdot 3H_2O$ in 70 mL of distilled water. Dilute to 100 mL with distilled water. Store in dropper bottles for student use.

Aluminum nitrate, 1.0 M: Dissolve 37.5 g of $Al(NO_3)_3 \cdot 9H_2O$ in 70 mL of distilled water. Dilute to 100 mL with distilled water. Store in dropper bottles for student use.

Copper (II) sulfate, 1.0 M: Dissolve 25.0 g of $CuSO_4 \cdot 5H_2O$ in 70 mL of distilled water. Dilute to 100 mL with distilled water. Store in dropper bottles for student use.

Safety Requirements

- Goggles and apron are required in the laboratory area.

- Solutions can be disposed of down the drain.

- Solid metals can be disposed of in the garbage.

- Wash hands and arms before leaving the laboratory area.

CHAPTER 6

Meeting the Needs of All Students
Differentiated Instruction

Augmentation and Accommodations

LEARNING ISSUE	REFERENCE	AUGMENTATION AND ACCOMMODATIONS
Expressing a chemical equation as a sentence	*Investigate* 1.c)-d)	**Augmentation** • Teach students to work left to right to convert the equation to a sentence one symbol at a time in the same way they previously used this strategy to write a definition in their own words. Ask students to think of their own words to begin the sentence and replace the arrow. • Specifically point out the theoretical format of a single-replacement reaction given in *Section 4*, A + BC $\longrightarrow$ B + AC. • Help students see the connection between the chemical formulas in 1.d), the sentence, and the symbolic structure of the single-replacement reaction. **Accommodations** • Give students the page and paragraph in *Section 4, Chem Talk* where single-replacement reactions are explained. • Give students a word such as "combining" to begin the sentence and a phrase such as "results in the formation of" that replaces the arrow separating reactants and products.
Describing a reaction	*Investigate* 1.e)	**Augmentation** • Ask students to think of strategies they used in the previous steps to write good descriptions of this reaction. (See strategies above.) **Accommodation** • Have students write a description and compare their descriptions with a partner. Did they have the same events happening? Was the order similar? They should consolidate their descriptions into one good description that states everything that happened in the order it occurred.
Organizing the ideas in a passage for problem solving Reading comprehension	*Chem Talk* *Chem Words* *Chem Essential Questions* *Chem to Go*	**Augmentation** • Careful reading of the *Chem Talk* and *Chem Words* sections will allow students to create a frame for what they have learned about oxidation and reduction reactions. One way to organize the information is as follows: <table><tr><td></td><td>Oxidation</td><td>Reduction</td></tr><tr><td>Mnemonic device</td><td>LEO</td><td>GERrr</td></tr><tr><td>Change in number of electrons</td><td>Loses electrons</td><td>Gains electrons</td></tr><tr><td>Result of change</td><td>+ ion created</td><td>– ion created</td></tr><tr><td>Examples from equation: 4Fe + 3O$_2$ $\longrightarrow$ 2Fe$_2$O$_3$</td><td>4Fe^{3+}</td><td>6O^{2-}</td></tr></table> Students should add a row to the chart for each example they examine and problem they solve. **Accommodations** • Give students a chart to use. Model its use. • Have students use it when completing the *What does it mean?* question and *Chem to Go*.

Strategies for Students with Limited English Language Proficiency

LEARNING ISSUE	REFERENCE	AUGMENTATION AND ACCOMMODATIONS
Background knowledge	*What Do You Think?*	Students might benefit from an example of an object that is rusted, such as a bicycle wheel or a BBQ tool.
Vocabulary	*Investigate*	Have students work in partners or in small groups. Suggest that one student dictate the directions while the others read along and then take turns performing the various tasks.
Background knowledge Vocabulary Comprehending text	*Chem Talk*	Have students add the bold-face words to their *Active Chemistry* logs or personal dictionaries. Check sidebar text for further elaboration. Explain the prefix "*poly*" as in "*polyatomic* and give other examples of its use.
Background knowledge	*What Do You Think Now?*	Students might benefit from a small group discussion of the bullet item.
Background knowledge Vocabulary Comprehending text	*Chem Essential Questions*	In the *How do you know?* section, there is a yes or no question that might be good for discussion to reinforce the concepts taught.
Comprehension Vocabulary	*Chem to Go*	Check for understanding of the term "*galvanized*" and provide other uses to help build background knowledge.
Application Comprehension	*Inquiring Further*	Students may not have the term "*renovation*" in their expressive vocabulary. Other examples will be useful.

NOTES

_____

_____

_____

_____

_____

_____

_____

_____

_____

_____

_____

_____

CHAPTER 6

Section 8
Teaching Suggestions and Sample Answers

What Do You See?

The *What Do You See?* section is an opportunity to engage the students and not to worry about whether the student responses are correct. Listen for evidence of prior knowledge, conceptions and misconceptions.

In viewing the color illustration, students may comment that it appears to be a magic show based on the formal clothing and the white rabbit. They may anticipate that the section involves color changes.

What Do You Think?

Students should have a pretty good idea what rust is but what causes it to form may be more difficult. While some may know that oxygen from air is necessary, most may not be aware that moisture must be present in order for rust to form. If iron is stored in a dry environment, it will not rust even though oxygen is present.

Cool Chemistry Show

Section 8 — Oxidation and Reduction of Metals

Learning Outcomes

In this section you will

- Cause different metals to rust by oxidation-reduction (redox) reactions.
- Determine what materials can react with metals, causing the metals to corrode.
- Write the word equations and chemical equations for redox reactions.
- Identify the materials that react, and the materials that are simply spectators, in a redox reaction.
- Learn how to impede corrosion.

⚠️ Safety goggles and a lab apron must be worn at all times in a chemistry lab.

What Do You See?

What Do You Think?

A scratch on a car that is not repaired will rust. The same thing will happen to metal barbecue tools that get left out in the rain for a few weeks.

- What is rust and what causes it?

Record your ideas about these questions in your *Active Chemistry* log. Be prepared to discuss your responses with your group and the class.

Investigate

1. Half fill a test tube with copper (II) sulfate solution ($CuSO_4$(aq)). Add a small amount of zinc powder to the test tube. Stopper the test tube, and shake carefully. Then remove the stopper.

   a) Record your observations. Dispose of the products as directed by your teacher.

   b) The reaction you just observed was a single-replacement reaction. The zinc replaced the copper. Use this information and your observations to complete the following equations:

   zinc + copper (II) sulfate → _____ + _____

532

What Do You Think?
A CHEMIST'S RESPONSE

Rust is formed by the oxidation of iron in the presence of moisture. It is a reddish, flaky substance with the formula, Fe_2O_3. While many metals will corrode and form an exterior layer of oxide, rust becomes a serious problem because it flakes off from the metallic iron underneath. This exposes more unreacted iron to oxygen and moisture, allowing the process to continue until the iron loses its strength and its usefulness.

STUDENTS' PRIOR CONCEPTIONS

Antoine-Laurent Lavoisier originally defined oxidation as a reaction involving oxygen where oxides are formed. The modern definition describes these reactions as causing electron transfer between atoms, or a change in oxidation numbers of the atoms.

This difference can cause confusion. Although the process was named after oxygen, oxygen is not a required participant in all oxidation reactions.

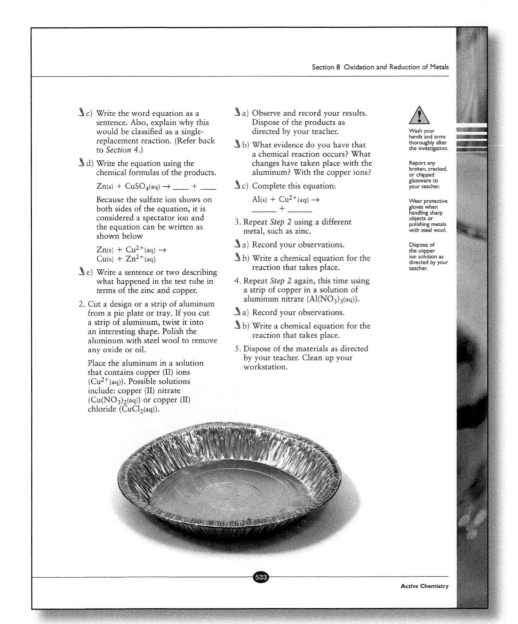

Section 8 Oxidation and Reduction of Metals

c) Write the word equation as a sentence. Also, explain why this would be classified as a single-replacement reaction. (Refer back to *Section 4.*)

d) Write the equation using the chemical formulas of the products.

$$Zn_{(s)} + CuSO_{4(aq)} \rightarrow \_\_\_\_ + \_\_\_\_$$

Because the sulfate ion shows on both sides of the equation, it is considered a spectator ion and the equation can be written as shown below

$$Zn_{(s)} + Cu^{2+}_{(aq)} \rightarrow$$
$$Cu_{(s)} + Zn^{2+}_{(aq)}$$

e) Write a sentence or two describing what happened in the test tube in terms of the zinc and copper.

2. Cut a design or a strip of aluminum from a pie plate or tray. If you cut a strip of aluminum, twist it into an interesting shape. Polish the aluminum with steel wool to remove any oxide or oil.

Place the aluminum in a solution that contains copper (II) ions ($Cu^{2+}_{(aq)}$). Possible solutions include: copper (II) nitrate ($Cu(NO_3)_{2(aq)}$) or copper (II) chloride ($CuCl_{2(aq)}$).

a) Observe and record your results. Dispose of the products as directed by your teacher.

b) What evidence do you have that a chemical reaction occurs? What changes have taken place with the aluminum? With the copper ions?

c) Complete this equation:

$$Al_{(s)} + Cu^{2+}_{(aq)} \rightarrow$$
$$\_\_\_\_ + \_\_\_\_$$

3. Repeat *Step 2* using a different metal, such as zinc.

a) Record your observations.

b) Write a chemical equation for the reaction that takes place.

4. Repeat *Step 2* again, this time using a strip of copper in a solution of aluminum nitrate ($Al(NO_3)_{3(aq)}$).

a) Record your observations.

b) Write a chemical equation for the reaction that takes place.

5. Dispose of the materials as directed by your teacher. Clean up your workstation.

⚠

Wash your hands and arms thoroughly after the investigation.

Report any broken, cracked, or chipped glassware to your teacher.

Wear protective gloves when handling sharp objects or polishing metals with steel wool.

Dispose of the copper ion solution as directed by your teacher.

533

Active Chemistry

Investigate

1.a)

Students should note the original solution was blue. After the addition of the zinc granules, they will notice a change in the surface of the zinc as it reacts with the copper ions in the solution. The solution may become a lighter blue color or completely colorless, depending on how much zinc was added.

1.b)

zinc + copper (II) sulfate $\rightarrow$ copper + zinc sulfate

1.c)

The zinc replaces the copper in the copper sulfate solution to form a solution of zinc sulfate. This is an example of a single-replacement reaction.

1.d)

$$Zn_{(s)} + CuSO_{4(aq)} \rightarrow$$
$$Cu_{(s)} + ZnSO_{4(aq)}$$

1.e)

The copper (II) ions gain electrons and are being reduced to copper metal. The zinc metal is losing electrons as it is oxidized to zinc ions. The blue color of the solution becomes lighter due to the decrease in the number of copper ions remaining in solutions.

2.a)

The solution will again become lighter as the copper plates out on the aluminum.
(Note: The aluminum should have been polished with steel wool before inserting it in the copper solution.)

2.b)

Evidence of a reaction is shown by the precipitation of copper metal and the aluminum metal being consumed. Also, the color of the solution becomes a lighter blue. The aluminum is being oxidized and dissolving in the solution as aluminum ions. The copper ions are being reduced and coming out of solution as copper metal.

2.c)

$$2Al_{(s)} + 3Cu^{2+}_{(aq)} \rightarrow$$
$$3Cu_{(s)} + 2Al^{3+}_{(aq)}.$$

In this reaction the total electron transfer is six electrons. Here are the half-cell reactions:

$$2Al_{(s)} \rightarrow 2Al^{3+}_{(aq)} + 6e^-[\text{Oxidation reaction}]$$

$$3Cu^{2+}_{(aq)} + 6e^- \rightarrow 3Cu_{(s)} [\text{Reduction reaction}]$$

If you add the two equations you see that the electrons subtract out and the net ionic equation is obtained. The sulfate ions are spectator ions and do not appear.

Active Chemistry **359**

3.a)

The reaction is the same as that of the aluminum with the copper, but with zinc taking the role of the aluminum. The copper plates out on the zinc metal and the solution becomes a lighter blue. The zinc particles decrease in size as they are oxidized to zinc ions.

3.b)

$Zn_{(s)} + Cu^{2+}{}_{(aq)} \longrightarrow Cu_{(s)} + Zn^{2+}{}_{(aq)}$

4.a)

No apparent reaction has taken place.

4.b)

There is no chemical reaction and no chemical equation. The Metal Activity Series chart tells us that copper cannot be oxidized in a solution of aluminum nitrate.

Chem Talk

This section discusses redox reactions in terms of oxidation and reduction. The process of rust formation is covered in detail. Other examples of oxidation are introduced.

Cool Chemistry Show

Chem Talk

REDOX REACTIONS

When zinc metal reacts with copper ions in solution, a reaction occurs. Atoms of zinc lose electrons to form zinc ions (Zn^{2+}) that dissolve in the solution. Copper ions (Cu^{2+}) gain the electrons from the zinc atoms to form copper atoms that plate out as a solid. Whenever an atom or ion becomes more positively charged in a chemical reaction, as in the case of zinc atoms forming positive zinc ions, the process is called **oxidation**. Oxidation is the process of losing electrons. Whenever an atom or ion becomes less positively charged in a chemical reaction, as in the case of the copper ions forming copper atoms, the process is called **reduction**. Reduction involves a gain of electrons. The processes of oxidation and reduction happen together and as such are commonly referred to as **"redox" reactions**. An easy way to remember which is oxidation and which is reduction is by remembering "LEO the lion says GERrr,"—Lose Electrons Oxidation; Gain Electrons Reduction.

Chem Words

oxidation: the process of a substance losing one or more electrons.

reduction: the process of a substance gaining one or more electrons.

redox reaction: a chemical reaction where both oxidation and reduction occur simultaneously.

The formation of rust is a redox process. Water and oxygen are necessary for the iron metal to corrode (rust). Iron atoms lose electrons to form mostly Fe^{3+} ions with the help of the moisture in the air and the heat of the Sun. Because the atoms have given up electrons to become more positively charged, oxidation of iron has taken place. Molecules of oxygen gain electrons to form O^{2-} ions. The oxygen has accepted electrons and is said to have been reduced. Corrosion can be prevented by painting a surface of iron to prevent moisture and air from coming in contact with the metal.

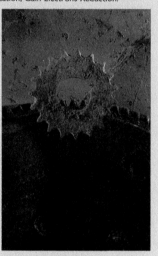

To summarize what you have learned about atoms and ions:

The term atom means that the element is neutral; this means that it has the same number of protons and electrons.

Ions mean that the atom (or ion) has gained or lost electron(s). When an atom gains or loses one or more electrons, an ion results.

Examples are

$Na \rightarrow Na^+ + e^-$ (Sodium atom loses one electron and now has a net charge of +1.)

$Cl_2 + 2e^- \rightarrow 2Cl^-$ (The two chlorine atoms gain one electron each and the net charge is −1 for each chloride ion.)

Polyatomic ions like the sulfate ion ($SO_4{}^{2-}$) imply that there are two more electrons than protons in the entire structure.

In some cases you will find that an ion can gain or lose an electron and form a new ion. An example of this type is $Fe^{2+} \rightarrow Fe^{3+} + e^-$ (The iron in the +2 state loses 1 more electron and now will be in a +3 state.)

Checking Up

1. What change in charge does an ion have when it is oxidized?

2. What change in charge does an ion have when it is reduced?

3. Explain what happens in a redox reaction.

What Do You Think Now?

At the beginning of this section you were asked the following:

• **What is rust and what causes it?**

How has your understanding of rusting changed from when you first answered these questions?

How do you think you could slow down the oxidation process involved in the corrosion and destruction of things made from metal?

535

Checking Up

1.

An ion will have a positive charge on it as a result of oxidation. If it had a charge on it before oxidation, the new charge will be more positive (less negative).

Examples: $Na \rightarrow Na^+ + e^-$
and
$Fe^{2+} \rightarrow Fe^{3+} + e^-$

2.

An ion will have a negative charge on it as a result of reduction. If it had a charge on it before reduction, the new charge will be more negative (less positive).

Examples: $Cl_2 + 2e^- \rightarrow 2Cl^-$
and
$Fe^{3+} + e^- \rightarrow Fe^{2+}$

3.

In a redox reaction, two processes are occurring simultaneously. One substance is losing electrons and is being oxidized. A second substance is gaining those electrons and is being reduced.

What Do You Think Now?

This is an opportunity to return to the illustration of *What Do You See?* and *What Do You Think?* questions and review the original responses. Students will be able to respond to the illustration and the questions at a higher level than before. This realization will enhance their understanding and their confidence in making progress.

"How do you think you could slow down the oxidation process involved in the corrosion and thus the destruction of things made from metal?"

The simplest way to avoid oxidative processes would be to prevent the oxidizing agent (oxygen) from reaching the reducing agent (metal). Sealing, painting, and oiling all prevent oxidation. Using knowledge from other chapters and other sections, students may suggest that oxidation could be slowed by changing the rate of reaction through a lower temperature or by removing the oxygen. In essence, painting a metal object is the same as removing the oxygen. For iron, specifically, removal of all moisture will stop the reaction.

CHAPTER 6

Chem Essential Questions

What does it mean?

MACRO — When the oxidation-reduction reaction occurred, there were changes in the solution color and in the appearance of the metal.

NANO — Oxidation is the loss of electrons from a reactant during a chemical reaction. Reduction is the addition of electrons to a reactant during a chemical reaction.

Electron flow is from the substance being oxidized (the reducing agent) to the substance being reduced (the oxidizing agent).

SYMBOLIC —

$Na \longrightarrow Na^+ + e^-$ oxidation

$Cl + e^- \longrightarrow Cl^-$ reduction

$4Fe + 3O_2 \longrightarrow 2Fe_2O_3$

Both oxidation (Fe) and reduction (O_2)

$2Al_2O_3 \longrightarrow 4Al + 3O_2$

Both oxidation (O) and reduction (Al)

How do you know?

Metals have extra electrons (positive oxidation numbers) and thus tend to lose electrons. An example is how iron is easily oxidized to form iron oxide (rust). Nonmetal elements do not normally oxidize as they can achieve the stable gas electron configuration by gaining electrons (reduction).

Why do you believe?

Student answers will vary. Examples are rust, color change in foods (such as apples), batteries, the burning of fuels and metabolic processes.

Why should you care?

Student answers will vary. A good example that is interesting is the corrosion of aluminum when placed in a solution of copper (II) chloride.

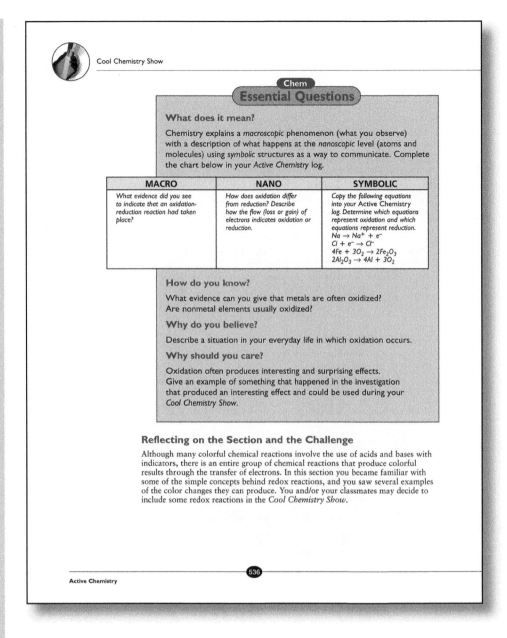

Cool Chemistry Show

Chem Essential Questions

What does it mean?

Chemistry explains a *macroscopic* phenomenon (what you observe) with a description of what happens at the *nanoscopic* level (atoms and molecules) using *symbolic* structures as a way to communicate. Complete the chart below in your *Active Chemistry* log.

MACRO	NANO	SYMBOLIC
What evidence did you see to indicate that an oxidation-reduction reaction had taken place?	How does oxidation differ from reduction? Describe how the flow (loss or gain) of electrons indicates oxidation or reduction.	Copy the following equations into your Active Chemistry log. Determine which equations represent oxidation and which equations represent reduction. $Na \rightarrow Na^+ + e^-$ $Cl + e^- \rightarrow Cl^-$ $4Fe + 3O_2 \rightarrow 2Fe_2O_3$ $2Al_2O_3 \rightarrow 4Al + 3O_2$

How do you know?

What evidence can you give that metals are often oxidized? Are nonmetal elements usually oxidized?

Why do you believe?

Describe a situation in your everyday life in which oxidation occurs.

Why should you care?

Oxidation often produces interesting and surprising effects. Give an example of something that happened in the investigation that produced an interesting effect and could be used during your *Cool Chemistry Show*.

Reflecting on the Section and the Challenge

Although many colorful chemical reactions involve the use of acids and bases with indicators, there is an entire group of chemical reactions that produce colorful results through the transfer of electrons. In this section you became familiar with some of the simple concepts behind redox reactions, and you saw several examples of the color changes they can produce. You and/or your classmates may decide to include some redox reactions in the *Cool Chemistry Show*.

536

Active Chemistry

Reflecting on the Section and the Challenge

At the conclusion of the section and its various parts, it is useful for the students to pause and review what has been learned and how the chemistry could be integrated into the *Chapter Challenge*. You might wish to do this as a group exercise so that the teams could work together. If time permits, the students could briefly report back to the class and potentially generate new ideas.

Section 8 Oxidation and Reduction of Metals

Chem to Go

1. Aluminum metal can react to form an ion with a charge of +3. Does the aluminum atom gain or lose electrons to form the Al^{3+} ion?

2. A copper ion with a charge of +2 can react to form an atom of copper. Does the copper ion have to gain or lose electrons in this reaction?

3. The element iron can form two different ions. The iron (II) ion (Fe^{2+}) is commonly called a ferrous ion while the iron (III) ion (Fe^{3+}) is called a ferric ion. When ferrous ions undergo a chemical change to become ferric ions, what process has taken place, oxidation or reduction? Explain your answer.

4. In the reaction you did with zinc metal reacting with copper ions, which substance gains electrons? Which loses electrons?

5. What must take place for copper metal to be oxidized?

6. Galvanized iron nails are used to fasten materials that will be exposed to the outdoors. A galvanized nail is a regular iron nail that is coated with zinc.

   a) Why would a zinc coating be an advantage here? What do you think is the purpose of the zinc?

   b) What two reactants could you use to test this in the laboratory? What results would you expect if you were right about the purpose of the zinc?

7. When a zinc metal strip is placed in a blue copper (II) nitrate solution, the blue solution disappears. Explain why this is happening.

8. Which reaction is not an example of an oxidation-reduction reaction?

   a) $AgNO_3 + KI \rightarrow AgI + KNO_3$ b) $Cu + 2AgNO_3 \rightarrow Cu(NO_3)_2 + 2Ag$

   c) $Fe_2O_3 + 2Al \rightarrow Al_2O_3 + 2Fe$ d) $Ba + 2HCl \rightarrow BaCl_2 + H_2$

Inquiring Further

The Statue of Liberty

In the 1980s the Statue of Liberty in New York harbor underwent extensive renovation. Research the involvement of oxidation-reduction reactions in this renovation. Identify what the problem was and its solution.

537

Active Chemistry

Chem to Go

1.

The aluminum metal must lose three electrons and this is called oxidation. The oxidation equation:

$$Al_{(s)} \rightarrow Al^{3+}_{(aq)} + 3e^-$$

2.

The copper ion must gain two electrons in order to become copper metal and this process is called reduction. The reduction equation is:

$$Cu^{2+}_{(aq)} + 2e^- \rightarrow Cu_{(s)}$$

3.

The ferrous ion must lose one electron in order to form ferric ions. This process is oxidation. The oxidation equation is:

$$Fe^{2+}_{(aq)} \rightarrow Fe^{3+}_{(aq)} + e^-$$

4.

The copper ions gains two electrons and the zinc metal loses two electrons. The half reactions are:

$$Zn_{(s)} \rightarrow Zn^{2+}_{(aq)} + 2e^-$$
[Oxidation]

$$Cu^{2+}_{(aq)} + 2e^- \rightarrow Cu_{(s)}$$
[Reduction]

$$Zn_{(s)} + Cu^{2+}_{(aq)} \rightarrow Cu_{(s)} + Zn^{2+}_{(aq)}$$
[Overall ionic equation]

5.

The copper must be in an environment where it can lose electrons. The metal solution must be a solution that has a metal that is less active than copper. Silver nitrate solution would cause copper metal to oxidize.

6.a)

Zinc metal is more susceptible to oxidation than iron, but it does not flake off. It will protect the iron nail as long as it remains intact on the surface of the iron.

6.b)

Place a galvanized nail in a beaker of water with a nail which is not galvanized. Determine which nail rusts more quickly.

7.

The blue color of the copper (II) nitrate solution is caused by the hydrated Cu^{2+} ion. As the copper is reduced to metallic copper, these ions are removed from solution, decreasing the intensity of the color. If enough zinc is added, eventually the solution will no longer be blue. The hydrated Zn^{2+} ion is colorless.

CHAPTER 6

8.

Answer a) is not an example of an oxidation-reduction reaction. It is a double-replacement reaction.

Inquiring Further

The Statue of Liberty

The restoration of the Statue of Liberty from 1984 to 1986 showed that oxidation-reduction (redox) reactions were an important factor in the need for this restoration. However, it was not the copper surface of the statue that suffered long-term effects from the environment. Due to the protective coating of copper compounds, the copper "skin" of the statue lost only 0.005 inches in the first 100 years.

Greater damage was done in the interior structure where copper and iron came in contact. Due to galvanic corrosion, up to one-half of the iron was oxidized to non-supportive iron salts. In the restoration, the iron was replaced by less-reactive steel. Also, Teflon was used to insulate the steel from the copper to prevent the corrosion process.

Galvanic corrosion is a spontaneous process when two metals of differing activity are in contact. The more reactive metal (iron) will be oxidized while trace salts of the less reactive metal (copper) are deposited through reduction.

SECTION 8 – QUIZ

| 6-8a | Blackline Master |

1. Is the corrosion of a metal an oxidation reaction or reduction reaction? Explain.

2. What conditions will make an iron nail rust?

   a) Heating it to 500°C or more

   b) Leaving it out in the rain

   c) Covering it with a coating of zinc

   d) Painting it

3. What is the complete equation for the oxidation of iron metal to the +3 oxidation state with oxygen?

4. Which of the follow reactions shows aluminum being used as a reducing agent?

   a) $2Al + 3Cl_2 \rightarrow 2AlCl_3$

   b) $Al_2O_3 + 6HCl \rightarrow 2AlCl_3 + 3H_2O$

   c) $3K + Al(NO_3)_3 \rightarrow 3KNO_3 + Al$

   d) $Al_{(s)} \rightarrow Al_{(l)}$

SECTION 8 – QUIZ ANSWERS

❶ Metal corrosion is an oxidative process. The atoms go from a state of 0 charge to ions with positive charges. An example is:

$2Mg_{(s)} + O_{2(g)} \rightarrow 2MgO_{(s)}$

❷ b) Leaving it out in the rain.

❸ $4Fe_{(s)} + 3O_{2(g)} \rightarrow 2Fe_2O_{3(s)}$

❹ a) $2Al + 3Cl_2 \rightarrow 2AlCl_3$

NOTES

Chem You Learned

The chemistry content covered in this chapter is listed in the *Student Edition* at the end of the chapter. This could be a good time to evaluate your students' comprehension of the material. You may then want to suggest that they help each other in reviewing those concepts that may need reinforcement. You may also want to point out to students that the *Chem You Learned* section is a handy checklist of the chemistry concepts they might want to incorporate into their *Chapter Challenge*.

Cool Chemistry Show

Chem You Learned

- In general, a **physical change** is a process where a substance's chemical properties have not changed.
- A **chemical change** occurs when new substances or materials are produced that have different chemical properties from the reactants.
- **Chemical tests** are used to identify substances and also to confirm that a chemical reaction has taken place.
- A typical **single-replacement reaction** occurs when an active metal reacts with a strong acid to produce hydrogen gas.
- Formation of a **precipitate** is commonly seen in **double-replacement reactions** and is a method to identify the presence of specific ions in a solution.
- Using **acid-base indicators** is a simple, quick method to determine the **pH** of a solution.
- The periodic table aids in writing **chemical formulas** by organizing the symbols for elements, as well as providing information about **oxidation states**.
- **Polyatomic ions**, such as **carbonate** (CO_3^{2-}), carry an overall **ionic** charge but internally the atoms are **covalently** bonded.
- **Chemical equations** are a shorthand method of writing the **reactants** and **products** of a reaction. **The law of conservation of mass** requires that the equation be **balanced**.
- **Endothermic** and **exothermic** reactions are commercially used in cold and hot packs.
- **Chemical kinetics** or **chemical rates of reactions** are dependent on several factors: **surface area** of reactants, **temperature**, **concentration**, and presence of a **catalyst**.
- **Strong acids** and **strong bases** are 100% ionized while **weak acids** and **weak bases** are partially ionized.
- **pH** is used to determine the concentration of **hydrogen ions (hydronium ions)** of a solution.
$$pH = -\log[H^+]$$
- When several indicators covering the entire **pH** range are mixed together they form a **universal indicator** solution.
- The definition of acid and base has evolved from that of **Arrhenius** who defined an acid as a compound that releases hydrogen ions and a base as releasing hydroxide ions.
- **Brønsted-Lowry** defined acids as proton donors and bases as proton acceptors.
- Finally, **Lewis** provided the most general definition, stating that acids are electron pair acceptors and bases are electron pair donors.
- **Oxidation-reduction** or **redox reactions** involve the equal transfer of electrons between the elements. If iron is in the presence of oxygen and moisture it will **oxidize** (commonly called rust) while the oxygen is correspondingly **reduced**.
- A **single-replacement reaction** is another example of an oxidation-reduction reaction.

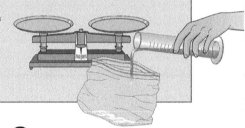

Chem
Chapter Challenge

As you assemble ideas and information for your *Chapter Challenge* you will be completing a second round of the *Engineering Design Cycle*. The *Goal* and criteria remain unchanged; however, your list of *Inputs* has grown. You now have much more chemistry information and new concepts that may help you complete your *Cool Chemistry Show*. You also have the *Feedback* you received during the *Mini-Challenge* to help guide your efforts. Your class may want to revise the way it coordinates the contribution from each group depending on how well the *Mini-Challenge* presentations went.

Goal

You have already outlined one *Cool Chemistry Show* as a class. As you complete the *Chapter Challenge* you will use the *Engineering Design Cycle* to improve and complete that show or create a brand new one. The *Goal* is the objective you are trying to reach or the problem you need to solve in the *Engineering Design Cycle*. Go back and quickly read the challenge description at the start of the chapter. You will find all of the details for completing the entire challenge there. You should also review the rubric your class generated to determine the way your group's contribution to the show

will be graded. Now that you have a deeper understanding of the chemistry involved, your class and your instructor may want to revise the rubric to emphasize specific aspects of each demonstration. You will want to make sure you address each aspect of the rubric completely so your team can earn the highest possible grade.

Each demonstration in the *Cool Chemistry Show* will need to meet the same criteria:

• An entertaining and informative demonstration of acids, bases, or colorful chemical reactions for fourth- and fifth-graders

• A set of written instructions including complete list of materials, expected observations, and safety considerations

• An explanation of the chemistry for the target audience

• A thorough explanation of the chemistry in your demonstration including reaction equations, other example reactions, and additional observations or background materials.

Inputs

The *Inputs* for the *Engineering Design Cycle* include all of the resources you have to help you complete the *Chapter Challenge*. The constraints for this challenge are also *Inputs* for your *Engineering Design Cycle*. Each of the chapter sections has provided you with information on physical and chemical properties or about chemical reactions that will help you to explain your chemistry demonstrations. The section activities also provided you with some colorful examples of chemical reactions to include in your show. Your team will have to supply some creativity to ensure that your demonstration is not only informative but also entertaining.

All of the *Inputs* for this challenge will help determine the success of the *Cool Chemistry Show* your class produces. As your group

539

Cool Chemistry Show Chapter Challenge

A brief review of the *Chapter Challenge* reminds students that the chemistry show they will be creating must be geared for fourth-or-fifth grade students and address the specific subject matter that is outlined. Although the demonstration and presentation target a younger audience, the written directions and explanation of the chemistry concepts are for the teacher and should be at a high-school level.

Chemistry Content

A list reviewing the various sections contained in this chapter provides a useful summary of the chemical concepts that were covered by these investigations. This list can be helpful in generating ideas for the *Cool Chemistry Show* and as a map to help students locate material related to specific concepts.

CHAPTER 6

Criteria for Success

Now that students have completed the *Mini-Challenge* and are preparing to start the *Chapter Challenge*, they will need to determine how their projects will be graded by developing a comprehensive assessment rubric. It is essential that students actively participate in deciding the criteria so they are in agreement as to the expectations and how they will be graded. Their involvement in determining the criteria will also instill a sense of ownership in most students, thereby boosting enthusiasm and commitment.

On the next page is a sample assessment rubric for the *Chapter Challenge*. This rubric is also provided as a Blackline Master on the *Teacher Resources CD*. You can copy and distribute the rubric as a foundation for developing scoring guidelines and expectations that suit your needs. For example, you might wish to ensure that core concepts and abilities derived from your local or state science frameworks also appear on the rubric.

Students may choose a scoring system as simple as ascribing points to each of the types of criteria. For example, Content value could be worth 50 points, Presentation value 30 points, and Group Interaction value worth 20 points. Although there is likely to be some differences among the students, it is important to get a majority to agree on the criteria for

evaluation, the guidelines for scoring and the general point distribution for the rubric.

However you decide to evaluate the *Chapter Challenge*, keep in mind that all expectations should be communicated to students at the start of their work.

Cool Chemistry Show

reviews the chemistry you have learned, be sure to pay special attention to the *Reflecting on the Section and the Challenge, Chem Essential Questions*, and *Preparing for the Chapter Challenge* portions of the text. You should also review your *Active Chemistry* log for notes that you recorded during each section. The brief section summaries listed here will give you an overview of the information you have learned to help get you started.

Section 1 You discussed chemical and physical changes.

Section 2 You learned about more chemical changes, including tests for gases and indicator tests for acids and bases.

Section 3 You studied how to use chemical names and formulas properly, as well as the difference between ionic and molecular compounds.

Section 4 You investigated four types of reactions (synthesis, decomposition, single-replacement, and double-replacement).

Section 5 You observed energy changes when matter changed and identified the change as either exothermic endothermic.

Section 6 You discovered conditions that make a reaction proceed faster or slower and explained this at the molecular level.

Section 7 You investigated acids and bases, read about different definitions of acids, and categorized acids and bases using the pH scale.

Section 8 You demonstrated oxidation-reduction reactions and wrote word and chemical equations for redox reactions.

Process

The *Process* step of the *Engineering Design Cycle* is where you turn your ideas into products. Your product for this challenge will be a dramatic presentation of chemical reactions for fourth- and fifth-graders. Your team must provide an entertaining and informative demonstration for your young audience. Teaching anyone involves giving them information in a way that allows them to use it later on. Teaching

younger students to understand something you have learned will require you to simplify the information for them, which is harder than it sounds.

Teachers, like engineers, use models to help organize and present information. One model teachers may use is the 7E instructional model. There are seven E's to remind teachers to address each of the seven steps that help students learn, so that when they present information they know they are presenting it in a way that is proven to help students. The 7E model is a process for teaching much the same way the *Engineering Design Cycle* is a process for solving design problems.

Because this design challenge requires you to become the teacher, try to use the 7E model to build your presentation. The first E is for *engage*—get the learners attention focused on the subject. Your demonstration should get their attention, some type of drama usually well received. The second E is *elicit*, which means finding out what students already know about the topic. The third E is for *explore*. This is the time to introduce new information related to your demonstration. *Explain* is the next E, so you make connections and explain the observations that were made during your demonstration. *Elaborate* is the next E; you can elaborate by giving examples where students may see a similar reaction in their daily lives. The next E stands for *extend*. Put forward some idea or concept for students to investigate or ponder that is related but beyond the scope of your presentation (usually an open-ended question that requires some effort to answer). The final E is for *evaluate*, which means finding out if your message is reaching the audience. You might ask them to "remind" you of one of the important steps or some other important piece of the information you have presented. Evaluation can take place throughout the lesson; it does not have to be the final step. Like the *Engineering Design Cycle*, which can send you back to the *Input* phase to find a better solution, sometimes an evaluation will trigger the instructor to go back and review an idea that is confusing to the audience.

You might use an evaluation question to see if you have presented your message at the right

Active Chemistry

540

The *Sample Assessment Rubric* is also provided as a Blackline Master on the *Teacher Resources CD*.

6b	Blackline Master

SAMPLE ASSESSMENT RUBRIC FOR CHAPTER 6

	MEETS THE STANDARD OF EXCELLENCE	APPROACHES THE STANDARD OF EXCELLENCE	MEETS AN ACCEPTABLE STANDARD	BELOW ACCEPTABLE STANDARD
CONTENT CRITERIA				
Chemistry Concepts	At least six chemistry concepts are accurately incorporated into the show. **30**	At least four chemistry concepts are accurately incorporated into the show. **20-29**	At least three chemistry concepts are accurately incorporated. **10-19**	One or two chemistry concepts are applied. **0-9**
Explanation	Clear explanations detailing how each chemical procedure works are provided. **15**	Explanations are provided, but they lack somewhat in clarity. **10-14**	Explanations are incomplete or unclear. **5-9**	Explanations are inaccurate or are not provided. **0-4**
Written Summary	A thorough and well-written summary of all procedures and related chemical principles is provided. **15**	A summary of all chemical procedures is provided, but it is not clear or is not complete, or has some grammatical errors. **10-14**	The summary provided lacks some important information or is inaccurate or is not well written. **5-9**	A summary is not provided or is missing vital information, is inaccurate or poorly written. **0-4**
PRESENTATION CRITERIA				
Procedure/ Design	Procedures for the chemistry show are safe, accurate, and effectively demonstrate the chemical principles. **15**	Procedures are safe, accurate, and adequately demonstrate the chemical principles. **10-14**	Procedures are theoretically sound, but need to be redesigned to effectively demonstrate the chemical principles. **5-9**	Procedures are inaccurate and do not effectively demonstrate the chemical principles. **0-4**
Demonstration	Chemistry show demonstration is creative, well-crafted, and has high entertainment value. **15**	Demonstration is well-conceived and has good entertainment value. **10-14**	Demonstration lacks somewhat in effect but has some interest value. **5-9**	Demonstration is ineffective and/or does not have interest value. **0-4**
GROUP INTERACTIONS				
Group Interaction	Group members work together productively in a joint cooperative effort, each member contributing equally. **10**	Group members showed effort to work constructively, but interactions lacked cooperative teamwork. **6-9**	Some group members worked constructively, but overall effort lacked teamwork effectiveness. **3-5**	There is no indication of group interaction to work together constructively or cooperatively. **0-2**

CHAPTER 6

Preparing for the Chapter Challenge

The *Chapter Challenge* is the opportunity for students to review all the material in the chapter and find a creative way of interpreting that content. The *Preparing for the Chapter Challenge* sections in the text guide the students toward a successful project and the pages in the front matter of this *Teacher's Edition* provide the instructional rationale for this problem-based learning model.

In the *Chapter Challenge* preparations, remind students that the best presentations will not only be entertaining and effective, but they should also demonstrate a working knowledge of the chemistry content. The more chemistry concepts that can be successfully included in their chemistry show, the stronger their presentation.

Prior to students beginning the *Chapter Challenge*, you should repeat the discussion you had at the start of the chapter and have the class agree on the rubric and standards for excellence.

Allow time for students to review the *Manage Your Time* section at the end of the chapter and make sure that they allow enough time to accomplish the tasks and that all members of each group actively participate. Also remind them that they will only have five minutes for the demonstration so their show should be well rehearsed, with all components labeled and arranged in order of use.

No doubt many of the *Cool Chemistry Show* projects created by the students will be highly entertaining as well as informational. You may want to put together a presentation of some of the most impressive projects to be viewed by a larger audience so that other students, teachers, and administration members can enjoy the effort, creativity, and knowledge shown.

NOTES

_____

_____

_____

_____

_____

_____

_____

_____

_____

_____

_____

level for the fourth- or fifth-graders. You may want to have a simpler explanation ready, or a tougher question ready in case you misjudged slightly. A live audience is always full of surprises and unexpected responses. The better you are prepared, the better you can respond to the unexpected.

Outputs

The products that you deliver during an *Engineering Design Cycle* are the *Outputs*. The *Outputs* for this challenge is your demonstration in the *Cool Chemistry Show*. Your presentation will need to address four distinct components to be successful:

- The entertaining and informative presentation
- Written instructions and safety precautions
- The explanation that is targeted for the student audience
- A written explanation of the chemistry principles for the teachers

Your group should make sure that you have included each component listed in the class rubric for your presentation. The rubric will clearly describe the products you must deliver to earn the points associated with that component. Plan to have each person of your group contribute equally to the final project. Because time will be limited, make sure that everyone has a role that allows them to be working during the entire time. Set deadlines for each product so that you will have time to review everybody's work as a group and make any necessary corrections prior to your final presentation. If someone is having difficulty getting their part done, ask how you can share the work to get the job done. Assisting a struggling teammate is part of teamwork. Make sure you follow a plan for success!

Feedback

Your instructor and your classmates will give you *Feedback* on your demonstration based on the criteria of the *Cool Chemistry Show*. This *Feedback* will likely become part of your grade, indicating how successful your group was at meeting the *Chapter Challenge*, but could also be useful for additional design iterations. Don't forget, you will be viewing other design solutions for the same challenge. The different group presentations may represent *Feedback* in the form of presenting alternatives you may have included in your show design. The variety of design solutions should reflect the fact that there are endless ways to satisfy the challenge criteria.

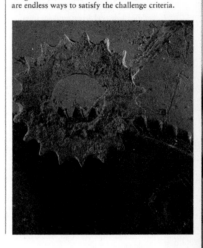

541

the first time it is tried. Students will have to troubleshoot and experiment, and in some cases will need to make adjustments and modifications. For example, their first try at putting on a show may take too long or may not have all the desired results. Their efforts at this point would be to modify the procedure so that it goes faster, or is more effective. It would then be appropriate to rehearse the show to ensure that their modifications did in fact effect improvements.

Students should be well equipped to do this because they will understand some of the underlying chemical principles, and so will be able to make intelligent predictions and approach modifications with a deeper understanding of why results will change when conditions are altered.

Engineering Design Cycle

Have students revisit the *Engineering Design Cycle* they applied to the *Mini-Challenge* for their first-try chemistry shows. What adjustments will they need to make to achieve success in the *Chapter Challenge*? Now that students know more about chemical reactions and have a better understanding of the chemical principles behind them, they can incorporate this information to improve their design by beginning the design cycle again.

The *Chapter Challenge* asks students to design a process in order to develop a chemistry show based on the chemistry they have learned in this chapter. Rarely will students conceive of a process that works perfectly

Chem Connections to Other Sciences

Students gain understanding of the interdisciplinary aspects of chemistry when they are actively engaged in thinking about the connections between the sciences. This section provides a glimpse of the interconnections between the content in this chapter and other scientific disciplines. Brief sketches relate students' study of chemistry concepts to biology, physics, and Earth science.

Encourage students to draw analogies with science connections they are familiar with while discussing the science connections. The chemistry concepts discussed in this chapter hold true in every branch of science, and can provide scientists in other fields with new insights. Emphasize the growing interdisciplinary approach to science and the need for scientists who have a broader view of science. Discuss how scientists try to understand phenomena by studying a problem from different points of view. Encourage the appreciation for chemistry in relation to the broader framework of science by describing the increase in demand for scientists with interdisciplinary backgrounds (for example, geochemistry, biochemistry, and chemical physics).

Consider developing an interdisciplinary lesson plan that investigates how key chemistry concepts are applied in different sciences. Groups would select

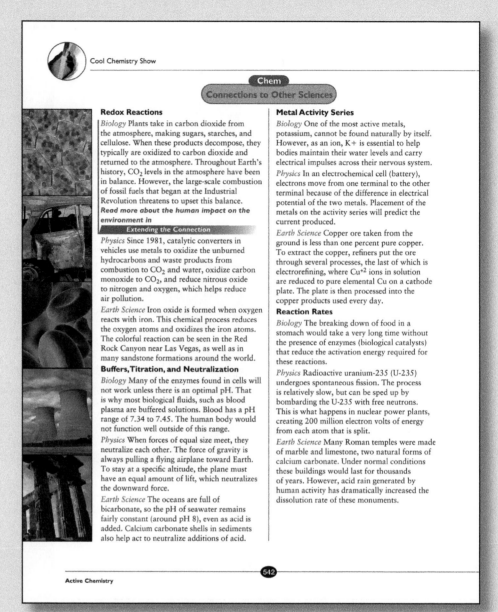

Cool Chemistry Show

Chem Connections to Other Sciences

Redox Reactions

Biology Plants take in carbon dioxide from the atmosphere, making sugars, starches, and cellulose. When these products decompose, they typically are oxidized to carbon dioxide and returned to the atmosphere. Throughout Earth's history, CO_2 levels in the atmosphere have been in balance. However, the large-scale combustion of fossil fuels that began at the Industrial Revolution threatens to upset this balance. **Read more about the human impact on the environment in**

Extending the Connection

Physics Since 1981, catalytic converters in vehicles use metals to oxidize the unburned hydrocarbons and waste products from combustion to CO_2 and water, oxidize carbon monoxide to CO_2, and reduce nitrous oxide to nitrogen and oxygen, which helps reduce air pollution.

Earth Science Iron oxide is formed when oxygen reacts with iron. This chemical process reduces the oxygen atoms and oxidizes the iron atoms. The colorful reaction can be seen in the Red Rock Canyon near Las Vegas, as well as in many sandstone formations around the world.

Buffers, Titration, and Neutralization

Biology Many of the enzymes found in cells will not work unless there is an optimal pH. That is why most biological fluids, such as blood plasma are buffered solutions. Blood has a pH range of 7.34 to 7.45. The human body would not function well outside of this range.

Physics When forces of equal size meet, they neutralize each other. The force of gravity is always pulling a flying airplane toward Earth. To stay at a specific altitude, the plane must have an equal amount of lift, which neutralizes the downward force.

Earth Science The oceans are full of bicarbonate, so the pH of seawater remains fairly constant (around pH 8), even as acid is added. Calcium carbonate shells in sediments also help act to neutralize additions of acid.

Metal Activity Series

Biology One of the most active metals, potassium, cannot be found naturally by itself. However, as an ion, K+ is essential to help bodies maintain their water levels and carry electrical impulses across their nervous system.

Physics In an electrochemical cell (battery), electrons move from one terminal to the other terminal because of the difference in electrical potential of the two metals. Placement of the metals on the activity series will predict the current produced.

Earth Science Copper ore taken from the ground is less than one percent pure copper. To extract the copper, refiners put the ore through several processes, the last of which is electrorefining, where Cu^{+2} ions in solution are reduced to pure elemental Cu on a cathode plate. The plate is then processed into the copper products used every day.

Reaction Rates

Biology The breaking down of food in a stomach would take a very long time without the presence of enzymes (biological catalysts) that reduce the activation energy required for these reactions.

Physics Radioactive uranium-235 (U-235) undergoes spontaneous fission. The process is relatively slow, but can be sped up by bombarding the U-235 with free neutrons. This is what happens in nuclear power plants, creating 200 million electron volts of energy from each atom that is split.

Earth Science Many Roman temples were made of marble and limestone, two natural forms of calcium carbonate. Under normal conditions these buildings would last for thousands of years. However, acid rain generated by human activity has dramatically increased the dissolution rate of these monuments.

542

Active Chemistry

a topic and determine how it relates to biology, physics, and Earth science based on their reading of *Chem Connections to Other Sciences*, and how it relates to the key chemistry concepts. A set of questions can be constructed for students to focus on, allowing them to build a constructive inquiry. A group member could write down the highlights of their discussion. Once students have recorded the focal points of their group discussions, bring together the whole class and have a volunteer from each group share the major points of their discussion of science connections.

Extending the Connection

THE HUMAN TOLL ON THE ENVIRONMENT

Redox Reactions that Change Our World

Matter is neither created nor destroyed in chemical reactions, but it can be transferred, rearranged, and transformed. One example of this phenomenon is the biogeochemical cycling of carbon dioxide gas (CO_2) as it moves between rocks, water, living organisms, and the atmosphere. Naturally occurring CO_2 is released into the atmosphere from animal and plant respiration, organic decay, ocean processes, and volcanic eruptions. These sources have been releasing CO_2 into the atmosphere over geologic time. There also are naturally occurring sinks that remove CO_2 from the atmosphere. The most significant of these processes is photosynthesis, which is performed by land and ocean plants and certain bacteria.

The cycling of CO_2 between sources and sinks has been going on for millions of years and is linked to global climate cycles. Increases in the concentration of atmospheric CO_2 cause increases in the average temperature of Earth because CO_2 acts as a greenhouse gas, trapping the heat energy given off by Earth.

What is causing these increased levels of CO_2 in the atmosphere? The burning of fossil fuels (coal and petroleum for example) for industry, electricity, and transportation is one of the most significant sources of increased atmospheric CO_2 concentrations, with almost 1.4 metric tons per person per year released to the atmosphere.

This statistic is especially staggering when taking into consideration the environmental effects of increased CO_2 levels. Some scientists believe that as the temperature of Earth's atmosphere (and thus the oceans) increases, there could be changes in wind and climate patterns, growing seasons, ocean currents, and rainfall patterns.

Melting polar ice caps are another very serious consequence of increasing global temperatures, because ice reflects the Sun's energy and helps keep Earth cool. Fresh water from melted ice may alter global ocean circulation patterns. Flooding would be a serious problem because nearly 10 percent of the world's population lives in areas that are considered low-lying.

The long-term effects of the global climate change are not yet well understood. Not everyone feels the increase in atmospheric CO_2 is caused by humans or that the increase in Earth's temperature is other than the normal cycle that Earth has experienced many times before. Many factors other than the amount of CO_2 need to be taken into account when understanding Earth's climate system. →

Extending the Connection

The *Chem Connections to Other Sciences* show students that the chemistry concepts they studied in each chapter are also basic to many other sciences. The chemistry they are learning is fundamental in the understanding of the concepts that they will study in all the other sciences. *Extending the Connection* delves deeper into one or two of these connections. It gives students an opportunity to examine a particular relationship to another science in greater depth.

CHAPTER 6

Cool Chemistry Show

Ozone Depletion

Over the course of several decades, people released large amounts of chlorofluorocarbons (CFCs) into the atmosphere. The most common uses of CFCs are as refrigerants in air conditioners and propellants in aerosol cans and fire extinguishers. The original refrigerants were highly toxic, so they were replaced with the CFCs that are so harmless to humans that a person can inhale them without any negative effects. They are also very stable, which makes them easy to handle and last a long time. Society did not realize the effect these synthetic molecules would have on the environment, but scientists now know they destroy ozone molecules. Stratospheric ozone plays an important role in absorbing high-energy ultraviolet (UV) radiation from the Sun. UV radiation causes skin cancer, eye damage, and can damages cells, plants, and the DNA molecule required for cellular reproduction.

However, this protective shield is being destroyed. The bonds that hold the CFCs in place are extremely strong and will remain in the atmosphere a long time before decomposing. UV radiation coming from the Sun has enough energy to break those bonds, releasing atomic chlorine radicals, which break down the ozone molecules. Over the decades, enough CFCs have escaped into the atmosphere to create a hole in the ozone over Antarctica.

Human Activity and the Waterways

The atmosphere is not the only place on Earth that has experienced large-scale environmental effects from human activity. Waterways have been affected as agriculture and industry use them as part of their waste system. There has been increased use of pesticides and fertilizers, which run off the land and into streams, rivers, lakes, and eventually oceans. At the mouth of the Mississippi river there is a "dead zone" where no animals can survive. Fertilizer runoff from the Mississippi drainage system caused algae to grow so much it robbed the water of oxygen. Marine life can no longer thrive there, and a once-robust fishing industry in the region has been drastically reduced.

Industrial waste and unintentional spills have released toxins into the water system that can never be contained. Many toxic synthetic chemicals and heavy metals also seep into the groundwater, polluting the surrounding environment and draining into the water system. Some of these toxins bioaccumulate, causing damage to whole food chains. The story of Love Canal is an example. In the early 1950s, several thousand tons of toxic waste was buried in a New York canal. The property was later sold for housing. Unknown to the residents, the toxins were seeping into the water system. There were an unusual number of miscarriages and birth defects reported among the residents in the 1970s. The Love Canal disaster became a story of local activism, and a mass environmental cleanup.

Chem at Work

Dr. Bassam Shakhashiri

Professor of Chemistry—University of Wisconsin–Madison, Chairman for the Wisconsin Idea

"Science is Fun" reads the T-shirt of Dr. Bassam Shakhashiri. It appears fun when he works with Bucky Badger, the 6-foot tall mascot of the University of Wisconsin, at his annual Christmas science show. But if you talk to Dr. Shakhashiri candidly, he will probably tell you that demonstrating science is all about preparation and hard work (in spite of his T-shirt).

Over the last 35 years, Dr. Shakhashiri has demonstrated science to over 1,100 audiences worldwide. On several occasions his shows have been nationally televised. He has put on large public demonstrations at the National Academy of Sciences, the Smithsonian Museum in Washington, and Boston's Museum of Science.

He is an educator for all ages. People from age 5 to 85 enjoy his displays. On stage, the principles of chemistry come to life through smoking beakers and chemiluminescence. "Young kids are especially curious. They see changing colors and bubbles and they want to know 'why is that?' They are seeking explanations."

Careful planning is at the heart of every show. "When I do a demonstration, I follow a carefully designed plan. I remember my professor who failed in a demonstration in front of a hundred students. I don't want that to happen to me." It's that memory that fuels the doctor's need for careful planning.

He doesn't have a secret. He is not overly dramatic or flamboyant. Dr. Shakhashiri is an educator. He goes on stage armed with science knowledge and genuine enthusiasm. These are the powerful tools he uses to reach an audience. His audiences react in kind. "I feed off the expressions on their faces. I tell them I wish I could take their picture."

Cathy Culver

Chemist, Tarrytown, NY

Cathy Culver, a chemist, is the resident expert on drink colors at the Pepsi Cola Corporation. One of Cathy's favorite activities is to give color demonstrations to students. The students help her create new flavors of soda (like peanut butter and jelly, buttered popcorn, mint chocolate-chip and bubble gum) and then use chemistry to color them accordingly.

Ken Furstoss

Event Coordinator, Pyrotecnico, New Castle, PA

Ken Furstoss is trained as a jet pilot, not a chemist. However, his current job is all about oxidation reactions. Ken is a salesperson and a producer at Pyrotecnico, Inc. The company produces some of the biggest and best fireworks displays in the country, including the fireworks at the Philadelphia Eagles home games.

543

Active Chemistry

Chem at Work

Some of the chemical procedures prescribed in the previous sections are performed every day by average people doing their jobs. This section provides some examples of how the chemical principles learned in this chapter are applied in the everyday workplace.

As the *Chem at Work* profiles demonstrate, chemistry is relevant to a wide range of professions and an equally wide range of professionals. There are no geographic, ethnic, or educational specifications for people using chemistry. They do not all wear white lab coats or have advanced degrees; many are average people whose jobs may not seem to be related to chemistry at all.

For example, one may not think that an event coordinator for a fireworks production company would have much to do with chemistry. Students may also be surprised to learn that the colors of the carbonated beverages that they drink are determined by someone applying chemical principles. You may want to have students discuss how chemistry might be involved in some of the occupations that they are interested in.

For your convenience, all three full-length *Chem at Work* profiles are provided as Blackline Masters on the *Teacher Resources CD*.

6c Blackline Master

6d Blackline Master

6e Blackline Master

CHAPTER 6

Chem Practice Test

The *Chemistry Practice Test* is provided as a Blackline Master on your *Teacher Resources CD*.

6f　**Blackline Master**

Content Review

1. b

2. d

3. b

4. d

5. a

6. d

7. c

8. c

9. c

10. d

Cool Chemistry Show

Chem
Practice Test

Content Review

On a separate sheet of paper answer the following.

1. Which one of the following is classified as a chemical change?
   a) evaporating water
   b) burning gasoline
   c) shredding paper
   d) crushing solid coal

2. A block of dry ice (CO_2) is placed on a lab table. You observe that carbon dioxide gas is released by sublimation (solid vaporizes to a gas). Which of the following is correct?
   a) This is an exothermic process.
   b) This is an irreversible reaction.
   c) A chemical change takes place.
   d) This is an endothermic process.

3. When equal volumes of two different solutions are mixed together a precipitate forms. Based on this information, you conclude that

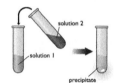

solution 2

solution 1

precipitate

   a) a physical reaction has taken place.
   b) a chemical reaction has taken place.
   c) solids form when excess volumes are added together.
   d) when common ions combine, they will solidify.

4. The correct formula for potassium bromide is
   a) KBr_2.
   b) K_2Br.
   c) K_7Br.
   d) KBr.

5. The correct formula for aluminum nitrate is
   a) $Al(NO_3)_3$.
   b) $AlNO_3$.
   c) Al_3NO_3.
   d) $Al_3(NO_3)_3$.

6. Total number of atoms contained in iron (II) ammonium sulfate, $Fe(NH_4)_2(SO_4)_2$, is
   a) 5.
   b) 11.
   c) 19.
   d) 21.

7. The correct formula for ammonium hydrogen carbonate is
   a) NH_4CO_3.
   b) $(NH_4)2HCO_3$.
   c) NH_4HCO_3.
   d) $NH_4(CO_3)_2$.

8. What are the correct coefficients needed in order to balance the following equation?
   $$\_Zn(s) + \_HCl(aq) \rightarrow \_H_2(g) + \_ZnCl_2(aq)$$
   a) 1, 1, 1, 1
   b) 1, 1, 2, 1
   c) 1, 2, 1, 1
   d) 1, 1, 1, 2

544

9. Oxygen and hydrogen react with an explosion to form water when they are mixed together and ignited with a spark. Which of the following potential energy diagrams best represents this reaction?

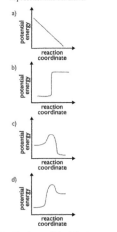

a)

b)

c)

d)

10. Which one of the following processes is exothermic?
   a) $H_2O(l) \rightarrow H_2O(g)$
   b) $H_2O(s) \rightarrow H_2O(g)$
   c) $H_2O(s) \rightarrow H_2O(l)$
   d) $H_2O(l) \rightarrow H_2O(s)$

11. Which of the following factors should not have any effect on the rate of the reaction?
   a) temperature
   b) density
   c) concentration
   d) catalyst

12. When carbon dioxide is dissolved in water, the pH of the solution will
   a) become more basic.
   b) become neutral.
   c) become greater than the pH of water.
   d) become acidic.

13. When hydrochloric acid is added to zinc metal, what gas is released?

HCl

Zn

   a) H_2
   b) Cl_2
   c) HCl
   d) $ZnCl_2$

14. Red litmus will turn blue when the solution being tested is
   a) acidic.
   b) neutral.
   c) basic.
   d) saturated.

15. If a strong acid is added to a buffer system, it reacts with the _____ to maintain a constant _____.
   a) weak base; pH
   b) weak acid; pH
   c) strong base; volume
   d) weak base; volume

16. If the pH of a solution is 1 and the solution is then diluted to a pH of 2, the hydrogen ion concentration of the diluted solution becomes
   a) 2 times greater than the original hydrogen ion concentration.
   b) 2 times weaker than the original hydrogen ion concentration.
   c) 10 times weaker than the original hydrogen ion concentration.
   d) 10 times greater than the original hydrogen ion concentration.

545

Active Chemistry

11. b

12. d

13. a

14. c

15. a

16. c

17. d

18. b

19. a

20. b

CHAPTER 6

Critical Thinking

21.a)

To change the pentahydrate form to the anhydrous form you will need to dehydrate the compound.

21.b)

Students will probably classify this as a physical change. They may state that since both compounds are solids and only the formula has been changed, the change should be classified as a chemical reaction. A good defense should receive credit.

21.c)

$Cu^{2+} \, SO_4{}^{2-}$

22.a)

$Ba(NO_3)_2(aq) + Na_2SO_4(aq) \rightarrow 2NaNO_3(aq) + BaSO_4(s)$

22.b)

Barium sulfate forms a precipitate because it is insoluble in water.

22.c)

Barium nitrate is soluble because all nitrates are soluble.

23.

10 mL of 0.1 M NaOH will neutralize the 10 mL of 0.1 M HCl. The pH will be 7 because a strong base is being added to a strong acid.

24.a)

As the nature of the solid is broken up, it allows for more surface area to be able to react favorably.

24.b)

An increase in the temperature increases the kinetic energy of the particles in the system, which in turn increases rate of the reaction.

24.c)

If the concentration of the reactants is increased, it will increase the chance for a successful collision, leading to reaction.

25.

The overall equation is
$Zn(s) + Cu^{2+}(aq) \rightarrow Zn^{2+}(aq) + Cu(s)$
The copper is reduced, and as the copper ion concentration decreases, the blue solution gradually fades. The blue color is a result of the concentration of the hydrated copper ions present in the solution.

Cool Chemistry Show

Practice Test *(continued)*

For *Questions 17–19*, use the following net ionic equation:

$\_ Zn(s) + \_ Cu^{2+}(aq) \rightarrow \_ Zn^{2+}(aq) + \_ Cu(s)$

17. When the equation is balanced, the correct coefficients are
    a) 1, 1, 1, 2.
    b) 1, 1, 2, 1.
    c) 1, 2, 1, 1.
    d) 1, 1, 1, 1.

18. In this reaction, you can say that the zinc metal
    a) gained two electrons.
    b) loses two electrons.
    c) gained two protons.
    d) loses two neutrons.

19. In this reaction, you can say that copper was
    a) reduced.
    b) oxidized.
    c) acidified.
    d) neutralized.

20. A strong acid reacts with a strong base. Choose the equivalence point from the graph below.

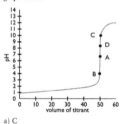

    a) C
    b) A
    c) D
    d) B

Critical Thinking

On a separate sheet of paper answer the following.

21. Copper (II) sulfate changes from sulfate pentahydrate ($CuSO_4 \cdot 5H_2O$) to anhydrous copper (II) sulfate ($CuSO_4$).
    a) Explain how you would accomplish a change from one form to the other.
    b) Would this be a physical or a chemical change?
    c) Write the chemical formula for the ions present in $CuSO_4$.

22. When clear solutions of barium nitrate and sodium sulfate are mixed together, a white precipitate forms.
    a) Write a balanced equation for the reaction.
    b) Which products forms a precipitate and why?
    c) Is barium nitrate soluble in water? Explain your answer.

23. How many milliliters of 0.1 M NaOH must you add to 10 mL of 0.1 M HCl in order to neutralize the acid? What pH would the neutral solution have? Explain your answer.

24. Certain factors usually affect reaction rates. Discuss how each of the following factors can affect the reaction rate.
    a) size of solid reactant particles
    b) increase in temperature
    c) increase in the concentration of the reactants

25. If a strip of zinc metal is placed in a test tube that contains a blue solution of copper nitrate and allowed to stand, the copper will plate out on the zinc strip and the solution will lose its blue color. Explain what occurs in this reaction and why the solution loses its blue color.

546

Active Chemistry

COOKIN' CHEM

Chapter 7

CHAPTER 7
COOKIN' CHEM
Chapter Overview

Chapter Challenge

This chapter challenges students to create a segment of a television cooking show that explores the chemistry behind the cooking involved. Their presentation can be live action, a videotape, or a voice-over of an actual cooking show. In addition, students will submit scripts for their presentations that include descriptions of the chemistry involved. This chapter introduces a number of chemical concepts that students could include in their segment.

Cookin' Chem begins with an investigation into methods of heat transfer using a light bulb and pinwheel. After this investigation, students design and conduct an experiment that demonstrates the flow of thermal energy into a cooking potato. The remaining activities take students through topics such as combustion reactions, calorimetry, phase changes, specific heats of metals (and how they relate to cookware), protein denaturation, and understanding the structure of organic molecules. These topics can all be directly related to cooking and therefore, are key to the *Chapter Challenge*.

Chapter Summary

- Learn how chemical concepts are involved in cooking and how the explanation of these concepts can enhance a cooking show.

- Learn how to use scientific inquiry and how to develop conclusions from the data and evidence collected.

- Learn how to use instruments and make precise measurements.

- Understand how to carry out mathematical calculations.

- Gain awareness that chemistry is involved in everyday activities and that an understanding of chemical principles can enrich our lives.

KEY SCIENCE CONCEPTS

SECTION SUMMARIES	CHEMISTRY PRINCIPLES
Section 1: Heat Transfer: What Is Heat? By studying the heat from a light bulb, the three ways in which heat can be transferred are explored. A distinction is made between heat and temperature. Heat transfer is also discussed by examining a partially cooked potato. Examples that demonstrate convection, conduction, and radiation in the home are identified.	Heat and heat transfer Convection, Conduction Radiation, Heat energy Kelvin scale, Absolute zero Calories, Temperature Joules, Celsius
Section 2: Combustion Reactions and Hydrocarbons By observing an unlit and lit candle, the necessary features that support combustion are shown. This knowledge is used to discuss the control of combustion reactions.	Balancing chemical equations Combustion reactions, Catalysts Hydrocarbons, Chemical change Law of Conservation of Mass Reactants, Products
Section 3: Thermochemistry and Cooking Fuels Using an insulated container containing water, the heat content of several fuels are measured. This leads to a discussion of how energy is stored in fuels and how it is released.	Thermochemistry Exothermic, Endothermic Activation energy Bond energy, Joules Mole concept, Energy diagram Hydroxyl group, Alcohols Specific heat capacity System, Surroundings
Section 4: Phase Changes and the Heating Curve of Water By taking data and graphing a heating curve, the heat of vaporization and phase changes are explored. The effect of pressure on the boiling point is examined.	Energy of phase changes Heat of vaporization, Condensation Boiling point, Heating curves Physical change, Endothermic Exothermic, States of matter
Section 5: Phase Changes and the Cooling Curve of Water By taking data and graphing a cooling curve, the heat of fusion and phase changes are explored. The section also provides graphing skills practice.	Cooling curves Heat of fusion/crystallization Melting point Energy of phase changes
Section 6: Calorimetry and Specific Heat Capacity The properties of several substances (Cu, Fe, Al, plastics, glass, and ceramics) are examined. The section also explores specific heat and principles of heat transfer.	Specific heat capacity Calorimetry Conduction Alloys
Section 7: Denaturation: How Do Proteins in Foods Change? Raw egg protein is denatured in two ways—with heat by boiling in water and by pH change with acid. The structures of primary, secondary, and tertiary proteins are examined.	Organic molecules Denaturation Proteins, Amino acids Primary, secondary, tertiary structure Molecular formula Structural formula Functional group
Section 8: Modeling Organic Molecules: Soap Using model kits, organic molecules of increasing complexity are constructed, and the VSEPR Theory is used to determine the geometry of these structures. A soap molecule is modeled and the micelle is introduced.	Molecular models, Lewis diagrams Organic molecules, Double bond Triple bond, Covalent bonding Valence electrons, Isomers Functional groups, VSEPR Theory Carboxylic acid group, Cis/trans Bonding electrons Nonbonding electrons Line bond structures Saturated and unsaturated hydrocarbons Micelle, Tetrahedron

Chapter Concept Map

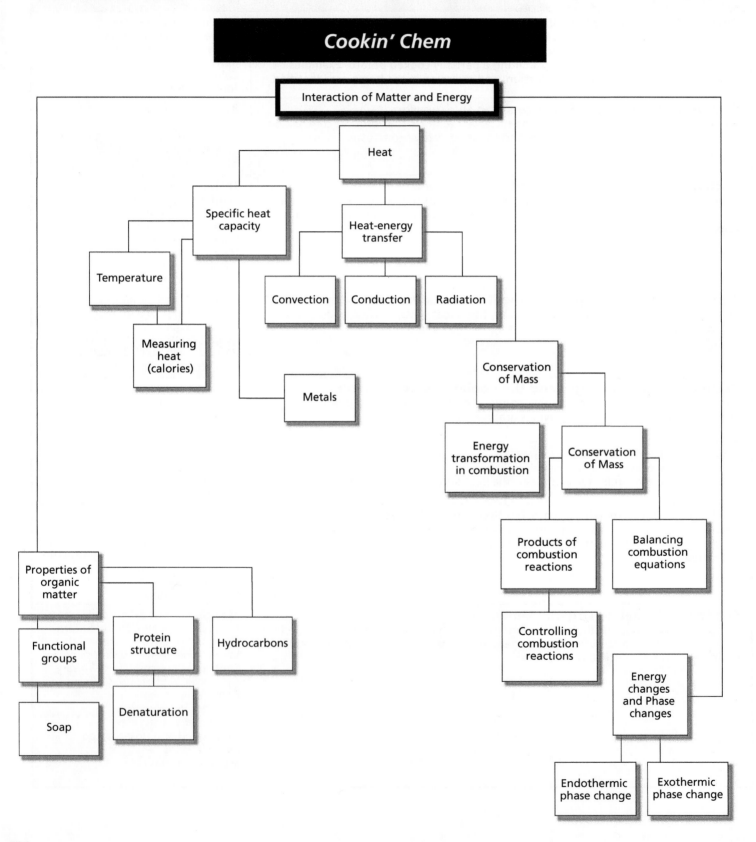

Cookin' Chem

Interaction of Matter and Energy

Heat

Specific heat capacity

Temperature

Measuring heat (calories)

Metals

Heat-energy transfer

Convection

Conduction

Radiation

Conservation of Mass

Energy transformation in combustion

Conservation of Mass

Products of combustion reactions

Balancing combustion equations

Controlling combustion reactions

Energy changes and Phase changes

Endothermic phase change

Exothermic phase change

Properties of organic matter

Functional groups

Soap

Protein structure

Denaturation

Hydrocarbons

UNDERSTANDING BY DESIGN*

The *Understanding by Design* template focuses on the three stages of backward design:
- **Identify desired results**
- **Determine acceptable evidence**
- **Plan learning experiences**

What overarching understandings are desired?

- Cooking involves chemistry.
- Different fuels release varied amounts of energy.
- Pots and pans are constructed of different materials to aid in our cooking.
- Cooking involves heat and requires safety.
- Organic molecules have specific shapes that relate to their function.

What are the overarching "essential" questions?

- What kind of chemistry is involved in cooking?
- What safety issues are common to chemistry and cooking?
- How can cool acids "cook" foods?
- What happens to food when we cook it?
- Why do we need so many types of pots and pans?
- What is unique about the shape of a soap molecule?

What will students understand as a result of this chapter?

- Cooking involves numerous chemical principles.
- The nature of heat energy.
- The differences between convection, conduction and radiation.
- The effect of heat on matter.
- How to write and balance combustion reaction equations.
- The role of oxygen and carbon dioxide in combustion reactions.
- How to measure the energy content of various fuels.
- Heating curves for ice, water and vapor.
- Safe practices in the lab and in the kitchen.
- Choice of cookware is determined by the properties of matter.
- How a soap molecule is able top clean grease and dirt.

What "essential" questions will focus this chapter?

- What is heat energy?
- How do convection, conduction and radiation heat food?
- What is the difference between heat and temperature?
- What safety issues are involved in cooking?
- How can one compare the energy of different cooking fuels?
- What temperature changes take place as ice turns to water and water turns to steam?
- Why do we use cast-iron pans or copper-clad pans for cooking?
- How does a soap molecule cause grease to dissolve in water?

* Grant Wiggins and Jay McTighe, *Understanding by Design* (Merrill/Prentice Hall, 1998), 181.

Pacing Guide

This chapter may take 4–5 weeks to complete, assuming a full 5-day school week. Keep in mind that a *Pacing Guide* is merely a suggestion and that you should adjust your pace to your students' needs and the school schedule.

A sample outline is shown below. It assumes that you will assign homework every day and that class time will be used to discuss homework and special topics. *Inquiring Further* activities, if assigned, will allow students to do research or investigations outside regular class time.

Note: Each "Day" assumes a 45-minute class period, or one-half of a 90-minute block.

DAY	SECTION	HOMEWORK
1	Discuss *Scenario, Your Challenge,* and *Criteria for Success* Develop a scoring rubric. **Section 1** Discuss *What Do You See?* and *What Do You Think?* Students complete *Investigate* Parts A and B. Review the results of the investigation.	Read *Chem Talk* and answer *Checking Up* questions. Answer *What Do You Think Now?* questions.
2	Discuss *Chem Talk* and review *Checking Up* answers. Discuss *What Do You Think Now?* Discuss *Chem Essential Questions.* Answer *Chem to Go* questions 1-3 in class.	Answer *Chem to Go* problems 4-11. Read *Reflecting on the Section and the Challenge.*
3	Review *Chem to Go* answers. **Section 2** Discuss *What Do You See?* and *What Do You Think?* Students complete *Investigate.* Review results of investigations.	Read *Chem Talk* and answer *Checking Up* questions. Answer *What Do You Think Now?* questions.
4	Discuss *Chem Talk* and review *Checking Up* answers. Discuss *What Do You Think Now?* responses. Discuss *Chem Essential Questions.* Answer *Chem to Go* problems 1 and 3.	Answer *Chem to Go* problems 2, 4-10. Read *Reflecting on the Section and the Challenge.* Read Section 3 *Investigate* Part A and design a procedure.
5	Review *Chem to Go* answers. **Section 3** Discuss *What Do You See?* and *What Do You Think?* Students complete *Investigate* Part A (or B) and C. Review results of the investigation.	Read *Chem Talk* and answer *Checking Up* questions. Answer *What Do You Think Now?* questions.
6	Discuss *Chem Talk* and review *Checking Up* answers. Discuss *Chem Essential Questions* and *What Do You Think Now?* responses. Answer *Chem to Go* problems 1 and 3.	Answer *Chem to Go* problems 2, 4-11. Read *Reflecting on the Section and the Challenge.* Read *Chapter Mini-Challenge.*
7	Review answers to *Chem to Go.* Discuss the *Chapter Mini-Challenge* and have groups work on presentations.	Student groups work on *Chapter Mini-Challenge* presentations.
8	Students present *Chapter Mini-Challenges* and receive feedback on their presentations. **Section 4** Discuss *What Do You See?* and *What Do You Think?* Students complete *Investigate.* Review results of investigation.	Read *Chem Talk* and answer *Checking Up* questions. Answer *What Do You Think Now?* question.

DAY	SECTION	HOMEWORK
9	Discuss *Chem Talk* and review *Checking Up* answers. Discuss *Chem Essential Questions* and *Reflecting on the Section and the Challenge*. Answer *Chem to Go* problem 1 in class.	Answer *Chem to Go* problems 2-8. Read *Reflecting on the Section and the Challenge*.
10	Review *Chem to Go* answers. **Section 5** Discuss *What Do You See?* and *What Do You Think?* Students complete *Investigate* Part A. Review results of investigation.	Read *Chem Talk* and answer *Checking Up* questions. Answer *What Do You Think Now?* questions.
11	Students complete *Investigate* Part B. Review the results of the investigation. Discuss *Chem Talk* and review the *Checking Up* answers. Answer *Chem to Go* problem 1.	Answer *Chem Essential Questions* and *Chem to Go* problems 2-9. Read *Reflecting on the Section and the Challenge*.
12	Discuss *Chem Essential Questions* and review *Chem to Go* answers. **Section 6** Discuss *What Do You See?* and *What Do You Think?*	Read *Investigate* and outline the procedure.
13	Students complete *Investigate*. Discuss the results of the investigation.	Read *Chem Talk* and answer *Checking Up* questions. Answer *What Do You Think Now?* questions.
14	Discuss *Chem Talk* and review *Checking Up* answers. Discuss *What Do You Think Now?* responses and *Chem Essential Questions*. Answer *Chem to Go* problems 1 and 3.	Answer *Chem to Go* problems 2, 4-10. Read *Reflecting on the Section and the Challenge*.
15	Review *Chem to Go* answers. **Section 7** Discuss *What Do You See?* and *What Do You Think?* Students complete *Investigate*. Discuss results of the investigation.	Read *Chem Talk* and answer *Checking Up* questions. Answer *What Do You Think Now?* question.
16	Discuss *Chem Talk* and review *Checking Up* answers. Discuss *What Do You Think Now?* responses and *Chem Essential Questions*. Answer *Chem to Go* problem 1.	Answer *Chem to Go* problems 2-5. Read *Reflecting on the Section and the Challenge*.
17	Review *Chem to Go* answers and discuss *Reflecting on the Section and the Challenge*. **Section 8** Discuss *What Do You See?* and *What Do You Think?* Students complete the *Investigate* Parts A and B. Review the results of the investigation.	Read *Chem Talk* through **Valence Shell Electron Pair Repulsion Theory** and answer *Checking Up* questions 1 and 2.
18	Discuss *Chem Talk* and review the *Checking Up* answers. Students complete *Investigate* Parts C, D, and E. Review the results of the investigations.	Read the remaining *Chem Talk* and answer *Checking Up* question 3. Answer *Chem to Go* problems 1-3.
19	Discuss *Chem Talk* and *Chem Essential Questions*. Review the *Checking Up* and *Chem to Go* answers. Discuss the *What Do You Think Now?* question.	Answer *Chem to Go* problems 4-10. Read *Reflecting on the Section and the Challenge*. Read *Preparing for the Chapter Challenge*.
20	Review *Chem to Go* answers. Discuss *Preparing for the Chapter Challenge*. Work on the *Chapter Challenge*.	Work on the *Chapter Challenge* in groups.
21	*Chapter Challenge* presentations by students.	

Chapter 7
Materials, Equipment, and Chemicals

The following tables contain lists of materials, equipment, and chemicals needed to do all of the activities. The tables are organized as follows:

- **Table 1:** Durables per group (4 Students)
- **Table 2:** Durables per class
- **Table 3:** Consumables per group (4 Students)
- **Table 4:** Consumables per class
- **Table 5:** Chemicals

Durables are items which are not consumed during the activity and which can be used for several classes over several years. **Consumables** are items that are used up during each class and must be resupplied for future classes. Both the durables and consumables are broken down by group and by class. A **Group** consists of four students. While the group size will be determined by the teacher based upon logistics and availability of equipment, the information in Table 1 and Table 3 is based upon the recommended group size of four students.

Materials and Equipment

The first table contains the **durable** items needed **per group.** The right-hand column, **Quantity,** contains the number of items needed per group. The left-hand column, **Section,** gives the section number(s) in which each item will be used.

The item quantities given are considered to be a minimum but, in some cases, if more are available, that would be ideal.

The second table contains the information on **Durables** needed **per class** (recommended class size is 24 students). In some cases, these will be items that are shared by the class. For example, a balance with a precision of 0.01 g. Two balances (or more) are recommended to avoid long wait times and students lining up to use a balance. If necessary, a single balance will do.

The third and fourth tables contain the items which are **consumable.** The third table contains **consumables per group** (recommended group size is four students) and the fourth table contains **consumables per class.**

TABLE 1: DURABLES PER GROUP (4 STUDENTS)		
Section	**Materials and Equipment (Durables)**	**Quantity**
All	Lab aprons	4
All	Safety goggles	4
1	25-watt incandescent bulb	1
1	75-watt incandescent bulb	1
1	Bulb socket with electrical plug	1
1, 3	Burette clamp	1
1	Pencil with eraser, pkg of 10	1
1	Straight pin	1
1	Pinwheel pattern (see Blackline Master)	1
1, 2, 3, 8	Scissors	1
1	Knife (plastic okay)	1
1, 2, 6	Crucible tongs	1
1, 3, 4	Ringstand	1
1, 3, 4, 5, 6	Thermometer or temperature probe	1
1, 4, 5, 6, 7	Hot plate	1
1, 4, 5, 6, 7	Wire gauze squares for hot plate	2
1, 7	Beaker, 1 L	1
1, 2, 8	Ruler	1
2	Scoopula	1
2	Cardboard squares (4" x 4") covered with foil	1
2	Graduated cylinder, 50 mL	1
2, 4	Beaker, 250 mL	1
2, 5	Test tube, large	1
2, 5	Test-tube rack	1
3	Alcohol burner	1
3	Extension clamp for burner	1
3	Glass stirring rod, 12"	1
3	Support ring, $2\frac{1}{2}$"	1
3, 4, 5, 6	Graduated cylinder, 100 mL	1
5	Beaker, 400 mL	1
6	Set of metals: iron, copper, aluminum, zinc, other	1

TABLE 2: DURABLES PER CLASS

Section	Materials and Equipment (Durables)	Quantity
6	Screen support for metal slugs	1
3, 6	Balance, 0.01 g	2
8	Molecular model classroom set	1

TABLE 3: CONSUMABLES PER GROUP (4 STUDENTS)

Section	Materials and Equipment (Consumables)	Quantity
1	Small potatoes, 2-3" diameter	5
2, 3	Candle with holder	1
2	Modeling clay or candle holder	1
3	Alcohol burners	1
3	Empty soda cans, 12 oz	2
5	Heating/Cooling Curve of water graph, blank (see BLM)	1
5, 6	Styrene foam cups, large	2
7	Rubber gloves, pairs	4
7	Raw egg	1
7	Hard-boiled egg	1
7	Raw egg soaked in HCl	1

TABLE 4: CONSUMABLES PER CLASS

Section	Materials and Equipment (Consumables)	Quantity
1, 2	Roll of aluminum foil	1
1, 4, 5	Pack of graph paper, 50 sheets	1
1	Tracing paper, pad	1
2	Box of wooden splints	1
2, 3	Box of matches	1
5	Bucket of crushed ice	1
5	Roll of paper towels	1
8	Ball of string	1

Chemicals

In this fifth table, the **Chemicals** required for each activity are listed. By their nature, most chemicals are consumable, of course.
The amounts given in the right-hand column under **Quantity** are calculated for 5 classes of 24 students, or 120 students. Most teachers will find that these amounts (when divided by 5 to give the amount needed for one class), will still provide ample excess for repeat experiments or student error.

TABLE 5: CHEMICALS FOR FIVE CLASSES (24 Students per class)		
Section	**Chemicals**	**Quantity**
2	Manganese dioxide, MnO_2	12.5 g
2	Hydrogen peroxide, 3%	250 mL
3	Fuels: ethanol, kerosene, lamp oil, etc.	100 mL each
5	Sodium choride, NaCl (table salt)	1250 g
7	Hydrochloric acid, HCl, 3.0 M	1 L
2	Sodium bicarbonate	200 g
2	Acetic acid	2 L

NOTES

_____

_____

_____

_____

_____

_____

_____

_____

_____

_____

Teacher Resources

Blackline Masters

- Blackline Masters
Available on the *Teacher Resources* CD.

- Color Overheads
Available on the *Teacher Resources* CD.

Blackline Masters

Chapter Supports

	POINT OF USE	BLACKLINE MASTER LABEL
Sample Criteria for Excellence	*Chapter Challenge* Introduction	7a
Sample Assessment Rubric	*Chapter Challenge* Conclusion	7b
Chem at Work: Profile 1	*Chem at Work*	7c
Chem at Work: Profile 2	*Chem at Work*	7d
Chem at Work: Profile 3	*Chem at Work*	7e

Section Quizzes

Section 1 Quiz	Section 1	7-1c
Section 2 Quiz	Section 2	7-2b
Section 3 Quiz	Section 3	7-3b
Section 4 Quiz	Section 4	7-4b
Section 5 Quiz	Section 5	7-5c
Section 6 Quiz	Section 6	7-6b
Section 7 Quiz	Section 7	7-7d
Section 8 Quiz	Section 8	7-8a

Activity Supports

	POINT OF USE	BLACKLINE MASTER LABEL
Pinwheel pattern	Section 1	7-1a
Sample Data Table – Potato Cooking	Section 1	7-1b
Chem Poetry	Section 2	7-2a
Data Table – Bond Energies	Section 3	7-3a
Kinetic Energy of Water Molecules Diagram: Heating	Section 4	7-4a
Kinetic Energy of Water Molecules Diagram: Freezing	Section 5	7-5a

	POINT OF USE	BLACKLINE MASTER LABEL
Heating/Cooling Curve of Water Graph	Section 5	7-5b
Specific Heat and Molar Heat Capacity Table	Section 6	7-6a
Protein – Primary Structure Diagram	Section 7	7-7a
Protein – Secondary Structure Diagram	Section 7	7-7b
Protein – Tertiary Structure	Section 7	7-7c

Chapter Assessment

Chem Practice Test	Chapter Conclusion	7f

Color Overheads

	POINT OF USE
What Do You See?	Section 1
What Do You See?	Section 2
What Do You See?	Section 3
What Do You See?	Section 4
What Do You See?	Section 5
What Do You See?	Section 6
What Do You See?	Section 7
What Do You See?	Section 8

NOTES

Chapter Challenge

Scenario

Read, or have a student read this section aloud. Pause after each paragraph and ask a question to test for their understanding and to generate interest. Ask students about their favorite foods and how to prepare them. Encourage them to share experiences they have had with cooking. Discuss various cooking techniques that they practice at home or enjoy. Food, food preparation, and cooking can easily get students wanting to talk. It is your responsibility as a teacher to engage them but not to devote too much time to this discussion.

You may wish to expand on the *Scenario* by using videos of cooking shows, or by asking your school's cooking teacher to give a talk. You could also invite a restaurant chef, a cookware salesperson, or any other cookery professional to make a presentation.

7

Chapter Challenge

Cookin' Chem

Scenario

Everyone enjoys good food! That is probably why cooking shows are so very popular. However, if you want to know why you can cook hard-boiled eggs or which pan to use, don't turn to your cookbook. Pick up your chemistry book instead. The Cooking Science Foundation knows this. That is why the Foundation wants to add a chemistry segment to a cooking show. One of the goals of the Foundation is to make the public aware of the chemistry involved in cooking. Your *Active Chemistry* class has been asked to help by creating a chemistry segment for a cooking show.

548

Your Challenge

Your challenge is to create a five-minute chemistry segment for a cooking show. The segment should provide the audience with a detailed explanation of the chemistry involved. Your presentation could be live action, a videotape, or even a voice-over of an actual show.

You can bring your cultural heritage into play by focusing on ethnic food. Your show might be humorous or serious. It could deal with cafeteria food or gourmet food from a five-star restaurant. The show should be interesting and entertaining. It must include correct chemistry content. In addition to the presentation, you will submit a script for the show that includes a discussion of the chemistry involved.

This challenge has an almost unlimited number of possibilities because there is so much chemistry that goes on in the kitchen. You may find it difficult to limit the number of chemical principles that you discuss!

Think of all the possibilities!

Chem Corner
Chemistry in *Cookin' Chem*

- Heat transfer
- Combustion reaction
- Balanced equations
- Quantitative analysis
- Qualitative analysis
- Heat energy of fuels
- Thermochemistry
- Boiling point
- States of matter
- Heating curve

- Freezing point
- Heat of fusion
- Alloys
- Amino acids
- Protein structure
- Denaturation
- Lewis dot structures
- Saturated and unsaturated
- Tetrahedral structure of carbon

- Soaps and detergents
- *cis-* and *trans-* double bonds
- Triple bonds
- Molecular geometry
- Valence-shell-electron-pair-repulsion theory
- Functional group
- Micelles

549

works on a consistent basis. In order to do this, students will want to take full advantage of planning and trouble-shooting at the *Chapter Mini-Challenge* level.

When you come to the section *Reflecting on the Section and the Challenge*, point out how each section contributes to the challenge in some way. As you discuss the challenge, reassure students that while they may feel overwhelmed by the demands of the assignment now, by the end of the chapter they will have the necessary skills and understanding to succeed.

Chem Corner

This section contains a preview of the basic science principles and skills that will be presented in this chapter. You may wish to see how many of these terms are familiar to your students. At the end of the chapter, it will be worthwhile to return to this list so that students can gauge their growth in understanding. The *Chem Corner* is a good opportunity to remind students that the chemistry concepts and skills they learn in each new activity will be the building blocks they will need at the end of the chapter to complete the *Chapter Challenge*.

Your Challenge

You may wish to lead a class discussion about the challenge and the expectations.

Review the titles of the activities in the Table of Contents at the front of the *Student Edition*. Point out that the content of the sections aligns with the content expected for the *Chapter Challenge* and ask students for ideas as to how these kinds of activities might relate to the challenge at hand.

Stress the importance of recording each step of the design process (results, successes, and failures) since the students will be required to explain their cooking procedure in detail. Another key to success for the challenge will rely on testing to make sure the design process is reliable and

Chapter Challenge

Criteria for Success

After the class has read the *Scenario* and the *Chapter Challenge*, you can take a few moments as a class to develop the assessment. Students should be asked, "What should your cooking show segment be like to earn an A?" Remind them that their presentation must help people understand certain chemical principles. One way to get started is to make a list of the important criteria that must be included in the *Chapter Challenge*. List some suggestions they might consider, including the number and variety of chemical principles incorporated in the presentation, the accuracy and clarity of the explanation, the quality, entertainment value, and originality of the segment and the script, etc. (As they volunteer ideas, it is important that all suggestions be recognized, so consider this a brainstorming session.) By soliciting the students' opinions, the class will create an assessment tool that is written in language the students can understand. When you have a thorough description of each part of the *Chapter Challenge*, you can have the class vote on how much each part is worth.

After having this 10-minute discussion with the students, you can now read aloud the

Criteria for Success. This section will reinforce the discussion that you have had with the students. It may also add some interesting points that did not emerge in class. Students will be able to better understand this section after their own discussion.

Students should try to develop a rough rubric for the grading of the chapter. This can be as

simple as ascribing points to each of their criteria. For example, the visual presentation could be worth 40 points, the chemical content worth 30 points and the written script another 30 points. A sample rubric for assessing the *Chapter Challenge* is provided at the end of this chapter. You can copy and distribute it as is, or use it as a baseline for developing scoring

---

Chapter Challenge

Criteria for Success

How will you present your cooking-show segment? Will it be performed live in your classroom, video taped, or will you create a voiceover of an existing show? Discuss the types of shows with which you are familiar. Your teacher may show you video clips from one or two shows. Discuss with your classmates the attributes of a successful segment and how your cooking show segment might be graded. You may want to consider some or all of the following in your discussion:

Visual Presentation
- Multiple chemical principles explained
- Accuracy of explanation
- Creative, engaging, fun
- Overall quality of presentation
- All group members contribute

Written Script
- Multiple chemical principles explained and highlighted
- Accuracy of explanation
- Mechanically correct
- All group members contribute
- Script matches presentation

Once you have determined how to evaluate the cooking show segments, you and your class should decide how many points should be given for each criterion. Should creativity of the presentation be awarded more points than the clarity and accuracy of the script? How many different chemical principles should be addressed in the segment? How many points should be given for each chemical principle? For each criterion you should decide how excellence is defined and how it compares with a satisfactory effort. Determining grading criteria in advance will help you focus your time and effort on the important parts of the challenge.

Engineering Design Cycle

However you choose to do it, your group will create a five minute segment revealing the chemistry behind the cooking for a TV show. The simplified *Engineering Design Cycle* you have been using for each *Chapter Challenge* will help you complete this design challenge. Understanding the *Goal* is the first step in any *Engineering Design Cycle*. The *Goal* for your chemistry cooking show is clear, so you are already on the path to success. During the chapter sections you will learn the chemistry you need to include in your television debut.

As you proceed, each section will provide *Inputs* to use in the *Engineering Design Cycle*. These *Inputs* will include new chemistry concepts, new chemical reactions, and explanations of common cooking techniques—important information you can use to explain the cooking taking place in your show. When your group prepares the *Mini-Challenge* presentation and the *Chapter Challenge*, you will be completing the *Engineering Design Cycle Process* step. During the *Process* step you will consider different potential formats for your cooking segment, compare and contrast potential ideas, and, most importantly, make decisions about the way you will demonstrate the chemistry involved in cooking.

The *Outputs* of your *Engineering Design Cycle* will be your cooking segment and the chemistry explanations that go with it. Your *Goal* is to provide a thorough explanation of the chemistry involved in creating your culinary concoction. Finally, you will receive *Feedback* from your class and your instructor about which parts of your cooking segment are good and which parts need to be refined. You will repeat the *Engineering Design Cycle* two times during the course of the chapter— when you complete the *Mini-Challenge* and after you have completed the second half of the chapter, gain more *Inputs*, finalize your presentation, and complete your script and cooking segment.

550

---

guidelines and expectations that suit your needs. For example, you might wish to ensure that core concepts and abilities derived from your local or state science frameworks also appear on the rubric. However you decide to evaluate the *Chapter Challenge*, keep in mind that all expectations should be communicated to the students at the start of their work.

The *Sample Criteria for Excellence* is also provided as a Blackline Master in your *Teacher Resources* CD.

7a	Blackline Master

SAMPLE CRITERIA FOR EXCELLENCE

It is important for students to decide on the criteria for grading the *Chapter Challenge* themselves. This will give them a voice in determining how their projects will be judged. You can help them arrive at a list of criteria by outlining those aspects of the project that would need to be rated. Some aspects that could be considered are the entertainment value of the cooking presentation, the creativity of the written script, and the number of chemical concepts addressed. You may want to share the list of sample criteria provided below as a source of inspiration. Remember that the primary purpose for having the students establish the criteria for earning a top grade is to motivate them to succeed.

As the *Chapter Challenge* approaches, you will need to develop a more comprehensive assessment rubric for evaluating the projects. For an example, you can refer to the *Sample Assessment Rubric for Chapter 7* at the end of the chapter in this *Teacher's Edition*.

MEETS THE STANDARD OF EXCELLENCE FOR CHAPTER CHALLENGE

Aspect	Criteria of Excellence
Visual Presentation	• The presentation thoroughly demonstrates the cooking techniques and the related chemical concepts. • The presentation is well rehearsed, entertaining, and creative.
Written Script	• The script is well-written and creative. • The script accurately and clearly explains the cooking techniques and the chemistry concepts involved.
Chemical Concepts	• At least seven chemistry concepts are applied in the cooking techniques and in the cookware utilized.
Group Interaction	• All group members participate equally. • Project is executed by coordinated teamwork.

SECTION 1
Heat Transfer: What Is Heat?

Section Overview

In this section, students will explore three methods of heat transfer. They experience conduction by brief contact with a 25-watt light bulb. They experience radiation by sensing the heat from a 75-watt light bulb. They then assemble a pinwheel, place it over a 75-watt bulb, and observe convection from the rotation of the pinwheel. Students should be able to identify each type of heat transfer in their light bulb/pinwheel model and similarly, apply the three aspects of heat transfer to the process of cooking peas in boiling water. Finally, students will design a mini-investigation to model conduction in a potato. By observing and measuring the growth of the opaque ring in the potato, they will graph and explain heat flow.

Background Information

We cook our food for a variety of reasons. Cooking extends the range of foods we can eat. Some raw foods are indigestible. The starch found in raw potatoes, for example, is in a form that our stomachs cannot process. However, heating a potato to a high enough temperature alters the starch, and it becomes digestible. Some raw foods contain toxins (e.g., pork) and these toxins can often be destroyed by the application of heat. So, cooking food can lead to a reduced risk of food poisoning. Cooking can also change the texture of foods, making the food more appealing and chewable. It can even lead to chemical reactions that change the flavor of foods by breaking down large molecules, which we cannot taste, into smaller molecules that we can taste.

Cooking involves heat, of course, and thermal energy is the energy possessed by a substance due to the movement of its atoms, ions and molecules. Heat is defined as the amount of kinetic energy transferred from one object to another as a result of a temperature difference between them. On the molecular level, more rapidly moving molecules in the hotter object collide with the more slowly moving molecules in the colder object. Kinetic energy is transferred between molecules. The faster-moving molecules give up some of their kinetic energy and slow down while the slower-moving molecules speed up.

The temperature of a substance is a measure of the average kinetic energy of its particles. The kinetic energy of molecular motion of a substance is measured by its temperature. If the molecules of a substance are moving rapidly and colliding forcefully with the bulb of a thermometer, the substance is considered "hot" and it has a higher temperature compared to some other substance. If its molecules are moving slowly and colliding less forcefully with the thermometer, the substance has a lower temperature relative to another substance.

This *relative* hotness or coldness of a substance is an important concept. An object with a temperature of 100° C is not twice as hot as one with a temperature of 50°C. In order to directly relate the temperature and average kinetic energy of the particles of a substance, the Kelvin scale must be used. Absolute zero, or 0 K, is where the particles of a substance have minimum motion. An object with a temperature of 100 K has molecules with twice the kinetic energy of the same object at 50 K.

	LEARNING OUTCOMES	
LEARNING OUTCOMES	**LOCATION IN SECTION**	**EVIDENCE OF UNDERSTANDING**
Demonstrate the three ways that heat is transferred.	*Investigate* Parts A-B *Chem to Go* Questions 1-3,11 *Inquiring Further* 1-3	Students can correctly identify and define the processes of conduction, convection and radiation.
Distinguish between heat energy and temperature.	*Chem Talk, Chem to Go* Questions 6-10	Students can determine temperature in kelvins or Celsius and convert from one to the other. Students' answers match those provided in this *Teacher's Edition*.

NOTES

Section 1
Materials, Chemicals, Preparation, and Safety

("per Group" quantity is based on group size of 4 students)

Materials and Equipment

Materials (and Equipment)	Quantity per Group (4 students)
25-watt incandescent bulb	1
75-watt incandescent bulb	1
Bulb socket with electrical plug	1
Ringstand	1
Clamp for ringstand	1
Pencil w/eraser*	1
Straight pin*	1
Pinwheel pattern* (Blackline Master)	1
Scissors*	1
Ruler	1
Crucible tongs	1
Hot plate	1
Wire gauze squares for hot plate	2
Beaker, 1000 mL	1
Knife (plastic okay)	1
Thermometer	1
Small potatoes, 2"-3" diameter	5

Materials (and Equipment)	Quantity per Class (24 students)
Roll of aluminum foil*	1
Pack of graph paper, 50 sheets	1
Tracing paper, pad	1

*if ready-made pinwheels are available, these items are not necessary

Chemicals

Chemicals	Quantity per Class (24 students)
None	None

Teacher Preparation

If ready-made pinwheels are not available, you may want to prepare the pinwheels for Part A, Step 3 in advance, or at least cut out the paper or foil using the pattern provided in Blackline Master 7-1a.

7-1a   **Blackline Master**

Safety Requirements

- All activity in the laboratory area requires goggles and aprons.

- All waste can be disposed of in the trash or down the sink.

- Wash hands and arms before leaving the laboratory area.

NOTES

Meeting the Needs of All Students
Differentiated Instruction

Augmentation and Accommodations

LEARNING ISSUE	REFERENCE	AUGMENTATION AND ACCOMMODATIONS
Envisioning the final presentation	*Chapter Challenge Criteria*	**Accommodations** • Model project expectations by showing students a videotaped presentation with a voiceover.
Dexterity	*Investigate* Part A, 3.	**Accommodations** • Pair students who are having difficulties creating the pinwheels with partners who can compensate. • Provide students with completed pinwheels.
Reading and following directions	*Investigate* Part A, 3. Part B	**Accommodations** • Pair students having difficulties with partners who can compensate. • Create a table or flow chart for students that has the sequence of directions clearly labeled. **Augmentation** • Teach students to follow directions by showing them where the directions are in the text and helping them read them one at a time, completing each task as they go. Use a model to demonstrate each step.
Understanding cause-and-effect relationships	*Investigate* Part A	**Accommodations** • Provide three choices. Make each student provide a reason for his choice. • Provide two or three choices and reasons worded simply.
Applying new learning to written expression	*Investigate* Part A, 4.	**Augmentation** • Lead students through the rewrite step-by-step following a prescribed sequence: 1) describing a particular part of the original text, 2) labeling the type of transfer, and 3) stating a reason for their answer. • Teach students that convection applies to heat transfer via gas OR liquid. At the point in the lesson when they are asked to identify convection in the boiling peas example, they may not be able to make the association with the earlier example of convection through air with the light bulb. **Accommodations** • Divide each type of heat energy transfer into a separate copy block. Then ask students to identify the type of transfer in each block.
Graphing variables	*Investigate* Part B, 1.,2.	**Accommodations** • Provide students with graphs they can label and use to record data.
Reading comprehension Note-taking	*Chem Talk*	**Augmentation** • Teach students how structure affects meaning. Each paragraph identifies a type of transfer, and includes a definition, medium and an example. Teach students to recognize this pattern and use it to guide their note-taking. • Have the students write their own definitions of each type of heat-energy transfer including the medium through which it transfers, and an example.
Conceptualization of the difference between heat energy and temperature	*Chem Talk*	**Accommodations** • Use an animated illustration of the movement of molecules as heat is transferred into kinetic energy. • Refer students to the boiling potatoes example to help them think about the relationship of mass to heat energy. Were all the potatoes the same size? Which took longer to turn translucent? What is the effect of mass?

LEARNING ISSUE	REFERENCE	AUGMENTATION AND ACCOMMODATIONS
Written expression	*Chem Essential Questions*	**Accommodations** • Answering the question, "What evidence do you have that heat energy can be used to cook a potato?" may take more scaffolding. Some students may think it is self-evident that it is cooked or that it is hot, but may not describe the process. This may require providing an example that the students did not study, but which illustrates the format of the answer they should provide.
Written expression Application of prior knowledge	*Preparing for the Chapter Challenge*	**Accommodations** • Some students may require a scaffold similar to the one used for the peas example. Others may need nothing, or just a reminder to look at the peas example as a model.

Strategies for Students with Limited English Language Proficiency

LEARNING ISSUE	REFERENCE	AUGMENTATION AND ACCOMMODATIONS
Background knowledge	*Scenario*	It may be helpful to have an excerpt from a TV cooking show so students understand what a "*segment*" is. Help students with the meanings of words in the *Chem Corner*. A general discussion of the criteria for the segment will be helpful, and will provide some oral language development. Having students describe what they see in the illustration will also be helpful.
Background knowledge	*What Do You Think?*	Facilitate a discussion where each student has to contribute. A nonverbal or visual representation may serve to stimulate a discussion of the questions about "*heat*."
Vocabulary	*Investigate*	Check for understanding of the word, "*conduction*" and of the nature of a "*pinwheel*." In Part B, where students are asked to construct a data table, references can be made to previous tables they have worked with. For questions about recipes, students may benefit from seeing some examples of recipes.
Background knowledge Vocabulary Comprehending text	*Chem Talk*	Check for understanding of bold-type words. Multiple uses of the words are helpful to apply understanding, such as in the various uses of the word "*radiation*." Check for understanding of the term, "*convection*." Help students with the correct pronunciation of the terms, "*Fahrenheit*" and "*Celsius*." Refer students to sidebar material for further explanations of the isolated words.
Background knowledge	*What Do You Think Now?*	Have students discuss their answers prior to writing them down.
Background knowledge Vocabulary Comprehending text	*Chem Essential Questions*	In three of the questions the students are asked to "*describe*" a solution and in another question, they are asked to "*suggest*" an answer. These words may require clarification.
Comprehension Vocabulary	*Chem to Go*	Make sure students can distinguish questions that are stacked, where there is more than one response, from those that are multiple-choice questions.
Application Comprehension	*Inquiring Further*	In the first task, ensure that students understand when they are asked to "*determine*" an equation. Give them an analogy or synonym that explains the action. For the second and third tasks, it may be helpful to supply an example of a pamphlet.

Section 1
Teaching Suggestions and Sample Answers

What Do You See?

This colorful illustration serves several purposes. The first is to engage the students' interest. Additionally, you can use the illustration to elicit information about students' prior knowledge.

Students' reactions will vary, which is good. Some may notice that the hot dog is burning. Others may attempt to analyze the illustration and combine the temperature effects (hot to cold) with the tape measure in the foreground. "Hey, the closer they are to the light bulb, the warmer they are!" All reactions are to be valued. This is not the time to make judgments about their responses although you might wish to draw out additional information from a student if a response is vague or if you sense that it can lead to important information for the class.

Later, the class will have an opportunity to return to the illustration and their initial responses to it.

What Do You Think?

Let students freely share their ideas and clarify that you are not looking for right answers, just open expression. Encourage them to participate in this discussion.

Have students share key ideas for future reference. Ask students to brainstorm about various methods of cooking–boiling, frying, baking, for example–so they can begin to think of a variety of energy transfers.

Pay careful attention to statements that students make in attempting to answer these questions. These can reveal misconceptions and limited understandings they might have about heat. Note students' impressions about cooking as they will be developed further as the chapter unfolds.

You will find numerous occasions in this section and several that follow to reinforce the concept of the transfer of energy to matter.

STUDENTS' PRIOR CONCEPTIONS

Some representative student misconceptions about heat include ideas such as:

- Heat makes things rise. In many cases, this is correct. "Heat rises" is a common phrase, especially as applied to fluids such as water and air.
- Cold is opposite to heat. Again, there is a grain of truth here but "cold" and "hot" are simply two points on a continuous scale.
- Heat acts as a fluid. It accumulates in one spot until that spot is full. Then that spot "bursts" and heat overflows to other parts of a substance.
- Everything contains air bubbles, and some bubbles contain cold air and others hot air.
- Heat is a material substance like air or steam. It is made up of fumes that can transfer into and out of an object.

On the difference between heat and temperature:

- Temperature is used to measure heat, and heat is "hot."
- There is no difference between heat and temperature. (This is false.)

- Heat is something that is started and maintained by a source.
- Heat moves around and rises. (This is a simplification based on gases, including air.)
- Heat is a substance which could be added to or removed from an object. For example, when a metal rod is heated, a substance from the flame enters the rod and then moves on.
- Larger ice cubes have a colder temperature. (They do have the same temperature as small ice cubes but a greater cooling capacity.)
- Metal is colder than plastic because cold passes through it more quickly than plastic. (Actually, metals feel colder because they conduct heat more efficiently.)
- Metal is colder because it absorbs more cold than plastic.
- The reason metals get hotter than other substances is because they can attract heat better than other substances.

Section 1

Heat Transfer: What Is Heat?

What Do You See?

Learning Outcomes

In this section you will

• Demonstrate the three ways that heat energy is transferred

• Distinguish between heat energy and temperature.

What Do You Think?

When you think of cooking, you think of heat. Good cooks have an understanding of how heat interacts with food (matter).

• **What is heat?**

• **What is the difference between heat and temperature?**

The *What Do You Think?* questions are meant to get you thinking about what you already know or think you know. Don't worry about being right or wrong. Discussing what you think you know is an important step in learning.

Record your ideas about these questions in your *Active Chemistry* log. Be prepared to discuss your responses with your group and the class.

Investigate

To help you understand how heat interacts with food (matter), you will investigate the heat from a light bulb. Heat energy can be transferred in several distinct ways. Each way has its own characteristics, and all are used in cooking.

What Do You Think?
A CHEMIST'S RESPONSE

Heat is a form of energy contained in the kinetic energy of the particles of a substance. When two particles at different temperatures interact, heat flows from the hotter to the cooler particle.

Temperature is related to heat but is not identical. Temperature is a measure of the average kinetic energy of all of the particles of a substance.

CHAPTER 7

Investigate

Part A: Transferring Heat Energy

1.

Safety precaution: Warn students that the 25-Watt bulb may get very hot. They should be very cautious when touching it lightly and quickly with one unprotected finger.

1.a)

Students will answer "Yes."

1.b)

Students may select any number of foods that can be cooked in a frying pan—hot dogs, hamburgers, French toast, stir-fry vegetables, eggs, etc. Favorites will vary.

2.a)

Students should be able to easily feel the heat emanating from the bulb. Make certain that they position their hand on the side of the bulb, not above it. The sensation of heat when the hand is below the bulb is even more pronounced.

3.

A Blackline Master of a pattern for creating a pinwheel is available on the *Teacher Resources CD*.

7-1a **Blackline Master**

Cookin' Chem

Safety goggles and a lab apron must be worn at *all times* in the laboratory.

Use caution when touching 25-W light bulbs.

Use caution when handling sharp objects.

Part A: Transferring Heat Energy

1. Use care in this investigation to avoid skin burns. Turn on a light which contains a 25-Watt incandescent light bulb. After 1-2 minutes, touch the bulb quickly with a finger tip.

   a) Did you feel the heat?

   Unplug the light and let the bulb cool. You have just investigated one way *heat* energy is transferred—through contact. This form of heat-energy transfer is also called *conduction.*

   b) Conduction is often used in cooking by placing food in contact with a frying pan. List three foods that can be cooked by conduction. Which of these is your favorite?

2. After the 25-Watt bulb has cooled, replace it with a 75-Watt bulb. Turn on the light. After a few minutes, put your hand as close to the side of the bulb as you can without touching it.

   a) Can you feel the heat from the bulb without touching the bulb? Is it more or less intense than touching a 25-Watt bulb?

   You have just investigated a second way heat energy is transferred—by *radiation.* The heat energy from the bulb passed from the bulb through space and came in touch with your hand. Radiation is often used in restaurants by placing heat lamps above food to keep it warm.

3. Using a pattern and a piece of paper from your teacher, construct a pinwheel to demonstrate the third way in which heat energy is transferred. Cut on the diagonal of a square piece of paper from each corner to about 2.5 cm from

the center point. Starting with one corner, fold every other corner to the center.

Push a straight pin through the center point, making sure to catch the tip of every folded corner as shown. Secure the pinwheel to the rubber end of a pencil.

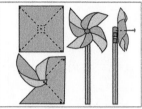

Blow on the pinwheel to make certain that it spins freely. Now construct a cylinder from paper or aluminum foil which can serve as a chimney. This chimney can be 20–30 cm long (8–12 in.) and about 8 cm in diameter (3 in.). A standard sheet of paper will work well.

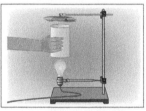

Set up the light bulb, chimney, and pinwheel as shown in the diagram.

   a) Turn on the light. What is causing the pinwheel to move? Write down your hypothesis in your *Active Chemistry* log.

552

You can demonstrate how to make a pinwheel from a sheet of 8 ½" × 11" paper. Tracing paper works best. Aluminum foil can be used but it tends to be difficult.

- Make a 5" square from the foil or paper so that all sides are of equal measure.

- Determine the center point by drawing the diagonal from one corner, through the center, to the opposite

corner and repeat for the opposite diagonal.

- Cut on the diagonal from each corner to about 1" from the center point When complete, you should have eight corners instead of four.

- Starting with one corner, fold every other corner to the center.

- Push the straight pin

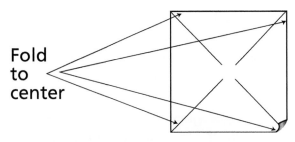

Fold
to
center

through the center, making sure to catch every corner, and secure in the cork or rubber stopper.

- The pinwheel should spin freely on the stopper or pencil eraser.

The chimney can be constructed from another 8 ½" × 11" sheet of paper by simply making a cylinder of it along its long axis and taping the edge. A cardboard cylinder will also work well, as will one made of aluminum foil. If a candle is used as the heat source, a chimney from aluminum foil is required.

The chimney is placed above the bulb as shown so that it can direct the hot air to the pinwheel. Students can clamp the chimney and pinwheel or simply hold them in place.

3.a)

The movement of the pinwheel is caused by the movement of upward air currents from the heating of the air by the bulb. Hot air is less dense than cold air and will move upward. Have students discuss and explain how this movement occurred. You may also have them note the speed of the pinwheel at various distances from the bulb. Another option is to have the students measure the time required for the

pinwheel to begin to move once the light bulb is turned on.

3.b)

Students should diagram the way heat is being transferred in their log. Convection occurs as air above the bulb is heated and will rise. The rising air pushes against the non-symmetric surface of the pinwheel blades, causing it to turn.

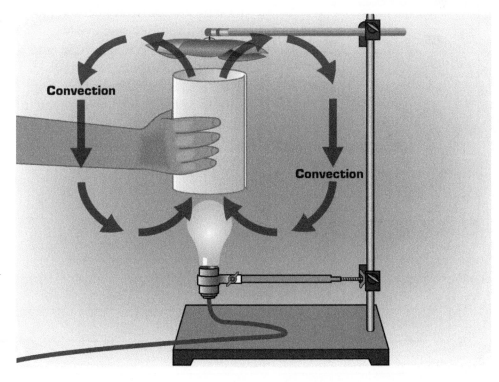

Students can record temperature readings from 1 to 15 cm from the bulb. A temperature probe works nicely for this, since it reads temperature changes automatically and immediately. Students should notice a marked decrease in temperature as they get further from the bulb. However, they should note that the air surrounding the bulb is warmer than air away from the bulb. They should be able to explain this pattern using the idea of radiation and convection.

Sample Data:
Distance from bulb vs. Temperature

Distance (cm)	Temperature (°C)
0	110
1.5	68
3	66
4.5	61
7.5	58
9.0	52
10.5	48
12	41
15	37

Part B: Observing the Transfer of Heat Energy

1.

Safety precaution: Remind students to use tongs when removing potatoes from the boiling water and to use caution around a hot plate or flame. Remind students to allow the beaker to cool before cleaning it.

You may suggest that students check their potatoes at regular time intervals and not to exceed 15 to 20 minutes for small potatoes. The translucent ring should be obvious and easy to measure. Students should decide to start all potatoes at the same time and remove one every three minutes, cut it in half, and measure the translucent ring. The ring, or evidence of heating, should appear to be fairly even all around the potato. Measurements are from the outside skin inward.

2.a)

The following table and graph using sample data are provided as a Blackline Master in your *Teacher Resources* CD.

7-1b **Blackline Master**

Sample Data Table

Time (min)	Ring (mm)
0	0
3	4
6	7
9	10
12	13

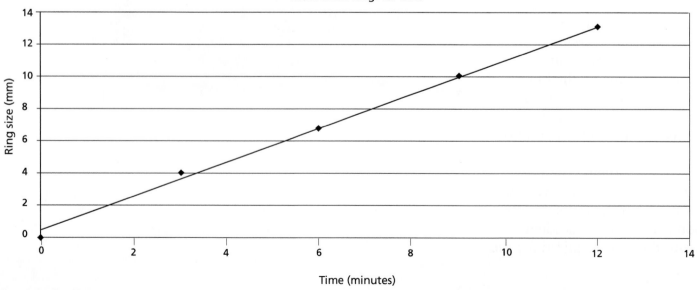

Translucent Rings vs. Time

(y-axis: Ring size (mm), x-axis: Time (minutes))

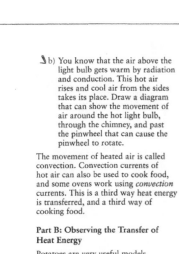

b) You know that the air above the light bulb gets warm by radiation and conduction. This hot air rises and cool air from the sides takes its place. Draw a diagram that can show the movement of air around the hot light bulb, through the chimney, and past the pinwheel that can cause the pinwheel to rotate.

The movement of heated air is called convection. Convection currents of hot air can also be used to cook food, and some ovens work using *convection* currents. This is a third way heat energy is transferred, and a third way of cooking food.

Part B: Observing the Transfer of Heat Energy

Potatoes are very useful models for observing how heat energy is transferred when cooking food. When you heat a potato to 60°C (or higher), there is a change in its appearance. The potato changes from an opaque, white texture and becomes translucent.

If you put some potatoes into boiling water for various lengths of time, and then remove them and cut them open, you will see the increase in size of a

ring of translucent material. (Note: It is easier to see the ring of translucent material if you do not peel the potato.)

1. Design an experiment using five different potatoes and boiling water. Use time as the independent variable and the growth of the translucent ring of cooked potato as your dependent variable. Have your teacher approve your experiment before you begin.

2. Construct a data table for recording the width of the ring in millimeters and the cooking time in minutes. Graph the data.

a) Include your data table and graph in your *Active Chemistry* log.

b) What conclusions can you draw about cooking time and heat-energy transfer?

c) How is this kind of data useful for developing recipes?

3. All three types of heat-energy transfer occur when you are boiling the potatoes in your experiment.

a) Diagram and label the three types of heat-energy transfer (include a hot plate, beaker, water, and potatoes).

⚠️

Use extreme caution around boiling water. It can cause very serious burns.

The potatoes will be very hot. Remove them very carefully using tongs.

Wash hands and arms thoroughly before leaving the lab area.

Active Chemistry

2.c)

Cooking time is an important part of any recipe. This kind of data is useful for determining the exact amount of time needed to cook any type of food. In this particular case, the data could be expanded to include potatoes of varying size.

3.a)

In their diagrams, students should note that radiation is occurring from the hot plate, conduction is occurring within the potato, from the water to the potato, and where the beaker is in contact with the hot plate or flame, and convection is occurring in the boiling water. Radiation would be the least important mode of transfer because of the amount of energy that is lost and not transferred to the potato. The ring grows from the outside inward due to conduction.

2.b)

Students should note that the ring grows from the outside towards the inside, suggesting heat flow from the water to the surface of the potato by conduction. They should note the very obvious trend that as the cooking time increases, so does the width of the ring. They should speculate that they could use their data to predict when the potato will be cooked all the way through by extrapolating from their graph.

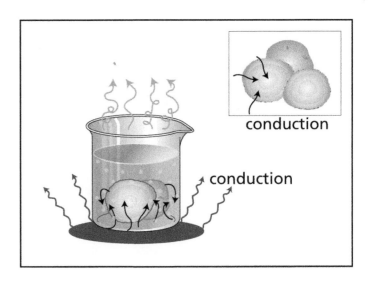

conduction

conduction

Chem Talk

The reading addresses heat energy and the three methods of transferring heat (conduction, convection, and radiation). An explanation of the difference between heat energy and temperature is reviewed. In addition, an outline of methods for measuring temperature explains the procedure for conversion between the Celsius scale and the Kelvin scale.

Cookin' Chem

Chem Talk

HEAT ENERGY

How Heat Energy Is Transferred

Heat energy is transferred to matter (food) in three ways. One way is conduction. **Conduction** is the movement of heat energy through matter by the transfer of vibrational energy between atoms and molecules that are in contact with each other. The transfer of heat energy inside of any solid occurs by conduction. You experienced this when you touched the light bulb. Another example of conduction is an egg cooking in a frying pan. The key to conduction is contact.

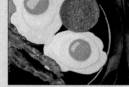

Another method of heat-energy transfer is convection. **Convection** is the transfer of heat energy by the physical motion of masses of fluid. (A fluid can be a liquid or a gas.) Convection describes a movement of heat energy through the transfer of a fluid medium from one place to another. When peas are boiling in a pot of water, thermal energy is being transferred by convection. As hot water is heated at the bottom of the pot on the stove, the hot water circulates around the pot, heating the peas.

Finally, there is radiation. **Radiation** is the transfer of heat energy by electromagnetic radiation. This is the only form of heat-energy transfer that does not require atoms or molecules. All bodies, when hot, radiate heat energy. The most important source of radiation is the Sun.

When you held your hand close to the light bulb, the heat you felt was due (in part) to radiation and (in part) to convection. In this case, the convecting substance was air. When you touched the light bulb, the heat you felt was due to conduction.

Chem Words

conduction: the transfer of heat energy from particle to particle between substances through contact or within a substance.

convection: the transfer of heat through the movement of air or liquid currents.

radiation (of heat): transfer of heat energy by emission of electromagnetic radiation in all directions.

554

Active Chemistry

The Difference Between Heat Energy and Temperature

What is heat? **Heat** is a form of energy that results from the motion of atoms and molecules. (Random motion means that the atoms and molecules are moving in no specific pattern.) Moving particles have kinetic energy. This kinetic energy is transferred to other particles through collisions on the atomic or nanoscopic scale. In this way, heat energy is transferred.

It is not uncommon for people to confuse heat and temperature. Temperature is a property of matter that is measured with a thermometer. You can use your sense of touch to judge temperature. However, a thermometer is a more accurate and precise tool than your skin. At the molecular or nanoscopic level, temperature is a measure of the average kinetic energy (energy of motion) of a substance's molecules. Some molecules will be moving faster than average and some will be moving slower than the average. If one could measure the temperature of individual molecules, the faster, more energetic molecules would be hotter, but of course, this is impossible. When you watch the temperature on a meat thermometer inside a roast increase steadily as the roast cooks, you know that the molecules of meat are absorbing heat energy and, as a result, these molecules are vibrating faster.

Heat energy is a measure of both the amount of matter and the temperature of that matter. A cup of coffee at 90°C is very hot. A swimming pool at 25°C is quite cool by comparison. The coffee has a higher temperature. The swimming pool has more heat energy. That is because of the enormous amount of water present. Think about how much heat energy would be required to raise the temperature of the coffee by 1°C and the amount of heat energy required to raise the temperature of the entire swimming pool by 1°C. Think about what would happen if the hot coffee in a closed container were thrown into the pool. The coffee would cool off and its temperature would drop to 25°C. The swimming pool's temperature would rise only the tiniest amount. The swimming pool has much more heat energy, even though it is at a cooler temperature.

Temperature determines the exchange of heat energy. Heat energy is transferred as a result of a temperature difference between bodies that are in contact. Heat energy always travels from a hotter to a colder →

Chem Words

heat: a form of energy that results from the motion of atoms and molecules.

temperature: a measure of the average kinetic energy of a substance's atoms and molecules, or how fast they are moving.

555

Active Chemistry

Cookin' Chem

body. A colder body always gets warmer when placed in contact with a hotter body. The fast-moving molecules of the hotter substance collide with the slow-moving molecules of the cooler substance and both substances reach an intermediate temperature.

When a molecule vibrates it transfers some of its energy to neighboring molecules and they begin to vibrate more vigorously. As their motion starts to increase, the first molecule now vibrates a little less because some of its energy has been passed on. This is how heat energy spread through your potatoes as they were cooked. The physical property known as **thermal conductivity** is the ability of an object to move heat energy from one part of itself to another. Metals are used in cookware because they spread heat energy very quickly.

Measuring Temperature

Temperature is measured in units called degrees. You are probably familiar with degrees Fahrenheit or Celsius. There is also a kelvin temperature scale. Heat energy, on the other hand, is measured in units such as calories, or **joules**.

One **calorie** (cal) is the amount of heat energy required to raise the temperature of 1 g of water 1 degree Celsius.

$$1000 \text{ cal} = 1 \text{ kcal (kilocalorie)}$$
$$1 \text{ cal} = 4.184 \text{ J (joules)}$$

Celsius is a metric temperature scale based on water freezing at 0°C and boiling at 100°C. Kelvin is another metric scale. It is also called the absolute temperature scale. When a temperature is 0 K (kelvin), this is called **absolute zero**. This is the temperature at which molecular motion is brought to a minimum. (Note: Temperatures on this scale are called kelvins, not degrees kelvin.)

Chem Words

thermal conductivity: the ability of an object to move heat energy from one part of itself to another. This is a result of atomic or molecular motion.

joule: a unit of energy that is equal to Newtons × meters, or kg · m²/s²

calorie: the amount of heat energy required to raise the temperature of 1 g of water 1°C. 1 cal = 4.184 J.

absolute zero: 0 K or –273°C. Molecular motion is minimum.

The size of a Celsius degree is equal to the size of a kelvin. The only difference is where the zero point is set. Absolute zero on the kelvin scale is equal to −273°C.

To convert from Celsius degrees to kelvins, add 273. To convert from kelvins to Celsius degrees, simply subtract 273.

Although there are equations for converting from Fahrenheit to Celsius and vice versa, it is more important to be able to approximate temperatures in both units. To do this, it's useful to know some common temperatures in each scale. It is also useful to know that 1° change in Celsius is almost a 2° change in Fahrenheit.

Event	Celsius temperature (°C)	Fahrenheit temperature (°F)
water freezes	0	32
room temperature	20	68
body temperature	37	99
water boils	100	212

If you have reason for a precise conversion, you can refer to a table showing sets of both temperatures, create a spreadsheet, or use the algebraic equations given below.

To convert Fahrenheit to Celsius $°C = \frac{5}{9} (°F - 32)$

To convert Celsius to Fahrenheit $°F = \frac{9}{5} °C + 32$

Cooking Food in a Microwave Oven

How does a microwave oven work? A microwave oven emits electromagnetic waves of a frequency identical to the frequency that causes water molecules to vibrate and rotate. The microwaves enter the food and the water molecules within the food move and vibrate against one another at the rate of over a billion times a second. The heat from the vibrating molecules moves throughout the food by conduction.

Summary of Heat-Energy Transfer

Conduction is the transfer of heat energy throughout a material or through contact between different materials. When you cook pancakes in a frying pan, the flame never touches the pancake batter. The frying pan gets hot because part of it is in contact with the flame or →

557

Active Chemistry

Checking Up

1.

Heat energy can be transferred by conduction, convection, or radiation. Conduction is the transfer of heat energy from particle to particle through contact. This will occur within a substance or between substances and always from greater heat energy to lower heat energy. Convection is the transfer of heat through the movement of a fluid, either a gas or a liquid. Radiation transfers heat energy by emission of electromagnetic radiation in all directions.

2.

An example of conduction is cooking an egg in a frying pan. The transfer of heat occurs primarily by direct contact of the metal frying pan with the egg. An example of cooking by convection is peas cooking in a boiling pot of water. The water, heated by the bottom of the metal pot, moves upward in a convection current to cook the peas. Lastly, heating a TV dinner in a microwave oven is an example of cooking by radiation.

3.

Heat is a form of energy that results from the motion of atoms and molecules. It encompasses both the temperature and the amount of matter. Temperature is a measure of the average kinetic energy of the particles.

4.

Thermal conductivity is the ability of a substance to move heat energy from one part of itself to another. Some substances, such as copper, are more efficient in this process than others, such as glass.

5.

Temperature is measured in units called degrees. The three temperature scales used are Celsius, Fahrenheit, and Kelvin (absolute temperature scale).

6.

Heat energy is measured in units of calories or joules. 1000 cal = 1 kcal and 1 cal = 4.184 Joules.

7.

a) Swimming might be appropriate when the air temperature is above 70° Fahrenheit or 21° Celsius.

b) Ice skating might be appropriate when the air temperature is below the freezing point, which is 32° Fahrenheit or 0° Celsius.

Cookin' Chem

the hot electric coils. The molecules of the pan that are in direct contact with the coils or flame vibrate faster and this heat energy is transferred to neighboring molecules through collisions. Before too long, the entire pan is hot. This movement of the heat energy throughout the metal pan is conduction.

Convection is the transfer of heat energy through the movement of air or liquid currents. Hot air rises because it is less dense than cool air. When the hot air rises, other air must come in from the sides to take up the space of the rising hot air. This sets up a flow of air that is called convection. The currents of moving air are called convection currents. The shape of a candle flame gives you a sense of the convection currents. The hot air rises and cool air comes in from the sides. Similar convection currents are set up when you have a pot of water on the stove. The hot water at the bottom of the pot begins to rise and cooler water takes its place. This creates a convection current and gradually all the liquid heats up.

Radiation is the transfer of heat energy by emission of electromagnetic radiation in all directions. The Sun is a source of electromagnetic radiation. This includes visible light, infrared rays, ultraviolet rays, and radio waves. Your eyes detect the visible light. Your skin detects the infrared radiation. You call it "heat." These electromagnetic waves are able to travel through empty space as well as through air and other materials. When a heat lamp is used to keep foods warm, the expectation is that the food will gain the energy from the infrared radiation (heat energy).

Checking Up

1. Explain three ways that heat energy can be transferred.

2. Give an example for each method of heat-energy transfer as it relates to cooking.

3. What is the difference between heat energy and temperature?

4. Define thermal conductivity.

5. How is temperature measured? Identify the three temperature scales used.

6. What units can be used to measure heat energy?

7. At which approximate temperatures would you do the following activities? Give the temperatures in degrees Fahrenheit and degrees Celsius.

   a) go swimming

   b) go ice skating

conduction

convection

radiation

Active Chemistry

NOTES

What Do You Think Now?

Have students refer to their original responses to the questions from the beginning of the section. Their responses should now be more accurate and informed. You may want to share the answer provided in *A Chemist's Response* and discuss their reactions.

Also, ask them to revisit the *What Do You See?* illustration. They should be able make better connections between what they see and the knowledge they gained from the investigation they performed.

The following are some additional questions that you may want to pose to students:

1.

Are the three types of heat transfer mutually exclusive? Ask students to come up with real life examples. (See the next question for examples.)

2.

What type of heat transfer occurs when you:

- grab the handle of a hot pan and it burns you? (conduction)

- warm your hands over an open fire? (convection, radiation)

- steam vegetables? (convection, conduction)

Chem Essential Questions

What does it mean?

MACRO — Temperature is measured with a thermometer by immersing a thermometer in a substance and waiting until the temperature reading stabilizes. At this point, the temperature is recorded. Temperature changes due to radiation were observed by feeling the heat from the side of a 75-watt light bulb. Temperature changes due to conduction were observed by touching a 25-watt light bulb. Temperature changes due to convection were not observed directly but inferred from the motion of the pinwheel.

NANO — Temperature is a measure of the average kinetic energy of the particles in a substance. When the temperature rises, the particles in that substance are moving faster.

SYMBOLIC —

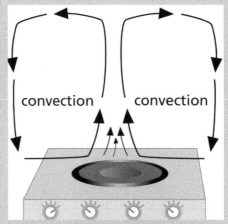

convection   convection

How do you know?

In a controlled experiment, the translucent ring of cooked potato was found to have a direct relationship with cooking time. The longer the potato was cooked by conduction, the thicker the translucent ring grew.

Why do you believe?

Cooking hot dogs by frying is done primarily by the heat from conduction from the hot pan directly to the meat. Cooking hot dogs by boiling them is accomplished by convection currents from the pan to the water and by conduction in the contact of hot water with the meat. Cooking hot dogs on the barbecue uses all three modes of heat transfer: radiation through space from the hot coals to the meat; convection of hot air from the hot coals to the meat; and conduction from the hot grill directly to the meat. Microwave cooking occurs through radiation.

Why should you care?

Students' answers will vary. Make certain that their descriptions are accurate and include all relevant modes of heat transfer. Example: Students may describe the preparation of scrambled eggs by radiation. As the microwave radiation heats and cooks the egg, the egg will transfer some of the heat to the container (dish) by conduction. As the container becomes hot, it may transfer some heat back to cooler portions of the egg by conduction.

What Do You Think Now?

At the beginning of the section you were asked the following:

• What is heat?

• What is the difference between heat and temperature?

Now that you have completed this section on heat-energy transfer, how would you explain the difference between heat and temperature?

Chem
Essential Questions

What does it mean?

Chemistry explains a *macroscopic* phenomenon (what you observe) with a description of what happens at the *nanoscopic* level (atoms and molecules) using *symbolic* structures as a way to communicate. Complete the chart below in your *Active Chemistry* log.

MACRO	NANO	SYMBOLIC
Describe how to take measurements using a thermometer. In this investigation, how did you observe temperature changes due to radiation, conduction, and convection?	Explain what is happening to the particles (or molecules) in the object that causes the temperature to rise.	In convection, the movement of the air is invisible. Draw a picture showing how the air moves.

How do you know?

What evidence do you have that heat energy can be used to cook a potato? Describe what was happening to your potatoes as they cooked. Include the method(s) of heat transfer, and evidence that thermal energy was absorbed.

Why do you believe?

You can cook hot dogs by frying them, boiling them, barbecuing them, or microwaving them. Describe where in each of these methods there is conduction, convection, and/or radiation.

Why should you care?

It is very likely that you will want to discuss conduction, convection, and radiation as you cook foods or choose typical kitchen equipment in your cooking show. Suggest one food preparation that you may use in your cooking show.

559

Reflecting on the Section and the Challenge

This section provides an opportunity for students to begin thinking about how to transfer what they have learned into a useful part of their project for the *Chapter Challenge*. You might want to have them do this individually in their *Active Chemistry* logs or informally in their working groups. If time permits, they may benefit from sharing their ideas with the class and getting feedback.

Chem to Go

1.

a) convection

b) conduction

c) radiation

2.

In a solid, an increase in heat energy causes the particles to vibrate more vigorously. In liquids and gases, they gain velocity in their movements in space. Another way that students may answer this question is that when heat energy is absorbed, the particle's kinetic energy is increased, indicated by an increase in temperature.

3.

At absolute zero, the temperature is 0 K and, theoretically, all molecular motion ceases. 0 K = −273.15° C.

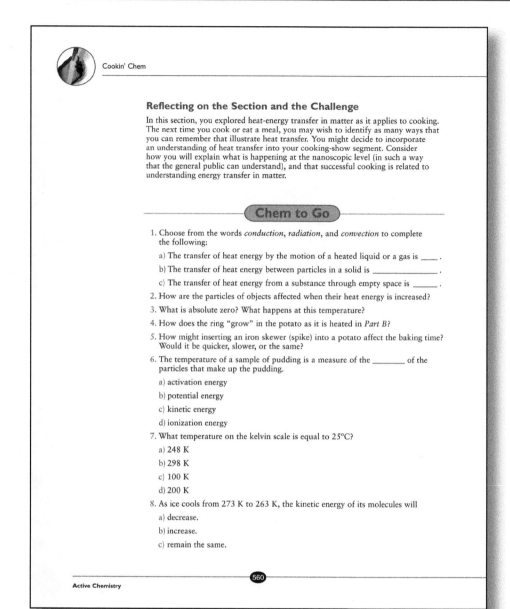

Cookin' Chem

Reflecting on the Section and the Challenge

In this section, you explored heat-energy transfer in matter as it applies to cooking. The next time you cook or eat a meal, you may wish to identify as many ways that you can remember that illustrate heat transfer. You might decide to incorporate an understanding of heat transfer into your cooking-show segment. Consider how you will explain what is happening at the nanoscopic level (in such a way that the general public can understand), and that successful cooking is related to understanding energy transfer in matter.

Chem to Go

1. Choose from the words *conduction*, *radiation*, and *convection* to complete the following:
   a) The transfer of heat energy by the motion of a heated liquid or a gas is ____ .
   b) The transfer of heat energy between particles in a solid is _____ .
   c) The transfer of heat energy from a substance through empty space is _____ .
2. How are the particles of objects affected when their heat energy is increased?
3. What is absolute zero? What happens at this temperature?
4. How does the ring "grow" in the potato as it is heated in *Part B*?
5. How might inserting an iron skewer (spike) into a potato affect the baking time? Would it be quicker, slower, or the same?
6. The temperature of a sample of pudding is a measure of the _____ of the particles that make up the pudding.
   a) activation energy
   b) potential energy
   c) kinetic energy
   d) ionization energy
7. What temperature on the kelvin scale is equal to 25°C?
   a) 248 K
   b) 298 K
   c) 100 K
   d) 200 K
8. As ice cools from 273 K to 263 K, the kinetic energy of its molecules will
   a) decrease.
   b) increase.
   c) remain the same.

560

Active Chemistry

4.

The potato cooks from the outside inward due to transfer of heat by conduction within the potato. The uncooked portion (the ring) at the center of the potato grows smaller.

5.

The baking time would be reduced by inserting an iron skewer into a potato. The iron skewer would conduct heat and transfer that heat directly to the inside of the potato. Thus, the potato would cook from the outside inward as well as from the inside outward.

6.

c) average kinetic energy

7.

b) 298 K

8.

a) decrease

9.

b) *X* is 10°C and *Y* is 5°C

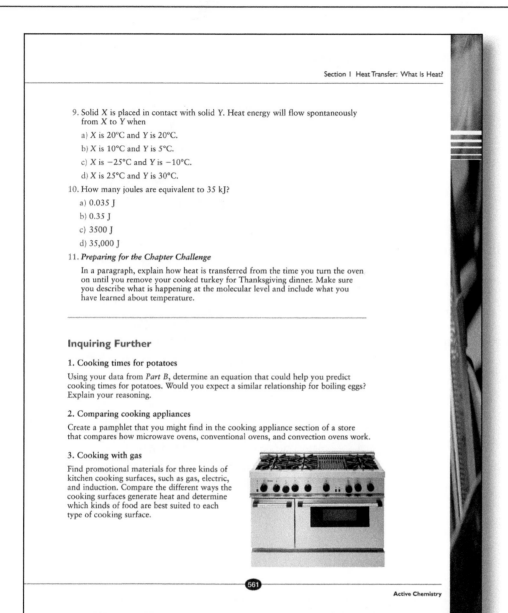

9. Solid *X* is placed in contact with solid *Y*. Heat energy will flow spontaneously from *X* to *Y* when

   a) *X* is 20°C and *Y* is 20°C.

   b) *X* is 10°C and *Y* is 5°C.

   c) *X* is −25°C and *Y* is −10°C.

   d) *X* is 25°C and *Y* is 30°C.

10. How many joules are equivalent to 35 kJ?

    a) 0.035 J

    b) 0.35 J

    c) 3500 J

    d) 35,000 J

11. *Preparing for the Chapter Challenge*

   In a paragraph, explain how heat is transferred from the time you turn the oven on until you remove your cooked turkey for Thanksgiving dinner. Make sure you describe what is happening at the molecular level and include what you have learned about temperature.

Inquiring Further

1. Cooking times for potatoes

Using your data from *Part B*, determine an equation that could help you predict cooking times for potatoes. Would you expect a similar relationship for boiling eggs? Explain your reasoning.

2. Comparing cooking appliances

Create a pamphlet that you might find in the cooking appliance section of a store that compares how microwave ovens, conventional ovens, and convection ovens work.

3. Cooking with gas

Find promotional materials for three kinds of kitchen cooking surfaces, such as gas, electric, and induction. Compare the different ways the cooking surfaces generate heat and determine which kinds of food are best suited to each type of cooking surface.

561

Active Chemistry

10.

d) 35,000 J

11.

Preparing for the Chapter Challenge

Students' answers will vary but all should include accurate use of the terms for heat transfer – conduction, convection, and radiation. Most ovens will use at least two of these modes, and some all three. Heat transfer from the surface of the turkey to its center takes place by conduction. Knowing how heat is transferred is a key part to understanding how foods and cookware can be used to prepare the final product for their cooking show.

Inquiring Further

1. Cooking times for potatoes

The data table and graph students prepared in the *Investigate*, Part B: Step 2, will be most helpful here. If the graph appears to be linear, a line can be drawn through the points and pass through zero. The equation for a straight line is $y = mx + b$, where m is the slope of the line and b is the y intercept. Because the line passes through the origin, the equation becomes $y = mx$. Using the data from the table and graph,

$$m = (y_2 - y_1)/(x_2 - x_1)$$
$$= (13 - 0)/(12 - 0)$$
$$= 13/12 = 1.1$$

The equation becomes $y = 1.1x$.

If the graphing of the data does not result in a straight line, the data can be entered into a graphing calculator to find a best fit with equation.

The equation for cooking an egg would be similar because it has about the same shape (oval) as a potato. It should cook more quickly because it is smaller and is more liquid, but like the potato, will cook from the outside inward.

2. Comparing cooking appliances

You might want to have the students provide sketches as well as word descriptions.

3. Cooking with gas

Students may be surprised to learn that a induction cooking surface remains cool to the touch and only heats the cookware, which must contain ferromagnetic materials. Unlike gas or electric stovetops, induction does not heat the surrounding air which is a benefit, especially in summer. You might ask them to include a comparison of safety and air conditioning costs in considering the cooking surfaces.

SECTION 1 – QUIZ

| 7-1c | **Blackline Master** |

1. Define heat and its relationship with temperature.

2. What are the three ways that heat can be transferred?

   a) Absorption, convection, and thermation

   b) Absorption, convention, and radiation

   c) Conduction, convection, and radiation

   d) Conduction, absorption, and radiation

3. Convert 25°C to Kelvin and show your work.

4. Convert 100°C to Fahrenheit and show your work.

5. Identify and describe the types of heat transfer involved when:

   a) You cook a hot dog over a camp fire.

   b) Spaghetti is cooked in a pot of water.

SECTION 1 – QUIZ ANSWERS

❶ Heat is a form of energy that results from the motion of particles–atoms and molecules. It is transferred as a result of a temperature difference between two particles. Temperature is a measure of the average kinetic energy of the particles of a substance.

❷ c) Conduction, convection, and radiation

❸ $K = °C + 273$, $25°C + 273 = 298$ K

❹ $°F = 9/5(°C) + 32$, $9/5(100°C) + 32 = 212°F$

❺ a) Convection from the hot air rising and heating the hot dog, radiation from the hot coals directly to the hot dog, conduction from the hot air to the hot dog.

   b) Convection from the hot water currents as they rise from the bottom of the pot, conduction from the hot pot to the water and from the hot water directly to the spaghetti.

NOTES

_____

_____

_____

_____

_____

_____

_____

_____

NOTES

SECTION 2
Combustion Reactions and Hydrocarbons

Section Overview

This section allows students to explore combustion reactions and make qualitative observations. They will use candles to learn about combustion and to determine the requirements for starting and maintaining a fire. Some of the chemical properties of CO_2 and O_2 gases will be examined and students will practice balancing equations of combustion reactions.

Background Information

Long before anyone knew anything about the existence of atoms and elements, people were applying chemistry by lighting fires and cooking food. The creation and controlling of fire was perhaps the first of many chemistry-related discoveries that has led civilization to where it is now.

An English chemist, Joseph Priestly, isolated oxygen gas in 1774 and soon afterwards, French chemist Antoine Lavoisier showed that oxygen is the key substance in combustion reactions. Lavoisier also demonstrated that when combustion is carried out in a closed container, the mass of the combustion products is equal to the mass of the starting reactants. This is true of all chemical reactions and is known as the law of conservation of mass.

Combustion is the rapid combination of oxygen with another material. When hydrocarbons, such as propane, are burned in air, oxygen combines with carbon and hydrogen to form CO_2 and H_2O. Combustion is generally an exothermic reaction that is accompanied by release of energy in the form of heat and light. The combustion of paraffin candles may be represented as:

$$2C_{20}H_{42} + 61O_2 \longrightarrow 40CO_2 + 42H_2O$$

What is happening when a candle burns? It is known that the fuel is the wax, but why isn't it possible to ignite and burn the wax directly? That is, why doesn't the flame from the wick extend down to the pool of liquid wax below and set it on fire?

The answer is that it is actually the vapor of the wax that undergoes combustion instead of its liquid or solid form. The heat produced by the combustion started by the flame of a match melts some of the wax at the top of the candle. Some of this liquid makes its way up the wick where it is evaporated by the flame's heat and this gas is then ignited.

	LEARNING OUTCOMES	
LEARNING OUTCOMES	**LOCATION IN SECTION**	**EVIDENCE OF UNDERSTANDING**
Discover what a combustion reaction is and what the products of a combustion reaction are.	*Investigate* Steps 2-8 *Chem Talk, Checking Up* Questions 2, 6 *Chem to Go* Questions 1, 3-5, 7	Successfully complete the *Investigate* steps and correctly describe the reactants and products of combustion reactions based upon observations. Students' answers match those provided in this *Teacher's Edition*.
Form carbon dioxide and oxygen gases and understand their role in the combustion process.	*Investigate* Steps 7-8. *Chem Talk*	Successfully complete the *Investigate* steps and correctly describe the role of CO_2 and O_2 in combustion reactions.
Practice balancing chemical equations.	*Chem Talk, Checking Up* Question 6 *Chem to Go* Questions 2-6, 8-9	Students' answers match those given in this *Teacher's Edition*.

NOTES

_____

_____

_____

_____

_____

_____

_____

_____

_____

_____

_____

_____

_____

_____

_____

Section 2
Materials, Chemicals, Preparation, and Safety

("per Group" quantity is based on group size of 4 students)

Materials and Equipment

Materials (and Equipment)	Quantity per Group (4 students)
Crucible tongs	1
Candle	1
Cardboard squares (4"x 4") covered with foil	1
Box of matches	1
Beaker, 250-mL	1
Scoopula	1
Graduated cylinder, 50-mL	1
Test-tube, large	1
Test-tube rack	1
Modeling clay or candle holder	1
Ruler	1
Scissors	1
Materials (and Equipment)	Quantity per Class
Box of baking soda	1
Box of wooden splints	1
Ball of string	1
Scissors	1

Chemicals

Chemicals	Quantity per Class (24 students)
3% hydrogen peroxide	50 mL
Manganese dioxide, MnO_2	2.5 g
Acetic Acid	400 mL
Sodium bicarbonate	40 g

Teacher Preparation

None.

Safety Requirements

- Goggles and aprons are required for all activity in the laboratory area.

- All waste can be disposed of in the trash or down the drain.

- Wash hands and arms before leaving the laboratory area.

NOTES

Meeting the Needs of All Students
Differentiated Instruction

Augmentation and Accommodations

LEARNING ISSUE	REFERENCE	AUGMENTATION AND ACCOMMODATIONS
Making qualitative and quantitative observations	*Investigate*	**Augmentation** • Circulate among students who need guidance during the investigation. **Accommodations** • Some students' observations may not pertain to combustion (e.g, "The candle is red.") while others may make only qualitative observations. Check for understanding by asking students to share their observations with the class, providing qualitative and quantitative models for students who have difficulty.
Descriptive and interpretive writing	*Investigate*	**Augmentation** • At the beginning of the investigation, clearly explain the difference between a brief description of an activity, their observations from it, and their interpretations to come later. When students reach Step 9, model expectations by reading a well-written description and some observations. Ask them to compare that writing with interpretive writing and give examples students might use.
Interpreting equations and symbols	*Chem Talk*	**Augmentation** • Ensure that students know that O, C and H are symbols for oxygen, carbon and hydrogen and that the number after each letter indicates the number of atoms of that element. Check for understanding of the use of the plus sign and arrow. The names and functions will need to be directly taught to individuals or groups who do not have this knowledge already. **Accommodations** • Allow students to work in small groups, with at least one skilled writer in each.
Interpreting symbolic drawings	*Chem Talk*	**Augmentation** • Despite the equations and ball-and-stick representations, some students may need practice with manipulatives they can actually arrange to mimic the reactions and balancing.
Determining whether an equation is balanced	*Chem to Go*	**Augmentation/Accommodations** • For students with math difficulties, determining balance is considerably easier than actually balancing an equation. Determining balance requires that students know that the arrow divides the reactants from the products and that the number of atoms on the reactant side must be equal to the number of atoms on the product side. For students having difficulty, prepare a table that separates reactants and products as well as elements. Any problems that they have in counting the atoms should be clearly evident for you to resolve.
Balancing a combustion reaction equation	*Chem to Go*	**Augmentation** • Model the cognitive process of balancing an equation: counting a particular type of atom on each side, adjusting the coefficient to balance those atoms, looking for imbalance produced by that change, and repeating this procedure until the equation is balanced. Your students may need to be shown the procedure and told that if they repeat this procedure, the equation will eventually balance. Remind them that successful problem solvers are persistent. **Accommodations** • Some equations require only one or two steps to balance. For example, Question 3.a) requires students to simply double the number of water molecules and then adjust the number of hydrogen molecules accordingly. Question 9.a), however, is more complex – involving several steps in proper sequence. You may choose to divide the questions and assign the less challenging ones to those students having difficulties.

Strategies for Students with Limited English Language Proficiency

LEARNING ISSUE	REFERENCE	AUGMENTATION AND ACCOMMODATIONS
Background knowledge	*What Do You Think?*	Students may want to start with a description of what is in the illustration for oral language development. Check for understanding of the prefix "*un*" as in "*unwanted*."
Vocabulary	*Investigate*	Check for understanding of the idea of "*quantitative*" and "*qualitative*." When students are asked to write a brief description, they might benefit from an example. In Step 4, students are asked to "*invert*," which may be an unfamiliar word for some students.
Background knowledge Vocabulary Comprehending text	*Chem Talk*	Check for understanding of the term "*coefficients*." Refer students to sidebar material for further explanations of the isolated words. Check for pronunciation of the term "*acetic*" as it may be new to them.
Background knowledge	*What Do You Think Now?*	Have students discuss their answers prior to writing them.
Background knowledge Vocabulary Comprehending text	*Chem Essential Questions*	"*Soot*" may be a new term for some students. Discuss the word, "*extinguished*" and share some of the different uses of this word to provide different contexts and build background knowledge.
Comprehension Vocabulary	*Chem to Go*	Make sure students can distinguish between those questions that are stacked, where there is more than one response, and those that are multiple choice.
Application Comprehension	*Inquiring Further*	The word "*devise*" may be a new term for some students. Have students discuss possible answers in small groups.

NOTES

_____

_____

_____

_____

_____

_____

_____

_____

_____

_____

_____

Section 2
Teaching Suggestions and Sample Answers

What Do You See?

The colorful illustration that begins the section offers a way to capture students' interest and get them thinking and talking about the topic of this section. This is a good opportunity to promote active participation and the responses should help you to evaluate prior knowledge and possible misconceptions. The accuracy of the students' comments is not important at this stage.

Some of their comments may focus on the obvious or incidental features of the illustration, such as "Look at that fire burn!" or "That cat is really moving!" Others may find some greater meaning in the picture and suggest that "It looks like carbon dioxide is putting the fire out." Both types of responses are valid and should be recognized.

 Cookin' Chem

Section 2   Combustion Reactions and Hydrocarbons

What Do You See?

Learning Outcomes

In this section you will

- Discover what a combustion reaction is and what the products of a combustion reaction are.
- Generate carbon dioxide and oxygen gases.
- Practice balancing chemical equations.

What Do You Think?

Humans have been using fire to cook food for thousands of years.

- **What is necessary for a fire?**
- **What can be used to put out an unwanted fire in a kitchen?**

Record your ideas about these questions in your *Active Chemistry* log. Be prepared to discuss your responses with your group and the class.

Investigate

Many of the investigations of science involve making observations with your senses—mainly sight, but to a lesser extent smell, touch, and sound. Observations can be either qualitative or quantitative. *Qualitative observations* are descriptions of what is occurring. *Quantitative observations* involve the use of measurements. Interpretations are based on your observations. They are an explanation of the observations.

In this lab investigation, you will make qualitative and quantitative observations about a candle before, during, and after it is lit. You will then interpret several of your observations. This will give you information that could be used as a part of your cooking show.

For each step in the procedure, write a brief description of what you are doing, followed by your observations in your *Active Chemistry* log. Leave room for interpretations (three or four lines), but do not attempt to make interpretations yet.

562

What Do You Think?

Like the illustration, the questions posed here are intended to elicit student responses for the purpose of assessing prior knowledge and conceptions. Students may suggest that a fire needs something to burn (fuel) and air (oxygen) and that controlling the amount of fuel or air can control fires. They might also say that a flame (heat) is necessary. For putting out kitchen fires, they might suggest that a fire extinguisher is needed. Some may think that only water is necessary. Accept all reasonable responses; you are not looking for accuracy at this point. You will be returning to these questions later in the activity.

What Do You Think?
A CHEMIST'S RESPONSE

The necessary elements for a fire are fuel and an oxidizer. Common fuels are coal, wood, methane, propane, butane, kerosene, and gasoline. The most common oxidizer is, of course, the oxygen found in air. Almost all fires also need a source of heat – a flame or spark – in order to begin the combustion process. Once started, a fire will provide its own heat to maintain the process.

An unwanted kitchen fire in the kitchen must be treated carefully. If it is a grease fire on the stove, water is not a good choice. Water will cause spattering and perhaps even exacerbate or spread the fire. For this type of fire you would want to use a solid chemical fire extinguisher or simply smother the fire using a lid. If it is an electrical fire, water is again a poor choice. A solid chemical fire extinguisher would be best.

Substances and/or procedures that are effective in putting out fires fall into three categories:

- Removal of the oxidizer
- Removal of the fuel
- Removal of the heat source that maintains the combustion process

Water is sometimes a good choice for extinguishing fires because it can do all three things. By coating the fuel (wood, coal) with water, the fuel and oxygen are separated. Also, any water evaporated by the heat will provide a transient blanket of nonflammable gas. Finally, the water will lower the temperature of the fuel and thus require the fire to use its heat to evaporate the water rather than continue the combustion process.

On the other hand, there are many types of fires that would be aggravated by the use of water. Burning liquids, for instance, will usually float on top of water and actually be spread further. A kitchen grease fire is best extinguished with a CO_2 fire extinguisher, a dry chemical extinguisher, or simply by placing a lid on the frying pan. A fire involving sodium or potassium also should not be extinguished with water. These elements react with water to form hydrogen gas. In addition, electrical fires should not be treated with water. While it might extinguish the blaze, the use of water risks the danger of electrocution since it conducts electricity.

As shown in the activity, carbon dioxide is an excellent extinguisher of fires. It separates the fuel from the oxygen with a layer of nonflammable CO_2 and has the advantage of being heavier than air so it will stay on top of the fuel.

STUDENTS' PRIOR CONCEPTIONS

Students will generally agree that oxygen is necessary for combustion, but do not see it as something interacting with the combustible reactant. They have a hard time believing that water is one of the products of the candle burning.

Students will probably be uncertain about the source of fuel for a burning candle and what physical state this fuel is in when burning. They may believe that the wick is burning and that the wax is simply present to slow down the burning.

They may say that water can be used to smother a fire, but not be aware of the fact that it lowers the heat available for the combustion reaction.

NOTES

1. Obtain a ruler, a candle, and a foil-covered cardboard square. Place the candle in a holder on the square, or fix it to the square using putty. Make between six and ten observations about the unlit candle.

🖎 a) Record your observations in your *Active Chemistry* log.

2. Light the candle. Make an additional six to ten observations. Be sure to make observations about the flame.

🖎 a) Record your observations.

3. Light a match. Blow out the candle and quickly bring the lit match into the smoke. Repeat once or twice and make observations.

🖎 a) Record your observations.

🖎 b) Leave room in your log for the interpretations that you will make later.

4. Light the candle and then invert a clean, dry 250-mL beaker over the flame. Slowly lower the beaker over the flame. Repeat once or twice and make observations. Be sure to look carefully into the beaker, too. (Note: The beaker will become hot over time!)

🖎 a) Record your observations.

🖎 b) Leave room for your interpretations.

5. Hold a piece of string with forceps over the table. Light the string.

🖎 a) Record your observations.

🖎 b) Leave room for your interpretations.

6. Place a foil collar around the wick of the candle. Light the candle.

🖎 a) Record your observations.

🖎 b) Leave room for your interpretations.

7. The reaction between vinegar and baking soda releases carbon dioxide gas. Place a small scoop of baking soda with about 50 mL of vinegar in a 250-mL beaker. Observe the reaction. Carefully 'pour' the gas (but not the liquid) over the flame of the candle.

🖎 a) Record your observations.

🖎 b) Leave room for your interpretations.

8. The decomposition of hydrogen peroxide releases oxygen gas. The reaction is catalyzed (sped up) by adding manganese dioxide to the hydrogen peroxide. Fill a test tube one third of the way with hydrogen peroxide and add a rice grain-sized amount of manganese dioxide. Test the resulting gas by lighting a splint and blowing it out.

Investigate

Begin by brainstorming the differences between observations and interpretations. Have students come up with a list of what makes a good observation. Then begin the activity by reminding the students that their first task is to make only observations – interpretations will come later.

1.

Observations of the candle may be both qualitative and quantitative.

Qualitative observations may include color, feel, color of wick, odor, shape, and any designs or irregularities on the surface of the candle.

Quantitative observations may include the mass (g) as well as the length, diameter, circumference, and length of wick (cm).

Explain that scientific observations should describe objectively what is present (e.g., there is a black, 1-cm string in the center of the top of the wax cylinder) and should not interpret or try to make sense of what is seen (e.g., the candle has been burned).

2.

Observations of the lit candle will be mostly qualitative and could include colors, shape and size of flame, location of flame, what it is doing, e.g., formation of a "bowl-shaped" area at top of candle, liquid in the bowl, particles moving in the liquid.

3.

The candle should relight as flame from the match jumps to the wick.

4.

The beaker should be clean and dry. Students should see the candle flame increase in size before going out; smoke fills the beaker, a black deposit forms on the bottom of the beaker, and a "fog" of water vapor forms on the sides of the beaker.

5.

The string burns up quickly; ashes remain.

6.

Use a 2–3 cm square of aluminum foil with a slit to the center. Apply snugly around the wick. Students should see the candle flame gradually get smaller and eventually go out.

7.

If poured directly over the flame, the gas should put the flame out. This may need to be repeated. Since carbon dioxide is heavier than air, it should pour out over the flame.

8.

The splint will reignite in the mouth of the test tube.

> ### TEACHING TIP
>
> You may want to assign the interpretations of Steps 3-8 as homework and discuss them during the next class period. Remind students about the distinction between interpretations and observations:
>
> Interpretations are explanations of observations. That is, they should explain why a particular reaction occurred and what was formed. Interpretations should be supported by the observations. Students may find that their interpretations are not the "correct" ones upon further investigation.

9.

- Step 3: It is not the candle wax or the wick that is burning in the flame. An invisible gas around the wick provides the fuel and relights. If not done quickly, the candle does not relight.

- Step 4: The beaker cut off the oxygen that is needed for the flame. It could also be that there was a buildup of carbon dioxide that put out the flame. The black deposit was unburned carbon from the fuel. The fog was water that formed and condensed on the beaker.

- Step 5: The string is made of the same material as the wick. It burns quickly and doesn't leave much behind. This shows that the wick is not a significant source of fuel for the flame.

- Step 6: The aluminum foil collar cut off the supply of wax (fuel) to the flame. It is also possible that it absorbed the heat needed to maintain the flame. It did not cut off the oxygen supply.

- Step 7: The carbon dioxide put out the flame. It must have cooled the flame so that it could not be maintained or it removed the supply of oxygen.

- Step 8: The oxygen accelerated the combustion process.

10.a)

Two methods used to put out the fire were:

- inverting a beaker over the lit candle

- pouring carbon dioxide over the lit candle.

Cookin' Chem

The end should be glowing. Quickly insert and remove the glowing splint into the mouth of the test tube.

a) Record your observations.

b) Leave room for your interpretations.

9. For *Steps 3* through *8*, write a sentence to interpret your observations. These should be an explanation of what you observed. Why do you think each observation occurred? How can you explain what you saw?

10. There are three things necessary for combustion—fuel, oxygen, and a source of heat. The fuel in this case is the candle, which is made of wax and a string. The source of heat was from the match. The oxygen is found in the air. Answer the following questions in your *Active Chemistry* log, based upon your observations and interpretations.

a) What are two methods that you used to put out the fire? Explain how each one worked in terms of the three necessities for combustion.

b) What is the actual fuel for the combustion of the burning candle? What are the functions of the wax and the string? What evidence do you have to support your response?

c) Suppose you were to let the candle burn until the wick was completely gone. Describe what would be left and how it would compare to the original candle. What happened to the wax? Could you make a new candle from what remained?

d) Clean up your workstation as directed by your teacher. Save the candle for future use.

> ⚠️ Wash hands and arms thoroughly before leaving the lab area.

Chem Words

chemical change: a process in which new materials with different properties are formed.

reactants: the materials that you initially start with in a chemical reaction.

products: the materials that are the result of a chemical reaction.

Chem Talk

THE COMBUSTION REACTION

The Equation for Combustion

Food is all about eating! Cooking food is all about heat. Fire is one way of producing heat. Creating a flame was certainly one of the great advances in the history of humankind. The first fire may have been from lightning, but some human decided to maintain the flame and use it to begin other fires. Eventually, someone invented a means to create a spark and start fires at will.

When a substance burns in the presence of oxygen, a chemical change takes place. In a **chemical change**, new substances are produced. The substances you start with are called **reactants**, and the substances that form are called **products**. The key part of a chemical reaction is that the products are different substances from the reactants.

564

Active Chemistry

Both methods separated the oxygen from the fuel long enough to extinguish the flame.

10.b)

The actual fuel for the flame is a gas, possibly vaporized wax. The evidence for the fuel being a gas was provided by the behavior of the flame (moving more like a gas than a liquid or solid) and by its re-ignition with a match.

The function of the wax is to provide a constant source of fuel. The wax first melts; it then moves up the wick by capillary action. The evidence for this is the decreasing size of the candle with time as the candle burns. The wick provides no significant fuel because, by itself, it burns quickly with little total heat or light. When it reaches the flame, it is vaporized and burns.

The function of the string (wick) is to provide a place for the liquid wax to contact excess air as it is vaporized for burning. The evidence for the wick being a transport device is the extinguishing of the flame when an aluminum foil collar is placed on it.

10.c)

A puddle of solid wax would be left after the wick was completely gone. It would represent a small portion (perhaps 10%) of the original candle and have an entirely new form. The remainder of the wax (90%) burned to provide light and heat. Yes, you could make a new candle from the remaining wax but it would be much smaller and require a new wick.

TEACHING TIP

At this point you may want to have a class discussion.

You can begin by having students read their descriptions from the first two procedures as you attempt to draw what they describe on an overhead. (Their descriptions will probably lack the appropriate qualifiers and quantitative information.) A student observation may be that the candle is round with a burned wick in it. A more descriptive observation might be that the candle is a cylinder about 10 cm tall and 1 cm in diameter with a piece of black string about 1 cm tall protruding from the center of the top. The same is true for the lit candle. Descriptions of the flame are usually limited to the fact that there is a flame on top of the candle.

More descriptive observations would include the colors (orange and blue), the shape (teardrop), size (about 2 cm), location (surrounding the string) and other properties (e.g., the flame is moving, smoke can be seen coming from the top, there is a bowl-shaped depression at the base of the string where liquid wax is forming, the tip of the string is glowing red). Questioning the students should lead them to the understanding that good observations include both descriptive adjectives and quantitative information and are different from interpretations.

Each of the discussion questions should offer an opportunity to reinforce the differences between observations and interpretations. Have students review the interpretations they did for homework. They may realize that they had too narrow a focus when looking for evidence to support an interpretation, which could lead to an incorrect interpretation. Questions that are designed to help them focus on the "big picture" will help them to find broad support for an interpretation.

NOTES

When a **hydrocarbon** (a compound composed of hydrogen and carbon) reacts with oxygen (O_2), a **combustion reaction** occurs. The products of a complete combustion reaction are carbon dioxide (CO_2) and water (H_2O). There are lots of materials you can burn. Candles, wood, gasoline, and natural gas are some. Candle wax is made of relatively long-chain hydrocarbons ($C_{20}H_{42}$ and larger). Other hydrocarbon fuels that you might be familiar with are methane (CH_4, the chief component of natural gas), propane (C_3H_8), butane (C_4H_{10}), and octane (C_8H_{18}, a component of gasoline). When any of these compounds are burned in the presence of sufficient oxygen, the products are CO_2 and H_2O.

Consider the complete combustion of propane gas

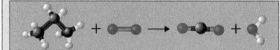

$$C_3H_8 \quad + \quad O_2 \quad \rightarrow \quad CO_2 \quad + \quad H_2O$$

propane   oxygen   carbon dioxide   water

reactants

(total of 3 C atoms, 8 H atoms, 2 O atoms)   products

(total of 1 C atom, 2 H atoms, and 3 O atoms)

The propane gas and the oxygen reacts to produce carbon dioxide and water.

The chemical equation is one way you can describe the reaction. Another symbolic representation (ball-and-stick models) is shown in the diagram. The products are carbon dioxide and water.

Balancing the Combustion Equation

Look closely at the chemical equation for the combustion of propane. You can see that there are different numbers of atoms on both sides of the equation. On the reactant side, there are 3 carbon atoms (shown in black), 8 hydrogen atoms (shown in white), and 2 oxygen atoms (shown in red). On the product side of the equation, there is only 1 carbon atom, 2 hydrogen atoms, and 3 oxygen atoms. This violates the **law of conservation of mass**. The law states that the total mass of the products of a chemical reaction is the same as the total mass of the reactants entering into the reaction. Since there are different numbers of atoms before and after the reaction, the total mass of atoms involved is not equal. To fix this, you need to **balance** the equation. →

Chem Words

hydrocarbon: an organic compound that contains only hydrogen and carbon atoms.

combustion reaction: a chemical reaction that involves the burning of a hydrocarbon in presence of oxygen.

law of conservation of mass: a law that states that the total mass of the products of a chemical reaction is the same as the total mass of the reactants entering into the reaction.

balanced chemical equation: an equation in which the number and kind of atoms of the reactants equals the same number and kind of atoms of the products.

Chem Talk

The reading provides a detailed summary of combustion and the equations that describe the process. The relationship of the chemical change, the reactants and the products are detailed by those equations. Balancing equations using the concept of the law of conservation of mass is explained, and important understandings and skills relating to balancing equations are outlined. Finally, the roles of oxygen and carbon dioxide in the reactions encountered in this activity are reviewed.

CHAPTER 7

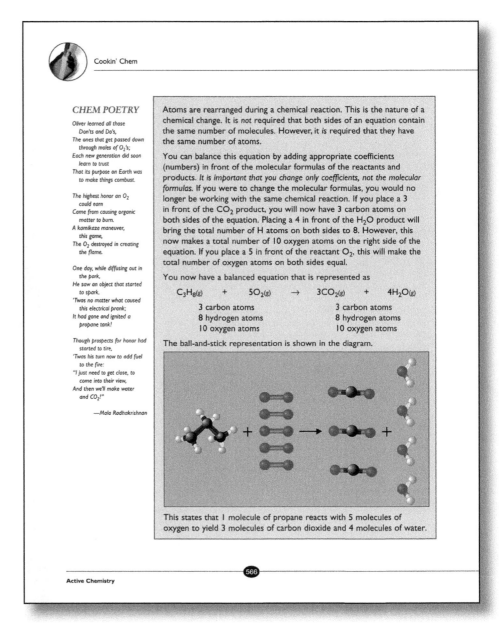

CHEM POETRY

Oliver learned all those
  Don'ts and Do's,
The ones that get passed down
  through moles of O_2's;
Each new generation did soon
  learn to trust
That its purpose on Earth was
  to make things combust.

The highest honor an O_2
  could earn
Came from causing organic
  matter to burn.
A kamikaze maneuver,
  this game,
The O_2 destroyed in creating
  the flame.

One day, while diffusing out in
  the park,
He saw an object that started
  to spark.
'Twas no matter what caused
  this electrical prank;
It had gone and ignited a
  propane tank!

Though prospects for honor had
  started to tire,
'Twas his turn now to add fuel
  to the fire:
"I just need to get close, to
  come into their view,
And then we'll make water
  and CO_2!"

—Mala Radhakrishnan

Atoms are rearranged during a chemical reaction. This is the nature of a chemical change. It is *not* required that both sides of an equation contain the same number of molecules. However, it *is* required that they have the same number of atoms.

You can balance this equation by adding appropriate coefficients (numbers) in front of the molecular formulas of the reactants and products. *It is important that you change only coefficients, not the molecular formulas.* If you were to change the molecular formulas, you would no longer be working with the same chemical reaction. If you place a 3 in front of the CO_2 product, you will now have 3 carbon atoms on both sides of the equation. Placing a 4 in front of the H_2O product will bring the total number of H atoms on both sides to 8. However, this now makes a total number of 10 oxygen atoms on the right side of the equation. If you place a 5 in front of the reactant O_2, this will make the total number of oxygen atoms on both sides equal.

You now have a balanced equation that is represented as

$$C_3H_{8(g)} \quad + \quad 5O_{2(g)} \quad \rightarrow \quad 3CO_{2(g)} \quad + \quad 4H_2O_{(g)}$$

3 carbon atoms	3 carbon atoms
8 hydrogen atoms	8 hydrogen atoms
10 oxygen atoms	10 oxygen atoms

The ball-and-stick representation is shown in the diagram.

This states that 1 molecule of propane reacts with 5 molecules of oxygen to yield 3 molecules of carbon dioxide and 4 molecules of water.

Chem Poetry

The *Chem Poetry* provides an additional opportunity to engage students' imagination and curiosity about chemistry. You may want to read the poem aloud and briefly discuss ideas on how it might relate to the chemistry. There is no need for analysis now; you will have a chance to return to the poem after the activity is complete to reassess its relevance.

The *Chem Poetry* provided in the Student Edition is only an edited version of the longer, complete poem as it was originally published. For your convenience, the unabridged versions of all the *Chem Poetry*

7-2a   **Blackline Master**

There are two important understandings for balancing equations that you should have:

- You need to understand that you can balance equations because mass is conserved during a chemical reaction. The mass before the reaction must be identical to the mass after the reaction.

- You need to understand that you can balance equations because atoms are conserved during a chemical reaction. For example, the oxygen atoms entering the reaction must be the same oxygen atoms after the reaction.

There are two skills concerning balancing equations that you should also develop:

- You should be able to recognize whether a chemical equation is balanced by checking if the numbers of each atom are identical in the product and reactant sides of the equation.

- You should be able to balance the equations so the numbers of each atom are identical in the product and reactant sides of the equation. This skill has more to do with solving a "math puzzle" than the essence of chemistry and chemical principles.

All chemists understand why equations must be balanced. They can check to see if an equation is balanced. Some chemists enjoy balancing equations, while others do not.

The Role of Oxygen and Carbon Dioxide in Combustion

In *Step 4* of this *Investigate*, you placed a beaker over the candle flame. This reduced the amount of O_2 entering into the reaction. Without a source of O_2, the combustion reaction eventually stops.

In addition to the requirement that oxygen be present for fuel to burn, energy must be provided in order to start the reaction. In lighting a candle, a burning match provides the energy required to initiate the reaction.

In *Step 7*, you prepared CO_2 gas by reacting vinegar with baking soda. This happens in two steps. Vinegar contains acetic acid. This acetic acid reacts with baking soda (sodium hydrogen carbonate), and produces carbonic acid and sodium acetate. The carbonic acid is an unstable compound. It decomposes into CO_2 and H_2O.

→

567

Checking Up

1.

A qualitative observation is an observation of features that do not involve measurement. On the other hand, a quantitative measurement is an observation of features that involve the use of measurements.

2.

A chemical change is a process in which new chemical materials with new chemical properties are formed.

3.

The reactants in a combustion reaction are a fuel–commonly a hydrocarbon–and oxygen. The products are carbon dioxide and water.

4.

Examples of hydrocarbons include candle wax ($C_{20}H_{42}$), methane (CH_4), propane (C_3H_8), butane (C_4H_{10}), and octane (C_8H_{18}).

5.

The law of conservation of mass states that the total mass of the products of a chemical reaction is the same as the total mass of the reactants entering into the reaction. Therefore, one can balance a chemical reaction by equating the number and kind of atoms in the reactants with the number and kind in the products.

6.

Yes, the equation is balanced. The reactants and products both contain 1 carbon atom, 4 hydrogen atoms, and 4 oxygen atoms.

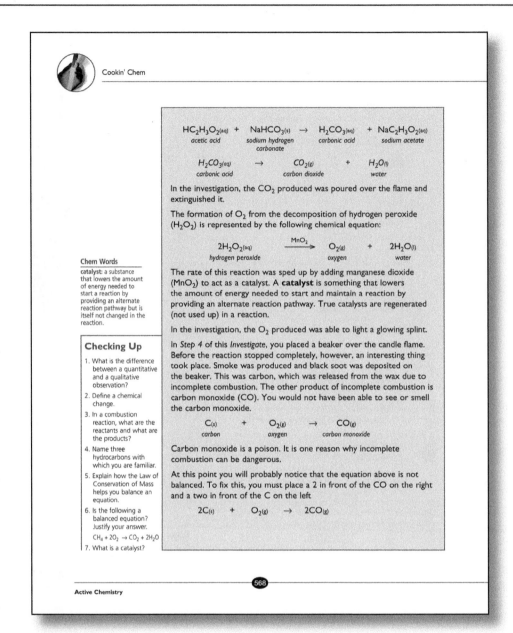

Cookin' Chem

$$HC_2H_3O_{2(aq)} + NaHCO_{3(s)} \rightarrow H_2CO_{3(aq)} + NaC_2H_3O_{2(aq)}$$

acetic acid   *sodium hydrogen carbonate*   *carbonic acid*   *sodium acetate*

$$H_2CO_{3(aq)} \rightarrow CO_{2(g)} + H_2O_{(l)}$$

carbonic acid   *carbon dioxide*   *water*

In the investigation, the CO_2 produced was poured over the flame and extinguished it.

The formation of O_2 from the decomposition of hydrogen peroxide (H_2O_2) is represented by the following chemical equation:

$$2H_2O_{2(aq)} \xrightarrow{MnO_2} O_{2(g)} + 2H_2O_{(l)}$$

hydrogen peroxide   *oxygen*   *water*

The rate of this reaction was sped up by adding manganese dioxide (MnO_2) to act as a catalyst. A **catalyst** is something that lowers the amount of energy needed to start and maintain a reaction by providing an alternate reaction pathway. True catalysts are regenerated (not used up) in a reaction.

In the investigation, the O_2 produced was able to light a glowing splint.

In *Step 4* of this *Investigate*, you placed a beaker over the candle flame. Before the reaction stopped completely, however, an interesting thing took place. Smoke was produced and black soot was deposited on the beaker. This was carbon, which was released from the wax due to incomplete combustion. The other product of incomplete combustion is carbon monoxide (CO). You would not have been able to see or smell the carbon monoxide.

$$C_{(s)} + O_{2(g)} \rightarrow CO_{(g)}$$

carbon   *oxygen*   *carbon monoxide*

Carbon monoxide is a poison. It is one reason why incomplete combustion can be dangerous.

At this point you will probably notice that the equation above is not balanced. To fix this, you must place a 2 in front of the CO on the right and a two in front of the C on the left

$$2C_{(s)} + O_{2(g)} \rightarrow 2CO_{(g)}$$

Chem Words

catalyst: a substance that lowers the amount of energy needed to start a reaction by providing an alternate reaction pathway but is itself not changed in the reaction.

Checking Up

1. What is the difference between a quantitative and a qualitative observation?
2. Define a chemical change.
3. In a combustion reaction, what are the reactants and what are the products?
4. Name three hydrocarbons with which you are familiar.
5. Explain how the Law of Conservation of Mass helps you balance an equation.
6. Is the following a balanced equation? Justify your answer. $CH_4 + 2O_2 \rightarrow CO_2 + 2H_2O$
7. What is a catalyst?

568

Active Chemistry

7.

A catalyst is a substance that lowers the amount of energy needed to start a reaction by providing an alternate reaction pathway but is, itself, not changed in the reaction.

What Do You Think Now?

At the beginning of the section you were asked the following:

- What is necessary for a fire?
- What can be used to put out an unwanted fire in a kitchen?

Now that you have completed this section on heat-energy transfer, what are the three things required for a fire? Once a fire has started, what should you remove in order to put the fire out?

Chem Essential Questions

What does it mean?

Chemistry explains a *macroscopic* phenomenon (what you observe) with a description of what happens at the *nanoscopic* level (atoms and molecules) using *symbolic* structures as a way to communicate. Complete the chart below in your Active Chemistry log.

MACRO	NANO	SYMBOLIC
List three observations that you made about the burning candle.	In a combustion reaction, describe why the equation must be balanced.	Use chemical formulas in a balanced chemical equation to represent the combustion of propane, C_3H_8.

How do you know?

In an incomplete combustion reaction, carbon (soot) is formed. Where did you observe this in the investigation?

Why do you believe?

Fires need to be controlled or extinguished. These include campfires, fires in the kitchen, and large-scale fires in the burners of an electrical power plant. Explain the importance of controlling the fire in each of these cases.

Why should you care?

You may choose to use fire in your cooking-show segment. Allowing the fire to rage out of control might not go over well with the TV executives. Being able to explain the chemical reaction responsible for the fire might be of interest to your viewers.

569

Active Chemistry

What Do You Think Now?

Have students return to the *What Do You Think?* questions. They should be able now to name the necessary components of a fire and make suggestions as to what might be suitable for extinguishing a kitchen fire. You may share the answer provided in *A Chemist's Response* and have them discuss their reactions. Also have them refer to their original responses at the beginning of the section. It is a useful exercise for them to realize how their understanding has grown as a result of their investigations.

Additionally, the illustration will be more meaningful to them now. Ask them to return to the *What Do You See?* exercise and identify those features that are significant and have relevance to the section.

Chem Essential Questions

What does it mean?

MACRO — Students' answers will vary. They may include the following: Light is emitted, heat is emitted, wax is melted and forms a pool at the base of the wick, melted wax runs down the side of the candle and solidifies.

NANO — Matter cannot be either created or destroyed. This principle requires that the reactants and products must match in terms of numbers of atoms and types of atoms.

SYMBOLIC —

$$C_3H_8 + 5O_2 \longrightarrow 3CO_2 + 4H_2O$$

How do you know?

Soot was observed when the candle was extinguished with a beaker.

Why do you believe?

It is important to control the fire in a campfire because unless contained, it could cause a forest fire.

Fires in a kitchen are controlled to regulate proper temperature and cooking time for food preparation. Any kitchen fire that is out of control could burn down the house.

Fires in an electrical power plant are controlled for the efficient production of electricity. An out-of-control fire in an electrical power plant could spread to surrounding areas and cause power outages.

Why should you care?

Students' answers will vary. If they decide to have a fire, they should have a fire extinguisher present and emphasize safety.

Reflecting on the Section and the Challenge

Students should read this section for a specific connection between the section and the *Chapter Challenge*. It is quite possible that flame is going to play an important role in their challenge presentation. Stressing safety when using fire could easily be implemented as a part of their presentation.

Chem to Go

1.

Students' answers will vary, depending on the type of extinguisher.

a) Possible fire extinguishers:

• CO_2

• Dry chemical

• Water

b) Modes of operation:

• CO_2 – cuts off oxygen supply, smothers

• Dry chemical – separates fuel from heat source; cuts off oxygen supply

• Water – reduces the temperature so that the fire cannot maintain itself

2.

Reactant side – 16 carbon, 36 hydrogen and 50 oxygen atoms

Product side – 16 carbon, 36 hydrogen and 50 oxygen atoms

 Cookin' Chem

Reflecting on the Section and the Challenge

In this section, you learned about the combustion of fuels and what is required to keep the fuel burning. In a kitchen, natural gas (which is mostly methane) is often used as a source of fire for cooking. You may want to discuss the combustion of methane (natural gas) that allows you to cook during the segment. You may find a creative way of describing the need for balancing the equations that describe the combustion. You may also consider some other possible sources of combustion that might be found in a kitchen or used in cooking. There are many precautions that a cook should take when working in the kitchen. You might also want to include some fire safety issues in your cooking-show segment.

Chem to Go

1. Locate the fire extinguisher in your lab or in some other location at your school.

   a) What substances are in the extinguisher?

   b) How do they put out a fire?

2. Prove to yourself that the following equation is balanced by determining the total number of atoms on both sides of the equation:

   $$2C_8H_{18} + 25O_2 \rightarrow 16CO_2 + 18H_2O$$

   (Remember that $25O_2$ means that there are 25 molecules of oxygen. Each molecule of O_2 has two oxygen atoms.)

   How many carbon atoms on the reactant side? How many carbon atoms on the product side?

   Repeat for the H and O atoms.

3. Balance the following reactions:

   a) ___H_2 + ___O_2 → ___H_2O

   b) ___C_3H_8 + ___O_2 → ___ CO_2 + ___ H_2O

4. Show whether the following reactions are balanced.

   a) $2C_3H_8 + 7O_2 \rightarrow CO_2 + 4CO + 8H_2O + C$

   b) $2CH_3CH_2OH + 7O_2 \rightarrow 4CO_2 + 6H_2O$

5. The products of the balanced equation for the complete combustion of butane $(2C_4H_{10} + 13O_2)$ are

   a) $4CO_2 + 10H_2O$

   b) $4CO + 10H_2O$

   c) $8CO_2 + 10H_2O$

   d) $8CO_2 + 5H_2O$

3.

a) $2H_2 + O_2 \rightarrow 2H_2O$

b) $C_3H_8 + 5O_2 \rightarrow 3CO_2 + 4H_2O$

4.

a) Balanced. Both sides have 6 carbon, 16 hydrogen, and 14 oxygen.

b) Not balanced. The reactant side has two more oxygen atoms than the product side.

Reactants: 4 carbon, 12 hydrogen, 16 oxygen

Products: 4 carbon, 12 hydrogen, 14 oxygen

5.

c) $8CO_2 + 10H_2O$

Section 2 Combustion Reactions and Hydrocarbons

6. Which of the following must be the same before and after a chemical reaction?

   a) The sum of the masses of all substances involved.

   b) The number of molecules of all substances involved.

   c) The number of atoms of each type involved.

   d) Both (a) and (c) must be the same.

7. Describe the combustion process to someone who has not studied chemistry.

8. Balance the following equations with whole-number coefficients:

   a) $CH_3OH + O_2 \rightarrow CO_2 + H_2O$

   b) $CH_4 + O_2 \rightarrow CO_2 + H_2O$

   c) $HCl + NaOH \rightarrow NaCl + H_2O$

   d) $C_5H_{12} + O_2 \rightarrow CO_2 + H_2O$

9. Determine which of the following equations are balanced.

   a) $NaHCO_3 + HCl \rightarrow NaCl + H_2O + CO_2$

   b) $Al + S \rightarrow Al_2S_3$

   c) $CH_3COOH + NaOH \rightarrow CH_3COONa + H_2O$

   d) $CH_2CH_2 + 6O_2 \rightarrow 2CO_2 + 2H_2O$

10. *Preparing for the Chapter Challenge*

   In your cooking show, how might you include a segment about fire safety? Other than the stove and oven, what are some other possible sources of combustion (expected and unexpected) in the kitchen? How can you make this segment both entertaining and informative?

Inquiring Further

Generic balanced chemical equation

Devise a generic balanced chemical equation for the combustion of those hydrocarbons that have the general formula C_nH_{2n+2}.

571

Active Chemistry

6.

d) Both a) and c) must be the same.

7.

In order for a substance to burn it must have oxygen (air) to support combustion. It must also have a fuel, such as wood, to support combustion. Finally, it must have a heat source to start the combustion process going.

8.

a) $2CH_3OH + 3O_2 \rightarrow 2CO_2 + 4H_2O$

b) $CH_4 + 2O_2 \rightarrow CO_2 + 2H_2O$

c) $HCl + NaOH \rightarrow NaCl + H_2O$

d) $C_5H_{12} + 8O_2 \rightarrow 5CO_2 + 6H_2O$

9.

Both a) and c) are balanced equations.

10.

Preparing for the Chapter Challenge

Students' answers will vary. Segments about fire safety should demonstrate an understanding of the various methods for preventing and extinguishing kitchen fires. Besides the stove and oven, other kitchen appliances, such as toasters, can generate accidental kitchen fires by the heat they generate or by faulty wiring.

Another point that could be discussed is why one would not want to have an open flame in a tightly sealed room. Eventually, all of the oxygen would be consumed and it would be a very dangerous environment. This could lead to a discussion of carbon monoxide poisoning.

Inquiring Further

Generic balanced chemical equation

The generic chemical equation is:

$C_nH_{2n+2} + 1.5\ (n+1/3)\ O_2 \rightarrow nCO_2 + (n+1)\ H_2O$

or, the equivalent,

$C_nH_{2n+2} + 0.5\ (3n + 1)\ O_2 \rightarrow nCO_2 + (n+1)\ H_2O$

When n is an even number, the moles of oxygen involve a fraction, ½. While one can have 0.5 moles, one cannot have 0.5 molecules. Students may be more comfortable with an equivalent form of the equation that doubles all of the reactants and products when n is an even number.

$2C_nH_{2n+2} + (3n + 1)\ O_2 \rightarrow 2nCO_2 + (2n+2)\ H_2O$

SECTION 2 – QUIZ

7-2b | **Blackline Master**

1. What is meant by a combustion reaction? What are the requirements for combustion?

2. If the fuel does not have enough oxygen to burn completely to CO_2 and H_2O, there can be two additional products. What are they?

3. Why is CO_2 used in fire extinguishers?

4. Balance the following chemical equation.
   $$\_\_ CH_3OH + \_\_ O_2 \rightarrow \_\_ CO_2 + \_\_ H_2O$$
   a) 1, 2, 1, 1
   b) 2, 3, 2, 4
   c) 1, 2, 1, 2
   d) 2, 2, 2, 3

5. Can you change the coefficients when balancing a chemical equation? Can you change the molecular formula when balancing a chemical equation?
   a) both
   b) neither
   c) the coefficients can be changed, but not the molecular formula
   d) the molecular formula can be changed, but not the coefficients

SECTION 2 – QUIZ ANSWERS

1. A combustion reaction occurs when a substance is burning (rapid oxidation with heat and light) in the presence of oxygen. The requirements are fuel, oxygen, and an initial heat source.

2. Incomplete oxidation of a fuel source yields carbon monoxide (CO) and carbon (soot).

3. The CO_2 smothers the fire by cutting off the oxygen supply. It is relatively safe, cheap, and heavier than air so it will form a blanket over the fuel.

4. b) 2, 3, 2, 4

5. c) the coefficients can be changed, but not the molecular formula

NOTES

NOTES

SECTION 3
Thermochemistry and Cooking Fuels

Section Overview

This section provides the students with an introduction to thermochemistry. Students will first make predictions as to which of several fuels releases the most energy upon combustion. They will then design experiments to test their predictions. Their experiments will measure the heat energy released by various fuels using a simple calorimeter.

Background Information

The heat and light given off in an exothermic reaction comes from the formation of new bonds in the products. In an exothermic reaction, bonds are broken (in the reactants) and stronger bonds are formed (in the products). The energy difference is released into the surroundings. At constant pressure, the heat of reaction is equal to the change in the enthalpy ($\Delta H°$) of the system. One can estimate the enthalpy of reactions by using a table of average bond dissociation energies (D_o). For instance, in the combustion of methane:

$$CH_{4(g)} + 2O_{2(g)} \longrightarrow CO_{2(g)} + 2H_2O_{(g)}$$

The bonds broken in the reactants:

4 mol C-H bonds $\times$ 413 kJ/mol = 1652 kJ

2 mol O=O bonds $\times$ 495 kJ/mol = 990 kJ

By adding these two numbers, the total potential energy of reactants is obtained: 2642 kJ

The bonds formed in the products:

2 mol C=O bonds $\times$ 799 kJ/mol = 1598 kJ

4 mol O-H bonds $\times$ 463 kJ/mol = 1852 kJ

Total potential energies of products: 3450 kJ

At constant pressure, the change in enthalpy for this reaction as written is the sum total bond energies of the reactants minus the sum total bond energies of the products:

$$\Delta H° = \Sigma D_{o \text{ reactants}} - \Sigma D_{o \text{ products}}$$

$$= 2642 \text{ kJ} - 3450 \text{ kJ} = -808 \text{ kJ}$$

is released, for the reaction as written, that is, one mole of CH_4.

The estimated value is in close agreement with the experimentally determined (by calorimetry) heat of reaction of −802 kJ. The small amount of discrepancy is primarily due to the fact that the estimated value is arrived at using *average* bond energies.

This method assumes that the heat of reaction is due entirely to changes in bond energy, which requires that all reactants and products be gases. When liquids or solids are present, the additional heat involved in changing physical state must be taken into account.

Energy is required to break the bonds of the reactants and energy is released as new bonds form in the products. Alternatively, this calculation can be carried out as the sum of all the bond energies, as long as there is a negative sign put in front of the bond energies of those bonds formed.

In summary, a negative $\Delta H°$ indicates an exothermic reaction and a positive $\Delta H°$ indicates an endothermic reaction.

The table on the facing page is provided as a Blackline Master in your *Teacher Resources* CD.

7-3a | **Blackline Master**

BOND ENERGIES OF COVALENT COMPOUNDS			
Bond	**Bond Energy (kJ/mol)**	**Bond**	**Bond Energy (kJ/mol)**
H-H	436	C-F	442
H-C	413	C-Cl	328
H-N	393	C-Br	276
H-O	463	C-I	240
H-S	368	N-N	193
H-F	563	N=N	418
H-Cl	432	N≡N	941
H-Br	366	N-O	176
H-I	298	N=O	607
C-C	348	O-O	146
C=C	620	O=O	495
C≡C	812	O-P	502
C-O	356	O-Si	452
C=O	724 (799 in CO_2)	O=S	469 (532 in SO_2)
C≡O	1072	F-F	157
C-N	276	Cl-Cl	243
C=N	615	Br-Br	192
C≡N	891	I-I	151

LEARNING OUTCOMES		
LEARNING OUTCOMES	**LOCATION IN SECTION**	**EVIDENCE OF UNDERSTANDING**
Make quantitative observations about different fuels.	*Investigate* Part B, Steps 3-7	Students successfully complete investigation steps.
Understand where the energy comes from when a fuel is burned.	*Chem Talk,* *Checking Up* Questions 7-9 *Chem to Go* Questions 3, 8, 10 *Inquiring Further*	Students' answers are similar to those provided in this *Teacher's Edition*.
Understand the relationship between heat and temperature change.	*Investigate* Part C *Chem Talk,* *Checking Up* Questions 1-2 *Chem to Go* Questions 1, 5-7, 9	Students successfully complete investigation steps and provide answers similar to those outlined in this *Teacher's Edition*.
Determine the amount of heat released from the combustion of various fuels.	*Investigate* Part B Steps 1-7 Part C Steps 1-2	Students successfully complete investigation steps.

Section 3
Materials, Chemicals, Preparation, and Safety

("per Group" quantity is based on group size of 4 students)

Materials and Equipment

Materials (and Equipment)	Quantity per Group (4 students)
Soda can (empty)	1
Glass stirring rod, 12"	1
Graduated cylinder, 100 mL	1
Thermometer or temperature probe	1
Ringstand	1
Support ring, $2\frac{1}{2}$"	1
Burette clamp	1
Alcohol burner	1
Extension clamp for burner	1
Jellied camp fuel	1
Candle with holder or base	1
Scissors	1
Materials (and Equipment)	Quantity per Class
Balance, 0.01 g	1
Box of matches	1

Chemicals

Chemicals (and Equipment)	Quantity per Class (24 students)
Fuels: ethanol, isopropyl alcohol, lamp oil, kerosene, etc.	(enough for 2- 3 different per group)

NOTES

_____

_____

_____

_____

_____

_____

Teacher Preparation

You can prepare the "calorimeters" in advance out of the empty soda cans. Use a can opener to make two holes on opposite sides near the top of the can. The holes are for the insertion of a glass stirring rod to balance the can on a ringstand over the heat source. (See diagram in the *Student Edition*.)

Safety Requirements

- Goggles and aprons must be worn for all activity in the laboratory.

- Flammable liquids must be handled carefully.

- Alcohol burners should be secured to lab tables so they cannot be knocked over.

- Make sure flammable liquids are stored in clearly labeled, proper containers.

- Place used fuels in containers that are clearly labeled "used fuels" to prevent accidental contamination by mixing with pure fuels. Used fuels can be used again for this type of experimentation.

- Make sure to replace caps on jellied camp fuel securely for reuse.

- Wash hands and arms before leaving the laboratory area.

NOTES

_____

_____

_____

_____

_____

_____

_____

_____

_____

_____

_____

_____

_____

Meeting the Needs of All Students
Differentiated Instruction

Augmentation and Accommodations

LEARNING ISSUE	REFERENCE	AUGMENTATION AND ACCOMMODATIONS
Synthesis of content and process to design an experiment	*Investigate,* Part A, 3.	**Accommodations** • Students having difficulty can work backwards by first reading through the experiment described in Part B of the text. Go through it with them asking questions about how the first six steps correspond to the bulleted list. Point out ways in which variables are controlled. Then have students attempt to design their own experiment. **Augmentation** • If students cannot get started, help them determine what the first step should be. • Tell them the first step, have them complete it and give them one direction at a time or ask questions that move them through the process. • Model your own thought process for designing an experiment.
Creating an organizer for recording data	*Investigate,* Part B, 2.-6.	**Accommodations** • Provide a blank form for students to collect the data. **Augmentation** • Appoint a capable student in each group to be responsible for the organization and accuracy of data, but do not let him record it himself. He may only help other members of the group create and complete a form. That student becomes a turnkey trainer for others in the group.
Using a formula to calculate the heat energy and understanding the meaning of this data	*Investigate* Part C, 1.-2.	**Augmentation** • Students' approaches will vary. Concrete learners want to identify the data corresponding to each symbol, and memorize the sequence of steps to substitute numbers in the formula and solve. They tend to need repeated practice to learn. Variations in the process may throw them off and should be explained. • Other students rely on their reasoning to solve problems. Those students need to understand the meaning of the symbols and their relationships. When the formula makes sense to them, they can solve a variety of problems. • Those students who have difficulty understanding the symbols may need to examine them using the sensory data from the experiment and their predictions to understand the relationships in the formula. • Check each student's table in Step 2 to make sure they are calculating correctly. Those who aren't may need to be guided through a problem in small groups.
Drawing conclusions by comparison of results /written expression of those ideas	*Investigate* Part C, 3.	**Accommodations** • For students who don't understand their data, explain how *Heat per gram of fuel burned* (the last column of the table) can be used for comparison because of the built-in controls for changes in temperature, mass of water and mass of fuel. Point out that the greater the cal/g, the greater the heat energy generated. Then they should be able to complete b), c), and d). • Some students may have writing difficulties. Those students might be allowed to use a computer, dictate their answers or work with a partner.

Finding information in the text	*Checking Up*	**Augmentation**
		• The following advice may help students improve the quality of their written responses:
		   o Do not guess. Look back in the text unless you are absolutely sure your answers are correct. This exercise is to help you remember the correct information, not to test your skills.
		   o The order of the questions generally follows the order of the text. Therefore, the answer to the first question can probably be found at the beginning of the text.
		• Students should use key words in the question to locate the information, but once they find those words, they should start reading from the beginning of the paragraph and keep reading until they understand the answer and can write it in *their own* words.

Strategies for Students with Limited English Language Proficiency

LEARNING ISSUE	REFERENCE	AUGMENTATION AND ACCOMMODATIONS
Background knowledge	*What Do You Think Now?*	Students may benefit from an explanation of the different uses of the word "*fuel*" as both a noun and a verb. Have them describe what they see in the illustration for oral language development.
Vocabulary	*Investigate*	Make sure that students understand the idea that to "*compare*" means to find similarities. Make sure that students understand the term "*characteristic*." For Step 3, students may need to have the instructions shared verbally, by the teacher or by another student. In Part C, Step 2.a), check to see that students recognize the signal word "*since*" as a sign that a result is being explained.
Background knowledge Vocabulary Comprehending text	*Chem Talk*	Check for understanding of the term "*capacity*." Refer students to sidebar material for further explanations of the isolated words. Check for pronunciation of the term "*acetic*" as it may be a new word. Review the prefix, "*exo*" as in "*exothermic*," and "*endo*" as in "*endothermic*."
Background knowledge	*What Do You Think Now?*	Have students discuss their answers prior to writing them.
Background knowledge Vocabulary Comprehending text	*Chem Essential Questions*	In the *How do you know?* section, there is reference to "*partially oxygenated fuels*." The term "*partial*," or the derivative "*partially*" might be a new term for some students.
Comprehension Vocabulary	*Chem to Go*	Make sure students are able to distinguish questions that are stacked, where there is more than one response, from those that are multiple-choice. In Question 11., students are asked to "*explain*" and may need some further direction.
Application Comprehension	*Inquiring Further*	Students may need direction to determine methods of investigating fuel costs, and to identify the various types of fuels to research.

NOTES

_____

_____

_____

_____

_____

_____

_____

_____

_____

Section 3
Teaching Suggestions and Sample Answers

What Do You See?

Allow students a few minutes to contemplate the illustration. It represents the artist's conception of some of the key elements of this section and provides an early opportunity to engage the students and to elicit some responses.

Some students may point out the smoke pouring from the charred hamburger on the grill. Others may see a trend in the use of various fuels for cooking. All responses are valid and should be acknowledged as such. The students' responses also provide you with the opportunity to assess prior knowledge and potential misconceptions. Later in the activity, this section will be revisited for the students to review their initial reactions.

Section 3

Thermochemistry and Cooking Fuels

What Do You See?

Learning Outcomes

In this section you will:

• Make quantitative observations about different fuels.

• Understand where the energy comes from when a fuel is burned.

• Understand the relationship between heat and temperature change.

• Determine the amount of heat released from the combustion of various fuels.

What Do You Think?

Cooks use different fuels for different reasons.

• Which fuel do you think will cook foods the fastest?

• Where does the energy in the fire come from?

Record your ideas about these questions in your *Active Chemistry* log. Be prepared to discuss your responses with your group and the class.

Investigate

In this investigation, you will compare the energy content of various fuels. Fuels that you may be testing may include methanol, ethanol, kerosene, lamp oil, butanol, paraffin (candle wax), and jellied petroleum.

Part A: Designing Your Own Investigation

1. A common characteristic of most fuels is that they are compounds made of carbon and hydrogen (hydrocarbons) or carbon, hydrogen, and oxygen (*alcohols*). The amount of energy that a fuel releases has to do with how much and how completely the fuel is burned. But where do you think this energy comes from? You discussed this with your class in the *What Do You Think?* section.

572

STUDENTS' PRIOR CONCEPTIONS

Students' thoughts about chemical change tend to be naturally focused on the visible features of the change. Some students think that when something is burned in a closed container, it will weigh more because they see the smoke that was produced.[1] The concept that changes in configurations of atoms in molecules result in the absorption or release of energy is a fairly sophisticated concept. They do not understand that substances can be formed by the recombination of atoms in the original substances. Rather, they see chemical change as the result of a separate change in the original substance, or changes—each one separate—in several original substances. Some students will think that smoke formed from the burning of wood is somehow driven out of the wood by the flame.[2] Or they may believe that a combustible material must be composed of water and carbon dioxide since these substances eventually appear as products of combustion reactions. Some students will proclaim that a fuel plus oxygen yields fire—indicating a lack of understanding of the difference between matter and energy.

1. Driver, R., Guesne, E., Tiberghien, A. Beyond appearances: The conservation of matter under physical and chemical transformations. *Children's ideas in science*, 1985, Open University Press.

2. Atlas of Science Literacy, Project 2061. American Association for the Advancement of Science and the National Science Teachers Association, 2001.

2. To determine the amount of energy released from the combustion of a fuel, you will heat some water. By measuring the amount of fuel used and the change in temperature of the water, you will be able to make conclusions about the energy of each fuel.

Consider the fuels that your teacher will be asking you to test. Predict which fuel will have the best heating ability.

a) Record your prediction in your *Active Chemistry* log.

3. Using this strategy, design an experiment that can be conducted to determine the amount of energy released from the combustion of a fuel.

Include in your design:

• What apparatus and supplies you will need.

• What measurements you will make.

• What data you will record.

• How you will analyze the data.

• How you will draw a conclusion based on the data.

4. If your teacher has the materials in your design and approves your design, then you may proceed to carry out your investigation. Your teacher may decide to give you credit for your design and ask you to use the steps outlined in *Part B*.

Part B: Energy Content of Various Fuels

If your teacher does not have the supplies you need to do the investigation you designed, follow this procedure. In this procedure, you will use a soda can as a container for the water. While the soda can will not provide completely accurate results

(some heat energy will be lost to the *surroundings*), it will give you some idea of the energy content of fuels. A cook will want to choose the right fuel for the job.

1. Your teacher will provide you with a soda can that has two holes at the top. Set up a ringstand and ring. Place a glass stirring rod through the holes in the can. Set the can and stirring rod on the ring, as shown in the diagram.

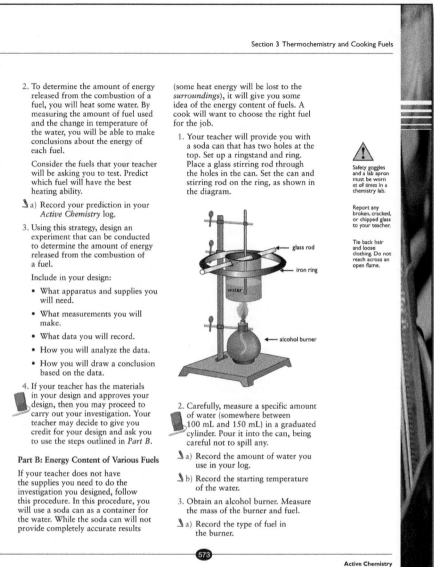

glass rod

iron ring

water

alcohol burner

⚠️

Safety goggles and a lab apron must be worn *at all times* in a chemistry lab.

Report any broken, cracked, or chipped glass to your teacher.

Tie back hair and loose clothing. Do not reach across an open flame.

2. Carefully, measure a specific amount of water (somewhere between 100 mL and 150 mL) in a graduated cylinder. Pour it into the can, being careful not to spill any.

a) Record the amount of water you use in your log.

b) Record the starting temperature of the water.

3. Obtain an alcohol burner. Measure the mass of the burner and fuel.

a) Record the type of fuel in the burner.

573

What Do You Think?

The students will most likely be guessing as to which fuel will cook foods the fastest. The accuracy of their answers is not an issue at this point; it is more important to listen to their rationale for selecting one fuel over another to get an understanding of their preconceptions and misconceptions regarding the subject matter.

Thinking macroscopically, students may suggest that the energy comes from the burning of the fuels which, of course, it does. They may think that bonds are like a vessel that contains energy and that when bonds are broken, the energy is released. Actually, breaking bonds requires energy but energy is released when new bonds of the reactants form.

What Do You Think?
A CHEMIST'S RESPONSE

The answer to the question, "Which fuel do you think will cook foods the fastest?" is too general to be answered with certainty. Factors such as type of food, mass, water content, and design of the cooking device will all play an important part. The illustration shows four ways of heating food–propane, wood, a toaster, and charcoal. If each cooking device shown is used to cook a hot dog, probably the propane would cook it the fastest.

The energy in a campfire comes from the formation of chemical bonds between oxygen in the air and the carbon and hydrogen in the wood. The energy in a typical grill (barbecue) fire comes from the formation of bonds between oxygen in the air and the carbon in the charcoal. The energy from a gas (e.g., propane) fire comes from the formation of chemical bonds between oxygen in the air and the carbon and hydrogen in the propane gas.

Investigate

Part A:
Designing Your Own Investigation

1. _____

This is a good time to introduce and briefly discuss the various fuels that students will be using in this activity. Provide students with the formula for each:

Jellied camp fuel – CH_3CH_2OH (ethanol with some methanol)

Candle – $C_{30}H_{62}$ (a mixture of hydrocarbons from C-25 to C-60)

Propanol – $CH_3CH_2CH_2OH$

CHAPTER 7

Isopropanol – $CH_3CHOHCH_3$

Kerosene – $C_{10}H_{22}$ to $C_{16}H_{34}$
(mixture of hydrocarbons)

2.

The predictions are not important, but making predictions should heighten interest and give students a sense of investment in the outcome.

3.

Remind students of safety issues, especially with regard to the alcohol burners. Have the burners ready and clearly marked as to fuel type. Do not change fuels during the lab. Rotate the burners among groups and have students share data.

Some important design elements students should consider are:

- the mass of water in the can (The same quantity of water does not have to be used each time, as long as the mass is carefully recorded each time.)

- the temperature of the water before and after heating

- the mass of the fuel before and after heating

CHEM TIP

A coffee can open at both ends and placed around the burner can help control heat loss. Another can open at only one end may be used to snuff out the burner, which may be preferable to blowing it out.

Procedure for jellied camp fuel cans: Find the mass before and after with the lid on. The lid should be used to snuff out the flame and prevents further loss of the alcohol due to evaporation.

Cookin' Chem

!
Be sure that the burner setup is secure.

Follow all precautions required around an open flame.

Be aware of the location of the fire extinguisher.

Wash hands and arms thoroughly before leaving the lab area.

b) Record the total mass of the burner and fuel as "mass before."

4. Set the burner under the can of water. Adjust the height of the ring so only the flame tip will hit the bottom of the can. This should be about 2–3 cm from the wick.

5. Light the burner and readjust the height of the can, if necessary. Let the fuel burn for four minutes. Blow out the flame. Measure the temperature of the water using a thermometer or temperature probe.

a) Record the color of the flame.

b) Record the highest temperature of the water.

6. Let the burner cool for a while and then measure its mass again.

a) Record this as "mass after."

7. Now that you have learned the techniques, you can complete the investigation. Design an experiment, using the apparatus available, to compare three fuels and their heating ability.

Each group will now work with one fuel and then the class will share data.

a) You may want to prepare a table similar to the one below in your *Active Chemistry* log. Record your measurements for each fuel in the table.

8. Clean your workstation as directed by your teacher. Save leftover fuels for future use.

(Note: If you use a candle, record the mass of the candle and foil-covered square base. For the jellied petroleum, record the mass of the open can.)

Part C: Analyzing Your Data

The thermal energy required to change the temperature of a given amount of water by 1°C is the *specific heat capacity*. The specific heat capacity of water is one calorie per one gram per one degree Celsius. It is written as

$$\frac{1\,cal}{g\cdot{}^{\circ}C} \quad \text{or} \quad 1\ cal\ g^{-1}\ {}^{\circ}C^{-1}$$

In other words, it takes one calorie of heat energy to raise the temperature of one gram of water by one degree Celsius.

If you know the amount of water and the change in temperature through which it goes, the specific heat capacity allows you to determine how much heat energy the water absorbs.

1. The equation to determine heat energy is

Heat = (mass of water) × (specific heat capacity of water) × (temperature change of water)

Using mathematical symbols, this equation can be written as

$$Q = mc\Delta T$$

Where Q = the change in heat
m = the mass of water (in grams)
c = the specific heat capacity of water
ΔT = the change in temperature ($T_{final} - T_{initial}$)

Fuel and flame color	Amount of water (mL)	Temp. before (°C)	Temp. after (°C)	Mass before (g)	Mass after (g)

574

Active Chemistry

Part B:
Energy Content of Various Fuels

1.

Make sure students clamp the alcohol burner to the ringstand for safety.

2.

The water should be at or near room temperature.

3.

Students should prepare a data table to record their data.

4.

Advise students that they will have to readjust the height after the flame is lit.

5.

The wick may have to be adjusted after lighting to burn efficiently.

6.

The mass of the fuel and burner should have decreased after the fuel burned.

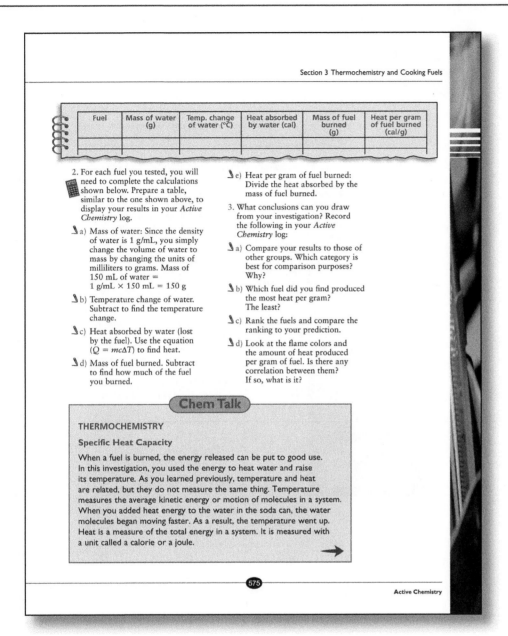

2. For each fuel you tested, you will need to complete the calculations shown below. Prepare a table, similar to the one shown above, to display your results in your *Active Chemistry* log.

a) Mass of water: Since the density of water is 1 g/mL, you simply change the volume of water to mass by changing the units of milliliters to grams. Mass of 150 mL of water = 1 g/mL × 150 mL = 150 g

b) Temperature change of water. Subtract to find the temperature change.

c) Heat absorbed by water (lost by the fuel). Use the equation ($Q = mc\Delta T$) to find heat.

d) Mass of fuel burned. Subtract to find how much of the fuel you burned.

e) Heat per gram of fuel burned: Divide the heat absorbed by the mass of fuel burned.

3. What conclusions can you draw from your investigation? Record the following in your *Active Chemistry* log:

a) Compare your results to those of other groups. Which category is best for comparison purposes? Why?

b) Which fuel did you find produced the most heat per gram? The least?

c) Rank the fuels and compare the ranking to your prediction.

d) Look at the flame colors and the amount of heat produced per gram of fuel. Is there any correlation between them? If so, what is it?

Chem Talk

THERMOCHEMISTRY

Specific Heat Capacity

When a fuel is burned, the energy released can be put to good use. In this investigation, you used the energy to heat water and raise its temperature. As you learned previously, temperature and heat are related, but they do not measure the same thing. Temperature measures the average kinetic energy or motion of molecules in a system. When you added heat energy to the water in the soda can, the water molecules began moving faster. As a result, the temperature went up. Heat is a measure of the total energy in a system. It is measured with a unit called a calorie or a joule.

575

Active Chemistry

a) Mass of water (m)
   130.0 mL (1.00 g/mL) = 130.0 g water

b) Temperature change of water (ΔT) 47.5°C – 22.5°C = 25.0°C

c) Heat absorbed by water (ΔQ)
   (130.0 g) (1 cal g^{-1} °C^{-1}) (25.0°C) = 3250 cal

d) Mass of fuel used
   78.60 g – 76.40 g = 2.20 g

e) Heat/gram fuel
   3250 cal/2.20 g = 1480 cal/g

3.

There are many factors that affect the heat transfer from the fuel to the water (loss of heat to air, distance between the flame and can, accuracy in measurements). The heat per gram for each fuel may vary from the accepted values. The point is to show that heat is produced in these exothermic reactions and that the amount of heat can be calculated.

3.a)

The data in the column "Heat per gram of fuel burned (cal/g)" is the best to use for comparisons of fuels. This data removes the variations in fuel mass loss.

3.b)

Group data may show that hydrocarbons produce the most heat per gram. The alcohols produce less heat per gram than the hydrocarbons. Energy is released as bonds form to make carbon dioxide and water. Since the alcohols already have a carbon to oxygen bond, less energy will be released during their combustion.

7.

Rotate the fuels among the groups and share data. Students can record their data in the table they prepared in Step 3.

Part C: Analyzing Your Data

1.

After data collection, students may need help in calculating heat and heat per gram. You may go through a sample calculation with them.

2.

You might suggest that students add a column in their data tables for the specific heat capacity of water (c). It should be situated between the column for mass of water (m) and the column for temperature change (ΔT). That way, the equation for determining the heat energy ($mc\Delta T$ = heat absorbed by water) appears in proper sequence in their tables, making it easy for them to complete the calculations. Some typical calculations follow:

3.c)

Answers will vary, depending on heat losses and the fuels used. In most cases, heat loss will amount to up to 50%.

3.d)

Blue and colorless flames are hotter, more efficient and have higher cal/g values. Yellow and orange flames are cooler and less efficient.

Chem Talk

The first part of this section covers specific heat capacity and terms commonly used in thermochemistry. These include calories, joules, and the equation, $Q = mc\Delta T$. Exothermic and endothermic reactions are reviewed in detail, augmented with reaction energy diagrams. The diagrams show that in order for a chemical reaction to take place, enough activation energy (E_a) must be supplied to break the bonds of the reactants. The atoms then combine to form the product bonds and either release or absorb energy. The combustion reactions of fuels are exothermic reactions but may differ from each other depending on the atoms contained in the fuel.

 Cookin' Chem

A calorie is the amount of heat needed to raise the temperature of one gram of water by one degree Celsius. You are probably familiar with the term Calorie as it relates to foods. A food Calorie (note the capital C) is equal to 1000 cal (calories) or 1 kcal (kilocalorie). It is also a measure of the energy available from the food. The joule is also used as the unit of energy.

In chemistry, as in all science, the international community has agreed to use joules as a unit of energy. However, in this investigation, you used calories in your calculations. In the United States, the energy content of foods is still given in kilocalories (kcal or C). A food that is 100 C (Calories) has an energy content of 100,000 cal (calories). Since 1 cal is equal to 4.184 J (joules), 100 C food has an energy content of 418,400 J.

To calculate the heat per gram of fuel consumed you needed to use the energy required to raise the temperature of 1 g of water by 1°C. This is the **specific heat capacity** of water. The **specific heat capacity** of water is one calorie per one gram per one degree Celsius. It is written as

$$\frac{1 \text{ cal}}{\text{g} \cdot °\text{C}} \quad \text{or} \quad 1 \text{ cal g}^{-1} °\text{C}^{-1}$$

In other words, it takes one calorie of heat to raise the temperature of one gram of water by one degree Celsius.

In the investigation, you measured the amount of water and the change in temperature of the water. Then, using specific heat capacity, you determined how much heat energy the water absorbed using the following equation:

Heat = (mass of water) × (specific heat capacity of water) × (temperature change of water)

Using mathematical symbols, this equation can be written as:

$$Q = mc\Delta T$$

Where Q = the change in heat
m = the mass of water (in grams)
c = the specific heat capacity of water
ΔT = the change in temperature
$(T_{final} - T_{initial})$

Terms Used in Thermochemistry
Thermochemistry is the study of heat effects that accompany chemical reactions. When you measure the quantities of heat gained or lost in chemical reactions, you are investigating the thermochemistry of

Chem Words

specific heat capacity: the heat energy required to raise the temperature of 1 g of a substance by 1°C.

thermochemistry: the study of heat effects that accompany chemical reactions.

576

Active Chemistry

CHAPTER 7

those reactions. In studying thermochemistry, you use the term **system** to describe the reactants, solvent, and products of a reaction. You use the word **surroundings** to indicate everything outside of the chemical reaction: the can, the room, building, and so on, out into the universe.

When energy is released from the system to the surroundings, it is called an **exothermic reaction**. An **endothermic reaction** is where energy is absorbed by the system from the surroundings. In the investigation, energy was released as the fuel burned in an exothermic reaction.

When energy is released in an exothermic reaction, where does the energy come from? To understand exothermic reactions, you have to look at the same events from the viewpoint of the molecules and atoms. In *Active Chemistry*, we refer to this as the nanoscopic scale. That is because one nanometer is the size of some molecules. The energy in exothermic and endothermic reactions relates to the chemical bonds of the reactants. It takes energy to break a chemical bond. Consequently, when a chemical bond is formed, energy is released to the surroundings. Energy *in* to break a bond; Energy *out* to create a bond.

When your fuel was burned in the presence of oxygen, it underwent a combustion reaction. Combustion of any hydrocarbon is an exothermic process, which produces carbon dioxide and water. The combustion of candle wax you observed earlier was the same exothermic reaction.

Methane is the chief component of natural gas used in kitchens for cooking. Methane undergoes combustion according to the following balanced equation:

$$CH_{4(g)} + 2O_{2(g)} \rightarrow CO_{2(g)} + 2H_2O_{(g)} + \text{energy}$$

You see that + energy has been added to this reaction. It indicates that this is an exothermic process. The energy that is released from this reaction comes from the stored energy in the molecular bonds. The energy to break the bonds of the reactants is less than the energy released to create the bonds in the products. The extra energy is released to the surroundings in this exothermic process.

All molecules have potential energy resulting from the bonds that hold the atoms together. In this reaction, if 1 mol of CH_4 were used, the potential energy of the reactants is equal to 3450 kJ. The total potential energy of the products is equal to 2642 kJ. The heat energy that is released from this reaction is the difference between the potential energies of the reactants and products

$$2642 \text{ kJ} - 3450 \text{ kJ} = -808 \text{ kJ}$$

These 808 kJ of heat energy are released in this exothermic reaction. ➔

Chem Words

system: the chemical reaction being studied; in this case, the reactants, solvent, and products of a reaction.

surroundings: everything outside of a chemical reaction.

exothermic reaction: a reaction in which energy is released from the system to the surroundings.

endothermic reaction: a reaction in which energy is absorbed by the system from the surroundings.

Active Chemistry

Checking Up

1.

Temperature measures the average kinetic energy or motion of particles in a system. Heat, however, is a measure of the total energy in a system and includes temperature and mass.

2.

Heat energy can be measured in either joules or calories.

3.

The specific heat capacity of a substance is the heat energy required to raise the temperature of 1 g of that substance by 1°C.

4.

The specific heat capacity of water is exactly 1 cal g^{-1} °C^{-1}.

5.

Thermochemistry is the study of heat changes that accompany chemical reactions.

6.

An exothermic reaction is a reaction in which energy is released from the system to the surroundings. An endothermic reaction is a reaction in which energy is absorbed by the system from the surroundings.

7.

In an exothermic reaction, the energy it takes to break the bonds of the reactants is less than the energy released to create the bonds in the products. Therefore, the extra energy from bond formation is the source of the heat energy released to the surroundings.

Cookin' Chem

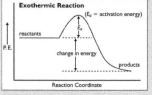

Checking Up

1. Explain again the difference between heat energy and temperature.
2. What two units can be used to measure heat energy?
3. Define the specific heat capacity of a substance.
4. What is the specific heat capacity of water?
5. What does thermochemistry study?
6. Explain the difference between an exothermic and an endothermic reaction.
7. From where does the energy released in an exothermic reaction come?
8. In the exothermic reaction, is the potential energy of the products *lower* or *higher* than that for the reactants?
9. In the endothermic reaction, is the potential energy of the products *lower* or *higher* than that for the reactants?
10. What type of reaction occurs when the weaker bonds of the reactants are broken and stronger bonds in the products are formed?
11. What is activation energy?
12. What is the difference between methane and methanol?

Energy Change in Exothermic and Endothermic Reactions

One way to graphically represent the energy changes of a reaction is with an **energy diagram**. Typical energy diagrams for both an exothermic reaction and an endothermic reaction are shown below.

In the exothermic reaction, the potential energy (P.E.) of the products is *lower* than that for the reactants. The energy difference (in the form of heat energy, or Q) is negative because it leaves the system and is given off to the surroundings.

In the endothermic reaction, the P.E. of the products is *higher* than that of the reactants. Energy must be supplied to the reaction to make it occur. The energy difference is positive because it is provided to the system from the surroundings.

When weaker bonds (less stable, higher energy) of the reactants are broken and stronger bonds (more stable, lower in energy) in the products are formed, energy is released to the surroundings in an exothermic reaction. This is because the potential energy of the system (the substances involved in the reaction) has been lowered. A chemical reaction where stronger bonds of the reactants are broken and weaker bonds are formed in the products is an endothermic reaction that requires energy in order to take place.

In both cases, there is an energy that must be supplied in order for the reactants to have the proper collision energy for the reaction to occur. This is called the **activation energy** (E_a). When you light the propane burner of a camp stove, a spark is needed to start the reaction, supplying the activation energy. Even though the combustion of propane gas is an exothermic reaction, the spark must be supplied before the reaction will proceed. An exothermic reaction can be sustained by the heat liberated by the reaction.

8.

In an exothermic reaction the potential energy of the products is lower than the potential energy of the reactants.

9.

In an endothermic reaction the potential energy of the products is higher than the potential energy of the reactants.

10.

When weaker bonds of the reactants are broken and stronger bonds in the products are formed, energy is released to the surroundings in an exothermic reaction.

11.

Activation energy is the energy that must be supplied in order for the reactants to have sufficient collision energy for the reaction to occur.

Alcohol Fuels

Alcohol fuels contain the hydroxyl group (–OH). If you replace one of the hydrogens of methane with a hydroxyl group, you will now have a compound that is called an **alcohol**. In this case, the alcohol is called methanol or methyl alcohol. Methane is CH_4 and methanol is CH_3OH.

The combustion of methanol is shown as

$$2CH_3OH_{(l)} + 3O_{2(g)} \rightarrow 2CO_{2(g)} + 4H_2O_{(g)} + energy$$

As in the combustion of methane, energy is released as the strong carbon-oxygen bonds are formed in CO_2. As a general rule, the fewer carbon-oxygen bonds in the reactants, the more energy released. Larger hydrocarbon compounds with no oxygen present should release more heat on burning than smaller, partially oxygenated hydrocarbons.

Here are the formulas of some possible fuels.

Name	Molecular formula	Condensed structural formula
methanol	CH_4O	CH_3OH
ethanol	C_2H_6O	CH_2CH_2OH
1-propanol	C_3H_8O	$CH_3CH_2CH_2OH$
2-propanol (isopropyl alcohol)	C_3H_8O	$CH_3CH(OH)CH_3$
n-butanol	$C_4H_{10}O$	$CH_3CH_2CH_2CH_2OH$
kerosene	A mixture averaging $C_{10}H_{22}$	
lamp oil	A mixture of paraffin and kerosene	
candle wax (paraffin)	A mixture of $C_{20}H_{42}$ and larger	

Balanced equations show relationships in molar quantities. A **mole** is a specific number of particles (6.022×10^{23} particles). The combustion of methanol shown in equation above can also be described in words as

> Two moles of methanol react with three moles of oxygen to produce two moles of carbon dioxide and four moles of water, with a certain amount of energy released.

In the investigation, you determined the amount of heat per gram of fuel. In the equation just described, the heat released would be per mole(s) of fuel burned. For methanol, one mole is about 32 grams.

Chem Words

energy diagram: a way to represent graphically the energy changes of a reaction.

activation energy: the energy that must be supplied in order for the reactants to have the proper collision energy for the reaction to occur.

alcohol: a hydrocarbon in which a hydrogen atom is replaced with a hydroxyl group (—OH).

mole: a specific number of particles (6.022×10^{23} particles).

12.

The difference between methane and methanol is that one of the hydrogens in methane is replaced with a hydroxyl group (–OH). Methane has a molecular formula of CH_4 while methanol is CH_3OH.

What Do You Think Now?

Have students refer to their original responses to questions about the rankings of fuels and their ideas about the source of energy in fire. Their answers should be more accurate and sophisticated now and they will realize this. Also have them re-examine the *What Do You See?* illustration. They should now be able to make more and better connections with the intentions of the artist.

Reflecting on the Section and the Challenge

Following the *Chem Essential Questions*, it is useful to have the students pause and consider how they might incorporate the information learned in this activity into their *Chapter Challenge*. Knowing how to control a reaction is an important part of understanding chemistry. You might want to have the students reflect on this individually in their *Active Chemistry* logs. If time permits, they could meet in their groups for a few minutes of discussion and then report back to the class.

Cookin' Chem

What Do You Think Now?

At the beginning of the section you were asked the following:
- Which fuel do you think will cook foods the fastest?
- Where does the energy in the fire come from?

Now that you have completed this section, where does the energy released in the exothermic process of burning fuels come from?

Chem Essential Questions

What does it mean?

Chemistry explains a *macroscopic* phenomenon (what you observe) with a description of what happens at the *nanoscopic* level (atoms and molecules) using *symbolic* structures as a way to communicate. Complete the chart below in your *Active Chemistry* log.

MACRO	NANO	SYMBOLIC
What did you observe in this investigation that led you to believe that the combustion of a fuel is an exothermic reaction?	When a fuel burns, compare the bonds of the molecules on the product and reactant sides.	Use an energy diagram as a symbolic structure to describe what happens during an exothermic reaction.

How do you know?

Take a look at the class data for the energy content of the different fuels used. In the *Chem Talk* section, you read the hypothesis that partially oxygenated fuels (those with some carbon-oxygen bonds present) will release less heat than similar hydrocarbons without oxygen. Does the class data support this hypothesis?

Why do you believe?

Your everyday experiences make it easy to accept that when a fuel is burned, it is an exothermic process. What examples of fires would you use to explain to someone that fires require fuel?

Why should you care?

Consider some of the fuels that are sources of heat for cooking. You cannot always use fuels with the highest heat output per gram. Consider why not in terms of cost, convenience, and safety.

Reflecting on the Section and the Challenge

Think about the advantages of gas and electric stoves in terms of the control of the amount of heat, the response to the change in heat, and safety. You may want to describe these as well as the combustion reaction of the gas stove in your show. Making the discussion entertaining is one of the tougher parts of your cooking show because it requires creativity.

580

Active Chemistry

Chem Essential Questions

What does it mean?

MACRO — The combustion of fuels released heat, which is a definite sign of an exothermic reaction.

NANO — In an exothermic reaction, the total energy of all the reactant bonds is greater than the total energy of all the product bonds. This difference in energy appears as the light and heat that is given off.

SYMBOLIC —

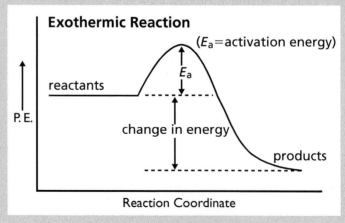

Exothermic Reaction

Chem to Go

1. How would your data be different if you used only 50 mL of water instead of 150 mL in this experiment?

2. Write balanced chemical equations for the fuels that you tested.

3. a) Explain the difference between an endothermic and an exothermic reaction.

   b) List some technologies that use endothermic and some that use exothermic reactions.

4. Convert the following heat quantities, recalling that 1 cal = 4.184 J:

   a) 350 cal to joules   b) 515 J to calories   c) 1.6 kcal to joules

5. Suppose you have two containers of water. One contains 150 mL at 80°C and the other has 75 mL at 60°C. Is the heat content of both containers equivalent? If not, which has the lesser heat content?

6. How much heat is required to change the temperature of 150 g of water by 20°C?

7. How much heat will be given off when 1500 g of water cools down by 20°C?

8. Which statement describes the characteristics of an *endothermic* reaction?

   a) The sign of Q is negative, and the products have less potential energy than the reactants.

   b) The sign of Q is positive, and the products have less potential energy than the reactants.

   c) The sign of Q is negative, and the products have more potential energy than the reactants.

   d) The sign of Q is positive, and the products have more potential energy than the reactants.

9. What is the total number of joules of heat energy absorbed by 15 g of water when it is heated from 30°C to 40°C?

   a) 10   b) 63   c) 150   d) 630

10. Whenever bonds between atoms are broken and rearranged to form new bonds,

    a) energy is involved.   c) melting has occurred.

    b) an exothermic reaction has taken place.   d) energy is supplied to the system.

11. *Preparing for the Chapter Challenge*

    In preparing for your *Chapter Challenge*, you may want to explain what source of heat is used for cooking and why it is used. Make a list of possible sources in your *Active Chemistry* log.

Inquiring Further

Cost of fuels and energy content

Investigate whether the cost of fuels is related to the energy content of the fuels.

581

Active Chemistry

How do you know?

Yes, the data supports the hypothesis that oxygenated fuels such as alcohols release less energy upon combustion than do hydrocarbons.

Why do you believe?

Examples of fires that require fuels:

• Forest fires (trees – wood)

• Kitchen gas stove (gas)

• Campfires (wood)

• Barbecue grills (charcoal)

Why should you care?

Typical cooking fuels include natural gas, propane, charcoal, and wood. Of these, wood may be the least costly but may not have the energy per gram as the others. Charcoal is also convenient but does not have the energy per gram as propane or gas, which also present greater safety risks. Hydrogen as a fuel would have a higher energy output per gram but is not used because it would have serious safety and cost restraints.

Chem to Go

1.

The temperature would increase faster and the increase would probably be greater; less fuel would be used but the heat per gram would not be affected.

2.

Assuming complete combustion, CO_2 and H_2O are the only products.

a) methanol
$$2CH_3OH + 3O_2 \rightarrow 2CO_2 + 4H_2O$$

b) ethanol
$$CH_3CH_2OH + 3O_2 \rightarrow 2CO_2 + 3H_2O$$

c) propanol
$$2CH_3CH_2CH_2OH + 9O_2 \rightarrow 6CO_2 + 8H_2O$$

d) kerosene
$$2C_{10}H_{22} + 31O_2 \rightarrow 20CO_2 + 22H_2O$$

e) paraffin
$$2C_{20}H_{42} + 61O_2 \rightarrow 40CO_2 + 42H_2O$$

f) Sterno® fuel – alcohol-based (use ethanol equation)

3.

Exothermic reactions release energy to the surroundings. The products have less energy than the reactants. Endothermic reactions require energy from the surroundings. The products have more energy than the reactants.

3.b)

Very few technologies depend upon endothermic reactions. One use of endothermic reactions is a cold pack for treating injuries. Technologies that use exothermic reactions are automobile engines, power plants and iron manufacturing.

4. a)

350 cal × (4.184 J/cal) = 1.5 kJ

b) 515 joules (1 cal/ 4.18 J) = 123 cal

c) 1.6 kcal (1000 cal / 1 kcal) (4.18 J/1cal) = 6.7 kJ

5.

No, the heat content is not equivalent. There is less heat in the 75 mL of water. Each gram of water has to absorb 1 calorie of heat to go up one degree Celsius. The beaker with 150 mL of water contains more heat energy than the beaker with 75 mL of water.

6.

(150 g) (1 cal/1 g•1°C) (20°C) = 3.0 kcal = 13 kJ

7.

(1500 g) (1 cal/1 g•1°C) (−20°C) = 30 kcal is given off (or 130 kJ).

8.

d) The sign of Q is positive, and the products have more potential energy than the reactants.

9.

d) 630

10.

a) Energy is involved.

11.

Preparing for the Chapter Challenge

Cooking fuels obviously play an important role in preparing foods. The combustion of fuels should be discussed as well as the types of fuel that are most efficient and provide the greatest amount of energy. Safety and cost are also important considerations. Combustion reactions should be demonstrated with chemical equations.

Inquiring Further

Cost of fuels and energy content

An investigation of fuel costs should include source availability and processing costs. Unless the literature suggests otherwise, students should always assume complete combustion of each fuel.

NOTES

_____

_____

_____

_____

_____

_____

_____

SECTION 3 – QUIZ

| 7-3b | **Blackline Master** |

1. What is the specific heat capacity of water (include the units) and what does it mean?

2. What is a hydrocarbon? Provide an example.

3. What structural feature makes a molecule an alcohol?

4. Whether you are using natural gas in your home, propane for a gas grill, or charcoal for a barbecue, energy must be supplied in order to start the combustion reaction. What is this energy called?

   a) starting energy

   b) activation energy

   c) catalyst

   d) exothermic energy

5. In a combustion reaction, compare the potential energy of both the reactants and the products.

SECTION 3 – QUIZ ANSWERS

❶ 1 cal/g °C (or 4.184 J/g°C) is the specific heat of water. The specific heat of a substance is the number of calories (or joules) it takes to raise the temperature of 1 g of the substance by 1° Celsius.

❷ A substance made of only carbon and hydrogen, such as methane, CH_4, or propane, C_3H_8.

❸ All alcohols possess at least one hydroxyl group (–OH).

❹ b) activation energy

❺ Combustion reactions are exothermic, so the potential energy of the products is lower than that of the reactants.

NOTES

_____

_____

_____

_____

_____

_____

_____

_____

_____

_____

_____

Chapter Mini-Challenge

The students have been introduced to new concepts in the first three sections of this chapter. Now is a good time for them to review these principles and consider how they can be applied to their *Chapter Challenge* projects. The *Mini-Challenge* provides an opportunity for students to implement and test some of their ideas. Any problems or obstacles they encounter with this smaller project will better prepare them for the bigger challenge ahead.

This *Mini-Challenge* will also give you an opportunity to coach students in the creation of their five-minute chemistry segments for the cooking show. Encourage students to refer to the criteria decided upon by the class for grading the *Chapter Challenge* projects in the design of their cooking show segments.

As students decide on the form of presentation for their projects, you can give pointers on videotaping techniques, voice-overs and script-writing. Remind students that the scripts are to include a discussion of the chemistry, so now is a good time to address any misconceptions that may arise as students attempt to explain the chemistry of their cooking presentations.

The *Mini-Challenge* should take about one hour for preparation and about 20 minutes for all teams to share their one-minute

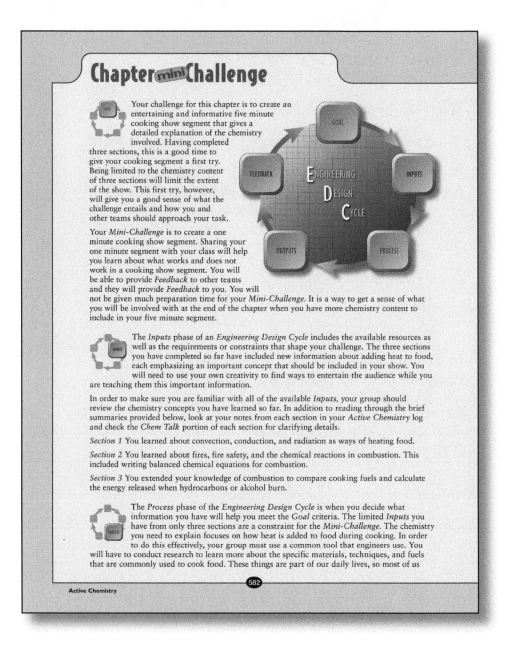

segments. All teams should receive written feedback from the class after their presentations. One method for encouraging helpful feedback is to require each individual to write down two positive comments and one suggestion for improvement.

take them for granted and don't think about them. Creating your *Mini-Challenge* cooking segment will be a great opportunity to explore these underappreciated technologies that rely on chemistry principles.

In the *Process* step of the *Engineering Design Cycle* the design work gets done and decisions are made. As you learn about the common materials used to make pots and pans and the different ways heat is generated and transferred to food, you will find that you can describe the chemistry behind virtually any cooking process. Combining your research and your new chemistry knowledge in your cooking segment is essential to the *Process* step. Your choice of format for your cooking segment is also part of your *Process* step. You may choose to showcase the preparation of your favorite ethnic dish or to infuse comedy through the personalities you represent in your segment. Even if you choose to use a straightforward, just-the-facts approach, these decisions are all part of the *Process* step of the *Engineering Design Cycle*.

 The *Outputs* of an *Engineering Design Cycle* are the products that you created during the *Process* step. Your product for the *Mini-Challenge* will be your one minute cooking segment about adding heat during the cooking process. Your *Outputs* must include written chemistry explanations in the form of a script and additional details that support the script. Depending on your group's choices, your *Outputs* may include acting out a cooking demonstration, showing video footage of a real cooking show, or recording your group cooking. You will have a very limited amount of time to prepare your presentation, so be sure to spend most of your time getting the explanations perfected. You will have more time to perfect the cooking steps or video presentation for your full *Chapter Challenge*.

 The *Feedback* phase of the *Engineering Design Cycle* is the final phase of one cycle and simultaneously *Inputs* for the next design cycle. Your instructor and your classmates will give you *Feedback* on the format of your cooking segment and how well you described the chemistry involved. This *Feedback* will become the *Inputs* you will use in the final *Chapter Challenge* presentation because you will need to include information about the ways heat is added to your food no matter what format you use. You will have enough time to make corrections and improvements before the *Chapter Challenge*, so pay attention to the valuable information they provide.

Remember to make any necessary changes to the chemistry explanation that received *Feedback*. Also note any ideas you may have gotten by viewing other cooking segments. Your group may want to revise the format of your segment for the *Chapter Challenge*, and seeing others may spark your own creativity. In many cases your group will be able to simply add on to your *Mini-Challenge* cooking segment to create your *Chapter Challenge* cooking segment. If you do that you will be able to focus all of your efforts on incorporating chemistry from the remaining chapter sections.

You will learn about new chemistry concepts in each of the remaining chapter sections. Each section will teach you new information about the role of heat and molecular structures in cooking. Pay careful attention to the *Chem Talk* presented in each chapter section, because they are the key to creating a high-quality chemistry explanation in your challenge presentation.

583

Active Chemistry

Engineering Design Cycle

Remind students that this is a first try and that they should use the feedback from the class to improve upon their projects for the *Chapter Challenge*. After all the presentations are completed, review the *Engineering Design Cycle* to help students see other ways to put their chemistry knowledge to use.

They do not have to have their cooking segment ready, but they should have some firm plans for the procedures that they will perform and be able to describe them. They should also be able to explain what chemical principles they are going to emphasize in their cooking processes. At the end of the chapter, you can ask students to reflect on the successes and disappointments from the *Mini-Challenge*. This experience and information will be vital for making the necessary modifications to their design cycles in order to succeed with the *Chapter Challenge*.

CHAPTER 7

SECTION 4
Phase Changes and the Heating Curve of Water

Section Overview

Students create a graph recording the heating of water from room temperature to boiling. The graph is based on readings taken every 30 s. The data from the graph is then analyzed. Water molecules are drawn to represent cool water, hot water, and steam.

Background Information

The boiling point of liquid is conventionally defined as the temperature at which its vapor pressure equals atmospheric pressure, as determined under standard conditions. However, it must be understood that a liquid like water can also evaporate at temperatures lower than its boiling point. To explain this phenomenon, it must be understood that not all molecules in a liquid are moving at the same speed. Hence, the temperature of the liquid is based on the average kinetic energy. This means that some of the molecules have enough energy to overcome the surface tension and to escape the liquid phase, i.e., to evaporate. For this reason, the volume slowly decreases during this slow evaporation process. However, when the liquid is at the boiling point, the molecules anywhere in the liquid may be vaporized, resulting in the formation of vapor bubbles.

Molar heat of vaporization is the amount of energy required to vaporize 1 mol of a liquid into a vapor. The molar heat of vaporization of water is 40.67 kJ/mol at 100°C and pressure of one atmosphere. In this activity, students will complete a table containing both molar heat of vaporization and the molar heat of fusion.

LEARNING OUTCOMES		
LEARNING OUTCOMES	**LOCATION IN SECTION**	**EVIDENCE OF UNDERSTANDING**
Determine the boiling point of water.	*Investigate* Steps 1-3	Students' data support their determination of the boiling point.
Show graphically what happens to the temperature as water is heated to boiling and while the water is boiling.	*Investigate* Step 4	Students' graphs are similar to those outlined in the *Teacher's Edition*.

NOTES

_____

_____

_____

_____

_____

Section 4
Materials, Chemicals, Preparation, and Safety

("per Group" quantity is based on group size of 4 students)

Materials and Equipment

Materials (and Equipment)	Quantity per group (4 students)
Ringstand	1
Thermometer or temperature probe	1
Beaker, 250 mL	1
Hot plate	1
Wire gauze squares for hot plate	1
Graduated cylinder, 100-mL	1
Graph paper, sheet	1

Chemicals

Chemicals	Quantity per Class (24 students)
None	None

Teacher Preparation

None.

Safety Requirements

- All activity in the laboratory area requires goggles and aprons.
- All materials can be disposed of in the trash or down the drain.
- Students should take precautions when working with boiling water.
- Wash arms and hands before leaving the laboratory area.

NOTES

Meeting the Needs of All Students
Differentiated Instruction

Augmentation and Accommodations

LEARNING ISSUE	REFERENCE	AUGMENTATION AND ACCOMMODATIONS
Graphing change of temperature over time	*Investigate* 4.	**Augmentation** • Group together students who need help making a graph. Teach them the skills while the other groups continue with the activity. Give the students who are able to graph independently an extension assignment to do while the others finish. **Accommodations** • Allow students to choose between creation of their own graph and using the temperature probe and software. • Pair students who need help with students who are proficient with graphing. • Give the students a ready-made graph they can use to plot their data.
Understanding the effect of heat on molecules	*Investigate* 5.f) *Chem Talk, Checking Up* 1.	**Augmentation** • Students may need to learn the effects of heat on the relative distance between molecules before they can complete 5.f). Have them read the first four paragraphs of the *Chem Talk* text, highlighting the words in the paragraphs that describe the relative distances between molecules in each state. Then have them return to the problem and draw the picture. This will also help those who get stuck with the first *Checking Up* question.
Reading comprehension and writing observations	*What does it mean? Macro, Nano, Symbolic, Chem Talk*	**Augmentation** • Students may need help with the reading to complete the *Macro, Nano,* and *Symbolic* exercises. Have them read the first four paragraphs of the *Chem Talk* text, highlighting the words in the paragraphs that describe what happened to the water as heat was applied. (They should use a different highlighting color than they used in the previous reading.) They should also refer to the first paragraph of the Heat of Vaporization and Condensation section which describes the effects of a change of phase on molecules. • It may be useful to point out to students that in all three states, the symbolic formula for water remains constant. This will help them understand that no new materials are created; only phases are changed. **Accommodations** • Students may not understand what is meant by the reference to two equations in the *Symbolic* question. Remind them that they learned the equation to determine heat energy in the previous activity, and the equation for determining energy needed for a change in phase in the *Chem Talk* section of this activity.
Practice with word problems and calculations	*Chem to Go* 2.-4.	**Augmentation** • Teach students to recognize key words or phrases in problems, such as *"vaporize," "raise the temperature"* and *"remove heat,"* that often provide clues as to which equation to use. • Help students having difficulty plugging in the values or making the calculations **Accommodations** • Provide students having difficulty solving the word problems with three models, one for vaporization, one for raising the temperature and one for lowering the temperature. Mix up the word and problem order so that students are forced to think about the strategy to use for each of their problems.

Strategies for Students with Limited English Language Proficiency

LEARNING ISSUE	REFERENCE	AUGMENTATION AND ACCOMMODATIONS
Background knowledge	*What Do You Think?*	Use a description of the illustration to explain possible answers to the question about water and temperature.
Vocabulary	*Investigate*	Check students' understanding of the term, "*graduated cylinder*" and discuss uses of the terms "*graduate*" and "*gradual*." Use of the word "*note*" may require an explanation as well. Explain the use of the signal word, "*alternatively*" to mean another choice or possibility. Students may require some help in determining what to do when they are asked to "*describe the relationship*."
Background knowledge Vocabulary Comprehending text	*Chem Talk*	Check for understanding of the "*ize*" verb ending, as in "*vaporize*," and the noun form, "*vaporization*." Also refer to the "*ation*" noun ending in "*condensation*" and share derivatives to build background and vocabulary knowledge.
Background knowledge Application	*What Do You Think Now?*	Have students discuss answers prior to writing their own.
Background knowledge Vocabulary Comprehending text	*Chem Essential Questions*	Help students understand what they do when they are directed to "*describe*" something, as in the *How do you know?* section. Point out the use of the "*ation*" ending again in the term "*preparation*."
Comprehension Vocabulary	*Chem to Go*	Make sure students understand what they have to do when they are asked to "*determine*" an amount, as in Questions 2. and 3.

NOTES

_____

_____

_____

_____

_____

_____

_____

_____

_____

_____

_____

Section 4
Teaching Suggestions and Sample Answers

What Do You See?

The colorful illustration is an early opportunity to engage the students' interests and to elicit responses. Students will see various things in the illustration and each student will make different connections. Some may see the clouds of steam while others may comment on the bellows. All responses are valid and not to be judged. You will have an opportunity to revisit this section with your students at a later time.

What Do You Think?

Students will probably say that the temperature of the water will steadily increase from its original temperature until it is boiling. Some may know that the temperature of the water cannot increase beyond its boiling temperature, while others may not. Listen carefully for prior conceptions – especially misconceptions – but it is not useful to correct students at this point. Simply take note of their responses and ask for their explanations; it will help you to assess your students' understanding before you begin the section.

What Do You Think?
A CHEMIST'S RESPONSE

The temperature of boiling water does not change and remains at the boiling point. Any time a substance undergoes a phase change, the temperature remains constant until all of the substance has undergone the phase change.

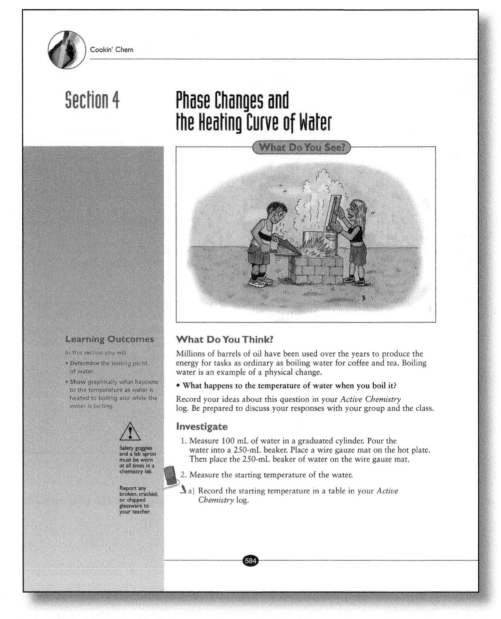

STUDENTS' PRIOR CONCEPTIONS

Students are familiar with solids and liquids because these are concrete and visible states of matter. The most common liquid is water, and therefore many students believe that all liquids are watery. Students have less familiarity with the gas state because gases are usually invisible and odorless. It is especially difficult to attribute mass to something invisible, and therefore many students have difficulty seeing gases as having material character. Some students attribute "negative weight" to gases, since it is common experience that gases tend to rise or float.

The behavior of water is one of the most confusing concepts for students. Many high school students are unable to distinguish between a physical and a chemical change, thus making it difficult for them to understand the ability to change state. Students tend to have a static rather than kinetic conception of the particulate model of matter.[1] They sometimes think that molecules of the same

Investigate

Note: These procedures could also be done with a temperature probe and software. The resulting graphs could be saved to a computer, printed, and analyzed. If a hot plate is going to be used, it should be turned on a few minutes before the start of the investigation. This will give a more constant amount of heat being applied to the water.

1.

The volume of water is not critical. However, if the students all start with the same amount of water, they should all finish the activity at about the same time.

2.

Room temperature is fine. Hot water should not be used because the heating time, and thus the graph, will be shortened.

NOTES

_____

_____

_____

_____

_____

_____

_____

_____

substance can change shapes in different phases.[2] Among the changes of state, melting is the most difficult for students to understand. This is because they confuse melting with dissolving, even though two materials are required for dissolving to occur. Experience has shown that students often believe the attraction between atoms gets weaker when a substance melts or boils.

Another common misconception is that the bubbles in boiling water are either "heat," "air," or "oxygen and hydrogen atoms."[3] The key to understanding vaporization (and sublimation) is for students to understand that the liquid is not being destroyed and that no mass is lost. This comes back to understanding conservation of matter.

Students see that it takes a long time to completely convert liquid water to vapor, but they have difficulty understanding that the change of state occurs at a constant temperature. Most students will believe that the longer a pure substance boils, the higher the temperature will rise. This activity addresses this point.

1. Driver, R., Guesne, E. Tiberhien, A. (eds), *Children's Ideas and the learning of science*, Children in Science, pp 124-144, 1985, Milton Keynes, UK: Open University Press.

2. Anderson, B. *Pupils Conceptions of Matter and its Transformations (ages 12-16)*, Studies in Science Education, 18, pp 53-85, 1990.

3. Osborn, R,. Cosgrove, M. *J. Res. Sci. Teach*, 1983, 20, 825.

3.

The water temperature will increase steadily until it reaches 100° C (or close) and then will stabilize. No amount of additional heat or time will increase the temperature (under normal conditions). At the boiling point, remind students to continue making readings and then to stop after 6-8 readings.

4.

The *x*-axis can have gradations every minute and cover at least 30 minutes. The *y*-axis of the graph should have at least 13 gradations and be labeled every 10 degrees from 0° C to 120° C.

5.a)

The graph of the boiling water should show two sections – one with a rising slope and then a leveling-off section.

5.b)

The temperature was rising, as shown by the inclined line.

5.c)

The leveled-off, or plateau section of the graph represents the temperature of the water while it was boiling.

5.d)

As the water boils, there is no visible relationship between the heat and the temperature. The temperature stays constant. There would be an inverse relationship between heat and the volume of water, however.

5.e)

No, the water could not be heated to 120°C. The water could not be heated beyond 100°C because, at 1 atmosphere, that is the boiling point.

5.f)

A copy of the diagrams below is provided as a Blackline Master in your *Teacher Resources* CD.

7-4a **Blackline Master**

Kinetic Energy of Water Molecules

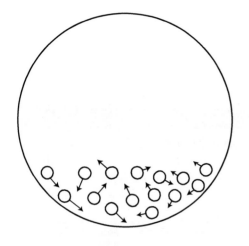

Cool Water

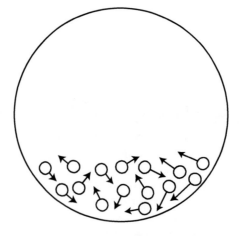

Hot Water

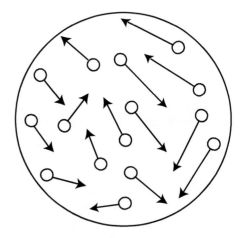

Steam

3. Turn on the hot plate to the highest setting to heat the water. Measure the temperature of the water every 30 s. Try to heat the water to 120°C and then stop. You may need to stop heating the water when your teacher instructs you to do so.

a) Record the temperature of the water every 30 s.

b) Note the temperature when the water begins to boil.

4. Graph the temperature versus time in your *Active Chemistry* log. Plot time on the *x*-axis and temperature on the *y*-axis. With good planning, your lab group may be able to complete the graph as you record the data.

Alternatively, you may use a temperature probe and software in *Steps 2* and *3*. In this case, the graph will be generated for you.

a) Place a copy of the graph in your *Active Chemistry* log.

5. Answer the following questions in your *Active Chemistry* log:

a) Describe the graph of the boiling water. How many sections are present?

The *x*-axis of the graph is time. Since you were heating the water at a constant rate, you can also refer to the *x*-axis as heat energy.

b) The water gained heat energy the entire time to get it to boil. What happened to the temperature while the water gained heat energy?

c) Which section of the graph shows where the water is actually boiling? What happens to the temperature while the water is *boiling*?

d) Describe the relationship between heat and temperature as water boils.

e) The instructions were to heat the water to 120°C. Were you able to do this? Why do you think that the water could not be heated beyond 100°C?

f) Make three sketches showing the water molecules in the cool water, the hot water, and the steam.

Make certain that the ringstand, ring, beaker, and burner are secure.

Caution! Hot plates may remain hot for several minutes after being unplugged.

Wash hands and arms thoroughly before leaving the lab area.

585

Active Chemistry

TEACHING TIP

At this point, you might want to go back to the heating curve and discuss what is occurring at the molecular (particle) level for each portion of the graph.

As the liquid or gas heats, the temperature rises. The particles of the liquid or gas are absorbing energy and moving faster. This increase in kinetic energy is seen as a rise in temperature (temperature measures the average kinetic energy of the particles). The rate at which the substance absorbs heat and changes temperature is its Specific Heat Capacity.

As the liquid boils, the temperature remains constant. The particles of the liquid are absorbing heat, but not changing kinetic energy. The energy is used to overcome the attractive forces between the molecules. An increase in potential energy is seen at the phase change. The energy needed to change phase is the Heat of Vaporization.

The opposite is true if the heating/cooling curve is read backwards (cooling). Heat is lost in the gas or liquid and a temperature drop is seen as the kinetic energy of the particles decreases. During the phase change from steam to water, heat is still lost, but it is lost as potential energy, not kinetic energy. With cooling, the gas particles slow down and move closer together as the attractive forces between the liquid particles become dominant. Water condenses and forms a liquid. The energy lost as the phase changes is the Heat of Condensation.

Chem Talk

The physical properties of solids, liquids, and gases are reviewed. The students learn why they cannot reach a temperature above the boiling point under conditions of approximately one atmosphere. Finally, the similarities and differences between the heat of vaporization and the heat of condensation are examined.

 Cookin' Chem

Chem Talk

HEAT ENERGY AND THE CHANGES OF STATE: BOILING AND CONDENSATION

The States of Matter

Chem Words

plasma: a high-energy state of atoms and molecules, such as those found in solar wind and Earth's ionosphere.

Solids, liquids, and gases are three of the states, or phases, of matter. The fourth state of matter is **plasma**, but this will not be discussed here. The following definitions will help you to identify a substance's state of matter and to describe the changes from one state to another.

Solids have a definite shape and volume. True solids retain their shape and take up a definite volume for a given amount of mass. The particles are close together in solids. They are locked into a fixed position. For the most part, they cannot be compressed and they are unable to flow. All materials become solid if their temperatures are reduced enough or the pressure exerted on them becomes high enough. Many people will mistakenly believe that the particles of a solid are not moving. They do move. They vibrate slightly around a fixed position. The solid state of H_2O (water) is ice. You will study ice in the next section.

Liquids do not have a definite shape and will flow to take the shape of the container they are in. The particles are close together in liquids. Liquids do have a definite volume for a given mass. All liquids are not easily compressed. At the same temperature, there is less attraction between the particles of a liquid substance than those of a solid. Therefore, they are able to move more than the particles of a solid. They are able to slip and slide over and around one another. The liquid state of H_2O is water.

Gases have no definite shape or volume of their own. Therefore, if the volume of a gas container changes, so does the volume of the gas. The particles are very far apart in a gas. Individual molecules do not change size when they are vaporized (or undergo any phase change). Gases are also easily compressed. All of these characteristics of gases are due to the fact that at room temperature the particles of a gas have almost no attraction for one another. The gas state of H_2O is water vapor.

Change of State: A Physical Change

In this investigation, you explored **boiling**, also called **vaporization**. Boiling is a change from a liquid to a gas phase. The temperature at which this occurs for a given substance is the **boiling point**.

Condensation is the change from a gas to a liquid. The temperature at which this occurs for a given substance is the **condensation point**. The condensation point and the boiling point are the same.

When water boils or steam condenses, a **physical change** takes place. A physical change is one that involves changes in the state or phase of a material. It does not involve the creation of new materials. The water boils and turns to water vapor (steam) and water vapor condenses to form liquid water. However, there is no change to the molecular structure or size of the water molecule. It is still H_2O. The phase change does involve changes in heat though. **Endothermic changes** occur when heat is absorbed. **Exothermic changes** occur when heat is removed. Vaporization is endothermic and condensation is exothermic. You can remember this by recalling the investigation you completed. To boil water, the water must gain heat energy. Boiling is therefore an endothermic process. A phase change can also take place with a change in pressure.

Heat of Vaporization and Condensation

When you added heat energy to water, at first, the water's temperature increased. As you supplied more heat energy, the water got hotter and hotter. At a certain point, the water no longer got hotter. At 100°C, the liquid water began to become a gas of water vapor. The molecules of water were no longer in contact with the other water molecules and were able to move about the room. You can try to get water in an *uncovered* pot to reach temperatures higher than 100°C, but you cannot do it! →

Chem Words

boiling (vaporization): a change from a liquid to a gas phase.

boiling point: the temperature at which vaporization occurs for a given substance.

condensation: a change from a gas to a liquid.

condensation point: the temperature at which condensation occurs for a given substance.

physical change: a process that involves changes in the state or phase of a material.

endothermic change: a change that occurs when heat is absorbed by a system.

exothermic change: a change that occurs when heat is released from a system.

Checking Up

1.

Solids have a definite shape and volume. The particles in a solid are close together and locked in a fixed position. However, the particles of a solid move, vibrating slightly around a fixed position. For the most part, they cannot be compressed and they are unable to flow except under very high pressure. The attraction between particles of a solid is a greater force than their kinetic energy, and so they are fixed in place.

Liquids do not have a definite shape and will flow to take the shape of their container. Liquids do have a definite volume for a given mass. Liquids are not easily compressed. The particles are close together in liquids. Kinetic energy overcomes some of the attraction of one particle for another. Therefore, particles in liquids can move more freely than those of solids.

Gases have no definite shape or volume of their own; therefore, they must take the shape and volume of their container. The particles are relatively far apart in a gas. Because of the large amounts of empty space between particles, gases are easily compressible. All of these characteristics are due to the fact that the kinetic energy of the particles of a gas overwhelms the attraction of one particle for another.

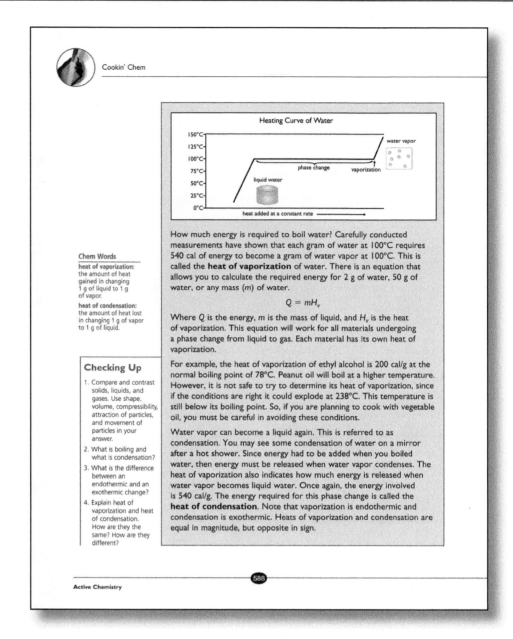

Cookin' Chem

Heating Curve of Water

How much energy is required to boil water? Carefully conducted measurements have shown that each gram of water at 100°C requires 540 cal of energy to become a gram of water vapor at 100°C. This is called the **heat of vaporization** of water. There is an equation that allows you to calculate the required energy for 2 g of water, 50 g of water, or any mass (m) of water.

$$Q = mH_v$$

Where Q is the energy, m is the mass of liquid, and H_v is the heat of vaporization. This equation will work for all materials undergoing a phase change from liquid to gas. Each material has its own heat of vaporization.

For example, the heat of vaporization of ethyl alcohol is 200 cal/g at the normal boiling point of 78°C. Peanut oil will boil at a higher temperature. However, it is not safe to try to determine its heat of vaporization, since if the conditions are right it could explode at 238°C. This temperature is still below its boiling point. So, if you are planning to cook with vegetable oil, you must be careful in avoiding these conditions.

Water vapor can become a liquid again. This is referred to as condensation. You may see some condensation of water on a mirror after a hot shower. Since energy had to be added when you boiled water, then energy must be released when water vapor condenses. The heat of vaporization also indicates how much energy is released when water vapor becomes liquid water. Once again, the energy involved is 540 cal/g. The energy required for this phase change is called the **heat of condensation**. Note that vaporization is endothermic and condensation is exothermic. Heats of vaporization and condensation are equal in magnitude, but opposite in sign.

Chem Words

heat of vaporization: the amount of heat gained in changing 1 g of liquid to 1 g of vapor.

heat of condensation: the amount of heat lost in changing 1 g of vapor to 1 g of liquid.

Checking Up

1. Compare and contrast solids, liquids, and gases. Use shape, volume, compressibility, attraction of particles, and movement of particles in your answer.
2. What is boiling and what is condensation?
3. What is the difference between an endothermic and an exothermic change?
4. Explain heat of vaporization and heat of condensation. How are they the same? How are they different?

2.

Boiling, otherwise known as vaporization, is a change from a liquid to a gas phase and is endothermic. Condensation is a change from a gas to a liquid, and is exothermic.

3.

An endothermic change is a change that occurs when heat is absorbed by a system from the surroundings. An exothermic change is a change that occurs when heat is released from a system to the surroundings.

4.

The specific heat of vaporization is the amount of heat gained when changing 1 g of liquid to 1 g of vapor. Conversely, the specific heat of condensation is the amount of heat lost when changing 1 g of vapor to 1 g of liquid. Thus, heats of vaporization and condensation are equal in magnitude but opposite in sign. A key difference between the two is that vaporization is endothermic while condensation is exothermic.

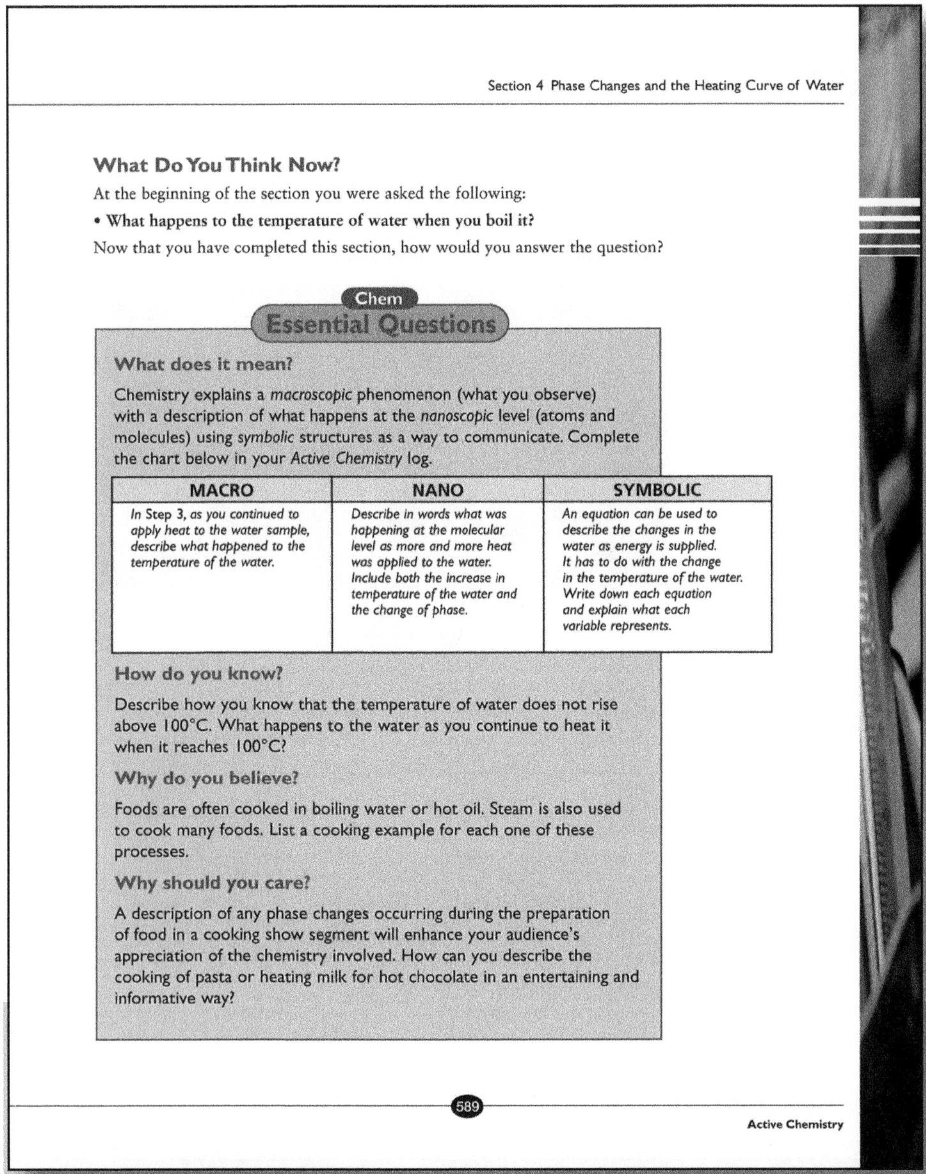

What Do You Think Now?

Have students revisit the *What Do You See?* illustration and the *What Do You Think?* question. They should now have a better understanding of the content that the artist wished to convey in the illustration. Students should also have a more sophisticated, in-depth response to the *What Do You Think?* question. They should understand what happens at a phase change and why the temperature remains constant. They should also know that under the conditions that were used in the investigation, it would be impossible to raise the temperature to 120° C.

You may choose to share the answer provided in *A Chemist's Response* and ask students to discuss their reactions and opinions.

The following reproduces the student page shown at left:

What Do You Think Now?

At the beginning of the section you were asked the following:

• **What happens to the temperature of water when you boil it?**

Now that you have completed this section, how would you answer the question?

Chem
Essential Questions

What does it mean?

Chemistry explains a *macroscopic* phenomenon (what you observe) with a description of what happens at the *nanoscopic* level (atoms and molecules) using *symbolic* structures as a way to communicate. Complete the chart below in your *Active Chemistry* log.

MACRO	NANO	SYMBOLIC
In Step 3, as you continued to apply heat to the water sample, describe what happened to the temperature of the water.	Describe in words what was happening at the molecular level as more and more heat was applied to the water. Include both the increase in temperature of the water and the change of phase.	An equation can be used to describe the changes in the water as energy is supplied. It has to do with the change in the temperature of the water. Write down each equation and explain what each variable represents.

How do you know?

Describe how you know that the temperature of water does not rise above 100°C. What happens to the water as you continue to heat it when it reaches 100°C?

Why do you believe?

Foods are often cooked in boiling water or hot oil. Steam is also used to cook many foods. List a cooking example for each one of these processes.

Why should you care?

A description of any phase changes occurring during the preparation of food in a cooking show segment will enhance your audience's appreciation of the chemistry involved. How can you describe the cooking of pasta or heating milk for hot chocolate in an entertaining and informative way?

589

Active Chemistry

Chem Essential Questions
What does it mean?

MACRO — Initially, the temperature of the water rose steadily in a straight line. At 100° C the temperature stopped rising and the water began to boil.

NANO — Prior to 100° C, the temperature rose steadily and the water molecules moved faster and faster as their average kinetic energy rose. At 100° C the temperature no longer increased, but the water began to boil. Water in the gas phase is steam and the continued application of heat went into providing the heat of vaporization to the water molecules as they went into the gas phase.

SYMBOLIC—

Equation 1: $Q = mc\Delta T$;
Q = heat, m = mass, c = specific heat, ΔT = change in temperature

Equation 2: $Q = mH_v$
Q = heat, m = mass,
H_v = specific heat of vaporization

How do you know?

The temperature of water at 100° C does not rise any higher with added heat because at this point, all the heat goes into evaporating the water. Eventually all the water enters into the gas phase (becomes steam).

Why do you believe?

Pasta and potatoes generally are boiled.
French fries (potatoes) are cooked in oil.
Vegetables, such as broccoli, can be steamed.

Why should you care?

Cooking of pasta: Heat is applied to water to bring it to the boiling point (100°C). The pasta is added, which cools the water. More heat brings the water back to 100°C, where it remains as the water cooks the pasta.

Heating milk for hot chocolate: Heat is applied to the milk gently to raise its temperature. The powdered hot chocolate mix is added, with stirring, and heating continues until the powder is evenly dispersed.

Reflecting on the Section and the Challenge

Following the *What Do You Think Now?* question is an opportunity to pause and have students think about how they will incorporate the information in this section into their challenge. In order for food to be cooked using water, the temperature of the water must be at a certain temperature. Water will remain at 100° C throughout the cooking process as long as it does not all evaporate away. The cook needs to understand that water boils when it reaches the atmospheric pressure of the environment. For that reason, cooking at high altitudes may require greater than one atmosphere of pressure in a pressure cooker, or longer times in an oven.

Chem to Go

1.

Increasing the heat to a pot of boiling water will do nothing to its temperature. The water boils at a constant temperature (100° C at one atmosphere). The heat is being used to change phase (providing the heat of vaporization-potential energy) and does not change the temperature (kinetic energy).

2.

500 g (540 cal/g) = 270,000 cal or 270 kcal.

3.

It will require a total of 140 kcal of heat energy. It takes 5 kcal to raise the temperature of 250 g of water by 20° C to reach 100° C (20°C × 250 g × 1.00 cal/g° C) and an additional 135 kcal of heat energy to vaporize the water (250 g × 540 cal/g).

4.

It will require the removal of 240 kcal of heat energy. To condense the vapor it will require the removal of 220 kcal of heat energy (400 g × 540 cal/g). To cool the water from 100°C to 50°C will require the removal of 20 kcal of heat energy. The total is 240 kcal (20 kcal + 220 kcal).

Cookin' Chem

Reflecting on the Section and the Challenge

In this section, you learned that energy is required to change a liquid into a gas and that a gas must lose heat energy in order for it to condense into a liquid. Boiling water is used to cook different foods. Vegetables, potatoes, and eggs are all examples that can be cooked in boiling water. If you include cooking in boiling water in your segment it will be informative for your audience.

Chem to Go

1. You have a pot of water boiling on the stove. What will happen to the temperature of the water if you increase the heat?

2. Determine the amount of heat needed to vaporize 500 g of water at 100°C.

3. Determine the amount of heat needed to vaporize 250 g of water starting at 80°C.

4. How much heat must be removed from 400 g of steam at 100°C to bring it down to 50°C?

5. Draw a heating curve (temperature versus time) for 100 mL of water where heat is added at 50 cal/min. Start at 0°C and continue to the boiling point.

6. Draw a heating curve (temperature versus time) for 500 mL of water where heat is added at 50 cal/min. Start at 0°C and continue to the boiling point.

7. Draw a heating curve (temperature versus time) for 1.0 L of ethyl alcohol where heat is added at 5.0 cal/min. The heat of vaporization of ethyl alcohol is 0.200 cal/g. The boiling point of ethyl alcohol is 78°C. Start at 78°C and continue until evaporation is complete. The density of ethanol is 0.79 g/mL.

8. *Preparing for the Chapter Challenge*

   List three instances where there are condensation/evaporation phase changes occurring in everyday cooking. Describe the processes as either endothermic or exothermic.

590

Active Chemistry

5.

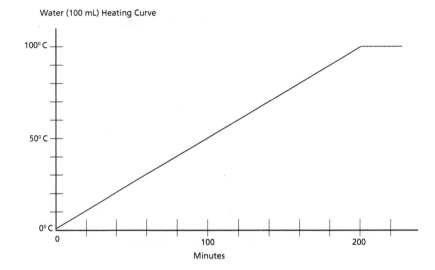

Water (100 mL) Heating Curve

6.

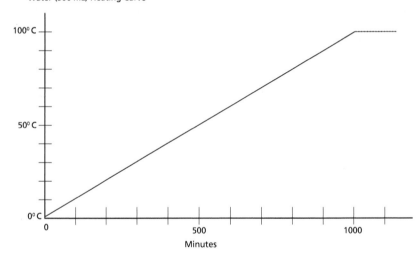

Water (500 mL) Heating Curve

7.

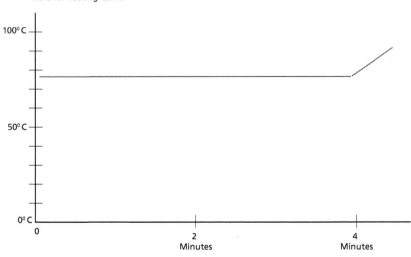

Ethanol Heating Curve

8.

Preparing for the Chapter Challenge

Steaming vegetables	endothermic – vegetables absorb heat
Poached eggs	endothermic – eggs absorb heat
Steamed salmon	endothermic – the salmon absorbs heat
Steamed rice	endothermic – the rice absorbs heat

In the examples above, the food is cooked in an endothermic process although the condensation of steam is an exothermic process.

In food preservation, water is often removed using heat. This is also an endothermic process.

SECTION 4 – QUIZ

7-4b	Blackline Master

1. When water is at 100° C, which phase change is exothermic? Which is endothermic?

2. The heat of vaporization of substance X is calculated at 250 cal/g. Explain what this means.

3. Will increasing the heat under a pot of boiling water increase its temperature? Explain your answer.

4. How are the particles in a solid moving?

   a) They are not moving.

   b) They are vibrating slightly in place.

   c) They slide over one another.

   d) They are relatively far apart and moving rapidly.

5. How are the particles in a gas moving?

   a) They are not moving.

   b) They are vibrating slightly in place.

   c) They slide over one another.

   d) They are relatively far apart and moving rapidly.

SECTION 4 – QUIZ ANSWERS

❶ Exothermic: condensing
   Endothermic: boiling or vaporization

❷ It takes 250 cal to vaporize 1 g of substance X at its boiling point.

❸ No. Once the water is boiling, you cannot raise its temperature by supplying more heat. Temperature remains constant during a phase change.

❹ b) They are vibrating slightly in place.

❺ d) They are relatively far apart and moving rapidly.

NOTES

_____

_____

_____

_____

_____

_____

_____

_____

NOTES

SECTION 5
Phase Changes and the Cooling Curve of Water

Section Overview

In this section, students will take temperature readings of water as it cools and freezes. They will use this data to make a graph and will combine it with the data from *Section 4* to create an energy curve. They will also calculate the heat of fusion of ice by determining the amount of heat energy added to a certain quantity of ice as it melts.

In this investigation, students should find that the temperature remains constant during a phase change.

Background Information

The atoms or molecules of a solid tend to vibrate quickly in place and are generally spaced as closely together as possible. Because of this close packing, solids can't be significantly compressed. The atoms or molecules of a liquid are also generally spaced as closely together as possible but they tend to slide by one another, allowing the liquid to take the shape of its container. Since the molecules of a liquid are closely packed, they too cannot be significantly compressed. Gases have relatively large distances between their atoms or molecules and are therefore easily compressed.

When the heating of ice is considered, molecules that were once well-ordered and vibrating around relatively fixed positions now begin to vibrate more vigorously. When the temperature is high enough, the solid begins to melt and the particles slide by each other, forming a liquid. Continuing the addition of heat, the molecules overcome the intermolecular forces of attraction completely and become a gas.

As frozen water is heated to boiling, a plot of temperature vs. time yields a **heating curve**. As heat is added, the temperature of the ice increases to 0°C and the melting point of ice is reached. At 0°C, the temperature remains constant for a period of time, even though heat is continually added. The temperature remains at 0°C until all the ice is melted. The energy that is absorbed as heat and is required to melt one mole of any substance is called the molar enthalpy of fusion or the **molar heat of fusion** and is denoted by ΔH_{fus}, and has a value of 6.01 kJ/mol for water. Once the temperature of the ice reaches 0°C, the addition of further heat goes into disrupting hydrogen bonds and other intermolecular forces rather than into increasing the temperature, as indicated by the plateau at 0°C on the heating curve. At this temperature (the melting point) solid and liquid coexist in equilibrium as molecules break free from their positions in the ice crystals and enter the liquid phase.

After all the ice is melted, the temperature will rise continuously until 100°C, which is the boiling point. Again, the temperature remains constant for a period even though heat is being added at a constant rate. The heat being absorbed at 100°C is vaporizing the liquid water into water vapor. The temperature remains at 100°C as the heat goes into overcoming intermolecular forces until all the water is vaporized. The amount of energy necessary to convert one mole of a liquid to a gas is called the molar enthalpy of vaporization or **molar heat of vaporization**, ΔH_{vap}, and has a value of 40.7 kJ/mol at 100°C for water. Only after the liquid is completely vaporized will the temperature again begin to rise.

The opposite of a heating curve is a cooling curve. In this case, you start with a gas and continually cool it – removing heat at a constant rate – until you have reached a solid. The curve looks very much like the opposite of a heating curve.

A table of heats of vaporization and fusion for various substances is listed below.

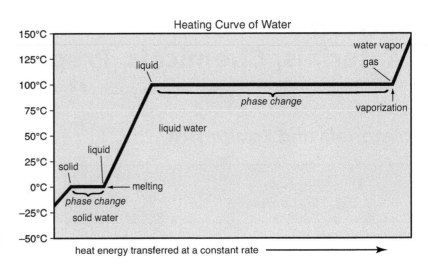

Heating Curve of Water

heat energy transferred at a constant rate

MOLAR HEATS OF FUSION AND VAPORIZATION AT 1 ATM		
Substance	ΔH_{fus} kJ/mol	ΔH_{vap} kJ/mol
Aluminum	10.50	230.00
Ammonia	5.66	23.40
Argon	1.11	6.54
Chlorine (Cl_2)	6.41	20.10
Ethane	2.86	14.70
Ethanol	5.03	38.60
Helium	0.021	0.084
Hydrogen (H_2)	0.117	0.905
Iron	1.29	380.00
Methane	0.943	8.19
Methanol	3.17	35.30
Nitrogen (N_2)	0.721	5.58
Oxygen (O_2)	0.444	6.83
Platinum	22.20	520.00
Silver	9.52	250.00
Sodium chloride	28.90	180.00
Water	6.02	40.69

LEARNING OUTCOMES		
LEARNING OUTCOMES	LOCATION IN SECTION	EVIDENCE OF UNDERSTANDING
Determine the freezing point of water.	*Investigate* Part A, Step 3 *Chem Talk,* *Chem to Go* Questions 1.3.	Students are able to successfully complete this part of the activity and provide answers that match those provided in this *Teacher's Edition.*
Show graphically what happens to the temperature as water is cooled to freezing and while it is freezing.	*Investigate* Part A, Step 4 *Checking Up* Question 2. *Chem to Go* Questions 1.-8.	Students' answers and calculations are similar to those outlined in this *Teacher's Edition.*

Section 5
Materials, Chemicals, Preparation, and Safety

("per Group" quantity is based on group size of 4 students)

Materials and Equipment

Materials (and Equipment)	Quantity per Group (4 students)
Beaker, 400 mL	1
Thermometer or temperature probe	1
Hot plate*	1
Wire gauze for hot plate	1
Test tube, large	1
Test tube rack	1
Styrene foam cups, large	2
Graduated cylinder, 100 mL	1
Materials (and Equipment)	**Quantity per Class**
Bucket of crushed ice	1
Roll of paper towels	1
Pack of graph paper, 50 sheets	1

* or Bunsen burner, ringstand, and iron ring

Chemicals

Chemicals	Quantity per Class (24 students)
Sodium chloride, NaCl (table salt)	250 g

Teacher Preparation

Print out copies of the *Heating/Cooling Curve* graphs from the Blackline Master (7-5b) and provide one to each group.

7-5b Blackline Master

Safety Requirements

- Goggles and aprons are required for any activity in the laboratory area.

- Ice, water, and saltwater can be disposed of in a sink.

NOTES

Meeting the Needs of All Students
Differentiated Instruction

Augmentation and Accommodations

LEARNING ISSUE	REFERENCE	AUGMENTATION AND ACCOMMODATIONS
Graphing temperature change over time	*Investigate* Part A, 4.	• See suggestions for a similar exercise in the previous section.
Labeling a graph	*Investigate* Part A, 6.	**Accommodation** • Refer to the graph on the last page of *Chem Talk* in *Section 4* for a model graph.
Completing a data table	*Investigate* Part B, 1.	**Augmentation** • Check for understanding of completion of this more complex graph in class. • Subsequently, the class could do one line of their graphs together using one group's materials if needed. This would provide all groups with a model. **Accommodations** • Move to a group and do the first line with them after making sure the graph and experiment are correctly set up. • Consider heterogeneous grouping to allow weaker students to participate.
Calculating with equations	*Investigate* Part B, 7.	**Augmentation** • Make sure students know which equations to use. • For students having difficulty, re-teach meanings of symbols in the equation corresponding to the values in the table. Point out that the table was set up to give them information from calculations they would need later. Then, model solving a similar problem using the data collected from a different substance so they can apply the learning to their problem. Students who can independently use the equation to determine heat of fusion could be given a completed table for other substances and practice determining heat of fusion for them. **Accommodations** • Show students a heat of fusion table which includes the symbols used in the equation shown under the column headings.

Reading comprehension
 	
Analysis of a diagram
 	
Summarizing
	Chem Talk	**Augmentation**
		• Students will tend to overlook the completed diagram without analysis necessary to synthesize their learning.
		  ○ Give students a graph with only the ice, water and vapor included. Have them use the *Chem Talk* text which precedes the diagram to illustrate the relationships described there.
		  ○ Give them the entire diagram without labels and have them label it.
		• Point out and explain the terms "*sublimation*" and "*deposition*" on the diagram. They will need to understand these terms during the *Checking Up* section and the terms that do not appear elsewhere in the chapter.

Graphing phase changes of water Summarizing an experiment	*Chem Essential Questions*	**Accommodations** • Provide a graph for students to label. • Have students use the steps of the experiment that appear in the text as the outline for writing a summary explaining how they know the amount of heat it takes to melt ice.

LEARNING ISSUE	REFERENCE	AUGMENTATION AND ACCOMMODATIONS
Practice with word problems and calculations	*Chem to Go* 4.-8.	**Augmentation** • Teach students to recognize the key words and phrases such as *"vaporize,"* *"raise the temperature,"* and *"remove heat"* that tell them which equation to use. • Help students plug in the values and make the calculations. **Accommodations** • Provide students with three models – one for vaporization, one for raising the temperature, and one for melting ice. • Give students the equation and a legend which defines the symbols in the equation, or show them where to find that information in the text.

Strategies for Students with Limited English Language Proficiency

LEARNING ISSUE	REFERENCE	AUGMENTATION AND ACCOMMODATIONS
Background knowledge	*What Do You Think?*	Use a description of the illustration to explain possible answers to the question about water and temperature. Explain the sentence "Slow freezing permits large ice crystals to form." This use of the word *"permits"* may be unfamiliar.
Vocabulary	*Investigate*	Students may benefit from working in small groups or as a team. Point out that the first part of the *Investigate* section includes activities, and the second part beginning with Step 5 of Part A requires students to answer questions. Students may require clarification of the phrase *"heat of fusion."*
Background knowledge Vocabulary Comprehending text	*Chem Talk*	Review the concept of *"capacity."* Check *Chem Words* for further explanation of new vocabulary. Students might benefit from pointing out the *"ize"* form of the word *"crystallize"* as well as the noun form of the word *"crystallization"* as the *"ation"* noun suffix is added, to give them additional vocabulary knowledge.
Background knowledge Application	*What Do You Think Now?*	Have students discuss answers prior to writing their own.
Background knowledge Vocabulary Comprehending text	*Chem Essential Questions*	Point out the use of the *"de"* prefix to mean *"not"* as in *"defrost"* in the *Why do you believe?* section.
Comprehension Vocabulary	*Chem to Go*	Students can work in teams or small groups. Make sure that students know that when they *"compare"* something, they are finding likenesses and not differences.

NOTES

_____

_____

_____

_____

_____

_____

_____

Section 5
Teaching Suggestions and Sample Answers

What Do You See?

This is an opportunity for you to capture students' interest in the section. You can ask them what they see in the illustration that represents a scientific concept. They may be able to identify the concept of temperature at the freezing point but at this time you are not looking for correct answers. Listen for the expression of ideas, conceptions, and interpretations that may be critical in students' understanding of the investigation ahead of them.

What Do You Think?

Again, you should not be concerned with correct answers now. You will want to elicit responses from the students in order to assess their prior knowledge and conceptions. Students will probably say that the temperature of the water will steadily decrease as it cools from the tap to form ice in the freezer.

| *What Do You Think?* |
| **A CHEMIST'S RESPONSE** |
| The temperature of water is constant at 0°C during the period that the liquid is becoming a solid. When there is no liquid left, the temperature of the ice can then decrease. |

Investigate

Part A: Freezing Water

| **TEACHING TIP** |
| These procedures could also be done with a temperature probe and software. The resulting graphs could be printed and analyzed. |

1.

An ice-salt-water mixture will have a temperature below 0°C.

2.

The water temperature will decrease steadily until it reaches 0°C (or close) and then will stabilize. It will remain at constant temperature for several readings and then begin to drop again.

STUDENTS' PRIOR CONCEPTIONS

Students are familiar with solids and liquids because these are concrete and visible states of matter. The most common liquid is water, and therefore many students believe that all liquids are watery. Students have less familiarity with the gas state because most common gases are usually invisible and odorless. It is especially difficult to attribute mass to something invisible, and therefore many students have difficulty seeing gases as having material character. Some students attribute "negative weight" to gases, since it is common experience that gases tend to rise or float.

The behavior of water is one of the most confusing concepts for students. Many high school students are unable to distinguish between a physical and a chemical change, thus making it difficult for them to understand that changes in state do not change the substance. Students tend to have a static rather than kinetic conception of the particulate model of matter.[1] They sometimes think that molecules of the same substance can change shapes in different phases.[2] Among the changes of state, melting is the most difficult for students to understand. This is because they confuse melting with dissolving, even though two materials are required for dissolving

Section 5

Phase Changes and the Cooling Curve of Water

What Do You See?

Learning Outcomes

In this section you will

• Determine the freezing point of water.

• Show graphically what happens to the temperature as water is cooled to freezing and while it is freezing.

Safety goggles and a lab apron must be worn *at all times* in a chemistry lab.

Report any broken, cracked, or chipped glassware to your teacher.

What Do You Think?

Fast freezing rates promote the formation of many small ice crystals. Slow freezing permits large ice crystals to form. This is important when freezing delicate foods or when making ice cream.

• **What happens to the temperature of water as it freezes?**

Record your ideas about this question in your *Active Chemistry* log. Be prepared to discuss your responses with your group and the class.

Investigate

Part A: Freezing Water

1. Half fill a test tube with water. Place the test tube in a polystyrene cup containing an ice and salt mixture.

2. Use a temperature sensor or thermometer to measure the starting temperature of the water in the test tube.

 a) Record the starting temperature in a table in your *Active Chemistry* log.

591

Active Chemistry

---

to occur. It has been shown that students often believe the attraction between atoms gets weaker when a substance melts or boils. In fact, the attractions remain the same but they are overcome by the increase in kinetic energy.

Another common misconception is that the bubbles in boiling water are either "heat," "air," or "oxygen and hydrogen atoms."[3]

The key to understanding vaporization (and sublimation) is for students to understand that, while the liquid is disappearing, no mass is lost. This comes back to not understanding the conservation of matter.

Students see that it takes a long time to completely convert liquid water to vapor, but they have difficulty understanding that the change of state occurs at a constant temperature. Most students will believe that the longer a pure substance boils, the higher the temperature will rise. This section addresses that point.

1. Driver, R., Guesne, E. Tiberhien, A. (eds), *Children's Ideas and the Learning of Science*, Children in science, pp 124-144, 1985, Milton Keynes, UK: Open University Press.

2. Anderson, B. *Pupils Conceptions of Matter and its Transformations (ages 12-16)*, Studies in Science Education, 18, pp 53-85, 1990.

3. Osborn, R., Cosgrove, M. J. *Res. Sci. Teach*, 1983, 20, 825.

3.

Be sure to remind students not to stir with the thermometer or try to loosen the thermometer, as it may break. Students will be tempted to ignore readings as the temperature stabilizes; remind them to continue the readings until they see a change.

4.

If a temperature probe and data collection instrument is used, students may need access to a computer and printer.

5.a)

The graph of the freezing water shows three sections – the temperature decreases, then levels off, and then decreases again.

5.b)

While the water is becoming a solid (freezing), the temperature is constant.

5.c)

The middle section when the temperature is constant shows where the water is freezing. The temperature does not change during this time.

5.d)

As water freezes, heat energy is being removed and potential energy is decreasing. The average kinetic energy of the water molecules, as shown by the temperature, is not changing.

5.e)

For your convenience, the following diagram is also provided as a Blackline Master in your *Teacher Resources* CD.

7-5a | **Blackline Master**

Cookin' Chem

3. Measure the temperature of the water in the test tube every 30 s as it freezes. Continue until you reach a temperature of –5°C.

   a) Record the temperature of the water every 30 s.

   b) Note the temperature at which *freezing* begins.

4. Graph the temperature versus time in your *Active Chemistry* log. Plot time on the *x*-axis and temperature on the *y*-axis. With good planning, your lab group may be able to complete the graph as you record the data.

   Alternatively, you may use a temperature probe and software in *Steps 2* and *3*. In this case, the graph will be generated for you.

   a) Place a copy of the graph in your *Active Chemistry* log.

5. Answer the following questions in your *Active Chemistry* log.

   a) Describe the graph of the temperature of water as it cools and freezes. How many sections are present?

   b) The water loses heat energy the entire time it is freezing. What happened to the temperature during this time?

   c) Which section of the graph shows where the water is actually freezing? What happens to the temperature while the water is freezing?

   d) Describe the relationship between heat and temperature as water freezes.

   e) Draw three pictures showing the water molecules in the cool water, the colder water, and the frozen water.

6. From the results of the previous *Investigate* and *Part A* of this *Investigate*, you can see that temperature remains constant during a phase change. The temperature of a solid, liquid, or gas changes as it gains or loses heat energy. Using the graph you created as a guide, sketch a new temperature versus time graph if ice at –5°C were heated on a hot plate until it boils.

   a) Label the portion of the graph that shows a solid, liquid, and a gas.

   b) Label the portion of the graph that shows *melting*, freezing, boiling, and condensing.

   c) Draw two arrows and label each arrow as exothermic or endothermic.

592

Active Chemistry

Kinetic Energy of Water Molecules

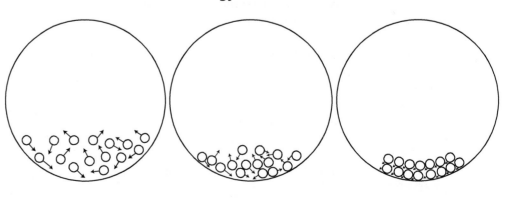

Cool Water   Colder Water   Frozen Water

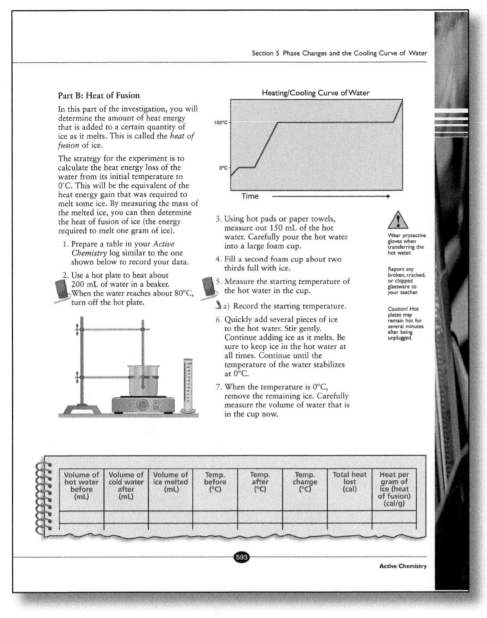

Part B: Heat of Fusion

In this part of the investigation, you will determine the amount of heat energy that is added to a certain quantity of ice as it melts. This is called the *heat of fusion* of ice.

The strategy for the experiment is to calculate the heat energy loss of the water from its initial temperature to 0°C. This will be the equivalent of the heat energy gain that was required to melt some ice. By measuring the mass of the melted ice, you can then determine the heat of fusion of ice (the energy required to melt one gram of ice).

1. Prepare a table in your *Active Chemistry* log similar to the one shown below to record your data.

2. Use a hot plate to heat about 200 mL of water in a beaker. When the water reaches about 80°C, turn off the hot plate.

Heating/Cooling Curve of Water

3. Using hot pads or paper towels, measure out 150 mL of the hot water. Carefully pour the hot water into a large foam cup.

4. Fill a second foam cup about two thirds full with ice.

5. Measure the starting temperature of the hot water in the cup.

   a) Record the starting temperature.

6. Quickly add several pieces of ice to the hot water. Stir gently. Continue adding ice as it melts. Be sure to keep ice in the hot water at all times. Continue until the temperature of the water stabilizes at 0°C.

7. When the temperature is 0°C, remove the remaining ice. Carefully measure the volume of water that is in the cup now.

⚠️ Wear protective gloves when transferring the hot water.

Report any broken, cracked, or chipped glassware to your teacher.

Caution! Hot plates may remain hot for several minutes after being unplugged.

Volume of hot water before (mL)	Volume of cold water after (mL)	Volume of ice melted (mL)	Temp. before (°C)	Temp. after (°C)	Temp. change (°C)	Total heat lost (cal)	Heat per gram of ice (heat of fusion) (cal/g)

593

Active Chemistry

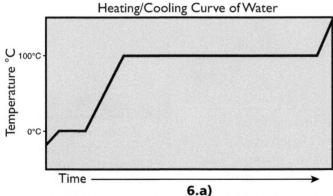

Heating/Cooling Curve of Water

6.

The preceding diagram is also provided as a Blackline Master in your *Teacher's Resources* CD.

7-5b **Blackline Master**

6.a)

The portions of the graph that represent solid, liquid, and gas are the three sections of the line in which temperature is increasing.

6.b)

The portions of the graph that represent melting, freezing, boiling and condensation are the two sections where temperature is constant.

6.c)

The arrow going to the right shows the endothermic processes. The arrow going to the left shows the exothermic processes.

Part B: Heat of Fusion

1.

It may save time to give the students the chart and have them copy it into their log later.

2.

The starting water temperature should be 70-75°C. If too hot, the ice melts too quickly.

3.

Leave room for at least 200 mL of additional water.

4.

The use of a foam cup for the ice is optional.

5.

The temperature should be about 70-75°C.

6.

Keep ice in the hot water at all times until temperature reaches about 0°C (or very close).

7.

Remove excess ice as soon as the temperature stabilizes. If ice is left in the cup after the temperature stabilizes, the ice will continue to melt but it is absorbing heat from the environment, not the water.

CHAPTER 7

8.a)

The total volume will be about 290 mL and so the volume due to added ice is about 140 mL.

8.b)

The temperature change will be about 75°C, from 75°C to 0°C.

8.c)

Sample calculation:

$\Delta Q = mc\Delta T =$
$150 \text{ g} \times 1.00 \text{ cal/g}\bullet°C \times 75°C$

8.d)

Sample calculation:

heat of fusion =
(total heat)/(mass of ice melted)
heat of fusion =
11.2 kcal/140 g = 80 cal/g

9.

The data table only needs one more cell than the number of groups in the class.

9.b)

The class average is usually closer to the true value of 79.6 cal/g than any of the groups.

10.a)

Any further melting would be from the heat of the surroundings and would cause an error in the final value. The error would be on the low side (< 79.6°C).

10.b)

Yes, ice would continue to melt.

10.c)

The heat would be coming from the surroundings.

11.a)

Student answers will vary. Results within a calorie or two are expected.

 Cookin' Chem

⚠ Wash hands and arms thoroughly before leaving the lab area.

8. Calculate the heat of fusion using the following steps. Show all your calculations in your *Active Chemistry* log.

a) Determine the volume of water from ice that melted.

b) Find the temperature change of the hot to cold water.

c) Determine how much heat the hot water lost by using the heat equation. Remember that the volume of hot water is also the mass of hot water (density of water = 1g/mL).

$$\Delta Q = mc\Delta T$$

d) Because the hot water lost heat energy, the ice gained the same amount of heat energy (assuming no loss to the surroundings). This is a statement of the conservation of energy. The volume of water from melted ice is equal to the mass of ice that melted. (Recall the density of water again.) Determine the heat of fusion of ice by dividing the total heat the ice absorbed by the mass of ice that melted. The unit will be cal/g.

$$\text{Heat of Fusion} = \frac{\text{total heat}}{\text{mass of ice melted}}$$

9. Prepare a class data table in your *Active Chemistry* log.

a) Record the heat of fusion of ice from the other groups.

b) Find the average for the class.

10. You stopped the investigation when the temperature stabilized.

a) Why do you think you stopped the investigation at this point?

b) Would the ice continue to melt?

c) Where would the ice be getting the heat from?

11. When experiments similar to the one that you have done are completed with extreme care and many, many times, chemists publish their work and arrive at a value for the heat of fusion of ice. The accepted heat of fusion of ice is 79.6 cal/g. This means that it takes 79.6 cal of heat to melt one gram of ice.

a) How close to the accepted value was your heat of fusion of ice?

b) How close was the class average?

11.b)

The class average value is expected to be closer than the value of any of the groups. The class average for the heat of fusion of ice should be close to the accepted value of 79.6 cal/g. You might want the students to find their percent error

$$\frac{79.6 - \text{class value}}{79.6} \times 100$$

TEACHING TIP

At this point, you might want to go back to the heating/cooling curve and discuss what is occurring at the molecular (particle) level for each portion of the graph.

Chem Talk

CHANGES OF STATE

Melting and Freezing

In the previous investigation, you explored boiling and condensation. Recall that boiling was also called vaporization. It is the change of state from a liquid to a gas. Condensation is the change of state from a gas to a liquid. Boiling is an endothermic change because water had to gain heat energy in order to boil. Condensation is an exothermic change.

In this investigation, you explored freezing and melting. **Melting** is the change from a solid to a liquid phase. Melting is also called **fusion**. The temperature at which this occurs for a given substance is the **melting point**. At the melting point there is enough kinetic energy to cause particles in the crystal structure to break free from the forces holding them together in the crystal structure. This required energy for a given mass is the **heat of fusion**.

Freezing is the change from a liquid to a solid phase. Freezing is also called crystallization. The temperature at which this occurs for a given substance is the **freezing point**. The freezing point occurs at the same temperature as the melting point. The energy lost when a substance freezes is the **heat of crystallization**. Fusion (melting) is endothermic and crystallization (freezing) is exothermic. The heats of fusion and crystallization are equal in magnitude, but opposite in sign.

Chem Words

melting (fusion): the change from a solid to a liquid phase.

melting point: the temperature at which a solid changes to a liquid.

heat of fusion: the amount of energy that a substance must gain in order for a solid to change to a liquid.

freezing: the change from a liquid to a solid phase.

freezing point: the temperature at which a liquid changes to a solid.

heat of crystallization: the energy released when a unit liquid mass of a substance freezes.

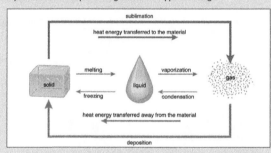

Recall also, that changes of state are physical changes. If you apply heat to the bottom of a candle, the wax will melt. As it cools, the wax will harden again. This is an example of a physical change. In *Section 2*,

Active Chemistry

Chem Talk

Changes of state are discussed in relation to melting (or fusion) and freezing (or crystallization). A diagram depicting energy transfers from vaporization, condensation, melting and freezing introduces the concepts of sublimation and deposition. Phase changes in terms of endothermic and exothermic heat energy and the relationship between temperature and intermolecular bonding are also reviewed.

Checking Up

1.a)

Melting or fusion is the change from a solid to a liquid phase. The reverse is freezing (crystallization), the change from a liquid to a solid phase. Melting is endothermic, whereas freezing is exothermic. The heats of fusion and crystallization are equal in magnitude, but opposite in sign.

1.b)

Vaporization is the change from a liquid to the gas phase. The reverse is condensation, the change from a gas to the liquid phase. Vaporization is endothermic, whereas condensation is exothermic. The heats of vaporization and condensation are equal in magnitude, but opposite in sign.

1.c)

Sublimation is the change directly from a solid to the gas phase. The reverse is deposition, the change from a gas to a solid phase. Sublimation is endothermic, whereas deposition is exothermic. The heats of sublimation and deposition are equal in magnitude, but opposite in sign.

2.

The temperature of a material does not change during a phase change.

3.

The heat energy that is absorbed by a material during an endothermic phase change like melting or evaporation is used to overcome the intermolecular forces of attraction between particles (molecules or atoms). The heat energy that is released during an exothermic phase change like freezing or condensation is due to the formation of interactions between the particles.

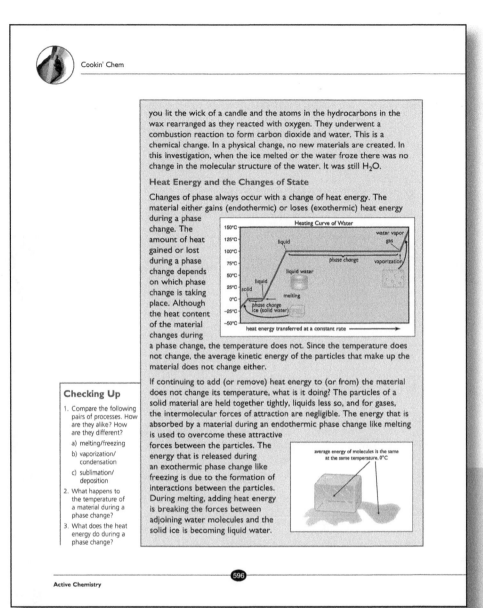

Cookin' Chem

you lit the wick of a candle and the atoms in the hydrocarbons in the wax rearranged as they reacted with oxygen. They underwent a combustion reaction to form carbon dioxide and water. This is a chemical change. In a physical change, no new materials are created. In this investigation, when the ice melted or the water froze there was no change in the molecular structure of the water. It was still H_2O.

Heat Energy and the Changes of State

Changes of phase always occur with a change of heat energy. The material either gains (endothermic) or loses (exothermic) heat energy during a phase change. The amount of heat gained or lost during a phase change depends on which phase change is taking place. Although the heat content of the material changes during a phase change, the temperature does not. Since the temperature does not change, the average kinetic energy of the particles that make up the material does not change either.

If continuing to add (or remove) heat energy to (or from) the material does not change its temperature, what is it doing? The particles of a solid material are held together tightly, liquids less so, and for gases, the intermolecular forces of attraction are negligible. The energy that is absorbed by a material during an endothermic phase change like melting is used to overcome these attractive forces between the particles. The energy that is released during an exothermic phase change like freezing is due to the formation of interactions between the particles. During melting, adding heat energy is breaking the forces between adjoining water molecules and the solid ice is becoming liquid water.

Checking Up

1. Compare the following pairs of processes. How are they alike? How are they different?
   a) melting/freezing
   b) vaporization/ condensation
   c) sublimation/ deposition
2. What happens to the temperature of a material during a phase change?
3. What does the heat energy do during a phase change?

596

Active Chemistry

Chem Essential Questions

What does it mean?

MACRO — The ice melted and the temperature of the hot water went down.

NANO — As the ice is heated, the water molecules vibrate faster and begin to overcome the intermolecular forces of attraction. Eventually, the heat energy allows the molecules of water to overcome the forces which hold the solid together and the ice melts. As a liquid, the molecules can move past one another but are still affected by forces of attraction which hold the liquid together.

What Do You Think Now?

Section 5 Phase Changes and the Cooling Curve of Water

What Do You Think Now?

At the beginning of the section you were asked the following:

• What happens to the temperature of water when it freezes?

Now that you have completed this section, how would you answer this question?

Chem
Essential Questions

What does it mean?

Chemistry explains a *macroscopic* phenomenon (what you observe) with a description of what happens at the *nanoscopic* level (atoms and molecules) using *symbolic* structures as a way to communicate. Complete the chart below in your Active Chemistry log.

MACRO	NANO	SYMBOLIC
What did you observe when hot water was mixed with ice?	When ice melts, the solid H_2O becomes liquid H_2O. Explain the relationship between the addition of heat to the solid ice and the change in the way the molecules move relative to one another.	You can represent the melting of ice, the heating of the water, and the creation of vapor with a graph to better illustrate what is happening. Draw a temperature vs. time graph for these phase changes of H_2O.

How do you know?

How do you know that the amount of heat required to melt a quantity of ice is 80 calories per gram of ice? Describe the experiment that can determine this heat of fusion.

Why do you believe?

Foods are frozen and then defrosted. Estimate the time to defrost a specific food from your freezer. List one food that can turn from a solid to a liquid when defrosting and one food that remains a solid after defrosting.

Why should you care?

Adding ice to a warm drink can be a part of your cooking show. How would you describe this in an entertaining way for a 10-second part of your cooking-show segment?

597

Active Chemistry

Students' answers will vary. They should compare their findings to their predictions at the start of the investigation. You might ask them to include an explanation for the differences in their findings and their predictions.

Now is also a good time to return to the illustration at the beginning of the section and ask if students can find more significance in the depiction. Do they now understand the relevance of the salt in the image? You might want to share the answer provided in *A Chemist's Response* and invite students to share their opinions and responses.

SYMBOLIC —

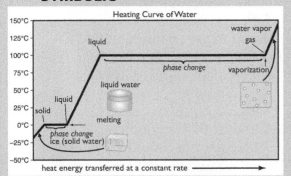

Heating Curve of Water

How do you know?

By knowing the specific heat of water (1.00 cal/g°C), the heat of fusion of water can be determined. A known quantity of hot water of known temperature is cooled to 0°C with ice. From this, the heat energy given up by the ice in melting can be determined.

$\Delta Q = mc\Delta T$, m, c and ΔT are all known quantities. By measuring the final volume of the water and subtracting the original volume, the mass of the ice can be determined. Finally, by dividing value for ΔQ by the mass of the ice, the heat of fusion for water can be determined experimentally.

Why do you believe?

Student answers will vary. You should expect answers from 1 minute to more than 10 minutes

to defrost food. Students should know that larger food items will take longer. Soup, when defrosted, will become a liquid. A burrito, when defrosted, will remain a solid.

Why should you care?

Student answers will vary. Example: [Set: Chef, microwave, glass of steaming hot chocolate in the gloved hand of the chef]. "Now that I've microwaved the hot chocolate with the energy from radiation, [raising it to lips] it's DEeee...Ow! Much too hot to drink. Let me cool it with ice." [Set glass down, take up bowl of ice cubes. Back away about 3-4 feet. Begin tossing ice cubes at glass of hot chocolate] "Now let's talk about accuracy and precision. To avoid adding too much ice to the drink, make it a game. For every hit, swirl the hot chocolate and taste. Or burn lips. This is a win-win situation, because the longer it takes to hit the target, the hot chocolate cools anyway through conduction, convection, and radiation."

Reflecting on the Section and the Challenge

In *Section 4*, students learned how to generate the data to graph a heating curve for water. One key point was the absence of temperature change during the phase change from liquid to gas. In this activity, students learned how to generate data for making a graph for the cooling of water. They also were able to determine the heat of fusion for water by experimentation. Again, a key point was the absence of temperature change during the phase change from water to ice. Determining the heat of fusion and comparing it to the accepted value will help them understand the potential errors involved in the experimentation and how the averaging of data can improve the data.

Chem to Go

1.

You would set the temperature below zero. To freeze water, you need to remove heat while the water is at its freezing point (heat of crystallization). Setting it at zero will result in cold water, not ice.

2.a)

The amount of heat needed to melt ice at 0° C or freeze water at 0° C is the same – 80 cal/g. One is exothermic (freezing) and the other is endothermic (melting). To melt 100 g of ice, 8000 cal of added heat energy is required. To freeze 100 g of water at 0° C, 8000 cal needs to be removed.

Cookin' Chem

Reflecting on the Section and the Challenge

You have now learned that heat energy is gained or lost as a solid, liquid, or gas changes temperature. You have also learned that during a phase change, energy is gained or lost, but the temperature remains the same. Freezing foods is an important process that is used in food preparation. It is primarily used to preserve foods but it also can be used to make special desserts and salads. Including descriptions of phase changes in your cooking segment will be informative for your audience.

Chem to Go

1. If you put water in the freezer to make ice, would you set your freezer thermostat at zero Celsius or at a temperature below zero Celsius? Explain why.

2. Use the information on the Heating and Cooling Curve to answer the following questions below.

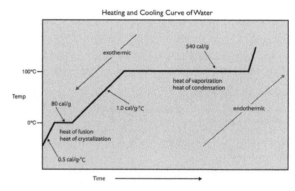

Heating and Cooling Curve of Water

Compare the amount of heat needed to

a) melt 100 g of ice or freeze 100 g of water if both are at 0°C.

b) change the temperature of 50 g of ice and 50 g of water by 20°C.

2.b)

The amount of heat needed to change 50 g water by 20°C is greater than that needed to change the same amount of ice by the same temperature (it takes 1 cal to change 1 g of water by 1° C and only 0.5 cal to change 1 g of ice by 1° C).

3.a)

Water vapor (steam) at 100° C contains 540 cal/g more heat energy than water at 100° C.

3.b)

Water at 0° C contains 79.6 cal/gram more heat energy than ice at 0° C. 100 g of ice has 7.96 kcal less heat energy than 100 g of water at the same temperature.

Section 5 Phase Changes and the Cooling Curve of Water

3. Compare the amount of heat in

   a) water at 100°C or water vapor (steam) at 100°C.

   b) 100 g of ice and 100 g of water at 0°C.

4. Determine the amount of heat needed to melt 50 g of ice at 0°C.

5. Determine the amount of heat needed to vaporize 500 g of water at 100°C.

6. Determine the amount of heat needed to raise the temperature of 350 g of water from 20°C to 100°C.

7. How much heat must be removed from 600 g of water at 80°C to bring it down to 0°C?

8. This question will require several steps. Determine the total amount of heat needed to take 200 g of ice at –25°C to water vapor at 100°C.

9. *Preparing for the Chapter Challenge*

   Prepare a list of three instances where there are melting/freezing phase changes occurring in everyday cooking. Describe the processes as either endothermic or exothermic.

599

Active Chemistry

- Heat 200 g of water from 0°C to 100°C = 200 g × 1 cal/g°C × 100 = 20 kcal.

- Vaporize 200 g of water at 100°C = 200 g × 540 cal/g = 108 kcal.

Total heat energy required: 150 kcal

9.

Preparing for the Chapter Challenge

Below is a list of examples of acceptable answers:

Melting chocolate	endothermic – the chocolate absorbs heat
Making popsicles	exothermic – the flavored water gives off heat
Chilling gelatin	exothermic – the flavored water gives off heat
Making ice cream	exothermic – the sugar-cream-flavoring mixture gives off heat
Cooling fudge	exothermic – the liquid fudge mixture gives off heat
Making fondue	endothermic – the solid cheese absorbs heat
Roasting marshmallows	endothermic – the solid marshmallows absorb heat
Grilling cheese sandwiches	endothermic – the solid cheese absorbs heat

---

4.

4000 cal is required to melt 50 g of ice at 0°C.

5

2.7×10^5 cal is required to vaporize 500 g of water at 100°C. Or, 2.7×10^2 kcal.

6.

The specific heat of water is 1.00 cal/g. To raise the temperature of 350 g of water by 80°C will require 28,000 cal or 28 kcal.

7.

600 g × 1.00 cal/g °C × 80°C = 48 kcal must be removed.

8.

This will require several steps as illustrated by the heating curve of water.

- Heat the ice at –25°C to 0°C = 200 g × 0.5 cal × 25°C = 2500 cal.

- Melt 200 g of ice at 0°C = 200 g × 79.6 cal/g = 16 kcal.

SECTION 5 – QUIZ

7-5c	Blackline Master

1. When water is at 0°C which phase change is exothermic?

    a) freezing

    b) vaporizing

    c) melting

    d) condensing

2. When water is at 0°C which phase change is endothermic?

    a) freezing

    b) vaporizing

    c) melting

    d) condensing

3. Define the heat of fusion of water.

4. Compare the heat of fusion of ice to the heat of crystallization of water.

5. How much heat is needed to melt 35 g of ice at 0°C?

6. If 30 g of a solid at its melting point requires 4200 calories of heat to melt, what is the heat of fusion of this solid?

SECTION 5 – QUIZ ANSWERS

❶ a) freezing

❷ b) vaporizing

❸ The heat of fusion of water is the amount of heat energy needed to melt 1 g of ice at 0°C (80 cal/g).

❹ They have the same magnitude, 79.6 cal/g, but are of opposite direction. Heat is supplied, +79.6 cal/g, to melt (fusion) ice which is an endothermic process. Heat is removed, −79.6 cal/g, from water to freeze (crystallize) which is an exothermic process.

❺ 2800 cal is needed.

❻ The heat of fusion is 140 cal/g.

NOTES

_____

_____

_____

_____

_____

_____

_____

NOTES

CHAPTER 7

SECTION 6
Calorimetry and Specific Heat Capacity

Section Overview

In this section, students will investigate and measure the specific heat capacity of several different materials. By comparing their findings, students will draw conclusions about the properties that make these different materials useful as cookware.

(While specific heat capacity is not the only factor that influences absorbency, conductivity, and heat retention, it is fairly easy to measure and provides useful information for experimental purposes.)

Background Information

In order to change the temperature of a substance, heat energy must be added or removed. The amount of heat energy required to change the temperature of one gram of a substance by one degree Celsius is known as the specific heat capacity of that substance, or c_p. This amount of energy is measured in joules (J). A total of 4.18 joules are required to raise the temperature of 1 g of water by 1° C. The specific heat capacity of a substance is given in joules per g•° C. The specific heat capacity of water is 4.18 J/g•° C. Note that 4.18 J = 1 cal.

Molar heat capacity is another heat measurement. It refers to the amount of heat needed to raise the temperature of one mole of a substance by 1° C.

The calorimeter uses changes in water temperature to measure the heat released or absorbed by a substance or a process. The heat energy released or absorbed by the water is calculated using the following equation:

(heat gained or lost) = (mass in grams) × (specific heat capacity) × (change in temperature)

$$Q = mc\Delta T$$

For water, $Q = $ (g of water)(4.18 J/g •°C) $\times \Delta T$

The Law of Conservation of Energy states that energy is neither created nor destroyed. Because it is assumed that calorimeters do not absorb energy and do not let it escape, once the energy transfer between water and another substance is completed, the amount of energy transferred represents that of the components in the mixture. It can be exemplified as follows:

Heat flows from warmer regions to colder regions, so when two substances with different temperatures come into contact with each other, heat will flow from the "hot object" to the "cold object" until a condition of thermal equilibrium exists. This means that they are now at the same temperature; the "hot object" is now cooler than when contact first occurred and the "cold object" is now warmer than when contact first occurred.

Since the amount of energy is conserved, this means that the amount of heat lost by the "hot object" is equal to the amount of heat gained by the "cold object." In thermodynamics, heat loss is designated with a negative sign while heat gain is positive. In a simple equation:

(heat lost)$_{\text{hot object}}$ = −[(heat gained)$_{\text{cold object}}$]

In a calorimeter using water, $Q_{\text{water}} = -Q_{\text{substance}}$

(g of water)(4.18 J/g•°C)(ΔT_{water}) = −(g of substance)($c_{\text{substance}}$) ($\Delta T_{\text{substance}}$)

The specific heat capacity of a substance can be determined by placing measured amounts of water and the substance in a calorimeter and then determining the temperature changes for both.

Since the specific heat capacity of water is known, the only unknown is the specific heat capacity of the substance being tested.

The specific heat capacity of a material is represented by c_P and the change in temperature of a material is represented by ΔT, where ΔT = final temperature – initial temperature

In another form,
$(c_P \times \text{mass} \times \Delta T)_{\text{hot object}} =$
$-[(c_P \times \text{mass} \times \Delta T)_{\text{cold object}}]$

The table on the right provides the specific heat capacity and molar heat capacity for various substances at constant pressure. For your convenience, it is provided as a Blackline Master on your *Teacher Resources CD*.

7-6a **Blackline Master**

Substance	c_p in J/g K	Molar c_p J/mol K
Aluminum	0.900	24.3
Copper	0.386	24.5
Gold	0.126	25.6
Lead	0.128	26.4
Silver	0.233	24.9
Tungsten	0.134	24.8
Zinc	0.387	25.2
Mercury	0.140	28.3
Alcohol(ethyl)	2.4	111
Water	4.184	75.3
Ice (−10°C)	2.05	36.9
Granite	0.790	...
Glass	0.84	...
Dry air	0.24	1005

LEARNING OUTCOMES

LEARNING OUTCOMES	LOCATION IN SECTION	EVIDENCE OF UNDERSTANDING
Explore the concept of specific heat capacity.	*Investigate, Chem Talk, Checking Up* Question 2. *Chem to Go* Questions 4.-10.	Students successfully complete the activity investigation. Students' answers match those found in this *Teacher's Edition*.
Experimentally determine the specific heat capacity of various substances.	*Investigate*	Students' calculated values are different for each substance, but similar to accepted values.
Distinguish between materials used in cookware.	*Investigate* Step 9 *Checking Up* Question 3. *Chem to Go* Questions 1.-3.,9.	Students' investigation conclusions and answers are similar to those outlined in this *Teacher's Edition*.

Section 6
Materials, Chemicals, Preparation, and Safety

("per Group" quantity is based on group size of 4 students)

Materials and Equipment

Materials (and Equipment)	Quantity per Group (4 students)
Hot plate	1
Wire gauze squares for hot plate	1
Screen support for metal slugs	1
Beaker, 1 L	1
Crucible tongs	1
Thermometer or temperature probe	1
Graduated cylinder, 100 mL	1
Styrene foam cups (large)	2
Set of metals: tin, iron, copper, aluminum, stainless steel, zinc, etc.	approx. 50 g each
Materials (and Equipment)	Quantity per Class
Balances, 0.01 g	2

Chemicals

Chemicals	Quantity per Class (24 students)
None	None

Teacher Preparation

In the beaker or a large container, create a screen table for the metal slugs to rest on while they are boiling. Before the class starts, have the metal samples already submerged in boiling water. Because of the large difference in the specific heat of metals and water, the metals should have a mass between 25 g and 75 g; for good results, 50 g is a good middle ground.

If there is time and if thermometers are being used, test them for calibration.

The foam cups must be large enough to contain 400 mL of water. They should also be nested to improve the insulation properties.

Safety Requirements

- All activity in the laboratory area requires goggles and aprons.

- Make sure that students take extra precautions and wear gloves when handling boiling water.

- All metal samples can be saved for use in a future class.

- Wash arms and hands before leaving the laboratory area.

NOTES

Meeting the Needs of All Students
Differentiated Instruction

Augmentation and Accommodations

LEARNING ISSUE	REFERENCE	AUGMENTATION AND ACCOMMODATIONS
Recording data in a data chart	*Investigate* 6.,8.a), d)	**Augmentation** • Check to see that students are recording the information in the right boxes of the table. • Using an overhead projection of the table, place the symbols from the equations with the appropriate headings and explain why they correspond to the labels in those heading boxes. • Create different tables with headings that correspond with the symbols in the equations. For example, to calculate the heat absorbed by the water, label the columns from left to right beginning with heat and continuing with mass of water, specific heat of water, temperature change of water. Then create another table with headings that correspond to the formula given for finding specific heat – specific heat of the material, heat lost, mass of material, and temperature change of material. This should make it easier for students to plug the values into the equations and solve them.
Calculating the amount of heat absorbed by water	*Investigate* 8.c)	**Augmentation** • Model plugging values from the tables into equations to solve problems by doing a sample from the values in a table. • Have students practice a common problem and then check answers to make sure they are calculating correctly.
Reading comprehension Analysis of information	*Chem Talk*	**Augmentation** • Have students read the *Chem Talk* and make a chart that lists each significant property of cookware, gives its practical effect on cooking, and rates each cookware material. For example, one property is thermal conductivity. The higher the thermal conductivity, the more evenly the substance distributes heat to the food being cooked. Copper and aluminum have high conductivity. Iron and steel are low by comparison. Completing a table will enhance comprehension of this information by highlighting the structure and relationships, while helping students prepare for their cooking demonstration through organization of the criteria they will use to choose their cookware material. There are eight properties in the text and four basic materials to compare. **Accommodations** • Give students a table that is partially completed and ask them to add the other information by finding the information in the *Chem Talk* section.
Summarizing the learning	*Chem Essential Questions, How do you know?*	**Accommodations** • Although students are expected to answer this question, you may provide the answer to help students understand the process of data collection, table building and calculations. • Give two or three alternative answers to this question; allow students working in groups to determine which one is the best summary. A discussion of the rationales for their choices should follow in which the aspects of a good summary are illuminated.

Strategies for Students with Limited English Language Proficiency

LEARNING ISSUE	REFERENCE	AUGMENTATION AND ACCOMMODATIONS
Background knowledge	*What Do You Think?*	Use a description of the illustration to explain possible answers to the question about water and temperature. Students may need examples of *"cookware"* as it may be a new term for some students.
Vocabulary	*Investigate*	Check for understanding of the term *"proceeding."* Point out what *"crucible tongs"* are if they do not recognize this term. In Step 7.a), have a volunteer student who knows algebra explain to the class how to do the calculation. In Step 9.b), check for recognition of the word *"prefer."*
Background knowledge Vocabulary Comprehending text	*Chem Talk*	Review the concept of *"capacity."* Check sidebar material for further explanation of new vocabulary.
Background knowledge Application	*What Do You Think Now?*	Have students discuss their answers prior to writing them.
Background knowledge Vocabulary Comprehending text	*Chem Essential Questions*	Make sure students realize that there are stacked questions in this section. Clarify the meaning of the word *"utensils"* in the *Why do you believe?* section.
Comprehension Vocabulary	*Chem to Go*	Students can work in teams or small groups. In Question 3 the term *"confectioners"* may be a new term for some. Point out how the application of the suffix *"-ers"* to the word *"confection"* changes the meaning.

NOTES

_____

_____

_____

_____

_____

_____

_____

_____

_____

_____

_____

Section 6
Teaching Suggestions and Sample Answers

What Do You See?

The purpose here is to engage students' interest and elicit reactions to the illustration. All responses are acceptable and can be valuable as indicators of misconceptions or misinterpretations of established concepts. Allow students to share their ideas and thoughts. After the investigation, you will revisit the illustration to assess how their interpretations have changed.

Most students will notice the difference in the sizes of the holes in the ice in the two images. The more thoughtful students may relate the "orange slab" going from a sauna to the water as the reason for the ice melting and the bigger hole. It is unlikely students will recognize that the slab represents a piece of metal. They will realize this after completing the *Investigate* section and they should be able to identify the significance of the metal upon returning to the illustration following the *Investigate* section.

What Do You Think?

Students' initial attempts to answer this question may not be accurate but can be helpful in determining their level of understanding. To the question, "Which cookware would you choose to fry an egg and why?" you can only expect general answers from the students and these will be based on their experience and on their opinions. Encourage students to share their thoughts. There are no right or wrong answers at this point. What can be more interesting are the students' explanations for their choices. This is a good chance to identify misconceptions. Also be alert for language interpretations, especially with the words "cookware" and "fry." Later on, students will return to the question to apply the knowledge that they gained from the activity.

Cookin' Chem

Section 6 — Calorimetry and Specific Heat Capacity

What Do You See?

Learning Outcomes

In this section you will

- Explore the concept of specific heat capacity.
- Experimentally determine the specific heat capacity of various substances.
- Distinguish between materials used in cookware.

What Do You Think?

You want to fry some eggs. There are many choices for cookware. Pots and pans can cost anywhere from a few dollars to hundreds of dollars. Some frying pans are steel with a copper bottom, some are steel with a steel bottom, and some are iron.

- **Which cookware would you choose to fry an egg and why?**

Record your ideas about this question in your *Active Chemistry* log. Be prepared to discuss your responses with your group and the class.

Investigate

In this investigation, you will explore and measure the heating ability of different materials, and decide which ones are suitable for cookware.

For each material to be tested, the general procedure involves taking a hot object and placing it in cold water. You then measure the final temperature of the object and water. Recognizing that the heat energy gained by the water is equal to the heat energy lost by the object, you can calculate the specific heat of the object. You want to investigate whether all materials will bring the water to the same final temperature.

600

What Do You Think?
A CHEMIST'S RESPONSE

Almost any reasonable cookware can be used to fry eggs. The term "fry" implies that intense heat is used, so a list of suitable materials would include ceramic, copper, aluminum, steel, iron, and perhaps nonstick-coated metals. Some desirable properties to consider for a frypan might include: quick heating, good heat retention, even heating, easy to clean, nonstick, etc.

1. Before proceeding, make a list of what measurements you will have to record in the experiment.

2. Your teacher will have a large container of boiling water with the different metal samples submerged and sitting on a screen support.

a) Record the temperature of the boiling water. This will be the starting temperature of the substance.

3. Carefully measure 200 mL of water and pour it into a double foam cup.

a) Record the beginning temperature of the water in the cup.

4. Using crucible tongs, quickly lift a metal sample out of the boiling water and transfer it to the double foam cup. Try not to transfer any of the hot water. Gently agitate the cup to distribute heat.

a) Record the highest temperature that the water reaches.

5. Remove the metal sample from the foam cup and after drying it off, determine the mass of the sample. Save the metal samples for future use.

a) Record the mass of the metal sample in your *Active Chemistry* log.

6. Now that you know a procedure, you can create an investigation for the other samples. You may want to use a data chart similar to the one shown below to keep track of all the measurements.

7. The law of conservation of energy states that the energy gained by the cold water must be equal to the energy lost by the hot sample. You know how to calculate the energy change by using the equation

$$Q = mc\Delta T$$

You can calculate this Q gain for cold water because you know the mass of the cold water, the specific heat of water (1 cal/g·°C), and the change in temperature. You also know the mass of the sample and the change in temperature of the sample. The unknown is the specific heat c of the sample. Knowing all other values, you can solve for this unknown.

a) If you are confident with your algebra skills, calculate and record the specific heat of each sample. Skip *Step 8*.

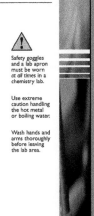

Safety goggles and a lab apron must be worn *at all times* in a chemistry lab.

Use extreme caution handling the hot metal or boiling water.

Wash hands and arms thoroughly before leaving the lab area.

Substance	Mass (g)	Start temp. of substance (°C)	Start temp. of cold water (°C)	End temp. of substance and water (°C)

STUDENTS' PRIOR CONCEPTIONS

At this point, students will generally have no concept of specific heat capacity. When asked, for example, to explain why a lake is warmer than the land around it in the winter, they may suggest that liquids cool more slowly. In this case, it would be true. They will not know, however, that the specific heat capacity of water is greater than the land and that it contains more heat energy per unit volume. Similarly, the lake will warm more slowly, staying cooler than the land mass long into summer.

Investigate

1.

Students should list mass (volume) of water, starting temperature of water (probably room temperature), mass of metal sample, temperature of metal sample (temperature of boiling water), final temperature of both water and metal sample. You may also have them provide a description of the metal sample, including at least the color.

2.

Make certain that the metal samples are submerged in the boiling water at all times, but not touching the bottom of the container, which is why a screen support is needed. (If touching, they may have a higher temperature than the water.) Have a minimum heating time for all metal samples tested. Five minutes in the boiling water should be enough time for the temperature of the metal to rise to the temperature of the water. If you need to add more water, allow enough heating time for the water to return to boiling.

2.a)

Temperature of boiling water should be close to 100°C. This will depend upon the atmospheric pressure that day and the accuracy of the thermometer. If the accuracy of the thermometer is suspect, find one that reads 100°C. Students' thermometers should be kept calibrated.

3.

The 200 mL of tap water should be measured carefully; the metal should still be in the boiling water.

3.a)

All temperatures should be recorded as accurately as possible, to 0.5°C, if possible.

4.

Transfer the slugs to the water as quickly as possible. The small amount of hot water on the slugs should not be a significant factor.

4.a)

Again, have students read thermometers as accurately as possible, preferably to 0.5°C.

5.

Make sure students are wearing gloves. The mass of the metal sample should be between 25 g and 75 g. (To save time, you can weigh the metal samples before heating and simply provide those numbers to the students.)

6.

You might want to prepare and provide a data chart for students that already includes rows for the metal samples you are using.

7.a)

Some students may be able to calculate the specific heat of each sample without help. They may proceed to Step 9. Those that need direction should continue with Step 8.

8.b)

The temperature change of the water is based on the difference between the beginning temperature of the water in the foam cup and the temperature after the metal's heat has been transferred to the water.

Cookin' Chem

Temp. change of water (°C)	Heat absorbed by water (lost by substance) (cal)	Substance tested	Mass of substance (g)	Temperature change of substance (°C)	Specific heat capacity of substance (cal/g·°C)

8. If you need more assistance, continue with the steps shown below.

a) Make a table similar to the one shown above to record your calculations.

b) Determine the temperature change of the water in the polystyrene cup and record it in the chart.

c) Use the heat equation to determine the amount of heat the water absorbed from the hot object used.

heat = (mass of water) (specific heat of water) (temperature change of water)

or

$Q = mc\Delta T$

Specific heat of water is 1 cal/g·°C.

d) Because the heat energy from the hot metal was gained by the water, the quantity of heat energy lost is identical to the amount gained.

Knowing the quantity of heat the material lost, the mass of the material, and the temperature change it underwent, the specific heat of the material can be calculated

$$c = \frac{Q}{m\Delta T}$$

The temperature change of the material is from the boiling water temperature to the high temperature of the cold water after the hot substance has been transferred to it.

The units for your specific heat will be in cal/g·°C or cal g⁻¹·°C⁻¹

9. Answer the following questions in your *Active Chemistry* log.

a) Which substance had the lowest *specific heat capacity*? Which had the highest?

b) Explain why you would prefer a substance with a higher or lower specific heat capacity for cookware.

$\Delta T = T_{final} - T_{start}$

Example:
$\Delta T = 28°C - 24°C = 4°C$

8.c)

$Q = mc\Delta T$

Example:

$Q_{water} = 210 \text{ g} \times 1.00 \text{ cal/g°C} \times 4°C = 800 \text{ cal}$

8.d)

$Q_{metal} = Q_{water} = 800 \text{ cal}$

$Q_{metal} = mc\Delta T_{metal}$ or $c_{metal} = Q_{metal} / m\Delta T_{metal}$

Example:
$\Delta T_{metal} = T_{start} - T_{final} = 100°C - 28°C = 72°C$

$c_{metal} = 800 \text{ cal}/(25g \times 72°C) = 0.5 \text{ cal/g°C}$

Chem Talk

A pizza hot from the oven provides a good example for an explanation of specific heat capacity when compared to the aluminum foil that it is wrapped in. A review of the various considerations for suitable cookware materials develops into an analysis of the properties of various types of common cookware materials, such as aluminum, copper, and iron. The advantages of using alloys are reviewed, as well as the reaction of some metals with foodstuffs.

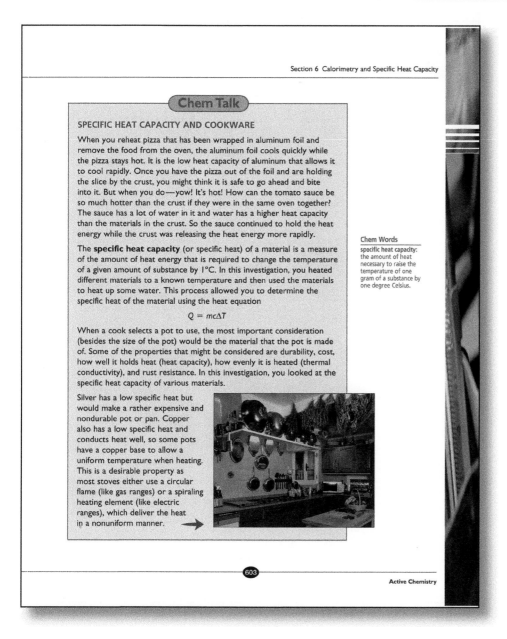

Section 6 Calorimetry and Specific Heat Capacity

Chem Talk

SPECIFIC HEAT CAPACITY AND COOKWARE

When you reheat pizza that has been wrapped in aluminum foil and remove the food from the oven, the aluminum foil cools quickly while the pizza stays hot. It is the low heat capacity of aluminum that allows it to cool rapidly. Once you have the pizza out of the foil and are holding the slice by the crust, you might think it is safe to go ahead and bite into it. But when you do—yow! It's hot! How can the tomato sauce be so much hotter than the crust if they were in the same oven together? The sauce has a lot of water in it and water has a higher heat capacity than the materials in the crust. So the sauce continued to hold the heat energy while the crust was releasing the heat energy more rapidly.

The **specific heat capacity** (or specific heat) of a material is a measure of the amount of heat energy that is required to change the temperature of a given amount of substance by 1°C. In this investigation, you heated different materials to a known temperature and then used the materials to heat up some water. This process allowed you to determine the specific heat of the material using the heat equation

$$Q = mc\Delta T$$

When a cook selects a pot to use, the most important consideration (besides the size of the pot) would be the material that the pot is made of. Some of the properties that might be considered are durability, cost, how well it holds heat (heat capacity), how evenly it is heated (thermal conductivity), and rust resistance. In this investigation, you looked at the specific heat capacity of various materials.

Silver has a low specific heat but would make a rather expensive and nondurable pot or pan. Copper also has a low specific heat and conducts heat well, so some pots have a copper base to allow a uniform temperature when heating. This is a desirable property as most stoves either use a circular flame (like gas ranges) or a spiraling heating element (like electric ranges), which deliver the heat in a nonuniform manner.

Chem Words
specific heat capacity: the amount of heat necessary to raise the temperature of one gram of a substance by one degree Celsius.

603

Active Chemistry

9.a)

The ranking will depend on the metal substances used and individual results. The purpose of the activity is to experimentally determine specific heat capacities, not necessarily to get "right" answers. Accept what the students' data shows. If something is obviously askew, find out why and correct it.

9.b)

Students' answers will vary, depending upon results. Higher heat capacity will lead to slower cooking initially, but a longer retention of heat. A lower heat capacity will facilitate faster cooking, but heat will not be retained as long after the heat source is removed.

Checking Up

1.

Equal masses of aluminum foil and of pizza, at the same temperature, have very different heat capacities, and therefore, contain very different amounts of heat energy. Per gram, aluminum, given the same temperature, contains much less heat than pizza and cools much more quickly. This is due to the low heat capacity of aluminum relative to pizza.

2.

No, the crust and the sauce on top of the pizza will not stay at the same temperature. The tomato sauce will be much hotter than the crust after being removed from the oven because the sauce is mostly water and water has a higher heat capacity than the substances making up the crust. Therefore, the sauce continues to hold the heat energy longer. Both the sauce and the crust are cooling but the crust contains less heat energy and will release it more rapidly.

3.

Copper is used for making cookware because it has a low specific heat (it gets hot fast) and conducts heat well and uniformly. It is also unreactive with most foods and will not cause contamination, as aluminum can.

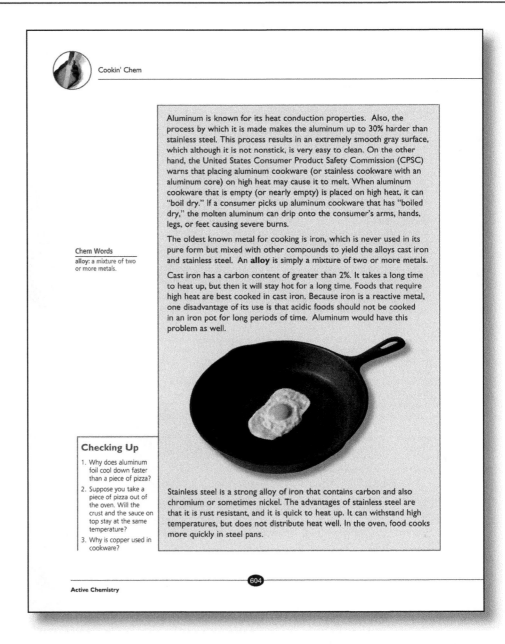

Cookin' Chem

Aluminum is known for its heat conduction properties. Also, the process by which it is made makes the aluminum up to 30% harder than stainless steel. This process results in an extremely smooth gray surface, which although it is not nonstick, is very easy to clean. On the other hand, the United States Consumer Product Safety Commission (CPSC) warns that placing aluminum cookware (or stainless cookware with an aluminum core) on high heat may cause it to melt. When aluminum cookware that is empty (or nearly empty) is placed on high heat, it can "boil dry." If a consumer picks up aluminum cookware that has "boiled dry," the molten aluminum can drip onto the consumer's arms, hands, legs, or feet causing severe burns.

The oldest known metal for cooking is iron, which is never used in its pure form but mixed with other compounds to yield the alloys cast iron and stainless steel. An **alloy** is simply a mixture of two or more metals.

Cast iron has a carbon content of greater than 2%. It takes a long time to heat up, but then it will stay hot for a long time. Foods that require high heat are best cooked in cast iron. Because iron is a reactive metal, one disadvantage of its use is that acidic foods should not be cooked in an iron pot for long periods of time. Aluminum would have this problem as well.

Chem Words
alloy: a mixture of two or more metals.

Stainless steel is a strong alloy of iron that contains carbon and also chromium or sometimes nickel. The advantages of stainless steel are that it is rust resistant, and it is quick to heat up. It can withstand high temperatures, but does not distribute heat well. In the oven, food cooks more quickly in steel pans.

Checking Up

1. Why does aluminum foil cool down faster than a piece of pizza?
2. Suppose you take a piece of pizza out of the oven. Will the crust and the sauce on top stay at the same temperature?
3. Why is copper used in cookware?

604

Active Chemistry

Chem Essential Questions

What does it mean?

MACRO — The metal object had a temperature change from the boiling water (near 100°C) to a few degrees above the starting temperature of the cold water. This was a large temperature change. The cold water had a temperature change from its original temperature (near room temperature) to an elevated temperature a few degrees higher.

Due to the relatively high specific heat capacity of water compared to the metal, the water will have a small change in temperature.

NANO — The kinetic energy of the "cooler" solid substance is reflected in its temperature. For a solid, the particles (atoms or molecules) are vibrating with a defined energy. When these come into direct contact with particles (atoms or molecules) which are "hotter," their kinetic energy increases and they become "hotter," as reflected in their temperature increase. The particles of the "hotter" material lose energy

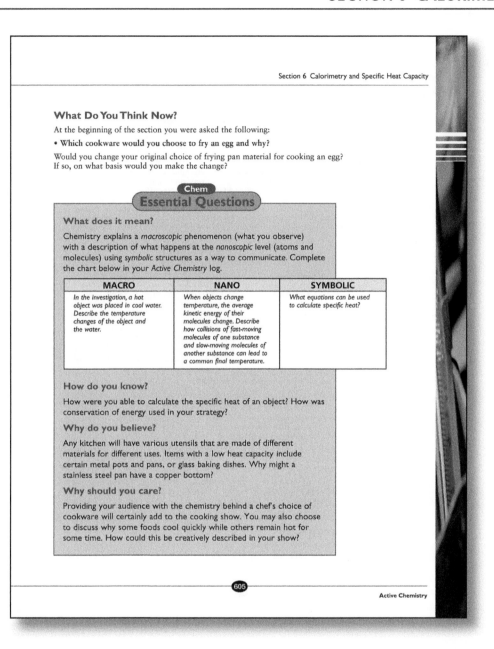

Section 6 Calorimetry and Specific Heat Capacity

What Do You Think Now?

At the beginning of the section you were asked the following:

• Which cookware would you choose to fry an egg and why?

Would you change your original choice of frying pan material for cooking an egg? If so, on what basis would you make the change?

Chem
Essential Questions

What does it mean?

Chemistry explains a *macroscopic* phenomenon (what you observe) with a description of what happens at the *nanoscopic* level (atoms and molecules) using *symbolic* structures as a way to communicate. Complete the chart below in your *Active Chemistry* log.

MACRO	NANO	SYMBOLIC
In the investigation, a hot object was placed in cool water. Describe the temperature changes of the object and the water.	When objects change temperature, the average kinetic energy of their molecules change. Describe how collisions of fast-moving molecules of one substance and slow-moving molecules of another substance can lead to a common final temperature.	What equations can be used to calculate specific heat?

How do you know?

How were you able to calculate the specific heat of an object? How was conservation of energy used in your strategy?

Why do you believe?

Any kitchen will have various utensils that are made of different materials for different uses. Items with a low heat capacity include certain metal pots and pans, or glass baking dishes. Why might a stainless steel pan have a copper bottom?

Why should you care?

Providing your audience with the chemistry behind a chef's choice of cookware will certainly add to the cooking show. You may also choose to discuss why some foods cool quickly while others remain hot for some time. How could this be creatively described in your show?

605

Active Chemistry

What Do You Think Now?

Now that students have had a chance to test various types of materials used for cookware, they should be able to name a suitable metal and explain their selection based on their findings in the investigation. You can also return to the *What Do You See?* illustration and ask students to reconsider the artist's intent. Their answers should be more accurate and more informed now. They should also recognize the figure in the sauna as a piece of metal and be able to explain the significance of the metal and the melting ice.

through these collisions and become cooler. The particles of the "cooler" material gain energy through these collisions and become hotter. Ultimately, the temperature of both arrive at the same temperature.

SYMBOLIC — The relevant equations are:
$Q = mc\Delta T$ and $Q_{water} = Q_{metal}$

How do you know?

The conservation of energy is a fundamental scientific principle as energy can be neither created nor destroyed, although it can be transformed. In this activity, heat energy is transferred from the metal object to the water in the calorimeter. The careful measurement of this heat transfer was the basis for the calculation of the specific heat of the metal object.

Why do you believe?

A stainless steel pan might have a copper bottom for several reasons. One is that copper is less reactive than iron and will last longer. Also, copper transfers heat energy more efficiently to the iron pan. Lastly, because of its superior conductivity, copper tends to provide more uniform heating of the base of the pan.

Why should you care?

Students' answers will vary. Foods with a higher heat capacity, like cheese, will retain high temperatures longer than others, including bread or dough. This explains why the cheese on a pizza will be so much hotter than the crust. Students can use a large "ouch" factor to make their presentation more creative and interesting.

Reflecting on the Section and the Challenge

Cookware plays an important part in all cooking. Understanding how heat is conducted and the specific heat of metals is essential in selecting proper cookware and in succeeding at the *Chapter Challenge*.

Students should read this section for a specific connection between the activity and their response to the *Chapter Challenge*. While students do not answer any questions in this section, it will provide them with valuable direction in their projects. You may want to provide some class time for students to read this paragraph and discuss their ideas or questions.

Chem to Go

1.

Copper would be the hottest because it has the lowest specific heat capacity. It absorbs heat the fastest, meaning that its temperature increases at the quickest rate.

2.a)

(1000.0 g)(0.380 J/g•°C)(60°C)= 22,800 J (1 cal/ 4.18 J)=5.50 kcal

2.b)

(1000.0 g)(0.44 J/g•°C)(60°C)= 28,000 J (1 cal/4.18 J) = 6.4 kcal

---

 Cookin' Chem

Reflecting on the Section and the Challenge

Knowing how well a material conducts heat is the first step in making a cookware choice. Heat conductivity is most important for pots and skillets used on the stovetop, where uniform heating helps to prevent hot spots that burn food before it's completely cooked. The low specific heat capacity of metals means that it does not take much heat to increase the temperature of the metal. Consider how information such as this might be used in your cooking-show segment. For instance, you could describe why a chef might choose a copper-coated steel pan over an iron skillet for frying eggs. Your cooking show may also point out how some materials from the oven quickly cool to room temperature while others stay hot. A good restaurant must ensure that all foods are the right temperature when the food is served. This may be something that you want to highlight in your cooking show.

Chem to Go

1. If you had pans (of identical mass) made of each of the following metals—Al, Cu, and Fe—which would be the hottest after sitting on a burner for 1 min? Explain your answer.

Material	Specific heat (J/g·°C)
copper	0.38
iron	0.44
aluminum	0.9
glass	0.840
stainless steel	0.500
water	4.18

2. a) If you had a 1000.0 g copper pot, how many calories of heat energy would it take to raise its temperature by 60.0°C?

   b) How many calories of heat energy would it take to raise an iron pot with the same mass by 60.0°C?

3. Given that the specific heat of a marble slab (like glass) is about twice that of iron or steel, what is the advantage of using a marble slab to pour very hot fudge on when making candy?

4. Folklore says that a metal spoon should be placed in a china cup before pouring boiling water into the cup to make tea. Using the difference between the properties of metal and ceramic (glass), explain the reasoning behind this belief.

5. If you had water in either of the pots in *Question 2*, would the same amount of heat need to be supplied in order to bring about the same temperature change?

6. The heat capacity of a substance depends on

   a) temperature only

   b) mass only

   c) temperature and mass

   d) mass and specific heat

 606

Active Chemistry

3.

The marble slab is better for making candy because it will absorb more heat than steel, cooling the hot candy more quickly. Then, the marble slab holds the heat better than steel because it is less conductive, and the warm fudge can be worked at the lower temperature without cooling quickly to room temperature.

4.

A metal spoon will absorb the heat quickly due to its low specific heat and transfer the energy to the entire spoon quickly, due to its conductivity. As the entire spoon becomes hot, the heat energy is radiated to the surrounding air. The brittleness of ceramic materials sometimes causes them to break with sudden changes in temperature.

Section 6 Calorimetry and Specific Heat Capacity

7. Consider the graph of temperature (°C) vs. time (minutes) showing the cooling curve of metal A. If 100 g of metal A loses 840 J of heat in the first 6 min, the specific heat capacity of metal A is about _____ J/g·°C.

a) 0.21

b) 0.84

c) 2.1

d) 8.4

8. If the temperature of a certain mass of an aluminum alloy (which has a specific heat capacity of 0.8 J/g·°C) is lowered by 10°C and the heat lost is 80 J, then the mass of the aluminum alloy is

a) 8 g.

b) 80 g.

c) 100 g.

d) 10 g.

9. What properties would you want to see in your pots and pans that would make them good for cooking. Include a list of different materials that are used for cookware and rank the usefulness or suitability of these based on the properties that you listed.

10. *Preparing for the Chapter Challenge*

You have investigated the specific heat capacity of various materials and *Section 1* led you to an understanding of conduction. You should now have some idea why certain materials are selected for use in cookware (and other kitchen utensils) due to their ability to hold different quantities of heat. Prepare a listing of kitchen utensils that have (a) high specific heat capacities; and (b) low specific heat capacities. Include the functions of the pots and pans in the list. Discuss with your group how this might be incorporated into your cooking segment.

607

Active Chemistry

9.

Students' answers will vary. A list of properties may include the following:

A. Corrosion resistance

B. Heat retention

C. Even heating

D. Lightweight

E. Nonstick

F. Good heat conductivity

A sampling of cookware materials and their properties:

Copper—A, C, F

Iron—B, C, F

Steel—A, B, C, F

Aluminum—C, D, F

Ceramic—A, B

Polymer-coated steel— A, B, C, E, F

10.

Preparing for the Chapter Challenge

Since cookware will play an important part in their *Chapter Challenge* cooking show, students should be able to categorize cookware and utensils according to their specific heat capacity:

- High specific heat capacity: rubber/nylon/plastic utensils

- Low specific heat capacity: metal pans/pots, glass cookware.

5.

The heating of the iron pot would always require more heat than the copper pot. The transfer of heat with copper is always more efficient.

6.

d) mass and specific heat.

7.

a) 0.21

8.

d) 10 g

SECTION 6 – QUIZ

7-6b   Blackline Master

1. Define the term "specific heat capacity."

2. Given that the specific heat capacity of copper is 0.092 cal/g°C and aluminum is 0.215 cal/g°C:

   a) Given equal masses of each, which metal will be hotter to the touch after 5 minutes on a hot burner?

   b) If equal masses of both metals are heated to 150°C and allowed to cool, which one will stay hotter longer?

   c) If you have a 1500 g aluminum pot, how much heat energy is needed to raise its temperature by 100°C?

   d) If you have a 1500 g copper pot, how much heat energy is needed to raise its temperature by 100°C?

3. Why would a chef sometimes use a copper-bottomed stainless steel pot as opposed to just a stainless steel pot? (Stainless steel has a specific heat capacity of 0.50 cal/g°C.)

4. Explain the safety risks of leaving a stainless steel spoon in a pot while cooking.

5. Calculate the specific heat capacity of unidentified material X if 310 g of this material causes the temperature of 150 g of water to increase by 8°C while material X itself undergoes a 75°C temperature change.

SECTION 6 – QUIZ ANSWERS

1 Specific heat capacity is the amount of heat required to raise (or lower) the temperature of exactly 1 g of a substance by 1°C.

2   a) Copper will be hotter.
   b) Aluminum will stay hotter longer.
   c) $Q = 1500 \text{ g} \times 0.215 \text{ cal/g°C} \times 100 °C = 32,250 \text{ cal}$.
      This will require 32 kcal of heat energy.
   d) $Q = 1500 \text{ g} \times 0.092 \text{ cal/g°C} \times 100°C = 13,800 \text{ cal}$.
      This will require 14 kcal of heat energy.

3 The copper heats up more quickly and will transfer the heat to the steel by conduction. The steel will then hold the heat longer.

4 The spoon will get hot enough to burn when touched.

5 Heat absorbed by water = heat lost by metal
$Q = mc\Delta T$ $Q = mc\Delta T$
$= 150 \text{ g})(1 \text{ cal/g°C})(8°C)$
$1200 \text{ cal} = (310 \text{ g})(c)(75°C)$
$= 1200 \text{ cal}, c = 0.052 \text{ cal/g°C}$

NOTES

SECTION 7

Denaturation: How Do Proteins in Foods Change?

Section Overview

This section focuses on the effect of energy transfer on matter. Students will design an investigation to determine how an egg changes when it is cooked. In effect, they will be examining the effects of temperature change and pH change on the proteins in eggs. They will note the change in translucence as the temperature increases and as the pH becomes more acidic. From these observations, students will generalize the effect of heat on egg proteins. After reading and discussing the *Chem Talk*, students will understand that protein denaturation is due to changes in the secondary and tertiary structures of the proteins, which in turn affects their function.

Background Information

Proteins are macromolecules. They are constructed from very long chains of amino acids, which means they are a type of polymer. A typical protein contains 200-300 amino acids but some are smaller (the smallest, containing 2-20 amino acids, are often called peptides) and some much larger. The largest to date is titin, a protein found in skeletal and cardiac muscle. It contains some 27,000 amino acids in a single chain.

Proteins are the working tools of biology. As enzymes, proteins are the driving force behind many biochemical reactions. As structural elements, proteins are important constituents of our bones, muscles, hair, skin, and blood vessels. As antibodies, they recognize invading elements and cause the immune system to eliminate unwanted "invaders" from our bodies.

In order to carry out their specific functions (e.g., as enzymes or antibodies), different proteins have particular shapes. Anything that interferes with this shape will alter a protein's function and cause it to be inactive. Mad Cow Disease is an extreme example of detrimental effects caused by the altered shape of proteins in the brain.

The **primary structure** of a protein is its linear sequence of amino acids and the location of any disulfide (–S–S–) bridges. The sequence is characterized by the **amino terminal** or "N-terminal" ($-NH_3^+$) at one end; and the **carboxyl terminal** or "C-terminal" ($-COO^-$) at the other end.

7-7a   **Blackline Master**

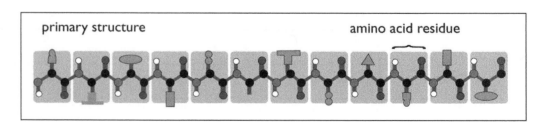

primary structure   amino acid residue

Most proteins contain one or more strands of amino acids that give rise to a characteristic three-dimensional structure. The most common of these are the **alpha helix** and the **beta conformation**. This is a description of the **secondary structure** of the protein.

7-7b | **Blackline Master**

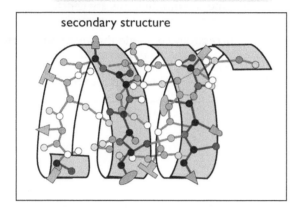

secondary structure

Tertiary structure refers to the three-dimensional structure of the entire protein chain. This can be very complex and not obviously reflective of the primary and secondary structure.

7-7c | **Blackline Master**

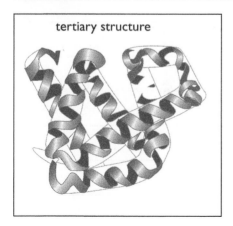

tertiary structure

For your convenience, the diagrams on both these pages are provided as Blackline Masters in your *Teacher Resources* CD.

The function of a protein (except when it is serving as a source of amino acids and nitrogen) is dependent on its shape or three-dimensional structure. A number of agents can disrupt this structure, thus denaturing the protein. When a protein is denatured, it loses its shape and, therefore, its function.

Protein denaturation can be defined in various ways. For example, denaturation can be simply a change in solubility or a result of more complex changes in chemical, physical and biological properties. A change in physical properties is due to configurational changes (changes in shape) in the polypeptide chains. The primary structure is not affected. The denaturation process involves an unfolding of the natural, folded structure. Most changes that cause denaturation consist of alterations in the forces of attraction– ion-dipole, hydrogen-bond and Van der Waals forces– and in the rotational positions around single bonds, which are controlled by these forces of attraction. The term denaturation means the response of the protein to heat, acid, alkali, and a variety of other chemical and physical agents that cause changes in the protein structure and function.

The denaturation process can be achieved by any one of the following methods: increasing temperature, changing pH, applying high pressure, or using denaturants (i.e., various amines and sulfur compounds), inorganic salts, organic solvents, or detergents. The temperature at which a particular protein will unfold varies. Most proteins unfold at elevated temperatures (e.g., 80°C), but some unfold at lower temperatures (e.g., 40°C). Many proteins unfold at temperatures only a few degrees higher than those at which they function. Others are stable at much higher temperatures, such as the gluten proteins.

Often, when a protein has been gently denatured and then is returned to normal physiological conditions of temperature, pH, salt concentration, etc., it can spontaneously regain its function (e.g., resume enzymatic activity or ability to bind its antigen). Protein denaturation by high temperature, however, is always irreversible.

LEARNING OUTCOMES		
LEARNING OUTCOMES	**LOCATION IN SECTION**	**EVIDENCE OF UNDERSTANDING**
Gain an understanding of proteins and what happens to them upon denaturation.	*Investigate* Steps 3, 5 *Chem Talk,* *Chem to Go* Questions 1, 3-5	Students observations and explanations are similar to those given in this *Teacher's Edition.* Students' models and explanations indicate understanding. Student's answers match those found in this *Teacher's Edition.*
Observe the effects of temperature on egg proteins.	*Investigate* Steps 3-4 *Inquiring Further*	Students successfully complete the investigation steps. Students' experimental findings are conclusive.
Observe the effects of changing pH on egg proteins.	*Investigate* Step 5 *Chem to Go* Questions 1, 4 *Inquiring Further*	Students successfully complete the investigation step. Students' answers match those found in this *Teacher's Edition.* Students' experimental findings are conclusive.

NOTES

Section 7
Materials, Chemicals, Preparation, and Safety

("per Group" quantity is based on group size of 4 students)

Materials and Equipment

Materials (and Equipment)	Quantity per Group (4 students)
Raw egg	as many as necessary
Hard-boiled egg	1
Raw egg soaked in HCl	1
Hot plate	1
Wire gauze square for hot plate	1
Beaker, 1 L	1
Rubber gloves, pairs	4
Materials (and Equipment)	**Quantity per Class**
None	None

Chemicals

Chemicals	Quantity per Class (24 students)
Hydrochloric acid, HCl, 3 M	1 L

Teacher Preparation

Hydrochloric acid, 3 M: In a fume hood, slowly and carefully, with stirring, add 250 mL of concentrated HCl (12 M) to 500 mL of distilled water. When cool, add water to make 1.0 L.

HCl-treated eggs: Place 6-12 raw eggs in a 1 L beaker and cover with 3 M HCl for 2 hours. Rinse well with water before allowing students to handle with gloves.

TEACHING TIP

If time allows, an attention-grabbing demonstration to start off this activity is to place a single egg in 3 M HCl and allow students to watch the shell dissolve.

Safety Requirements

- All activity in the laboratory area requires goggles and aprons.

- Disposal of eggs must follow school procedure.

- All solutions can be disposed of down the drain.

- Remind students not to eat anything in the laboratory area.

- Remind students to wash arms and hands before leaving the laboratory.

Meeting the Needs of All Students
Differentiated Instruction

Augmentation and Accommodations

LEARNING ISSUE	REFERENCE	AUGMENTATION AND ACCOMMODATIONS
Participation in class discussion	*What Do You See?* *What Do You Think?*	**Augmentation** • Pre-teach the essential concepts and knowledge to students who need it, either in class while other students are working on an extension, or before class in a supportive setting, such as a special education classroom. If other teachers are doing the pre-teaching, let them know what to emphasize so that you may call on those students during the lesson with the expectation that they are prepared to respond. **Accommodations** • Pair students strategically. Ask them to examine the picture and discuss their observations with each other. Then ask the more reticent student of the pair to comment on the picture. The information from his partner becomes his scaffold. • Have your weakest participants begin the discussion. This gives them more response options and challenges your stronger participants to extend the discussion. • Begin the discussion of the illustration by asking your most reluctant or weakest student what he sees. Accept almost any answer to encourage further participation. • When discussing how eggs change during cooking, begin by asking a weaker student the difference in color between a raw egg and a cooked egg. • To elicit student response, begin the discussion by asking opinion questions or open-ended questions related to eating raw eggs or eating a large number of hard-boiled eggs. • Instead of calling on students whose hands are up, regularly call on others to make sure students know that they are expected to participate. Use suggested accommodations to avoid humiliating shy students. Accept their answers regardless of the shaping required to make them appropriate.
Interpreting data Recalling units of measure	*Investigate* 1.a)	**Accommodations** • Remind students that mass is measured in grams and that usually the answer to the first question in a series is found at the beginning of a chart or text.
Calculating percentages	*Investigate* 1.b – d)	**Augmentation** • Review how to determine percentages on a calculator.
Designing an experiment	*Investigate* 4.	**Accommodations** • Provide struggling students with a basic design outline that they can elaborate upon.
Text analysis Reading comprehension	*Chem Talk*	**Augmentation** • Help students use the *Chem Talk* text to list the types of chemical changes embedded in it and describe what those changes involve. Changes in composition, shape, structure, and bonds could be included. This will pay off when students are asked how an egg changes when it is cooked and how they know, and when they are asked if denaturation is a chemical or physical change.
Interpreting diagrams	*Chem Talk*	**Augmentation** • Explain the difference and significance of primary, secondary and tertiary structure. • Show students how the structure may change during denaturation.
Reading comprehension Finding answers to questions in a textbook	*Checking Up* 1.-7.	**Augmentation** • Show students that while some answers to the *Checking Up* questions may be found in the preceding *Chem Words* sidebars, they will need to look back in their text for others. Their text is divided into several main sections: the introduction, *Investigate*, *Chem Talk* and the conclusion. The answers to the questions may be found in the *Chem Talk* section in the same order as the questions are asked.

Strategies for Students with Limited English Language Proficiency

LEARNING ISSUE	REFERENCE	AUGMENTATION AND ACCOMMODATIONS
Background knowledge	*What Do You Think?*	Students may not have background knowledge on the movies mentioned, so you may want to describe the scenes or play clips from the videos.
Vocabulary	*Investigate*	Check for understanding of the term "*bio-molecules.*" Students might benefit from working in small groups to complete the tasks, taking turns to read the directions and the questions.
Background knowledge Vocabulary Comprehending text	*Chem Talk*	Explain the word "*denaturation*" based on its linguistic parts. Have students make up some other words that utilize these linguistic structures to help build vocabulary (*e.g., "deforestation"*).
Background knowledge Application	*What Do You Think Now?*	Have students discuss answers prior to writing their own.
Background knowledge Vocabulary Comprehending text	*Chem Essential Questions*	Have students give examples of food that has been "*denatured*" as in the *Why do you believe?* section.
Comprehension Vocabulary	*Chem to Go*	Students can work in teams or small groups. The term "*minimal competence*" may be new for some students.
Application	*Inquiring Further*	Students may not have an understanding of the word "*foam,*" and may need some examples. Explain the phrase, "*The amount of fat in meat influences its flavor...*" as that may be an unfamiliar construction. Point out the prefix "*dis*" as in the term "*discoloration.*" Students may not have experience with recipes, and may benefit from seeing an example.

NOTES

Section 7
Teaching Suggestions and Sample Answers

What Do You See?

The colorful illustration introduces students to the section and is the first opportunity to engage the students' interest in the focus of the investigation – eggs. You can elicit their initial reactions to the illustration and learn which features interest them the most. A student may notice the egg on the floor and comment on the difference in form between that and what is being served. Other students may remark on the magnifying glasses. All answers are valid and should not be judged. The purpose here is to generate interest and responses, and to listen for prior knowledge and conceptions. You will be returning to the illustration later in the section.

What Do You Think?

Students may provide a variety of responses to this question. Steer them to consider physical and chemical changes that occur by the application of heat. Listen carefully and respectfully. The accuracy of their answers is not important at this point. Occasionally, you can uncover an important misconception by asking why they have a given opinion.

STUDENTS' PRIOR CONCEPTIONS

Students will have varying experiences with the cooking of eggs but few will be able to identify specific changes to protein structure. One common misconception you can listen for is that the cooking of eggs, especially hard-boiled eggs, involves the removal of water.

 Cookin' Chem

Section 7

Denaturation: How Do Proteins in Foods Change?

What Do You See?

Learning Outcomes

In this section you will

- Gain an understanding of proteins and what happens to them upon denaturation.
- Observe the effect of temperature on egg proteins.
- Observe the effect of changing pH on egg proteins.

What Do You Think?

In a movie called *Cool Hand Luke*, the main character eats 50 hard-boiled eggs in one hour as a bet. In the movie *Rocky*, the main character eats raw eggs for breakfast.

• **How does an egg change when cooked?**

Record your ideas about this question in your *Active Chemistry* log. Be prepared to discuss your responses with your group and the class.

Investigate

1. Your body is mainly composed of four elements: C, H, N, and O. The sources for these elements are carbohydrates, *proteins*, and fats with some trace elements being supplied by vitamins and minerals in the foods you eat. If you examine the food label on the next page, you'll notice important dietary information contains the amount of these molecules as well as Na, Ca, and vitamins. But what happens to these major bio-molecules (proteins, fats, and carbohydrates) as they are cooked?

608

What Do You Think?
A CHEMIST'S RESPONSE

The changes between a raw egg and a cooked egg are almost entirely due to changes in the protein structures. Essentially, the proteins are denatured by the heat and change irreversibly from a gelatinous liquid to a solid. If cooked in a frying pan, the temperature will exceed 100°C and chemical reactions involving proteins, carbohydrates and fats will occur.

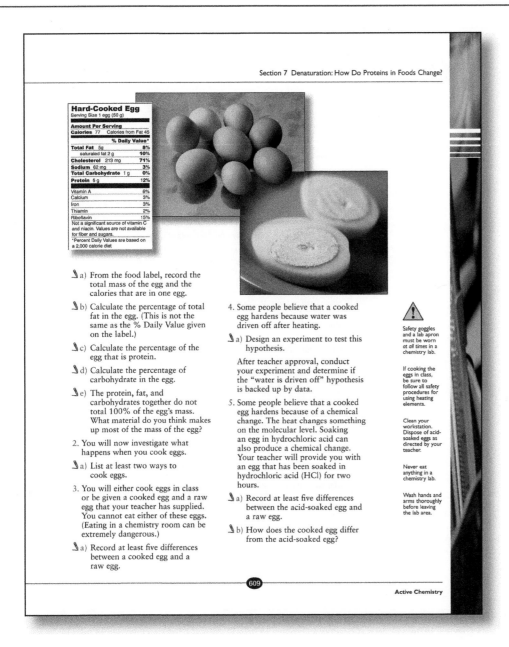

Section 7 Denaturation: How Do Proteins in Foods Change?

Hard-Cooked Egg
Serving Size 1 egg (50 g)

Amount Per Serving	
Calories 77	Calories from Fat 45

	% Daily Value*
Total Fat 5g	**8%**
saturated fat 2 g	**10%**
Cholesterol 213 mg	**71%**
Sodium 62 mg	**3%**
Total Carbohydrate 1 g	**0%**
Protein 6 g	**12%**

Vitamin A	6%
Calcium	3%
Iron	3%
Thiamin	2%
Riboflavin	15%

Not a significant source of vitamin C and niacin. Values are not available for fiber and sugars.
*Percent Daily Values are based on a 2,000 calorie diet

a) From the food label, record the total mass of the egg and the calories that are in one egg.

b) Calculate the percentage of total fat in the egg. (This is not the same as the % Daily Value given on the label.)

c) Calculate the percentage of the egg that is protein.

d) Calculate the percentage of carbohydrate in the egg.

e) The protein, fat, and carbohydrates together do not total 100% of the egg's mass. What material do you think makes up most of the mass of the egg?

2. You will now investigate what happens when you cook eggs.

a) List at least two ways to cook eggs.

3. You will either cook eggs in class or be given a cooked egg and a raw egg that your teacher has supplied. You cannot eat either of these eggs. (Eating in a chemistry room can be extremely dangerous.)

a) Record at least five differences between a cooked egg and a raw egg.

4. Some people believe that a cooked egg hardens because water was driven off after heating.

a) Design an experiment to test this hypothesis.

After teacher approval, conduct your experiment and determine if the "water is driven off" hypothesis is backed up by data.

5. Some people believe that a cooked egg hardens because of a chemical change. The heat changes something on the molecular level. Soaking an egg in hydrochloric acid can also produce a chemical change. Your teacher will provide you with an egg that has been soaked in hydrochloric acid (HCl) for two hours.

a) Record at least five differences between the acid-soaked egg and a raw egg.

b) How does the cooked egg differ from the acid-soaked egg?

⚠

Safety goggles and a lab apron must be worn *at all times* in a chemistry lab.

If cooking the eggs in class, be sure to follow all safety procedures for using heating elements.

Clean your workstation. Dispose of acid-soaked eggs as directed by your teacher.

Never eat anything in a chemistry lab.

Wash hands and arms thoroughly before leaving the lab area.

609

Active Chemistry

Investigate

1.
Students' answers will vary but the only valid answer that some students might come up with is the denaturation of proteins.

1.a)
Mass = 50 g; Calories = 77.

If time permits, it would be interesting to weigh all the eggs in an egg carton and see how close the weight of each is to 50 g. (Also, the difference in mass between large and extra large eggs would be interesting. The students could determine which one is the better buy.)

1.b)
The total fat percentage of an egg is 10% (5 g/50 g × 100). The % Daily Value refers to the % of the recommended daily value each egg provides. For instance, one would have to eat about 12 eggs to obtain the daily recommended amount of fat.

1.c)
The protein percentage is 12% (6 g/50 g × 100).

1.d)
The carbohydrate percentage is 2%.

1.e)
The total of protein, fat, and carbohydrates amounts to 12 g, or 24% of the egg. The remainder is mostly water. Minerals and cholesterol will account for small amounts.

2.a)
Various ways of cooking eggs include boiling (in the shell), frying (e.g., scrambled, "sunny-side up," and "over easy"), poaching, and microwaving.

3.a)
Note: If still in the shell, the cooked egg must have been boiled and there will be little physical evidence of difference without breaking them. The cooked egg, however, will spin much easier than the raw egg.

If a comparison is made between a fried egg and a raw egg (out of the shell), a number of differences could be noted:

Raw	Fried
The white is translucent.	The white is opaque.
The white is a liquid.	The white is a solid.
The white is relatively uniform.	The white may vary in texture and coloring.
The yolk is liquid.	The yolk is solid.
The yolk cannot be perfectly separated from the white.	The yolk can easily be separated from the white.

4.a)

Some examples of experiments for testing the hypothesis by cooking an egg with heat could include the following:

• Use four test tubes of water containing the same quantity of water (10 mL). Heat each test tube to a different temperature. The temperature range should be from 10-15°C to 70-80°C. Drop 1 mL (or do it by mass) of egg white into each test tube and observe. Note the temperature at which this occurs. Since the egg white is cooked in water, cooking cannot be linked to water being driven off.

• Fill a beaker with 100 mL of water and add a measured volume of egg white. Begin heating, note the change in temperature and the changes in the appearance of the egg white. Denaturation is visible when the egg white changes from translucent to opaque. Note the temperature at which this occurs. Again, since the egg white is cooked in water, cooking cannot be linked to water being driven off.

• Obtain the mass of an egg (in shell) before and after boiling. The mass will be the same, which strongly indicates that no significant amount of water has been driven off.

• Obtain the mass of an egg before and after poaching. The mass will be the same, which strongly suggests that no significant amount of water has been driven off.

5.a)

Some differences between an acid-soaked egg and a raw egg could include:

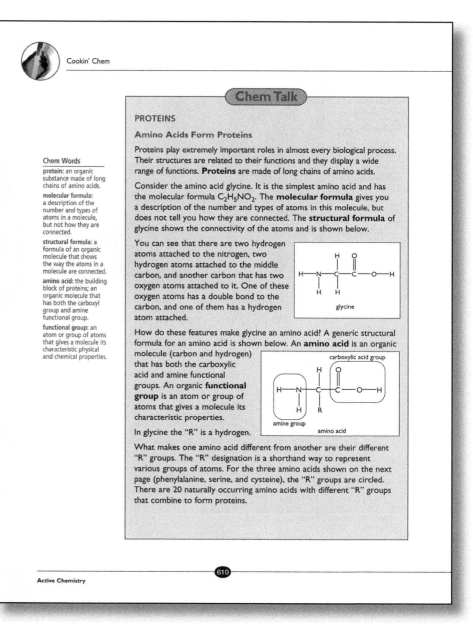

Raw egg	Acid-soaked egg
The white is gelatinous.	The white is solid and can be sliced.
The white is translucent.	The white is opaque.
The white is a liquid.	The white is a solid.
The yolk is liquid	The yolk is solid.
The yolk cannot be perfectly separated from the white.	The yolk can be easily separated from the white.

5. b)

The cooked egg holds the shape whereas the acid-soaked egg is more amorphous.

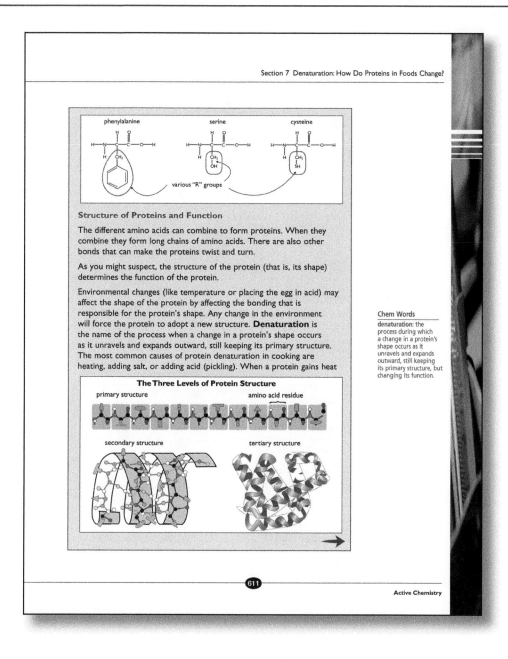

Structure of Proteins and Function

The different amino acids can combine to form proteins. When they combine they form long chains of amino acids. There are also other bonds that can make the proteins twist and turn.

As you might suspect, the structure of the protein (that is, its shape) determines the function of the protein.

Environmental changes (like temperature or placing the egg in acid) may affect the shape of the protein by affecting the bonding that is responsible for the protein's shape. Any change in the environment will force the protein to adopt a new structure. **Denaturation** is the name of the process when a change in a protein's shape occurs as it unravels and expands outward, still keeping its primary structure. The most common causes of protein denaturation in cooking are heating, adding salt, or adding acid (pickling). When a protein gains heat

Chem Words

denaturation: the process during which a change in a protein's shape occurs as it unravels and expands outward, still keeping its primary structure, but changing its function.

Chem Talk

Amino acids, the basic units of proteins, are introduced. They can form long polymer chains which can be defined by molecular and structural formulas. A brief explanation of organic functional groups and "R" groups is provided. The reading concludes with information about structure and function and how changes in pH and temperature can denature proteins.

CHAPTER 7

Checking Up

1.

A protein is an organic substance made of a long chain of amino acids.

2.

A molecular formula is a description of the number and types of atoms in a molecule, but not how they are connected. A structural formula contains the same information but also indicates how the atoms in that molecule are connected.

3.

An amino acid is an organic molecule that has both the carboxylic acid and amine functional groups. These groups are almost always connected to the same carbon atom.

4.

The functional group is an atom (or group of atoms) that gives a molecule its characteristic chemical properties.

5.

The structure of a protein (its shape) determines its function.

6.

Denaturation is the process during which a change in a protein's shape occurs as it unravels. It keeps its primary structure, but its secondary and tertiary structure are changed, and, thus, its function. When a protein gains sufficient heat energy, the forces of attraction that contribute to a protein's secondary and tertiary structure are broken. Denaturation can also be caused by pH changes, pressure changes, and changes in ionic strength.

7.

Proteins can be denatured in cooking either by heat, high pressure, adding salt, or by changing the pH.

Cookin' Chem

Checking Up

1. What are proteins made up of?
2. How are a molecular formula and a structural formula similar? How are they different?
3. What is an amino acid?
4. Define a functional group of a molecule.
5. What determines the function of a protein?
6. Describe the process of denaturation.
7. Give two ways in which proteins are denatured in cooking.

energy, the attractive forces contributing to its secondary and tertiary structure are broken. However, the sequence of the amino acids in the primary structure is unchanged. Those bonds are stronger and not broken. Denaturation is not a change in composition, only a change in structure. But since structure determines function, denatured proteins behave quite differently from their original or un-denatured form.

Proteins are denatured at temperatures of 40°C. At higher temperatures, they may begin to break up or bond with each other and form clumps. Your clear egg white became firm and opaque when the temperature was raised and more denaturation took place. Changing the pH also disrupts the bonds that give proteins their shapes.

When meat is cooked and the proteins in it are denatured, the proteins are extended and more vulnerable to attack by enzymes that aid in the digestion of your dinner.

What Do You Think Now?

At the beginning of the section you were asked the following:

• **How does an egg change when cooked?**

Look back at your answer at the beginning of the section. How would you change your original answer?

Chem
Essential Questions

What does it mean?

Chemistry explains a *macroscopic* phenomenon (what you observe) with a description of what happens at the *nanoscopic* level (atoms and molecules) using *symbolic* structures as a way to communicate. Complete the chart below in your Active Chemistry log.

MACRO	NANO	SYMBOLIC
What changes do you see when you cook an egg?	Describe the denaturation of an egg white at the molecular level. Remember that structure determines function.	You can use drawings of protein secondary structures as one way to represent this physical change. What symbolic structure do you use to describe amino acids?

612

What Do You Think Now?

Have students refer to their original responses to the *What Do You Think?* question. They may have said that the egg will change color or texture. Now, however, they should be able to make some generalizations about the effect of heat energy on the protein structure. Their revised responses may include references to the increased motion of molecules and the effects on intermolecular forces responsible for secondary and tertiary structure. They should also express an understanding of the effect of pH change on intermolecular forces and structure. Help students connect cooking conditions where the pH may be changed and the resulting effect on proteins (e.g., in some recipes, lime juice is used instead of heat for "cooking").

Chem Essential Questions

What does it mean?

MACRO — The entire egg becomes solid and the egg white, which was originally translucent, becomes opaque.

NANO — When egg white is denatured with heat, the various parts of the protein structure begin to gain kinetic energy and move more vigorously. At some point, this motion will overcome the forces of attraction that hold the protein in a specific shape. These forces include hydrogen bonds and dipole-dipole attractions. As these forces of attraction are broken, the protein begins to unravel and change its shape. As it changes shape, it loses its biological function.

SYMBOLIC — The symbolic structure used to represent amino acids is shown below.

primary structure

How do you know?

The answer will depend upon the method that the students used to test the hypothesis. If they denatured egg white protein in hot water, there is clear evidence that there is no loss of water. If they did it by measuring the mass before and after denaturation, they can show that there is no appreciable loss of water.

Why do you believe?

Uncooked meat proteins are tough and stringy. Cooked (denatured) meat is easier to chew (less tough and stringy). The proteins in milk remain dispersed as a colloid. When cooked, they precipitate out as a curd. Bean and peanut proteins are hard and flavorless. When cooked (roasted) they become softer and more flavorful.

Why should you care?

No answer is required here. Students should be familiar with the answer to the NANO question and the fact that heat energy causes proteins "to jiggle" out of their natural structural conformations is a key understanding. Denaturation due to pH change is more related to solubility, but also to the change in forces of attraction within the protein molecule. Students can prepare an informative and entertaining demonstration of the uncoiling of a protein.

NOTES

_____

_____

_____

_____

_____

_____

_____

_____

Reflecting on the Section and the Challenge

Students should identify some possible ways to use what they have learned about denaturation in a cooking show segment. They should consider how they would present the information to their viewers (i.e., by using models, animation, drawings, etc.). If time permits, students can discuss within their groups and then share with the class. This could help those groups without firm plans to get some ideas on ways to apply the knowledge gained by the sections.

Chem to Go

1.

Indicators of denaturation include clumping (precipitate forming), change in color, change in texture, change from translucent to opaque, etc.

2.

Students' answers may vary, but they should provide support for their methods. The temperature for boiling an egg is defined by the laws of physics. Basically, it will be around 100°C unless the atmospheric pressure is significantly different than 1 atmosphere, such as in areas like Denver or Death Valley. Generally, only the cooking time will be a variable. Students may find articles, recipes, information in cookbooks, or the Internet to help answer this question. They may find that a temperature of only 40°C is enough to cook (denature the proteins of) an egg.

3.a)

The heat from the butter-sugar-syrup mixture is enough to denature the proteins in the beaten eggs and cause instant denaturation of the egg proteins.

3.b)

The pie would probably be heterogeneous and lumpy. There would be lumps of egg white throughout the pie.

4.

Denaturation can be both a physical change and a chemical change.

Because the amino acid arrangement of protein composition is not affected and its primary structure is maintained, it is primarily a physical change. This is true especially during denaturation due to heating. When the pH is lowered, the negatively charged carboxyl ions are chemically converted to carboxylic acids, and the solubility is usually decreased. This will usually cause the precipitation of the protein and its loss of function. If the pH is raised significantly, many proteins are also denatured with a loss of function. This would be a result, in general, of the neutralization of the ammonium groups of the protein.

NOTES

_____

_____

_____

_____

_____

_____

How do you know?

The change in an egg during cooking is not due to a loss of water, but rather it is due to a chemical change. What evidence do you have for this?

Why do you believe?

Personal experiences tell you that raw foods are different from cooked foods in appearance, texture, and taste. Give examples of how other proteins such as meat change (denature) with cooking.

Why should you care?

Explaining the *nanoscopic* changes that occur during cooking foods containing proteins would be an exciting addition to your cooking show.

Reflecting on the Section and the Challenge

In this section, you designed a way of examining what happens to egg proteins when they are cooked. Since your challenge is to create a segment of a cooking show and provide a detailed explanation of the chemistry that is occurring, consider how you might use the knowledge gained from this section in your segment. Think about all of the information you would need to explain protein denaturation to your viewers. Consider how you would explain at the molecular level what happens when an egg cooks or when meat is cooked.

Chem to Go

1. What are some indicators that protein denaturation is occurring during cooking?

2. Although boiling an egg is often seen as a measure of minimal competence for a cook, there are actually many things to consider in producing a good hard-boiled egg. Based on your tests and the tests of your classmates, what advice could you give a cook about temperature and cooking conditions for boiling an egg? Provide a recipe for the best way to boil the perfect egg.

3. In one recipe for great Southern pecan pie, the directions state: *Combine butter, sugar, and corn syrup; cook over low heat, stirring constantly, until the sugar is dissolved. Cool. Add eggs, vanilla, and salt; mix well...*

   a) Why is the cook directed to allow the butter-sugar solution to cool before adding the beaten eggs?

   b) What might be the results if eggs are added before the solution cools?

4. Is protein denaturation a chemical or a physical change? Explain your reasoning.

613

5.

Preparing for the Chapter Challenge

Students' answers will vary, depending on how they choose to address the problem. You may want to have some odds and ends from a craft store available for students to use to create protein models. Some handy items might include pipe cleaners, beads, construction paper, clay, etc.

Inquiring Further

1. Egg white's foaming ability

When raw egg whites are beaten, air bubbles are incorporated into the water-protein solution. Adding air bubbles to egg whites causes the egg proteins to unfold (denatures them) just as heating does. Egg white proteins contain both hydrophilic and hydrophobic amino acids. When the protein is curled up, the hydrophobic amino acids are packed in the center away from the water and the hydrophilic ones are on the outside closer to the water. This is what makes the protein soluble in water. When the egg protein molecule is next to an air bubble, part of that protein is exposed to air and part is still in water. The protein uncurls so that its water-soluble parts are immersed in water. At the same time, its internal hydrophobic sections are forced into the air. This causes a dramatic change in the structure as the proteins uncurl, and the hydrophobic portions of the molecule connect with each other creating a network that can hold the air bubbles in

place. This is the foam. Various environmental factors, such as dirt, pH changes, extra moisture, etc., can disrupt this network formation, thus affecting the "foaming" ability of the egg whites. Students can design controlled tests to test the effect of one of these environmental factors on the denaturation process. Emphasis should be on their experimental design and the conclusions that they draw from their data.

2. Maillard reaction

The Maillard reaction occurs when the denatured proteins on the surface of the meat react with the sugars present. This combination creates the "meaty" flavor and changes the color. As many as six hundred components have been identified in the aroma of beef. Useful information about the Maillard reaction and browning of meat can be found on the Internet.

Cookin' Chem

5. Preparing for the Chapter Challenge

The main bio-molecules found in foods and required by the body are carbohydrates, fats, and proteins. In this section, you examined the behavior of proteins in eggs when cooked. Design and create a model that can be used to explain what happens to proteins as they are cooked. You might consider using a pipe-cleaner and bead model, or a cut-out "puzzle" model. Perhaps, you can use your computer skills and create a video or claymation that depicts protein denaturation. Use your imagination and be creative but clear in illustrating the process of cooking proteins. Work with your group to determine how you will model protein cooking and then create your model complete with an explanation of what is happening.

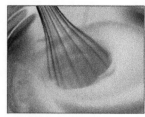

Inquiring Further

1. Egg white's foaming ability

Egg whites make excellent foams, however foams can be tricky to produce. Research what foams are and explain how egg whites can form foams. Humidity, dirty or greasy bowls, pH, and the age of the egg can affect egg white's foaming ability. Design a test to determine how one of these factors influences an egg white's foaming ability.

2. Maillard reaction

Most of meat's flavor develops when it is cooked. The amount of fat in meat influences its flavor, as does a process called the Maillard reaction. The Maillard reaction occurs when the denatured proteins on the surface of the meat recombine with the sugars present. The combination creates the "meaty" flavor and changes the color. Find out more information about the Maillard reaction. Explain how the same reaction could account for providing a meaty flavor in meats, browning meat, caramelizing, and even providing the flavor of toast.

3. Green egg yolks

Sometimes when boiling eggs, a greenish-gray discoloration appears on the surface of the yolk of an egg. This discoloration has been identified as iron sulfide. As the egg is heated, some of the sulfur atoms found in the egg white (albumen) are liberated and react with hydrogen ions in the albumen to form hydrogen sulfide (H_2S). In minute quantities, this gas is responsible for the characteristic and pleasant odor of cooked eggs and meat, but in larger quantities it is the odor associated with rotten eggs. As the gas diffuses, some of it reaches the yolk, where it encounters iron contained in the yolk. The hydrogen sulfide then reacts with the iron to form iron sulfide, which is a greenish-gray color. Design and conduct a test to determine the best way to reduce the formation of FeS in a hard-boiled egg. Write a recipe for making the best hard-boiled eggs, including tips for cooks so they can avoid having green yolks.

614

3. Green egg yolks

The formation of FeS is dependent upon cooking time. In order to reduce its formation, eggs should not be overcooked. Since heat will make the diffusion of the H_2S gas occur more quickly, plunging the eggs into cold water can help prevent the yolk from turning green. Students' tests should examine size or mass of the egg and determine the least amount of time needed to hard-boil an egg. They should then determine that overcooking the eggs is responsible for the greenish-gray discoloration around the yolk.

They might also suggest that putting the eggs into cold water after the optimal cooking time could limit the discoloration, because the drop in temperature slows down the diffusion of the H_2S and stops the cooking process. Useful information on hard-boiling eggs can be found on the Internet.

SECTION 7 – QUIZ

7-7d	Blackline Master

1. What is an amino acid?

   a) a substance that has both amine groups and carboxyl groups

   b) a substance that is the building block for proteins

   c) a family of substances in which only 20 occur naturally

   d) all of the above

   e) none of the above

2. Answer the following questions about protein denaturation.

   a) What are two ways a protein may be denatured?

   b) What happens when a protein is denatured?

   c) Is protein denaturation a chemical or physical change? Explain your answer.

SECTION 7 – QUIZ ANSWERS

❶ d) all of the above

❷ a) Exposure to heat, acid, high pressure, or salt will denature a protein.

   b) The protein's secondary and tertiary structure is destroyed during denaturation as the protein uncoils and changes shape. Biological function is lost because the protein's function is a result of its shape.

   c) Denaturation is mostly a physical change. The primary structure is not altered. However, when acid or base is used to denature a protein, some bonds are altered. Many consider this a chemical change.

SECTION 8
Modeling Organic Molecules: Soap

Section Overview

Students are introduced to a molecular model kit and learn to construct increasingly complex molecules using it. With the knowledge of how the kit can be used to build representations of organic molecules, students learn about double bonds, triple bonds, and isomers, including *cis-trans* isomers. Using four lengths of string, students predict molecular geometry using the principles of the Valence-Shell-Electron-Pair-Repulsion Theory (VSEPR). Finally, they build stearic acid, the sodium salt of which is sodium stearate, a common soap. Modeling this soap molecule with foam spheres and toothpicks, students show how soap can remove dirt and grease from dishes or clothing, leaving them clean.

Background Information

Properties of a chemical compound arise from its structure. So it's important to be able to determine a molecule's structure. For smaller compounds, once the atoms making up the compounds have been identified, a fairly simple set of rules determine the possible structures; sometimes there is only one. Larger molecules can be analyzed in terms of the subunits of which they are composed, because functional groups each contribute predictable properties to the molecule. Patterns of variations of properties corresponding to variations in functional groups can be determined and used for prediction. Drawing chemical structures allows us to predict the properties of those molecules and to relate them to the properties of other molecules with similar, but different, structures.

Cis and *trans* refer to a type of geometric isomer at a site containing a double bond. Consider the two molecules at the start of this *Investigate*. If we begin with an ethene ($CH_2=CH_2$) structure, we

obtain the molecules pictured by adding a methyl ($-CH_3$) group to each end. However, we can do this in two ways. We obtain a *cis* molecule by adding a methyl group to each carbon on the same side of the ethene double bond.

We obtain a *trans* molecule by adding a two methyl group to each carbon on opposite sides of the ethene double bond.

Because atoms connected by a double bond can't rotate around that bond (as atoms connected by a single bond can), these are two different molecules, and they cannot easily be converted from one to the other.

The process of hydrogenation adds a hydrogen atom to each side of a double bond, converting the double bond to a single bond. However, like many chemical reactions, this reaction is reversible. In commercial hydrogenation of fats and oils (e.g., $C_nH_{2n} + H_2 \rightarrow C_nH_{2n+2}$, which is the hydrogenation of a mono-unsaturated hydrocarbon to form a saturated hydrocarbon), conditions are controlled to minimize the reverse reaction. Nevertheless, some hydrogenated fats lose hydrogen atoms and regain a double bond. If the two hydrogen atoms leave from the same side of the double bond, they will produce a *cis* molecule. But if they leave from opposite sides of the bond, they will produce a trans molecule. About half of the fat molecules produced in this way will be *trans* (since the hydrogen atoms have a roughly equal chance of leaving from the same or opposite sides of the bond).

Living things produce *cis* fatty acids, but very few *trans* fatty acids. So human diets in the past have usually contained only small amounts of *trans* fat. However, food manufacturers now add hydrogenated fats (to increase shelf life) to a great many processed foods, including baked goods, crackers, chips, cereals, etc., and these products are likely to contain *trans* fats. The amount can be determined by comparing the total amount of fat to the sum of the amounts of saturated and unsaturated fat (if listed). The difference will be the amount of trans fat, because *trans* fat is not counted as unsaturated fat. In 2006, *trans* fat information was required on nutrition labels. The effects of trans fat are not completely clear, but among other things, *trans* fat increases the amount of LDL ("bad") cholesterol in your blood and decreases the amount of HDL ("good") cholesterol, both leading to increased risk of cardiovascular disease.

LEARNING OUTCOMES		
LEARNING OUTCOMES	**LOCATION IN SECTION**	**EVIDENCE OF UNDERSTANDING**
Connect the two-dimensional drawing of a simple organic molecule to the three-dimensional structure it represents.	***Investigate*** Parts A, B, C, D ***Checking Up*** Question 2 ***Chem to Go*** Questions 1, 3, 7, 8, 9	Students are able to infer the 3-D structure of an organic molecule from a provided 2-D structure.
Examine the differences in molecular shape that result from small differences in molecular structure.	***What Do You Think?*** ***Chem Talk*** ***Checking Up*** Question 2 ***Chem to Go*** Questions 1, 2, 8, 9	Students are capable of differentiating a *cis* arrangement from a *trans* arrangement.
Predict the shape and polarity of molecules by examining each atom's bonding (valence) electrons.	***Investigate*** Part B Steps 1-7; Part D Steps 1-4 ***Chem Talk*** ***Checking Up*** Question 1 ***Chem to Go*** Questions 4, 5, 6	Students have the ability to draw Lewis structures for atoms and molecules and apply the VSEPR theory to determine the shape and polarity of a molecule.
Model micelle formation during the process of dirt and grease removal by soap.	***Investigate*** Part E ***Chem Talk*** ***Checking Up*** Question 3 ***Chem to Go*** Question 10	Students can model micelle formation by aligning the polar and nonpolar ends of a simulated soap molecule into water and grease, respectively.

Section 8
Materials, Chemicals, Preparation, and Safety

("per Group" quantity is based on group size of 4 students)

Materials and Equipment

Materials (and Equipment)	Quantity per Group (4 students)
Scissors	1
Ruler, clear plastic, 30-cm	1

Materials (and Equipment)	Quantity per Class
String, ball	1
Molecular model class kit	1

Teacher Preparation

To save materials and class time, the four 20-cm strings for each group can be cut in advance and the molecular model kits can be divided up into sets for each group.

Safety Requirements

- All activity in the laboratory area requires goggles and aprons.

- Wash arms and hands with soap and water before leaving the lab area.

NOTES

NOTES

Meeting the Needs of All Students
Differentiated Instruction

Augmentation and Accommodations

LEARNING ISSUE	REFERENCE	AUGMENTATION AND ACCOMMODATIONS
Visual analysis of complex compounds	*What Do You Think?* *Investigate*	**Augmentation** • Some students have difficulty seeing the visual patterns in complex diagrams. The molecular diagrams at the beginning of the activity provide an opportunity to give students a process for analysis of these complicated molecules. • It is probably most useful to have students who struggle with visual analysis begin with the carbon atoms. Ask them how many there are and how they are connected in each molecule in *What Do You Think?* • Show students how to work from the center of each molecule, the double bonded carbons, work their way along one branch, then the others. Have students compare each branch for similarities and differences. • Ask students to use various colored markers to highlight similar subgroups within each molecule. Point out that this color-coding strategy is widely used by experts in the field as a way to visually differentiate groups, as demonstrated in Step 2.a) of this investigation. Students should also use the color-coding strategy when they are combining previous models to make new, more complex ones, as in Part D: Step 4.a). • Ask students to compare the shape, subgroups and number of atoms of each element in each subgroup. • Finally, help students to list strategies they can use to analyze subsequent molecule diagrams they encounter in this section.
Interpreting various representations of hydrocarbons	*Investigate*	**Augmentation** • In this section, students are asked to become familiar with organic molecules by analyzing and comparing two-dimensional and three-dimensional models of them, but there are several ways these molecules are represented: ball and stick models, ball and stick diagrams, letter and stick diagrams, "line-bond" drawings, and the properties of the substances and their names. Organizing their learning in a table will encourage further processing during their exploration of the molecules and provide a better reference for them in their *Active Chem* logs. Give students the categories above and the names of each molecule they will study. Ask each group to set up a table that shows each representation of the molecules they are modeling. • To avoid tedious copying of long molecules, have each group create one table to hand in. Tell them their group's table must be revised until it is as accurate as possible and satisfactory to all group members. • To ensure that each student is engaged, arrange the task so that each member has a role. Require that a different person be responsible for recording each type of representation. Allow students to choose assignments among themselves. Since they know the table will be strictly judged, they will initially differentiate the assignments appropriately or switch roles when they see a member of their group struggling. • Check for accuracy. When the tables are correct and finalized, return them to students with photocopies for each group member.

LEARNING ISSUE	REFERENCE	AUGMENTATION AND ACCOMMODATIONS
Comparing types of visual diagrams	*Investigate*	**Augmentation** • To avoid confusion, be sure to illustrate different types of the same molecule for the class on the board as is found in the *Student Edition* for stearic acid. Otherwise, students may think that different representations of the same molecule are illustrations of different molecules. • Check in with each group during the investigation and make sure each student can name and identify different representations of molecules. • Be sure to point out the comparison of the ball and stick model of methane with the model of the tetrahedron. Students need help to see the similarities because they may not be able to visualize the triangles when looking at the ball and stick figure or the understood carbon atom in the center of the tetrahedron.
Following directions Constructing molecular models	*Investigate*	**Augmentation** • Pair students heterogeneously so that they interpret the directions together and use each other's molecules as models. • To match learning style with the task, allow struggling students to copy someone else's completed construction instead of reading the directions, but then require them to write a summary of the steps they took and compare them to the directions in the *Student Edition*. Perhaps a third group could work from their instructions.
Dealing with input overload	*Chem Talk*	**Augmentation** • Before the class begins, divide the *Chem Talk* explanation into three or four segments that correspond with the steps in the investigation. If students become disengaged as the investigation moves forward from one model to the next, stop the activity and ask students to read the part of the *Chem Talk* section that corresponds to the model they just completed before beginning the next model. This will chunk the exploration and explanation segments into smaller, more palatable segments.

Strategies for Students with Limited English Language Proficiency

LEARNING ISSUE	REFERENCE	AUGMENTATIONS
Background knowledge	*What Do You Think?*	Have students describe what they see in the illustration in small groups or with partners to provide for oral language development and a discussion of content.
Vocabulary	*Investigate*	Students might not be familiar with the term, "*crucial*" and might benefit from some explanation of this signal word. The word "*interact*" will be a significant word in this section and may be unfamiliar to some students. Awareness of the "*co*" affix as in "*covalent*" will provide some vocabulary and language development. Students may need help in pronunciation of words such as "*tetrahedron*," "*stearic*," and "*glycerol*." They may also need supporting explanation of the direction, "*describe a skit.*"
Background knowledge Vocabulary Comprehending text	*Chem Talk*	Check for understanding of bold type words. Refer students to sidebar material for further explanations of the isolated words. Review the use of the "*un*" prefix as in "*saturated*" and "*unsaturated*" to show how meaning is altered.
Background knowledge	*What Do You Think Now?*	Allow students to discuss their answers. Check for understanding of the word, "*identical*" as this may not be in the students' expressive vocabulary.
Background knowledge Vocabulary Comprehending text	*Chem Essential Questions*	In the *Why should you care?* section, students are asked to explain aspects of their presentation. The word "micelle" might require some explanation. Students will benefit from discussing this section.
Comprehension Vocabulary	*Chem to Go*	Allow students to work in small groups or with a partner. Note that the picture gives an example of a model.

Section 8
Teaching Suggestions and Sample Answers

What Do You See?

The students may have no clear idea of what the illustration depicts, but it should be interesting to hear their suggestions as to why some of the water molecules are trying to escape the soap molecule and some are attracted to it. Allow them to share their ideas in a discussion; they will have a chance to return to the illustration after completing the investigation. All responses are valid and do not expect correct responses, but be alert for evidence of misunderstandings or misconceptions.

What Do You Think?

At this point, students probably do not have any idea of what geometric isomers are, but they should be able to note the difference between single and double bonds. They may note that the methyl groups in the *cis* configuration are adjacent to one another while they are on opposite sides in the *trans* configuration. The investigation should resolve any unanswered questions and they will have a chance to return to the question later.

What Do You Think?
A CHEMIST'S RESPONSE

The first structure is *cis*-2-butene and the second structure is trans-2-butene. These are isomers of butene, C_4H_8. Other isomers of butene are 1-butene and 2-methyl propene. In all cases it is noted that they have the same number of carbon and hydrogen atoms. The cis configuration shows that the two methyl groups are on the same side of the double bond (above it) and the trans shows that the two methyl groups are on opposite sides. The two carbons that contain the double bond are sp^2 hybrids and the geometry is described as triangular planar with bond angles of 120°.

STUDENTS' PRIOR CONCEPTIONS

Students may think that an atom can have numerous bonds and that geometric structure is by choice and not specific at this time. The activity should address these concepts and they will see how the valence electrons of an atom help to determine the number of bonds. The octet rule also is applied to the number of electrons needed to satisfy an atom's structure. Carbon can achieve an octet of electrons by either having four single bonds or multiple bonds (double or triple) between carbon atoms. They will have a better understanding of the geometry of sp^3 and sp^2 hybrid states that are found in carbon compounds.

NOTES

Section 8

Modeling Organic Molecules: Soap

What Do You See?

What Do You Think?

Here are the structures of two different four-carbon molecules that have the same numbers of carbon and hydrogen atoms and the formula, C_4H_8.

• **Describe the differences in these two molecules' shapes.**

Record your ideas about this question in your *Active Chemistry* log. Be prepared to discuss your response in your group and with the class.

Investigate

In this section, you will use molecular model sets to build some hydrocarbons and related molecules so that you can see what shapes molecules can take. Understanding the shapes of molecules is crucial to understanding how soap molecules interact with the dirt and grease that can build up in a kitchen or get on your hands while cooking.

615

Investigate

Part A: Getting Acquainted with the Models

1.

Instructions may vary with the type of molecular model kit available. In a standard kit, there are four colors of spheres that represent atoms. There are also two types of gray sticks, which represent bonds. Students should note that there are four colors of plastic spheres and two types of gray sticks. You might suggest that they begin to refer to the spheres as "atoms" and the gray sticks as "bonds."

1.a)

Students will record the following:

- black atom—4 holes, equally spaced
- blue atom—3 holes, similar spacing but missing one hole
- red atom—2 holes, similar spacing of the two holes
- white atom—1 hole

1.b)

Students will record the following:

- There are two types of bonds in the kit.
- Short gray bond—stiff, not flexible
- Long gray bond—flexible

2.

Tell students they can relate the color of the atom with its identity and the number of holes. Remind them of what they have learned about atomic structure and bonding.

 Cookin' Chem

These interactions of shape and polarity determine a soap molecule's behavior in water and grease. Chemists design soap molecules to have different shapes and polarities to serve a variety of purposes, including soaps for dishwashers, laundry detergents, bar soaps, and shampoos. Each of these soaps is specially engineered to function differently.

Part A: Getting Acquainted with the Models

1. Work individually or in pairs. Open a molecular-model set and organize the spheres and sticks in it. What kinds of different spheres and sticks do you see?

   a) Write down a description of each type of sphere. For example, a black sphere has four holes that appear to be equally spaced apart. (It can make four bonds with other atoms.)

   b) Are the sticks all the same? Describe them.

2. A hydrogen atom will make one bond, an oxygen atom will make two bonds, a nitrogen atom will make three bonds, and a carbon atom will make four bonds. (This can be remembered as HONC: 1, 2, 3, 4.)

   a) Given the number of holes, which color is associated with each of these elements? Of course, the

actual atoms are not red or blue or any color at all. The different colors make it easier to keep track of which atoms are where when making molecules.

The gray sticks are bonds. Each one represents the pair of electrons in a chemical bond. The longer sticks are more flexible and are used in double and triple bonds.

3. Use the short sticks and spheres to make a molecular structure containing no more than six spheres. Make sure that all the holes are filled with sticks that connect to other spheres. When you have completed the structure, then you have constructed a model of a molecule that could exist. (Hint: Only two molecules are possible. Oxygen rarely is bonded to another oxygen atom.)

   a) Sketch a copy of your model in your *Active Chemistry* log and record its formula. Describe the shape of the molecule at the intersection of the bonds at each carbon, oxygen, or nitrogen atom.

   b) Take two longer, flexible gray sticks for use as a double bond. Replace the middle short bond with a longer one. Then remove two hydrogen atoms from adjacent atoms. Fill the vacant holes with the second flexible gray stick.

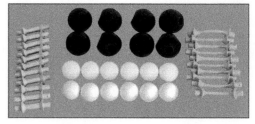

616

Active Chemistry

2.a)

A hydrogen atom (white) can form one bond, oxygen (red) forms two, nitrogen (blue) forms three, and carbon (black) forms four bonds.

Tell students that the more flexible bonds are used for double and triple bonds. It may help them understand if you show them an example of each.

3.

Students often start creating animal figures as soon as they open their model sets for the first time. Allowing this to occur early may be helpful in moving the class beyond that stage. Remind students of the constraints: only six atoms, short bonds, and all holes must be filled. You might want to add the further constraint that oxygen (red) cannot be bonded to oxygen. In real molecules, this is an unstable bond.

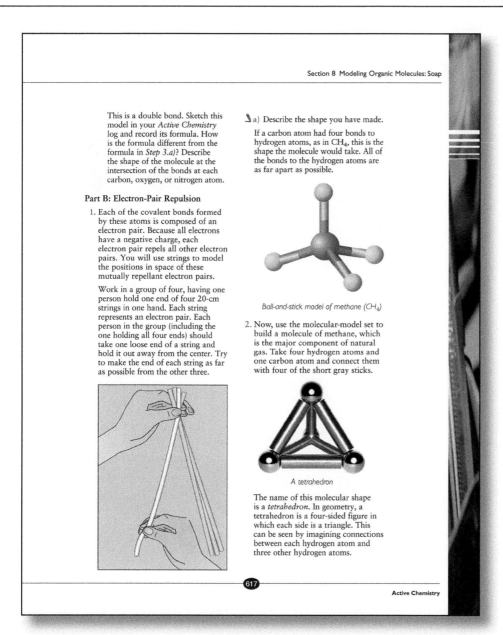

This is a double bond. Sketch this model in your *Active Chemistry* log and record its formula. How is the formula different from the formula in *Step 3.a)*? Describe the shape of the molecule at the intersection of the bonds at each carbon, oxygen, or nitrogen atom.

Part B: Electron-Pair Repulsion

1. Each of the covalent bonds formed by these atoms is composed of an electron pair. Because all electrons have a negative charge, each electron pair repels all other electron pairs. You will use strings to model the positions in space of these mutually repellant electron pairs.

   Work in a group of four, having one person hold one end of four 20-cm strings in one hand. Each string represents an electron pair. Each person in the group (including the one holding all four ends) should take one loose end of a string and hold it out away from the center. Try to make the end of each string as far as possible from the other three.

🔌 a) Describe the shape you have made.

If a carbon atom had four bonds to hydrogen atoms, as in CH₄, this is the shape the molecule would take. All of the bonds to the hydrogen atoms are as far apart as possible.

Ball-and-stick model of methane (CH₄)

2. Now, use the molecular-model set to build a molecule of methane, which is the major component of natural gas. Take four hydrogen atoms and one carbon atom and connect them with four of the short gray sticks.

A tetrahedron

The name of this molecular shape is a *tetrahedron*. In geometry, a tetrahedron is a four-sided figure in which each side is a triangle. This can be seen by imagining connections between each hydrogen atom and three other hydrogen atoms.

has two fewer hydrogen atoms. In terms of shape at the carbon, oxygen, and nitrogen atoms, students may suggest "flat," "stick-like," or "boomerang." The conventional terms used by chemists are "trigonal planar," "linear," and "bent."

Part B: Electron-Pair Repulsion

1.

Make certain that students understand that the hand holding four strings must be in the center and represents a carbon atom. Some groups will think that the four strings are farthest apart when held in a plane, intersecting at 90°. Show them that by moving one string out of the plane, it is now farther from the others. The actual angle they should arrive at is about 109° for each pair of strings.

1.a)

The students have seen this shape earlier in this *Investigate* and may remember to call it "*tetrahedral*."

2.

Students may have difficulty visualizing a methane model as a tetrahedron. Point out the picture of a tetrahedron in their text and explain to them that they should imagine each group of three hydrogen atoms as a plane. This plane is in the shape of a triangle.

3.a)

Students can only make two molecules if they adhere to the constraints. These are methanol (CH₃OH) and hydrazine (NH₂NH₂). They may describe the shape of the molecule at the carbon atom of methanol as a tripod; at the oxygen atom of methanol as "a boomerang;" at the nitrogen atom of hydrazine as "a pyramid." The accepted names that chemists use are: tetrahedral, bent (or angular), and trigonal pyramidal.

3.b)

Make sure that students first replace the bond between carbon and oxygen (in methanol) or between the two nitrogen atoms (in hydrazine). The reason for the flexibility of the longer gray stick will be obvious now that they have made a double bond. The methanol molecule is converted to methanal (H₂C=O, also called formaldehyde) and the hydrazine is converted to diazine (HN=NH). Students should note that the formula of each new compound

3.

As the students build an ethane molecule, emphasize to them that the bonds are covalent and represent two electrons each. To fill its valence shell, a carbon atom needs four electrons to complement its original four electrons. It does this by sharing electrons in four bonds.

3.a)

The formula of ethane is C_2H_6. Have students note that the bond between the two carbon atoms rotates freely. Tell students that free rotation is a characteristic of single bonds.

4.

Tell the students to make a double bond between the two carbon atoms of ethane. They should remember how to do this from their experience earlier in the *Investigate*. Ask students to try to gently rotate the two carbon atoms of ethene in the same way as ethane. Tell them that this rigidity is a characteristic of double bonds and leads to many interesting properties.

4.a)
The formula of ethene is C_2H_4.

4.b)

The shape of the ethene molecule at each carbon atom is called "trigonal planar."

5.

Have three students use four strings to define the geometry at each carbon atom of ethene. Make sure that the two strings representing the double bond are side-by-side.

Cookin' Chem

3. Next, join two carbon atoms from your molecular-model kit with a single bond, and add hydrogen atoms (six) to fill the valence shell with eight electrons (an octet) or four pairs of electrons. You will find there are two tetrahedrons connected by a single bond.

a) Write down the formula of the molecule you have made. This molecule is called ethane, a two-carbon hydrocarbon.

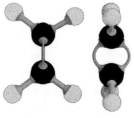

4. Replace the central bond of ethane with a longer, flexible gray stick. Remove one hydrogen atom from each carbon. Use another flexible gray stick to connect the remaining holes in each of the two carbon atoms. This makes a double bond.

a) Write down the formula of this compound. This is ethene, sometimes called ethylene.

b) Describe the shape of the atoms at either carbon atom (they are the same).

5. You have seen that the shape of a molecule containing a central carbon atom with four single bonds is tetrahedral. You have also seen that the shape of the molecule changes when a double bond is inserted.

With your group, take up the four strings again, but this time you will model a double bond. Two of the strings now form a double bond, and there are only three regions of valence shell electron repulsion to model. Make the four strings (two of them are side-by-side) as far apart as possible.

a) This geometry is called trigonal planar and is characteristic of double bonds. Why do you think it is called trigonal planar?

6. For carbon, there is one more simple arrangement of atoms containing two carbon atoms possible. Model this by removing one more hydrogen atom from each carbon atom in ethene. Then connect the two holes with another flexible gray stick. You should now have a triple bond.

a) Record the formula of this compound.

7. With your group, take up the four strings again, this time to model a triple bond. Three of the strings now form a triple bond and now there are only two regions of valence shell electron repulsion to model. Make the four strings (three of them are side-by-side) as far apart as possible.

a) Write down the formula of this compound and describe the geometry at each carbon atom.

This molecule is called ethyne, or acetylene. Acetylene is a gaseous hydrocarbon used in welding and in cutting metal.

b) The geometry is called linear and is characteristic of triple bonds. Why do you think it is called linear?

Active Chemistry

5.a)

With three strings, a planar geometry does give the greatest separation of the strings. The angle between the three strings symmetrically divides a circle into three equal sections of 120° each. It is called trigonal planar because the three regions of electrons lie in a plane which is divided into three equal parts.

6.

Have the students now make a triple bond and convert ethene to ethyne. This compound is

also often referred to by its old name, acetylene.

6.a)

Ethyne's formula is C_2H_2. Make sure the students have three of the strings side-by-side.

7.a)

The formula is C_2H_2. Students may say that the geometry of the strings describe a straight line.

7.b)

It is called linear because the carbon and hydrogen atoms are arranged in a line.

You have made several models containing carbon and recorded the three different geometries that carbon can have: tetrahedral, trigonal planar, and linear. Tetrahedral represents carbon with four single bonds, trigonal planar represents carbon with two single bonds and one double bond, and linear represents carbon with one single bond and one triple bond. Can you think of other possibilities for carbon?

Part C: Modeling Hydrocarbons

Hydrocarbons are a very large category of organic compounds containing only carbon and hydrogen. It is the unique character of the carbon atom and its many shapes and its ability to bond with itself to form very long chains of carbon atoms.

1. Build the C_2H_6 ethane molecule again. This is sometimes represented as CH_3CH_3.

2. Replace one of the hydrogen atoms with a third carbon atom. Fill in the holes of the new carbon atom with hydrogen atoms.

 a) Write down the formula of the compound you have modeled. This molecule is propane, the gas used in gas grills. It is sometimes called "bottled gas" in rural areas.

3. Replace another hydrogen atom with a carbon atom so that you have four carbons in a row. Fill in the new model with hydrogen atoms. This molecule is butane, the chemical used in cigarette lighters. Butane's boiling point is −1°C, so it will be a gas unless under pressure.

 a) Record the formula.

You could continue in this manner, removing one hydrogen atom and replacing it with a −CH_2− fragment. All compounds you make in this manner are valid, existing organic compounds. Carbon is truly amazing!

Part D: Modeling Soap Molecules

1. Take your molecule of butane and prepare to build a new molecule with your molecular-model set.

2. Remove a hydrogen atom from one of the two −CH_3 groups in your butane molecule. Replace it with only a carbon atom. Turn this bare carbon atom into a carboxyl group using the illustration shown.

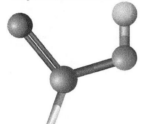

Carboxyl functional group

To do this, you need to add two oxygen atoms to the bare carbon atom. One of these will be attached with a single bond and the other will be attached with a double bond.

3. You will see that there is still one hole left unoccupied in the singly bonded oxygen atom. Add a hydrogen atom here. This is a very important oxygen atom because it makes this molecule an acid.

 a) Record the formula of this new organic compound.

may recognize that the formula increases by "CH_2" each time.

Students should be comfortable now in making an unbranched hydrocarbon of any length.

Part D: Modeling Soap Molecules

1.

Students will now make a model of the carboxylic acid functional group.

2.

The two added oxygen atoms make the carboxylic acid group very polar.

3.

The proton on the oxygen atom is highly polarized by the two oxygen atoms and forms hydrogen bonds with other electronegative groups, such as oxygen and nitrogen.

3.a)

The formula of this new organic compound is $C_5H_{10}O_2$. It is called pentanoic acid but its common name is valeric acid.

Part C: Modeling Hydrocarbons

1.

Using their kit, have students make the ethane molecule again. You might wish to have students draw ethane and attempt to render a 3-dimensional object in 2-dimensions. Most students will draw the carbon atom and its bonds as an "X." More ambitious students can attempt drawings which show some of the bonds projecting out of the paper, and other bonds extending into it. This is most often accomplished with shading or other "perspective" devices.

2.a)

The formula for this compound is C_3H_8, propane.

3.a)

The formula for butane is C_4H_{10}.

You may ask students if they see a pattern as the chain length of the hydrocarbons increases from methane through butane. Some

4.

Have students add –CH$_2$–
groups until there are 17 in a
row. Then they should complete
stearic acid with a terminal –H.

4.a)

The formula for stearic acid is
C$_{18}$H$_{36}$O$_2$, or it is sometimes
written as CH$_3$(CH$_2$)$_{16}$COOH
to emphasize that it has the acid
functional group.

Have the student play with their
model of stearic acid to show
how flexible it is and how many
shapes it can take on.

Cookin' Chem

This five-carbon acid is called
pentanoic acid, or valeric acid,
which is often found in goat cheese.
The –COOH group is one of
several functional groups in organic
chemistry. Ethanoic acid, or acetic
acid (CH$_3$COOH), is a very common
organic acid seen everyday as vinegar.

When the acid function of stearic
acid is neutralized with the base,
NaOH, it becomes sodium stearate,
a crude soap. It has a very polar
end where the oxygen atoms, the
negative charge, and the sodium
ion are located. The rest of the
molecule is simply a hydrocarbon
and very nonpolar.

Acetic acid

One unit of soap.

4. Next, construct a fatty acid by
replacing one of the hydrogen
atoms in the CH$_3$ group of
pentanoic acid with a carbon atom.
Continue this until you have a
molecule that has eighteen carbon
atoms in a row. This will create a
long chain of carbon atoms, ending
in a –COOH group. You probably
will need to combine atoms from
your kit with other groups' kits
in order to have enough.

a) This is stearic acid. Write its
formula and describe its shape.
Notice that it can be stretched
out in a long chain, or coiled in
many shapes, like a snake.

Part E: How Does Soap Work?

You are going to model how polar
and nonpolar molecules behave in the
presence of soap molecules.

1. Prepare the following models from
toothpicks and small foam spheres:
Take 20 toothpicks and 20 small
foam spheres. Attach the spheres to
the toothpicks as shown.

polar end   nonpolar end

The sphere represents the polar end of
the soap molecule, the carboxyl group.

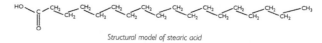
Structural model of stearic acid

Ball-and-stick model of stearic acid

620

Active Chemistry

**Part E:
How Does Soap Work?**

1.

Emphasize to students that
the soap molecule is unique in
having a small, polar group
attached to a long, nonpolar
hydrocarbon chain. These
features allow it to attract both
water, which is polar, and
grease, which is nonpolar.

Section 8 Modeling Organic Molecules: Soap

The longer toothpick portion of the molecule represents the long, non-polar hydrocarbon chain.

2. Take about 20 more foam spheres. These represent additional polar water molecules.

3. Take about 10 or 20 more toothpicks. These represent molecules on a greasy spoon or dish.

You will now use the models to figure out how soap can bring molecules of grease into soapy water. Remember, just as gasoline and water don't mix, neither do grease and water.

4. Place a large piece of white paper on your desk or lab bench. Take all of the polar "water molecules" that represent a sample of water and place them randomly all over the paper.

5. To show what happens in the absence of soap, place the non-polar "grease molecules" on the paper with the water. Put all the grease and water molecules together in a way that they have the least interaction with each other.

a) Sketch the pattern of your molecules in your *Active Chemistry* log. Label your sketch, "How water and grease molecules are arranged in a mixture of grease and water."

6. In this next step, you will model how water and grease behave in the presence of soap.

Add five "soap molecules" to your water and grease model on the sheet of paper. Using your knowledge of "like dissolving like," arrange the soap molecules as you think they would do. Start with the polar end of the soap molecule. Place this end in either the water molecules or the grease molecules.

7. Bring five molecules of grease into alignment with the nonpolar tail of the soap molecules. This helps them dissolve in the polar water molecules.

8. Continue to add more soap molecules and bring more grease molecules into solution. When you have used all 20 soap molecules, you should have a spherical arrangement with water—the solvent—all around the outside, the soap polar ends in the water, and the soap tails pointing inward, aligned with grease molecules. This structure is called a *micelle*. The grease is surrounded by soap molecules and suspended in water where it can be rinsed away.

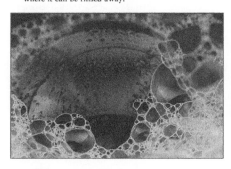

621

Active Chemistry

5.a)

Student sketches should show no mixing of water and grease. The grease molecules will be all together in one place.

6.

The polar end of the "soap molecules" should be surrounded by water molecules.

7.

The toothpicks representing grease should be brought into alignment with the nonpolar end of the soap molecules. The polar end of the soap molecules remain in water.

8.

The model of a micelle should be an oval of soap molecules surrounding the grease molecules and shielding them from the water molecules. The water molecules remain on the outside of the oval of soap molecules and attracted to the sphere of the soap molecule which represents the polar carboxyl group.

2.

Tell students that the foam spheres represent the polar water molecule. These will dissolve the polar end of the soap molecule.

3.

The toothpicks represent the nonpolar molecules found in grease and dirt. These will be attracted to the nonpolar portion of the soap molecule.

4.

Students should organize the foam spheres randomly and evenly around the paper but not use much time to do this.

5.

The "grease molecules" will be all together in one mass, not mixing with the "water molecules."

Chem Talk

The reading focuses on simple organic compounds, how to represent them in drawings, and how to interpret their shapes. The saturated hydrocarbons that are presented show that all of the carbon atoms contain four single bonds. Students also learn that hydrocarbons that contain double or triple bonds have their own unique shapes and are said to be "unsaturated." An introduction to isomers and geometric isomers is included. Since the atoms that bond to carbon are covalently bonded, there is a discussion of valence electrons and Lewis structures. Valence-shell-electron-pair-repulsion theory is used to determine geometry at each carbon atom.

The discussion concludes with an explanation of how soap interacts with both water and grease to clean clothes and dishes. The soap molecule has both a polar end as well as a nonpolar end. The nonpolar end attracts the grease and dirt while the polar end is dissolved in water. This dual nature of a soap molecule allows it to suspend dirt in water in a micelle so that the dirt can be rinsed away from the object being cleaned.

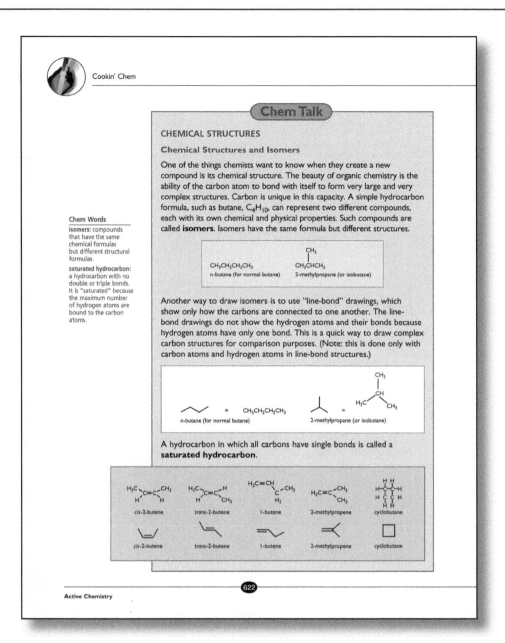

Cookin' Chem

Chem Talk

CHEMICAL STRUCTURES

Chemical Structures and Isomers

One of the things chemists want to know when they create a new compound is its chemical structure. The beauty of organic chemistry is the ability of the carbon atom to bond with itself to form very large and very complex structures. Carbon is unique in this capacity. A simple hydrocarbon formula, such as butane, C_4H_{10}, can represent two different compounds, each with its own chemical and physical properties. Such compounds are called **isomers**. Isomers have the same formula but different structures.

Another way to draw isomers is to use "line-bond" drawings, which show only how the carbons are connected to one another. The line-bond drawings do not show the hydrogen atoms and their bonds because hydrogen atoms have only one bond. This is a quick way to draw complex carbon structures for comparison purposes. (Note: this is done only with carbon atoms and hydrogen atoms in line-bond structures.)

A hydrocarbon in which all carbons have single bonds is called a **saturated hydrocarbon**.

Chem Words

isomers: compounds that have the same chemical formulas but different structural formulas.

saturated hydrocarbon: a hydrocarbon with no double or triple bonds. It is "saturated" because the maximum number of hydrogen atoms are bound to the carbon atoms.

540

Saturated Hydrocarbon Isomers Increase Geometrically In Number		
Number of Carbon atoms	Formula	Number of Isomers
One, Two, Three	CH_4, C_2H_6, C_3H_8	0
Four	C_4H_{10}	2
Five	C_5H_{12}	3
Six	C_6H_{14}	5
Seven	C_7H_{16}	9
Eight	C_8H_{18}	15
Nine	C_9H_{20}	35
Ten	$C_{10}H_{22}$	75

An **unsaturated hydrocarbon** contains one or more carbon–carbon double or triple bonds. (Remember, all carbon atoms must have four bonds!) As carbon atoms and functional groups are added, the number of isomers rises even faster. To convert butane, C_4H_{10}, into a simple unsaturated hydrocarbon, C_4H_8, two hydrogen atoms must be replaced with one double bond. To show the amazing versatility of carbon compounds, the formula, C_4H_8, represents five different isomers, each with its own physical and chemical properties. As a further example, the number of hydrocarbons with the formula C_6H_{12} is about 24.

Lewis Structures of Atoms and Molecules

Recalling the octet rule and the special stability attained in filling an electron shell, you can see that a carbon atom (in Group IVA) needs four more electrons. However, carbon almost never gives up electrons or takes on electrons. Because of this, nearly all carbon compounds are covalent and contain four bonds to other atoms. **Lewis structures** are diagrams that show only the outer-shell valence electrons. These are the electrons used in bonding. A look at the Lewis structures in the diagram of some common atoms (H, C, N, O, F) allows you to figure out how many electrons each needs to fully bond and how many bonds it will usually form. Hydrogen requires only two electrons to fill its shell for stability.

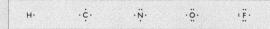

Look at a few simple molecules with full electron shells after bonding. The Lewis structures of water and methane would look as shown in the diagram. The hydrogen always has two electrons and the oxygen or carbon has eight electrons.

water   methane

Chem Words

unsaturated hydrocarbon: a hydrocarbon (organic compound) with one or more carbon-carbon double or triple bonds.

Lewis structure: a system of showing chemical structure in which the valence electrons of an atom are placed around the atom. Bonds are shown as a pair of dots or as a line. Non-bonding valence electrons are shown as dots that are not placed between the symbols or elements in the compound.

Active Chemistry

Cookin' Chem

Shared pairs of electrons between two atoms represent covalent bonds, while unshared pairs of electrons on one atom belong only to that atom. These are called "lone pairs" or "non-bonding pairs."

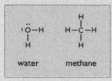

water   methane

One shorthand method for drawing structures uses a single line to represent a single bond. In this fashion, the two molecules can be drawn as shown.

You can draw very complicated structures, such as the structure of a fat molecule, in this way. As suggested previously, each atom will form a standard number of bonds, depending on how many valence electrons it has. Carbon always forms four bonds, while nitrogen forms three, oxygen forms two, and the halogens (F, Cl, Br, I), like hydrogen, form one bond. A **structural formula** of this type tells you the number of each kind of atom and how they are connected to one another. In molecules having **polar covalent bonds**, you can also deduce the polarity of the molecule by considering its geometry.

Double and Triple Bonds

Sometimes two or three bonds can form between two atoms. When double or triple bonds are formed, atoms share more than one pair of electrons. These fall into the unsaturated class of compounds and have their own unique physical and chemical properties. The two simplest of these organic compounds are ethene and ethyne, as shown in the diagram.

ethene   ethyne

Note that the "-ane" ending as in methane (ethane, propane, butane) indicates a saturated hydrocarbon. The "-ene" ending indicates an unsaturated molecule with at least one double bond. The "-yne" ending indicates an unsaturated molecule with at least one triple bond. The terms "saturated" and "unsaturated" are in reference to the total number of hydrogen atoms. An unsaturated hydrocarbon has fewer hydrogen atoms than it could have and can react to take on more hydrogens.

You observed during the investigation that single bonds allow free 360° rotation about the bond. The result of this is that the molecule can adopt many different shapes. When you made a C=C double bond, you found that it was rigid and could not be rotated without breaking the bond.

Chem Words

polar covalent bond: a bond between two atoms of different electronegativity. The center of electron density is found nearer to the more electronegative atom.

In the same way, the two carbons of a triple bond cannot be rotated without breaking the bond between them. Compounds with double and triple bonds in their structure have more rigid structures than saturated compounds. This generally results in higher melting and boiling points.

cis and trans Structures

In the *What Do You Think?* at the beginning of this section, you were shown two molecules. They had the same formula and name (C_4H_8 and 2-butene), and yet, they were clearly different molecules. The compound on the left is a **cis** isomer and the other isomer is called **trans**. Typically, a *trans* compound will be more stable than the *cis* isomer. Therefore, it is less reactive than the *cis* isomer. It will pack into a crystalline structure better and have a higher melting point.

cis-2-butene   trans-2-butene

You often hear on television that *trans*-fatty acids are bad for you and that *cis*-fatty acids are healthier in your diet. The *cis* compounds are the natural form of most fats. Enzymes can more easily digest them by breaking them into smaller molecules that your body can use.

Valence-Shell-Electron-Pair-Repulsion Theory—VSEPR

Each carbon bond is made of two shared electrons, just as with other elements' covalent bonds. As your group discovered by using the four strings representing the four bonds of methane, the molecule takes on the shape of a **tetrahedron**. This shape is formed by positioning the four bonds as far apart from each other as possible because of electrostatic repulsion by the electron pairs.

In this way, predicting the geometry of a molecule is done by using valence-shell-electron-pair-repulsion theory, or VSEPR. You modeled this when you used four strings to determine the geometry about the carbon atoms in methane (CH_4), ethene (C_2H_4), and ethyne (C_2H_2). This theory argues that the geometry of the atoms bonded to a central atom, such as carbon, is determined by the electrons found in the valence shell (bonding shell) of that carbon atom. Since bonds are composed of two electrons and all electrons are negatively charged,

Chem Words

cis- **double bond:** a geometric arrangement of a carbon to carbon double bond where the hydrogen atoms are located on the same side of the double bond.

trans- **double bond:** a geometric arrangement of a carbon to carbon double bond where the hydrogen atoms are located on opposite sides of the double bond.

tetrahedron: in geometry, a pyramid with four sides that are equilateral triangles. In chemistry, the term used for molecular structures in which there are four bonds at equal angles between each other (109.5°) around an atom.

Checking Up

1.

a) Magnesium – 2

b) Sulfur – 6

c) Neon – 8

d) Aluminum – 3

2.

cis-2-butene

trans-2-butene

3.

A micelle is a globular aggregation of molecules, including water, soap, and dirt. The dirt is suspended in the center of the micelle by its attraction to the nonpolar ends of the soap molecules. The bipolar soap molecules act as the transport medium since they are attracted to the dirt on the interior of the micelle and to water on the outside of the micelle. In this way, nonpolar dirt can be removed from clothes or dishes with the polar solvent, water, using soap as the interface between the two.

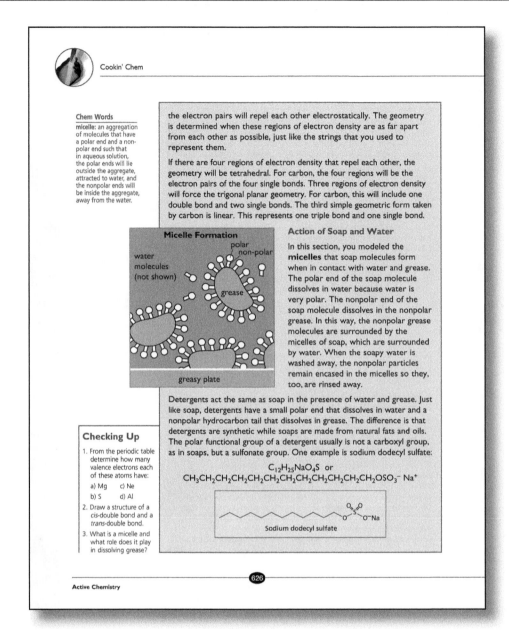

Cookin' Chem

Chem Words

micelle: an aggregation of molecules that have a polar end and a nonpolar end such that in aqueous solution, the polar ends will lie outside the aggregate, attracted to water, and the nonpolar ends will be inside the aggregate, away from the water.

the electron pairs will repel each other electrostatically. The geometry is determined when these regions of electron density are as far apart from each other as possible, just like the strings that you used to represent them.

If there are four regions of electron density that repel each other, the geometry will be tetrahedral. For carbon, the four regions will be the electron pairs of the four single bonds. Three regions of electron density will force the trigonal planar geometry. For carbon, this will include one double bond and two single bonds. The third simple geometric form taken by carbon is linear. This represents one triple bond and one single bond.

Micelle Formation

polar non-polar

water molecules (not shown)

grease

greasy plate

Action of Soap and Water

In this section, you modeled the **micelles** that soap molecules form when in contact with water and grease. The polar end of the soap molecule dissolves in water because water is very polar. The nonpolar end of the soap molecule dissolves in the nonpolar grease. In this way, the nonpolar grease molecules are surrounded by the micelles of soap, which are surrounded by water. When the soapy water is washed away, the nonpolar particles remain encased in the micelles so they, too, are rinsed away.

Detergents act the same as soap in the presence of water and grease. Just like soap, detergents have a small polar end that dissolves in water and a nonpolar hydrocarbon tail that dissolves in grease. The difference is that detergents are synthetic while soaps are made from natural fats and oils. The polar functional group of a detergent usually is not a carboxyl group, as in soaps, but a sulfonate group. One example is sodium dodecyl sulfate:

$C_{12}H_{25}NaO_4S$ or

$CH_3CH_2CH_2CH_2CH_2CH_2CH_2CH_2CH_2CH_2CH_2CH_2OSO_3^- \ Na^+$

Sodium dodecyl sulfate

Checking Up

1. From the periodic table determine how many valence electrons each of these atoms have:
   a) Mg   c) Ne
   b) S   d) Al
2. Draw a structure of a *cis*-double bond and a *trans*-double bond.
3. What is a micelle and what role does it play in dissolving grease?

626

Active Chemistry

What Do You Think Now?

Have the class reconsider the *What Do You See?* illustration and the *What Do You Think?* question. They should now draw greater insight from the water interaction with a soap molecule. Additionally, they should be able to describe the difference between the *cis* and *trans* forms of the molecules in concrete, chemical terms. The discussion should focus on the restriction that is placed on the double bond between the two carbons. The single bond between the carbon atoms allows free rotation between the carbon atoms and the double bond prevents this free rotation.

What Do You Think Now?

At the beginning of the section you were asked to describe the differences between two molecules that have the same numbers of carbons and hydrogens.

You now have made models of the two molecules. Building a model and holding it in your hand is the best way to become familiar with the shape of a molecule. The two molecules are not identical. What is it about the C=C double bond that makes it different from a C—C single bond?

Chem
Essential Questions

What does it mean?

Chemistry explains a *macroscopic* phenomenon (what you observe) with a description of what happens at the *nanoscopic* level (atoms and molecules) using *symbolic* structures as a way to communicate. Complete the chart below in your *Active Chemistry* log.

MACRO	NANO	SYMBOLIC
Describe two properties of soap that you have observed when washing dishes or washing your hands	Describe a soap molecule in terms of its structure	Draw a line-bond model for a soap molecule.

How do you know?

What are the different types of symbolic structures explored in this section? Which symbolic structure would be the best for predicting the number of bonds an atom will form? Which symbolic structure would be best for predicting the bond geometry about an atom?

Why do you believe?

Diamond is one of the hardest substances known, so it is very difficult to break. Graphite is so soft and slippery that it is often used as a lubricant. (This property makes graphite a good writing material because it helps the point of your pencil slide easily across the paper, leaving a trail of graphite bits behind.) Yet both diamonds and graphite are pure carbon. What do you think accounts for their different properties?

Why should you care?

For the completion of your cooking show you will want to wash up the dirty dishes. To do this, it will be helpful to have a solid understanding of soap's chemical structure and how it forms micelles. Explaining to your audience how dirt and grease are removed will help convince viewers that you are tidy and competent. Using models in your presentation will help the cooking show audience understand how soap works.

627

Chem Essential Questions

What does it mean?

MACRO — Two major properties that students may mention are "slippery" and "foamy in water." They may also note that it is soluble in water. Color and odor may be mentioned, but they are due to chemicals added and irrelevant to the question.

NANO — Student descriptions should mention a small, polar functional group at one end of the soap molecule and a long, nonpolar hydrocarbon chain which makes up the rest of the molecule.

SYMBOLIC —

$$Na^+ \; {}^-O - C \; \wedge\wedge\wedge\wedge\wedge\wedge$$

How do you know?

The symbolic structures used in this section include the simple formula, the condensed structure, the line-bond structure, the VSEPR model, and the Lewis dot structure. The best symbolic structure to use for predicting the number of bonds an atom will form is the Lewis dot structure. The best for predicting bond geometry is the VSEPR model.

Why do you believe?

Even though each substance is composed of the same set of identical atoms, those atoms are connected to each other in very different ways, and that difference produces enormous differences in properties of the materials. Diamond is composed of carbon atoms arranged in a very regular, rigid lattice structure, where each carbon atom is covalently bonded to four others, each bonded to four others. The crystal formed is extremely hard and strong, because each atom is surrounded and held in place by others surrounded and held in place by still others.

Graphite, in contrast, forms a similar lattice structure, but with each atom bonded to only three other carbon atoms. This change in structure produces flat (rather than three dimensional) sheets of carbon atoms, tightly attached to each other, but only very loosely held to adjoining sheets. These sheets of atoms slide past each other very easily, producing the lubricant properties of graphite.

The differences in these two materials are caused strictly by differences in the way that their atoms are connected to each other, i.e., their bonding. Understanding the structures of these materials is essential to understanding their properties and behavior.

Why should you care?

Answers will vary, but students should show the structure of soap and describe its polar and nonpolar parts. They should also show how micelles to carry dirt away and how micelle formation is due to the structure and polarity of soap.

Reflecting on the Section and the Challenge

Students review what they have learned about using models to represent molecules and molecular shapes and properties. They have learned several ways to draw molecules, depending on their purpose, and how to predict the bond geometry at each atom. They can use this information as they prepare to meet the Challenge later in the Section.

Chem to Go

1.

The shapes of the two molecules are different. In the first molecule, *trans*-2-pentene, the double bond has hydrogen atoms on opposite sides of the double bond. The second molecule, *cis*-2-pentene, has hydrogen atoms on the same side.

2.

The isomers are
$CH_2 = CHOH$

3.

The molecules are the same. Different orientation in space does not change the molecule.

4.

a)

b)

c)

d)

Cookin' Chem

Reflecting on the Section and the Challenge

The world is filled with millions of different organic compounds that serve a myriad of purposes. In order to fully understand the differences in function, you have to look at both the macroscopic properties of those compounds and the properties that arise at the atomic level. The ways that atoms are connected and the three-dimensional shape of the molecules contribute to the properties of a material. You can draw diagrams and build models of those molecules to better visualize and understand the structures of substances, and, in turn, their properties. Understanding the structure of a soap molecule can help you understand its properties and how it is an effective cleaning agent.

Chem to Go

1. Are the shapes of these two molecules different? If so, why?

2. Draw all reasonable structures for a compound with the formula C_2H_4O. Remember, isomers have the same formula but different structures. (Hint: There are three isomers.)

3. Are these two molecules different or the same? Explain.

4. Draw the Lewis structure of each of the following atoms. Use the Roman numeral group number in the periodic table for the number of valence electrons.
   a) N   b) S   c) F   d) Ar

5. How many bonds will each of the atoms in *Question 4* make to complete their octet? Which atom cannot form bonds?

6. a) Draw the Lewis dot structure of ammonia, NH_3.
   b) Make the model of ammonia, or draw the three-dimensional structure, using lines for bonds.
   c) In your own words, compare the geometry of ammonia with the geometry of methane, CH_4.

628

Active Chemistry

5.

All except argon can make bonds. N can make 3, F can make 1, and S can make 2 (although students may learn in higher levels of chemistry that through hybridization of orbitals S can make 4 if sp^3d hybridized and 6 if sp^3d^2 hybridized, but this is not the time to bring this up).

6.a-c)

The ammonia molecule has

trigonal pyramidal geometry while methane has tetrahedral geometry. Students' words will likely be different.

7.a)

Chemical structure of ethanol

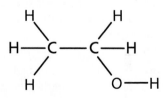

546

Section 8 Modeling Organic Molecules: Soap

7. The following problems are about ethanol (grain alcohol), CH_3CH_2OH.

   a) Using a line to represent each bond, draw the chemical structure for ethanol.

   b) How many bonds does each carbon atom make? Does carbon always make the same number of bonds? Why?

8. Explain why the presence of a carbon–carbon double bond makes it possible to have *cis/trans* isomers. Why cannot carbon–carbon single bonds or triple bonds have *cis/trans* isomers? Use your models to help answer this question, if necessary.

9. The structure below represents a fat that could be used to make a soap. Draw the chemical structure of one unit of soap in the *cis* form that would be created by reacting this fat with three units of NaOH.

10. *Preparing for the Chapter Challenge*

    In the *Chapter Challenge*, you might want to explain how grease and dirt are removed from your hands, kitchen tools and countertop. You can use models to represent the various molecules (water, soap, and grease) involved. Your audience should be reminded that "like dissolves like" in the same sense they understand "birds of a feather flock together" and "gasoline and water don't mix." They will make the connection that the long hydrocarbon portion of the soap molecule mixes well with the long hydrocarbon molecules found in grease. Also, the small polar end of the soap molecule will attract the very polar water molecules. It might be helpful to have a detailed sketch of a micelle or even a model using toothpicks and foam spheres.

629

Active Chemistry

7.b)

Carbon always makes four bonds, because it has four valence electrons, and needs four more to fill its second energy level with electrons and reach a stable state. Its four valence electrons pair with four valence electrons from other atoms to form four bonds with a total of eight electrons.

8.

The rigidity of the double bond makes it possible to have *cis-trans* isomers. The two ends of the double bond can be different and non-interchangeable. Carbon-carbon single bonds can rotate through 360° and therefore cannot have fixed positions. The carbon-carbon triple bond is symmetrical, no matter what is attached to it.

9.

10.

Preparing for the Chapter Challenge

Students can begin to prepare for their presentation for the *Chapter Challenge*.

SECTION 8 – QUIZ

| 7-8a | **Blackline Master** |

1. Why do these two molecules have different shapes?

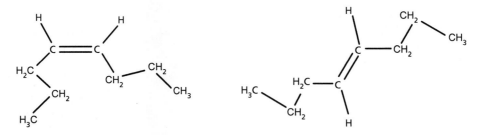

2. For each of the following, draw a Lewis structure.

   a) a neon atom

   b) C_2H_6

3. Why do carbon atoms form tetrahedral structures?

4. 2–methyl-2-propanol has three carbon atoms and an –OH group all connected to a central carbon atom. The chemical formula is C_4H_9OH. Draw a structural diagram of this molecule.

SECTION 8 – QUIZ ANSWERS

❶ The molecules have different shapes because the *cis* double bond in the first molecule causes a bend or kink in the molecule, and the *trans* double bond in the second molecule does not.

❷ a) b)

```
          H   H
          ..  ..
 ..    H : C : C : H
: Ne :    ..  ..
 ..       H   H
```

❸ Chemical bonds are made of electron pairs. Electrons are negative and these electron pairs repel each other. Carbon atoms have four single bonds and the most stable structure for four repelling electron pairs is the tetrahedral structure. In this 3-dimensional structure, the bonds are farthest apart in the tetrahedral geometry.

❹ 2-methyl-2-propanol alcohol, C_4H_9OH

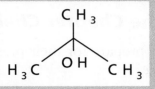

NOTES

Chapter Assessment

Chem You Learned

The chemistry content covered in this chapter is listed in the *Student Edition* at the end of the chapter. This is a good time to evaluate your students' comprehension of the material. You may want to suggest that they help each other in reviewing those concepts that may need reinforcement. You may also want to point out that the *Chem You Learned* section is a handy checklist of the chemistry concepts they might want to incorporate into their *Chapter Challenge*.

Cookin' Chem

Chem You Learned

- There are three ways in which heat energy is transferred: **conduction**, **convection**, and **radiation**. In real situations, these often occur in combination.

- Fuels undergo oxidation during a **combustion reaction**. The complete combustion of **hydrocarbons** results in two products: water and CO_2.

- In the combustion of a hydrocarbon, the reaction equation is **balanced** when there are the same number of C, H, and O atoms in the **reactants** and in the **products**.

- In a **quantitative analysis**, measurements are required. In a **qualitative analysis**, observations are sufficient.

- The **specific heat capacity** of a substance is the amount of heat energy required to raise 1 g of that substance by 1°C. For water this value is 1 cal/g·°C.

- The study of the **heat energy** contained in the chemical bonds of a fuel is called **thermochemistry**.

- When a substance is changing state, the temperature remains constant. This includes the processes of boiling and **condensation**, as well as **freezing** and **fusion (melting)**.

- A **heating-curve diagram** can be generated by graphing the temperature data vs. the time of heating, assuming the heat input to be constant.

- The **heat of fusion** of a substance is the heat energy required to change 1 gram from solid to liquid at constant temperature. For water, the value is 80 cal/g.

- An **alloy** is a solution of one or more substances in a metal to produce a hybrid substance with improved properties. Chromium in steel makes it more resistant to rust.

- **Amino acids** are organic compounds with at least two **functional groups**, the amine group and the carboxylic acid group. The 20 natural amino acids are the building blocks of the enormous biomolecules, **proteins**.

- The structure of proteins is described at three levels. The **primary structure** shows the sequence in which the amino acids are chemically bonded to form the protein. The **secondary structure** shows the coils and folds of the protein's segments. The **tertiary structure** shows the distinct three-dimensional structure of the protein.

- As the term relates to cooking, **denaturation** refers to changes in the secondary and tertiary structures, but not to the primary structure. This usually leads to a loss in solubility, as well as chemical and biological properties.

- **Organic chemistry**, or carbon chemistry, is an important aspect of cooking chemistry. Fats, oils, proteins, sugars, hydrocarbons, amino acids, and soap are all based on organic chemistry.

- When a small clump of soap molecules encircles a "dirt" particle, it is called a **micelle**.

- The **Lewis dot structure** of an atom or molecule represents the valence electrons of the atoms.

- The geometry of a molecule can be predicted using **valence-shell-electron-pair-repulsion theory**.

Chem Chapter Challenge

A brief review of the requirements for fulfilling the *Chapter Challenge* reminds students that the cooking show segment they will be producing can be either live action, a video tape, or a voice-over and can deal with any type of cuisine. It can be serious or humorous, but must be informative and provide a detailed explanation of the chemistry involved. Make sure that the students are very clear on the expectations and invite them to discuss any questions or uncertainties that they might have.

Chemistry Content

In addition, there is a complete listing of this chapter's sections with short descriptions of the investigations that were conducted in each one. This list is a very helpful summary that will remind students of the various experiments they completed during the course of this chapter. They can skim through their *Active Chemistry* logs to recount the various chemical concepts that were addressed in each section. This list can be used as a map to locate material related to specific principles and can inspire ideas for their cooking show segment.

Chem Chapter Challenge

As you assemble ideas and information for your five minute cooking segment you will be completing a second round of the *Engineering Design Cycle*. The *Goal* and criteria are slightly expanded from the *Mini-Challenge* and your list of *Inputs* has also grown. You now have more information about adding heat to food and the role of molecular structure in cooking and cleaning up, too. You also have the *Feedback* you received during the *Mini-Challenge* to get you started and help guide your efforts.

Goal

Each group has already tested out creating and presenting one cooking segment. As you complete the *Chapter Challenge* you will use the *Engineering Design Cycle* to improve and expand your segment or create a brand new one. Go back and quickly read the challenge description at the start of the chapter. You will find all of the details for completing the entire challenge there. You should also review the rubric your class generated to determine the way your group's presentation will be graded. You will want to make sure you address each aspect of the rubric completely so that your team can earn the highest possible grade.

The *Goal* is the objective you are trying to reach or the problem you need to solve in the *Engineering Design Cycle*. The *Goal* for this *Chapter Challenge* is to create an entertaining and informative five minute cooking show segment that gives a detailed explanation of the chemistry involved. Your segment can be live action, a video tape, or even a voice-over of an actual show. You can bring your cultural heritage into view by focusing on ethnic food. Your show may be humorous or serious. It could deal with cafeteria food or gourmet food from a five-star restaurant. The show should be interesting and entertaining. It must include correct chemistry content. In addition to the presentation, you have to submit a script for the show that includes a discussion of the chemistry involved.

Inputs

The *Inputs* for the *Engineering Design Cycle* include all of the resources you have to help you complete the *Chapter Challenge*. Each one of the chapter sections has provided you with information on adding heat to food or the role of molecular structures in the kitchen. You have a number of resources to draw on as inspiration for your segment format. You can use footage from any number of existing food shows, personal kitchen experiences, hands-on demonstrations, or even some form of reenactment of cooking to showcase the cooking process. When you decide on the format of your cooking segment you will be limited to the technology resources that you have available in your classroom, so be sure to check with your teacher if you need to show pre-recorded footage.

All of the *Inputs* for this challenge will help determine the success of the *Cookin' Chem* show your class produces. As your group reviews the chemistry you have learned, be sure to pay special attention to the *Reflecting on the Section and the Challenge, Chem Essential Questions,* and *Preparing for the Chapter Challenge* portions of the text. You should also review your *Active Chemistry* log for notes that

Active Chemistry

Criteria for Success

Students should be preparing to start their *Chapter Challenge* projects now that they have completed all the sections and the *Mini-Challenge*. They will need to develop a comprehensive assessment rubric to determine how their projects will be graded. It is critical that they be responsible for deciding the criteria and scoring system so they know exactly what is expected and how their projects will be judged before they start.

On the facing page is a sample assessment rubric for the *Chapter Challenge*. You can copy and distribute it as is, or use it as a foundation for developing scoring guidelines and expectations that suit your own particular needs. For example, you might wish to ensure that core concepts and abilities derived from our local or state science frameworks also appear on the rubric.

Students may decide to vary the point value of the different criteria categories. In the example, Content value is potentially worth 60 points, Presentation value is worthy 30 points and Group interaction is worth 10 points. Students may decide to change the balance and put a higher value on Group interaction.

However you decide to evaluate the *Chapter Challenge*, it is essential that all expectations be communicated to students before they begin work on the *Chapter Challenge*.

Cookin' Chem

you recorded during each section. The brief section summaries listed here will give you an overview of the information you have learned to help get you started.

Section 1 You learned about convection, conduction, and radiation as ways of heating food.

Section 2 You learned about fires, fire safety, and the chemical reactions in combustion. This included writing balanced chemical equations for combustion.

Section 3 You extended your knowledge of combustion to compare cooking fuels and calculate the energy released when hydrocarbons or alcohol burn.

Section 4 You investigated the change in temperature as water is heated to its boiling point and again while the water is boiling.

Section 5 You investigated the change in temperature as water is cooled to its freezing point and again while the water is freezing.

Section 6 You explored the concept of specific heat capacity and how it relates to materials used in cookware.

Section 7 You investigated the effect of temperature and pH on egg protein. This gave you an understanding of proteins and denaturation.

Section 8 You learned about molecular structure and Lewis dot diagrams. Understanding the shapes of molecules is crucial to understanding how the molecules interact with each other and how the interactions create the behavior of substances like soap.

Process

The *Process* step of the *Engineering Design Cycle* is where you turn your ideas into products. The first part of creating your cooking segment is a very creative one. Your group will need to agree on a format for your presentation. You will need to compare and contrast whether your group would prefer to create their own show or simply explain what is going on in a show that was created by someone else. Creating your own show will obviously be a much more

creative process, but it will also require much more discipline within your group because the possibilities are only limited by time and your imagination. Your group will have to schedule carefully to make sure that you allow plenty of time to complete the entire challenge, not just the creative portion.

The chemistry knowledge you have learned can be used to explain the straightforward process of boiling an egg, or the much more complicated process of creating an elaborate holiday entrée. Because the *Goal* of this challenge is thoroughly explaining cooking chemistry, most of your group's efforts should be focused on the details. You should complete a very methodical analysis of the cooking steps that are included in your show and ask your group "why do we do that?" and "how do we do that?" for each step in the cooking process. The chemistry you have learned will apply directly, but you will probably have to do some research to answer those two simple questions thoroughly. One question, for example, could be "What is a frying pan made of?" Look at several manufacturers' Web sites for the product details. What are those materials good for? Are they all the same? Cookbooks and cooking Web sites will offer good definitions for cooking terms and information about desired outcomes

632

Active Chemistry

Be sure that the students actively participate in deciding the criteria for evaluation and the guidelines for scoring.

The *Sample Assessment Rubric* is also provided as a Blackline Master on the *Teacher Resources* CD.

7b | **Blackline Master**

SAMPLE ASSESSMENT RUBRIC FOR CHAPTER 7

	MEETS THE STANDARD OF EXCELLENCE	APPROACHES THE STANDARD OF EXCELLENCE	MEETS AN ACCEPTABLE STANDARD	BELOW ACCEPTABLE STANDARD
CONTENT CRITERIA				
Chemistry Concepts	At least seven chemistry concepts are effectively applied in the cooking techniques, fuel, and/or cookware used. **30**	At least five chemistry concepts are applied in the cooking, fuel, or cookware. **20-29**	At least three chemistry concepts are effectively applied. **10-19**	Less than three chemistry concepts are effectively applied. **0-9**
Scientific Explanations	Clear explanations for each chemical concept are provided. **15**	Explanations of the chemical concepts are provided but they lack somewhat in clarity, or are not complete. **10-14**	Explanations of chemical concepts are unclear or incomplete. **5-9**	Explanations are inaccurate or are not provided. **0-4**
PRESENTATION CRITERIA				
Written Script	The script is well written, creative, entertaining, and effectively incorporates the chemistry explanations. **20**	The script is organized, entertaining, and covers most of the essential chemistry. **13-19**	The script doesn't effectively incorporate all of the chemistry concepts and/or needs better organization. **6-12**	The script does not address all the chemistry, is poorly written and disorganized. **0-5**
Demonstration	The cooking segment is well rehearsed, entertaining, and an effective demonstration of the chemistry concepts. **25**	The cooking segment demonstration is an acceptable demonstration of the chemistry. **17-24**	The cooking segment demonstration is a little disorganized or unclear. **8-16**	The segment is not effective. **0-7**
GROUP INTERACTIONS				
Teamwork	The project is executed by interactive teamwork, with all members of the group cooperating and actively engaged. **10**	Group members showed effort to work constructively, but interactions lacked cooperative teamwork. **6-9**	Some group members worked constructively, but project lacked teamwork interaction. **3-5**	There is little or no indication of group interaction or effort to work together as a team. **0-2**

Preparing for the Chapter Challenge

The *Chapter Challenge* is the opportunity for students to review all the material in the chapter and find a creative way of interpreting that content. The *Preparing for the Chapter Challenge* sections in the text guide the students toward a successful project and the pages in the front matter of this *Teacher's Edition* provide the instructional rationale for this problem-based learning model.

In the *Chapter Challenge* preparations, remind students that the best presentations will not only be entertaining and effective, they should also demonstrate a working knowledge of the chemistry content. The more chemistry concepts that can be successfully included in their chemistry show, the stronger their presentation.

Prior to students beginning the *Chapter Challenge*, you should repeat the discussion you had at the start of the chapter and have the class agree on the rubric and standards of excellence.

Allow time for students to review the *Manage Your Time* section at the end of the chapter and make sure that they allow enough time to accomplish the tasks and that all members of each group actively participate. Also remind them that the cooking show segment should only last five minutes so their show should be well rehearsed, with all components labeled and arranged in order of use.

No doubt many of the *Cookin' Chem* projects created by the students will be highly entertaining as well as informative. You may want to put together a presentation of some of the most impressive segments to be viewed by a larger audience so that other students, teachers, and administration members can enjoy the effort, creativity, and knowledge shown.

NOTES

_____

_____

_____

_____

_____

_____

_____

_____

_____

_____

for particular cooking techniques, like baking, frying, and roasting. Your research will require you to combine information from at least two sources to provide thorough explanations for your cooking segment.

The research you do will tell you the specifics of what materials are used in a particular cooking technique. Your group will need to use the chemistry you learned to explain why those materials are effective for creating the desired result. If comedy is your target, you could use your chemistry knowledge to explain why some "good" cooking ideas would not work, like baking bread in a microwave. You will be learning along the way and can be excited about how you will share what you have learned. If your excitement shows in your presentation it will add to the entertainment value of the segment you have designed.

Outputs

The products that you deliver during an *Engineering Design Cycle* are the *Outputs*. The *Outputs* for this challenge are your cooking show segment presentations. Along with the presentation you are also required to submit a written script that includes thorough explanations of the chemistry that is employed in your segment. The format that your group chooses for your segment will have a large influence on your *Outputs*. If you are doing a voice-over of a professionally produced video segment, you have much less production work to do than a group who actually cooks something in front of the class. However, your explanations will likely be more complicated because you can't modify the cooking process to align with all of your new chemistry cooking knowledge.

Your group should make sure to include each component listed in the class rubric for your presentation. The rubric will clearly describe the products you must deliver to earn the points associated with that component. Plan to have each person of your group contribute equally to the final project. Time will be limited, so make sure everyone has a role that allows them to be working during the entire time. Set deadlines for each product so you will have time to review everybody's work as a group and make any necessary corrections prior to your final presentation. If you are creating your own video footage, make sure you leave time to film and edit your footage. If you are giving a live presentation, make sure you set aside time to practice your presentation and make any necessary changes. When you change your presentation, make sure to make the same changes to the script you will submit to your instructor.

Feedback

Your instructor and your classmates will give you *Feedback* on your cooking segment presentation. This *Feedback* will likely become part of your grade, indicating how successful your group was at meeting the *Chapter Challenge*, but it could also be useful for additional design iterations. Do not forget that you will be viewing other design solutions for the same challenge. The different group presentations may represent *Feedback* in the form of presenting alternatives you may have considered in the design of your cooking segment. The variety of design solutions should reflect the fact that there are endless ways to satisfy the criteria of the challenge.

633

Active Chemistry

they have learned in this chapter. It is unlikely that students will conceive of a process that works perfectly the first time it is tried. They will have to troubleshoot and experiment, and in some cases, make adjustments and modifications. For example, their first try at putting together a cooking segment may take too long or may not have all the desired results. Their efforts at this point would be to modify the procedure so that it goes faster, or is more effective. It would then be advisable to rehearse the show to ensure that their modifications have the desired results.

Students should be well equipped to do this because they understand most of the underlying chemical principles. They should be able to make informed predictions and approach modifications with a knowledge of how results will change when conditions are altered.

Engineering Design Cycle

Have students revisit the *Engineering Design Cycle* process they applied to the *Mini-Challenge* for their first-try chemistry shows. What adjustments will they need to make to achieve success in the *Chapter Challenge*? Now that students know more about chemical reactions and have a better understanding of the chemical principles behind them, they can incorporate this information to improve their design by beginning the design cycle again.

The *Chapter Challenge* asks students to design a process in order to develop a cooking show segment based on the chemistry

Chem Connections to Other Sciences

Students gain understanding of the interdisciplinary aspects of chemistry when they are actively engaged in thinking about the connections between the sciences. This section provides a glimpse of the interconnections between the content in this chapter and other scientific disciplines. Brief sketches relate students' study of chemistry concepts to biology, physics, and Earth science.

Encourage students to draw analogies with science connections they are familiar with while discussing the science connections. The chemistry concepts discussed in this chapter hold true in every branch of science, and can provide scientists in other fields with new insights. Emphasize the growing interdisciplinary approach to science and the need for scientists who have a broader view of science. Discuss how scientists try to understand phenomena by studying a problem from different points of view. Encourage the appreciation for chemistry in relation to the broader framework of science by describing the increase in demand for scientists with interdisciplinary backgrounds (for example, geochemistry, biochemistry, and chemical physics).

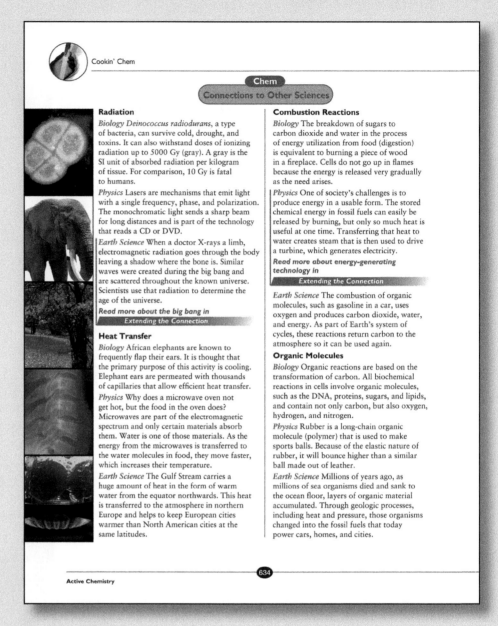

Cookin' Chem

Chem Connections to Other Sciences

Radiation

Biology Deinococcus radiodurans, a type of bacteria, can survive cold, drought, and toxins. It can also withstand doses of ionizing radiation up to 5000 Gy (gray). A gray is the SI unit of absorbed radiation per kilogram of tissue. For comparison, 10 Gy is fatal to humans.

Physics Lasers are mechanisms that emit light with a single frequency, phase, and polarization. The monochromatic light sends a sharp beam for long distances and is part of the technology that reads a CD or DVD.

Earth Science When a doctor X-rays a limb, electromagnetic radiation goes through the body leaving a shadow where the bone is. Similar waves were created during the big bang and are scattered throughout the known universe. Scientists use that radiation to determine the age of the universe.

Read more about the big bang in
> Extending the Connection

Heat Transfer

Biology African elephants are known to frequently flap their ears. It is thought that the primary purpose of this activity is cooling. Elephant ears are permeated with thousands of capillaries that allow efficient heat transfer.

Physics Why does a microwave oven not get hot, but the food in the oven does? Microwaves are part of the electromagnetic spectrum and only certain materials absorb them. Water is one of those materials. As the energy from the microwaves is transferred to the water molecules in food, they move faster, which increases their temperature.

Earth Science The Gulf Stream carries a huge amount of heat in the form of warm water from the equator northwards. This heat is transferred to the atmosphere in northern Europe and helps to keep European cities warmer than North American cities at the same latitudes.

Combustion Reactions

Biology The breakdown of sugars to carbon dioxide and water in the process of energy utilization from food (digestion) is equivalent to burning a piece of wood in a fireplace. Cells do not go up in flames because the energy is released very gradually as the need arises.

Physics One of society's challenges is to produce energy in a usable form. The stored chemical energy in fossil fuels can easily be released by burning, but only so much heat is useful at one time. Transferring that heat to water creates steam that is then used to drive a turbine, which generates electricity.

Read more about energy-generating technology in
> Extending the Connection

Earth Science The combustion of organic molecules, such as gasoline in a car, uses oxygen and produces carbon dioxide, water, and energy. As part of Earth's system of cycles, these reactions return carbon to the atmosphere so it can be used again.

Organic Molecules

Biology Organic reactions are based on the transformation of carbon. All biochemical reactions in cells involve organic molecules, such as the DNA, proteins, sugars, and lipids, and contain not only carbon, but also oxygen, hydrogen, and nitrogen.

Physics Rubber is a long-chain organic molecule (polymer) that is used to make sports balls. Because of the elastic nature of rubber, it will bounce higher than a similar ball made out of leather.

Earth Science Millions of years ago, as millions of sea organisms died and sank to the ocean floor, layers of organic material accumulated. Through geologic processes, including heat and pressure, those organisms changed into the fossil fuels that today power cars, homes, and cities.

634

Active Chemistry

Consider developing an interdisciplinary lesson plan that investigates how key chemistry concepts are applied in different sciences. Groups would select a topic and determine how it relates to biology, physics, and Earth science based on their reading of *Chem Connections to Other Sciences*, and how it relates to the key chemistry concepts. A set of questions can be constructed for students to focus on, allowing them to build a constructive inquiry. A group member could write down the highlights of their discussion. Once students have recorded the focal points of their group discussions, bring together the whole class and have a volunteer from each group share the major points of their discussion of science connections.

Extending the Connection

THE BIG BANG THEORY

The observation of the skies played an important role in all highly developed ancient civilizations. These celestial observations helped them begin to develop an understanding of the universe. Many, however, believed the observed skies were able to influence life on Earth and predict future events. For centuries the study of astrology, which connects celestial events with events on Earth, and astronomy, the study of the universe, were very closely related. Astrology and astronomy gradually came to be recognized as separate fields. Some people may still believe that the position of stars and other celestial bodies can provide explanations of events on Earth, but to the scientific community, astrology is a pseudoscience. It does not stand up to the test of observable evidence and repeatable data.

Astronomers, on the other hand, use scientific methods to investigate and develop explanations about the nature and origin of the universe. Like all other scientists, astronomers build on the work of others who came before them to increase their understanding.

Modern astronomy has benefited from modern physical science to form one of the most important, fundamental understandings to emerge in the twentieth century—that matter, energy, space, time, and the laws and rules that govern their behavior comprise the universe.

Astronomers and other physical scientists generally agree that the universe emerged from the very rapid expansion of a hot and infinitely dense "primordial atom" about 13.5 billion years ago. That event has become known as the "big bang." Unlike astrology, which does not stand up to either scientific or mathematical analysis, the big bang theory is well supported. It shows that the universe is still expanding and cooling, and will continue to do so long after the Sun has completed its life cycle.

Microwave Radiation as Proof of the Big Bang

An important piece of evidence for the big bang theory was discovered by accident when two scientists noticed their sensitive satellite-tracking telescope was plagued by a low-frequency background hiss. After carefully checking their instruments—including removing pigeon droppings from the telescope—they realized that they were actually measuring what is today known as Cosmic Microwave Background radiation (CMB). The CMB, which had been predicted by other astronomers, is the heat left over from the big bang.

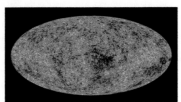

This image shows temperature fluctuations in the full sky. Red areas are zones of greater heat and blue areas are colder. The difference between the two is only about 0.0002°.

The big bang theory also predicts the formation and abundance of various atoms—particularly the lighter elements like hydrogen and helium. The creation of more massive elements allowed for the formation of the planets throughout the universe. Current observations confirm that the actual composition of the universe is consistent with what scientists predicted would have resulted from the big bang.

634A

Extending the Connection

The *Chem Connections to Other Sciences* show students that the chemistry concepts they studied in each chapter are also basic to many other sciences. The chemistry they are learning is fundamental in the understanding of the concepts that they will study in all the other sciences. *Extending the Connection* delves deeper into one or two of these connections. It gives students an opportunity to examine a particular relationship to another science in greater depth.

Cookin' Chem

Extending the Connection

THE ENVIRONMENTAL COSTS OF ENERGY-GENERATING TECHNOLOGY

As human populations increase, so does the demand for reliable and affordable energy. In the United States, power plants transform the potential energy in fossil fuels or radioactive uranium into electrical energy, which is distributed to users on a vast, interconnected network of electrical power transmission lines called the "power grid."

A modern electrical transfer station.

Water—a plentiful resource with a huge heat capacity—is the medium used to transfer energy from the fuel to electricity-generating turbines. The turbines' kinetic energy is transformed into electrical potential energy that is available to users connected to the power grid.

That system works, but those transfers and transformations are not very efficient. In a modern nuclear power plant, only one-third of the energy released in the reactor is actually transformed into electrical potential energy. The other two-thirds are considered "waste heat" that can harm nearby ecosystems. Nuclear power plants often are built alongside rivers and rely on the intake of large amounts of fresh, cool water. That water is circulated through heat exchangers inside the reactors to absorb and carry away any excess heat. When the heated water is released back into the river, many fish, microorganisms, plants, and animals are killed. It is estimated that over a billion fish are killed annually as a result of "thermal pollution."

Today, more power plants are using "closed" systems that get rid of waste heat by using cooling towers, where much of the heat is dissipated into the atmosphere through evaporative cooling. The cooled water is then recycled back into the reactor to pick up more heat rather than being discharged directly into the environment.

Nuclear power generation also results in small amounts of radioactive material escaping into the atmosphere and being distributed around the plant, particularly downwind of the plant. Slightly elevated levels of certain radio isotopes have been measured in the human population around some nuclear power plants. Efforts must be made to limit exposure to radioactive materials.

Retrofitting old plants and building new plants with closed cooling systems and new reduced-emissions technology is a costly process. Efforts to balance the economic, health, and environmental costs of providing energy to meet the ever-increasing demands of a growing population often result in heated political and legal conflicts among consumers, environmental groups, and the power industry.

are there any geographic, ethnic, gender, or educational specifications for people who use chemistry in their professions. As the *Chem at Work* profiles show, people from a wide variety of backgrounds use chemistry for an equally wide range of purposes as part of their jobs.

Many common occupations that don't seem related to chemistry actually are. For example, one wouldn't generally associate chemistry with a chef or a caterer, but obviously, there are connections.

You may want to open a discussion on various occupations that students are interested in and how chemistry might relate to some of them.

For your convenience, all three full-length *Chem at Work* profiles are provided as Blackline Masters on the *Teacher Resources* CD.

Chem at Work

René Fernandez
Chef/Restaurateur, San Antonio, TX

Most chefs use heat to prepare meat, poultry, and fish. Direct or indirect heat fuels a chemical process resulting in the denaturization of the protein. The result is sizzling meat that is ready to eat. But heat isn't the only way to cook protein. Protein can be "cooked" in another way—using acid.

René Fernandez is a chef and restaurateur. One of his specialties is a dish called "ceviche" (pronounced say-vee-chay). It is a traditional dish in many Latin American and Caribbean cultures. Ceviche uses the acid from citrus fruits to cook fresh fish into a spicy, fish stew. Usually served cold, it makes a juicy and refreshing meal perfect for lunch on a hot tropical beach.

The fish is placed in a marinade made of lime juice, which has a high concentration of citric acid. Spices and vegetables are added for flavor. Within hours, the acid breaks down the peptide bonds in the raw fish meat, just like heat would. Acid cooks the meat! Chef René says, "The concentration of acid in lime (or limónes) is just right for cooking. I have tried to make ceviche using other fruit juices like pineapple and lemon, but the concentration is either too weak or too strong. Acid can overcook, just like when using heat."

The fish is marinated with spices and vegetables in addition to the lime. When the time is right for the acid to stop cooking, he drains the marinade or adds a neutralizer. Water dilutes the acid enough to stop the stew from overcooking. More marinade is added for flavor and it is ready to serve.

Chef René developed his many ceviche recipes while he was traveling through the Caribbean and South America. He has worked for resort hotels in Puerto Rico, Brazil, Aruba, Guatemala, and all over Mexico. He varies the ingredients and flavors, but each dish is an example of chemical cooking.

Katricia Kelly
Caterer, Las Vegas, NV

Kat Kelly's dinner parties were a local legend in Las Vegas, NV. She parlayed that skill into a successful business, Top Kat Katering. She couldn't do her job without chemistry. "You can see it on the grill," she says, "when a steak turns from red to brown. Whatever you cook, a chemical change is going to take place."

Sarah Johnston
Executive Director, NOFA, Fultonville, NY

Pesticides are widely used by farmers around the world. Sarah Johnston, the Executive Director of the Northeast Organic Farmers Association (NOFA), is an advocate for farmers and consumers. She lobbies for more government research to investigate the harmful side effects of spraying crops with chemicals.

635

Active Chemistry

Chem at Work

The *Chem at Work* section provides students with examples of how chemistry is applied by working people in the real world. These profiles can help students realize that the same challenges they are attempting to master for their *Chapter Challenges* are often routine procedures for people who work in professions such as those featured here. As a matter of fact, most of the chemical procedures that students have performed in the previous activities are employed every day by average people like these.

Students should also note from these profiles that chemistry relates to many different kinds of people. Scientists and science teachers are not the only ones who practice chemistry. Nor

7c	Blackline Master
7d	Blackline Master
7e	Blackline Master

Practice Test

The *Practice Test* is provided as a Blackline Master in the *Teacher Resources* CD.

7f   **Blackline Master**

Content Review

1. c

2. a

3. a

4. b

5. d

6. c

7. c

8. b

9. c

10. d

11. d

12. c

13. a

14. b

15. c

16. d

17. a

18. a

19. b

20. a

 Cookin' Chem

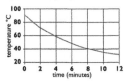
Chem
Practice Test

Content Review

On a separate sheet of paper answer the following.

1. Which of the following is not a method of heat transfer?
   a) conduction
   b) convection
   c) isotopic
   d) radiation

2. 0°C is equivalent to
   a) 273 K.
   b) 32 K.
   c) 100°F.
   d) 0 K.

3. Which of the following describes heat transfer by conduction?
   a) frying an egg in an iron skillet
   b) boiling water
   c) cooking toast in a toaster oven
   d) sun-drying tomatoes

4. Which of the following describes heat transfer by convection?
   a) frying an egg in an iron skillet
   b) boiling water
   c) cooking toast in a toaster oven
   d) sun-drying tomatoes

5. Carbon atoms usually make ___ bonds.
   a) 1
   b) 2
   c) 3
   d) 4

6. The graph below shows the cooling curve of a metal that loses 400 J of energy in the first 8 minutes. If the metal has a mass of 10 g, the specific heat capacity of the metal is

   a) 0.21 J/g •°C.
   b) 0.71 J/g •°C.
   c) 0.80 J/g •°C.
   d) 0.50 J/g •°C.

7. To balance a chemical equation, you can
   a) change the formulas of the chemicals involved.
   b) change the subscripts of each chemical involved.
   c) change the number of molecules on each side of the arrow.
   d) change both the formulas and amounts of each chemical involved.

8. Carbon dioxide puts out fires by
   a) cooling the fuel.
   b) keeping oxygen from the fuel.
   c) separating the fuel from the heat.
   d) removing the heat.

9. In exothermic chemical reactions, energy is
   a) required to keep the reaction going.
   b) stored in the products of the reaction.
   c) released by the system to the surroundings as the reaction occurs.
   d) absorbed by the system from the surroundings as the reaction occurs.

Active Chemistry

636

558

10. The energy required to start a reaction is called the

    a) energy of combustion.

    b) potential energy of reactants.

    c) potential energy of products.

    d) activation energy.

11. Which phase changes are exothermic?

    a) boiling and freezing

    b) condensing and melting

    c) boiling and melting

    d) condensing and freezing

12. The amount of heat needed to change one gram of a liquid at its boiling point to a gas at its boiling point is called

    a) heat of fusion.

    b) heat of condensation.

    c) heat of vaporization.

    d) heat of crystallization.

13. As water freezes, which of the following is true?

    a) heat is lost and temperature remains constant

    b) heat is lost and temperature decreases

    c) heat remains constant and temperature decreases

    d) heat remains constant and temperature remains constant

14. If 540 calories of heat are released as 1 g of steam at 100°C condenses, then

    a) it will take less heat to turn the liquid water back to steam.

    b) 540 calories of heat must be added to 1 g of water at 100°C to vaporize it.

    c) it will take more heat to turn the liquid water back to steam.

    d) water will boil at 90°C if it absorbs 550 cal of heat per gram.

15. Which of the following is true?

    a) steam at 100°C has the same heat energy content as water at 100°C

    b) water at 100°C has more heat energy than steam at 100°C

    c) water at 100°C has less heat energy than steam at 100°C

    d) none of these are true

16. The amount of heat needed to raise the temperature of one gram of a substance by 1 degree Celsius is

    a) its heat of fusion.

    b) its heat of vaporization.

    c) 1 calorie.

    d) its specific heat capacity.

17. Which of the following would require the least amount of heat to increase in temperature by 50°C?

    a) copper – specific heat capacity of 0.39 J/g•°C

    b) water – specific heat capacity of 4.18 J/g•°C

    c) aluminum – specific heat capacity of 0.90 J/g•°C

    d) iron – specific heat capacity of 0.47 J/g•°C

18. The sequence of amino acids in a protein determines

glycine

    a) its primary structure.

    b) its secondary structure.

    c) its tertiary structure.

    d) its peptide bonds.

637

Active Chemistry

Critical Thinking

21.a)

Line 2 represents the activation energy.

21.b)

Line 3 represents the change in energy.

21.c)

Line 4 represents the potential energy of the products.

21.d)

The reaction is exothermic.

22.a)

$$2C_2H_6 + 7O_2 \rightarrow 4CO_2 + 6H_2O$$

22.b)

$$C_5H_{12} + 8O_2 \rightarrow 5CO_2 + 6H_2O$$

22.c)

$$2C_3H_7OH + 9O_2 \rightarrow 6CO_2 + 8H_2O$$

23.a)

Heat is the transfer of energy from a warmer substance to a cooler substance, and is dependent on the total mass, the heat capacity, and the temperature of a substance. Its units are joules or calories.

23.b)

Temperature is a measure of the average kinetic energy of the molecules of a substance. Its units are degrees Celsius (°C), degrees Fahrenheit (°F), or Kelvin (K).

23.c)

The transfer of heat is dependant on a temperature difference between two objects. If there is no temperature difference, no heat will be transferred.

24.a)

$0°C + 273 = K$

24.b)

0 K is called absolute zero.

24.c)

At 0 K, molecular motion is brought to a minimum.

25.)

A micelle is a sphere of molecules arranged so that their polar ends are all on the outside, and their non-polar ends are on the inside when dissolved in water, which is a polar substance. Soap works by forming micelles that gather grease and other hydrophobic materials inside the micelles and wash it away when the water surrounding the micelles is washed away.

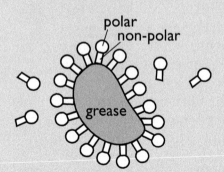

polar
non-polar

grease

 Cookin' Chem

Practice Test *(continued)*

19. Denaturation of proteins is caused by changes in

unfolding

a) the primary structure of the protein.

b) the tertiary and secondary structures of the protein.

c) peptide bonds holding amino acids together.

d) chemical content of the proteins.

20. Why do carbon atoms form tetrahedral structures when they form four single bonds?

a) The electron pairs of the bonds repel one another.

b) The protons are arranged tetrahedrally.

c) Every atom is arranged like this.

d) It doesn't form tetrahedral structures.

> **Critical Thinking**

On a separate sheet of paper answer the following.

21. An energy diagram is shown below.

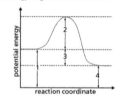

potential energy

reaction coordinate

a) Which line represents the activation energy?

b) Which line represents the overall change in energy?

c) Which line represents the potential energy of the products?

d) Is the reaction endothermic or exothermic?

22. Balance the following equations:

a) $\_C_2H_6 + \_O_2 \rightarrow \_CO_2 + \_H_2O$

b) $\_C_5H_{12} + \_O_2 \rightarrow \_CO_2 + \_H_2O$

c) $\_C_3H_7OH + \_O_2 \rightarrow \_CO_2 + \_H_2O$

23. Temperature and heat are related, but they are different physical quantities and do not have the same units.

a) What is heat and what is the unit of heat?

b) What is temperature and what is the unit of temperature?

c) What is the relationship between them?

24. Kelvin scale is a metric scale for temperature. Celsius is a metric scale as well.

a) How do you convert from degrees Celsius to Kelvin?

b) What is the significance of 0 K?

c) What happens to a substance at the molecular level, at 0 K?

25. How does soap (or detergent) work to clean grease from dishes? Explain what the molecules do. Draw a picture to illustrate and clearly label your picture.

638

Active Chemistry

CSI CHEMISTRY

Chapter 8

CHAPTER 8
CSI CHEMISTRY
Chapter Overview

Chapter Challenge

This chapter, *CSI Chemistry*, challenges students to focus on atoms, compounds, and reactions. For the *Chapter Challenge*, students will be asked to create a crime scene, much like the ones seen on the television show *CSI* and prepare evidence that requires the use of at least three forensic chemistry techniques. Students' crime shows should include a police report, description/story of the crime, a diagram of the crime scene, dossiers of suspects and any other evidence. This material will be presented to the class who will then use their chemistry knowledge to try and solve the crime-scene mystery.

Students will incorporate what they have learned about atoms, ions, single- and double-replacement reactions, redox chemistry, and qualitative analysis into their crime-scene mystery. They will also act as forensic chemists by using their chemistry knowledge about the structures of solids and liquids as they pertain to explaining how some analysis techniques work (serial-number restoration, chromatography) in order to solve other groups' crime-show mystery. Finally, the students will build deductive reasoning skills and learn how to use and create flowcharts as part of their *Chapter Challenge*. The goals of the chapter, which should be reflected in the *Chapter Challenge*, are that science is reproducible but evidence is not necessarily proof, chemicals have unique properties and structure (at the particle level) that inform those properties, and models are useful tools in predicting properties.

Chapter Summary

- Learn how to organize evidence from a crime scene.

- Learn how to use density to identify substances.

- Learn how to recover finger prints and how to interpret the prints.

- Understand how metals and metal ion solutions react with each other.

- Learn how to use the Metal Activity Series to recover serial numbers from metal plates.

- Learn how to separate mixtures using chromatography.

KEY SCIENCE CONCEPTS

ACTIVITY SUMMARIES	CHEMISTRY PRINCIPLES
Section 1: Groups, Periods, and the Properties of Elements: Clue Me In In this investigation, deductive reasoning skills are used to identify elements based on clues about their properties, names, position on the periodic table, and history. Next, collaboration is used to gather evidence and solve a crime using deductive reasoning.	Chemical families, Elements Periodic table, Categorization Group, period, series Deductive reasoning Halogens, Metals Nonmetals, Metalloids Alkali, Alkaline earth Transition metals Inner transition metals
Section 2: Physical Properties: Density of Glass In this investigation, the density of a glass sample is determined using the slope method. The density of one group's sample to another group's sample is compared to determine if the same type of glass was used.	Density, Measurements Graphing, Mass, Volume Chemical properties Physical properties Extensive properties Intensive properties
Section 3: Atomic Structure and Chemiluminescence: The Luminol Reaction In this section, the principles of chemiluminescence are explored while testing bovine hemoglobin with a luminol reagent. These principles include ground state, excited state, energy levels, and catalysis. The formation of ions examined through the gain or loss of electrons.	Atomic structure, Protons Neutrons, Electrons, Nucleus Atomic number, Spectroscopy Chemiluminescence, Ions Reactants, Products, Catalyst Ground state, Excited state Energy levels, Enzymes
Section 4: Solubility and Qualitative Analysis: White Powders This investigation shows how flowcharts are used and read. A flowchart is developed that will identify six white powders. The development of the flowchart is based on the chemical and physical properties of the six white powders.	Qualitative Analysis, Anions Word equations, Flowcharts Polyatomic ion, Ionic bonds Double-replacement, Cations Solubility Rules, Insoluble Acid-base chemistry Law of Conservation of Matter
Section 5: Double-Replacement Reactions and Fingerprints The investigation shows how to use a double-replacement reaction and an oxidation-reduction reaction to develop invisible fingerprints on paper.	Solvents, Solutes Oxidation Reduction Fingerprint analysis Crystalline structure
Section 6: Reactions with Transition Metals: Metal Activity Series Metals are added to different ionic solutions to develop a smaller version of the activity series.	Activity series of metals Oxidizing agent Reducing agent Single replacement Double replacement Oxidation number Valence electrons Transition metals
Section 7: Using the Metal Activity Series to Etch a Serial Number In this investigation, a serial number is stamped into a piece of metal, and then what is known about single-replacement reactions is applied to restore that serial number after it has been obliterated. Next, a clay model is built and manipulated in order to understand what happens to metal atoms when they are stamped and how the changes caused by stamping allow the restoration of serial numbers.	Metal properties, Luster Ductile, Malleable, Models Redox reactions, Etching Grain of metal Nanostructure of metals
Section 8: Paper Chromatography: Separating Molecules In Part A, a separation of black marker dye is performed. In Part B, a model of the separation process is developed to learn how it separates the different dyes in the ink. In this model, a felt board is used to represent the paper and different colored game chips represent the dyes in the marker ink. Finally, in Part C, a set of standard chromatograms R_f value of different black inks is developed. An unknown sample of black ink is provided and the brand of ink is asked to be determined.	Chromatography Mixtures Pure substances Separation methods Mobile phase Stationary phase R_f factor, Modeling

CHAPTER 8

Chapter Concept Map

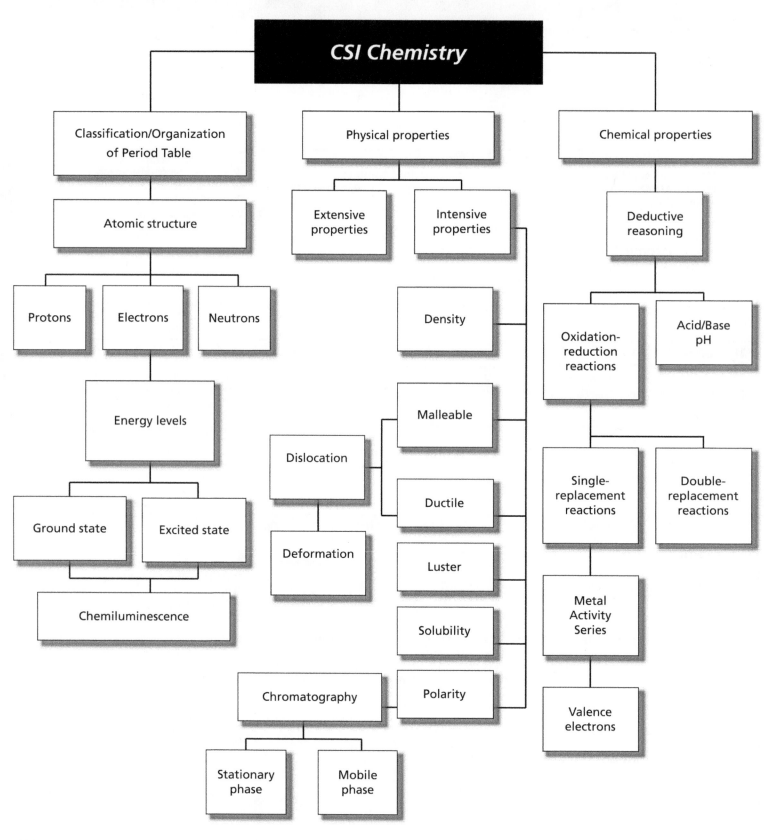

UNDERSTANDING BY DESIGN*

The *Understanding by Design* template focuses on the three stages of backward design:
- **Identify desired results**
- **Determine acceptable evidence**
- **Plan learning experiences**

What overarching understandings are desired?

- It is not possible to definitively prove anything in science. Rather, hypotheses can be strongly supported by evidence, similar to "proving" a verdict "beyond a shadow of a doubt" in law.
- The same scientific evidence can be used to support multiple explanations.
- Science is reproducible.
- Doing science involves using deductive reasoning to develop logical conclusions.
- Conclusions are stronger when supported by multiple lines of reasoning and evidence.
- Science, engineering and technology are pursued for different purposes. Engineering and technology have more apparent effects on society because their purposes include solving human problems, while science is driven by the desire to understand the natural world.
- A chemical can be identified by properties that are unique to that chemical.
- Microscopic structure informs macroscopic properties.
- Scientists use models to understand how mater behaves. However, all models have limitations.

What are the overarching "essential" questions?

- Is it possible to identify conclusively?
- What would it take to disprove a conclusion?
- What makes science different from engineering and technology?
- Who decides what is/and is not evidence? Or who decides what is to be considered as "evidence" and what is not?
- Is all evidence permanent?
- How is logic useful in drawing conclusions?
- How many lines of reasoning are necessary to convince someone that a conclusion is valid?
- Where do materials get their properties from?
- How do you know you'll get the same answer from the same test every time?
- How you do figure out the limitations of a model?
- How does one record observations?
- Why is it important for chemists to understand how tests work, in addition to being able to do them in the lab?

What will students understand as a result of this chapter?

- Different methods of investigation can be used to analyze evidence.
- It is possible to fit given evidence into more than one story line.
- Construct a logical argument to make a convincing conclusion.
- Specific properties of substances are useful in identifying them. Many tests are class identifiers. Some tests can be used to uniquely identify substances.
- Certain properties of materials permit the application of specific tests.
- In order for science to be reproducible, procedures must be standardized.
- Models can be used to describe and predict behavior of matter.

What "essential" questions will focus this chapter?

- Given some evidence, how do you decide which techniques will be valuable in analyzing it?
- Is it possible to arrive at more than one conclusion using the same evidence?
- How can you convince someone that your conclusion is the most probable one?
- What are some specific properties that will allow the unique identification of a chemical?
- What properties of the material allow the test to work?
- Would someone in a different location repeating your tests get the same results? What factors might contribute to results being different, even if the same procedure is followed?
- How do you figure out when a model useful to predict behavior, and when it breaks down?

* Grant Wiggins and Jay McTighe, *Understanding by Design* (Merrill/Prentice Hall, 1998), 181.

Pacing Guide

This chapter will take about 4 weeks to complete, assuming a full 5-day school week. Keep in mind that a *Pacing Guide* is merely a suggestion and that you should adjust your pace to your students' needs and the school schedule.

A sample outline is shown below. It assumes that you will assign homework every day and that class time will be used to discuss homework and special topics. *Inquiring Further* activities, if assigned, will allow students to do research or investigations outside regular class time.

Note: Each "Day" assumes a 45-minute class period, or one-half of a 90-minute block.

DAY	SECTION	HOMEWORK
1	Discuss *Scenario, Your Challenge, and Criteria for Success.* Develop a scoring rubric. **Section 1** Discuss *What Do You See?* and *What Do You Think?* Students complete *Investigate*. Review results of investigation.	Read *Chem Talk* and answer *Checking Up* questions. Answer *What Do You Think Now?* questions.
2	Discuss *Chem Talk* and review *Checking Up* answers. Discuss *What Do You Think Now?* responses and *Chem Essential Questions.* Answer *Chem to Go* problems 1 and 2.	Answer *Chem to Go* problems 3-7. Read *Reflecting on the Section and the Challenge.*
3	Review *Chem to Go* answers. **Section 2** Discuss *What Do You See?* and *What Do You Think?* Students complete *Investigate.* Review results of investigations.	Read *Chem Talk* and answer *Checking Up* questions. Answer *What Do You Think Now?* questions.
4	Discuss *Chem Talk* and review *Checking Up* answers. Discuss *What Do You Think Now?* responses. Discuss *Chem Essential Questions.* Answer *Chem to Go* problem 1 and 2.	Answer *Chem to Go* problems 3-6. Read *Reflecting on the Section and the Challenge.*
5	Review *Chem to Go* answers. **Section 3** Discuss *What Do You See?* and *What Do You Think?* Students complete Investigate. Review results of the investigation.	Read *Chem Talk* and answer *Checking Up* questions. Answer *What Do You Think Now?* questions.
6	Discuss *Chem Talk* and review *Checking Up* answers. Discuss *What Do You Think Now?* and *Chem Essential Questions.* Answer *Chem to Go* problems 1-4 in class.	Answer *Chem to Go* problems 5-8. Read *Reflecting on the Section and the Challenge.*
7	Review *Chem to Go* answers. **Section 4** Discuss *What Do You See?* and *What Do You Think?* Students complete the *Investigate* Part A. Review results of the investigation.	Read *Chem Talk* and answer *Checking Up* questions. Complete *Investigate* Part B.
8	Discuss *Chem Talk* and review *Checking Up* answers. Review Investigate Part B. Discuss *Chem Essential Questions* and *What Do You Think Now?* Answer *Chem to Go* problem 1 in class.	Answer the *Chem to Go* problems 2-11. Read *Reflecting on the Section and the Challenge* and the *Chapter Mini-Challenge.*

DAY	SECTION	HOMEWORK
9	Review the *Chem to Go* answers. Discuss the *Chapter Mini-Challenge* and work on presentation.	Work on *Chapter Mini-Challenge* with group.
10	Students present *Chapter Mini-Challenges* and receive feedback from peers. **Section 5** Discuss *What Do You See?* and *What Do You Think?*	Read *Investigate* and outline the procedure.
11	Students complete *Investigate* Parts A and B. Review results of investigation.	Read *Chem Talk* and answer *Checking Up* questions. Answer *What Do You Think Now?* questions.
12	Discuss *Chem Talk* and review *Checking Up* answers. Students complete *Investigate* Part C. Review results of investigation. Discuss *Chem Essential Questions* and *What Do You Think Now?* questions.	Answer *Chem to Go* problems 1-9. Read *Reflecting on the Section and the Challenge*.
13	Review *Chem to Go* answers. **Section 6** Discuss *What Do You See?* and *What Do You Think?* Students complete *Investigate*. Review results of investigation.	Read *Chem Talk* and answer *Checking Up* questions. Answer *What Do You Think Now?* questions.
14	Discuss *Chem Talk* and review *Checking Up* answers. Discuss *What Do You Think Now?* and *Chem Essential Questions*. Answer *Chem to Go* problems 1 and 2.	Answer *Chem to Go* problems 3-8. Read *Reflecting on the Section and the Challenge*.
15	Review *Chem to Go* answers. **Section 7** Discuss *What Do You See?* and *What Do You Think?* Students complete *Investigate* Part A. Discuss results of the investigations.	Read *Chem Talk* through **The Nanoscopic View of Metals** and answer *Checking Up* questions 1 and 2.
16	Discuss *Chem Talk* and review *Checking Up* answers. Students complete *Investigate* Parts B and C. Review results of investigation.	Read the rest of *Chem Talk* and answer *Checking Up* question 3. Answer *What Do You Think Now?* questions.
17	Discuss *Chem Talk* and review *Checking Up* answer. Discuss *What Do You Think Now?* and *Chem Essential Questions*.	Answer *Chem to Go* problems. Read *Reflecting on the Section and the Challenge*.
18	Review *Chem to Go* answers and discuss *Reflecting on the Section and the Challenge*. **Section 8** Discuss *What Do You See?* and *What Do You Think?* Students complete *Investigate* Parts A, B, and C. Review the results of the investigation.	Read *Chem Talk* and answer the *Checking Up* questions. Answer *What Do You Think Now?* questions.
19	Discuss *Chem Talk* and review the *Checking Up* answers. Discuss *What Do You Think Now?* and *Chem Essential Questions*. Answer *Chem to Go* problems 1 and 2.	Answer *Chem to Go* problems 3-8. Read *Reflecting on the Section and the Challenge*. Read *Preparing for the Chapter Challenge*.
20	Review *Chem to Go* answers. Discuss *Preparing for the Chapter Challenge*. Work on the *Chapter Challenge*.	Work on the *Chapter Challenge* as a group.
21	*Chapter Challenge* presentations by students.	

CHAPTER 8

Chapter 8
Materials, Equipment and Chemicals

The following tables contain lists of materials, equipment, and chemicals needed to do all of the *Investigates*. The tables are organized as follows:

- **Table 1:** Durables per group (4 Students)
- **Table 2:** Durables per class
- **Table 3:** Consumables per group (4 Students)
- **Table 4:** Consumables per class
- **Table 5:** Chemicals

Durables are items which are not consumed during the *Investigate* and which can be used for several classes over several years. **Consumables** are items that are used up during each class and must be resupplied for future classes. Both the durables and consumables are broken down by group and by class. A **Group** consists of four students. While the group size will be determined by the teacher based upon logistics and availability of equipment, the information in Table 1 and Table 3 is based upon the recommended group size of four students.

Materials and Equipment

The first table contains the **durable** items needed **per group.** The right-hand column, **Quantity,** contains the number of items needed per group. The left-hand column, **Section,** gives the section number(s) in which each item will be used. The item quantities given are considered to be a minimum but, in some cases, if more are available, that would be ideal.

The second table contains the information on **Durables** needed per class (recommended class size is 24 students). In some cases, these will be items that are shared by the class. In other cases, the item will be used for a demonstration.

The third and fourth tables contain the items which are **consumable.** The third table contains **consumables per group** (recommended group size is four students) and the fourth table contains **consumables per class.**

TABLE 1: DURABLES PER GROUP (4 STUDENTS)		
Section	**Materials and Equipment (Durables)**	**Quantity**
All	Lab aprons	4
All	Safety goggles	4
2,3,4,5	Graduated cylinders, 100-mL	2
2	Tweezers	1
2,6,8	Clear metric ruler, 30-cm	1
3	Light stick	1
3	Spray bottle, small, 100-mL capacity	1
4	Test tubes, large	4
4,5	Stirring rod	1
4	Spatula	1
4	Test-tube rack	1
4	Test-tube brush	1
5	Beakers, 250-mL	2
5	Long stem funnel	1

TABLE 1: DURABLES PER GROUP (4 STUDENTS)		
5	Ringstand	1
5	Funnel support	1
5,6,7,8	Hand lens	1
5	Soft bristle brush	1
6	12-well microplates	4
6	Diagonal cut pliers	1
7	Pair of rubber gloves	1
7	Black marker	1
7	Wood dowel, 1" diameter, 1 foot long	1
7	Cutting knife or razor blade	1
8	Binder clip, small	1
8	Felt board, approx 6' x 4"	1
8	2 colors of poker chips	10 each color
8	Meter stick	1
8	Beaker, 600-mL	1
8	Graduated cylinder, 250-mL	1

TABLE 2: DURABLES PER CLASS		
Section	Materials and Equipment (Durables)	Quantity
2	Balances (0.01g)	1
2	Glass tubing cutter (teacher prep)	1
4,6	Dropping bottles/dropper (at least 7 drops for silver nitrate)	300
5	UV light source	1
7	Set of metal dies	1
2, 7	Hammer	1
7	Electric drill with grinding wheel	1
8	Scissors	1
7	Beaker, 50-mL	1

CHAPTER 8

TABLE 3: CONSUMABLES PER GROUP (4 STUDENTS)		
Section	**Materials and Equipment (Consumables)**	**Quantity**
2	Microscope slides, glass, to make 40 pieces	2
2	Glass tubing, borosilicate glass, 2 ft.	40 pc
3	Disposable Beral pipettes	30
3, 5, 6	White paper sheets	10
3	Rusty iron nail	1
5	Copper penny	1
5	Black ink pad	1
6	Steel wool or sandpaper	1
7	Sheet of 100-grit sandpaper	1
7	Sheet of 150-grit sandpaper	1
7	Sheet of 220-grit sandpaper	1
7	Unsharpened pencil	1
7, 8	Sharpened pencil	1
8	Set of 5 different water-soluble black markers	1
8	Chromatography paper, large sheet	1
8	Large paper clip	1
8	Roll of cellophane tape	1

TABLE 4: CONSUMABLES PER CLASS		
Section	**Materials and Equipment (Consumables)**	**Quantity**
2	Pack of graph paper (50 sheets)	2
3,7	Wax paper, roll	1
3,5	Filter paper, box (100)	1
3	Bottle of ketchup	1
3	Jar of Horseradish	1
3	Red food coloring	1
5	Paper towels, roll	1
7	Ethanol (or isopropyl alcohol), 100 mL	2
7	Box of cotton balls (100)	1
7	Modeling clay-Color A	2-lb slabs
7	Modeling clay-Color B	2-lb slabs
8	Plastic wrap, roll	1

Chemicals

In the fifth table, the **Chemicals** required for each section are listed. By their nature, most chemicals are consumable. The amounts given in the right-hand column under **Quantity** are the amounts needed for five classes of 24 students (for a total of 120 students). These numbers were chosen

as reasonable estimates of the number of class sections that a teacher might have. Most teachers will find that these amounts, when divided by five (to reach the amount needed for one class), will still provide ample excess for repeat experiments or student error.

TABLE 5: CHEMICALS FOR FIVE CLASSES (24 Students per class)		
Section	**Chemicals**	**Quantity**
3	Bovine hemoglobin powder	6.0 g
3	Luminol reagent	1.0 g
3	Sodium carbonate, Na_2CO_3	50 g
3	Sodium perborate tetrahydrate, $NaBO_3 \cdot 4H_2O$	7.0 g
3	Household bleach solution	125 mL
3	0.1 M iron(II) chloride dihydrate, $Fe(Cl_2) \cdot 2H_2O$	8.0 g
3	0.1 M iron(III) chloride, hexahydrate, $Fe(Cl_3) \cdot 6H_2O$	13.5 g
4	Calcium carbonate, $CaCO_3$	200 g
4	Calcium sulfate, $CaSO_4$	200 g
4	Sodium carbonate, Na_2CO_3	200 g
4	Sodium hydrogen carbonate, $NaHCO_3$	200 g
4	Sodium chloride, NaCl	212 g
4	Sodium hydroxide, NaOH	200 g
4	Phenolphthalein solution	100 mL
4	1.0 M Acetic acid	500 mL
4,5	0.1 M Silver nitrate (store in dark bottle)	51.0 g
6	Aluminum metal strip, 9 x 1 x 0.2 cm	7
6	5 cm copper metal strip, 9 x 1 x 0.2 cm	7
6	5 cm iron metal strip, 9 x 1 x 0.2 cm	7
6	5 cm magnesium metal strip, 9 x 1 x 0.2 cm	7
6	5 cm tin metal strip, 9 x 1 x 0.2 cm	7
6	5 cm zinc metal strip, 9 x 1 x 0.2 cm	7
6	3.0 M hydrochloric acid	125 mL
6	Zinc nitrate hexahydrate, $Zn(NO_3)_2 \cdot 6H_2O$	7.4 g
6	Tin(IV) chloride pentahydrate, $Sn(Cl)_4 \cdot 5H_2O$	8.8 g
6	Magnesium nitrate, $Mg(NO_3)_2 \cdot 6H_2O$	6.4 g
6	Iron(III) nitrate nonahydrate, $Fe(NO_3)_3 \cdot 9H_2O$	10.1 g
6	Copper(II) nitrate trihydrate, $Cu(NO_3)_2 \cdot 3H_2O$	6.0 g
6	Aluminum nitrate nonahydrate, $Al(NO_3)_3 \cdot 9H_2O$	9.4 g
7	Aluminum metal bars, approx. 8 x 1 x 0.4 cm	35
7	Iron(III) chloride, hexahydrate, $Fe(Cl_3) \cdot 6H_2O$	125 g
7	Hydrochloric acid, HCl, 12 M	125 mL
7	Sodium hydrogen carbonate, $NaHCO_3$	420 g

Teacher Resources

Blackline Masters

- Blackline Masters

Available on the *Teacher Resources* CD.

- Color Overheads

Available on the *Teacher Resources* CD.

Blackline Masters

Chapter Supports

	POINT OF USE	BLACKLINE MASTER LABEL
Sample Criteria for Excellence	*Chapter Challenge* Introduction	8a
Sample Assessment Rubric	*Chapter Challenge* Conclusion	8b
Chem at Work: Profile 1	*Chem at Work*	8c
Chem at Work: Profile 2	*Chem at Work*	8d
Chem at Work: Profile 3	*Chem at Work*	8e

Section Quizzes

Section 1 Quiz	Section 1	8-1b
Section 2 Quiz	Section 2	8-2c
Section 3 Quiz	Section 3	8-3a
Section 4 Quiz	Section 4	8-4a
Section 5 Quiz	Section 5	8-5a
Section 6 Quiz	Section 6	8-6b
Section 7 Quiz	Section 7	8-7a
Section 8 Quiz	Section 8	8-8a

Section Supports

	POINT OF USE	BLACKLINE MASTER LABEL
Element Cards	Section 1 – *Investigate*	8-1a
Glass Density — Blank Data Table	Section 2 – *Investigate*	8-2a
Mass vs. Volume Graphs	Section 2 – *Investigate*	8-2b
Metal Activity — Blank Data Table	Section 6 – *Investigate*	8-6a

Chapter Assessment

Chem Practice Test	Chapter Conclusion	8f

Color Overheads

	POINT OF USE
What Do You See? Section 1	Section 1
What Do You See? Section 2	Section 2
What Do You See? Section 3	Section 3
What Do You See? Section 4	Section 4
What Do You See? Section 5	Section 5
What Do You See? Section 6	Section 6
What Do You See? Section 7	Section 7
What Do You See? Section 8	Section 8

NOTES

CHAPTER 8

Chapter Challenge

Scenario

Read, or have a student read this section aloud. Pause after each paragraph and ask a question to test for their understanding and to generate interest. Ask students about their favorite detective shows and how the various lead detectives solve the crimes. Encourage them to share experiences they have had solving a mystery or puzzle. Discuss various crime lab techniques they may have seen, such as fingerprinting, DNA testing, etc. Crime shows and detective work can easily get students wanting to talk. It is your responsibility as a teacher to engage them but not to devote too much time to this discussion.

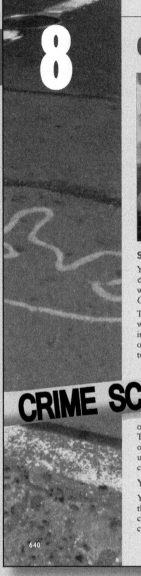

8

Chapter Challenge

CSI Chemistry

Scenario

You may have heard of detective shows, like *CSI*; *Murder, She Wrote*; *Law & Order*, or even *Scooby-Doo*. The producers of a popular crime show would like to develop several new episodes. They have asked your *Active Chemistry* class to participate in this process.

To put together an exciting and interesting show, the producers begin with a set of evidence that can be analyzed to solve the mystery. Then they introduce a creative story line and bring in intriguing characters. Every piece of evidence is a potential clue that can lead to solving the crime. However, to keep the plot interesting, writers

often include dead ends and puzzles along the way to solving the crime. The fact that evidence can lead you in multiple directions makes for some of the great drama in detective stories! Also, multiple pieces of evidence are usually needed to indicate whether a suspect is guilty. Conclusions are more convincing when supported by multiple lines of reasoning and evidence.

Your Challenge

Your challenge is to create a crime scene and prepare evidence that requires the use of at least three forensic chemistry techniques learned in this chapter in order to solve the crime. Before you develop your story for the crime-show episode, you will need to analyze the evidence you create in the

640

laboratory. Then, determine which pieces the star detectives in the show would use to figure out which suspect is guilty. Finally, based on the evidence, develop the crime story. Your crime story should include a police report, description of the crime, a diagram of the crime scene, a list of all the evidence found at the scene, and anything else that will make the story come to life.

Next, you will create dossiers (descriptions) for at least four different suspects. Each dossier will include personal information about the subject, such as a mug shot, fingerprint of right index finger, the suspect's name, occupation, clothing worn on the day of the crime and any other information that will be needed to link the suspect to the crime or eliminate him or her as a suspect. You may be as creative as you'd like with your characters (they are characters after all), but using names or lives of students is not allowed. It is very important that you develop the story and the characters of the suspects so that the evidence you were given logically points to a single guilty suspect. However, you may also want to include a piece of evidence that implicates more than one suspect so that the audience of the crime show cannot immediately guess who the guilty party is right away.

As a way of testing whether your story is solvable by forensic chemists in a crime show, you will present your police report, story of the crime, dossiers of four suspects, and evidence to another group of students, who will act as forensic chemists and try to solve the crime. You will write down the solution to the crime (which suspect is guilty), including a flowchart illustrating the expected outcomes of the analysis of evidence. Your solution should also address the chemical principles used within the crime by explaining the *macroscopic*, *nanoscopic*, and *symbolic* perspectives of each principle used in your crime scene. All of the solution material should be sealed in an envelope. Once the students testing your package have analyzed the evidence and

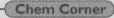

Chem Corner

Chemistry in *CSI Chemistry*

- Deductive reasoning
- Intensive property
- Extensive property
- Density
- Chemiluminescence
- Ground state
- Excited state
- Qualitative analysis
- Latent fingerprints
- Crystalline structure
- Oxidation number
- Ductile and malleable
- Etching
- Chromatography
- Stationary phase
- Mobile phase
- R_f
- Acid and base

CRIME SCENE

the design process is reliable and works on a consistent basis. In order to do this, students will want to take full advantage of planning and trouble-shooting at the mini-challenge level.

When you come to the section *Reflecting on the Section and the Challenge*, point out how each section contributes to the challenge in some way. As you discuss the challenge, reassure students that while they may feel overwhelmed by the demands of the assignment now, by the end of the chapter they will have the necessary skills and understanding to succeed.

Chem Corner

This section contains a preview of the basic science principles and skills that will be presented in this chapter. You may wish to see how many of these terms are familiar to your students. At the end of the chapter, it will be worthwhile to return to this list so that students can gauge their growth in understanding. The *Chem Corner* section is a good opportunity to remind students that the chemistry concepts and skills they learn in each new investigation will be the building blocks they will need at the end of the chapter to complete the *Chapter Challenge*.

Your Challenge

You may wish to lead a class discussion about the challenge and the expectations.

Review the titles of the activities in the *Table of Contents* at the front of the *Student Edition*. Point out that the content of the sections aligns with the content expected for the *Chapter Challenge* and ask students for

ideas as to how these kinds of activities might relate to the challenge at hand.

Stress the importance of recording each step of the design process (results, success, and failures) since the students will be required to explain their crime scene in detail. Another key to success for the challenge will rely on testing to make sure

Chapter Challenge

Criteria for Success

After the class has read the *Scenario* and the *Chapter Challenge*, you can take a few moments to develop the assessment. Students should be asked, "What should your crime scene/story be like to earn an A?" Remind them that their presentation must help people understand certain chemical principles. One way to get started is to make a list of the important criteria that must be included in the *Chapter Challenge*. List some suggestions they might consider, including the number and variety of chemical principles incorporated in the presentation, the accuracy and clarity of the explanation, the quality, entertainment value, and originality of the crime scene, police report and story, etc. (As they volunteer ideas, it is important that all suggestions be recognized, so consider this a brainstorming session.) By soliciting the students' opinions, the class will create an assessment tool that is written in language the students can understand. When you have a thorough description of each part of the *Chapter Challenge*, you can have the class vote on how much each part is worth.

After having this 10-minute discussion with the students, you can now read aloud the *Criteria for Success* section. This section will reinforce the discussion that you have had with the students. It may also add some interesting points that did not emerge in class. Students will be able to better understand this section after their own discussion.

Students should try to develop a rough rubric for the grading of the chapter. This can be as simple as ascribing points to each of their criteria. For example, the visual presentation could be worth 40 points, the chemical content worth 30 points and the written report and evidence another 30 points. A sample rubric for assessing the *Chapter Challenge* is provided at the end of this chapter. You can copy and distribute it as is, or use it as a baseline for developing scoring guidelines and expectations that suit your needs. For example, you might wish to ensure that core concepts and abilities derived from your local or state science frameworks also appear

---

Chapter Challenge

presented their case, they will open the envelope and compare what they decided to what you intended. They will also take a look at your chemistry reflection and provide you with feedback on your explanations.

Criteria for Success

How will your crime scene and investigations of another group's crime scene be evaluated? What qualities should a good crime scene have? What types of information need to be provided in the dossiers? How detailed does your analysis of the evidence need to be? Discuss these issues in small groups and with your class. You may decide that some or all of the following qualities should be graded:

- number of techniques used
- creativity of the story
- authenticity of police report
- originality of the dossiers of the suspects
- number of chemistry principles included
- accuracy of chemistry principles
- solvability of the crime
- logic of the crime story

Engineering Design Cycle

Your chemistry class will help you prepare to be a crime scene investigator. Scientists work to understand the world and figure out how to make better use of the resources it provides, including using clues to track down criminals. Your group will use the chemistry you learn to create a classic "whodunit" mystery. The simplified *Engineering Design Cycle* you have been using for each *Chapter Challenge* will help you complete this *Goal*. Understanding the *Goal* is the first step in any *Engineering Design Cycle*. The *Goal* for your *CSI Chemistry* challenge is to create your own crime scene drama that can be solved by your classmates. During the chapter sections you will be learning the chemistry you need to include in your crime scene.

As you experience each one of the chapter sections you will be gaining *Inputs* to use in the *Engineering Design Cycle*. These *Inputs* include new forensic chemistry techniques, new chemical reactions, information about identifying mystery samples, and practice using deductive reasoning. Each section of this chapter will help you learn important information you can use to create your crime scene and the dramatic story that will go with it. When your group prepares the *Mini-Challenge* presentation and the *Chapter Challenge* you will be completing the *Process* step of the *Engineering Design Cycle*. During the *Process* step you will prepare the evidence, create unique character dossiers, and create a dramatic mystery for your classmates to solve using their new forensic chemistry techniques.

The *Outputs* of your *Engineering Design Cycle* will be all of the components of your crime scene mystery. The *Outputs* will include the police report, the crime scene diagram, the evidence you create, the four character dossiers, and, most importantly, the solution envelope that includes your complete analysis of the evidence you have provided and the explanations of the forensic chemistry techniques that were required to accurately solve the crime. Finally, you will receive *Feedback* from your class and your instructor about what parts of your crime scene drama are good and which parts need to be refined. You will repeat the *Engineering Design Cycle* two times during the course of the chapter— when you complete the *Mini-Challenge* and after you have completed the second half of the chapter, gained more *Inputs*, finalized the crime scene drama, and completed your evidence and solution packets.

642

on the rubric. However you decide to evaluate the *Chapter Challenge*, keep in mind that all expectations should be communicated to the students at the start of their work.

The *Sample Criteria for Excellence* is also provided as a Blackline Master in your *Teacher Resources* CD.

8a	Blackline Master

SAMPLE CRITERIA FOR EXCELLENCE

It is important for students to decide on the criteria for grading the *Chapter Challenge* themselves. This will give them a voice in determining how their projects will be judged. You can help them arrive at a list of criteria by outlining those aspects of the project that would need to be rated. Some aspects that could be considered are the creativity and originality of the crime story and solution for the crime show, the authenticity of the police report and the dossiers of the different suspects, and the number of chemical concepts addressed.

You may want to share the list of sample criteria provided below as a source of inspiration. Remember that the primary purpose for having the students establish the criteria for earning a top grade is to motivate them to succeed.

As the *Chapter Challenge* approaches, you will need to develop a more comprehensive assessment rubric for evaluating the projects. For an example, you can refer to the *Sample Assessment Rubric for Chapter 8* at the end of the chapter in this *Teacher's Edition*.

MEETS THE STANDARD OF EXCELLENCE FOR CHAPTER CHALLENGE

Aspect	Criteria of Excellence
Content	• At least seven chemistry concepts are identified or applied in the evidence and the techniques used to solve the crime. • At least three different forensic techniques are correctly and effectively used in the solution of the crime. • The solution to the crime addresses the chemical principles used in the crime by explaining the macroscopic, nanoscopic, and symbolic perspectives.
Presentation	• The story is logical, well crafted, creative, entertaining, and effectively incorporates the evidence at the crime scene. • The police report is thorough, authentic and clearly documents and explains all evidence found at the crime scene. • There are at least four dossiers containing all the pertinent information regarding the various crime suspects; the suspect characters are original and creatively depicted.
Group Interaction	• The project is executed by interactive teamwork, with all members of the group cooperating and actively engaged.

Groups, Periods, and the Properties of Elements: Clue Me In

Section Overview

In this section, students play an intellectually stimulating game and hone their skills of deduction. Based on information in the periodic table, students try to guess the identity of an element based upon increasingly specific clues. In the context of this game, students learn facts from the periodic table and, at the same time, practice their reasoning powers to win the prize.

Background Information

Deductive Reasoning

Investigators and forensic scientists are often faced with a jumble of facts and evidence that seem to be unconnected.

It is the job of the investigator or forensic scientist to organize, analyze, and determine the relationship between different pieces of evidence to reconstruct the crime in order to solve it. The process that they use is known as deductive reasoning. Deductive reasoning can be considered a top-down approach to problem solving. In deductive reasoning, observations lead to a hypothesis. More information is systematically gathered and tested against the hypothesis. If the evidence agrees with the hypothesis, a theory is formed. If the evidence does not agree with our hypothesis, a new hypothesis is developed and the process repeats itself.

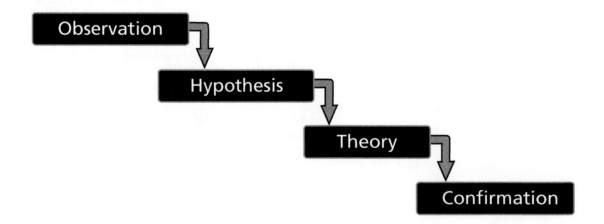

Trochim, William M.K. *Deduction and Induction*. Research Methods Knowledge Base, 2nd Edition. 29 June 2000. 10 Feb. 2004.

A simplified example of deductive reasoning is illustrated in every episode of *C.S.I* on television. First, Grissom (the lead forensic scientist) and his forensic team survey the crime scene and come up with a theory about how the crime happened. This occurs at the beginning of an episode when Grissom says to his investigators "Make the call." Then they take the available evidence and come up with a hypothesis. This hypothesis is tested against the evidence available and more evidence is sought to support the hypothesis. If the new evidence supports the hypothesis, then it is pursued. If the evidence doesn't support the hypothesis, a new hypothesis is proposed and the process repeats itself. Since the show is only 45 minutes long, Grissom and his team make the process seem relatively easy. In real life, this process can take months and the investigators can go through many hypotheses before they arrive at the correct one and apprehend the perpetrator. As illustrated in the next section, the process of deductive reasoning is also used to solve problems in chemistry.

The Elements and the Periodic Table

The chair you are sitting on, the book you are reading, the clothes you are wearing, and everything around you is made of matter. All matter is made of elements or combinations of different elements. Elements are the basic building blocks of matter. They cannot be broken down into simpler substances by using physical or chemical means.

Very few elements are found in the earth in a pure form as most are combined with other elements. As a result, very few elements were known to ancient civilizations. The unreactive elements that the ancients did know included gold, silver, and copper. It wasn't until the late 1700s that scientists had the knowledge and the methods to isolate previously undiscovered elements from their mineral sources. As the number of known elements increased, chemists noticed that some elements had similar properties. Scientific discussion revolved around the question of "Is there a pattern?" One of the first chemists to notice a pattern was Antoine Lavoisier. Lavoisier was a French chemist and is often referred to as the father of modern chemistry. In the late 18th century, he organized the known elements into two groups, metals and nonmetals. Then, in 1829, a chemist by the name of Johann Dobereiner arranged the elements into groups of three, called triads. Elements in each triad had similar chemical and physical properties. However, as more elements were isolated, there were many that would not fit in these triads. John Newlands organized the elements in order of increasing atomic weights. When this was done, he noticed that the properties repeated after every eighth element. That is, the first in his scheme was similar in chemical and physical properties to the ninth, the second to the tenth, and so on. His repeating pattern of eight was called the "Law of Octaves," due to its similarity to the musical scale.

However, it had blank spaces for elements that had not been discovered yet. In this way, it predicted new elements having similar properties. Then in 1869, two chemists simultaneously developed the first modern periodic table. The chemists were Lothar Meyer and Dimitri Mendeleev. Mendeleev was known to enjoy playing solitaire. One day, he wrote the properties for the known elements on cards. He used one card for each element. Then, much as one would arrange cards to play solitaire, he began to arrange the elements. He finally determined that if he placed the element cards in order of increasing atomic mass a pattern emerged. His arrangement was very convincing and he recognized that there were empty slots for elements that had not yet been discovered. He used the properties of the element around these blank spots in his arrangement to predict the properties of each missing element. Later, when these missing elements were discovered, their properties were very nearly what Mendeleev had predicted years before. Thus, the first modern periodic table evolved. The modern periodic table was developed by Henry Moseley in 1934. He arranged the elements in order of increasing atomic number instead of atomic mass. This eliminated some of the remaining discrepancies in Mendeleev's arrangement.

Currently, there are about 114 known elements. Each element is represented on the periodic table with a symbol. For example, the first element on the table, hydrogen, is represented by the symbol, H. The elements are arranged in 18 groups, or columns, and seven periods, or rows.

Elements in the same group have similar chemical and physical properties. This is because elements in the same group possess the same number of outer electrons known as *valence electrons*. Thus, groups are often referred to as families. The two groups on the left and the six groups on the right are known as the *representative* or *main group* elements. They include:

Group 1: **alkali metals**

Group 2: **alkaline earth metals**

Group 13: no common name

Group 14: no common name

Group 15: **pnictogens**

Group 16: **chalcogens**

Group 17: **halogens**

Group 18: **noble gases**

The alkali metals are shiny, soft metals that react rapidly with oxygen. When they are placed in water, they react to form metal hydroxides which make the resulting solution basic or alkaline. Due to their reactivity, the alkali metals are never found in nature in their pure elemental state.

The alkaline earth metals are also shiny but they are not as soft or reactive as the alkali metals. When the alkaline earth metals are placed in water they also form a basic or alkaline solution. Although they are not as reactive as the alkali metals, they are still not found (in their pure state) in nature by themselves.

The pnictogens are called such because their gases are often choking or suffocating. The name for the chalcogens comes from the Greek word for ore-former. The halogens, found in Group 17, are very corrosive nonmetals. They range in state from gas (fluorine and chlorine), liquid (bromine), and solid (iodine and astatine). They are found in nature bonded to other elements. Fluorine, chlorine, bromine, and iodine will also bond with themselves and are called diatomic elements.

The noble gases are called such because they are the most unreactive elements in the periodic table. They are all gases at room temperature and, due to their inert nature, they are often used as a "blanket" to keep other elements from reacting with oxygen. For example, incandescent light bulbs are often filled with a noble gas, such as argon, to prevent the filament from reacting with oxygen.

The groups located in between the representative elements are called the *transition metals*. The groups that lie below the others on the periodic table are called the *inner transition metals*.

Elements can also be classified as metals, nonmetals, and metalloids. The metallic elements are located to the left of the stair-step line. *Metals* are shiny, can be pounded into sheets (*malleable*), drawn into wires (*ductile*), and are good conductors of heat and electricity. Nonmetals are located to the right of the stair-step line. *Nonmetals* tend to be gases or brittle solids at room temperature. They are also poor conductors of heat and electricity. The shaded elements located on the stair-step line are called metalloids. *Metalloid* elements have both metallic and nonmetallic properties. Take, for example, the element silicon. Silicon is shiny like a metal but brittle like a nonmetal.

LEARNING OUTCOMES		
LEARNING OUTCOMES	**LOCATION IN SECTION**	**EVIDENCE OF UNDERSTANDING**
Use deductive reasoning to arrive at a conclusion.	*Investigate, Checking Up* Question 1	Students are able to identify an element correctly and then describe their line of reasoning.
Know and apply different ways in which the elements are classified and organized.	*Investigate, Checking Up* Questions 2-4	Students can identify the general location of elements based on a description as a metal, nonmetal, or metalloid.
Use references, including the periodic table, to learn more about individual elements.	*Investigate, Checking Up* Question 2 *Chem to Go* Questions 2-6	Students use the distinction between a group and a period to identify their element. Students identify elements in specific groups and periods.

NOTES

_____

_____

_____

_____

_____

_____

_____

_____

_____

_____

_____

_____

_____

_____

_____

_____

_____

_____

CHAPTER 8

Section 1
Materials, Chemicals, Preparation, and Safety

("per Group" quantity is based on group size of 4 students)

Materials and Equipment

Materials (and Equipment)	Quantity per Group (4 students)
Element cards (Blackline Masters)	2
Periodic table with groups numbered 1-18	1

Chemicals

Chemicals	Quantity per Class (24 students)
None	None

Teacher Preparation

Make sure all groups have one set of the element cards. There are plenty of cards so that each group has different elements. The element cards are provided as a Blackline Master.

Make sure each group has one periodic table. Have students refer to the inside back cover of the *Student Edition* for the periodic table.

Safety Requirements

- Goggles and aprons are required in the laboratory area.

NOTES

_____

_____

_____

_____

_____

_____

_____

_____

_____

NOTES

Meeting the Needs of All Students
Differentiated Instruction

Augmentation and Accommodations

LEARNING ISSUE	REFERENCE	AUGMENTATION AND ACCOMMODATIONS
Managing impulsivity Behaving appropriately in a competitive social situation	*Investigate*	**Augmentation** • Playing a game may seem so similar to other investigations your class has done that it may appear unnecessary to take precautions that help avert inappropriate behavior. However, the social interaction and competition among groups inherent in this section warrants establishment of protocols to help students manage impulsivity, maintain respect for others and behave courteously. Think through the way the game will work and your expectations for your students' behavior. • Explain the specific role of the group leader. What will he/she do? How should he/she be selected? • Should there be a person in each group designated to record the clues for use during the game or the post-game reflection? • How will the groups discuss the clue before they make their guess? **Accommodations** • Students with attention deficit issues can become over-stimulated in fun, interactive, competitive situations, but most such students are motivated to cooperate and comply. If you have impulsive students in your class, speak to them privately before this activity. Describe the circumstances of the section, acknowledge their motivation to do well, and make a plan that helps the students maintain perspective.
Developing clues	*Investigate*	**Accommodations** • Developing clues for this game is in great measure an issue of accessing prior understandings. Students may need cues and questions to help them recall what they know about identifying elements. • Thinking of the *Macro*, *Nano* and *Symbolic* descriptions of elements may help students develop good clues. Remind them that *Macro* clues would give information about how their element looked, smelled, felt, or what they observed in a reaction with another element. *Nano* clues would be those that give information about the atomic make-up of their element, and *Symbolic* clues would be those having to do with chemical symbols and formulas. Giving students this scaffold acts as a prompt for their thinking. • Refer students to the periodic table to develop clues about their element. • Suggest students use *Chem Talk* as a reference to develop clues.
Evaluating clues	*What Do You Think Now?*	**Augmentation** • The two questions in this section require students to reflect about which of their clues were appropriate. To fool the other group, students made clues that were intentionally vague; more than one element satisfied the parameters of the clue. However, if the group was trying to identify a mystery element, they would want to test it in ways that would give them the most specific information. Some clues mislead, others direct. Have students determine which purpose their clues served. This will help them analyze what they need to know to identify an element. • Ask students to compare the clues they gave to the information given in the *Chem Talk*. Ask them what other clues they might have used if they had read the *Chem Talk* before playing the game.
Using the periodic table to solve problems	*Chem to Go*	**Augmentation** • Students who may not process deeply when reading the *Chem Talk* description of how the periodic table of elements is organized may be more ready to grasp the organizational principles of the table when they need it to solve problems at the end of the section. Use this teachable moment to review the organization of the periodic table with students.

Strategies for Students with Limited English Language Proficiency

LEARNING ISSUE	REFERENCE	AUGMENTATIONS
Background knowledge	*Scenario*	Check to see that students are familiar with the TV shows mentioned. The expression *"multiple lines of reasoning and evidence"* may require some elaboration. Explain the idea of a crime scene and also the term *"forensic chemistry"* as well as the idea of a crime-show episode. Use the photograph as a bridge to building background knowledge. Students might benefit from a model of a storyboard. Note the word *"solvable"* in describing the storyline and explain the use of the *"able"* suffix for language development. Some students may need help with pronunciation of terms in *Chem Corner*.
Background knowledge	*What Do You Think?*	Students might discuss the questions to develop oral language proficiency.
Vocabulary	*Investigate*	Students will need to express clues orally and can benefit from working in small groups or teams.
Background knowledge Vocabulary Comprehending text	*Chem Talk*	Check for understanding of bold-type words. Refer students to *Chem Words* for further explanations of the isolated words. Students might benefit from some common examples of how people use *"deductive reasoning."*
Background knowledge	*What Do You Think Now?*	Students may need a model of a flowchart or a concept map. Note that *"deduce"* is a derivative of *"deductive."*
Background knowledge Vocabulary Comprehending text	*Chem Essential Questions*	Students might benefit from a model of the common use of *"deductive reasoning"* prior to explaining and writing their own. Ensure the understanding of the term *"Scenario."*
Comprehension Vocabulary	*Chem to Go*	Make sure students understand when a question is a multiple-choice response. Students may benefit from working with partners to discuss responses prior to writing their own answer.
Application Comprehension	*Inquiring Further*	Students might benefit from explanation of the significance of the timeline from *1829–1934* as noted in this section.

NOTES

_____

_____

_____

_____

_____

_____

_____

_____

CHAPTER 8

Section 1
Teaching Suggestions and Sample Answers

What Do You See?

The colorful illustration provides an opportunity to engage the students and to elicit their comments. The artist incorporates several components of the upcoming section, thus subtly introducing those to the students. This is an initial encounter for the students and their responses need not be accurate nor does the discussion need to come to closure. Some students may focus on the less relevant features of the illustration. Others may try to make sense of the various clues. All responses are valid.

What Do You Think?

Students will probably identify physical properties that they are familiar with, such as density, color, and metallic characteristics. Since this question can be answered at several levels (depending on what is meant by "identify" and "a material"), you should expect a variety of answers.

Since the term "element" was used, students will naturally be directed to use their knowledge of the periodic table. This is an excellent opportunity for you to be alert for misconceptions about elements and the organization of the periodic table. Again, there are no wrong answers. You will return to these questions later in the *What Do You Think Now?* section.

What Do You Think?
A CHEMIST'S RESPONSE

Without further definition of the terms "identify" and "material," it is difficult to give a satisfactory answer. The range can be from a density measurement of glass to a DNA match between two samples. To determine the identity of an element, a chemist would probably use mass spectrometry for gases and liquids. For solids, especially metals, atomic absorption spectroscopy would be used.

STUDENTS' PRIOR CONCEPTIONS

This is a minor component of this section, but students may have ideas on how to solve a mystery. Active participation in the "Mystery Elements" game described in the *Investigate* section may be dependent on student familiarity with games in general. You may want to consult the *Augmentation and Accommodations* section before you begin the game.

NOTES

_____

_____

_____

_____

_____

_____

_____

_____

1.

Give each group two element cards. If you are pressed for time, one card may be sufficient. A complete set of element cards is provided as a Blackline Master in your *Teacher's Resources* CD.

| 8-1a | **Blackline Master** |

2.

Each group must decide the order in which they will present their clues. Their goal should be to give less useful clues first so that other groups will not be able guess the element until three or four clues have been presented.

If your class has not had sufficient exposure to the organization of the periodic table in earlier chapters, you should have them first read through the *Chem Talk* before they start the competition. You could also give this as an assignment for the night before this game.

CHAPTER 8

Investigate

In this part of *Section 1*, the students use the periodic table and their prior knowledge to determine the identity of an unknown element. However, it should be noted that some of the information on the element cards will not help them, since they do not have the background at this time. Hopefully, it will caution them not to guess too quickly until they have enough information to make the right choice. Then, in front of the class, the first group that identifies an element will use a wall-sized periodic table to explain the logic they used to identify the element.

3.

The students will use their knowledge of groups, group names, periods, and properties to identify the elements. Most groups can figure the element out rather rapidly.

3.a)

Student answers will vary but their logic should be consistent.

3.b)

Student answers will vary. Typically, the year of discovery for an element is of little use.

Chem Talk

Learning how to organize facts and draw conclusions from this information is called deductive reasoning. In this discussion the students learn how the data on elements can be used to organize and classify elements into groups.

 CSI Chemistry

3. You will play a game with other groups in your class.

The rules of the game are as follows: When it is your group's turn, you will tell the other groups one of the properties of your mystery element. The leader of any group can then raise his or her hand and attempt to guess the element on the basis of the first property. If the group guesses correctly, it scores one point. If it guesses incorrectly, that group is out of this round.

Your goal is to give clues in such an order that nobody is able to identify your element until the last clue is given. You receive 1 point for every clue that you recite. If a team identifies your element after the first clue, you only get 1 point. If the first team to correctly identify your element requires 4 clues, then you score 4 points.

Each team gets a chance to provide clues to the first mystery element. After one round, each team gets to go again with their second element.

a) At the conclusion of the game, describe the properties that helped the teams identify your material.

b) Which properties did not help the team identify the element? Why?

 Chem Talk

DEDUCTIVE REASONING

Imagine you get up out of your seat to sharpen your pencil. You leave a candy bar on your desk. (Of course, you are not in the lab!) When you return, you notice the candy bar is missing and you wonder, "Where did it go?" Your partner, who sits next to you in class, has chocolate all over his face and an identical wrapper sticking out of his book bag. What do you conclude? Your partner took the candy bar and ate it!

The process you used to assemble and analyze clues that helped you answer the question is called **deductive reasoning**. So, in this case, you deduced that your partner ate your candy bar. You based this on the evidence at the scene (the chocolate on his face and the wrapper in his bag). In this investigation, you used deductive reasoning skills and a variety of reference materials to identify the mystery element's identity.

Often, investigators and forensic chemists are faced with a jumble of facts and evidence that seem to be unconnected. It is the job of the investigator or forensic chemist to organize, analyze, and determine the relationships between different pieces of evidence to reconstruct

Chem Words

deductive reasoning: organizing, analyzing, and determining the relationships between different pieces of information to construct a solution to the situation being investigated.

644

and solve the crime. They are also using deductive reasoning. Some techniques used to analyze information include making lists, making charts, and using the process of elimination.

The Elements and the Periodic Table

The chair you are sitting on, the clothes you are wearing, the air you are breathing, and you, yourself—everything around you is made of **matter**. All matter is made of elements or combinations of different elements. **Elements** are the basic building blocks of matter. They cannot be broken down into simpler substances by physical or chemical means. Currently, there are 114 known elements, each represented by a symbol. These symbols, or more specifically **atomic symbols**, are either one or more letters. The first letter is always capitalized, and the second or third letter, if there is one, is always lowercase. For example, the first element on the table, hydrogen, is represented by the atomic symbol H, and the second element on the table, helium, has the symbol He.

Long ago, data on the individual elements was presented to scientists in a jumble. Chemists sought out a way to organize this information. The result is one of the most marvelous references in science, the periodic table. Using the atomic number of each of the elements, scientists have organized the elements on the **periodic table of elements** into 18 **groups** (up-down columns) and seven **periods** (across rows).

Elements in the same group have similar chemical and physical properties. Because of this, they are often referred to as families. Some of the families have names. The two groups on the far left and the six groups on the far right are known as the **representative** or **main-group** elements.

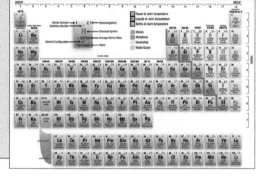

Chem Words

matter: anything that has mass.

element: any material that cannot be broken down into simpler materials.

atomic symbols: one or more letters that represent each element in the periodic table.

periodic table of elements: a tabular arrangement of the elements according to their atomic numbers so that elements with similar properties are in the same column.

group: a column of elements or family of elements in the periodic table. Example: alkali metals are Group 1A.

period: a row of the periodic table. Example: the second period starts with the element lithium and ends with neon.

representative or **main-group elements:** the elements of the periodic table in which the final electron is placed in either an *s* or *p* orbital. Example: All of the elements of the first and second periods are representative elements.

CHAPTER 8

Checking Up

1.

Answers will vary. Deductive reasoning is the kind of reasoning where a conclusion is reached from known data. The conclusion must be valid if the facts are valid.

2.

A group in the periodic table is a column of elements, top to bottom. A period is a row of elements, from left to right.

3.

a) Physical properties of metals are: shininess or luster, conductivity of heat and electricity, malleability, and ductility.

b) Physical properties of nonmetals are: dullness, nonconductive of heat and electricity, brittleness.

4.

Elements located on the "stair-step" line on the periodic table are the metalloids: boron, silicon, germanium, arsenic, antimony, tellurium, and polonium.

What Do You Think Now?

Returning to the *What Do You See?* and the *What Do You Think?* questions will provide students some insight into their greater understanding of the physical world and how to analyze it. Their answers to these questions should be more sophisticated than before.

A flowchart of questions to use to identify an unknown element can be quite simple. For example the following questions could be used:

 CSI Chemistry

Chem Words

transition metals: the elements between the representative elements in which the final electrons are contained in the *d* orbital.

inner transition metals: elements that contain *f* orbital electrons and are called the lanthanides and actinides series.

metalloid: an element that possesses both metal and nonmetal characteristics. Silicon, arsenic, and germanium are examples of metalloids.

The groups are:

Group 1: alkali metals, which include lithium

Group 2: alkaline earth metals, which include beryllium

Group 13: boron group, which has no common name

Group 14: carbon group, which has no common name

Group 15: pnictogens, which include nitrogen

Group 16: chalcogens, which include oxygen

Group 17: halogens, which include fluorine

Group 18: noble gases, which include helium

Groups 3-12 are located in between the representative elements and are called the **transition metals**. The groups that lie below the others on the periodic table are called the **inner transition metals**.

Elements can also be classified as metals, nonmetals, and **metalloids**. The metallic elements are located to the left of the stair-step line that starts between aluminum (Al) and silicon (Si) and ends between tin (Sn) and tellurium (Te). Metals are shiny, can be pounded into sheets (malleable), drawn into wires (ductile), and are good conductors of heat and electricity. Nonmetals are located to the right of the stair-step line. Nonmetals tend to be gases or brittle solids at room temperature. They are also poor conductors of heat and electricity. The elements located around the "stair-step" line on the periodic table are called metalloids. Metalloid elements have both metallic and nonmetallic properties. For example, the metalloid element silicon is shiny like a metal but brittle like a nonmetal.

Checking Up

1. Give an example of deductive reasoning.
2. What is the difference between a group and a period on the periodic table?
3. Describe three physical properties of:
   a) metals
   b) nonmetals
4. Where on the periodic table are the metalloids located?

What Do You Think Now?

At the beginning of this section, you were asked the following:

• What information would you need to identify a material?

• How would you decide which element the material is?

Review your thoughts in the *What Do You Think?* section of your *Active Chemistry* log. Now that you have worked specifically with deductive reasoning and have learned more about the properties of elements, create a simple flowchart or concept map of specific questions. Come up with questions about the material that will help you deduce the identity of an unknown element. Be sure your questions have a logical sequence to them that would lead you to the identity of an element.

 646

Active Chemistry

1.

Is it shiny? (Is it a metal or nonmetal/metalloid?)

2a.

If "yes," then what is its density? (Higher density metals are nearer the bottom of the periodic table; less dense metals are nearer the top of the periodic table.)

2b.

If "no," then what is its boiling point? (Is this nonmetal a liquid, gas or solid at room temperature?)

3a.

And so on. How many oxygen atoms appear in its oxide? If one, it is a Group I or II metal, such as MgO, CaO. If three, it is a Group III metal, such as Al_2O_3.

3b.

And so on. How many sodium ions appear in its sodium salt? If one, it is a halogen, such as NaCl. If two, it belongs in Group VI, such as Na_2O, and so on.

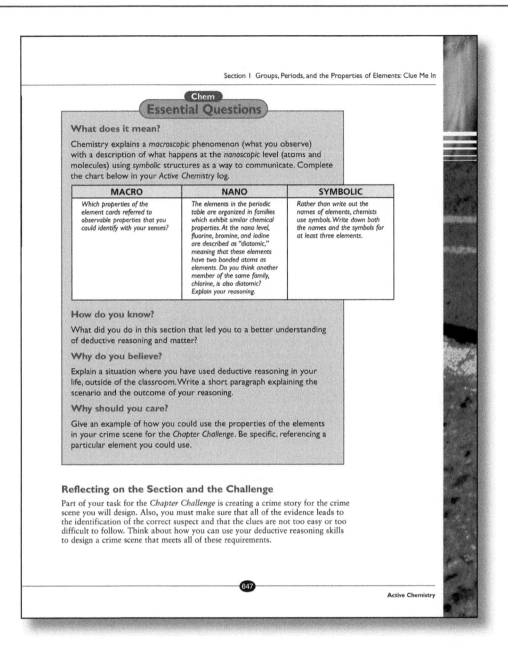

Reflecting on the Section and the Challenge

Following the *Investigate* and *Chem Talk* sections, it is appropriate to take a few minutes and think about how the new information can be used in the *Chapter Challenge*. You might want the students to do this in their small group and then report out to the entire class.

CHAPTER 8

Chem Essential Questions

What does it mean?

MACRO — Properties of the element cards that can be detected with one's senses are: color, odor, and state (solid, liquid, gas).

NANO — Yes, the element chlorine, Cl_2, is diatomic as are the other members of the halogen family. Having the same valence shell electronic configuration leads to having the same chemistry. This will be seen in the similarity in the formulas in compounds of the same family. In ionic compounds we have NaF, NaCl, NaBr and NaI. In organic compounds we have CH_3F, CH_3Cl, CH_3Br, and CH_3I.

SYMBOLIC — Student answers will vary. They should agree with the symbols on the periodic table.

How do you know?

Playing the element game leads to a better understanding of deductive reasoning and how conclusions are based on facts.

Why do you believe?

Student answers will vary. Read each one carefully to ensure that the student understands the step-wise logical nature of the process.

Why should you care?

Student answers will vary. Arsenic is often a popular choice at a crime scene.

Chem to Go

1.

Chlorine

2.

Alkali metals, Group I

3.

d) contains all transition elements, zinc, scandium, iron, and silver.

4.

b) contains elements that are all from the same group.

5.

metals: Lu, V, Ho, Co, La

nonmetals: I, C, Te (tellurium is a metalloid)

6.

Student answers will vary. Caution the students not to merely copy an existing element card.

7.

Preparing for the Chapter Challenge

Answers will vary. Check students' responses for accuracy and for misconceptions.

Inquiring Further

Timeline in the development of the periodic table

Students are asked to research the history that took place in the development of the modern periodic table. You should give them guidelines regarding the length of the paper and the time frame for completion.

 CSI Chemistry

Chem to Go

You will need to use the periodic table to help answer many of the questions below.

1. What element is in group 17 and period 3?

2. What is the name of the group that contains potassium?

3. Which of the following sets of elements contains all transition elements?

   a) vanadium, strontium, aluminum, titanium

   b) tungsten, gold, potassium, ruthenium

   c) tellurium, nickel, phosphorus, magnesium

   d) zinc, scandium, iron, silver

4. Which of the following sets of elements are all members of the same group?

   a) cobalt, rhodium, iridium, tin   b) silicon, germanium, lead, carbon

   c) iodine, xenon, antimony, indium   d) barium, calcium, radium, beryllium

5. Identify the metals and the nonmetals in the following list.

   I, Lu, V, C, Ho, Co, La, Te

6. Select an element from the periodic table that interests you. Create a mystery element card for it. Describe how a fellow student would use the clues you have listed to identify the element.

7. *Preparing for the Chapter Challenge*

   Flip through the entire *CSI Chemistry* chapter of your *Active Chemistry* book. Pay particular attention to the titles and goals of each section. Also, review your *Active Chemistry* log to identify any possible concepts from previous chapters you feel at this point may be useful in creating crime-scene evidence. In your log, prepare a list of possible evidence that you see you'll learn more about in this chapter. If possible, add to that list any topics you have already studied in previous chapters. For topics from other chapters, briefly write down your thoughts on why they may be useful in the crime-scene challenge.

Inquiring Further

Timeline in the development of the periodic table

In developing the periodic table of elements, as more knowledge was acquired about each of the elements, scientists began to ask, "Is there a pattern?" Between 1829 and 1934, chemists attempted to use deductive reasoning to answer this question. Research this period of time in chemistry and create a timeline explaining the history and evolution of the current model of the periodic table. Be sure to cite specific scientists and how they used reasoning skills to organize the elements into the current pattern.

648

Active Chemistry

SECTION 1 – QUIZ

8-1b **Blackline Master**

1. An element that is shiny, conducts electricity, and can be bent is most likely _____ the periodic table.

a) on the left side of   b) in the middle of

c) on the right side of   d) nowhere on

2. Elements are organized on the periodic table by _____ and _____.

3. Place the following elements in the appropriate categories listed below: H, Be, Cd, Ne, Sn, Sc, P, As, Rb, C, I, Sr

_____ Metals   _____ Halogens

_____ Nonmetals   _____ Noble gases

_____ Metalloids   _____ Transition metals

_____ Alkaline earth   _____ Inner transition metals

4. Identify the following element using the periodic table. Arrange the clues in descending order of importance for determining its identity.

- Transition metal
- Liquid at room temperature
- From a bright red mineral called cinnabar
- Used in dental fillings

- Period 6
- Extremely toxic
- Responsible for the "Mad Hatter"

SECTION 1 – QUIZ ANSWERS

❶ a) on the left side of the periodic table, since it is a metal.

❷ groups/families and periods

❸

Be, Cd, Sn, Sc, Rb, Sr	Metals	I	Halogens
H, Ne, P, C, I	Nonmetals	Ne	Noble gases
As	Metalloids	Cd, Sc, Sn	Transition metals
Be, Sr	Alkaline earth	none	Inner transition metals

❹ Most important:

- Liquid at room temperature—only two elements are liquid at room temperature
- Period 6—eliminates over 60 percent of the elements
- Used in dental fillings—gold, silver, mercury (somewhat obscure)
- From a bright red mineral called "cinnabar"—obscure, but HgS if known.
- Extremely toxic—many elements are toxic
- Transition metal—there are many transition metals
- Responsible for the "Mad Hatter"—obscure knowledge; least important.

CHAPTER 8

SECTION 2
Physical Properties: Density of Glass

Section Overview

In this section, students determine the density of a glass sample using the slope method. Different groups will then compare the densities of their samples to find out if they have the same type of glass.

Background Information

Glass fragments from windows, bottles, cars, or mirrors are a common form of evidence found at crime scenes. Forensic chemists need a way to determine if fragments found on a suspect are the same as those belonging to the crime scene. In looking for ways to identify glass fragments and other materials, scientists look to the properties of matter.

Glass

From bottles to windshields, glass is found everywhere. Glass is made from silicon dioxide which is commonly known as sand. When silicon dioxide is heated to temperatures greater than 1700°C, it melts and the silicon atoms bond to four different oxygen atoms creating a tetrahedral structure with the silicon atom in the middle between four oxygen atoms. Long chains of these tetrahedral structures are formed and are "frozen" into place when the material is cooled and crystallizes. This material is a very brittle form of glass known as quartz glass.

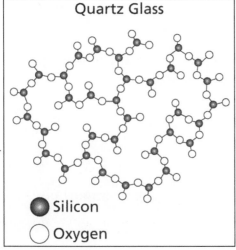

Quartz Glass

● Silicon
○ Oxygen

Besides being brittle, quartz glass also has a very high melting point. This makes it difficult to work with. To modify the properties of glass, different atoms are added that fit into the spaces between the silicon-oxygen chains. Soda-lime glass, one of the most common types of glass, has both calcium ions and sodium ions added to it. This makes it more difficult for the silicon chains to align themselves and creates irregularities in the crystal. The resulting glass has an amorphous structure which makes the glass less brittle and lowers its melting point.

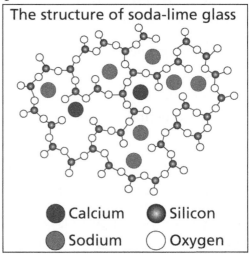

The structure of soda-lime glass

● Calcium   ● Silicon
● Sodium   ○ Oxygen

Notice how the calcium and sodium ions fit in the spaces between the silicon chains. The presence of sodium ions and calcium ions in these spaces makes soda-lime glass denser than quartz glass. Soda-lime glass is used for glasses, jars and windows. Below are some different types of glass; the tables list the different elements that are added to make these types of glass.

1. Commercial glass

2. Borosilicate glass–used for laboratory glassware, beakers, etc.

3. Lead glass > 24% lead

4. 96% Silica glass–used in applications needing great heat resistance such as oven sights, space orbiter windows, etc.

	Formula	1	2	3	4
Silica	SiO_2	73.6%	80.0%	35.0%	96.5%
Soda	Na_2O	16.0	4.0	--	--
Lime	CaO	5.2	--	--	--
Potash	K_2O	0.6	0.4	7.2	--
Magnesium	MgO	3.6	--	--	--
Aluminum	Al_2O_3	1.0	2.0	--	0.5
Iron oxide	Fe_2O_3	--	--	--	--
Boric oxide	B_2O_3	--	13.0	--	3.0
Lead oxide	PbO	--	--	58.0	--

Silica (sand, quartz pebbles)	silicon dioxide	SiO_2
Soda (soda ash ($Na2CO_3$): natron, marine plant ashes)	sodium oxide	Na_2O
Lime (chalk, limestone ($CaCO_3$))	calcium oxide	CaO
Potash (ashes of inland plants)	potassium oxide	K_2O
Lead (oxidized lead metal)	lead oxide	PbO
Boron (modern mineral)	boric oxide	B_2O_3
Magnesium (impurity)	--	MgO
Aluminum (impurity)	--	Al_2O_3
Iron (impurity)	--	Fe_2O_3

Physical and Chemical Properties

Size, color, flammability, mass, stability, and temperature are all properties of matter. Properties are characteristics used to describe matter. Properties can be classified in two categories: physical and chemical.

Physical properties are characteristics of matter that can be observed without changing the chemical identity of the substance. Glass is brittle, hard, odorless, and has a high melting point. It may also be transparent or opaque, colored or uncolored. Other examples of physical properties would include luster, mass, and volume.

Chemical properties describe how the substance reacts with other materials. Glass is a fairly unreactive material. However, it does react with hydrofluoric acid, HF. When forensic chemists are looking for properties to identify materials, they often use a combination of physical and chemical properties.

Intensive Properties of Materials

Because glass is an unreactive material, scientists rely on the physical properties of glass fragments to match them to a crime scene or to a suspect. But which physical properties are the most useful? If the glass fragments are large enough, they can be pieced back together to possibly fit the pieces found at the scene. However, many times the fragments are too small to be pieced back together.

A physical property used in identifying a material must be characteristic of that material and not depend on the quantity of the material. In other words, the property must have the same measurement no matter what amount of material is tested, as long as it is the same material. This kind of physical property is called **intensive**. You can think of an intensive property as one that doesn't change regardless of how small or how large the sample is. In fact, intensive properties are often called characteristic properties, because they can be used to characterize a material. Examples of intensive properties include melting point, freezing point, and temperature. Length and mass are not intensive properties; these are **extensive** properties.

Density

In this activity, students will determine the mass and the volume of four different-sized samples of the same glass. **Mass** is a measure of the amount of matter an object contains. It does not depend on gravity (like weight does) and will be the same no matter where it is measured. Since mass depends on the amount of matter present, it is not an intensive property. Similarly, volume, the amount of space occupied by an object, is not an intensive property. But, when the mass of a glass sample is plotted versus its volume, there is a linear (straight line) relationship. The ratio of mass to volume is constant and independent of sample size. Therefore, the relationship between the mass of a substance and its volume is an intensive property. And since it is an intensive property, it can be used to identify a substance. The relationship between the mass of an object and its volume is called the object's density.

Density is defined as the mass per unit volume. Density can be calculated using the equation:

$$Density = \frac{mass\ (grams)}{Volume\ (mL\ or\ cm^3)}$$

Density is reported in units of g/cm³ for a solid and g/mL for a liquid. For example, if the mass of a solid object is 15.0 grams and its volume is 25.3 cm³, the density of the object is equal to:

$$D = \frac{m}{V} = \frac{15.0\ g}{25.3\ cm^3} = 0.593\ g/cm^3$$

The density of a substance can also be determined by dividing the substance into four or more different-sized samples. Each sample is then massed and its volume is measured. Plotting the mass of an object versus its volume results in a straight line. The slope of the line will be equal to the density of the object. The volumes and the masses for the above example are given below.

Mass (g)	Volume (cm³)
3.01	5.08
7.01	11.8
11.0	18.5
15.0	25.3

Once the density of the substance is known, a table of known densities can be used to identify the substance. With glass fragments, the density of fragments found on a given suspect will be compared to glass fragments found at the scene. If the densities are identical, there is a chance that the suspect was at the scene, although there are many considerations to be checked. After all, if the glass in question is automobile glass from a popular car model, there could be thousands of that particular car model in the state, and hundreds in the area of the crime scene. This technique is not limited to glass but can be used for metals or any other materials for which the density can be measured.

Sources for Error in the Density Measurement

The greatest source of error in this experiment is due to the graduated cylinder. A 100-mL graduated cylinder is used and the minor scale division on this type of cylinder is the "ones" place. Therefore, for each reading, the "ones" place and those places to the left of it are known. However, the tenths place is estimated. The uncertainty of the tenths place can be estimated to be approximately ±0.2 mL. If a small sample size is used, the uncertainty associated with the volume reading will have a large effect on the calculated density. For example, if the volume of a 2.5 g sample is determined to be 1.4 mL, the actual volume is somewhere between 1.2 mL and 1.6 mL. Thus, the actual density would be between 1.6 g/cm³ and 2.1 g/cm³. This range is undesirable and can be limited by using larger sample sizes and by using a large number of samples.

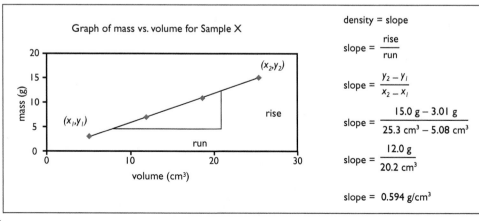

density = slope

slope = $\dfrac{rise}{run}$

slope = $\dfrac{y_2 - y_1}{x_2 - x_1}$

slope = $\dfrac{15.0\ g - 3.01\ g}{25.3\ cm^3 - 5.08\ cm^3}$

slope = $\dfrac{12.0\ g}{20.2\ cm^3}$

slope = 0.594 g/cm³

LEARNING OUTCOMES		
LEARNING OUTCOMES	**LOCATION IN SECTION**	**EVIDENCE OF UNDERSTANDING**
Experimentally determine the density of a solid without a definite shape.	*Investigate*	Students are able to measure the volume of four different sized samples of glass and determine the mass of each sample.
Understand the difference between *intensive* and *extensive* properties.	*Chem Talk,* *Checking Up* Questions 1-2 *Chem to Go* Questions 1, 3	Students find that mass and volume depend on amount present, whereas density does not. This highlights the difference between intensive and extensive properties.
Use an *intensive property* of matter to identify an unknown substance.	*Investigate,* *Chem to Go* Question 4	Students correctly determine the density of their glass sample using the slope of the best straight-line fit.

NOTES

_____

_____

_____

_____

_____

_____

_____

_____

_____

_____

_____

_____

_____

_____

CHAPTER 8

Section 2
Materials, Chemicals, Preparation, and Safety

("per Group" quantity is based on group size of 4 students)

Materials and Equipment

Materials (and Equipment)	Quantity per Group (4 students)
Graduated cylinder, 100-mL	1
Metric ruler, flexible	1
Tweezers	1
Glass tubing, borosilicate glass, 2 ft.	40
Materials (and Equipment)	**Quantity per Class**
Metric graph paper, package of 50	1
Glass tubing cutter, teacher prep	1
Balance, 0.01 g	1
Hammer, small, teacher prep	1
Microscope slides, glass	36

Chemicals

Chemicals	Quantity per Class (24 students)
None	None

Teacher Preparation

Because it is unsafe for students to break glass, you will need to prepare the two types of glass fragments used in the activity—the glass tubing and the microscope slides. Each group will need approximately 40 pieces of each glass sample. Use the glass cutter to cut 250-300 half-inch pieces of the borosilicate glass tubing. Follow the safety instructions provided with the cutter. Break two microscope slides for each group by wrapping each one in a paper towel or plastic bag and hitting it lightly with a hammer. With a few taps you should get about 20 fragments from each slide.

Safety Requirements

- All activity in the laboratory area requires goggles and aprons.

- Working with glass tubing requires special care. Glass cylinders should be handled using tweezers or forceps. If students are handling the glass, they must wear gloves and the glass must be fire polished.

- Glass fragments should be placed in a special container that is approved and clearly identified as an approved broken glass container. Do not throw broken glass into a garbage can.

- Use a broom and dustpan to sweep up any broken glass.

NOTES

CHAPTER 8

Meeting the Needs of All Students
Differentiated Instruction

Augmentation and Accommodations

LEARNING ISSUE	REFERENCE	AUGMENTATION AND ACCOMMODATIONS
Measuring volume and mass Following instructions	*Investigate* Part A	**Accommodations** • A physical task like measuring mass or volume may seem easy to an expert, but the precision of the visual motor skills, concentration, sequencing skills, and reading comprehension required to make accurate measurements can make this a daunting task for novice students with issues in these areas. • Observe students who have difficulty making these measurements to discern what their difficulties are. • If students' problems are due to visual motor coordination, concentration, or inability to follow a sequence, give one-on-one or small-group instruction to teach each step and allow time for practice. • If you discover some students not reading for detail or misreading, help them pick out each direction from the text and make procedure cards that can be followed. • For poor readers, consider adapting the pictures in the text to create a pictorial set of directions they can follow. • Extra time is not just for tests. Give these students extra time to complete the measurements in class.
Creating a data table	*Investigate* Part A, 2.a)	**Augmentation** • Show students who have difficulty copying tables how to create an appropriately sized border for their tables in their *Active Chemistry* logs by counting the number of columns and using a multiple of that measure to determine the width of the table. For example, five columns are needed to re-create the table in the text. Help students determine a measurement for each column that fits in their notebooks (An inch to an inch and a half would work for standard notebook pages.) They can see that the table has five rows. Have students with fine motor issues use three lines in their notebook for each box to make certain they have a large enough space to write their observations. Show them how to count out five multiples of three lines each down each side of the page, marking the lines as they go. Then they can connect the marks with a ruler. **Accommodations** • Provide students with a prepared table to complete.
Following instructions	*Investigate* Part B, 1.	**Augmentation** • Help students find each directive in the first paragraph and rewrite them as a bulleted list of directions. • An alternative would be to have students highlight or underline each step in this paragraph on a copy of the page. Explain how they might use this strategy on their own by copying the directions into a list in their notebooks the next time they encounter directions embedded in a text passage.
Determining a scale for a graph	*Investigate* Part B, 3.b)	**Augmentation** • Because the numbers involved are decimals carried out to the nearest thousandth, having students pick two points on the line which intersect with whole numbers of the grid and count rise over run is not a shortcut to find the slope. Therefore, at this point you will have to teach students a method for calculating slope or provide one or more of the accommodations below. **Accommodations** • Arrange groups so that at least one member in each group can calculate the slope and help other group members. • Show students how to plug the numbers to determine slope into their calculators. • Give students the formula for calculating slope from two or more points. • Refer students to the *Chem Talk* where they are shown how to calculate slope.

Strategies for Students with Limited English Language Proficiency

LEARNING ISSUE	REFERENCE	AUGMENTATIONS
Background knowledge	*What Do You Think?*	Students will benefit from an explanation of the illustration. Students may need an explanation of what it means to be a "*hero*" in a movie. Some examples solicited from the class might help to illustrate this idea.
Vocabulary	*Investigate*	Students might not have the word "*fragments*" in their expressive vocabulary. Provide a synonym for the word "*obtain*." Check for understanding of the idea of "*evidence*." Check that students know the term "*forceps*." Make sure that students understand what to do when directed to "*determine*" something. Check students' understanding of the term "*justify*."
Background knowledge Vocabulary Comprehending text	*Chem Talk*	Check for understanding of bold-type words. Refer students to *Chem Words* material for further explanations of the isolated words. Check for understanding of the term "*versus*." Point out the signal word "*therefore*" to indicate a concluding statement.
Background knowledge	*What Do You Think Now?*	Allow students to discuss some of the possible answers.
Background knowledge Vocabulary Comprehending text	*Chem Essential Questions*	In the *Why should you care?* section students are asked to write a scene. Some students may need to see an example of a scene from a screenplay and may need help with the writing of dialogue.
Comprehension Vocabulary	*Chem to Go*	Students may not know what a "*crystal goblet*" is and might benefit from a description or picture.
Application Comprehension	*Inquiring Further*	Students might need some help in their search for automakers. Check for understanding of the terms "*manufacturers*" and "*windshield*."

NOTES

_____

_____

_____

_____

_____

_____

_____

_____

_____

_____

CHAPTER 8

Section 2
Teaching Suggestions and Sample Answers

What Do You See?

Students will most likely deduce from the colorful illustration that broken glass is the focus of this section. However, they may have difficulty figuring out how they will be investigating broken glass, and to what end. Open a discussion to engage students and elicit responses. This is an opportunity for you to be alert for student misconceptions. Remember that all student responses at this point are valid and that you will return to this question following the *Investigate* and *Chem Talk*.

Some students may focus on the intentions of the artist and comment on the many types of broken glass. Other students may find the hammer-bearing raccoon the most interesting feature. All responses are to be honored and there is no need to come to a consensus or closure.

What Do You Think?

Again, this is simply a chance for you to gauge students' prior understanding and conceptions. All attempts to answer this question should be accepted. Some students may think that an equal volume of sand will do the job and not consider the difference in density between sand and gold. However, some may know that sand and gold do not have the same density and that it would be necessary to adjust the volume of sand so that its mass equals the mass of the gold statue.

What Do You Think?
A CHEMIST'S RESPONSE

As depicted in the movie, the hero spends little time considering the differences in density between sand and gold. In fact, the density of sand might be approximately 2 g/cm^3 while the density of gold is 19.3 g/cm^3.

A more thoughtful hero, perhaps in a lab coat and safety goggles, would carefully consider the density differential and realize that in order to replace gold, he could need 8-12 times the volume in sand. Since the density of sand depends considerably on how much water it contains (wet sand is considerably denser than dry sand), he would need to know how much water the sand contains.

STUDENTS' PRIOR CONCEPTIONS

There are many conceptions regarding the concept of density that you may encounter. Some examples of common misconceptions may include:

1. A bar of lead will displace more water that an aluminum bar of the same size.*

2. A kilogram of lead weighs more than a kilogram of water.*

3. Objects float because they are light (without regard to volume or density.)*

4. Air fills all space.*

5. Two samples of glass that have the same size and shape are the same.

6. The space between atoms is filled with air.

Such misconceptions may stem from students' incomplete understanding of the particle nature of matter. According to a report prepared for the Royal Society of Chemistry titled *Beyond Appearances: Students' misconceptions about basic chemical ideas* by Vanessa Barker Kind, younger students tend to view matter as continuous and describe matter by its bulk properties. This limited understanding probably stems from the fact that students tend to use sensory reasoning based on sensory experiences to formulate thoughts about what they cannot see. Reliance on sensory reasoning may also be due to students' limited exposure to the particle theory matter. In addition, when the particle theory is studied at the secondary level it is usually confined to a limited number of examples such as water. This may lead students to believe that the particle nature of matter is only true for these examples.

* Horton, Chris (2001), "Student Preconceptions and Misconceptions in Chemistry" Integrated Physics and Chemistry Modeling Workshop, Arizona State University, June 2001, Version 1.35

Section 2

Physical Properties: Density of Glass

What Do You See?

Learning Outcomes

In this section you will:

• **Experimentally determine** the density of a solid without a definite shape.

• **Understand** the difference between intensive and extensive properties.

• **Use an intensive property** of matter to identify an unknown substance.

Safety goggles and a lab apron must be worn at all times in a chemistry lab.

Report any broken, cracked, or chipped glassware to your teacher.

Wear protective gloves when working with glass pieces.

What Do You Think?

A good detective must be able to apply what he or she knows in any situation. In a well-known movie, *Raiders of the Lost Ark*, the hero replaces a gold statue with a bag of sand.

• How would the hero of the movie know how much sand to put in the bag to replace the gold statue?

Record your ideas about this question in your *Active Chemistry* log. Be prepared to discuss your responses with your group and the class.

Investigate

Many crimes result in broken glass fragments. Breaking a window, shattering a bottle, crashing through a glass table—the possibilities are endless because so many products are made of glass. In this investigation you are going to learn one way a forensic detective matches a piece of glass from the crime scene.

Part A: Collecting the Data

1. Obtain two samples of glass, labeled A and B, from your teacher. Be careful not to mix the two samples. Examine each sample through a hand lens or stereomicroscope.

 a) Record your observations in your *Active Chemistry* log.

649

Active Chemistry

Investigate

Part A: Collecting the Data

In this section students determine the density of a glass sample. They are given two samples of glass and asked to make observations. The students will then pick one of the two samples and determine its density by using the slope of the line on a mass versus volume graph. Finally they compare the density of their sample to the density of the sample they did not study. They learn that the two samples of glass have actually different densities.

TEACHING TIP

Advise students to use tweezers when handling glass.

1.

Provide students with any two samples of glass that have significantly different densities. If the two samples appear to be identical visually, all the better.

CHAPTER 8

2.a)

You may want to provide students with a copy of the data table. For your convenience, the table is provided as a Blackline Master in your *Teacher Resources* CD.

| 8-2a | **Blackline Master** |

3.

If mechanical balances are used, you may want to review the proper way to use and read them.

4.a)

Make sure that the students read the volume using the bottom of the meniscus. Also, make sure they record the proper number of significant figures. Most 100-mL graduated cylinders show markings for each mL (the "ones" place). All measurements should be estimated to 0.1 mL.

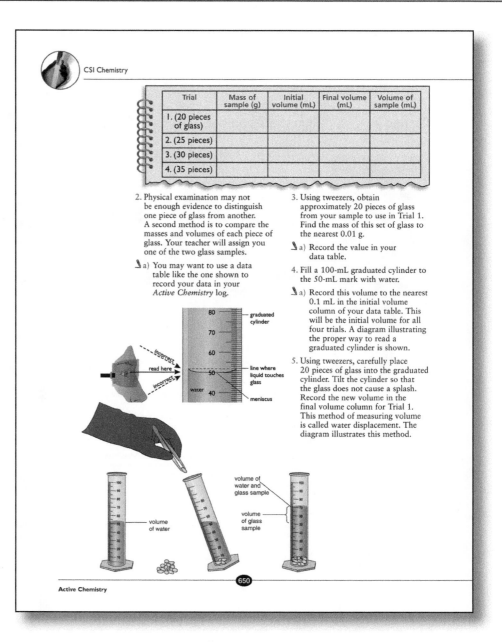

CSI Chemistry

Trial	Mass of sample (g)	Initial volume (mL)	Final volume (mL)	Volume of sample (mL)
1. (20 pieces of glass)				
2. (25 pieces)				
3. (30 pieces)				
4. (35 pieces)				

2. Physical examination may not be enough evidence to distinguish one piece of glass from another. A second method is to compare the masses and volumes of each piece of glass. Your teacher will assign you one of the two glass samples.

a) You may want to use a data table like the one shown to record your data in your *Active Chemistry* log.

3. Using tweezers, obtain approximately 20 pieces of glass from your sample to use in Trial 1. Find the mass of this set of glass to the nearest 0.01 g.

a) Record the value in your data table.

4. Fill a 100-mL graduated cylinder to the 50-mL mark with water.

a) Record this volume to the nearest 0.1 mL in the initial volume column of your data table. This will be the initial volume for all four trials. A diagram illustrating the proper way to read a graduated cylinder is shown.

5. Using tweezers, carefully place 20 pieces of glass into the graduated cylinder. Tilt the cylinder so that the glass does not cause a splash. Record the new volume in the final volume column for Trial 1. This method of measuring volume is called water displacement. The diagram illustrates this method.

650

Active Chemistry

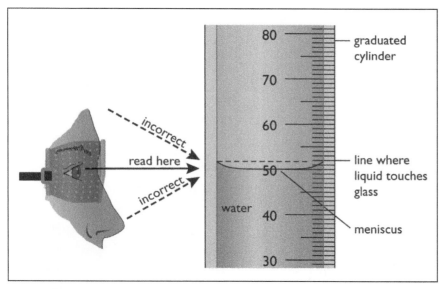

5.

Students should hold the cylinder at an angle and slide the pieces in carefully so that they pack well. If the pieces are tossed quickly into the graduated cylinder, air bubbles may get caught in the pieces of glass. Also, splashing may change the volume.

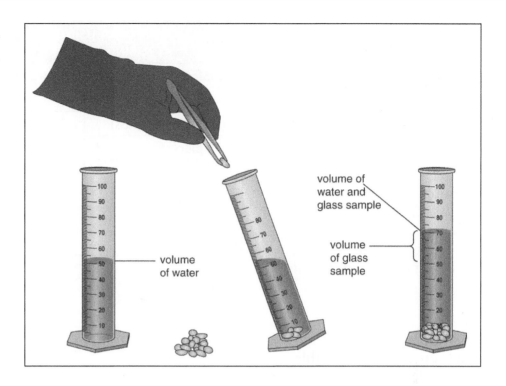

volume of water

volume of water and glass sample

volume of glass sample

CHAPTER 8

NOTES

6.

To calculate the volume of the sample, students should subtract the initial volume from the final volume and record their answer in the column labeled "Volume of Sample."

6.a)

The initial volume of the water for Trials 2-4 will be the same as the final volume from the previous trial. Some students may become confused by this fact.

7.a)

Mass five more pieces of glass. Make sure students add this mass to the mass of the previous trial and record it as the mass for Trial 2. It is important that students realize that they are adding more pieces of glass to the pieces that are already in the cylinder. The mass of the glass in the cylinder is the sum of the mass of original five pieces plus the mass of the five new pieces.

8. a-b)

Students should check to make sure that the volume of the glass is greater than the volume recorded for the previous sample. That is because there are now 25 pieces of glass in the cylinder instead of 20 pieces of glass.

9.

Repeat steps 7 and 8 for two more sets of glass, each set containing five pieces. In addition to their data points from Trials 1-4, it may be wise to include the point (0,0) to indicate that zero mass has zero volume. This data point has no error.

SAMPLE DATA USING HEAT-RESISTANT GLASS (SAMPLE #1) TUBING AND MICROSCOPE SLIDES (SAMPLE #2)		
Sample # 1	**Volume (cm³)**	**Mass (g)**
No glass	0.0	0.0
1 (20 pieces of glass)	11.0	16.4
2 (25 pieces)	13.0	20.47
3 (30 pieces)	15.0	23.01
4 (35 pieces)	17.0	26.0
Sample # 2	**Volume (cm³)**	**Mass (g)**
No glass	0.0	0.0
1 (20 pieces of glass)	1.5	3.04
2 (25 pieces)	2.25	4.53
3 (30 pieces)	2.75	5.27
4 (35 pieces)	3.0	5.81

10.

Have students wrap the wet glass samples in paper towels and shake them gently to get rid of the water. If the next class will be using the same samples, you may ask students to put them in a beaker and place it in a drying oven.

11.a)

Students should share their data with a group that measured a different sample. Remind students to document which groups shared their data.

Part B: Analyzing the Data

1.a)

The best straight-line fit is the second graph.

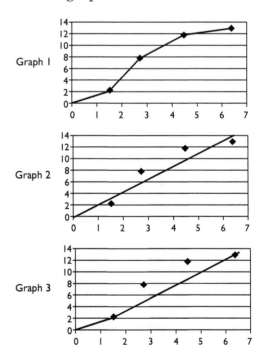

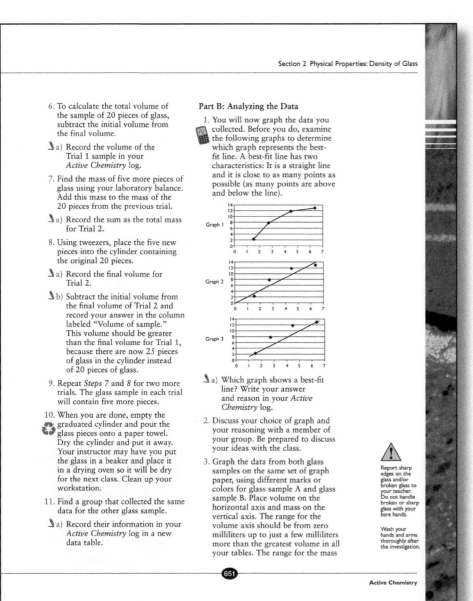

6. To calculate the total volume of the sample of 20 pieces of glass, subtract the initial volume from the final volume.

▲ a) Record the volume of the Trial 1 sample in your *Active Chemistry* log.

7. Find the mass of five more pieces of glass using your laboratory balance. Add this mass to the mass of the 20 pieces from the previous trial.

▲ a) Record the sum as the total mass for Trial 2.

8. Using tweezers, place the five new pieces into the cylinder containing the original 20 pieces.

▲ a) Record the final volume for Trial 2.

▲ b) Subtract the initial volume from the final volume of Trial 2 and record your answer in the column labeled "Volume of sample." This volume should be greater than the final volume for Trial 1, because there are now 25 pieces of glass in the cylinder instead of 20 pieces of glass.

9. Repeat *Steps* 7 and 8 for two more trials. The glass sample in each trial will contain five more pieces.

10. When you are done, empty the graduated cylinder and pour the glass pieces onto a paper towel. Dry the cylinder and put it away. Your instructor may have you put the glass in a beaker and place it in a drying oven so it will be dry for the next class. Clean up your workstation.

11. Find a group that collected the same data for the other glass sample.

▲ a) Record their information in your *Active Chemistry* log in a new data table.

Part B: Analyzing the Data

1. You will now graph the data you collected. Before you do, examine the following graphs to determine which graph represents the best-fit line. A best-fit line has two characteristics: It is a straight line and it is close to as many points as possible (as many points are above and below the line).

▲ a) Which graph shows a best-fit line? Write your answer and reason in your *Active Chemistry* log.

2. Discuss your choice of graph and your reasoning with a member of your group. Be prepared to discuss your ideas with the class.

3. Graph the data from both glass samples on the same set of graph paper, using different marks or colors for glass sample A and glass sample B. Place volume on the horizontal axis and mass on the vertical axis. The range for the volume axis should be from zero milliliters up to just a few milliliters more than the greatest volume in all your tables. The range for the mass

⚠️ Report sharp edges on the glass and/or broken glass to your teacher. Do not handle broken or sharp glass with your bare hands.

Wash your hands and arms thoroughly after the investigation.

651

3.

Have students include the point (0,0) in their data and on their graph. Depending on their previous experience with graphing, students may have some problems here. Their graphs may be too small. Encourage them to expand their scales so that the entire piece of paper is used; it minimizes error when calculating the slope. Students also tend to confuse the x-axis with the y-axis. When calculating the slope, students should choose points as far apart as possible to minimize error. The *Chem Talk* section contains more detailed information on graphing as well as a sample slope calculation. It may be helpful to direct students to read this section before starting their graph.

2.

Keep the discussion short. You may use an overhead of the graphs to facilitate the discussion. However, if you have student groups of widely varying ability, you may choose to have the groups individually conference with you about this as they reach this point.

The first graph is simply a "connect the dots" exercise and will not allow any prediction of density. The second graph is a best straight-line fit for the data and does go through (0, 0). The third graph is incorrect because it simply connects the first and last data points and ignores the other values. Impress upon the students the importance of using all the data to get the best straight line. All of the points contain some error and this can be minimized by averaging the data.

3.a)

The line should start at (0,0) since that point is known to contain no error. After that, the straight line should have two data points above it and two data points below it.

3.b)

Encourage students to choose points as far apart as possible. The difference in density should be large enough for them to distinguish the samples from one another.

For your convenience, a Blackline Master of the following graphs and table of glass densities is provided in your *Teacher Resources* CD.

8-2b | **Blackline Master**

CSI Chemistry

axis should be from zero grams up to just a few grams more than the mass in Trial 4.

a) For each sample, use a ruler to draw a straight line that best fits the five points you graphed.

b) Calculate the slope of each of the lines and record it in your *Active Chemistry* log. Slope = $\frac{y_2 - y_1}{x_2 - x_1}$. The slope of the line will be measured in g/mL. Since 1.0 mL is equal to 1.0 cm^3, the slope could also have the units g/cm^3. This is the *density* of the glass.

4. Graphing the data from two samples of glass has provided you with a second way to distinguish between the two samples. Review the table of glass densities provided by your teacher.

Using the table of glass densities, identify each sample of glass.

a) Write and justify your conclusions in your *Active Chemistry* log. If there are samples that cannot be identified, write what additional information you would need in order to match your sample of glass to a type of glass on the list.

5. You now have two related techniques to use to match glass samples from a crime scene. Given an unknown piece of glass, you can measure its density mathematically ($D = m/V$) or graphically by finding the slope of the mass vs. volume graph of multiple pieces of the same glass. You can then match the density of the unknown glass with other glass samples that you have investigated.

Chem Talk

PROPERTIES OF MATTER

Physical and Chemical Properties

Forensic detectives use properties of matter to identify an unknown object found at a crime scene. This chapter will focus on using properties of matter and deductive reasoning to construct and solve a crime scene. Size, color, flammability, mass, stability, and temperature are all examples of properties (characteristics) you can use to describe matter. Properties fall into two categories: physical and chemical.

Physical properties are characteristics of matter that can be observed without changing the chemical identity of the substance. Examples of physical properties include luster, color, mass, volume,

Chem Words

physical property: a property of matter that can be measured without causing chemical change or a change in the composition of the material. Density is a physical property of a substance.

652

Active Chemistry

Mass vs. Volume Sample #1 (Borosilicate Glass)

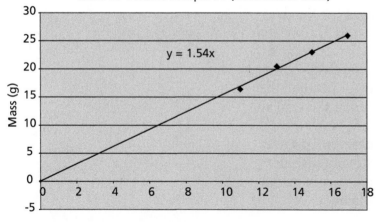

y = 1.54x

Mass (g) vs. Volume (mL)

and odor. Glass is brittle, hard, odorless, and has a high melting point. It may also be transparent or opaque, colored or uncolored. These are just some of the physical properties of glass.

Chemical properties describe how the substance reacts with other materials. Rusting is a chemical property of iron. It describes what happens to iron when in the presence of oxygen and moisture. Firefighters' suits are flame retardant; this is a chemical property. Glass is a fairly unreactive material. However, glass does react with hydrofluoric acid. Reactivity with hydrofluoric acid is a chemical property of glass. Forensic chemists often use a combination of physical and chemical properties to identify materials. In this chapter, you will always reflect on the chemical and physical properties of evidence in order to determine or confirm the identity of the matter.

Intensive and Extensive Properties of Materials

Glass fragments found at the crime scene or on a suspect can be large enough to be pieced back together into the original object, such as a broken glass vase. Then this can be examined for additional evidence such as fingerprints. Could you imagine trying to put the pieces you used today back together! It would probably be a hopeless task because the pieces are so small! In these cases, the properties of the glass itself must be used for identification. Since glass is a fairly unreactive material, scientists rely on the physical properties of glass fragments to match to a crime scene or a suspect. However, not all physical properties are equally useful. A physical property used in identifying a material must not depend on the quantity of the material. In other words, the property must have the same measurement no matter what amount of material is tested, as long as it is the same material. This kind of physical property is called an **intensive property.** You can think of an intensive property as one that doesn't change regardless of how small or how large the sample of a particular substance is. In fact, intensive properties are often called characteristic properties, because they can be used to characterize a material. Examples of intensive properties include melting point and freezing point. Length and mass are not intensive properties of a material because they depend on the amount of substance in a given sample. Properties like length and mass, which vary depending on the amount of material present, are called **extensive properties.** Extensive properties are not used to identify or match matter at a crime scene.

Chem Words

chemical property: a property that is displayed when matter undergoes a change in composition (it undergoes a chemical reaction). The burning of wood is a chemical property.

intensive property: a physical property that does not change (has the same measurement) no matter how much of the material is present.

extensive property: a physical property that varies depending on the amount of material (matter) present.

653

Active Chemistry

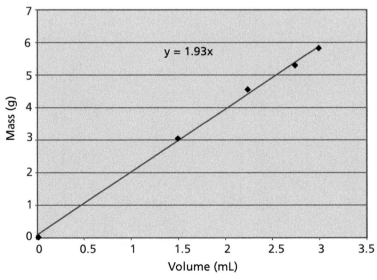

Mass vs. volume Sample #2 (Microscope Slide)

$y = 1.93x$

4.a)

Students should be able to identify, at least tentatively, the two glass samples. Other information they might consider are color, unique fragmentation pattern, and exterior contaminants (e.g., paint, tar, blood).

5.

Students should identify their group's glass sample and the other group's glass sample based on the correspondence between their calculated density values and the reference table values for soft glass and borosilicate glass densities, as long as their calculated values are close to those in the table. Any major discrepancies should be checked and examined for errors.

Type of Glass	Density (cm³)
quartz glass	2.2
borosilicate glass	2.3
soft glass	2.6
leaded glass	2.8

Chem Talk

A review of physical and chemical properties leads into an explanation of the differences between intensive and extensive properties. Density, which is mass per unit volume, relies on the extensive properties of mass and volume, but is itself an intensive property. The reading concludes with an examination of density and how it can be calculated from a mass and volume.

CHAPTER 8

Checking Up

1.

Two physical properties of glass: brittle and non-conductive.

Two chemical properties of glass: unreactive with oxygen, nitrogen, or water.

2.

An intensive property is a property that does not depend on the quantity of material. Density is an example of an intensive property. An extensive property depends on the quantity of material. Mass is an example of an extensive property, as are length and width.

3.

The equation to calculate the density of a material is:

$$\text{Density} = \frac{\text{mass}}{\text{volume}} = \text{g/cm}^3.$$

4.

The slope of a straight line in a graph of mass vs. volume is the density.

5.

No, density cannot be used to match two substances. However, density can be used to show that the two substances are not the same.

6.

No, many samples of glass will have the same density. However, if the density does match, it is a piece of evidence that the suspect might have been at the crime scene.

CSI Chemistry

Chem Words

mass: a measure of the amount of matter an object contains.

volume: a measure of the space occupied by matter.

density: the mass of a substance per unit volume.

Density

In this experiment, you determined the mass and the volume of four samples of the same glass. Each sample was a different size. **Mass** is a measure of the amount of matter an object contains. It does not depend on gravity (like weight) and will be the same regardless of where it is measured. Since mass depends on the amount of matter present, it is an extensive property. Likewise, **volume**, the amount of space occupied by matter, is also an extensive property. But, you may have noticed that when the mass of the glass sample was plotted against its volume, there was a linear (straight-line) relationship. The ratio of the mass to the volume was constant and did not depend on the sample size. Therefore, the relationship between the mass of a substance and its volume is an intensive property. And since it is an intensive property, you can use the mass versus volume relationship to identify a substance. The relationship between the mass of an object and its volume is called the object's **density.**

Density is defined as the mass per unit volume. Density can be calculated using the equation

$$\text{Density} = \frac{\text{mass (g)}}{\text{volume (mL or cm}^3)}$$

Density is reported in units of g/cm³ or g/mL. For example, if the mass of a solid object is 15.0 g and its volume is 25.3 cm³, the density of the object is equal to

$$\text{Density} = \frac{m}{V} = \frac{15.0 \text{ g}}{25.3 \text{ cm}^3} = 0.593 \frac{\text{g}}{\text{cm}^3} \text{ or } 0.593 \text{ g/mL}$$

Calculating Density from a Mass and Volume Data Set

The density of a substance can be found with a single calculation or by graphing a data set of mass versus volume. In this investigation, you used a graph to determine the density of your glass sample. Using this procedure for a sample "X," a data table below was created.

Checking Up

1. Give two physical and two chemical properties of glass.
2. In your own words, describe the difference between an intensive and extensive property.
3. What equation can be used to calculate the density of a material?
4. What does the slope of a mass versus volume graph represent?
5. If two unknown materials have exactly the same density, can you deduce that the two materials are the same?
6. If the density of glass fragments found on a suspect matches the glass fragments at the scene of a crime, can you prove without a doubt that the suspect was at the scene of the crime?

Sample X

Mass (g)	Volume (cm³)
3.01	5.08
7.01	11.8
11.0	18.5
15.0	25.3

The next step is to plot the mass versus the volume for all four samples on a graph. After plotting the data, a straight-line fit for the data is drawn. This line may not go through all of the data points. The slope of this line will be equal to the density of the substance. That's because the slope is equivalent to

---

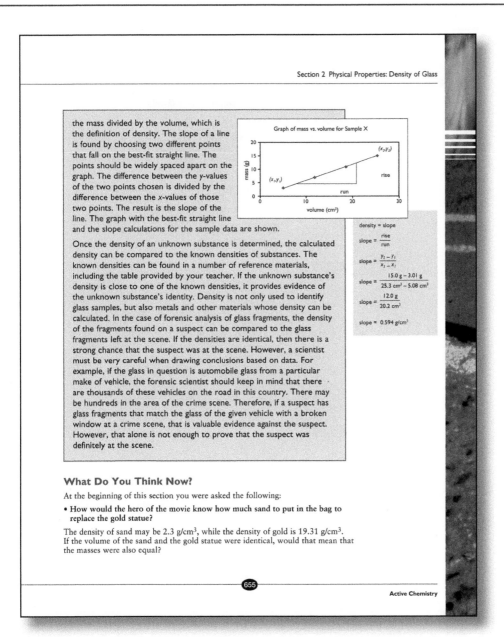

the mass divided by the volume, which is the definition of density. The slope of a line is found by choosing two different points that fall on the best-fit straight line. The points should be widely spaced apart on the graph. The difference between the y-values of the two points chosen is divided by the difference between the x-values of those two points. The result is the slope of the line. The graph with the best-fit straight line and the slope calculations for the sample data are shown.

Once the density of an unknown substance is determined, the calculated density can be compared to the known densities of substances. The known densities can be found in a number of reference materials, including the table provided by your teacher. If the unknown substance's density is close to one of the known densities, it provides evidence of the unknown substance's identity. Density is not only used to identify glass samples, but also metals and other materials whose density can be calculated. In the case of forensic analysis of glass fragments, the density of the fragments found on a suspect can be compared to the glass fragments left at the scene. If the densities are identical, then there is a strong chance that the suspect was at the scene. However, a scientist must be very careful when drawing conclusions based on data. For example, if the glass in question is automobile glass from a particular make of vehicle, the forensic scientist should keep in mind that there are thousands of these vehicles on the road in this country. There may be hundreds in the area of the crime scene. Therefore, if a suspect has glass fragments that match the glass of the given vehicle with a broken window at a crime scene, that is valuable evidence against the suspect. However, that alone is not enough to prove that the suspect was definitely at the scene.

What Do You Think Now?

At the beginning of this section you were asked the following:

• How would the hero of the movie know how much sand to put in the bag to replace the gold statue?

The density of sand may be 2.3 g/cm^3, while the density of gold is 19.31 g/cm^3. If the volume of the sand and the gold statue were identical, would that mean that the masses were also equal?

What Do You Think Now?

Now that students have completed the investigation, they should be able to answer the question at the introduction of the section. You may choose to read them the answer provided in A *Chemist's Response* and have students discuss their opinions. You may also want to return to the *What Do You See?* illustration for another look. Students' interpretations will be more accurate and insightful, which should bolster their confidence.

No, masses of equal volumes of sand and gold would not be the same. Gold would be many times more massive.

CHAPTER 8

Reflecting on the Section and the Challenge

Intensive properties play an important part in identifying the materials that are collected at a crime scene. Learning how to use density to include or exclude a substance in the compilation of evidence can be an important part in reconstructing a crime scene. You might want to take some class time to have the students meet in their groups and plan how they might use the knowledge gained in their *Chapter Challenge*. If time permits, an oral report to the class from each group may help improve their final presentations.

Chem Essential Questions

What does it mean?

MACRO — As the mass increased, the volume of the glass also increased linearly. However, since density is an intensive property, it did not change.

NANO —

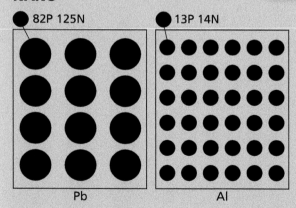

Pb   Al

SYMBOLIC — The units that represent density are typically g/cm³ for solids or g/mL for liquids. The equation that defines density is: $D = \frac{m}{V}$.

CSI Chemistry

Chem Essential Questions

What does it mean?

Chemistry explains a *macroscopic* phenomenon (what you observe) with a description of what happens at the *nanoscopic* level (atoms and molecules) using *symbolic* structures as a way to communicate. Complete the chart below in your *Active Chemistry* log.

MACRO	NANO	SYMBOLIC
How did increases in the mass of the glass affect the volume and the density of the glass?	In two separate diagrams, represent the densities of two different elements at the nanoscopic (molecular) level. Make one element lead, a very dense element, and the other aluminum, a less dense element.	What are the units you use to represent density? What is the equation you use to define density?

How do you know?

Making specific reference to your data, explain how a person can distinguish two types of glass.

Why do you believe?

Solid gold and gold-plated jewelry may look identical. How can density measurements be used to determine if a piece of jewelry is real gold or just gold-plated?

Why should you care?

You will be creating and solving a crime scene for your challenge in this unit. Write a short scene using glass fragments to clear one suspect of suspicion and indicate another suspect. In your short scene, explain how the glass fragments were found, analyzed, and interpreted.

Reflecting on the Section and the Challenge

You have learned how to experimentally determine the density of a glass sample. Because density is an intensive (or characteristic) property, this measurement can help determine the identity of a material that looks like glass found at the crime scene or on a suspect. If glass fragments remain as evidence of a crime, then you may need to measure the density of the glass to determine if the fragment is from the scene of the crime or if it is unconnected to the crime.

Active Chemistry

How do you know?

Two samples of glass were examined. The densities of each were calculated from the mass and volume measurements. The first had a density of 2.1 g/cm³. The second had a density of 2.4 cm³. This difference was great enough to distinguish between the two types of glass.

Why do you believe?

Jewelry made of pure gold (24 carat) is much denser than a gold-plated piece of jewelry. Therefore, it's heavier and easy to distinguish.

Why should you care?

Students' responses will vary widely. Check submissions carefully for logic and accuracy as well as for evidence of understanding of the relevant concepts.

Set	Mass (g)	Volume (cm³)
0	0.0	0.0
1	2.0	0.71
2	4.2	1.5
3	6.5	2.1
4	7.9	2.8

Type of Glass	Density (cm³)
quartz glass	2.2
borosilicate glass	2.3
soft glass	2.6
leaded glass	2.8

CHAPTER 8

Section 2 Physical Properties: Density of Glass

Chem to Go

1. Identify the following as physical or chemical properties.

   a) height   b) flammability   c) tarnishing   d) hardness

2. Calculate the density for an object that has a mass of 2.53 g and a volume of 4.54 cm³.

3. Give an example of an intensive physical property. Explain your choice.

4. A collection of glass fragments was found in the car of the prime suspect, Bob. The glass found at the crime scene was from a crystal goblet made of leaded glass. Using the data obtained by the forensic chemists and the graph-slope method, determine if the glass in Bob's car could be from the crime scene.

Glass Data from Bob's Car		
Set	Mass (g)	Volume (cm³)
0	0.0	0.0
1	2.0	0.71
2	4.2	1.5
3	6.5	2.1
4	7.9	2.8

Type of glass	Density (g/cm³)
quartz glass	2.2
borosilicate glass	2.3
soft glass	2.6
leaded glass	2.8

5. If different glass manufacturers use different window glass formulations, density measurements can be used to help identify the manufacturer of a particular glass fragment. How? Explain.

6. *Preparing for the Chapter Challenge*

   You will want your data used in the challenge's crime scene to be realistic. Look at the four types of glass presented in *Question 4*. Using any resource you choose, find an example of how each of these types of glass may be present at a typical crime scene, such as a kitchen, office, or bedroom. In your *Active Chemistry* log, create a table to organize your findings, including columns for type of glass, density, uses, and examples of crime scenes where you may find that type of glass.

Inquiring Further

Glass used by car manufacturers

Research the density of the glass used by three different automakers. Obtain and test a windshield sample from a local glass shop or car impound lot under the supervision of a responsible adult. Share this information with your classmates by creating a detailed profile document of each of the windshield types, including comparing your experimental results to the known data you researched.

657

Active Chemistry

Chem to Go

1.

a) height	*Physical*
b) flammability	*Chemical*
c) tarnishing	*Chemical*
d) hardness	*Physical*

2.

The density of an object that has a mass of 2.53 grams and a volume of 4.54 cm³:

$$D = \frac{m}{V} = 2.53 \text{ g}/4.54 \text{ cm}^3$$

$$D = 0.557 \text{ g/cm}^3$$

3.

Answers will vary but might include temperature, color, magnetism, melting point, or boiling point. Explanations should focus on the fact that intensive physical properties do not depend on the amount of material.

4.

The density of the glass in Bob's car is about 2.8 g/cm³, which is similar to the density of the leaded glass found at the crime scene. This can be used as evidence to establish that Bob was present at the crime scene.

5.

If each manufacturer has a unique formulation, then the density of any glass sample can be matched to a specific manufacturer. If the glass by that manufacturer is only sold in certain regions, it can help narrow the field.

6.

Preparing for the Chapter Challenge

There are specific types of glass for different things, like glass from a vehicle, glass from a window, tableware glass, etc. Students should realize that the density of glass could be a key factor in developing their crime scene. Answers will vary.

Inquiring Further

Glass used by car manufacturers

Make sure any students undertaking this project have adequate adult supervision. They may have success obtaining samples of windshield glass from car repair shops; they should not attempt to break any windshields to obtain samples. Much of the information they need could be available from Internet research.

SECTION 2 – QUIZ

8-2c	Blackline Master

1. What is the formula for calculating density?

2. Fill in the blanks in the following chart.

METAL	Mass	Volume	Density
Nickel	5.6 g	0.63 cm^3	
Copper	1.8 g		9.0 g/cm^3
Lead		0.56 cm^3	11 g/cm^3

3. Two spheres of the same volume are shown below. How do the masses of the spheres compare?

a) mass Pb sphere > mass Ni sphere

b) mass Pb sphere = mass Ni sphere

c) mass Pb sphere < mass Ni sphere

4. Which of the following is not a physical property?

a) color   b) mass

c) odor   d) rusting

SECTION 2 – QUIZ ANSWERS

❶ $D = \dfrac{m}{V}$

❷

METAL	Mass	Volume	Density
Nickel	5.6 g	0.63 cm^3	**8.9 g/cm^3**
Copper	1.8 g	**0.20 cm^3**	9.0 g/cm^3
Lead	**6.3 g**	0.56 cm^3	11 g/cm^3

❸ a) mass Pb sphere > mass Ni sphere.

❹ d) rusting.

NOTES

CHAPTER 8

SECTION 3
Atomic Structure and Chemiluminescence: The Luminol Reaction

Section Overview

In this section, students investigate chemiluminescence and its application to forensics. Students observe a lightstick, perform the luminol blood test, and then compare the two reactions. Lastly, they use the luminol blood test on other substances to determine if the test is specific for blood.

Background Information

Investigators use many different techniques to find evidence at a crime scene. One of the methods popularized by many of today's crime shows and movies uses a light-producing chemical reaction to visualize hidden bloodstains. In this activity, when light-producing chemicals (luminol and hydrogen peroxide) are sprayed on areas contaminated with blood, they produce a blue glow. Due to the sensitivity of this technique, even invisible blood splatters that have been supposedly "cleaned" off the surface will appear. To learn how the luminol test works, an understanding of the atom is needed.

Structure of the atom

The atom is composed of *protons*, *neutrons* and *electrons*. The protons and neutrons are located in the center of the atom known as the *nucleus*. Neutrons (n^0), are neutral particles located in the nucleus of the atom. Protons, (p^+), are positively charged particles also located in the nucleus.

Atoms of the same element contain the same number of protons. For example, every atom of iron has 26 protons. However, every atom of the element copper has 29 protons. The number of protons in a single atom of an element is equal to the element's *atomic number*. The atomic number is found above an element's symbol on the periodic table.

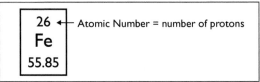

Electrons, (e^-), are negatively charged particles located outside the nucleus. The electrons exist outside the nucleus in certain allowable states called *energy levels*. If an atom has an equal number of electrons and protons, then the atom is neutral. For example, a neutral iron atom has 26 protons and 26 electrons. The positive charge of the protons is equal to the negative charge of the electrons. A neutral carbon atom contains 6 protons and 6 electrons.

Electrons can be lost or gained in chemical reactions. If an atom loses an electron, the number of protons is larger than the number of electrons and the atom becomes positively charged. The atom gets one positive charge for every electron it loses. If an iron atom loses two electrons, it will have a (+2) charge. If an iron atom loses three electrons, it will have a (+3) charge. The charges are written in the upper right corner above the element's symbol.

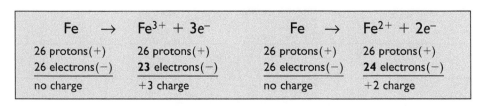

If a neutral atom gains an electron, it will become negatively charged. If a chlorine atom gains an electron, it will have a (–1) charge. If oxygen gains two electrons, it will have a (–2) charge.

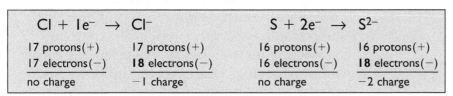

In each example, only the number of electrons changes. The number of protons in each atom will always remain the same. Atoms that have lost or gained electrons are called *ions*. In addition to blood, students will observe that the luminol solution also produces a blue glow with a number of different ions.

Light

Light is a form of energy known as electromagnetic radiation. Electromagnetic radiation includes x-rays, ultraviolet rays, microwaves, and radio waves. Visible light is the only portion of the electromagnetic spectrum that can be seen by the human eye.

Electromagnetic radiation, including visible light, can be characterized by its wavelength and its frequency. The wavelength of light is the distance from peak to peak or trough to trough. The number of wavelengths passing a point per second is called the frequency of the radiation. The frequency of a wave is inversely proportional to its wavelength.

The energy of light is inversely related to its wavelength and directly related to its frequency. Light that has a long wavelength has less energy than light that has a short wavelength. The wavelength of visible light ranges from 700 nm for red to 400 nm for violet. Red light has less energy than blue light. The energy of a given wavelength of light determines if it can interact with the electrons in an atom or molecule.

How Atoms Produce Light

Electrons exist outside the nucleus in certain allowable states called energy levels. As the distance from the nucleus increases, the energy difference between the two adjacent levels decreases. When an electron absorbs energy, it can move from a lower energy level to a higher level. However, the energy that the electron absorbs must be equal to the energy difference between the two levels. Think of the energy levels as the rungs of a ladder. If you only give your foot enough energy to make it halfway between one rung and the next, it is not going to reach the next rung. Instead, it will remain on the lower rung. If an electron does not get enough energy, it will not be promoted to a higher energy level. When the electron absorbs enough energy to get promoted to a higher state, it is considered to be in an *excited state*, to distinguish it from the *ground state* where the electron began. The energy the electron absorbs may come from heat, collisions, chemical reactions, light, or other forms of electromagnetic radiation. An electron does not remain in the excited state for very long. It moves to a lower energy state and loses energy in the process. In the hydrogen atom, transitions from higher energy levels to the first energy level result in the emission of UV radiation. Transitions from higher energy levels to the second energy level result in the emission of visible light and transitions to the third energy level result in infrared emissions.

It is important to remember that, while energy levels are often illustrated as circular orbits, the electrons are not actually traveling circular orbits but are located in regions in space around the nucleus of the atom. The electron can actually be in a number of places but when the most probable locations are plotted, a three-dimensional region in space is formed. Also, excited electrons do not have to return to their ground state in a single step. For example, an excited electron from the first energy level that is in the fifth energy level may return directly to the first energy level by releasing energy. Or, it may return to the first energy level in a series of steps. For example, it may drop to the third energy level by releasing energy. Then it may drop from the third to the first level, releasing energy again.

Incandescence, Fluorescence, Phosphorescence, and Chemiluminescence

Incandescence refers to light produced by an object when it is heated. The light produced by an incandescent bulb is an example. The filament in the incandescent bulb is made of tungsten metal. When the light is turned on, electricity travels through the wire, and the wire heats up. The wire is very thin and thin wires heat up faster than thick wires. When an object is heated, the atoms vibrate faster. The higher the temperature is, the faster the atoms vibrate. These vibrations excite the electrons in the tungsten atoms and they move to an excited state. When the excited electrons move down to a lower energy state, they release energy in the form of electromagnetic radiation. Initially, the first type of radiation is in the infrared portion of the spectrum. This cannot be seen, but it is felt as heat. As the wire continues to heat up, some of the electrons can jump up to higher levels. When the electrons move back down, they release more energy and the emitted radiation has a shorter wavelength. The wire now glows red. This is the source of the common expression, "red hot." As the wire continues to heat, more high-energy electron transitions occur and the wavelength of the radiation shifts from red, to orange, to yellow, and eventually to a bluish white (which is the derivation of the expression "white hot").

Another type of light emission that occurs is called fluorescence. *Fluorescence* is the emission of light at a lower energy and longer wavelength than the energy that was used to excite it. In fluorescence, the electrons in an atom or molecule absorb energy, such as UV light, and move to an excited state. In the excited state, the electron then loses some energy to vibrations before it drops down to a lower energy state. As a result, the color (wavelength) of the light emitted is shifted towards the red (longer wavelength, lower energy) end of the visible spectrum.

In *phosphorescence*, the electrons are excited in the same manner as fluorescence. Once the electron has been excited, it relaxes to an intermediate meta-stable state. Depending on the conditions such as temperature, the electron can get stuck in the intermediate state. The electrons relax back to the ground state at different times. As a result, the emission of light is delayed over a period of time ranging from seconds to hours. This delayed emission of light is known as the *persistence* and distinguishes phosphorescence from fluorescence.

The lightstick reaction and the luminol reaction are examples of *chemiluminescence*. Chemiluminescence is the production of light without heat by a chemical reaction. In chemiluminescence, the starting compounds react and their atoms rearrange themselves to form new compounds and light. The luminol spray consists of luminol, sodium perborate, sodium carbonate and water. The sodium carbonate provides the basic conditions necessary for the reaction to take place. The sodium perborate, when dissolved in water, provides hydrogen peroxide by the following reaction:

$$NaBO_3 \cdot 4H_2O \rightarrow NaBO_2 + H_2O_2 + 3H_2O$$

In the luminol blood test, luminol is oxidized by the hydrogen peroxide to form an excited compound called 3-aminopthalate. When the electrons in the 3-aminopthalate return to the ground state, blue light is released.

However, at room temperature, luminol and hydrogen peroxide do not react. A *catalyst* is needed to speed up the reaction. A catalyst is a substance that speeds up a chemical reaction without being consumed. It provides an alternate pathway for the reaction to take place. With every chemical reaction, there is an energy barrier that must be overcome for the reactants to be converted into products. For the luminol reaction, this energy barrier is too high and the reaction cannot take place. This explains why the luminol solution that you made does not glow in the spray bottle. A catalyst is needed. A catalyst works by lowering this energy barrier.

When the luminol-peroxide mixture comes into contact with blood, the Fe^{2+} ions in the center of the hemoglobin molecules catalyze the reaction and a visible blue glow is produced. Because other substances also catalyze the reaction and cause the solution to glow, the luminol test is not specific for blood. Examples of other ions that catalyze this reaction include Cu^{2+} and Co^{2+} ions. Different plant materials such as horseradish can catalyze the luminol reaction. These materials

contain *enzymes*. Enzymes are materials that catalyze biological reactions. Other tests need to be performed on the sample to confirm that the substance is blood. However, each substance speeds up the reaction to a different degree. For example, the cobalt II ion causes the reaction to glow intensely for a few seconds whereas hemoglobin causes the reaction to glow more uniformly, dimmer, and for a longer period of time. An experienced forensic investigator will have a good idea whether or not the glow is caused by blood. However, no matter how experienced the investigator, a sample will have to be taken back to the lab to determine if the substance is actually blood.

CHAPTER 8

LEARNING OUTCOMES		
LEARNING OUTCOMES	**LOCATION IN SECTION**	**EVIDENCE OF UNDERSTANDING**
Gain a basic understanding of atomic structure and its connection to the production of light.	*Chem to Go* Questions 5-7 *Checking Up* Questions 1-3	Students use knowledge about atomic structure to identify elements using the number of protons. Students can correctly write the symbols and charges for ions given the number of protons and electrons.
Define and explain chemiluminescence as it relates to luminol.	*Investigate* Parts A-B *Checking Up* Question 4	Students observe how compounds combine to create light. Students' answers match those provided in this *Teacher's Edition*.
Be able to apply a presumptive test to your crime scene.	*Investigate* Parts B-C	Students test different substances using luminol solution. Students use the procedure learned in Part C to determine if other substances cause the luminol solution to glow.

NOTES

_____

_____

_____

_____

_____

_____

_____

Section 3
Materials, Chemicals, Preparation, and Safety

("per Group" quantity is based on group size of 4 students)

Materials and Equipment

Materials (and Equipment)	Quantity per Group (4 students)
Lightstick	1
Spray bottle – 100-mL capacity	1
Beral pipettes, disposable	30
Iron nail (rusty)	1
White paper, sheets	10
Graduated cylinders, 100-mL	2

Materials (and Equipment)	Quantity per Class
Ketchup, bottle	1
Horseradish, jar	1
Red food-coloring, vial	1
Filter paper, box (100)	1
Wax paper, roll	1

Chemicals

Chemicals	Quantity per Class (24 students)
Luminol	0.2 g
Bovine hemoglobin, powder	1.25 g
Sodium carbonate, Na_2CO_3	10 g
Sodium perborate tetrahydrate, $NaBO_3 \cdot 4H_2O$	1.4 g
Bleach, NaOCl	25 mL
0.1 M iron (II) chloride dihydrate, $FeCl_2 \cdot 2H_2O$	1.6 g
0.1 M iron (III) chloride hexahydrate, $FeCl_3 \cdot 6H_2O$	2.7 g

NOTES

_____

_____

_____

_____

_____

_____

_____

Teacher Preparation

Luminol reagent—Dissolve 10.0 g of Na_2CO_3 in 500 mL of deionized water, followed by 0.2 g or luminol. On the day of use, add 1.4 g of $NaBO_3 \cdot 4H_2O$. Put 50-75 mL of the luminol reagent into each of 6 spray bottles, one for each group.

Bovine hemoglobin solution—Dissolve 1.25 g of bovine hemoglobin in 500 mL of deionized water. Treat all spills with dilute bleach solution. This is enough for 10 classes or more. If desired, this solution can be replaced with 0.1 M cobalt nitrate $(Co(NO_3)_2)$ solution.

Dilute bleach solution—Place 25 mL of household bleach solution in a 500 mL beaker and add 225 mL of deionized water. This can be placed in 1 or more labeled spray bottles for cleaning up bovine hemoglobin.

Iron (II) chloride solution, 0.1 M—Dissolve 1.6 g iron (II) chloride dihydrate $(FeCl_2 \cdot 2H_2O)$ in 75 mL of deionized water. Add water to make 100 mL and place in labeled dropper bottles for student use.

Iron (III) chloride solution, 0.1 M—Dissolve 2.7 g iron (II) chloride hexahydrate $(FeCl_3 \cdot 6H_2O)$ in 75 mL of deionized water. Add water to make 100 mL and place in labeled dropper bottles for student use.

Fake blood recipes:

- 5 drops red food coloring for every 1 drop of blue.

- 5 mL of 0.1 M $Co(NO_3)_2$ solution—Dissolve 2.91 grams $Co(NO_3)_2 \cdot 6H_2O$ in 70 mL of deionized water and adjust volume to 100 mL by adding water.

Rusty nails: soak iron nails in saltwater for 1-2 days

Safety Requirements

- Goggles and aprons are required in the laboratory area.

- Make sure that students rinse and clean their arms and hands with soap and water.

- All equipment that was used for the bovine hemoglobin solution must be rinsed in a dilute bleach solution. Hands should also be rinsed with dilute bleach solution.

- Small amounts of the metal solutions can be rinsed down the sink.

CHAPTER 8

Meeting the Needs of All Students
Differentiated Instruction

Augmentation and Accommodations

LEARNING ISSUE	REFERENCE	AUGMENTATION AND ACCOMMODATIONS
Using a control group in an experiment Answering "why?" questions	*Investigate* Part B, 4.b)	**Augmentation** • The *Investigate* is set up for students to explore the topic before the chemistry is explained; therefore, it is more appropriate for students to make reasoned predictions than it is for you to tell them answers. You should check students' responses to this question during the investigation and clarify the concept of using controls. • Understanding the semantics of responses to "why?" questions will help students write more clearly. Before students answer the question about why a control is needed, develop a rubric with them that includes the action taken, its purpose, and words/phrases from the text. An appropriate response to this question from a student might be, "Using a control allows a scientist to confirm that the reaction is caused when blood is present and does not occur when water is used." This response included words that describe the action taken, the purpose of the action, and the effects of not taking the action.
Copying a table Visual motor skills Spatial skills Using measures and proportions	*Investigate* Part C, 2.	**Augmentation** • Show students how to set up proportions they can use to fit this table into their notebooks and establish the width of each column. • Show students who need more space to write legibly how they can use proportions to enlarge their tables. • Show students with difficulties in math how to measure the table in the text, measure the space they have, and adjust the size by dividing the space they have by the number of columns they need without setting up proportions. **Accommodations** • Give students who have difficulties understanding proportions the measurements for the perimeter of the table and the width of each column. • Give students who have difficulties with spatial and visual motor skills a prepared table they can complete and attach to their logs.
Reading comprehension Receptive language Analysis Maintaining attention	*Chem Talk*	**Accommodations** • The concept that ions that lose electrons have a positive charge is difficult for students to understand, but it is explained very well in the *Chem Talk*. Read through the explanation with those students whose analytical, language or reading issues prevent comprehension of the text. • Use the diagrams from the text to reinforce your instruction. • Have kinesthetic learners create diagrams of the atoms with orbiting electrons, erase or add electrons, and count the resulting numbers of protons and electrons.
Explaining learned concepts	*Checking Up* 3.	**Accommodations** • Require students to use key words and phrases from the question in their explanations. • Refer students to the *Chem Talk* titled "How Substances Produce Light: The Nanoscopic Perspective." You may need to modify this reference further by having students read the first two sentences and then skipping to the next page in the text to the sentence that begins, "When an electron gains enough…" • Have students use the sentences above to explain the diagram to a partner. The partner should record the answer. They can then reverse roles. The recorder should ask clarifying questions of the explainer.

LEARNING ISSUE	REFERENCE	AUGMENTATION AND ACCOMMODATIONS
Explaining learned concepts	*Chem Essential Questions*	**Accommodations** • Help students select data they can use in their answers. • Provide a list of terms students should use in their answers. • To explain how they know, refer students to the appropriate section in the *Chem Talk* to find the three sentences that explain the topic. • Give students additional prompts: Have them explain why the luminol test is not specific for blood. Ask what other substances could cause glowing. Give students a definition of "*presume*" related to its use in this context.

Strategies for Students with Limited English Language Proficiency

LEARNING ISSUE	REFERENCE	AUGMENTATIONS
Background knowledge	*What Do You Think?*	Students may need further explanation of the phrase "*spray for blood.*"
Vocabulary	*Investigate*	In Part A, students might benefit from a tip that the word "*although*" is a signal word for an alternative example. When asked to "*describe in words*," students might need some specifics as to what they are to do. In Part B, The word "*alternatively*" might be noted as a signal word for another choice or direction. Later, when students are asked to compare and discuss differences, point out that the word "*compare*" suggests how they are alike. In Part C, students are given a direction, a question, and then asked to explain. You may need to specify what to do for each of those directions.
Background knowledge Vocabulary Comprehending text	*Chem Talk*	Check for understanding of bold-type words. Refer students to the *Chem Words* for further explanations of the isolated words. Check for understanding of the word "*sensitivity*" in the context used in first section. Some derivatives of the word will be helpful as well as some alternative meanings. Students may not have the word "*presumptive*" in their expressive vocabulary. Some derivations of that word will help build students' language development. When possible, explanation of the effect of the "*ity*" and the "*ive*" endings might promote language proficiency.
Background knowledge	*What Do You Think Now?*	Allow students to discuss possible answers. Check for understanding of the word "*assume*." A comparison to the word "*presume*" may advance understanding.
Background knowledge Vocabulary Comprehending text	*Chem Essential Questions*	In the *Why should you care?* section, students are asked to use the luminol test in their stories. Some discussion of examples might be helpful here.
Comprehension Vocabulary	*Chem to Go*	An explanation of the term "*false identification*" may be useful along with some other derivatives of the word, such as "*falsely*," "*falsify*," and "*falsification*."
Application Comprehension	*Inquiring Further*	Students may need help creating a design for their experiments. It could help to review the concepts of "*solution*," "*dilution*," and "*concentration*." Point out the common feature of the "*tion*" endings to signify a noun form.

CHAPTER 8

Section 3
Teaching Suggestions and Sample Answers

What Do You See?

The illustration depicts two detectives conducting a luminol test. Students may be able to figure this out from their experiences watching crime shows and movies. Encourage them to share their ideas about the illustration and the topic of the section. The purpose here is to engage students' interest and to elicit responses; you do not need to check for accuracy at this point.

What Do You Think?

Again, familiarity with crime shows may give students a head start on these questions. They might know about the luminol test but they probably will not realize that blood is not the only solution that will glow when the test is administered. Accept all answers and listen carefully for prior understanding and misconceptions.

What Do You Think?
A CHEMIST'S RESPONSE

Detectives often spray a luminol solution on suspicious areas at a crime scene. If there is no light given off under this procedure, then blood is definitely <u>not</u> present. If the sprayed spot gives off chemiluminescent light, there is only a possibility that blood could be present, since other materials will give a positive test as well. Additional tests are needed to determine if blood is definitely present.

 CSI Chemistry

Section 3

Atomic Structure and Chemiluminescence: The Luminol Reaction

What Do You See?

THE BLUE BLOOD MYSTERY

Learning Outcomes

In this section you will:
• Gain a basic understanding of atomic structure and its connection to the production of light.
• Define and explain chemiluminescence as it relates to luminol.
• Be able to apply a presumptive test to your crime scene.

Safety goggles and a lab apron must be worn *at all times* in a chemistry lab.

What Do You Think?

Every good episode of a crime show has some dealings with blood— what would a good murder be without it? In many episodes of murder mysteries, you can watch the investigators "spray for blood."

• What do detectives spray when they are spraying for blood?

• How do they know blood is present at the scene after spraying?

Record your ideas about these questions in your *Active Chemistry* log. Be prepared to discuss your responses with your small group and the class.

Investigate

Although it may sound like science fiction, the spraying of a chemical on blood can create light and make the invisible blood "glow." In this investigation, you will explore how the light is produced and whether any materials other than blood can produce the light.

Part A: Experiencing Chemiluminescence

1. The luminol reaction you'll use in the lab today has quite a bit in common with the typical crack-n-glow light stick you may have played with. Take a look at an uncracked light stick and complete the following questions.

 658

STUDENTS' PRIOR CONCEPTIONS

There are many common misconceptions that could arise during the course of this activity.

First, the Bohr model of the atom is used when describing atomic spectra. In this model, energy levels are represented as circular orbits around the nucleus. As a result, students think that electrons orbit the nucleus like planets orbit around the Sun.[1] In fact, even though circular orbits are used to represent energy levels, the electrons do not follow fixed circular paths around the nucleus and it is impossible to know exactly where an electron is.

Many students believe that energy is created or used up in chemical reactions, without regards to the Law of Conservation of Energy.[1] This conception is transferred to the production of light by the atom. Many students fail to see that the amount of energy that is absorbed by the electron to move to a higher energy level is equal to the total amount of energy that is released when it returns to the ground state.

Another common misconception is the assumption that an excited electron always returns to its ground state. In fact the electron may return to its ground state in a series of steps. It is also possible that it gets excited again before it reaches the ground state.

In addition, some students may think that the glowing occurs because the luminol causes something in the blood to "catch on fire."[2] Many students associate the production of light outside of light bulbs to be caused by fire, especially in chemistry classes where students anticipate labs and demos involving fire.

1. Arizona State University. Integrated Physics and Chemistry Modeling Workshop. *Student Preconceptions and Misconceptions in Chemistry* Comp. Chris A Horton. N.p.: Arizona State University, 2001.

2. Orna, Mary Virginia, James O. Schreck, and Henry Heikkinen, eds. "*Photochemistry*." ChemSource SourceBook. Version 2.1 ed. Vol. 3. Philadelphia: ChemSource, Inc., 1998. 18

CHAPTER 8

NOTES
_____

_____

_____

_____

_____

_____

_____

_____

_____

_____

_____

_____

_____

Investigate

Part A: Experiencing Chemiluminescence

1.

For the lightstick demonstration, you should use a number of lightsticks, so that they can be passed around to students. If they handle the lightsticks, they will be able to observe that the lightstick reaction does not produce heat since it does not get warm.

TEACHING TIP

You also may want to have a lightstick that has been cut in half on display for the students. Make sure the glass ampoule is at one end and cut the other end open with a razor blade. Carefully place the contents (liquid substance and glass ampoule) into a beaker for students to observe.

1.a)

Students' answers will vary. They should mention color, the presence of a liquid, and other features.

1.b)

The students should note that the lightstick produces a light, or glows.

1.c)

This will be a difficult task for most students. They are unlikely to be specific or accurate; be alert for misconceptions.

Part B: Using Luminol To Test for Blood

1.

You may obtain the luminol reagent in a different form and with different instructions. Make up enough for only one day as the reagent does not keep well. The luminol powder mixture is good for one year if kept tightly sealed. However, once the water is added, the solution is only good for one or two days. If it stops working, add more sodium perborate or 3% hydrogen peroxide solution. Sodium perborate decomposes in water to produce hydrogen peroxide.

2.

Instead of pipettes, students can use glass capillaries or disposable pipettes. Make certain that all equipment is cleaned with a dilute bleach solution.

2.a)

Students' observations will vary. They should notice that it is red, or reddish-brown.

3.

The wax paper is to prevent contamination of the lab bench.

4.

You can substitute 0.1 M cobalt (II) nitrate solution for the bovine hemoglobin. If you do this, add a tiny bit of red food-coloring so that it looks less magenta and more like blood.

4.a)

To speed up the process, students can dry the spots with a hair dryer or a warm hot plate. An alternative is to have students use fewer than 10 drops. The control paper with water should be invisible, but the hemoglobin test should leave a red or reddish-brown stain.

4.b)

The control is necessary to make certain that the filter paper itself or the water does not cause chemiluminescence when sprayed with the luminol reagent.

5.

If you can darken the room, you will get the best results. If you cannot darken the room, try turning off the lights and having students do the experiment in the sink. You can also paint the inside of a cardboard box black to minimize reflected light.

6.a)

The students should observe a glow from the bovine hemoglobin spot, but not from the control spot.

6.b)

The use of a control test that contains all of the same possible causes of chemiluminescence except for the bovine hemoglobin, ensures that the hemoglobin must be the cause.

6.c)

They are similar in the type of light that is produced. It is a glowing, eerie light. The two types of light are different in color as the hemoglobin produces a persistent blue glow.

7.

You might wish to collect all of the filter circles containing the hemoglobin in a separate plastic bag for disposal.

 a) Make some initial observations of the uncracked light stick. Write or draw these in your *Active Chemistry* log.

 b) Crack and shake the light stick. Write what you observe happening. These are observations on the macroscopic level.

 c) Describe what you think is happening at the nanoscopic level (to the atoms and molecules).

2. Dispose of the light sticks as directed by your teacher.

Part B: Using Luminol to Test for Blood

1. Obtain a spray bottle containing luminol reagent. The luminol reagent contains both luminol and hydrogen peroxide. Add 100 mL of distilled water to the spray bottle, then cap and mix. Allow it to sit for five minutes while occasionally shaking it. This solution will be good for one day.

2. While someone in your group is making the solution, have another group member obtain a small pipette of bovine hemoglobin solution. Bovine hemoglobin solution is made from the blood of cows. The red blood cells, which contain hemoglobin, are separated from the rest of the cow's blood, and then they are sterilized and crystallized. Make sure you wash your hands and clean your pipettes and beakers with a dilute bleach solution when you are done.

 a) Record your observations of the hemoglobin solution in your log.

3. Obtain a piece of wax paper and two medium circles of filter paper. Label one circle "blood solution: experimental group" and one circle "distilled water: control group."

Place the filter paper circles on the piece of wax paper at your lab bench.

4. Place 10 drops of bovine hemoglobin solution into the circle labeled "blood solution." Place 10 drops of distilled water in the second circle.

 a) Once the circles are dry, record your observations.

 b) Why does this experiment need a control? Record your answer in your *Active Chemistry* log.

5. Turn off the lights in the room and allow your eyes one minute to adjust to the dark. Alternatively, you can place the sample in a box.

6. In a dark room, or inside the box spray the luminol solution onto the test paper over each circle and observe. It will take 5–10 minutes to develop. While you are waiting, discuss your crime-scene story and how blood can be a creative element in your plot.

 a) Record your observations in your *Active Chemistry* log.

 b) What evidence is there that the hemoglobin causes the luminol to glow and not the paper or the distilled water? Record your answer after the lights are back on.

 c) Compare the light produced by the light stick to the light produced by the luminol-blood mixture. How are they alike? How are they different? Record your answers in your *Active Chemistry* log.

! CAUTION
If any solution comes in contact with your skin, wash the area with soap and water immediately. Report all accidents to your teacher.

Avoid breathing dust from the bovine hemoglobin.

Report any broken, cracked, or chipped glassware to your teacher.

CHAPTER 8

Part C: The Luminol Reaction

1.

To save time, you can have these sheets prepared in advance for the students to use.

2.a)

Again, for expediency, you can prepare tables in advance for students to use although it is best if they record the data directly into a table in their *Active Chemistry* log.

3.

Use fresh horseradish since the potency of horseradish diminishes with age. If you have the students use disposable pipettes, you can minimize the number of pipettes used by having groups share. Remember to rinse the hemoglobin pipette with a dilute solution of bleach.

4.

You may want to have students share spray bottles to minimize preparation time.

4.a)

The hemoglobin sample emits a persistent blue glow. Students' observations should be similar to those listed below:

0.1 M Fe^{2+}	Glows
0.1 M Fe^{3+}	No reaction
Bleach	Glows
Ketchup	No reaction
Horseradish	Glows
Rusty iron nail	Sometimes glows
Food coloring	No reaction

CSI Chemistry

7. Rinse the paper with the bovine solution in a small amount of dilute bleach solution before throwing it out. Dispose of the materials as directed by your teacher. Clean up your workstation.

Part C: The Luminol Reaction

As you have seen, in the presence of blood, luminol reacts to produce light. Can something other than blood produce a similar reaction?

1. Obtain a piece of wax paper, and a sheet of white paper with circles on it, similar to the one shown. Label each circle with one of the following labels: 0.1 M Fe^{2+}, 0.1 M Fe^{3+}, bleach, ketchup, horseradish, a rusty iron nail, hemoglobin mixed with food coloring, and plain food coloring.

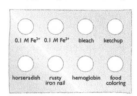

2. In this investigation you will observe how the luminol solution reacts with these different substances.

a) You may want to record your observations in a table like the one shown.

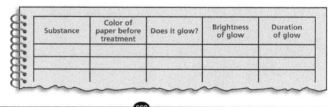

Substance	Color of paper before treatment	Does it glow?	Brightness of glow	Duration of glow

Safety note: Wash your hands and arms thoroughly after the investigation.

Bleach can stain clothing and irritate skin. Handle with caution.

Use caution when handling sharp objects.

Report any broken, cracked, or chipped glassware to your teacher.

3. Place three drops of each solution on the appropriately labeled circle. To save time, you may want to share pipettes with another group. Excess solutions should be disposed of as directed by your instructor. The hemoglobin pipette needs to be rinsed with a dilute solution of bleach before it is thrown away. All other pipettes may be rinsed with water and thrown out. The horseradish and iron nail can be placed directly on top of their circles.

4. In a dark room or inside a box, spray each circle with the luminol solution.

a) Record your observations in your data table in your *Active Chemistry* log.

b) Compare the results of tests on the different substances. Is the luminol test specific to blood? Explain.

c) Based on your results, describe what is meant by the statement that the luminol test is a presumptive test for blood.

5. Rinse the hemoglobin circle with a small amount of bleach solution before you throw the circle away. Clean your workstation as directed by your teacher.

4.b)

The luminol test is not specific to blood. This is evident because the luminol spray reacted with other substances such as horseradish and some iron ions.

4.c)

The luminol test is a presumptive test for blood since it cannot prove that blood is present but it indicates the possibility that it could be present. Other substances, such as Fe^{2+}, Cu^{2+}, Co^{2+} and horseradish will give a false positive. The test is necessary but not sufficient to prove that blood is present.

Chem Talk

HOW ATOMS PRODUCE LIGHT

There are many techniques investigators use to find evidence at a crime scene. One of the methods popularized by many of today's crime shows and movies uses a light-producing chemical reaction to visualize hidden bloodstains. As you observed in this investigation, when the light-producing molecules of luminol and hydrogen peroxide are sprayed on areas contaminated with blood, a blue glow is produced. Due to the sensitivity of this technique, even invisible blood splatters that have been supposedly "cleaned" off the surface will appear. To learn how the luminol test works, you need to understand the structure of an atom.

Structure of the Atom

The atom is composed of **protons**, **neutrons**, and **electrons**. The protons and neutrons are located in the center of the atom, known as the **nucleus**. Neutrons, n^0, are neutral particles located in the nucleus of the atom. Protons, p^+, are positively charged particles also located in the nucleus. Atoms of the same element contain the same number of protons. For example, every atom of iron has 26 protons. However, every atom of the element copper has 29 protons. The number of protons in a single atom of an element is equal to the element's **atomic number**. The atomic number is found above an element's symbol on the periodic table.

Electrons, e^-, are negatively charged particles located outside the nucleus. The electrons exist outside the nucleus in certain allowable states called **energy levels**. If an atom has an equal number of electrons and protons, then the atom is neutral. For example, a neutral iron atom has 26 protons and 26 electrons. The positive charge of the protons is equal to the negative charge of the electrons. A neutral carbon atom contains 6 protons and 6 electrons.

Atoms Lose or Gain Electrons to Form Ions

Electrons, e^-, can be lost or gained in chemical reactions. If an atom loses an electron, the number of protons is larger than the number of

Chem Words

proton: the positively charged subatomic particle contained in the nucleus of an atom. Proton mass is 1.672623×10^{-24} g.

neutron: a neutral particle located in the nucleus of an atom. Neutron mass is 1.674929×10^{-24} g.

electron: the negatively charged subatomic particle of an atom located outside the nucleus. Electron mass is 9.109389×10^{-28} g.

nucleus: the very small dense region in the center of an atom that contains all the positive charge and most of the atom's mass.

atomic number: the number of protons contained in an element.

energy level: the specific amount of energy that an electron possesses in an atom. The ground-state energy level of the hydrogen electron is -2.18×10^{-18} J/atom.

```
26  ← Atomic Number =
Fe      # of protons
55.85
```

Chem Talk

An explanation of how the luminol test works leads to an examination of the structure of an atom, ion formation, and the production of light as a result of electrons changing energy levels. Chemiluminescence is defined as the chemical production of light without heat, and the luminol test is an example of this process. The reading concludes with an explanation as to why the luminol test is a presumptive, as opposed to a definitive test. Because other substances besides blood can also test positive (i.e., cause the luminol to glow), the test can only be used to include blood as a possibility, but not to exclude all other substances.

CSI Chemistry

electrons and the atom becomes positively charged. The atom has one positive charge for every electron it loses. If an iron atom loses 2 electrons it will have a (+2) charge. If an iron atom loses 3 electrons it will have a (+3) charge. The charges are written in the upper right corner above the element's symbol.

$$Fe \rightarrow Fe^{3+} + 3e^- \qquad\qquad Fe \rightarrow Fe^{2+} + 2e^-$$

26 protons(+)	26 protons(+)	26 protons(+)	26 protons(+)
26 electrons(−)	23 electrons(−)	26 electrons(−)	24 electrons(−)
no charge	+3 charge	no charge	+2 charge

Chem Words

ion: an atom or molecule that has acquired a charge by either gaining (anion) or losing (cation) electron(s).

In both examples given, only the number of electrons changes. The number of protons in each atom always remains the same. Atoms that have lost or gained electrons are called **ions**. Atoms of most elements can form ions. Metal elements, like iron, lose electrons when they form ions, so they become positively charged. Nonmetal atoms form ions, too, but when they do, they gain electrons. Thus, they become negatively charged because they have more electrons than they do protons. If a chlorine atom gains an electron it will have a (−1) charge (shown as Cl^-). If sulfur gains 2 electrons it will have a (−2) charge.

$$Cl + 1e^- \rightarrow Cl^- \qquad\qquad S + 2e^- \rightarrow S^{2-}$$

17 protons(+)	17 protons(+)	16 protons(+)	16 protons(+)
17 electrons(−)	18 electrons(−)	16 electrons(−)	18 electrons(−)
no charge	−1 charge	no charge	−2 charge

Ions have very different properties than the neutral atoms they are formed from. For example, Fe atoms are very different from Fe^{2+} ions. Atoms of some elements, like iron, can form more than one type of ion, because atoms of those elements can lose varying numbers of electrons. Those different ions of the same element, such as Fe^{2+} and Fe^{3+}, not only have different properties from their neutral atoms, but they also are very distinct from each other. You observed one significant difference between Fe^{2+} and Fe^{3+}, that they have different effects on some chemical reactions. In this investigation, Fe^{2+} ions speed up the reaction between luminol and hydrogen peroxide, but Fe^{3+} ions do not.

How Substances Produce Light: The Nanoscopic Perspective

Electrons exist outside the nucleus in certain allowable states called energy levels. When an electron gains energy, it can move from a lower energy level to a higher level. However, the energy that the electron gains must be equal to the energy difference between the two levels.

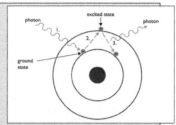

Think of the energy levels as the rungs of a ladder. If you only give your foot enough energy to make it halfway between one rung and the next, it is not going to reach the next rung. Instead, it will remain on the lower rung. If an electron does not gain enough energy, it will not be promoted to a higher energy level.

When an electron gains enough energy to move to a higher state it is in an **excited state**. This excited state has a higher energy level than the **ground state** where the electron began. The energy the electron gains may come from heat, collisions, chemical reactions, light, or other forms of electromagnetic radiation.

The electron does not remain in the excited state for very long. It quickly falls to a lower energy state and in the process loses the energy it gained. The energy lost from the electron's return to the ground state is emitted as light energy and so the atom gives off light. With this basic understanding of how some atoms are able to produce light, you can now make sense of the luminol reaction.

Production of Light with the Luminol Mixture

The light stick reaction and the luminol reaction are examples of **chemiluminescence**. As you observed in this investigation with the light stick, chemiluminescence is the production of light without heat through a chemical reaction. In chemiluminescence, the starting substances (**reactants**) react and their atoms rearrange to form new substance (**products**) and light. In the luminol blood test, luminol reacts with hydrogen peroxide to form a new compound (called 3-aminophthalate). The energy released in this reaction excites some of the electrons in the new compound. When the electrons in the new compound return to the ground state, blue light is released.

However, at room temperature, luminol and hydrogen peroxide molecules do not react at a significant rate. Some light may be emitted but not enough to easily observe. A **catalyst** is needed in order to speed up the reaction so that more light will be produced in a given time and the light can be more easily observed. A catalyst is a

Chem Words

excited state: a condition where an electron of an atom or molecule has absorbed energy so that the electron is now at a higher energy level than its ground state.

ground state: the lowest energy level that the electron of an atom or molecule can occupy.

chemiluminescence: a chemical reaction that releases energy as light or electromagnetic radiation.

reactants: the starting materials in a chemical reaction that are transformed into products during chemical reactions.

products: the substances formed from reactants as a result of a chemical reaction.

catalyst: a substance that speeds up a reaction without being consumed in the overall reaction.

CHAPTER 8

Checking Up

1.

The atomic number of an element indicates the number of protons in its nucleus. In the neutral atom, this is also the number of electrons in its orbitals.

2.

An ion is vastly different from a neutral atom because the atom has either gained or lost electrons and now carries an electrical charge.

3.

An electron in the excited state is at a higher energy level than an electron in the ground state.

4.

Chemiluminescence is the production of light without heat through a chemical reaction.

5.

An enzyme and a catalyst are different in that an enzyme is a biologically active protein but a catalyst is usually much smaller and often an ion or metal. They are similar in that they speed up a reaction without being consumed in the reaction.

6.

The luminol test for blood is called a presumptive test because it is not specific for blood. Other substances will also give a positive result.

 CSI Chemistry

Chem Words

mass: a measure of the amount of matter an object contains.

volume: a measure of the space occupied by matter.

density: the mass of a substance per unit volume.

Density

In this experiment, you determined the mass and the volume of four samples of the same glass. Each sample was a different size. **Mass** is a measure of the amount of matter an object contains. It does not depend on gravity (like weight) and will be the same regardless of where it is measured. Since mass depends on the amount of matter present, it is an extensive property. Likewise, **volume**, the amount of space occupied by matter, is also an extensive property. But, you may have noticed that when the mass of the glass sample was plotted against its volume, there was a linear (straight-line) relationship. The ratio of the mass to the volume was constant and did not depend on the sample size. Therefore, the relationship between the mass of a substance and its volume is an intensive property. And since it is an intensive property, you can use the mass versus volume relationship to identify a substance. The relationship between the mass of an object and its volume is called the object's **density.**

Density is defined as the mass per unit volume. Density can be calculated using the equation

$$\text{Density} = \frac{\text{mass (g)}}{\text{volume (mL or cm}^3)}$$

Density is reported in units of g/cm^3 or g/mL. For example, if the mass of a solid object is 15.0 g and its volume is 25.3 cm^3, the density of the object is equal to

$$\text{Density} = \frac{m}{V} = \frac{15.0 \text{ g}}{25.3 \text{ cm}^3} = 0.593 \frac{g}{cm^3} \text{ or } 0.593 \text{ g/mL}$$

Calculating Density from a Mass and Volume Data Set

The density of a substance can be found with a single calculation or by graphing a data set of mass versus volume. In this investigation, you used a graph to determine the density of your glass sample. Using this procedure for a sample "X," a data table below was created.

Checking Up

1. Give two physical and two chemical properties of glass.
2. In your own words, describe the difference between an intensive and extensive property.
3. What equation can be used to calculate the density of a material?
4. What does the slope of a mass versus volume graph represent?
5. If two unknown materials have exactly the same density, can you deduce that the two materials are the same?
6. If the density of glass fragments found on a suspect matches the glass fragments at the scene of a crime, can you prove without a doubt that the suspect was at the scene of the crime?

Sample X

Mass (g)	Volume (cm³)
3.01	5.08
7.01	11.8
11.0	18.5
15.0	25.3

The next step is to plot the mass versus the volume for all four samples on a graph. After plotting the data, a straight-line fit for the data is drawn. This line may not go through all of the data points. The slope of this line will be equal to the density of the substance. That's because the slope is equivalent to

654

Chem Essential Questions
What does it mean?

MACRO — When a blood sample is sprayed with luminol reagent and observed under an ultraviolet light, the sample will glow with a blue-white light.

NANO — An atom can produce light by first absorbing a specific energy from a photon which moves a ground state electron to an excited state. This excited state is unstable and the electron will return to the original ground state while simultaneously emitting a photon of the same energy.

SYMBOLIC —

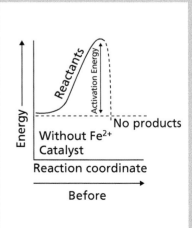

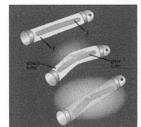

What Do You Think Now?

At the beginning of this section you were asked the following:

- What do detectives spray when they are spraying for blood?
- How do they know blood is present at the scene after spraying?

You explored the answers to these questions during the *Investigate*. Now, think about the light stick you looked at in *Part A*. The diagram shows how a light stick works. Assume luminol is causing the glow of this light stick. (There are other possibilities besides luminol.) What substances could be in the glass and plastic tubes?

Chem
Essential Questions

What does it mean?

Chemistry explains a *macroscopic* phenomenon (what you observe) with a description of what happens at the *nanoscopic* level (atoms and molecules) using *symbolic* structures as a way to communicate. Complete the chart below in your *Active Chemistry* log.

MACRO	NANO	SYMBOLIC
What are the observable changes when the luminol is sprayed onto blood?	Describe how light can be produced by an atom.	Graphically and symbolically, how can you represent the reaction you observed both before you sprayed (what is happening in the bottle) and after you sprayed the reaction mixture on your sample?

How do you know?

Making specific reference to your data and using terms from the *Chem Talk* section, explain why the luminol test is called a *presumptive test* for the presence of blood.

Why do you believe?

A neon sign is nothing more than electrodes, powered through the electrical socket of your house, in atoms of a gas, like neon. When you turn a neon sign on, electrical energy is gained and lost by the gas atoms, and the sign glows. When you stop the electricity, it doesn't glow. How does this relate to the luminol reaction studied in this section? How is it different?

Why should you care?

How could you use the idea that luminol is a presumptive test in your story? Give a specific example.

What Do You Think Now?

Have the class return to the *What Do You See?* illustration and the *What Do You Think?* questions and review their earlier answers. They probably originally did not know what detectives spray at the crime scene. Now they should be able to respond with the name of the reagent, luminol, and have some idea of the chemistry behind it. Also, they probably thought the presence of blood could be automatically deducted if the luminol spray produced a glow. Now, however, their answers should be more sophisticated and accurate.

Based on their experience and reading, students will probably guess that besides luminol, lightsticks can also contain hydrogen peroxide and Fe^{2+} in the glass and plastic tubes.

How do you know?

The luminol reaction is not specific for blood and can be catalyzed by other substances. The activity showed that substances in horseradish and bleach worked, as well as the Fe^{2+} ion by itself. Since the test is not specific, it is "presumptive" until further tests either prove or disprove the presence of blood.

Why do you believe?

The operation of a neon sign is similar to the luminol reaction in that electrons in atoms are excited by a source of energy to a higher state.

When they return to the ground state, a glowing light is given off. The operation of a neon sign is different in that the source of energy is electricity and can be controlled. The luminol reaction is chemical in nature and can't be turned on and off.

Why should you care?

Students' answers will vary. They might suggest that a beet-horseradish mixture on the floor would suggest blood and test as a false positive for blood.

Energy vs. Reaction coordinate diagram:
Reactants — Activation Energy — Products
With Fe^{2+} Catalyst
After

Reflecting on the Section and the Challenge

Following the *What Do You Think Now?* questions is an opportunity for students to pause and think about how they will incorporate the information in this activity into their *Chapter Challenge*. The students have learned that it is important to be able to identify the presence of blood in a crime scene and that luminol is a very effective reagent when testing for blood. However, they also have learned that the luminol test can be positive but can also be misleading. You might want to have students reflect on this individually or in their *Active Chemistry* logs. If there is time, they could meet in their groups for a short discussion and then report back to the class.

Chem to Go

1.

The chemicals are separated to prevent the reaction from occurring while lightsticks are on the store shelf. The reaction will stop producing light after a defined length of time.

2.

The reaction stops because it has consumed all of the reactants.

3.

This reaction will not begin until there is a catalyst present.

4.

The symbol for the element that has 16 protons is "S" for sulfur.

5.

a) 15 protons and 15 electrons is a neutral phosphorus atom.

b) 7 protons and 10 electrons is a negative nitrogen ion.

c) 3 protons and 2 electrons is a positive lithium ion.

6.

The ion with 16 protons and 18 electrons is the sulfide ion: S^{2-}.

7.

Group 1 was formed by the loss of electrons.

Group 2 was formed by the gain of electrons.

 CSI Chemistry

Reflecting on the Section and the Challenge

The powdered luminol reagent you used contains both luminol and hydrogen peroxide. The luminol reacts with the hydrogen peroxide once the reagent is dissolved in water, producing light. However, this reaction does not occur fast enough to produce enough light for your eyes to detect it until the hemoglobin comes in contact with the luminol and hydrogen peroxide. The hemoglobin in the blood contains a particular form of iron, and that iron speeds up the reaction. When that happens, the reacting luminol produces enough light for you to see a blue glow. The more blood present, the faster the reaction takes place and the brighter the glow is.

Part of the problem you are facing in creating a crime scene is how to observe something that is not initially visible. In this section you focused on how the chemiluminescence of luminol could be used to detect the presence of blood. You also examined other substances that caused the luminol to glow. A positive luminol test does not mean the substance is definitely blood. Think how this may mislead you when you are examining a crime scene. Finally, you can now use the concepts that you have learned to describe the chemistry behind this technique, another important element of the *Chapter Challenge*.

Chem to Go

1. Why are the two chemicals in a light stick separated by glass?

2. Why do light sticks eventually stop producing light?

3. What prevents the hydrogen peroxide and the luminol from glowing in the spray bottle?

4. What is the symbol for the element that has 16 protons?

5. Identify each as an atom or ion.

   a) 15 protons and 15 electrons   b) 7 protons and 10 electrons

   c) 3 protons and 2 electrons

6. Write the symbol for the element that has 16 protons and 18 electrons.

7. Examine Group 1 and Group 2 below.

   Group 1: Ti^{2+} Na^+ Mg^{2+} Al^{3+}

   Group 2: P^{3-} F^- As^{3-} O^{2-}

   Which group was formed when electrons were lost?

   Which group was formed when electrons were gained?

666

Active Chemistry

3. Other presumptive blood tests

Have students research other techniques that forensic scientists use to visualize blood. You may suggest that a good place to start may be the local police station. Many police stations now have special light sources that can be used to visualize blood splatters.

Section 3 Presumptive Blood Testing: The Luminol Reaction

8. *Preparing for the Chapter Challenge*

Using density to identify glass and using luminol to indicate blood, are two ways that can lead to a false identification of a suspect. In your *Active Chemistry* log, write two scenes; one that uses the properties in the last two sections to correctly identify a suspect as the criminal and one that uses both properties and falsely identifies a suspect as the criminal. In the false statement, give an explanation as to how it was a false identification. Use this process and your teacher's feedback to start thinking about how you'll make your crime scene have possible twists for the future investigators.

Inquiring Further

1. Other luminol reaction catalysts

Research the luminol blood test. Design an experiment to determine if other household chemicals will catalyze the luminol reaction. Under the supervision of your teacher perform your investigation.

Conduct the experiment you design only under adult supervision.

2. Sensitivity of the luminol test

Design an experiment to determine the sensitivity of the luminol test. Before designing your experiment research the concepts of solution, dilution and concentration. Under the supervision of your teacher perform your experiment and present your results to the class.

3. Other presumptive blood tests

There are many other types of presumptive blood tests. One of the more popular alternatives to the luminol test is the Kastle-Meyer test. In the Kastle-Meyer test, the reagent turns pink in the presence of blood. Research the Kastle-Meyer test. Under the supervision of your teacher, investigate the sensitivity and specificity of this test. Compare your results to the luminol test.

667

Active Chemistry

8.

Preparing for the Chapter Challenge

Students could describe broken glass at a crime scene that tested positive for blood. Later, the detective learns that the glass came form a broken bottle that contained horseradish.

Inquiring Further

1. Other luminol reaction catalysts

Make certain that the procedures are safe and that a control is used.

2. Sensitivity of the luminol test

Make certain that the procedures are safe and that a control is used.

SECTION 3 – QUIZ

| 8-3a | Blackline Master |

1. _____ and _____ are located in the nucleus of the atom.

    a) protons, neutrons   b) protons, electrons

    c) positrons, neutrons   d) positrons, protons

2. An atom of fluorine contains _____ protons.

    a) 8   b) 9

    c) 10   d) 11

3. If an atom of aluminum loses three electrons, it will have a charge of _____.

    a) −3   b) −1

    c) +1   d) +3

4. Are the following atoms or ions? Explain.

    a) 15 protons and 15 electrons

    b) 14 protons and 15 electrons

NOTES

_____

_____

_____

_____

_____

_____

_____

_____

_____

SECTION 3 – QUIZ ANSWERS

① a) protons, neutrons

② b) 9 protons

③ d) +3

④ a) This describes an atom because the number of protons and electrons are equal. There is no charge.

    b) This describes an ion, specifically an anion, because there are more electrons than protons. There is a −1 charge.

NOTES

SECTION 4
Solubility and Qualitative Analysis: White Powders

Section Overview

In this section, students develop a series of tests to identify some common white powders found in a typical home. They test the six powders with a set of reagents (water, phenolphthalein, silver nitrate solution, and acetic acid) looking for signs of physical or chemical change. They then learn how to represent the test results in flowcharts that chart the process of elimination. Finally, they test their flowcharts using the known white powders to ensure that they are accurate.

Background Information

Forensic scientists are often faced with the challenging task of identifying unknown compounds. With millions of possible compounds and mixtures of compounds to choose from, forensic scientists must develop tests that are specific to certain types of compounds. The use of tests to determine the identity of an unknown compound is called *qualitative analysis*. In this type of analysis, it is the identity of the unknown that is important and not the quantity. Once a substance has been identified, such as cocaine, a *quantitative analysis* will be performed to determine the amounts of different substances present. Quantitative analysis is used to determine the amount of cocaine and the amount of each material used to cut, meaning 'dilute,' the cocaine. In this experiment, students use the results from a series of tests performed on six different compounds to develop a flowchart. This flowchart will enable them to identify an unknown white powder.

The white powders that students test have different physical and chemical properties because they have different structures or formulas. The key to identifying a powder is to select properties that differentiate one white powder from another. For example, both sugar and salt dissolve easily in water. So testing a powder that may be sugar or salt by dissolving the powder in water would not help tell them apart. But sugar melts at a relatively low temperature, while salt melts at a much higher temperature, so if the white powder melts in a pan on the stove, it cannot be salt.

Solubility

In *Part A* of the experiment, students place a sample of each white powder in water to see if it would dissolve. This property of matter is called *solubility*. The powders that dissolved in water are said to be *soluble*. When a solid dissolves in water, the mixture of the dissolved solid and the water is called a *solution*. The powders that did not dissolve are said to be *insoluble*. Whether or not a powder dissolves in water is a complex matter. Fortunately, the solubility of many substances in water has been investigated. The results of some of the investigations are summarized in the list below.

Solubility Rules

Nitrates (NO_3^-)	All are soluble.
Chlorides (Cl^-)	All are soluble **except** those containing ions of silver, mercury (I), and lead (II).
Sulfates (SO_4^{2-})	All are soluble **except** those containing ions of barium, calcium, strontium, silver, lead (II), and mercury (I).
Carbonates (CO_3^{2-})	All are insoluble **except** those containing ions of the Group 1 metals or the ammonium ion.
Hydroxides (OH^-)	All are insoluble **except** those containing ions of the Group 1 metals or the ammonium ion.

This table can be used to predict if a given solid will dissolve in water. For example, sodium carbonate, Na_2CO_3, contains the carbonate ion, CO_3^{2-}. According to the table, all carbonates are insoluble except for the ones containing Group I metals. Sodium is a Group I metal, therefore sodium carbonate is soluble and will dissolve in water. Other examples are given below:

KCl – soluble, all Group I chlorides are soluble.

$Mg(OH)_2$ – insoluble, magnesium is not a Group I metal.

Phenolphthalein: An Acid-Base indicator

In the second test, students add phenolphthalein to each sample. Phenolphthalein is one of a class of compounds known as acid-base indicators. An indicator is a substance that changes color in the presence of an acid or a base. *Acids* are compounds that form H^+ ions in solution. Acids taste sour (citric and maleic acids are used in sour candies), react with metals (corrosive), neutralize bases, and react with some indicators to produce a color change. *Indicators* are substances that change color when exposed to an acid or a base. Acids do not cause phenolphthalein to change color. Some common acids and their uses include:

Name	Formula	Use
Acetic acid	$HC_2H_3O_2$	Vinegar
Carbonic acid	H_2CO_3	Carbonate sodas
Hydrochloric acid	HCl	Stomach acid, Serial-number etching

Bases are compounds that form hydroxide ions (OH^-) in solution. Bases taste bitter, are corrosive, feel slippery, saponify fats (turns fats into soaps), neutralize acids, and cause certain indicators to change color. Bases will cause phenolphthalein to turn bright pink. Some common bases and their uses are listed below.

Name	Formula	Use
Sodium hydroxide (Lye)	$NaOH$	Making soap, drain cleaners
Ammonia	NH_3	Fertilizers and cleaners
Magnesium hydroxide	$Mg(OH)_2$	Antacids
Sodium carbonate	Na_2CO_3	Luminol blood test

When an indicator is placed into an acidic or basic solution, it undergoes a change in structure. Primarily, it either loses or gains a hydrogen ion. This change in structure results in a change in color. It is this color change that gives the indicator its name. In acidic solutions, the indicator is one color and in basic solutions, the indicator is another color.

Regarding the indicator phenolphthalein, when the indicator is present in an acidic or neutral solution, the phenolphthalein exists primarily in its colorless HIn (In = indicator) form. However, when the indicator is added to a basic solution, the phenolphthalein donates its hydrogen ion to the hydroxide ion and the indicator is reduced to its In$^-$ form, which has a pink hue. As a result, the solution turns pink.

Ionic Compounds

The white powders used in this investigation all contain *ionic bonds*. Ionic bonds are formed when one element loses electrons, becoming a positive ion, and one element gains electrons, becoming a negative ion. For example, sodium will lose an electron to chlorine.

$$Na + Cl \rightarrow Na^+ + Cl^-$$

Since opposite charges attract, the positive sodium ion is attracted to the negative chloride ion. This attraction is called an ionic bond. In an ionic compound, the positively charged ions are called *cations* and take the name of the element. Negatively charged ions are called *anions*. They take the name of the element but the ending is changed to *–ide*. Notice that metals form positive ions and nonmetals form negative ions. Some common ions are listed below.

Formula	Name	Formula	Name
Na^+	Sodium ion	Cl^-	Chloride ion
K^+	Potassium ion	F^-	Fluoride ion
Ag^+	Silver ion	O^{2-}	Oxide ion
Ca^{2+}	Calcium ion	S^{2-}	Sulfide ion

CHAPTER 8

Groups of atoms may also form ions by losing or gaining electrons. This type of ion is called a *polyatomic ion*. The formulas and names for some common polyatomic ions are listed below.

Some Common Polyatomic Ions

Formula	Name	Formula	Name
NH_4^+	Ammonium ion	NO_3^-	Nitrate ion
OH^-	Hydroxide ion	SO_4^{2-}	Sulfate ion
CO_3^{2-}	Carbonate ion	$C_2H_3O_2^-$	Acetate ion
HCO_3^-	Hydrogen carbonate, or bicarbonate ion		

When ionic compounds dissolve in water they form hydrated ions. Water is a polar molecule. It has a positive and a negative end. In an overly simplistic view of the solution process, when a soluble ionic compound is placed in water the positive end of the water molecule pulls the negative ions out of the ionic crystalline lattice and surrounds them. The negative end of the water molecule pulls the positive ions out of the ionic crystalline lattice. The resulting solution contains positive and negative ions distributed throughout the solution. The presence of the positive and negative ions in solution are responsible for the conductivity of ionic solutions. An additional test you could add to this section would be conductivity. The solutions of the soluble ionic compounds will conduct electricity.

Ionic compounds will participate in chemical reactions. For example, when silver nitrate solution is added to sodium chloride solution a milky white solid is formed. The chemical reaction is shown below.

silver **nitrate** + sodium chloride ⟶ sodium **nitrate** + **silver** chloride

$AgNO_{3(aq)}$ + $NaCl_{(aq)}$ ⟶ $NaNO_{3(aq)}$ + $AgCl_{(s)}$

By examining the reaction, you can see that the metals exchange places to form two new compounds. This reaction is called a *double-replacement reaction*. You can determine the identity of the milky white solid, called a *precipitate*, by looking at the products and using the solubility rules. Sodium nitrate will dissolve in water because all nitrates are soluble. All chlorides are soluble with the exception of mercury (II), lead (II), and silver. So the milky white precipitate is silver chloride. More examples of double-replacement reactions are shown below.

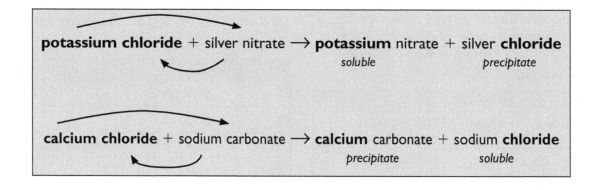

potassium **chloride** + silver nitrate ⟶ **potassium** nitrate + silver **chloride**
                                                soluble   precipitate

calcium **chloride** + sodium carbonate ⟶ **calcium** carbonate + sodium **chloride**
                                            precipitate   soluble

Another example of a double-replacement reaction is the reaction of acetic acid solution with sodium hydrogen carbonate solution.

$$HC_2H_3O_2 + NaHCO_3 \rightarrow NaC_2H_3O_2 + H_2CO_3$$

The hydrogen ion in acetic acid trades places with the sodium ion in the sodium carbonate. The carbonic acid, H_2CO_3, immediately decomposes to produce carbon dioxide gas (the bubbles in Activity B) and water.

$$H_2CO_3 \rightarrow H_2O + CO_2$$

So whenever carbonic acid is a product, it is replaced with water and carbon dioxide.

$$2HC_2H_3O_2 + Na_2CO_3 \rightarrow$$
$$2NaC_2H_3O_2 + H_2O + CO_2$$

Generally, acetic acid and other acids will react with carbonates and hydrogen carbonates to form carbon dioxide gas. The gas is the bubbles that form in the solution. A carbonate is a compound that contains the CO_3^{2-} ion. Some common carbonates include sodium carbonate (Na_2CO_3) and calcium carbonate ($CaCO_3$). Hydrogen carbonates are compounds that contain the hydrogen carbonate ion HCO_3^-. The most common hydrogen carbonate is sodium hydrogen carbonate, $NaHCO_3$, also known as baking soda. Bicarbonates will also react with acids in a similar manner.

CHAPTER 8

LEARNING OUTCOMES		
LEARNING OUTCOMES	**LOCATION IN SECTION**	**EVIDENCE OF UNDERSTANDING**
Create and use a flowchart to identify an unknown.	*Investigate* Part B	Students create and use a variety of different flowcharts that are based on the properties of different substances.
Identify an unknown ionic compound based on an understanding of its chemical and physical properties.	*Investigate* Part A *Chem to Go* Questions 1-2,5	Students correctly identify the ions and the precipitates that form in a test tube. Students can identify the insoluble compounds from a list of compounds and the precipitates in double-replacement reactions.
Identify limitations to white powder tests.	*Investigate* Part B *Chem to Go* Questions 6-7	Students use the flowchart to correctly identify white powders based on experimental data. Students' answers match those provided in this *Teacher's Edition*.

NOTES

_____

_____

_____

_____

_____

Section 4
Materials, Chemicals, Preparation, and Safety

("per Group" quantity is based on group size of 4 students)

Materials and Equipment

Materials (and Equipment)	Quantity per Group (4 students)
Test tubes, large	4
Scoopula	1
Test-tube rack	1
Test-tube brush	1
Stirring rod	1
Graduated cylinder, 100-mL	1
Materials (and Equipment)	**Quantity per Class**
Dropping bottles/droppers (at least 7 dark for silver nitrate)	21

Chemicals

Chemicals	Quantity per Class (24 students)
Calcium carbonate	30 g
Calcium sulfate	30 g
Sodium carbonate	30 g
Sodium hydrogen carbonate	30 g
Sodium chloride	30 g
Sodium hydroxide	30 g
Phenolphthalein, 1% solution	20 mL
1.0 M Acetic acid	100 mL
0.1 M Silver nitrate (in dark bottle)	10 mL

Teacher Preparation

Phenolphthalein—Dissolve 1 g of phenolphthalein in 70 mL of 95% ethanol and then adjust volume to 100 mL. This will make a 1% solution of phenolphthalein which can be put into dropper bottles for student use.

0.1 M Silver nitrate, $AgNO_3$—Dissolve 10.2 g of silver nitrate in 400 mL of distilled water and adjust volume to 600 mL. This solution will also be used in *Section 5* as well. Use caution when preparing solution, as it will stain skin and clothing. Store in dark dropper bottles for student use.

1.0 M Acetic acid, $HC_2H_3O_2$—Add 5 mL of concentrated acetic acid (17.4 M) slowly to 75 mL of deionized water and then adjust the volume to 100 mL. Store in dropper bottles for student use. As an alternative, use white vinegar.

Safety Requirements

- Goggles and aprons are required in the laboratory area.

- Safe handling of sodium hydroxide must be emphasized. Proper use of rubber gloves will prevent hand and skin burns and goggles must be worn securely to avoid contact with the eyes. In the event that a student's eyes are exposed to sodium hydroxide solution, immediate action is necessary. The eyes must be flushed with cold water for at least 15 minutes and an eye specialist should be consulted as soon as possible.

- Broken glass must be disposed of in a special container that is marked for broken glass. Do not allow it to be placed in a regular garbage container.

- The solutions produced are minimal and can be disposed of down the drain.

- Wash arms and hands before leaving the laboratory area.

Meeting the Needs of All Students
Differentiated Instruction

Augmentation and Accommodations

LEARNING ISSUE	REFERENCE	AUGMENTATION AND ACCOMMODATIONS
Copying a table Visual motor skills Spatial skills Using measures and proportions	*Investigate* Part A, 2.a)	**Augmentation** • Show students how to set up proportions that enable them to fit this table into their notebooks by establishing the width of each column. The width of the table in text should be modified to accommodate the width of the space available in their logs. • Show students who need more space to write legibly how they can use proportions to enlarge their tables. • Show students with difficulties in math how to measure the table in the text, measure the space they have and adjust the size by dividing the space they have by the number of columns they need without setting up proportions. **Accommodations** • Give students who have difficulties understanding proportions the measurements for the perimeter of the table and the width of each column. • Give students who have difficulties with spatial and visual motor skills a prepared table they can complete and attach to their logs.
Determining saliency and classifying observations	*Investigate* Part A, 5.a)	**Accommodations** • When asked to record their observations to 24 reactions, some students may predict appropriate color changes, formation of precipitates or no reaction at all. Other students may have expectations that are unrealistic and still others may have no expectations at all. Help these students access prior understandings by listing various forms of evidence of chemical change they have observed in the past. • Instead of a teacher-led discussion, have students use a think, pair, share strategy to make predictions about possible observations. Pair students having difficulty with others more capable, thus preparing weaker students to share during the class discussion.
Synthesizing information to make predictions Making a generalization from their investigation	*Investigate* Part A, 11.	**Augmentation** • Students are almost ready to design a process that will help them determine the identity of each white powder, but they need to see how all the parts of their evidence can be assembled. Step 11 is designed to help students see that each substance has specific properties that can be determined from the tests. Make sure all students have drawn this inference so they understand the general idea of what to do next. • Explain that since each substance has unique properties, they can use the observations made in the tests to systematically determine the identity of each substance (using their flowcharts).
Determining saliency and classifying observations	*Investigate* Part B,1.a)	**Augmentation** • Writing their thoughts about the first flowchart is much like recording observations with no context. Since this is a preliminary exercise, don't expect students to understand the salient characteristics of flowcharts yet. Using a think, pair, share exercise will begin to shape the students' learning. Silent study of the first flowchart and a brief discussion with their partners should only take two minutes. Be sure to observe students who tend to get off-task or take longer to process visual materials. Provide private cues to extinguish off-task behavior and do not end the "think" session before everyone is ready.

CHAPTER 8

LEARNING ISSUE	REFERENCE	AUGMENTATION AND ACCOMMODATIONS
Logical sequencing Visual analysis Imagining all consequences of an action	*Investigate* Part B	**Augmentation** • Help students create a legend to explain the symbols used in flowcharts. The arrows indicate possible next steps, but they can also indicate cause/effect relationships with the arrow pointing from the cause to the effect. The arrows in chemical reactions indicate the results of mixing two or more reactants. In the flowcharts in this activity, shapes are used to add meaning. The large oval indicates the topic; diamond shapes indicate questions to be answered, and circles are used to indicate each possible answer to the question. Words and phrases outside of the boxes along the arrows indicate actions taken or answers to questions. • After the legend is created, apply it to one of the flowchart samples in the text. Explicitly connect the content of the flowchart to the symbols and connectors used. • Give students a simple narrative that could be organized into a flowchart. Have them practice creating that flowchart before they create the more complex chart required in this investigation. • Teach students where to find information that they can reference to determine all possible consequences of an action. Many times it is embedded in their observations. **Accommodations** • Give students the actions, questions and possible consequences (like a word bank) for them to insert in their own flowcharts. • Give students a blank flowchart with a word/phrase bank they can use to fill it. • Help students locate specific information in the text and in their notes that they can transfer to their flowcharts. • Some students will find it much easier to use a computer to make a flowchart. *Inspiration* is an easy-to-learn software program that students can use for this purpose.

NOTES

_____

_____

_____

_____

_____

_____

_____

_____

Strategies for Students with Limited English Language Proficiency

LEARNING ISSUE	REFERENCE	AUGMENTATIONS
Background knowledge	*What Do You Think?*	Students may need some explanation or definition of the term *"forensic."*
Vocabulary	*Investigate*	Check for understanding of the term *"reagents."* Note that the word *"alternatively"* is a signal word indicating another choice. The phrase, *"taken into account"* may need some explanation. Check for understanding of the word *"scoop"* and share derivatives and multiple meanings to build vocabulary. Check for students' pronunciation of chemical names. Revisit the term *"validity."*
Background knowledge Vocabulary Comprehending text	*Chem Talk*	Check for understanding of bold-type words. Refer students to the *Chem Words* for further explanations of the isolated words. Check for understanding of the word *"notice"* as a verb. Check for understanding of the word *"dissociated."*
Background knowledge	*What Do You Think Now?*	Allow students to discuss some of the possible answers in small groups or teams for oral language development.
Background knowledge Vocabulary Comprehending text	*Chem Essential Questions*	In the *Why do you believe?* students are asked to explain a situation where they witnessed physical and chemical changes outside of the classroom. Some discussion might be helpful here, along with an example.
Comprehension Vocabulary	*Chem to Go*	Students might need an explanation of what a *"defense attorney"* does in order to make his or her case.
Application Comprehension	*Inquiring Further*	Students might need some assistance in researching instruments in a crime lab. A suggested website or a visit with a criminologist might promote understanding. A list of criteria would provide guidance in formulating their presentation.

CHAPTER 8

NOTES

_____

_____

_____

_____

_____

_____

_____

_____

_____

_____

_____

Section 4
Teaching Suggestions and Sample Answers

What Do You See?

This exercise is intended to spark interest and engage students' attention. Ask students what they think the students pictured in the illustration are doing and what the writings on the blackboard might represent. You can do this as a class discussion or by having students respond directly in their *Active Chemistry* logs. Their answers may not be accurate, but accept all responses and take note of misconceptions and evidence of prior learning. You will have a chance to return to this illustration after completing the investigation.

What Do You Think?

Students may guess that chemical testing would be necessary to identify white powders, but they may not know what kind of information to test for, or the kinds of methods used in the testing. Allow them to discuss the questions and share ideas. Be alert for misconceptions, but accept all responses and don't expect right answers at this point. You will come back to these questions again after the investigation is complete.

 CSI Chemistry

Section 4 | Solubility and Qualitative Analysis: White Powders

What Do You See?

Learning Outcomes

In this section you will
- Create and use a flowchart to identify an unknown entity.
- Identify an unknown ionic compound based on an understanding of its chemical and physical properties.
- Identify limitations to white powder tests.

Safety goggles and a lab apron must be worn at all times in a chemistry lab.

What Do You Think?

Forensic scientists and detectives often find traces of white powders at a crime scene.

- What information would you need to tell several different white powders apart?
- Can you think of any methods you could use to identify what they are?

Record your ideas about these questions in your *Active Chemistry* log. Be prepared to discuss your responses with your small group and the class.

Investigate

Part A: Identifying Household White Powders

In this part of the investigation, you will test each of six white powders with a set of reagents (water, phenolphthalein, silver nitrate solution, and acetic acid), looking for signs of a physical or chemical change. For safety reasons, you will use common white powders found around the house.

1. How would you design an experiment to carry out these tests? You can share your design with your teacher and you may be given permission to proceed. Alternatively, your teacher may suggest you use the procedure outlined here because the materials have all been prepared and safety considerations taken into account.

668

What Do You Think?
A CHEMIST'S RESPONSE

Some information that would help to differentiate between two or more white powders would include: solubility in water, solubility in hexane, melting point, reaction with acid, reaction with base and many more.
To actually identify the white powders would take more time and perhaps more sophisticated equipment. For organic compounds, a mass spectrum would identify the compound. For inorganic salts or elements, atomic absorption spectroscopy would provide key information

Due to the wide variety of topics covered in this section, there are many common misconceptions that teachers may encounter in this section. Examples of typical misconceptions are not limited to the following:

1. Dissolving and melting are the same thing.*
2. Matter is continuous but contains particles.*
3. Chemical reactions are caused by mixing of substances.*
4. Analysis is easy.

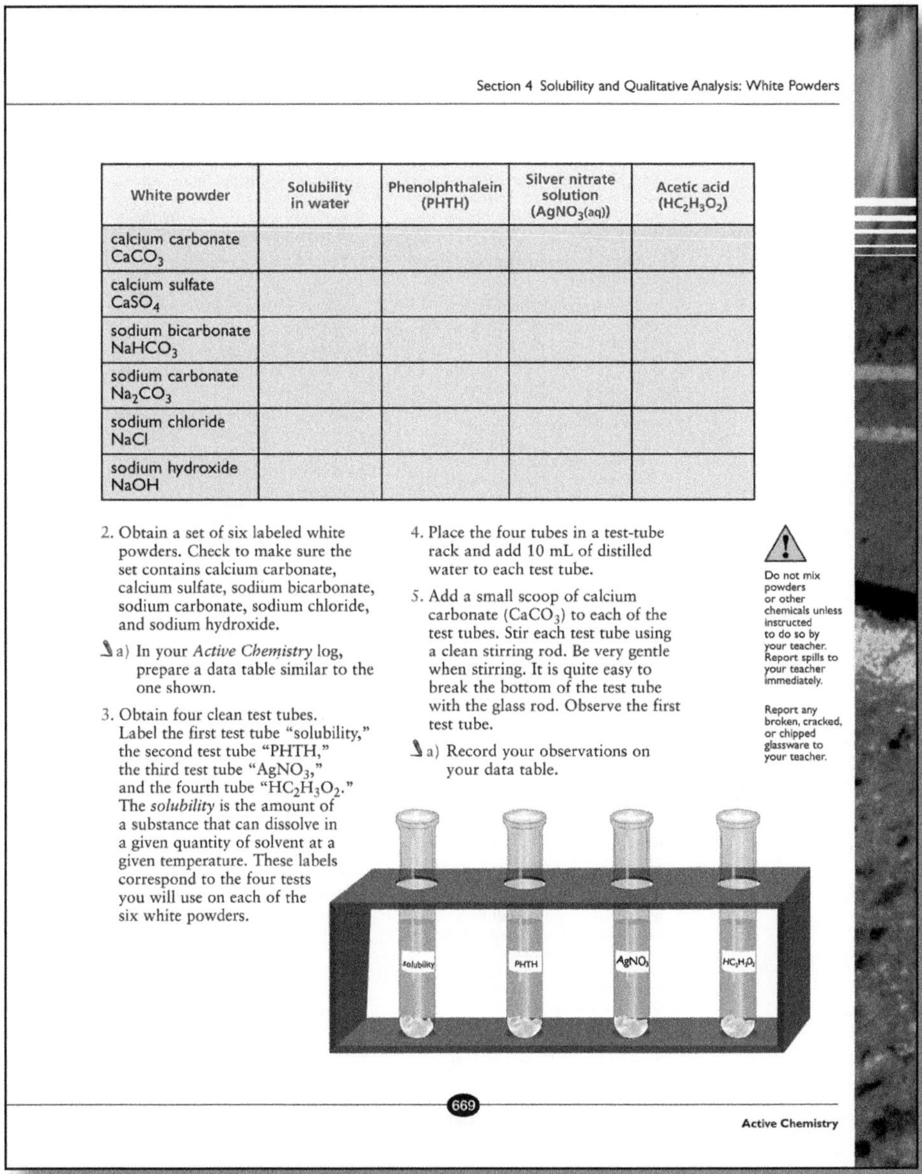

The left portion reproduces a student page:

White powder	Solubility in water	Phenolphthalein (PHTH)	Silver nitrate solution ($AgNO_3(aq)$)	Acetic acid ($HC_2H_3O_2$)
calcium carbonate $CaCO_3$				
calcium sulfate $CaSO_4$				
sodium bicarbonate $NaHCO_3$				
sodium carbonate Na_2CO_3				
sodium chloride $NaCl$				
sodium hydroxide $NaOH$				

2. Obtain a set of six labeled white powders. Check to make sure the set contains calcium carbonate, calcium sulfate, sodium bicarbonate, sodium carbonate, sodium chloride, and sodium hydroxide.

a) In your *Active Chemistry* log, prepare a data table similar to the one shown.

3. Obtain four clean test tubes. Label the first test tube "solubility," the second test tube "PHTH," the third test tube "$AgNO_3$," and the fourth tube "$HC_2H_3O_2$." The *solubility* is the amount of a substance that can dissolve in a given quantity of solvent at a given temperature. These labels correspond to the four tests you will use on each of the six white powders.

4. Place the four tubes in a test-tube rack and add 10 mL of distilled water to each test tube.

5. Add a small scoop of calcium carbonate ($CaCO_3$) to each of the test tubes. Stir each test tube using a clean stirring rod. Be very gentle when stirring. It is quite easy to break the bottom of the test tube with the glass rod. Observe the first test tube.

a) Record your observations on your data table.

⚠️
Do not mix powders or other chemicals unless instructed to do so by your teacher. Report spills to your teacher immediately.

Report any broken, cracked, or chipped glassware to your teacher.

669

Active Chemistry

Investigate

Part A: Identifying Household White Powders

Make sure your labels have the name of the chemical, the formula, and any safety warning to avoid confusion.

1.

If students design their own experiments, check to make sure their test designs are safe, practical, effective, and that all necessary equipment is available.

2.

The potential hazards of handling sodium hydroxide should be clearly emphasized. You may want to have each group test only one of the six powders. Then they can share their results. If you choose that option, make sure that the group handling the sodium hydroxide thoroughly understands the safety measures.

3.

Stress the importance of accurate labeling.

CHAPTER 8

STUDENTS' PRIOR CONCEPTIONS

5. Analysis will always give you a right answer.
6. All solutions are pure liquids.
7. When a precipitate forms, all that remains in the test tube is precipitate and pure water. The other ions cease to exist.
8. One test is conclusive.
9. There is one correct order to perform the tests.

Such misconceptions often stem from students' incomplete understanding of the particle nature of matter. According to a report prepared for the Royal Society of Chemistry titled *Beyond Appearances: Students' misconceptions about basic chemical ideas* by Vanessa Barker Kind, younger students tend to view matter as continuous and describe matter by its bulk properties. This limited understanding probably stems from the fact that students tend to use sensory reasoning based on sensory experiences to formulate thoughts about what they cannot see. Reliance on sensory reasoning may also be due to students' limited exposure to the particle theory matter. In addition, when the particle theory is studied at the secondary level it is usually confined to a limited number of examples such as water. This may lead students to believe that the particle nature of matter is only true for these examples.

*Horton, Chris (2001), "Student Preconceptions and Misconceptions in Chemistry" Integrated Physics and Chemistry Modeling Workshop, Arizona State University, June 2001, Version 1.35

4.

If the test tubes are clearly labeled, a 250-mL beaker can be used instead of a test-tube rack.

5.

A "small" scoop is a difficult concept. You may want to demonstrate what a small scoop is—roughly the tip of the scoopula, which should be approximately 0.5 g. You may choose to reduce the amount of white solid (calcium carbonate) used from 0.5 g to 0.2 or even 0.1 g.

5.a)

$CaCO_3$ is essentially insoluble.

6.a)

The phenolphthalein will turn the solution light pink.

7.

The students adding silver nitrate to the third test tube should wear rubber gloves. Caution them in advance about the risk of staining.

7.a)

Due to the slight solubility of $CaCO_3$, students should observe a light precipitate of white Ag_2CO_3.

$$CO_3^{2-} + 2Ag^+ \longrightarrow Ag_2CO_3$$

8.

The small pipette should amount to approximately 2-3 mL of acetic acid.

8.a)

Students will observe bubbles from the reaction of the acid with carbonate ions.

$$2HC_2H_3O_2 + CO_3^{2-} \longrightarrow H_2O + 2C_2H_3O_2^- + CO_2$$

CSI Chemistry

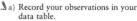

Silver nitrate can stain skin and clothing. Handle with care.

Wash your hands and arms thoroughly after the investigation.

6. Add 1-2 drops of phenolphthalein solution (PHTH) to the second test tube. Gently swirl the contents of the test tube.

   a) Record your observations in your data table.

7. Add a couple of drops of silver nitrate solution, $AgNO_3$(aq), to the third test tube. Gently swirl the contents and observe.

   a) Record your observations in your data table. Note the symbol (aq) following the chemical symbol. Recall that this stands for aqueous and means the compound is in a solution with water. Other symbols can be used to represent the states of matter for compounds including (s) for solids, (l) for liquids, and (g) for gases.

8. To the fourth test tube, add a small pipette full of acetic acid solution, $HC_2H_3O_2$. Gently swirl the contents.

   a) Record your observations in your data table.

9. Dispose of the contents of the test tubes as indicated by your teacher. Clean the test tubes using a test-tube brush. Rinse them twice with a small amount of distilled water.

10. Now that you are familiar with lab techniques for each material, repeat *Steps 4 to 9* for the remaining five powders, substituting the next white powder in your data table where the directions call for calcium carbonate, $CaCO_3$. Your teacher may have your sodium hydroxide samples already measured for you. In the event that your teacher wants you to do the preparation, you must be extremely careful with solid sodium hydroxide, as it will burn. (Chemically speaking, it will

saponify your skin, i.e., make soap). Use gloves in measuring out your solid sodium hydroxide for the different test tubes.

11. You are given a white powder.

   a) What test results would you expect if the white powder were NaCl?

   b) What test results would you expect if the white powder were $NaHCO_3$?

   c) Does each material have a unique set of properties?

Part B: Reading and Creating Flowcharts

Now that you can identify each compound based on its solubility in water and reaction with the other three reagents, you need a way to represent this simply. In this part of the investigation, you will learn how to use a type of map called a flowchart. Flowcharts can be used to illustrate a deductive reasoning process, so they are useful to a forensic scientist.

1. What does the first flowchart on the next page represent?

   a) Write down your thoughts in your *Active Chemistry* log and be prepared to share them with the class.

2. The next flowchart can be used to identify the six modes of transportation shown. Choose a mode of transportation and see if the flowchart identifies it correctly. Choose a second one and try it again.

   a) Copy the flowchart into your *Active Chemistry* log and fill in all the blanks. Is each blank unique? If so, the flowchart works.

(670)

9.

You may wish to keep the third test tube (containing silver ions) from each group in a special container for hazardous heavy metals.

10.

The sample data in the following table represents typical results you may expect students to collect:

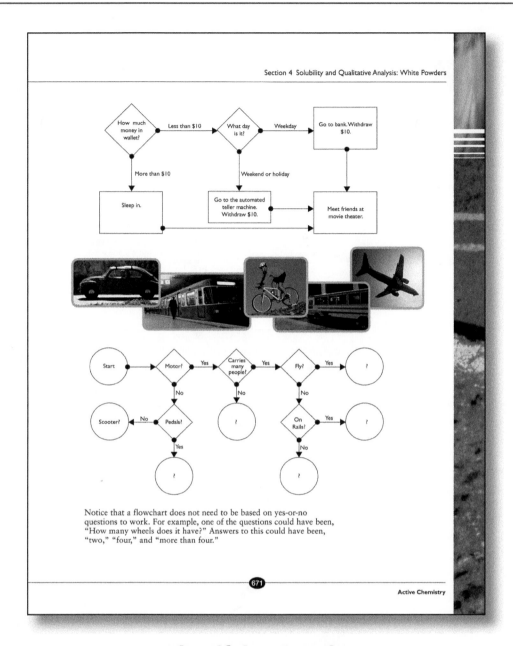

Notice that a flowchart does not need to be based on yes-or-no questions to work. For example, one of the questions could have been, "How many wheels does it have?" Answers to this could have been, "two," "four," and "more than four."

671

Active Chemistry

Identifying Powders

Powder	Solubility	Phenolphthalein	0.1 *M* AgNO$_3$(aq)	1 *M* HC$_2$H$_3$O$_2$
CaCO$_3$	Insoluble	Light pink	Very light, white precipitate	Bubbles
CaSO$_4$	Insoluble	Clear	Possible light precipitate	No visible change
NaHCO$_3$	Soluble	Light pink	White precipitate	Bubbles
Na$_2$CO$_3$	Soluble	Bright pink	White/brown precipitate	Bubbles
NaCl	Soluble	Clear	White precipitate	No visible change
NaOH	Soluble	Bright pink	Brown/silvery precipitate	No change, perhaps some heat

CHAPTER 8

11.a)

If the unknown were NaCl, the results would be as shown in the table below. A white crystalline solid that is soluble in water, has no change in color with phenolphthalein and gives a heavy white precipitate with silver nitrate. It also shows no reaction with acetic acid.

11.b)

If the unknown were NaHCO$_3$, the results would be as shown in the table. A white solid that is soluble in water, changes to a pink color with phenolphthalein and gives a white precipitate with silver nitrate. It also gives off bubbles with acetic acid.

11.c)

Each of these four compounds has a unique set of properties. The two salts which would be most difficult to distinguish are NaHCO$_3$ and Na$_2$CO$_3$.

Part B: Reading and Creating Flowcharts

Some students may be intimidated by the fact that there is no one "right" answer in the design of flowcharts. Many will struggle with the creation of a flowchart in the beginning. If possible, resist the temptation to help. As soon as one group figures it out, other groups should catch on.

1.a)

The flowchart represents what someone would have to do to ensure that he or she can finance a trip to the movies with friends.

2.a)

From bottom left to top right, the modes of transportation to fill in the blank circles in the chart are: bicycle, car, bus, train, airplane. Each blank (circle) is unique.

3.

Advise students to leave plenty of space on their flowchart sheets for expansion. The beginning of the flowchart that is provided in the text should be positioned on their page so as to allow for expansion below and out to either side.

4.

The silver nitrate solution turns out to be unnecessary and some students may figure this out. The phenolphthalein test can be used to distinguish the strong bases (Na_2CO_3, $NaOH$ – bright pink) from the weak base ($NaHCO_3$ – light pink color).

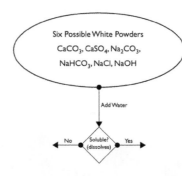

CSI Chemistry

Six Possible White Powders
$CaCO_3$, $CaSO_4$, Na_2CO_3,
$NaHCO_3$, $NaCl$, $NaOH$

Add Water

No ← Soluble? (dissolves) → Yes

3. Now that you've had some practice creating flowcharts, use your test results from *Part A* to create a flowchart for identifying the household white powders. Hint: You might want to start with whether the solid dissolves in water as your first decision. (See the example flowchart shown.)

4. Once you have created your chart, try it out using at least two of the white powders to test its validity. (See if it works!). If your flowchart does not correctly identify all six of the powders, revise it and test it again.

a) Once you have a flowchart that works, copy it into your *Active Chemistry* log.

Chem Talk

IDENTIFYING UNKNOWNS IN CHEMISTRY

Qualitative Analysis

Forensic chemists are often faced with the challenging task of identifying unknown compounds. There are millions of possible compounds and mixtures of compounds to choose from. Forensic chemists must develop tests that identify each one! The use of tests to determine the identity of an unknown compound is called **qualitative analysis**. In this type of analysis, it is the identity of the unknown—the qualities that make it unique—that is important and not the quantity, or amount, of the substance. In this experiment, you used the results from a series of tests performed on six different compounds to develop a flowchart. This flowchart will allow you to identify one or more unknown white powders found at the *Chapter Challenge* crime scene, if the powder or powders are the ones you have tested in this investigation.

The key to identifying a white powder is testing properties that allow one powder to be differentiated from another. For example, both sugar and salt dissolve easily in water. Therefore, testing a powder that may

Chem Words

qualitative analysis: the determination of which substances are present in the sample with little or no regard to the exact amount of each.

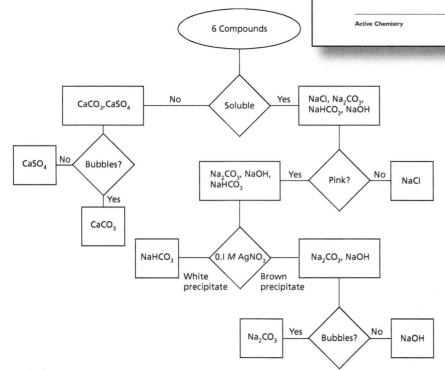

6 Compounds

Soluble

No → $CaCO_3$, $CaSO_4$

Yes → $NaCl$, Na_2CO_3, $NaHCO_3$, $NaOH$

Bubbles?

No → $CaSO_4$

Yes → $CaCO_3$

Pink?

Yes → Na_2CO_3, $NaOH$, $NaHCO_3$

No → $NaCl$

0.1 M $AgNO_3$

White precipitate → $NaHCO_3$

Brown precipitate → Na_2CO_3, $NaOH$

Bubbles?

Yes → Na_2CO_3

No → $NaOH$

be either sugar or salt by dissolving the powder in water would not help tell them apart. But sugar melts at a relatively low temperature, while salt melts at a much higher temperature, so if the white powder melts in a pan on the stove, you know that it cannot be salt. The tests used in a qualitative analysis depend on the properties of the possible unknown substances. If the number of possible substances is large or some of the possible substances have many physical and chemical properties in common, a scientist might have to conduct several different tests before accurately identifying the unknown substance.

Ionic Compounds

The white powders you used in this investigation are all **ionic compounds**. Ionic compounds are made of a combination of positive and negative **ions**. Sodium chloride is an ionic compound, so its chemical formula, $NaCl$, means there is one positive sodium ion (Na^+) for every one negative chloride ion (Cl^-).

Ionic compounds form on the basis that opposite charges attract. The positive sodium ion is attracted to the negative chloride ion. This attraction between the positive ion (also called a **cation**) and the negative ion (also called an **anion**) is called an **ionic bond**, and the substance formed by the bond is the ionic compound. The sodium ion and chloride ion join to form the ionic compound sodium chloride, $NaCl$, as shown.

$$Na^+ + Cl^- \rightarrow NaCl$$

In calcium chloride, $CaCl_2$, there is one positive calcium ion (Ca^{2+}) for every two negative chloride ions (again, Cl^-).

$$Ca^{2+} + 2Cl^- \rightarrow CaCl_2$$

Notice since there are two chloride ions for every one calcium ion there is a 2 in front of the chloride ion. You must always have the same number of ions or atoms of each element on both sides of a chemical equation. This is due to the **law of conservation of matter**. It states that matter cannot be created or destroyed. Chloride ions must be equal in the reactants and products, so there must be two on each side.

In an ionic compound the cations take the name of the element. The anions take the name of the element but the ending is changed to –*ide*. Notice that metals form positive ions and nonmetals form negative ions.

Chem Words

ionic compound: a compound that is composed of positive ions (cations) and negative ions (anions).

ion: an electrically charged atom or group of atoms that has acquired a net charge, either negative or positive.

cation: an ion that has a positive charge.

anion: an ion that has a negative charge.

ionic bond: the attraction between oppositely charged ions.

law of conservation of matter: the amount of matter present before and after a chemical change remains the same.

Chem Talk

Qualitative analysis is defined as the use of tests to determine the identity of an unknown substance and ionic bonds are reviewed. The nature of different ionic compounds, cations, anions and some common characteristics such as solubility, pH, and melting points are examined. A look at the reactions of ionic compounds leads to a review of double-replacement reactions and precipitates.

CHAPTER 8

CSI CHEMISTRY

CSI Chemistry

Some Common Ions

Formula	Name	Formula	Name
Na^+	sodium ion	Cl^-	chloride ion
K^+	potassium ion	F^-	fluoride ion
Ag^+	silver ion	O^{2-}	oxide ion
Ca^{2+}	calcium ion	S^{2-}	sulfide ion

Groups of atoms may act as a single ion in an ionic compound, like in calcium carbonate, $CaCO_3$. There is one calcium cation (Ca^{2+}) for every one carbonate anion (CO_3^{2-}). Ions like carbonate, (CO_3^{2-}), are called **polyatomic ions**. Sulfate (SO_4^{2-}), hydroxide (OH^-), nitrate (NO_3^-), acetate ($C_2H_3O_2^-$) and bicarbonate (HCO_3^-) are other polyatomic anions found in the white powders and reagents used in this section.

Solubility

In *Part A*, you placed a sample of each white powder in water to see if it would dissolve. This property of matter is called **solubility**. The powders that dissolved in water are **soluble**. When a solid dissolves in water the mixture of the dissolved solid and the water is called a **solution**. The powders that did not dissolve are **insoluble**. Whether or not a particular powder dissolves in water is a complex matter that depends on many factors. Fortunately, the solubility of many substances in water has been investigated. The results of some of the investigations are summarized in the table.

You can use the thousands of hours of work of chemists that resulted in this table to help you make identifications. Chemists don't memorize these tables, though some remember parts of the table. For example, some chemists through their repeated experiences with chlorides may remember which ones are not soluble.

This table can be used to predict if a given solid will dissolve in water. To determine if a solid is soluble, look at the chemical formula for the

Chem Words

polyatomic ion: an ion that consists of two or more atoms that are covalently bonded and have either a positive or negative charge.

solubility: the amount of a substance that can dissolve in a given quantity of solvent at a given temperature.

soluble: a property of a substance that dissolves in a liquid.

solution: a homogeneous mixture that consists of a solvent and at least one solute.

insoluble: a substance that will not dissolve in a liquid.

Solubility Rules

Nitrates (NO_3^-)	All are *soluble*.
Chlorides (Cl^-)	All are *soluble* **except** those containing ions of silver, mercury (I), and lead (II).
Sulfates (SO_4^{2-})	All are *soluble* **except** those containing ions of barium, calcium, strontium, silver, lead (II), and mercury (I).
Carbonates (CO_3^{2-})	All are *insoluble* **except** those containing ions of the Group I metals or the ammonium ion.
Hydroxides (OH^-)	All are *insoluble* **except** those containing ions of the Group I metals or the ammonium ion.

674

solid, and identify which of the five negatively charged ions listed in the table the solid contains. Then read the rule for solids containing that ion and the exceptions to the rule. For example, sodium carbonate, Na_2CO_3, contains the ion carbonate, CO_3^{2-}. According to the table, all carbonates are insoluble except for the ones containing Group I metals. Sodium is a Group I metal, so sodium carbonate is an exception to the general rule that carbonates are insoluble. Therefore, sodium carbonate is soluble and dissolves in water. Other examples are given below.

- KCl is soluble because all chlorides are soluble except those containing ions of silver, mercury (I), and lead (II). KCl does not contain any of the exceptions.

- $Mg(OH)_2$ is insoluble because hydroxides are insoluble except for those containing Group I metals, and magnesium is not a Group I metal.

Determining whether a given solid is soluble is another example of deductive reasoning using both the table of solubility rules and the periodic table.

Phenolphthalein: An Acid-Base Indicator

In the second test, you added phenolphthalein (PHTH) to your sample. PHTH is one of a class of compounds known as acid-base indicators. **Acids** are compounds that form H^+ ions in solution and strong acids are 100% dissociated in water. Acids taste sour (citric and maleic acids are used in sour candies), react with metals (corrosive), neutralize bases, and react with indicators to produce a color change. **Acid-base indicators** are substances that change color when exposed to an acid or a base. Some common acids and their uses are listed in the table. Unlike HCl, weak bases are only slightly dissociated in water.

Chem Words

acid: a solution that has a pH value lower than 7.

acid-base indicator: a substance that changes color when exposed to either an acid or a base.

base: a solution that has a pH value greater than 7.

Common Acids and Their Uses

Name	Formula	Use	Strength
acetic acid	$HC_2H_3O_2$	vinegar	weak
carbonic acid	H_2CO_3	carbonated sodas	weak
hydrochloric acid	HCl	stomach acid	strong

Bases are compounds that form hydroxide ions (OH^-) in solution. Bases taste bitter, are corrosive, feel slippery, saponify fats (turns fats into soaps), neutralize acids, and cause indicators to change color.

CHAPTER 8

CSI Chemistry

Bases cause phenolphthalein to turn bright pink. Some common bases and their uses are listed in the table.

Common Bases and Their Uses

Name	Formula	Use	Strength
sodium hydroxide (lye)	NaOH	drain cleaners	strong
ammonia	NH_3	window cleaners	weak
magnesium hydroxide	$Mg(OH)_2$	antacids	strong
sodium carbonate	Na_2CO_3	glass manufacture	strong

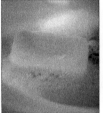

Reactions of Ionic Compounds: Double-Replacement Reactions

Ionic compounds can form insoluble solids in chemical reactions. For example, when silver nitrate solution is added to sodium chloride solution, a milky white solid is formed. The chemical equation for this reaction is shown below.

silver nitrate + sodium chloride → sodium nitrate + silver chloride

$$AgNO_{3(aq)} + NaCl_{(aq)} \rightarrow NaNO_{3(aq)} + AgCl_{(s)}$$

By examining the reaction, you can see that the metals, sodium (Na) and silver (Ag), exchange places to form two new compounds. This reaction is called a **double-replacement reaction**. You can determine the identity of the milky white solid, called a **precipitate**, by looking at the two products and using the solubility rules. The first product, sodium nitrate, dissolves in water because all nitrates are soluble. The second product, silver chloride, is insoluble because all chlorides are soluble with the exception of mercury (II), lead (II), and silver. Because of silver chloride's insolubility, instead of dissolving and being invisible like the sodium nitrate, the silver chloride that is formed is visible as a milky white precipitate.

Chem Words

double-replacement reaction: a reaction in which two elements or groups of elements in two different compounds exchange places to form new compounds.

precipitate: an insoluble salt that is formed when two solutions are mixed together.

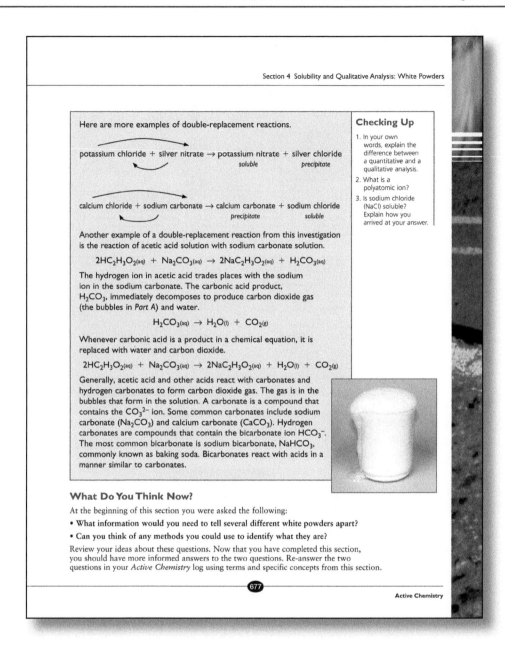

Section 4 Solubility and Qualitative Analysis: White Powders

Here are more examples of double-replacement reactions.

potassium chloride + silver nitrate → potassium nitrate + silver chloride
soluble   precipitate

calcium chloride + sodium carbonate → calcium carbonate + sodium chloride
precipitate   soluble

Another example of a double-replacement reaction from this investigation is the reaction of acetic acid solution with sodium carbonate solution.

$$2HC_2H_3O_{2(aq)} + Na_2CO_{3(aq)} \rightarrow 2NaC_2H_3O_{2(aq)} + H_2CO_{3(aq)}$$

The hydrogen ion in acetic acid trades places with the sodium ion in the sodium carbonate. The carbonic acid product, H_2CO_3, immediately decomposes to produce carbon dioxide gas (the bubbles in *Part A*) and water.

$$H_2CO_{3(aq)} \rightarrow H_2O_{(l)} + CO_{2(g)}$$

Whenever carbonic acid is a product in a chemical equation, it is replaced with water and carbon dioxide.

$$2HC_2H_3O_{2(aq)} + Na_2CO_{3(aq)} \rightarrow 2NaC_2H_3O_{2(aq)} + H_2O_{(l)} + CO_{2(g)}$$

Generally, acetic acid and other acids react with carbonates and hydrogen carbonates to form carbon dioxide gas. The gas is in the bubbles that form in the solution. A carbonate is a compound that contains the CO_3^{2-} ion. Some common carbonates include sodium carbonate (Na_2CO_3) and calcium carbonate ($CaCO_3$). Hydrogen carbonates are compounds that contain the bicarbonate ion HCO_3^-. The most common bicarbonate is sodium bicarbonate, $NaHCO_3$, commonly known as baking soda. Bicarbonates react with acids in a manner similar to carbonates.

Checking Up

1. In your own words, explain the difference between a quantitative and a qualitative analysis.
2. What is a polyatomic ion?
3. Is sodium chloride (NaCl) soluble? Explain how you arrived at your answer.

What Do You Think Now?

At the beginning of this section you were asked the following:

• What information would you need to tell several different white powders apart?

• Can you think of any methods you could use to identify what they are?

Review your ideas about these questions. Now that you have completed this section, you should have more informed answers to the two questions. Re-answer the two questions in your *Active Chemistry* log using terms and specific concepts from this section.

677

Active Chemistry

What Do You Think Now?

It is useful for students to return to the original *What Do You See?* illustration and the *What Do You Think?* questions to review their original responses. When they reconsider the questions, most will probably now say that the information needed would be the data from testing the powders with a variety of reagents. The illustration should be more meaningful to them now as it represents the investigation that they just performed. Ask students if they can now figure out the meaning of the writing on the blackboard.

This review should give them confidence in their growth and ability to use flowcharts correctly. Refer to the suggestions in *A Chemist's Response* for some examples of answers to the *What Do You Think?* questions and allow students to share their opinions.

Checking Up

1.

Qualitative analysis is primarily dedicated to the identification of substances while quantitative analysis focuses on the quantity of a known substance.

2.

A polyatomic ion is an ion that consists of two or more atoms that are covalently bonded and have either a positive or negative charge (Examples: NH_4^+ and CO_3^{2-}).

3.

Sodium chloride is soluble in water as demonstrated by either an experiment where $NaCl_{(s)}$ is mixed with 10 mL of water or by looking at the Solubility Rules table already created by many chemists.

Chem Essential Questions

What does it mean?

MACRO — Some of the macroscopic properties that were observed are: color, solubility, color with phenolphthalein, precipitate with silver nitrate and bubbles with vinegar.

NANO — At the nano level, KCl and $AgNO_3$ react by exchanging cations when AgCl forms a white precipitate.

SYMBOLIC —
The formula NaOH signifies that the substance has one sodium ion and one hydroxide ion. Chemists name the compound by using the element's name for the positive ion (sodium) and the "ide" ending on the negative ion.

How do you know?
The evidence for physical change was the dissolving in water. That is, when the sodium chloride (also, sodium bicarbonate, sodium hydroxide, and sodium carbonate) dissolved in water, a physical change took place.
The evidence for chemical change was the precipitate of silver chloride when silver nitrate was mixed with sodium chloride. Reactions with phenolphthalein (color change) and acetic acid (gas evolution) also constitute evidence of chemical change.

Why do you believe?
Students' answers will vary. Common examples are the use of salt to melt ice (physical), boiling water (physical), iron rusting (chemical), and combustion (chemical).

Why should you care?
Students' answers will vary. They may choose the flowchart concept for crime scene analysis and the concept of solubility. Students should explain their choices.

 CSI Chemistry

Chem Essential Questions

What does it mean?

Chemistry explains a *macroscopic* phenomenon (what you observe) with a description of what happens at the *nanoscopic* level (atoms and molecules) using *symbolic* structures as a way to communicate. Complete the chart below in your *Active Chemistry* log.

MACRO	NANO	SYMBOLIC
What are some of the macroscopic properties that you observed with the white powders in this investigation?	Explain what is happening at the nano level during a double-replacement reaction. You can use potassium chloride and silver nitrate as examples.	Chemists use formulas as symbols to represent elements and compounds. Explain the meaning of the formula NaOH. How do chemists name this ionic compound?

How do you know?

What was the evidence in the laboratory of physical and chemical changes? Explain.

Why do you believe?

Explain a situation where you have seen a chemical and physical change in your experiences outside of the classroom.

Why should you care?

List at least two concepts from this section that you think would be useful in analyzing a crime scene. Explain why you chose each concept.

Reflecting on the Section and the Challenge

You have learned how to identify white powders based on their chemical and physical properties. If your crime scene includes a white powder, you will need to analyze it to determine its identity. You will also need to assign different powders to different suspects so that the identity of the powder will help to identify the suspect.

Chem to Go

1. Use the list of ions below to answer the questions.
   Cl^-, Na^+, Al^{3+}, SO_4^{2-}, MnO_4^-, NH_4^+, O^{2-}, Fe^{2+}
   a) Which ions are cations? b) Which ions are anions?
   c) Which ions are polyatomic ions?
2. Which of the following compounds are insoluble in water?
   K_2CO_3, Na_2SO_4, $MgCO_3$, $Ba(OH)_2$, $FeCl_3$, $Cu(NO_3)_2$, $PbCl_2$

678

Active Chemistry

Reflecting on the Section and the Challenge

Students should read this section for a direct connotation between the section and the *Chapter Challenge*. While students do not answer any questions in this section, it will give them a chance to think about how to implement the information about qualitative analysis based on chemical and physical changes in the development of their crime scene.

You might want to have a short discussion.

Chem to Go

1.

a) Na^+, Al^{3+}, NH_4^+, Fe^{2+}

b) Cl^-, SO_4^{2-}, MnO_4^-, O^{2-}

c) SO_4^{2-}, MnO_4^-, NH_4^+

2.

$MgCO_3$, $Ba(OH)_2$, and $PbCl_2$ are insoluble in water.

3. Which of the following are double-replacement reactions?

   a) $AgNO_3 + NaBr \rightarrow NaNO_3 + AgBr$ b) $CaCO_3 \rightarrow CaO + CO_2$

   c) $FeCl_3 + 3KOH \rightarrow 3KCl + Fe(OH)_3$ d) $Zn + CuSO_4 \rightarrow ZnSO_4 + Cu$

4. Complete the word equations for the following double-replacement reactions.

   a) potassium chloride + lead (II) nitrate →

   b) iron (III) chloride + potassium hydroxide →

   c) sodium hydroxide + calcium nitrate →

5. Identify the precipitates formed in each of the reactions in *Question 4*.

6. Name one other physical property and one other chemical property you could use to identify any powdered chemical found at a crime scene.

7. How could a defense attorney prove that a white powder was NOT the chemical that the prosecutors claimed it to be?

8. In the reaction described in the *Chem Talk* section,

   $2HC_2H_3O_2 + Na_2CO_3 \rightarrow 2NaC_2H_3O_2 + H_2O + CO_2$

   a) Show that the number of H, C, O and Na atoms are identical on both sides of the equation.

   b) Why must the number of these elements be identical on both sides of the equation?

9. List a few properties of one of the white powders so another team can use their flowchart to identify the powder.

10. What is the minimum number of tests you must conduct to determine if the white powder is NaCl, if the only possibilities are the powders you used in the investigation?

11. **Preparing for the Chapter Challenge**

   Each of the chemicals in this lab was called a "household" chemical. Create a table with three columns: white powder, possible uses of the white powder, and crime scenes where you might find this chemical. Use the Internet and references suggested to you by your instructor to determine each chemical's possible use or uses.

Inquiring Further

Instrumental techniques

On many of the crime dramas, you will notice researchers using machines to identify samples from the crime scene, or more commonly, they send it off to the lab and get back a printed report. Research instrumental methods forensic chemists use to identify white powders found at a crime scene. Describe what criteria you used to determine the reliability of the sources you used in your research. Identify the name of one of these instruments and explain how it functions on the physical or chemical properties of the white powder.

Active Chemistry

5.

The precipitates formed are:

a) lead (II) chloride

b) iron (III) hydroxide

c) calcium hydroxide

6.

Answers will vary but students may suggest one of the following physical properties: color, melting point, or magnetism. For chemical properties, students may suggest that if the powder is soluble, it could be treated with other solutions to see if a replacement reaction takes place, which would help identify an anion or cation.

7.

The defense attorney could perform a series of tests showing that other chemicals could have the same results.

8.

a) Both the reactant and the product sides of the equation contain: 8 hydrogen atoms, 5 carbon atoms, 7 oxygen atoms, and 2 sodium atoms

b) The Law of Conservation of Mass dictates that the mass must be conserved. In a chemical reaction, matter can be neither created nor destroyed. Thus, the number of elements on both sides of an equation must be equal.

3.

The double-replacement reactions are:

a) $AgNO_3 + NaBr \rightarrow$
   $NaNO_3 + AgBr$

c) $FeCl_3 + 3KOH \rightarrow$
   $3KCl + Fe(OH)_3$

NOTE: b) is a decomposition reaction and d) is a single-replacement reaction.

4.

a) potassium chloride + lead (II) nitrate → lead (II) chloride + potassium nitrate

b) iron (III) chloride + potassium hydroxide → potassium chloride + iron (III) hydroxide

c) sodium hydroxide + calcium nitrate → calcium hydroxide + sodium nitrate

9.

Students' answers will vary. For an example, sodium carbonate is soluble in water, basic, releases bubbles when it reacts with an acid, and produces a precipitate with silver nitrate solution.

10.

Two tests would identify sodium chloride as the white powder:

• Solubility

• Reaction with phenolphthalein.

11.

Preparing for the Chapter Challenge

Students' answers will vary. Below is a sample chart that could be used to give students a head start.

White powder	Possible uses	Crime scene
Cocaine	Drug	Robbery
Arsenic	Poison	Murder

Inquiring Further

Instrumental Techniques

You may want to conduct some preliminary research to identify some of the instruments used by forensic labs for powder identification. This would narrow the field and provide more definition for students' research projects.

NOTES

_____

_____

_____

_____

_____

_____

_____

_____

_____

_____

_____

_____

_____

SECTION 4 – QUIZ

8-4a **Blackline Master**

1. Explain how a qualitative test is different from a quantitative one.

2. A bond that forms between a positive and negative ion is called _____.

   a) a covalent bond   b) an ionic bond

   c) a dynamic bond   d) grouping

3. Circle the elements below that are nonmetals.

   Na   H   P   Sn   Cu   Kr   Al

4. Use the list of ions to answer the questions.

   OH^-, Cl^-, Na^+, O^{2-}, NH_4^+, CO_3^{2-}, Ba^{2+}

   a) Which ions are anions?

   b) Which ions are cations?

   c) Which ions are polyatomic ions?

5. In the following double-replacement reaction, which product is a precipitate?

   $Na_2SO_4 + BaCl_2 \rightarrow BaSO_4 + 2NaCl$

   a) Na_2SO_4 b) $BaSO_4$

   c) $NaCl$ d) SO_4^{2-}

SECTION 4 – QUIZ ANSWERS

❶ A quantitative test measures the amount (quantity) of a specific substance. A qualitative test provides information about the identity of a substance but not amounts. Example: To say that a solution contains iron (II) ion is a qualitative statement. To say that a solution contains 100 ppm of iron (II) ion is a quantitative statement.

❷ b) an ionic bond

❸ H, Kr, and P are nonmetals

❹ a) OH^-, Cl^-, O^{2-}, CO_3^{2-} are anions

   b) Na^+, NH_4^+, Ba^{2+} are cations

   c) OH^-, NH_4^+, CO_3^{2-} are polyatomic ions

❺ b) $BaSO_4$

CHAPTER 8

Chapter Mini-Challenge

The students have been introduced to new concepts in the first four sections of this chapter. Now is a good time for them to review these principles and consider how they can be applied to their *Chapter Challenge* projects. The *Mini-Challenge* provides an opportunity for students to implement and test some of their ideas. Any problems or obstacles they encounter with this smaller assignment will better prepare them for the bigger challenge ahead.

The *Mini-Challenge* will also give you an opportunity to coach students in the creation of their crime stories, scenes, and evidence. Encourage students to refer to the criteria decided on by the class for grading the *Chapter Challenge* in the design of their projects.

As students decide on the methods to use for their projects, you can give pointers on writing crime stories, creating evidence, and composing dossiers and police reports. Remind students that they must also create flowcharts and a list of the relevant chemical concepts with the solution material they are to submit in sealed envelopes. Therefore, now is a good time to address any misconceptions as students attempt to explain the chemistry involved in the solutions to their crime scenes.

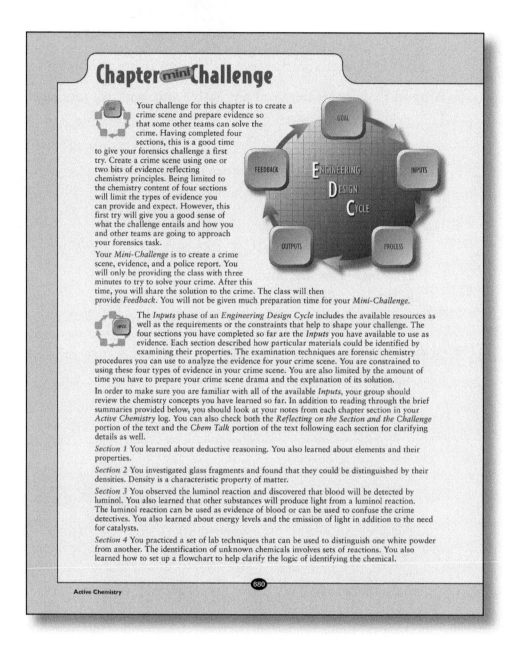

The *Mini-Challenge* should take about one hour for preparation and one half-hour period for all teams to share their crime scenes and evidence. All teams should receive written feedback from the class after their presentations. One method for encouraging helpful feedback is to require each student to write down two positive comments and one suggestion for improvement.

CHAPTER 8

Engineering Design Cycle

Remind students that this is a first try and they should use the feedback from the class to improve upon their projects for the *Chapter Challenge*. After all the presentations are completed, review the *Engineering Design Cycle* to help students see other ways to put their chemistry knowledge to use.

Because there are still four more activities to go, students should expect that their final *Chapter Challenge* presentations will incorporate more chemical concepts in the solving of the evidence, and the feedback from their *Mini-Challenge* presentations should enable them to improve upon their crime stories and scenes. At the end of the chapter, you can ask students to reflect on the successes and disappointments from the *Mini-Challenge*. This experience and information will be vital for making the necessary modifications to their design cycles in order to succeed with the *Chapter Challenge*.

The *Process* phase of the *Engineering Design Cycle* is where you decide what information you have will help you meet the criteria of the *Goal*. Your group has to create a crime scene drama that involves some combination of the following evidence: a mystery chemical element, an unidentified white powder, a sample of glass that can be tested for density, and evidence that may or may not catalyze the luminol reaction. The primary vehicle for your drama will be the police report, which should also list and describe any known suspects since you will not be producing dossiers for the *Mini-Challenge*. Your task will require you to use deductive reasoning to create a logical—though hopefully not obvious—chain of evidence that implicates a single suspect. Using a flowchart like you did in *Section 4* can help you organize the detailed information, visualize the path to your criminal, and create a dramatic story.

Engineers use flowcharts to troubleshoot a complicated process that is not functioning properly. They often can identify the source of a problem by identifying where in the process the products do not match the steps in the chart. In your flowchart, each piece of evidence will have a block for analysis. The analysis block will have two or more possible results, each of which should be linked to one or more of the suspects. Once all of the evidence is analyzed, the guilty suspect should match *all* of the analytic outcomes. All of the other suspects should *not* match at least one piece of analytic evidence; otherwise your deductive reasoning would be inconclusive. You might alternatively draw your flowchart to start with "suspect" and have each decision block lead toward the final "guilty" block using yes or no options (two choice paths). Any negative decision results would deviate from the linear path and then lead to a "not guilty" block.

Your drama does not need to be realistic; you might have to exaggerate or over-emphasize some details to link the evidence and the suspects clearly in the police report. The chemistry, however, must be real. You will have to explain how forensic detectives process the evidence to connect the suspects to the crime. You are welcome to use your imagination; make the context of the story as silly or scary as you like as long as it includes a crime and suspense as the evidence is analyzed. The decisions your group makes are all part of the *Process* step of the *Engineering Design Cycle*.

The *Outputs* of an *Engineering Design Cycle* are created during the *Process* step. Your product for the *Mini-Challenge* will be your crime scene diagram presentation, your written police report explaining the known details, and a description of the analyzed evidence. You must provide a brief explanation of the solution of your crime scene drama to reveal after students have had three minutes to consider the given information. You will have very limited time to prepare your presentation, so be sure to focus on each product you need to deliver. You will create a more involved crime scene drama for the full *Chapter Challenge*.

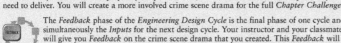

The *Feedback* phase of the *Engineering Design Cycle* is the final phase of one cycle and simultaneously the *Inputs* for the next design cycle. Your instructor and your classmates will give you *Feedback* on the crime scene drama that you created. This *Feedback* will become the *Inputs* you will use in the final *Chapter Challenge*. You will not be able to use the same mystery twice, but you can use the presentation techniques that created the most drama and the evidence that was the most challenging to connect to a suspect. You will create a more detailed scene in the *Chapter Challenge*, so pay attention to the information *Feedback* provides.

Make any changes to the chemistry explanation that received *Feedback*. Note any ideas you may have gotten by viewing other presentations. Your group will need to create a new crime scene, and seeing others may spark your creativity. Add your own perspective to create your *Chapter Challenge* scene. You are using *Feedback* for creative inspiration, not copying what another group has done.

You will learn new chemistry concepts in each of the remaining sections. Each section will teach you new forensic chemistry techniques. Pay careful attention to the *Chem Talk* presented in each chapter section; they are the key to creating a high-quality chemistry explanation in your final presentation.

681

Active Chemistry

SECTION 5
Double-Replacement Reactions and Fingerprints

Section Overview

Students learn about the chemical properties of silver nitrate and develop an image of a coin in silver chloride. This represents an example of a double-replacement reaction followed by an oxidation-reduction reaction. They will then learn how to make images of their own fingerprints and analyze patterns they see. Finally, they will develop a method for visualizing latent (hidden) fingerprints using the chemistry that they have learned.

Background Information

Fingerprint Patterns and General Classification

The ridge patterns that form fingerprints can generally be categorized as loops, whorls, or arches, and each of these three categories is further divided into subcategories. Fingerprints can easily and accurately be assigned to one of the three broad groups based upon visual inspection, and individuals practiced at fingerprint classification can further classify prints into more specific subcategories.

Loops are the most common type, representing about 65% of all fingerprints. In a loop pattern, the ridges enter and exit from the same side of the finger. They are classified as radial if the ridges come from and leave toward the thumb side of the finger, and ulnar if the loop opens toward the pinkie finger.

Whorls, the second most common ridge pattern, representing about 30% of fingerprints, contain two deltas, which are triangular patterns of ridges. They are identified as one of four subtypes: plain, central pocket loop, double loop, or accidental. Plain whorls contain at least one ridge that makes

a complete loop and rejoins itself. Also, the deltas are oriented around the loop such that a straight line connecting the two deltas would intersect the loop. A central pocket loop also contains a complete loop, but the deltas surrounding the loop are oriented differently, and a line connecting them would not touch the closed loop. A double loop contains two distinct loops, which can be either plain whorls or complete pocket loops or one of each. An accidental whorl is either a print that contains two or more of the other subcategories, or a print that cannot be properly categorized into any of the other subcategories.

The least common type of pattern, arches, is found in about 5% of all prints. Arches do not contain deltas or loops. Rather, they contain ridges that enter one side of the print and exit the other side, rising in the center to form a hill pattern. Arches are either plain or tented. In a plain arch, the ridges rise and fall gradually and smoothly at the center of the print, while in tented arches, there is at least one ridge that spikes upward very sharply in the center.

Fingerprint Identification

Fingerprints are unique as far as science has been able to determine – no two fingerprints studied have been found to be indistinguishable from each other. Positive identification of a fingerprint as that of one particular individual, as is desired in forensic cases, relies not upon the general categorization scheme outlined above but rather on the systematic comparison of the type and location of very small features of the latent print and a reference print taken from a person of interest. A fingerprint typically contains about 150 of these features, known as minutiae. Fingerprint experts usually declare a conclusive match if they find 10 to 16 minutiae in common, and no minutiae that are present in either the latent or the reference print but not the other. Minutiae are of five distinct types. See if you can find some of these in the following sample prints.

1. *bifurcations*, where one ridge splits to become two

2. *short ridges*, which are, as the name implies, very short lines

3. *enclosures*, where a ridge bifurcates and then immediately rejoins itself

4. *islands*, which are ridges that are just tiny dots

5. *ridge endings*, which are the point at which a ridge ceases.

Latent Fingerprint Visualization Techniques

In addition to the silver nitrate method utilized in this section, there are several other ways that latent fingerprints can be visualized. In fact, these methods are often preferred over the silver nitrate method for reasons of DNA preservation (DNA is destroyed in the silver nitrate method), ability to be used in conjunction with other fingerprinting techniques (once silver nitrate has been applied, other methods can not be used), and quality of visualized prints. These alternate methods, which include dusting, iodine fuming, and cyanoacrylate fuming, are described in the *Inquiring Further* section at the end of this section.

Double-Replacement Reactions

Double-replacement reactions, sometimes referred to as double-displacement reactions, represent one large category of chemical reactions. Double-replacement reactions generally occur between ionic compounds dissolved in solution, typically aqueous solution. In such a reaction, the two compounds exchange positive ions (cations), forming two new ionic compounds. Such reactions are of the general form:

$$AB + CD \rightarrow AD + CB$$

A and C and are metallic cations while B and D are nonmetallic anions (negative ions).

However, such reactions do not occur any time two ionic compounds in aqueous solution are mixed. Only when one of the products (AD or CB in the above example) is insoluble, forms a gas, or forms a water molecule, does a double-replacement reaction occur. In this section, an aqueous solution of silver nitrate dissolves the sodium chloride found in a latent fingerprint. Because one of the new combinations resulting from cation exchange, silver chloride, is insoluble in water, a double-replacement reaction occurs.

$$AgNO_{3(aq)} + NaCl_{(aq)} \rightarrow AgCl_{(s)} + NaNO_{3(aq)}$$

The silver ions in silver chloride then undergo a subsequent chemical reaction to form metallic silver, which is the substance that is visualized in the section. The chemistry of that second reaction is explored below.

Oxidation-Reduction Reactions

Oxidation-reduction reactions, sometimes called redox reactions, represent another important group of chemical reactions. Oxidation is the loss of one or more electrons, while reduction is the gain of one or more electrons. These two processes always occur simultaneously (in an oxidation-reduction reaction), because in order for one substance to lose electrons, another substance must accept those electrons and thus experience a gain in electrons. In an oxidation-reduction reaction, the reactant that loses electrons is said to be oxidized in the reaction, while the reactant that gains electrons is said to be reduced. Somewhat confusingly, the substance or ion that is oxidized is referred to as the reducing agent, because it causes the reduction of the other reactant. Likewise the reactant or ion that is reduced is called the oxidizing agent, because it causes the oxidation of the other reactant.

A^+	B^-	$\rightarrow$	A	+	B
A^+ is already **oxidized:** A^+ is the **oxidizing agent**	B^- is already **reduced:** B^- is the **reducing agent**		A is the reduced form of A^+		B is the oxidized form of B^-

In this activity, silver chloride, an ionic compound, undergoes an oxidation-reduction reaction to form the pure elements silver and chlorine. The silver ions are reduced to silver metal, and are the oxidizing agent. The chlorine ions are oxidized to form chlorine gas, and are the reducing agent. As this example demonstrates, a single substance, silver chloride in this case, can contain both the reducing agent and the oxidizing agent.

$2AgCl_{(s)}$	$\rightarrow$	$2Ag_{(s)}$	+	$Cl_{2(g)}$
Ag^+ ions are the oxidizing agent Cl^- ions are the reducing agent		Product resulting from reduction of Ag^+ ions		Product resulting from oxidation of Cl^- ions

LEARNING OUTCOMES		
LEARNING OUTCOMES	**LOCATION IN SECTION**	**EVIDENCE OF UNDERSTANDING**
Learn how to identify fingerprints.	*Investigate* Parts A-B *Chem Talk, Chem to Go* Question 8	Students are able to develop a procedure that allows them to visualize their own prints. Students are able to distinguish fingerprints on the basis of ridge characteristics. Students' answers match those provided in this *Teacher's Edition*.
Develop latent (invisible) fingerprints using the silver nitrate method.	*Investigate* Part C, Steps 2-3 *Chem Talk, Chem to Go* Question 1	Students successfully complete Part C of the investigation. Students' answers match those provided in this *Teacher's Edition*.
Learn the difference between accuracy and precision in experimental measurements.	*Investigate* Parts A-C *Checking Up* Question 3 *Chem Essential Questions, Chem to Go* Questions 1-5	Students are able to describe the chemistry behind the method and correctly utilize identified vocabulary terms. Students' answers match those provided in this *Teacher's Edition*.

CHAPTER 8

NOTES

_____

_____

_____

_____

_____

_____

_____

_____

_____

_____

_____

_____

Section 5
Materials, Chemicals, Preparation, and Safety

("per Group" quantity is based on group size of 4 students)

Materials and Equipment

Materials (and Equipment)	Quantity per Group (4 students)
Beaker, 250-mL	2
Long-stem funnel	1
Ringstand	1
Graduated cylinder, 100-mL	1
Funnel support	1
Copper penny	1
Black ink pad	1
Soft bristle brush	1
Stirring rod	1
White paper sheet	4
Graduated cylinders, 100-mL	2
Hand lens	1

Materials (and Equipment)	Quantity per Class
Paper towels, roll	1
UV light source	1
Filter paper, box	1

Chemicals

Chemicals	Quantity per Class (24 students)
Sodium chloride, NaCl	2.0 g
Silver nitrate, $AgNO_3$ (in dark bottle)	10.2 g

Teacher Preparation

0.1 M sodium chloride, NaCl—Dissolve 2.0 g of NaCl in 300 mL of deionized water and dilute to 350 mL.

0.1 M silver nitrate, $AgNO_3$—(See preparation for Activity 4.) Dissolve 10.2 g of silver nitrate in 400 mL of distilled water and adjust volume to 600 mL. Use caution when preparing solution, as it will stain skin and clothing.

Safety Requirements

- Goggles and aprons are required in the laboratory area.

- Broken glass must be placed in a special container that is marked for broken glass. Do not allow it to be placed in a regular garbage container.

- Silver nitrate solution should be stored in a dark bottle properly labeled for later use.

- Silver chloride should be deposited in a waste disposal container for heavy metals.

- The sodium chloride solution can be disposed of down the drain.

- Wash hands and arms before leaving the laboratory area.

NOTES

Meeting the Needs of All Students
Differentiated Instruction

Augmentation and Accommodations

LEARNING ISSUE	REFERENCE	AUGMENTATION AND ACCOMMODATIONS
Recording salient observations	*Investigate* Part A, 2.a)	**Augmentation** • Continue to remind students who have difficulties making observations that they should: 　o Predict what they think they will see. 　o Develop a list containing evidence of chemical changes they have seen previously, categorized by color precipitates, and other types of change. **Accommodations** • Give students the categories of observations you want them to consider when observing this reaction. • In addition to the above categories, give students many examples of each category which include the observations they will observe in this reaction.
Translating observations into word equations Accessing prior understandings	*Investigate* Part A, 3.a)	**Augmentation** • To write the double-replacement reaction between silver nitrate and sodium chloride, students must consider several concepts they have previously studied: 　o What is a double-replacement reaction? Assign students to work in heterogeneous groups or review double-replacement reactions with the class. 　o Make sure students understand they must look up nitrates and chlorides in the solubility table because they are named in the reactants. 　o Make sure students refer to the solubility table to apply the solubility rules to this reaction because success will be easy, providing reinforcement for those who have difficulty integrating references and understanding chemical reactions.
Classifying information from words and pictures	*Investigate* Part B, 2.	**Augmentation** • To identify the ridge pattern of a fingerprint, students are required to differentiate between the arch, loop, and whorl using the pictures on the page. Creating categories from the examination of visual images will be an easy task for learners dependant on visual processing, while others will need word explanations to understand the critical design features that differentiate these images. Refer the latter group to the explanation of each type of ridge pattern found in the *Chem Talk*.
Evaluation of minutiae in fingerprints Comparing two substances for similarities	*Investigate* Part B, 3.e) *Investigate* Part C, 3.d)	**Augmentation** • Noticing tiny details in a complex pattern is not easy for students who tend to process more globally. They need to be taught this process explicitly. Clarify the importance of paying attention to tiny details: 　1) Attention to detail is an important and critical skill practiced by good students. 　2) Noticing detail enhances memory and the ability to reflect on acquired knowledge. 　3) Often, critical features are found in the tiniest details. First show students the critical features of the ridge patterns and examples of minutiae in the two prints being compared. When students are able to distinguish minutiae, give them a starting place from which to begin to find tiny features that make one print distinct. Students should compare each feature to the same area of the other print to see if the prints are alike or unique. Ask students to summarize the strategy they used before trying to compare prints independently.

LEARNING ISSUE	REFERENCE	AUGMENTATION AND ACCOMMODATIONS
Designing a procedure to develop an invisible fingerprint	*Investigate* Part C, 2. *Chem Essential Questions*	**Accommodations** • Tell students the procedure must begin with an invisible fingerprint on a piece of paper and end with a step that makes that print visible to the naked eye. • Give students the steps in random order and ask them to sequence them.
Extending the learning Making inferences	*Chem To Go*	**Augmentation** • Explain what is meant by extending the learning; students must apply the concepts they learned to new situations. In this case, students must think about the action described in the question and how it would affect the chemical reaction they studied or fingerprints they made. Be sure students understand that with inferences, the answers will not be found in the book or their *Active Chemistry* logs, but only in their minds.

Strategies for Students with Limited English Language Proficiency

LEARNING ISSUE	REFERENCE	AUGMENTATIONS
Background knowledge	*What Do You Think?*	Students may need some explanation or definition of the term, *"UV."* An explanation of the illustration may be helpful and would be good for oral language development.
Vocabulary	*Investigate*	Check for understanding of the term, *"latent."* Note the word *"filter"* as a verb. Check for word identification of the term, *"spatula."* Mention is made of *"ridges"* and *"valleys."* Check students' understanding of those terms in this context. Check understanding of the word, *"devise."* Make sure students understand the terms, *"loop," "whorl,"* and *"arch."*
Background knowledge Vocabulary Comprehending text	*Chem Talk*	Check for understanding of bold-type words. Refer students to the *Chem Words* for further explanations of the isolated words. Check for understanding of the word, *"disputed"* and share derivatives for vocabulary development. Check for understanding of the term *"If all else fails..."* as this may not be in the students' expressive vocabulary.
Background knowledge	*What Do You Think Now?*	Allow students to discuss some of the possible answers. Students might work together to construct their detailed paragraph. Explain what is meant by the description, *"detailed."*
Background knowledge Vocabulary Comprehending text	*Chem Essential Questions*	In the *Why do you believe?* explain the use of the word "else" as additional choices. In the *Why should you care?* section, allow for some discussion to consider creative uses for fingerprints in their own crime scenes.
Comprehension Vocabulary	*Chem to Go*	As students are directed to create characters, some criteria might be helpful. Explain that the term *"upcoming"* means something in the near future if this is an unfamiliar word.
Application Comprehension	*Inquiring Further*	Check for word identification of *"previous"* and the use of *"relies," "relied,"* and *"rely."* Some derivatives will advance vocabulary development. Explain how students will present their findings.

Section 5
Teaching Suggestions and Sample Answers

What Do You See?

Allow students a few minutes to contemplate the illustration. It represents the artist's conception of some of the key elements of this activity and provides an early opportunity to engage the students and elicit some responses.

Some students may point out the cookie jar; others may suggest a connection between the fingerprint and the jar of silver nitrate. All responses are valid and should be acknowledged as such. The students' responses also provide you with the opportunity to assess prior knowledge and potential misconceptions. Later in the activity, this section will be revisited for the students to review their initial reactions.

What Do You Think?

The students will most likely be guessing as to the changes that occurred in the dish of silver chloride after exposure to UV light. The accuracy of their answers is not an issue at this point. Students may assume that the object reacts with the silver chloride or maybe it just makes an indentation on the silver chloride. They may also conclude that object did not react with the silver chloride, but somehow the exposed silver chloride changed color due to a chemical reaction. Be alert for any misconceptions and evidence of prior learning.

 CSI Chemistry

Section 5 — Double-Replacement Reactions and Fingerprints

What Do You See?

Learning Outcomes

In this section you will

- **Learn** how to identify fingerprints.

- **Develop** latent (invisible) fingerprints using the silver nitrate method.

- **Explain,** using specific terms and concepts, the chemistry behind the silver-nitrate method from the *macroscopic, nanoscopic,* and *symbolic* perspectives.

What Do You Think?

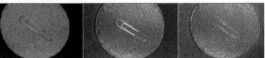

The picture above shows a dish of silver chloride with a paper clip on top of it. The picture in the middle shows the same dish after exposure to ultraviolet light. The picture on the right shows the dish after the paper clip is removed.

- **What changes do you observe after silver chloride has been exposed to UV light?**
- **Why have these changes occurred?**

Record your ideas about these questions in your *Active Chemistry* log. Be prepared to discuss your responses with your small group and the class.

Investigate

In this *Investigate* section you will explore how one chemical—silver chloride—and its properties aid forensic chemists in their discovery and identification of fingerprints at a crime scene. First, you will learn

682

What Do You Think?
A CHEMIST'S RESPONSE

After the silver chloride was exposed to ultraviolet light, one could see the image of the paper clip in the dish of silver chloride. This image shows that the paper clip had some impact on the silver chloride underneath it. The clip protected the silver chloride from the effects of exposure to ultraviolet radiation.

Exposure of silver chloride to UV light changed the silver chloride on the surface to a darker color. This darker color is due to the presence of metallic silver, which is black in finely divided form. That change did not occur where the radiation did not strike the silver chloride, which means the area under the paper clip.

STUDENTS' PRIOR CONCEPTIONS

One important theme of this section is that double-replacement and oxidation-reduction reactions can be distinguished and understood by their characteristic features and components. The following conceptions may be stumbling blocks along the path to learning this:

1. *Double-replacement products can be any combination of the four ions present in the reactants.* Double-replacement reactions are often referred to as "switching partners." While this analogy can be helpful in recognizing double-replacement reactions, it can lead to confusion in terms of which new combinations of ions are possible. In reality, the positive ions (cations) in the two reactants cannot join to form a compound, nor can the negative ions (anions) in the two reactants join to make a substance. The only new combinations that are possible are the cation of the first compound paired with the anion of the second, and the cation of the second compound with the anion of the first. It will be helpful to remind students that ionic compounds must be electrically neutral, and thus require a negative ion and a positive ion in order to balance charges to zero. Also emphasize that the cation is always given first in chemical formulas and names, making it easier to identify which ion is positive and which is negative.

2. *Any two ionic compounds will undergo a double-replacement reaction when combined.* Students often have not had experience considering situations in which substances are combined but do not react, because instruction typically focuses on situations where reactions do occur when substances are mixed. Thus, many students assume that if some ionic compounds will switch cations to form new substances in a double-replacement reaction, then any two ionic compounds will do that. To facilitate learning that double-replacement reactions only occur when one of the products formed is an insoluble compound, a gas, or water, students can be given a set of examples of possible double-replacement reactant pairings and asked to predict which pairings will react and which pairings will not react.

3. *Double-replacement reactions will occur regardless of the phase of the reactants.* The idea that the phase that substances are in has an impact on their ability to react chemically is generally new to students. It is critical that you emphasize that double-replacement reactions will only occur when reactants are in solution or are liquid. A demonstration showing the mixing of two ionic compounds in crystal (solid) form alongside the mixing of the same two compounds dissolved in aqueous solution can help students understand this idea. One pairing that could be used in this demonstration is the one used in this section— silver nitrate and sodium chloride.

4. *Oxidation means oxygen must be involved.* This point of confusion is certainly most understandable, given the common root in "oxidation" and "oxygen". However, while oxygen is a common oxidizing agent in oxidation-reduction (redox) reactions, many oxidation-reduction reactions involve no oxygen. One example is the conversion of silver chloride to its elements as seen in this activity. Other examples of redox reactions that do not involve oxygen can be discussed, and the key idea that "oxidation" means the loss of electrons by any chemical species should be emphasized.

5. *Reduction is a loss of electrons.* Because students are taught that the defining feature of a redox reaction is the transfer of electrons from one species to another, they frequently assume that "reduction" means a reduction in the number of electrons. In fact, the opposite is true – reduction is the gain of electrons. It is helpful to provide students with several examples of redox equations and help them to identify what is reduced in the reaction. Another important theme of this section has to do with the capabilities and limitations of scientific techniques in general and the silver nitrate method of obtaining fingerprints in particular.

6. *Perfect fingerprints can be taken off anything.* Students' impressions from television shows, movies, and books that depict forensic science and fingerprinting often lead them to believe that high-quality fingerprints can be visualized on any surface. Such media portrayals rarely include mention of the limitations of any technique used in forensic science, and fingerprinting is no exception. Discussion of the quality of prints students obtained in Parts A and C of the *Investigate* (some will be quite blurry) can lead to the conclusion that even the best forensic fingerprint analyst is often unable to extract usable prints from rough surfaces like stone. In addition, variations in the amount of skin oil deposited by a person's fingers can affect print quality.

7. *Identical twins have the same fingerprints.* Students learn in biology that identical twins have the same genes, and most students know that the physical similarities between identical twins can be startling. This awareness often results in the belief that all physical traits are exactly the same for each identical twin. Thus, students may be surprised to learn that even identical twins have unique fingerprints.

CHAPTER 8

Investigate

You may want to cut the amount of silver nitrate and sodium chloride used in *Part A* in half. The procedure outlined in the *Student Edition* will produce about 0.75 g of silver chloride. However, cutting that amount in half may still produce enough to spread across the paper for the experiment to work. This measure would be less costly and reduce the waste disposal. Another alternative is to conduct Part A of the *Investigate* as a teacher demonstration to reduce even further the amount of silver nitrate solution used.

Part A: Properties of Silver Chloride

1.

Silver nitrate should always be stored in a brown bottle as it decomposes when exposed to light.

2.a)

Caution the students not to cross-contaminate the two reagents.

3.

Try to minimize the exposure of the silver chloride to light. Lights can be turned off and the windows can be partially shaded. You may want to demonstrate the correct method for filtering.

3.a)

The word equation is "silver nitrate + sodium chloride $\rightarrow$ sodium nitrate + silver chloride (precipitate)."

Solubility Rule: All chlorides are soluble except those containing ions of silver, mercury (I), and lead (II). If the equipment is available, vacuum filtration will be much quicker than gravity filtration. In addition, the students will obtain a flat, circular bed of AgCl.

4.a)

The precipitate is a moist white solid. Depending on the brightness of the lights, it may already be turning gray.

5.

Students should try to make the silver chloride into a uniform surface which is larger than the object to be placed on it.

6.a)

A penny is convenient, but any small, solid object will do. Students should not look directly at the ultraviolet light.

7.a)

The precipitate under the penny should be white, while the exposed precipitate on the paper should be dark gray.

Part B: Types of Fingerprints

1.

When fingerprinting with ink, roll finger slowly from left to right.

2.a)

A print represents the ridges of the finger.

NOTES

___

more about silver chloride and its synthesis. Then, you will investigate the properties of fingerprints and determine how forensic scientists make their identifications. Finally, you will create your own procedure to analyze fingerprints using silver chloride. Be sure to ask plenty of questions in the first two parts of this investigation, so you create the most effective procedure to identify *latent prints* (fingerprints that cannot be seen by the naked eye)!

Part A: Properties of Silver Chloride

1. Using a clean, graduated cylinder measure 50 mL of 0.1 *M* silver nitrate solution and place it in a 250-mL beaker. Recall that the symbol *M* stands for molarity and represents the concentration of the ionic compound that is dissolved in the water.

2. Using a second clean graduated cylinder, add 50 mL of 0.1 *M* sodium chloride solution to the beaker containing the silver nitrate solution.

🔖 a) What happens? Record your results in your *Active Chemistry* log.

3. Filter the white precipitate.

🔖 a) Write the word equation for the double-replacement reaction between silver nitrate and sodium chloride. Use the solubility rules in *Section 4* to identify which product is a precipitate.

4. When you finish separating the precipitate from the solution, remove the filter paper from the funnel, unfold it and place it on a paper towel.

🔖 a) What does the precipitate look like? Record your observations in your *Active Chemistry* log.

5. Using a spatula or a stirring rod spread the precipitate evenly over the surface of the filter paper.

6. Place a penny in the center of the paper and expose the paper to UV light for about three to five minutes.

🔖 a) Record your observations in your *Active Chemistry* log.

7. Remove the penny from the center of the paper.

🔖 a) How does the precipitate that was under the penny compare to the precipitate that was exposed to UV light?

Part B: Types of Fingerprints

1. Ink your right index finger on an inkpad. Place the left side of the inked finger onto a sheet of white paper. Slowly roll the finger to the right using even pressure. If your print is blurry, try again. Wash your finger with soap and water.

2. Examine your fingerprint with a magnifying glass. Using the figure below, classify your print as an arch, loop, or whorl.

Safety goggles and a lab apron must be worn at all times in a chemistry lab.

Silver nitrate will irritate skin and eyes. Be careful when handling it. Keep silver nitrate away from flames.

Report any broken, cracked, or chipped glassware to your teacher.

Silver chloride is a heavy metal. Dispose of it as directed by your teacher.

arch   loop   whorl

683

Active Chemistry

CHAPTER 8

3.a)

Students' answers will vary depending on what they observe.

3.b)

Students' answers will vary depending on what they observe.

3.c)

No two prints are exactly the same although some may be somewhat similar.

3.d)

A person cannot be identified based only on the type of print because the ridge pattern categories are too general to identify a person. Just because two prints have loops does not mean they are the same.

3.e)

Students' answers will vary.

Part C: Developing Latent Prints

1.

When students are making an invisible fingerprint on paper for *Part C*, have them rub their nose, ears, or forehead with the finger they are going to use. This will place oils and salts on their finger in case they have naturally dry hands or have recently washed them.

2.

Sample Procedure:

- Wipe finger against nose.
- Make print on paper by rolling finger.
- Dip paper with print in a bath of 0.1 *M* AgNO₃ solution until it is fully submerged.

CSI Chemistry

a) When a print is made, does the print represent the ridges of the fingerprint or the valleys? Record your observations and answers in your *Active Chemistry* log.

3. Compare your print to your classmates' prints.

a) Are there any similarities between prints?

b) How many of the index prints are arches, loops, or whorls?

c) Are any two prints exactly the same?

d) Can a person be identified based only on the type of print (arch, loop, or whorl)? Explain.

e) When identifying a person based on fingerprints, scientists often look for tiny features within the print itself. These features are called *minutiae*. Compare whorls from two people. How do they differ?

Part C: Developing Latent Prints

In *Part A* of this investigation you observed that silver chloride, AgCl, is a light-sensitive compound. It turns from white to dark gray when it is exposed to UV light. Can this property of silver chloride be used to visualize hidden prints?

1. One way to observe latent prints is the silver-nitrate method. Silver nitrate solution contains silver nitrate dissolved in water. When silver nitrate is placed on a print, a double-replacement reaction occurs between the silver nitrate in the solution and the sodium chloride

(salt) in the print. You saw this type of reaction before in *Section 4*. A double-replacement reaction is a reaction in which the positive ions in the compounds switch places.

As you observed in *Part A*, silver nitrate will react with sodium chloride to form the precipitate silver chloride, AgCl.

2. Devise a procedure to develop invisible fingerprints on a piece of paper. (Hint: Before making a fingerprint on paper, wipe your index finger against your nose or behind your ear to ensure your print contains an ample amount of oils and salt.)

3. When you have created a procedure, have it approved by your teacher before you begin.

a) Record your procedure and your observations in your *Active Chemistry* log. Place the developed print in your *Active Chemistry* log.

b) How does your developed print compare to the print you made in *Part B*?

c) Can you tell if the developed print is an arch, loop, or whorl?

d) Can you see the fine details (minutiae) in the print?

e) How did your image compare to those made by the other groups in class? How did your procedure compare to the other groups' procedures?

4. Dispose of the materials as directed by your teacher. Clean up your workstation.

- Allow the print to dry by warming gently on a hot plate.
- Expose to UV light for 5 minutes.

3.a-b)

Answers will vary, but generally the developed print will be of poorer quality than the inked print.

3.c)

Answers will vary.

3.d)

Answers will vary.

3.e)

Answers will vary.

4.

Silver chloride should be placed in a "heavy metal" hazardous waste container for safe disposal.

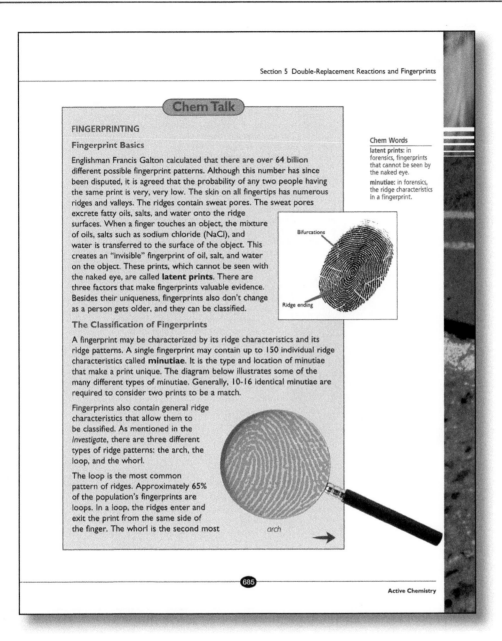

Chem Talk

FINGERPRINTING

Fingerprint Basics

Englishman Francis Galton calculated that there are over 64 billion different possible fingerprint patterns. Although this number has since been disputed, it is agreed that the probability of any two people having the same print is very, very low. The skin on all fingertips has numerous ridges and valleys. The ridges contain sweat pores. The sweat pores excrete fatty oils, salts, and water onto the ridge surfaces. When a finger touches an object, the mixture of oils, salts such as sodium chloride ($NaCl$), and water is transferred to the surface of the object. This creates an "invisible" fingerprint of oil, salt, and water on the object. These prints, which cannot be seen with the naked eye, are called **latent prints**. There are three factors that make fingerprints valuable evidence. Besides their uniqueness, fingerprints also don't change as a person gets older, and they can be classified.

The Classification of Fingerprints

A fingerprint may be characterized by its ridge characteristics and its ridge patterns. A single fingerprint may contain up to 150 individual ridge characteristics called **minutiae**. It is the type and location of minutiae that make a print unique. The diagram below illustrates some of the many different types of minutiae. Generally, 10-16 identical minutiae are required to consider two prints to be a match.

Fingerprints also contain general ridge characteristics that allow them to be classified. As mentioned in the *Investigate*, there are three different types of ridge patterns: the arch, the loop, and the whorl.

The loop is the most common pattern of ridges. Approximately 65% of the population's fingerprints are loops. In a loop, the ridges enter and exit the print from the same side of the finger. The whorl is the second most

Chem Words

latent prints: in forensics, fingerprints that cannot be seen by the naked eye.

minutiae: in forensics, the ridge characteristics in a fingerprint.

Bifurcations

Ridge ending

arch

Active Chemistry

Chem Talk

Fingerprints normally cannot be seen by the naked eye and thus, are called latent fingerprints. Silver nitrate solution reacts with the sodium chloride that is present in all finger prints to produce a precipitate that shows the outline of the fingerprint. All fingerprints have unique characteristics that are used to distinguish them from one another and to identify individuals.

The reading concludes with an explanation of the chemistry behind the oxidation-reduction reaction of silver chloride when it is exposed to UV light.

CHAPTER 8

CSI Chemistry

common pattern at 30%. A whorl must have two deltas (triangular patterns of ridge lines) on either side of the center of the print. Finally, the arch is the least common type of fingerprint at 5%. Arches look like little tents or hills in the middle of the print. It is important to remember fingerprints cannot be considered a match based on the ridge patterns alone. A match is determined by the position and type of minutiae.

Developing Latent Prints

As you have probably seen on television and in the movies, there are numerous ways to develop latent prints. They include dusting, iodine fuming, superglue fuming, and silver nitrate developing. All the methods work by interacting with one of the three components in the print: the fatty oils, the salts, or the water. In this investigation you studied the silver-nitrate method.

If all else fails when looking for latent prints, one of the last methods to be used is the silver-nitrate method. Silver nitrate solution contains silver nitrate dissolved in water. When silver nitrate is placed on a print, a double-replacement reaction occurs between the silver nitrate in the solution and the sodium chloride (salt) in the print. Recall that a double-replacement reaction is a reaction in which the positive ions in the compounds switch places.

As you observed in *Part A*, silver nitrate will react with sodium chloride to form the precipitate silver chloride, AgCl. This same reaction happens on the surface of a latent print when it is painted with silver nitrate solution

$$AgNO_{3(aq)} + NaCl_{(s)} \rightarrow AgCl_{(s)} + NaNO_{3(aq)}$$

| *painted on the print* | *salt in the print* | *precipitate formed on the print* |

Silver chloride is formed on the surface of the print. However, at this point the print is still invisible.

Why Silver Chloride Turns Gray

Silver chloride is an ionic compound. Ionic compounds are composed of positive and negative ions attracted to each other. They are arranged in an orderly repeating pattern to maximize the attractive forces between the oppositely charged ions and to minimize the repulsive forces between the like-charged ions. This regular repeating pattern is called the **crystalline structure** of the compound. The crystalline structure for silver chloride is shown in the diagram.

Notice the alternating pattern of positive silver ions and negative chloride ions. When a crystal of silver chloride is exposed to light, the light has enough energy to promote electrons in the crystal to a higher energy level. When electrons are in the higher level (called an "excited state," remember *Section 3* and the luminol reaction) they can undergo reactions that do not usually occur. Ultimately, a chloride ion in the crystal loses one of its electrons to a silver ion. The silver ion gains the electron and becomes silver metal. The chlorine atom combines with another chlorine atom that has lost an electron to form chlorine gas. Silver metal is gray; its presence explains why the precipitate turns gray. This process is repeated throughout the crystal and the net reaction is

$$\overbrace{2Ag^+_{(aq)} + 2Cl^-_{(aq)}}^{\text{oxidation}} \rightarrow \underbrace{2Ag^0_{(s)} + Cl_2^0_{(g)}}_{\text{reduction}}$$

When an atom or ion loses an electron we say that it has been **oxidized**. In this reaction the chloride ion loses an electron and is oxidized. The silver ion takes the electron and becomes silver metal. When an atom or ion gains an electron we say that it has been **reduced**. This type of reaction is an **oxidation-reduction reaction**. Keep these basic terms in mind, because you will learn more about oxidation-reduction reactions in the next section.

Upon exposure to UV light, the silver ion in the silver chloride is converted into silver metal and the print turns gray. This creates a visible image of the print in much the same manner as photography. Also, silver nitrate reacts with the proteins in your skin. If you were to spill silver nitrate on your skin, then go outside, a similar developing reaction would occur. The UV light from the Sun would end up leaving a black or brown stain on your skin. As a last note, if the silver-nitrate method is used by forensic chemists when analyzing evidence, it is one of the last methods used to visualize the prints. This is because silver nitrate destroys other forms of evidence, such as DNA.

Chem Words

crystalline structure: the regular arrangement of the oppositely charged ions of the compound, geometric bonding pattern, and the packing of the metal atoms in the structure in solid salts, compounds, and metals.

oxidized: an atom, molecule, or ion that has lost one or more electrons to gain a certain positive charge.

reduced: an atom, molecule, or ion that has gained one or more electrons to gain a certain negative charge.

oxidation-reduction (redox) reaction: a chemical reaction in which an atom, molecule, or ion transfers electron(s) to another atom, molecule, or ion.

Checking Up

1. Why are fingerprints valuable pieces of evidence in forensics?

2. What are three components of a fingerprint that are used in developing latent prints?

3. Why does silver chloride turn gray when exposed to UV light?

687

Checking Up

1.

Fingerprints are a valuable piece of evidence in forensics because their characteristics are unique to the individual. Also, fingerprints do not change as a person gets older, which means they can still be used for identification long after a crime is committed.

2.

The three components from every fingerprint that are used to develop a latent print are fatty oils, salt, and water.

3.

Silver chloride undergoes a double-displacement reaction with sodium chloride to produce a white silver chloride precipitate. In the presence of UV light, an oxidation-reduction reaction occurs producing a precipitate of elemental silver. The individual particles of silver metal are black, which gives the characteristic gray color observed.

CHAPTER 8

What Do You Think Now?

Revisiting the *What Do You See?* illustration and *What Do You Think?* questions now will help students integrate their new knowledge. It will also demonstrate how they have actually progressed along the learning curve. This accomplishment should give them greater confidence in their abilities. Refer them to the answer provided in *A Chemist's Response* and ask them to share their opinions.

Reflecting on the Section and the Challenge

This section provides an opportunity for students to start thinking about how to transfer what they have learned into a useful part of their *Chapter Challenge* projects. Learning how to make hidden evidence visible is an important aspect of forensics and silver nitrate is one of numerous techniques that can be used to identify fingerprints. Showing how this technique is used can be a part of the crime scene solution.

You may want to have students reflect on this individually in their *Active Chemistry* logs. If time permits, you may want to have students meets in their groups for a short discussion and then report back to the class.

CSI Chemistry

What Do You Think Now?

At the beginning of this section you were asked the following:

- What changes do you observe after silver chloride has been exposed to UV light?
- Why have these changes occurred?

Read the answers you gave to these questions. In a detailed paragraph, write what happened from the picture on the left to the picture on the right. Use the vocabulary from this section as you write your response.

Chem
Essential Questions

What does it mean?

Chemistry explains a *macroscopic* phenomenon (what you observe) with a description of what happens at the *nanoscopic* level (atoms and molecules) using *symbolic* structures as a way to communicate. Complete the chart below in your *Active Chemistry* log.

MACRO	NANO	SYMBOLIC
What was required to observe latent prints?	Describe the reaction of silver nitrate and the salt in your sweat in developing latent prints.	Draw a picture of an NaCl crystal.

How do you know?

How could you demonstrate that it is the salt from your skin that reacts with the silver nitrate when "lifting" latent fingerprints?

Why do you believe?

What else might involve oxidation or reduction that you've experienced outside this class? Provide a positive and negative consequence of having everybody's fingerprints on file.

Why should you care?

Fingerprinting has always been considered an excellent way in which to determine the identity of a person. How can you use fingerprints in a creative way as part of the crime scene that you develop?

Reflecting on the Section and the Challenge

Part of the problem you are facing in creating a crime scene is to understand how to observe something that is not initially visible. In this section you focused on how to develop hidden prints. Think about how you can use hidden prints to enhance your crime scene. Also, think about the types of surfaces that will work best with the silver-nitrate method. Finally, keep in mind the limitations of the silver-nitrate test and how you can use those limitations in your crime scene.

Chem Essential Questions

What does it mean?

MACRO — In order to observe latent prints, it was necessary to use a silver nitrate solution. When placed on a print, a double-replacement reaction occurs between the solution and the sodium chloride (salt) that is naturally in a fingerprint. The reaction results in the formation of the precipitate, silver chloride, on the surface of the print. Once exposed to UV light, the silver ion in the silver chloride is converted into silver metal and the print turns gray. This gray color makes the fingerprint visible.

NANO — Silver nitrate is soluble in water as is the sodium chloride found on the surface of the skin. However, when these two salts are mixed in solution, a precipitate of silver chloride forms. This leaves sodium nitrate behind as the soluble product of this double-replacement reaction.

SYMBOLIC —

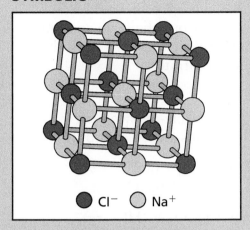

● Cl^- ○ Na^+

How do you know?

One way to demonstrate that the salt that reacts with the silver nitrate comes from your skin is to try to "lift" fingerprints left by someone wearing rubber gloves. When applied to the latent print, the silver nitrate should not react, and no precipitate of silver chloride should form. This indicates that the gloves prevented the natural salts from the skin to attach to the print, thus preventing any reaction from taking place when the silver nitrate was applied.

Why do you believe?

The rusting of iron is an example of an oxidation-reduction reaction that occurs outside of class.

Having everyone's fingerprints on file could make it easier to identify those involved in criminal behavior when fingerprints are left behind. However, it could also constitute a violation of the personal rights of those who have not engaged in crime.

Why should you care?

Students' answers will vary. Encourage a discussion of creative ways for students to use fingerprints as part of their *Chapter Challenge* crime scenes.

CHAPTER 8

NOTES

Chem to Go

1.

The silver nitrate reacts with sodium chloride to form silver chloride. Ultraviolet rays excite the electrons in the chloride ions to higher energy levels. The electrons are picked up by the silver ion, causing it to turn into silver (which appears gray).

2.

Oxidation is the loss of one or more electrons and is accompanied by a more positive charge on an ion, atom or molecule. Reduction is the corresponding gain of electrons and results in a more negative charge. The two processes occur simultaneously.

3.

A print not exposed to proper amounts of UV light will not develop properly and will be too light. A print overexposed to UV light may be so dark that the fine features of the print are obscured.

4.

Ionic crystalline structures alternate cations and anions because:

1. This arrangement maximizes the bond strength from electrostatic attraction of opposite charges.

2. This arrangement minimizes the repulsion of like charges (anion-anion and cation-cation).

5.

No, a fingerprint soaked in water would have no sodium chloride left to react with the silver nitrate.

6.

The double-replacement reactions are a), c) and d).

a) $CuSO_4 + BaCl_2 \rightarrow$
   $CuCl_2 + BaSO_4$

c) $Na_2CO_3 + 2HCl \rightarrow$
   $2NaCl + H_2O + CO_2$

d) $CaCl_2 + Na_2SO_4 \rightarrow$
   $2NaCl + CaSO_4$

Reaction b) is a synthesis reaction.

7.

a) copper (II) sulfate +
   sodium carbonate $\rightarrow$
   sodium sulfate +
   copper (II) carbonate

b) cadmium (II) chloride +
   sodium hydroxide $\rightarrow$
   sodium chloride +
   cadmium (II) hydroxide

c) lead (II) nitrate +
   sodium sulfate $\rightarrow$
   sodium nitrate +
   lead (II) sulfate

d) nickel (II) chloride +
   sodium carbonate $\rightarrow$
   sodium chloride +
   nickel (II) carbonate

8.

No, the ridge patterns are not specific enough. For example, many people have loops. Forensic experts must examine beyond the ridge patterns and look at the minutiae.

9.

Preparing for the Chapter Challenge

Responses will vary. Crime scenes generated by students should definitely make use of fingerprints as part of their evidence. Using fingerprints and combinations of white powders, glass fragments, and blood samples, students should be able to devise an original plot and solution.

Chem to Go

1. In your own words, describe how the silver-nitrate technique works in developing latent prints.

2. Describe oxidation and reduction in terms of electron transfer and electrical charge.

3. What would happen to the image if the print was not left under the UV light long enough? What would happen to the image if you left the print under the UV light too long? Explain.

4. Give two reasons that ionic crystal structures alternate cations and anions.

5. Would the silver-nitrate technique work on a piece of evidence that had been soaked in water? Explain. (Hint: think back to the solubility rules in *Section 4*.)

6. Which of the following reactions are double-replacement reactions?

   a) $CuSO_4 + BaCl_2 \rightarrow CuCl_2 + BaSO_4$

   b) $Mg + Cl_2 \rightarrow MgCl_2$

   c) $Na_2CO_3 + 2HCl \rightarrow 2NaCl + H_2O + CO_2$

   d) $CaCl_2 + Na_2SO_4 \rightarrow CaSO_4 + 2NaCl$

7. Complete the following double-replacement word equations. Circle the precipitates.

   a) copper (II) sulfate + sodium carbonate →

   b) cadmium (II) chloride + sodium hydroxide →

   c) lead (II) nitrate + sodium sulfate →

   d) nickel (II) chloride + sodium carbonate →

8. Can a suspect be identified as a criminal based on his ridge patterns? Explain.

9. *Preparing for the Chapter Challenge*

   Fingerprints need fingers to create them. It is time to begin to create some of your characters for your crime scene. Look through your original table from the first *Preparing for the Chapter Challenge* from *Section 1* at the types of evidence throughout this entire chapter. Reflect back on the details of the evidence from the first five sections. After thinking back on your work this far and the possibilities from the upcoming sections, create at least four characters for your crime scene. For each character create a brief biography, a picture, and of course, a unique fingerprint!

CHAPTER 8

Inquiring Further

Methods of identifying fingerprints

You may need to provide some guidance for students in this assignment. Three additional methods for visualizing latent fingerprints are described below. This information can be helpful for those students eager to explore other methods used to develop prints.

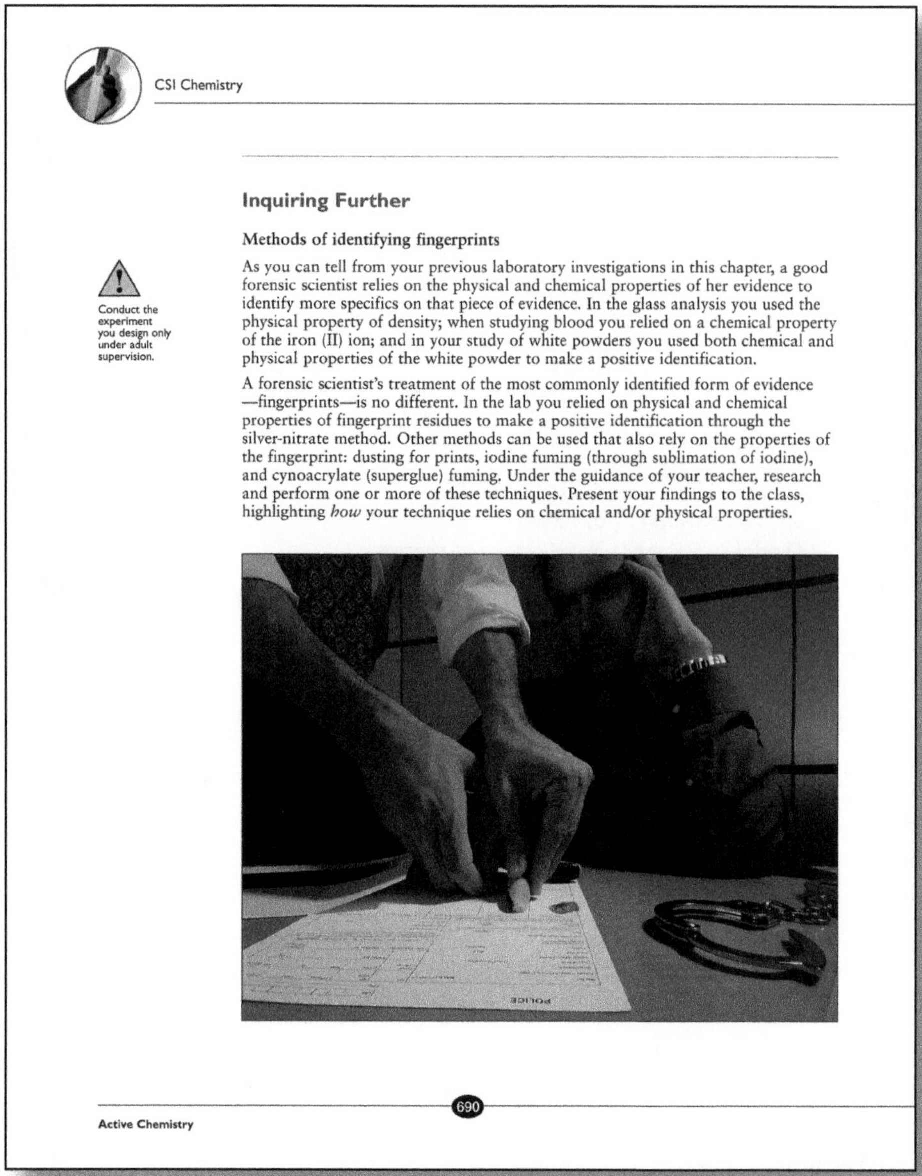

CSI Chemistry

Inquiring Further

Methods of identifying fingerprints

Conduct the experiment you design only under adult supervision.

As you can tell from your previous laboratory investigations in this chapter, a good forensic scientist relies on the physical and chemical properties of her evidence to identify more specifics on that piece of evidence. In the glass analysis you used the physical property of density; when studying blood you relied on a chemical property of the iron (II) ion; and in your study of white powders you used both chemical and physical properties of the white powder to make a positive identification.

A forensic scientist's treatment of the most commonly identified form of evidence —fingerprints—is no different. In the lab you relied on physical and chemical properties of fingerprint residues to make a positive identification through the silver-nitrate method. Other methods can be used that also rely on the properties of the fingerprint: dusting for prints, iodine fuming (through sublimation of iodine), and cynoacrylate (superglue) fuming. Under the guidance of your teacher, research and perform one or more of these techniques. Present your findings to the class, highlighting *how* your technique relies on chemical and/or physical properties.

690

Active Chemistry

Dusting for Prints

Dusting is the simplest and the most commonly used method to develop latent prints. When the dusting powder is placed over a print, the dust sticks to the oils in the print. Brushing or blowing from the surface removes excess dust. This technique requires a soft brush to prevent damage to the pattern of the print. Powders commonly used for dusting include aluminum for dark colored surfaces, and carbon for light colored surfaces. Dusting works best on nonporous surfaces such as metal or glass. Porous surfaces such as paper contain tiny holes. These holes trap the powder on the surface, which obscures the print.

Iodine fuming — Using sublimation to develop latent prints

At room temperature, iodine is a reddish, brown nonmetallic solid that is unique because it sublimates at room temperature. Sublimation is the change from the solid state to the gaseous state without becoming a liquid. In iodine fuming, the print is placed into a chamber with iodine crystals. The iodine crystals sublimate to form violet-colored iodine gas. When the iodine gas comes into contact with the print, a chemical reaction occurs between the fatty oils in the print and the iodine gas. The unsaturated fats in the fatty oils contain double bonds or two shared pairs of electrons. The iodine destroys the double bond and bonds with the oil. This turns the oil a reddish brown color, making the print visible. Over time, however, the color of the print will fade and eventually become invisible. This occurs because the oils eventually evaporate and because light breaks down the oil-iodine bond. When iodine fuming is used to develop a print, the visible print is photographed immediately. Another way to preserve the image is to treat the iodine print with starch. Starch reacts with the iodine to form a blue compound. This fixes (makes permanent) the print on the surface. Iodine works best with fresh prints on porous surfaces. As the print ages, the oils evaporate and degrade, preventing them from reacting with the iodine. One of the advantages of iodine fuming is that it does not interfere with other methods of fingerprint developing.

Developing Latent Prints on Smooth Surfaces using Cyanoacrylate Fuming

Sometimes it is difficult to dust a nonporous surface because of its shape or location. Superglue fuming offers an excellent alternative to dusting. Superglue fuming can be done with a chamber like the one used in this activity or it can be done using a portable wand and a plastic bag. Superglue consists of cyanoacrylate ester.

In this method, superglue is heated to form gaseous cyanoacrylate ester. When the ester comes into contact with the water in the print, it polymerizes. Polymerization is a process in which individual molecules link up to form a long chain. Making a paper clip chain is a simple model of polymerization. Each clip represents a single molecule or monomer. As they are linked, the chain gets longer. This chain of monomers is called a polymer. Polymers are an extremely important part of our lives because plastics are made of polymers.

Water in the fingerprint causes the gaseous cyanoacrylate molecules to link to each other. Eventually, the polymer chain gets large enough to see. Superglue fuming works well on nonporous surfaces. However, when superglue fuming is used, it destroys all DNA evidence that may be contained within the print.

CHAPTER 8

NOTES

_____

_____

_____

_____

_____

_____

_____

_____

_____

_____

_____

SECTION 5 – QUIZ

8-5a **Blackline Master**

1. Why does silver chloride turn gray?

2. Which of the following reactions are double-replacement reactions?

   a) $KCl + AgNO_3 \rightarrow KNO_3 + AgCl$

   b) $Mg + 2HCl \rightarrow MgCl_2 + H_2$

   c) $2KClO_3 \rightarrow 2KCl + 3O_2$

   d) $MgCl_2 + 2NaOH \rightarrow Mg(OH)_2 + 2NaCl$

3. Complete the following double-replacement reactions:
   a) silver nitrate + sodium chloride $\rightarrow$

   b) barium chloride + potassium hydroxide $\rightarrow$

   c) copper (II) chloride + sodium carbonate $\rightarrow$

4. Identify the precipitates for each reaction in *Question 3*.

5. What is oxidation and what is reduction?

SECTION 5 – QUIZ ANSWERS

1 Silver compounds are sensitive to visible and ultraviolet (UV) light. UV light causes a decomposition of AgCl by the excitation of a chloride ion to an unstable state where it is transferred to a silver ion. This reduces Ag^+ to Ag metal which is gray.

2 a) and d) represent double-replacement reactions.

3 a) silver nitrate + sodium chloride $\rightarrow$ *silver chloride + sodium nitrate*
b) barium chloride + potassium hydroxide $\rightarrow$ *barium hydroxide + potassium chloride*
c) copper (II) chloride + sodium carbonate $\rightarrow$ *copper (II) carbonate + sodium chloride*

4 a) silver chloride
b) barium hydroxide
c) copper (II) carbonate

5 Oxidation is the loss of electrons and reduction is the gain of electrons.

NOTES

CHAPTER 8

SECTION 6
Reactions with Transition Metals: Metal Activity Series

Section Overview

The key idea in this section is that metals exist in two very different forms—neutral metals and metallic ions in compounds—and they can be converted from one form to the other through a reduction-oxidation (redox) reaction. In a redox reaction, one metal is converted from ionic form to neutral form, while a second metal simultaneously undergoes the opposite change, from neutral to ionic.

In the *Investigate*, students add metals to different ionic solutions to observe single-replacement reactions. The data is collected and organized to replicate a partial version of the Metal Activity Series.

Background Information
Single-Replacement as Oxidation-Reduction Reactions

In a previous section, silver chloride, an ionic compound, underwent an oxidation-reduction decomposition reaction, forming the pure elements silver metal and chlorine gas. (A more complete discussion of this type of oxidation-reduction reaction as well as a general introduction to all oxidation-reduction reactions can be found in the *Background Information* section for *Section 5*.) In this section, a different kind of oxidation-reduction, or redox, reaction occurs—one in which a metal element reacts with an ionic compound. This type of reaction is of the general form that follows:

$$A \quad + \quad BX \quad \rightarrow \quad B \quad + \quad AX$$

A	+	BX	→	B	+	AX
Neutral form of A		Ionic compound consisting of B cation and a nonmetal anion X		Neutral form of B		Ionic compound consisting of A cation and a nonmetal anion X

A and B are metal species of different elements and X is a nonmetal anion. Prior to the reaction, metal A is a free element and metal B is the cation in an ionic compound with the nonmetallic anion X. During the reaction, A atoms transfer one or more electrons to each B ion, causing B to become a neutral metal, while A, because it has lost the electrons it gave to B, becomes positively charged and forms an ionic bond with X. In effect, A has replaced B in the ionic compound with X, and thus reactions of this type are considered single-replacement reactions.

More specifically, reactions that are of the form described above are single-replacement oxidation-reduction reactions. Because the reaction involves the transfer of electrons from one chemical species (A in this case) to another (B), it is an oxidation-reduction reaction. It is worth noting that not all single-replacement reactions involve electron transfer (though most do), and thus not all are considered oxidation-reduction reactions. Nor are all oxidation-reduction reactions single-replacement reactions, as the oxidation-reduction reaction studied in *Section 5* demonstrates.

In the specific example below, magnesium (metal A) replaces silver (metal B) in a compound with nitrate as the nonmetallic anion. Magnesium metal loses two electrons and thus is oxidized, while two silver ions each gain one electron and are reduced:

$$Mg \quad + \quad 2AgNO_3 \quad \rightarrow \quad 2Ag \quad + \quad Mg(NO_3)_2$$

Mg	+	2AgNO₃	→	2Ag	+	Mg(NO₃)₂
Neutral form of Magnesium		Ionic compound consisting of silver cation and nitrate anion		Neutral form of silver		Ionic compound consisting of magnesium cation and nitrate anion

Metal Reactivity and the Activity Series

All metal elements undergo oxidation, forming positive ions. However, different metal elements undergo oxidation with varying levels of ease. In other words, some metals are oxidized very easily, while others are comparatively resistant to oxidation. In fact, metal elements can be ranked in order of most to least easily oxidized. Such a list has been determined experimentally, and is referred to as the Activity Series of Metals. The activity series ranks the most easily oxidized at the top and the least easily oxidized at the bottom. Because oxidation is the characteristic reaction that metal elements undergo, ease of oxidation is synonymous with chemical reactivity. Thus, it is accurate to say that the activity series ranks metals in pure form from most to least reactive.

There are many common misconceptions about the activity series, even among scientifically informed people. It is important to note that according to the activity series, not all of the Group I metals are more active than the Group II metals. Nor is there a strong correlation between atomic radius and reactivity or electrical conductivity and reactivity. In addition, although some metals such as sodium react strongly, they are actually less reactive than other metals. For example, calcium is notably "calmer" when reacting with water, but is more reactive than sodium. This apparent contradiction is the result of different rates of reaction between calcium and sodium (sodium reacting much faster with water than calcium); the rate of reaction does not necessarily correlate with reactivity. These statements may conflict with many conventional understandings about reactivity and activity.

Reactivity is actually determined experimentally by measuring the reduction potential of metal elements. Reduction potential is the voltage produced when a metal reduces hydrogen ions under standard conditions. It is a measure of how forcefully a metal "pushes" or "gives" electrons to hydrogen ions. This is considered the true measure of a metal's reactivity or activity.

For example, because calcium has a greater (more negative) reduction potential than sodium (-2.87 V compared to sodium's -2.71 V), it is more reactive than sodium and is thus higher on the activity series. It should also be noted that the activity series ordering does not take into account factors that can impact the reactivity observed under common laboratory conditions, such as the tendency of very reactive metals to form an oxide coating by reacting with oxygen in air. This oxide coating can then reduce the sample's reactivity with other substances, like ionic compounds.

Because a metal is oxidized more easily than all of the metals below it in the activity series, it follows that a metal element will undergo a single-replacement oxidation-reduction reaction of the type seen in this activity. But that is only true if the metal ion in the ionic compound is below the metal element on the activity series. This indicates that the metal element is more easily oxidized than the metal ion in the compound, and therefore will undergo oxidation, replacing the metal ion in the compound and simultaneously reducing the metal ion. For example, the following reaction occurs because magnesium, the metal element, is more reactive than silver, the metal ion:

$$Mg + 2AgNO_3 \rightarrow 2Ag + Mg(NO_3)_2$$

Consequently, this places magnesium higher in the activity series than silver. The superior placement of magnesium in the activity series indicates that magnesium is more easily oxidized than silver, and therefore magnesium will oxidize in the presence of silver ions. Simultaneously, with the transfer of electrons, the silver ions are reduced to neutral silver metal. Note that the opposite redox reaction, the reduction of magnesium ions by neutral silver atoms, does not occur spontaneously.

$$Ag + Mg(NO_3)_2 \rightarrow NO\ RXN$$

The activity series is useful in that it allows one to predict whether a particular metal and ionic compound combination will react with each other in a single-replacement oxidation-reduction reaction.

CHAPTER 8

Half-Reactions and Balancing Electrons

Oxidation and reduction always occur simultaneously, because electrons lost by one species must be accepted by another instantly. However, the oxidation and reduction components of a redox reaction can be considered separately in the form of half-reactions. These show either the oxidation portion or the reduction portion of a complete redox reaction. It should be emphasized that half-reactions are a convenient way of analyzing oxidation-reduction reactions and keeping track of electrons transferred in the reaction. But it should be remembered that a half-reaction never occurs independent of a complementary half-reaction of the other type. The oxidation half-reaction for the general form single-replacement reaction outlined above is:

$$A \longrightarrow A^{y+} + ye^-$$

| A will be oxidized in the reaction | Oxidized form of A | Number of electrons lost by each atom of A in the reaction |

The reduction half-reaction for the general form single-replacement reaction outlined above is:

$$B^{z+} + ze^- \longrightarrow B$$

| B will be reduced in the reaction | Number of electrons gained by each atom of B in the reaction | Reduced form of B |

Note that the anion does not appear in either the reduction or the oxidation half-reaction because it does not lose or gain electrons and thus remains unchanged during the reaction. Because the anion does not take part in the reaction, it is called a **spectator ion**.

The symbols y and z represent the number of electrons lost by one atom of A and gained by one atom of B, respectively, in the oxidation-reduction reaction. These numbers are characteristic of the particular metals involved in the reaction. So, as in our example above, if A is magnesium, y will be +2, because magnesium atoms always lose two electrons when they are oxidized (and conversely,

Mg^{2+} ions always gain two electrons when they are reduced). Thus the oxidation half-reaction would be:

$$Mg \longrightarrow Mg^{2+} + 2e^-$$

Continuing with the reaction between magnesium and silver nitrate, each silver atom gains one electron and is reduced, so the reduction half-reaction would be:

$$Ag^+ + 1e^- \longrightarrow Ag$$

Silver atoms always lose one electron when oxidized. Thus, silver ions always gain one electron when reduced.

Note that the oxidation and reduction half-reactions contain different numbers of electrons as they are written above. In a chemical reaction, all electrons lost by one element's atoms must be gained by another element's atoms. Therefore, the number of electrons in the two half-reactions must be equal in order to accurately represent the ratio of reduced ions and oxidized atoms. In this particular example, because of their charges, for every one oxidized magnesium atom there must be two reduced silver ions. This ratio is represented symbolically by multiplying the silver half-reaction by a factor of two.

$$2Ag^+ + 2e^- \longrightarrow 2Ag$$

Now the electrons in the two half-reactions are equal, and when the half-reactions are added together (representing the **net ionic equation** for the reaction), the electrons cancel out.

$$Mg \longrightarrow Mg^{2+} + 2e^-$$
$$\underline{2Ag^+ + 2e^- \longrightarrow 2Ag}$$
$$Mg + 2Ag^+ \longrightarrow Mg^{2+} + 2Ag$$

It is important to note that most transition metals form more than one type of ion, because their atoms can lose different numbers of electrons. For example, neutral copper atoms, when oxidized, can lose one electron:

$$Cu \longrightarrow Cu^+ + 1e^-$$

Or they can lose two electrons:

$$Cu \longrightarrow Cu^{2+} + 2e^-$$

Several factors determine which one of these two ions is formed from copper atoms in a redox reaction where copper metal is oxidized. Those factors include reaction conditions, like pH, as well as the identity of the metal being reduced in the reaction.

Oxidation Numbers

Oxidation numbers are another symbolic convention, like half-reactions, used by chemists to help keep track of electrons in oxidation-reduction reactions. Oxidation numbers represent the charge on a chemical species. In the case of atoms in covalent compounds (or polyatomic ions), where atoms are sharing electrons, the oxidation number is assigned based on the number of shared and unshared electrons surrounding the atom, as well as how the electrons are being shared by the covalently bonded electrons. The following general rules govern the assignment of oxidation numbers (also called oxidation states). Note that there are exceptions to most of these rules. Each rule below is followed by a specific example.

- Free elements have oxidation number 0.
  Mg atoms have oxidation number 0.

- Monatomic ions have oxidation numbers equal to their charge.
  Mg^{2+} ions have oxidation number +2, Al^{3+} ions have oxidation number +3.

- Halogens usually have oxidation number −1 in compounds.
  Cl^- ions have oxidation number −1 in $MgCl_2$.

- Oxygen usually has oxidation number −2 in compounds.
  O^{2-} ions have oxidation number −2 in Al_2O_3.

- Hydrogen usually has oxidation number +1 in compounds.
  H^+ ions have oxidation number +1 in H_2SO_4.

- The sum of oxidation numbers of all the atoms in a compound is zero.
  In H_2SO_4, 2 H ions have +1 oxidation numbers, the S atom has oxidation number +6, and each of 4 O atoms has oxidation number −2. The sum of +1, +1, +6, -2, -2, -2, and -2 is 0.

- The sum of oxidation numbers of all the atoms in a polyatomic ion is the charge on the ion.
  In SO_4^{2-} the S atom has oxidation number +6, and each of 4 O atoms has oxidation number −2. The sum of +6, −2, −2, −2, and −2 is −2, which is the charge on the ion.

In any chemical reaction, the sum of all atoms' oxidation numbers on the reactant side must equal the sum of all atoms' oxidation numbers on the product side. The species oxidized in a redox reaction always experiences an increase in oxidation number. Likewise, the species reduced in the redox reaction always experiences a decrease in oxidation number. Thus, assigning oxidation numbers can help to identify whether a reaction is a redox reaction, and if so, what is being oxidized and what is being reduced.

CHAPTER 8

NOTES

_____

_____

_____

_____

_____

_____

LEARNING OUTCOMES		
LEARNING OUTCOMES	**LOCATION IN SECTION**	**EVIDENCE OF UNDERSTANDING**
Use chemical properties and deductive reasoning to identify a pattern in metal reactions.	*Investigate* Steps 5-6, 8-9 *Chem to Go* Question 3	Students successfully complete the activity and identify which pairings of metal and ionic solution will react. Students' answers match those provided in this *Teacher's Edition*.
Compare and contrast single-replacement and double-replacement reactions.	*Investigate* Steps 5-6, 8 *Chem Talk, Checking Up* Question 4	Students can identify which combinations of metals and ionic solutions react in the lab. Students' answers match those provided in this *Teacher's Edition*.
Define and explain the concepts of oxidation and reduction.	*Chem Talk, Checking Up* Questions 3-4 *Chem to Go* Questions 5, 7	Students can identify which combinations of metals and ionic solutions react in the lab. Students can identify redox reactions based on descriptions and chemical equations. Students' answers match those provided in this *Teacher's Edition*.
Gain an understanding of the Activity Series of Metals.	*Investigate* Step 6 *Checking Up* Question 5 *Chem to Go* Questions 1-3	Students are able to rank metals tested in the lab from most to least active. Students' answers match those provided in this *Teacher's Edition*.

NOTES

_____

_____

_____

_____

_____

_____

_____

_____

_____

_____

NOTES

Section 6
Materials, Chemicals, Preparation, and Safety

("per Group" quantity is based on group size of 4 students)

Materials and Equipment

Materials (and Equipment)	Quantity per Group (4 students)
Sandpaper sheet or steel wool pad	1
Reaction plates, 24-well	2
White paper, sheets	4
Scissors	1
Clear metric ruler	1
Magnifying glass	1
Materials (and Equipment)	Quantity per Class
Dropping bottles/droppers	50

Chemicals

Chemicals	Quantity per Class (24 students)
Aluminum metal strips, 5 cm	7
Copper metal strips, 5 cm	7
Iron metal strips, 5 cm	7
Magnesium metal strips, 5 cm	7
Tin metal strips, 5 cm	7
Zinc metal strips, 5 cm	7
Hydrochloric acid (HCl), 3.0 M	100 mL
Zinc nitrate, 0.2 M	100 mL
Tin (IV) chloride, 0.2 M	100 mL
Magnesium nitrate, 0.2 M	100 mL
Iron (III) nitrate, 0.2 M	100 mL
Copper (II) nitrate, 0.2 M	100 mL
Aluminum nitrate, 0.2 M	100 mL

NOTES

_____

_____

_____

_____

_____

_____

_____

_____

Teacher Preparation

3.0 *M* HCl—In a fume hood, slowly and while stirring, add 25.0 mL of concentrated hydrochloric acid (HCl, 12 *M*) to 50 mL of distilled water. Adjust volume to 100 mL.

0.20 *M* Al(NO$_3$)$_2$—Dissolve 7.5 g of aluminum nitrate nonahydrate (Al(NO$_3$)$_3$•9 H$_2$O) in 75 mL of distilled water and adjust the volume to 100 mL.

0.20 *M* Cu(NO$_3$)$_2$—Dissolve 4.84 g of copper (II) nitrate trihydrate (Cu(NO$_3$)$_2$•3H$_2$O) in 75 mL of distilled water and adjust the volume to 100 mL.

0.20 *M* Fe(NO$_3$)$_3$—Dissolve 8.08 g of iron (III) nitrate nonahydrate (Fe(NO$_3$)$_3$•9 H$_2$O) in 75 mL of distilled water and adjust the volume to 100 mL.

0.20 *M* Mg(NO$_3$)$_2$—Dissolve 5.12 g of magnesium hexahydrate (Mg(NO$_3$)$_2$•6H$_2$O) in 75 mL of distilled water and adjust the volume to 100 mL.

0.20 *M* SnCl$_4$—Place 75 mL of distilled water in a 250-mL beaker and put the beaker in an ice bath and allow the water to cool. Then add 7.0 g of tin (IV) chloride pentahydrate (SnCl$_4$•5H$_2$O) and stir to dissolve all of the tin (IV) chloride. Remove the beaker from the ice water bath, and allow it to warm to room temperature. After it has reached room temperature, adjust the volume to 100 mL.

0.20 *M* Zn(NO$_3$)$_2$—Dissolve 5.94 g of zinc nitrate hexahydrate (Zn(NO$_3$)$_2$•6H$_2$O) in 75 mL of distilled water and then adjust volume to 100 mL.

Safety Requirements

- There may be some pieces of metal strips remaining in the wells that should not be flushed down the drain. Except for magnesium, they can be collected and placed in the general garbage container. Magnesium metal should be treated with dilute HCl and the clear solution flushed down the drain.

- The solutions are not a hazard and can be rinsed down the drain.

- Goggles and aprons are required in the laboratory area.

- Wash arms and hands before leaving the laboratory area.

CHAPTER 8

NOTES

_____

_____

_____

_____

_____

_____

_____

_____

Meeting the Needs of All Students
Differentiated Instruction
Augmentation and Accommodations

LEARNING ISSUE	REFERENCE	AUGMENTATION AND ACCOMMODATIONS
Copying tables Visual motor skills Spatial skills Using measures and proportions	*Investigate* 3.a), 8.	**Augmentation** • Show students how to set up proportions they can use to fit this table into their notebooks and establish the width of each column. • Show students who need more space to write legibly, how to use proportions to enlarge their tables. • Show students with difficulties in math how to measure the table in the text, measure the space they have and adjust the size by dividing the space they have by the number of columns they need. **Accommodations** • Give students who have difficulties understanding proportions the measurements for the perimeter of the table and the width of each column. • Give students who have difficulties with spatial and visual motor skills a prepared table they can complete and attach to their logs.
Finding patterns among complex data Interpreting written directions	*Investigate* 6.	**Augmentation** • The purpose of the investigation is for students to see the relative reactivity of metals. Having observed the reactions, students must look for a pattern. They are to rewrite their tables or results only if they cannot find a pattern. Not wanting to rewrite a table of this complexity could be an incentive for students who do not see a pattern to ask others for the pattern. Clarify the directions and check for understanding that each student must be able to explain the pattern. **Accommodations** • Some students who do not see the pattern will have difficulty understanding what the directions are asking them to do. Help them dissect the first paragraph into two parts, the directive that they look for a pattern and what to do if they do not see one. Once they understand the first two sentences, have them make a simple flowchart of the directions.
Explaining what they learned Writing with accuracy and precision	*Investigate* 8.	**Augmentation** • Students reading the *Chem Talk* will probably not refer to their periodic tables Ask students to work in groups to develop a list of words they should incorporate in their summaries. They should consider including the following phrases and terms: pattern, greatest number of reactions, least number of reactions, elements at the top, elements at the bottom, and metals. **Accommodations** • Give students the list of words above. • Refer students to the last section of the *Chem Talk* for help in summarizing their grid.

NOTES

_____

_____

_____

_____

_____

LEARNING ISSUE	REFERENCE	AUGMENTATION AND ACCOMMODATIONS
Constructing differentiated representations of a reading passage Gaining an understanding of the Activity Series of Metals	*Chem Talk*	**Augmentation** Use a class period to look closely at the *Chem Talk* as a reading passage for the purpose of improving reading skills through construction of meaningful representations of the information in the text. The following series of activities could be a fun way to reinforce the chemistry as well: o Ask students to read the first segment of the *Chem Talk*. Discuss with the class how the passage is organized. What is the main idea? How many groups of elements are discussed? Point out that groups of metals are being compared and ask students to work in groups to illustrate those similarities visually. Groups should first construct the framework for the comparisons by determining the names of each group compared and the type of information given about each group. o As a follow-up activity, ask the groups to create an organizer for the next *Chem Talk* section, Single Reactions. This passage is also a comparison of single-replacement reactions and double-replacement reactions. Students are being asked to notice the structural similarities and design an organizer that shows their similarities and differences. o Explain that representing information in ways that illustrate the relationships among concepts and examples helps students create meaning, which helps students remember and use new information. The most meaningful representations are those created by students themselves. Encourage each group to think of creative ways to illustrate their comparisons in a table, an outline, a cartoon, or other visual organizers. Creating a poem or song may appeal to some groups. Show students models of these types of representations. o After students have read the next-to-last section of the *Chem Talk*, use a Socratic dialogue format to discuss the following question, "What is the most meaningful way to organize the essential understandings of this section?" **Accommodations** • Give students a template for their comparisons that includes the name of the group, its characteristics, general reactivity level, type of ions formed, examples of elements from that group and location on the periodic table. • Give students a framework and word list for representing the Single-Replacement Reactions passage of the *Chem Talk*.

CHAPTER 8

NOTES

_____

_____

_____

_____

_____

_____

_____

Strategies for Students with Limited English Language Proficiency

LEARNING ISSUE	REFERENCE	AUGMENTATIONS
Background knowledge	*What Do You Think?*	Explanation of the illustration could be used to build oral language development as well as segue into the content. The word "*impress*" may not be in students' expressive vocabulary. Use of derivatives and multiple meanings will build students' knowledge of the word.
Vocabulary	*Investigate*	Students may benefit from working in small groups or with partners. Discussion of each of the questions prior to answering will build oral language and help with content.
Background knowledge Vocabulary Comprehending text	*Chem Talk*	Check for understanding of bold-type words. Refer students to the *Chem Words* for further explanations of the isolated words. Check for understanding of the word, "*reactivity*" and share derivatives for vocabulary development to demonstrate how the "*ity*" suffix changes the meaning of the word.
Background knowledge	*What Do You Think Now?*	The word "*scarcity*" may not be in the students' expressive vocabulary. This also allows for an additional reference to the "*ity*" suffix to alter word meaning.
Background knowledge Vocabulary Comprehending text	*Chem Essential Questions*	In the *Why should you care?* section, there is an example of how the prefix "*dis*" affects meaning in the word "*disadvantages*" as contrasted with "*advantages*."
Comprehension Vocabulary	*Chem to Go*	As students are directed to share scripts, they might benefit from a review of how to portray dialogue in writing and how to describe scenes. Formatting for the script may also require some review.
Application Comprehension	*Inquiring Further*	Ask students to isolate the important question that is being asked in this section as it is embedded in the middle of the paragraph. Ensure that students know what to do when they are asked to "*reflect*."

NOTES

NOTES

Section 6
Teaching Suggestions and Sample Answers

What Do You See?

To begin the section, ask students to study the illustration featured on the first page of the section. You might ask if they recognize the chemistry that is depicted. Can they determine what process the metal figures are undergoing? By listening to your students' responses, you may be able to assess their prior understanding about the concepts. Accept all answers; you will have a chance to return to the illustration after completing the section.

What Do You Think?

Let students freely share their ideas and clarify that you are not looking for correct responses, just open expression. Encourage them to participate in this discussion. Pay careful attention to statements that students make in attempting to answer these questions. These can reveal misconceptions and limited understandings they might have about metals.

The students will most likely point out that aluminum is much lighter than gold. They might also be aware that gold is scarcer than aluminum, which would explain why it is more expensive. They probably will not be able to explain why the value of aluminum has decreased over the years.

What Do You Think?
A CHEMIST'S RESPONSE

A thorough discussion of the differences between aluminum and gold could fill a book. For the purposes of providing an answer, only the reasons for the cost differential will be considered.

In terms of availability, gold is scarcer than aluminum, which is one reason it is more expensive. Also, the fact that gold is a stable and decorative metal used in making jewelry increases its value to our society.

The cost of aluminum has decreased over the years because relatively inexpensive methods of mass production have been developed.

STUDENTS' PRIOR CONCEPTIONS

Some representative conceptions that students might have about metals include ideas such as:

1. *Oxidation means oxygen must be involved.* See the *Students' Prior Conceptions* section in the previous section.

2. *Reduction is a loss of electrons.* See the *Students' Prior Conceptions* section in the previous section.

3. *There is no difference between metal atoms and metal ions.* The distinction between metal atoms and metal ions is a topic that students often have several interrelated misconceptions about. Students generally think of metal elements as only having one form—that of a pure, uncombined metal. This belief is a result of their familiarity with common properties of pure (and alloyed) metals, such as malleability, luster, and hardness; their extensive experience with objects

made of these substances; and their knowledge that these substances are generally referred to as "metals" in everyday usage. Ionic compounds that contain metal ions have very different observable properties than do pure metals and are never referred to as "metals" in everyday conversation, so the reality that such compounds contain metal elements, albeit in a different form, is difficult for students to internalize. Further, because metal ions do not exist in isolation, but rather are always combined with an anion, it is not possible to study the macroscopic properties of a sample of an ion, like color and density, as students have done with samples of different pure metals, like aluminum foil and zinc squares. Aluminum ions appear different on the observable level depending on what anion they are paired with. Thus, a clear connection

Section 6

Reactions with Transition Metals: Metal Activity Series

What Do You See?

Learning Outcomes

In this section you will:

• Use chemical properties and deductive reasoning to identify a pattern in metal reactions.

• Compare and contrast single-replacement and double-replacement reactions.

• Define and explain the concepts of oxidation and reduction.

• Gain an understanding of the activity series of metals.

Safety goggles and a lab apron must be worn *at all times* in a chemistry lab.

What Do You Think?

Aluminum was once so valuable that kings used to impress their guests with aluminum forks and spoons. Aluminum now sells for 20¢ per pound. Gold sells for over $1,200 per ounce.

• **What is the difference between aluminum and gold?**

• **Why has the value of aluminum decreased over the years?**

Record your ideas about these questions in your *Active Chemistry* log. Be prepared to discuss your responses with your group and the class.

Investigate

A piece of metal is left at the crime scene. Could this be a clue? In this investigation, you'll look at a way of identifying a pure metallic element.

1. Obtain small strips of aluminum (Al), copper (Cu), iron (Fe), magnesium (Mg), tin (Sn), and zinc (Zn). Other forms of metal can be used (shavings or filings, like steel or copper "wool," shot), but strips work best. Use sandpaper or steel wool to clean off the surface of the strips as thoroughly as possible.

   a) Why is it necessary to clean the strips? Record your thoughts in your *Active Chemistry* log.

691

Active Chemistry

---

between something concrete like aluminum foil with the idea of individual aluminum atoms (Al) is possible. On the other hand, the connection with the concept of individual aluminum ions (Al^{3+}) is not so clear.

Because of this confusion on the macroscopic or observable scale, it is not at all surprising that the distinction between ions and neutral atoms of metals is difficult to grasp on the symbolic level of equation-writing and the microscopic scale of individual particles. Therefore, students often have trouble understanding that when a metal is changed from either its ionic form or its pure form to the other form via oxidation or reduction, it is a significant and often dramatic change.

To help overcome this common misunderstanding, it is important that the connection linking the observable reactions between pure metals and ionic solutions, the microscopic transfer of electrons during those reactions, and the symbols for the atoms and ions, be emphasized as often as possible.

4. *The two metal elements in a single-replacement reaction can join to form a compound product.* This idea stems in part from confusion about the difference between atoms and ions, as described above. It may be helpful to remind students that ionic compounds must be electrically neutral, and thus require a negative ion and a positive ion in order to balance charges to zero. Metals can only form cations, and therefore it is impossible for them to join to create a neutral ionic species. Also emphasize that the cation is always given first in chemical formulas and names, making it easier to identify which ion is positive and which is negative.

Investigate

1.a)

Most metals will have a surface coating of oxide from reaction with air. This coating could prevent a reaction in some instances. Also, some metal strips may have a surface oil from the machining process. This must be removed to prevent contamination of the procedure.

2.

If a 48-well plate is not available, two 24-well plates will suffice. Any combination of plates that provide 35 wells could also be used.

3.

The size of the square of each metal isn't important but the key is to have a good deal of surface area for reaction.

3.a)

A Blackline Master of the grid featured in the *Student Edition* is available in your *Teacher Resources* CD.

8-6a	Blackline Master

4.

Only the copper (II) and iron (III) ions will have color— blue and yellow-orange, respectively.

5.a)

Some of the reactions will take five minutes or longer. As a general rule of thumb, the closer together the metal and the ion it is replacing are in the activity series, the slower the reaction will be.

CSI Chemistry

Color	Al(NO₃)₃	Cu(NO₃)₂	Fe(NO₃)₃	Mg(NO₃)₂	SnCl₄	Zn(NO₃)₂	HCl
Al							
Cu							
Fe							
Mg							
Sn							
Zn							

Mix chemicals only as instructed by your teacher.

Hydrochloric acid is corrosive. Handle with caution.

Wash your hands and arms thoroughly after the investigation.

2. Set up a 6 × 7 grid on a 48-well reaction plate or a combination of well plates. Place a piece of blank white paper underneath the reaction plate. This will make it easier to observe the reactions that will occur.

3. Make sure the wells are as clean as possible. Cut seven 3 mm squares from the aluminum strip and place one in each well of the first row. Repeat with the other five metals in the next six rows of wells. A sample grid is provided above. Each box represents one well on your well plate.

   a) Draw the grid in your *Active Chemistry* log.

4. Make a note of the color of each original solution above its column. These colors are characteristic of the metal ions in these solutions. For example copper (II) nitrate, Cu(NO₃)₂, is blue. The blue is due to the Cu²⁺ ion in solution.

5. Add 10 drops of the specific 0.2 *M* ionic solution to each well in the column, starting with aluminum nitrate, Al(NO₃)₃ in the first column. Many of these solutions are called nitrate solutions, because they have the anion nitrate, NO₃⁻. Instead of tin (IV) nitrate, tin (IV) chloride is used. In the last column of wells, add 10 drops of 1.0 *M* HCl.

a) Record what you see in each well on the corresponding square of your grid. Look for color changes in the solutions or the metals. You may also see precipitates, bubbles, or other evidence of the occurrence of a reaction. You may want to use a magnifying glass to help you see very small changes. (Hint: Some of these changes take longer than others, so be patient.)

b) If after a second look you still see no changes, then write "N.R." in that box to represent no chemical reaction has happened.

6. Once you stop seeing new evidence of chemical reactions, look for a pattern in the results you have recorded. If you can't find one, try rewriting your table of results.

a) First, next to the metal's atomic symbol, write the number of solutions each metal reacted with.

b) Next, beside the solution's chemical formula, write the number of metals each solution reacted with.

7. Rinse and save metal pieces for future use. Dispose of solutions containing heavy metals (Cu, Fe, Sn, Zn) as directed by your teacher. Clean up your workstation.

692

5.b)

The following grid contains sample data that may be similar to students' findings.

Sample Grid

	Al(NO₃)₃	Cu(NO₃)₂	Fe(NO₃)₃	Mg(NO₃)₂	SnCl₄	Zn(NO₃)₂	HCl
Al	N.R.	Al turns red brown	Al turns dark	N.R.	Al turns dark	Al turns dark	bubbles
Cu	N.R.	N.R.	N.R.	N.R.	N.R.	N.R.	N.R.
Fe	N.R.	Very slow, Fe turns red brown	N.R.	N.R.	Slow reaction	N.R.	Very slowly bubbles
Mg	Mg dissolves	Black precipitate on Mg	Mg disappears, reddish precipitate	N.R.	Mg disappears, gray precipitate	Mg disappears	bubbles
Sn	N.R.	Very slow reaction	N.R.	N.R.	N.R.	N.R.	Extremely slow. May not notice it at all.
Zn	N.R.	Zn turns black	Zn slowly dissolve, reddish- brown precipitate	N.R.	Zn slowly disappears	N.R.	bubbles

6.a-b)

The following sample grid contains sample data that may be similar to students' findings. Students should look for a pattern.

Sample Grid

	Al(NO₃)₃ 1	Cu(NO₃)₂ 5	Fe(NO₃)₃ 3	Mg(NO₃)₂ 0	SnCl₄ 4	Zn(NO₃)₂ 2	HCl 5
Al-5	N.R.	Reaction	Reaction	N.R.	Reaction	Reaction	Reaction
Cu-0	N.R.	N.R.	N.R.	N.R.	N.R.	N.R.	N.R.
Fe-3	N.R.	Reaction	N.R.	N.R.	Reaction	N.R.	Reaction
Mg-6	Reaction	Reaction	Reaction	N.R.	Reaction	Reaction	Reaction
Sn-2	N.R.	Reaction	N.R.	N.R.	N.R.	N.R.	Reaction
Zn-4	N.R.	Reaction	Reaction	N.R.	Reaction	N.R.	Reaction

7.

Dispose of any leftover magnesium by treating it with dilute HCl.

8.

The following sample grid reflects a change in the order of the metals and solutions. The metals are aligned according to the greatest to the least number of reactions.

Second Results Grid

	$Mg(NO_3)_2$	$Al(NO_3)_3$	$Zn(NO_3)_2$	$Fe(NO_3)_3$	$SnCl_4$	HCl	$Cu(NO_3)_2$
Mg	---	Reaction	Reaction	Reaction	Reaction	Reaction	Reaction
Al	N.R.	---	Reaction	Reaction	Reaction	Reaction	Reaction
Zn	N.R.	N.R.	---	Reaction	Reaction	Reaction	Reaction
Fe	N.R.	N.R.	N.R.	---	Reaction	Reaction	Reaction
Sn	N.R.	N.R.	N.R.	N.R.	---	Reaction	Reaction
Cu	N.R.	N.R.	N.R.	N.R.	N.R.	N.R.	----

8.a)

Students should note that the pattern indicates a decrease in activity from Mg > Al > Zn > Fe > Sn > Cu. This is confirmed by the mirror image results from the metal cations where Cu^{2+} > H^+ > Sn^{4+} > Fe^{3+} > Zn^{2+} > Al^{3+} > Mg^{2+}. Of these, Cu^{2+} is the most easily reduced and the most difficult to oxidize. Magnesium is the most difficult to reduce but the most easily oxidized.

9.a)

Copper and silver metal atoms are shown in the diagrams.

9.b)

Like ionic compounds, metal atoms are arranged in rows and columns in the solid state. They differ, however, in that metal atoms have no charges while ionic compounds have a cation and an anion.

9.c)

At the macro level, copper atoms are a solid and part of a coil of the metal. Copper (II) ions are charged, hydrated cations with a blue color.

Chem Talk

This section explores the basis for variations in the activity of metals. An explanation of single replacement reactions leads to a discussion of the oxidation-reduction process of these reactions and concludes with a review of the activity series of metals.

8. Make a second results grid, but this time you will change the order of the metals and solutions. Order the metals from the greatest number of reactions at the top row to the least number of reactions as the bottom row. Order the solutions from the greatest number of reactions in the first column to the least number of reactions in the final column. Then fill in your results in the new grid. Write a brief summary of the pattern you see now.

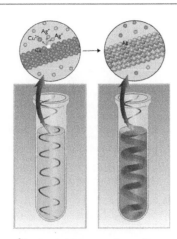

🖎 a) Record your arrangement and your answer in your *Active Chemistry* log.

9. The analysis of diagrams is just as important as being able to draw them. Take a look at the diagrams shown here. Analyze the diagrams carefully and discuss them with your partners before tackling the questions below.

🖎 a) What metal elements are represented in these diagrams?

🖎 b) How is the structure of a metallic element similar to that of an ionic compound? How is it different?

🖎 c) What is the difference between Cu and Cu^{2+} at the macroscale (in the test tubes)?

METAL ACTIVITY SERIES

Metals and Transition Metals

Metals vary in their reactivity. Some metals lose their outer electrons so easily that they rarely are seen in their pure form. They react with too many common substances, like water. Metals that are in Group I of the periodic table, such as sodium and potassium, fall into this category. Group II metals tend to be slightly less reactive. However, not all Group I metals are more reactive than Group II metals. Other metals are so unreactive that they are found in nature in their pure state. Gold and silver fall into this category. This property accounts in part for the high value placed upon them.

693

CSI Chemistry

Gold and silver, along with many of the metals you tested in this investigation, are transition metals. Transition metals are located in the center section of the periodic table, making the "transition" from the metals on the left side of the periodic table to the nonmetals on the right side.

Iron is an example of a transition metal. Like many transition metals, iron can form cations with different charges and properties. As you saw in the luminol reaction from *Section 3*, iron (II) and iron (III) ions had different chemical properties. When naming most transition metals, a roman number is used, following the metal name. The numeral represents the charge on the metal ion in the compound. For example, you used $SnCl_{4(aq)}$ in this investigation. This is called tin (IV) chloride, since tin is a transition metal and in this compound the tin ions have a charge of +4. Tin (II) is another possible cation of tin. It has a charge of +2.

Single-Replacement Reactions

In this investigation, you placed a piece of metal into a solution of an ionic compound in order to observe a possible chemical reaction. This type of reaction is called a **single-replacement reaction**. An example of a single-replacement reaction you didn't observe is the reaction between copper metal and silver nitrate solution.

copper + silver nitrate → copper (II) nitrate + silver

$$Cu_{(s)} + 2AgNO_{3(aq)} \rightarrow Cu(NO_3)_{2(aq)} + 2Ag_{(s)}$$

It is called a single-replacement reaction because a free element replaces an ion in the compound. The ion in the compound becomes a free, neutral element. In the example, the metal copper replaces the silver metal ion in the compound silver nitrate, forming copper (II) nitrate. The silver ions that are replaced become neutral silver atoms. This type of reaction is similar to the double-replacement reaction you studied in the last section. In a double-replacement reaction, ions from two different compounds exchange places. In a single-replacement reaction, a free element replaces an ion in a compound. An example of each type of reaction is shown below.

Single replacement $\quad Zn_{(s)} + Cu(NO_3)_{2(aq)} \rightarrow Zn(NO_3)_{2(aq)} + Cu_{(s)}$

Chem Words

single-replacement reaction: a chemical reaction in which a free element replaces an ion in a compound.

694

Double replacement $NaCl_{(aq)} + AgNO_{3(aq)} \rightarrow AgCl_{(s)} + NaNO_{3(aq)}$

Other examples of single-replacement reactions include

zinc + copper (II) sulfate → zinc sulfate + copper

$$Zn_{(s)} + CuSO_{4(aq)} \rightarrow ZnSO_{4(aq)} + Cu_{(s)}$$

aluminum + sulfuric acid → aluminum sulfate + hydrogen gas

$$2Al_{(s)} + 3H_2SO_{4(aq)} \rightarrow Al_2(SO_4)_{3(aq)} + 3H_{2(g)}$$

Single-replacement reactions differ from double-replacement reactions in that electrons are transferred in single-replacement reactions but not in double-replacement reactions. In double-replacement reaction ions are switching places. In a single-replacement reaction the free metal is losing electrons (thus becoming a positively charged ion) and the metal ion is gaining electrons (thus becoming a neutral atom). Because of this electron transfer, single-replacement reactions are classified as oxidation-reduction reactions.

Oxidation and Reduction

Atoms that have an equal number of protons and electrons are neutral and have no charge. Any metal in its natural state, when it is not combined with any other element, such as copper metal, aluminum metal, and iron metal, is neutral. So, iron metal $Fe_{(s)}$, copper metal $Cu_{(s)}$, and aluminum metal $Al_{(s)}$ are all neutral. If the metal loses electrons, it becomes a cation, an ion with a positive charge.

In *Section 4*, you learned that when a metal forms a compound, it loses electrons. So, in a single-replacement reaction, the free metal loses electrons to the cation in the compound. Look at the reaction you did in this investigation between aluminum metal and iron (III) nitrate

$$Al_{(s)} + Fe(NO_3)_{3(aq)} \rightarrow Fe_{(s)} + Al(NO_3)_{3(aq)}$$

In this reaction, aluminum metal loses three electrons to iron ions, forming aluminum ion.

$$Al_{(s)} \rightarrow Al^{3+}_{(aq)} + 3e^-$$

When a substance loses electrons it has been oxidized. Oxidation is the loss of electrons. In this case, aluminum metal has been oxidized to form aluminum ion. Also, in oxidation, the charge, or **oxidation number** as it is called, is becoming more positive, 0 to +3.

Chem Words

oxidation number: a positive or negative number assigned to each atom in a compound to help keep track of the electrons in a chemical reaction.

695

CHAPTER 8

CSI CHEMISTRY

 CSI Chemistry

However, electrons cannot just be lost. Another element has to accept them. In this case, iron (III) ions from the iron nitrate accept the electrons from aluminum to form iron metal.

$$Fe^{3+}_{(aq)} + 3e^- \rightarrow Fe_{(s)}$$

When a substance gains electrons, it has been reduced. In this case, iron (III) ion has been reduced to form iron metal. Notice that in reduction, the oxidation number, or charge, gets smaller, $+3$ to 0. The net reaction is (nitrate, NO_3^-, is omitted because it is not changed in the reaction)

$$\overset{\text{oxidation}}{Al_{(s)} + Fe^{3+}_{(aq)} \rightarrow Al^{3+}_{(aq)} + Fe_{(s)}}$$
reduction

Another example is the reaction between zinc and a copper (II) solution

$$\overset{\text{oxidation}}{Zn_{(s)} + Cu^{2+}_{(aq)} \rightarrow Zn^{2+}_{(aq)} + Cu_{(s)}}$$
reduction

An easy way to remember oxidation and reduction is the saying "**LEO** *the lion says* **GER**"– **L**oss of **E**lectrons is **O**xidation, **G**ain of **E**lectrons is **R**eduction. Since oxidation does not occur without reduction, these types of reactions are called oxidation-reduction reactions.

The Activity Series of Metals

As you observed in this investigation, not all metals will react to replace all of the metal ions. Some elements do not lose their **valence electrons** in single-replacement reactions as easily as other elements. Some elements are not

Chem Words

valence electrons: electrons in the outermost shell or outermost energy level of an atom.

activity series of metals: a list of the metals based on their ability to be oxidized. The easier it is to oxidize the more active the metal is in comparison to other metals.

Metal Activity Series	
Name	Symbol
lithium	Li
potassium	K
calcium	Ca
sodium	Na
magnesium	Mg
aluminum	Al
zinc	Zn
iron	Fe
tin	Sn
lead	Pb
hydrogen*	H
copper	Cu
mercury	Hg
silver	Ag
platinum	Pt
gold	Au

* Hydrogen is not a metal but it behaves like a metal in some chemical reactions so it is included in the activity series.

oxidized as easily as others. The **activity series of metals** ranks the metals in order of ease of oxidation. The elements at the top of the activity series lose their electrons in single-replacement reactions more easily than elements at the bottom of the list. The activity series can be used to predict if a single-replacement reaction will take place. For a single-replacement reaction to occur, the free, neutral metal must be higher on the list than the metal ion it is trying to replace. For example, the following reaction will not occur:

$$Au_{(s)} + FeCl_{3(aq)} \rightarrow \text{no reaction}$$

No reaction will occur in this case, meaning that Au, the free atom, is lower than Fe, the metal ion, on the activity series. Another example is below. This reaction will take place

$$3Mg_{(s)} + 2FeCl_{3(aq)} \rightarrow 3MgCl_{2(aq)} + 2Fe^{3+}_{(aq)}$$

This reaction will occur and therefore Mg, the free atom, is higher on the activity series than Fe, the metal ion. Magnesium is oxidized more easily than iron, and magnesium will transfer its outer electrons to iron.

Checking Up

1. Are all Group I metals more reactive than Group II metals?

2. Where are the transitional metals found on the periodic table? Why are they called transitional metals?

3. Explain the difference between single-replacement reactions and double-replacement reactions.

4. Is an oxidation-reduction reaction an example of a single-replacement or double-replacement reaction?

5. How would you use the activity series of metals as a student chemist?

What Do You Think Now?

At the beginning of this section you were asked the following:

• What is the difference between aluminum and gold?

• Why has the value of aluminum decreased over the years?

What have you learned about these metals and their reactivity from this section? Finding pure gold may be difficult because of its scarcity but not because it reacts with other substances. How might this explain why the value of aluminum has changed so drastically over time?

Active Chemistry

---

reactions are classified as oxidation-reduction reactions. Most double-replacement reactions have products that are solid, gas, or water.

4.

An oxidation-reduction reaction is an example of a single-replacement reaction.

5.

The activity series is used to predict if a single-replacement reaction will take place.

What Do You Think Now?

This is a good time to have your class reconsider the *What Do You See?* illustration and the *What Do You Think?* questions. They should now be able to identify the process that the artist is depicting. Their answers to the original questions should be more sophisticated and accurate than their initial responses. Recognizing the knowledge they have gained should increase their confidence in the learning process of *Active Chemistry*.

Students' answers regarding the dramatic change in the value of aluminum may vary. In addition to the new and cheaper methods of mass production, some students may also suggest that recycling (of aluminum) might have contributed to the decrease in value.

Checking Up

1.

No. Sodium (Na), which is a Group I metal, is less reactive than barium (Ba) and calcium (Ca), which are Group II metals.

2.

Transition metals are located in the center section of the periodic table. They are called transition metals because they transition from the metals on the left side of the periodic table to the nonmetals on the right side.

3.

A single-replacement reaction is a chemical reaction that involves a free element replacing another ion in a compound. In a double-replacement reaction, ions from two different compounds exchange places. Single-replacement reactions differ from double-replacement reactions in that electrons are transferred in single-replacement reactions but not in double-replacement reactions. Therefore, single-replacement

CHAPTER 8

Chem Essential Questions

What does it mean?

MACRO — Single-replacement reactions were observed between the metals and the nitrate solutions. Elements higher in the Metal Activity Series replaced the metal ions which were lower.

NANO — At the nanoscopic level, the metals of higher activity gave up electrons to the metal ions of lower activity. This is an oxidation-reduction process in which the more active element releases electrons (is oxidized) to the metal ion, which becomes the corresponding elemental substance (is reduced).

SYMBOLIC — Starting with the solution of a metal ion and its spectator anion, any metal above the metal ion in the Metal Activity Series will replace it. For example:

$$Mg(s) + 2AgNO_3(aq) \longrightarrow$$
$$Mg(NO_3)_2(aq) + 2Ag(s)$$

Using the activity series chart, one can predict that magnesium will replace silver ion. Other single-replacement reactions can be easily predicted using the chart.

How do you know?

In the investigation, the iron metal was oxidized and replaced copper ions, which were reduced. However, copper metal did not replace iron ions.

Why do you believe?

The iron in the exposed steel alloy is oxidized by oxygen to iron cations. This is what appears as reddish-brown rust. The iron is oxidized and the oxygen is reduced.

Why should you care?

Students' answers will vary. An advantage to using chemical properties to identify metals from a crime scene is that valuable information can be gained about the identity of the metal. A disadvantage, however, is that sometimes the chemical methods used will destroy or alter the sample.

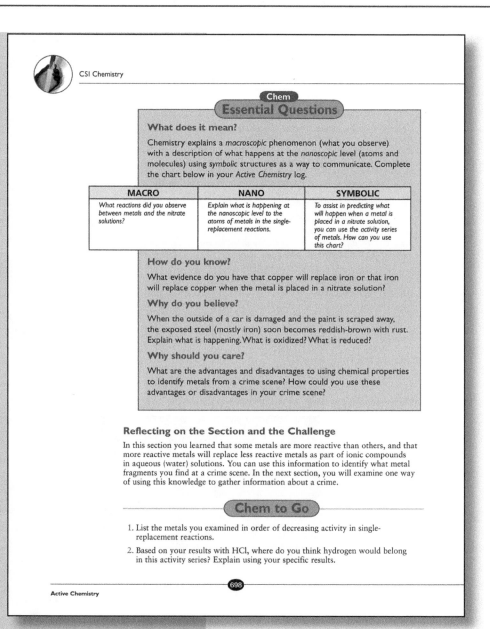

CSI Chemistry

Chem Essential Questions

What does it mean?

Chemistry explains a *macroscopic* phenomenon (what you observe) with a description of what happens at the *nanoscopic* level (atoms and molecules) using *symbolic* structures as a way to communicate. Complete the chart below in your *Active Chemistry* log.

MACRO	NANO	SYMBOLIC
What reactions did you observe between metals and the nitrate solutions?	Explain what is happening at the nanoscopic level to the atoms of metals in the single-replacement reactions.	To assist in predicting what will happen when a metal is placed in a nitrate solution, you can use the activity series of metals. How can you use this chart?

How do you know?

What evidence do you have that copper will replace iron or that iron will replace copper when the metal is placed in a nitrate solution?

Why do you believe?

When the outside of a car is damaged and the paint is scraped away, the exposed steel (mostly iron) soon becomes reddish-brown with rust. Explain what is happening. What is oxidized? What is reduced?

Why should you care?

What are the advantages and disadvantages to using chemical properties to identify metals from a crime scene? How could you use these advantages or disadvantages in your crime scene?

Reflecting on the Section and the Challenge

In this section you learned that some metals are more reactive than others, and that more reactive metals will replace less reactive metals as part of ionic compounds in aqueous (water) solutions. You can use this information to identify what metal fragments you find at a crime scene. In the next section, you will examine one way of using this knowledge to gather information about a crime.

Chem to Go

1. List the metals you examined in order of decreasing activity in single-replacement reactions.

2. Based on your results with HCl, where do you think hydrogen would belong in this activity series? Explain using your specific results.

Active Chemistry

698

Reflecting on the Section and the Challenge

Students should read this section for a direct connotation between the section and the *Chapter Challenge*. This is a chance for them to think about how they can integrate their new knowledge about identifying unknown metals into the crime scenes for their *Chapter Challenge* projects. You may want to let students reflect and share their ideas in a class discussion

Section 6 Reactions with Transition Metals: Metal Activity Series

3. Use the metal activity series to determine which of these combinations you would expect to produce a reaction. For each, explain why.

a) aluminum with iron (III) sulfate   b) zinc with copper (II) sulfate

c) calcium with zinc sulfate   d) magnesium with zinc nitrate

4. Complete the word equations for the single-replacement reactions in *Question 3*.

5. The chemical formula for rust is Fe_2O_3. Iron metal is simply Fe. When iron is converted to iron (III) oxide, what chemical process occurs?

6. Sometimes a piece of zinc metal is attached to a steel pipe. Why?

7. Which reactions are redox reactions? For the redox reactions identify the reactant that is oxidized and the reactant that is reduced.

a) $Sn(s) + Cu^{2+}(aq) \rightarrow Sn^{2+}(aq) + Cu(s)$

b) $2Zn(s) + Sn^{4+}(aq) \rightarrow 2Zn^{2+}(aq) + Sn(s)$

c) $Cu^{2+}(aq) + 2OH^{-}(aq) \rightarrow Cu(OH)_2(s)$

8. **Preparing for the Chapter Challenge**

Now that you have practiced writing a crime scene story and received feedback on it, it is time to begin drafting your group's story with the cast of characters you created in the previous sections. With your group, spend some time talking about a possible story, not forgetting the pieces of evidence we have yet to investigate (serial number recovery and ink identification). A good place to start may be to share your *CSI Chemistry* scripts. In your group, have a recorder write down your ideas and hold them for the group, and a leader to keep the conversation on task and moving. After the discussion, write your reflection of the conversation in your *Active Chemistry* log. Be sure to include any final decisions made on the direction or plot of the story.

Inquiring Further

1. Removing oxidation

One of the first steps you used in this investigation was to sand or use steel wool on each metal strip. You were asked to respond to why this was important. With the guidance of your teacher, design an experiment to determine if the sanding really was an important step. Report your results. Explain your observations, reflecting on the *nanoscopic* and *symbolic* meanings presented in this and other sections.

2. Brass or bronze

Locate advertisement data from two or more metal-polishing liquids and, if possible compare them with regard to cost, types of metals each will clean, speed and thoroughness of cleaning, and toxicity of ingredients. Determine which would be best for cleaning a metal object in your classroom.

699

Active Chemistry

Chem to Go

1.

In order of decreasing activity in single-replacement reactions, the metals tested fall into the following order:

Mg, Al, Zn, Fe, Sn, Cu

2.

Hydrogen ions reacted with all metals but copper. Therefore, it belongs between tin and copper.

3.

Each of these examples will complete the reaction because in each example, the neutral metal is higher on the activity series than the metal ion. Thus, the metal atom will readily give its electrons to the metal ion in the compound, in the process becoming an ion itself.

4.

a) aluminum + iron (III) sulfate $\rightarrow$ iron + aluminum sulfate

b) zinc + copper (II) sulfate $\rightarrow$ copper + zinc sulfate

c) calcium + zinc sulfate $\rightarrow$ zinc + calcium sulfate

d) magnesium + zinc nitrate $\rightarrow$ zinc + magnesium nitrate

5.

Fe is oxidized; oxygen is reduced.

$Fe \rightarrow Fe^{3+} + 3e^-$, $O_2 + 4e^- \rightarrow 2O^{2-}$

or

$4Fe + 3O_2 \rightarrow 2Fe_2O_3$

6.

Zinc is attached to a steel pipe to protect the steel from oxidation. Since zinc is more reactive than iron, it will be oxidized while the iron (in the steel) will not.

7.

a) $Sn(s) + Cu^{2+}(aq) \rightarrow Sn^{2+}(aq) + Cu(s)$

Sn is oxidized:
$Sn \rightarrow Sn^{2+} + 2e^-$

Cu is reduced:
$Cu^{2+} + 2e^- \rightarrow Cu$

b) $2Zn(s) + Sn^{4+}(aq) \rightarrow 2Zn^{2+}(aq) + Sn(s)$

Zn is oxidized:
$Zn \rightarrow Zn^{2+} + 2e^-$

Sn is reduced:
$Sn^{4+} + 4e^- \rightarrow Sn$

c) $Cu^{2+}(aq) + 2OH^-(aq) \rightarrow Cu(OH)_2(s)$

This is not a redox reaction.

8.

Preparing for the Chapter Challenge

The Metal Activity Series can be of significant value in crime detection, and the knowledge gained from this section should generate some ideas about how to use metals and metal activity in a crime detection story. Group discussions should help students figure out how to incorporate those ideas into their *Chapter Challenge* projects. Make sure groups record their discussion results.

Inquiring Further

1. Removing oxidation

Check students' proposed procedures for safety and effectiveness. Remind them of the importance of using controls in experiments.

2. Brass or bronze

Locate advertisement data from two or more metal polishing liquids and compare them with regard to cost, types of metals each will clean, speed and thoroughness of cleaning and toxicity of ingredients (if possible). Determine which would be best for cleaning a metal object in your classroom.

NOTES

_____

_____

_____

_____

_____

_____

_____

_____

_____

_____

_____

_____

_____

SECTION 6 – QUIZ

8-6b	Blackline Master

1. The following reaction is called a single-replacement reaction. Why is it called that?

   $$2Al + 3CuSO_4 \rightarrow Al_2(SO_4)_3 + 3Cu$$

2. Why must oxidation always be accompanied by reduction?

3. Single-replacement reactions are a type of redox reactions. In the following reaction, _____ is being reduced, and _____ is being oxidized:

   $$Zn^0 + 2Ag^+ \rightarrow Zn^{2+} + 2Ag^0$$

   a) Zn^0, Ag^+ b) Ag^+, Zn^0

   c) Ag^0, Ag^+ d) Zn^{2+}, Zn^0

4. Use the activity series to determine if the following reactions will take place.

   a) $Mg + HCl \rightarrow$

   b) $Ni + MgCl_2 \rightarrow$

   c) $Na + Al(NO_3)_3 \rightarrow$

SECTION 6 – QUIZ ANSWERS

❶ It is called a single-replacement reaction because the element Al is replacing the copper ion in copper (II) nitrate.

❷ For an atom to lose its electrons (be oxidized), there has to be another atom to accept the electrons (be reduced).

❸ b) Ag^+, Zn^0
Ag^+ is being reduced, and Zn^0 is being oxidized: $Zn^0 + 2Ag^+ \rightarrow Zn^{2+} + 2Ag^0$

❹ a) Yes – $Mg + 2HCl \rightarrow H_2 + MgCl_2$

b) No, the reaction will not take place.

c) Yes – $3Na + Al(NO_3)_3 \rightarrow Al + 3NaNO_3$

CHAPTER 8

SECTION 7
Using the Metal Activity Series to Etch a Serial Number

Section Overview

In this section, students stamp a serial number into a piece of metal and then apply what they have learned about single-replacement reactions to restore that serial number after it has been obliterated. Next, they build and manipulate a clay model in order to understand what happens to metal atoms when they are stamped and how the changes caused by stamping allow restoration of serial numbers.

Background Information

Metallic Properties and Microscopic Structure

Materials made of metals in uncombined form have properties that make them extremely useful in a wide range of applications, from electrical wiring to jewelry to support beams for huge buildings, as well as countless others. These properties include malleability, ductility, luster, and the ability to conduct both heat and electricity well. All of these properties can be understood through examination of the microscopic properties of metals as they exist in the solid phase, including the arrangement of atoms and the attractions between the atoms. These microscopic properties differ significantly from those seen in other types of solids, and these differences explain why metals' properties are not shared by other solids such as ionic salts.

A metal sample is composed of tiny individual grains, and within each grain the atoms are arranged in very orderly rows that extend linearly in all three dimensions, with occasional slight disruptions called **dislocations**. The metal atoms are strongly attracted to each other through their shared, movable valence electrons and are closely packed together in this crystalline structure. In fact, they are so near to each other that the outer energy shells of the atoms' electron clouds actually overlap. Because of these overlapping regions, the valence (outer-shell) electrons inside a metal grain are actually free to move from one atom to another. In other words, these outer electrons are shared between all of the atoms in the grain. The effect of metallic bonding is to create a giant molecule with flexible bonds that allow the movement of atoms within a "sea of electrons."

Some of the macroscopic properties of metals are easily explained by the model of metallic structure and bonding outlined above. Since electrical conduction is simply the movement of electrons through a substance, the ability of the valence electrons to move confers this property. Malleability, the ability to bend or stretch without shattering, requires that atoms in the structure be able to move with respect to one another without breaking the attraction between them. The arrangement of the atoms in ordered layers in metals allows this movement. In effect, one layer can slide slightly past another layer in response to stress. Because all of the atoms are equally attracted to all of the other atoms in the metal grain, when the layers move, atoms simply experience attractions with their new atomic neighbors.

When metals are oxidized, they combine to form compounds with negatively charged nonmetal ions. These compounds are called **ionic salts**. Ionic salts in the solid phase are similar to metals in that the particles are arranged in an orderly, three-dimensional geometric pattern within each individual grain or crystal; ionic salts are considered crystalline solids just as uncombined metals are. However, unlike metal grains, in which all of the particles are attracted to each other, ionic salts contain two distinct types of particles, positively charged cations (often metal ions) and negatively charged anions. Cations and anions are attracted to each other because of their opposite electrical charges, and so the ionic crystalline structure consists of alternating cations and anions. This arrangement minimizes cation-cation and anion-anion repulsions, which result from their like electrical charges. In contrast to metals, ionic crystals do not conduct electricity, despite containing charged particles, because the charged particles are not free to move within the crystal. Like metals, ionic compounds have atoms (as ions) arranged in crystalline, orderly patterns. However, ionic solids are brittle, meaning they shatter in response to stress. This is because when a stress is applied, **ions** with like charges are forced near each other, causing electrical repulsions that cause the crystal to break.

Oxidation-Reduction and Single-Replacement Reactions

See the *Background Information* section for *Section 5* and *Section 6*.

LEARNING OUTCOMES		
LEARNING OUTCOMES	**LOCATION IN SECTION**	**EVIDENCE OF UNDERSTANDING**
Apply the chemical and physical properties of metals to serial-number stamping and recovery.	*Investigate, Chem to Go*	Students restore an obliterated serial number in the lab. Students describe the changes in their clay models when they are stamped. Students identify that $FeCl_3$ is used to etch Al because Fe is lower on the activity series than Al, and identify other solutions that could etch Al because their metallic cations are also lower on the series than Al. Students describe how metals are affected by stamping.
Explain what happens at the nanoscopic level when serial numbers are stamped and recovered.	*Investigate, Chem to Go*	Students hypothesize about the mechanism of serial-number restoration after completing the restoration lab activity. Students describe situations in which etching would not work to restore a serial number and explain why it would not work.
Use and create models to represent the nanoscopic, physical, and chemical changes of metals.	*Chem to Go*	Students identify that $FeCl_3$ is used to etch Al because Fe is lower on the activity series than Al; identify other solutions that could etch Al because they are also lower on the series; choose which of two opposite redox reactions between Al and Fe will occur spontaneously, and select the two of four reactions given that will occur based on the location of reactants on the activity series.

NOTES

_____

_____

_____

_____

_____

Section 7
Materials, Chemicals, Preparation, and Safety

("per Group" quantity is based on group size of 4 students)

Materials and Equipment

Materials (and Equipment)	Quantity per Group (4 students)
Sheet of 100-grit sandpaper	1
Sheet of 150-grit sandpaper	1
Sheet of 220-grit sandpaper	1
Pair of rubber gloves	1
Black marker	1
Wood dowel	1
Cutting knife	1
Unsharpened pencil	1
Sharpened pencil	1
Magnifying glass	1
Materials (and Equipment)	**Quantity per Class**
Set of metal dies	1
Hammer	1
Bottle of ethanol or isopropyl alcohol	1
Box of cotton balls	1
Electric drill/grinding wheel	1
Sculpey modeling clay-2 colors	2 packages
Roll of wax paper	1

Chemicals

Chemicals	Quantity per Class (24 students)
Aluminum metal bars	7
Iron(III) chloride	25.0 g
Concentrated hydrochloric acid	25.0 mL
1.0 M sodium hydrogen carbonate	1.0 L

NOTES

_____

_____

_____

_____

Teacher Preparation

Etching solution: In a fume hood, slowly and carefully, with stirring, add 25.0 mL of concentrated hydrochloric acid (HCl, 12 M) to 100 mL of deionized water. Allow solution to cool and then add 25.0 g of iron(III) chloride hexahydrate (FeCl$_3$•6H$_2$O) with stirring until dissolved. Dilute to 125 mL.

1.0 M Sodium bicarbonate solution—Dissolve 84.0 g of sodium hydrogen carbonate (baking soda, NaHCO$_3$) in 800 mL of distilled water and then adjust the volume to 1.0 L. This solution can be used for neutralizing acid spills in this section and other sections.

Aluminum metal bars—If necessary, cut strips of 8 mm aluminum sheet to pieces 7.5 cm long, one for each group, with a few extras in case students stamp too deeply. You might find this at a hardware store (where they might do the cutting for you). Talk to your Industrial Arts teacher and they may be able to provide the materials for you.

Do **not** use aircraft aluminum. It has magnesium and other metals in it. It does not etch well.

Safety Requirements

- Goggles and apron are required in the laboratory area.

- When using the dies on the aluminum strips this should be done on a surface that cannot crack from the blows of the hammer. Make sure that your lab tables can withstand this.

- The etching solution contains hydrochloric acid and will cause burns if it comes in contact with the skin. Instruct students to use rubber gloves in this procedure.

- Wash arms and hands before leaving the laboratory area.

CHAPTER 8

NOTES

_____

_____

_____

_____

_____

_____

_____

_____

_____

Meeting the Needs of All Students
Differentiated Instruction

Augmentation and Accommodations

LEARNING ISSUE	REFERENCE	AUGMENTATION AND ACCOMMODATIONS
Matching learning styles with kinesthetic, visual and language tasks	*Investigate*	**Accommodations** • Kinesthetic learners, artists and others with an affinity for hands on tasks may appreciate the chance to use their talents during this investigation. The task also requires students to read and follow directions carefully, a role which may fit the talents or comfort zones of others. For some it is an opportunity to actively increase their involvement; for others, the same visual motor tasks may be intimidating. • You may already know your students well enough to predict which ones are well-matched for this section and which are not, or you could survey the class informally to determine who may enjoy playing a greater role and who may need more help. • Arrange groups so that normally quiet students who happen to prefer drawing or stamping and sanding the aluminum can emerge in leadership roles. • Be sure that the group work is structured so that reluctant students get some experience out of their preferred style stamping, sanding or drawing. For example, reluctant students could read the directions and keep the group moving or help rolling out the clay. • Create a classroom climate where student differences are appreciated, where it is safe for students to take risks to try something they may not be good at, and where others will help them. • Be aware that students who do not find a productive role within their group are likely to be off task during this long activity. Structured roles within each group and clear direction that they begin their models.
Making three dimensional drawings	*Investigate*	**Augmentation** • Each student must draw a three dimensional box in their Chem Logs, but many students may not be able to draw this shape. Teach students to draw a box by drawing a horizontal line of about two inches along the bottom of a space for the drawing in their logs. They should then draw two perpendicular lines straight up from the ends of the horizontal line to points along another rule line in their log half way up the space reserved for the drawing. Finish the face of their box by connecting the two perpendicular lines with a second horizontal line. From the two top corners and the right bottom corner, extend three lines of equal length out from the corners at 45o angles. Connect the lines to finish the box. Every student should learn to draw this. • While this activity is in progress, invite one student from each group to meet with you. Teach the students this method and have them return to their groups and teach the others.
Developing vocabulary	*Chem Talk*	**Augmentation** • The *Chem Talk* is rich with new vocabulary words. Some have been highlighted and defined in the *Chem Words* others such as "cold-worked," stamped, anneal and compression have not. • Review strategies such as skipping the word, looking it up in *Chem Words*, and stopping to figure out its meaning from context, which students should use when they encounter unfamiliar words. • Have students make picture representations of the meanings on index cards they can use to practice during any group down time. • Divide the unfamiliar words into essential and enrichment words. Emphasize that all students learn the essential words. Differentiate for students who struggle to learn vocabulary.

LEARNING ISSUE	REFERENCE	AUGMENTATION AND ACCOMMODATIONS
Explaining a series of events Making a flow chart	*Chem Essential Questions*	**Augmentation** • Have students illustrate their explanations using a flow chart to capture each event in sequence. Be sure to clarify that this flow chart will be simpler than the ones they made in the previous section because there are no questions or options, just events in the order they happened. Use this flow chart as a basis for writing a narrative explanation. **Accommodations** • Allow students to explain their flow charts orally.
Writing precise answers to questions	*Chem To Go*	**Augmentation** • Teach students to use a part of the question to begin their answer. Using this strategy will help them think more carefully about what the question asks.
Understanding mathematical symbols	*Chem to Go*	**Augmentation** • Be sure all students understand the greater than and less than symbols, one of which is used in Question 5.
Writing word equations	*Chem to Go*	**Accommodation** • Refer students to the *Chem Talk* to see a model of an equation similar to the one in which magnesium and zinc exchange ions.

Strategies for Students with Limited English Language Proficiency

LEARNING ISSUE	REFERENCE	AUGMENTATIONS
Background knowledge	*What Do You Think?*	The opening illustration provides a storyline for this activity and could generate an introductory discussion. Examples of the multiple meanings of the word *"serial"* will help build background knowledge and provide more meaning.
Vocabulary	*Investigate*	Students may benefit from working in small groups or partners. Make sure students understand the term *"die"* in this context. Also explain the plural of the noun *"dies."* Check for understanding of the term *"ground off"* as this may be a new term when the word is used as a derivative of the word *"grind."* In Part B, the word *"etching"* may be unfamiliar. The word *"grit"* may be a new term as is the plural form *"grits."* The word *"discern"* might be unfamiliar.
Background knowledge Vocabulary Comprehending text	*Chem Talk*	Check for understanding of bold type words. Refer students to sidebar material for further explanations of the isolated words. Students may require help with the pronunciation of the word *"malleable."* The word *"deformation"* provides an example of how the prefix *"de"* can alter a word's meaning.
Background knowledge	*What Do You Think Now?*	Students may need an explanation of the word *"critiquing"* and other forms of the word (*critique, criticize, etc*).
Background knowledge Vocabulary Comprehending text	*Chem Essential Questions*	In the *How do you know?* section the word *"retrieved"* may not be in the students' expressive vocabulary.
Comprehension Vocabulary	*Chem to Go*	The word *"obscured"* may not be part of the students' expressive vocabulary. The phrase *"link the evidence"* may be unclear to some students and may require some explanation.
Application Comprehension	*Inquiring Further*	The phrase *"serial number restoration"* may require some explanation. Reference to earlier meanings of serial will reinforce the concept. Students may need assistance on resources to conduct this research. Point out how the prefix *"non"* alters word meaning in such words as *"nonmetallic"* for English language development.

CHAPTER 8

Section 7
Teaching Suggestions and Sample Answers

What Do You See?

The *What Do You See?* illustration is meant to engage students' interest and imagination. Additionally, you can use the illustration to elicit information about student's prior knowledge. Students' reactions will vary, and all reactions are to be valued. This is not the time to make judgments about their responses, although you might wish to draw out additional information from students if you sense that it will lead to an important class discussion.

What Do You Think?

Student responses will vary, but they may think that the atoms move out of the way to allow the imprint to be produced or they may think that the atoms compress to form an alloy-type metal. Another response might be that the atoms will be closer together since they may think, based on what they know about gases, that the atoms have a large amount of empty space between them. Students' illustrations will also vary.

A CHEMIST'S RESPONSE
What Do You Think?

The atoms in the surface of a metal bar are distorted by being "stamped" with a number or letter with a die. The actual surface evidence of the "stamp" can be filed off, but the underlying atoms still have the impression of the "stamp."

An accurate student picture would show a regular array of metal atoms, in columns and rows, with the distortions from the force of the "stamp" evident in the spacing of atoms.

Investigate

To save time, materials, and frustration, make examples of badly and well-stamped metal to show students. Hitting the die too hard or too softly will make indentations difficult to later visualize through etching.

Part A: Stamping a Serial Number

1. _____

The dimensions provided in the *Student Edition* are only a suggestion. Other dimensions for the aluminum metal will work.

If necessary, cut strips of 8 mm aluminum sheet to pieces 7.5 cm long, one for each group, with a few extras in case students stamp too deeply. Get the sheet at a hardware store and they might also do the cutting for you. Talk to your Industrial Arts teacher and they may be able to provide the materials for you.

Do **not** use aircraft aluminum. It has magnesium and other metals in it. It does not etch well.

STUDENTS' PRIOR CONCEPTIONS

The two key areas to focus on in this section are how metals' microscopic crystalline structure allows serial-number etching to work and single-replacement oxidation-reduction reactions, the latter being a continuing topic from the two previous activities.

1. *When you hit or scrape a piece of metal, only the surface atoms are affected.*

Students will likely believe that only the area of the metal sample that shows macroscopic observable effects after stamping were affected by the stamps. Thus they will infer that once the stamped area of the metal is removed by grinding, it will be impossible to determine what the serial number was. This inference is logical, of course, because students have usually not had an experience where they have seen evidence that metals are affected beyond the area where the effects of a stressor can be visually observed. In fact, however, the metal layers below the evidently stressed area are affected when the metal surface is scraped or hit. Evidence for these effects includes the faster rate of reaction of the area of the metal below the stressed area compared with other areas of the metal in a single-replacement reaction with a suitable ionic solution. This phenomenon is observed in serial-number etching.

In addition, the clay modeling section provides more evidence that layers far below the surface are compressed during stamping. Both of these sections will directly address the original misconception, and the teacher can draw students' attention to the cause and effect relationship between the surface stamping and the evidence of deeper effects in both the metal and the clay model.

2. *Strength and concentration mean the same thing.*

In this activity, as a caution, students are told that the acid they are using is fairly concentrated acid. Concentration is often interpreted as strength by students, probably because the two terms are used interchangeably in many everyday contexts, particularly in advertising for consumer products. Also, students have been warned about the dangers of acids and "acid" is a term that is used in everyday language to refer to any dangerous, reactive solution, whether it is actually dangerous or not.

In chemistry, the terms strength and concentration have distinct meanings. Concentration refers to the ratio of solute (dissolved substance) particles to solvent (dissolving medium) particles in the solution, while strength means relative ability to react in a reaction of interest. As a result of their confusion of these two words, students may believe that a concentrated solution of hydrochloric acid is "stronger" or more reactive with uncombined metals then an ionic solution containing a metal ion that is lower on the activity series than hydrogen. The preceding statement is not correct, because metal ions below hydrogen on the activity series will react with more uncombined metals than will acids, which contain hydrogen ions. For example, a dilute solution of silver ions will react with copper metal in a single-replacement reaction, but concentrated hydrochloric acid will not react with copper metal, because silver ions can oxidize copper but hydrogen ions can not. Note that for metal ions, their reactivity, or ability to be reduced in a single-replacement reaction, decreases as one proceeds from top to bottom on the activity series. This is the opposite of the reactivity (ability to be oxidized) of uncombined metals, which increases as one proceeds down the table. To help students to understand this distinction, it is helpful to discuss the two terms explicitly and to discuss the example described above.

2.

Show students examples and make sure they don't stamp metal too deeply. To help students gain practice, give them a practice piece of metal to get the idea of how deeply to stamp it.

3.a)

Eight numbers is not required. Two or three numbers or letters will enable the students to work with the aluminum and understand the techniques. If you have access to letter (rather than number) dies, it's fun to have students write secret messages.

4.a)

This is optional. If the aluminum bars are too thick, the students will not see any impression on the back of the aluminum bar. Make sure you get the expensive dies back before students leave the class.

5.

Students should write the number, letters, or combinations on the back of the aluminum piece before turning it in for grinding.

6.

Care must be taken in grinding the numbers off. If you go too deep, the numbers cannot be regenerated. Use the minimum grinding to visually remove the evidence of numbers and letters. Your Industrial Arts teacher may be able to help you.

INSTRUCTIONS FOR TEACHER ON GRINDING

1. There are two important reasons the teacher should do this, not the students: first, students will gouge the metal and that will hold acid – you need the surface to be as smooth as possible. Second, it takes too much class time and there will be a shortage of equipment.

2. Clamp or tape the metal to a flat surface. Move the grinding wheel evenly back and forth across the surface until the serial number is visually removed but go no further. Do not press down, let the tool do the work, because if you press down, you'll get "potholes."

Part B: Etching to Recover Serial Numbers

1.a)

Student sketches, ideally, will show nothing.

2.

Have students try to sand the metal surface as smoothly as possible. This is so the acid won't pool and cause problems in etching.

Make sure the students don't touch the surface of the metal after sanding it because that will leave oils on the surface which will hinder the action of the acid.

3.a)

Students may see nothing with a hand lens but some may see the beginnings of the serial number reappearance.

2. Before proceeding consider what will happen if you hit the die too hard. If you hit the die too hard it will take a long time to obliterate the number. If you hit the die too softly, it will not penetrate far enough under the metal's surface to allow the number to be restored later. Your instructor may have you practice stamping a scrap piece of aluminum a few times.

3. Using a hammer and dies, carefully stamp eight different numbers into the aluminum bar to create a serial number like the one in the diagram. Do not use the same number more than twice. Also, make sure to hit the die evenly.

 a) Important: Record the serial number you have stamped and its position on the aluminum bar in your *Active Chemistry* log because you may not remember these things exactly later on.

SPM

65478901

4. In the upper left corner, stamp your initials or your group's identification number by hitting it extremely hard with the hammer. Look at the back side of the metal where you put your initials. What do you see? Try to explain why this has happened.

 a) Record your observations and your answers in your *Active Chemistry* log.

5. Record the number or combination of letters written on the back of your piece of aluminum using a black marker. This number is there for your instructor to match and for you to know which side formerly had the serial number!

6. Turn your sample in to your teacher so that the serial numbers can be ground off.

Part B: Etching to Recover Serial Numbers

1. Examine the front of the aluminum piece under a hand lens or stereoscope.

 a) Sketch your observations in your *Active Chemistry* log.

2. You must first prepare the surface for the *etching* process (a process of reproducing an engraving on the surface of a metal plate with acids) by sanding the surface until it is perfectly smooth. Any rough surface will cause the powerful etching solutions to pool, giving you poor results. Sand the surface first using 100-grit sandpaper, followed by 150-grit, and finally 220-grit, wiping the surface with a damp towel between each of the grits. Sand the bar in an up and down motion as shown in the diagram.

3. Again examine the front of the aluminum piece under a hand lens or stereoscope. Even at this early stage, you may start to see the beginnings of a serial number.

 a) Sketch your observations in your *Active Chemistry* log.

Be very careful when using the hammer. Strike the dies gently and keep your fingers out of the way.

Report any spills of the etching solution to your teacher immediately.

CHAPTER 8

4.

Other alcohols, such as methanol or isopropyl alcohol (rubbing alcohol) will work as well as ethanol.

5.

Remember that etching solution is an acid. Caution students not to get this on hands. Also, the FeCl₃ will stain clothing and possibly skin.

6.

When students apply etching solution, make sure they give it time (about 2 minutes) to react before making another application.

7.

This part is deceiving – the process of restoration can take 30-40 minutes because of the many applications of etching solution required. 10-20 applications may be needed.

Sometimes it's easier to see the serial number through the solution. The etching solution reacts faster where the metal has been stamped, and more bubbles form there. Look at it through a magnifying glass to help see the number.

It's okay to wipe off previous applications before applying new etching solution. In fact, this may help because old (reacted) solution dilutes the new application.

8.

Remind students to dip metal in neutralization solution before they return it to you at end of class.

CSI Chemistry

4. Using gloves, wipe the metal thoroughly with a cotton ball soaked in ethanol. This removes all of the oils from the surface. Oil and the aqueous solutions you'll use do not mix. A layer of oil will keep the etching solution from reacting with the surface of the metal evenly, so it is very important to keep the surface oil free.

5. Still using gloves (keep them on throughout the first portion of this investigation), use a cotton ball to evenly apply the etching solution of hydrochloric acid and iron (III) chloride.

6. Repeat *Step 5* every two minutes.

7. This process is not quick, so be patient. While working on the applications (which may take up to 40 minutes), begin the next portion of the laboratory investigation. Occasionally you may want to look at the metal with a hand lens or under the stereoscope to see what is happening. Be sure that only the gloved person uses the etching solution and touches the bar. The gloved person should not touch the material in the next portion of the lab.

8. When you are finished, rinse the bar in a solution of sodium bicarbonate.

⚠️ a) Sketch your observations in your *Active Chemistry* log.

⚠️ b) What happened? Were you able to discern the serial numbers? How long did it take? Record your answers in your *Active Chemistry* log.

⚠️ c) A metal is made of atoms packed in a regular repeating pattern, called a lattice. Based on the figure and your observations,

⚠️ **Wear protective gloves when handling chemicals hat can burn skin.**

The etching solution contains a concentrated strong acid, so you must be careful not to get any on your skin or clothing.

what do you think happened to the atoms when you hit the die to create a serial number? What do you think the solution did to restore the serial number?

Dispose of corrosive substances as directed by your teacher. Clean up your workstation.

Part C: Making a Model

1. Obtain two different colored blocks of modeling clay. Working on a piece of wax paper, cut 20 thin layers, approximately 1 mm thick (about the thickness of a penny), from the rectangular end of each block of clay. Each of these layers will represent a layer of metal atoms in the sample.

2. Using 10 layers of each color, create two stacks of alternating colors.

3. Take the wooden dowel and carefully roll out each stack so that it is about ¾ of its original thickness. Carefully trim the edges so that you can see each layer and it is rectangular again.

8.b)

It is important to reassure students that a full recovery is often not possible, but that partial recovery of a serial number is quite useful and realistic in forensic chemistry. It may take 20-40 minutes.

8.c)

Student answers will vary. The die distorts the crystal lattice of the metal and the site of the distortions are more easily "attacked" by the etching solution. Reaction is faster at these sites.

Part C: Making a Model

1.

When cutting the polymer modeling clay, have students make sure the blade is as vertical as possible to cut slices evenly. Instruct students that layers need to be as uniform (horizontal) as possible.

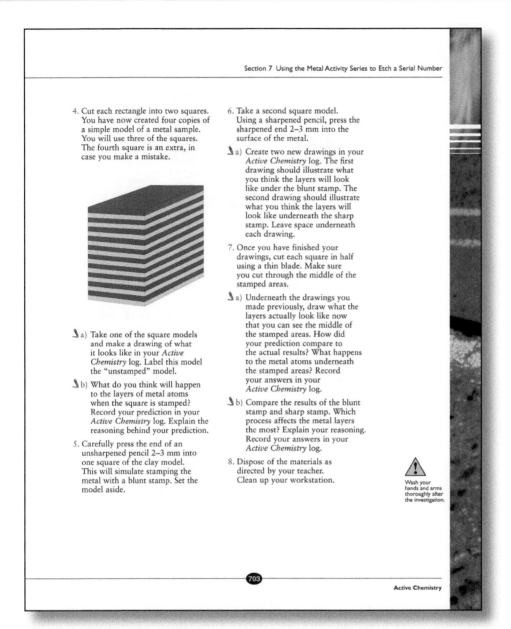

4. Cut each rectangle into two squares. You have now created four copies of a simple model of a metal sample. You will use three of the squares. The fourth square is an extra, in case you make a mistake.

a) Take one of the square models and make a drawing of what it looks like in your *Active Chemistry* log. Label this model the "unstamped" model.

b) What do you think will happen to the layers of metal atoms when the square is stamped? Record your prediction in your *Active Chemistry* log. Explain the reasoning behind your prediction.

5. Carefully press the end of an unsharpened pencil 2–3 mm into one square of the clay model. This will simulate stamping the metal with a blunt stamp. Set the model aside.

6. Take a second square model. Using a sharpened pencil, press the sharpened end 2–3 mm into the surface of the metal.

a) Create two new drawings in your *Active Chemistry* log. The first drawing should illustrate what you think the layers will look like under the blunt stamp. The second drawing should illustrate what you think the layers will look like underneath the sharp stamp. Leave space underneath each drawing.

7. Once you have finished your drawings, cut each square in half using a thin blade. Make sure you cut through the middle of the stamped areas.

a) Underneath the drawings you made previously, draw what the layers actually look like now that you can see the middle of the stamped areas. How did your prediction compare to the actual results? What happens to the metal atoms underneath the stamped areas? Record your answers in your *Active Chemistry* log.

b) Compare the results of the blunt stamp and sharp stamp. Which process affects the metal layers the most? Explain your reasoning. Record your answers in your *Active Chemistry* log.

8. Dispose of the materials as directed by your teacher. Clean up your workstation.

⚠ Wash your hands and arms thoroughly after the investigation.

703

Active Chemistry

students not to stamp all the way through the modeling clay, but only 2-3 mm.

6.a)

It may be helpful to put a mark on the pencils 3 mm from the end to help the students avoid "over-stamping" the clay.

If you want to make the point that you cannot recover engraving, but only recover stamping, have students try engraving clay with pencil tip (this just removes clay, does not alter lower layers, which they will discover when they make cross section).

7.

Again, when cutting polymer modeling clay after stamping, be careful to make even, clean slices with a vertical blade.

7.a)

Student answers will vary depending on what they see and what they predicted.

The crystal lattice of the metal atoms under the stamp is distorted.

7.b)

The blunt stamps affect the metal layers the most.

2.

The two stacks should be as nearly identical as possible and about 20 mm high (a little more than $\frac{3}{4}$ inch).

3.

When rolling it, make sure the students stop when thickness is $\frac{3}{4}$ original or about 15 mm (about $\frac{5}{8}$ inch). If rolled too thinly, students won't be able to see layers.

4.

Use a sharp blade for cutting the rectangles to avoid flattening the clay down.

4.b)

Student answers will vary. Many will think that the layers of clay will be pushed down uniformly.

5.

To simulate blunt and sharp objects, use unsharpened and sharpened pencils. Instruct

Chem Talk

The discussion reminds students of the physical properties of metals, such as, ductility, malleability, etc. From this it leads them through a nano scale of the metal substance and shows them that the atoms are arranged in a certain pattern and will have some natural defects. When the metal is hit with a die it causes a shaped deformation and it is this characteristic that we take advantage in recovering the lost serial number. They are using the single-replacement reaction when they treat aluminum metal with a solution of iron(III) chloride which is dissolved in concentrated hydrochloric acid.

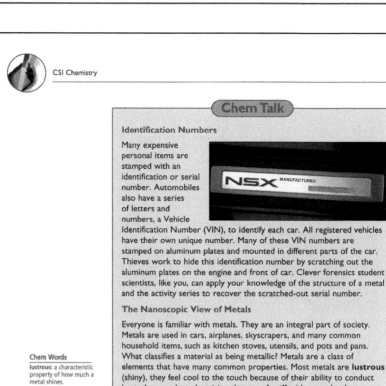

CSI Chemistry

Chem Talk

Identification Numbers

Many expensive personal items are stamped with an identification or serial number. Automobiles also have a series of letters and numbers, a Vehicle Identification Number (VIN), to identify each car. All registered vehicles have their own unique number. Many of these VIN numbers are stamped on aluminum plates and mounted in different parts of the car. Thieves work to hide this identification number by scratching out the aluminum plates on the engine and front of car. Clever forensics student scientists, like you, can apply your knowledge of the structure of a metal and the activity series to recover the scratched-out serial number.

The Nanoscopic View of Metals

Everyone is familiar with metals. They are an integral part of society. Metals are used in cars, airplanes, skyscrapers, and many common household items, such as kitchen stoves, utensils, and pots and pans. What classifies a material as being metallic? Metals are a class of elements that have many common properties. Most metals are **lustrous** (shiny), they feel cool to the touch because of their ability to conduct heat, they conduct electricity, they are **ductile** (they can be drawn into wires), and they are **malleable** (they can be hammered into thin sheets). And as you learned earlier, metals are located on the left side of the stair-step line in the periodic table of the elements.

But why does serial-number etching work? To understand this you need to take a much closer look at the metal, zooming in on its nanoscopic structure. In a metal, the atoms are arranged in tiny regions called **grains**. These grains range in size from 0.01 mm to 0.1 mm.

Chem Words

lustrous: a characteristic property of how much a metal shines.

ductile: a characteristic property of how easy it is to pull metal into the form of a wire.

malleable: a characteristic property of how easy it is to flatten a piece of metal.

grain: a small piece of metal that shows how the atoms are arranged.

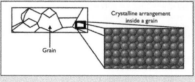

Crystalline arrangement inside a grain

Grain

Within each grain, the metal's atoms are arranged in an orderly or crystalline arrangement. Within the crystalline structure of the grain, however, there are tiny irregularities called **dislocations**.

When a metal is bent repeatedly, the dislocation moves inside the crystal creating other dislocations. This increases the stress inside the metal until the metal becomes brittle and breaks. You can try this yourself by bending a paper clip or a coat hanger back and forth numerous times. Eventually, the paper clip or the coat hanger will break. If you were to heat the metal and allow it to cool slowly, the metal will anneal, that is, the metal atoms will rearrange themselves to relieve the stress and the metal will be malleable (bendable) again. High temperatures and slow cooling are needed for annealing to give the metal atoms sufficient energy to move and rearrange.

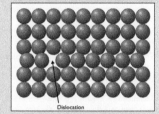

Dislocation

The Chemistry behind Serial Numbers in Metals

Serial numbers are usually stamped into metal with hard, blunt metal dies. When this is done at a fairly low temperature, such as room temperature, the metal is said to be "cold-worked" or "work-hardened." The die strikes the surface of the metal with a strong force, causing the die to penetrate the metal. The atoms just below the surface of the metal undergo a **plastic** (permanent) **deformation**. This creates a huge number of dislocations in the metal beneath the surface of the stamp. As you saw in your model, the layers of the clay were compressed directly underneath the stamped area, with the blunt "stamp" compressing more area than the sharp "stamp." The compression in your clay model is an example of plastic deformation. The further away from the stamp, the less compressed the layers were.

The same kind of physical deformation happens in the metal when it is stamped. In metals there are grains instead of layers like in the clay. The dislocations force the electrons of the atoms in the stamped grains to get closer together. This creates a lot of stress in the crystalline structure of the grain and hardens the material in that region.

Chem Words

dislocations: atoms misplaced in a crystalline structure especially in metals.

plastic deformation: a permanent dislocation of atoms in an area of a metal that has been struck with a strong force.

CHAPTER 8

705

Active Chemistry

CSI CHEMISTRY

Checking Up

1.

A crystalline structure of a solid metal refers to the regular arrangement or the packing of atoms.

2.

Dislocations are tiny irregularities in the regular crystalline structure of the grain.

3.

The etching reaction is a single-replacement chemical reaction.

What Do You Think Now?

Have your class return to the *What Do You See?* illustration and the *What Do You Think?* questions at the beginning of the section. It will be instructional to review their earlier answers.

CSI Chemistry

In these stressed areas, some of the energy used to make the deformation is stored in the stressed (stamped) grains. This stored energy gives the stressed (stamped) grain a higher energy than the unstamped grains. As a result, when an etching solution is applied to the surface, the stamped areas react faster than the unaltered metal. The products of this reaction have a different appearance than does the unreacted metal, so the serial number reappears as impressions, made of the reaction products, in the metal.

The **etching** method works by using single-replacement chemical reactions. As you learned in *Section 6*, a single-replacement reaction is a type of oxidation-reduction reaction. The etching solution used for aluminum was made of hydrochloric acid and iron (III) chloride. Aluminum (Al), being higher on the activity series than iron and hydrogen, will donate some electrons to the iron (III) ions and the hydrogen ions in the etching solution. Since the iron (III) ions and the hydrogen ions are gaining electrons from the aluminum, they are being reduced and the aluminum is being oxidized (see equations below). This results in the formation of iron metal atoms, hydrogen gas, and aluminum ions. Remember, the stamped aluminum atoms have a higher energy than the unstamped atoms, so the stamped atoms will react faster with the two compounds than the unstamped aluminum atoms.

Reaction 1 from the etching solution
$$Al_{(s)} + Fe^{3+}_{(aq)} \rightarrow Al^{3+}_{(aq)} + Fe_{(s)}$$

Reaction 2 from the etching solution
$$2Al_{(s)} + 6H^+_{(aq)} \rightarrow 2Al^{3+}_{(aq)} + 3H_{2(g)}$$

If you wanted to etch a metal other than aluminum, such as iron, you would need to consult the activity series for an appropriate replacement for the iron (III) chloride solution.

Chem Words

etching: the removal of metal atoms from a metallic surface using a corrosive liquid.

Checking Up

1. What is a crystalline structure?
2. What are dislocations in a crystalline structure?
3. What type of reaction is the etching reaction?

What Do You Think Now?

At the beginning of this section you were asked the following:

• What do you think happens to the atoms in a piece of metal when a serial number is stamped into the metal?

• Without referencing any sources, draw a picture to illustrate your idea.

Look back at your answers. Write a paragraph critiquing your original response. Comment on what was correct, what was incorrect, and how you would change your answers and diagram now that you've completed the lab.

706

Active Chemistry

Chem Essential Questions
What does it mean?

MACRO — Sanding the aluminum bar removed the scratches left in the aluminum from the grinder and made the surface very smooth. Etching produced a reaction with bubbles, which allowed the original stamped letters/numbers to be seen.

NANO — The single-replacement reaction which took place during etching was the replacement of aluminum atoms with iron atoms.

SYMBOLIC —

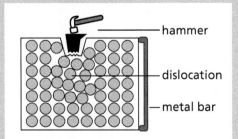

hammer — dislocation — metal bar

Chem Essential Questions

What does it mean?

Chemistry explains a *macroscopic* phenomenon (what you observe) with a description of what happens at the *nanoscopic* level (atoms and molecules) using *symbolic* structures as a way to communicate. Complete the chart below in your *Active Chemistry* log.

MACRO	NANO	SYMBOLIC
Explain what events took place at the macroscopic level when you sanded, etched, and reconstructed the serial numbers.	What oxidation-reduction reaction was able to reconstruct the serial numbers?	Draw a structure for the metal and the serial-number etching to explain why you were able to retrieve the numbers once they were "gone."

How do you know?

What evidence do you have from this section that the serial numbers can still be retrieved after they have been sanded off the metal?

Why do you believe?

In tracking stolen cars, the police often use the serial numbers to identify the vehicles. What other items can be tracked using serial numbers etched in metal?

Why should you care?

How can you increase the interest in your crime-scene drama by adding a serial-number component?

Reflecting on the Section and the Challenge

Part of the problem you are facing in creating a crime scene is to understand how to observe something that is not initially visible. To restore an obliterated serial number, you used knowledge developed from a model and from reading about the microscopic structure of metals, combined with knowledge about the metal activity series from the last section. There are many different metals and you should begin thinking of ways to etch different metal samples. You can now also use the concepts that you have learned to describe the chemistry behind the technique.

Chem to Go

1. Describe two ways that the original serial number could be obscured so that the etching method would not be useful to reveal the serial number. Use your model to explain why it would keep the etching process from working.

2. Based on what you learned in the previous section on the activity series, why is iron (III) chloride used to etch aluminum instead of magnesium chloride?

3. Based on the activity series, what other metals could be etched by a hydrochloric acid and iron (III) chloride mixture?

 707

Active Chemistry

How do you know?

In this section, the serial numbers were ground away until they were no longer visible. By carefully sanding the aluminum bar until it was smooth, and then etching the surface, the serial numbers became visible again.

Why do you believe?

In addition to stolen cars, police can trace other stolen property, such as computers, televisions, and audio equipment, by means of serial numbers.

Why should you care?

Student answers will vary. Different metals will require different etching solutions and this will allow students to show their knowledge of chemistry.

Reflecting on the Section and the Challenge

This section ties together with *Section 6*. Understanding metal activity and crystalline structure will help students being able to recover a serial number that supposedly has been removed. This can play an important part in their crime scene.

Chem to Go

1.

Stamping over the serial number with new numbers before filing off the serial number, or grinding the metal below the serial number down so far that all of the layers deformed by the stamp were removed would prevent the serial number from being restored.

Stamping over the serial number would make it impossible to tell what the original numbers were because both the old and new numbers would appear during etching. Grinding the metal down far enough would remove all of the higher energy atoms that react faster and appear as the serial number during etching.

2.

The reaction between aluminum and magnesium chloride will not occur because aluminum is less reactive than magnesium. However, aluminum is more reactive than iron, so this reaction will take place creating iron and aluminum chloride.

3.

Any metal which is higher than iron in the activity series. For example, magnesium or zinc.

CHAPTER 8

4.

The bubbling results from the oxidation reaction of aluminum, specifically the production of hydrogen gas.

$$2Al + 6H^+ \rightarrow 2Al^{3+} + 3H_2$$

5.

$Mg > Al > Zn > Fe > Pb > H^+ > Cu > Hg > Ag.$

a) Magnesium is the most active of these metals.

b) Silver is the least active of these metals.

c) $Mg_{(s)} + Zn^{2+}_{(aq)} \rightarrow Mg^{2+}_{(aq)} + Zn_{(s)}$

d) Zn^{2+}, Sn^{2+}
 or anything below Al in the Metal Activity Series.

6.

a) zinc + sodium nitrate $\rightarrow$ no reaction

b) zinc + silver nitrate $\rightarrow$ silver + zinc nitrate

c) tin + zinc nitrate $\rightarrow$ no reaction

7.

Preparing for the Chapter Challenge

Student answers will vary. The students have a strong background in metal activity series and now understand that a serial number that is imprinted with a die is better than scratching a serial number on a piece of metal. They also know how to recover a serial number that has been sanded down. Metal chemistry can certainly play an important part in their crime scene.

CSI Chemistry

4. Why did the etching solution bubble? Explain.
   (Hint: You can start to explain by writing the reaction that occurs.)

5. A more complete activity series is
   $Mg > Al > Zn > Fe > Pb > H > Cu > Hg > Ag.$
   Answer the following questions using this information.

   a) Which is the most active of these metals?

   b) Which is the least active of the metals?

   c) If a magnesium ion has a +2 charge and a zinc ion has a +2 charge, write the reaction that occurs spontaneously between them when one is a metal and the other is an ion. Be sure to write the aqueous or solid information in parentheses.

   d) Name two other metal ion solutions, besides Fe^{3+} (which you used), that could be used to restore a serial number in aluminum.

6. Complete the word equations for the following reactions. If a reaction does not occur, write "N.R."

   a) zinc + sodium nitrate →

   b) zinc + silver nitrate →

   c) tin + zinc nitrate →

7. *Preparing for the Chapter Challenge*

   Using the chemistry and techniques in this chapter, you must create a crime scene, analyze the evidence, and link the evidence so that it implicates one of the four suspects. Write a paragraph describing how you can use what you learned in this section to analyze a metal piece of evidence. In addition, write a paragraph that describes how you can link that piece of evidence to one of your characters.

Inquiring Further

1. Etching other metals

Pick a common metal other than aluminum, such as iron or copper. Using the activity series, predict what might be a good reagent to use with that metal. Research serial-number etching further to determine a method for etching the metal you select. Under the supervision of an adult, test the method.

2. Restoring serial numbers on nonmetallic materials

Research serial-number restoration methods that are used on nonmetallic materials. Begin by reading the article titled, *A Compilation of Techniques and Chemical Formulae used in the Restoration of Obliterated Markings*, by Ernest E. Massiah, in the *AFTE Journal*, volume 8, number 2, 1976. Under the supervision of an adult, experiment with one of the methods you read about.

Inquiring Further

1. Etching other metals

Check student procedures for safety and workability. If they select a metal too low in the Metal Activity Series, the number of types of metal ions to use is diminished.

2. Restoring serial numbers on nonmetallic materials

Check student procedures for safety and workability.

SECTION 7 – QUIZ

8-7a	**Blackline Master**

1. Silicon is a bright, shiny element that is brittle and conducts heat and electricity poorly. Would you classify silicon as a metal, a nonmetal, or a metalloid? Explain.

2. What are dislocations and how do they affect the malleability of a metal? Why does a paper clip break when you repeatedly bend it back and forth?

3. In the following serial-number recovery reaction what is being oxidized and what is being reduced? Why are you using a Fe^{3+} solution?

   $$Al + Fe^{3+} \longrightarrow Al^{3+} + Fe$$

4. Which reaction below will NOT occur?

   a) $2Na + Ca^{2+} \longrightarrow 2Na^+ + Ca$

   b) $Ca + Cu^{2+} \longrightarrow Ca^{2+} + Cu$

   c) $3Mg + 2Al^{3+} \longrightarrow 3Mg^{2+} + 2Al$

SECTION 7 – QUIZ ANSWERS

❶ Silicon is classified as a metalloid. It is brittle and nonconductive like nonmetals, but it is bright and shiny like metals.

❷ Dislocations are imperfections in the crystalline structure of metals. When a metal is bent, a dislocation is created in its crystalline structure. As you bend the metal more and more of these imperfections are created, making it more difficult for the metal atoms to move. Eventually they can no longer move and the metal breaks.

❸ Al is being oxidized. It is losing electrons and becoming more positive. Fe^{3+} is being reduced. Iron is below aluminum on the activity series and so the aluminum is replacing the iron in the solution.

❹ a) $2Na + Ca^{2+} \longrightarrow 2Na^+ + Ca$

CHAPTER 8

NOTES

_____

_____

_____

_____

_____

_____

_____

_____

_____

_____

SECTION 8
Paper Chromatography: Separating Molecules

Section Overview

In the first part of the investigation, students perform a separation of black marker dye. In the second, they create a model of the separation process seen in chromatography using a felt board and poker chips to represent the paper and the ink dyes. Finally, students create a standard chromatogram of different black inks and learn how to identify a particular brand of ink from an unknown sample.

Background Information

Intermolecular Attractions

All particles experience intermolecular forces or attractions as a result of the electrical attraction between the particles. The degree of polarity determines the level of intermolecular attractions between particles. **Polar** molecules contain localized areas of positive and negative charge as a result of the unequal distribution of electrons in the bonds and also from the asymmetric arrangement of atoms in the particle. The most extreme case of polarity is an ionic compound, where fully charged ions exist. At the other end of the spectrum are completely **non-polar** substances, where the valence electrons are distributed within the molecule symmetrically, so that there are no areas that have a permanent partial electrical charge. Between these two extremes are particles with a valence electron distribution such that some atoms or regions within the molecule have a fractional negative charge and others have a fractional positive charge. The overall charge of such polar compounds is zero, just as ionic compounds are neutral, because the positive and negative regions cancel each other out. Thus, substances exist along a continuum of polarity from ionic at the most polar end to entirely nonpolar at the least polar end, with substances of varying degrees of polarity in between.

Intermolecular forces, also know as **van der Waals** forces (named after Dutch physicist J.D. van der Waals), are of two types. The first type is a **dipole-dipole** attraction. Polar particles experience significant attraction to other polar particles. These dipole-dipole attractions result from the attraction of the negative region of one particle with the positive region of another particle. Polar (and ionic) substances thus generally mix with each other readily because of these attractions. Polar particles do not experience this same type of attraction with non-polar substances because the non-polar particles do not have charged regions. As a result, polar substances generally will not mix with non-polar substances. The polar substances' particles are strongly attracted to each other so they remain together, physically excluding non-polar particles. This explains the common observation that water (a very polar substance) and oil (a non-polar substance) do not mix.

A particular kind of dipole-dipole interaction is known as **hydrogen bonding**. In hydrogen bonding, very polar particles that contain a hydrogen atom bonded to either a nitrogen (N—H), an oxygen (O—H), or a fluorine (F—H) atom form **hydrogen bonds** with other such particles. Hydrogen bonds are not real bonds (covalent or ionic) but are the strongest intermolecular attractions, much stronger than other intermolecular forces. Water is an important example of a substance that forms hydrogen bonds with other substances, as well as with itself.

The second type of van der Waals force is a weaker, transient force evident in all particles. These intermolecular forces are often called **London dispersion forces,** or simply, dispersion forces. They result from the unequal distribution of surface electrons that exist between two adjacent molecules or atoms. Dispersion forces are directly related to surface area and thus, to a particle's size. Larger particles experience larger dispersion forces than do smaller particles.

Van der Waals forces have an effect on the separating ability observed in paper chromatography. The degree of polarity, and, to a far lesser extent, the size, of the particles in the components of a mixture determine how "fast" the molecules will travel. The actual rate of travel is due to a complex interaction of the molecules, the mobile phase, and the stationary phase.

Theory of Paper Chromatography

Chromatography is the collective term for a range of laboratory techniques for the separation and analysis of complex mixtures. Chromatography takes advantage of the attraction that each substance has for the particles of other substances. Each component in a mixture interacts with a minimum of two other substances during chromatographic separation. One of these is the stationary phase and the other is the mobile phase. The choice of materials used as the mobile phase and the stationary phase are very important because they determine how well a mixture will be separated. There needs to be a significant difference in the components' interactions with at least one of the chromatographic phases in order for the components to be separated, which is the ultimate goal of chromatography. If the phases do interact differently with each component of the mixture, then each component will travel at a different rate over the stationary phase. In addition, the mobile and stationary phases are interacting with each other and these interactions can play an important role in the separation.

The sum of a component's interactions with the mobile phase and with the stationary phase plays a large role in determining the rate of travel of the component in the stationary phase. If a component has strong attractions for the stationary phase and little attraction for the mobile phase, it travels slowly and will thus be close to the original starting spot when the chromatogram is removed from the mobile phase. This slow movement corresponds to a low R_f value (~0).

$$R_f = \frac{\text{Distance (cm) compound traveled}}{\text{Distance (cm) mobile phase traveled}}$$

On the other hand, if a component has little attraction for the stationary phase but is very attracted to the mobile phase, it will travel quickly in the mobile phase and will thus be near or at the mobile front when the chromatogram is removed. The fast rate of travel results in a high R_f value (near 1.0). Other combinations of attractions to the two phases result in intermediate distances traveled from the original spot.

In the section, this theory is presented to students in slightly simplified form. In order to facilitate understanding and avoid confusion, the interactions between the two phases are not discussed. Rather, the role of both phases in interacting with the mixture components is explored and explained. Note that the model that students build to explore intermolecular attractions in chromatography only approximates the stationary phase interactions with the component. While this is a significant limitation, the model is a useful one for understanding the predominant force at work in the method.

Other Types of Chromatography

This section centers on paper chromatography, the simplest example of chromatographic separation methods. Paper chromatography is most commonly used as it is here, to separate a mixture of colored dyes. There are several other types of chromatography, including gas, high-performance liquid, and thin-layer chromatography. All of them share a common method of separation—the dissolving of a mixture in a gas or liquid substance referred to as the mobile phase, followed by the distribution of the components of the mixture over another, immobile substance, which is known as the stationary phase. All forms of chromatography rely upon the different levels of interactions of each mixture component with the mobile and stationary phases to effect the separation.

Gas chromatography (GC) is a fast and precise chromatographic method useful for a wide variety of separations, including forensic analyses of liquid and solid evidence. Such analyses permit the identification of samples of materials like paint chips, fibers, and plastics, which are often useful in investigations. In this method, the mobile phase is gaseous, and it travels through a fine glass tube containing a liquid stationary phase. The glass tube is contained within an instrument called, predictably, a gas chromatograph. The mixture to be analyzed is injected via syringe into one end of the glass tube, where it is heated to vaporize it. The mobile gas phase flows through the tube, carrying the vaporized mixture components over the stationary phase at different rates depending on their attraction to the mobile and stationary phases. As the components emerge from the tube, they are ignited by a detector, which sends an electrical signal. The signal is recorded on a piece of paper by the chromatograph, which keeps a continuous record of the signals received throughout the mixture's separation. This written record, the chromatogram, is then analyzed by comparison with chromatograms of known substances and mixtures to determine the composition and the relative amounts of component in the mixture. A sample chromatogram is shown below.

High-performance liquid chromatography (HPLC) is also a fast method of analysis. Because HPLC is conducted at room temperature, it is often chosen when the mixture to be separated and analyzed contains components that are heat-sensitive and thus will not survive analysis by gas chromatography, as is often true of explosives and street drugs. In this method, the mixture is dissolved in a liquid mobile phase, which is pumped through a column containing a solid stationary phase. Because different components will travel

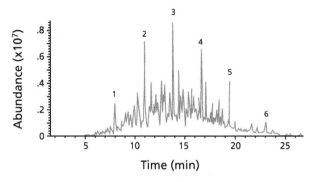

A gas chromatogram of a lighter fluid from a forensics laboratory

through the column at varying rates, the fastest traveling components will exit the column before slower components. The mobile phase is analyzed by a detector as it exits the column. There are several different types of detectors, but typically, they measure the wavelength of the light and other radiation absorbed by the sample. The detector records the information on a graph, just as the gas chromatograph does in GC, and this graph is used to identify the components present in the mixture.

A third important type of chromatography, *thin-layer chromatography* (TLC), uses a liquid mobile phase and a thin layer of solid gel laid down on a glass plate as the stationary phase. One advantage of this method over paper chromatography is that it more easily allows colorless components to be analyzed. However, it is generally less quantitative and precise than either GC or HPLC. The setup for this method is very similar to that used in paper chromatography. The mixture sample is spotted near one end of the plate and then the plate is placed upright in a container with the sample spot near the bottom of the container. A small amount of the mobile phase is added, and it travels up the gel via capillary action. After the process is complete, the plate is analyzed by viewing it under UV light, which causes fluorescent components to glow, or by treating the plate with chemicals that react with the components to produce colored spots. The R_f values of components are then calculated and compared to known values.

LEARNING OUTCOMES		
LEARNING OUTCOMES	**LOCATION IN SECTION**	**EVIDENCE OF UNDERSTANDING**
Identify an unknown ink based on a set of standards.	*Investigate* Parts B-C *Chem to Go* Questions 4,7	Students successfully complete Parts B and C of the activity. Students use their observations of the model to hypothesize about the mechanism of separation. Students' answers match those provided in this *Teacher's Edition.*
Explain, from the macroscopic, nanoscopic, and symbolic perspectives, how the components of a mixture are separated in chromatography.	*Chem Talk, CheckingUp, Chem Essential Questions*	Students analyze differences between the chromatography model and reality. Students' answers match those provided in this *Teacher's Edition.*
Calculate, compare, explain, and predict R_f values for substances.	*Chem to Go* Questions 5-6	Students' answers match those provided in this *Teacher's Edition.*

NOTES

CHAPTER 8

Section 8
Materials, Chemicals, Preparation, and Safety

("per Group" quantity is based on group size of 4 students)

Materials and Equipment

Materials (and Equipment)	Quantity per Group (4 students)
Water-soluble black markers, set of 5 different	1
Chromatography paper, large sheet	1
Paper clip, large	1
Binder clip, small	1
Felt board, 6' x 4'*	1
Poker chips, 2 colors	10 of each
Meter stick	1
Beaker, 600-mL	1
Cellophane tape, roll	1
Graduated cylinder, 250-mL	1
Metric ruler, clear plastic, 30-cm	1
Pencil, sharpened	1
Magnifying glass	1
Materials (and Equipment)	Quantity per Class
Plastic wrap, roll	1
Scissors	1

*The felt board must be prepared in advance. The size and composition of the board isn't fixed and can vary.

Chemicals

Chemicals	Quantity per Class (24 students)
None	None

Teacher Preparation

Poker chips—all chips of one color must have one side sanded smooth so that they have less friction on the felt board than the chips of the other color.

The chromatography paper must be cut in advance to fit the 250 mL graduated cylinder and the 600 mL beaker.

Safety Requirements

- Goggles and aprons are required in the laboratory area.

NOTES

CHAPTER 8

Meeting the Needs of All Students
Differentiated Instruction

Augmentation and Accommodations

LEARNING ISSUE	REFERENCE	AUGMENTATION AND ACCOMMODATIONS
Determining how black ink can be used as evidence	*What Do You Think?*	**Augmentation** • Expect some students to be confused about whether the detective can directly determine from the ink who wrote the threatening letters, or whether it is only possible to determine the brand of ink used, which might help connect the notes to a limited number of suspects. • Ensure students that misinterpretations are common and should not cause embarrassment. • Make sure all students understand the benefit of knowing the brand of ink before they begin the investigation. Otherwise, they will not understand the purpose of the investigation, which is to understand how ink can be used as evidence.
Interpreting directions from text and diagrams	*Investigate*	**Augmentation** • Students may be confused by the multi-step directions. • Refer students to the diagrams provided in the text. • Model each step in Parts A and B.
Creating a chromatogram Designing a multi-step process	*Investigate* Part C, 1.c)	**Accommodations** • Refer students to the directions for analyzing ink in Part A, and have them re-create that procedure, but make the adjustments required for testing more than one ink described in Part C. • Require that students write their directions as a bulleted list. • Have each group do a dry run to evaluate their procedure themselves before submitting it for approval.
Understanding R_f factor Using ratios to solve problems	*Chem Talk* *Chem to Go* 5.-6.	**Augmentation** • Some students will understand this section easily, but others will not learn it from just reading it. For those who need more help, show students how to find R_f factors of the chromatographs they made in the investigation. • Have each student practice making the measurements and determining R_f factors. • Help students work backward to draw a chromatograph when they are given the R_f factors. **Accommodation** • Have students use calculators.
Classification of substances as mixtures	*Chem to Go* 1.	**Accommodation** • Refer students to the definition in the *Chem Words* section and the explanation of mixtures in the first paragraph of the *Chem Talk*. Have them underline the key words in the definition and use those as criteria to evaluate each substance in the *Chem to Go* question.

NOTES

_____

_____

_____

_____

_____

Strategies for Students with Limited English Language Proficiency

LEARNING ISSUE	REFERENCE	AUGMENTATIONS
Background knowledge	*What Do You Think?*	The opening illustration provides a storyline for this section and could generate an introductory discussion. Check that students understand the "*un*" prefix in the word "*unsigned*"
Vocabulary	*Investigate*	Students may benefit from working in small groups or with partners. Help students with the pronunciation of "*chromatography*" and share root "chrom" for language development. Reference root again in "*chromatogram.*" Other derivatives in this section will also help with language development.
Background knowledge Vocabulary Comprehending text	*Chem Talk*	Check for understanding of bold-type words. Refer students to the *Chem Words* for further explanations of the isolated words. Check for understanding of the term "*stationary*" and differentiate from "*stationery*" to build language development.
Background knowledge	*What Do You Think Now?*	Have students brainstorm with partners prior to answering the questions on their own.
Background knowledge Vocabulary Comprehending text	*Chem Essential Questions*	In the How do you know? section the word "*identical*" may not be in the students' expressive vocabulary. In the *What do you believe?* section, check for understanding of the term "*component ingredients.*" In the *Why should you care?* section, the term "*creative fashion*" may be an unfamiliar phrase.
Comprehension Vocabulary	*Chem to Go*	Check students' understanding of the task when asked to write a descriptive paragraph. Students may need some assistance with what it means to "*analyze.*"
Application Comprehension	*Inquiring Further*	The phrase "*factors that influence*" may require some explanation. Students may need assistance on resources to conduct this research. Check for understanding of the terms "*applicable*" and "*mobile.*"

CHAPTER 8

NOTES

_____

_____

_____

_____

_____

_____

_____

_____

_____

Section 8
Teaching Suggestions and Sample Answers

What Do You See?

This colorful illustration serves several purposes. The first is to engage the students' interest. Additionally, you can use the illustration to elicit information about students' prior knowledge.

Students' reactions will vary, which is good. All reactions are to be valued. This is not the time to make judgments about the responses although you might wish to draw out additional information from a student if a response is vague or if you sense that it can lead to important information for the class. Later, the class will have the opportunity to return to the illustration and their responses to it.

What Do You Think?

Students will probably rely on their art knowledge of colors and think that black is a mixture of colors and the inks consists of a mixture of colors. They may also assume that each brand has characteristic colors in their inks and this would help to identify the ink source. Listen carefully for prior conceptions—especially misconceptions—but it is not useful to correct students at this point. Simply take note of their responses and ask for their explanations; it will help you to assess your students' understanding before you begin the section.

What Do You Think?
A CHEMIST'S RESPONSE

A detective can use black ink as evidence by analyzing it and proving that its components are identical to those from a suspect's pen. Black ink can be analyzed because it usually is composed of several discrete components of specific color, structure, and percentage.

STUDENTS' PRIOR CONCEPTIONS

The most important area to emphasize is the role of particle-level interactions between the separated components, the mobile phase, and the stationary phase, which result from the characteristic properties of each substance. These interactions determine the observed separation on paper, and this microscopic-to-macroscopic connection should continually be called to students' attention.

1. *Intermolecular bonds are the same as intramolecular bonds.*

Use of the word "bond" to describe both the relatively weak attractions between different particles and the far stronger covalent and ionic attractions that hold individual particles together leaves students understandably confused. Because they have probably learned about intramolecular covalent and ionic bonding previously and almost certainly more extensively than they have intermolecular bonds, they are likely to believe that intramolecular bonds are very similar to their conception of covalent and ionic bonds. To help students develop an understanding of these two distinct types of microscopic interactions, point out the differences in relative strength between the two using representative examples, such as the intermolecular and intramolecular bonds seen in water. Also, you may want to avoid using the word "bond" to describe intermolecular attractions and substitute the term "intermolecular forces". This could help students develop a conception of the idea as distinct from intramolecular bonds.

2. *Materials have color.*

When students read that colorless substances can be separated via chromatography in the *Chem Talk* section, they may be skeptical. This response likely results from a belief that substances are separated by chromatography because of color differences. This conception makes sense for two reasons: first, because color was the distinguishing feature of the components they were able to observe on the chromatogram, and second, because they often believe that materials have color at the molecular level. When students see that substances' colors result from their interaction with the light that strikes them, they should also understand that color is an observation tool in chromatography rather than the property of the substance that determines its rate of travel over the chromatogram. It will be helpful to explain that white light contains all of the colors in the rainbow, and different substances, because of their particular microscopic structures, absorb particular colors of light from the white light and reflect back others. What is seen is the blending of the reflected colors. Without light, the substance has no color, and in light other than white light, it may have a different color.

3. *Separations are perfect and all the particles of each substance travel through the column at the same rate.*

Students may have a "black-and-white" conception of separation in general and may thus believe that complete separation of components of a mixture is possible. In fact, typically, some degree of

Section 8

Paper Chromatography: Separating Molecules

What Do You See?

The WHO-WROTE-The-RANSOM-LETTER MYSTERY

Learning Outcomes

In this section you will

- Identify an unknown ink based on a set of standards.

- Explain, from the *macroscopic, nanoscopic,* and *symbolic* perspectives, how the components of a mixture are separated in chromatography.

- Calculate, compare, explain, and predict R_f values for substances.

Safety goggles and a lab apron must be worn *at all times* in a chemistry lab.

What Do You Think?

A detective searches a crime scene, looking for pieces of evidence and comes across a stack of threatening letters written in black ink. Each is unsigned and has no fingerprints except the victims', but the detective still knows they can be used as evidence.

- How can a detective use black ink as evidence?

- What properties of black ink make it possible evidence at a crime scene?

Record your ideas about these questions in your *Active Chemistry* log. Be prepared to discuss your responses with your group and the class.

Investigate

In this investigation you will explore one way forensic scientists identify inks—paper chromatography.

Part A: Analyzing Ink

1. Your teacher will give you a piece of *chromatography* paper (a paper used to separate mixtures) with a small spot of black ink at one end.

2. Tape a large paper clip to the top of the paper and attach a binder clip to the bottom of the paper to weigh down the paper once it's resting in the water as pictured in the diagram on the next page.

709

Active Chemistry

Talk section can be a starting point for this discussion and students can be asked to generate illustrations of this idea to reinforce learning.

4. *"Pure" products (e.g., aspirin, soap, bottled water) contain only one substance.*

Many commercial products are labeled pure when in fact they do not meet the technical definition of pure substance – composed of only one element or compound. It is important to draw students' attention to this point and to emphasize that the common usage of the term does not correspond to its meaning in chemistry class. It may be helpful to take an example such as bottled spring water and show students the names and chemical formulas of several substances found in the product.

5. R_f *factor changes with the length of the column/paper.*

R_f factor is a constant ratio for a particular substance in a given mobile-stationary phase combination. Thus a substance will travel further on a longer column than on a shorter one, but the ratio of the distance traveled by the component to the distance traveled by the mobile front will be the same. Because students often have difficulty understanding the underlying concept of ratios or proportions, they may in turn be confused by this specific application of ratios. It will be helpful to discuss how two chromatograms of the same substance that are different lengths appear and to measure and calculate Rf values for the components on those chromatograms.

---

intermingling of components will remain. Chromatography is no exception to this general principle. To help students understand and internalize this idea, it will be helpful to emphasize one of the reasons for imperfect separation of components in chromatography – that all of the particles of one component do not travel through the column at the same rate. For every component, there is a distribution of speeds of particle travel, which leads to an indistinct spot on the resulting chromatogram rather than the tiny dot that would result if all of the particles moved at the same rate. The R_f value represents the average of the particle speeds and thus the measurement of the distance traveled by the component is measured from the middle of the dot on the chromatogram. Because there is a range of speeds within each component's particles, the ranges of different particles can overlap even though they have different averages. The slower particles of a component with a faster overall average speed (and thus a higher R_f value) can be moving at the same rate as the faster particles of a component with a slower average speed (and thus a lower R_f value). Particles moving at the same speed will be intermingled on the chromatogram. The *Chem*

Investigate

Part A: Analyzing Ink

1.-2.

Water-soluble overhead markers work the best. In addition, you will need four other (different) black water-soluble markers for *Part C*. You may also want to add a permanent marker. It will raise some interesting questions when the students see that the spot doesn't move.

3.

The students should add no more than 12-15 mm ($\frac{1}{2}$ inch) of water to the graduated cylinder. The water line should be well below the ink spot (20 mm).

4.

Make sure the sides of the paper do not touch the walls of the graduated cylinder or beaker.

5.

If the colors separate clearly before the water reaches the top of the paper, the students can stop the process. This will save some class time.

6.

Drying time can be reduced by using a hair dryer or a warm hot plate.

7.a)

Have the students measure the "distance traveled" for the center of each spot and calculate the R$_f$ values.

The colors came from the mixture in the ink which gave it a black color. The spots of various colors are composed of different molecules having different polarities.

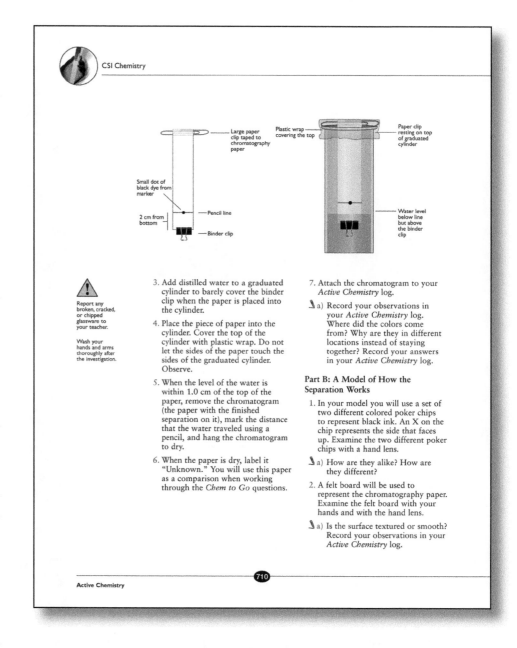

They moved at different rates on the stationary phase because of intermolecular attractive forces. The slower spots spent more time with the stationary phase and the faster spots spent more time in the mobile phase.

Part B: A Model of How the Separation Works

1.

Be sure that one side of each of the "A" poker chips has been sanded so it is very smooth.

If you find they are still as slow as the "B" chips, then sand the bottom edge so that it is rounded upwards.

1.a)

They are alike in size and shape. They are different because one type of poker chip has a smooth surface while the other type is ridged on both sides.

2.a)

The felt board is rough and fuzzy.

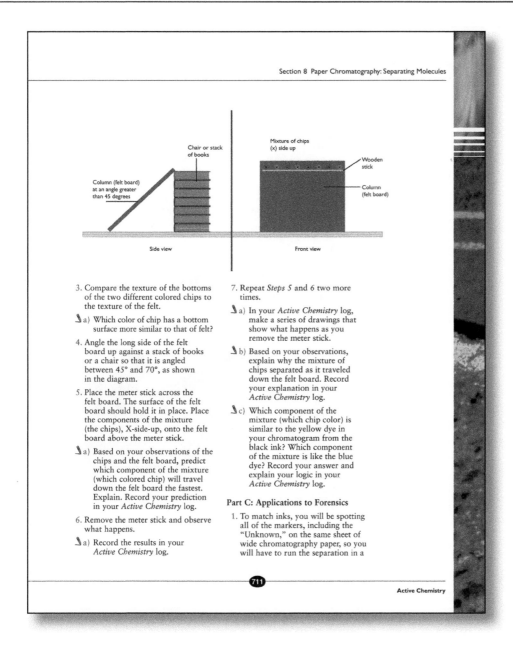

7.a)

Students should show the "A" poker chips leading the "B" chips. You might provide them with colored pencils for their sketches.

7.b)

The students can mention that one type of poker chip had a smooth surface but you should make them take the model one step further. They should understand that the "B" chips had more interaction with the felt board (stationary phase) than the "A" chips did.

7.c)

Students' answers will vary, depending on their results.

CHAPTER 8

Within the figure (student book page 711):

Section 8 Paper Chromatography: Separating Molecules

Chair or stack of books

Mixture of chips (x) side up

Wooden stick

Column (felt board) at an angle greater than 45 degrees

Column (felt board)

Side view

Front view

3. Compare the texture of the bottoms of the two different colored chips to the texture of the felt.

▲a) Which color of chip has a bottom surface more similar to that of felt?

4. Angle the long side of the felt board up against a stack of books or a chair so that it is angled between 45° and 70°, as shown in the diagram.

5. Place the meter stick across the felt board. The surface of the felt board should hold it in place. Place the components of the mixture (the chips), X-side-up, onto the felt board above the meter stick.

▲a) Based on your observations of the chips and the felt board, predict which component of the mixture (which colored chip) will travel down the felt board the fastest. Explain. Record your prediction in your *Active Chemistry* log.

6. Remove the meter stick and observe what happens.

▲a) Record the results in your *Active Chemistry* log.

7. Repeat *Steps 5* and 6 two more times.

▲a) In your *Active Chemistry* log, make a series of drawings that show what happens as you remove the meter stick.

▲b) Based on your observations, explain why the mixture of chips separated as it traveled down the felt board. Record your explanation in your *Active Chemistry* log.

▲c) Which component of the mixture (which chip color) is similar to the yellow dye in your chromatogram from the black ink? Which component of the mixture is like the blue dye? Record your answer and explain your logic in your *Active Chemistry* log.

Part C: Applications to Forensics

1. To match inks, you will be spotting all of the markers, including the "Unknown," on the same sheet of wide chromatography paper, so you will have to run the separation in a

711

Active Chemistry

3.a)

The "B" poker chips have a surface more similar to that of the felt board.

4.

Test this in advance so that you can find the correct angle quickly.

5.

Alternate the chips as depicted in the student book, but don't allow them to touch.

5.a)

Students may predict that the chips with the smoother bottom will travel faster.

6.a)

The "A" chips will separate from the "B" chips and reach the bottom of the felt board first.

Part C: Applications to Forensics

1.

If you do not have wide chromatography paper, you can have students run the standards for comparison and the unknown on separate pieces of the same chromatography paper used in the other parts. Be sure to emphasize that the conditions must be identical for all of the standards as well as the unknown.

1.a)

It is important to run them all at the same time on the same sheet of paper so that the conditions (i.e., mobile and stationary phases) for all samples will be identical.

Sample Procedure:

- Draw a pencil line 2 cm from the bottom of a wide piece of chromatography paper.

- Spot "Known" marker inks in a row on the pencil line. Keep the spot as small as possible (1-2 mm) and well-separated (~1 cm) from adjacent spots. Spot the "Unknown" ink somewhere in the middle of the "Known" inks. Using a pencil, label each spot at the top of the chromatogram.

- Obtain a 600-mL beaker and add distilled water to a depth of about 1 cm.

- Tape the top of the paper to a pencil. Clamp the bottom of the paper with a binder clip and then place the binder clip in the water in the beaker.

- Cover the beaker with plastic wrap and allow the chromatogram to develop.

- When the mobile phase is about 1 cm from the top of the paper, remove the paper from the beaker. Mark the leading edge of the mobile phase with a pencil line.

- Allow the chromatogram to dry.

CSI Chemistry

large 600-mL beaker. Also, you will attach the paper to a pencil instead of a paper clip because the pencil will reach across the mouth of the beaker.

a) Why do you think it is important to run all of the samples on the same sheet?

b) Using what you have learned about paper chromatography separations, write down the procedure you will use for creating the chromatogram in your *Active Chemistry* log.

Report any broken, cracked, or chipped glassware to your teacher.

Wash your hands and arms thoroughly after the investigation.

2. Show your procedure to your teacher for approval before proceeding.

a) After you have completed your chromatogram, identify the "Unknown." Record and justify your answer in your *Active Chemistry* log.

3. Dispose of the materials as directed by your teacher. Clean up your workstation.

Chem Words

mixture: a combination of two or more substances.

Chem Talk

SEPARATING MIXTURES USING CHROMOTOGRAPY

Mixtures

In this investigation you explored a method for separating mixtures. Mixtures are all around you and make up many common household items, such as soda, baking powder, cleaning solutions, and of course, black ink. A **mixture** is defined as a physical combination of two or more substances. Mixtures can be separated based on differences in their physical properties. Salt water is a mixture of salt and water. The salt can be separated from the water by evaporating the water. The salt will remain in the container and the water vapor (steam) can be collected above the container. Chromatography is another means that chemists can separate mixtures.

712

Active Chemistry

2.

When you check the groups' procedures, be sure students label the chromatogram with the initials of the marker brand above each spot.

2.a)

- One of the "Known" inks will match the "Unknown" ink in pattern and in R_f values. Identify it.

Chem Talk

Chromatography is a technique that can be used to separate mixtures. The discussion leads students through what is meant by the stationary phase and mobile phase. They also learn that the different components within the mixture have different polarities and hence will not move the same distance as the mobile phase. Being able to calculate the R_f value allows a semi-quantitative measurement for comparison of different substances.

Chromatography

Chromatography is a method of separation that was originally invented for separating different colored plant pigments. Its name derives from the Greek words *chroma*, meaning "color," and *graphein*, meaning "write." In this experiment you used chromatography to separate the components in black ink. However, this technique is not limited to colored materials. It may be used to separate colorless mixtures of gases, solids, or liquids. It is important to note that chromatography does not separate materials because of their different colors, but because of their different properties. In this investigation you used components of different colors because this makes them easy to see as they separate. However, color has nothing to do with the way chromatography works.

In chromatography you have two different phases: the **stationary phase** and the **mobile phase**. In your experiments, the chromatography paper was the stationary phase because it does not move. The mobile phase was the water that moved up the paper. In chromatography, the components of the mixture interact with both the mobile and stationary phases. The higher the polarity of a component, the more it will interact with the mobile phase (the water) and the faster it will travel. The more a component interacts with the stationary phase (the paper) the slower it travels. Since every component has a different polarity, each will interact with the mobile and stationary phases to different degrees. Therefore, each different chemical in the mixture will pass through at different rates, thus separating the substances in the mixture.

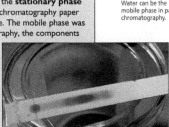

In *Part B* of this investigation you modeled the chromatography process. The stationary phase was represented by the felt board and the mixture was made of two different substances—represented by the different surfaces on the chips. The poker chips with a rough surface interact with the felt board more than the smooth poker chips. The chips with the rough bottoms attach and detach on the fuzzy surface of the board. This slows them down as they travel down the board. The smooth chips do not catch on the surface as much as the rough chips, so they travel down the board at a much faster rate. The difference in the attraction to the stationary phase causes the separation of the different poker chips in the mixture.

Chem Words

chromatography: an experimental technique that separates a mixture by the speed at which they migrate over a stationary phase.

stationary phase: the absorbent in chromatography. In paper chromatography, the paper is the stationary phase.

mobile phase: the fluid that contains the mixture that is analyzed in chromatography. Water can be the mobile phase in paper chromatography.

713

Active Chemistry

CHAPTER 8

Checking Up

1.

Some examples of common mixtures are black ink, baking powder, toothpaste, gasoline, milk and floor cleaner. There are many more examples as there are very few pure substances.

2.

In the experiments performed, the stationary phase was the chromatography paper. The mobile phase was water.

3.

$$R_f = \frac{\text{distance "A" traveled}}{\text{distance mobile phase traveled}}$$

$$= \frac{5.0 \text{ cm}}{10.0 \text{ cm}} = 0.50$$

CSI Chemistry

Application of Chromatography to Forensic Chemistry

In forensics, chromatography has a wide variety of applications, such as ink analysis, toxicology, and arson investigations. As you saw in *Part C* of the *Investigate* section, chromatography can be used to identify different brands of black ink by separating them into their individual components. In toxicology it can be used to separate mixtures of different drugs and other chemical substances, such as a mixture of heroin and baking soda. In arson investigations, samples taken from the site of the fire can be analyzed for the presence of gasoline or other flammable substances.

Unknown components in mixtures can be identified by comparing the chromatogram of the unknown sample to a set of standard chromatograms. Standard chromatograms are made using the same stationary phase and mobile phase that were used for the "Unknown." In addition to comparing the chromatogram of the Unknown to the standard, a quantitative measure known as the R_f can be used to identify components. The **R_f factor** is defined as the distance traveled by the component divided by the distance traveled by the solvent. An example is shown in the diagram.

$$R_f = \frac{\text{distance traveled by component}}{\text{distance traveled by solvent (mobile phase)}}$$

Chem Words

R_f factor: the retention factor and the ratio of the distance a component traveled compared to the distance the mobile phase moved.

Distance traveled by Component X 8.0 cm

Distance traveled by the solvent 11.0 cm

For Component X
$R_f = \frac{8.0 \text{ cm}}{11.0 \text{ cm}} = 0.73$

For Component Y
$R_f = \frac{3.0 \text{ cm}}{11.0 \text{ cm}} = 0.27$

For Component Z
$R_f = \frac{0.0 \text{ cm}}{11.0 \text{ cm}} = 0$

Checking Up

1. Give two examples of mixtures you use every day.

2. What was the stationary phase and what was the mobile phase in the chromatography experiments you did?

3. In a chromatography test, Component A traveled 5.0 cm. The solvent (mobile phase) traveled 10.0 cm. Calculate the R_f factor of Component A.

For a given stationary-mobile phase combination, the R_f factor of a compound is constant. So if a yellow dye in the unknown has R_f factor different from the R_f factor of the yellow dye in the standard chromatogram, then it can be assumed the two dyes are not the same.

Finally, the relative quantities of each component can be qualitatively determined by comparing their intensities. The more intense the color the higher the concentration of the component with that color is in the mixture. If the intensities of all of the spots are the same, the components are present in nearly equal quantities in the mixture.

714

Active Chemistry

What Do You Think Now?

Have the students revisit the *What Do You See?* illustration and the *What Do You Think?* questions and discuss how their responses have changed as a result of what they have learned. They should now have a better understanding of the content that the artist tried to convey. They should also have more sophisticated and in-depth responses to the questions. You may want to share the answers provided in *A Chemist's Response* and have them discuss their opinions.

Section 8 Paper Chromatography: Separating Molecules

What Do You Think Now?

At the beginning of this section you were asked the following:

• How can a detective use black ink as evidence?

• What properties of black ink make it possible evidence at a crime scene?

Answer the two questions again, this time using the theory and chemistry words you learned in this investigation.

Chem
Essential Questions

What does it mean?

Chemistry explains a *macroscopic* phenomenon (what you observe) with a description of what happens at the *nanoscopic* level (atoms and molecules) using *symbolic* structures as a way to communicate. Complete the chart below in your *Active Chemistry* log.

MACRO	NANO	SYMBOLIC
What did you observe with your sense of sight during the chromatography investigation?	Explain why some molecules are able to travel larger distances on the paper.	You used poker chips as a model to explain how chromatography works. How is this model of poker chip motion not like the movement of the molecules?

How do you know?

What evidence do you have that all black inks are not identical?

Why do you believe?

Ink makers often change the component ingredients of their inks. How would this add a complication to a crime investigation?

Why should you care?

Notes at the crime scene can now be a chemical tool for investigation. Create a part of a crime scene that fits in with your general story that uses ink marks in a creative fashion.

Chem Essential Questions

What does it mean?

MACRO — Students could observe the mobile phase move up the paper by capillary action. They could also see the black ink separate into its component colors as they moved with the mobile phase.

NANO — Molecules which are more polar interact with the polar mobile phase more and thus travel farther than less polar molecules.

SYMBOLIC — The poker chips moved according to their interaction with the rough felt surface, not due to intermolecular attractive forces. Also, there was no model for the mobile phase unless one considers gravity as representative of that phase.

How do you know?

Several different black inks were analyzed by paper chromatography and found to have different components upon comparison.

Why do you believe?

If the ink manufacturer changed the composition of an ink which was evidence in a crime scene, it would be difficult to prove that the evidence was identical to the standard ink.

Why should you care?

Students' answers will vary.

Reflecting on the Section and the Challenge

Now is an opportunity for students to pause and think about how they will transfer what they have learned in this section into their crime scenes. You might want to have them do this individually in their *Active Chemistry* logs or informally in their working groups. If time permits, they may benefit from sharing their ideas with the class and getting feedback.

Chem to Go

1.

Classify the following as mixtures or pure substances:

a) (sugar water) *mixture*

b) (copper wire) *pure substance*

c) (ammonia cleaning solution) *mixture*

d) (table salt) *pure substance*

2.

Answers will vary depending on the marker used. The dye interacting more with the mobile phase will travel farthest and the dye interacting more with the stationary phase will travel the shortest distance.

3.

If a longer piece of chromatography paper is used, the mobile phase will move further as will the component spots. Better separation of the mixture should be observed. The R_f value for each spot would remain the same.

CSI Chemistry

Reflecting on the Section and the Challenge

In this section you separated various colored mixtures using chromatography. Consider the types of evidence that paper chromatography would be good for analyzing. Black ink used in a ransom note may be the same as the ink in the pen of one of the suspects. Think of how you can use standards and R_f values to determine the type of ink used.

Chem to Go

1. Classify the following as mixtures or pure substances:

   a) sugar water   b) copper wire

   c) ammonia cleaning solution   d) table salt (sodium chloride, NaCl)

2. Based on your knowledge of chromatography, which dye in *Part A* interacted more with the mobile phase than the stationary phase? Explain your reasoning.

3. How would varying the size of the piece of paper change your results? What would remain the same? Explain your answers to both questions.

4. Why is it important to use a pencil when making any markings on the chromatogram?

5. What is the maximum possible value for R_f? Where would the component be on the column when R_f is the maximum value?

6. Calculate the R_f factors for the Unknown from *Part A* of the *Investigate*. How do these values compare to the R_f factors of the dyes in each of the standards and the same Unknown in *Part C*? Explain your findings.

7. In this investigation, you constructed a model to illustrate how chromatography works. While you were able to explore some of the factors that affect the separation of components in chromatography using this model, the model is not effective for explaining everything about chromatography. Where are some areas in which the model is inaccurate? Consider what in the model represents each of the components and the two phases (mobile and stationary).

8. *Preparing for the Chapter Challenge*

   Consider how you could use chromatography as a part of your *Chapter Challenge*. In a few sentences, describe the types of evidence that you could analyze in class using chromatography. In a paragraph, describe how chromatography works and how it can be used to analyze a piece of evidence retrieved from a crime scene.

716

Active Chemistry

4.

Pencils do not have dye in them, so the pencil mark will not travel on the chromatogram as the ink would.

5.

The maximum R_f value is 1.0. At this value, the component would appear on the solvent front (at the top of the paper).

6.

Answers will vary depending on the marker used.

7.

Answers will vary. It is a good idea to review this question as a class brainstorming session. The key is that the interaction of the "B" poker chips with the felt mimics the interaction of the molecules with the chromatography paper. However, the model is lacking in at least two ways. First, there is no mobile phase represented in the model (unless gravity is considered). Also, the interactions

Section 8 Paper Chromatography: Separating Molecules

Inquiring Further

1. Investigating factors influencing chromatography

There are many different factors that can influence your chromatogram. Some of these include the length of the stationary phase, the size of the original sample, and the types of mobile phases that you can use with paper chromatography. Choose one of these variables to change. If applicable, research the variable to develop a hypothesis. Under the supervision of an adult, investigate how changing specific variables affects the separation of black ink.

2. Investigating permanent inks

In this investigation you used water-based black inks. Can permanent black ink be separated using paper chromatography? Research the properties of permanent inks. Under the supervision of an adult, investigate what types of mobile phases are needed to separate permanent ink.

717

Active Chemistry

Inquiring Further

1. Investigating factors influencing chromatography

Check students' proposed procedures for conducting experiments by changing specific variables for safety and feasibility.

2. Investigating permanent inks

Check students' procedures for safety and feasibility. For permanent black ink separation, students may need to use an organic solvent, such as ethanol or acetone, mixed with the water as a mobile phase.

CHAPTER 8

between the poker chips and the felt board are due to friction, whereas intermolecular attractions are based on polarity.

8.
Preparing for the Chapter Challenge

Students' answers will vary. Many will suggest that if a crime scene has a ransom note or writing on a pad that gives an address, the ink could be analyzed for comparison to the ink from a pen that a suspect was carrying. If the R_f values are determined, they can be used to tentatively identify the source that produced them. This is the type of evidence that can be used in a crime scene.

SECTION 8 – QUIZ

8-8a | **Blackline Master**

1. Chromatography is a technique used to _____.

    a) make solutions   b) determine solubility

    c) separate mixtures   d) color different materials

2. Using the diagram in *Question 3* (below), calculate the R_f of component b from its midpoint. The R_f is:

    a) 0.40   b) 0.32   c) 0.90   d) 0.10

3. In the diagram, which component, *a*, *b*, or *c*, interacts with the stationary phase the most? Which component interacts with the stationary phase the least? Explain.

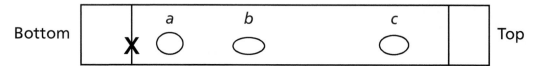

Bottom   X   a   b   c   Top

4. Using the diagram above as a reference, where in relation to your starting material X would you want to have your mobile phase at the beginning of your experiment? Explain.

SECTION 8 – QUIZ ANSWERS

1   c) separate mixtures

2   a) 0.40

3   Component *a* interacted with the stationary phase the most, which is why it did not travel very far. Component *c* interacted with the stationary phase the least, which is why it traveled the farthest.

4   The solution would have to be between the bottom of the sheet and X because otherwise, the separation would be flawed. Very likely, some of the components would dissolve in the reservoir of mobile phase and disappear.

NOTES

Chapter Assessment

Chem You Learned

The chemistry content covered in this chapter is listed in the *Student Edition* at the end of the chapter. This could be a good time to evaluate your students' comprehension of the material. You might suggest that they help each other in reviewing those concepts that may need reinforcement. You may also point out to students that they can use the *Chem You Learned* section as a handy checklist of the chemistry concepts they might want to incorporate into their *Chapter Challenge*.

CSI Chemistry

Chem You Learned

- **Deductive reasoning** involves the use of observable data and the use of that data to solve a problem.
- **Transition metals** include many of the more common metals (Cu, Zn, Fe, Sn, and so on), and often have similar chemical properties.
- **Physical properties** and **chemical properties** help to characterize the various **elements** and **compounds** in our physical world.
- Every pure **substance** has a **density**, a physical property that is characteristic of that substance under standard conditions.
- In **forensics**, blood testing at a crime scene is always **"presumptive."** A **luminol** reagent is used to show the possibility of the presence of blood residue.
- With the **catalyst** of hydrogen peroxide, the **luminol** reagent will show a **chemiluminescent** yellow-green color in the presence of blood.
- **Electrons** can exist at several **energy levels**, depending upon the situation. Normally, they occupy the lowest energy level, the **ground state**. When an electron absorbs energy, it can rise to higher energy levels, called **excited states**.
- An excited electron will return to the **ground state** with the emission of energy, typically light energy of a very specific **wavelength**.
- **Qualitative analysis** is used to determine *whether* a substance is present in a sample whereas **quantitative analysis** is required to determine *how much* of that substance is present.
- **Ionic compounds** always contain a **cation** and an **anion**, and are formed by the complete transfer of one or more electrons.
- **The law of conservation of matter** is a key concept in chemistry and it makes possible the balancing of chemical equations.
- Some ions are composed of two or more atoms which are **covalently** bonded together. These are called **polyatomic ions**. Two examples are NH_4^+ and CO_3^{2-}.
- A **solution** is a homogeneous mixture of two or more substances. The substance in greater concentration is called the **solvent** and those in lesser concentrations are called **solutes**.
- Predictions about **solubility** can be made by using a table of **solubility rules**.
- **Double-replacement reactions** always involve the formation of a **precipitate** or a gas.
- **Oxidation** and **reduction** occur simultaneously as one substance loses electrons (is oxidized) and another substance gains those electrons (is reduced).
- **Single-replacement reactions** always involve the reduction-oxidation process (**redox**).
- Copper can be oxidized to the (I) state or the (II) state with the corresponding **oxidation numbers** of +1 and +2.
- Most metals have the physical properties of being **lustrous**, **ductile**, **malleable**, and have the ability to **conduct** heat and electricity well.
- The technique of **chromatography** is used for the separation of mixtures based on differing physical properties.
- In a chromatographic separation, a **mobile phase** carries the mixture through a **solid phase**.

718

Active Chemistry

Chem Chapter Challenge

As you assemble ideas and information for your *CSI Chemistry* crime scene drama you will be completing a second round of the *Engineering Design Cycle*. The goals and criteria are slightly expanded from the *Mini-Challenge* and your list of *Inputs* has grown. You now have access to more forensic chemistry techniques. You also have the *Feedback* you received during the *Mini-Challenge* to get you started and help guide your efforts.

Goal

Your group has already created its first *CSI Chemistry* crime scene. Now you will use the *Engineering Design Cycle* to help you create an even more intricate and dramatic scene. Go back and quickly read the challenge description at the start of the chapter. You will find all of the details for completing the entire challenge there. Review the rubric your class generated to determine the way your group's presentation will be graded. Make sure you address each aspect of the rubric completely so that your team can earn the highest possible grade.

The *Goal* is the objective you are trying to reach or the problem you need to solve in the *Engineering Design Cycle*. The *Goal* for this *Chapter Challenge* is to create a crime scene, write a police report, and prepare evidence so that another team can solve the crime. The crime scene must include evidence that can be analyzed using chemistry techniques learned in this chapter. Your crime story should include a police report, description of the crime, a diagram of the crime scene, a list of all the evidence found at the scene, and anything else that will make the story come to life. Each piece of evidence should point to more than one suspect while the totality of evidence should link the crime to only one suspect.

You will create dossiers (descriptions) for at least four different suspects, including the suspect's name, occupation, and any other information that will be needed to link the suspect to the crime or eliminate him or her as a suspect. You may be creative with your characters, but using names or lives of students is not allowed. It is important that you develop the story and the characters of the suspects so that the evidence you provide logically points to a single guilty suspect. However, you may also want to include a piece of evidence that implicates more than one suspect so the audience of the crime show cannot immediately guess the guilty party.

Your classmates will have to solve your crime. You will write down the solution to the crime (which suspect is guilty), including a flowchart illustrating the expected outcomes of the analysis of evidence. All of the solution material should be sealed in an envelope. Once the students testing your evidence have analyzed it and presented their case, they will open the envelope and compare their decision to what you intended.

Inputs

The *Inputs* for the *Engineering Design Cycle* include all of the resources that have helped you complete the *Chapter Challenge*. Each section taught you a new forensic chemistry technique. Some of the techniques are very specialized, while others rely on observable material properties and deductive reasoning. You also have a number of resources to use as inspiration for your crime

719

Active Chemistry

Chem Chapter Challenge

A brief review of the *Chapter Challenge* reminds students that the crime scene that they create must include physical evidence that can be analyzed using chemistry techniques that were learned in this chapter. The crime scene should be derived from an original crime story that can be solved from the evidence and information they provide.

Each piece of evidence should point to more than one suspect, but the combined data should pinpoint only one culprit. The supporting information is to be provided in various documents. There should be a police report, a description of the crime, a diagram of the crime scene, and a list of all evidence.

In addition, at least four dossiers detailing the particulars of four different imaginary suspects must be provided. These dossiers should include personal data such as background information and descriptions, mug shots or fingerprints, etc. Using names or identities of students is not allowed.

The solution to the crime should be logical and based only on the evidence and information provided. The solution material should include a flowchart that illustrates and explains the progressive elimination of all suspects except one. It should be sealed in an envelope and opened after the students who are challenged to solve the crime have reached their own conclusion.

Chemistry Content

A list reviewing the various activities contained in this chapter provides a convenient summary of the chemical concepts that were covered by these investigations. This list can be useful in generating ideas for creating the crime scene and for locating material related to specific concepts.

CSI CHEMISTRY

Criteria for Success

Now that the students have completed the *Mini-Challenge* and are preparing to start the *Chapter Challenge*, it is time to develop a more comprehensive assessment rubric that will determine how the projects will be graded. It is important that the students be involved in deciding the criteria for the rubric so they know exactly what is expected of them and how they will be assessed.

On the facing page is a sample assessment rubric for the *Chapter Challenge*. You can copy and distribute it as is, or use it as a foundation for developing scoring guidelines and expectations that suit your own particular needs. For example, you might wish to ensure that core concepts and abilities derived from your local or state science frameworks also appear on the rubric.

Students may decide to vary the point value of the different criteria categories. In the example, Content value is equal to Presentation value, but they may decide it should be worth more. They may also think that Group Interaction value should have a higher value.

However you and your students decide to evaluate the *Chapter Challenge*, it is essential that all expectations be communicated to students before they begin work on the *Chapter Challenge*. Be sure that the students actively participate in deciding the criteria for evaluation and the guidelines for scoring.

CSI Chemistry

scene drama—detective novels, illustrated novels, mystery movies, and TV police shows that depict the type of drama you are trying to create. One constraint on your crime scene will be the type of evidence you will be able to include, which must take advantage of the forensic chemistry techniques included in this chapter. Plan on using the materials from the chapter activities as evidence unless you have permission from your teacher to include additional materials.

The dramatic quality of your *CSI Chemistry* crime scene will depend on your team's use of the available *Inputs*. As your group reviews the chemistry you have learned, be sure to pay special attention to the *Reflecting on the Section and the Challenge, Chem Essential Questions*, and *Preparing for the Chapter Challenge* portions of the text. Review your *Active Chemistry* log for notes that you recorded during each section. The brief section summaries listed here will give you an overview of the information you have learned to help get you started.

Section 1 You learned about deductive reasoning. You also learned about elements and their properties.

Section 2 You investigated glass fragments and found that they could be distinguished by their densities. Density is a characteristic property of matter.

Section 3 You observed the luminol reaction and discovered that blood will be detected by luminol. You also learned that other substances can produce light from a luminol reaction. The luminol reaction can be used as evidence or can be used to confuse the crime detectives. You also learned about energy levels and the emission of light in addition to the need for catalysts.

Section 4 You practiced a set of lab techniques that can be used to distinguish one white powder from another. The identification of unknown chemicals involves sets of reactions. You also learned how to set up a flowchart to help clarify the logic of identifying the chemical.

Section 5 You learned how to develop latent prints and investigated the double-replacement reaction of sodium chloride and silver nitrate.

Section 6 You investigated single-replacement reactions and redox reactions in order to develop the metal activity series.

Section 7 As investigators, you learned how to lift the serial numbers from sanded pieces of metal. The explanation for why this is possible required you to look at metals at the molecular or *nanoscopic* level.

Section 8 You practiced chromatography techniques in order to analyze different inks that may be present at a crime scene.

Process

The *Process* step of the *Engineering Design Cycle* is when you turn your ideas into products. The *CSI Chemistry* crime scene has more products than any other *Chapter Challenge*, so your team has a lot of work to coordinate. Your group will draw on all of the techniques you have developed during the *Process* step of previous challenges. There are so many interconnected parts to this challenge that you will need to use brainstorming, decision matrices, research, and good time management to complete it. Select a "leader" for each product required for this challenge so that any decisions or changes can be made quickly on each of the interconnected products. Spend a small amount of time organizing the roles of your group members before making decisions and your efforts will go much more smoothly.

Some crimes lend themselves to a crime scene investigation because there are no available witnesses: theft, murder, destruction of property, and kidnapping. Your group may start by choosing a crime category and then building evidence and characters around it. You may also choose a compelling or classic crime scene drama and carefully select your evidence to support that story, building the characters last. You could also select evidence, create characters that would closely match the evidence, and then craft a crime drama that matches that information. The format you choose will depend solely on the preference of your group, but the last method might be the most straightforward approach if you are having trouble getting started.

The details of your drama do not need to be realistic. In fact, you might have to exaggerate or over-emphasize some details of the story to link the evidence and the suspects clearly in the story. The chemistry, however, must be real. You

720

Active Chemistry

The *Sample Assessment Rubric* is also provided as a Blackline Master in your *Teacher Resources* CD.

8b   Blackline Master

SAMPLE ASSESSMENT RUBRIC FOR CHAPTER 8

	MEETS THE STANDARD OF EXCELLENCE	APPROACHES THE STANDARD OF EXCELLENCE	MEETS AN ACCEPTABLE STANDARD	BELOW ACCEPTABLE STANDARD
CONTENT CRITERIA				
Chemistry Concepts	At least seven chemistry concepts are accurately identified or applied in the evidence and the techniques used to solve the crime. **15**	At least five chemistry concepts are correctly identified or used in the evidence and forensic techniques. **10-14**	At least three chemistry concepts are accurately identified or used. **5-9**	Less than three chemistry concepts are correctly identified or used. **0-4**
Techniques	At least three different forensic techniques are effectively applied to solve the crime. **15**	At least two different forensic techniques are correctly applied to solve the crime. **10-14**	One forensic technique is effectively used to solve the crime. **5-9**	No specific techniques are applied, or techniques are not correctly and effectively applied in the solution. **0-4**
Solution	The solution to the crime addresses the chemical principles used in the crime by explaining the macroscopic, nanoscopic, and symbolic perspectives. **15**	The solution is logical and addresses the chemical principles but does not provide adequate explanations. **10-14**	The solution is not airtight and lacks clear explanations. **5-9**	The solution is missing or lacks logic and clear explanations. **0-4**
PRESENTATION CRITERIA				
Crime Story	The story is logical, well crafted, creative, entertaining, and effectively incorporates the evidence. **15**	The story is logical and incorporates the evidence, but may lack in originality and creativity. **10-14**	The story does not account for all the evidence and/or lacks somewhat in logic. **5-9**	The story is not well thought out and lacks crucial important elements. **0-4**
Police Report	The police report is thorough, authentic and clearly documents and explains all evidence found at the crime scene. **15**	The report is unclear and/or misses a few significant points that would not be overlooked in an authentic police report. **10-14**	The report has some important facts but is not complete and needs clarification. **5-9**	The report is missing or is not authentic and lacks many important elements. **0-4**
Dossiers	There are at least four dossiers containing all pertinent information regarding various crime suspects; the suspect characters are original and creatively depicted. **15**	There are less than four dossiers or dossiers do not contain thorough descriptions. **10-14**	There are less than three dossiers and/or dossiers are missing some essential information necessary to identify the culprit. **5-9**	There are no dossiers or there is only one dossier and it is missing much essential information. **0-4**
GROUP INTERACTIONS				
Group Interaction	The project is executed by interactive teamwork, with all members of the group cooperating and actively engaged. **10**	Group members showed effort to work constructively, but interactions lacked cooperative teamwork. **6-9**	Some group members worked constructively, but project lacked teamwork interaction. **3-5**	There is little or no indication of group interaction or effort to work together as a team. **0-2**

CHAPTER 8

Preparing for the Chapter Challenge

The *Chapter Challenge* is the opportunity for students to review all the material in the chapter and find a creative way of interpreting that content. The *Preparing for the Chapter Challenge* section in the text guide the students toward a successful project. The pages in the front matter of this *Teacher's Edition* provide the instructional rationale for this problem-based learning model.

In the *Chapter Challenge* preparations, remind students that the best crime-show episodes will not only be entertaining and effective, but they should also demonstrate a working knowledge of the chemistry content. The more chemistry concepts that can be successfully included in their evidence and crime scene, the stronger their crime-show episode.

Prior to students beginning the *Chapter Challenge*, you should repeat the discussion you had at the start of the chapter and have the class agree on the rubric and standards for excellence.

Allow time for students to review the *Manage Your Time* section at the end of the chapter and make sure that they allow enough time to accomplish the tasks and that all members of each group actively participate. Also remind them that they must also include the solution to their crime scenes complete with an explanation of the chemical principles involved and a flowchart illustrating the steps to the solution, in a sealed envelope.

No doubt many of the crime-show episodes created by students will be highly entertaining as well as instructional. You may want to put together a collection of some of the most impressive projects to share with other students, teachers, and administration members so that others can enjoy the effort, creativity and knowledge shown.

NOTES

_____

_____

_____

_____

_____

_____

_____

_____

_____

_____

_____

Rarely will students conceive of a process that works perfectly the first time. Students will have to troubleshoot and experiment, and in some cases will need to make adjustments and modifications. For example, their first try at putting together evidence may focus too much on one suspect instead of posing a challenge for detection. Their efforts at this point would be to modify some of the crime scene evidence and/or some of the information in the dossiers so that each piece of evidence implicates more than one suspect.

Students should be well equipped to do this because once they grasp the underlying chemical principles, they will be able to make intelligent predictions and approach modifications with a deeper understanding as to why results will change when conditions are altered.

must explain how forensic detectives process the evidence to connect the suspects to the crime. Make the story as silly or scary as you like as long as it includes a crime and some suspense as the evidence is analyzed.

No single clue should indicate the guilty suspect; instead, each clue should implicate at least two suspects and only eliminate one suspect or make one suspect seem less guilty. The drama in your story will have to come from the deductive reasoning that is required to put all of the facts together and connect them with a suspect. All of the necessary evidence must be included in the crime scene. You will need to choose suspects that have more similarities than differences, with only a single piece of differentiating or identifying evidence linked to their profession or known personal habits. For example, a baker and a janitor could both leave a white powder at the scene of a crime, though the powders would likely be different based on the materials they routinely handle at their job. Similarly, some professions may allow a suspect to "easily" provide glass replicas for stolen glass items. Some suspects may even use glass items as part of their profession or a hobby, broken pieces of which could be inadvertently left as evidence at the scene of a crime. Some types of ink or marking pens are particular to special trades or professions, like a red grading pen.

Creating a *CSI Chemistry* crime scene drama requires your group to work creatively and analytically simultaneously. This is not easy for anyone, and most people prefer one of those modes over the other. Ask yourself and your group members which mode is more appealing and try to assign your group's tasks accordingly. Your group's *Outputs* will benefit from the skills and interests of your members if everyone enjoys the task they are assigned. You will need everyone's full participation to be outstanding!

 Outputs

The products you deliver during an *Engineering Design Cycle* are the *Outputs*, and this challenge has a lot. You will be providing a short story setting the scene and describing the crime, a crime scene diagram, a police report detailing the information collected at the scene that is related to the crime,

dossiers of at least four known suspects, carefully prepared evidence samples for analysis by the investigating team, and your crime solution packet. The solution packet must include an explanation of all of the forensic chemistry techniques that will be required to analyze the evidence and a flowchart detailing how that analysis leads to the guilty suspect.

Make sure you have included each component listed in the class rubric for your presentation. The rubric will describe the products you must deliver to earn the points associated with that component. Each person in your group should contribute equally to the final project. Time will be limited, so make sure that everyone has a role that allows them to be working during the entire period. Set deadlines for each product so that you will have time to review everybody's work as a group and make any necessary corrections prior to the investigation date. Your group may want to make duplicate evidence samples so you can test the analyses before the investigation date. If you find problems or make changes to the final products, make sure that the change is reflected in the story, the diagram, the police report, the dossiers, the evidence samples, and the solution packets. A single inconsistency could lead to a mistrial, a false arrest, or a criminal free on the streets! You don't want a small change to undermine your group's hard work.

 Feedback

Your instructor and classmates will give you *Feedback* on your *CSI Chemistry* crime scene presentation based on the rubric your class developed. You will directly compare the results of the "investigators" with the results your group intended. This *Feedback* will become part of your grade, indicating how successful your group was at meeting the *Chapter Challenge*, but could also be useful for refining your dramatic scene if it were selected to create a television script. The *Feedback* may reveal missing information you considered and forgot to include in the crime scene, or even conflicting evidence that was included in the crime scene unintentionally. Remember, every design can be refined based on the *Feedback* you receive in the *Engineering Design Cycle*.

(721)

Active Chemistry

Engineering Design Cycle

Have students revisit the *Engineering Design Cycle* they applied to the *Mini-Challenge* for their first-try crime scenes. What adjustments will they need to make to achieve success in the *Chapter Challenge*? Now that students know more about chemical reactions and

have a better understanding of the chemical principles behind them, they can incorporate this information to improve the design of their crime scenes by beginning the design cycle again.

The *Chapter Challenge* asks students to design a process in order to develop a crime-show episode based on the chemistry they have learned in this chapter.

Chem Connections to Other Sciences

Students gain understanding of the interdisciplinary aspects of chemistry when they are actively engaged in thinking about the connections between the sciences. This section provides a glimpse of the interconnections between the content in this chapter and other scientific disciplines. Brief sketches relate students' study of chemistry concepts to biology, physics, and Earth science.

Encourage students to draw analogies with science connections they are familiar with while discussing the science connections. The chemistry concepts discussed in this chapter hold true in every branch of science, and can provide scientists in other fields with new insights. Emphasize the growing interdisciplinary approach to science and the need for scientists who have a broader view of science. Discuss how scientists try to understand phenomena by studying a problem from different points of view. Encourage the appreciation for chemistry in relation to the broader framework of science by describing the increase in demand for scientists with interdisciplinary backgrounds (for example, geochemistry, biochemistry, and chemical physics).

CSI Chemistry

Chem Connections to Other Sciences

Chemical Families

Biology Similar to the grouping of chemicals into families, biological molecules can be grouped into families based on their sequences. Proteins from the same family are thought to have evolved from a common ancestral protein and typically have similar three-dimensional structures, functions, and sequences.

Physics The chemical family that includes the semiconductors, silicon, and germanium are of particular importance to the computer industry. Their ability to selectively conduct electrons and their uses in amplification have made them important in thousands of applications in the electronic industry.

Earth Science Polychlorinated biphenyls (PCBs) are a family of organic compounds that came into use in the 1930s as synthetic lubricants and coolants. Their surprisingly high thermal conductivity and high dielectric constant made them useful in industrial processes. In the 1970s, PCBs were determined to cause cancer, and they were subsequently banned in 1979.
Read more about technology's effect on the environment in
Extending the Connection

Chromatography

Biology Chromatography is one of the most common methods used to separate one biological molecule from one another. For example, size exclusion chromatography can tell whether a protein molecule exists as a monomer or a dimer in solution. Affinity chromatography can be used as a powerful method for isolating specific molecules out of complex mixtures.

Physics Gas chromatography linked with mass spectrometry is used to "fingerprint" the source of oil pollution. Geochemists can use the composition of hydrocarbons found in an oil slick to determine where the oil originated.

Earth Science The Environmental Protection Agency (EPA) uses chromatography to test drinking water and to monitor air quality. Liquid chromatography and gas chromatography can be used to measure levels of dangerous contaminants in water and air.

Crystalline Structure

Biology X-ray diffraction is used to determine the three-dimensional structure of proteins. A concentrated protein solution is slowly evaporated until crystals of pure protein are formed. The information gathered provides clues to how the protein functions in cells.

Physics Most crystals in nature are symmetrical and repeat their patterns. Quasi-crystals are ordered but do not repeat and were thought to be impossible until recently. It is interesting to note that there are instances of Islamic mosaic work that display these intricate structures.

Earth Science Ulexite is also known as "television stone" or "fiber optic rock" because of its crystalline structure. The hydrated sodium calcium borate mineral forms a set of parallel fiber optics so clear that, when properly polished, you can read through it.

Chemiluminescence

Biology Certain small crustaceans use bioluminescent chemical mixtures or bioluminescent bacterial slurries the same way many squid use ink. When threatened, they distract their predators by flashing colors and light. Many species of firefly has larvae that glow to repel predators.

Physics Chemiluminescence is a phenomenon that occurs at the molecular level when two compounds react, forming a product in an excited state. The product returns to the ground state by emitting light, either by fluorescence (a quick reaction) or phosphorescence (a slow reaction).

Earth Science Many deep-sea organisms express bioluminescence when the enzyme luciferase oxidizes luciferin pigments. This light helps organisms find mates or blind and confuse predators in the darkness of their environment.

722

Active Chemistry

Consider developing an interdisciplinary lesson plan that investigates how key chemistry concepts are applied in different sciences. Groups would select a topic and determine how it relates to biology, physics, and Earth science based on their reading of *Chem Connetions to Other Sciences*, and how it relates to the key chemistry concepts. A set of questions can be constructed for students to focus on, allowing them to build a constructive inquiry. A group member could write down the highlights of their discussion. Once students have recorded the focal points of their group discussions, bring together the whole class and have a volunteer from each group share the major points of their discussion of science connections.

Extending the Connection

Extending the Connection

TECHNOLOGY AND ENVIRONMENTAL QUALITY

Polychlorinated biphenyls (PCBs) are a group of synthetic chemicals that contain chlorinated molecules. Their production and release is an example of technology that has had a negative effect on the environment. PCBs can be either oily liquids or solids, are odorless and tasteless, and are mostly colorless. PCBs do not occur in nature, but are the product of science's ability to create new materials. They are stable, nonflammable compounds that were used widely as lubricants and as coolants in transformers and other electrical equipment.

In 1977, the United States stopped production of PCBs when evidence was found that the buildup of PCBs in the environment was having harmful effects on people's health. Before that time there was no control over disposal because no one knew the ill effects produced. PCBs do not break down easily, are not soluble in water, and are now found widely in our environment. Although their measured concentrations in the environment generally are low, they accumulate in river and lake sediments where they enter into and then bio-accumulate up the food chain. The highest levels are found in large predator fish, birds, and humans. In the United States, 2 million lake acres and 130,000 miles of rivers have PCB advisories urging people to limit the amount of fish they consume from these waterways.

Ultraviolet (UV) radiation causes skin cancer, eye damage, and, in larger doses, damages the DNA molecules required for cell reproduction. Agriculture in areas of higher UV radiation is less productive. Stratospheric ozone (O_3) plays an important role in absorbing high-energy UV radiation from the Sun, which limits the amount reaching Earth. However, this protective shield is being destroyed. Man-made chlorofluorocarbons (CFCs) that at first were thought to be harmless are actually harmful, and are destroying ozone molecules in the stratosphere. The bonds that hold the CFCs in place are extremely strong,

722A

Active Chemistry

The *Chem Connections to Other Sciences* show students that the chemistry concepts they studied in each chapter are also basic to many other sciences. The chemistry they are learning is fundamental in the understanding of the concepts that they will study in all the other sciences. *Extending the Connection* delves deeper into one or two of these connections. It gives students an opportunity to examine a particular relationship to another science in greater depth.

CHAPTER 8

CSI Chemistry

which means they will remain in the atmosphere for a long time before decomposing. UV radiation from the Sun has enough energy to break those bonds, releasing atomic chlorine radicals. The chlorine radicals react with O_3 molecules, breaking them down to oxygen (O_2). The chlorine radical is then regenerated, breaking down many more O_3 molecules before it is removed from the stratosphere. Over the decades, enough CFCs have escaped into the atmosphere to create a large hole in the ozone layer over Antarctica and a smaller hole over the Arctic region.

More Production Means More Waste

As the human population increases, demand for household goods and consumer products also increases. Enjoying a lifestyle of convenience and comfort is the result of technological advances, but there is always a tradeoff. The technology that created our TVs, computers, automobiles, air conditioning, fast food, and high-yield agriculture methods has also produced contaminated groundwater, rivers, lakes, and soil, air pollution, noise pollution, acid rain, and many other harmful and unhealthy environmental problems. The waste products of the industries that create the goods and the disposal of the items themselves all contribute to environmental damage.

Americans consume over 100 billion plastic shopping bags every year. These bags, developed to be strong and lightweight, frequently are used only once and then spend decades in a landfill. Plastic water and drink containers take hundreds of years to decompose and over 38 million of them end up in Unites States landfills every year.

Millions of cell phones are thrown away every year in the United States. Lead, nickel, and cadmium in the battery pose threats to the environment if they are not properly managed in the waste stream. Before plasma screens and liquid crystal displays, all televisions contained a cathode ray tube (CRT). The CRTs contain lead, and as new technology replaces them, millions of these now-outdated TVs are being placed in landfills. Lead is a serious water and soil pollutant and a health hazard to humans and animals.

Do the positive aspects of technological advances outweigh the damage to our environment? What risks are we willing to live with to have the products that support our lifestyle? These are questions our society must wrestle with now and in the future.

backgrounds use chemistry for many different purposes as part of their jobs.

The *Chem at Work* profiles also demonstrate that many professions that do not seem to be related to chemistry, actually are. For example, one might not think there would be a strong connection linking chemistry with the U.S. Fish and Wildlife Service. You may want to open a discussion on how chemistry relates to some occupations that students in your classes are interested in.

For your convenience, all three full-length *Chem at Work* profiles are provided as Blackline Masters in your *Teacher Resources* CD.

CHAPTER 8

8c	Blackline Master
8d	Blackline Master
8e	Blackline Master

Chem at Work

Jacqueline Leith

Forensic Chemist, Miami Dade Crime Lab, Miami, FL

One of the most popular shows on television today is *CSI: Miami*. The show features a team of criminologists who solve crimes by gathering evidence and analyzing it with state-of-the-art forensic technology. Jacqueline Leith's job is like a real-life version of the show. She is a forensic chemist in Miami's crime lab.

Jacqueline is an expert at identifying unknown substances. "We mostly deal in analyzing controlled substances like drugs. Later, we present the evidence at trial to a jury." She feels that this is the most satisfying part of her job.

Jacqueline does three tests when a controlled substance comes into the lab. First, she conducts a "spot test" or "color test," in which a chemical reagent is added to a sample of the unknown substance. If there is a color change, Jacqueline can usually identify it as heroin or cocaine. Next, she performs a "micro-crystalline test" which involves another chemical reagent. Jacqueline then views the sample under a light microscope. If she sees "feathered crystals" form, the unknown substance is cocaine. The last test utilizes a complex machine with a robotic arm. This machine, called a gas chromatograph mass spectrometer, breaks the sample apart chemically. "Just like on TV," Jacqueline adds with a smile.

Jacqueline finds her job fulfilling in many ways. She loves the work she does because she has always been fascinated by science and always wanted a career that involved science.

Doug Lerner

Arson Investigator, Sheriff's Dept., Rockland County, NY

Doug Lerner and his "K-9" partner, Scooter, are arson investigators with the Rockland County Sheriff's Department in New York. Their job is to determine the causes of fires. Lerner knows melted aluminum means the fire exceeded 1200°F. Scooter, a yellow Labrador, can sniff out fire accelerants like gasoline and kerosene.

Dr. Ed Espinoza

Chief Forensic Scientist at U.S. Fish and Wildlife Service, Ashland, OR

Ed Espinoza plays an important part in the fight to protect and preserve wildlife by solving crimes against endangered species and protected animals. His lab uses techniques rooted in chemistry to identify, for example, animal species from blood samples. The evidence he gathers helps to track down smugglers, poachers and illegal hunters.

Active Chemistry

Chem at Work

Chem at Work relates the material covered in each chapter with the real world by providing students with some examples of professions that make use of the chemical principles they have just learned. Many of the chemical procedures that students have performed in the previous sections and/or plan to incorporate into their *Chapter Challenge* projects are employed every day by average people, such as those featured here.

Students should note from these profiles that chemistry is embedded in a wide range of professions practiced by an equally broad range of people. There are no geographic, ethnic, gender, or educational specifications for people who apply chemistry in their professions. It should also be apparent that it's not necessary to have an advanced degree or be a scientist in order to practice chemistry. As the *Chem at Work* profiles show, people from all

Chem Practice Test

The *Chem Practice Test* is provided as a Blackline Master on your *Teacher Resources CD*.

8f	Blackline Master

Content Review

1. d

2. a

3. a

4. c

5. b

6. c

7. c

8. b

9. c

10. d

CSI Chemistry

Chem Practice Test

Content Review

On a separate sheet of paper answer the following.

1. Use deductive reasoning to determine the element that has the following properties:

   • Diatomic
   • Sublimes at room temperature
   • Violet-black solid
   • Halogen
   • Found in large quantities in ocean water
   • Period 5
   • Antiseptic

   a) sulfur   b) bromine
   c) nitrogen   d) iodine

2. An O^{2-} ion has _____ protons and _____ electrons.

   a) 8, 10   b) 10, 8
   c) 8, 8   d) 10, 10

3. The slope of a straight line can be obtained by

   a) rise divided by the run.
   b) the run divided by the rise.
   c) the rise plus the run.
   d) the rise minus the run.

4. If you have two spheres of equal volume, one made of carbon and the other made of strontium, what is the relationship of their masses?

   a) mass of C sphere = mass of Sr sphere
   b) mass of C sphere > mass of Sr sphere
   c) mass of C sphere < mass of Sr sphere

5. All of the following are units of density except

   a) g/cm^3.   b) kg/cm^2.
   c) lb/ft^3.   d) g/mL.

6. Which ion in hemoglobin catalyzes the luminol reaction?

   a) Fe^{3+} b) Ca^{2+}
   c) Fe^{2+} d) He^{2+}

7. Identify the precipitate in the following chemical formula:

   barium nitrate + sodium hydroxide →
   barium hydroxide + sodium nitrate

   a) barium nitrate   b) sodium hydroxide
   c) barium hydroxide   d) sodium nitrate

8. Which of the following compounds are insoluble in water?

   $CaCl_2$, $(NH_4)_2CO_3$, $AgCl$, K_2SO_4, $Mg(OH)_2$, KNO_3, $NaOH$

   a) $Mg(OH)_2$, $NaOH$
   b) $Mg(OH)_2$, $AgCl$
   c) $(NH_4)_2CO_3$, $AgCl$
   d) $(NH_4)_2CO_3$, $CaCl_2$

9. Which of the following reactions are double-replacement reactions?

   I. $KCl + AgNO_3 \rightarrow KNO_3 + AgCl$
   II. $2NaHCO_3 \rightarrow Na_2CO_3 + H_2O + CO_2$
   III. $MgCl_2 + Na_2CO_3 \rightarrow MgCO_3 + 2NaCl$
   IV. $3Zn + 2Fe(NO_3)_3 \rightarrow 3Zn(NO_3)_2 + 2Fe$

   a) I
   b) IV
   c) I, III
   d) I, II, III
   e) I, II, IV

10. What happens to a Br atom when it becomes a Br^- ion?

    a) The bromine atom gains an electron and is oxidized.
    b) The bromine atom loses a proton and is reduced.
    c) The bromine atom loses a proton and is oxidized.
    d) The bromine atom gains an electron and is reduced.

724

Active Chemistry

11. Two stains at a crime scene are sprayed with luminol reagent. Stain A glows but Stain B does not. This means

a) A is blood and B is not.

b) A may be blood, but B cannot be.

c) A is blood; nothing can be said about B.

d) A may be ketchup but B cannot be.

12. Which of the following ions are polyatomic anions?

CO_3^{2-}, Ca^{2+}, S^{2-}, Ag^+, NH_4^+, PO_4^{3-}, Br^-, SO_4^{2-}

a) CO_3^{2-} and Ca^{2+}

b) PO_4^{3-}, SO_4^{2-}, CO_3^{2-}, Ca^{2+}, and S^{2-}

c) only NH_4^+

d) CO_3^{2-}, PO_4^{3-}, SO_4^{2-}, and NH_4^+

13. What are three insoluble compounds that could be made from the following chloride, sulfate, and hydroxide ions?

a) calcium chloride, magnesium sulfate, and silver carbonate

b) silver chloride, magnesium hydroxide, and calcium carbonate

c) Barium hydroxide, potassium carbonate, and ammonium sulfate

d) Magnesium chloride, ammonium hydroxide, and magnesium carbonate

14. Would the silver nitrate technique work best on a piece of glass, a brass doorknob, or an envelope? (Hint: The technique works best on absorbent surfaces.)

a) piece of glass

b) brass doorknob

c) envelope

d) it would not work on any of them

15. Can oxidation occur without reduction occurring at the same time?

a) Yes, oxidation occurs when there is a loss of electrons.

b) Yes, oxidation is a special type of reaction.

c) No, oxidation and reduction occur at the same time.

d) No, oxidation and reduction are the same thing.

16. Use the activity series to determine which of the following reactions will take place.

I. $Mg + NaNO_3 \rightarrow$

II. $K + CaCl_2 \rightarrow$

III. $Cu + HCl \rightarrow$

a) I

b) II

c) III

d) I, III

e) I, II, III

17. A serial number has been removed from a piece of iron (Fe) metal. Which solution should a forensic chemist use to recover the serial number?

a) $FeCl_3$

b) $MgCl_2$

c) $CuCl_2$

18. An example of the formation of dislocations in a metal's crystal structure is

a) the presence of surface oxides.

b) oils from fingers on the surface.

c) heating the metal to red hot and then cooling slowly.

d) bending the metal back and forth.

19. Which of the following is a pure substance?

a) salad dressing

b) iron nail

c) copper chloride in water solution

d) black transparency marker

20. Given that substance A has an $R_f = 0.17$ and substance B has an $R_f = 0.51$, which substance moved farther in the chromatography experiment? Which substance interacted most with the stationary phase?

a) A, B   b) B, A

c) A, A   d) B, B

725

Active Chemistry

11. b

12. d

13. b

14. c

15. c

16. b

17. b

18. d

19. b

20. b

CHAPTER 8

Critical Thinking

21.

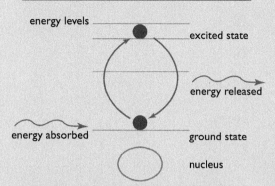

energy levels

excited state

energy released

energy absorbed

ground state

nucleus

When an electron in an atom absorbs energy equal to the difference between two energy levels, it is promoted to a higher energy level. This is called an excited state. When the electron drops down to its starting energy level, or ground state, energy is released. If the energy released is in the visible spectrum, it is observed as light.

22.a)

The volume is 20 mL.

22.b)

The metal's density is

d=54 g/20 ml = 2.7 g/cm^3

22.c)

The metal is aluminum.

22.d)

A piece of gold with a mass of 86 g would have a volume of 4.6 mL because 89 g/(19.3 g/cc) = 4.6 cc or mL.

23.a)

A positive luminal test is considered presumptive because it cannot confirm that the sample tested was blood.

23.b)

The test is called presumptive until further tests can prove or disprove that blood is present.

23.c)

Other substances that have Co^{2+} ions, or rust and horseradish, can give a positive test.

CSI Chemistry

Practice Test *(continued)*

Critical Thinking

On a separate sheet of paper answer the following.

21. Label the diagram below. Use the terms ground state, excited state, energy absorbed, energy released, nucleus, and energy levels and explain how atoms emit light.

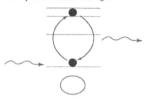

22. Diagram A below shows a graduated cylinder with a liquid. A 54-g sample of metal is added to the graduated cylinder and the volume of the liquid reaches the level illustrated in diagram B. Using the table provided, answer the following questions:

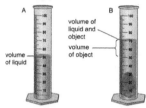

A

B

volume of liquid and object

volume of object

volume of liquid

Metal	Density at 25°C (g/cm³)
Gold	19.3
Mercury	13.5
Lead	11.4
Copper	8.92
Iron	7.87
Aluminum	2.70

a) What is the volume of the metal?

b) What is the density of the metal?

c) What is the identity of the metal?

d) How would the volume of graduated cylinder B change if an 86-g sample of gold were added to the cylinder A instead?

23. When the luminol-peroxide mixture comes into contact with blood, the Fe^{2+} ions in the center of the hemoglobin molecule catalyze the reaction, producing a visible blue glow.

a) Why is a positive luminol test considered a presumptive test for blood?

b) What is the test called presumptive?

c) Can substances other than blood give a positive test?

24. Using the data given below, create a flowchart to separate the following white powders; sucrose, CaCO₃, MgSO₄, starch.

Powder	Solubility	Iodine	Phenolphthalein	NaOH	HC₂H₃O₂
sucrose	yes	brown	clear	no change	no change
CaCO₃	no	brown	pink	no change	bubbles
MgSO₄	yes	brown	clear	white precipitate, very cloudy	no change
starch	no	dark blue/black	clear	no change	no change

25. Identify the reactants and products in the following chemical reactions and balance the equations where necessary:

a) CuOH + H₂SO₄ → 2H₂O + _____

b) _____ + AgNO₃ + AgCl + Ba(NO₃)₂

c) KOH + HCl → _____ + H₂O

d) CaSO₄ + NaOH → Na₂SO₄ + _____

726

24.

There are many possible answers. The following flowchart is an example.

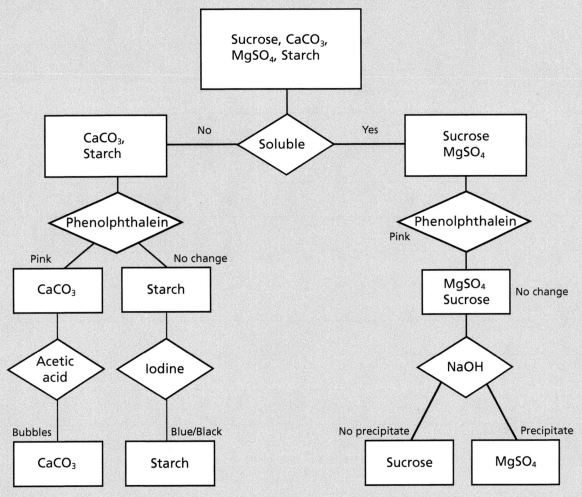

25.

a)

$$2CuOH + H_2SO_4 \rightarrow 2H_2O + Cu_2SO_4$$

copper(I) hydroxide   *sulfuric acid*   *water*   *copper(I) sulfate*

b)

$$BaCl_2 + 2AgNO_3 \rightarrow 2AgCl + Ba(NO_3)_2$$

barium chloride   *silver nitrate*   *silver chloride*   *barium nitrate*

c)

$$KOH + HCl \rightarrow KCl + H_2O$$

potassium hydroxide   *hydrochloric acid*   *potassium chloride*   *water*

d)

$$CaSO_4 + 2NaOH \rightarrow Na_2SO_4 + Ca(OH)_2$$

calcium sulfate   *sodium hydroxide*   *sodium sulfate*   *calcium hydroxide*

NOTES

84 Business Park Drive, Armonk, NY 10504
www.its-about-time.com

Publishing Team

President
Tom Laster

**Director of
Product Development**
Barbara Zahm, Ph.D.

Managing Editor
Maureen Grassi

Project Development Editor
Ruta Demery

Project Managers
Gary Hickernell
Sampson Starkweather

Editors
Gary Hickernell
Tamara Kathwari
Zhiren Qin
Marti Davidson Sichel

Proofreaders
Alexander Charles
John Fuller

Editorial Coordinator
Susan Gibian

Indexer
Caryn Sobel

Creative Director, Design
John Nordland

Assistant Art Director
Mauricio Gonzalez

Quality Control Editor
Alexander Mari

Safety Reviewer
Ed Robeck

Equipment Kit Developers
Dana Turner
Joseph DeMarco
Henry Garcia

**Staff Photographer/
Videographer**
Jason Harris

Creative Artwork
Tomas Bunk

**Production/Studio
Manager**
Robert Schwalb

**Production Studio
Coordinator**
Marie Killoran

Illustrators
Sean Campbell
Richard Ciotti
Doreen Flaherty
Marie Killoran
Louise Landry
Cora Roman
MaryBeth Schulze
Jason Skinner

Layout Artists
Richard Ciotti
Frank Fallon
Mauricio Gonzalez
Marie Killoran
Cora Roman
Lorraine Schwartz

Prepress
Richard Ciotti

NOTES

NOTES

NOTES

NOTES

NOTES